THE OXFORD HANDBOOK OF

LEGAL HISTORY

THE OXFORD HANDBOOK OF

LEGAL HISTORY

Edited by

MARKUS D. DUBBER

and

CHRISTOPHER TOMLINS

OXFORD

UNIVERSITY PRESS

OXFORD
UNIVERSITY PRESS

Great Clarendon Street, Oxford, OX2 6DP,
United Kingdom

Oxford University Press is a department of the University of Oxford.
It furthers the University's objective of excellence in research, scholarship,
and education by publishing worldwide. Oxford is a registered trade mark of
Oxford University Press in the UK and in certain other countries

Published in the United States of America by Oxford University Press
198 Madison Avenue, New York, NY 10016, United States of America

British Library Cataloguing in Publication Data
Data available

Library of Congress Control Number: 2018940691

ISBN 978-0-19-879435-6

EDITORS' PREFACE

....

For much of its editorial gestation period, this *Handbook of Legal History* went by the name *Handbook of Historical Legal Research*. Although the title eventually changed, the content did not. The handbook is not, in other words, an encyclopedic guide to 'topics' in legal history. It is not a collection of essays in chronological order, perhaps divided into geographic or systemic (common law vs. civil law?) clusters, and further subdivided into legal subjects (criminal law? landlord-tenant?), perhaps travelling from East to West, or North to South, or from centre to periphery, from what matters to what is marginal, or even the other way around. If you are looking for 'The History of Contract Law: Germany, 1900-1914' or for 'American Tort Law: The Age of the Restatement Masters', you will be disappointed.

Our goal was never a handbook of law across time and space. What we were after instead was a volume that would capture the glorious variety of research on legal history going on around the world today. What we are proud to offer is a general methodological handbook on legal history as a mode of legal scholarship (i.e., on the enterprise of historical analysis of law in all its multifaceted breadth and depth).

Some of the most exciting and innovative legal scholarship of the past fifty years has been driven by historical curiosity. Legal history today comes in a wonderful spectrum of shapes and sizes, flavors and tones. Legal historical inquiry extends from short-range, micro social history to global intellectual history over the *longue durée*. Legal historical discourse has expanded beyond traditional national/ parochial boundaries to become international and comparative in scope and orientation, and in ambition.

Legal history—like law and like history—is in the midst of a 'methodological moment'. Several ongoing projects are currently devoted to exploring varieties of legal historiography and legal history's relationship to other approaches to legal scholarship. Here, we investigate the current state of the art in legal history around the world. We examine the variety of modes of historical analysis of law, past, present, and future. Our ambition for this book has been to bottle the ambition of legal history as historical analysis of law.

Projects as big as this one tend to experience quite a bit of mission creep, as the weeks stretch into months and months into years, tens of chapters turn into dozens, then scores, and authors come and authors go, as life goes on outside the two covers of the growing book, across disciplines and countries and through academic seasons and professional—and personal—developments. And yet, comparing the list of chapters and contributors now to our initial wish list of subjects and authors then, we're delighted that the book in your hands bears a close resemblance to the book we envisioned. We are grateful that so many admirable scholars were willing to devote their scarce time to a wide-ranging and flexibly-conceived project that (quite a few must have expected) had a decent chance of petering out before seeing the light of publication day.

The book is not *exactly* the book we had in mind when we started this project. We think that is a good thing. A handbook that doesn't deviate from its original plan is a handbook not worth making. It is a collection of chapters written on spec that may impart (soon-to-be-outdated) information rather than inspiration. Inspiration is precisely what drew us to legal historical scholarship, and the ever-curious people who produce it, in the first place. Inspiration is what we believe this *Handbook* successfully conveys.

The handbook takes a broad and inclusive approach to its subject matter. Its list of contributors includes scholars from several countries and legal systems, ranging from current to future research leaders and representing a variety of methodological approaches, areas of expertise, and research agendas. Its content is similarly wide and diverse in scope and substance, covering a broad range of perspectives and topics. The handbook's fifty-seven chapters are divided into five parts: I. Contexts: Locating Legal History, II. Approaches: Conceptualizing Legal History, III. Perspectives: Legal History in Modern Legal Thought, IV. Traditions: Tracing Legal History, and V. Illustrations: Doing Things with Legal History.

Part I explores the relationship between legal history as historical analysis of law and other scholarly projects, including history unmodified and legal history as a subspecies of historical—rather than of legal—scholarship, as well as other modes of critical analysis of law, such as philosophical, economic, comparative, literary, and rhetorical approaches.

Part II considers various approaches to legal history as a scholarly enterprise, ranging from legal history as social and political history to archival and quantitative legal history.

Part III homes in on the interrelation between legal history and jurisprudence by investigating the role and conception of historical inquiry in various models, schools and movements of legal thought, from Historical Jurisprudence to Critical Legal Studies to Queer Legal History.

Part IV traces the place and pursuit of historical analysis in various legal systems and traditions across time, culture, and space, including, among others, Roman Law, Jewish Law, and Imperial Law.

Finally, Part V narrows the handbook's focus to explore several illustrations of legal history in action, including its use in various legal doctrinal contexts (e.g., constitutional law), during times of national, and supranational, community building (e.g., 'Europe'), and in various modes of legal intervention in specific disputes (e.g., Indigenous title claims).

Enjoy!

Markus D. Dubber and Christopher Tomlins

Contents

III. PERSPECTIVES: LEGAL HISTORY
IN MODERN LEGAL THOUGHT

IV. TRADITIONS: TRACING LEGAL HISTORY

V. ILLUSTRATIONS: DOING THINGS
WITH LEGAL HISTORY

Notes on the Contributors

Clifford Ando is the David B. and Clara E. Stern Professor and Professor of Classics, History, and Law at the University of Chicago.

Leora Bilsky is Professor at the Tel Aviv University Faculty of Law, and Director of the Minerva Center for Human Rights at Tel Aviv University.

Richard P. Boast QC is Professor at the School of Law, University of Wellington.

Alfred L. Brophy holds the D. Paul Jones Chair in Law at the University of Alabama, School of Law.

Emilios Christodoulidis holds the Chair of Jurisprudence at University of Glasgow, School of Law.

Marianne Constable is Professor of Rhetoric at the University of California, Berkeley.

Elizabeth Dale is Professor of History at the University of Florida.

Maksymilian (Maks) Del Mar is Reader in Legal Theory and a founding co-director of the Centre for Law and Society in a Global Context (CLSGC) at Queen Mary University of London.

Justin Desautels-Stein is Associate Professor of Law at the University of Colorado.

Shaunnagh Dorsett is Professor of Law at the University of Technology, Sydney.

Maria Drakopoulou is Reader in Law at the University of Kent.

Thomas Duve is Managing Director of the Max-Planck Institute for European Legal History and Professor of Comparative Legal History at Goethe University, Frankfurt.

Laura F. Edwards is Peabody Family Professor of History at the Trinity College of Arts and Sciences, Duke University.

Sam Erman is Associate Professor of Law at USC, Gould School of Law.

Samera Esmeir is Associate Professor of Rhetoric at the University of California, Berkeley.

Angela Fernandez is Associate Professor of Law at the University of Toronto.

Catherine L. Fisk is the Chancellor's Professor of Law at the School of Law, University of California, Irvine.

Anne Fleming is Associate Professor of Law at Georgetown University.

Günter Frankenberg is Professor at Goethe University, Frankfurt.

Joshua Getzler is Professor of Law and Legal History at the University of Oxford.

Paul D. Halliday is Professor of Law and the Julian Bishko Professor of History at the University of Virginia.

Ron Harris is Professor of Legal History at Tel Aviv University.

Tom Johnson is a lecturer in Late Medieval History at the University of York.

Rachel Klagsbrun is a member of the Tel Aviv University, Faculty of Law.

Daniel Klerman is the Edward G. Lewis Chair in Law and History at the Gould School of Law, University of Southern California.

Roy Kreitner is a Professor at Tel Aviv University.

Tahirih V. Lee is Associate Professor of Law at Florida State University.

Gerald Leonard is Professor of Law at Boston University, School of Law.

Assaf Likhovski is Professor of Law and Legal History at Tel Aviv University.

Peter Lindseth is the Olimpiad S. Ioffe Professor of International and Comparative Law at the School of Law, University of Connecticut.

Michael Lobban is Professor of Legal History at the London School of Economics and Political Science.

Martin Loughlin is Professor of Public Law at the London School of Economics and Political Science.

Arlie Loughnan is Professor of Criminal Law and Criminal Law Theory at the School of Law, University of Sydney.

H. Timothy Lovelace Jr. is Associate Professor in Law at the Maurer School of Law.

Doreen Lustig is a fellow of the Tel Aviv University Faculty of Law.

Renisa Mawani is Professor, Sociology at the University of British Columbia.

Paul G. McHugh is Professor of Law and Legal History at the University of Cambridge.

David Minto is an assistant professor in the department of History at Durham University.

Noga Morag-Levine is Professor of Law and the George Roumell Faculty Scholar at Michigan State University.

John V. Orth is the William Rand Kenan Jr. Professor of Law at UNC, School of Law.

Kunal M. Parker is Professor of Law and Dean's Distinguished Scholar at the University of Miami School of Law.

Nathan Perl-Rosenthal is Assistant Professor of History and Spatial Sciences at Dornsife College, University of Southern California.

Heikki Pihlajamäki is Professor of Comparative Legal History at the University of Helsinki.

Dan Priel is an associate professor at Osgoode Law School.

Mathias Reimann is the Hessel E. Yntema Professor of Law at the University of Michigan.

Anat Rosenberg is a fellow of Radzyner Law School, IDC Herzliya.

Lena Salaymeh is Associate Professor at Tel Aviv University, Faculty of Law.

John Henry Schlegel is Distinguished Professor and the Floyd H. and Hilda L. Hurst Faculty Scholar at the University at Buffalo, the State University of New York.

Katharina Isabel Schmidt is a J.S.D. candidate at Yale Law School.

Philip Schofield is Professor of the History of Legal and Political Thought and Director of the Bentham Project at University College London.

David B. Schorr is director of the Berg Institute for Law and History and the Law and Environment Program at Tel Aviv University, Faculty of Law.

Mitra Sharafi is Associate Professor of Law at the University of Wisconsin.

Karl Shoemaker is Associate Professor of History and Law at the University of Wisconsin.

Norman W. Spaulding is the Nelson Bowman Sweitzer and Marie B. Sweitzer Professor of Law at Stanford Law School.

Simon Stern is an associate professor and co-director of the Centre for Innovation Law and Policy both at the University of Toronto.

Carolyn Strange is a senior fellow of the Australian National University College of Arts and Social Sciences.

Johan van der Walt is Professor and Head of the Law faculty at the University of Luxembourg.

Bryan Wagner is an associate professor in the English department at the University of California, Berkeley.

Steven Wilf is the Anthony J. Smits Professor of Global Commerce at the School of Law, University of Connecticut.

PART I

CONTEXTS: LOCATING LEGAL HISTORY

CHAPTER 1

PHILOSOPHICAL ANALYSIS AND HISTORICAL INQUIRY

THEORIZING NORMATIVITY, LAW, AND LEGAL THOUGHT

MAKSYMILIAN DEL MAR*

I. INTRODUCTION

WHAT is the relationship between philosophical analysis and historical inquiry? Why is a partnership or tension between the two beneficial for the practice of theory? What specific virtues does historical inquiry bring, and thus what is lost when theorizing is restricted to philosophical analysis? And why does all this matter specifically for theorizing law and legal thought? It is the task of this chapter to offer some suggestive answers to these questions.

* Versions of this chapter have been given before a variety of audiences, including at the National University of Singapore, University of Cartagena in Colombia, Jagellonian University in Poland, and the University of Edinburgh. I thank all my hosts and discussants. Special thanks to Michael Lobban, who has been my most patient and long-suffering interlocutor on these issues.

The questions themselves are not new. They have flared up at different times and places, and it would be a matter of interest to investigate why that occurs. The fight to establish the autonomy of philosophical analysis and the pushback against this—from history, but also other disciplines—seems to be a recurring debate that each generation rediscovers for itself. It was there in the efforts of Jeremy Bentham and John Austin on behalf of analysis, and Sir Henry Maine and others on behalf of history, anthropology, and comparative studies. It was there in H. L. A. Hart's 'perennial questions' and the armchair philosophy of his concept of law and in Brian Simpson's, William Twining's, and others' emphasis on law-in-context. And it is there in recent times, with some standing up for not only the autonomy but also priority of analysis (e.g., John Gardner), and others pushing back against this in various ways—sometimes via the history of ideas (e.g., Gerald Postema, Michael Lobban, Roger Cotterrell, Jeremy Waldron) and sometimes via a more general historical approach, often in tandem with sociology and anthropology or the humanities (e.g., see Nicola Lacey, Christopher Tomlins, Robert Gordon, Brian Tamanaha, Patrick Glenn, Fernanda Pirie).[1] Some areas of the law have seen particularly heated debates on the value and importance of history—international law is the stand out contemporary example[2]—and it would again be interesting to ask why some areas of law attract this debate more than others.

Some of these debates occur against the background of quarrels between philosophy and history—or, as some think of it, between analysis and context—outside of the legal domain. Even if we just limit ourselves to the twentieth century and mention but a few names—e.g., Isaiah Berlin, Alasdair MacIntyre, E. P. Thompson, Bernard Williams, and Quentin Skinner—we can see this debate has been alive and well in the last century. Arguably, all these thinkers sought to find ways of showing how philosophy and history, analysis and context, can and ought to work together, sometimes collaborating and at other times generatively challenging each other. In addition, these, and other, thinkers have all offered powerful arguments for what is at stake—morally and politically—in not losing sight of the crucial value of historical inquiry (for both theory and practice).

And yet, within the legal academy, there continues to be resistance to history. Legal history is often sidelined in legal education, and most if not all topics in the legal syllabus are taught either without any historical sensitivity (e.g., often jurisprudence) or with but a passing nod to the 'origins' of some area of doctrine that is only ever at best recommended reading. How can this be, especially for a subject that so clearly lends itself to historical inquiry, and where there is arguably so much overlap between legal thought and the practice of history?

---

[1] See the Bibliography at the end of this chapter for some references.
[2] Bardo Fassbender, Anne Peters (eds.), *The Oxford Handbook of the History of International Law* (2012).

Part of the answer may be that a good many arguments for the value of historical inquiry for theorizing law (both in general jurisprudence and in more doctrinally-oriented legal scholarship) are negative in character. We can challenge philosophical hypotheses historically, or history shows us the time-boundedness, and thus also dispensability, of what we might otherwise treat as perennial or universal questions and concepts. History thus becomes a bit of a spoilsport, a party pooper—it deflates and defuses philosophical enthusiasm. No wonder it is then avoided at all costs by hard-nosed philosophers, who feel anxious their assertions and systems will become but granules of sand and disperse into winds of dust in the glare of history. The challenge, then, is to show the theoretically generative character of historical inquiry. We must ask how thinking historically can both create objects of inquiry and explore them in particular ways—these being ways that cannot be reproduced through philosophical analysis. We must consider how the history of historical inquiry is itself a repository of theoretical insight and just how much there is to gain—in terms of substance, but also in terms of acquiring certain virtues of thought—by theorizing with historical sensitivity.

Needless to add, this is easier said than done. One of the shoals to be avoided in making the case for history is divorcing it too much from philosophy. Thus, it has sometimes been argued that history offers its own kind of irreducible explanation, but one that is essentially incommensurable with the kind of explanation offered by philosophy—e.g., the historical mode of knowing is 'configurational', which requires treating objects as elements in a single complex of concrete relationships, and this is entirely different to, and distinct from, the philosophical mode of knowing, which is 'theoretical', and according to which there are universal types, such that individual entities can be identified as instances of them.[3] Another version of this would be to say that whereas history deals with particulars—including, or perhaps especially, accidental particulars, the world of a million chance encounters—philosophy deals with universals or necessities (Platonic forms, changeless substances). The danger with these approaches is that at the cost of demonstrating the uniqueness of history, they move it further and further away from theoretical significance, including being unable to articulate how both philosophy and history can fruitfully relate to each other.

In what follows, then, I attempt to articulate how historical inquiry is generative theoretically and how it can exist, as part of the broader activity of theorizing, in fruitful tension with philosophical analysis. The approach is based on a particular concept of historical inquiry and its resulting historical insights, which I shall present in the first part of the chapter. Having done so, the second part will then offer some suggestive and necessarily sketchy illustrations of the value of historical inquiry for theorizing law and legal thought.

---

[3] See Louis Mink, 'The Autonomy of Historical Understanding', in William Dray (ed.), *Philosophical Analysis and History* (1966). See also Thomas Kuhn, *The Essential Tension* (1977).

II. Historical Inquiry

I begin with two stipulative models (stipulative because I acknowledge this to be just one possible model of philosophical analysis and historical inquiry, respectively):

1. By philosophical analysis, I mean: the creation of an object of inquiry via the pursuit and identification of predominantly (though often exclusively)[4] necessary and sufficient features, which distinguish an object from amongst a pool of objects evaluated to be relevant comparators;

2. By historical inquiry, I mean: 1) the creation of an object of inquiry that a) exists in time and (at least potentially and sometimes) b) persists through time (across times and places); and 2) a treatment of that object of inquiry as variable both internally and externally, where those variables are a) acknowledged to be contingent and b) explored via multiple temporalities.

Broadly speaking, then, on these models, whereas philosophy is an art of distinction, of breaking apart and disassociating but also systematizing, history is the art of variation, combining change and persistence in time, as well as associating and relating. The general argument, then, is that the practice of theory requires both—without analysis, we lose certain theoretical virtues, e.g., of some degree of consistency (in our language), and without historical inquiry, we lose other virtues, e.g., the reflexivity that comes with recognition of the complexity, including relationality, of an object. Without historical inquiry, the practice of theory is impoverished in all kinds of ways—it loses certain objects of inquiry, it misses out on various aspects of exploring them, and it operates without the benefit of certain theoretical virtues.

In what follows, I focus on unpacking this rather dense model of historical inquiry. In order to facilitate this and not make it too abstract and obtuse, I will interweave a running example: normativity. This choice is hardly innocent—explaining normativity has been a prominent problem of theorizing law. A treatment of this problem from the perspective of philosophical analysis would involve identifying the (necessarily and sufficiently) distinctive features of normativity by distinguishing it from, e.g., naturalism. Thus, as H. L. A. Hart proposed, one may seek to carve out a distinctive space for the normative by distinguishing rules from habits, coercive orders, and predictions. One might then argue that only normative, rule-governed behaviour is characterized by the presence of a critical reflective attitude, which consists in persons being aware of the standard of behaviour prescribed

---

4 For a defence of (legal) philosophical method that includes both necessary and contingent features, see Michael Giudice, *Understanding the Nature of Law: A Case for Constructive Conceptual Explanation* (2015).

or proscribed by the rule, a disposition to criticize those who breach it, and an acknowledgement by others of the legitimacy of that criticism (on the occasion it is made). This attitude is missing from habits, coercive orders, and predictions. The evidence for this would consist of, for instance, our ordinary use of the terms, e.g., 'rule' and 'habit', and several well-crafted examples that generate and support the associated intuition. The philosophical insight, generated by this philosophical analysis, is that normativity, unlike the naturalism of, say, habit, is distinguished by the existence of this critical reflective attitude.

It is important to see that there are various judgments at work in the above philosophical analysis. One is that rule-governed behaviour is somehow paradigmatic of the normative. When historicized, however, we realize that rules are a particular kind of expression of the normative, with their own progeny and cultural associations.[5] For example, we may readily associate (as Hart in fact does) rules with games. Contrast that with norms or values—to speak of norm-governed or value-governed behaviour is already quite different to speaking of rule-governed behaviour, e.g., norms are less likely to be written down than rules, and one might also expect looser inter-personal agreement on what a norm is than on what a rule is.[6] There is, therefore, a judgment being made here (perhaps not very reflexively) as to the importance of rules for the understanding of normativity. Similarly, there is a judgment that the relevant pool of comparators (for rules) are habits, coercive orders, and predictions. It is important to see this pool could be quite different, and that the choice of objects to be included in the pool influences what one asserts is distinctive about rules. Once one also sees that this is a choice, one also comes to acknowledge the incompleteness of any philosophical analysis, e.g., comparing rules to, for instance, dispositions or desires, would generate other features one would then present as distinctive about them. Philosophical analysis, then, is an incomplete process of comparisons judged to be relevant.[7]

The acknowledgment of these limitations of philosophical analysis already opens the door to other modes of inquiry, including historical. Let us then ask: what could historical inquiry bring to the study of normativity? To answer this, let us consider and unpack each of the elements in the stipulative model above.

One element of the above model of historical inquiry is that it involves the creation of an object that exists in time. By this I mean, for instance, that the object

---

[5] Lorraine Daston is at present at work on a history of rules—for a taste, see Lorraine Daston, 'The Premodern Rule: History of an Epistemic Category' 2016 Working Paper <http://www.humcenter.pitt.edu/sites/default/files/PittsburghPremodernRulesNov2016.pdf> (accessed 11 May 2017).

[6] See Neil MacCormick, *Institutions of Law* (2007), who works with the example of a norm of queuing.

[7] Of course, the very selection of normativity as a problem requiring explanation is already a judgment—this too is one that can and ought to be historicized. For instance, this language of normativity arguably comes to the fore in the context of methodological debates as to the status of philosophy in a world of science.

of inquiry is temporally extended—it is not assumed to be merely existing, but is constructed as existing for a certain length of time, however short or long. Further, it would mean seeing that object as having a before-and-after, i.e., as situated in the course of time.

It is instructive to see how this might work with normativity. Something may be temporally extended in many different ways, for example as (potentially recurring) flickers or moments or as a longer process involving various distinct stages. If we treat normativity as temporally extended in the latter sense, we already begin to raise the possibility of its variability—thus, for example, normativity can come in degrees, which vary over time, whether that means being fragile early on and strengthening with time, or as burning with enthusiasm early on and waning with time. If we think of stages, we might further see aspects of normativity we might not see otherwise, e.g., contestability. Thus, at a first stage, someone might propose or signal something as unacceptable or as taboo; at a second stage, others may agree or not agree, or leave this undecided for some time; at a third stage, there may be a clash over what is to count as unacceptable or there may be tacit agreement, with silence being treated by most as acquiescence to the original proposal. The point is that if we treat our object of inquiry as temporally extended—and, once again, there is a multiplicity of ways in which that temporal extension can be modelled— then this is already theoretically generative. We no longer assume something merely exists—we now consider how it exists in time, whether it can be stretched out over time into distinct stages, or whether it comes to exist ephemerally at ad hoc moments and, if so, why.

Similarly, by creating an object of inquiry that exists in time, we do not take for granted its existence, but consider its before-and-after. What comes before normativity? What comes after it has expired? What does normativity tend to be preceded by, i.e., what collection of circumstances tends to create conditions in which it comes to be a question for a group of persons? For instance, do we ask questions about what is acceptable or not, what ought to be, after a period of violence amongst in-group members, or more when a newcomer enters an already stable world of ways of doing? How do these different 'before-s' affect the character of the normativity that arises or might arise? What might it mean to ask about the 'after-s' of normativity? How does normativity expire? How does, say, a certain set of values come to be seen by members of a group as no longer relevant or helpful, or how are norms simply forgotten? Again, the point here is to see that creating an object as existing in time generates possibilities and questions, all of which is theoretically generative.

The creation of objects in historical inquiry involves not only constructing them as existing in time, but as persisting through time and thus existing across times and places. These are, of course, compatible. Thus, one can treat normativity as (for example) a process with distinct stages, while also treating it as something that takes on a different character in different times and places. This latter task has not always been a feature of historical inquiry—for instance, some historians claim that they are providing a portrait of a particular time and place. On the model I am proposing, historical inquiry involves treating something as variable over time. To historicize is, then, to variabilize, for it is to treat something as having a history, in such a way that its character changes. This, naturally, raises the question of what about it changes and the ways in which it does so (internal variables), and what affects that (external variables). It is further important to see that the internal variables of an object of inquiry are not—in historical inquiry—its necessary and sufficient features (the features it must have to be what it is). They are merely contingent aspects of an object that are subject to change.

Thus, with respect to normativity, one of the internal variables may be the size and pool of normative forms, e.g., whether members of community speak only of values, or whether they also speak of (for instance) rules, norms, conventions, standards, and principles. This is itself a question one is likely only to ask if one treats normativity as something that changes over time. The pool of relevant possible normative forms is not something static or forever etched into some Platonic heaven. How large that pool is and what kinds of distinctions between forms in the pool are made is contingent—it changes over time. Having proposed this as an internal variable of normativity, one can then explore its external variables, i.e., the variables that affect the size and pool of normative forms. For example, it may be that the size and heterogeneity of a population is likely to affect the size and pool of normative forms. Or it may be that the presence of writing affects (slowly or rapidly?) the emergence of a greater range of normative forms—for instance, we now begin to make distinctions between so-called 'implicit norms' and 'explicit rules'.

The thought that must be resisted here is that there is some underlying, changeless concept (composed of necessary and sufficient features) that enables this kind of variability. Thus, someone might argue: but all this assumes that normativity is essentially about, say, 'oughtness'. Your very grouping of rules, norms, values, etc. has something in common which enables you to treat them as a group that can then vary across time. The problem with this is that 'oughtness' is itself a language that comes into being at a particular time and place and has no more universal standing than any other attempt to identify what is necessary or essential about normativity. In other words, to think historically is, in the negative sense, to be conscious of the historicity of any allegedly universal language, and, more positively, to variabilize all the way down. We may, of course, in the process of that inquiry treat something as paradigmatic or exemplary of the object—in the case of normativity, we may think of the rules of games or the virtues of saints—and this will help us in our variabilizing. But these associations at the level of examples do not equate to, and are also not inferior (for instance, as a beginning point of theoretical inquiry) to any more systematic analysis of an object (e.g., something that, from the beginning, distinguishes normativity from, say, habits, coercive orders, and predictions). On the contrary, beginning with a more systematic analysis already closes down what can be theorized (it takes as given or static certain distinctions, which in fact are not stable). To begin with systematic analysis may have the virtue of internal consistency, but, in the end, it is a less reflexive way of creating an object of inquiry. This does not mean a more systematic analysis cannot be a valuable part of theorizing something—it can—but there is no priority here: it is not that analysis comes first, and then an exploration of variability comes second. When, in thinking historically, we treat an object as existing in time and persisting through time, we are also creating an object of inquiry. Further, we do so by treating it as variable over time, without having necessary and sufficient conditions that guarantee its diachronic identity. Historical inquiry resists the search for or need for those kinds of guarantees—instead, it begins with loose associations of examples and then, by variabilizing, creates objects of inquiry.

Let me say more about how historical inquiry is sensitive to variability. Here, we come to the last two elements of the model, namely, to the acknowledgment of contingency and to the awareness of multiple temporalities. Both of these are key to the practice of history and to its unique epistemic virtues.

The acknowledgement of contingency in historical inquiry is best approached by what it is not. It is not a view of the past as 'one damn thing after another', i.e., the acknowledgement of contingency is at odds with a chronicle view of the past. In a sense, this involves resistance to the very talk of 'the past', and a disposition to explore the multiplicity of pasts, including awareness that one can never exhaust that multiplicity. It is an attitude to the past that finds a middle path between two extremes: 1) the over-determination of the past and 2) the under-determination of the past. To over-determine the past is to treat the past as already prefiguring the present, or a later time as already being implicit or emergent in an earlier time. It is, in short, to treat the past as not being able to have been other than it was. To under-determine the past is effectively to think that how the past occurred does not matter—that there could have been any number of ways in which the past was, but that differences between those ways do not affect our understanding of the present (or some later time). Acknowledgment of contingency steers between over-determination and under-determination, recognizing that how the past has been matters, but that there is no way it had to be. This does not necessarily mean identifying chance, accident, or coincidence (though it may sometimes); mostly, it means exploring how the past might have been—identifying the possible futures in the past. This attitude to the past comes along with a certain style of describing the past: a subjunctive style, which is attentive to what might have been, what almost occurred, what was nearby causally, what seemed possible and impossible.

If we return to our running example, if we think of normativity as something that exists in time and thus has a before-and-after, and if we add the element of contingency, we become sensitive to describing how normativity might not have emerged and what else may have been possible. Again, the benefits of this sensitivity consist in large part in avoiding over-determination and under-determination.

Thus, if one is sensitive to contingency, one will not describe the before of normativity by saying that some norm, say, was already implicit in some practice or activity, waiting only to be made explicit. To do that would be to over-determine the past—to describe an earlier time from the exclusive perspective of a later time. As a result, one will also notice, for instance, the power dynamics involved in the fragile emergence of normativity: someone, somewhere, at someplace, makes an initial judgment that something is unacceptable; that judgment may or may not be accepted by others; even if it is accepted, others may understand the object of the judgment in different ways; a lot needs to happen before a norm of sufficient interpersonal agreement comes to settle in a group of persons—and none of these things are bound to happen. In this context, to be sensitive to contingency—and to the many possible futures of an initial judgement—is to learn something about normativity, e.g., that it depends on certain power (perhaps also affective) dynamics within a group, that there is some arbitrariness to the initial judgment, and that various enabling social circumstances assist in the making of a norm. This element of the model of historical inquiry, then, is also theoretically generative.

It is important to see that acknowledgement of and sensitivity to contingency has come in many varieties in the practice of history and that there have also been times when historians have been more prone to the over-determination of the past. It would be an interesting exercise to historicize this variation in the practice of history[8]—and thus to examine why, at certain times and places, languages of 'fate' or 'destiny' come to be popular, or why various civilizational or progress-based narratives dominate, or why genres such as prophecy or the apocalypse catch on. Similarly, the acknowledgement of contingency in historical practice can take on different forms, e.g., what-if or as-if histories, counter-factuality, precisely the use of subjunctive language when describing the past, and the self-undermining of the authority of the historian. I mention this because I want to make clear that the model of historical inquiry I propose, although a somewhat ideal model, nevertheless makes room for historical variation.

The final element of the model of historical inquiry is that of awareness of the multiplicity of temporality. Again, this is a crucial part of the model, for thanks to it, we can see the history of historical practice as a rich depository of different ways of modelling time, each of which is theoretically generative in its own way.[9] I cannot describe all these possible ways here, nor give each the attention it deserves—the list below is therefore but indicative and suggestive. Here, then, are some different ways in which time has been and may be modelled for the purposes of historical inquiry:

[8] For the Victorian period and its ways of historicizing international law in this over-deterministic way, see Jennifer Pitts, 'International Law', in Mark Bevir (ed.), *Historicism and the Human Sciences in Victorian Britain* (2017).

[9] For a similar way of presenting the theoretical significance of history, see William Sewell, *Logics of History: Social Theory and Social Transformation* (2005). See also Reinhart Koselleck, *The Practice of Conceptual History: Timing History, Spacing Concepts* (2002).

1. Spatialization of time: we can think of time as linear, cyclical, or simultaneous/parallel—and, in the context of normativity, we could thus ask: what are the cycles of normativity? Do norms, in order to be efficacious, need to get renewed within the social dynamics of a group every now and then, and how does that occur? Are there parallel processes that occur alongside normativity—for instance, institutionalization?

2. Speed of time: whether variable or stable, or fast or slow, and whether accelerating or decelerating. Here, we have many languages of speed that are also quite familiar to legal theorists, e.g., gradualism and incrementalism, the use of various organic metaphors. We might then ask: what is it to think about the variable speeds of the normative? How might we compare the diffusion of conventions as distinct from values along this dimension of time? If conventions take longer to spread across a population, then what does this tell us about them? How does the spread of norms compare to, say, the spread of rumour or gossip?

3. Degree of occurrence: what happens only once, and what recurs? What needs to recur? Again, how might we map this dimension of time onto various normative forms, e.g., do reminders of norms (for instance, in the form of nudges) require a higher degree of occurrence within a community than reminders of values? Or is it the other way round: a community needs regular spectacles that remind them of what the values of the community are?

4. Direction of time: we can speak of progression or regression of processes, or processes in which there are two steps forward and one step back. Thus, we might speak of the conventionalization of some practice or discourse, but we might also speak of de-conventionalization. When does this occur and why? When does the normative space of some discourse tighten, so that the members of that discourse come to be highly judgmental and disciplined about the use of language, and when does it loosen?

5. Duration of time: do we speak of micro or macro time—of short-term actions and events or long-term processes? Do we speak of flickers of normativity or its *longue durée*? What do we learn about normativity when we experiment with different lenses of duration?

I have only mentioned a few possibilities here—one may speak, for instance, of models of time that are not easily captured along one dimension, e.g., bucolic or summer time, or emotional time (the time of regret or hope), and there are aspects of time that are not easily classifiable under any one dimension, e.g., provisionality or potentiality. Here, the languages in which we model time outstrip any analytical model of time and its dimensions—e.g., the associations that members of a culture may have with turns, ages, or moments (or, in law, with the 'time immemorial') will themselves influence both the writing and reading of history. To notice this is also to say—as above with contingency—that an interesting exercise here would be to historicize the dominance or popularity of certain ways of modelling time in historical practice in certain times and places. Thus, to give but one example, when Fernand Braudel emphasized the *longue durée* during the Nazi occupation in France, part of the reason for this may have been the desire to de-emphasize the significance of the occupation in the perspective of a longer stretch of time.

I have now articulated the various elements of the model of historical inquiry. On this model, historical inquiry is a highly reflexive mode of both creating objects of inquiry and investigating them. It is highly theoretically generative: it makes us consider aspects of what we study and how we study it that arguably no other mode of inquiry does or does not do as well. This does not mean it is incompatible with other modes, including the mode of philosophical analysis. When we think of normativity as existing in time and over time, and we do that in a way that acknowledges the contingency of the pasts of normativity, and we model the temporalities of normativity in multiple ways, we raise all kinds of questions about what to compare normativity to and how to distinguish it from those comparators. But we do more than that, for we then begin to relate and associate normativity to a wider range of phenomena, e.g., by thinking about the *longue durée* of normativity, we ask what are the factors (external variables) that affect the persistence of certain forms of normative expression over long lengths of time (e.g., in the form of maxims or sayings), and we then set up a theoretically generative relation, namely between language and memory. Historical inquiry, then, as an art of variation, generates theoretically valuable associations or relations—and it does that in a way that is irreplaceable by, but also compatible with, the art of distinction and disassociation that characterizes philosophical analysis.

III. Theorizing Law and Legal Thought Historically

Let me now briefly illustrate the value of historical inquiry for theorizing law and legal thought. What follows is not systematic, but rather suggestive—my aim is to offer some illustrations of the possibilities on offer when we theorize law and legal thought along the lines of the model of historical inquiry I have sketched above.

We can begin with law and ask: what might it mean to treat law as existing in time and across times and places in a way that acknowledges its contingency and explores it in a multiplicity of temporalities? We might contrast this with an approach that is at odds with it, e.g., H. L. A. Hart's account of the concept of law. On the face of it, it may seem that Hart's (in)famous fable of the emergence of law is a historical one, or at least pseudo-historical. After all, Hart speaks of how as a result of the 'defects' that characterize certain 'primitive communities'—i.e., uncertainty about what the rules are, inefficiency in the resolution of disputes, and the difficulty of changing the law—law emerges by 'curing' those 'defects' in the form of secondary rules, i.e., the rules of recognition, adjudication, and change, respectively. Further, at times in his *The Concept of Law* (1961), Hart cites a range of historical sources, including from both historical anthropology (via the work of Malinowski, Diamond, Llewellyn and Hoebel, Evans-Pritchard, and Gluckman) and Roman legal history (Schulz). He also occasionally makes claims like the following: 'there are many studies of primitive communities which not only claim that this possibility [of societies without secondary rules] is realised but depict in detail the life of a society where the only means of social control is that general attitude of the group towards its own standard modes of behaviour in terms of which we have characterised rules of obligation'.[10]

The problem with this approach—from the perspective of the model of historical inquiry I have proposed—is the absence of an acknowledgement of contingency. The very language used here of 'defects' and 'cures' or 'remedies', and of a former society 'lacking'[11] what a later society has, belies an attitude to the past that I have characterized as over-determined. On Hart's approach, the present (a legal system in the form of a union of primary and secondary rules) is already prefigured in the past, for the past is lacking that which the present will fill. Theorists writing after Hart—including those sympathetic to him—have recognized the historical awkwardness of Hart's account, and have sought to characterize it in a different way, biting the bullet on its a-historicism. Thus, Neil MacCormick said:

Hart's treatment of the emergence of the 'remedies' to cure the 'defects' of the pre-legal social order is thematic and schematic rather than historical. . . It is perhaps best seen as a kind of ex post facto argument. We now have criteria for 'valid law'; we now have legislatures; we now have courts and associated law-enforcement agencies. How would we fare without them? Badly indeed; for we would have to fall back on uncertain emanations of positive morality to ground our common life, our standards would freeze into a static pattern, and we would have less efficiency methods of solving disputes of right, and no method of enforcing such conclusions as we reached.[12]

MacCormick here recognizes that Hart's approach is historically problematic and he asks us to treat it as a thought experiment about the present: What if we take X, Y, and Z away? How would we, in the present, then fare? MacCormick, however, does not leave matters there and goes on to argue that 'it remains more than a pity that he [Hart] did not take more account of the history of legal institutions

---

[10] H. L. A. Hart, *The Concept of Law* (1961) 91 ff.   [11] Hart (n. 10) 291 ff.
[12] Neil MacCormick, *H. L. A. Hart* (2008) 136 ff.

in piecing together his story of the emergence of rules of recognition, change, and adjudication'.[13]

I will return in a moment to MacCormick's suggestions for how to conduct this more historical account. Let me first, however, note two other characterizations of Hart's position—ones that not only characterize it as a-historical, but that also (unlike MacCormick) defend its a-historicism. Thus, Peter Hacker has argued that Hart deploys a 'time-honoured' method—the 'genetic-analytic method'.[14] According to Hacker, this method—which he also catalogues under the banner of 'conceptual analysis'—is liable to be misinterpreted if thought of as in any way subject to empirical verification. Instead, the method asks us 'to envisage a purely notional situation in order to perceive what crucial features characterize our own complex situation, and to understand the structure of the concepts with which we describe it'.[15] History, in this view, is entirely unnecessary to conceptual analysis—in fact, it might introduce irrelevant distractions, which make it harder to see 'crucial features' or the 'structure of concepts'. More recently, John Gardner put matters this way:

Hart's story is a fable, an imaginary tale of the birth of a possible legal system. He does not care, and has no reason to care, whether this is how actual legal systems in general emerge, or whether even one legal system has ever so emerged. Nor does he care, or have reason to care, whether the 'pre-legal' conditions that he presents as obtaining at the start of the story, before law emerges, have ever obtained anywhere.[16]

History, once again, is irrelevant to this imaginary exercise. Constructing such fables is independent from historical consciousness—and rightly so, says Gardner. Elsewhere, Gardner has gone further to assert the priority of philosophy over history (and other kinds of empirical inquiry), saying that 'one must already know what counts as law before one can make either empirical or evaluative observations of it *qua* law'.[17]

But let us consider for a moment what is obscured from view—and what is taken for granted—as a result of this a-historical approach to law. I mentioned above MacCormick's lament that Hart did not take history more seriously. For MacCormick, Hart takes for granted or assumes as necessary a certain amount of formalism for the existence of secondary rules. MacCormick gives the following example:

Suppose it is against our primary social standards for anyone to use or eat a cow unless it is his own, it being understood that anyone who has had and openly used a cow for two

---

[13] Ibid.

[14] Peter Hacker, 'Hart's Philosophy of Law', in Peter Hacker, Joseph Raz (eds.), *Law, Morality, and Society: Essays in Honour of H. L. A. Hart* (1977) 11 ff.

[15] Ibid., at, 12 ff.

[16] John Gardner, 'Why Law Might Emerge: Hart's Problematic Fable', in Luis Duarte d'Almeida, James Edwards, Andrea Dolcetti (eds.), *Reading HLA Hart's The Concept of Law* (2013) 82 ff.

[17] John Gardner, *Law as a Leap of Faith* (2012) 273–4 ff.

years owns it and also its offspring, and that anyone who has been given a cow by its owner becomes in turn the owner of it. Especially where general social pressure and self-help are the only 'sanctions' behind such standards, there would be good reason for any 'giving' of a cow to be attended by public solemnities and formalities to let everyone know whose cow it now is. Otherwise the recipient may have fear of being subsequently accused of stealing it. Primitive legal ceremonies like the elaborate Roman procedure of *mancipatio* which had to be performed to transfer ownership of domesticated animals have all the look of practices descended from remote antiquity and quite probably from a time when the Latins lived 'pre-legally'. There is no reason at all to suppose that such formal requirements cannot arise by simple custom and convention hallowed by tradition and usage.[18]

MacCormick here questions the idea that primary rules must have preceded secondary rules, showing how some primary rules might in fact be dependent on certain secondary-rule-like customs. This further suggests that there need not be a deliberate, formal introduction, e.g., in writing, of a secondary rule to cure defects of primary-rule-only communities. By thinking historically, then, MacCormick opens up the question of how law is related to its expression—observing that the relationship between law and language can be contingent. Law may also be expressed in the performance of certain gestures or in communal bodily rituals. To his credit, Hart did in fact mention that his own approach to the transition from the pre-legal to the legal world could mean that a necessary distinguishable stage in that process was 'the mere reduction to writing of hitherto unwritten rule'.[19] Note, however, the difference between the two approaches: MacCormick's is more historical, for he treats law as something capable of existing across times and places, such that the expression of law becomes one of law's internal variables; Hart's, on the other, is a-historical, for he treats law as existing (in some mythical time, or out-of-time) as a union of primary and secondary rules, which leads him to make certain problematic historical assumptions, in this case that law would need to be written down first for secondary rules to emerge (after primary rules). On the MacCormick approach, we can study the variability of law's forms of expression across times and places, also identifying external variables that may affect how law is expressed, e.g., the size and heterogeneity of the population, the degree of professionalization and bureaucratization, perhaps the degree of the centralization of power, and so on.

I return briefly to the variable of law's expression below, as it is generative also for theorizing legal thought. For now, let me mention something else that is taken for granted historically by Hart's a-historicism in theorizing law. Consider the following from Brian Simpson:

To a historian, a critical stage in the evolution of a form of society governed by law as we now understand it seems to involve the development not so much of rules but of institutions, which have come to be called courts, which enjoy the power of adjudication.

---

[18] MacCormick (n. 12) 128 ff.   [19] Hart (n. 10) 95 ff.

It is out of such institutions that legislation, originally not clearly differentiated from adjudication, emerges.[20]

Simpson's observation here reminds us that, in theorizing law, we cannot take for granted the separation of powers. Further, in thinking about the history of power, we cannot assume that the institutions of power, divided or not, were deliberately and strategically established by rules first. On the contrary, the more likely sequence is for exercises of power, some more or less institutionalized, to have come first, with rules at some point entering into the story for various particular purposes, introduced by particular persons or groups at particular times. In other words, rather than beginning with an account that already assumes certain well-established distinctions—for instance, between legislation and adjudication (as Hart's secondary rules arguably do)—we must inquire into the messy, contingent history of conflicts and struggles over power (including precisely the fragile emergence of such distinctions as between law-making, law-administering, and law-applying), and think about law's relation to those conflicts and struggles.

Let me add just a little more historical detail here. We know, for instance, that the very word 'statute' does not appear in England until later in the thirteenth century.[21] Even when it does come into usage, and we can speak of officials applying them, it would be misleading to say that these are judges interpreting statutes, for, as Neil Duxbury points out, 'no real distinctions were made' at that time 'between enactment and adjudication. The king's justices were not mere officers of law but important members of his council with responsibility for drafting, or at least assisting with the drafting of, statutes.'[22] Thus, not only was there no distinction between the legislative and the adjudicative, but also the officials involved in both kinds of power were very much in the service and control of the king. Peter Cane, in his recent book on *Controlling Administrative Power: A Comparative History* (2016), puts the point very clearly:

In the period from the late 11th century to the turn of the 17th, the English system of government is aptly described as monarchical. In theory, at least, all public power resided ultimately in the Monarch, who was chief legislator, chief administrator and chief judge. The main institutions of Central government—The Council . . . Parliament and the courts—developed out of and were, in a significant sense, extensions of the group of hand-picked advisers and supporters—the Curia Regis (King's Court, the ancestor of the Privy Council)—that early Monarchs summoned as the need was felt. Membership of the various manifestations of the Curia was quite fluid. For instance, judges were active in Parliament. No sharp distinctions were drawn between legislating, administering and adjudicating. Parliament was the highest 'court' in the land; and in modern terms, much of its business was judicial rather than legislative.[23]

---

[20] Brian Simpson, *Reflections on 'The Concept of Law'* (2011) 176 ff.
[21] Neil Duxbury, *Elements of Legislation* (2012) 23 ff.   [22] Duxbury (n. 21) 23 ff.
[23] Peter Cane, *Controlling Administrative Power: A Comparative History* (2016) 25.

As Cane goes on to describe, during the seventeenth century, we see a series of conflicts and struggles over the scope of the King's power, including the well-known cases of *Prohibitions* (1607), *Proclamations* (1611), and *Bonham's case* (1610). The first two challenge 'the power of the Monarch to participate personally in the administration of justice', and establish 'the nature, scope and limits of prerogative powers'.[24] *Bonham's Case* (1610) again seeks to limit power, this time holding 'that an Act of Parliament contrary to common law would be void'.[25] Important here—in terms of challenging the power of the Monarch—are not only statements made by judges, but also the Parliament, e.g., the *Petition of Right* (1628), 'which challenged royal assertions of prerogative power to raise loans, and impose taxes and imprisonment'.[26]

Let me now return to Hart. Recall that Hart wants to say that law emerges when we have the union of primary and secondary rules, with the majority of the population obeying the primary rules and the officials accepting (in Hart's sense) the secondary rules. Hart's secondary rules are, as we all know, power-conferring rules. According to Hart, it is the introduction of these rules that is supposed to distinguish the pre-legal society from the legal. This looks plausible until it is looked at historically. When we think historically, we see that taken for granted in this picture is an already-existing class of officials and their practices (here, precisely, are the institutions before the rules) as well as divisions between powers. Taking this for granted obscures matters of theoretical significance to law, both descriptively and normatively. Descriptively, we see how law changes, and is thus affected by, changes in the structure of power relations (for instance, precisely their fact and degree of separation). We see, too, the importance of the process of professionalization, in which a certain class of persons is involved in a struggle to establish their own (relative) autonomy. Power is in many ways already being exercised, and the rules that are introduced are less about conferring power, and more about limiting it. Normatively, what is at stake is whether and how, and of course whose, power is limited. Both descriptively and normatively, then, we might inquire into the importance of power-limiting rules (or, perhaps more broadly, power-limiting practices). Further, rather than presenting this as an inevitable, progressive narrative (of law limiting power ever more successfully, or worse, finally taming power), we see the contingency and fragility of law's capacity to limit power, with law adapting (though sometimes also misadapting) to new forms of power (including of course being used by power as an instrument).

I have now given a sense of the dangers of theorizing law a-historically, as well as indicating some of the benefits of the model of historical inquiry for theorizing law. Something similar could be done for theorizing legal thought. Given constraints of space, let me simply make a few suggestions for how this might be done.

Recall that on the model I have proposed, an object of inquiry can be created by treating it as existing in time. This can be done by seeing it as temporally extended,

---

[24] Ibid., 29 ff.   [25] Ibid., 32 ff.   [26] Ibid., 30 ff.

though this temporality can be modelled in various ways. Theorizing legal thought can benefit greatly from treating its operations as temporally extended in different ways, for example, by looking over long spans of time, we can ask about the lifecycles of certain kinds of operations and expressions in legal thought, such as metaphors. If we focus only on the use of a metaphor in an instant case, we can miss both its function and its value, which often only come into view over a long period. For instance, with metaphor, part of its value is its memorability (obtained, for example, through its surprising clash of images), and another is the way it can both suggest a direction of legal change while also making room for a good deal of disagreement (for the semantic tension inherent in metaphor can be resolved in different ways by different persons on different occasions). Metaphor is a feature of legal thought that must be studied as it exists in time, not only because a metaphor will generate different kinds of cognitive resources at different times in its lifecycle or career (both of these metaphors have been popular in the literature on metaphor), but also because the use of particular metaphors is related to changes in other aspects of social life, including cultural, literary, and technological innovations.

Treating legal thought as temporally extended already suggests a broader object of inquiry than the traditional focus on the use of justifying reasons in particular cases. It might result, for instance, in modelling legal thought as a diachronic process of communicative inquiry into normative relevance, accompanied by reason-giving in resolving disputes or advising on particular occasions. This broader object will then enable both the identification, as well as investigation into the value, of a group of cognitive operations that one might not otherwise notice, e.g., precisely metaphorical communication over time, or a range of devices that enable decision-making while withholding generalization (such as, arguably, personified tests).

Historical inquiry creates object of inquiry by also sometimes treating them as persisting through time, going on to explore the internal and external variables that characterize how it changes across times and places. Such internal variables—i.e., features that one may, but need not necessarily, find in the practice of legal thought— may include the resolution of disputes, the giving of advice, the provision of reasons, communication with future courts, drawing on materials from past courts, proving and disproving of claims, interpreting social actions, events, and utterances, and so on. To these internal variables we add the external variables that may affect their character, e.g. reason-giving or interpreting may be affected by the presence and development of archival depositories and information technology,[27] by whether reasons are given orally or in writing, by the visual design of the materials,[28] by the

---

[27] See e.g., Paul Halliday, 'Authority in the Archives' (2014) 1(1) *Critical Analysis of Law* 1 ff.

[28] See e.g., Manuel Hespanha, 'Form and Content in Early Modern Legal Books' (2008) 12 *Rechtsgeschichte* 12 ff. See also Ian MacLean, *Interpretation and Meaning in the Renaissance: The Case of Law* (1992) and Nils Jansen, *The Making of Legal Authority* (2010).

architecture of the places where reasons are given, and by the emotional culture of that time and place. Each of the above internal and external variables would be approached as contingent, and thus capable of being otherwise—legal thought may not have developed reason-giving, and so it is interesting to ask when and why it does, and what other possible futures there were in times past. Similarly, each of these variables can be modelled with different temporalities, e.g., we could speak of recurring cycles of intense pressure to justify by precedent, followed by just as intense pressure to justify by policy.

I mentioned above the theoretically generative feature of variable legal expression and, particularly, the importance of the changes wrought by writing. There have, of course, been studies of the history of legal language,[29] but more could be done to theorize the impact on legal thought of continuities and discontinuities in the transition from an oral to a literate culture.[30] What survives and what does not survive in that transition—for example, how much of the language of law continues, even after the turn to writing, to be influenced by the arts of memory, e.g., some laws continue to take the form of sayings (one thinks of the maxims of equity), and legal knowledge is in many respects comprised of archetypal characters and certain genre-specific kinds of narrative.[31] What is lost and what is gained in (arguably) less emphasis on gesture or visuality as a carrier of legal meaning? The point here is simply to raise these questions, at once pointing to their theoretical generativity.

IV. CONCLUSION

Louis Mink, who contributed greatly to the question of the epistemic benefits of historical inquiry, said once that 'the historian must in act of judgement hold together in thoughts events which, by the destructiveness of time, no one could experience together'.[32] On the model of historical inquiry I have proposed, to think historically is to experiment with modelling pasts in ways that do not necessarily overlap with what is experienced. It is, further, to recover much that almost was or could have been, but was not, experienced, i.e., to return and give back to the past its possible futures. In this respect, it is quite different to other modes of inquiry,

---

[29] See e.g., Peter Goodrich, *Languages of Law* (1990) and Peter Tiersma, *Legal Language* (1999).

[30] See Jack Goody, *The Logic of Writing and the Organisation of Society* (1986), chapter 4 on 'The Letter of the Law'.

[31] Indeed, the very idea of the 'case' may be thought to be a literary form—see e.g., Andres Jolles, *Simple Forms* (2017), chapter 6.

[32] Mink (n. 3) 187.

e.g. those for which the anchor to experience matters, such as phenomenology, some traditions of sociology, and anthropology. Historical inquiry, then, is a distinct mode of inquiry, with distinct virtues and vices. But its distinctiveness need not be incompatible with other modes of inquiry, nor neither superior or inferior to them. Theory need not be thought of as a practice that has winner-takes-all stakes. What we have, instead, are modes of inquiry, which themselves shift and change over time and which carry their own benefits and dangers. To theorize, then, would be to create objects of inquiry via different modes, exploring their complexity—and to enter into dialogues between modes and their relative strengths and weaknesses. And, surely, that is the kind of engagement that complex phenomena such as normativity, law, and legal thought call for and deserve.

BIBLIOGRAPHY

Roger Cotterrell, *The Politics of Jurisprudence* (Oxford University Press, 2003)

Maksymilian Del Mar, Michael Lobban (eds.), *Legal Theory and Legal History* (Ashgate, 2014)

Maksymilian Del Mar, Michael Lobban (eds.), *Law in Theory and History: New Essays on a Neglected Dialogue* (Hart Publishing, 2016)

Sean Patrick Donlan, Lukas Heckendorn Urscheler (eds.), *Concepts of Law: Comparative, Jurisprudential and Social Science Perspectives* (Ashgate, 2014)

William Dray (ed.), *Philosophical Analysis and History* (Harper & Row, 1978)

Patrick Glenn, *Legal Traditions of the World* (Oxford University Press, 2004)

Robert Gordon, *Taming the Past: Essays on Law in History and History in Law* (Cambridge University Press, 2017)

M. J. Horowitz, 'Why is Anglo-American Jurisprudence Unhistorical?' (1977) 17 *Oxford Journal of Legal Studies* 551

Nicola Lacey, 'Jurisprudence, History and the Institutional Quality of Law' (2015) 101 *Virginia Law Review* 919

Andrew Lewis, Michael Lobban (eds.), *Law and History* (Oxford University Press, 2004)

Fernanda Pirie, *The Anthropology of Law* (Clarendon Press, 2013)

Gerald Postema, 'Jurisprudence, The Sociable Science' (2015) 101 *Virginia Law Review* 869

Gerald Postema, 'Melody and Law's Mindfulness of Time' (2004) 17(2) *Ratio Juris* 203

Richard Rorty, Quentin Skinner, J. B. Schneewind (eds.), *Philosophy in History: Essays in the Historiography of Philosophy* (Cambridge University Press, 1984)

Brian Tamanaha, *A Realistic Theory of Law* (Cambridge University Press, 2017)

Christopher Tomlins, 'After Critical Legal History: Scope, Scale, Structure' (2012) 8 *Annual Review of Law and Social Science* 31

CHAPTER 2

THE HISTORY AND HISTORICAL STANCE OF LAW AND ECONOMICS

RON HARRIS*

LAW and Economics is arguably the most influential scholarly movement in law schools in the U.S. in the last half a century. It is also the most controversial of jurisprudential movements of recent decades. How did it become so rapidly so influential? What made it so controversial from the start? Why didn't it interact with legal history? What are the prospects for future interactions? This chapter addresses these questions. It first presents the pre-1970 intellectual bedrock of the movement. The next section analyses the ways in which the formative period of the movement in Chicago, in the period 1970–1985, shaped the particular interaction between law and economics that the movement embraced—namely economic analysis of legal rules. This section also lays the foundations for understanding the a-historical stance of economic analysis of law. The next two sections survey the expansion of law and economics beyond Chicago, as it became more pluralistic and more global, and the challenges to its coherence and its viability in law schools. The chapter then backtracks in time in order to explain the static and a-historical nature of law and

* School of Law, Tel Aviv University. I would like to thank Oz Pinhas for the excellent research assistance and Oren Bar-Gill, Markus Dubber, Omri Ben-Shahar, Ariel Porat, and participants in the Berg Institute for Law and History Oxford Handbook workshop for advice and direction.

economics as these were shaped in the formative period in Chicago. Lastly, the prospects for more historical orientation, given internal challenges and external opportunities, such as the turn to empirical legal studies and the institutional turn in economics, are evaluated.

I. THE PRE-1970 PRECURSORS

Some of the most influential thinkers of the modern era, from Adam Smith and Jeremy Bentham to Karl Marx and Max Weber, studied both law and economics and explored the various intersections between the two. But none of them had direct impact on the formation of the modern Law and Economics movement (hereafter L&E in this chapter). It is debated whether its intellectual origins are in the pre-Second World War or the post-war period. Some historians suggest a peculiar connection between the L&E movement and early twentieth-century institutional economics or else 1920s and 1930s legal realism, or a combination of the two in the form of the 'first great law & economics movement'.[1] The prominent first generation L&E scholars renounce such pre-war intellectual origins.[2] They argue that the story began in Chicago in the late 1940s and 1950s and the key figures were all economists working within the neo-classical school of economics and not manifestly inspired by the older institutional school.

The Chicago School of Economics galvanized around Frank Knight, who was able to attract Milton Friedman in 1947, Fredrich Hayek in 1950, and George Stigler in 1958 to join The Economics Department at the University of Chicago. That department became the bedrock of the Chicago School of Economics that formulated more purely neoclassical, highly mathematical, anti-interventionist, and more conservative economic theory and policy recommendation than earlier economics schools.

The connections between the University of Chicago Law School and the Chicago Economists began on a personal and contingent basis. In the 1930s, the law school initiated a four-year program that intended to attract candidates without an undergraduate degree and offered as substitute introductory courses in the social sciences, including in economics. Henry Simons was the first to offer such courses, beginning in 1934, and upon his death in 1946 Aaron Director joined the law school. He taught basic price theory courses in parallel to his

[1] Herbert Hovenkamp, 'The First Great Law & Economics Movement' (1990) 42 *Stanford L.R.* 993 ff.
[2] Edmund W. Kitch, 'The Fire of Truth: A Remembrance of Law and Economics at Chicago, 1932–1970' (1983) 26 *J.L. & Econ.* 163 ff.

brother-in-law Friedman and to Walter Bloom. Director developed, with Edward Levi, Dean of the Law School (and future President of the university and U.S. Attorney General) an anti-trust course syllabus that combined legal and economic approaches and resulted in the formulation of an integrated anti-trust theory that was influenced by economic price theory and the non-interventionist stance of the Chicago School of Economics.[3] Their students included Robert Bork, Henry Manne, and Kenneth Dam. In 1958, Director founded the *Journal of Law & Economics*.

The two persons that contributed most to the expansion of economic analysis of law beyond anti-trust and taxation were Ronald Coase and Gary Becker. Coase moved from Britain to the U.S. in 1951. While a faculty member in Virginia in 1960, he published his seminal article 'The Problem of Social Cost'. He asserted that in the absence of transaction costs, parties will engage in market transactions up to the state in which the resource entitlement ends up in the hands of whoever values that resource most.[4] However, as Coase pointed out—and this is a crucial point for Coase and for the future of law and economics—transaction costs in the real world are not zero. Prohibitive transactions costs will preclude some otherwise efficient transactions, and thus in the real world, the initial allocation of legal entitlements of all sorts determines the allocation of resources, the costs of this allocation, and the performance of the economy. Interestingly, despite being an economist by training, Coase illustrated his theorem by using four nineteenth-century English common law court cases.

Coase defended his theorem successfully in a memorable seminar in Chicago in which he overcame harsh criticism by the leading economists of the time. Coase eventually convinced the Chicago economists in his view, which they initially totally dismissed, that law matters for the functioning of markets and for economic performance.[5] The presence of transaction costs, the allocation of property rights, and the nature of liability regimes should be taken into account in the fashioning of the institutions which make up the economic system.[6]

Coase published 'The Problem of Social Cost' in the third volume of the *Journal of Law & Economics*, moved to the University of Chicago Law School in 1964, and became the co-editor of the *Journal*. Coase's seminal theorem, his personal prestige, and his presence in Chicago convinced economists to support the infant

---

[3] James R. Hackney, 'Law and Neoclassical Economics: Science, Politics, and the Reconfiguration of American Tort Law Theory' (1997) 15(2) *Law & Hist. Rev.* 275 ff; Nicholas Mercuro and Steven Medema, *Economics and the Law, From Posner to Post Modernism* (Princeton University Press, 1997) 54–6 ff; Neil Duxbury, *Patterns of American Jurisprudence* (Clarendon Press, 1995).

[4] Subject to a few relatively conventional assumptions: perfect competition, full information, strict definition of property rights.

[5] Samuel Ferey, 'Law and Economics and the Coase Theorem: A View from Coase's Papers and Correspondence' (2015) 23(3) *History of Economic Ideas* 45–60 ff.

[6] Ronald Coase, 'The Problem of Social Cost' (1960) 3 *J.L. & Econ.* 1 ff.

legal field at the stage at which it was most fragile. Further, his work motivated the formation of new fields in economics, such as property rights economics and transaction costs economics, that later overlapped and interacted with law and economics. More directly, 'The Problem of Social Cost' demonstrated to lawyers how the efficiency of legal rules can be evaluated using economic criteria. Remarkably, despite being an economist, Coase's article became canonical in legal scholarship beyond L&E, as reflected in its being the most cited law review article of all time.[7]

Becker, after completing his economics doctoral dissertation in 1955 (published in 1957), extended the realm of neo-classical theory by deploying it in the analysis of non-market behaviour. His application of economic theory to the non-market setting began with the study of racial discrimination; he then proceeded to the family, and by the late 1960s, arrived at crime and punishment.[8] Becker's assumption that criminals are rational, his examination of level of crime as a matter of economic efficiency, and his policy recommendation to reduce enforcement expenditure and instead introduce harsher sanctions were subject to severe criticism by lawyers. But this criticism did not preclude the expansion of Becker's new methodological framework beyond criminal sanctions to the enforcement of all sorts of regulations. On a more profound level, Becker demonstrated the potential of applying economic theory to non-market contexts. Becker joined the University of Chicago in 1968 just as he was making academic progress and reputation. The legitimacy he and his work achieved amongst economists in Chicago paved the way to a specific version of L&E, namely, economic analysis of the law. Applying economics to the analysis of the law was part of a wider imperialistic trend among economists, spearheaded by Becker, and their followers in other social science disciplines of applying price theory to non-market legal behaviour that included, beyond law, also family decision making, criminal behaviour, the behaviour of politicians, and of state agencies.

Thus the work of Coase and Becker planted the roots of the modern incarnation of L&E in Chicago and in the neo-classical tradition. Both Coase and Becker, the intellectual founders of L&E, were economists by training and really more interested in the study of the economy than the study of legal rules. Ironically, the new field of law and economics that their work launched focused mainly on legal rules. Their own scholarly work was not within that field as later defined by Posner, and they failed to shift the field's research agenda to studying the effects of the law on the economy or the economy on the law. They provided the theoretical approach, but it was Posner that set the research agenda.

---

[7] Fred R. Shapiro and Michelle Pearse, 'The Most-Cited Law Review Articles of All Time' (2012) 110 *Michigan L.R.* 1483 ff. Though not one of the top cited.

[8] Gary Becker, *The Economics of Discrimination* (University of Chicago Press, 1957); Gary Becker, 'Crime and Punishment: An Economic Approach' (1968) 76 *J. Pol. Econ.* 169 ff.

Guido Calabresi was an untenured professor at Yale Law School when he published 'Some Thoughts on Risk Distribution and the Law of Torts' in 1961.[9] In the following decade, he developed a new economics-inspired theory of torts in a series of articles and a notable book, *The Costs of Accidents* (1970). When he embarked on his project, Calabresi did not have any affiliation with Chicago or with an economics department, or evident exposure to the groundbreaking contributions of Becker and Coase. His contribution seems to have been intellectually independent and original. Somewhat inspired by welfare economics, Calabresi criticized torts scholarship of his time. He argued that costs of injuries should be borne by the activities that caused them and reflected in the price of such activities. In order to achieve this proper pricing, liability should be imposed on the performers of these activities. When probable damages are reflected in prices, he argued, the allocation of resources will be more efficient. Otherwise, inefficient activities would be performed and resources would not be optimally allocated. He recommended imposing liability on those who could avoid damage most cheaply (the so-famously-called cheapest-cost avoiders). He believed that the proper imposition of liability would create proper incentives for the cheapest-cost avoiders and promote aggregate social welfare. He acknowledged the limits of judges and juries in evaluating avoidance costs and performing cost-benefit analysis and believed that legislation could better perform such tasks.[10]

Calabresi built on Coase's framework, moving from the issue of initial allocation of entitlements to protection of entitlements. Beyond the direct theoretical contribution, Calabresi's contributions were important in that they demonstrated the advantage of an economically informed analysis of tort law over that of traditional legal scholarship. It brought new perspectives to the ongoing debate between supporters of a negligence regime and those of a strict liability regime. Unlike Becker's and Coase's work, Calabresi's was immediately relevant for and comprehended by legal scholars.

As we have already seen about the intellectual unfolding in Chicago and shall see more strikingly when moving to Posner in the next section, Calabresi did not share the same intellectual background with the Chicago School of economic analysis of law, did not work within its price theory paradigm, had different policy recommendations, and often criticized the Chicago version of law and economics. Calabresi's scholarship shows that the Chicago School's path was not the only possible historical path to economic analysis of law.

---

[9] Guido Calabresi, 'Some Thoughts on Risk Distribution and the Law of Torts' (1961) 70(4) *The Yale L.J.* 499 ff.

[10] In a classic article co-authored with A. Douglas Melamed in 1972, 'Property Rules, Liability Rules, and Inalienability: One View of the Cathedral', Calabresi moved beyond tort law to offer a unified theory of legal entitlements and remedies. See Guido Calabresi, and A. Douglas Melamed, 'Property Rules, Liability Rules, and Inalienability: One View of the Cathedral' (1972) *Harvard L.R.* 1089 ff.

ii. The Chicago Formative Period 1970–1985

The Chicago school of economic analysis of law became the dominant approach within L&E not only because of its intellectual persuasiveness, but also because of contingencies and personal and institutional factors that marginalized the research agendas of Coase and Calabresi and followed that of Becker. I examine this period closely not only because it shaped L&E in the following decades, but also it is a key period in understanding the a-historical attitude of the movement.

Richard Posner graduated from Harvard Law School in 1962, Clerked for Justice Brennan of the U.S. Supreme Court, worked in the Federal Trade Commission and for Solicitor General Thurgood Marshall, and in 1968 took a teaching position at Stanford Law School. There he met the leading Chicago School economists Stigler and Director and in the next year, under their auspices, moved to the University of Chicago Law School. Posner was distinct from the earlier contributors to the emerging field of L&E in that he was not trained as an economist and that he had not only legal education but also significant experience in legal practice. With the publication of his *Economic Analysis of Law* in 1973 Richard Posner in fact formed and designed L&E as economic analysis of legal rules and positioned it securely in the Chicago Law School. He went beyond the earlier focus on taxation and antitrust that was led by Director and Levy and that he shared in his first scholarly years. He analysed specific legal rules, compared to the abstract analysis of Coase and Becker.[11]

Posner pronounced the jurisprudential justification of economic analysis of the law and its main normative criterion: wealth maximization. A shift from one legal rule to another is justified if the second is Kaldor-Hicks superior even if it is not Pareto superior to the first. In other words, Posner believed that the normative criterion for change should not be whether at least one party affected by the change was made better-off and no one was made worse-off. Such a requirement is impractical and would preclude most beneficial changes. It is sufficient that wealth was maximized (the pie was enlarged) in a manner that created the potential, if compensation was implemented, to make no one worse-off, while still making at least one party better-off.

The early editions of Posner's book also made a far-reaching positive claim that was backed by several examples, speculations, and intuitions that the common law had an inherent drive towards efficiency. Posner's contribution was three-pronged: (i) normative support for the methodology; (ii) an array of policy recommendations

---

[11] Ron Harris, 'The Uses of History in Law and Economics' (2003) 4(2) *Theoretical Inquiries in Law* 659 ff.

in a variety of fields of law; and (iii) a positive observation with respect to the development of the common law. The various chapters of his book analysed the basic doctrines of the core common law fields of torts, contracts, and property law using price theory. With every future edition of the book, 1977, 1986, 1992, he made inroads into additional fields of law, criminal law, constitutional law, regulation, the legal process, family law, and more. The book set out a research agenda, some would say a manifesto.

In the same year Posner established the *Journal of Legal Studies* with an intention to distinguish it from the *Journal of Law and Economics*. Though Stigler and Demsetz were invited to write the lead articles of the first issue, Posner aimed at drawing legal scholars as contributors and readers. The economist William Landes joined the University of Chicago Law School in 1974 and became a frequent co-author of Posner.

The University of Chicago Law School became the powerhouse of law and economics in the second half of the 1970s. By 1980 Chicago economic analysis of law had acquired all its familiar characteristics: reliance on the neo-classical assumption that individuals are rational maximizers; equating change in legal rules with change in relative prices; and adoption of Kaldor-Hicks efficiency ('potential Pareto efficiency', in more obscure terms) in the sense of wealth maximization as a standard of evaluation. Posner's approach to L&E marginalized and may even have prevented other potential connections between law and economics, such as the ones envisioned by Coase, for example the study of the effects of legal rules and institutions on economic growth and on the functioning of markets. Limiting the boundaries of law and economics made sense for a newly formed field, as it enabled the concentration of research resources and rapid advancement of learning on a narrow front. Moreover, law and economics was institutionalized as a discipline in law schools rather than in economics departments. This institutional home shaped the agenda. By analysing legal rules and providing prescriptions for legal reforms, law and economics scholars could participate in the major areas of discourse within legal academia. By focusing initially on the core fields of the common law they entered high profile debates and challenged centuries-old common wisdom about the desirability of specific legal rules. They could even demonstrate the power of their coherent and rigorous theory over what they perceived as the confused intuitions of other legal scholars. This further expanded their sphere of activity within the law schools. For economics departments, this was just one more sub-field of applied economics and not the most sophisticated or attractive of them.

Because Posner's work was highly visible and quite provocative in style and content, it attracted a lot of attention to economic analysis of law and harsh criticism of it. Law and economics scholars were engaged in intense normative and policy debates with critics from rival jurisprudential and doctrinal schools. These debates revolved around the imperialistic tendencies of economics, its unrealistic assumptions (e.g., of rationality), and its ideological bias in favour of efficiency considerations at the expense of distributive considerations. The general normative call of L&E was criticized primarily by legal and moral philosophers. Its positive assertions were ridiculed by legal historians. Its specific doctrinal recommendations were disapproved of by legal scholars in the respective fields. Its expansion into criminal law was rejected by criminologists and sociologists. It faced strong political and methodological opposition within the law schools in the form of the emerging Critical Legal Studies movement. Indeed, the 1970s and 1980s were a heyday of ideological and jurisprudential debates in American law schools. The criticism and debates served the field well. In this atmosphere Posner and his lawyer colleagues in Chicago were not open to Coase's calls to show interest in the economy and solidified their research agenda around the analysis of legal rules.

III. The Expansion Beyond Chicago

While Chicago was the powerhouse of economic analysis of law, developments took place elsewhere as well. Henry Manne, a 1952 graduate of the University of Chicago Law School, made a seminal contribution to the field and then became one of its apostles. His groundbreaking article, 'Mergers and the Market for Corporate Control', published in 1965, showed that mergers are not only means for advancing market monopoly, and as such should be reviewed suspiciously by anti-trust regulators. They also serve as an important device to discipline corporate controllers, mitigate agency problems, protect non-controlling shareholders, and promote general welfare. This article is credited with opening the field of corporate law to economic analysis. In that article Manne also advance Chicago School ideological positions, as it questioned the rationale for regulation and exemplified the welfare advantages of allowing the expansion of the free market for corporate control.[12]

Manne became a leading entrepreneur in the emerging field of economic analysis of law.[13] He was indispensable to the expansion of law and economics beyond Chicago at that crucial moment of mounting criticism. He organized numerous academic conferences in law and economics that were generously funded by the Liberty Fund. He began a summer Economics Institute for Law Professors in 1971. In 1974 he initiated programs for training federal judges in economics and in law and economics. He held positions at St. Louis University, the University of

---

[12] Henry G. Manne, 'Mergers and the Market for Corporate Control' (1965) 73(4) *J. Pol. Econ.* 110 ff.

[13] Henry G. Manne, 'How Law and Economics was Marketed in a Hostile World: A Very Personal History', in Francesco Parisi, Charles K. Rowley (eds.), *The Origins of Law and Economics: Essays by the Founding Fathers* (Edward Elgar, 2005) 309 ff.

Wisconsin, George Washington University, the University of Rochester, University of Miami, and Emory University, bringing the message of L&E to all these places. Upon becoming dean of the George Mason Law School in 1986, he transformed that school's curriculum and faculty to a blatant law and economics orientation.

The expansion of law and economics beyond Chicago intensified with the hiring of prominent scholars having PhDs in economics by leading law schools. Between 1977 and 1983 eight such faculty members were hired.[14] In the years 1986 to 1989 five more were hired.[15] The scholars in the field in its first two decades were predominantly white men, not an atypical trend in many disciplines in American academia of the time. The expansion was manifested also by the creation of additional journals in the field: the *International Review of Law and Economics* (1981), initially edited in England and catering for European contributors and in 1988 relocated to Berkeley, the *Journal of Law, Economics and Organization* at Yale (1985), the *American Review of Law and Economics* (1999) as the journal of ALEA, and the *Review of Law and Economics* (2005).

A key factor in the expansion of L&E beyond Chicago is the financial support of conservative charitable foundations: the Liberty Fund and later the Olin Foundation. The Liberty Fund was instrumental in pioneering the field of law and economics. A series of conferences during the 1970s and 1980s were funded by the Liberty Fund at the initiation of its founder Pierre Goodrich and academically organized by Henry Manne. In the mid-1980s the Olin Foundation, whose President was William Simon, Secretary of the Treasury in the Nixon and Ford administrations, embarked on a program of massive support for law and economics throughout the elite universities.[16] By the end of the decade, John M. Olin Programs in Law and Economics were established at the law schools of California at Berkeley, Chicago, Columbia, Duke, Georgetown, Harvard, Pennsylvania, Stanford, Toronto, Virginia, Yale, Emory, Miami, George Mason, and in the following decade, also in Cornell and Michigan. A few Olin professorships were also endowed by the Foundation, and Olin Fellowships were offered by various law schools. In 1991 the American Law and Economics Association was formed with the support of the Olin Foundation. Altogether, around $50 million were granted by the Olin Foundation (and other foundations including the Sarah Scaife and Bradley Foundations) for law- and economics-related purposes in the period between 1985 and its dissolution in 2005 (as envisioned by John Olin).[17] It was argued that the foundations made these grants

[14] Dan Rubinfeld—Michigan, Mitch Polinsky—Stanford, Steven Shavell—Harvard, Robert Cooter—Berkeley, Jeff Strand—USC, Kip Viscusi—Duke, Lewis Kornhauser—New York, Fred, McChesney—Emory. Based on Robert Cooter, 'The Mortar between Stones' (working paper) Table 2.

[15] Avery Katz—Michigan, John Donohue—Northwestern, Ian Ayres—Northwestern, Thomas Ulen—Illinois, David Hadock—Northwestern.

[16] Manne (n. 12) 309 ff.

[17] Ron Harris, 'Law and Economics', in Stanley Katz (ed.), *The Oxford International Encyclopedia of Legal History* (Oxford University Press, 2009).

as part of a wider effort to advance neo-conservative ideology and a right-wing political agenda through magazines, think-tanks, institutions, and universities.

L&E expanded beyond academia also to the judiciary. Richard Posner and one of his colleagues at Chicago, Frank Easterbrook, were appointed to the U.S. Court of Appeals for the Seventh Circuit in 1981 and 1985, respectively, and Guido Calabresi was appointed to the U.S. Court of Appeals for the Second Circuit in 1994; other law and economics adherents have also been appointed to the judiciary. A growing percentage of federal judges studied in the program, initiated by Henry Manne, for training the judiciary in law and economics. The expansion to the judiciary made an impact on court decisions and on the actual development of the common law. It also made an impact on the legal profession, as litigating attorneys had to be able to understand the opinions of Posner, Easterbrook, Calabresi, and their likes and had to be able to argue effectively in their courtrooms.

The granting philanthropic foundations were able to advance law and economics programs at the expense of competing movements at law schools but were not able to fully dictate the methodological or ideological content of such programs. Scholars outside Chicago were not as committed to the dogmas of neoclassical economics or to the Posnerian coupling of the normative, positive, and policy facets of economic analysis of the law. They were more open to influences from other quarters of economics—including some that were initially considered heterodoxies by the Chicago School of Economics—and much of the change in law and economics in the late 1980s and 1990s resulted from advances and trends in economics. I will refer here to three of the most influential trends: public choice, game theory, and behavioural economics.

Public choice economics, developed by Arrow, Buchanan, Downs, Olson, and others in the 1950s to the 1970s, used economic theory in order to study group decision making, the functioning of political organizations, voting, interest groups, rent-seeking behaviour, and other related issues. Law and economics scholars used these tools to go beyond the common law into legislation and regulation. Game theory was originally developed in mathematics and used in economics to study interactions between rational individuals and the cooperation, conflicts, and strategic behaviour that result from these interactions. Nash, Selten, and Harsanyi won the Nobel for their contribution to the field in 1994, and Schelling and Aumann in 2005. Game theory enabled L&E scholars to analyze interactions in contractual negotiation and litigation. Tversky and Kahneman constructed bridges between behavioural psychology and economics in the 1970s and 1980s. These led to the emergence of the burgeoning field of behavioural economics that questioned and revised the assumption of full rationality and substituted it with bounded rationality and integrated prospect theory, cognitive biases, and heuristics into the analyses. By the 1990s the trend reached L&E in the form of behavioural law and economics. The behavioural scholarship in economics and in L&E increasingly uses experimental research methods.

Members of this 'younger generation' of law and economics scholars that used public choice, game theory, and behavioural economics reached policy recommendations that were often in conflict with those of Posner and his colleagues at Chicago. Interest in distributive consequences increased. L&E became less coherent in its agenda, methodology, institutional affiliations, and politics. One can find anti-interventionist recommendations together with pro-interventionist calls and agnostic-scientific analysis. More scholars began to view their approach as nonexclusive, as one that could or even should be accompanied by non-economic considerations.

The field of L&E has expanded beyond the U.S. from the 1980s. A European Law and Economics Association was founded in 1984, a Latin American and Caribbean Law and Economics Association in 1995, and an Asian Law and Economics Association in 2005. Country level associations were established in Australia, Brazil, Canada, Finland, Greece, Israel, Italy, Japan, Korea, Mexico, New Zealand, and Scandinavia. Centres for L&E were created in as distant places as the University of Amsterdam and Gujarat National Law University in India, the Max Planck Institute for Research on Collective Goods in Bonn, and the Summer School in Law and Economics for Chinese faculty members held in Chicago. The research agendas, the promotion and pay incentives, and the encounters with economics outside the U.S. were often influenced by domestic concerns, institutions, and ideologies, and thus different from the Chicago paradigm.[18]

iv. Into the Twenty-First Century

A good way to identify developments in the field of L&E in the twenty-first century is through short essays written by ten eminent University of Chicago Law School scholars on the future of the field. Indeed, this is a view from Chicago, and not elsewhere, and is based on observations made in 2011, and not earlier or later. But this virtual roundtable offers a plurality of opinions by very active players in different sub-fields with different backgrounds and ages. Two repeated and related observations are that the field is becoming more formal, technical, and mathematical and that the field is experiencing a split between lawyers and economists. One version is that while in its early years at Chicago the field established itself in law schools, and in recent years economics departments in the U.S. are also willing to entertain it (in Europe

---

[18] Oren Gazal-Ayal, 'Economic Analysis of Law & (and) Economics' (2006) 35 *Capital University L.R.* 787 ff; Thomas S. Ulen, and Nuno Garoupa, 'The Market for Legal Innovation: Law and Economics in Europe and the United States' (2008) 59 *Alabama L.R.* 1555–6 ff.

such a willingness was present from the start). Another is that law schools are hiring economics PhDs in growing numbers. Recent studies report that as many as 48 per cent of the new hires in top US law schools in 2011–2015 and 67 per cent in 2014–2015 had PhDs and as many as 25–30 per cent of the PhD hires were of economics PhDs.[19] Now the question is to what extent do these economists turn L&E into a sub-field of applied economics that shares theoretical and methodological tools with economics and converse with the other subfields of applied economics? To what extent do lawyers that are not fully trained in economics and are using economic analysis more intuitively feel that they are irrelevant for the field and desert it? And does L&E remain an active field in both law schools and economics departments? After all, for a split to occur, lawyers have to stay in the L&E business. In that event a split can occur not only on the level of methodology and research agenda but also on the level of journals, conferences, and the like.

As we have seen, Chicago L&E scholars claimed to be interested not only in legal rules but also in how legal incentives affect individuals' behaviour. However, their research did not focus on studying the behaviour of individuals, and the behaviour of societies, basic social structures, and trends was entirely beyond the scope of their research agenda. The behaviour of individuals was assumed to be affected by changes in legal rules that altered individual incentives. Law and economics aimed at changing behaviour but, in fact, studied rules and their change. As its other name, economic analysis of the law, implies, it mainly aspired to normatively evaluate legal rules and prescribe their modification.

Over the last two decades empirical legal studies became a burgeoning field, with economists, political scientists, sociologists, psychologists, and lawyers trained in these disciplines as the leading researchers. The availability of Big Data, computational resources, and skilled scholars contributed their share to the meteoric rise of empirical legal studies. The rise was enhanced by the establishment of journals and an association. Law and economics became much more empirical as well. This is partly a result of the hiring of empirically trained economists by law schools. The empirical preoccupation is reflected in the change in article composition of the leading L&E journals in recent decades.

Now it will be interesting to see to what extent will empirical L&E follow the footsteps of other empirical fields in the discipline of economics, using similar econometric tools and talking to other economists. Or alternatively, will empirical scholars in the field collaborate with lawyers, psychologists, and political scientists in law schools and be active within empirical legal studies institutional frameworks and blur the lines between empirical L&E and other empirical approaches in law schools that deal with similar topics, ranging from

---

[19] Lynn M. LoPucki, 'Dawn of the Discipline-Based Law Faculty' (2016) 65(3) *J. Legal Educ.* 506 ff; Joni Hersch, W. Kip Viscusi, 'Law and Economics as a Pillar of Legal Education' (2012) 8(2) *Rev. L. & Econ.* 487 ff.

the impact of law on medical malpractice, to crime, to judicial behaviour, and to board decision-making.

v. The A-Historical Nature of L&E

Law & Economics was shaped as an a-historical field for three main reasons: (i) the a-historical nature of economic theory in the 1950s and 1960s; (ii) the focus of the field on the analysis of legal rules to the exclusion of the study of economic performance; and (iii) the failed endeavour at arguing for the common law's drive to efficiency.

For economics, the 1950s was a decade of high theory. It was one of markets, allocation, and equilibrium; of abstraction and deduction; of analysis of marginal utilities and costs and incremental change; and of optimization and mathematization. It was one in which the basic assumptions of neo-classical theory still held strong. This decade was a low point in economic theory in terms of interest in history and change over real time. Theory was mainly static, not dynamic. Change over time was neglected or discussed as a shift from time t^0 to time t^1 with no real reference to the measurements units, the time dimension, and the historical process. There was also a perception that the past of any given economic state had no bearing on its present and certainly not on its future. Since any given current regime of functions, allocations, and equilibria is not burdened by its past, it can serve as a good starting point for future predictions. Imagining change over time was confined to the two-dimensional classroom blackboard curves and left real history out of the analysis.

This static state of economic theory was applied in the late 1960s and early 1970s by Richard Posner and his colleagues at the University of Chicago Law School to the analysis of legal rules. Well into the 1980s and beyond, L&E was still engaged in the static application of price theory to the specific contours of the law. Theory thus hindered the development of dynamic analysis and contributed to the a-historical nature of law and economics. The a-historical, neoclassical characteristics of law and economics dominated the field.

Three potential outcomes of the interaction between the disciplines of economics and law appeared around 1960: (i) the study of the effects of law on the economy; (ii) the study of the effects of the economy on legal change; and (iii) the application of economic methodology to the analysis of law (assuming that law has no methodology of its own to contribute to the study of economics). The Chicago School of Law and Economics as defined by Posner in the formative 1970s advanced primarily the third and least historical of these possible research agendas. The first and second agendas, the study of the effect of law on economic change or vice versa, deal with change over time, economic and legal development, aggregate social inequality, and historical causation. They could lead to more historical L&E. The narrow research agenda of L&E as economic analysis of legal rules as it was shaped by Posner and the Chicago School enhanced its a-historical nature and its lack of interaction with legal history. Both Coase and Becker, who provided the theoretical tools of law and economics and legitimized it in the discipline of economics, were economists by training and much more interested in the study of economic performance than legal rules. Coase reiterated on various occasions that he was interested in the part of L&E that used economics to analyse the law. Coase was disappointed by his failure to shift the field's research agenda to studying the effects of the law on the economy or the economy on the law.[20] Coase's failure was also the failure of more historical L&E.

As early as the very first edition of his book *Economic Analysis of Law*, Posner added to his normative jurisprudence and to his economic analysis of specific legal rules a thesis that common law exhibits a tendency towards efficiency. His positive theory was that the logic of common law litigation and judicial decision making leads to decisions that promote economic efficiency by the systematic upholding of precedents that promote efficiency and the overruling of decisions that don't. Over time, case-based common law will develop towards growing efficiency. The normative implication is that regulators and legislators should not intervene in the functioning of the common law because this will drive law away from efficiency and often tilt it in the service of vested interests. He illustrated and supported his positive theory based on a few stylized historical examples from nineteenth-century America, including: enterprise liability for faulty products; industrial accidents; railroad-crossing accidents; damage caused by train engine sparks; and the impossibility doctrine in contracts. It is interesting to note that Posner's positive theory was not directly based on economic theory. It was based on Hayek's libertarian ideology and predisposition towards the decentralized admiration of the common law and on the general notion that judges must maximize a utility of some sort.[21]

Posner's theory of the logic of development of common law was too deterministic and simplistic for most legal historians. It is not surprising that several legal historians, in response to this challenge, criticized Posner for misunderstanding

[20] For the debates about the proper agenda of L&E see Richard Posner, 'The New Institutional Economics Meets Law and Economics' (1993) 149 *J. Institutional and Theoretical Econ.* 73 ff; Kenneth Scott, 'The New Institutional Economics Meets Law and Economics: Comment' (1993) 149 *J. Institutional and Theoretical Econ.* 92 ff; Ronald Coase, 'Coase on Posner on Coase' (1993) 149 *J. Institutional and Theoretical Econ.* 96 ff; Oliver E. Williamson, 'Transaction Cost Economics Meets Posnerian Law and Economics' (1993) 149 *J. Institutional and Theoretical Econ.* 99 ff; Richard Posner, *Overcoming Law* (1995) 426 ff.

[21] For alternative economically based theories see George Priest, 'The Common Law Process and the Selection of Efficient Rules' (1977) 6 *J. Legal Stud.* 65 ff; Paul Rubin, 'Why Is the Common Law Efficient?' (1977) 6 *J. Legal Stud.* 51 ff.

the history of legal doctrines and their social and economic effects. They criticized him for cherry-picking examples that supported and refined his efficiency thesis. They downplayed the value of Posner's historical scholarship because it avoided archival historical research and was based on a selective free ride of the secondary legal history literature. In each of the editions of *Economic Analysis of Law*, Posner's discussion of the positive theory of common law's tendency towards efficiency grew in length.[22] The prolongation of the sections on common law's tendency towards efficiency were not the result of more historical studies conducted to test and potentially rebut the efficiency theory. Rather, greater space was devoted to criticizing legal historians for not understanding economic theory. Legal historians became more critical of Posner, and Posner became more critical of legal historians, particularly those critical legal historians who viewed the law as subsidizing business, redistributing wealth, and oppressing the weak. The debate about the efficiency of the common law destroyed the reputation of law and economics historical studies in the eyes of legal historians—quite a bad start for a shift towards history in law and economics, specifically, and for any empirical and comparative studies in general. This weak start at positive research, coupled with the a-historical nature of economic theory and the research agenda that was confined to analysis of legal rules, further removed law and economics scholars from engaging in historical research.

vi. Prospects for Historical L&E

In 2003 I recognized nascent inclination towards resort to history in the L&E literature. I offered a typology, based on five types of resort to history.[23] The first is the literature that supported, criticized, and refined Posner's thesis of the common law's tendency towards efficiency. The second is the resort to historical examples in order to illustrate a theory. This includes the examples of the English commons, the ownership of a lighthouse, beaver hunting rights, the acquisition of Fisher Body by General Motors, and more. The third is the use of the past as a laboratory for testing economic theory. The fourth is a public choice analysis that aims at uncovering the origins and intents of legislation. The fifth and related type is aimed at understanding how we ended up at the present state of law. The sixth and last is scholars of social

---

[22] Richard Posner, *Economic Analysis of Law* (Little Brown, 1st edn., 1972) 98–102 ff; Richard Posner, *Economic Analysis of Law* (Little Brown, 2nd edn., 1977) 179–85 ff; Richard Posner, *Economic Analysis of Law* (Little Brown, 3d edn., 1986) 229–38 ff.

[23] Harris, (2003) 4(2) *Theoretical Inquiries in Law* 659 ff.

norms that wanted to study them in pre-state and pre-modern contexts in which they could evolve organically.

A decade later Dan Klerman was able to report that economic analysis of legal history is a sprawling field. He offered a somewhat different five genres typology.[24] Law as a dependent variable explains why societies have the laws they have and why laws change over time. Law as an independent variable explains how law affects human behaviour and economic performance. The third genre holds the causal relationship between law and society/economy as bi-directional and interactional. The fourth deals with private ordering and social norms. The fifth focuses on litigation and contracts, namely not on legal rules but rather on legal behaviour in the shadow of the legal rules.

I would like to explore here the prospects for a more meaningful future integration of history into L&E in three arenas: (i) the history of capitalism, (ii) empirical legal studies, and (iii) institutional economics. Historians were pushed out of economic history by the cliometric revolution of the 1960s. Economists took over the field asserting that without the all-powerful theoretical and econometric tools they were trained in, a historian cannot really research and understand economic history. Economists also took over the journals, associations, positions, and the training of the young generation of economic historians. In the departments of history, Marxist history, social history, and annals school history were in decline by the 1970s. Cultural history, history of identities, and histories inspired by post-structuralism were on the rise. The subprime mortgage crisis of 2007–2010 was a wakeup call for historians that they cannot neglect materialistic history, the history of the economy, or of economics as a discipline. The result was that a few historians began studying and teaching these issues and were at the right time and place to attract huge crowds of students, and by 2013 these new beginnings were enthusiastically named the new history of capitalism.[25] Programs for the study of capitalism were established at Harvard and Cornell, and a new monograph series was launched by Columbia University Press.

Does history of capitalism offer better opportunities for meeting places of L&E scholars with history? Its leading historians say that unlike the historians of the previous generation they are interested in capitalist entrepreneurs and executives, in business corporations and financial institutions, and in economics. So is there place for optimism? The recent literature fashionably labelled history of capitalism can be

---

[24] Daniel Klerman, 'Economics of Legal History', in Francesco Parisi (ed.), *Oxford Handbook of Law and Economics* (Oxford University Press, 2017) ff.

[25] Jennifer Schuessler, *In History Departments, It's Up With Capitalism*, The New York Times (6 April 2013), <http://www.nytimes.com/2013/04/07/education/in-history-departments-its-up-with-capitalism.html>. See also Jeremy Adelman, Jonathan Levy, *The Fall And Rise Of Economic History*, The *Chronicle Of Higher Education* (1 December 2014), <http://www.chronicle.com/article/The-FallRise-of-Economic/150247>; Louis Hyman, *Why Write the History of Capitalism?*, Symposium Magazine, (8 July 2013), <http://www.symposium-magazine.com/why-write-the-history-of-capitalism-louis-hyman>.

classified into at least three categories. As it is still in a dynamic and burgeoning stage, a time perspective may offer more categories or different classificatory schemes—(i) one category examines standard economic history topics from a critical perspective that looks for exploitation, oppression, and inequality; (ii) another category is that of critical study of the history of economic ideas and their diffusion; (iii) and the third category deals with issues that are taken by economists as given as exogenous, that are blind spots for economists, such as the shaping of tastes, fashions, and preferences, the attitude towards risk taking, and the attitude towards speculation and fraud.[26]

A few endeavours were made to connect the history of capitalism to law. Ajay Mehrotra published a programmatic essay suggesting ways for bridging between intellectual legal history and the history of capitalism, demonstrating this on the history of tax law and policy.[27] Christine Desan and Roy Kreitner wrote a political and constitutional history of money.[28] The American Bar Foundation recently organized a conference on 'Law in the History of Capitalism'.[29] The intellectual history of economic analysis of capitalism is only beginning to be written and this direction is promising. But the conversation between the history of capitalism and economic history is still at the stage of ignoring each other and passing by each other.[30] And the conversation between the history of capitalism and economic analysis of law is still two steps removed and unlikely to develop anytime soon.

As we have seen, economic analysis of law became more empirical over the last two decades. Empirical legal studies were possibly the fastest growing field within the discipline of law over the same two decades. The two trends may intermesh. Now, the open question is to what extent will this empirical turn express itself in historical research. No doubt it will. But will it just use historical data for the sake of presentism, or will it show interest in history for the sake of history or in an attempt to study change over time as such? Will L&E scholars overcome the trauma of the failed attempt to assert the common law's tendency towards efficiency and redevelop theories of legal change? I am somewhat sceptical.[31] It devotes much more energy these days to experimental empirics than to purely historical ones.

---

[26] 'Interchange: The History of Capitalism' (2014) 101(2) *The Journal of American History* September 503 ff.

[27] Ajay K. Mehrotra, 'A Bridge Between: Law and the New Intellectual Histories of Capitalism' (2016) 64 *Buffalo L.R.* 1 ff.

[28] Christine Desan, *Making Money Coin, Currency, and the Coming of Capitalism* (Oxford University Press, 2014); Roy Kreitner, 'Legal History of Money' (2012) 8 *Annual Review of Law and Social Science* 415 ff; Roy Kreitner, 'Money in the 1890s: The Circulation of Politics, Economics and Law' (2011) 1 *U.C. Irvine L.R.* 975 ff.

[29] <http://www.americanbarfoundation.org/events/571>.

[30] Eric Hilt, 'Economic History, Historical Analysis, and the "New History of Capitalism"' (2017) 77(2) *The Journal of Economic History* 1 ff.

[31] Gillian Hadfield, *Rules for a Flat World: Why Humans Invented Law and How to Reinvent It for a Complex Global Economy* (Oxford University Press, 2016) offers an alternative thesis to Posner's that stresses law's non-responsiveness to changes.

Generally speaking historical research does not yield itself to experimental research as its actors are often long dead and they and their generational counterparts cannot take part in experiments. Will legal history become more empirical beyond the sense in which every historical research is empirical? As Klerman has shown, so far it did not display real inclination towards quantitative and statistical analysis.[32] So empirical studies in L&E are generally speaking not interested in historical questions as such and in the dynamics of change over time, and legal history is not interested in statistically based empirical studies.[33]

I see more prospects in institutional economics as a bridge between L&E and legal history. As we saw, the field of economic history was taken over by economists, at the expense of historians, in the clinometric revolution of the 1960s. These economists soon realized that economic theory of the time that was dominated by the static price theory constrained their ability to utilize theory when studying historical dynamics.[34] The critique from within on the exclusive reliance on price theory came primarily from Douglass North and the consolidating historical new institutional economics school. This school aimed to bring history and time back into economic theory. It aimed at the integration of history into economic theory by emphasizing the explanation of change as a core task of the theory, by allowing for historical contingencies, and by exposing the ways in which the past is relevant to an understanding of the present. North was also among those that asserted that institutions are crucial for economic development. The institutional turn received symbolic recognition and impetus by the award of the Nobel Prize in Economics to Coase in 1991, Becker in 1992, and Douglass North in 1993.[35] Institutional economics became more attractive to young economists. Economics departments and business schools were willing now to hire economists working in this field. Economists advanced a research agenda that studied institutions of all sorts, viewing the market as only one end of a continuum of institutions whose other end is the state. The market was now viewed as a historically-created institution, not a state of nature. Great attention was paid to legal and enforcement institutions and their historical development. Institutional economists aimed at treating institutions as endogenous, not exogenous, in their models of change; that is, they tried to explain them, not to take them as given.[36]

---

[32] Dan Klerman, 'Quantitative Legal History', in Markus Dubber, Christopher Tomlins (eds.), *Oxford Handbook of Legal History* (2018).

[33] For an exception that proves the rules see Giuseppe Dari-Mattiacci (ed.), *Roman Law and Economics* (Forthcoming).

[34] Ron Harris, 'The Encounters of Economic History and Legal History' (2003) 21(2) *Law & Hist. Rev.* 297 ff.

[35] Others associated with the field were Nobel laureates in later years: Elinor Ostrom and Oliver Williamson in 2009, Oliver Hart and Bengt Holmström in 2016.

[36] Douglass C. North, *Structure and Change in Economic History* (Norton, 1981); Douglass C. North, *Institutions, Institutional hange and Economic Performance* (Cambridge University Press,

A good opportunity for the move that combined history and institutions was created with the 1993 awarding of the Nobel Prize to two of the dominant figures in the cliometric revolution and in the practice of economic history in the four decades that followed—Robert Fogel and Douglass North. The dynamic and institutional trends in economic history enhanced each other and the historical new institutional economics school as the one offering the greatest potential for interaction with legal history within the discipline of economics, more than law and economics.

vii. Conclusion

The methodology, normative stance, and research agenda of L&E resulted from both internal disciplinary dynamics and external ideological and political influences. The field was shaped particularly as Economic Analysis of Law out of historically well recorded and traceable contingent and personal interactions between economists and lawyers in the University of Chicago in the 1950s and 1960s. The effects of the wider historical context of the cold war, the rise of free market economic policy, and libertarian ideology on the shaping of L&E cannot be traced as easily. This intellectual history is awaiting more research by historians. These factors impacted the nascent field in its formative period in the 1970s and moulded the field for decades to come as a field that is focused on legal rules and not on economic performance or on historical change. In the following decades L&E became much more pluralistic and diverse. This might explain its successful expansion beyond Chicago and beyond the U.S. This expansion also created unresolved tensions that threaten to split the field between economists and lawyers or between policy-oriented scholarship and empirical scholarship. What to some is a crisis is an opportunity for others. The a-historical nature of the theory and a-historical research agenda of the field from its inception still holds strong. But now there are prospects for change due to the empirical turn and to the possible interaction with more historically oriented scholarly fields.

1990); Thrainn Eggertsson, *Economic Behavior and Institutions* (Cambridge University Press, 1990); Avner Greif, 'Micro Theory and Recent Development in the Study of Economic Institutions through Economic History', in David M. Kreps, Kenneth F. Wallis (eds.), *Advances in Economics and Econometrics: Theory and Application* (Cambridge University Press, 1997), 79 ff; Symposium, 'The New Institutional Approach to Economic History' (1989) 145 *J. of Institutional and Theoretical Econ.* ff; Avner Greif, *Institutions and the Path to the Modern Economy: Lessons from Medieval Trade* (Cambridge University Press, 2006).

Bibliography

Neil Duxbury, *Patterns of American Jurisprudence* (Clarendon Press, 1995)

Oren Gazal-Ayal, 'Economic Analysis of Law & (and) Economics' (2006) 35 *Capital University L.R.* 787

James R. Hackney, 'Law and Neoclassical Economics: Science, Politics, and the Reconfiguration of American Tort Law Theory' (1997) 15(2) *Law & Hist. Rev.* 275

Ron Harris, 'The Uses of History in Law and Economics' (2003) 4(2) *Theoretical Inquiries in Law* 659

Ron Harris, 'The Encounters of Economic History and Legal History' (2003) 21(2) *Law & Hist. Rev.* 297

Joni Hersch, W. Kip Viscusi, 'Law and Economics as a Pillar of Legal Education' (2012) 8(2) *Rev. L. & Econ.* 487

Herbert Hovenkamp, 'The First Great Law & Economics Movement' (1990) 42 *Stanford L.R.* 993

Edmund W. Kitch, 'The Fire of Truth: A Remembrance of Law and Economics at Chicago, 1932–1970' (1983) 26 *J.L. & Econ.* 163

Daniel Klerman, 'Economics of Legal History', in Parisi, Francesco (ed.), *Oxford Handbook of Law and Economics* (Oxford University Press, 2017)

Henry G. Manne, 'How Law and Economics was Marketed in a Hostile World: A Very Personal History', in Francesco Parisi, Charles K. Rowley (eds.), *The Origins of Law and Economics: Essays by the Founding Fathers* (Edward Elgar, 2005)

Nicholas Mercuro, Steven Medema, *Economics and the Law, From Posner to Post Modernism* (Princeton University Press, 1997)

Thomas S. Ulen, Nuno Garoupa, 'The Market for Legal Innovation: Law and Economics in Europe and the United States' (2008) 59 *Alabama L.R.* 1555

CHAPTER 3

CRITICAL HISTORIES OF COMPARATIVE LAW

GÜNTER FRANKENBERG

I. INTRODUCTION

COMPARATIVE law has a history of oscillating between marginalization and megalomania—a movement that resonates, on the part of its protagonists, in a minority complex and delusions of grandeur.[1] The tensile counter-pull exerted by the two poles and the unstable self-image it creates points to a disciplinary unease that hides behind a peculiar mindset characterized by 'the innocence of method'.[2] Critique and critical approaches might work as a therapy.

A. The Birth of Comparative Law as a Discipline

Disciplines lend protection: they cover up the historically contingent way in which various ideas and practices are gathered and ordered into fields of study and research and then essentialized as philosophy, medicine, or law. More

---

[1] In this chapter I draw on Günter Frankenberg, *Comparative Law as Critique* (2016) and 'Critical Comparisons: Re-Thinking Comparative Law' (1985) 26 *Harvard I.L.J.* 411 ff.

[2] Frankenberg, *Comparative Law as Critique* (n. 1) ch. 1.

importantly, only disciplines, as institutionalized formations, are recognized as legitimately arranging the procedures and communication for the production of knowledge in ways that lend themselves to be qualified as truth. As such, they may become the basis of funding, reputation, and power;[3] they generate jobs, influence, and prestige; they mastermind the way that knowledge is produced and how the information for study, research, and education is processed by establishing schemes of perception, concepts of interpretation, and criteria of relevance.

Methods and explanatory theories are essential disciplinary tools to elucidate 'normal science' (Thomas Kuhn) and reproduce scientific standards as well as the accepted conventions of an epistemic community. Jointly, methods and theories guide scientific analysis of a discrete subject-matter or field of thought, like law or, for that matter, comparative law. In addition, they usually provide both scholarship and (university) education, based on and structured by a curriculum, with a disciplinary orientation ascertaining the reproduction of knowledge within a given domain, and sustain the fantasy of disciplinary unity.

Boundary-work is a prerequisite of disciplinary activity: it ascertains that the scientific practice in a bounded field is performed by professionals and, more so, specialists. Moreover, it helps establish a disciplinary identity—comparative law—and distinguish intra- from interdisciplinary work. The identity lends itself to creating over time an orthodoxy or mainstream that defines and monitors the accepted standards of normal science. Their serial appearance and dominance are discussed below.

The birth of Comparative Law as a discipline can be located quite exactly: it happened in Paris in the year of 1900. Whoever invokes the venerable tradition of the discipline may enlist Aristotle as one of its founders, distinguish Montesquieu's *Spirit of the Laws* as one of its founding documents, and praise Henry Sumner Maine and Max Weber as comparative law's heroes of the nineteenth century. And there were others who maintained a practice in comparative legal studies. Yet, it took the *Congrès International de Droit Comparé* in Paris to raise comparative law above the level of singular, disparate, albeit remarkable studies and treatises to a collective, concerted venture[4] guided by theories, methods, and projects. Before 1900 there was little interest in systematic legal comparison, notably the jurisprudence of natural law, conceptual jurisprudence, and the nationalist

---

[3] Michel Foucault, *The Order of Things: An Archeology of the Human Sciences* (Tavistock: Routledge, 1970).

[4] For an account of the different schools and orientations, see Édouard Lambert, 'Conception générale et définition de la science du droit comparé, sa méthode, son histoire; le droit comparé et l'enseignement du droit', in Konrad Zweigert, H. J. Puttfarken (eds.), *Rechtsvergleichung* (1978) 30 ff. See also Ralf Michaels, 'Im Westen nichts Neues?' 100 Jahre Pariser Kongreß für Rechtsvergleichung— Gedanken einer Jubiläumskonferenz in New Orleans' (2002) 66 *RabelsZ* 97 ff.

frame of mind that drew inspiration from codifications could rarely be enticed to embark upon comparative studies.

The Congress privileged a scientific approach to foreign laws that included an intense occupation with the foundations of legal comparison. It was dominated by the motivation of the French organizers, Raymond Saleilles and Édouard Lambert, to overcome the sterile 'école de l'exégèse' and direct the epistemic community towards new horizons—the 'droit commun de l'humanité' (Saleilles) and the 'droit commun de l'humanité civilisée' (Lambert). By contrast, the German faction led by the immensely productive Josef Kohler tended to be more inspired by Herder's and Hegel's philosophy of history and, assuming that different legal cultures follow the same pattern of development, therefore reached out to a 'Weltrecht' (world law). After the Paris Congress these traditions disembogued into the delta of attempts to recapture the pre-modern and early modern concepts of universal jurisprudence and to re-imagine them as updated scientific frameworks for a universal jurisprudence of comparative law.

B. Cinderella as Queen

Comparative law was marked, in the Western comparative community, by a significant inferiority syndrome. Comparatists felt neither adequately recognized by their academic peers nor sufficiently represented in the law school curriculum. Comparative law, some argued, enjoyed little prestige in the inner circles of the academy, was regarded as peripheral,[5] their field of research and study in search of an audience—in short the 'Cinderella of the legal sciences'.[6]

Over the years, the Cinderella complex[7] has become more knotty and perplexing. More recently, the discipline was said to have moved swiftly 'from a long infancy to teenage maturity' and now has to cope with the problems of 'a healthy adolescence'.[8] Today, Cinderella-in-the-attic has been replaced by royalties. The (changing) reality of curricular marginality and comparative law's growing popularity appears

[5] See Harold Gutteridge, *Comparative Law* (1949); James Gordley, 'Comparative Law in the United States Today: Distinctiveness, Quality, and Tradition' (1998) 46 *American Journal of Comparative Law* 607 ff.

[6] Gutteridge (n. 5) 26. An 'atmosphere of hostility [. . .] at best the chilly environment of indifference' was reported by Pierre Lepaulle, 'The Function of Comparative Law' (1922) 35 *Harvard L.R.* 838 ff. The more recent development is analysed by Mathias Reimann, 'The Progress and Failure of Comparative law in the Second Half of the Twentieth Century' (2002) 50 *American Journal of Comparative Law* 671 ff.

[7] Regarding the complex, see Frankenberg 'Critical Comparisons' (n. 1) 416 ff.

[8] Alan M. Watson, *Legal Transplants: An Approach to Comparative Law* (Scottish Academic Press, 1974).

to nourish fantasies of liberation and, ultimately, the hope for the well-deserved invitation as princess to the academic dance or to the coronation of Queen of the legal sciences.

The queen of the legal sciences brings to mind the spirit of naïve enthusiasm (or lack of awareness of the intricacies of comparative research) that led comparatists to embrace the *méthode Montesquieu* featuring the *highest* possible standard for the *widest* scope and *most complex* complexity of their task and committing them to an endless search for phenomena related to law:

The student of the problems of law must encompass *the law of the whole world, past and present*, and *everything that affects the law*, such as geography, climate and race, developments and events, shaping the course of a country's history—war, revolution, colonization, subjugation—religion and ethics, the ambition and creativity of individuals, the needs of production and consumption.[9]

In the same vein, the still-leading textbook commands, albeit with too much of a vengeance: '[N]o study deserves the name of a science if it limits itself to phenomena arising within national boundaries. For a long time lawyers were content to be insular in this sense, and to some extent they are so still. But such a position is untenable, and comparative law offers the *only* way by which law can become international and consequently a *science*.'[10]

Despite the porous boundaries demarcating the subject-matter and the methodological problems, comparatists no longer appear as 'intellectual nomads',[11] bereft of a genuine field of research. Many would indeed subscribe to the conclusion 'that comparative law has developed into a respectable body of actual knowledge'.[12] Moreover, the typical genres of literature covering fields of research, their genealogy and tools—encyclopaedias, handbooks, monographic studies, and elaborate introductions[13]—as well as intensive debates about theory and method[14] provide comparative law with the widely recognized credentials of

[9] Ernst Rabel, *Aufgabe und Notwendigkeit der Rechtsvergleichung* (1925) 3, emphasis added; see Hein Kötz, 'Comparative Law in Germany Today' (1999) 51 *Révue internationale de droit comparé* 753, 754 ff. In a similar vein: Albert Kocourek, John H. Wigmore, *Sources of Ancient and Primitive Law* (1915).

[10] Konrad Zweigert, Hein Kötz, *An Introduction to Comparative Law* (3rd edn., 1998) 15—emphasis added. See also Reimann (n. 6) 677.

[11] Vivian Grosswald Curran, 'Cultural Immersion, Difference and Categories in U.S. Comparative Law' (1998) 46 *A.J.C.L.* 657 ff.

[12] Reimann (n. 6) 672 ff.

[13] See the seventeen volumes of René David et al. (eds.), *International Encyclopedia of Comparative Law* (1972 seq.); and Jan Smits (ed.), *Elgar Encyclopedia of Comparative Law* (2012); Mauro Bussani, Ugo Mattei (eds.), *The Cambridge Companion to Comparative Law* (2012); Mathias Reimann, Reinhard Zimmermann (eds.), *Oxford Handbook of Comparative Law* (2006); David Nelken, Esin Örücü, *Comparative Law—A Handbook* (2007).

[14] See Pier G. Monateri (ed.), *Methods of Comparative Law* (2012); Frankenberg (n. 1); Grosswald Curran (n. 11).

science, which comes with a peculiar feature, though, because many comparatists argue that method and subject-matter are co-extensive in comparative law. In other words: there is *only method*.

c. The Veil of Innocence

The mantra 'comparative law is nothing but a method' serves as a veil of innocence for most of the mainstream practices. It is supported by the claim that comparative law, by necessity, counts for a science—objective, ethically neutral, and politically agnostic. Those who follow this mantra are obviously unaware of Evans-Pritchard's famous dictum that 'there is only one method in social anthropology, the comparative method—and that is impossible'. One may assume this mantra explains the Cinderella complex as well as the more recent turn to royalty.

After the intense and controversial debates in the other human and social sciences about objectivity and positivism, comparative law's mainstream basically holds on to the belief that their practice consists of the methodologically controlled production of knowledge and has no political or ethical implications. No wonder then that this pose of innocuousness and virginity would ultimately foster the image of a collateral science and a 'ubiquitous angst about the disciplinary identity'.[15]

The prominent figures of the *belle époque* of comparative law, before and in the aftermath of the 1900 Congress, were neither Cinderellas nor claiming innocence, however. They came across as men with projects and earned respect and also admiration for introducing and applying methods and, more importantly, for translating their dream of a better world into treatises of comparative law.[16] Their universalistic agenda came with ethical claims to neutrality, not always sufficiently explicit, provided by philosophies of history or the idea of a universal jurisprudence. It may be doubted whether they would have described their mindset and cosmopolitan project as politically agnostic. Yet, innocence was also transmitted by the disciplinary program supported not only by French and German but also other European protagonists of what was innocently referred to as the 'école de vérité'. The virginal search for inspiration in other countries, whether driven by humanism or reformism, was invariably guided by the ambition—untainted by bias or interest, it seemed—to promote comparative law as a science, thus linking comparative legal studies with the overall nineteenth-century project of scientism.

---

[15] Annelise Riles, *Rethinking the Masters of Comparative Law* (2001) 3 ff.
[16] See David Kennedy, 'The Methods and the Politics of Comparative Law', in Pierre Legrand, Roderick Munday (eds.), *Comparative Legal Studies: Traditions and Transitions* (2003); and Riles (n. 15).

After the Second World War had exhausted—and compromised—the vocabulary of comparative law's universalism, the discipline went through a phase of significant re-orientation. It had been prepared during the 1920s when it had reinvented itself as a pragmatic science and remained preoccupied, for the greater part of the century, with functionalist, structuralist, and taxonomic approaches.[17] While at times reproducing the rhetoric and retaining some of the themes of the founding generation, comparatists were no longer predisposed to dream of a better world. Mainstream comparative law moved away from a historical, anthropological, or philosophical alignment to the narrower purposes of charting the laws of the world (taxonomy) or probing into doctrine and legislation to come up with 'better solutions' to social problems (functionalism) by producing 'politically neutral' knowledge to sustain their belief in legal comparison as unrelated to power.[18] *Knowledge* turned into comparatists' magic bullet and anchor for their innocent mindset.

II. White Universalism

A. Universal Law and Jurisprudence

The protagonists of the Golden Era of comparative law deserve credit for propagating a normative and political, interdisciplinary project with an ambitious design, namely to follow the aspiration for a more human and just society and world by tapping 'un certain nombre de grands courants juridiques . . . auxquels [le comparatiste] ne saurait résister impunément'.[19] Comparative law was geared towards the discovery of the spirit that informs the laws of all 'civilized nations'. What could be more laudable and innocuous—against the backdrop of wars, nationalism, and imperialism—than searching for the element of unity in foreign laws? Accordingly, the discipline was widely understood, among universalists, as an instrument for releasing a common ground shared by all (civilized) peoples.

What is more, by invoking universal science[20] and jurisprudence, comparatists sought to establish the academic discipline of law, distinguished by strict methods

---

[17] Gutteridge (n. 5); Zweigert, Kötz (n. 10); Rodolfo Sacco 'One Hundred Years of Comparative Law' (2000) *Tulane L.R.* 1159 ff.

[18] Gutteridge (n. 5) 26 and 72–87; Zweigert, Kötz (n. 10) 15.

[19] Louis Josserand quoted by Édouard Lambert 'Conception générale et définition de la science du droit comparé, sa méthode, son histoire; le droit compare et enseignement du droit', (1978) in Zweigert, Puttfarken (n. 4) 30 ff.

[20] Giorgio Del Vecchio, *Sull'idea di una scienza del diritto universale comparato* (1909). See also Kocourek, Wigmore (n. 9); Riles *Rethinking the Masters* (n. 15).

that could measure up to mathematics and the natural sciences. And they gave their project a peculiar twentieth-century twist: the seemingly innocent-because-scientific preoccupation with method.

B. The Silence of the Lambs

The innocence of the all-male academy of masters permitted most comparatists to remain silent over colonialism and imperialism and thus entertain a 'white universalism' with a hegemonic touch and a racist subtext. First, comparative law's universalism was implicitly limited to the civilized members of the common-civil law family. Other legal cultures were invited to join and assimilate. Second, the term human universalism had appeared roughly one hundred years before the Paris Congress. As a theological doctrine it had strong religious connotations, meaning that all human beings will eventually be saved, as long as they accept the culture and ways (and laws) of the 'civilized nations'. Third, at the turn of the century, universalism was anything but genuinely universal. The erudite universalists present at the Paris Congress assumed, however discretely, that all non-whites were inherently like them and needed only a little assistance in order to take part in the highest expression of universalism, which, of course, was and still is Western civilization. For example, they would not return to the widely forgotten 1805 *Constitution of Haiti* and value this document of post-slavery, egalitarian constitutionalism as measuring up in its way to the French *Déclaration des Droits de l'Homme et du Citoyen* of 1789.

The universalism of the Golden Era was etched into relief against the backdrop of the greedy 'scramble for Africa' and other ugly colonial-imperial adventures of the non-gentle European 'civilizers'.[21] Rather than addressing and confronting the law's role in sustaining or at least facilitating colonialism and imperialism, the heroes of the discipline invoked what they understood to be the faultless program of humanism and—some of them—cosmopolitanism. Generally they would neither directly assist the powers that be in subjugating tribes, countries, and continents, nor openly justify the civilizing mission of the imperialist European powers. Instead, *fin de siècle* comparatists set out to look at legal phenomena in the modality of philosophical speculation to 'feel the pulse that trembles through all peoples'.[22] The political implications of their academic enterprise were hidden behind their clean-handed humanitarian rhetoric and noble claims to truth and objectivity.[23]

---

[21] See Martti Koskenniemi, *The Gentle Civilizers of Nations: The Rise and Fall of International Law 1870–1960* (2001).

[22] Eduard Gans, *Naturrecht und Universalrechtsgeschichte: Vorlesungen nach G. W. F. Hegel* (2005); Josef Kohler, *Philosophy of Law* (1914).

[23] Kohler (n. 22).

III. THE TURN TO PRACTICAL KNOWLEDGE

Post-First World War comparatists and their disciples followed the objectivist and positivist trend in the social sciences at the time and later.[24] Their dualist mantra of 'comparative law as method' and 'method as science' reflected the rise of the natural-science paradigm and the corresponding fall of the philosophical-speculative epitome of comparative studies.

A. The Triumph of the Functionalist Method

After a phase of ataraxy during which comparatists remained stoically indifferent to the intense debates on methodology in the neighbouring sciences, they woke up innocent, in the 1920s and again after the Second World War, with a frame of mind epitomized by functionalism.[25]

They sought refuge in the Weberian realm of value-freedom, where science was believed to operate in the domain of ethical and political neutrality. There they hoped to exorcise political influence and socio-economic interests and then be able to work—detached from passions, political ideologies, and social conflicts as well as economic imperatives and cultural particularities—in the service of purely scientific comparative discovery.

The turn to practical knowledge superseded the former interest in foundational and theoretical ideas. The comparative law of ideas and grand projects was displaced by 'applied comparative law',[26] privileging a functionalist design. By consequence, the comparative gaze focused on systems rather than sources and was geared towards finding solutions rather than the origins of law. The innocence of method came under a different guise and triumphed throughout the twentieth century as a pragmatic mindset. The focus on (social) problems and their legal solutions fostered a new realism without a critical edge, by some authors also referred to as 'factual approach'.[27] The functionalist would not question what entitled a comparatist to define 'problems' and decide about 'better solutions', because the functional approach appeared commonsensical and without alternative.

---

[24] Critical: Jürgen Habermas *Knowledge and Human Interests* (1972); Theodor W. Adorno (ed.), *The Positivist Dispute in German Sociology* (1976).

[25] For a comprehensive overview of the logical varieties of functionalism see Ralf Michaels, 'The Functional Method of Comparative Law', in Reimann, Zimmermann (n. 13) 339 ff.

[26] Ernst Rabel (1925), 'Aufgabe und Notwendigkeit der Rechtsvergleichung'—republished in Zweigert, Puttfarken (n. 4) 85 ff; Gutteridge (n. 5) 9 ff.

[27] Michaels (n. 25) 339; Rodolfo Sacco, 'Legal Formants: A Dynamic Approach to Comparative Law' (1991) 39 A.J.C.L. 1–34 and 343–401 ff.

In consequence, functionalists presumed similarity and allowed only for differences in detail. They oscillated between instrumentalism and reformism, thereby rearranging comparative law's veil of innocence: whatever their brand, they defined the utility of comparative law preferably in cognitive terms and practised comparison as cognitive control, while their instrumentalism lent itself to all sorts of (legislative) reforms.

B. Searching for Common Cores

Functionalists supported theories of legal transplants, structural analyses, and political initiatives for the unification of (private) law, notably in the European Union. For over two decades the Trento (now Torino) Group has relentlessly searched for the common core of European private law, all the while modestly claiming they only wanted to 'obtain at least the main lines of a *reliable* geographical "map" of the law of Europe'.[28] Quite strikingly, this group combined Rudolf Schlesinger's factualist functionalism with Rodolfo Sacco's structural investigation of legal formants by gathering facts (without questioning their social construction) and exploring those 'formants' that shape the principles of contract law or torts in the different legal regimes of the European member states.

By all means, they held on to the functionalist credo of political agnosticism: 'In using, at the beginning of our journey, the metaphor of cartography we have certainly tried to convey a message of neutrality and skepticism, locating our comparative work in the domain of the "is" rather than of the "ought".[29] They actually claimed that the politics of harmonization had 'nothing to do with the common core research in itself, which is devoted to produce reliable information, *whatever its policy use may be*'.[30]

Producing reliable information, gaining more knowledge, 'whatever its policy use may be,' objectivity, neutrality, factual approach, etc. point towards the innocent aspiration of comparatists, in particular functionalists, who lean over backwards to establish their work as purely scientific, neither ethical, nor political, nor ideological.

---

[28] Mauro Bussani, Ugo Mattei, 'The Common Core Approach to European Private Law' (1997) 3 *Columbia Journal European Law* 339, 340 ff; Mauro Bussani, Ugo Mattei (eds.), *Opening Up European Law* (2007).

[29] James Gordley, one of the leading members of the Trento Group, admitted to a more demanding goal: 'The Trento Common Core Project is an ambitious search for unity in private law.' Gordley, 'Mapping Private Law', in Bussani, Mattei (eds.), *The Common Core of European Private Law* (2002) 43 ff.

[30] Bussani, Mattei, 'Preface' in Bussani, Mattei (n. 29) 4, emphasis added

iv. The Tragic History of Taxonomy

While functionalists buried the spirit and ideas of the Golden Era, a few post-war French authors doggedly pursued the concept of a universal jurisprudence and investigated the possible contributions of comparative legal studies to a better understanding among nations.[31] They were led by their desire, anything but uncommon in comparative law, to classify foreign laws and legal regimes—as a matter of fact, all of them.

Looking at the world of laws from Archimedes' imaginary outpost, unmarked and never called into question, exercises a temptation comparatists do not find easy to overcome. Who would not fancy a complete grasp of a field of research? Besides, comparative law invites comparatists, almost by definition, to study, understand, classify, and compare *any* familiar and unfamiliar legal phenomenon that may cross the researcher's path and mind.

Therefore, taxonomy—the practice of classifying phenomena, including the principles and criteria that underlie such classification—has always been a preoccupation, not to say an obsession, in comparative legal practice.[32] If one reads—and, alas, often yawns—through the comparative classifiers' work, one is moved by a sense of tragedy and, on the other hand, the impression of futility.

A. The Tragedy of *Grands Systèmes*, Families, and Traditions of Law

Comparative law sports a venerable history of taxonomy, coming to us from as far back as Aristotle's classification by definition via Montesquieu's taxonomy of three forms of government and the different laws derived from nature and Maine's terse classification of status and contract-based societies, and reaching a high point in the 1950s with René David's *grands systèmes* and Arminjon's, Nolde's, and Wolf's treatise on legal families.[33] It was followed by a turn to legal traditions[34] that ended,

---

[31] René David, 'Le droit comparé – Enseignement de culture générale', and André Tunc, 'La contribution possible des études juridiques comparatives à une meilleure compréhension entre nations', both in: Zweigert, Puttfarken (n. 4) 205, respectively 334 ff.

[32] Regarding taxonomy I am indebted to Russell Miller, 'The Taxonomy in Comparative Law' (unpublished manuscript on file with the author). See Mariana Pargendler, 'The Rise and Decline of Legal Families' (2012) 60 *A.J.C.L.* 1043 ff; Grosswald Curran (n. 11).

[33] René David, John E. Brierley, *Major Legal Systems in the World* (3rd edn., 1985); Arminjon et al., *Traité de Droit Comparé* (1951).

[34] Mary Ann Glendon et al., *Comparative Legal Traditions in a Nutshell* (3rd edn., 2008).

for the time being, with H. Patrick Glenn's much praised and also harshly criticized *Legal Traditions of the World*.[35]

René David's taxonomy of legal systems and also Patrick Glenn's legal traditions echo the universalistic spirit of the founding era. In David's treatise, it is reduced to the legal geographer's mindset and tropes, whereas Glenn places national laws in the broader context of major legal strands, those of chthonic (or indigenous—oral and written) law, Talmudic law, civil law, Islamic law, common law, Hindu law, and Confucian law. He examines each tradition primarily in terms of its institutions, substantive law, and its founding concepts and methods, which could arguably be related to Sacco's 'legal formants'. His difference-oriented approach to traditions distinguishes the category from the somewhat hermetic concept of legal families by the openness of traditions to new and inclusive forms of logic. Whatever the flaws of his work may be, Glenn deserves credit for, unlike legal positivism, looking beyond the end of norms.

Classifying the world of laws or all laws and legal regimes of the world seems tragic, though.[36] However the comparatist tackles the task of classification, things comparative seem to end in a bad way. Resisting the taxonomic temptation means passing on (to colleagues with fewer qualms) the grand and fascinating experience of exploring and arranging the global varieties of law, for classifying done well is like travelling and collecting the spoil of the trip. Giving in to the taxonomic temptation may indeed make complexity more manageable.[37]

Invariably, the taxonomic practice entraps the comparatist in a mire of problems. The arbitrariness of taxonomic ordering is only one of them. It was pinned down and exposed to ridicule by Jorge Luis Borges' in his 'Celestial Emporium of Benevolent Knowledge', a fictitious taxonomy of animals.[38] Three more problems are discussed below.

B. Taxonomy as an Exercise in Futility

Three aspects a taxonomist (like functionalists) may want to take care of, but usually does not, convey a sense of futility. First, *positionality* is the topos that is meant to turn the comparatist's attention to her position in the comparative space and to both her role as observer of the foreign and participant in her own legal culture/setting. To discuss positionality implies that comparative law is understood as a practice

---

[35] H. Patrick Glenn, *Legal Traditions of the World—Sustainable Diversity in Law* (2014).

[36] See Csaba Varga's survey: 'Taxonomy of Law and Legal Mapping' (2010) 51 *Acta Juridica Hungarica* 253 ff.

[37] Ugo Mattei, 'Three Patterns of Law' (1997) 45 *A.J.C.L.* 5 ff.

[38] Jorge Luis Borges, *The Analytical Language of John Wilkins* (*El idioma analítico de John Wilkins*) (1942). See also Foucault (n. 3).

geared towards studying the foreign (laws, decisions, institutions, or whatever) and relating them to more familiar ones. It is crucial to know whether the comparatist sees herself as detached from or committed to one or the other context and bent on coping with settled knowledges and experiences, whether s/he is a male WASP, a feminist from Utah, or a postcolonial theoretician from India.

Such information may help to comprehend and cope with pre-understandings and biases, commitments, and research interests that may privilege areas of study and account for disparities in the representation of the materials that are deemed to be relevant.

Second, taxonomists have to—but hardly do—discuss *selectivity* because no one can seriously be expected to 'encompass the law of the whole world, past and present, and everything that affects the law'—from geography and climate to the needs of production.[39] It is quite common in the school of comparative taxonomy that authors appropriate most of their attention and pages to the Common and Civil, and less than half to other families or traditions or legal contexts.[40] While proclaiming to classify the laws of the world, they focus on continental European and US and relegate the other families, interesting as they may be, to the margin.

Finally, *perspectivity* shifts the attention to the cognitive orientation a comparatist brings into the field where she sets out to study, evaluate, and relate foreign legal phenomena to each other and to the familiar. Perspectivity also to pins down her interpretative dilemma. If all goes well in comparative practice, that is, if the comparatist manages to reflect upon who she is (see above) and also what kind of work she does, which methods she uses to what end, and how she can disengage herself from settled knowledges, she may succeed in elucidating the hermeneutic and political pitfalls that threaten to entrap her.

Taxonomists, however, tend to avoid such discussion and soul-searching. In stark contrast, the scholarly discourse reiterates with never tiring energy the similarity versus difference debate and the varieties of—at bottom—related classification within the narrative of Anglo-European philosophical prejudices about 'the other' that have developed into a distinctively American-European ideology of empire.[41] Whether Cinderella or queen, taxonomies are far from innocent—they have included a good deal of chauvinism, legal-cultural imperialism and hegemony—the West and the rest—that come under the guise of harmless denominations as 'families' or 'systems' or 'traditions', convergence theories and unitary projects. Rarely are taxonomies submitted to a rigorous audit and critique of cognitive control.

---

[39] This Montesquieuian standard was reset by Anselm von Feuerbach, *Blick auf die deutsche Rechtswissenschaft* (1810) and confirmed by Ernst Rabel, *Aufgabe und Notwendigkeit der Rechtsvergleichung* (1925) 3 ff.

[40] E.g., David, Brierley (n. 33); Uwe Kischel *Rechtsvergleichung* (2016). Glenn (n. 35) presents a distinctly more even-handed allocation.

[41] See Pierre Legrand 'The Same and the Different', in Legrand, Munday (n. 16) 240 with further references and Teemu Ruskola, *Legal Orientalism—China, the United States, and Modern Law* (2013).

V. THICK COMPARISON

For comparative law to leave the tracks of cognitive control and universal constructions and try what in the Geertzian spirit could be called thick comparison,[42] a self-critical practice is called for. The first step would be to remove the veil of innocence and address the ethical and political implications of comparative law as well as the intimate relation between knowledge and power. Recognition of the social construction of facts and taxonomies would be a good start.

A. Provincializing Anglo-Europe—Orientalizing the Mainstream

To make legal comparison accessible as an expression of cultural experience, I introduced the following grid to chart different dimensions—(1) method, (2) ethics, and (3) politics—and styles of comparative law and submit the various strands of mainstream comparative law to a practice one may call provincializing Anglo-Europe and orientalizing the mainstream.[43]

For that purpose I bundle up the various theories, methods, or styles of comparative law into four basic tracks or vocabularies, each covering a spectrum of approaches. These tracks are venues where constitutive comparison produces, from a specific perspective, commensurable legal systems, norms, institutions, and practices. The grid represents them graphically as four discrete and adverse comparative practices: the infinite horizontal axis is meant to encompass the comparatist's scientific identity and *position* towards the other—prompting, in the extreme, *Detachment* or *Commitment*. The equally infinite vertical axis illustrates the tension in *interpretation* between *Similarity* and *Difference*. Within the intra-disciplinary debates, these polar opposites are endlessly reiterated with regard to the perception and comparative interpretation of familiar and unfamiliar/strange legal phenomena. *Similarity* and *Difference* are to capture the perspective and the interpretive dilemma that results when comparatists set out to investigate and evaluate how the other—unfamiliar, foreign, strange, unknown etc.—legal artefacts correspond to and compare with their own experience, training, and practice.

The horizontal axis, delimited by the polar opposites of *Detachment* and *Commitment*, digresses from the standard self-descriptions advanced by

---

[42] Clifford Geertz, *The Interpretation of Cultures* (1973) ch. 1; Geertz, *Local Knowledge: Further Essays in Interpretive Anthropology* (1983).

[43] The term I borrow is from Teemu Ruskola, *Legal Orientalism—China, the United States and Modern Law* (2013).

comparatists, who routinely qualify their work as objective or neutral—either explicitly or by implication when they accentuate the search for truth and nothing but the truth, knowledge, or (reliable) information. *Detachment* I consider more illuminating, here rather than featuring the comparatist's bearing and position as 'objective' or 'neutral'. While neutrality as disinterestedness or the absence of bias—and innocence—can hardly be claimed for comparative law (after what sociology, legal realism, and critical hermeneutics discovered about preconceptions, bias, etc.), objectivity[44] entertains a complex relationship with representing reality and truth that cannot easily be paired with commitment.

Similarity/Difference and *Detachment/Commitment* mark the border zones of the comparatist's professional skill of distancing and differencing. They also indicate her/his willingness to call into question preconceptions and stereotypes, as well as to criticize biases that fall within the framework of one's own legal culture.

The extreme poles of both axes demarcate dangerous shores to be navigated, binary oppositions to be transcended, as briefly outlined below. The intersection of the axes allows for the registering in each quadrant the methodological, ethical, and political dimension of the different comparative styles, more precisely: *first*, the comparatist's cognitive disposition to take for granted or deal critically with one's positionality, 'situated knowledges',[45] and with uncertainty (the dimension of method); *second*, the readiness to meet what is unknown and strange on its own terms and on an equal footing and grant it access (or not) to the same moral-ethical community (the dimension of ethics); and, *third*, the critical awareness of the consequences of comparative law as science: the operators of power at work, especially in the distinction of similarities and differences, the classification of relevant and not so relevant legal systems, and the definition of 'problems' as common and 'solutions' as better (the dimension of politics).[46]

1. *Cognitive Control 'Country and Western'-Style*

A preoccupation with *Cognitive Control* distinguishes the first track of comparative law. It is more or less coextensive with the 1920s and post-Second World War pragmatism.[47] This track features the combination of a *detached* scientific attitude

---

[44] Jacques Derrida, *Of Grammatology* (1976) 158: 'There is nothing outside of the text.'

[45] The concept was introduced by Donna Haraway, 'Situated Knowledges' (1988) 14 *Feminist Studies* 575 ff.

[46] The grid shares the typical shortcomings of modelling: it is comprehensive in scope and very penurious in detail. Looking on the bright side, it allows for transition and transfer between the different tracks and therefore hybrid modalities of comparison.

[47] 'Cognitive control is characterized by the formalist ordering and labeling and the ethnocentric interpretation of information, often randomly gleaned from limited data.' Frankenberg (n. 1); William Twining 'Globalisation and Comparative Law', in David Nelken, Örücü (eds.), *Comparative Law* (2007) 75–7 ff.

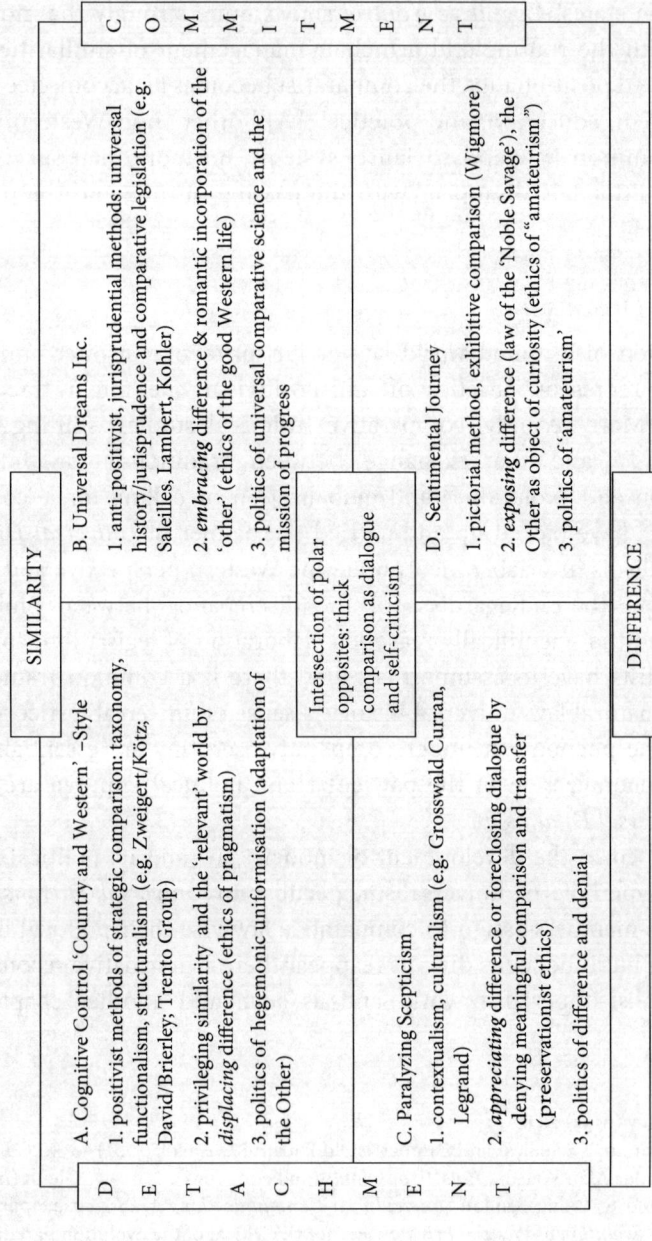

Figure 3.1 Basic structure of the grid for legal comparison

The figure content (read as arranged):

SIMILARITY

DEPTH (left axis)

A. Cognitive Control 'Country and Western' – Style

1. positivist methods of strategic comparison: taxonomy, functionalism, structuralism (e.g. Zweigert/Kötz; David/Brierley; Trento Group)

2. privileging similarity and the 'relevant' world by *displacing* difference (ethics of pragmatism)

3. politics of hegemonic uniformisation (adaptation of the Other)

B. Universal Dreams Inc.

1. anti-positivist, jurisprudential methods: universal history/jurisprudence and comparative legislation (e.g. Saleilles, Lambert, Kohler)

2. *embracing* difference & romantic incorporation of the 'other' (ethics of the good Western life)

3. politics of universal comparative science and the mission of progress

Intersection of polar opposites: thick comparison as dialogue and self-criticism

C. Paralyzing Scepticism

1. contextualism, culturalism (e.g. Grosswald Curran, Legrand)

2. *appreciating* difference or foreclosing dialogue by denying meaningful comparison and transfer (preservationist ethics)

3. politics of difference and denial

D. Sentimental Journey

1. pictorial method, exhibitive comparison (Wigmore)

2. *exposing* difference (law of the 'Noble Savage'), the Other as object of curiosity (ethics of "amateurism")

3. politics of 'amateurism'

COMMITMENT (right axis)

DIFFERENCE

with a *similarity*-orientation in interpretation—an alliance that lends itself to a preference for establishing order and sustaining Western hegemony by submitting what is different to adaptation. William Twining's irony aptly characterizes these diverse approaches as being 'over-concerned with the domestic law of [European] "parent" nation states'. *Cognitive Control* shows quite strongly the moral deficit that comes with the routine and armchair management of similarities. Due to the non-reflected positionality, the comparatist becomes an accomplice of his/her own legal system, education, and practice: '[A]ll other [non-Western, Romano-Germanic, Common Law and socialist] systems, no more than survivors from the past, will ultimately disappear with the passing of time and the progress of civilization.'[48]

2. *Universal Dreams Inc.*

The combination of a united world law or jurisprudence inspired universalistic dreams[49] that represent varieties of anti-positivism one might trace back to Montesquieu. More recently, comparative historical studies, shifting the focus on 'transplants'[50] and the 'exchange between traditions',[51] on intercultural communication and evolution,[52] and globalization or calling for a 'comparative jurisprudence'[53] have picked up and carried the banner of *Universal Dreams Inc.* Their universalisms invariably incorporate the Western perspective and construct the world from there. Regardless of the discrepancy between philosophical speculation and the scientifically reasoned elaboration of legislation, comparative law's universalists have to assume that, first, there is a common framework for comparison—natural law, universal history, a sense of universal justice, etc.—and, second, that the phenomena under comparative scrutiny are essentially similar. Hence, over-generalization of the particular and political amnesia are the main pitfalls of *Universal Dreams Inc.*

Once inscribed in the development of modern law and its political-economic context, the hyperbole of universalism, peculiar to *Universal Dreams Inc.*, and the mission its members assign to comparative law lose their political innocence. Their anything but innocuous dreams reappear there as normative reconstructions of the colonialist-imperialist world and as such add another chapter to the

---

[48]   David, Brierley (n. 33) 26 ff.

[49]   Christophe Jamin, ' "Saleilles" and Lambert's Old Dream Revisited' (2002) 50 *A.J.C.L.* 701 ff.

[50]   See in particular Alan Watson, *Legal Transplants* (2nd edn., 1993).   [51]   Glenn (n. 35).

[52]   R. Scollon and S. Wong Scollon, *Intercultural Communication: A Discourse Approach* (1995); Alan Watson, *The Evolution of Western Private Law* (1985); Critical of the evolution paradigm: P. Sack, J. Aleck, 'Introduction', in P. Sack, J. Aleck (eds.), *Law and Anthropology* supra note 82 at xiii, xvii ff.

[53]   William Ewald, 'Comparative Jurisprudence (I): What Was It Like to Try a Rat?' (1995) 143 *University of Pennsylvania L.R.* 1888, and 'Comparative Jurisprudence (II), The Logic of Legal Transplants' (43) *American Journal of Comparative Law* 489 ff.

'White Mythologies'[54] that rely on generally unquestioned, culturally embedded assumptions concerning Western civilization.

3. *Sentimental Amatourism*

Diametrically opposed to influential mainstream varieties of *Cognitive Control*, where confidence of the hegemonic message abounds, and in contrast to *Universal Dreams Inc.*, which conjoins a minority faction of the discourse still subscribing to the once glorious jurisprudential mission of comparative law, fewer comparatists inhabit the quadrant demarcated by *Commitment/Difference*. From afar, they seem like sentimental travellers—the last amateurs—touring the field of comparative law. They are congenially committed to respecting, at times essentializing and orientalizing,[55] difference.

Again, Montesquieu may be called down as a representative of amateurism and a source of inspiration for latter-day travellers. *The Spirit of the Laws* is replete with short vignettes of foreign countries and peoples, with bizarre observations and odd inferences, as for instance of the laws in relation to the sobriety of the people, as well as other touristic exhibits.[56] The *amatour*-comparatists eschew the anthropologist's theoretical overhead and travel instead with camera and treasure box to capture, collect, and bring home the impressions from the 'Panorama of the World's Legal Systems'[57] or 'a more sophisticated "Cook's tour" of the great legal families of the world—as if one has been upgraded from an ordinary package tour to a luxury cruise ship with a more sophisticated guide to the standard sights'.[58] They are committed to the difference of the other which they explore not infrequently through immersion from the armchair. Such commitment grows out of fascination with the exotic, primitive, culturally remote, or radically different. What seems attractive in the *amatourist's* gaze is likely to be rejected as a candidate for integration in the domestic legal order. In terms of politics, *amatourism* does not come with a clear political message or mission. Therefore it is not easy to identify a political project underneath the exhibitive style.

---

[54] Robert Young, *White Mythologies* (1990). See also Upendra Baxi, *The Future of Human Rights* (3rd edn., 2012); and Mahmood Mamdani, *Citizen and Subject: Contemporary Africa and the Legacy of Late Colonialism* (1995).

[55] Edward Said, *Orientalism* (1978); Ruskola (n. 43).

[56] Montesquieu, *The Spirit of the Laws* (Cambridge University Press, 1989) 57–8, 104, 103, 105, and 107 ff.

[57] John H. Wigmore, *Panorama of the World's Legal Systems* (1928); John H. Wigmore, 'Jottings on Comparative Legal Ideas and Institutions' (1931–1932) 6 *Tulane L.R.* 48 ff. See also John H. Barton et al., *Law in Radically Different Cultures* (1983).

[58] William Twining, 'A Comment on the First and Second Edition of H. P. Glenn' (n. 35) in Pierre Legrand, 'A Fresh Start for Comparative Legal Studies?' (2006) 1 *Journal of Comparative Law* 100/108 ff.

4. *Paralysing Scepticism*

The motley group of approaches and authors one could co-register in the *Detachment/Difference* track represents varieties of comparative-legal scepticism. They range from appreciation of the other (legal norms, practices, and institutions) as deserving equal treatment to a certain paralysis that forestalls a comparative view and evaluation altogether.[59] Though divided internally, the group's common programmatic platform could be to disturb the good conscience or even (in the case of the more ambitious and optimistic members) redirect the course of the mainstream, and to prevent a person's particular legal experience from masquerading as the universally legitimate and applicable, hegemonic legal system, culture, or practice.

Contextualism contravenes the (formalist) assumption that perfect comparison and, by the same token, the easy transfer of norms are possible. In consequence, the protagonists of *Detachment/Difference* appear estranged from comparative law tracks where taxonomies, similarities, and universals are constructed from a Western point of view. In fact, they rather avoid comparison altogether so as not to run head on into a methodological ambush or ideological trap of ethnocentrism. In stark contrast to the *Universal Dreams Inc.*, sceptics do not embrace (and choke) the foreign but champion radical versions of difference. Moderate sceptics are more confident that they may be or may become skilled cultural navigators.

Despite the internal diversity on methodological-theoretical grounds, sceptics share what one might characterize as a politics of tragic denial. They are motivated by three main concerns: *first*, that designations and classification are internally related to structures of power and sustain hegemony, in particular when allied with archetypical figures, like the primitive society; *second*, they believe with good cause that comparisons are almost never merely descriptive but more often both evaluative and expository; and, *third*, they claim that the real-existing divergence in the world of legal systems, families, and traditions requires a focus on difference rather than convergence or uniformization.

B. Thick(er) Comparison

The centre of the grid delineates, if tentatively, the methodological, hermeneutic, ethical, and political minefield where polar opposites might intersect and inform a

---

[59] Pierre Legrand, *Fragments on Law-as-Culture* (1999); Baxi (n. 54); Frankenberg (n. 1); Kennedy (n. 16); Pier G. Monateri, 'Black Gaius: A Multicultural Quest for the "Western Legal Tradition"' (2000) 51 *Hastings L.J.* 479 ff; Horatia Muir Watt, 'La fonction subversive du droit comparé' (2000) 52 *Revue International du Droit Comparé* 503 ff; Grosswald Curran (n. 11).

comparative practice that uneasily, dialectically, and dynamically transgresses the borders and limitations, the idiosyncrasies and pitfalls marking the four discrete tracks or vocabularies of legal comparison.

If at all possible, the transformative work would possibly have to be done jointly by dialogue, criticism, and self-criticism, as well as 'thick comparison'.[60] Thick—or rather, productive—comparison favours context and narrative and addresses the normative and political aspects of comparative practice.

A good start could be to stop the production and the recursive validation of inferior others. That is why the self-delusion about the objectivity and neutrality of comparative legal research needs to be discontinued. Next, one would have to de-Westernize the concepts, assumptions, and biases and consider the ethical and political implications of the different venues. One should bear in mind that no concept as such is universal, but requires translation, and '[t]ranslations are more delicate than heart transplants'.[61]

A turn to thicker comparison—enriched with context information—rather than thin taxonomies, meagre functional analyses, or bony factual positivism—may generate new insights and exciting perspectives. And who would not end the deceiving romance with 'innocent knowledge' for an alluring Cinderella who meets other laws and legal practices at eye-level and pursues a conversation with quite-different and quite-similar legal cultures on their own terms? A walk across the hermeneutic, ethical, and political minefield of the intercultural may not lead out of the dilemma of comparative law—how the deeply different can be deeply known without becoming any less different[62]—but could yield greater adventure in comparative legal studies.[63]

BIBLIOGRAPHY

Günter Frankenberg, *Comparative Law as Critique* (E. Elgar Publ., 2016)
David Kennedy, 'The Methods and the Politics of Comparative Law', in Pierre Legrand, Roderick Munday (eds.), *Comparative Legal Studies: Traditions and Transitions* (Cambridge University Press, 2003)

[60] The complexity of the hermeneutic operations is elucidated by Geertz (n. 42); and Thomas Scheffer, Jörg Niewöhner (eds.), *Thick Comparison—Reviving the Ethnographic Aspiration* (2010).

[61] Raimon Panikkar, 'Is the Notion of Human Rights a Western Concept?' (1982) 30 *Diogenes* 389 ff. The same applies to legal transfer; see Günter Frankenberg 'Constitutions as commodities' in Frankenberg (ed.), *Order from Transfer* (2013) 1 ff.

[62] According to Geertz, *Local Knowledge* (n. 42) at 48, ethnographers try to bring 'the enormously distant enormously close without becoming less far away'.

[63] On the same note: Sally Falk Moore, 'Legal Systems of the World' (1986) in L. Lipton, S. Wheeler (eds.), *Law and the Social Sciences* (1986) 11–62 ff.

Pier G. Monateri (ed.), *Methods of Comparative Law* (E. Elgar Publ., 2012)

Horatia Muir Watt, 'Globalisation and Comparative Law', in Mathias Reimann, Reinhard Zimmermann (eds.), *Handbook of Comparative Law* (Oxford University Press, 2006) 579

David Nelken, Esin Örücü, *Comparative Law—A Handbook* (Hart, 2007)

Teemu Ruskola, *Legal Orientalism—China, the United States, and Modern Law* (Harvard University Press, 2013)

CHAPTER 4

....

LITERARY
ANALYSIS OF LAW

....

SIMON STERN[*]

LEGAL historians often turn to literary examples to show how doctrines, practices, or institutions were perceived at a certain a time. Imaginative works sometimes serve as representative illustrations of legal phenomena, sometimes as alternatives to dominant legal ideas or assumptions (voicing dissent or presenting figures and perspectives that escape the law's comprehension), sometimes as evidence for the dissemination of legal thought or folk wisdom about the law, and sometimes as a kind of parallel formation that uses, or reflects on, legal methods and modes of explanation, even if the work does not expressly address legal issues.[1] Recent scholarship continues to use all of these methods, but there has been a shift towards the last two approaches over the last ten or twenty years, and this chapter will suggest ways of pursuing each.

As to the spread of legal ideas, new digital databases have made it possible to see how legal terms and doctrines are taken up in various genres of factual and imaginative writing. To give a sense of how legal historians might use these databases, this chapter shows what digital resources can reveal about the prehistory

* Thanks to Markus Dubber, Dan Priel, Bob Spoo, and Chris Tomlins for comments on an earlier draft.
[1] Although the discussion here focuses on imaginative writing, the same can be said of film. I use 'imaginative writing' and 'literature' interchangeably in this discussion, in part to avoid creating the impression that research on law and literature should be concerned only with literary classics.

of the *Miranda* warning. By searching for the terms in which the warning is articulated and looking at the role it plays in various narratives, we can gain a fuller understanding of the meanings and functions that laypersons associated with it. The first part of the chapter, then, offers an extensive, database-driven survey that takes novelistic representation as its focus. Conversely, by studying a particular work, and focusing not only on its content but also on how it uses plot and character, we can ask about its animating logic, posing questions about how a text works rather than what it says or shows overtly.[2] Imaginative writings often engage with legal concepts by remodelling or dismantling them, and these are modes of engagement that we will miss if we attend only to what narratives explicitly depict or describe. The second part of this chapter takes a more intensive approach, asking how Oscar Wilde's novel *The Picture of Dorian Gray* (1890/1891) uses various techniques of representation to explore the logic of obscenity law—a logic, I will suggest, that also applies to the legal regulation of language in other contexts, such as libel and sedition.

1. The *Miranda* Warning

American judges and lawyers have long recognized the importance of the *Miranda* warning as 'part of our national culture',[3] and this awareness has led scholars to study the warning's prehistory and its place in popular culture. Albert Alschuler notes that well into the nineteenth century, 'magistrates and judges in both England and America expected and encouraged suspects and defendants to speak during pretrial interrogation and again at trial'.[4] These expectations began to change towards the middle of the century: in *R v. Arnold* (1838), the King's Bench stated that a magistrate conducting a pre-trial hearing should tell the suspect 'that what he thinks fit to say will be taken down, and may be used against him on his trial'.[5] Ten years later, Sir John Jervis's Act (1848) provided that after presenting the accused with the Crown's evidence, the magistrate or Justice of the Peace 'shall say to him these words, or words to the like effect: . . . "[Y]ou are not obliged to say anything unless you desire to do so, but whatever you say will be taken down in writing, and may be given in evidence against you upon your trial." '[6] Alschuler observes that in New York

---

[2] For an excellent introduction to such questions, see John Mullan, *How Novels Work* (2008).

[3] *Dickerson v. United States*, 530 U.S. 428, 443 (2000).

[4] Albert W. Alschuler, 'A Peculiar Privilege in Historical Perspective: The Right to Remain Silent' (1996) 94 *Michigan L.R.* 2625, 2660–61.

[5] *R v. Arnold*, 173 Eng Rep 645, 645–6 (K.B. 1838).   [6] 11 & 12 Vict., ch. 42, § 18 (1848).

City, 'magistrates began routinely to caution defendants in 1835, [and] the number of defendants who declined to submit increased thereafter'.[7] Following up on this research, Wesley Oliver has shown how the practice of cautioning suspects arose out of concerns that a confession might be ruled inadmissible if a court regarded it as having been coerced. Oliver notes that '[t]he benefits of giving cautions were . . . widely publicized by [British and American] treatise writers in the early nineteenth century', and that an 1829 New York statute provided that magistrates should caution defendants in much the same way that Sir John Jervis's Act would later specify. As Oliver explains, New York City police officers adopted a similar practice in 1845, but changes to the law in the late 1860s made coercively obtained confessions much more likely to be admitted, and the police soon abandoned the practice of cautioning suspects—as, evidently, did the magistrates, whose warnings, in any case, were belated given this change in the habits of the police.[8]

Although scholars have also discussed the *Miranda* warning's place in American popular culture since the late 1960s, there has not been any research on how these earlier versions figured in the popular culture of the time.[9] Until recently, anyone interested in that question would have had few options short of an extended search through a massive print archive. The legal prehistory of the warning could be studied by turning to sources such as Westlaw and Lexis, the English Reports, and any treatises on criminal law and procedure that the library could offer. Heinonline has made the English Reports available digitally, and the treatise literature has become much easier to search with the advent of Gale's database 'The Making of Modern Law, 1800–1926'. These resources have greatly facilitated the kind of work that accounts for much of the conventional research on legal history. A study of how judicial statements relate to others' beliefs and attitudes, however, would move beyond the realm of legal doctrine and outside the register of lawyers talking to lawyers. Various newer digital resources, such as the Gale collections 'Wright American Fiction, 1774–1920' and 'Crime, 1790–1920' (which includes both British and American materials), have expanded the range of cultural reference that such a search might encompass.[10] Imaginative writing can help us understand the meanings, purposes, and effects that non-lawyers associated with the warning.

---

[7] Alschuler (n. 4) 2661; see also Mike McConville and Chester Mirsky, 'The Rise of Guilty Pleas: New York, 1800–1865' (1995) 22 *J.L. & Soc'y.* 443, 452.

[8] Wesley MacNeil Oliver, 'Magistrates' Examinations, Police Interrogations, and *Miranda*-Like Rules in the Nineteenth Century' (2007) 81 *Tulane L.R.* 777, 790, 792, 798–9, 810–28.

[9] Ronald Steiner et al., 'The Rise and Fall of the *Miranda* Warnings in Popular Culture' (2011) 59 *Cleveland State L.R.* 219; George C. Thomas III and Richard A. Leo, 'The Effects of *Miranda v. Arizona*: "Embedded" in Our National Culture?' (2002) 29 *Crime and Justice* 203.

[10] Google Books also has some use in this kind of research, but its value is limited because many titles are not available for full-text searching, and even when they are, the results are erratic. Few of the results obtained by searching Gale's Wright collection can be replicated on Google Books. The Wright bibliography is incomplete, but it offers by far the most comprehensive coverage of American novels published between 1774 and 1920 (more than 17,500 titles).

The results cannot provide statistical proof about the prevalence of its use or about social attitudes concerning the warning, but they can give us a sense—not available in the legal sources—of what contemporaries thought was required and of what they thought it achieved, practically and symbolically. Given that imaginative writing not only reflects existing views but can also help, often subtly and tacitly, to shape readers' attitudes, this kind of investigation is useful as a means of indicating a range of attitudes that were available at the time.

My approach here has been to limit the choice of search terms to a verbal formula based on the one adopted in *Miranda* (namely 'may/will/can/could . . . be used against'), whereas a fuller investigation would proceed iteratively, taking the various linguistic formulations that these searches reveal in the sources and using those results to seek further examples and variations. Moreover, the terminal point has been set at 1920, not because of any relevant historical event but because that is the last date in Wright's bibliography. As Robin Valenza notes, searching text databases for particular phrases yields limited results, because 'keyword techniques depend . . . on specific verbal configurations, [whereas] natural languages (such as English) depend on significant variability in the way that similar ideas can be expressed'. Valenza contrasts literary critical reading with 'indexical reading, in which the focus is the rapid processing of information'.[11] These are crucial considerations for a careful and thoroughgoing analysis of the way the prophylactic warning functioned in nineteenth-century fiction. My aim here is to indicate the potential for this approach rather than to present a comprehensive analysis, and even with the limitations described above, the results are suggestive.

To summarize briefly before turning to specific examples: the searches produced seventy-three results, including sixty-eight novels (after eliminating duplicates and irrelevant results),[12] supplemented by five of Conan Doyle's *Sherlock Holmes* stories. Most of the novels are American; there is, at present, no digital collection of nineteenth-century British fiction that rivals the Wright database, so these results reflect the current state of the resources rather than a greater American emphasis on criminal procedure. The searches yielded two novels in the late 1840s and another two in the 1850s, four or five novels per decade in 1860–1889, seven in the 1890s, seventeen in the first decade of the twentieth century, and twenty-five in the next decade. Most notably, then, this investigation shows that novelists had already begun to refer to the prophylactic warning in the middle of the nineteenth century, and that American writers did so increasingly during a period in which the warning seems no longer to have been required. Although the total number of examples

---

[11] Robin Valenza, 'How Literature Becomes Knowledge: A Case Study' (2009) 76 *ELH* 215, 225.

[12] Among the results that do not involve a legal authority's warning, however, some nevertheless bespeak a legal mindset. For example, in George Lincoln Walton's *Oscar Montague—Paranoiac* (1919), the protagonist believes that his friend's mother is conspiring with a lawyer: 'He would carefully choose his words so that nothing could be used against him' (167). For other telling results that were excluded from the totals given in the text, see the comments accompanying note 25.

remains small, it is significant that writers invoked the warning at all in this era. It seems to have acquired the status of a literary convention, a signal—even if used only rarely—of the law's integrity.

One pattern the search reveals is a tendency towards greater fanfare in the earlier references to the warning: writers draw more attention to its invocation, sometimes by introducing it with more legal pomp, sometimes by highlighting the drama accompanying its articulation, and sometimes by commenting narratively on its deployment. One of the earliest examples—just a year after Sir John Jervis's Act— appears in *The Forgery, or Best Intentions* (1849), by the prolific British novelist and historian G. P. R. James. The novel features a dramatic scene in which the hero, Henry Hayley, is examined by a set of magistrates on a charge of forgery. When the case begins to take on a serious cast, one of the magistrates asks Hayley for a 'clear and explicit explanation', but another quickly intervenes: 'Remember . . . that you are not obliged to make any statement, and that whatever you say will be taken down, and may be used against you at any other period.' The scene is replete with hearsay objections and other evidentiary intricacies, but despite all this legal wrangling, it is the delivery of the warning that first impresses the heroine with the gravity of the situation ('terribly agitated at the serious turn which affairs seemed to be taking, [she] closed her eyes and bent down her head'). Hayley, however, does not hesitate to proceed with his tale, which ultimately vindicates him.[13]

In another wildly popular British narrative published around the same time, *The Mysteries of the Court of London*, by George W. M. Reynolds, the warning is rendered in comic form, by a seasoned police officer who has no qualms about battering down a suspect's door without announcing himself, but then makes a show of standing upon form: 'Now, mind, genelmen . . . anything you say here will be used against you elsewhere, according to the stattit in that case made and purwided.'[14] The formulaic nature of the utterance, already evident from the mock-legalese that enfolds it, is underscored by his penchant for repeating the Pickwickian phrase ('according to the stattit . . .') whenever affirming the validity of some proceeding.[15] Here, the seemingly mechanical recitation, garnished with his cockney accent, conveys a sense that the warning (although only recently required by statute) is already so routine as to constitute a mere form of words, unlikely to serve its ostensible purpose—if one takes it to be concerned with protecting defendants' rights rather than ensuring the admissibility of any statement that follows.

A rather different effect is produced in one of the first fictional detective 'memoirs' in Britain, *Recollections of a Detective Police Officer*, originally published serially in

---

[13] G. P. R. James, *The Forgery: A Tale* (1849) 138.

[14] George W. M. Reynolds, *The Mysteries of the Court of London* (1849) 1:166. The narrative appeared serially, in weekly 'penny numbers', from 1848 to 1856.

[15] The officious, formula-spouting Mr. Grummer, in *The Pickwick Papers*, uses the same phrase, and indeed Reynolds's officer, Grumley, appears to be named after him. Charles Dickens, *The Posthumous Papers of the Pickwick Club* (1837) 251.

the early 1850s. The protagonist charges and arrests a wronged woman, interrupting her to say, 'If this . . . be a confession, let me warn you that all you say may be—' but he is cut off by the suspect herself: ' "Used against me hereafter," broke in the infuriate woman, whose eyes glared with a fiery rage that cast a light as of insanity over her white, haggard countenance,' and she rapidly proceeds to unburden herself.[16] The readiness of her answer suggests that she is repeating what is already well known, and her ability to repeat it suggests that she takes the warning seriously. That she nevertheless incriminates herself does not show that she regards the recitation as a mere form of words; rather, it underscores her role as a melodramatic victim intent on proclaiming her status. The officer's generous reminder bespeaks a sincere concern on the part of the law, one that remains admirable in spite of her refusal to heed it. These three British examples all highlight the drama that accompanies the delivery of the warning, even as they assign different meanings to the utterance.

The early American examples are equally dramatic. For instance, in Dillon O'Brien's *The Dalys of Dalyston* (1866), a gang of Irish criminals is destroyed when one of the malefactors, Bernard Casey, turns state's evidence and agrees to testify in court. Warned by the magistrate that 'what you say now, will be taken down, and may be used against you, if the government refuses to accept of you as an informer', Casey responds gamely, 'I'm not afraid of that, your honor. What would they hang me for, I'm not worth it?' Indeed, his evidence proves instrumental in convicting the main villain, who also receives a warning ('anything you have to say, I advise you to keep for your defence'), but is rapidly reduced to utter abjection when the full dimensions of the case against him become apparent.[17] Again, in G. J. A. Coulson's *The Ghost of Redbrook* (1879), the warning fails to deter a hapless victim, bent on clearing his name and seemingly aware of his own status as a fictional character. Rather than accepting the advice 'not [to] criminate yourself' because a confession 'may be used against you in your trial', he responds, 'I am willin' to print it—every word!' and proceeds to unfold a highly improbable tale that prompts his questioner to ask whether he has 'ever writ[ten] any novels'.[18] In *A Fool's Errand* (1879), the best-known work of the lawyer-novelist Albion Tourgée, a guilt-ridden ex-Klan member confesses to his participation in a lynching: told that 'any thing you may say here may be used against you upon trial for any crime', he answers, 'It makes no difference . . . I can not keep still any longer. I haven't had a good night's rest since it occurred.'[19]

---

[16] 'Waters' (pseudonym of William Russell), *Recollections of a Detective Police-Officer* (1856) 305. Offering what is thought to be the earliest fictional account of professional policing in Britain; these stories first appeared in *Chambers's Edinburgh Journal* in 1849 to 1853.

[17] Dillon O'Brien, *The Dalys of Dalystown* (1866) 265, 274.

[18] George James Atkinson Coulson, *The Ghost of Redbrook* (1879) 248, 249.

[19] Albion W. Tourgée, *A Fool's Errand: By One of the Fools* (1879) 280. Tourgée is better known as Homer Plessy's lawyer. See Mark Elliott, *Albion Tourgée and the Quest for Racial Equality from the Civil War to* Plessy v. Ferguson (2006).

In all of these instances (and in nearly every example from the nineteenth century) the warning is a mere formality, in the sense that hardly anyone chooses to exercise the right to remain silent. As we have seen, this is not simply a function of their confidence that it will help to secure their acquittal: the guilty are just as eager to talk. It is hardly surprising that the warning does nothing to stop the flow of the narrative; after all, unless the aim were to furnish a pretext for strategically husbanding some crucial detail to be produced later, a novelist would hardly be likely to include this bit of legal punctilio at all, if it signalled that an exciting revelation was about to be cut short. Rather, its insertion marks the seriousness of the occasion and shows how writers—and perhaps readers as well—associated the law's procedural commitments with a kind of self-abnegating scrupulousness, which could be regarded as admirable precisely because the culprits could also be counted on to see it that way and to refuse to take advantage of it. That is also the function it serves in its various reiterations in the *Sherlock Holmes* stories, as Doyle shows in 'The Adventure of the Dancing Men' (1903), when he proves unable to refrain from commenting explicitly on the practice: '"It is my duty to warn you that [any confession] will be used against you," cried the inspector, with the magnificent fair play of the British criminal law.'[20]

A warning that led the suspect to clam up would not only frustrate the progress of the narrative, but would also frustrate the judicial process, showing that culprits might actually avail themselves of the opportunity (as Alschuler and Oliver suggest they did, in fact) instead of recognizing it as an invitation to speak honestly and openly. Thus, Reynolds's *Mysteries of the Court of London* is an outlier: it belongs to the genre of 'city mysteries', describing a world suffused by vice and corruption, and in such a world, procedural safeguards may seem useless.[21] In most of these narratives, by contrast, the warning serves as a language in which legal professionals speak to laypersons and actually make themselves understood. At precisely the moment when legal officialdom interferes with a citizen's freedom, the law expresses itself not in the Latinate, multi-syllabic jargon that so often renders it eligible for satire, but in a clear and direct fashion that elicits a response in kind, showcasing for the reader a legal system that protects the rights of defendants and thereby earns their respect.

---

[20] A. Conan Doyle, 'The Adventure of the Dancing Men' (1903) in Leslie S. Klinger (ed.), *The New Annotated Sherlock Holmes* (2005) 2:895. On the only occasion when Holmes himself comments on the practice, he points out that his efforts have rapidly precipitated a result that the police, with their 'compulsory warning', could not have achieved, but significantly, the inspector is for once allowed to defend himself without contradiction: 'Perhaps not. But we get there all the same, Mr. Holmes'. 'The Adventure of the Retired Colourman' (1926) in ibid., 2: 1452. See also *A Study in Scarlet* (1887) in ibid., 3:175; *The Sign of Four* (1890) in ibid., 3:275; 'The Adventure of Wisteria Lodge' (1908) in ibid., 2:1236.

[21] On the genre, see Stephen Knight, *The Mysteries of the Cities: Urban Crime Fiction in the Nineteenth Century* (2011).

Among the narratives published during the nineteenth century, only a few are detective stories. Insofar as this scene of interaction between citizen and police officer (or magistrate) was becoming a literary convention, it was not restricted to a particular subgenre. Over time, however, mysteries increasingly account for these references to the prophylactic warning, and the repeat examples come exclusively from writers of detective fiction. The warning appears in three novels by Rodrigues Ottolgenui, a dentist-turned-detective writer of the 1890s.[22] The warning also appears in three of the four tales collected in Oswald Crawfurd's *The Revelations of Inspector Morgan* (1907).[23] Indeed, by the first decade of the twentieth century, not only do we see a significant increase in the number of detective stories using some version of the warning, but increasingly, the function is not to emphasize the legal system's dedication to 'fair play', but in fact to allow the suspect to remain silent—even when the suspect is innocent.[24] The highly dramatic and elaborately blazoned examples of the mid-to-late nineteenth century give way to a more perfunctory treatment after the turn of the century. That tendency suggests that writers of these early twentieth-century mystery stories—the precursor of the modern-day procedural—recognized the value of drawing on legal formalities and exploiting their narrative potential, particularly those formalities that had sufficiently entered the vernacular as to be readily intelligible to laypersons. No longer serving only symbolically, as a means of trumpeting the law's decorousness and impartiality, the warning could indeed help to justify the narrative deferral of information, a function it could achieve only after becoming sufficiently well-known that readers could take its symbolic meaning for granted.

Another indication that this language was increasingly familiar to readers comes from its use outside the legal context. In several early twentieth-century novels with courtship plots, writers place the warning in the mouths of female characters who jokily advise their suitors to be on their guard. In Alice Brown's *Margaret Warrener* (1902), one of the characters tells a male caller, 'This is an interview, you know. . . . Remember that anything you say may be used against you'.[25] The importation of the warning into the arena of sexual conflict signals the characters'

---

[22] Rodrigues Ottolengui, *An Artist in Crime* (1892) 103–4; *A Conflict of Evidence* (1893) 77; *A Modern Wizard* (1894) 415.

[23] Oswald Crawfurd, *The Revelations of Inspector Morgan* (1907) 246, 251, 328. See also Natalie Sumner Lincoln's two novels *The Trevor Case* (1912) 291–2; *C.O.D.* (1915) 300.

[24] The warning results in silence in Burford Delannoy, *The Margate Mystery* (1901) 79; Arthur Henry, *The Unwritten Law* (1905) 173; Jean Webster, *The Four-Pools Mystery* (1908) 149; Jacques Futrelle, *The Diamond Master* (1909) 192; Wells Hasting and Brian Hooker, *The Professor's Mystery* (1911) 182.

[25] Alice Brown, *Margaret Warrener* (1902) 58. For similar examples, see Frank H. Spearman, *Merrilie Dawes* (1913) 33; Eugene Manlove Rhodes, *The Desire of the Moth* (1916) 11.

urbane perspective on what they recognize as an adversarial relationship, but for the statement to have the desired effect, the writer must assume that the warning is already so well-known as to require no further translation.

It may seem tempting to ask about the kinds of law enforcement officers these stories portray—federal, state, county, or municipal—but writers are not likely to have been sensitive to such distinctions. What matters is not which authorities they thought were apt to utter a prophylactic warning, but rather that they thought it was apt to be uttered at all—let alone that an officer might consider it his 'duty' to issue the warning, or that 'the statute' provides for it, or that it would be recited 'like a lesson well learned'.[26] Again, the reactions of suspects who greet the statement as a platitude ('The old phrase!'),[27] are open to various interpretations—are these characters revealing their own experience with the law, or commenting cynically on the warning's uselessness? Even if these scenes offer a very inaccurate picture of contemporary practice or public knowledge, they suggest that readers would at least have been willing to indulge the premise that such a warning was a matter of routine.

As we have seen, over a period of about fifty years, what began as an event requiring elaborate narrative staging could become relatively mundane and could even be shown as resulting in the very response that the prophylactic warning allows. The development of this literary convention is all the more remarkable given that criminal defendants in the early twentieth century could hardly take it for granted that they would not be questioned without counsel and pressed to confess. Perhaps novelists were learning from each other, or perhaps they were responding to a treatise literature that continued to make reference to the rights of the accused. Further research may disclose that in some American jurisdictions, the practice of cautioning suspects persisted even after the New York City police abandoned it. In any case, its use in fiction seems to have become a convenient means of praising the even-handedness of a legal system dedicated to protecting the rights of all. In that way, long before the *Miranda* decision, the invocation of the right to remain silent joined other frequently rehearsed legal mottos that make up the language of America's civic religion.[28]

[26] For 'duty' see Saqui Smith, *Back from the Dead: A Story of the Stage* (1892) 54; Earle Ashley Walcott, *The Open Door: A Romance of Mystery* (1910) 75, 317; a District Attorney cites 'the statute' to an ignorant judge who speaks substandard English in T. P. Buffington, *Green Valley* (1900) 138–9; a corporal in the 'Mounted Police' recites the 'lesson' in Bertrand W. Sinclair, *Raw Gold* (1908) 171.

[27] Oswald Crawfurd, *The Revelations of Inspector Morgan* (1907) 328; William Russell, *Diary of a Detective Police Officer* (1864) 116.

[28] See Robert L. Tsai, 'Legal Language: Expansion, Consolidation, Resistance', in Nan Goodman and Simon Stern (eds.), *The Routledge Research Companion to Law and Humanities in Nineteenth-Century America* (2017) 150–62.

II. REFLECTING ON OBSCENITY
IN *DORIAN GRAY*

Having considered how fictional portrayals of legal actors and practices can inform historical research, I turn in this section to questions that have more to do with the logic and methods by which fiction operates. What novels say about the law can provide a useful perspective on the beliefs and attitudes of contemporary writers, but as every lawyer knows, judicial decisions are often telling not only because of what they assert, but also because of what they leave out or take for granted—and the same applies to imaginative works. Fiction explores legal modes of thought and argument as well as legal rules and doctrines, and we will miss those more conceptual kinds of engagement with the law if we focus only on what writers say directly or on particular verbal formulations (as Valenza notes).[29]

Oscar Wilde's *The Picture of Dorian Gray*, published in *Lippincott's Magazine* in 1890 and revised for book publication in 1891, raises a number of legal questions by way of the events it describes explicitly. Dorian commits a murder (arguably while under diminished capacity), and then uses blackmail to make an acquaintance get rid of the body. As the painting becomes increasingly repulsive, reflecting his increasingly depraved character, Dorian himself worries about blackmail, raising questions about privacy that may recall the concerns of Warren and Brandeis in their famous article on the subject, published at precisely the same time.[30] The premise that Dorian's crimes would be reflected on his face, if the picture were not there to keep him unblemished as it enacts this process, might recall the contemporary theories—usually associated with Cesare Lombroso—that delinquency can be read off the body.[31] *Dorian Gray*, then, engages with various legal questions relating to crime, coercion, and privacy, and a historical investigation might treat some of these episodes in the plot as evidence of how contemporaries thought about these issues. I will suggest that the novel also reflects on legal questions by means of the implicit logic that governs its plot.

Although *Dorian Gray* does not refer explicitly to obscenity, in the version published in 1890, Wilde repeatedly hints at the subject. Dorian Gray asserts that he has been 'poisoned' by a decadent French novel lent to him by Lord Henry Wotton (poison was already, at this, time, a common metaphor for obscenity), and the various scenarios involving blackmail, as well as the deliberately vague references to the experiences that result in 'the signs of sin' on the painting, suggest that Dorian's secrets are sexual in nature.[32] On its original publication, the story was attacked by

---

[29]   See (n. 11) above.

[30]   Samuel D. Warren and Louis D. Brandeis, 'The Right of Privacy' (1890) 4 *Harvard L.R.* 193.

[31]   Daniel Pick, *Faces of Degeneration: A European Disorder, c.1848–c.1919* (1989) 165.

[32]   Oscar Wilde, *The Picture of Dorian Gray* (ed.), Joseph Bristow (2008) 109.

some reviewers as obscene; for instance, the *Scots Observer* asserted that it dealt in 'matters only fitted for the Criminal Investigation Department or a hearing *in camera*'.[33]

Answering this review, Wilde wrote, 'Each man sees his own sin in Dorian Gray. What Dorian Gray's sins are no one knows. He who finds them has brought them.' To endow the tale with that reflective capacity, Wilde claimed, was 'the aim of the artist who wrote the story' and he pronounced the effort a success.[34]

Wilde responded further to these accusations when he revised the novel in 1891. In the preface, he wrote that '[t]hose who find ugly meanings in beautiful things are corrupt.' Continuing in the same vein, he explained that 'there is no such thing as a moral or an immoral book' and added that the 'dislike of realism is the rage of Caliban seeing his own face in a glass'.[35] Whereas in the magazine version, Lord Henry makes no answer to Dorian's complaint about having been poisoned, in the 1891 book version Lord Henry ridicules the idea: '[Art] is superbly sterile. The books that the world calls immoral are books that show the world its own shame.'[36] The novel was not prosecuted for obscenity in Britain,[37] but after Wilde's conviction for 'gross indecency', *Dorian Gray* was the only one of his publications to vanish from the literary marketplace: Wilde's publishers had prepared a second edition, which they sold off to a dealer in second-hand books, and the novel was not reprinted in Britain for eighteen years (save for a single, surreptitious piracy). Commentators celebrated Wilde's conviction as a verdict on the novel, observing, for example, that although *Dorian Gray*'s 'abominable immoralities' were aimed at 'the upper circles of the reading world', they had the same kind of 'corrupting influence' as more popular works 'which incite a less cultivated section of the reading public to even more dangerous crimes'.[38]

In some related research, I have discussed the history of obscenity prosecutions in Britain, arguing that a concern with the work's effects, rather than the author's intentions, was not a product of the 1868 decision in *R v. Hicklin* (as some scholars have thought), but has provided the basis for these prosecutions ever since obscenity became a matter for the criminal law, in the late seventeenth century.[39] In explaining

[33] 'Reviews and Magazines,' *Scots Observer* 4 (5 July 1890) 181. Another reviewer speculated that 'the Treasury or the Vigilance Society [might] think it worth their while to prosecute Mr. Oscar Wilde'. Samuel Henry Jeyes, 'A Study in Puppydom,' *St. James's Gazette* (24 June 1890) 3. The National Vigilance Association often initiated obscenity prosecutions.

[34] Oscar Wilde, 'To the Editor of the *Scots Observer*' (9 July 1890), in Merlin Holland and Rupert Hart-Davis (eds.), *The Complete Letters of Oscar Wilde* (2000) 439.

[35] Wilde (n. 32) 3.   [36] Ibid., 183.

[37] However, it was removed from library shelves in St. Louis and Newark and was banned in Russia. Evelyn Geller, *Forbidden Books in American Public Libraries, 1876–1939* (1984) 51; Marianna Tax Choldin, *Russian Censorship of Western Ideas under the Tsars* (1985) 111.

[38] Hugh Chisholm, 'How to Counteract the "Penny Dreadful"' (1895) 58 *Fortnightly Review* 765.

[39] Simon Stern, 'Cleland and the "Laws of Decency": Investigating Obscenity in Eighteenth-Century England', *Eighteenth-Century Life* (forthcoming); Simon Stern, 'Wilde's Obscenity Effect: Influence and Immorality in *The Picture of Dorian Gray*' (2017) 68 *Review of English Studies* 756.

that 'the test of obscenity is . . . whether the tendency of the matter . . . is to deprave and corrupt those whose minds are open to such immoral influences, and into whose hands [the] publication . . . may fall',[40] *Hicklin* merely summarized the logic that had long governed the analysis of obscenity. Indeed, *Hicklin* is notable less for what it says than for what it implies. Its concern with 'those whose minds are open to such immoral influences' was understood to be directed at 'the young person', who had also been a perennial object of the law's protection in this area since the late seventeenth century; and the attention to works that were likely to 'fall' into the hands of such readers was understood to refer to cheap books and prints, as opposed to expensive publications billing themselves as limited editions, intended for medical professionals or bibliophiles.

If this way of framing the aims of obscenity law was not particularly new, *Hicklin's* language was nevertheless helpful because it expressed these ideas so succinctly, furnishing an eminently quotable axiom that both British and American judges quickly adopted. Besides its concise, if tacit, specification of the objects of obscenity law, *Hicklin* also gestured implicitly towards the law's subject—namely, the reasonable man, whom the test relies on as the agent charged with recognizing 'the tendency . . . to deprave and corrupt'. In the second half of the nineteenth century, the reasonable man increasingly furnished the means by which the law oriented its objective standards in numerous areas,[41] and this kind of guidepost was particularly useful for language crimes, such as obscenity, sedition, and blasphemy, which were concerned with the words' effects rather than the speaker's intentions. Whenever language is regulated on the basis of its effects, the authorities may opt to prosecute after the injury has occurred and proof of the harm can be offered up, or may insist that a publication has an inherently harmful tendency, according to the kind of objective observer who is capable of discerning it—the reasonable man. The latter approach has the great advantage of eliminating the need to produce victims of these crimes (who are often hard to find), thereby translating the problem of proof into an entirely different register—one that infers the criminal effect from the text itself, based on a legal standard that judges can apply without any difficulty. *Hicklin* operates, then, in a Janus-like fashion, hinting at one kind of individual (the young person) as its object and another (the reasonable man) as its subject. That is precisely the way in which Wilde's protagonist operates, to similar effect.

As suggested above, *Dorian Gray* refrains from depicting any illicit conduct in particular and, in doing so, the novel courts the accusation that it depicts immorality; the story proceeds by inference and implication rather than by direct representation. Its cultivation of this reflective capacity is most salient in the character of Dorian Gray himself. The artist Basil Hallward completes the painting

---

[40] *R v. Hicklin*, (1868) LR 3 QB 360, 371.

[41] See Simon Stern, '*R. v. Jones* (1703): The Origins of the Reasonable Person', in Henry Mares, Ian Williams, and Phil Handler (eds.), *Landmark Cases in Criminal Law* (2017) 59–79.

of the twenty-year-old Dorian at the very moment when the latter is meditating on Lord Henry's provocative and hedonistic precepts, uttered in language that Dorian finds utterly captivating: 'Words! Mere words! How terrible they were! How clear, vivid, and cruel! One could not escape from them! And yet what a subtle magic there was in them!'[42] Dorian's expression during this reverie (he stands silently, 'with parted lips, and eyes strangely bright') is charged with an erotic force that Basil and Lord Henry register and that both of them find enchanting. Thus when Dorian wishes to change places with the painting and has his wish granted, the countenance he shows to the world, for the remainder of the story, is the one that Basil has captured during those crucial, reflective moments. People who meet him have various reactions—most of them are charmed, some are horrified, and more than a few see him as 'the true realization of a type of which they had often dreamed'.[43] The face they see reflects back their own dispositions, and it does so through the erotically charged medium of a young man discovering within himself the impulses awakened by a decadent philosophy. It is not his youth alone, but also this peculiarly reflexive erotic power, that makes him such an absorbing object of attention wherever he goes.

Dorian may appear to recall the 'young person' whom the law seeks to protect: not quite at the age of majority when he has his portrait painted, he falls unhesitatingly under the spell of Lord Henry's words, seemingly confirming the fear that one whose mind is 'open to . . . immoral influences' will go immediately from innocence to depravity and corruption. As if to underscore the point, Wilde informs us that Lord Henry, as he watches Dorian's reaction (and reflects on it, in turn) is reminded of 'a book that he had read when he was sixteen, a book which had revealed to him much that he had not known before', making him wonder 'whether Dorian Gray was passing through a similar experience'.[44] Two 'young persons', then—one who is twenty, one who is sixteen, both of them captivated and corrupted by an immoral influence.

At the same time, Dorian Gray's name might also conjure up the sombre, impersonal figure, shaded in neutral tones, that exemplifies the standard of the reasonable man—a standard, as Oliver Wendell Holmes explained in 1881, that 'should correspond with the actual feelings and demands of the community'.[45] Dorian would, undoubtedly, repudiate any suggestion that he is 'reasonable,' but his status as a model for the community is evident: some regard him as the exemplification of 'a type that . . . combine[s] . . . the real culture of the scholar with all the grace and

---

[42] Wilde (n. 32) 19.   [43] Ibid., 109.   [44] Ibid., 19.

[45] Oliver Wendell Holmes, *The Common Law* (1881) 41. On the tendency to be reasonable, the novel offers no kind words. Told that Americans 'are absolutely reasonable' and that this trait is 'their distinguishing characteristic', Lord Henry translates the statement into a claim about rationality and justification, which he finds abhorrent: 'How dreadful! . . . I can stand brute force, but brute reason is quite unbearable. There is something unfair about its use. It is hitting below the intellect.' Wilde (n. 32) 36.

distinction and perfect manner of a citizen of the world', and his mode of dressing and deportment leads 'the young exquisites of the Mayfair balls and Pall Mall club windows' to 'cop[y] him in everything'.[46] Dorian's dual mode of existence, making him at once a member of the fashionable London world and an external observer (frequently described, in the text, as an idealization), nicely exemplifies the means by which the 'reasonable man' standard operates. Dorian serves the same mirror-like function within the plot that the novel claims for itself. He embodies the Janus face that we saw in the *Hicklin* test, figuring both as the object of the law's concern and the abstracted subject that deploys a test for discerning others' tendencies.

Yet in serving these two functions, Dorian ironizes both of them. The speed of his reaction, and the amplification that Wilde achieves by offering Lord Henry as a second, younger example of a young person, have the effect of undermining the logic of *Hicklin*, caricaturing it through exaggeration rather than reproducing it. Dorian's rapid transformation mocks the supposition that corrupting influences operate so quickly and directly; according to the theories that Wilde elaborates throughout his writing, influence proceeds circuitously and indirectly.[47] The same applies to the novel's driving conceit, namely, that the portrait instantaneously changes with each new act of depravity that Dorian commits, undergoing an alteration that would otherwise—equally rapidly—have been discernible on his body.[48] Finally, the agent who applies the *Hicklin* standard is caught up in the same process of self-recognition, denial, and condemnation that Wilde attributes to the novel's other readers. In asserting that 'immoral' books are the ones that 'show the world its own shame', Wilde suggests that all who pronounce this verdict—book reviewers and legal actors alike—are inadvertently indicting themselves, exposing their own sins, and hence that instead of viewing the matter objectively, the wielder of the law's 'reasonable man' standard is implicated in the very process that he claims to discern. In Wildean paradox, then, obscenity law comes to stand in a contradictory relation to the harmful results it guards against: if (as Wilde implies) the effect's source is in the observer, then the law is looking in the wrong place when it attends to the text, and if the text actually has the power ascribed to it, then it can ensnare even the ideal observer of legal analysis, the 'true realization of a type' of which the jurists have 'often dreamed'.

Dorian Gray presents itself as a challenge to the logic of *Hicklin*, not by criticizing the law or taking on the subject of obscenity, but by holding itself up to the law's suppositions. Observing the result is akin to watching sunlight ricochet in the Hall of Mirrors at Versailles. Yet these are effects we can recognize only if we ask

---

[46]   Ibid., 110.

[47]   See, e.g., Valerie Rohy, 'Strange Influence: *The Picture of Dorian Gray*', in *Lost Causes: Narrative, Etiology, and Queer Theory* (2014) 56–79.

[48]   On the painting's cinematic ability to 'recor[d] real-world events in real time', see Aaron Worth, 'James, Marsh, Wilde: Uncanny Kinetics in the 1890s' (2016) 44 *Victorian Literature and Culture* 363, 368.

what the novel does rather than what it asserts. It is evident that many of Wilde's contemporaries considered it obscene and that—whether or not he meant to provoke that response, in particular—Wilde hoped that the novel would act as a touchstone. Henry James observed that '[e]verything Oscar does is a deliberate trap for the literalist', and that nevertheless, nothing was more common than 'to see the literalist walk straight up to it, look straight at it and step straight into it'.[49]

In this chapter I have sought to display two ways of studying the connections between law and literature, one focused on the explicit, and the other on the implicit, proposing that both approaches can inform legal history by suggesting new avenues of research and presenting legal doctrines and decisions in a new light. Mining textual corpora for legal language can complement the efforts that legal scholars typically undertake, using databases of cases and treatises. Because the search procedures are largely transposable, the turn to literary databases may seem the more appealing option. One might think that imaginative writing invites attention to how it works, as opposed to what it says, in a way that legal sources do not; however, this kind of investigation can remind us that the difference is, at most, a matter of degree rather than kind. Legal history is often, necessarily, concerned with the literal—with the explicit grounds of lawyers' arguments and judicial decisions, writs and verbal formulae, and quantifiable data about legal institutions and actors. But legal sources, no less than the other materials that historians study alongside them, often reveal similarly rich layers of meaning when we ask how they work, what they say implicitly, and what they avoid saying. If one of the rewards of reading law with literature is to reveal new perspectives on legal institutions and actors, another is to bring fresh insights to the study of conventional legal materials.

BIBLIOGRAPHY

Elizabeth Anker, Bernadette Meyler (eds.), *New Directions in Law and Literature* (Oxford University Press, 2017)

Stephen Best, *The Fugitive's Properties: Law and the Poetics of Possession* (University of Chicago Press, 2004)

Jeffory A. Clymer, *Family Money: Property, Race, and Literature in the Nineteenth Century* (Oxford University Press, 2012)

Bradin Cormack, *A Power to Do Justice: Jurisdiction, English Literature, and the Rise of Common Law, 1509–1625* (University of Chicago Press, 2007)

Gregg Crane, *Race, Citizenship, and Law in American Literature* (Cambridge University Press, 2002)

Jeannine Marie DeLombard, *In the Shadow of the Gallows: Race, Crime, and American Civic Identity* (University of Pennsylvania Press, 2012)

[49] Letter of 23 February 1892, in Leon Edel (ed.), *The Letters of Henry James* (1974–1984) 3:373.

Rex Ferguson, *Criminal Law and the Modernist Novel: Experience on Trial* (Cambridge University Press, 2013)

Jonathan Grossman, *The Art of Alibi: English Law Courts and the Novel* (Johns Hopkins University Press, 2002)

Lorna Hutson, *The Invention of Suspicion: Law and Mimesis in Shakespeare and Renaissance Drama* (Oxford University Press, 2008)

Lorna Hutson (ed.), *The Oxford Handbook of English and Literature, 1500–1700* (Oxford University Press, 2017)

John O'Brien, *Literature Incorporated: The Cultural Unconscious of the Business Corporation, 1650–1850* (University of Chicago Press, 2015)

Beth Piatote, *Domestic Subjects: Gender, Citizenship, and Law in Native American Literature* (Yale University Press, 2013)

Caleb Smith, *The Oracle and the Curse: A Poetics of Justice from the Revolution to the Civil War* (Harvard University Press, 2013)

Christopher Warren, *Literature and the Law of Nations, 1580–1680* (Oxford University Press, 2015)

Alexander Welsh, *Strong Representations: Narrative and Circumstantial Evidence in England* (Johns Hopkins University Press, 1992)

Edlie Wong, *Racial Reconstruction: Black Inclusion, Chinese Exclusion, and the Fictions of Citizenship* (New York University Press, 2015)

CHAPTER 5

RHETORIC AND THE POSSIBILITIES OF LEGAL HISTORY

MARIANNE CONSTABLE
AND SAMERA ESMEIR

WHAT do history and law signify in the work of legal historians? What does the enterprise of legal history assume the relations of history and law to be? Such questions are matters of rhetoric. Their answers inform the practice of legal history. By qualifying the history they investigate as 'legal,' historians aim to recover legal content. They distinguish words and acts of law from other matters of history, such as politics, economy, theology, and literature. Most legal historians posit law as an object in some historical past. They track law's content and transformations over time and explore law's fate. To them, history presents the temporal unfolding, law offers the substance; history gazes backward, law appears in the past. According to such historians, history constitutes a larger movement of past time; legal history makes up a sub-story.

A number of assumptions inform this kind of legal historian's relation to law and history. One assumption is that history's domain is that of temporality and that law endures over time, as an object of or for history. Another assumption is that law can be distinguished from other matters. Such historians believe that law can be revealed through words and perceived to exist (or to have existed). Law, however powerful or ineffective, may exist in relation to other forces and texts or independently of them, but it is always conceived as to some extent distinct.

From the point of view of rhetoric, these assumptions are neither wrong nor right. They are productive of the labour of many legal historians and constitute the conditions of possibility of much legal history. A rhetorical approach to legal history attends to such assumptions while doing something other than judging them. In attending to the assumptions of law and history, that is, the rhetoric of legal history attempts to release law from its status as explicit object of or for history—even as rhetoric somewhat paradoxically takes legal history to be the object of rhetoric.

History, to be sure, is not alone in treating law as an object. Most interdisciplinary studies of law posit law this way. Both social scientific and literary knowledges of law presume the hierarchy of subject over object and locate themselves, along with their knowers, in a position of disciplinary authority over law. Sociology of law, for instance, is a subfield of sociology; whatever the differences within the field, it studies law as an institution of social control. Likewise, literary scholars bring particular approaches, such as critical theory, psychoanalysis, and so forth, to bear on the legal texts that they take as their object.

Rhetoric does not reverse the hierarchy of subject over object, however, as do many within the legal professoriate. The latter in some sense reverse the historians' approach, by taking for granted that law, as subject, governs the things and relations of the world as its objects. In contrast, the historically-oriented legal rhetorician seeks neither to affirm nor to reverse the hierarchy between a subject with mastery over its object of knowledge. Instead, the rhetorician working in legal history takes up and interrogates this fascinating split, itself characteristic of modern disciplines and knowledges, to explore how it shows up vis-à-vis law. The issues that emerge in such explorations allow law to show itself otherwise than as object or subject.

The legal rhetorician may begin, as do we, with the observation that contemporary legal historians, like legal practitioners, to some degree privilege writings and documents. Both legal historians and practitioners attend to language in one form or another as source and evidence of law (even if only to claim, in the manner of socio-legal scholars, that 'law' is observed in the breach or in the so-called gap between law-in-action and law-on-the-books). In this context, the rhetorician may then wonder whether law, rather than being a readily available past object that can be located in written words, texts, or documents, may not also be unwritten or unrecorded, its words inaccessible to our modern eye or ear. The rhetorician wonders: suppose law had been neither written nor declared, its imprints never left or even made. Suppose there had been no words or records with which to locate law. Or suppose law had been declared and written, but its archive had been displaced or destroyed by negligence, by accidents, or by wars of conquest, colonization, and expansion. Suppose that an archive had survived, but that the memory of the legal universe which prompted that archive did not. How then would one read law's remains? Could one do so without a memory of the world contemporaneous with those remains? Must one rely on our present legal universe to chart a journey into the legal past? Might this reliance yield some law where none existed? Or render invisible a law that might otherwise appear? And if one were to locate law through a properly-remembered archive, what would one make of the unremembered laws that were shed along the way?

Conundrums of source and archive, of material and interpretation, of memory and forgetfulness, do more than complicate the classifications of law as an object of history occurring within a temporal context. They also suggest that law may be silent. Silence may be an obstacle to understanding or an invitation to further exploration of legal universes. When incorporated—through rhetoric—into writing about legal history, historical conundrums and legal silences incite one to a different kind of search into law. They show how sources and memories of law enable particular readings of the past and foreclose others, thereby opening up reflection on the very sources and memories that inform more conventional searches for law in our present.

Working concurrently in rhetoric, in law, and in history, the two of us find that making the sorts of issues that we articulate above into an explicit focus of our work distinguishes our concerns from that of many other—excellent—legal historians. Such focus allows us to ask different sorts of questions, to question what counts as law, and to challenge—in the name of what may be another law—injustices that may pass as justice.

The question for one of us, currently working with late nineteenth- to early twentieth-century U.S. materials, has become: how is it possible to write a history of 'unwritten' law, given the reliance of both law and history on writings as sources, evidence, and authority? Non-officially recognized practices of what came to be called 'new unwritten law' ostensibly exonerated women who killed their husbands in turn-of-the-century Chicago. Tracing the emergence of such practices shows how even the unwritten, for the legal historian, is a matter of records and writings. The naming of formerly unarticulated practices and their recognition as law privileges the standing and authority of explicit or formal law. In the context of the much earlier medieval practice of mixed juries, too, law formally recognized what had previously been local practices of allowing aliens on juries as law. This recognition reinforced the authority of the king's courts and of official law over those practices. Both in medieval mixed jury cases and in much later exonerations of husband-killers, formal articulation of practices and their official appropriation render suspect the status as law of unarticulated practices or customs. New questions emerge: what is it to acknowledge what was nameless? What was before the name? What does naming do to unwritten law? What does writing do? How do naming and writing relate to existence? What could a legal history of an unarticulated 'new unwritten law' be? How does one know or how can there be a history of something that was unnamed, unwritten, or in some ways did not exist?

For the other of us, working on nineteenth-century Ottoman-Islamic materials, the challenge concerns the attempt to narrate a legal history of rebellions, whose signifier, *isyan* (disobedience), conveys illegality. Furthermore, unlike the modern concept of revolution, *isyan*'s objective is not the constitution of a new legal order. In Islamic jurisprudence, *isyan* is first and foremost disruptive. The difficulty of relating the legal history of *isyan* is compounded when studying a particular *isyan* in Palestine whose events concluded in the defeat of the rebels, with no Ottoman state legal records articulating law's relationship to the event, not even as an agent of repression. Instead, the archival records of the rebellion narrate a history of military victory, the killing of the rebels, and the conscription of their children. How can one write a legal history of a defeated rebellion, which neither engendered a new legal order nor incited a counter-legal response? What account is possible absent legal theories or documents carving out some potential legal space for rebellion and in the presence of records of the execution and the exiling of the rebels? Does this absence necessitate writing off the failed rebellion as an extra-legal event, or as an event rendered illegal by state law? Might there be another law that informs the rebels' action—a law that does not consist of the written text of legal history, but of the unwritten claims of justice that are the background for political action, or of a divine law that does not belong to the historical era but informs ethical and political judgment? Might a rebellion have a place in law, even as it does not aspire to constitute a new legal order, but restricts itself to disruption? And if so, what is that law and why capture it through the "law"?

In what follows, we draw on our own concerns and those of others to show how rhetorically-inflected legal histories may integrate into their work questions about sources and archives, destruction and silences, and the many temporalities of law. The work we propose renders visible the hold of state law, or of authoritative positive law, on our current historical imaginary. In challenging conventional wisdom about the questions to be asked in doing legal history, we aim to open up possibilities of law.

I. Sources and Archives

Historians often presume that law refers to the law of the state or, at least in part, to the more-or-less discrete social or speech acts of formal institutions. Such acts include Congressional enactments, trial instruction, verdicts, exonerations, and pardons, as well as marriages, contracts, and so forth, material evidence of which can be found in official documents, files, and archives. Indeed, state archives often serve as model sources of law. Acts of state in effect comprise the statements of rules of Hartian legal positivism, which conceives of the modern municipal legal system as a unified system of primary rules that citizens obey and secondary rules that officials accept.[1] When historians do consider the nonverbal conduct or behaviour of officials and institutions to be expressions or manifestations of state law, they look to non-state documents primarily for contacts, overlaps, and contradictions with official state records. The value of such non-state documents becomes secondary or derivative. Knowledge of their existence often becomes known only coincidentally. Hence when the state offers the dominant model of archiving, the contingency and reliability of private writings becomes an issue. How authoritative are the writings of non-state entities or authors? How valid are they for determining law? What sort of law? How do differences in author-reader relationships, in diaries, and in letters, matter? In what senses can journals and other writings be considered public— or reveal everyday norms?[2] (Even setting aside questions about the neutrality or 'objectivity' of a person's perceptions—and how we presume that these are different than those of an institution—how might acts of writing themselves transform practices and words?)

Working within the methods of social science to approach state law, many legal historians ask such questions as: what are the appropriate sources for this study? How reliable are they? To what degree can they support the particular inferences to be made in, and the generalizations to be suggested by, the account to be offered? The methods of these historians parallel those of the legal practitioner who inquires into the sources and authority for the position that the practitioner posits and maintains. A legal historian concerned with rhetoric however will also ask: how have particular sorts of evidence become privileged as sources? How is it that the renderings of this particular institution have come to be considered authoritative? What produces standards of reliability? How have some kinds of documents come to be considered authentic? To what extent can such matters of authoritativeness and authenticity be related to the particular story being told?

Just as social scientists characteristically abstract from concrete examples, formulating general statements that then govern their inquiry into other examples or areas of law, so too do some historians. General theorization takes over, and the concrete facts and sources are lost to abstract theorization and readings. The source appears as a source, that is, from within a framework of research that abstracts from a document's earlier use; its actual life or use and meanings are lost to method and theory. The rhetorical approach, in response, translates or transforms the inquiry, making the question of what appears to be an appropriate source itself the focus of interrogation. For a historical study of land holdings in a particular region, for instance, one might assume that forged deeds should not count as evidence. How

---

[1] Hart, *Concept of Law* (1961).

[2] For a brilliant reading of a journal, including implications for law, see Laurel Ulrich, *A Midwife's Tale: The Life of Martha Ballard, Based on her Diary, 1785–1812* (1990).

is it, then, that at one time in England what we now consider forgeries served as authoritative evidence in legal disputes? Are they not forgeries? Or might ostensible forgeries have established—reliable—records of sales after the fact? Why might such documents have been created? Did similar practices occur elsewhere? In our own era of near-universal literacy and of duplication, photographic reproduction, and instantaneous communication, those questions—and their answers—point to now-unfamiliar ways of validating and determining ownership claims. Insights into such alternative ways of proving the truth of ownership arise in asking not only what a document reveals, but also how it has come to be, and to be conceived as, an unreliable or an inappropriate—or non-authoritative—source, and how other documents have not.

One way of interrogating documents or sources is to ask to what sort of discourse they belong. Here Foucault's 'order of discourse' or 'discourse on language' offers some helpful ways of thinking about how the sources of disciplines such as law and history are both developed by and rely on particular practices.[3] In their 'will to truth,' particular knowledges make various sorts of exclusions, allow only particular kinds of commentaries, and train their initiates through their own fellowships and associations of knowledge. It has become commonplace to say that there are different ways of reading, but it is not any the less true for being repeated. In U.S. law schools, for instance, students learn to identify what law 'is' by reading authoritative texts—by judges and others—and commentary. They learn to decontextualize and recontextualize what they read as law in particular ways, extracting statements of rules from a limited set of texts, which they then bring to bear on analogous fact situations, irrespective of chronology or periodization.[4] Students learn that, although in some sense infinitely malleable, the statements of rules and the stories of cases they can tell are constrained by the possibilities of the authoritative archive and its categories, just as an appellate court's consideration of the facts of a case is constrained by what occurred at trial and appears in the transcript. Asked to imagine another sort of story than the one told by the Court in a textbook case on evidence law, for instance, one law student asked 'You mean a torts story?'[5]

If law students learn to circumscribe legal acts, history students, by contrast, learn to situate the institutional acts and events that they take law to be in much broader social and cultural context. They study—or skim—long books full of details that provide accounts of matters that are classified not by particular authorities as such, but by historical periods and regions. In treating divorce, the lawyer (or law

---

[3] Michel Foucault, 'Order of Discourse' also translated as 'The Discourse on Language', in *Archaeology of Knowledge* (1972).

[4] Elizabeth Mertz, *The Language of Law School: 'Learning to Think Like a Lawyer'* (2007); Jennifer Andrus, *Entextualizing Domestic Violence* (2015).

[5] West Academic's 'Law Stories Series' offers some behind-the-scenes accounts of famous U.S. court decisions that exemplify limits of the formal archive.

student) offers rules as to what to do and how, while the legal historian provides an explanation in terms of the society, culture, and institutions of a period.

Foucault adapts the phrase 'will to truth' from Nietzsche, who writes of explanation that 'The banker thinks at once of "business," the Christian of "sin," the girl of her love.'[6] Nietzsche and Foucault suggest that what 'counts' as true in any particular discourse links to the desires, needs, and habits of particular subjects. One can imagine oneself as another kind of subject than one is (to some degree), however, by reading with or against a text, as does, for instance, Upendra Baxi.

The counter-reading Upendra Baxi offers in his reflections on colonial law in India releases one from the confines of the discursive order to which the source belongs. Baxi examines one archival source in a case concerning a rebellion against the colonial state: a testimony by a Shakiri who appears in the records as the Approver, that is, he whose testimony verifies for the prosecution the facts of violence enabling the sentencing of the participants. But rather than read Shakiri's testimony as an instrument of colonial justice, as a 'sealed text' in a colonial discursive field that secures the source as an 'Approver's Testimony,' Baxi offers an imaginative reading of the testimony. His reading exceeds the written words of the testimony and inquires into the possible motivations of Shakiri's words, transforming an act of reneging into a possible act of solidarity with ex-comrades. Baxi's imaginative reading is an example of a rhetorical reading that releases subjects, like Shakiri, and sources, like the Approver's Testimony, from their status as 'vessels, or discursive fields, into which history—colonial or subaltern—pours content'.[7]

Baxi shows how one can move between the surface of words and their depths, arriving at an interpretation that exceeds both or that stands arrested in between. Reading this way can reveal the 'legal theory' that frames a document as a source and that mediates its words, showing how particular ways of thinking have become taken-for-granted by particular sorts of subjects, in areas of law, or in periods of history. Cornelia Vismann in *Files*, for instance, attends precisely to what makes particular sources authoritative and what that authoritativeness can do.[8] She shows how different forms of record-making and record-keeping correspond to different forms of governance and constitute different kinds of subjects. If papyrus scrolls were used for the imperial administration of territories, the development of more durable parchment and loose leaf files, which could be updated, corresponded to Rome's 'eternal empire'. As modes of transfer, storage, manipulation, and deletion change, so too do the roles of files in law. An often-hidden basis for the bureaucratic administration of subjects of modern state law, the file itself—as in East Germany after the fall of the Berlin Wall—has now become the subject of administration.

---

[6] Nietzsche, *Twilight of the Idols*, trans. R. J. Hollingdale, 'Four Great Errors' (1968) section 5.

[7] Upendra Baxi, 'The State's Emissary: The Place of Law in Subaltern Studies', in Partha Chatterjee and Gyanendra Pandey (eds.), *Subaltern Studies* VII (1992) 247 ff.

[8] Vismann, *Files: Law and Media Technology* (2008).

Key to what we are calling the 'rhetorical' approach to legal history is the way that its interrogation of assumptions and methods about law allows us to take up a perspective on state law. Rhetorical legal history maintains that there are other—perhaps radically different—possibilities of law than those that are today taken for granted. Modern state law offers only one set of histories of law. Competing and intertwined accounts of law, of governance, of practices, of knowledge of what to do, or of how to act, or how to live, can be found. Even when involving what is called 'religion,' they need not involve throwbacks to natural law. The rhetorical approach need not seek to secure a definition or singular 'concept' of law. It may take Hart's 'concept' of the modern legal system as one, perhaps the predominant, understanding of contemporary law, most compatible with modern state law, but it does not exclude other kinds of law, such as *shari'a* or custom. Just as a rhetorical approach does not aim to simply reverse the subject-object dynamic of history-law, so too it does not aim to expand the logic of state law to where no state existed. Rather, it explores formations in non-Western traditions which others have translated into English as 'law,' whether to render them legible or to facilitate comparisons. Rhetoric recognizes that such acts of productive, failed translation divest other orders of some of their distinctiveness, even before the inquiry into their history begins.

Consider the modern translation of *shari'a* into the concept of 'Islamic law'. This translation renders *shari'a* legible as law comparable to other systems of law. Yet this legibility is possible only by offering *shari'a* the English language concept of law, which by the time of the translation has itself undergone transformations that generated it out of, and separated it from, ethics and theology. This translation, in other words, makes the jural forms characteristic of *shari'a*, which are comparable but distinct from the modern concept of law, more difficult to appreciate. In 'What is Shari'a?' Wael Hallaq suggests that the modern translation of *shari'a* into 'Islamic law' reveals the difficulties in linguistically representing non-Western traditions. He notes that 'our [English] language fails us in our endeavour to produce a representation of that history,' which he adds 'articulated itself conceptually, epistemically, morally, socially, culturally, and institutionally in manners and ways utterly different from those material and non-material cultures that produced modernity and its Western linguistic cultures'. At issue, however, is not only the possible loss of the sign *shari'a* through its assimilation into the concept of Islamic law, with its modernist, state-centred connotations. At issue is also how the modern concept of law takes over as the model according to which *shari'a* is evaluated, disciplined, and reformed. One instance of such evaluation is when the absent distinction between law and morality constitutive of *shari'a* qualifies it as an imperfect law, necessitating overcoming or reform. For Hallaq, therefore, 'the very use of the word law is *a priori* problematic; to use it is to project, if not superimpose, on the legal culture of Islam notions saturated with the conceptual specificity of nation-state law'.[9] For us, however, the

---

[9] Wael Hallaq, *Shari'a: Theory, Practice, Transformation* (2009) 2 ff.

task of the legal rhetorician-cum-legal historian is not only to rescue the translation of *shariʿa*, or other legal orders, from the concept of law, but to open up 'law' beyond both its positivist concept and its English definition.

The challenge is to write histories of law that at once open law up to different traditions and legal forms, that is, and at the same time to not collapse them all into the English word, law. The danger resembles that which Hayden White points out for history and modern historiography. How is it possible to write a (narrative) history of the way in which history has come to be narrative without excluding precisely those non-narrative modes of recording events (such as annals and chronicles) of which one would have history take account?[10]

Moving beyond *shariʿa*, a number of works suggest that categories of 'religious law' and religion emerge with nineteenth-century secularization in Europe. Anglo traditions themselves have also supported practices, phenomena, or ways of life that have bound persons in ways that state law has not adequately captured—or perhaps has, in another sense, captured only too well. The mixed or half-alien jury *de medietate linguae* of the past, for instance, brought together alien and local jurors who represented the laws of other places when they rendered a verdict or 'speaking of truth' in lawsuits involving alien parties. Works on Native American, First Nations, and aboriginal law, too, show the existence of non-state communities, traditions, groups, and collectives that have or have had ways of living that resist or refuse state law, have tried to negotiate with it on their own terms, or have otherwise challenged the monopoly of the state law model for understanding law.[11]

The state archive not only tempts one to understand law as state law, but its own internal divisions and classifications tempt one to follow law as it appears in these divisions: under court cases, in the general prosecutor's office, as legislative material, and so forth. The divisions that archivists generate to assist in efficient research thus generate boundaries of law and indeed materialize law as a limit concept, with an inside that is distinct from other laws and other matters and materials of history. The archive also seduces us into believing that it is the medium for recovery of a legal past.

Unconventionally presented legal histories draw attention to such issues. Having found local East German court archives that had not been discarded as called for, Inge Markovits, in *Justice in Lüritz*, acknowledges that she speculates as to transformations in 'her' court and its judges.[12] By introducing matters of serendipity and speculation that are not always explicitly addressed, her work invites readers to wonder about the fortuitousness of preservation and encounter. How does

---

[10] Hayden White, 'The Value of Narrativity in the Representation of Reality' (1980) 7:1 *Critical Inquiry* 5 ff.

[11] Vine DeLoria, Jr., *Behind the Trail of Broken Treaties* (orig. 1974, rev. 2010); Audra Simpson, *Mohawk Interruptus* (2014); Kirsten Anker, *Declarations of Interdependence* (2014).

[12] Inge Markovits, *Justice in Lüritz* (2010).

preservation differ from protection? What could have been protected? Under what terms? By whom and why? What was considered worthy of protection? And for what human purposes? And what, by contrast, may (as here) have been preserved by being forgotten? In Markovits' hands, documents and archives are not so much the records of static rules as they are traces of dynamic events, even when they testify to a failure to discard.

In sum, rhetorically-inflected legal history interrogates legal and historical assumptions, exploring how sources are taken as 'authoritative' or foundational and suggesting, importantly, that perhaps they need not have been so. It expands the domain of what counts as law while also questioning its categories. Rhetorical legal history connects law with an inquiry into the will to truth that ultimately critiques the ways in which particular relations—between subjects who know and objects of knowledge, as well as among subjects of law—are presumed to be foundational.

II. Destruction and Silences

In approaching documents and archives as sources of legal history, many legal historians treat absences in records as unfortunate gaps. They presume that a more complete archive is a better archive. Here again, historians' expectations and desires conform to those of modern state law, with its drive towards codification and, in the U.S., federal rules and model codes. Even codification and the expectation that codes contain a complete statement of law, however, has a history worth exploring. Early codes did not presume exhaustiveness.[13] Hammurabi's 'Code,' for instance, though later treated as a model by other so-called legal systems, seems to be a collection of supplementary judicial decisions. The laws there record resolutions of disputes by abstracting from them, thereby settling issues that were apparently in flux, against a background of law that was not articulated and presumably not (yet) contested. The nineteenth-century Anglo-American drive towards codification and its reinforcement of the authoritativeness of writing and particular sorts of state action has been written about, but bears further exploration of what it aimed to leave out and why.

Rather than considering records exclusively for what they say, that is, one can deal affirmatively with what they don't say. One can also consider the absence of records productively. What is not said—or not written—can of course be interpreted

---

[13] David Daube, 'Code and Codas', in *Collected Works of David Daube, vol. III: Biblical Law and Literature* (2003).

different ways: as unnecessary to say (as in Hammurabi's code), as nonexistent (such as cyberlaw in earlier centuries or written records of some disputes), as unthought (before 'new' law emerges or in Foucault's usage), as forgotten (for a time) and then remembered, as denied (as in some legal fictions), as repressed or suppressed (as in Peter Goodrich's work on legal images or Maria Aristodemou's on psychoanalysis of law), or as destroyed, which we consider below. Just as silences of law may be read in various ways, so too the absences of records or sources encountered by the legal historian offer different sorts of opportunities for doing history.

Several legal traditions offer readings of silence as generative and integral to law. Michel Chodkiewicz argues that for Ibn 'Arabi, a twelfth-century Muslim Sufi theologian, the silences of law are part of its plentitude. They are not gaps, lacunas, or an occasion for an exception that must be filled up and clarified; they are no more fortuitous than the pronouncements of law. In Ibn 'Arabi's writings, the silences of law are related to its ambiguities. The Quran, the law, is a treasure 'whose abundance is truly infinite'. Knowing the Quran, or the law, does not entail knowing its words, but the 'generation of an immeasurable sweetness that surpasses all joy'. The Quran/law descends upon tongues but more profoundly upon the hearts, a descent that 'brings comprehension with it'. To understand the Quran's allusions to divine secrets, one must travel within the revealed word, its surface and its depth, its visible signifier and the invisible signified, or, to use Ibn Arabi's own metaphor, the depths of the oceans and the surfaces of the shore. And since all language and all words have a divine origin, the divine both reveals itself through language and hides itself by what it says; many of its secrets transcend the limits of language. Hence all words return to their principle, to their primordial silence, inviting a journey of perpetual discovery and perpetual revelation.[14]

Here silence emerges as the background of law's explicit words, generative of them and of attempts to comprehend them. While this hermeneutics may appear to best fit the believer or the scholar working from within the Islamic tradition, the rhetorician also finds it useful in thinking about silence as that out of which speech—of law or of history—may come.[15]

If there is a silence which is generative of law or speech that one may attend to from within law, there are also legal silences that come from without. The destruction of sources and archives through accidents of history, such as fires or robberies, or through colonization, occupation, and genocide provoke different kinds of histories. They follow destruction and occur in the ruins, when the 'facts' of legal history (or at least its documents and archives) no longer exist. Silences

---

[14] Michel Chodkiewicz, *An Ocean Without Shore: Ibn Arabi, the Book, and the Law* (1993).

[15] Marianne Constable, *Just Silences: Limits and Possibilities of Modern Law* (2005), arguing in the context of Anglo-American law that justice lies (in all the various meanings of the term 'lie') in the silences of law and legal texts. See also ' "Response" to Review by John Conley, of Just Silences' (2010) 33:1 *PoLAR: Political and Legal Anthropology Review* 148–51 ff.

need not be read simply as gaps in the sources, as absences to be ignored or that lack filling in. Destruction often triggers counter-excavation efforts, activating state and non-state machineries to collect more sources, reprint documents, and rebuild archives. One complements fragments of written records with oral words, archiving them too. The more destruction, the more archiving, as legal historians collect scattered evidence to rebuild a world from the fragments that remain.

In the work of legal historians who work on occupied countries, where archives have either been destroyed or sealed off by occupying powers, the task becomes the search for hidden truth. These are histories of worlds and laws turned inaccessible not only through the passing of time, but also because of the destruction of the written documents pertaining to their existence. Like historians of war-torn countries, historians of traditions lost to modern state law encounter the challenge of stitching together a world destroyed, to render it visible and to save it, in words, from oblivion.

In such historians' valiant attempts to reconstruct a law lost, law emerges ever more intensely as an object of excavation. The more loss and destruction, the more objectification of law, and paradoxically the more distanced that law becomes, thereby entrenching the subject-object relationship. It becomes all the more important to acknowledge the tentativeness of the effort and its incompleteness.

Out of such tentativeness may come recognition that some destructions do more than lose sources and cannot be met with counter-excavation efforts. Even archival traces of the occurrence of some kinds of destruction may themselves be lost. In histories of genocide or of ethnic cleansing, for instance, historians may find evidence and establish facts of mass murder and of mass exile, but fail to find evidence of intentions to commit such acts. As a matter of law, however, intentions and designs define such monstrous events as genocide. Without evidence of intention and designs, the legal decision and naming of genocide as fact does not occur, Marc Nichanian argues in relation to the Armenian genocide. Absent the legal decision and absent an archive, he writes, genocide 'is not a fact'. It is, rather, the destruction even of fact, of the notion of fact, of 'the factuality of fact'. If historians can only study evidence in archives, then they cannot account for an event founded on the destruction of that which defines their discipline: the archive or the fact. And if courts of law rely on the work of historians, or on similar facticity to establish genocidal will or intent, then genocide cannot be definitively established. Both legal proceedings and historiography limit the establishment of the fact of a genocide. The proliferation of testimonies aiming to prove genocide do not overcome these limits; rather, as Nichanian argues, they remain captive to the genocidal logic of factuality and doubt.[16]

Can one escape what Nichanian calls the logic of factuality and will (which relates back to Nietzsche and Foucault's 'will to truth' above)? For Nichanian,

---

[16] Marc Nichanian, *The Historiographic Perversion*, trans. Gil Anidjar (2009), p. 70.

concerned with the Armenian genocide, the first task is to understand how the legal category of genocide enhances the impossible desire to secure a meaning for an otherwise indefinable event, transforming it into a criminal category and an object of intensified doubt that requires factual evidence. The next task, he argues, is to move away from the legal category of genocide, to think 'catastrophe,' and to liberate the event 'of everything that transforms [the event] into an object, an instance, or a fact, that gives a delusory *meaning* to it'.[17] For Nichanian, the objectification of genocide is accomplished through the complicity of law and history; testimony that is ostensibly outside law and history must become (the new) document and archive.

A rhetorically inflected legal history will likewise think with and against legal categories. It will articulate testimonies without necessarily subjecting them to legal and historiographic validity tests; it will recall witnesses without turning them into authoritative archival sources or material; it will narrate without filtering out legally irrelevant evidence and events. A rhetorical legal history, following Nichanian, may write the history of a crime, without attempting to prove that it occurred. It may write the history of an unwritten law and of its disappearance. Such histories open up events, releasing them from the disciplinary and temporal confines of what is cognizable in modern law and historiography.

III. TIME AND LAW

The static view of law as object belonging to a subject corresponds to an understanding of time as a series of present moments or as a linear chronology. Future events come into a present or take place now, then fade into the past. Conversely, things may endure from the past into the present and then into the future. From the historian's perspective of time as a series or flow of moments, law, like all else, passes through time, whether as an object whose qualities or attributes evolve or change through time or as an event that after coming to be fades into the past.

Law can indeed be perceived this way, as indebted to a past or as producing a future. But law is not only like other objects or events of history. Law itself is a historicizing force that establishes temporal relations. Law may authoritatively declare something ostensibly present to be legally past, for instance, by overcoming or dismembering it. The overruling of past cases in the common law tradition leads in the direction of departure from the past, while legal declarations may establish

17 Marc Nichanian, *Writers of a Disaster: Armenian Literature in the Twentieth Century* (2002).

states of affairs that have not yet been. Such legal acts may hasten or retard the unfolding of events.

Law's indebtedness to the past is itself complex. The 'traditions' of both common law and *shari'a* constitute threads, in Hannah Arendt's words, that guide communities and individuals through the vast realms of the past. For Arendt, this thread is 'also the chain fettering each successive generation to a predetermined aspect of the past'.[18] Yet Arendt suggests that modern progressive temporality no longer navigates a way to the past through tradition. Rather, positivist legal orders legitimate themselves through the authority of the written word of the legal present. Such legal orders, as Hayden White also points out of modern histories, dismember the pre-positivist past and the continuity between present and future. The law of the privileged present variously authorizes or overcomes its own past. Positivist jurisprudence textbooks, for instance, present readers with self-referential legal narratives that constitute the law they describe. The historical references in these narratives do not acknowledge their indebtedness to the past so much as they signal their independence or distance from it.[19]

Legal orders may also reach out to a future utopia for their present grounds and arguments, conceiving of past and present in terms of a progressive future. In revolutionary legal orders, as in utopian human rights regimes, the objective is to accelerate time and to bring about a better future.[20] By contrast, some legal orders valorize the immediate (present) and conceive of the (more distant) future as a threat. Post-Cold War individual human rights projects manifest this temporality.[21]

Finally, some law appears a-historical, not simply in the sense that its texts have no sense of history, like presentist positivism, but insofar as they function with or within an expansive sense of time. They subject human beings to infinite law or to a law, whether divine or mystical, natural or supernatural, beyond human authorship and control.

In short, the language of legal texts reveals that laws and legal orders offer, make use of, and produce different relationships in and with time. They temporalize and periodize past, present, and future in different ways. Further, insofar as law is known to the historian through language, and insofar as language cannot divorce itself from past meanings or possible future mutations, the rhetorically-aware historian encounters yet another relation of law to time. Language itself carries on from the past and includes within it future possibilities.

---

[18] Hannah Arendt, *Between Past and Future: Eight Exercises in Political Thought* (1961) 94 ff. For the articulation of this relation in *shari'a*, see Wael Hallaq, *Authority, Continuity and Change in Islamic Law* (2005).

[19] For the relationship between positivism and presentism, see Samera Esmeir, *Juridical Humanity: A Colonial History* (2012).

[20] Reinhart Koselleck, *Futures Past: On the Semantics of Historical Time*, trans. Keith Tribe (2004 [1979]).

[21] Stefan Ludwig Hoffmann, 'Human Rights and History' (2016) 232:1 *Past Present* 279 ff.

Language itself is temporally layered. Through words, law stores and anticipates. Memories of previous legal orders guide analyses in new ones. Judges from older orders populate new courts and interpret new laws. Even after revolutions and independence, following ostensibly wholesale adoption of new laws in colonial, post-socialist, or modernizing legal orders, previous words and texts continue to occupy shelf space in law libraries. Law thus holds within itself what Koselleck calls the 'contemporaneity of the non-contemporaneous' or layers of co-extensive times and temporalities.

To the historian, the functions of law and legal language—temporalizing and periodizing, on the one hand, and storing and anticipating, on the other—may appear to conflict. The first set reveals ruptures, detachments, and breaks, as well as classifications and categorizations; the second reveals the co-presence of that which lies in the sediments of law and language. Holding these functions together enables one to note how different legal orders shape experiences of time which extend beyond strict periodizations and ruptures and whose potentially subversive legacies await activation.

From very different fields and perspectives, Jacques Derrida and H. L. A. Hart make what can be taken to be related rhetorical points about the temporality of law. Both treat of what is, in effect, the grammatical future perfect tense, namely, what 'will have been' once a particular act that takes place in a present is completed. The 'fabulous retroactivity' that Derrida accords to the signing of the Declaration of Independence of the very people whom the U.S. Declaration ostensibly brings into being through its signing, applies also to the authorization of any legal act. An act is not authorized as such until it is completed, and yet it must be made or performed to become authorized. Likewise Hart writes of English judge-made law that in deciding questions that arise as to the applicability of a statement of a rule to a particular instance, one 'shall have rendered more determinate our initial aim' and 'shall . . . have settled' questions as to the meaning of the earlier rule. A legal holding too comes to serve as precedent, as has often been pointed out, only if and after a new analogous case arises; at that moment, the first case will have become precedent—or will be recognized as having been such an event. The future perfect tense thus both ruptures linear time and offers the possibility of closure in a more determinate identification of what count as acts or events.

Law not only consists of distinct acts or events; it also constitutes the more amorphous background against which acts and events occur. This temporal background can be likened to the imperfect aspect of verbs in some languages. In sentences such as 'we *were speaking* English when we made the agreement' or 'we *are in the habit of dating* our drafts', the use of the gerund ('ing') marks a background or context of activity or of practical knowledge (of what to do), against which a particular event or act (in the form of an active verb, such as 'made' in the first example) occurs (or could occur). The temporality of law is imperfect, not only because shared background knowledges of law are incomplete and overlapping, but also in a manner akin to grammatically imperfect activity, insofar as law is continuous and habitual—as well as interruptible. As in the grammatical use of the imperfect, law is an ongoing, yet interruptible, activity which serves as a background against which more specific legal acts or events may stand out or occur.

These formulations and others suggest that a rhetorically-inflected legal history must be attentive to the ways that different legal orders contribute to different experiences of time and construe temporality differently. To accept this means that history can no longer be conceived as a container of time within which law proceeds chronologically. One cannot retrieve a past nor 'return' to it, but showing the strangeness of the past or that there has been a radically different past than what we know or take for granted (as in our own rhetorical legal histories) opens the possibility of an unpredictable future. Moving away from conceptions of history in which the past is detached from or authorized by a present that only progresses into the future, rhetorical legal history finds resources in the past that may constitute a check on our present or expand our imagination of law and of the just. This is not entirely a gaze backward; the past persists as potentiality.[22]

IV. CONCLUSION

Rhetorically-oriented legal histories foreground issues that today's legal histories sometimes forego. Rhetorically-inflected legal histories make explicit and render problematic the ways in which law is an object of study for the scholar of history, a subject who draws on and interprets legal records to recount how law has changed over time. Rather than aiming to reverse this subject-object relation and to make history the object of law, rhetoric dwells on the ways in which legal historians' assumptions (as to the sources, the silences, and the temporalities of legal history) correspond to knowledge of the positivist law of the modern state. Rhetoric, in making legal history its object, challenges legal historical scholarship to interrogate itself and to present its work in ways that destabilize the status of law as object.

---

[22] In the words on Alexandra Lianeri reflecting on Koselleck's conceptual history and the work of translation, there is 'an accumulated memory of past meanings inscribed into a concept as possibilities of future signification, but also as traces of a recurring silencing associated with the past'. Alexandra Lianeri, 'A Regime of Untranslatables: Temporalities of Translation and Conceptual History' (2014) 53 *History and Theory* 477 ff.

Bibliography

Hannah Arendt, *Between Past and Future: Eight Exercises in Political Thought* (Viking, 1961)

Upendra Baxi, 'The State's Emissary: The Place of Law in Subaltern Studies', in Partha Chatterjee, Gyanendra Pandey (eds.), *Subaltern Studies VII: Writings on South Asian History and Society* (OUP India, 1992)

Michel Chodkiewicz, *An Ocean Without Shore: Ibn Arabi, the Book, and the Law* (SUNY, 1993)

Marianne Constable, *The Law of the Other: The Mixed Jury and Changing Conceptions of Citizenship, Law, and Knowledge* (Chicago, 1994)

Marianne Constable, *Just Silences: The Limits and Possibilities of Modern Law* (Princeton, 2005)

Marianne Constable, *Our Word is Our Bond: How Legal Speech Acts* (Stanford, 2014)

David Daube, 'Codes and Codas', in *Collected Works of David Daube, vol. III: Biblical Law and Literature* (Robbins Collection, 2003)

Samera Esmeir, *Juridical Humanity: A Colonial History* (Stanford, 2012)

Reinhart Koselleck, *Futures Past: On the Semantics of Historical Time*, trans. Keith Tribe (MIT Press, 2004 [1979])

Wael Hallaq, *Shari'a: Theory, Practice, Transformation* (Cambridge, 2009)

Inga Markovits, *Justice in Lüritz: Experiencing Socialist Law in East Germany* (Princeton, 2010)

Marc Nichanian, *The Historiographic Perversion*, trans. Gil Anidjar (Columbia, 2009)

Laurel Thatcher Ulrich, *A Midwife's Tale: The Life of Martha Ballard, Based on Her Diary, 1785–1812* (Knopf, 1990)

Cornelia Vismann, *Files: Law and Media Technology* (Stanford, 2008)

Hayden White, 'The Value of Narrativity in the Representation of Reality' (1980) 7:1 *Critical Inquiry* 5 ff

PART II

APPROACHES: CONCEPTUALIZING LEGAL HISTORY

CHAPTER 6

LEGAL HISTORY AS LEGAL SCHOLARSHIP

DOCTRINALISM, INTERDISCIPLINARITY, AND CRITICAL ANALYSIS OF LAW

MARKUS D. DUBBER*

LEGAL history is having a methodological moment. So is law (and, as it turns out, history as well)—and not just in one country or legal system, but across the common law/civil law divide.

In this chapter I try to capture some aspects of this methodological moment—or moments—and then to add some reflections of my own that locate legal history within the enterprise of legal scholarship. More specifically, I will outline an approach to legal history that regards historical analysis as one mode of critical analysis of law, along with other modes of 'interdisciplinary' analysis (economical, philosophical,

* Professor of Law & Director, Centre for Ethics, University of Toronto. Thanks to the Alexander-von-Humboldt Foundation, the Royal Society of Canada, and the Social Sciences and Humanities Research Council of Canada for financial support, to Klaus Günther (Goethe-University Frankfurt/Excellence Cluster 'Normative Orders') and Tatjana Hörnle (Humboldt-University Berlin) for their kind hospitality, and to Simon Stern and Chris Tomlins for comments and encouragement.

sociological, literary, etc.) and 'doctrinal' analysis. In this way, legal history plays a key role in the general effort to move beyond the long-standing and rhetorically useful, but ultimately unproductive, distinction between 'modern' and 'traditional' legal scholarship, and that between 'common law' and 'civil law' scholarship besides.[1] According to this view of legal history, it is a mode of jurisprudence (in fact, we might call it New Historical Jurisprudence), rather than a subspeciality of law or a form of applied history.

But, first, let's take a look at the recent methodological stirrings in law and legal history. This will be an incomplete overview, highlighting certain features of a large and varied interdisciplinary and international literature. I'll draw examples primarily from the U.S. and Germany, as familiar—and familiarly imperfect— stand-ins for 'common law' and 'civil law' perspectives, with side glances at other countries, including Britain (England and Scotland) and France.

Since I'm interested here in locating legal history within legal scholarship, I'll move from the latter to the former. Sections I and II focus on two recent developments in legal methodology, one in the U.S. literature, the other in the civil law sphere. At first glance, these trends appear to point in opposite directions; upon closer inspection, however, they can be seen to converge. They mark out a space for a broadly contextual and interdisciplinary view of legal scholarship as *critical analysis of law*.

The U.S. trend is all about the rediscovery of law as the subject of legal scholarship and of doctrinalism as a respectable, even important, way of going about the academic study of law. This conversation is largely about the legacy of American Legal Realism which, fairly or not, has been blamed for the disappearance of law and legal doctrine from serious legal scholarship in the U.S. and the establishment of a now decades-long interdisciplinary orthodoxy.

In the civil law world, the move has been away from legal doctrine, not towards it. Interdisciplinarity is the name of the game, to open up legal scholarship beyond the parochial and solipsistic pursuit of legal dogmatics associated with traditional legal science (or *Rechtswissenschaft* as *Rechtsdogmatik*) since Savigny and the origins of historical jurisprudence (*historische Rechtswissenschaft*) in the early nineteenth century. Much like the U.S. discussion is about the (almost century-long) legacy of American Legal Realism, then, the civil law discussion is about the (almost two-centuries-long) legacy of Historical Jurisprudence.

Legal scholarship as critical analysis sits at the point of convergence of these trends, from interdisciplinarity to law and from law to interdisciplinarity.

---

[1] See Special Issue, Critical Analysis of Law and the New Interdisciplinarity (2014) 1:1 *Critical Analysis of Law* 1 ff. <http://cal.library.utoronto.ca/index.php/cal/issue/view/1458> (accessed 14 June 2017); Markus D. Dubber, 'Critical Analysis of Law: Interdisciplinarity, Contextuality, and the Future of Legal Studies' (2014) 1:1 *Critical Analysis of Law* <http://cal.library.utoronto.ca/public/journals/99/ CAL.pdf> (accessed 15 June 2017).

Critical analysis of law embraces both because it welcomes any methodological approach that makes critical analysis of the subject of legal scholarship, law, possible, including any interdisciplinary perspective and law's own disciplinary method: doctrinal analysis. Starting from opposite ends of the spectrum, (no-law, no-doctrine) American Legal Realism and (all-law, all-doctrine) German Historical Jurisprudence, both common law and civil law approaches end up in the same place: critical analysis of law (which from one side may appear as New Legal Realism and from the other as New Historical Jurisprudence[2]).

Section III moves from law to legal history, with a stopover at history, more specifically the revival of *longue durée* historiography proposed by Jo Guldi and David Armitage in their *History Manifesto* (2014). I am particularly interested in the vision of 'engaged scholarship' that drives Guldi and Armitage, in which methodological reflection goes beyond the usual navel-gazing to serve the end of critical engagement with the world (as it does in the work of contemporaries in other fields, including notably Thomas Piketty). In the end, then, the approach to legal history I outline in this chapter regards it as one mode of critical analysis of law, understood as a project of engaged legal scholarship that overcomes the rhetorical juxtaposition of doctrinal and interdisciplinary analysis in the service of a comprehensive critique of state power through law in a modern liberal democracy. Legal history plays a central role in this critical project by historicizing, and thereby both substantiating and complicating, the notion of 'modern' law that drives the normative project of critical analysis and, at the same time, defines the contours of the project of critical analysis of law: countries, or jurisdictions, that regard—or portray—themselves as committed to the modern legal-political project of a democratic law state/state under the rule of law.

I. BACK TO LAW

In U.S. legal academe, everyone is a legal realist, and has been for some time. What this means isn't clear, and that's no accident. The legal realists didn't know what a legal realist was, and they liked it that way. They were simply too idiosyncratically clever and innovative to fit a single mould, or so their story went; after all, they were trying to break the mould (of 'Formalism', usually), not to replace it with another. The very mouldness of jurisprudential orthodoxy struck them as un-realist; they

---

[2] It's a little more complicated than that, of course. American Legal Realism and German Historical Jurisprudence don't fit neatly on opposite ends of a spectrum, or at least not as neatly as their caricatures. On New Legal Realism, see Section I below.

preferred to face bravely the unvarnished messiness of law as it really was, and lived, and breathed, rather than force law into a pre-existing set of conceptual categories.

For not quite as long, but also for decades now, everyone in U.S. law academe has been an interdisciplinarian as well. That doesn't actually mean that everyone is doing interdisciplinary scholarship—any more than saying everyone is a legal realist means that everyone is doing legal realist scholarship—but it does mean that interdisciplinary scholarship carries a certain prestige, with the percentage of faculty members with a graduate degree (which is to say, usually, a doctorate) in a subject other than law taken to reflect the faculty's general level of scholarly sophistication. 'Traditional' or 'doctrinal' scholarship, if it is considered scholarship at all, instead tends to be regarded as a less complex task, reflecting an outdated conception of legal scholarship and, ultimately, of law itself.

More recently, however, law has been making a comeback, ironically partly as a result of interdisciplinary engagement. I don't mean the often mentioned, conveniently pre-packaged and labelled, complaints by 'the judiciary' (though, interestingly, not the legislature, never mind the executive!) that the law professoriate has detached itself from its long-standing grounding in doctrinal analysis and no longer does its job of making the lives of federal appellate judges (or their clerks) easier by supplying them with 'doctrine'. This criticism has a point, just not the one it tries to make. Apart from being oddly self-serving, it is myopic in another, more significant, sense: it misconstrues and underestimates the contribution legal academics might make to public scrutiny of state power through law in a modern liberal democracy.

Consider, for instance, the phenomenon of New Doctrinalism, recently the subject of a two-day symposium at the University of Pennsylvania Law School and an accompanying special issue of the *University of Pennsylvania Law Review*. The symposium wears the rediscovery of legal doctrine on its sleeve; in the fine print, however, it turns out that the new doctrinalism is, in fact, an old doctrinalism, the persistence of which is framed as a 'puzzle': the New Doctrinalism is about 'the role that legal doctrine *continues to play* in different areas of American law, *despite the continuing influence of American Legal Realism*' (emphasis added). Doctrine can't be brought back because it had never left, despite the best efforts of 'American Legal Realism' and 'the growing influence of interdisciplinary ideas':

Since the 1930s, American Legal Realism has argued that law is not an autonomous discipline and that traditional legal materials—legislation, regulation and judicial precedent—are not, themselves, sufficient to determine the outcome of the most interesting legal disputes. How that gap is filled, with moral philosophy, industry practice, the idiosyncratic preferences of the judges, economics, etc., has been debated ever since. Yet legal practice and legal discourse remain stubbornly doctrinal. What explains this? It is this puzzle that the symposium hopes to uncover.[3]

---

[3] 'The New Doctrinalism' at Penn Law, *Legal History Blog* (26 September 2014) <http://legalhistoryblog.blogspot.ca/2014/09/the-new-doctrinalism-at-penn-law.html> (accessed 14 June 2017);

Among the participants in this symposium was Hanoch Dagan, a sympathetic historian of legal realism and exponent of another new methodological venture, *Reconstructing American Legal Realism*.[4] Dagan's reconstructed version of legal realism also insists on taking doctrine seriously, but not too seriously. Once again, this turns out not to be an innovation, but merely a recovery, for the not-yet-reconstructed original version of legal realism already had been eager to give doctrinalism its due, just not 'pure Doctrinalism'.[5]

Reconstructed Legal Realism (RLR) is not to be confused with another methodological intervention, New Legal Realism.[6] New Legal Realism (NLR), as its name suggests, also styles itself as revision rather than as invention; in fact, it can be seen as a double revision in the sense that it appears to be a revision of sociolegal ('law & society') scholarship as empirical legal studies on a global scale. At any rate, New Legal Realism, too, insists that doctrine must be taken seriously, though perhaps not quite as seriously, or in quite the same way or for the same reason, as in Reconstructed Legal Realism, not to mention in New Doctrinalism (ND). New Legal Realism's insistence that law and legal doctrine matter appears to grow out of its desire to distance itself from what *it* regards as the methodological orthodoxy in U.S. legal scholarship, which traffics in the 'language of law and economics and rational choice'[7] and, in its empirical variant, uses 'microeconomic or behavioral methods to identify the nonlegal independent variables causing or determining law defined as a dependent variable'. By contrast, NLR pays attention to 'law itself'.[8]

At the other end of our imaginary doctrinalist spectrum (from ND to RLR to NLR) sits another methodological project, the New Private Law (NPL).[9] NPL does not shy away from the view that OLR (Old Legal Realism) had no (constructive) use for doctrine and, in fact, defined itself in large part through its rejection of doctrinalism. To the contrary, NPL sees itself as throwing off the realist

see also Shyamkrishna Balganesh, 'Foreword: The Constraint of Legal Doctrine' (2015) 163 *U. Pa. L. R.* 1843 ff.

[4] Hanoch Dagan, *Reconstructing American Legal Realism & Rethinking Private Law Theory* (2013). As the title of Dagan's book makes clear, however, he is after more than methodology; he puts that methodology to work in 'rethinking private law theory'. See generally Book Forum (2014) 1 *Critical Analysis of Law* 199 ff.

[5] Hanoch Dagan, 'Doctrinal Categories, Legal Realism, and the Rule of Law' (2015) 163 *U. Pa. L. R.* 1889 ff., 1890.

[6] New Legal Realism (NLR)—like Old Legal Realism (OLR)—can be hard to pin down. Dagan and Kreitner provide a convenient overview of the literature, though with the ultimate aim of positioning Reconstructed Legal Realism (RLR) in relation to NLR. Hanoch Dagan, Roy Kreitner, 'The New Legal Realism and the Realist View of Law' (forthcoming 2017) *Law & Soc. Inquiry*. To be precise, Dagan and Kreitner refer to their approach as 'the realist view of law'.

[7] Mary Anne Case, 'Is There a Lingua Franca for the American Legal Academy?' in Elizabeth Mertz et al. (eds.), *The New Legal Realism: Volume 1: Translating Law-and-Society for Today's Legal Practice* (2016) 289 ff., 291–2.

[8] Michael McCann, Preface to 'The New Legal Realism, Volumes I and II', in ibid. xv ff., xvii.

[9] Symposium, 'The New Private Law' (2012) 125(7) *Harv. L. R.*

anti-doctrinalist orthodoxy by rediscovering doctrinalism and, after decades of neglect and disrespect, taking doctrine seriously again and giving it its due. NPL, then, is not a revision of legal realism (once or twice over), but a revision of the sort of doctrinal scholarship that legal realism not only rejected, but destroyed. It is a rebirth of private *law*, not a reconstruction of legal realism or, even worse, a global expansion of the legal realist project that, according to NPL, has dominated U.S. legal scholarship.

Again, what matters for present purposes is not whether any of these 'new' methodological projects get legal realism righter than the next or hits the precise Goldilocksian middle between too much or too little, too pure or too diluted, doctrinalism. They all acknowledge that legal doctrine (if only as a 'language/ discourse'[10]) must find a place in legal scholarship, even if they may disagree on what that place is and how much of a status upgrade for doctrine is required (roughly, from NLR on one end to NPL on the other). They all also identify themselves as addressing questions of *legal* methodology, as legal scholars engaged in scholarship on law, for its own sake and on its own terms. For the NPLer, this may mean throwing off the yoke of interdisciplinarity and reaffirming the study of legal doctrine; for the NLRer, this may mean throwing off the yoke of a particular interdisciplinary approach to legal scholarship that in fact fails to engage with law as such.

There is something artificial about this call for the rediscovery of doctrine, at least insofar as it relies on a line-up of strawmen, several rows deep, to dramatize the need for a turn, or return, one way or another. But such is the 'language/ discourse' of methodological interventions, and many other academic 'turns' (or 'returns') besides, and seems particularly appropriate given the legal realists' own penchant for casual if entertaining caricature. To the extent anything turns on the question of whether the legal realists, or even some subset of them, did or did not reject doctrine, or assigned it (or law) some more or less significant place in the jurisprudential firmament, this seems like a distraction for methodological (and even for historiographical) purposes. Focusing on American Legal Realism also, on the face of it, looks like an unpromisingly parochial start to a project of framing the future of 'legal scholarship' unmodified or globalized.[11]

At the same time, it's worth noting that the mentioned methodological prescriptions are, without exception, framed not as radical breaks from the past (unlike, again, the legal realists in certain moods), but as revivals or revisions of roads less travelled. If law wants to participate in an interdisciplinary dialogue, rather than serve as the playground for other disciplines, it would do well to develop a habit of reflecting on its methodology over time, rather than as occasional episodes of reinvention, hopefully while retaining a healthy disdain for navel-gazing, avoiding

---

[10] McCann (n. 8) xvii.

[11] Unless, perhaps, it's seen as one starting point of a convergence of approaches, the other being the traditional methodology of civil law scholarship: (historical) legal science. See Section II.

unproductive taxonomic and genealogic squabbles (say, about 'legal realism' and 'its' view of 'doctrine'), and—above all—heeding Holmes's admonition: 'For lack of imagination, five dollars.'

That legal scholarship should be about law certainly would seem to be obvious enough without engaging in extensive methodological archaeology or debunking myths about American Legal Realism. And if 'Legal Realism' had declared categorically that it was *not* 'law-centred' and that whatever it was taking seriously, it certainly would not be law, and had made clear, just to remove any remaining ambiguity, that this meant (also?) that it had no interest whatsoever in legal doctrine or 'doctrinalism' in any shape or form, then it would be absurd: a discipline practised by law professors at law schools teaching law students and publishing in law reviews that would not be about law. Put another way, if 'Legal Realism' were not law-centric in the end, anyone who dismissed it as a fit of juvenile (even quintessentially American) contrariness that should be ignored in polite scholarly society[12] would have been right. In other words, we'd have discovered another reason to detach reflection about legal methodology from thinking about 'Legal Realism' (in fact or fiction).

Interestingly, one of the clearest reminders of the lawness and the doctrinalism of legal scholarship arises from interdisciplinary engagement, i.e., from outside legal scholarship rather than from within. Anyone who has participated in interdisciplinary dialogue about law will be familiar with the phenomenon of the 'interdisciplinary jurist'. The interdisciplinary jurist is a law professor whose role in interdisciplinary discourse is reduced to that of an expert witness or legal consultant; anticipating a rich and stimulating exchange of ideas across disciplinary boundaries, interdisciplinary jurists instead find themselves fielding questions about what the law is, which—depending on the topic and the context—usually call for an answer in the form of a citation to an authoritative legal text (a statute preferably, though a court decision might do in a pinch), conveniently accompanied by a canned summary of its content.

The point here is not to capture the disappointment of the interdisciplinary jurist at being reduced to a human hornbook,[13] but to note that non-lawyer participants in interdisciplinary discourse about law very much expect lawyer participants to know—and care—a great deal about law in general and about legal doctrine in

[12] For a sympathetic version of this sentiment by someone who otherwise might have been mistaken for a proto-Realist, see Hermann Kantorowicz, 'Some Rationalism About Realism' (1934) 43 *Yale L.J.* 1240 ff. Ironically, Kantorowicz's own provocative foray into Free Law, Gnaeus Flavius (pseud.), *Der Kampf um die Rechtswissenschaft* (Winter, 1906), was dismissed by German Legal Science for the same reason. German jurisprudence simply kept going about its formalist-doctrinalist business and, by and large, has been happily going about it ever since. See Section II.

[13] Or to record the law professor's shock at an unsophisticated (and vaguely insulting) understanding of law and, more important, legal scholarship. Cf. Julie Stone Peters, 'Law, Literature and the Vanishing Real: On the Future of an Interdisciplinary Illusion' (2005) 120 *Pubs. Mod. Language Assoc.* 442 ff.

particular. Of course, more than doctrinal expertise is needed for interdisciplinary exchange, most importantly the curiosity to go beyond the boundaries of law as a discipline, and of doctrinal analysis of law, in the first place. A familiarity with other disciplinary enterprises and approaches, and perhaps even expertise in one of them (as indicated by a graduate degree, possibly), would be helpful as well, of course; but, unlike intellectual curiosity and doctrinal expertise, it's not a prerequisite.

Law is what lawyers bring to the interdisciplinary table, whether they like it or not. In this way, embracing law and doctrinal analysis of law as the subject matter and distinctive mode of analysis of law scholarship and teaching, far from being anathema to interdisciplinary scholarship, instead makes true interdisciplinarity possible. By true interdisciplinarity, I mean the bilateral interdisciplinarity, in contrast to a unilateral mode of interdisciplinarity that 'applies the tools of established disciplines (again, primarily in the social sciences) to the raw material of "law", which had remained unprocessed in the hands of amateur lawyer-scholars':

Bilateral interdisciplinarity requires two disciplines, rather than using the subject matter of one discipline as a testing ground for the other. This approach captures the sparks that fly when two disciplines come into contact (and perhaps even collide), each benefitting from the other, and in the end generating more light (and perhaps heat) together than each could by itself. It is a horizontal, rather than hierarchical, interdisciplinarity, reflecting mutual respect among equals rather than application of one's superior wisdom, sophistication, expertise, or experience to another realm.[14]

There is no reason, of course, why one's expertise in law, and facility with doctrinal analysis of law, has to match the expectations of newcomers to the interdisciplinary conversation. Just because a sociologist expects law professors to contribute some 'law' stuff by citing chapter and verse of this or that piece of legislation doesn't mean that law professors can't have a nuanced appreciation of doctrinal analysis itself[15] or of its place in the toolkit of modes of critical analysis. Doing law, and doing doctrinal analysis of law, doesn't mean doing law badly or doing doctrinal analysis exclusively. Taking law, and doctrinalism, seriously doesn't mean taking it too seriously.

After all, the point of interdisciplinary dialogue is precisely to expand the repertoire of mutually complementary modes of critical analysis of law to make possible a multifaceted, both multi- and inter-disciplinary, contextual enterprise of legal scholarship. This means not only nurturing a variety of modes of critical analysis, but also militating against the dominance of one mode at the expense of others. Doctrinal analysis of law is not the only game in town. At the same time, simply replacing it with another dominant, or even exclusive, mode of critical analysis of law is problematic as well. New Legal Realism adherents, for instance, would rightly object to 'law and economics and rational choice' as the *lingua franca*

---

[14] Dubber (n. 1).
[15] Duncan Kennedy, 'Legal Education and the Reproduction of Hierarchy' (1982) 32 *J. Legal Educ.* 591 ff.

of—U.S., and increasingly global—legal scholarship, even if law and economics had paid closer attention to legal, rather than nonlegal, variables.

II. Away from Law

So far we have focused on the rediscovery of law and of its doctrinal analysis in U.S. legal scholarship. Legal scholarship turns out to be about law, after all, and doctrinal analysis finds its rightful place among a palette of modes of critical analysis of law. We've encountered two other modes of critical analysis: economic analysis of law (or 'law and economics') and sociological analysis of law (or 'law and society'), with empirical analysis of law ('empirical legal studies') as a possible third (if it is conceived as a mode apart from the previous two). There are many others, of course, historical analysis of law among them (plus psychological, philosophical, literary, anthropological, ethnographic, archaeological, cultural, social, feminist, Marxist, and so on).

While U.S. legal scholarship has been busy reminding itself of the significance of law as its subject and of doctrinalism as one of its modes of critical analysis, legal scholarship in the civil law world has begun to realize that there is a world beyond law and beyond doctrinal analysis. Untouched by American Legal Realism and the interdisciplinary revolution that swept doctrinalism out of the halls of (high status) U.S. law schools, legal scholarship in the civil law world—'legal science'—recently has started to reflect on its law- and doctrinalism-centred *modus operandi*.

Legal scholarship in civil law countries has remained largely unchanged methodologically since at least the beginning of the nineteenth century. At the risk of oversimplification, if not caricature, legal scholarship in the civil law world remains committed to a self-conception as legal science, so much so that legal scholarship and legal science are frequently treated as synonyms. The idea of a science of law has a long history (which is difficult to trace since both of its constituent ideas—law and science—are moving parts), but it's fairly common to locate the beginning of 'modern' legal science, in the civil law world, at the turn of the nineteenth century, and more specifically, in the emergence of Friedrich Carl von Savigny's project of 'historical legal science' (*historische Rechtswissenschaft*). The law in Savigny's legal science was *Roman law* (and, more specifically, Roman civil law); the science was both law and history, not necessarily in that order. History was needed to discover the original, pure, sources of Roman law, which the acid of historical research had stripped of the accumulated distortions of centuries of copying, editing, commenting by more or less competent scholars (*The Law of Possession* (1803)). Law, thus having been revealed in its unvarnished fundamental building blocks through a thorough historical cleansing with the help of a detailed method for assessing the purity and reliability of sources and their human handlers, could now be scientifically assembled into a comprehensive coherent system (*System of Contemporary Roman Law* (1840–1848)). This construction was not a historiographical reconstructive exercise, as one might imaginatively assemble a complete dinosaur's skeleton out of properly dated and classified individual archaeological discoveries. It was instead a work of contemporary legal science, in Savigny's case, of contemporary German (civil) law, which eventually undergirded the German Civil Code of 1900.

Now, to say that civil law scholarship, or at least German legal scholarship, continues to pursue this project of legal science to this day is true enough, but also misleading in several interesting ways. First, it's not clear whether there is one project here, or two. By the middle of the nineteenth century, historical legal science had lost its history. Just as Savigny had turned his attention from the legal archaeology of *The Law of Possession* to the doctrinalism of *System of Contemporary Roman Law*, so historical legal science became legal science first, and history a remote second. By 1884, when one of its most prominent exponents, Rudolf von Jhering, had a change of heart and ridiculed the 'Heaven of Legal Concepts' in a bit of holiday satire,[16] historical legal science had long been consumed by, and identified with, an all-encompassing doctrinalist project that from one professorial generation to the next progressed, through scientific discovery, ever closer to an ideal of systematic perfection (if not juridical truth).

For our purposes, this evolution of historical legal science is both interesting and ironic: what started out as an exercise in historical analysis of law turned not only into an exercise in doctrinal analysis of law, but into a radically a-historical exercise in doctrinal analysis of law. The pursuit of purely doctrinal legal science has no use for historical context; in pursuit of an ideal measured in terms of rationality, systematicity, correctness, even truth, legal science has no more use for history than physics has for the history of science. It's not surprising, perhaps, that historical legal science could so quickly and easily morph into an a-historical legal science. After all, Savigny's historical method was not interested in context, either; Savigny's aim was to remove context, to turn back the hands of time to reveal the purity of Roman law norms that could then be used to assemble the contemporary system of law.

At any rate, to say that civil law scholarship continues to pursue Savigny's historical legal science is to say that it pursues its later incarnation of a-historical legal science, that to common law eyes looks very much like the (almost cartoonish) sort of formal-conceptual-abstract doctrinalism that the American Legal Realists enjoyed butting up against. In fact, a reference to Jhering's 'dream' of the Heaven

---

[16] Rudolf von Jhering, 'Im juristischen Begriffshimmel: Ein Phantasiebild', in *Scherz und Ernst in der Jurisprudenz* (1884) 245 ff.

of Legal Concepts populated by his fellow master doctrinalists of historical legal science opens Felix Cohen's well-known contribution to the American Legal Realist canon, his 1935 article 'Transcendental Nonsense and the Functional Approach'.[17]

Second, Jhering's methodological turn suggests another reason why we might take with a grain of salt the general observation that civil law scholarship has been stuck in the same legal scientific rut (or continuous progress towards systemic perfection, depending on your point of view) since 1803 or thereabouts. Even if we ignore the remarkable shift from the centrality to the irrelevance of historical analysis, from history as guarantor of scientific legal scholarship to history as distraction (or non-essential diversion) from proper legal scientific research, and focus exclusively on the later, a-historical, version of modern legal science, the path of its orthodoxy, and therefore the progressive pursuit of legal scientific discovery, was not quite as straight as it may appear in hindsight. The dominance of doctrinal legal science was challenged at regular intervals: for instance, around the turn of the twentieth century, by Jhering and the sociological jurisprudes and Free Lawyers after him (including Hermann Kantorowicz),[18] then, over a half century later, in the late 1960s, by Rudolf Wiethölter and others.[19]

These methodological interventions, however, remained just that: momentary disruptions that failed to knock the legal scientific project off its stride. Once the moment, however brief, of methodological experimentation had passed, the legal scientific complex went back to business as usual. In fact, legal science's resilience to such ill-conceived and half-baked excitements only confirmed to its practitioners its superiority to legal scholarship in other countries, say, in common law countries, where modern legal science never managed to establish itself—never mind to progress, institutionally and substantively—as it did in civil law countries, and notably in Germany.[20]

If viewed in a different light (or even from the outside in), however, the story of German legal science may not differ as radically from that of U.S. legal scholarship as is generally supposed. If one takes the purported moments of deviation seriously, the story of German legal science might appear as the story of road(s) not taken. At the turn of the twentieth century, formalist doctrinalism faced an interdisciplinary and self-critical challenge. In Germany, it survived unscathed. In the U.S., it did not.

What's more, these supposed divergences—the original history-centric vision of *historical* legal science and the later recurrent moments of interdisciplinarity

---

[17] Felix Cohen, 'Transcendental Nonsense and the Functional Approach' (1935) 35 *Colum. L. R.* 809 ff., 809.

[18] See n. 12.

[19] See, in particular, this remarkable book based on a series of public radio programs on law (or 'legal science'): Rudolf Wiethölter, *Rechtswissenschaft [Legal Science]: Funk-Kolleg Recht* (1968).

[20] The similarities between the critical response—measured in German law journal reviews (or their absence)—to Kantorowicz's *The Struggle for Legal Science* (1906) and Wiethölter's *Legal Science* (1968) are instructive.

and intradisciplinary critique (or self-doubt and personal reorientation, as in Jhering's case)—help frame the current turn towards interdisciplinarity in civil law scholarship. Is the call for interdisciplinary (and international) engagement to escape the solipsism, irrelevance, and parochialism of orthodox doctrinalism a radical deviation from the project of civil legal science, a point of innovative departure? Or is it instead an opportunity to recover submerged facets of that project which have been dismissed as misguided and luckily inconsequential methodological nuisances? These questions, of course, mirror the questions that have framed the recent methodological discussion in the U.S., which asks similar questions, but in reverse (where doctrinalism is awaiting rediscovery after a long period of interdisciplinary orthodoxy, rather than the other way around).

Then again, instead of uncovering an alternative interdisciplinary strand in civil law scholarship, perhaps the current willingness to consider alternatives to what is regarded as the long-standing norm of formalist doctrinalism is merely the most recent addition to the list of divergent interludes that in the end, rather than challenge the legal scientific status quo, merely affirm its strength and thereby justify and extend its dominance.

In German legal science, the current (re)discovery of interdisciplinarity has treaded lightly, without the provocative texts that marked previous methodological interventions (Kantorowicz's *Struggle for Legal Science* and Wiethölter's *Legal Science*, for instance). The *locus classicus* of the interdisciplinary turn in German legal scholarship is instead very much an establishment document, a lengthy report (available in English translation) on 'Prospects of Legal Scholarship in Germany: Current Situation, Analyses, Recommendations' (2012), produced by the 'German Council of Science and Humanities'—a large blue-ribbon commission that 'provides advice to the German Federal Government and the State (Länder) Governments on the structure and development of higher education and research'.[21] Designed to 'provide an impetus for the advancement of law as an academic subject', the 114-page report addresses a wide range of audiences, including 'legal scholars, . . . decision makers in higher education, and . . . the federal and state governments of Germany', 'the Ministries of Education and Research on the federal and state levels as well as the Ministries of Justice on either level', and 'all the relevant legal professions and their respective associations (lawyers, notaries, public prosecutors and judges)'.[22] The document begins, somewhat ominously, by declaring that '*[l]ike theology and medicine*, law belongs to the so-called professional disciplines'.[23] Much is at stake: we learn, for instance, that law 'is embedded in a long academic tradition and is considered important both with regard to its quality and in numerical terms', as '[b]oth higher education policy makers and

---

[21] Wissenschaftsrat, *Prospects of Legal Scholarship in Germany: Current Situation, Analyses, Recommendations (Drs. 2558-12)* (2014) (original German edn., 2012).

[22] Ibid., at 12.   [23] Ibid., at 11 (emphasis added).

representatives of other disciplines have high expectations for its achievements.' To meet these expectations:

the German Council of Science and Humanities considers it necessary to strengthen legal scholarship in Germany both with regard to research and teaching. In particular, this entails strengthening the foundational subjects, intensifying exchanges within and outside the discipline and opening up legal scholarship towards other academic disciplines and the wider system of higher education and academic research.[24]

More specifically, the report makes four recommendations, including:

[T]he discipline should become more interdisciplinary. To achieve this, legal scholarship in Germany should be opened up to the alternative perspectives of neighbouring disciplines. Intensifying the exchange with the humanities and social sciences will render legal research, study and teaching more dynamic.[25]

Whether this recommendation, if implemented, will have the desired effect remains to be seen. The report's endorsement of interdisciplinarity for the sake of injecting 'dynamism' into German legal scholarship (and teaching), however, is plain enough. And yet, it elicited nothing like the systemic rejection prompted by Kantorowicz's or Wiethölter's critical interventions. Which is not to say that, in the end, it may not have the same impact, or rather the lack of one. The report is an exercise in moderate establishment self-analysis with modest suggestions for adjustment further softened by deep appreciation for both the long and illustrious tradition of German legal science and the unique, complex, and unbending constraints it faces in light of its official duty to train future German lawyers, judges, and state officials.

France, by contrast, does have a manifesto-like text that fired a critical broadside at the French version of positivist doctrinalism, appropriately entitled *La Doctrine* (2004).[26] France, in fact, has produced an institution that defines itself as the locus of this critical perspective, the (fairly) new law school at *Sciences-Po*. Perhaps, over time, a non-doctrinalist (if not anti-doctrinalist) approach will take hold across French legal scholarship, as the critical ('theoretical') exception becomes the institutional norm.

Elsewhere in Europe, traditional (and often Germano-centric) doctrinalism has been drawn into question as well. Jan Smits, a leading private law scholar at Maastricht University in Holland, has noted that European 'legal studies are increasingly becoming less doctrinal and more interdisciplinary', a development that he attributes, sensibly if somewhat prosaically, to 'the institutional change in how public universities are funded' as a result of which 'law faculties increasingly

---

[24] Ibid., at 13. Legal history is among the 'foundational subjects', along with legal philosophy, legal theory, legal sociology. Foundational subjects are strictly distinguished from 'doctrinal subjects'. All doctrinal subjects are mandatory; some foundational subjects are required electives.

[25] Ibid., at 14.

[26] For an earlier piece by the same authors that is available in English translation, see Philippe Jestaz, Christophe Jamin, 'The Entity of French Doctrine' (1998) 18 *Legal Stud.* 415 ff.

have to compete with other faculties, which puts their traditional way of doing things under considerable pressure'.[27]

We could continue our survey of signs of a turn away from (what is generally taken to be) a monolithic and unidirectional tradition of doctrinalism, as straight as it is uncontested and so deeply rooted and long-standing as to have (almost) no past, analysing samples from other countries in the civil law realm. We could even expand our search to England and other common law countries that were latecomers to the interdisciplinary party and remained largely untouched by American Legal Realism, but where legal scholarship has become better integrated into a web of other academic pursuits over the past few decades, extending beyond the sort of common law doctrinalism traditionally pursued by 'proper lawyers'.

Instead, in the interest of space and time, let's stipulate at this point that such a move towards interdisciplinary, and away from doctrinalism, has occurred, or at least has been advocated, in various ways, by various people, for various reasons, in a number of civil law countries, and—earlier—also in common law countries outside the U.S.

Having captured a move towards law and doctrinalism in the U.S. (in Section I) and a move towards interdisciplinarity elsewhere (in Section II), we're left with the impression that legal scholarship in the U.S. and elsewhere is headed in opposite directions. That's true enough, but given their starting points at opposite ends of a spectrum from doctrinalism to interdisciplinarity, moving in opposite directions translates into convergence at a point where doctrinal and interdisciplinary analysis are no longer treated as radically different, but instead are viewed as different modes of inquiry, without privileging one mode over another.

The notion of critical analysis of law marks that spot.[28] It regards doctrinal and interdisciplinary analysis as modes of critical analysis of law. And legal history, as historical analysis of law, is one instance of interdisciplinary analysis (along many others, economic, sociological, philosophical, etc.[29]) within this general contextual account of legal studies.

---

[27] Jan M. Smits, 'Law and Interdisciplinarity: On the Inevitable Normativity of Legal Studies' (2014) 1 *Critical Analysis of Law* 75 ff, 77–8.

[28] There are other ways of capturing this methodological pluralism, for instance, Dagan's Reconstructed Legal Realism and Smits's view of legal studies revolving around the 'inevitable normativity' of law. The differences between these views aren't trivial; the choice, however, is not between doctrinalism and interdisciplinarity, but between different accounts of their interplay.

[29] The focus of this chapter is the place of historical analysis of law within legal scholarship, or discourse, as critical analysis of law. On the recently much-explored relation between historical analysis and other modes of interdisciplinary analysis, in particular philosophical (or 'theoretical') analysis, see, e.g., Maksymilian Del Mar, Michael Lobban (eds.), *Law in Theory and History: New Essays on a Neglected Dialogue* (2016); Symposium, 'Jurisprudence and (Its) History' (2015) 101(4) *Va. L. R.* 849 ff.; Maksmylian Del Mar, 'Philosophical Analysis and Historical Inquiry: Theorising Normativity, Law and Legal Thought', in this handbook.

iii. Legal History as Critical Analysis of Law

What, then, is the place of legal history in legal scholarship regarded as critical analysis of law? To address this question, in the remainder of this chapter I discuss the role of historical and doctrinal analysis in the project of critical analysis of law against the backdrop of recent methodological reflections in history and legal history.[30]

Critical. Critical analysis of law takes a broadly contextual and interdisciplinary approach to legal studies, moving beyond entrenched distinctions and self-imposed limitations, pursuing critique and analysis, theory and doctrine, because both are essential interdependent aspects of the enterprise of legal studies as a discipline. It regards critique without analysis as baseless, and analysis without critique as pointless.

It might be useful, though not necessary, to differentiate between internal (horizontal) and external (vertical) critique.[31] Internal critique draws on formal norms like consistency, comprehensiveness, and coherence. Traditional doctrinalism exemplifies a form of internal critique that, in many (positivist) versions, insists on its pure internality, rejecting any attempt to subject legal norms to what it regards as external, i.e., 'non-legal', norms (justice, right). In this sense, traditional doctrinalism equates critique with internal critique.

External critique subjects legal norms, practices, and institutions to critique in light of external (or substantive) norms, the very norms that traditional doctrinal critique has long declared out of bounds, i.e., extra- or supra-legal norms that leave the comfort of positivistic analysis and serve to critique, and not merely to elucidate, legal norms. The choice, and formulation, of the relevant norms is obviously crucial to this critical exercise. Since we're concerned here with the critical analysis of *law*, everything turns on the operative conception of law, on the fundamental normative commitments implied by a critique of a norm *qua* law.

Historical analysis can play a key role in helping us address the question of the normativity of lawness. Rather than taking a conception of law as given (and constant, if not timeless), or deducing it from some given principle or other, historical analysis can illuminate the genealogy of a conception as constitutive of

---

[30] See generally Markus D. Dubber, 'New Historical Jurisprudence: Legal History as Critical Analysis of Law' (2015) 2 *Critical Analysis of Law* 1 ff; Dubber (n. 1).

[31] This is one way (or perhaps two), not meant as groundbreaking, to flesh out the frequent claim that law is a 'normative' science, rather than, say, an 'empirical' one. See, e.g., Hermann Kantorowicz, 'Some Rationalism About Realism' (1934) 43 *Yale L.J.* 43 1240 ff.

a particular legal-political project of governance. (More on this shortly, when we consider the 'lawness' of an object of critical analysis of law.)

As essentially contextual, historical analysis of law also expands the scope of critical analysis beyond traditional parochial limits and, as a result, makes room for comparative analysis and, more specifically, comparative historical analysis. Legal history, then, is no longer a patchwork of domestic legal histories, but extends through, and beyond, comparative analysis to systemic legal history (e.g., European legal history) and even global legal history (not to be confused with legal history unmodified).[32]

Analysis. Analysing law as the object of critical analysis of law from a variety of perspectives, inter- and intra-disciplinary, promises to reveal different features of 'law' in the abstract and in operation, as a set of norms and as a cluster of practices, as a social enterprise and a bureaucratic institution. These analytic projects may be undertaken for their own sake (whatever that might mean). In critical analysis of law, they are pursued as the means to the end of critique. It makes no sense to critique an aspect of law without appreciating its conception and operation, which includes a thorough and imaginative analysis of its doctrinal design and context. It makes just as little sense to treat one mode of critical analysis as exclusive or as inherently superior to another. For instance, a critical analysis of contemporary U.S. criminal law (and in similar, though not identical, ways also of criminal law in other countries to the extent they regard themselves as committed to the liberal legal-political project) would benefit from a careful contextual and multidisciplinary (e.g., doctrinal, historical, comparative, and administrative) analysis of the complex regime of possession offences (in substantive and procedural criminal law and their interplay) as the modern, far more sophisticated and powerful, version of the centuries-old sweep and incapacitation 'offence' of vagrancy.[33]

Legal history as historical analysis of law here might be contrasted with legal history as antiquarianism, on the one hand, and as 'social history' or 'economic history', on the other. The point of historical analysis is not, as in Savigny's antiquarian jurisprudence, to dig up and dust off shards of pure law from a particular, great 'age' of (Roman) law, when it had reached 'maturity' but had not yet descended into the feebleness of old age. The point of historical analysis of law is to trace the genealogy of law, or legality, over the *longue durée* in a particular legal-political project in order to bring into clearer relief its normative features, which then drive the critical analysis of legal norms and practices within that (temporally and spatially limited) project.

---

[32] See, e.g., Thomas Duve, 'European Legal History: Concepts, Methods, Challenges' in Thomas Duve (ed.), *Entanglements in Legal History: Conceptual Approaches* (2014) 29 ff.; Thomas Duve, 'Global Legal History: A Methodological Approach' in *Oxford Handbooks Online* (2017) (DOI: 10.1093/oxfordhb/9780199935352.013.25).

[33] See Markus D. Dubber, 'Policing Possession: The War on Crime and the End of Criminal Law' (2002) 91 *J. Crim. L. & Criminology* 829 ff.

In other words, historical analysis of law is relentlessly presentist. It is, to cite Guldi and Armitage again, an exercise in 'engaged scholarship'; it uses legal history as one tool of critical analysis of state action in the name of law (for instance, the modern penal state characterized by racially discriminatory mass incarceration). At the same time, historical analysis of law does not lose sight of the 'lawness' of its object, unlike the analysis of law (critical or not) in terms of 'nonlegal independent variables', whether these variables are economic, social, cultural, or of some other nonlegal ilk.[34]

Law. Critical analysis of law is a mode of legal scholarship or, more generally, of legal discourse. In this, not particularly helpful yet not necessarily obvious, sense it is law-centric (just like the various recovered, or traditional, methodologies discussed in Sections I and II).[35] The question is what this means. Historical analysis is key to framing the question and therefore can help us answer it. It does not provide a definitive answer, and certainly not an answer that is somehow more definitive and less subject to fundamental disagreement than any other answer, despite frequent attempts to portray historical analysis as objective, empirical, factual, 'merely' descriptive, etc. And even if historical analysis somehow could authoritatively reveal the lawness of law, this would still leave the crucial question of the application of law's normative commitments to the legal norms, practices, or institutions under scrutiny.[36]

I've suggested elsewhere[37] that taking a broad and long historical view locates the relevant, contemporary conception of law[38]—and what I really mean is 'liberal' law, or law characteristic of the legal-political project in Western liberal democracies— within a specific historical context: the critical, and (in some cases literally and self-consciously) revolutionary, promulgation, at the long turn of the nineteenth century (the 'Enlightenment'), of a modern conception of *law* (Recht, droit) as a mode of state governance in contradistinction to the 'orthodox' mode of state governance, *police* (Polizei, police).

---

[34] Cf. Lindsay Farmer, *Making the Modern Criminal Law* (2016) (historical analysis of criminal law that proceeds from 'an institutional theory of law' and aims to 'retain sight of the distinctive social and legal character of law').

[35] Unlike other methodological projects in law and in legal history (from nineteenth-century Historical Jurisprudence to twenty-first-century New Private Law), critical analysis of law and historical analysis of law as a mode of critical analysis of law are not private-law-focused, but public-law-centric. If contract law is the paradigm of legal studies (and legal history) in these other projects, criminal law is the paradigm of critical analysis of law (and historical analysis of law).

[36] American constitutional law, for instance, is littered with (perfunctory) supposedly determinative invocations of 'history'. See, e.g., *Bowers v. Hardwick*, 478 U.S. 186, 197 (1986) (Burger, C.J., concurring) ('proscriptions against sodomy have very "ancient roots"').

[37] See generally Markus D. Dubber, *The Police Power: Patriarchy and the Foundations of American Government* (2005).

[38] 'Contemporary', or 'modern', in the sense of being the currently operative conception, i.e., the conception of law in the light of which it is appropriate to critique contemporary norms and practices.

This radical, and rhetorical, distinction between law and police, and between the law state (*Rechtsstaat, état de droit*) and the police state (*Polizeistaat, état de police*), in turn reflects the long-standing tension between autonomy and heteronomy that can be traced back to the (decidedly pre-liberal) origins of Western legal-political life and, in particular, the interrelation between (autonomous, public, democratic) city-government by citizens of citizens, on one side, and (heteronomous, private, oeconomic) household-governance by citizen-householders of household resources (human and otherwise), on the other. Law governance, in this genealogy of the contemporary (liberal, Western) conception of law, is defined by autonomy (now of persons as such, not merely of householders); by contrast, police governance is characterized by heteronomy, the radical distinction between governor and governed, between subject and object of governmental power.[39]

To critique state (or state-sanctioned) norms and practices therefore is to test them against autonomy, as the *Grundnorm* of legitimacy, justice, right, etc.; to assess them from the perspective of police is to measure them against police's basic advisory maxim of good—or prudent, wise, competent, effective, efficient, etc.— governance, while keeping in mind that policial power, as ultimately patriarchal (or 'oeconomic') and thus unlimited, discretionary, and undefinable, cannot be subject to critique in the same sense that legal power can. (The distinction between law and police plays into a host of other formal and substantive contrasts and tensions beyond the scope of this chapter.[40])

There are any number of ways in which one might apply historical analysis to frame the question of law's lawness and therefore sharpen its critical potential (if any). What matters in the end is not how one frames the question, never mind how one then goes about answering it (and eventually applying that answer across the legal system as a whole). What matters is that the question is asked and addressed at all.[41] Without a sense of what law is about—pick any sense— legal scholarship, or public legal discourse, is not about law, which is fine as a matter of academic practice, of course, but threatens to drain legal scholarship of its critical potential, as a form of engaged scholarship that holds up state (and state-sanctioned) action against norms of law, i.e., the norms that fall within the

---

[39] Insofar as historical analysis of law, in this version, traces the genealogy of 'conceptions', norms of legitimacy, modes of governance, and the like, it is also conceptual, or intellectual, history—as well as doctrinal, comparative, institutional, etc. history. See generally Assaf Likhovski, 'The Intellectual History of Law', in this handbook.

[40] See Dubber (n. 37).

[41] For a comparative legal history of the principle of legality in U.S. and German criminal law arguing that the foundational question of the legitimacy of state *legal* punishment was not asked in the U.S., see Markus D. Dubber, 'The Legality Principle in American and German Criminal Law: An Essay in Comparative Legal History' in Georges Martyn et al. (eds.), *From the Judge's Arbitrium to the Legality Principle: Legislation as a Source of Law in Criminal Trials* (2013) 365 ff; see generally Markus D. Dubber, *The Dual Penal State: The Crisis of Criminal Law in Comparative-Historical Perspective* (forthcoming, 2018).

area of competence, or at least the training, of legal scholars.[42] Law, in this sense, is not only normative in general, but normative in the specific 'modern' critical sense of problematizing and challenging the legitimacy of state power employed in its name. To contribute, at various points and in various ways, to this enterprise of critical analysis of state power through law in modern liberal democracies is the point of legal history as historical analysis of law.

BIBLIOGRAPHY

Hanoch Dagan, *Reconstructing American Legal Realism & Rethinking Private Law Theory* (Oxford University Press, 2013)

Maksymilian Del Mar, Michael Lobban (eds.), *Law in Theory and History: New Essays on a Neglected Dialogue* (Bloomsbury, 2016)

Thomas Duve (ed.), *Entanglements in Legal History: Conceptual Approaches* (Max Planck Institute for European Legal History, 2014)

Jo Guldi, David Armitage, *The History Manifesto* (Cambridge University Press, 2014)

Philippe Jestaz, Christophe Jamin, *La doctrine* (Dalloz, 2004)

'Jurisprudence and (Its) History' (2015) 101(4) *U. Va. L. R.* (symposium)

'"Law As . . .": Theory and Method in Legal History' (2011) 1(3) *U.C. Irvine L. R.* (symposium)

'New Historical Jurisprudence and Historical Analysis of Law' (2015) 2(1) *Critical Analysis of Law* (symposium)

'The New Doctrinalism' (2015) 163(7) *U. Pa. L. R.* (symposium)

'The New Private Law' (2012) 125(7) *Harv. L. R.* (symposium)

Jan M. Smits, 'Law and Interdisciplinarity: On the Inevitable Normativity of Legal Studies' (2014) 1 *Critical Analysis of Law* 75 ff

Rudolf Wiethölter, *Rechtswissenschaft: Funk-Kolleg Recht* (Fischer, 1968)

Wissenschaftsrat (German Council of Science and Humanities), *Prospects of Legal Scholarship in Germany: Current Situation, Analyses, Recommendations* (Drs. 2558-12) (2014)

---

[42] See, e.g., the wide range of conceptions of law explored in the recent ambitious and stimulating symposium on the future of 'sociolegal history' as 'Law As . . .' (consciousness, enchanted ritual, spectacle, sovereignty, economic/cultural activity, fetish, framework, grace). Catherine L. Fisk, Robert W. Gordon, '"Law As . . .": Theory and Method in Legal History' (2011) 1 *U. Irvine L. R.* 519 ff.; Christopher Tomlins, John Comaroff, '"Law As . . .": Theory and Practice in Legal History', ibid., 1039 ff.

CHAPTER 7

LAW AS SOCIAL HISTORY

LAURA F. EDWARDS

I discovered legal history when working on my dissertation, which focused on social and political change in North Carolina during Reconstruction. Actually, I first discovered legal sources, namely, local court records that contained evidence of conflicts that I never expected to find: not just racial violence and disputes over labour arrangements, but also domestic violence, sexual assault, and a wide range of other issues that spilled over the borders of households, farms, and neighbourhoods and into the courts—often told in graphic terms that shattered my preconceptions about Victorian America. But while the resulting dissertation was based in those legal sources, it did not engage legal history. That came later, at the urging of legal historians—including one of the editors of this volume—who pointed out how problematic it was to use legal sources as a direct window onto social relations. Doing so missed the mediating power of the law and, ultimately, the significance of the material. They were right. The law changed what I was seeing in the sources, revealing the ways that people not only constructed their stories to fit within the legal process, but also understood their conflicts in legal terms, even before they entered a court. Legal history, in other words, changed the way I saw social history. But there was more to it than that, because people's use of the law also reshaped it. As I came to realize, social history and legal history are inseparable.

It is difficult to write about legal history as a field, because it covers so many areas and time periods and the focus on the law is just one aspect of legal historians' work. Those who work on colonial North America also define themselves as Early Americanists, just as those who focus on the administrative state or legal change connected to the Civil Rights Movement also define themselves as twentieth century

U.S. historians. All these parts of the field move in different directions, even as they remain in conversation with each other. With that caveat, this chapter explores two related themes embedded within the relationship between legal history and social history, focusing on the long nineteenth century to highlight conceptual points that apply more generally to other periods as well. First, it argues that the field of legal history takes a broader understanding of the law than do other historical fields. Moving beyond the written records, legal officials, and designated institutions usually associated with the law's presence and influence, legal historians extend law into the realm of social history. As that scholarship shows, law flourished in a variety of institutional contexts and even in rural byways and city streets, where it structured broad-reaching economic and cultural dynamics, as well as the ordinary relationships of daily life. Second, the chapter argues that legal history then changes our view of social history, by exposing the law's presence in places and relationships that most historians imagine to be far distant from anything remotely legal. The trajectory of my own scholarship is illustrative. When I was writing my dissertation, critiques of social history were folding that field into cultural and political history. I now have abandoned the label 'social history', as have most other historians. But I still do that kind of work in the context of legal history, which has provided the conceptual space to explore social relationships in ways that I would otherwise be unable to do.

Where is the law? Outside the field of legal history, the scholarship in U.S. history tends to locate the law within the governing institutions of the state—which, in the context of U.S. history, includes the governments of individual states as well as the federal government, the institutions that make up 'the state' and share governing authority within it according to the U.S. Constitution. That conception of law follows from the outsized role that the state has played in the historiography of the United States. The republic's first histories placed the new state at the centre of their analyses, identifying the end of the Revolution as its chronological beginning and, in the process, separating U.S. history from its colonial past. Subsequent scholarship continued within that paradigm through the nineteenth and much of the twentieth centuries. While historians have now moved on, the remnants of those narratives remain, particularly in conceptions of the law.

The resulting scholarship has given more weight to texts—statutes and appellate decisions as well as published treatises produced by trained legal professionals—than to practice, which involves the law's operation. Limiting the sources of legal authority in this way makes the law seem more simplistic than it actually was in practice. It also directs scholarly attention to people's interactions with governing institutions at the state and federal level, even though the vast majority of the American population lacked the standing to access these institutions for most of the nation's history. The long shadow of this view of law hangs over work on all those people who were excluded—particularly in women's history as well as African American and labour history. The focus of that scholarship has been on efforts to change those corners of the law deemed authoritative, particularly on struggles to obtain the rights assumed necessary to access the law. Otherwise the weight of the historiography has made it difficult to imagine most Americans as anything other than outside, looking in, subject to the law's disciplinary power, but unable to use it to pursue their own interests.

In the field of legal history, however, questions about the law's location are far more complicated. To be sure, legal historians have had a particularly strong investment in paradigms that focus on the state. The field of law has connections to the project of state formation that go back to the post-Revolutionary era, when the new republic's first historians were lawyers and state leaders. And the field's concern with the state has continued long after practitioners in the field ceased identifying with the project of state-building themselves. At the same time, though, legal historians' long-standing engagement in questions of state formation have given them critical insight into the law's relationship to the state, which has led them to look outward, beyond the state's boundaries. The study of law *and* society is a well-established approach in the field, with roots in the first half of the twentieth century. To be sure, the work that focuses on law and society has taken many forms and generated considerable debate. One effect, as outlined in Robert Gordon's trenchant critique, 'Critical Legal Histories', has been to reify the very divide that the approach sought to breach, not only drawing a sharp line between 'society' and the 'law', but also positing 'society' as the place that generates change to which 'law' responds.[1]

Critique, however, comes from within a field in which conceptions of law were more expansive and, if anything, were becoming more so. Hendrik Hartog's classic article, 'Pigs and Positivism', for example, follows the law from legal institutions into the streets of New York City in the early nineteenth century, exploring the relationship between formal law and popular legal culture through the attempted regulation of pigs, the favoured livestock of many city residents at that time. Custom allowed pigs to roam free and wallow about, a practice that New Yorkers with aspirations to refinement found distasteful. Challenged in court, the pigs and their owners lost. But that outcome made no dent whatsoever in practice: even as the prohibition against pigs entered into the law books, pigs remained on the streets. Hartog's analysis, however, is not about the failure of law, but its power and capaciousness: the conversations about the legal status of pigs extended beyond the borders of formal legal institutions and the decisions of designated lawmakers. Law was made through practice, on the streets of New York City, as well as in its courthouses.[2]

'Pigs and Positivism' anticipated developments within the field that uncoupled law from states and moved it into places associated with social history. Early American legal historians led the way in this conceptual shift, buoyed by historiographical

---

[1] Robert W. Gordon, 'Critical Legal Histories' (1984) 36 *Stanford L.R.* 56 ff.
[2] Hendrik Hartog, 'Pigs and Positivism' (1985) 4 *Wisconsin L.R.* 899 ff.

currents within that field in the 1990s that provided space for reimagining the institutional context of law. As long ago as 1984, Stanley Katz called on historians of colonial American law to drop their prevailing concerns with the ultimate emergence of the state. In 1993, *The William and Mary Quarterly* offered a special edition devoted solely to 'Law and Society in Early America' that featured scholarship calling for a broader view of law as well as its integration into the field more generally. In his introduction, Katz commended the writers' attention to the early American law as 'a complex, pluralistic, asymmetrical, gendered, and multicultural set of systems—messy systems, if indeed the term "system" can be applied . . . at all'. As the scholarship from that forum suggests, those legal systems were messy because they were so firmly rooted in context, highlighting the impossibility of separating law from society.[3]

That forum was part of a larger movement that opened up early American history chronologically and geographically, connecting the North American colonies to other parts of the globe and pushing the temporal boundaries of colonial history into the nineteenth century. Working in this context, one that focused on the exchange of goods, people, and ideas across borders, legal historians added law to the mix. In *Law and Colonial Cultures*, for instance, Lauren Benton argues that legal pluralism characterized colonialism before the nineteenth century, mixing together the legal regimes of colonizers and colonized. For many U.S. historians unfamiliar with legal history, the term 'pluralism' is linked to conceptual paradigms that posit a false equivalency among vastly unequal parties and obscure the operation of power. In the context of legal history, though, pluralism refers to the simultaneous operation of different legal frameworks. Benton's handling of pluralism focused on power relations, revealing new elements in the dynamics that underlay colonial rule. Mixed legal regimes did not indicate the weakness of colonial powers. To the contrary, they shored up colonial authority. Law, moreover, was not a cudgel that colonial powers could pick up, use, and put down. It was part of the terrain on which they moved.[4]

More recent work has elaborated on these points, locating law in places associated with social history by further loosening the longstanding monopoly that the state has had on the law in the historiography. As Philip Stern shows in *The Company-State*, corporations exercised the kind of legal authority that historians usually associate with states. The sovereignty in which legal authority was based travelled with corporations, because law was not necessarily tied to the territorial boundaries of states, as Benton shows in *A Search for Sovereignty*. Law followed a different kind of geography: the 'vectors' of roads and rivers along which people travelled. The idea that states could claim sovereignty within certain

---

[3] Stanley N. Katz, 'The Problem of Colonial Legal History', in Jack P. Greene and J. R. Pole (eds.), *Colonial British America: Essays in the New History of the Early Modern Era* (1984) 457 ff. Quote from Katz, 'Explaining the Law in Early American History: Introduction' (1993) 50 *William and Mary Quarterly* 6 ff.

[4] Lauren Benton, *Law and Colonial Cultures: Legal Regimes in World History, 1400–1900* (2002).

geographic bounds developed slowly, over time, as did the notion that law was defined through treaties and other documents, not practice. Even so, the territorial borders of nation states remained porous in the early modern period, resulting in overlapping legal regimes, connected to different governing authorities operating in the same place.[5]

At the same time, other scholars were tracing the layers of law within states. The work on early modern England, for instance, has emphasized the dispersion of legal authority and overlapping jurisdictions, with estates, municipalities, corporations, the military, Parliament, the Church, and the King all supporting legal institutions that generated different bodies of law. These jurisdictions operated simultaneously, resulting in legal forums that handled similar issues, using different principles—a situation analogous to the kind of legal pluralism that other scholars describe in the colonial context, although involving different legal frameworks within nations. In this context, there was no singular, definitive set of rules that applied universally in all like matters. Law took form in particular historical moments, amidst particular social configurations. Even as it reflected context, it also constituted it. That institutional context travelled to the North American colonies, where—to use Katz's terminology—the law was a 'set of systems', if 'the term "system" applied at all'.

These historiographical currents framed *The Many Legalities of Early America*, edited by Christopher Tomlins and Bruce Mann. In the introduction, Tomlins takes aim at historiographical frameworks that had separated legal history from colonial history, echoing Katz's points and arguing that colonial legal history was a central element of early America, not just a precursor to the history of the new state that emerged after the Revolution. But the larger point, both of the introduction and the essays that the volume brought together, was that law was essential to understanding the colonial past more generally. Tomlins and Mann used the term 'legalities' to distinguish the underlying conceptual framework of new work in the field from that of previous scholarship, which focused on a formalistic study of law and its development within the governing institutions of states—be they colonial powers or the United States. By contrast, legalities encompassed an array of ideas and practices that involved both state institutions and daily life. Yet, even as legalities informed a range of social, economic, and cultural relationships, they did not disappear into those dynamics. Legalities maintained a coherence and authority that still identified them as law. The concept was slippery, although purposefully so, with the intent of capturing the complexity and ambiguities that characterized the law's operation in the context of early America.[6]

---

[5] Philip J. Stern, *The Company-State: Corporate Sovereignty and the Early Modern Foundation of the British Empire in India* (2011); Benton, *A Search for Sovereignty: Law and Geography in European Empires, 1400–1900* (2011).

[6] Christopher L. Tomlins, Bruce H. Mann (eds.), *The Many Legalities of Early America* (2001).

Recent scholarship on women's economic status in early America suggests how profoundly legal history has changed the terrain of social history of this period. For decades, historians—particularly historians of the nineteenth century United States—have characterized coverture as a rigid set of legal rules with such deep roots that they had acquired a life of their own even before the Revolution. But, as Holly Brewer argues in 'The Transformation of Domestic Law', that situation owes, in large part, to the reliance of nineteenth-century legal professionals and later historians on legal texts taken out of context, particularly the writings of Sir William Blackstone. Writing in the 1760s, Blackstone characterized coverture as the suspension of 'the very being or legal existence of the woman . . . during the marriage.' According to Brewer, however, Blackstone's infamous invocation is best understood as a historically specific rendering of coverture, linked to political conflicts within England. Blackstone produced innovation under the guise of tradition, selecting the principles that suited his purposes and fashioning them into a new synthesis that significantly elevated the power of all patriarchs—husbands, fathers, and masters as well as kings. But it was not an accurate description of either past or current practice.[7]

Until these new conceptions of domestic relations acquired traction, coverture had different meanings in practice, varying widely across geographic space and legal jurisdictions. Cornelia Hughes Dayton's *Women Before the Bar* and Linda L. Sturtz's *Within Her Power* underscore the incredible variations that existed in the application of coverture over time and place. So do Ellen Hartigan-O'Connor's *The Ties That Buy* and Serena Zabin's *Dangerous Economics*. While Hartigan-O'Connor and Zabin are concerned with women's economic status, not their legal status, both incorporate a pluralistic view of law, one that accepts the presence of different legal principles, often conflicting, operating in multiple arenas. While under more restrictive definitions of coverture in some areas of law, women could still act as traders in others. It is too simplistic to say that the law restricted women's social and economic options—options that, somehow, existed outside of law. Law, in its multiple forms, shaped all the options.[8]

In *Robert Love's Warnings*, Cornelia Hughes Dayton and Sharon V. Salinger embed law so deeply in the relations of daily life that many readers might not recognize the book as legal history at all. The title refers to the legal process whereby officials like Robert Love sought out strangers and gave them public, verbal warnings to depart in fourteen days. The warning out system is often identified as evidence

---

[7] Holly Brewer, "The Transformation of Domestic Law", in Christopher L. Tomlins, Michael Grossberg (eds.), *Cambridge History of American Law* (2008) 288 ff.

[8] Cornelia Hughes Dayton, *Women Before the Bar: Gender, Law, and Society in Connecticut, 1639–1789* (1995); Linda L. Sturtz, *Within Her Power: Propertied Women in Colonial Virginia* (2002); Ellen Hartigan-O'Connor, *The Ties That Buy: Women and Commerce in Revolutionary America* (2009); Serena Zabin, *Dangerous Economics: Status and Commerce in Imperial New York* (2009).

of a particularly Puritan form of provincialism, illustrating the lengths to which Bostonians were willing to go to rid themselves of outsiders. But, as Dayton and Salinger show, the text of the law did not capture the institutional context that gave it meaning. In practice, warnings did not mean that strangers had to depart or even that they were unwelcome. Rather, they provided legal evidence that the individual in question did not have a 'settlement' in Boston—meaning that the person did not have a legal connection, usually established by birth, to Boston and, therefore, was not entitled to poor relief and other social services funded by the town. That evidence mattered, because those without settlements in the city became the legal responsibility of the colony of Massachusetts, not the city of Boston. As such, the warning-out system was about inclusion, not exclusion. Bostonians could accommodate more outsiders because of it, which explains why Robert Love warned people out and then lingered for a chat. Everyone involved understood the law's importance as well as its limits, because it was so thoroughly integrated into daily interactions.[9]

Thanks to scholarship from early America that has uncoupled law from the state and extended its chronological reach beyond the Revolution, law in the nineteenth century now appears more connected to its colonial past. Exemplary in chronological sweep is Christopher Tomlins's *Freedom Bound*, which moves from the colonial period to the Civil War era. As Tomlins argues, law framed the colonial project, justifying the seizure of property, the expropriation of the labour needed to work it, and the governing institutions necessary to maintain it. Law kept freedom bound, denying to the vast majority of Americans what it purported to protect. Separation from Britain did not alter those legal structures, which continued to haunt the new republic and proved resistant to alteration, except through violence. In the literature of U.S. history, the Civil War has been characterized as a social conflict, an economic conflict, a political conflict, or some combination thereof. But, in Tomlins's hands, the Civil War becomes the nation's confrontation with its legal past.[10]

Attention to the colonial past has rendered the nineteenth century state far less coherent than it once appeared to be. The number of jurisdictions and the extent of overlap among them diminished after the Revolution, but did not disappear entirely. The U.S. Constitution divided legal authority between the federal government and the states, leaving states with broad powers over the legal status of individuals and matters involving the public welfare. New state constitutions, in turn, made counties and municipalities subordinate to state authority. In practice, however, legitimacy of the various jurisdictions within the state and the balance of power

[9] Cornelia Hughes Dayton, Sharon V. Salinger, *Robert Love's Warnings: Searching for Strangers in Colonial Boston* (2014).

[10] Christopher Tomlins, *Freedom Bound: Law, Labor, and Civic Identity in Colonizing English America, 1580–1865* (2010).

among them remained unsettled, particularly in the period between the Revolution and the Civil War.

The resulting conflicts among various legal jurisdictions in the nineteenth century United States reflected and reinforced the era's key social, economic, and political struggles, just as they did in the colonial era. The scholarly literature tends to focus on the tensions between the federal government and states because they culminated in secession—and as a result have long comprised one of the thorniest nettles in American historiography. But, as Greg Ablavasky argues in 'Savage Constitution', the framers were thinking about people outside the legal jurisdiction of the United States as well as those within. Specifically, they were concerned about the power of Indian nations, which was constantly in play because of American settlers' persistence in ignoring federal policy, moving onto Indian lands, and igniting conflict. Framers buttressed the power of the federal government in the U.S. Constitution accordingly. Economic dynamics also altered the operation of federal authority, resulting in jurisdictional tensions involving economics and localities, which insisted on following longstanding practices that had acquired the force of law. As Gautham Rao argues in *National Duties*, the collection of customs duties was both essential to the federal government and well beyond its ability to control. Merchants expected federal officials to adhere to longstanding practices at ports that had acquired the force of law through use, despite the adoption of new rules by the federal government that were supposed to be applied uniformly. Federal officials complied with local practices well into the nineteenth century, because they knew they could never enforce the new rules without losing legitimacy—and revenue— altogether. As Karen M. Tani shows in *States of Dependency*, the jurisdictional conflicts persisted well into the twentieth century when it came to social welfare, where localities resisted federal efforts to wrest power from them.[11]

Not only did the layers of legal authority that characterized the colonial period persist, but so did the law's presence in a range of economic and social relationships. In *The People's Welfare*, William Novak takes issue with the notion that the *laissez faire* characterized the period between Revolution and the Civil War. To make his case, he shifts the focus from the federal government to states and localities, which engaged in extensive regulation of the economy in this period. The economic expansion of this period did not unfold of its own accord; it was guided by the law. Christopher Tomlins's *Law, Labor, and Ideology in the Early Republic* makes a similar point, although focusing on the development of labour law. Tomlins also adds another complication, showing how judges recast the labour relationship by resuscitating conceptions of patriarchal authority that gave employers extensive powers over their workers. The workplace became the private domain of employers,

---

[11] Gregory Ablavsky, 'The Savage Constitution' (2014) *Duke L.J.* 999 ff; Gautham Rao, *National Duties: Custom Houses and the Making of the American State* (2016); Karen M. Tani, *States of Dependency: Welfare, Rights, and American Governance, 1935–1972* (2016).

beyond the reach of the law. Markus Dubber roots modern police powers in similar conceptions of patriarchal authority in *The Police Power*. When translated to government, those powers allowed expansive authority while shielding it from public regulation. Not only did the law shape social dynamics, but those social dynamics also shaped the law, often in surprising ways.[12]

At the same time, though, the layers of law made it more accessible than portrayed outside the field of legal history. It was not just Blackstone that explains the persistence of a particular view of coverture in the historiography of nineteenth-century United States. As Mary Ritter Beard argued in her classic *Women as Force in History*, the emphasis on women's legal incapacity is traceable to the women's rights movement, which elevated the acquisition of rights and downplayed women's legal access through other means, particularly through the body of law known as equity. Reformers' use of coverture as a useful straw man has proven difficult to dispel, but legal historians have gradually reached a consensus on the subject, pointing to married women's access to law, despite restrictions on their rights. In *Governing the Hearth*, for instance, Michael Grossberg traces the erosion of the patriarchal authority of husbands and fathers in the decades following the Revolution. He attributes those changes, in part, to Revolutionary ideology, which challenged all forms of unchecked power and elevated women's roles as mothers. But throughout that era, women made important legal claims in the context of family law, including marriage settlements, divorce, and child custody. Grossberg elaborates on those dynamics in *A Judgment for Solomon*, which traces one woman's skilful legal manoeuvering to extract herself from a difficult marriage. Such actions were not limited to the elite, as Hendrik Hartog shows In *Man and Wife in America*. Married women, rich and poor, found legal openings to pursue their own interests, despite the rules of coverture that subordinated them to their husbands. Even within the bounds of coverture, women in the nineteenth century were remarkably savvy legal operators, moving a range of issues usually denominated as the stuff of social history into the ambit of law. Indeed, as Reva B. Seigel argues in ' "The Rule of Love" ', the private sphere that kept married women and marital relations outside the law did not take shape until the nineteenth century. Married women's subordination, in other words, did not cut off their legal access completely. The history of women's legal standing did not follow a straightforward trajectory from repression to liberation.[13]

---

[12] William J. Novak, *The People's Welfare: Law and Regulation in Nineteenth-Century America* (1996); Tomlins, *Law, Labor, and Ideology in the Early American Republic* (1993); Markus Dirk Dubber, *Police Power: Patriarchy and the Foundations of American Government* (2005).

[13] Mary Ritter Beard, *Women as Force in History: A Study of Traditions and Realities* (1946); Michael Grossberg, *Governing the Hearth: Law and Family in Nineteenth-Century America* (1985); Michael Grossberg, *A Judgment for Solomon: The d'Hauteville Case and Legal Experience in Antebellum America* (1996); Hendrik Hartog, *Man and Wife in America: A History* (2000); Reva B. Seigel, ' "The Rule of Love": Wife Beating as Prerogative and Privacy' (1996) *Yale L.J.* 105 2117 ff.

Legal institutions at the local level offered more options to those on society's margins. As I show in *The People and Their Peace*, municipalities and counties maintained considerable discretion in the area of public law, particularly in the decades immediately following the Revolution. That institutional context meant that a range of people—even those without the legal standing necessary to access other areas of law —had access to local legal venues, where they sought redress for grievances as members of the public order. Local legal venues also figure prominently in Martha Jones's *Birthright Citizens*, which explores free blacks' efforts to exploit the complicated legal relationships between localities, states, and the federal government to solidify their claims to rights and citizenship—which were far from secure in the period between the Revolution and the Civil War. Each layer of government was certain that questions regarding the legal status of free blacks lay within their jurisdiction. More than that, their laws conflicted, creating a muddle of contradictory outcomes that went unresolved until the ratification of the Fourteenth Amendment. That muddle, however, also had the effect of limiting the implications of restrictions in one jurisdiction by countering them with laws from another.[14]

Law continued to flourish in many locations in the nineteenth century, because legal principles circulated widely outside legal forums. As William Novak argues in 'The American Law of Association', law regulated a wide range of associations, 'ranging from towns, municipal corporations, and churches to business corporations, charities, and fraternal and benefit associations'. 'Law and politics' he concludes, 'thoroughly . . . penetrated even the most seemingly private of American fellowships'. Kevin Butterfield follows up on this idea in *The Making of Tocqueville's America*, arguing that voluntary associations encouraged a culture of interaction based in legalistic relations and procedural fairness. Constitutions and by-laws outlined the rules that an organization's members had to follow as well as the disciplinary measures that were invoked when they failed to do so. Butterfield's argument turns conventional wisdom on its head, locating legal practices usually associated with higher levels of government in the lives of ordinary of Americans. Those practices grew out of Americans' efforts to regulate their relationships with each other and then migrated into governing institutions—a kind of law from the bottom up.[15]

Law was even implicated in religion. Disestablishment removed the Anglican Church from its perch within the state and transferred issues it once handled— including poor relief, family disputes, and moral offences—to civil authorities in local jurisdictions. But many denominations retained church courts, which

---

[14] Laura F. Edwards, *The People and Their Peace: Legal Culture and the Transformation of Inequality in the Post-Revolutionary South* (2009); Martha Jones, *Birthright Citizens: A History of Race and Rights in Antebellum America* (forthcoming).

[15] Novak, 'The American Law of Association: The Legal-Political Construction of Civil Society' (2001) 15 *Studies in American Political Development* 163 ff; Kevin Butterfield, *The Making of Tocqueville's America: Law and Association in the Early Nineteenth Century United States* (2015).

continued to adjudicate conflicts among their members, using the same legalistic procedures that such courts had always followed, even though those courts no longer had the backing of the state. Disestablishment, moreover, did not really sever the ties between church and state, as Sarah Barringer Gordon argues in 'The African Supplement'. Religious communities regularly used the law to protect their interests, just as individuals did: to defend land, buildings, and assets from creditors, to resolve conflicts among congregants, to incorporate, and to obtain exemptions from taxes and other fees. The extent to which religion and state authority were intertwined comes through most dramatically in the ways that dispossessed people, particularly free blacks, accessed the law through their religious organizations. For those who could not claim full civil and political rights, religious organizations were the most stable, most direct route to state authority, and the most friendly to their interests because of their primary concern with free blacks as Christians. Not only did such actions result in state regulation of religion, but the state also began to identify religion as an appropriate way to achieve public ends. The results remade the relationship between church and state, embedding religion in the state, while reinforcing the place of law in religion.[16]

As the work on law and voluntary associations suggests, legal historians have moved law well beyond the boundaries that once contained it. Ariela Gross, for instance, has focused on the close relationship between formal law and cultural context in defining race. Statutes made strong statements about race, defining those with some African heritage as black, not white. But, as Gross argues in *What Blood Won't Tell*, blood percentages were impossible to determine in practice and, thus, provided little legal guidance. As a result, cases depended on local cultural practices that people used to assess racial identity in their daily lives, such as voting or reputation. *What Blood Won't Tell* reveals the dependence of law on cultural context, which supplied meanings that made the law work. In Gross's work, it is impossible to understand the law without attention to the many quotidian ways that people interacted with it.[17]

Other work emphasizes the legal qualities of practices that operated outside formal governing institutions—practices that the historiography outside legal history tends to characterize as social, not legal. As Dylan Penningroth has shown in *The Claims of Kinfolk*, enslaved people established claims to property that were recognized in their communities, even by their white masters and neighbours. Those legal conceptions could have significant power within legal institutions, as I argue in my new book project, *Only the Clothes on Her Back*. People with tenuous claims to property rights could make legal claims to some forms of property, particularly food and textiles, in local courts. That was true, even for enslaved people. Those forms of property

---

[16] Sarah Barringer Gordon, 'The African Supplement: Religion, Race, and Corporate Law in Early National America' (2015) 72 *William and Mary Quarterly* 385 ff.

[17] Ariela Gross, *What Blood Won't Tell: A History of Race on Trial in America* (2008).

were closely connected to the people who relied on their sustenance and coverage. But people without resources and the full range of property rights also solidified claims to these items through their own efforts: use, display, and trade. Local courts regularly adjudicated claims to such property based on such claims, suggesting the power of legal principles that people made through their own efforts.[18]

Similar dynamics emerge in Yvonne Pitts's *Family, Law, and Inheritance in America* and Susanna Blumenthal's *Law and the Modern Mind*. Pitts focuses on the ways that ordinary people inserted their own ideas about legal capacity—that is, the ability to make one's own decisions—into the adjudication of inheritance cases. The law's definition of a sane, capable individual did not necessarily work in context, because the deviations from sanity and capability were so often the point of conflict in such cases. When people brought their claims to court, they wanted the law to mediate those conflicts, which in turn had the effect of changing the law. As Blumenthal shows, the question of capacity had profound political implications. The founders built a republic in which authority lay in law, which assumed the presence of an autonomous individual with the soundness of mind to make rational decisions. Such individuals, however, were theoretical constructs. So jurists were regularly confronted with cases where litigants presented conflicting views of individual responsibility and new scientific concepts that explained deviant behaviour in terms of disease, not conscious choice. The resulting body of law shored up the legal assumptions that were so central to the new republic's political order by carving out a separate category for the insane and likening them to other people whom the law characterized as incapacitated, namely children, married women, and the enslaved. Even free white men had difficulty meeting the criteria demanded by the theoretical, autonomous individual. Like Gross, both Pitts and Blumenthal emphasize the way the law actually worked. Legal principles were not the same as popular conceptions of either race or individual capacity, but the relationship between them ultimately described the process of law.[19]

As the nineteenth century has become more connected to its colonial past, the Civil War has taken on more significance as a watershed. That emphasis underscores the continued importance of the state in legal history: the Civil War did what the Revolution did not, consolidating the legal authority of the state. At the same time, though, the scholarship is also attentive to social context, emphasizing the law's meaning in Americans' lives even as the focus shifts to the institutions of the state. The work on citizenship is particularly revealing in this regard, revealing dramatic changes in the operation of citizenship on the ground as well as in the law. As William

---

[18] Dylan C. Penningroth, *The Claims of Kinfolk: African American Property and Community in the Nineteenth-Century South* (2003). Edwards, *Only the Clothes on Her Back: Textiles, Law, and Commerce in the Nineteenth-Century United States* (manuscript in progress).

[19] Yvonne Pitts, *Family, Law, and Inheritance in America: A Social and Legal History of Nineteenth-Century Kentucky* (2012); Susanna Blumenthal, *Law and the Modern Mind: Consciousness and Responsibility in American Legal Culture* (2016).

Novak argues in 'The Legal Transformation of Citizenship in Nineteenth-Century America', citizenship did not confer much in the way of legal status in the first half of the nineteenth century. It was only later, when the authority over citizenship migrated to the federal government after the Reconstruction Amendments after the Civil War, that citizenship assumed more legal weight. Kunal Parker approaches that same issue from another perspective in *Making Foreigners*. As he argues, the legal designation 'foreigner' and its restrictions could apply to people, white and black, already within the country, as well as those who entered from outside—as it did to those 'strangers' from other parts of Massachusetts in *Robert Love's Warnings*. It was only later, when the federal government consolidated authority over citizenship in the late nineteenth and early twentieth centuries, that a clear divide emerged between citizens and foreigners, with foreigners becoming immigrants from outside the nation's borders.[20]

Central to the work on citizenship are analyses that focus on the efforts of those on the social margins—particularly African Americans, white women, and the labouring poor—to alter their own legal status. Barbara Welke's *Law and the Borders of Belonging in the Long Nineteenth-Century United States* reveals the profound difficulties they faced. Uncoupling rights from citizenship, Welke distinguishes the positive claims that individuals could make on the state through the legal system and the various demands that the state could make on individuals. Women in the nineteenth century did not have the full array of individual rights even though they were citizens. For them and for other Americans who were not white and male, as Welke argues, citizenship implied only responsibilities, restrictions, and regulations. The acquisition of rights resulted not in citizenship, but in legal personhood—the legal identity based in the theoretical, autonomous individual in Blumenthal's *Law and the Modern Mind*. Yet citizenship still gave meaning to legal personhood, because rights alone did not always guarantee the state's protection or support. Welke's approach emphasizes the relationship between the positive and negative elements of individuals' relationship to the state—the dynamic to which the term 'borders of belonging' refers. That term, however, is a purposefully ambiguous concept, rendering unstable what the scholarship now tends to treats as definitive. For, as Welke shows, neither legal personhood nor citizenship determined the borders of belonging. It was a mix of the two that mattered. Even then, possession of both did not always guarantee belonging.[21]

Like other recent work in legal history on the long nineteenth century, *Law and the Borders of Belonging* upends a progressive narrative of legal change, in which rights and citizenship were extended over time to those initially denied them, creating the

---

[20] William J. Novak, 'The Legal Transformation of Citizenship in Nineteenth-Century America', in Meg Jacobs, William J. Novak, Julian Zelizer (eds.), *The Democratic Experiment: New Directions in American Political History* (2003) 85 ff. Kunal Parker, *Making Foreigners: Immigration and Citizenship Law in America, 1600–2000* (2015).

[21] Barbara Young Welke, *Law and the Borders of Belonging in the Long Nineteenth Century United States* (2010).

conditions for greater equality in social and economic terms. In contrast, Welke emphasizes a deep-seated commitment to conceptions of rights and citizenship that privileged the status of white men at the expense of other, marginalized people. The emphasis is different, but compatible with scholarship that focuses on the efforts of marginalized people to use law and the legal system, despite all the barriers in their way. They are two sides of the same coin: both emphasize the pervasiveness of law in people's lives and its power in constituting relationships often denominated as purely 'social.' Law does not control society, forcing either repressive or progressive change on it. Nor does society drag the law along behind it, changing legal rules as necessary to reflect changing realities. The two are inseparable.

As the work in legal history shows, people in the nineteenth century did not see law as something abstract, arcane, and inaccessible. Instead, law infused all aspects of life, even the lives of those without resources and with tenuous claims to rights. The scholarship on the twentieth century follows the law's changing context: its professionalization, its consolidation at the state and federal levels, and its movement into a proliferating area of bureaucratic administrations. But legal histories of this period still tend to define law broadly and explore its implications for the key issues and relationships in American life.

Given the law's pervasiveness, it is historically inaccurate to separate it out and place it to one side, as a specialized body of rules, lodged in distant institutions. The recent work in legal history does emphasize the law's integrity and power, as a set of rules with its own logic and the ability to shape the people and issues that came within its purview. But the scholarship also embeds law within the social, economic, and cultural life of all Americans. Locating law in multiple sites only magnifies the implications, making its presence more ubiquitous, its power more profound, and its implications more resistant to easy categorization. This view makes it difficult to characterize law solely as an expression of those in authority: law could take even the privileged places they never intended. It also makes it difficult to site particular cases or statutes as definitive statements of 'the rules': the rules in one governing arena might not coordinate with those in another and, even then, those rules were always changing precisely because they were always in the process of revision through use. Law was not the authority to which people deferred. It was the authority they made. As such, it is impossible to understand American society without it.

BIBLIOGRAPHY

Lauren Benton, *Law and Colonial Cultures: Legal Regimes in World History, 1400–1900* (Cambridge University Press, 2002)

Susanna Blumenthal, *Law and the Modern Mind: Consciousness and Responsibility in American Legal Culture* (Harvard University Press, 2016)

Holly Brewer, 'The Transformation of Domestic Law', in Christopher L. Tomlins, Michael Grossberg (eds.), *Cambridge History of American Law* (Cambridge University Press, 2008) 288

Cornelia Hughes Dayton, Sharon V. Salinger, *Robert Love's Warnings: Searching for Strangers in Colonial Boston* (University of Pennsylvania Press, 2014)

Laura F. Edwards, *The People and Their Peace: Legal Culture and the Transformation of Inequality in the Post-Revolutionary South* (University of North Carolina Press, 2009)

Sarah Barringer Gordon, 'The African Supplement: Religion, Race, and Corporate Law in Early National America' (2015) 72 *William and Mary Quarterly* 385

Ariela J. Gross, *What Blood Won't Tell: A History of Race on Trial in America* (Harvard University Press, 2008)

Michael Grossberg, *A Judgment for Solomon: The d'Hauteville Case and Legal Experience in Antebellum America* (University of North Carolina Press, 1996)

Hendrik Hartog, 'Pigs and Positivism' (1985) 4 *Wisconsin L.R.* 899

Martha Jones, *Birthright Citizens: A History of Race and Rights in Antebellum America* (Cambridge University Press, forthcoming 2018)

William J. Novak, *The People's Welfare: Law and Regulation in Nineteenth-Century America* (University of North Carolina Press, 1996)

Yvonne Pitts, *Family, Law, and Inheritance in America: A Social and Legal History of Nineteenth-Century Kentucky* (Cambridge University Press, 2012)

Reva B. Seigel, ' "The Rule of Love": Wife Beating as Prerogative and Privacy' (1996) *Yale L.J.* 105 2117

Christopher L. Tomlins, Bruce H. Mann (eds.), *The Many Legalities of Early America* (University of North Carolina Press, 2001)

Christopher L. Tomlins, *Freedom Bound: Law, Labor, and Civic Identity in Colonizing English America, 1580–1865* (Cambridge University Press, 2010)

Barbara Young Welke, *Law and the Borders of Belonging in the Long Nineteenth Century United States* (Cambridge University Press, 2010)

CHAPTER 8

LEGAL HISTORY AS POLITICAL HISTORY

ROY KREITNER*

I. INTRODUCTION

LEGAL History as Political History has an unfamiliar ring, but one that calls up a number of related phrases that have peppered legal theory and its forays into interdisciplinarity for decades. To list a few, in acknowledgment that some readers will hear resonances where others may not: law and history; law and politics; law and literature; law in literature; law as literature; law as economy; law is politics; critical legal histories. This title, then, could be an invitation for serious reflection on how legal history and legal theory might be positioned, with political history as an axis for that positioning. I will respond to that invitation only obliquely and, I am afraid, not very deeply. I will have next to nothing to say about interdisciplinarity and very little to say about theory per se. And while 'legal history as political history' might refer us to a wide range of theoretical questions, I will limit the range rather severely. In what follows, I will take the phrase as gesturing at two existing, perhaps by now classic, debates. One is the question of political history's meaning, or its differentiation from social or cultural history. The other is the relationship between law and politics, especially regarding the Critical Legal Studies (CLS) view of that relationship. The latter question would arise

* Professor, Tel Aviv University Faculty of Law. For helpful conversations on the ideas that became this chapter, I am grateful to Yishai Blank, Christine Desan, Markus Dubber, Ron Harris, Shai Lavi, Assaf Likhovski, Doreen Lustig, David Schorr, and Chris Tomlins.

in any case by virtue of the inclusion of the term *political* in the title, and it takes on additional weight because of the impact of critical legal history for the field generally.[1] The chapter opens by waving briefly at these preliminary questions, continues by asserting an abstract claim, and then moves to explanation by example for the heart of the chapter. It concludes with some questions.

One way to take up the issue of legal history as political history would have been to trace an opposition between political history and its others, particularly social history and cultural history. This contrast, while somewhat outdated, still frames some historiographical discussion. Without allowing for nuance, political history is typically top down; its characters are drawn from elites and especially office holders and leaders of political parties (or in the case of the law, appellate judges); it focuses on signal events, major moments like regime change, revolution, war, conquest, elections, and in law, particularly great constitutional cases. Social history is typically less involved in hero-worship, oriented towards exploring broad processes and ways of life rather than discrete events; its characters are often groups, mostly unrecognized and sometimes nameless people who show up as evidence of regularities of life more often than as exemplars of greatness. This division, prevalent among historians (in history departments) for half a century or more (and in many ways already passé) still has some currency, and one hears a bit of it even at legal history conferences, sometimes with hints of animosity. Perhaps not many working historians were professionally active when the contest between political and social history was heated in the 1960s, but the distinction still generates discussion and at times even impassioned exchange. Recently, two historians published an Op-Ed in *The New York Times* bemoaning the decline of political history and suggesting that students and families lobby university administrators to make political history a priority, urging benefactors to endow professorships in the field, and calling on lawmakers and schoolboards to support political history.[2] And at least within law faculties, there are still conversations in which legal history is treated as valuable only when it traces, relatively closely, major political developments, usually on the constitutional plane. Despite its staying power, I will not chart a picture of legal history as political history onto this map of political history. Instead, the goal will be to stake out a somewhat different definition for political history, at least insofar as legal history is concerned. I return to the sense of political history I have in mind below.

The second preliminary issue is the relationship of political history in the title to critical legal histories and to CLS more generally. The reason this relationship

---

[1] Christopher Tomlins, 'What is Left of the Law and Society Paradigm after Critique? Revisiting Gordon's "Critical Legal Histories"' (2012) 37 *Law & Soc. Inquiry* 155 ff; Christopher Tomlins, 'After Critical Legal History: Scope, Scale, Structure' (2012) 8 *Ann. R.L. & Soc. Sci.* 31 ff.

[2] Fredrik Logevall, Kenneth Osgood, *The End of Political History? The New York Times*, 29 August 2016, at A17. The Op-Ed spurred a relatively heated exchange that appeared in *Perspectives on History* in January 2017. Available at <https://www.historians.org/publications-and-directories/perspectives-on-history/january-2017/political-history-an-exchange> (accessed 29 April, 2018).

begs some treatment is the basic CLS claim that denies the distinction between law and politics. If one takes this slogan at face value and accepts a complete collapsing of the categories law and politics, then any legal history is as a matter of course political history. There is no denying that this kind of manoeuvre granted CLS much of its energy in the late 1970s and early 1980s. The point was that the distinction between law and politics, a distinction that was central for a great deal of decision-making and for even more legal scholarship throughout the twentieth century, was itself ideological. It served, in essence, to lend greater legitimacy to positions staked out in the legal terrain than they ought to have been accorded. Much CLS work was focused on tearing down the veneer of legitimacy that the insulation from politics provided for legal argumentation. Easy examples came from the constitutionalization of freedom of contract in the Lochner era. But those were targets that had been critiqued as political in real time, at least since Charles Beard's *Economic Interpretation of the Constitution*.[3] In that sense, the easy targets were actually less thoroughgoing claims.

The deeper issue came out when CLS scholars used the same methods in critique of the development of doctrinal argumentation in pure private law. Characterizing the basics of property, tort, and contract as political took the claims to a different plane with more analytical bite. The idea was not simply that private law adjudication determined outcomes that had implications for the distribution of societal benefits. Rather, these analyses raised the question of whether the basic legal structure of market society was more or less given, so that the legal analyst (especially the judge) could find it existing in the law as 'neutral coordination', rather than politicized distribution.[4] The CLS claim of indeterminacy of legal materials was a three-pronged attack on standard legal analysis: first, it claimed that standard analysis mystified; second, that it gave 'inordinate power to the jurists' at the expense of democratic decision-making; and third, that it inhibited the imagination for social change.

Now, in the big picture, I think CLS had it right. The mainstream theorizing of law as working itself pure has a strong tendency to limit what Roberto Unger repeatedly refers to as 'institutional imagination' with the potential for large-scale social change. This was a claim about how lawyers and elite policymakers generally are taught to think about how societal arrangements ought to be managed, and about the ways expertise ought to be shielded from political morality. At both the scholarly level and at the educational bedrock, there is great value in undermining the sharp distinction that standard legal analysis employs. At the same time, at least for my purposes here, the broad cloth claim that law is politics is less useful. This is not because I would like to re-establish a firm line between law and politics as a general matter (I have no stake in that). The intuition I advance here is modest and local: when the claim about law and politics is drawn globally, it tends to be

---

[3] Charles A. Beard, *An Economic Interpretation of the Constitution of the United States* (1913).
[4] Robert Unger, *The Critical Legal Studies Movement: Another Time, A Greater Task* (2014) 10 ff.

understood as a matter of definition, and the stakes of the insight get lost. When the claim is narrowed to particular settings, the question of politics reasserts its urgency. As my examples will show, my sense of the political is still fairly capacious, so that perhaps the nuance is only of minor interest. That said, I will try to clarify at this point: in what follows, I argue for a narrower version of legal history as political history than would seem to flow from CLS, if CLS stands for the proposition that all law is politics, and thus all legal history simply is political history.

II. The Argument, Abstracted

In lieu of a developed analytic, I would like to advance a suggestion about what to look for when trying to understand legal history as political history. I suggest that there is a body of legal history being written and published today, not generally considered as a group or in any way related, that would be considered profitably as political history. The common feature for this work is that it shows change over time in the way law functions. This is history that shows not simply changes in the content of the law, but more specifically, changes in the forms and tools the law employs. A shorthand for this conception might claim that law as political history traces the way *jurisprudential* change varies the terms of social interaction. That may seem like a simple enough formulation, but it is potentially a can of worms because none of its terms is uncontroversially fixed.

A hypothetical example might bring us somewhat closer to analytical clarity. Assume for a moment that a city council or state highway commission changes the speed limit from 100 km/ph to 110 km/ph. I take it as uncontroversial that this establishes a change in the law, but at the same time, it has not changed the way law functions. On the other hand, if the same administrative body installs cameras that monitor every centimetre of the road at every second and eliminates all specific infractions but authorizes prosecution for anything the machines identify as unsafe driving, including automatic fines that work like present-day tolls and an automatic licence suspension that remotely shuts off your car at the nearest rest stop, I imagine most of us will think the highway commission has changed the way law functions. Indeed, in addition to traffic law, the right to freedom of movement and the right to privacy will also have been materially affected. Additionally, if this were not an isolated change, but rather one that characterized the lawmaker's entire attitude to low level 'crime', then even more people would be willing to admit a change in the functioning of law. None of this would be political history as traditionally conceived, but it would change the terms of social interaction and establish new tools of governance, making it obviously political. Of course, the starkness of the hypothetical distinction leaves open questions about the way-stations in between changing the speed limit to changing the entire mechanism, not to mention the attitude and basis of enforcement. Now, for any person actually doing the history, the need to draw lines may not be trivial, but as a theoretical matter it is not of much consequence, especially since classification is not a big concern. At least until people begin heeding Op-Eds from *The New York Times*, no historian's funding depends on labelling her work, *legal history as political history*.

The more significant difficulties with this idea of legal history as political history are less a matter of line drawing and more a matter of conceptual analysis. I bypassed these problems without comment in the fantasy/nightmare of automated enforcement, but they merit some attention. First, to accept the claim about locating change in the functioning of law is to reject (or at least significantly qualify) some of the standard approaches to analytical jurisprudence. Those approaches tend to frame issues of pure theory as questions that must be answered conceptually, in order to define law, anywhere anytime. Under the conception advanced here, on the other hand, a changing role of law or a change in law's function mean, at least potentially, that law changes its nature. The conception of law changing its core mode of functioning, or its very nature, is of course deeply familiar for those steeped in the sociology of law. The possibility of such change is a motivational necessity for Max Weber's ideal types ranging from the ordeal, through khadi justice to the substantive rationality of princely codes all the way to the formal rationality of legal science, or for Roscoe Pound's *Interpretations of Legal History*. Many historians are open to this as a matter of research, but they often do not elaborate it as a matter of theory. When they do, the results are the more self-conscious articulations of legal history as political history. A change in the way law functions, or a shift in the fundamentals of jurisprudence, is a change in (some of) the mechanisms by which people in a society live together; it is a change in the linguistic and conceptual tools through which governance means are given effect. While that is far from a comprehensive definition, it ought to suffice for present purposes as a working definition of politics.

An additional problem is methodological. It is probably easier to locate different 'natures' of law as an anthropologist who studies distant cultures and compares them to one's own than it is to see different natures where continuity is ingrained. Sometimes, this is an avenue open to the historian as well: comparisons of the present to the distant past can often do just what the anthropologist does in presenting a foreign culture—thus the quip that the past is a foreign country. The problem arises when our interest lies not only in showing some once-existing past in which something was different, but in examining a transition from one situation to the next. Granted, there might be a revolution: a regime might decide to scrap its old law for an entirely new system, with a new mode of functioning. Those moments are rare. In most of the cases that interest most of us, something much more delicate is going on. Tracing change within a particular legal area, or within a group of sufficiently related areas, will often entail leaps of interpretive faith. We are unlikely to see the vanishing of one mode of functioning and its total replacement by another. Systems that are no longer dominant are likely to have staying power in many details. If we draw on the analogy between the nature of law and the modes of governance, it is likely that we never really leave the past behind completely. Modes of governance layer on top of one another, with a new one becoming dominant while the old one survives in what may seem like random details. In addition, deciding how much to rely on new mechanisms that are institutionally or materially visible and how much to rely on the words jurists use to describe them will also be challenging tasks, both for the historian and for the readers. Some hint of that should come through in the discussion of examples, which this chapter now explores.

III. Examples

At times, portraying a shift in the nature of law's operation as a change in politics is an overarching theme in a grand narrative. Indeed, taken alone, this description is apt for much of the common (typically liberal) narrative of a shift from a patriarchal to a contractarian social order. In that narrative, traditional hierarchies embedded in thick communal relations give way to a world of free individuals whose connections, social, commercial, and civic, are based in consent. Against this background, we can begin to get a sense of the way recent legal history has developed new modes of engagement regarding the relationship between legal and political change. I begin with the example of legal history as political history that is perhaps the most self-conscious and theoretically engaged of the past decade, Chris Tomlins's *Freedom Bound*.[5] Tomlins sets the stage for a complex theoretical-methodological intervention by noting the particular form of combining law and social structure in varying interpretations (or evaluations) of what turn out to be progress narratives:

These interlocked themes—escape from subsistence, the decomposition of patriarchy, the appearance of discourses of consent in polity and economy, the freeing of labor and the changing contours of exploitation and distribution, the emergence of law as supreme social mediator and the consequent 'rethinking of all human communities' in contractarian terms—have been accepted as fundamentals of mainstream Anglo-American history, whether of liberal or . . . radical bent.[6]

---

[5] Christopher Tomlins, *Freedom Bound: Law, Labor, and Civic Identity in Colonizing English America, 1580–1865* (2010).

[6] Ibid., at 341.

Against this background, Tomlins sets out to tell a different story, too rich for summary here. However, two elements that distinguish it from traditional histories merit special attention. First, when unpacking the operation of law, the dominant narrative of Anglo-American labour turns out to be wrong: the historian discovers 'a world that simply does not comply with "the implied Whiggism of standard labor history" or with that of its traditional radical alternatives'.[7] Service does not morph into employment, because the category of service is only being constructed, at just the same time that more and more workers are governed by regimes that will eventually be organized by consent. The traditional narrative is not reversed, but undermined by breaking apart its coherence and pointing instead to its plurality.

What this suggests is that, prior at least to the early eighteenth century in England, the early nineteenth in America, work as an activity cannot be allowed to imply a single conceptualization of labor as a form of social action, such that *labor* can be understood as an expression of common-denominator social and legal characteristics reproduced across of a diversity of relationships. To encounter labor in English and American history is to encounter not a single form of relationship but multiple forms . . . .[8]

Second, even when the world of covenants, contracts, and free labour does eventually mature, it never ranges to 'encompass the full extent of the world of work'.[9] Instead, the contract world is built atop the social and legal relations of the household, a set of relations whose model of patriarchal authority extends in quite direct fashion from the slaveholder vis-à-vis his slaves straight through to the household proprietor's domestic relations. That form of authority shares organizing force with the model of the profit-oriented freely contracting individual, never to be wholly replaced.[10] The upshot of this kind of history is that there is historical development (though it would be fairly perverse to see it as progress), but it always holds together competing forms. The new, or newly recognized, or newly dominant legal forms are the language for contestation. A legal regime holds together tools of social discipline and perhaps enhances their effectivity. But it does not entail the necessity of all that has actually come about; it is not a system with an ineluctable logic, but a framing for a play of forces.

The shifts in the functioning of law in Tomlins's work stretch a broad canvas, so this section now looks to a more localized example from Shai Lavi's *The Modern Art of Dying*.[11] Like Tomlins, Lavi is deeply engaged with a theory or even a philosophy of history as well as with an account of jurisprudential change. His is a complex work that traces shifts in the meaning of euthanasia as the word and concept move through several stages. At the story's beginning (in colonial America and the early republic), euthanasia signified a blessed death, governed by a protestant religious tradition of the art of dying. During the nineteenth century, euthanasia changed into

---

[7] Ibid., at 355.   [8] Ibid., at 357.   [9] Ibid., at 358.

[10] Ibid., at 395ff. For a related account of interaction between rights-based legality and patriarchal authority, see Markus Dubber, *The Police Power: Patriarchy and the Foundations of American Government* (2005).

[11] Shai J. Lavi, *The Modern Art of Dying: A History of Euthanasia in the United States* (2005).

a new task for the medical profession, whose role it was to ease the pain of the dying person. But the medical profession had little to offer when relieving pain did not align with curing disease, leading the profession into an understanding of euthanasia as hastening death for the incurable. At this point legality enters the stage. The legal action of the book runs from the late nineteenth through the mid-twentieth century and traces the attempts to legalize the medical hastening of death. Attempts to legalize euthanasia did not succeed, but the attempts themselves are instructive. They show, in a span of less than half a century, a major shift in attitude. At the beginning of the period, the criminal prohibition on murder applied in direct fashion to hastening death and thus could be overcome only by direct legislation removing that ban. However, euthanasia advocates eventually took a different tack: rather than attempting simply to remove the ban, they proposed a regulatory regime. Lavi's language here resonates with the terms of jurisprudential change described above:

In the move from common law to a regulatory regime, the role of law was reimagined. Law's mission was no longer simply to prevent such a death but to regulate it . . . [T]he legal status of euthanasia involved more than the simple prohibition on the taking of life. In the case of self-wished death, this principle was changing, and emphasis was increasingly put on regulating such desires rather than on preventing the act itself . . . The legal intervention devised to solve the challenge [of unregulated medical practice] called for more than a mere removal of the legal barrier. The new legislation had to become part of the medical practice and redesign it from within . . . Thus law, through its agents, legal experts and legal codes, was called in to make the decision medicine, through its agents . . . could not make on its own.[12]

For Lavi, two stories are intertwined: the development that moves dying from art to technique is intertwined with the movement from common law prohibition to regulatory public policy, from a sovereign command to a problem of rational and scientific governance of ever-growing aspects of human conduct. The failure of mid-twentieth century campaigns to legalize euthanasia does not undermine the claim; instead, the very fact that such campaigns could be articulated and entertained shows how legal language had expanded and that the possible forms of law had been transformed.

Barbara Welke's *Recasting American Liberty*[13] offers another angle on the way cultural and technological changes coalesce with a shift in basic legal understanding. Welke's book uses an unusually rich array of sources to make a sweeping claim. During the period covered by the book (1865–1920), American society experienced a dramatic transformation in 'the cultural meaning of accidents and in turn the understanding of the relationship between individual autonomy and liberty'.[14] Railroads and streetcars, since their inception, had been markers of individual

---

[12] Ibid., at 87–91.
[13] Barbara Young Welke, *Recasting American Liberty: Gender, Race, Law, and the Railroad Revolution, 1865–1920* (2001).
[14] Ibid., at 8.

mobility, and thus of individual liberty. The expansion of railroad use, and the technological advances that made the cars more powerful, larger, faster, and more widely available, went hand in hand with an explosion in accidents and especially accidents involving serious injury. The response to the rising tide of accidents was to limit individual autonomy, subjecting the behaviour of riders and employees to a disciplinary regime that put 'safety first', as the campaigns dedicated to the regime's inculcation were called.

What makes this quintessentially a *legal* history is that Welke shows how central law was in this transformation. Much of the detail of the book comes from courtroom testimony and lawyers' briefs before trial courts. But a great deal of the action plays out in municipalities, before state regulators, legislatures, and most importantly, in railroad commissions that arose to provide 'the continuous, expert oversight which the emerging corporate-industrial order would require'.[15]

At the heart of state safety regulation was the recognition that the assumptions underlying the ethos of a nation of free men no longer reflected, if they ever had, the reality of daily life. In a world alive with danger, giving due warning was not enough. Human vulnerability, not mastery, marked men's encounters with technology. Safety could not be left to individual choice. State safety regulation offered a trade of one vision of liberty for another.[16]

The alignments of liberty and autonomy were significantly different from one another. When the railroad was an emerging phenomenon, courts divided responsibility, limiting the liberty of corporations where the risks created were unavoidable, but placing responsibility on individuals in situations where reasonable men could have avoided the risks. In the face of the rising tide of accidents and of the significant variance between assumed reasonable men (presumptively genderless) and actual, gendered people, the law shifted gears and began curtailing the autonomy of individuals in order to protect them. Assumed capabilities were no longer simply assumed. In what would be attacked as class legislation by its opponents, state action took certain kinds of risk taking off the table, as 'commissions substituted their regulatory judgment for individual judgments of safety and danger'.[17] In doing so, legal language infused gender and racial status directly into realms where the law had typically seen itself as paradigmatically neutral. Crucially, regulatory action took up new means to effect this change in outlook, mandating everything from speed limits, to procedures for boarding and alighting, prohibitions geared especially to women, and reaching down to specific standards for safety devices that railroads and streetcars were required to install. In other words, the mechanisms at hand for legal regulation were transformed, and those mechanisms were themselves portable. Law was proceeding on the basis of new kinds of knowledge, and it was mandating action at levels of detail unfamiliar to ideologues of the free market.

Welke's history shows law changing its character by shifting its orientation to law's very subjects, indeed blurring the line between treating them as subjects and

---

[15] Ibid., at 113.   [16] Ibid., at 120.   [17] Ibid., at 116.

as objects, or at the very least as patients. A different kind of shift in orientation towards the subject of law takes centre stage in Doreen Lustig's history of the private corporation in international law.[18] Lustig's book challenges the dominant narrative of international law's failure to regulate business enterprises during the century from their emergence as key players in late nineteenth-century globalization until their 'discovery' by lawmakers since the 1990s, primarily in the context of imputing responsibility to corporations for violations of human rights. The dominant narrative assumes that international law, working under Westphalian premises, always focused on sovereign states and only came to recognize the importance of business corporations when popular outcries regarding human rights violations gathered steam, first in the mid-1970s and with more energy in the 1990s. It assumes, in other words, that international law was simply a latecomer to the realization or even the possibility that the business corporation could or should fall within its ambit.

Lustig upends this narrative at every turn. She opens by showing that when international law emerged as a recognized discipline in the late nineteenth century, it did not simply find sovereign states as the sole subject of international law. The question of whether private corporations were subjects of international law was in flux. International lawyers actively positioned themselves as *public* lawyers by conceptualizing the business enterprise as private and, in a sense, marginal to international law. But this division did not actually lead to a vacuum of international law where private corporations were concerned. Instead, it created a 'global regulatory space' characterized by a dynamic and mutually enforcing division of labour, a 'legal space for strategic maneuvering among imperial, commercial, settler, and indigenous actors which carried the potential for resistance as well as violence and expropriation.'[19] Her case studies then analyse in detail the co-development of state and private powers, divided in ways that increased the capacities of strong (imperial) states and strong (multinational) corporations at the same time.

Lustig's history elucidates an important point about the changing form of international law. New forms were developed in response to particular challenges, and their creators often intended particular results. But the forms did not settle once and for all the place of the corporation vis-à-vis the state or the international order. Instead, development of new forms created the legal vocabulary for an ongoing contestation among multiple actors. The new vocabulary would make some arrangements intuitive while others would be uphill battles.[20]

[T]he supposed marginality of the business enterprise in international law, ingrained in the commonly accepted narrative, is *a conceptual bias* that facilitated (rather than prevented)

---

[18] Doreen Lustig, *The History of International Law and the Private Business Corporation, 1886–1980* (forthcoming 2018).

[19] Ibid., at fn. 52.

[20] E.g., one element that would become intuitive was the idea that states were responsible in the international arena for eliminating slavery, but shielded from international scrutiny regarding labour relations, which were conceived as the state's private realm. Lustig (n. 9) chs. 1 and 2.

the emergence and reach of the private business corporation and legitimized the elements in the international legal order that enabled it to thrive.[21]

But those forms do not make subsequent developments inevitable. They set the stage for ongoing contestation and conflict.

Finally, an older, but to my mind groundbreaking instance of legal history as political history may be found in Dirk Hartog's *Public Property and Private Power*.[22] The story of *Public Property and Private Power* is that of a shift

from a government insistent on governing through its personal, private estate, to one dedicated to using a public bureaucracy to provide public goods for public consumption.[23]

This is a story, then, of two different visions of governance: one links property in a direct sense with responsibility (so, for example, the City grants waterlots, and the grantees must build and maintain public wharfs and roads—responsibility to the public is entailed in ownership). The second is bureaucratic management, legislatively dictated, financed by taxation. Moving from one to the other means giving up much of the autonomy of the City vis-à-vis the state, even as it gains certain powers to administer life in the City more independently. If once the City had property, in the new vision, it will have jobs.

The role of law in these visions of governance is different. For the property-based vision, law is deep sub-structure, a sort of constitutional bedrock. It is a mode of ensuring the autonomy of corporate communities, while at the same time limiting the ways they can activate people. This is property as propriety, or property 'as the material foundation for creating and maintaining the proper social order, the private basis for the public good'.[24] These property-holding communities can offer people responsibilities; they are much less apt to innovate new tasks on their own. In contrast, the bureaucratic managerial city and state see tasks for improvement all around them, and they create new instrumentalities to deal with them. They build new structures on their own, funding themselves with taxes, and setting up a regulatory apparatus to ensure that what has remained under private initiative is run in accordance with their imposed rules.

For the nineteenth-century state moving into liberalism, and ever more so for the twenty-first century neo-liberal state, this is law as regulation writ large. To get a sense of the stakes of this kind of transformation and to understand its broad political import, consider the workings of transnational rulemaking (WTO, Basel Accords, IFRS Accounting Standards, Financial Action Task Force, environmental

---

[21] Ibid., at Conclusion.

[22] Hendrik Hartog, *Public Property and Private Power: The Corporation of the City of New York in American Law, 1730–1870* (1983).

[23] Ibid., at 8.

[24] Gregory S. Alexander, *Commodity and Propriety: Competing Visions of Property in American Legal Thought, 1776–1970* (1997) 1 ff. See also Carol M. Rose, *Property and Persuasion: Essays on the History, Theory, and Rhetoric of Ownership* (1994).

soft law): thoroughly rule based, hierarchical to the core, accountable to internally defined procedures, answerable to no one in particular. This is not to say that early nineteenth-century New Yorkers imagined transnational regulation, or even to hint that such regulation is a logical unfolding or necessary entailment of the changes that characterized local government in the early republic. It is, however, an opportunity to locate certain moments in the development of a legal vocabulary with which new forms of governing could develop.

In some of the cases discussed here, the type of shift I am highlighting is accompanied by a shift in the normative commitments or the values advanced by legal decision-makers. This might be termed a shift in juridical ideology. Such concurrence may well be common, and it may even be the main feature that makes such changes salient. But the shifts in conscious normative commitments are neither a necessary nor a sufficient condition for the changes that interest me here: the shifts I am drawing attention to are in large measure formal and institutional. They change the way the law works. They may also slant the types of normative commitments that can be worked into the law, but that seems to be a separate question. Indeed, it may well be that a shift in jurisprudence is instigated by a normative or ideological program; however, once the jurisprudential shift has taken place, it becomes open to drift or outright takeover by opposing ideological forces.[25]

Before concluding, a word on the generality of the examples is in order. While some readers will no doubt object that the spatial, temporal, or thematic range of the examples here is too narrow, others may think the collection eclectic and all-encompassing. That might lead any one of them to ask whether there is, in fact, any legal history that is not, under the generous terms of definition offered here, legal history as political history. I will answer a bit inelegantly, again by example. Jean-Christian Vinel's *The Employee: A Political History*[26] would seem at first glance to be a classic case of legal history as political history. Its title points directly to political history, while its theme is the legal definition of the category of employee. Again, on the face of things, what could be more apt for this title? Vinel's book is a rich and nuanced account of the political struggles that gave the legal category of employee its meaning, highlighting ideologies of harmony, loyalty, and workplace democracy. The category of employee was the focal point in workers' attempts to organize, and in the employers' resistance to those efforts. In the course of that history, Vinel analyses shifts in the capacity to exercise workplace discretion and in the modes of demanding and ensuring workplace discipline. However, while different workers move in and out of the category of employee (depending, in large measure, on the judiciary's attitude toward organized labour), the legal category itself always does the same work: it is the gate to organizing. All this makes for excellent legal

---

[25] J. M. Balkin, 'Ideological Drift and the Struggle Over Meaning' (1993) 25 *Conn L.R.* 869 ff.
[26] Jean-Christian Vinel, *The Employee: A Political History* (2013).

history and excellent political history. In fact, it is excellent *law and politics* in an historical vein. It is not, however, what I mean by legal history as political history, because while the content of a legal term changes through this history, its workings, function, and form remain intact.

IV. CONCLUSION

I have made an argument for an idiosyncratic yet quite general view of legal history as political history. That view holds that when legal history is attentive to changes in the forms of law and legal reasoning, rather than the law's content, it is legal history as political history. Changes in the form and function of law take different shapes, but they all change the language available for decision-makers who imagine, design, apply, and justify legal arrangements. The regulator, say, at the Occupational Health and Safety Administration who relies on expert assessments of risks in determining a safety standard, is speaking a different language from the judge who decides whether a danger created by a factory owner was reasonable. Modern social and economic analyses, internalized by the policy analysis familiar to lawyer-scholars, have taught us to see these two actors as analogues. They determine the same societal stakes by setting up the rules of engagement for people who may encounter one another. On some level, noting their common function allows us to understand deep continuities in our social arrangements. But those continuities obscure significant differences. The tools, material and cognitive, available to these decision-makers are different; the role of affected individuals in shaping the rules is different; the avenues for participating in the design of the rules is different; and the social vision that animates the decisions is probably different as well. These differences set the terms of political engagement. They give different weight and form to participation, offer different avenues for exploitation and resistance, and reinforce differing visions and valuations of worthy and well-lived lives.

Historical inquiry that is sensitive to these kinds of changes is legal history as political history. It is of course somewhat accidental that the examples adduced in this chapter to support this claim deal mostly with the emergence of a regulatory view of law. A scholar with different temporal or spatial interests would surely have amassed a very different set of examples. One might imagine, for instance, that an historian of the early modern period, or of countries transitioning from state socialism to market domination, might be fascinated by the emergence of rights' consciousness. And an historian with a different theoretical orientation might see the nineteenth or even the twenty-first century in completely different terms.[27] It is my hope that my limitations as a reader of history need not cloud the conceptual claims made here. The language of law is one of the main arenas of political engagement for people in modern societies. When that language changes, our political horizons change with it.

What then, if any, are the advantages and disadvantages of conceptualizing legal history as political history in this way? I will first point to one major potential pitfall and then suggest three modest advantages. The weakness of this vision of legal history as political history is that it says nothing about the issues that make politics urgent: nothing about domination or exploitation, race, gender, class, distributive justice, the north and the south, war, famine, hunger, deprivation, the erosion of democratic participation, nothing about whether the law is part of the problem or part of the solution. It says nothing about whether the role of the historian is to chronicle change or to jar the reader into different experiences of political possibility or political necessity. Perhaps it is enough to say that these issues would have to be addressed otherwise, in the question of whether a particular instance of legal history as political history is successful, good, or worthwhile.

The benefits of such a view are speculative. The first advantage is that this view makes better sense of where the political is located than the traditional views of political history. World leaders and political parties are not meaningless, but they surely do not exhaust the field of meaningful political contestation. Piecemeal processes that make up structural change are invisible for that kind of political history, which is one reason it has been besieged in the scholarly community for decades. Second, my account distinguishes between general political action and the type of engagement that is a core concern for legal history, because the change in the conception or use of law is the key issue. For many general readers, this may be of no concern. For scholars and readers who believe, on the other hand, that law is a crucial and oft-ignored element of politics, this is an advantage. Third and finally, concentrating on the changing language and forms of law throws a spotlight on both the power and the limitations of legal change. The engineers of a change in legal form often (always?) have particular, content-oriented goals as their main priority. But changes in legal form often outlast those goals and those engineers (or at least their hold on decision-making power). New legal forms change what can be said and justified in a legal forum, but they do not determine once and for all the direction of development of the law or of the law's objects. That remains the work of a reframed politics.

---

[27] E.g., see Charles R. Epp, *The Rights Revolution: Lawyers, Activists and Supreme Courts in Comparative Perspective* (1998).

Bibliography

Charles L. Barzun, Dan Priel, 'Jurisprudence and (Its) History' (2015) 101 *Virginia L.R.* 849 ff

Maksymilian Del Mar, Michael Lobban (eds.), *Law in Theory and History: New Essays on a Neglected Dialogue* (Hart Publishing, 2016)

Markus D. Dubber, *The Police Power: Patriarchy and the Foundations of American Government* (Columbia University Press, 2005)

Markus D. Dubber, 'New Historical Jurisprudence: Legal History as Critical Analysis of Law' (2015) 2 *Critical Analysis of Law* 1 ff

Hendrik Hartog, *Public Property and Private Power: The Corporation of the City of New York in American Law, 1730–1870* (University of North Carolina Press, 1983)

Shai J. Lavi, *The Modern Art of Dying: A History of Euthanasia in the United States* (Princeton University Press, 2005)

Jessica K. Lowe, 'Radicalism's Legacy: Developments in American Legal History Since 1998' 36 *Zeitschrift für Neuere Rechtsgeschichte* (2014) 288 ff

'Symposium Issue: "Law As . . .": Theory and Method in Legal History' (2011) 1 *U.C. Irvine L.R.* 519 ff

'Symposium on "Critical Legal Histories": Robert W. Gordon. 1984' 'Critical Legal Histories' *Stanford Law Review* 36: 57–125 (2012) 37 *Law & Soc. Inquiry* 147 ff

Christopher Tomlins, *Freedom Bound: Law, Labor, and Civic Identity in Colonizing English America, 1580–1865* (Cambridge University Press, 2010)

Christopher Tomlins, 'After Critical Legal History: Scope, Scale, Structure' (2012) 8 *Ann R.L. & Soc. Sci.* 31 ff

CHAPTER 9

THE INTELLECTUAL HISTORY OF LAW

ASSAF LIKHOVSKI[*]

I. INTRODUCTION

INTELLECTUAL historians of law are interested in the history of legal ideas and concepts. These ideas may be embodied in legal doctrines or found in theories about law developed by legal scholars in universities and other institutions of learning. Intellectual historians of law are also interested in the history of legal education and the production of academic and other legal texts, in changes in the abstract structures that underlie the thought and discourse of lawyers in a given era, and in the history of legal consciousness—that is, the study of the ideas that laypersons have about law and its institutions. Intellectual historians of law examine these topics to recover legal ideas produced in the past. They also seek to place these ideas in their historical contexts, to provide causal explanations for the appearance (and disappearance) of these ideas, to trace the influence of a given idea over time, and to de-familiarize current ideas and concepts about law as a first step in the process of reforming them.[1]

In this chapter I discuss ten historiographical trends that I believe characterize many recent works written by intellectual historians of law. I also discuss some

* Tel Aviv University Faculty of Law. I thank Joseph Mali, Nader Hakim, and the participants of the May 2017 Tel Aviv University Oxford Handbook workshop for their suggestions, Katarzyna Czerwonogóra for her assistance with the German sources, and Amanda Dale for her editorial assistance. Research for this chapter was supported by the Israel Science Foundation (grant no. 405/15).
[1] For a somewhat different definition see Frédéric Audren, 'Introduction: l'histoire intellectuelle du droit ou la fin du "Grand partage"' (2015) 9 *Clio@Thémis* 1 ff.

future directions of research that I believe should be pursued in the coming decades.[2] I mainly focus on histories dealing with western law in the modern era, but I will also mention works on non-western legal systems and pre-modern periods. Obviously, both the notion of 'trends' and the number of trends I identify are open to critique. One might object that it is impossible to talk about trends (or fashions, or styles) in vast disciplinary fields such as history, intellectual history, or even the intellectual history of law. These are large bodies of knowledge, and most of the trends I identify as recent actually existed, in various forms, prior to the last few decades. One possible response to such an objection would be that, like any general historiographical article, this chapter is also, by definition, inaccurate. A related objection could be to ask: 'why talk about ten trends and not nine, or eleven?' My answer would be to admit that the categories I use are not always clear-cut. Some of the trends I discuss can be broken into sub-categories. Other trends could arguably be aggregated or replaced by alternative categories. My choice of ten themes is merely meant to provide convenient scaffolding for the discussion. In the following pages I first discuss five general historiographical trends and their implications for the intellectual history of law (sections II–VI of this chapter). I then focus on five trends that are more specific to intellectual history and, again, discuss their relevance to the intellectual history of law (sections VII–XI of this chapter).

II. Frameworks I: Space

Over the last twenty years or so, many historians and legal historians, and also some intellectual historians of law, have become interested in expanding the spatial frameworks used to study the past. Nineteenth-century historiography was linked to the nation-state and its institutions (national universities, archives, museums, and so on), and the boundaries of the nation-state determined the boundaries of the stories told by historians, certainly those interested in modern history. This was also the case for legal historians. Students of ancient or medieval law, as well as those studying religious legal systems such as canon law, Islamic law, or Jewish law, have often used transnational frameworks to tell their stories (much like historians

---

[2] For recent discussions of future trends in legal historiography generally, as well as the intellectual history of law, see the series of 'Law As . . .' symposia published by the *U.C. Irvine L.R.*; Jacques Krynen, Bernard d'Alteroche (eds.), *L'Histoire du droit en France: Nouvelles tendances, nouveaux territoires* (2014); Markus D. Dubber, 'New Historical Jurisprudence: Legal History as Critical Analysis of Law' (2015) 2.1 *Critical Analysis of Law* 1 ff; '[Symposium]: Opportunities for Law's Intellectual History' (2016) 64 *Buffalo L.R.* 1 ff.

of philosophy, science, or music).[3] However, many of those working on the history of nineteenth- and twentieth-century law have tended to focus on the history of national legal systems. The positivist definition of law, which equates law with the norms produced by the 'sovereign', has also helped keep the work of historians of modern law within national boundaries. Standard works on the intellectual history of modern law therefore often discuss the history of national schools of legal thought.

Recently, however, a series of interrelated turns—the global, transnational, comparative, and colonial/postcolonial turns—have revolutionized historiography.[4] They have also led to a growing interest in writing global or transnational intellectual histories.[5] Scholars interested in the intellectual history of law have also been influenced by these turns. One type of transnational legal history, long-pursued, has been that of legal transplants. Some works on transplants seek to answer questions posed by comparative lawyers (e.g., about the proper classification of a given legal system), rather than questions about the causes, context, or conditions for the movement of legal ideas across national boundaries (questions that intellectual historians are inclined to investigate).[6] However, some works on the history of legal transplantation are more focused on questions that interest intellectual historians of law, for example studies examining the influence of legal thinkers belonging to one legal system on the thought of legal thinkers belonging to another system.[7] Another variety of works in this genre are studies that analyse *mutual* influence, or interactions, within circles or networks of scholars in two or more countries, or those that compare similar intellectual developments in two or more jurisdictions without reference to the problematic concept of influence. There are also transnational histories of specific regions, for example, of European legal thought.

There have also been some attempts to write global histories of legal thought. Here the aim is not to study the flow of legal ideas between two or more jurisdictions, but to provide a bird's-eye view of developments in legal thought that appeared simultaneously in many jurisdictions across the globe. Such an approach is found in Duncan Kennedy's influential article on 'three globalizations' of modern legal thought. In this article, Kennedy analysed the emergence of new structures of legal thought in one or another western metropolitan centre in the last two centuries,

---

[3] See, e.g., J. M. Kelly, *A Short History of Western Legal Theory* (1992); John W. Cairns, 'Intellectual History and Legal History', in Richard Whatmore, Brian Young (eds.), *A Companion to Intellectual History* (2016) 213, 220–2; Thomas Duve, 'German Legal History: National Traditions and Transnational Perspectives' (2014) 22 *Rechtsgeschichte/Legal History* 16, 22.

[4] On the promises (and perils) of these turns, which, like many historiographical fashions, are cyclical and therefore rise, but also wane, see Lynn Hunt, *Writing History in the Global Era* (2014).

[5] See, e.g., Samuel Moyn, Andrew Sartori (eds.), *Global Intellectual History* (2013).

[6] One collection of articles that seeks to straddle the divide between comparative lawyers and legal historians is 'Histories of Legal Transplantations' (2009) 10 *Theoretical Inquiries in Law* 299 ff.

[7] See, e.g., Katharina Isabel Schmidt, 'Law, Modernity, Crisis: German Free Lawyers, American Legal Realists, and the Transatlantic Turn to 'Life', 1903–1933' (2016) 39 *German Studies Review* 121 ff.

and the reception of these structures of thought in other western and non-western jurisdictions.[8]

Kennedy's narrative is based on the assumption that legal thought is western in origin and that non-western countries were essentially passive receivers of intellectual innovations that first appeared in the West. However, it seems that the relationship between the West and its periphery was sometimes one of interaction, mutual influence, or independent (but parallel) development.[9] Peripheries—provinces or colonies distant from national or imperial centres—were often places of experimentation and innovation, including legal innovation. For example, the codification of English law was first undertaken in nineteenth-century India, then in places influenced by the Indian codes, such as the African colonies of Empire, and finally in the United Kingdom itself. French colonies, too, were sometimes used as laboratories for legal experimentation.[10] We should therefore seek to de-centre the intellectual history of law and rethink the centre–periphery structure that underlies existing transnational and global histories of modern legal thought, devoting more attention in the future to the history of legal thought and legal education in the peripheries of the West.[11]

A promising topic for such future research would be the history of legal thought and legal education in the colonies of western empires. In recent years, there has been heightened scholarly interest in the legal history of European empires, influenced by the growing interest in post-colonial studies generally.[12] Many of these new works examine the political, social, and cultural aspects of colonial law. We know

[8] Duncan Kennedy, 'Three Globalizations of Law and Legal Thought: 1850–2000', in David M. Trubek, Alvaro Santos (eds.), *The New Law and Economic Development: A Critical Appraisal* (2006) 19 ff. On Kennedy's historiographical approach, see Justin Desautels-Stein, 'Back in Style' (2014) 25 *Law and Critique* 141 ff. For recent European discussions on the global history of law (and legal thought) see Jean-Louis Halpérin, *Profils des mondialisations du droit* (2009); Jean-Louis Halpérin, *Five Legal Revolutions Since the 17th Century: An Analysis of a Global Legal History* (2014); Thomas Duve (ed.), *Entanglements in Legal History: Conceptual Approaches* (2014).

[9] See, e.g., William Twining, *General Jurisprudence: Understanding Law from a Global Perspective* (2009) 269–92. For an earlier work on an earlier period, see Pier G. Monateri, 'Black Gaius: A Quest for the Multicultural Origins of the "Western Legal Tradition"' (2000) 51 *Hastings L.J.* 479 ff. For a non-legal discussion, see Suzanne Marchand, 'Has the History of the Disciplines Had its Day?' in Darrin M. McMahon, Samuel Moyn (eds.), *Rethinking Modern European Intellectual History* (2014) 130, 143–4.

[10] See, e.g., Pierre Singaravélou, *Professer l'Empire: Les 'sciences coloniales' en France sous la IIIe République* (2011) 300, 312–13. See generally Eric De Mari, Florence Renucci, 'Dépasser les frontières, Déplacer le regard: Les enjeux de l'histoire du droit et des institutions coloniales dans les facultés de droit', in Krynen, d'Alteroche (n. 2) 495 ff.

[11] See, e.g., Assaf Likhovski, 'Czernowitz, Lincoln and Jerusalem and the Comparative History of American Jurisprudence' (2003) 4 *Theoretical Inquiries in Law* 621 ff; Arnulf Becker Lorca, *Mestizo International Law: A Global Intellectual History 1842–1933* (2015).

[12] See, e.g., Shaunnagh Dorsett, John McLaren (eds.), *Legal Histories of the British Empire: Laws, Engagements and Legacies* (2014); 'Dossier: Chantiers de l'histoire du droit colonial' (2011) 4 *Clio@Thémis* 1 ff; Horst Hammen, 'Kolonialrecht und Kolonialgerichtsbarkeit in den ehemaligen deutschen Schutzgebieten—Ein Überblick' (1999) 32 *Verfassung und Recht in Übersee* 191 ff.

relatively less about the intellectual history of colonial law. For example, how was colonial law studied and taught in different metropoles and colonies? What role did colonial law play in the formation of modern legal disciplines, such as comparative law and legal anthropology? How was western legal self-understanding shaped by the study of non-western law, generally, and non-western religious legal systems, in particular? What role did colonial legal texts (codes, legal periodicals, textbooks) play in changes in the nature of both colonial law and the law of the metropole?

III. Frameworks II: Time

The expansion of the spatial frameworks used by some historians in recent decades was accompanied by the expansion of temporal ones. In the mid-twentieth century, historiography was dominated by social history. Historians focused on entities (society, social classes, the family) in which changes occur over centuries rather than decades. The broad time frames used by historians were especially evident in the work of the mid-twentieth-century French *Annales* School. Historians influenced by the *Annales* approach sought to analyse *longue durée* changes and also to use social science techniques, including quantification, appropriate for measuring such changes. But by the 1970s, broad temporal frameworks and social-science methodologies lost their appeal. The research focus of many historians shifted to micro-history, to singular events, to anecdotes, or to the biographies of specific individuals (no longer the biographies of unique leaders or geniuses, but rather those of ordinary people). Quantitative analysis of large data sets also went out of fashion.

In the last few years, a revival of the interest in studying *longue durée* change can be observed. Such interest is evident, for example, in Jo Guldi and David Armitage's *History Manifesto*, published in 2014.[13] There have also been calls for a return to writing intellectual histories that use *longue durée* frameworks, similar to that used by one of the major intellectual historians of the early twentieth century, Arthur Lovejoy.[14]

In the nineteenth century, legal historians too wrote works that spanned centuries and even millennia.[15] A contemporary call to return to such broad

---

[13] Jo Guldi, David Armitage, *The History Manifesto* (2014). For the lively debate created by the arguments made in this book, see, e.g., 'AHR Exchange: On *The History Manifesto*' (2015) 120 *American Historical Review* 527 ff.

[14] See Darrin M. McMahon, 'The Return of the History of Ideas?' in McMahon, Moyn (n. 9) 13 ff.

[15] One early, and very influential, example is Henry Sumner Maine, *Ancient Law: Its Connection with the Early History of Society and its Relation to Modern Ideas* (1861).

frameworks can be found in an article by Markus Dubber, who recently wrote a 'legal history manifesto', inspired by Guldi and Armitage's work. In this manifesto, Dubber calls for a new comparative–historical approach to the study of legal history, which he terms 'New Historical Jurisprudence'—an approach that is broad both spatially and temporally.[16] Dubber also provides some concrete examples of how such new historical jurisprudence might be produced, for example by analysing the histories of two competing concepts of government, 'law' vs. 'police' (that is, a government based on rule of law vs. a government based on discretionary power), over wide ranges of space and time: the West from ancient Athens to today.[17]

In addition to *longue durée* histories of deep legal structures of thought, of the type analysed by Dubber, one can think of additional topics that would benefit from a *longue durée* approach. One example would be histories of specific types of legal texts, such as codes or constitutions, that would explore the changing nature of these texts over centuries rather than decades.[18] A second example would be histories of legal education that would connect the modern history of western academic legal education to the longer history of both western and non-western legal education. One can think, for example, of a history of legal education that could trace similarities and differences between the modern legal academia and legal studies in non-western institutions, such as Islamic or Jewish religious schools (*madrasas* and *yeshivas*), in the distant and recent past.[19]

Finally, a *longue durée* approach to the history of legal ideas would allow historians to discover long-term trends in the history of legal thought, identifying various types of trajectories: continuity and rupture, linear progress, 'rise and fall', and cyclical patterns that repeat themselves over periods spanning decades or even centuries.[20] One such possible project would compare similarities and differences between, for example, the various nineteenth-century historical approaches to the study of law found in many European legal systems and their twentieth-century manifestations.[21] Such a comparison could raise some 'big questions' about these approaches that we do not ask today, for example: what were the external—political

---

[16] Dubber (n. 2).

[17] Markus D. Dubber, 'The Schizophrenic Jury and Other Palladia of Liberty: A Critical Historical Analysis' (2015) 3 *Comparative Legal History* 307 ff.

[18] See, e.g., Thomas Duve, 'Global Legal History—A Methodological Approach', Max Planck Institute for European Legal History Research Paper Series No. 2016-04, 3 ff.

[19] On the importance of the study of non-western legal systems generally see Ron Harris, 'Is it Time for Non-Euro-American Legal History?' (2016) 56 *American Journal of Legal History* 60 ff.

[20] For an interesting (a-historical) discussion see Jeremy K. Kessler, David E. Pozen, 'Working Themselves Impure: A Life-Cycle Theory of Legal Theories' (2016) 83 *University of Chicago L.R.* 1819 ff.

[21] On nineteenth-century historical approaches see, e.g., Philippe Sturmel, 'L'école historique française du droit a-t-elle existé?' (2002) 1 *Rechtsgeschichte/Legal History* 90 ff; David M. Rabban, *Law's History: American Legal Thought and the Transatlantic Turn to History* (2013).

and cultural—circumstances that led, over time, to the rise, demise, and resurgence of such approaches to the study of law? Another possible project could ask why certain legal systems prove receptive to specific jurisprudential approaches at certain points in time, but not at others, for example: why did the UK proved receptive to non-analytical approaches to law during Henry Maine's time, but less so during the 1930s?[22]

IV. POLITICAL RELEVANCE

The recent return to broad spatial and temporal frameworks seems to be connected to a deep unease with the political irrelevance of many current modes of writing history (and legal history). Thus, the interest in transnational or global history and the resurgence of interest in *longue durée* approaches is sometimes accompanied by a call to historians to use these frameworks to pose questions that would be relevant to contemporary political or policy debates. Guldi and Armitage's manifesto, for example, argues that the focus of historians since the 1970s on narrow, short-term events made their work irrelevant and that by returning to a more ambitious type of historiography devoted to mapping broad historical trends, historians would be able to influence politicians and policymakers dealing with problems such as global governance, climate change, or wealth inequality.[23]

Markus Dubber's legal history manifesto (inspired by works such as Thomas Piketty's *Capital in the Twenty-First Century*, as well as by Guldi and Armitage) also calls on historians (in his case, legal historians) to actively engage in current political controversies by pursuing topics that have normative and publicly significant implications.[24] For Dubber, being 'political' is also understood as being 'critical' or 'progressive'. This is also the case with Kennedy's 'three globalizations' thesis. In Kennedy's article he claims that one of his goals is to enable 'progressive elites in the periphery' to resist neo-liberal western hegemony.[25] Somewhat similar arguments about the need for legal historians to become politically relevant again can be found in Christopher Tomlins' recent work.[26]

---

[22] See, e.g., Neil Duxbury, 'English Jurisprudence between Austin and Hart' (2005) 91 *Virginia L.R.* 1, 54–69; William Cornish, Michael Lobban, Keith Smith, 'Theories of Law and Government', in William Cornish et al. (eds.), *The Oxford History of the Laws of England: Vol XI: 1820–1914: English Legal System* (2010) 72–131.

[23] Guldi, Armitage (n. 13) 61–87.   [24] Dubber (n. 2) 11.   [25] Kennedy (n. 8) 24.

[26] Christopher Tomlins, '"Be Operational, or Disappear": Thoughts on a Present Discontent' (2016) 12 *Annual Review of Law and Social Science* 1 ff.

In the past, works on the intellectual history of law based on broad spatial and temporal frameworks have been at the forefront of attempts to make legal history politically relevant. For example, in the 1970s and early 1980s, American Critical Legal Studies scholars sought to reconstruct the deep structures underlying liberal legal thought as a first step in the process of undermining liberal ideology—a project with which, one would assume, many progressive historians would identify. However, as Katharina Isabel Schmidt has recently pointed out, the political implications of such 'Big Legal History' may sometimes not be progressive but, in fact, retrograde.[27] Nineteenth-century legal history in the *longue durée* mode, as practised by the German historical school or its offshoots in England and the United States, was sometimes used to buttress nationalist, colonialist, and racist ideas by supposedly connecting concepts such as 'liberty' or 'democracy' with the law or customs of the Germanic tribes or the Aryan race. The recent resurgence of nationalist sentiments in many western democracies, accompanied by old–new notions about the uniqueness of 'western civilization' (and its law), can perhaps serve as a warning sign that the desire to make legal history (including the intellectual history of law) politically relevant may be a double-edged sword.

V. Beyond Traditional Sources

Historians are always looking for new sources with which to reconstruct the past. Sometimes these are newly-discovered sources, and sometimes they are existing sources suddenly put to a new use by having new questions asked about them.[28] Legal historians, too, are always on the lookout for fresh sources. One, cyclical, phenomenon evident in the work of legal historians is the movement between using elite and non-elite legal texts. Thus, American legal historians in the middle of the twentieth century moved their research focus from the decisions of appellate courts to those of lower ones, only to return to appellate court decisions in the 1970s with the rise of Critical Legal Studies.[29]

---

[27] Katharina Isabel Schmidt, '[Book Review]: Rethinking Modern Intellectual History' (2016) 3 *Comparative Legal History* 196 ff.

[28] An interesting example taken from the history of science is Lorraine J. Daston, Peter Galison, *Objectivity* (2007) (using scientific atlases to reconstruct the history of scientific objectivity).

[29] See, e.g., Angela Fernandez, 'Future(s) of American Legal History' (2012) 62 *University of Toronto Law Journal* 439 ff.

However, the research focus of legal historians also sometimes moves sideways—to new places in which law (and, in our case, legal ideas) may be found. An example of such a move is evident in a recent issue of the journal *Critical Analysis of Law*, which was devoted to 'Arts and the Aesthetic in Legal History'. Articles published in this issue discussed topics such as the use of nineteenth-century English novels as a source for the study of the history of imprisonment for debt, or the use of nineteenth-century impressionist paintings as a way to explore changing attitudes to pollution and environmental regulation.[30] The use of the arts as a source for the study of past ideas about law is not the only possible nexus between art and the intellectual history of law. An additional intersection is the use of literary theory to study the rise and decline of legal genres, for example codes, abridgments, digests, textbooks, dictionaries, case-notes, syllabi, maps (or categorization schemes), letters, autobiographies, inaugural lectures, book reviews, or obituaries.[31]

VI. THE DIGITAL REVOLUTION

In the last few decades, the digital revolution has changed the nature of historical research. The mass-scanning of books and archival sources, the growing interest in the use of big data to study the past, and the development of tools to mine these data (tools such as Google Ngrams that allow one to quickly perform searches that would have taken months of intensive work in the past) are transforming how historians work.

At first glance, it may appear that the use of digital tools to mine big data is more relevant to topics such as climate history, economic history, the history of demographic changes, or similar topics based on the use of quantitative data.

[30] See Anat Rosenberg, 'The Realism of the Balance Sheet: Value Assessments Between the Debtors Act and *The Picture of Dorian Gray*' (2015) 2.2 *Critical Analysis of Law* 363 ff; David B. Schorr, 'Art and the History of Environmental Law' (2015) 2.2 *Critical Analysis of Law* 322 ff. Another recent example of the creative use of non-conventional sources is Peter Goodrich, *Legal Emblems and the Art of Law: Obiter Depicta as the Vision of Governance* (2014).

[31] On legal genres see the section on 'Genres littéraires des juristes' from Issue 31 onwards of the *Revue d'histoire des Facultés de droit et de la culture juridique, du monde des juristes et du livre juridique*. See also Frédéric Audren, 'Alma mater sous le regard de l'historien du droit: Cultures académiques, formation des élites et identités professionnelles', in Krynen, d'Alteroche (n. 2) 145, 169; Laetitia Guerlain, 'Culture et usages des savoirs anthropologiques chez les juristes. De quelques apports de l'étude des recensions bibliographiques (XIXᵉ–XXᵉ siècles)', 35 (2015) *Revue d'histoire des Facultés de droit et de la culture juridique, du monde des juristes et du livre juridique* 233 ff.

However, since legal records were one of the earliest types of records to have been digitized, it seems that the use of digital tools is also relevant to legal historians— both historians interested in the social history of law (e.g., the history of crime) and also intellectual historians who can use digital databases to follow changes in legal and political discourse.[32] Indeed, in *The History Manifesto*, Guldi and Armitage remark that the use of big data is especially appropriate 'in law and other forms of institutional history'.[33] It is not surprising, therefore, that a recent issue of the *Law and History Review* was devoted to the ways in which historians of law have made use of digital resources.[34]

No one can doubt that the digital revolution has greatly increased the efficiency of historical research. It has also perhaps led to greater emphasis on theoretical discussion of the sources rather than mere compilation. However, one might certainly ask whether this revolution has also led to major methodological breakthroughs in the study of history and legal history.[35] Often the use of digital sources and tools, it seems, does not lead to new questions and arguments. Rather, the digital sources or tools are merely used to illustrate arguments that could have been made without them.

Perhaps a more promising aspect of the digital revolution is therefore not the use of big data, or the use of new tools to mine this data, but more modest projects: the creation of databases on, for example, the law professors of the past, or the opportunity that digitization provides to visualize our data in new ways (for instance to graphically track the rise or decline of legal keywords over time, or create maps of networks of scholars).[36] Digitization can also allow us to create new teaching tools: curated digital archives that could be used by students studying the intellectual history of law. Such digital archives could link, for example, passages from books produced by specific legal thinkers to cases or legislation in which the ideas of these thinkers appeared, to newspaper articles using these ideas politically, to the works of later scholars relying or trying to refute these ideas, etc.

---

[32] See, e.g., Assaf Likhovski, '"Tyranny" in Nineteenth-Century American Legal Discourse: A Rhetorical Analysis' (1997) 28 *Journal of Interdisciplinary History* 205 ff.

[33] See Guldi, Armitage (n. 13) 94 ff.

[34] '[Special Issue]: Digital Law and History' (2016) 34.4 *Law and History Review* 831 ff.

[35] See, e.g., Christiane Birr, 'Die geisteswissenschaftliche Perspektive: Welche Forschungsergebnisse lassen Digital Humanities erwarten?' (2016) 24 *Rechtsgeschichte/Legal History* 330 ff. On the problems created by digitization see generally Lara Putnam, 'The Transnational and the Text-Searchable: Digitized Sources and the Shadows they Cast' (2016) 121 *American Historical Review* 377 ff.

[36] On databases see, e.g., Audren (n. 31) 160; Annamaria Monti, '"Interdisciplinary" Legal Studies and the Emergence of New Academic Teachings: A Research Project on Law Courses in 19th–20th Century Italy' (2016) 19 *CIAN-Revista de Historia de las Universidades* 91, 95–6 (discussing databases of French, Spanish and Italian law professors). On new visualization and publishing opportunities enabled by the digital revolution see Stephen Robertson, 'Searching for Anglo-American Digital Legal History' (2016) 34 *Law and History Review* 1047, 1066–8.

VII. ACTORS I: INDIVIDUALS, COMMUNITIES, AND NETWORKS OF KNOWLEDGE

In the past, intellectual historians working on the history of the natural sciences, the social sciences, or the humanities often pursued their topics using a biographical approach. Perhaps under the influence of Romantic-era notions of individual genius, historians sought to reconstruct the history of their chosen scientific discipline by focusing on the life of 'great minds'. They thus imagined the history of their field as a relay race in which the baton of knowledge was passed in a linear fashion from one genius to the next.

Beginning in the 1960s and 1970s, historical interest shifted from the study of individual scientists, philosophers, and other thinkers to the study of communities of knowledge.[37] Two important milestones in this evolution were the publication of Thomas Kuhn's *The Structure of Scientific Revolutions* in 1962 and the publication of Michel Foucault's *The Order of Things* (first published in French in 1966).[38] This trend intensified in the following decades under the influence of sociological accounts of academic communities (found, e.g., in works such as Pierre Bourdieu's *Homo Academicus*) and of Science, Technology, and Society (STS) scholarship.[39]

Related developments were the linguistic and cultural turns in historiography. These turns led to the awareness that language, discourse, mental structures, and similar clusters of ideas shared by large groups were not natural and static, but socially-constructed and dynamic. Historians therefore began to study the history of ideas shared by communities of thinkers, rather than studying individuals. Sometimes the focus was on the ideas of groups of elite thinkers (local but also transnational groups such as the early modern 'Republic of Letters'), as was the case with the contextualist histories of political thought produced by scholars belonging to the Cambridge School. Sometimes, historians sought to recover ideas prevalent among larger collectives that included ordinary people, as was the case with the French *histoire des mentalités* approach.[40] Interest in the study of groups and their structures of thought was also reflected in works on the intellectual history of law. Such an approach, influenced by Kuhn's work, was

[37] See, e.g., John Tresch, 'Cosmologies Materialized: History of Science and History of Ideas', in McMahon, Moyn (n. 9) 153 ff.

[38] Thomas S. Kuhn, *The Structure of Scientific Revolutions* (1962); Michel Foucault, *Les mots et les choses: Une archéologie des sciences humaines* (1966).

[39] See Pierre Bourdieu, *Homo academicus* (1984); Tresch (n. 37) 158.

[40] See, generally, 'AHR Forum: Historiographic "Turns" in Critical Perspective' (2012) 117 *American Historical Review* 698 ff.

especially evident in the works produced by Critical Legal Studies scholars in the 1970s and 1980s.[41]

Both approaches—the biographical, which analyses the intellectual history of law by focusing on individual actors and the approach that focuses on ideas shared by whole communities of legal scholars—are, of course, perfectly legitimate. There are also intermediate points on the spectrum between these two extremes, for example prosopographic studies that paint a collective portrait of a given group of legal scholars but do not necessarily focus on paradigms or structures of thought that *all* the members of the given group share. A related category of works are those that examine scholarly circles and networks, whether national or transnational. Such circles or networks could be informal, such as those connecting academic legal scholars, or institutional, such as those created by international organizations and western governments in the post-Second World War period to train legal experts in the developing world.[42]

While works by intellectual historians of law are found on all points of the spectrum between the individual and the community, there are still promising avenues for further research that seem not to have been fully explored to date, and again much of the work that can be done in the future seems to be comparative. One can learn much about the nature of modern dictators by reading a biography of Hitler or a biography of Stalin, but a joint biography, juxtaposing and comparing their lives (as in Alan Bullock's *Hitler and Stalin: Parallel Lives*), is of particular value.[43] In a similar way, if one were to write a dual biography of, for example, Roscoe Pound and François Gény, such a biography would probably provide insights that cannot be gained from biographies of each of these thinkers separately.[44] A similar promising avenue of research may be found in comparisons of two or more communities of legal knowledge, networks, or structures of legal thought.

One final observation on this topic is that while intellectual historians of political thought, influenced by the ideas of the Cambridge School, seek to place the ideas of the major thinkers of the past in the context of their place and time and therefore often devote much attention to reconstructing this context by studying minor or forgotten thinkers, intellectual historians of law seem to be less interested in such minor figures. Thus, for example, if we examine works

[41]   See, generally, Robert W. Gordon, 'Critical Legal Histories' (1984) 36 *Stanford L.R.* 57 ff; William W. Fisher III, 'Texts and Contexts: The Application to American Legal History of the Methodologies of Intellectual History' (1997) 49 *Stanford L.R.* 1065 ff.

[42]   For informal networks of legal scholars in the Anglo-American world see, e.g., Richard A. Cosgrove, *Our Lady the Common Law: An Anglo-American Legal Community, 1870–1930* (1987). Legal networks involving the developing world are discussed in Yves Dezalay, Bryant G. Garth, *The Internationalization of Palace Wars: Lawyers, Economists, and the Contest to Transform Latin American States* (2002); Yves Dezalay, Bryant G. Garth, *Asian Legal Revivals: Lawyers in the Shadow of Empire* (2010).

[43]   Alan Bullock, *Hitler and Stalin: Parallel Lives* (1992).

[44]   See, e.g., Likhovski (n. 11); Phillipe Sands, *East West Street: On the Origins of 'Genocide' and the 'Crimes Against Humanity'* (2016); Charles L. Barzun, 'Jerome Frank, Lon Fuller, and a Romantic Pragmatism' (2017) 29 *Yale J. L. & Human.* 129 ff.

on late-nineteenth-century or early-twentieth-century English jurisprudence, thinkers such as Henry Maine have been relatively well studied.[45] We also know much about structures of legal thought supposedly shared by all English legal scholars during this period.[46] By contrast, we know relatively little about the authors of textbooks on jurisprudence such as Sheldon Amos, and even less about English-colonial jurisprudence textbook writers such as William Markby, William Henry Rattigan, or Frederic Goadby.

VIII. ACTORS II: CONCEPTS

The linguistic turn and the contextualist approach to intellectual history were related to the rise of conceptual history—that is, the study of the history of the meaning of such keywords as 'honour' or 'liberty' over extended periods of time. In the German-speaking world, the main advocates of this approach in the middle- and late-twentieth century were historians such as Reinhart Koselleck. In the Anglo-American world, it was identified with figures belonging to the Cambridge School, including Quentin Skinner or J. G. A. Pocock, but also with some of the pioneers of cultural studies such as Raymond Williams.[47]

Today, conceptual history is a flourishing sub-field of intellectual history, as is evident in journals such as *Contributions to the History of Concepts*. While some of the work conducted by conceptual historians looks at topics such as 'emotion concepts' and other themes that are closer to social and cultural history, much of the research in this field has been on the history of key political concepts such as 'citizenship' or 'liberalism.' This interest in political concepts makes conceptual history relevant to the work of legal historians.

Conceptual historians often pursue lexicographical projects based on large collaborative groups of scholars. In the German-speaking world, we find, for example, projects such as the historical dictionary of legal terms, the *Deutsches Rechtswörterbuch*, or the historical lexicon of political terms, the *Geschichtliche Grundbegriffe* (a lexicon which includes some legal terms as well).[48] I would suggest there is a need for similar projects dealing with Anglo-American legal

[45] See, e.g., the references in Rabban (n. 21) 115–49.

[46] See David Sugarman, 'Legal Theory, the Common Law Mind and the Making of the Textbook Tradition', in William Twining (ed.), *Legal Theory and Common Law* (1986) 26 ff.

[47] See, e.g., Jan-Werner Müller, 'On Conceptual History', in McMahon, Moyn (n. 9) 74 ff.

[48] See, e.g., Rolf Grawert, 'Gesetz', in Otto Brunner, Werner Conze, Reinhart Koselleck (eds.), *Geschichtliche Grundbegriffe: Historisches Lexikon zur politisch-sozialen Sprache in Deutschland* (1975) 863–922. See, generally, Duve (n. 3) 19–20.

keywords. In addition, collaborative projects exploring the history of key legal concepts comparatively, both within the western legal tradition and globally, are also needed.

IX. SITES OF KNOWLEDGE-PRODUCTION AND DISSEMINATION

Traditional intellectual historians studied relatively few canonical texts produced by relatively few elite thinkers. The paradigmatic example of such an approach has, perhaps, been the history of philosophy of the type taught in introductory courses, based on the study of a number of leading texts ordered in a linear chronological series and imagined as being in dialogue with each other.

Intellectual historians today, however, are interested not only in canonical texts but also in the contexts out of which these texts emerged. They also use sociological and anthropological tools to discuss the sites, conditions, and attitudes associated with the production of knowledge—topics on the borders of intellectual history and cultural and social history. These include: the fashioning (and self-fashioning) of scientific and scholarly personae; the relationship between teachers and students; daily life in the spaces where knowledge is produced (e.g., monasteries or laboratories); and the material tools, institutions, and intermediaries used to produce, represent, and disseminate knowledge (such as books, encyclopaedias, atlases, scientific collections, libraries, archives, museums, publishing houses, learned societies, and so on), as well as the audiences of knowledge.[49]

Intellectual historians of law too study the sites where legal knowledge is produced and disseminated. They obviously study legal research and law teaching in universities. However, they are also interested in law teaching in various non-academic sites.[50] Other channels for legal knowledge-production and communication are also

---

[49] See, e.g., Antoine Lilti, 'Does Intellectual History Exist in France?' in McMahon, Moyn (n. 9) 56, 61–65; Tresch (n. 37) 159 ff; 'Special Issue: Scientific Personae', *Science in Context* 16.1-2 (2003) 1 ff; Samuel Moyn, Andrew Sartori, 'Approaches to Global Intellectual History', in Moyn, Sartori (n. 5) 3, 9–16; 'Special Issue: Scholarly Personae: Repertoires and Performances of Academic Identity' (2016) 131.4 *Low Countries Historical Review* 1 ff.

[50] It seems that in France there is more institutional interest in the study of the history of legal education and legal research than there is in the Anglo-American world. This fact is evident from the existence of the *Revue d'histoire des Facultés de droit et de la culture juridique, du monde des juristes et du livre juridique* (a French journal established in 1984 specifically devoted to the study of the history of legal education and legal literature). See also *Quaderni fiorentini: per la storia del pensiero giuridico moderno* (an Italian journal established in 1972). See generally, Audren (n. 31).

studied. These include public and private law libraries or academic law societies, but also the material objects used to disseminate knowledge, such as professional and popular law books, legal periodicals, or non-legal literature. Related issues such as the history of law and print, the history of the book trade, translation, censorship, and plagiarism are studied as well, although the nexus between legal history and book history still contains, it seems, many unexplored areas.[51]

There are many other topics in this category that require additional research. For example, one potentially interesting topic, already mentioned, would be a broad-brush comparative study of the history of legal education and research in religious legal systems and its relationship to modern legal education. Recently, for example, a fascinating body of work on Jewish law studies in Talmudic academies (ranging from the late-antique period to the nineteenth and twentieth centuries) has appeared. These works discuss issues such as the nature of the curriculum, everyday scholarly life, academic hierarchies and leadership, relationship with lay persons, the formation of scholarly prestige (and scholarly shame), and the interaction or entanglement of these religious systems and modern ones.[52]

Another topic, on the borderline between intellectual and cultural history, is the study of the personae of legal scholars. The study of scientific and scholarly personae has thrived in recent years. We need more studies examining the images associated with specific legal scholars, and also ones analysing the criteria required in order to be considered a 'proper' or 'exemplary' legal scholar in a given place and time.[53]

Finally, more attention needs to be paid to the history of sites where legal knowledge was disseminated to lay persons. This topic is connected with a broader category—the history of legal consciousness: what did ordinary people know about law in different places in different times? How did people imagine law, and how did they talk about it? What ideas about law appeared in non-traditional sites and texts such as the public square, the coffeehouse, the theatre or the cinema, and

---

[51] See, e.g., Richard J. Ross, 'The Commoning of the Common Law: The Renaissance Debate over Printing English Law, 1520–1640' (1998) 146 *University of Pennsylvania L.R.* 323 ff; Patrick Polden, 'The Education of Lawyers', in Cornish (n. 22) 1201–11 ff; Angela Fernandez, Markus D. Dubber (eds.), *Law Books in Action: Essays on the Anglo-American Legal Treatise* (2012); Laura Beck Varela, 'The Diffusion of Law Books in Early Modern Europe: A Methodological Approach', in Massimo Meccarelli, Maria Julia Solla Sastre (eds.), *Spatial and Temporal Dimensions for Legal History: Research Experiences and Itineraries* (2016) 195 ff; Michael Stolleis, Thomas Simon (eds.), *Juristische Zeitschriften in Europa* (2006); Jean-Louis Halpérin, 'For a Renewed History of Lawyers' (2016) 56 *American Journal of Legal History* 53, 58–9; Joseph L. Gerken, *The Invention of Legal Research* (2016).

[52] See generally Assaf Likhovski, 'Recent Trends in the Study of the Intellectual History of Law and Jewish Law Scholarship' *Diné Yisrael* (forthcoming).

[53] See, e.g., Shaun McVeigh, 'Afterward: Office and the Conduct of the Minor Jurisprudent' (2015) 5 *U.C. Irvine L.R.* 499 ff.

newspapers and magazines (those with a broad readership, but also those targeting specific audiences such as women or children)? All such questions, which arise at the intersection of social, cultural, and intellectual history, have not been fully explored yet.[54]

x. Beyond Traditional Legal Fields

Historians of science are no longer exclusively interested in the history of 'science' as a whole or in the analysis of paradigmatic scientific fields such as physics or chemistry. They are also devoting attention to more 'marginal' areas such as the social sciences. A related process has been the movement from a western understanding of what 'science' is to a broader definition that also includes non-western science-like practices, replacing the notion of the 'history of science' with a more capacious term—'the history of knowledge'.[55]

In recent decades, legal historians, too, have begun to move beyond 'core' fields of law (such as constitutional, contract, tort, or criminal law) to less-explored fields, for example international law, tax law, or intellectual property law. Recent histories of these fields deal with their doctrinal, economic, and social history, but they also explore their intellectual history. There is now a growing body of works on the intellectual history of international law, analysing the works of early modern and modern scholars who shaped the field. Similarly, there are new works exploring the intellectual history of tax law or intellectual property law.[56]

Other legal fields whose intellectual history is still relatively unexplored include, for example, conflict of laws. In addition, even in those areas mentioned earlier, such as international law or intellectual property law, there is still significant progress to be made. For example, the focus of much of the new work to date has been on elite legal thinkers in the West, and therefore further research is needed on non-elite or lay ideas related to these topics, on how these ideas actually made an impact on

---

[54] See, e.g., Steven Wilf, *Law's Imagined Republic: Popular Politics and Criminal Justice in Revolutionary America* (2010).

[55] See Jürgen Renn, 'The Globalization of Knowledge in History and its Normative Challenges' (2014) 22 *Rechtsgeschichte/Legal History* 52 ff.

[56] See, e.g., Bardo Fassbender, Anne Peters (eds.), *The Oxford Handbook of the History of International Law* (2012); Ajay K. Mehrotra, *Making the Modern American Fiscal State: Law, Politics, and the Rise of Progressive Taxation, 1877–1929* (2013); Oren Bracha, *Owning Ideas: The Intellectual Origins of American Intellectual Property, 1790–1909* (2016).

non-academic actors (such as corporations), or on the ideas associated with these fields in non-western legal systems.[57]

XI. Exploring Law's Boundaries

One major factor that has long driven the study of legal history forward is the willingness to expand our definition of law beyond the traditional positivist definitions used by some legal philosophers and the adoption of more fluid, broader definitions closer to the ones often used by social scientists. The Hurstian revolution in American legal history, for example, was based on a willingness to define law in a way that included not just the doctrines created by higher courts, but also rules produced by lower courts, by state legislatures, and by administrative agencies. Similarly, in the last decade, much of the interesting work produced by legal historians has been inspired by a rejection of state-based, positivist, definitions of law, and on attention to non-state norms and legal pluralist notions of litigation.[58]

A specific aspect of this broader approach is the scholarly interest in 'boundary' work. The anthropology and sociology of the professions, and STS scholarship, have influenced work on intellectual history by drawing our attention to the importance of studying the effort of academic disciplines to mark and police disciplinary divisions, to maintain the social prestige of those belonging to a given discipline, and to deploy knowledge as power. One example of the study of such boundary work can be found in the history of endeavours to distinguish science from magic, technology, religion, and other types of knowledge classified as inferior.[59] In a similar way, sociologists and anthropologists of law also have become interested in how modern law has gradually assumed tasks that had been carried out in previous eras by other professions, such as the clergy or physicians.[60] There is a whole gamut of disciplines and practices that border law. We need more critical, external, non-evolutionary, and non-celebratory works that explore the shifting boundaries between law and

---

[57] See, e.g., Doreen Lustig, 'Governance Histories of International Law' (ch. 45 in this volume); Neil Weinstock Netanel, *From Maimonides to Microsoft: The Jewish Law of Copyright Since the Birth of Print* (2016).

[58] See Renn (n. 55).   [59] Tresch (n. 37) 163–6; Marchand (n. 9).

[60] See, e.g., Shai J. Lavi, *The Modern Art of Dying: A History of Euthanasia in the United States* (2007); Orna Alyagon Darr, *Marks of an Absolute Witch: Evidentiary Dilemmas in Early Modern England* (2011).

magic, religion, philosophy, political thought, accounting, economics, anthropology, and other related disciplines.[61]

XII. Conclusion

Many of the trends I have discussed here are not new but, in fact, cyclical. For example, 'Big Legal History' based on a global scale and on the *longue durée* is not new; we already encountered it in Henry Maine's work. Other trends may indeed be novel. For example, the digital revolution provides us with tools that the legal historians of the past could only dream of.

One can adopt a sceptical or cynical approach to the desire for progress in our discipline, but, at the risk of seeming naïve, I would like to conclude by arguing that there is indeed some progress in the study of the intellectual history of law over time. Looking to the future, I believe that one major avenue of progress in the next few decades could be the coalescing of the various national legal historians' communities that currently exist into a more global, unified community engaged in comparative and transnational collaborative studies of the history of legal ideas, both in the West and in non-western legal systems.

Bibliography

Frédéric Audren, 'Alma mater sous le regard de l'historien du droit: Culture académiques, formation des élites et identités professionnelles', in Jacques Krynen, Bernard d'Alteroche (eds.), *L'Histoire du droit en France: Nouvelles tendances, nouveaux territoires* (Classiques Garnier, 2014) 145

John W. Cairns, 'Intellectual History and Legal History', in Richard Whatmore, Brian Young (eds.), *A Companion to Intellectual History* (Wiley Blackwell, 2016) 213

Thomas Duve (ed.), *Entanglements in Legal History: Conceptual Approaches* (Max Planck Institute for European Legal History, 2014)

---

[61] See, e.g., Christopher Tomlins, 'Framing the Field of Law's Disciplinary Encounters: A Historical Narrative' (2000) 34 *Law and Society Review* 911 ff; Ajay K. Mehrotra, Joseph J. Thorndike, 'From Programmatic Reform to Social Science Research: The National Tax Association and the Promise and Perils of Disciplinary Encounters' (2011) 45 *Law and Society Review* 593 ff; Maksymilian Del Mar, Michael Lobban, 'Introduction', in Maksymilian Del Mar, Michael Lobban (eds.), *Legal Theory and Legal History* (2014) xi–xxxv; 'Symposium: Jurisprudence and (Its) History' (2015) 101 *Virginia Law Review* 849 ff.

Neil Duxbury, *Patterns of American Jurisprudence* (Clarendon Press, 1995)

Angela Fernandez, Markus D. Dubber (eds.), *Law Books in Action: Essays on the Anglo-American Legal Treatise* (Hart Publishing, 2012)

William W. Fisher III, 'Texts and Contexts: The Application to American Legal History of the Methodologies of Intellectual History' 49 (1997) *Stanford L.R.* 1065

Nader Hakim and Fatiha Cherfouh, 'L'histoire de la pensée juridique contemporaine. Hétérogénéité et expansion', in Jacques Krynen, Bernard d'Alteroche (eds.), *L'Histoire du droit en France: Nouvelles tendances, nouveaux territoires* (Classiques Garnier, 2014) 117

Duncan Kennedy, 'Three Globalizations of Law and Legal Thought: 1850–2000', in David M. Trubek, Alvaro Santos (eds.), *The New Law and Economic Development: A Critical Appraisal* (Cambridge University Press, 2006) 19

Darrin M. McMahon, Samuel Moyn (eds.), *Rethinking Modern European Intellectual History* (Oxford University Press, 2014)

Samuel Moyn, Andrew Sartori (eds.), *Global Intellectual History* (Columbia University Press, 2013)

David M. Rabban, *Law's History: American Legal Thought and the Transatlantic Turn to History* (Cambridge University Press, 2014)

CHAPTER 10

....

LEGAL HISTORY AS DOCTRINAL HISTORY

....

JOSHUA GETZLER

How do we account for the rules of law governing particular areas of social life changing over time? Scholars debate whether rule change reflects internal shifts of view within the legal profession, or external pressure from powerful groups seeking to advance their sectional ideas and interests, or else deeper currents in the surrounding society, for example demographic or economic transformations. Accounts that focus on the first perspective, the internal discourse of the lawyers, are often described as 'doctrinal history'. Such history will use formal legal materials such as reports of decisions, texts of statutes and codes, and evidence of lawyers' argumentation and reflections, in order to reconstruct the mind of the professional legal collective as it understands its own activity in guiding conduct and resolving disputes. In the English common-law tradition alone there are excellent doctrinal histories of agency,[1] charity,[2] contract,[3] crime,[4] equity,[5]

---

[1] Samuel J. Stoljar, *The Law of Agency: Its History and Present Principles* (1961).

[2] Gareth Jones, *History of the Law of Charity, 1532–1827* (1969).

[3] Brian Simpson, *A History of the Common Law of Contract: The Rise of the Action of Assumpsit* (1975); Patrick Atiyah, *The Rise and Fall of Freedom of Contract* (1979); Catharine MacMillan, *Mistakes in Contract Law* (2010).

[4] James Fitzjames Stephen, *A History of the Criminal Law of England* (1883); Percy Winfield, *The History of Conspiracy and Abuse of Legal Procedure* (1921).

[5] Frederic William Maitland, *Equity; Also The Forms of Action at Common Law* (1909); David Yale (ed. & intro.), *Lord Nottingham's Chancery Cases* (1957–1961); Chantal Stebbings, *The Private Trustee in Victorian England* (2002).

evidence,[6] family law,[7] land law,[8] torts,[9] obligations as a unified field,[10] native title,[11] unjust enrichment,[12] water rights,[13] company law,[14] and constitutional law;[15] the list is long indeed. Some doctrinal historians zero in on leading cases and write micro-histories charting small increments to doctrine:[16] in the hands of the late Brian Simpson, the acknowledged master of this technique, the effect is to cast an ironic eye at the pretensions of the common law and show how arbitrary and absurd doctrine can be.[17] At the other end of the scale there are some impressive survey histories of doctrine spanning the many subjects of the law across lengthy time periods[18] and exhibiting doctrine as an imposing achievement of the juristic collective, with William S. Holdsworth's monumental *History of English Law*[19] still holding the field, though its place is now being challenged by a new *Oxford History of the Laws of England*.[20]

This chapter will not survey and discuss the many fine examples of doctrinal history. It is too large and too varied a field really to form a unity, even within the confines of England; indeed, such writings could be said to make up a good

---

[6] Julius Stone, *Evidence: Its History and Policies* (1991); Michael Macnair, *The Law of Proof in Early Modern Equity* (1999).

[7] Rebecca Probert, *Marriage Law and Practice in the Long Eighteenth Century: A Reassessment* (2009); Stephen Cretney, *Family Law in the Twentieth Century: A History* (2003).

[8] S. F. C. Milsom, *The Legal Framework of English Feudalism* (1976); Brian Simpson, *A History of the Land Law* (1961); John Hudson, *Land, Law, and Lordship in Anglo-Norman England* (1994); Michael Taggart, *Private Property and Abuse of Rights in Victorian England* (2002); Stuart Anderson, *Lawyers and the Making of English Land Law 1832–1940* (1992).

[9] S. F. C. Milsom, *Studies in the History of the Common Law* (1985) esp. 1–103; Paul Mitchell, *The Making of the Modern Law of Defamation* (2005), and Paul Mitchell, *A History of Tort Law 1900–1950* (2015).

[10] David Ibbetson, *A Historical Introduction to the Law of Obligations* (1991); Cecil Fifoot, *History and Sources of the Common Law: Tort and Contract* (1949); Albert Kiralfy, *The Action on the Case* (1951).

[11] Paul McHugh, *Aboriginal Societies and the Common Law* (2004).

[12] Eltjo Schrage (ed.), *Unjust Enrichment: The Comparative Legal History of the Law of Restitution* (1995).

[13] Joshua Getzler, *A History of Water Rights at Common Law* (2004).

[14] Colin Cooke, *Corporation, Trust and Company* (1950); Bernard Rudden, *The New River* (1985).

[15] Frederic William Maitland, *The Constitutional History of England* (1908); John Allison, *The English Historical Constitution* (2007).

[16] See the Landmark Cases essay series edited by Charles Mitchell and Paul Mitchell (2006–2012).

[17] Brian Simpson, *Leading Cases in the Common Law* (1995); Joshua Getzler, 'Brian Simpson's Empiricism' (2012) 3 *Transnational Legal Theory* 127.

[18] Frederick Pollock and Frederic William Maitland, *The History of English Law Before the Time of Edward I* (2 vols., 1895; 2nd edn., 1898); T. F. T. Plucknett, *A Concise History of the Common Law* (5th edn., 1956); S. F. C. Milsom, *Historical Foundations of the Common Law* (2nd edn., 1981); John Baker, *An Introduction to English Legal History* (4th edn., 2002); John Langbein et al., *History of the Common Law: The Development of Anglo-American Legal Institutions* (2009).

[19] 17 vols. (1903–1972).

[20] Richard Helmholz, *Vol. I: The Canon Law and Ecclesiastical Jurisdiction from 597 to the 1640s* (2004); John Hudson, *Vol. II: 871–1216* (2012); John Baker, *Vol. VI: 1483–1558* (2003); William Cornish et al., *Vols. XI, XII, XIII: 1820–1914* (2010).

part, perhaps the major part, of historical writing about law in the past century, in both common-law and civilian jurisdictions.[21] Instead, here we will investigate the *idea* of doctrine as a focus of historical scholarship, asking how the doctrinal mentality arose and how historical approaches to doctrine emerged strongly in both common-law and civilian or Romanistic legal cultures. This enquiry may help to place all the riches of doctrinal legal history into due perspective.

We must first define our subject more accurately and set out a guiding thesis. An important dimension of doctrine, it will be argued, is communication; and jurists become fascinated by the history of doctrine when social and political conditions necessitate an expansion or transfer of the legal system, with concomitant transfers of doctrinal thought.

I. What is Doctrine?

Doctrine for lawyers expresses authoritative juridical ideas that may direct the course of legal decisions. Doctrine can be embodied in positive legal texts, as with statutes, constitutions, reports of leading case law, codes, and restatements; however, in all instances the normative content of any doctrine will fall to be determined by the dynamic interpretation of the legal community. Law in books does not signify without a reader; doctrine is a history of reading and speaking and not just of writing.[22] Doctrine can also take the form of *lex non scripta*, unwritten norms that command broad assent, even if no one jurist would agree with another's interpretation of that norm. The fact that much of common-law doctrine is embodied in a loose consensus amongst lawyers as to what the key case law has decided, with no definitive written texts, led Jeremy Bentham to claim that the

---

[21] American doctrinal historiography before the 1970s will be discussed alongside English scholarship for our purposes; indeed, American scholars tended to focus on English doctrine as a direct ancestor of American law and so belonged to a unified Anglo-Commonwealth intellectual community. Distinctly, American doctrinal history was often described as the adoption of English doctrine into America, as in Roscoe Pound, *Readings on the History and System of the Common Law* (1904, 2nd edn., 1913), or was linked to overt law reform exercises, as in Grant Gilmore, *Security Interests in Personal Property* (1965). Sociological and critical histories of American doctrine have since emerged, with seminal contributions from Lawrence Friedman, *A History of American Law* (1973) and Morton J Horwitz, *The Transformation of American Law, 1780–1860* (1977). Some fine doctrinal monographs have followed, often positioned for or against Friedman and Horwitz's methods: cf. Gregory Alexander, *Commodity and Propriety: Competing Visions of Property in American Legal Thought, 1776–1970* (1997) and Peter Karsten, *Heart Versus Head: Judge-Made Law in 19th Century America* (1997).

[22] Roman doctrine in fact formally identified *interpretatio* by jurists as a major source of doctrine: Peter Birks, Grant McLeod (eds.), *Justinian's Institutes* (1987) J.1.2.8, 38–9.

common law had no doctrines. This was a provocation that the common lawyers effortlessly ignored.[23]

The notion of doctrine derives from the classical Latin term *doctrina*, denoting teachings or communicable knowledge. Doctrine has been associated in the history of the West with theology, and its outgrowths of moral and political philosophy, as much as with law. In our postmodern era of scepticism about moral foundations, the very idea of authoritative legal doctrine can arouse suspicion as an attempt to impose a pseudo-theology, an unwarranted claim to wisdom or power protected from criticism. Or worse: doctrine with its semblance of neutrality can serve as ideology, constituting identities and enforcing power relations, and then concealing its work behind the carapace of scientific justice.[24] This critique of doctrine as ideology may have bite, but it cannot succeed if the appraisal of doctrine does not grapple with the internal conceptual world of the lawyers, or else it declines into an attack on the meta-concept of legalism without telling anything much about the actual law and its operation in society. One cannot well deconstruct doctrine if one does not know how doctrinalists think.

From the internal legal viewpoint, doctrine may be congruent with certain ethical or political principles, but its immediate task is more prosaic: to define general legal rules and principles solving disputes and constraining social behaviour and to regulate the jurisdictional powers of governing agencies such as courts and executives that issue and enforce the rules. The roots of legal doctrinalism go back very far and are a major achievement of Western culture, worthy of historicizing in the quest for self-knowledge.

II. Classical Origins—Gaius to Justinian

The second-century Roman jurist Gaius can be counted one of the great founders of the doctrinal tradition, notably in his *Institutes* written around AD 170 as a thematic summary of Roman jurisprudence. This work was probably composed as a teaching text for use in Gaius' *studium* and did not form part of the mainstream casuistic law-making of the time. Much of the content of the Gaian text was available to scholars from late antiquity via its reproduction in edited form in the sixth-century legal

---

[23] Gerald Postema, *Bentham and the Common Law Tradition* (1986) 191–262.

[24] See, e.g., Duncan Kennedy, *A Critique of Adjudication (fin de siècle)* (1997), building on his essay 'The Structure of Blackstone's Commentaries' (1979) 28 *Buffalo L.R.* 205.

codifications of the emperor Justinian. In 1816 an overwritten fifth-century copy of the complete text was discovered in the Verona cathedral library, giving direct access to Gaius' thought independent of any editorial hand. Gaius' *Institutes* emerges as probably the most important law book ever written, even if its content for long had to be surmised from other works. His achievement was to develop a highly rational and original doctrinal taxonomy of Roman jurisprudence, characterizing the varied sources of law, dividing the substantive and procedural laws subject by subject, and pointing out the relationships between the parts. He drew method and vocabulary from Aristotelian ethics, science, and biology and Ciceronian rhetoric, filtered through the schools debates of his day; yet his contribution to legal thought had no real precedent.[25]

Gaius' classification of sources divided the terrain between the law of all peoples (loosely, international and natural laws), and the civil laws of a particular community. He identified distinct types of law-making by different legal actors, for example by emperors, officials, jurists, and legislative assemblies, with customary law being seen as a type of implicit legislation promulgated through the voluntary conduct of the people. Some law was *lex*, a spoken or verbal command; some was *ius*, normative principles not decided by any person but extant in the society. Doctrine, such as the interpretation of skilled jurists, could be said to identify and interpret the content of both *ius* and *lex*, though when doctrine was officially endorsed through legislative statement it became *lex* in itself.[26]

Gaius drew a three-fold division of the doctrines of private law, being the rules governing relations between individuals.[27] There were *persons*, the subjects of the law; *things*, being the assets or interests that they claimed from each other; and *actions*, being the legal methods by which persons asserted their status or claimed their things. This triad encompassed all of the law. The law of persons tracked the distinction between freemen and slaves, as well as describing patriarchal authority and the subordinate place of women, children, and foreigners. The law of things included the valuable assets of property and contract, and the elements of this class were described first in terms of modes of acquisition, and secondly by their due actions for enforcement—Gaius was ambiguous as to whether property was ultimately an acquisition or a claim. Tortious or delictual obligations (embracing much of what would now be seen as crime) and remedies for debt and unjust enrichment sat uneasily between the categories of things as obligations complete in themselves and actions as remedies correcting breach of some prior interest. Succession or inheritance, dealt with at length, were a hybridized category straddling the three great divisions.[28] Some frictions and inconsistencies were to be expected

---

[25] Tessa Leesen, *Gaius Meets Cicero: Law and Rhetoric in the School Controversies* (2010); Birks and McLeod, 'Introduction' to *Justinian* (n. 22) 12–18.

[26] Francis de Zulueta (ed.), *The Institutes of Gaius* (1946) 3–5, §1.1.-7.   [27] Ibid., 5, §.1.8.

[28] Ibid., *passim*.

in any attempt to reduce a sprawling legal system into some doctrinal order and may even have been useful in fomenting experimentation with later doctrinal classifications.[29]

Gaius' achievement was to take a voluminous body of historical law and identify it as an integral system that could be understood, applied, criticized, reformed, extended, taught, and, ultimately, codified. Gaius' work is thus the foundation of legal doctrinalism. He legitimated the workings of the law by showing how any claim fitted into the extant legal order so that the particular remedy granted might be consistent with the logic of the entire system. This doctrinalism was not only intellectually inviting, but also highly practical, for it allowed legal problems to be broken into parts through juristic characterization, aiding the process of judgment. For example, where a person gave to another some goods, one could investigate if the deal involved a gift, outright or reversible, or a contractual loan or bailment, a sale, or a conditional conveyance by way of security. There might be delictual (tortious or criminal) claims for abuse or loss of the transferred or bailed object. Accessory and third-party claims could be layered onto the bilateral relationship. The status of the actors as competent persons within jurisdiction and without disability might also be legally relevant. Gaius' Institutional method was largely confined to the materials of private law; by eschewing more political subjects such as crime and constitutional law, the doctrinal system could be presented as a self-sufficient machinery driven by its own internal logic. Such doctrine presented itself as morally and politically neutral—a quality of Roman law that aroused both fascination and horror in later generations.[30]

Gaius was also remarkable in that he paid great heed to doctrinal history even as he carved out his novel rationalistic order. He constantly referred to laws belonging to past phases of Roman history and often observed that the legal forms of his own day could not be understood without observing how archaic laws were adapted and pressed into service to meet new social needs. A salient example was the use of notional formal delivery for incorporeal or dematerialized forms of property in the agrarian economy, such as watercourses and pathways, which had once been dealt with as defined physical objects; another was the use of fictitious contested court claims to effect the transfers of usufructs, necessitated by their roots in inalienable relationships within the family.[31] Thus, historical consciousness was an essential element of classical juristic science.

There was also a sociology of knowledge attached to the new legal science. Doctrinal skill for Gaius and many 'new men' who followed him turned out to be a passport to livelihood and professional repute. By the third century AD, the zenith of Roman juristic achievement, the well-born jurists who had dispensed legal

---

[29] George Gretton, 'Ownership and its Objects' (2007) 71 *RabelsZ* 802.

[30] James Whitman, 'Long Live the Hatred of Roman Law!' (2003) 2 *Rechtsgeschichte* 40.

[31] *Gaius* (n. 26) 73, §2.28.-33.

wisdom had been displaced by professionalized legal intellectuals working directly in the service of the Severan emperors as career attorneys and chancellors. The greatest of these jurists were three who likely came to Rome from Greek-speaking Syria or Phoenicia, where they may have grown up in contact with Judeo-Christian legal and theological ideas. The three were Paul, Ulpian, and Papinian, and each produced doctrinal commentaries of the greatest power and elegance, and their work makes up the greater part of the later Digest of Justinian, another key source of the Western legal tradition.[32]

Ulpian (c. AD 170–223) was particularly concerned with restating doctrine as a universalistic jurisprudence expressed in natural law terms. This transformation would make the law suitable for export across a multinational empire, loosening its links with the particular history and society of the Roman city state. Ulpian as a lawyer in the circle of the emperor may have helped launch the *Constitutio Antoniniana* of AD 212, also known as also Edict of Caracalla, extending equal Roman citizenship and equal legal competence and access to Roman justice for all free subjects of the emperor.[33] This was partly a fiscal measure, uniting the tax base of the empire, but it was also an historic act of statesmanship, postulating a supranational jurisdiction founded on natural law or refined common sense contained in evolved legal norms. Ulpian took it upon himself to write an elaborate code of all the important laws with commentary in the immediate wake of the Edict. His elaborations of Roman doctrine were now to be applied to all persons in the civilized world whatever their ethnicity, religion, or history. If the apostle Paul severed Judaic religious doctrine from its ethnic roots and made it available as a new Christian faith to all nations, then Ulpian achieved a similar feat with Roman legal doctrine. Ulpian's universalism also found expression in his suspicion of slavery, which he described as against nature, and he sought out ways to limit and extinguish slave status by creative readings of doctrine.

Non-Romanic legal cultures continued alongside the high Roman doctrinal science, and there was often a choice of universal or local laws in any locale. Indeed, Romanist law and government could be resented and resisted, as attested by the constant rebellions of component peoples of the empire. An alternative multicultural and pluralistic legal order probably existed under the skin of Roman legal science, and 'vulgar' or locally adapted versions of Roman doctrine were more likely to be followed in real transactions and disputes than Ulpianic or later Justinianic law.[34]

The Digest of the Emperor Justinian, collated in five short years from 528 and completed in 533, redacted the bulk of classical doctrine into fifty manageable books

---

[32] Fritz Schulz, *History of Roman Legal Science* (1946) 99–123; James Gordley, *The Jurists: A Critical History* (2013) 1–27.

[33] Anthony Honoré, *Ulpian* (1982) 25–9.

[34] Ernst Levy, *Western Roman Vulgar Law: The Law of Property* (1951); Maurizio Lupoi, *The Origins of the European Legal Order* (1994; trans. Adrian Belton, 2007); Pier Monateri, 'Black Gaius: A Quest for the Multicultural Origins of the "Western Legal Tradition"' (2000) 51 *Hastings L.J.* 479.

covering unified doctrinal themes of the law. It achieved this feat of compression and organization by adapting the teaching materials of the Eastern empire's law schools, arranging these on the old framework of the formulary and praetorian actions. Supplementary codifications covered legislation together with corrective decrees, bringing the new *Corpus Juris* up to date in 534. The project was in effect a massive exercise in historical doctrinal study; Justinian's jurists had to master the tangled history of past laws in order to surpass and escape them. A new edition of Gaius' *Institutes* was prepared for Justinian by his chief jurist Tribonian toward the end of the codification project in 533 as an appendix to the larger work, overtly dedicated to students broaching the mass of now-codified edicts, decisions, legislation, and commentary for the first time. Almost as an afterthought, Gaian doctrinalism survived into post-Roman Europe as a map and compass guiding readers into the treasures of classical law made available in a single legislative package bearing the authority of imperial legislation.[35]

III. DOCTRINAL HISTORY FROM THE *IUS COMMUNE* TO THE CODES

The Digest, or in Greek, the Pandects, may in fact have made little impact on the vulgar (that is, actually practised) laws of the fragmenting empire in the centuries following Justinian's reign. However, from the eleventh century, lawyers in Northern Italy and then in France, Germany, Spain, and England began poring over newly made copies of the Digest and the *Institutes*, cultivating their own glosses and commentaries and fitting national, imperial, and ecclesiastical laws around the inherited Romanistic framework. Romanist doctrinalism and its history came to be studied in the high Middle Ages and Renaissance as an object of learning in its own right, leading to the foundation of schools of historical jurisprudence at Bologna, Montpellier, Paris, and Oxford. It is no exaggeration to say that the very concept of a university was born from the need to create schools of skilled lawyers adept at historical study of doctrine, both as a prestigious form of new learning and as a handmaiden for state formation and administration.[36] A seminal figure in this intellectual movement was Bartolus of Sassoferrato (1331–1357), whose writings on the 'learned laws' (as post-classical Romanist law was often described) had enormous prestige across Europe as the perfection of the work of preceding

---

[35] Anthony Honoré, *Justinian's Digest: Character and Compilation* (2010).
[36] Gordley (n. 32) 28–81.

commentators. Bartolus deployed doctrine cleverly to investigate how the capacity to apply and enforce law—that is, jurisdiction—could be divided into concentric, overlapping, and intersecting circles, with free cities, principalities, feudal estates, church, and empire each interacting in an intricate balance. Doctrinal history here developed into a complex political science.[37]

Lawyers after Bartolus, and especially in the wake of the Reformation, busied themselves importing Romanist doctrine into their local laws, in a great process known as the Reception. The *ius commune* or common legal heritage of Roman doctrine now came to be divided into national wings.[38] There was also an internationalist dimension, as natural law, theology, and ethics were infused into the learned laws by Spanish and Dutch scholars, notably Suarez and Grotius, who both emphasized the equal and intrinsic rights of all peoples independent of jurisdiction, including aboriginal peoples in the new overseas empires—an echo of Ulpian's humanism.[39] French and German doctrinal scholarship in the modern era pressed down these historical paths of national codification in the garb of Romanist doctrine. Post-revolutionary France produced the elegant *Code civil* in 1804 as a liberalizing, anti-feudal legal programme, resting heavily on the hallowed Gaian taxonomies. This was such an elegant and lucid doctrinal restatement that it could easily travel, and in the wake of Napoleon's conquests it had very great influence across Europe and outwards to European colonies. The early production of a useful and attractive code in France perhaps diminished further interest in historical doctrine amongst the legal elites, who could instead concentrate on adapting the authoritative codal text to new social conditions. The concomitant loss of historical consciousness rendered the French system conservative, inviting imports of more questing German jurisprudence to maintain its effectiveness.[40]

By contrast, in Germany a community of legal historians led by Friedrich von Savigny argued that deep knowledge of classical legal doctrine would help Germans build their own civic culture, with the national spirit of the German people finding refined expression in the historically-minded jurisprudence of their leading professors (such as Savigny himself). This elitist attitude fused with the romantic

[37] Joseph Canning, 'Ideas of the State in Thirteenth and Fourteenth-Century Commentators on Roman Law' (1983) 33 *Transactions of the Royal Historical Society 5th ser.* 7; Magnus Ryan, 'Bartolus of Sassoferrato and Free Cities' (2000) 17 *Transactions of the Royal Historical Society 6th ser.* 65.

[38] Harold Berman, *Law and Revolution II: The Impact of the Protestant Reformations on the Western Legal Tradition* (2003); Peter Stein, *Roman Law in European History* (1999); Franz Wieacker, *A History of Private Law in Europe* (1952, trans. Tony Weir, 1995).

[39] Theodor Meron, 'Common Rights of Mankind in Gentili, Grotius and Suarez' (1991) 85 *American J. Int. L.* 110.

[40] Carl Zachariae, *Handbuch des französischen Civilrechts* (7 edns., 1808–1894), a highly influential Pandectist interpretation of the *Code civil*, was followed in the next century by Germanic transplants into French law by direct legislation: see Timothy Guinnane and Jean-Laurent Rosenthal, 'Adapting Law to Fit the Facts: the GmbH, the SARL, and the Organization of Small Firms in Germany and France, 1892–1930' (working paper, August 2012).

nationalism of the post-Napoleonic period, leading to the founding or revitalizing of law schools devoted to historical doctrine, covering not only Roman law and the *ius commune* but also native German customary and municipal laws.[41] Rival schools of scholarship emerged. Some jurists, known as the Pandectists, deepened the historical inquiry into Romanistic law, seeking to get behind Justinian and the learned lawyers and recover the form and spirit of Severan classical jurisprudence as an expression of Roman civics at its zenith in the era of the good emperors. Kantian and Hegelian philosophy could be added to the mix, with classical principles held to foreshadow a theory of freedom of the will and voluntary assumption of duties as the basis of society. The Pandectists also saw doctrinal history as a staging post towards codification of civil law as a unifying project for the German states, with Bernard Windscheid, the reigning expert on Roman classical procedure, as their leader. The codification movement, with its turn to centralized state legislation as the bearer of private law doctrine, was a departure from Savigny's romantic vision of juristic law as an *imitatio* of the classical world. But Savigny would have approved of the more scientific work of the Pandectists, culminating in the astonishing work of Otto Lenel (1849–1935), who reconstructed the Digest texts by returning them to their unredacted classical form through reassembly of the fragments and assignment to the original authors. Lenel's *Edictum Perpetuum* of 1883 and the *Palingensia juris civilis* of 1887–1889 were the *ne plus ultra* of Romanistic doctrinal scholarship and attained the highest prestige.

Not all scholars followed the dictates of Pandectism, and opposition began to emerge with devotees of German native laws resisting the course of Romanistic codification. The undoubted leader was Otto von Gierke (1841–1921), whose historical work concentrated on the medieval law of associations, from partnership and corporation to foundation and state. His dense historical work can be read as a rejoinder to the Pandectists who largely neglected the law of collectivities. Gierke also wrote searching studies of core private law doctrines of persons, property, and obligations from a Germanist perspective. Other leading Germanists steeped in an alternative non-Roman doctrinal history included Heinrich Brunner, Lujo Brentano, Rudolph Gneist, Andreas Heusler, and Felix Liebermann. These scholars postulated a Teutonic customary legal order of Northern Europe, resistant to centralizing Roman legal culture and attentive to the needs of local communities. They rejected the Kantian individualism implicit in much Pandectist research and turned instead to Norse, Icelandic, Anglo-Saxon, and Anglo-Norman law, myth, and literature in the search for an alternative tradition. Formidable doctrinalists themselves, in modern jurisprudence they devoted their energies

---

[41] Hermann Kantorowicz, 'Savigny and the Historical School of Law' (1937) 53 *L.Q.R.* 326; James Whitman, *The Legacy of Roman Law in the German Romantic Era* (1990); Joshua Getzler, 'Law, History and the Social Sciences: Intellectual Traditions of Late 19th and Early 20th Century Europe', in Andrew Lewis, Michael Lobban (eds.), *Law and History* (2003) 215 ff.

to areas neglected by the Pandectists, such as family law, associational law, and public law.[42]

The conflicting traditions of the German historical school were reflected in the turbulent and influential career of Rudolf von Jhering (1818–1892). He was a skilled Roman legal historian capable of the most virtuosic doctrinal analysis, who had early emphasized the universal applicability of Roman jurisprudence to the modern world, as an *echt Pandektist* should. But Jhering later came to reject the abstract Romanism of his youth and instead developed a theory of 'free law', seeing jurisprudence on the one hand as a tool to meet social needs, and on the other as the product of raw struggle between interest groups. The role of law was to hold the ring as strong individuals and groups asserted themselves and to accord due power to the core groups of society. Law was certainly not a neutral system of order as conceived by the elite doctrinalists around him. His theory could be associated with a political economy of free markets and social Darwinism, as well as showing some affinity with the law of social groups propounded by Gierke. But unlike the Germanists, Jhering's theories derived intellectually from novel readings of Roman doctrinal history, emphasizing those parts of the canon that could be harnessed for the purposes of regulating a modern economy and state. One such was the doctrine of *culpa in contrahendo*, repressing unfairly bargained contracts and redressing inequalities in market power through procedural controls. Another was Jhering's celebrated theory of possession, emphasizing physical control as a basis for *dominium* and so returning juridical power to those who occupied and worked with assets rather than absentee rentiers. Jhering advocated the free use of legislation to carry out his doctrinal programme, but recused himself from the Pandectist codification project, partly because he knew his presence would be provocative, partly because he disliked the conservatism of the mainstream Pandectists, who unanimously rejected his social reading of private law doctrines. He could well afford to stand outside the German legal establishment; his doctrinal and speculative works were translated widely and read across the world, and as an exciting speaker he communicated his ideas to large audiences through constant touring of the European capitals. The power of his work lay in his double status as a doctrinal superstar and a charismatic public figure tinged with rebellion.

The prestige of the German doctrinal-historical school reached its apogee with the promulgation of the Civil Code in 1900, the practical fruit of Pandectism and also a guarantor of the unity of the pan-German Bismarckian state. It was far more elaborate than the French Code, with great care taken by the drafters to explain how the basic doctrinal ingredients of the private law fitted together as a system. Versions of this code were adopted in one form or another across north, central, and eastern Europe, in the Near and Middle East, and indeed just about wherever

---

[42] Michael John, *Politics and the Law in Late Nineteenth-Century Germany: The Origins of the Civil Code* (1989).

the French code or English common law had not taken root. Meiji Japan took to the German code as an expression of modernity and progress, permitting Pandectist doctrine to spread through Japanese influence (and later, military conquest) to much of East Asia including China. Thus the Gaian doctrinal code, mediated by German doctrinalism, had become a global legal language, highly adaptable for national circumstances yet providing a *lingua franca* for transnational trade and also offering a blueprint for successful state formation.[43]

IV. THE COMMON-LAW TRADITION

Between the 1066 Conquest and the reigns of the Angevin kings Henry I and Henry II in the twelfth century, the common law developed a unique set of doctrines borrowing from Anglo-Saxon and Norman precedents, driven by the unique position of the English Crown at the apex of the post-Conquest feudal hierarchy. The kings sent out royal justices to supervise the due enforcement of tenants' rights in the manorial economy, partly to keep the peace and partly to enhance Crown revenues. These legal protections of tenure formed the core of the common law, 'common' because every freeholder in England enjoyed equal and unmediated access to the justice of the king's courts, leapfrogging (and ultimately displacing) intermediate feudal jurisdictions. The royal justice was cultivated by lawyers with a good awareness of Roman models and legal language. Treatises were written describing the doctrines and operation of the nascent common law, the two main ones being issued under the names of the royal justices Glanvill (*c*.1188)[44] and Bracton (*c*.1235).[45] The authors of these works used Romanist doctrinal language heavily to describe and organize the common-law actions. Samuel Thorne, through painstaking sifting of the text, has shown how Bracton deeply imbibed doctrinal ideas from Justinian and the learned laws, though Glanvill's more superficial Romanism may have derived from earlier Visigothic vulgar laws. Notwithstanding this deployment of Gaian or Justinianic

---

[43] Duncan Kennedy, 'Three Globalizations of Law and Legal Thought: 1850–2000', in David Trubek, Alvaro Santos (eds.), *The New Law and Economic Development: A Critical Appraisal* (2006) 19 ff, contrasting the liberal thought of nineteenth-century Pandectism based on the individual will with a twentieth-century wave of more communitarian regulatory law, followed by today's neo-liberalism associated with judicial review. For critique: Christopher Tomlins, 'The Presence and Absence of Legal Mind: A Comment on Duncan Kennedy's Three Globalizations' (2015) 78 *Law and Contemporary Problems* 1.

[44] Derek Hall (ed.), *The Treatise on the Laws and Customs of the Realm of England, Commonly Called Glanvill* (1965).

[45] Samuel Thorne (ed.), *Bracton on the Laws and Customs of England* (1968–1977).

doctrinal analysis, there was only a very limited adoption of Roman structural ideas direct into the substance of the law. For example, the drafters of the writs launching Henry II's Assizes of Novel Disseisin, designed to reverse wrongful dispossessions, may have borrowed language from the Roman possessory interdicts, yet no general vindication of absolute property rights emerged as a doctrinal correlate of the new possessory actions. The point of the assizes was to intervene from above where local feudal obligation had failed, imposing a royal remedy to correct the immediate mischief whilst ordering lords to do right by their tenants, to restore broken personal relations of tenure and so shore up local governance. A similar story could be told of early common-law enforcement of covenants or 'specialty' contracts designed and formalized by the parties as self-executing promises based on the honouring of relationships. Common law procedures could be invoked to ensure those bonds were executed; the law did not constitute the rights and duties under the bond.[46]

The early common law can thus be seen as a form of judicial review of subordinate jurisdictions and private law-making, not as a complete legal system covering the space of civil society. Only later, as feudal jurisdiction withered, did the common law take over the entire juridical space of English society.[47] One major technique, hastened by the unrest caused by the Black Death after 1349, was to expand the trespass jurisdiction of the Court of King's Bench, which had a paramount concern of keeping the peace.[48] By focusing on the wrong committed by breach of a relationship and offering a ready corrective justice, the court could start defining and enforcing the claims generated by that relationship; the result in time was the regular, direct common-law recognition and enforcement of rights as an exercise in distributive justice. Local relational justice was maintained through continuing reliance on the jury, which controlled forensic discovery and ultimate moral decision as to responsibility and liability. However, the jury system lost its qualities as local peer justice as jurisdiction was centralized in London. Pleading to fit causes within the correct form of action became the main focus of litigation, and doctrinal debate revolved around procedure rather than the substance of claims. Doctrine had to be extracted from a deep knowledge of the Year Book reports of legal jousting in court, and much treatise literature basically listed the array of writs and referenced the most important case law describing how and when each writ could be used.

By the late medieval period it was becoming clear that common-law rights of property and contract, stripped of relational content and embodied in the highly proceduralized discourse of the writs, led to widespread abuse and denial of justice to those who could not manipulate the system successfully. One solution was to set

[46] John Salmond, 'The History of the Law of Prescription', in J. Salmond, *Essays in Jurisprudence and Legal History* (1891) 73 ff.

[47] Milsom (n. 8) opened a lengthy debate over the purposiveness of Angevin legal reform; see further Paul Brand, 'The Origins of English Land Law: Milsom and After', in P. Brand, *The Making of the Common Law* (2012) 203 ff.

[48] Robert Palmer, *English Law in the Age of the Black Death, 1348–1381* (1993).

up or expand jurisdictions to supervise the operation of common law rights so as to protect relationships and the public good. If the common law had emerged as a type of judicial review of inferior feudal jurisdictions, there must now be jurisdictions to supervise the common law. On the side of criminal and public affairs including taxation, the main such courts were Star Chamber and various other prerogative tribunals. On the private side, administering property, contract, and inheritance, the main supervisory court was Chancery, afforced by the Court of Exchequer. The Court of King's Bench hovered between the two poles, controlling the conduct of public officials and affording new summary remedies for tort and contract with swifter procedure and more robust forensics than the old writs, especially in the all-important fields of contract enforcement and debt collection, where Chancery lacked powers or itself had become dilatory.

The modern common-law system emerging by the seventeenth and eighteenth centuries was thus quite distinct in Europe, as the product of tiered interlocking jurisdictions which had evolved adjacently, or one on top of the other, affording justice to litigants through an arcane system of writs regulated by cross-court review. This yielded a doctrinal culture of remarkable complexity, focused on forms of action, choice of forum, and forensic strategy. Until the nineteenth century law was learnt not in university but through apprenticeship to practising lawyers, participation in moots and debates at the Inns of Court in London, and laborious private study of writs and precedents. Substantive rights were not authoritatively proclaimed by judge and jurists, but 'secreted in the interstices of procedure', as Henry Maine put it.[49] This means that understanding the common law before 1800 consists of unlocking or decoding the nature of rights emerging from within procedure, when the jurisprudential, moral, and political suppositions of the main actors are rarely made plain in their arguments. For example, in the 1725 case of *Reynolds v. Clerke*, concerning harm caused by draining water onto a property in excess of a licence, the judges argued over the distinctions between direct and indirect infliction of harm and immediate and consequential loss. This was necessary in order to determine whether the plaintiff had pleaded the correct type of trespass writ to have the facts of the case assessed by a jury. After lengthy rounds of debate Raymond CJ convened the court a second time and warned that 'We must keep up the boundaries of actions, otherwise we shall introduce the utmost confusion'. The plaintiff succeeded; but stating the nature of property rights protecting unmolested enjoyment in the wake of that case proved impossible for later courts and commentators—because that was not the type of doctrine the court was deciding.[50]

In such a system, doctrine could fall into complete dysfunction. Solutions might then be sought by transplants of substantive Romanistic doctrine into the common law, sometimes via adoption of Scots law. These insertions have been described as

---

[49] Henry Maine, *Early Law and Custom* (1883) 389.
[50] (1725) 1 Strange 634; 93 ER 747; 2 Ld. Raym. 1399; 92 ER 40 (KB).

'inoculations'—the taking of a minor dose from a foreign body to prevent wholesale reception at a later date. Examples of Roman entryism included the great bulk of the law of servitudes or incorporeal property rights; causal rules for tort; rules for terms, conditions, and mistake in contract; standards of care in bailments, trusts, and assumed tort duties; and much of the law of restitution. There was also a constant stream of correcting and reforming statutes issued by Parliament, with the judges often initiating and drafting the legislative text in order to solve pressing problems in the law that they had grappled with in court. As a concomitant to the legislative process, senior lawyers at the Inns of Court would give 'readings' or lectures offering a critical historical disquisition on the impact of ancient and modern statutes. Such readings were an important element in doctrinal training of barristers and students, though they were rather random as a method of grasping and analysing the legal order.

The common law until well into the eighteenth century may be described as a type of tacit or craft knowledge, learnt by doing, and resistant to formal or rational doctrinal statement. This craft quality could be advanced as a political virtue leading to separation of powers and rule of law virtues, for overt attempts at political control of common-law justice could be rebuffed as ignorant interference. In a famous confrontation in 1607 Sir Edward Coke, Chief Justice of the Court of Common Pleas and the most learned common lawyer of his or perhaps any age, told King James I that the king could not exercise a personal power of judging in the royal courts, even though he was the sovereign source of law in his political person and a formidable intellect in his private person. The reasoning he offered to the king was this:

[T]he Lawes of his Realm of England . . . are not to be decided by naturall reason, but by the artificiall reason and judgment of Law, which Law is an art which requires long study and experience.[51]

It was a matter of constitutional convention that the judicial powers of the Crown had irreversibly been delegated to judges, though the king could exercise judgment in other more properly political fori, such as Star Chamber or the House of Lords. This jurisdictional distinction between prerogative and legal justice was itself a prime example of doctrine at work, defining its own sphere of exclusive operation.

Coke was himself a prolific legal author, preparing many volumes of well-edited and widely read law reports, many representing Coke's estimation of what the judges and counsel ought to have said; and also issuing four volumes of *Institutes of the Lawes of England* (1628–1644). These volumes offered an historical *summa* of all the ancient doctrines of the common law that Coke deemed important to understand the common law. The historical erudition of the work was staggering, and its authority (when it could be understood) was unquestioned. Coke by his title and four-part structure was clearly arguing that the common law could rival

---

[51] *Prohibitions Del Roy* (1607) 12 Co. Rep. 63, 65; 77 ER 1342, 1343.

Justinian's law as an imperial self-sufficient jurisprudence. But despite his gift for lapidary phrases and his political and constitutional importance as a Parliamentary opponent of the Crown, his institutional writings were too opaque to be followed easily by later lawyers.[52] Coke's contemporary John Selden also wrote deeply learned historical studies of early feudal and ecclesiastic law, including a widely read (and controversial) history of tithes as a civil institution, as well as a history of parliamentary privilege. A younger judicial contemporary, Sir Matthew Hale, wrote *A History and Analysis of the Common Law of England*, which had a limited circulation in manuscript, but was not published until 1713. More influential still was Hale's *History of the Pleas of the Crown*, published in 1736 and really the foundation of criminal law jurisprudence in English law. Hale was in turn important as a role model for Sir William Blackstone, whose *Commentaries on the Laws of England*, being elegant synoptic lectures on the history, philosophy, and doctrines of the common law published between 1765 and 1769, sought to exhibit common-law doctrine as both comprehensible and congruent with the values and needs of eighteenth-century England.

Blackstone's analyses were followed more by lay readers in England than by the profession. Blackstone was far more highly prized in America, and perhaps a neo-Blackstonian tradition is really to be found there, with an outstanding series of common-law treatises produced in the early republic by James Kent, Chief Justice and the Chancellor in New York,[53] and Joseph Story, Justice of the Supreme Court of the United States.[54] Sadly, nothing so good was produced in England until the *fin de siècle*. Doctrinal scholarship in the century after Blackstone in England typically clung to the severely practical, arranging precedents without chronological order or even much critical analysis, simply as collations of authority relevant to some subject area of law. Typical topics included bankruptcy, equity and trusts, commercial contracts, vendor and purchaser law, and conveyancing.[55] Historical learning about the sources of the ancient writs and the operation of old statutes gradually became less relevant, as major legislative reforms from the 1830s diminished the importance of the forms of action and procedural proprieties. The fusing of the complex of civil courts into one unified system in 1873, inspired in part by the 1850 Field Code of New York, led to significant rationalization of doctrine. The lead was taken by the new Court of Appeal, whose role was to state authoritative doctrine guiding the entire hierarchy, replacing the old judicial review system. Judges after 1873 were

---

[52] See the radically redacted edition with extensive commentaries of *Coke's First Institutes* published by J. H. Thomas in 1818; this glossed version swiftly displaced the urtext.

[53] With his *Commentaries on American Law* in four volumes published 1826–1830, and going into six editions in his lifetime.

[54] With his series of treatises issued from 1832 to 1846 on bailment, the constitution, conflicts of laws, equity, agency, partnership, bills, and notes.

[55] Brian Simpson, 'The Rise and Fall of the Legal Treatise: Legal Principles and the Forms of Legal Literature' (1981) 48 *U. Chicago L.R.* 632.

also keen to elaborate more substantive doctrine in their judgments in order to take away decisional power from the mute lay jury. Lord Mansfield in the 1760s had empanelled special juries of expert merchants to advise on trade custom as he reconstructed much of commercial law; judges a century later were at least as concerned to create articulate doctrine hospitable to industry and finance, but they turned away from juries to rely upon their own sense of policy direction, often informed by natural law and political economy theories that favoured an ideal of individual autonomy and contractarian social relations. Sir George Jessel MR, leading the Court of Appeal, and Lord Blackburn in the Judicial Committee of the House of Lords extensively reformed business law along these lines, extending the work of James Parke, George Bramwell, and other mid-Victorian judges. Such august judges could be less tender to consumers and labourers, and by the end of the century some of their number protested that doctrine risked becoming an ideological cloak for industrial and finance capital against labour, with prominent interventions from Lord Herschell in England,[56] echoed in America by Justice Holmes.[57]

The later nineteenth-century period is now counted the 'classical' period of English common-law doctrine. Much of the power of this culture lay in its judicial personnel, a remarkable cohort of elite figures, many active in party politics and cultural life in London, who vied with each other to produce effective and lasting jurisprudence. The *rationes decidendi* of the classical period in turn provided the raw material for a burst of superb new systematic treatises, really codifications of core areas of law produced by ambitious sole authors, ranging from contract, tort, and land law to conflict of laws and constitutional principle.[58] Many of those authors now taught at Oxford, Cambridge, and London as professors in prestigious chairs, devoted to the science of doctrine and building English law as an academic discipline as well as a professional training.

The expansion of the British empire from the 1870s was a major external influence on the making of doctrine in the new legal academy. Jurists were confronted with the same basic problem faced by Ulpian—how to make the local law of the metropole seem a fit and rational law for a multicultural empire. It was a matter of pride that the Dominions had reproduced local common-law systems as if by cellular division, in Australia, Canada, New Zealand, and southern Africa, with much trading of personnel with London as well as participation in Privy Council jurisdiction as an empire-wide supervisory court of appeal. But this devolved imperial system was splintering, for example as colonial jurisdictions diverged in their constitutional practice and began experimenting with such basics as Crown immunities and land title systems; here the separated American common law provided an opposing gravitational pull to London. At

[56] *Allen v. Flood* [1898] AC 1 (House of Lords).   [57] *Lochner v. New York* 198 U.S. 45 (1905).
[58] Simpson (n. 55).

least partial codification and rationalization of English law seemed mandated in order to project that law securely into the directly ruled imperial lands, mainly the Indian subcontinent. Historical consciousness of the law was a complement to codification and juridical expansionism in England as in Germany, but legal history as a branch of moral and political science could further offer a justificatory ideology supporting imperial hegemony. Oxford became the epicentre of this movement for a while. Bishop William Stubbs (1825–1901) wrote acclaimed constitutional and ecclesiastical histories celebrating the rise of limited government and a balanced and liberal public order; he also initiated the editing and publication of charters and other primary records through the Roll Series. Henry Maine (1822–1888) offered broad anthropological models of comparative legal and social development, making lofty claims about the move 'from status to contract' in 'progressive' societies (such as England, as opposed to imperialized India). Paul Vinogradoff (1854–1925), a Russian emigré, produced rather more careful work on English manorialism and the comparison of feudal orders in western and eastern Europe. The leading treatise writers Frederick Pollock (1845–1937) and John Salmond (1862–1924) each managed to combine proficiency in medieval and modern legal history with doctrinal analysis and legal philosophy of the highest order. Pollock developed his doctrinal work on contract and tort into important model codes for India in the 1880s, matching the evidence and criminal law statutes written a decade earlier for India by Sir James Fitzjames Stephen.

In this time of technocratic and imperial experimentation with doctrine, the German historical schools had considerable impact on the common-law world. Some English lawyers were influenced by the systemic thought of the German Romanists; an early adept was John Austin (1790–1859), the founder (after Bentham) of modern legal analysis, whose major work, *The Province of Jurisprudence Determined* (1832), was really a refraction of Pandectist Gaianism.[59] In the next generation Nathaniel Lindley (1828–1921) studied Pandectism in Bonn and then published *An Introduction to the Study of Jurisprudence; Being a Translation of the General Part of Thibaut's System des Pandekten Rechts* in 1855, presenting Thibaut's classic as an exemplary work of Gaian analysis for the education of common lawyers. Lindley went on as judge and author to become the leading company lawyer of the late Victorian period and a powerful appellate judge, responsible for hardening companies' doctrine around a contract-tort axis, pushing out the relational trust and status elements of older corporate law.

Straight-out systematizing Pandectism, as practised by Austin and Lindley, was rare in England however, and practically non-existent in America. More were influenced by the rival German-Teutonic historical school, and the most gifted jurists flocked to study Anglo-Saxon and medieval English law rather than

---

[59] Michael Lobban, *The Common Law and English Jurisprudence 1760–1850* (1991) 223–56.

classical Rome. Especially impressive work was produced in the 1870s and 1880s by American scholars led by John Adams, Melville Bigelow, Oliver Wendell Holmes Jr., James Barr Ames, and James Thayer. Part of their motivation was professional and elitist: close study of early English and other Teutonic laws would provide a vocabulary to deepen the unlearned and sparse common-law culture of the United States and bring prestige to legal scholars in the academy. There may also have been an ideological element joining American to German interests in *Volksrecht und Gemeinschaft*: like Gierke and Jhering, these scholars were looking for ways to soften and constrain the individualism and harsh competition of emergent American capitalism, and linking the law to a supposed communitarian Teutonic ancestry was a pleasing strategy. David Rabban, in a major study of this group of doctrinalists, observes that the love of ancient law passed with time, and almost all moved away from historical work to embrace law reform via treatise-writing and preparation of legislation and codes.[60]

The sense of doctrinal history as a handmaid of law reform was caught in an 1899 retrospective by the greatest jurist emerging from the American group, Justice Oliver Wendell Holmes (1845–1931). In 'Law in Science—Science in Law' he wrote:

[S]ome rules are mere survivals. Many might as well be different, and history is the means by which we measure the power which the past has had to govern the present in spite of ourselves . . . by imposing traditions which no longer meet their original end. History sets us free and enables us to make up our minds dispassionately whether the survival we are enforcing answers any new purpose when it has ceased to answer the old.[61]

Holmes' great work *The Common Law* (1881) offered a 'general view' of the development of liability from before the Conquest to modern times and proposed that objectification of duty standards was the true *telos* of private law doctrine, as societies matured into complex mechanical forms of solidarity. Holmes favoured ad hoc and continuous legislative and judicial reform of the law to clear away archaic elements, rather than codification *tout court* that would freeze the law into a new stasis.[62]

Like his contemporary Holmes, the English legal historian Frederic William Maitland (1850–1906) still has a hold on the legal imagination, combining expressive style and scholarly acumen in a manner comparable to or exceeding the greatest of the Germans and Americans. Maitland, like Holmes, read the

---

[60] David Rabban, *Law's History: American Legal Thought and the Transatlantic Turn to History* (2013).

[61] (1899) 12 *Harvard L.R.* 443, 452.

[62] Morton Horwitz, 'The Place of Justice Holmes in American Legal Thought', in Robert Gordon (ed.), *The Legacy of Oliver Wendell Homes Jr.* (1992) 51–71; Matthias Reimann, 'Holmes's *Common Law* and German Legal Science', ibid., 72–104; Matthias Reimann, 'Nineteenth Century German Legal Science' (1990) 31 *Boston College L.R.* 837. The German influence on Llewellyn's twentieth-century codificatory work is also of crucial importance: Julie Grise, Martin Gelter, Robert Whitman, 'Rudolf von Jhering's Influence on Karl Llewellyn' (2013) 48 *Tulsa L.R.* 93.

German historical schools avidly and at the end of his life published Anglo-German comparative work showing a complete mastery of the sources.[63] Like Holmes, Maitland eschewed the systematizations of the Pandectists and did not share their belief in the transcendental power and contemporary relevance of Roman law. Maitland instead embraced Gierke, Brunner, Heusler, and the Teutonic Germanist school and in his zealous advocacy translated much of Gierke's associational law for an English audience.[64] His own major contribution comprised a study of Anglo-Norman doctrines and practices constituting fees, feuds, homage and fealty, vills, manors, boroughs, towns, seigneuries, co-tenancies, marriages, kinships, and all the other complex associations and group identities yielded by medieval law, viewed alongside Germanic institutional forebears and analogues. Roman law by contrast had an underdeveloped law of groups beyond the family unit or the partnership; the Gaian doctrinal vocabulary could not easily accommodate multital claims between property and obligation. The Anglo-Norman common law was a new growth in the history of north European law because of the overlay of royal power adapting and transforming local custom and jurisdiction.[65]

In 1887 Maitland founded and directed the Selden Society dedicated to publishing scholarly editions of English primary materials of historical law; within that series he pioneered the study of the Year Books with his work on the reign of Edward II. He also worked on the earliest history of Parliament, modes of legal writing and thought in Angevin and Renaissance England, and in influential Cambridge lectures offered studies in the evolution of modern law, equity, and constitutionalism.[66] At the end of his relatively short life he published reflective works on the political and moral ideas thrown up by his doctrinal histories, returning to the philosophical interests of his youth.[67]

Maitland shared Holmes' view that doctrinal history served as a necessary prelude to law reform. In his lecture on 'The Making of the German Civil Code' of 1906 he praised the Pandectist codification project as a model for English reform, noting that deep understanding of historical doctrine had given the German jurists the confidence to decide when rules should be discarded or adapted as society moved.[68] But Maitland in his 1888 inaugural lecture at Cambridge entitled 'Why

---

[63] Frederic William Maitland, *State, Trust and Corporation* (ed., David Runciman, Magnus Ryan, 2003); Joshua Getzler, 'Frederic William Maitland—Trust and Corporation' (2016) 35 *U. Queensland L.J.* 171.

[64] Otto von Gierke, *Political Theories of the Middle Ages* (trans. Frederic William Maitland, 1900).

[65] Frederic William Maitland, *Domesday Book and Beyond* (1897); Pollock, Maitland (n. 18) (written almost entirely by Maitland).

[66] See Mark Philpott, 'Bibliography of the Writings of F W Maitland', in John Hudson (ed.), *The History of English Law: Centenary Essays on 'Pollock and Maitland'* (1996) 261–78, and other essays in that collection.

[67] Maitland (n. 63).

[68] *The Collected Papers of Frederic William Maitland* (Herbert Fisher (ed.), 1911) vol. III 474 ff.

the History of English Law is Not Written' had also cautioned that the historical analysis of doctrine required imaginative recreation of the thought of the past, and not just a relentlessly pragmatic search for the ancestry of current rules as a guide to evaluation. He contrasted the lawyer's 'logic of authority', tracing the evolution of rules through changing conditions to reach modern conclusions, and the historian's 'logic of evidence', looking for the oldest and most authentic material possible to portray of the legal past, unrefracted by later developments and mentalities. The historian's logic gave the advantage of giving strangeness and distance back to the past: 'The lawyer must be orthodox otherwise he is no lawyer; an orthodox history seems to me a contradiction in terms.'[69]

Maitland's quest for unorthodoxy is the leitmotif of his work as he uncovers fresh and disruptive ideas lurking within old doctrine. He stood the legal sociology of his own German and English mentors on their heads, arguing that medieval institutions, despite a 'thin cloak' of 'communalism', really exhibit in doctrinal terms 'a rough and rude individualism . . . communal liability . . . is merely a joint and several liability. . . . This is not communalism; it is individualism *in excelsis*.'[70] He notes that English law is poor in terms to distinguish the status of men, preferring to analyse tenurial relations to establish subjective capacities that in turn shape the legal will.[71] The revelation he finds is that through co-ownerships, title-splitting, and all the other irreducible ideas of old English doctrine, the law identifies aggregate *personae* based on shared purpose across a group, such that the group purpose feeds back to reshape individual personal identity. The orthodoxy of modern liberal individualism had repressed the earlier richness of ideas about what it meant to be an individual embedded in multiple communities.[72] The medieval Crown as a personification of the 'body politic' (and not a metaphysical state or corporation) was a good example of this older perspective.

Maitland here stood back from his close historical analysis of doctrine to help create a fresh moral and political science, that *fin de siècle* 'New Liberalism' whose implications and prospects we still explore today.[73] He decoded doctrinal stories about expansion and adaptation of legal jurisdictions to find something even larger. No doubt there are equally great discoveries awaiting future doctrinal historians. One just needs to start decoding.

---

[69] Ibid., 480, 490–1.   [70] Pollock and Maitland (n. 18) vol. II, 616–23.

[71] Ibid., vol. I, 430–1.

[72] Ibid., vol. II, 486–97, analysed in Joshua Getzler, 'Plural Ownership, Funds, and the Aggregation of Wills' (2009) 10 *T.I.L.* 241.

[73] The post-Maitland debate on aggregation of minds and group purpose is explored in Samuel Stoljar, *Groups and Entities: An Inquiry into Corporate Theory* (1973); David Runciman, *Pluralism and the Personality of the State* (1997); Christian List, Philip Pettit, *Group Agency: The Possibility, Design, and Status of Corporate Agents* (2011); Janet McLean, *Searching for the State in British Legal Thought: Competing Conceptions of the Public Sphere* (2012); David Seipp, 'Formalism and Realism in Fifteenth Century English Law: Bodies Corporate and Bodies Natural', in Paul Brand, Joshua Getzler (eds.), *Judges and Judging in the History of the Common Law and Civil Law* (2012) 37 ff.

Bibliography

John Baker (gen. ed.), *Oxford History of the Laws of England* (Oxford University Press, 2003–)

John Baker, *An Introduction to English Legal History* (4th edn., Butterworths, 2002)

Peter Birks, Grant McLeod (eds.), *Justinian's Institutes* (Duckworth, 1987)

Morton Horwitz, *The Transformation of American Law, 1780–1860* (Harvard University Press, 1977)

David Ibbetson, *A Historical Introduction to the Law of Obligations* (Oxford University Press, 1991)

Frederic William Maitland, *State, Trust and Corporation* (David Runciman, Magnus Ryan (eds.), Cambridge University Press, 2003)

S. F. C. Milsom, *Historical Foundations of the Common Law* (2nd edn., Butterworths, 1981)

Frederick Pollock, Frederic William Maitland, *The History of English Law Before the Time of Edward I* (2 vols., Cambridge University Press, 1895; 2nd edn., 1898)

David Rabban, *Law's History: American Legal Thought and the Transatlantic Turn to History* (Cambridge University Press, 2013)

Brian Simpson, *A History of the Land Law* (Oxford University Press, 1961)

Brian Simpson, *Leading Cases in the Common Law* (Oxford University Press, 1995).

Francis de Zulueta (ed.), *The Institutes of Gaius* (Oxford University Press, 1946)

CHAPTER 11

....

HISTORICAL METHOD IN THE STUDY OF LAW AND CULTURE

....

BRYAN WAGNER

To research law and culture, or to research legal history as cultural history, to discover the law in culture, or the culture in law, is always and inevitably to engage with the mythology of the state, a mythology that was given its most comprehensive expression by Max Weber. In contrast to earlier approaches that treated the law as the organic expression of national or universal culture, Weber helped to consolidate a modernist paradigm that emphasized the developmental tension between law and culture, a tension that resulted over time in the gradual disembedding of the state from a cultural environment conceived as a total ensemble of knowledge, principle, and practice. Weber was building upon a narrative of world history furnished by a previous generation of evolutionary anthropologists, most notably polymaths like Henry Sumner Maine and Edward Burnett Tylor, who believed that political authority was dispersed throughout primitive culture to an extent that made it impossible to divorce the law from traditional organization based on kinship, religion, and ritual. Modern societies, on the other hand, were supposed to be distinguished by the fact that they had evolved state institutions that were autonomous from culture, a development that made their laws more rational and predictable, finally reaching a point where the state could persuasively claim a monopoly on the violence by which the law was legitimately produced, maintained, and enforced.[1]

This myth of modern government has influenced thinking about law and culture in two main ways. First, it provided a framework for universal comparison, a way to measure the difference between traditional societies where law remained embedded in culture and modern societies where the law had separated from culture. Second, it suggested that law and culture in modern societies needed to be conceived in relationship. In both instances, culture is supposed to denote law's outer edge. Where law ends, culture begins. At the very least, critical engagement with this relational scheme needs to extend back to the decades in the late nineteenth century when many disciplines in the human sciences, including those concerned with law and culture, were professionalized. Clearly, many of the ideas introduced during these decades, particularly ideas about the universal stages of historical development, have been abandoned. We cannot forget, however, that we still retain methods, source materials, and an entire system of disciplinary organization influenced by these old ideas, an influence that is shown not least in our continuing sense that it is possible to know ahead of time how to classify evidence—as law, as culture, or as some amalgam ('legal culture') that derives from pre-existing social domains ('law and culture') that are otherwise incompatible.

This chapter explores some of the ways that legal historical research has been conditioned by the concept of culture. Above all, it argues for the importance of understanding key terms of analysis in light of their intellectual history. No matter how we draw the distinction between law and culture, legal historical research becomes skewed when we presume that we are able to distinguish law from culture without attending to the intellectual and institutional history that made law and culture understandable as opposed entities separated into distinct domains. The resulting methodological problems are only compounded by empirical approaches that treat the conventions in legislation, court records, and ethnography as positive attributes immanent to historical documentation rather than as framing concepts with their own wide-ranging, complicated existence in the world. Legal historians need to proceed inductively, but they also need to expand their analysis dialectically through a genealogy that conceives law and culture not as natural kinds, but as inherited ideas.

During the twentieth century, as social science began to lose the inclination to equate differences in culture with differences in development, anthropologists began to experiment with new ways to conceptualize the relationship between law and culture. Some of their claims were unprecedented in their time. In *Crime and Custom in Savage Society* (1926), for example, Bernard Malinowski suggested that

---

[1] Max Weber, 'Politics as a Vocation', in *From Max Weber*, trans. H. H. Gerth and C. Wright Mills (1946) 77; Henry Sumner Maine, *Ancient Law: Its Connection with the Early History of Society, and Its Relation to Modern Ideas* (1861); Edward Burnett Tylor, *Primitive Culture: Researches into the Development of Mythology, Philosophy, Religion, Language, Art, and Custom*, 2 vols. (1871).

primitive people actually had laws, an argument that he supported by looking not to law's form but to its function in society, an approach that was later elaborated in another classic study, *The Cheyenne Way* (1941), an interdisciplinary collaboration between Karl Llewellyn, a law professor, and Edward Hoebel, an anthropology graduate student, which took the case method from legal education and applied it to a society that was supposed to have no legal institutions.[2]

It would be hard to overstate the impact that these two books had first on legal anthropology and subsequently on legal history. In turning their attention to the Cheyenne, for example, Llewellyn and Hoebel's objective was not merely to explicate the law as it was practised in one society, it was to propose a general argument about how law functioned in all societies, an argument that would support the idea that law everywhere had to be analysed in relation to local circumstances. For Llewellyn, as for other scholars committed to legal realism, it was impossible to divorce legal principles from the imperfect and contingent process through which they were expressed. In *The Cheyenne Way*, Llewellyn and Hoebel press their commitment to understanding law in context to an extreme in which law dissolves back into culture, as all attention to legal principles disappears during the encounter with a people whose practical and intuitive 'law-ways' illustrate the general truth that law's functional significance is not available in the abstract, but only in concrete details. Although Llewellyn believed his approach to the Cheyenne was continuous with his work in legal realism, it is unquestionable that when one turns to Llewellyn's writing on the common law or his contributions to the uniform commercial code, there is an abiding interest in the tension between formal rules and their practical expression, a tension that is never resolved to the degree that it is with the more-or-less imaginary example of the Cheyenne, a people that, in Llewellyn's analysis, remains fully integrated as a culture, standing in contrast to the self-division of modern society.

Books like *The Cheyenne Way* attempted to attack colonialism at its intellectual foundations by debunking the myth that people like the Cheyenne had no laws, breaking with earlier generations of anthropologists who believed that colonialism was beneficial to primitive societies that had yet to establish modern political institutions on their own. Again, however, we need to recognize that the new approach to legal anthropology pioneered by *The Cheyenne Way* was profoundly and in many respects unavoidably conditioned by colonialism, a fact that has not always been apparent either to readers or the authors themselves. Llewellyn and Hoebel, for example, encountered the Cheyenne on the Tongue River Reservation in eastern Montana, an area demarcated in 1884 by the United States Bureau of Indian Affairs after the forced removal of the Cheyenne to Oklahoma had proven a failure. Llewellyn and Hoebel hoped to bypass this history, asking Cheyenne elders to

---

[2] Bernard Malinowski, *Crime and Custom in Savage Society* (1926); Karl Llewellyn, Edward Hoebel, *The Cheyenne Way: Conflict and Case Law in Primitive Jurisprudence* (1941).

explain how disputes (or 'trouble cases') were resolved long ago when the Cheyenne were still ranging widely and hunting buffalo on the plains. *The Cheyenne Way* does not bother to ask how these stories about legal process, cast in retrospect, were shaped by the intervening conflicts with colonial authorities, nor does it ask how its own interpretation of these stories is made possible by legal institutions established in the wake of colonial warfare. Llewellyn and Hoebel describe their encounter with the Cheyenne as if it were unmediated by colonial history, failing to consider how their access to the Cheyenne was facilitated by the reservation system, first by state officials and then by tribal representatives recognized by the state. The artificial conditions on the reservation undoubtedly helped to reinforce the appearance of functional integration among the Cheyenne. By binding the Cheyenne to a remote and partitioned site seemingly isolated from modern history, the reservation makes an important if unremarked contribution not only to Llewellyn and Hoebel's ethnography, but also to their general argument about the relationship between law and culture.

This issue is not unique to *The Cheyenne Way*. Indeed, it is a familiar topic in legal anthropology. In a well-known analysis, Michel-Rolph Trouillot proposes that the culture concept is inextricable from colonialism. Trouillot observes that in the year when Edward Tylor published the first general anthropology textbook in the English language—1881—Barbados had been settled by the British for two centuries, Cuba had been settled by the Spanish for four centuries, and Haiti had already been independent for generations following more than a century of French rule. Trouillot's point is that from the start anthropology has approached its reference communities in the exact same way Llewellyn and Hoebel approach the Cheyenne— treating them as insulated, if not wholly isolated, from the encroaching influence of modernity, committed in their daily routines to autochthonous principles that represent either the best or the last vestige of local resistance to outside influence, an approach that ignores the recent history and present conditions that compose these societies. Through these Caribbean examples, Trouillot argues that anthropology has tended to abstract its reference communities, distorting them to the point where their modern characteristics, including their mongrel demographics and staple-crop export economies, are impossible to distinguish.[3]

Even in the wake of this critique of anthropology, many researchers have remained committed to an idea of culture whose consequences are not fully understood. This is especially clear in cases where culture is invoked as an antidote or alternative to formal jurisprudence. Whenever culture's immanent or embodied practices are set against law's abstraction, whenever culture's sprawling heterogeneity is set against law's homogeneity, whenever culture's fluidity is set against law's rigidity, whenever culture's enchantment is set against law's secular reason, whenever culture's

---

[3] Michel-Rolph Trouillot, *Silencing the Past: Power and the Production of History* (1995); Edward Burnett Tylor, *Anthropology: An Introduction to the Study of Man and Civilization* (1881).

particularity is cast against law's pretence to inhabit an omniscient or universal point of view, we are under the influence of an old idea of culture that carries more than a trace of primitivism, as shown in the premium it places on the supposed immediacy of face-to-face communication. This influence has persisted despite several waves of disciplinary self-critique focused on complicity with colonialism and on the methodological assumption that culture is bounded and integrated. Ironically enough, the influence of this old thinking about culture can appear strongest in cases where the culture concept is being explicitly jettisoned, as in Lila Abu-Lughod's celebrated essay, 'Writing Against Culture', where we are instructed that the way to write against culture is to write 'ethnographies of the particular', a methodological imperative that paradoxically insists upon the strict application of the culture concept in research practice even as it disavows 'culture' in name.[4]

These methodological challenges are evident not only in comparative research but also in studies that seek to understand the relation between law and culture within modern society. In contrast to primitive cultures, which were supposed to be cohesive, there has been a longstanding emphasis on internal division in modern society. In this context, law's autonomy from culture has sometimes been understood as a procedural norm that encourages the uniform application of doctrine across cases. Other times, it has been described as the symptom of the unfortunate but inevitable chasm between legal doctrine and the dynamism of the social world. Both these perspectives ultimately derive from the same general approach to the study of law and culture, an approach committed to seeing law and culture as discontinuous but contiguous social domains whose shadowy proximity is best understood through metaphors of power, influence, penetration, and mutual determination.

This approach evolved during a time when researchers were overtly concerned with the relations among economic, political, and cultural domains in society. The separation of these domains was believed to be one of the hallmarks of modernization. The state's monopoly on legitimate violence brought new security and predictability to modern society that in turn encouraged an increasingly layered cultural and commercial interdependence. In the process, aspects of society previously integrated into a common mode of life were first segregated and then subdivided, as 'culture', for example, began to refer simultaneously to several things at once: folk culture (originally conceived as the decaying remnants from symbols and practices that were previously functional in society), mass culture (including a range of formula entertainment that relied on technological innovation), and art culture (which took elite rank in a new hierarchy even as it claimed a universal purpose).

Researchers working in a range of disciplines have endeavoured to understand law as it relates to culture in all of these senses. In each case, however, they have tended to begin from the premise that there is at base something counter-intuitive, or even

---

[4] Lila Abu-Lughod, 'Writing Against Culture', in Richard Fox (ed.), *Recapturing Anthropology: Working in the Present* (1991) 137 ff.

something forced, about the coupling of law and culture given that these terms have so often been conceived in opposition to one another. Whether we conceive of culture in the humanistic sense, as 'the general body of the arts', or in the anthropological sense, as 'a whole way of life', we are dealing with something that was originally separate from law, whether culture is defined as a non-purposive domain standing apart from society's mundane business; as a formulaic and repetitious distraction from rational deliberation; or as a glittering fragment with a forgotten purpose retrieved from some disappearing tradition.[5]

Rather than attempt a comprehensive survey of law's relation to culture in each of these various modes, this chapter will emphasize a historiographical problem that is relevant to all of them—the problem of legitimacy—a problem inherited from the classical tradition of political philosophy and particularly from the early modern discourse on natural law. In the twentieth century, legitimacy is recast as a question of culture, as research attempted to determine, on the one hand, how culture encourages people to consent to be governed, and on the other hand, how culture interrupts tacit consent by providing an intuitive and immediate alternative to political identification with the state.

Conventionally, the first step in addressing the legitimacy of the rule of law is breaking down the ways in which discipline is imposed on a population. First, discipline is imposed through churches, families, schools, trade unions, political parties, and communications media. Second, discipline is imposed by the military and police. This distinction—between indoctrination by cultural institutions and the threat of violence wielded by the state's legal apparatus—is longstanding in research on the problem of political legitimacy, as shown in classic works like Karl Marx's *Eighteenth Brumaire of Louis Bonaparte*, which interprets the rise of French authoritarianism after the 1848 Revolution, and Antonio Gramsci's prison writings, which examine the rise of Italian fascism after the defeat of the factory councils. Both of these works were precedents for the crucial interdisciplinary research on law and governmental legitimacy produced in the 1960s and 1970s at the Birmingham Centre for Contemporary Cultural Studies, a research unit whose most enduring contribution is arguably the collectively authored *Policing the Crisis: Mugging, the State, and Law and Order* (1978).[6]

The research team behind *Policing the Crisis* was led by Stuart Hall, a thinker with a commitment to overcoming reductive approaches that portray the law as a tool of elites, culture as an industry of mass deception, and the entire social superstructure (including law and culture) as a projection of the economic mode of production.

---

[5] Raymond Williams, *Culture and Society, 1780–1950* (1958).

[6] Karl Marx, The *Eighteenth Brumaire of Louis Bonaparte* (1991); Antonio Gramsci, *Selections from the Prison Notebooks*, trans. Quintin Hoare, Geoffrey Nowell Smith (1971); Stuart Hall, Chas Critcher, Tony Jefferson, John Clarke, Brian Roberts, *Policing the Crisis: Mugging, the State and Law and Order* (1978).

Following the precedents set by Marx and Gramsci, *Policing the Crisis* addresses a particular moment (or 'conjuncture') in history, in their case, the moment in Great Britain in 1972–1973 when police and media turned public attention to a purported epidemic of street crime. *Policing the Crisis* treats 'mugging' not as a problem needing a policy solution (as statistics show there was actually no increase in crime) but instead as a moral panic that arose in response to a breakdown in government legitimacy that followed a decade of economic instability. Following not only Gramsci but also Louis Althusser and Nicos Poulantzas, *Policing the Crisis* is committed to the fundamental distinction between government by consent, which is the 'normal mode' of the liberal state, and government by violence, which is reserved for moments of crisis. In normal times, we are informed, everything in society 'works spontaneously' to sustain equilibrium through consent, but in moments when this equilibrium is disturbed, we see 'a tilt in the operation of the state away from consent toward the pole of coercion', in which there is increased reliance on violence to manage the class struggle, both directly, through police and prisons, and indirectly, through the consolidation of a new authoritarian consensus that bolsters support for government as necessary defence against the threat posed by outsiders. In *Policing the Crisis*, the outsiders in question are predominantly recent immigrants from former British colonies represented in the communications media by a racial archetype (the 'mugger') imported from the United States.[7]

A classic example of the interdisciplinary methodology associated with cultural studies, *Policing the Crisis* illustrates how the relationship between culture and law has been represented through the distinction between consent and coercion, a distinction at times defined more systematically as the difference between 'hegemony' (rule by indoctrination) and 'domination' (rule by violence). This distinction was also fundamental to early work in anti-colonial and post-colonial studies where it was applied directly by thinkers like Frantz Fanon to distinguish the situation of the metropolitan working classes (who were brainwashed) from the plight of the colonized (who were brutalized). In subsequent decades, postcolonial historians like Ranajit Guha would develop this approach by pointing out that unlike in European societies, where the transition to capitalism tended to involve the creation of a new consensus between merchants and workers about the operation of markets and rights to property, capitalism arrived in the colonies with no such assent from the peasantry, which meant among other things that culture took on a different political meaning in the colonies. Because colonial peasants were ruled by violence, their vernacular traditions continued without becoming assimilated to capitalism, which meant that culture remained a source of resistance in the colonies, whereas in metropolitan states culture became associated with the dreamwork that

---

[7] Louis Althusser, 'Ideology and Ideological State Apparatuses (Notes towards an Investigation)', in *Lenin and Philosophy and Other Essays*, trans. Ben Brewster (1971) 121 ff.; Nicos Poulantzas, *Political Power and Social Classes* (1973).

prevented exploited segments of society from recognizing the real conditions of their existence.[8]

Since the 1970s, historians have become increasingly sceptical about this binary characterization of legal systems. The costs associated with this type of analysis have become clear as historians have become more flexible in looking for law in unconventional, nongovernmental settings. Rather than oppose primitive and modern societies, or metropolitan and colonial societies, or state-based and culture-based societies, they have looked for points of similarity as well as difference across a variety of legal situations, observing, for instance, the law-like character of the informal norms and dispute-resolution procedures among raft fishermen, zanjera farmers, and other social groups that have invented ways to govern themselves without recourse to a formal, state-based legal process. By looking carefully at how common pool resources are allocated among self-governing societies, political economists like Elinor Ostrom have specified design principles such as open rule-making, mutual monitoring, and graduated sanctions that have made for sustainable social arrangements in the absence of government institutions. These principles are examples of 'jurisgenesis', a term coined by Robert Cover to refer to the creation of 'legal meaning' through an 'essentially cultural medium.' Cover contrasts this jurisgenesis, which happens continually in many different ways in many different times and places, to the 'courts of the state', whose basic purpose is 'jurispathic.' According to Cover, courts exist to suppress the cultural proliferation of legal meaning, producing a hierarchy of legal codes whose functions are centralized and systematized in state institutions.[9]

This new approach to legal pluralism builds on some old ideas, including Malinowski's argument for the existence of law among savage societies. It differs from these older approaches, however, in its principled, though I believe mostly implied, refusal to use the concept of culture as a wedge to facilitate comparative analysis between state and non-state societies. Without this wedge, it is difficult to characterize the grievance procedures among nomadic groups like the Cheyenne as different in kind—as more intuitive, more contextual, more superstitious—from the legal process institutionalized in government bureaucracies. Again the first principle of legal pluralism is that law comes from many places and not merely from the state. The implication is that community rules should be accorded the same degree of legitimacy and analysed with the same seriousness as constitutional law. As if by fiat, legal pluralism dispenses with the old mythology of modernization, demanding that we see policies based in religion, status, kinship, and obligation not

---

[8] Gramsci (n. 6); Althusser (n. 7); Frantz Fanon, *The Wretched of the Earth*, trans. Richard Philcox (2005); Ranajit Guha, *Elementary Aspects of Peasant Insurgency in Colonial India* (1983).

[9] Elinor Ostrom, *Governing the Commons: The Evolution of Institutions for Collective Action* (1990); Robert M. Cover, 'The Supreme Court, 1982 Term—Foreword: Nomos and Narrative' (1983) 97 *Harvard L.R.* 4 ff.

as instances analogous to law but literally as examples of law that are not only coeval but consubstantial with the secular and bureaucratic government institutions that are supposed to have superseded them.

Historians and anthropologists dedicated to investigating legal pluralism have looked in particular to settler colonial societies such as Australia and the United States. Unlike approaches in cultural studies and the new social history, which narrate the process by which native culture is subsumed by the state, or where established customs are interdicted and thereby incorporated into the legal system as crimes, the research methods associated with legal pluralism emphasize, first, that the procedures of native self-rule need to be analysed not merely as custom but as law, and second, that these established procedures do not fade away but persist under colonialism, resulting in an uneven situation in which, as Sally Engle Merry writes, 'two or more legal systems coexist' within the same territory, a situation that provokes complicated questions of overlapping jurisdiction.[10]

It is fair to say that legal pluralism has succeeded more as a provocation than as a method. It has done away with an old definition of law, in other words, but it has not been able to provide a new definition in its place. Legal pluralism has brought many things into the law that would once have been considered aspects of culture, but it does not offer any criterion that can help us understand which aspects of culture should count as law and which aspects should count as something else. The easy answer to this question—that everything should count as law—is an approach that has been tried by a number of other self-regarding interdisciplinary enterprises intent on transforming everything into an instance of their chosen object of study. Whether this means turning everything into text, or into culture, or into performance, the results have not been sustainable, often enough leading to a crisis of faith in which the object's very existence is brought into question, with literary critics, for instance, rejecting the category of literature, and anthropologists rejecting the category of culture. It would seem that the same potentially holds true for law, as legal pluralism's success in expanding legal inquiry has been not only accompanied by but predicated upon its failure to offer a working definition of law. This point is made not only by critics of legal pluralism but also by its advocates. Both recognize that it is difficult to define law without making reference to the state. Their disagreement is whether this ambiguity undermines legal pluralism as a research programme.

In my view, this ambiguity results partly from the way in which the admittedly problematic concept of culture has been diminished and even eliminated in the effort to level the field of legal analysis. Given the core ambiguity in legal pluralism, it may be good to think again about how it deals with culture. Consider, for example, the distinction that William Sewell draws between culture as a domain of society

---

[10] Peter Linebaugh, *The London Hanged: Crime and Civil Society in the Eighteenth Century* (1991); Sally Engle Merry, 'Legal Pluralism' (1988) 22 *Law and Society Review* 869 ff.

and culture as a dimension of analysis. In the first sense, culture is a 'concrete and bounded world of beliefs and practices.' Culture in this first sense always exists in the plural, as in the examples 'Philippine culture' and 'Samoan culture.' The implied contrast in these cases is not between culture and nature or culture and anarchy, but between cultures that exist together in the world. In the second sense, however, culture has no concrete existence. It refers not to one particular province of a particular society but to a common dimension that is found in all societies. Culture in the second sense is a theoretical term of analysis, as in Claude Levi-Strauss's account of culture as a semiotic system. It is always used in the singular. Sewell's claim is that the critique of the culture concept has frequently conflated these two senses of culture, resulting in confusion.[11]

This distinction may be useful to legal historical scholarship as it suggests that culture can appear in research not as a name for something—for society or one of its parts—but rather as the aspect of analysis concerned with the creation and circulation of meaning. One way to illustrate the value of this way of thinking about culture is to return to questions raised at the beginning of this chapter about the state's monopoly on legitimate violence. As we have noted, these questions have been important to research on law and culture both in a positive sense, for scholars who have seen the achievement of this monopoly as a turning point in world history, and also in a negative sense, for critics whose vision of culture is explicitly opposed to this grand narrative of political development. In both instances, the state's monopoly on legitimate violence is defined in relation to culture. Whether it is conceived as the organizational principle that distinguishes modern civilization from backward and culture-bound tribes or as a military and police infrastructure that is simultaneously supported and contested by culture in various senses—formal education, mass communications, sectarian and dissident urban style—the state's monopoly on legitimate violence is conceived not as an example or as an extension of culture but as the institutional organization of brute force.

Critical attention to the cultural dimension of the state's monopoly on legitimate violence has been diminished by the longstanding preoccupation with legitimation, a preoccupation that is central not only to Weber's exposition but also to the alternatives proposed by critics like Gramsci, Althusser, and Hall, for whom 'consent' and 'coercion' stand as irreducible aspects of modern government. In all of these accounts, culture orients people to the state's actually existing capacity for violence. Culture is a way to win consent or stir dissent. The problem with this instrumental approach is that it fails to take into account the ways in which culture inevitably outstrips the state's actual powers, attributing powers to the state that the state does not actually have. Critics have tried to get at the cultural constitution of legal authority in discussions about the 'state idea' or the 'state effect', but the

---

[11] William H. Sewell Jr., *Logics of History: Social Theory and Social Transformation* (2005).

dominant impression left by these discussions is how profoundly difficult it is to tell where law ends and culture begins, a difficulty that throws every attempt to relate law to culture into disarray.[12]

This difficulty is apparent, for example, when we look to the years in the nineteenth century when modern police departments were established for the first time in cities like London and New York. These departments were championed by advocates, like Robert Peel, who justified the 'indefinite force' accorded to the London Metropolitan Police by invoking scenarios from political philosophy in which society emerges from chaos through the achievement of the state's monopoly on violence. Given the intense controversy surrounding the London Metropolitan Police, especially its right to use force against the citizenry as if it were a standing army, Peel's defence reads like an attempt to defend the police from its critics, but that is only part of the story, given that the police cannot muster anything like the 'indefinite force' that Peel attributes to them. Without firearms, without modern technology for communication, surveillance, and forensic analysis, with not much more than several hundred constables to patrol a metropolis whose population would soon reach two million, it requires imagination to describe the London Metropolitan Police as an indefinite force, and this imagination, indulged not only by Peel but also by his adversaries, remains inseparable from the institutional consolidation of modern government authority in London in 1829. Crucially, the same holds true in later centuries. Even as the police increase their ranks, even as weapons and technology continue to advance, the fact remains that the modern state will never arrive at the theoretical apogee at which claims about its authority have been pitched since the beginning.[13]

When we think more expansively about the rule of law as it is instantiated in the state's monopoly on legitimate violence, we confront a situation that is less stable than it previously appeared. This is a situation in which law's reach always exceeds its grasp, a situation in which the stories we tell swerve above the law into vigilantism or below the law into an underworld of collateral institutions. This is evident, for example, in cinema, from *Birth of a Nation* to *Batman*, and it is no less evident in legislation and jurisprudence. From Bentham to 'Broken Windows', commentators have turned to the same situations to explore the limit cases for legitimate violence. Cast in law or culture, these stories characteristically begin and end the same way, with society intact and the state in control, but in between they unfold in ways that reveal the flexibility of legal legitimacy, marking the occasions in which personal violence remains not only permissible, but necessary. More often than not, the rule of law is honoured in the breach as heroic individuals confront ticking time bombs and terrorist scenarios that legitimate exceptional measures to

---

[12] Philip Abrams, 'Notes on the Difficulty of Studying the State' (1988) 1 *Journal of Historical Sociology* 58 ff.

[13] Wilbur R. Miller, *Cops and Bobbies: Police Authority in New York and London, 1830–1870* (1977).

protect the greater good. Whether standing their ground against their enemies or defending their castles against intruders, whether stealing from the rich to feed the poor or lying to the authorities to protect the innocent, individuals are continually forced to confront the choice between following the rules and doing the right thing, a situation that brings archetypal dilemmas from discourse on natural law into policy discussions even as it also projects them into stories, songs, newspapers, novels, cinema, and television.[14]

My point is not that culture and law are merely related or continuous. My point is that they are *the same* in working together to compose the virtual reality of state authority, an authority whose real effects in the world are inseparable from their meaning. Reckoning with this complexity requires us to refuse the false clarity that results when we contrast modern states and primitive cultures, or when we divide society into parts in order to sort its functions. If recent attempts to overcome the inherited opposition between law and culture have not accomplished, and may never achieve, the promise of a unified field theory, our work can continue nevertheless without such guarantees.

BIBLIOGRAPHY

Louis Althusser, 'Ideology and Ideological State Apparatuses (Notes towards an Investigation)' *Lenin and Philosophy and Other Essays*, trans. Ben Brewster (Monthly Review Press, 1971) 121–76

Lauren Benton, *Law and Colonial Cultures: Legal Regimes in World History, 1400–1900* (Cambridge University Press 2000)

Bradin Timothy Cormack, *A Power to Do Justice: Jurisdiction, English Literature, and the Rise of the Common Law* (University of Chicago Press, 2007)

Robert M. Cover, 'The Supreme Court, 1982 Term—Foreword: Nomos and Narrative' (1983) *Harvard Law Review* 97 4–68.

Antonio Gramsci, *Selections from the Prison Notebooks*, trans. Quintin Hoare and Geoffrey Nowell Smith (International Publishers, 1971)

Ranajit Guha, *Elementary Aspects of Peasant Insurgency in Colonial India* (Oxford University Press, 1983)

Stuart Hall, Chas Critcher, Tony Jefferson, John Clarke, Brian Roberts, *Policing the Crisis: Mugging, the State and Law and Order* (Macmillan, 1978)

Hendrik Hartog, 'Pigs and Positivism' (1985) *Wisconsin Law Review* 899–935

Karl Llewellyn, Edward Hoebel, *The Cheyenne Way: Conflict and Case Law in Primitive Jurisprudence* (W. S. Hein and Company, 1941)

---

[14] D. W. Griffith, (dir.), *Birth of a Nation* (1915); Tim Burton, (dir.), *Batman* (1989); W. L. Twining, P. L. Twining, 'Bentham on Torture' (1973) 24 *Northern Ireland Law Quarterly* 305 ff. George L. Kelling, James Q. Wilson, 'Broken Windows: The Police and Neighborhood Safety' (1982) 249 *Atlantic Monthly* 29 ff.

Bernard Malinowski, *Crime and Custom in Savage Society* (Harcourt Brace and Company, 1926)

Sally Engle Merry, 'Legal Pluralism' (1988) *Law and Society Review* 22 869–96.

William Ian Miller, *Bloodtaking and Peacemaking: Feud, Law, and Society in Saga Iceland* (University of Chicago Press, 1990)

Elinor Ostrom, *Governing the Commons: The Evolution of Institutions for Collective Action* (Cambridge University Press, 1990)

William H. Sewell Jr., *Logics of History: Social Theory and Social Transformation* (University of Chicago Press, 2005)

Michel-Rolph Trouillot, *Silencing the Past: Power and the Production of History* (Beacon Press, 1995)

CHAPTER 12

LEGAL HISTORY AS ECONOMIC HISTORY

ANNE FLEMING*

OVER the past century, legal history and economic history developed as separate fields of scholarship. Their separation reflects an understanding of law and economy as distinct objects that may be pulled apart and each analysed apart from the other. Yet, even assuming that law and economy are separable, it is undeniable that they interact; laws govern economic actors, and these actors interpret, apply, and sometimes shape the law. More than four decades ago, historian Harry Scheiber described studies of this interaction as occupying a 'borderland' between the disciplines of law and economic history.[1] With the growth over the past half-century of legal history as a field distinct from law, the boundary between legal history and economic history has become its own borderland, which this chapter explores.

In a well-known article, historian Robert Gordon divided approaches to legal history into two broad categories: 'internal' and 'external.' Internal approaches explain law's history through legal sources and focus on charting the progression of legal doctrine and the development of legal ideas and institutions. For example, Marylynn Salmon's deeply-researched study of the formal colonial and state-level rules about women's property rights generally follows this approach, while also

* The author thanks Miri Gold and Patricia Jerjian for their helpful comments on earlier drafts of this chapter.
[1] Harry N. Scheiber, 'At the Borderland of Law and Economic History: The Contributions of Willard Hurst' (1970) 75 *American Historical Review* 744–56 ff.

acknowledging the influence of external events like the American Revolution on the law. Similarly, Roy Kreitner's *Calculating Promises* presents a narrative about changes in legal doctrine that is grounded in case law and the ideas of legal scholars. Gordon's external approaches, on the other hand, engage more deeply with non-legal sources and ask questions directed at understanding law's impact on society and vice versa. The legal history explored in this chapter falls into this external category. It focuses on the interaction between law and the economic dimensions of society—namely, a society's processes for the production, sale, and consumption of goods and services, as well as the social welfare institutions designed to address the risks and inequalities that those processes produce.[2]

Gordon credited Willard Hurst of the University of Wisconsin with breaking out of the then-traditional, internal approach to legal history in the 1950s and 1960s, becoming 'the leading exponent and practitioner of an external historiography'. Prior studies written by economic historians in the 1940s and 1950s—including a series supported by the Social Science Research Council's Committee on Research in Economic History—provided the foundation for Hurst's research on the role of law in economic development. These works showed how the states intervened in the nineteenth-century economy and, according to Harry Scheiber, 'disposed of the myth that the range and impact of 19th century governmental interventions had been only minimal'. Hurst introduced this research into legal scholarship and, by at least one account, 'essentially created the legal history of economic change'.[3]

In one of his best-known works, on the legal history of the Wisconsin lumber industry, Hurst made two important moves that would influence future scholarship. First, Hurst looked to law as a key factor in explaining a pattern of economic development—specifically, the deforestation of Wisconsin within the span of a few decades. Second, he adopted a broad understanding of 'law' that encompassed not only appellate court decisions and common law reasoning, but also legislative and executive action and the work of trial courts. Using a diverse set of legal materials, Hurst concluded that law fostered the 'release of private energies of mind and will' in nineteenth-century Wisconsin and 'channeled economic action in directions which promised quick and substantial multiplier effects on total output'.[4]

---

[2] Robert W. Gordon, 'Introduction: J. Willard Hurst and the Common Law Tradition in American Legal Historiography' (1975) 10 *Law & Society Review* 9–55 ff; Marylynn Salmon, *Women and the Law of Property in Early America* (1986); Roy Kreitner, *Calculating Promises: The Emergence of Modern American Contract Doctrine* (2007).

[3] Gordon (n. 2) 12 ff; James Willard Hurst, *Law and the Conditions of Freedom in the Nineteenth-Century United States* (1956) 112 n. 20 (citing Handlin and Handlin, *Commonwealth: Massachusetts, 1774–1861* (1947), Hartz, *Economic Policy and Democratic Thought: Pennsylvania, 1776–1860* (1948), Kirkland, *Men, Cities and Transportation* (1948)); Harry Scheiber, 'Federalism and the American Economic Order, 1789–1910' (1975) *Law & Society Review*, 59 ff; Victoria Saker Woeste, *The Farmer's Benevolent Trust: Law and Agricultural Cooperation in Industrial America, 1865–1945* (1998) 2 ff.

[4] James Willard Hurst, *Law and Economic Growth: The Legal History of the Lumber Industry in Wisconsin, 1836–1915* (1964) 608 ff.

Since then, legal historians have continued to revisit and revise Hurst's conclusions, while also rethinking the separation of 'law' and 'economy' that characterized the early work of Hurst and others in this field.

The remainder of this chapter proceeds in three parts. The first part maps the state of the field over the past several decades, identifying two major questions that have guided much of the scholarship on the border between legal and economic history. The second part describes two of the theoretical frameworks available to legal historians for conceptualizing the relationship between law and economy. Finally, the last part argues that future work on the history of political economy should put aside measuring the impact of law on economy (and vice versa) and instead explore how the boundary between law and economy has been constructed and maintained over time.

1. Law's Impact on Economy and Vice Versa

Two questions run through much of the work in this field. The first is whether law is 'autonomous' from economic developments and, if so, how much. In other words, how much of legal history can be explained by economic imperatives? In the 1970s, when the field of socio-legal history was still in its infancy, historians Lawrence Friedman and Morton Horwitz both addressed this question, but reached slightly different conclusions. Friedman found that law was not autonomous, but rather a 'mirror' of society, while Horwitz granted law a greater measure of independence, finding law to be 'autonomous to the extent that ideas are autonomous, at least in the short run'.[5]

Yet, even though Horwitz did not treat law as founded upon and wholly determined by the mode and relations of economic production, he emphasized the importance of economic interests in the transformation of American private law prior to the Civil War, finding that common law judges acted at the behest of merchants and entrepreneurs and their lawyers, to 'protect those groups that stood to benefit from an expanding market economy.' By 1850, as a consequence of these judicial decisions, the legal system advantaged 'men of commerce and industry' and 'actively promoted a legal redistribution of wealth' away from the least powerful, Horwitz argued.[6]

---

[5] Lawrence M. Friedman, *A History of American Law* (1973) 10 ff; Morton J. Horwitz, *The Transformation of American Law, 1780–1860* (1977) xiii ff.

[6] Ibid., 212, 253–4 ff.

The Horwitz thesis proved influential in shaping the agenda of the field. A number of subsequent studies described how the economic interests of elites transformed American law in the nineteenth century. In particular, historians scrutinized the role of slaveholders in shaping early American law, including constitutional law and fiscal policy. Subsequent work also reinforced Horwitz's claim that law was neither fully autonomous nor strictly a functional response to economic developments. Historian R. W. Kostal, for example, described law and industry as 'locked together in a powerful dialectical exchange' in his work on nineteenth-century English railroads. Ron Harris adopted a similarly 'pragmatic', 'dialectic', and contextual approach in his work on the English law of business organizations in the eighteenth and nineteenth centuries, finding law to be relatively autonomous in some contexts but also sometimes functionally responsive to the demands of a changing economy.[7]

Horwitz's provocative argument also spurred work critiquing and refining his concept of 'economic interests' and their relationship to law. In his study of a South American region in transition during the nineteenth century, Jeremy Adelman argued that economic interests did not stand apart from law, but were 'socially constructed', shaped by legal institutions and ideas 'in the course of state- and market-formation' in Argentina. As Adelman explained in a subsequent article, the aim of his work has been to 'historicize' the economy 'in part by attending to the fuzzy and shifting boundaries between the economic and noneconomic'. To do so, he questioned 'the neat and tidy divisions' between the legal, political, and economic dimensions of society. William Forbath's study of American law and labour unions similarly concluded that labour's adoption of the language and conceptual categories of the law at the turn of the twentieth century ultimately narrowed workers' understanding of their own interests and of the proper role of the state in industrial relations. In her work on agricultural cooperatives and their recourse to law, Victoria Saker Woeste likewise found that 'law furnished both a malleable tool and a formal restraint' on her subjects. Her story revealed 'the vagaries, the unintended effects and consequences, of recourse to law'. By showing that law shaped economic actors' understanding of their own material interests and how they made legal demands on the state in furtherance of those interests, these historians complicated the project of determining economy's impact on law over time.[8]

---

[7] On the economic interests of elites, see Charles Grier Sellers, *The Market Revolution: Jacksonian America, 1815–1846* (1991); John Lauritz Larson, *Internal Improvement: National Public Works and the Promise of Popular Government in the Early United States* (2001). On the role of slaveholders, see Sean P. Adams, *Old Dominion, Industrial Commonwealth: Coal, Politics, and Economy in Antebellum America* (2004); Robin L. Einhorn, *American Taxation, American Slavery* (2006); George Van Cleve, *A Slaveholders' Union: Slavery, Politics, and the Constitution in the Early American Republic* (2010). Rande W. Kostal, *Law and English Railway Capitalism, 1825–1875* (1994) 359 ff; Ron Harris, *Industrializing English Law: Entrepreneurship and Business Organization, 1720–1844* (2010) 4, 9 ff.

[8] Jeremy Adelman, *Republic of Capital: Buenos Aires and the Legal Transformation of the Atlantic World* (1999) 9, 13, 15 ff; Jeremy Adelman, Jonathan Levy, 'The Fall and Rise of Economic History'

Other scholars affirmed the difficulty of measuring economy's impact on law once other variables came into play, such as economic ideas. If ideas shaped how various actors defined their legal and economic interests, then tracking the influence of economy on law became even more complex. Robert Johnston's work on the 'radical middle class' in Portland, Oregon, for example, revealed that this group's political economic vision was rooted in an older populist and republican ideology. Several historians, including Alice Kessler-Harris and Linda Gordon, noted the importance of ideas about work and the gendered division of labour in shaping the rules governing the American welfare state. More recently, Ajay Mehrotra claimed a central role for ideas in the transformation of American income tax policy. In Mehrotra's telling, ideas 'were critical weapons and blueprints for building powerful political coalitions' in the struggle over tax policy between the late nineteenth century and the onset of the Great Depression. Daniel W. Hamilton's study of property confiscation during the American Civil War similarly placed legislative debates alongside ascendant ideologies of property, finding cause for the Union's rejection of confiscation in the increasing dominance of an 'individualized, rights-oriented' conception of property. Herbert Hovenkamp likewise explained the development of the law governing business in this period as a reflection of classical economic theory. Thus, historical studies of the relationship between economic ideas and law further stymied attempts to determine the degree of law's autonomy from economy. These findings supported the claim that law is not autonomous, but pointed to something other than economic interests as the limit on law's independence.[9]

The second question that has guided scholars working on the border between legal and economic history is the inverse of the first: what has been the impact of law on economy? In posing the question, legal historians have implicitly critiqued economic and business historians who have ignored law and instead explained change over time based on advances in technology or the bold decisions of significant entrepreneurs. Law played no role, for example, in Alfred Chandler's 1977 prize-winning narrative about the ascendance of modern managerial capitalism, *The Visible Hand*. Chandler, the inventor of modern business history, argued that technology and expanding markets created the conditions necessary

Chronicle of Higher Education, 1 December 2014 ff; William E. Forbath, *Law and the Shaping of the American Labor Movement* (1991); Woeste, *The Farmer's Benevolent Trust* 234–5 ff.

[9] Robert D. Johnston, *The Radical Middle Class: Populist Democracy and the Question of Capitalism in Progressive Era Portland, Oregon* (2003); Alice Kessler-Harris, *In Pursuit of Equity: Women, Men, and the Quest for Economic Citizenship in 20th-Century America* (2001); Linda Gordon, *Pitied but Not Entitled: Single Mothers and the History of Welfare, 1890–1935* (1994); Ajay K. Mehrotra, *Making the Modern American Fiscal State: Law, Politics, and the Rise of Progressive Taxation, 1877–1929* (2013) 9 ff; Daniel W. Hamilton, *The Limits of Sovereignty: Property Confiscation in the Union and the Confederacy during the Civil War* (2007); Herbert Hovenkamp, *Enterprise and American Law, 1836–1937* (1991).

for the rise of the large, modern business enterprise, which came to dominate major sectors of the economy. The visible hands of salaried managers then guided those enterprises and their decisions about how to produce and distribute their goods. Another study from the same decade, Robert Fogel and Stanley Engerman's *Time on the Cross*, likewise placed law in the background in its exploration of the economics of American slavery in the nineteenth century. More recently, Kenneth Pomeranz's *The Great Divergence* also emphasized non-legal factors, such as the location of coal and other natural resources, in explaining the divergent paths of economic development in Western Europe and East Asia in the nineteenth century.[10]

A number of legal and business historians have emphasized the importance of law and the state in explaining economic change, however. Richard John's *Network Nation*, for example, stressed the 'influence' of the 'structuring presence of the state' on the development of the telegraph and telephone industries, arguing that network builders in both systems devised strategies to develop their business within the context of each era's political economy. America's shift from an 'antimonopoly' to a 'progressive' political economy spurred the invention of new organizational tactics that would best serve the business within the new constellation of regulatory ideas. Sally Clarke's *Trust and Power* similarly chronicled how developments in tort law shaped the growth of the American automotive industry over the first six decades of the twentieth century. She showed how law influenced automotive design in both direct and indirect ways, including how regulation pushed insurance companies to pressure the car manufacturers they insured to invest in safety research and incorporate this research into design improvements. Other historians charted the state's influence on the major transportation industries—trucks, airlines, and rails—over the twentieth century, while Louis Hyman chronicled the federal government's role in the growth of consumer lending in the same period. More recently, Christopher Beauchamp found that patent law played a significant part in 'the transformation of the industrial economy'. Richard John nicely summarized the central theme of these works of business history in the conclusion to *Network Nation*: 'Politics always mattered.'[11]

---

[10] Alfred D. Chandler, *The Visible Hand: The Managerial Revolution in American Business* (1977); Robert William Fogel, Stanley L. Engerman, *Time on the Cross: The Economics of American Negro Slavery* (1974); Kenneth Pomeranz, *The Great Divergence: Europe, China, and the Making of the Modern World Economy* (2000).

[11] Sally H. Clarke, *Trust and Power: Consumers, the Modern Corporation, and the Making of the United States Automobile Market* (2007); Mark H. Rose, Bruce E. Seely, Paul F. Barrett, *The Best Transportation System in the World: Railroads, Trucks, Airlines, and American Public Policy in the Twentieth Century* (2006); Louis Hyman, *Debtor Nation: The History of America in Red Ink* (2011); Christopher Beauchamp, *Invented by Law: Alexander Graham Bell and the Patent That Changed America* (2015) 7 ff; Richard R. John, *Network Nation: Inventing American Telecommunications* (2010) 410 ff.

A related vein of scholarship stressed the importance of the state in economic development, particularly in early America, challenging the claim made by some scholars of American Political Development that the nineteenth-century state of 'courts and parties' played a minor role in the American economy. The Commonwealth studies conducted in the 1940s and 1950s were among the earliest works to emphasize how often state governments intervened in the early American economy. More recently, William Novak's *The People's Welfare* (1996) critiqued several enduring myths about the role of the American state in the nineteenth-century marketplace, finding regulation of economic and social life to be pervasive at the state and local levels in this period. Brian Balogh and Richard John likewise challenged the myth of the weak nineteenth-century American state, showing how the federal government furthered economic development and shaped markets despite the absence of a large, modern bureaucracy. Others described how the federal state expanded during and after the American Civil War in order to meet the material needs of the war effort and, later, to combat the economic threat of the Great Depression. In these studies, law is often defined as the 'language of the state' and a means through which the state has exerted power over the economy.[12]

Some scholars have found less use for the 'state' as a category of analysis, however. They have instead documented how economic behaviour may develop independently from formal legal rules and outside the reach of state power. Dylan Penningroth's research on slavery and property ownership, for example, revealed the existence of a 'system of property ownership and trade' that 'scarcely registered on the statute books,' but yet was deeply woven into the fabric of everyday life in the antebellum South. Writing about travellers on the overland trail in the American West during the same era, John Phillip Reid similarly discovered a society in motion that was governed by the legal norms the voyagers carried with them from home, despite the absence of formal law enforcement or legal institutions on the trail. These studies raised two critical questions for those seeking to measure the impact of law on economy: what is 'law'? And how do we separate 'law' from what is not law, in order to understand the relation of one to the other?[13]

---

[12] Ajay K. Mehrotra, 'A Bridge Between: Law and the New Intellectual Histories of Capitalism' (2016) 64 *Buffalo L.R.* 14 ff; William J. Novak, *The People's Welfare: Law and Regulation in Nineteenth-Century America* (1996) 3 ff; Brian Balogh, *A Government out of Sight: The Mystery of National Authority in Nineteenth-Century America* (2009); Richard R. John, 'Ruling Passions: Political Economy in Nineteenth Century America' (2006) 18 *Journal of Policy History* 1–20 (introducing essays in special issue on nineteenth-century political economy) ff; Mark R. Wilson, *The Business of Civil War: Military Mobilization and the State, 1861–1865* (2006); Jason Scott Smith, *Building New Deal Liberalism: The Political Economy of Public Works, 1933–1956* (2006).

[13] Dylan C. Penningroth, *The Claims of Kinfolk: African American Property and Community in the Nineteenth-Century South* (2003) 6 ff; John Phillip Reid, *Law for the Elephant: Property and Social Behavior on the Overland Trail* (1997).

ii. Conjunctions and Theoretical Frameworks

As the preceding summary of the existing literature illustrates, legal historians writing about the economy have often adopted a 'law and economy' framework, which treats law and economy as separate variables that interact over time. The researcher's task is to track this interaction, determining the impact of each variable on the other. Questions related to the autonomy of law from economy, or the autonomy of economy from law, fit easily into this framework. These questions have not generated satisfying answers, however. As Robert Gordon and Catherine Fisk recently observed, 'Theories of causal regularities in law/society relations were elusive and unstable; they tended to break down under critique into indeterminacy marked by complexity and contingency.' In Fiske's own work on employment and intellectual property ownership, she concluded that her findings do not support 'any single or elegant theory of the relationship between legal, social, and economic change'. Rather, she found 'heavy traffic back and forth across the bridge of causation between the legal and the material'. If law shapes economic actors' understanding of their own material interests, or if there are always multiple variables at play in addition to law and economy, then the project of separating law from economy and tracking the impact of each on the other seems doomed.[14]

An alternative approach is to apply a 'law as' framework. Rather than 'and,' which conjoins two variables understood as otherwise separate and distinct, the alternative formulation—'law as economy' and 'economy as law'—describes a singular phenomenon. As scholar Ritu Birla has explained, the approach emphasizes the embeddedness of law within economy and vice versa. Drawing on Foucault's concept of governmentality, she urged scholars to conceptualize law and economy not as separate domains, but as two modes of governing human bodies and populations. The approach entails 'a rigorous attention to law's role in the political rationalities *and* codings of culture that produce and are legitimized by the modern abstraction we call "the economy"'. Christopher Tomlins summarized the problem with 'law and economy', as well as 'law and capitalism', in a similar way: 'the *and* powerfully enforces a requirement that we think of 'law' and 'capitalism' as referencing ontologically distinct phenomena'. Tomlins suggested that we might instead think of studying law as a way of studying capitalism or any other system

---

[14] Catherine L. Fisk, Robert W. Gordon, ' "Law As…": Theory and Method in Legal History: Foreword' (2011) 1 *U.C. Irvine L.R.* 522 ff; Catherine L. Fisk, *Working Knowledge: Employee Innovation and the Rise of Corporate Intellectual Property, 1800–1930* (2009) 5 ff.

of political economy. Indeed, he argued, capitalism is made real through law and is 'knowable only through the operations of law'.[15]

Historian and political theorist Timothy Mitchell likewise has argued that attempts to separate law and economy are founded on a false distinction, taking at face value the claims of each domain to be separate and distinct from the other. As Mitchell explained, the abstraction of 'the economy' first appeared in the twentieth century, as the object of the state's power, while the state defined itself in opposition to the economy and the market, which it managed through law. Like Tomlins, Mitchell called for studying the ways in which the state seeks to separate itself from economy, how a line is drawn 'within the network of institutional mechanisms through which a certain social and political order is maintained'. 'Rather than searching for a definition that will fix the boundary' between state and non-state, Mitchell wrote, 'we need to examine the detailed political processes through which the uncertain yet powerful distinction between state and society is produced'. For Mitchell, this exploration must be grounded in a particular time and place, rather than occurring at a high level of theoretical generality.[16]

III. FUTURE DIRECTIONS

Legal historians should heed Mitchell's call for focusing on the specific and the technical, cracking open systems that might otherwise be left unexplored—among them, 'capitalism'. Instead of starting with a theory of how law relates to economy and finding evidence for its support, scholars might instead begin with primary source materials and construct a narrative about how law operated within the context of particular people, institutions, ideas, and material things. People, institutions, ideas, and the material world all shape and are shaped by law, as Fiske and others have found. Law is neither entirely determined by, nor wholly autonomous from, its material context—and vice versa. Furthermore, scholars need not adopt a singular understanding of how law works. As Christopher Tomlins demonstrated in his study of American colonization over the course of almost three centuries, law may

---

[15] Ritu Birla, 'Law as Economy: Convention, Corporation, Currency' (2011) 1 *U.C. Irvine L.R.* 1018–19 ff; Christopher Tomlins, 'Organic Poise: Capitalism as Law' (2016) 64 *Buffalo L.R.* 62, 76 ff; Christopher Tomlins, 'Law "And", Law "In", Law "As": The Definition, Rejection and Recuperation of the Socio-Legal Enterprise' (2013) 29 *Law in Context: A Socio-Legal Journal* 154 ff.

[16] Timothy Mitchell, *Rule of Experts: Egypt, Techno-Politics, Modernity* (2002); Timothy Mitchell, 'The Limits of the State: Beyond Statist Approaches and Their Critics' (1991) 85 *American Political Science Review* 78, 90 ff.

simultaneously serve as a technology for organization, a discourse of legitimation, and a modality of governance. Rather than attempt to find support for a generalized theory about how law and economy interact, historians might instead ask how the boundary between these two domains—law and economy—has been constructed over time, creating a sense of one's separation from the other.[17]

Historians might also look behind abstract labels, such as 'capitalism,' which may obscure more than they reveal about how a society's law relates to its economy. (The tendency of recent work to disaggregate capitalism into its many varieties—such as war capitalism and corporate capitalism—indicates that the analytic work done by 'capitalism' alone is limited.) Undermining the idea of capitalism as a singular thing requires drilling down to the specifics, setting aside the abstraction of 'capitalism,' and instead focusing on how particular capitalist societies operate and especially on how law allocates decision-making authority among economic actors. As historian Edward Purcell recently observed, although 'capitalist forms' may 'tend to create certain kinds of risks and results, it is the specific form of capitalism in its specific context—not "capitalism in general"—that determines the scope, extent, and impact of those risks and results'.[18]

Building on Tomlins' idea that capitalism is 'knowable only through the operations of law', legal historians might posit that the structure and substance of a society's law tell us something about how that society seeks to govern economic relations, and they would therefore look first to law to understand the economic order. It is insufficient, however, to study law in isolation, much as looking at an architectural blueprint of a structure is insufficient to understand how it functions in the world. To fully understand law requires looking within it and also outside it. People build and inhabit the structure and may move through it in surprising ways. External constraints on its size and shape also explain its form and the resulting paths of human activity. Rather than ascribing power over a society's economic life to 'capitalism', legal historians might instead dig deeper into how particular laws structure relations of exchange and interactions between people and the material world.

One line of research would explore the question of how the boundary between state and market, law and economy, has been constructed over time in particular societies. The goal is not to measure the impact of each variable on the other, but to deconstruct how these two modes of governing human behaviour came to be understood as separate and distinct in a particular time and place. Jeremy Adelman and Jonathan Levy have already advocated for economic historians to adopt

[17] Christopher L. Tomlins, *Freedom Bound: Law, Labor, and Civic Identity in Colonizing English America, 1580–1865* (2010).
[18] On varieties of capitalism, see Sven Beckert, *Empire of Cotton: A Global History* (2014); Peter A. Hall, David W. Soskice (eds.), *Varieties of Capitalism: The Institutional Foundations of Comparative Advantage* (2001); Edward A. Purcell, Jr., 'Capitalism and Risk: Concepts, Consequences, and Ideologies' (2016) 64 *Buffalo L.R.* 37 ff.

this approach in their writing of 'a history of economic life' that 'historicizes the economy itself, in part by attending to the fuzzy and shifting boundaries between the economic and noneconomic'.[19] Given that law has played a major role in drawing this boundary between the legal and the economic, legal historians are well equipped to explore its construction and movement over time.

Some historians have already begun to show how law and economy work to separate themselves from one another, and the challenges that have undermined this boundary. Gautham Rao's *National Duties*, for example, argues that in the late eighteenth century, the belief 'that the state and the marketplace must be distinct simply did not exist'. Brian Phillips Murphy's study of public works programmes in the early American republic similarly claims that the public and private spheres were never truly separate, in practice. According to Murphy, 'American capitalism instead grew out of collaborations between political and economic interests', creating 'a dynamic in which business strategies and institutions were shaped by political strategies and institutions, and vice versa'. Rafe Blaufarb's recent work likewise finds no clear dividing line between the public and private realms in France before 1789, when public power could be held as private property. He argues that the French Revolution brought about a major change in the system of property-holding, creating a new and 'radical distinction between the political and the social, state and society, sovereignty and ownership, the public and private'. My own research, on early twentieth-century America, finds that courts played a key role in defining the boundary between the state and the market in this period and that the state's obligation to care for the poor complicated judicial efforts to decide where the state's regulatory reach ended and the sphere of constitutionally-protected, private contractual freedom began. Only after much consideration did courts permit states to expand their oversight of private household borrowing, in order to protect the public interest in preventing a poor person from becoming 'a public charge' who was dependent on the state for support.[20]

A separate line of research would not explore how the separate spheres of law and economy have been constructed, but rather would critique the common understandings of the two domains that are the products of this process. It would look for law where law seems to be absent and examine the legal underpinnings of economic processes that seem to unfold organically. Although this might seem like old wine in new bottles, a way of reframing the old projects of measuring law's impact on economy and vice versa, this approach differs in one critical respect.

---

[19] Adelman, Levy, 'The Fall and Rise of Economic History'.

[20] Gautham Rao, *National Duties: Custom Houses and the Making of the American State* (2016), 11 ff; Brian Phillips Murphy, *Building the Empire State: Political Economy in the Early Republic* (2015) 12 ff; Rafe Blaufarb, *The Great Demarcation: The French Revolution and the Invention of Modern Property* (2016) 1 ff; Anne Fleming, 'The Borrower's Tale: A History of Poor Debtors in Lochner Era New York City' (2012) 30 *Law and History Review* 1095–8 ff.

It does not assume the separation of law and economy, but rather conceptualizes law 'as' economy and economy as law. Indeed, this approach seeks to undermine claims of separation by revealing the many ways in which law guides economic behaviour, including how law endows material objects with value and allocates the consequences of unexpected changes in those values.

The biggest target for such analysis is 'capitalism', the historical study of which has taken on new urgency in the wake of the global financial crisis of 2008. As Samuel Moyn urged in his review of Thomas Piketty's *Capital*, there is a danger in treating capitalism or any economic system as though it were guided by an intrinsic law or logic that exists apart from legal institutions. Although 'we now talk about "capitalism" as a matter of convenience', Moyn explained, 'we cannot make the mistake of regarding it as a domain where necessary laws like those of gravity or thermodynamics apply'. Rather than treating capitalism as a self-governing system that is merely channelled by law, Moyn encouraged scholars instead to 'recover the legal choices that created the illusion of a monolithic capitalism with its inexorable necessities in the first place'.[21]

Within capitalism or any other political economic system, there are also smaller targets for critical historical study, which include objects and ideas that are so foundational to modern economic exchange that they may appear to be creatures of the market, existing apart from law. Recent work on the history of money exemplifies how historians can undermine such appearances. Christine Desan's research on the 'reinvention' of money in early modern England, for example, chronicles a revolution that has since 'disappeared from view'. It aims to puncture the 'myth' that money emerges from exchange, rather than from legal engineering. Money is 'neither public nor private in a categorical sense', Desan concludes. In her study of 'stuff and money' during the French Revolution, Rebecca Spang similarly finds that the value of money depended on the relationships between its users, rather than inhering in the item deemed to be currency. Her goal is 'to estrange and denaturalize money, thereby restoring it to history'. Jonathan Levy's recent work likewise estranges economic 'risk' and gives it a history, showing along the way how nineteenth-century American law provided a means for individuals to manage fluctuations in the value of the stuff of capitalism, such as cargo, commodities, land, and labour. These projects all show the value of cracking open systems that, as Spang described, now appear 'fixed or made once and for all', but that were not always so.[22]

---

[21] Jennifer Schuessler, 'In History Departments, It's Up With Capitalism', *The New York Times*, 6 April 2013; Samuel Moyn, 'Thomas Piketty and the Future of Legal Scholarship' (2014) 128 *Harvard L.R. Forum* 51–2 ff.

[22] Christine Desan, *Making Money: Coin, Currency, and the Coming of Capitalism* (2015) 1, 6–8 ff; Jonathan Levy, *Freaks of Fortune: The Emerging World of Capitalism and Risk in America* (2012); Rebecca L. Spang, *Stuff and Money in the Time of the French Revolution* (2015) 6 ff.

Future work on the history of political economy could move in a variety of productive directions, including those discussed in this chapter. For legal historians undertaking work at the border between legal and economic history, it is not imperative that they seek to answer one of the questions presented here. What will best advance the field is research that clearly identifies the questions it seeks to answer and explains why the answers to those questions matter. The common thread running through the projects described above is that they aim to break down the law/economy distinction that structures contemporary thinking about the relationship between the state and the market and guides some policy-making. Although animated by concerns about the present, these projects are not 'presentist'—they do not use modern values and perspectives in interpreting the past. Rather, they seek to answer questions about the past that could unsettle present-day thinking about the relationship between law and the economic dimensions of society. The answers will matter to those working in the borderland between legal and economic history. As importantly, they may also matter to those who are not.

Bibliography

Jeremy Adelman, *Republic of Capital: Buenos Aires and the Legal Transformation of the Atlantic World* (Stanford University Press, 1999)

Rafe Blaufarb, *The Great Demarcation: The French Revolution and the Invention of Modern Property* (Oxford University Press, 2016)

Sally H. Clarke, *Trust and Power: Consumers, the Modern Corporation, and the Making of the United States Automobile Market* (Cambridge University Press, 2007)

Christine Desan, *Making Money: Coin, Currency, and the Coming of Capitalism* (Oxford University Press, 2015)

Catherine L. Fisk, *Working Knowledge: Employee Innovation and the Rise of Corporate Intellectual Property, 1800–1930* (University of North Carolina Press, 2009)

William E. Forbath, *Law and the Shaping of the American Labor Movement* (Harvard University Press, 1991)

Ron Harris, *Industrializing English Law: Entrepreneurship and Business Organization, 1720–1844* (Cambridge University Press, 2010)

Morton J. Horwitz, *The Transformation of American Law, 1780–1860* (Harvard University Press, 1977)

James Willard Hurst, *Law and Economic Growth: The Legal History of the Lumber Industry in Wisconsin, 1836–1915* (Belknap Press of Harvard University Press, 1964)

Richard R. John, *Network Nation: Inventing American Telecommunications* (Belknap Press of Harvard University Press, 2010)

Ajay K. Mehrotra, *Making the Modern American Fiscal State: Law, Politics, and the Rise of Progressive Taxation, 1877–1929* (Cambridge University Press, 2013)

William J. Novak, *The People's Welfare: Law and Regulation in Nineteenth-Century America* (University of North Carolina Press, 1996)

Dylan C. Penningroth, *The Claims of Kinfolk: African American Property and Community in the Nineteenth-Century South* (University of North Carolina Press, 2003)

Christopher L. Tomlins, *Freedom Bound: Law, Labor, and Civic Identity in Colonizing English America, 1580–1865* (Cambridge University Press, 2010)

Victoria Saker Woeste, *The Farmer's Benevolent Trust: Law and Agricultural Cooperation in Industrial America, 1865–1945* (University of North Carolina Press, 1998)

CHAPTER 13

FEMININITIES AND MASCULINITIES

LOOKING BACKWARD AND MOVING FORWARD IN CRIMINAL LEGAL HISTORICAL GENDER RESEARCH

CAROLYN STRANGE

I. INTRODUCTION

LAW demarcates. Law bifurcates, slicing the impermissible from the permissible; simultaneously it designates who may and may not enjoy its protections and suffer its consequences. Certain laws on the books make explicit sex distinctions, but gender norms find their way into law's application and its language of putative neutrality. In polities that adhere to the rule of law, criminal statutes and codes narrate the preamble to this fundamental fiction each time they proclaim: 'everyone' who commits X prohibited act is guilty of offence Y and subject to punishment Z. Feminists began in the late eighteenth century to call out this fiction and to identify the disparities of sex, which law both imposed and obscured. Every branch of law has been attacked subsequently on grounds of sex discrimination; despite this, feminists and their allies continue to look to the law to rectify inequity. Their opponents, meanwhile, cling to law as an anchor in the gender order of male domination, even though that anchor drags along the policing and punishment of men, often more intense and severe than the surveillance and sanctions women face. Law is awash with gender.

Through its texts and technologies, law imagines and acts on men and women, and in this sense law also produces gender. Accordingly, when scholars uncover and interrogate the distinctions legal processes bring about between the feminine and the masculine and the very conjuring of these categories, we produce gender history. Feminists of the 1970s were the first to erode certainty in the biological and cultural naturalness of male and female characteristics and the unequal distribution of power that attended it. Working in a variety of disciplines, academics blazed trails that have exposed and critiqued the artificiality of these assumptions and the variability of 'masculinity' and 'femininity' across time and place. Critical race theorists and Marxist scholars enriched this analysis by integrating cross-cutting social and economic stratifications. From nowhere on the academic map, gender seemed to be everywhere by the late-twentieth century, sprouting up in new specialist journals devoted to the study of its composition. Women's history lent a solid shoulder to this scholarly turn, leading with studies of family and private life. When the cross-disciplinary study of masculinity emerged in the 1990s it turned an eye to manhood's meanings in crime and greatly enriched the field by questioning the masculine norm in every field of law. The rise of critical legal studies provided an amiable companion along the way, as it nurtured modes of analysis that have prized open the gender politics of law.

Although the legal regulation of marriage, divorce, and child custody has always touched more lives than the criminal law and its connections to policing, prosecution, and punishment, this chapter focuses on the history of criminal justice and the directions future research might take. Family law, with its cast of wives and mothers, husbands and fathers, adulteresses and adulterers, provides a shop of ready-made categories for gender analysis. Historians, such as Michael Grossberg and Jacqueline Jones, have treated them like garments, sold and traded in legal fora, and their superb studies trace the legal regulation of the family to the fabric of economic and social relations, and to the deep dyes of race and religion.[1] Criminal law is different, since with few exceptions, 'anyone' can commit crime. Tracing gender's history calls for scepticism towards criminal law's neutrality and it requires researchers to ask how, why, and to what effect its constitution and applications manifest gender.

Studies of abortion, prostitution, and infanticide have used this approach to great effect, but in this chapter I concentrate on intimate murder and rape

[1] Michael Grossberg, *Governing the Hearth: Law and the Family in Nineteenth-Century America* (1985); Jacqueline Jones, *Labor of Love, Labor of Sorrow: Black Women, Work, and the Family, from Slavery to the Present* (2009).

and compare their study in British and U.S. history. The reason for this tack is threefold. First, research on these crimes pre-dated the feminist shake-up of academic studies, which highlights how this political lens changed the focus from offences to changing configurations of gender. The challenge remains, however, to push beyond identifying sexual differences in law breaking and punishment to address the question: how has the criminal law made gender? Second, since sex is integral to understandings of rape but not to the offence of murder, we can see most clearly how criminal law reads perpetrators and victims in gender terms by focusing on the history of inter-gender homicide and the ways in which historians have interpreted those readings. Third, both of these offences involve violence against the body and call into question the permissible and criminal nature of human aggression and victimhood, a subject enriched in studies that incorporate the concept of multiple masculinities and femininities.

The first section (I) reviews the foundational works and thinking that inserted gender into the study of criminal legal history, setting an ambitious research agenda that remains inspirational. The topic of fatal femininities and masculinities is explored in the second section (II), which considers how feminist scholars and masculinity researchers have shaped our analysis of men and women who murder intimates, in some cases wishing too strongly to identify women killers as gender warriors. The historiography of rape appears in the third section (III), which examines how historians, beginning in the 1970s, came to consider the enduring and historically variable contexts of the crime's perpetration, policing, and punishment. The last section discusses American exceptionalism—among Western advanced democracies the most murderous, and the nation in which race is held out to explain its unique history of rape. The conclusion identifies the challenges that remain and the need to review researchers' reliance on the now-standard intersectional model of gender analysis. A more dynamic analytical approach, better suited to historical research, merits serious consideration as we ponder how best to capitalize on digitized historical sources.

II. The Spade Work of Exploring Criminal Law's Sex Differences and Gender Dimensions

Provocative politics scented the air of the academy in the late-1960s. In this atmosphere historians of Europe and Britain became prime contributors to social history's rise. Founded in 1967, the *Journal of Social History* began to publish work about 'ordinary' people of the past, whose lives could be glimpsed in slave ship bills of lading, medieval burial records, and factory inspectors' reports. Six years after it appeared the journal featured an issue on criminal justice history, and three of the articles focused on the criminal law and expressly considered men's and women's roles. Although none of them referred to 'gender', it would be wrong to strike these early works from its appearance in the building blocks of its legal historiography.[2]

The publication of those works in 1975 marked a turning point when criminal justice historians began in earnest to tackle two new objectives: to contest the mythic timelessness of 'men's crimes' as opposed to women's, and the 'nature' of female versus male criminality; and to attack social, scientific, and behavioural claims about fixed 'sex-roles'. Historians played their part in this era of questioning what it meant to be men and women, and records produced through police reports, criminal indictments, and jail registers left nuggets that could be turned into solid evidence of women's and men's distinct offences and the punishment inflicted upon them or modified through mercy. Some of this material was amendable to quantitative analysis, and historians of the 1970s and 1980s produced ground-breaking studies that showed sex differentiations in offending, prosecutions, and punishments. How could these differences be explained? The question was critical. Prior to the emergence of feminist interventions in the academy, criminal justice historians had simply taken for granted women's innate 'difference' and they failed to question men's near-monopolization of crime, especially violent crime.

Historians made further headway in the 1980s with the journal *Gender and History*, whose founders proclaimed that the 'compensatory phase' of women's history, which gave womanhood a past and affirmed the significance of women actors (on the right side as well as the wrong side of the law), had lost its analytical edge. The feminist history project had to push further and harder if historians were to refine the analysis of gender in the past. Momentum could be revived if historians fully integrated the history of 'race, class, religion, and sexual orientation' and approached men as a sexed category of actors and manhood as a cultural construct. The editors called on this new brand of gender historian to discover and comprehend 'the creation and preservation of feminine and masculine identities, social roles, images, institutions and belief systems . . .'. Deconstructing the binary categories of masculinity and femininity as the means

---

[2] Guido Ruggiero, 'Sexual Criminality in the Early Renaissance: Venice 1338–1358', Carol Z. Wiener, 'Sex Roles and Crime in Late Elizabethan Hertfordshire', and John M. Beattie, 'The Criminality of Women in Eighteenth-Century England'—each appeared in (Summer 1975) 8 *The Journal of Social History* 4 ff.

through which 'gendered identities' were constructed in the past became the prime objective.[3]

Joan Wallach Scott's work, particularly her landmark essay of 1986, 'Gender, a Useful Category of Historical Analysis', informed much of the research that appeared in the field of gender history, which quickly flourished across many sub-disciplines, including criminal justice history. Scott's modest title obscured a proposition that upset many historians averse to her argument: gender discourse was a primary way of lending meaning to all hierarchical relationships. For Scott, gender was a constitutive element of social relationships based on perceived differences between the sexes, and gender was a primary way of 'signifying relationships of power'. The writing of gender history could and did stir up fields (such as diplomatic or military history) that had previously ignored gender. Law was one of those fields, and Scott urged legal historians, no less than others, to approach law as a 'set of practices and doctrines that categorically and unequivocally asserts the meaning of male and female, masculine and feminine'.[4] In the sections that follow I test how far and how effectively legal scholars have followed that prescription for gender history.

III. FATAL FEMININITIES AND MASCULINITIES IN INTIMATE INTER-GENDER HOMICIDE

The history of murder perpetrated by females has always intrigued popular writers, but it took feminist scholars to seek out what it can reveal about femininities of the past. Prior to the 1970s, popular accounts of 'women who kill' portrayed perpetrators as female Bluebeards or criminals 'deadlier than the male'. Then, in 1977, Mary S. Hartman applied academic skills to demonstrate how gender history could be written through the analysis of women accused of murder.[5] 'The Victorian murderess', like her modern counterpart, typically killed within a circle of intimacy. Although they were rare, Hartman used cases of women accused of murder to probe the domestic conditions and economic circumstances their

[3] The Editorial Collective, 'Why Gender and History?' (Spring 1989) 1 *Gender and History* 1, 1–6, 1; 2–3 ff.

[4] Joan W. Scott, 'Gender: A Useful Category of Historical Analysis' (1986) 91 *The American Historical Review* 5, 1053–75, 1073, 1067 ff.

[5] Mary S. Hartman, *Victorian Murderesses* (1977).

crimes exposed in nineteenth-century France and England. The hidden lives and troubles that ordinary women encountered came into view as Hartman examined the private writings and public representations of women accused of killing children, lovers, husbands, and rivals, and she carved out a new way to analyse the salience of sex, class, age, and respectability (masculine as well as feminine) in the Victorian period. Another study of homicidal women, Ann Jones' book on the U.S. from colonial times to the 1970s modified Hartman's approach, based on the premise that women who killed were seen as and treated as 'different' because masculine biases inherent in the criminal law rendered them so.[6] But these killers violated social, cultural, and religious expectations of women as the bearers and nurturers of life, which made them defiant and rebellious in Jones' view. Most provocatively, she claimed that murderesses of the past were akin to the feminists of her own day, who railed against patriarchy. Digging up evidence of the lives and lethal crimes of women in history was also, for Jones, another act of defiance.

Until the intersection of feminist and masculinities studies, histories of murder failed to make a question of gender and its changing constitution and meanings. The impact of feminist analysis on murders perpetrated by men cross-fertilized with the rise of masculinities studies in the 1980s and 1990s, with path-breaking results. Using case studies, historians have clearly shown that legal latitude towards men who killed wives who disobeyed or deserted them hinged on the sort of man a defendant appeared to be in the eyes of the men who judged him. Angus McClaren set a landmark in this field when he published *The Trials of Masculinity*, which integrated feminist approaches to the study of sexual deviance with R. W. Connell's explication of hegemonic and subordinated masculinities.[7] Adapting this plural model, McLaren argued that 'dominant forms of masculinity were constituted out of a set of "negative" varieties', which the criminal law, alongside medical and psychiatric authorities, defined, providing a foil for the normal man, whom men were meant to be.[8] The chivalrous feelings male jurors often expressed when they considered cases of females charged with murder found their parallel in masculine sympathies towards the cuckold, but not so much the coward or the brute. Gender impressions mattered as much for men as for women.

Longitudinal analysis of murder and its prosecution proves that the frequency and standards of judgment of murder have changed over time, even if statutory definitions of the legal criteria for judgment have remained essentially the same. Randolph Roth's mammoth study of murder in U.S. history showed that rates of

---

[6] Ann Jones, *Women Who Kill* (1980). The book has been republished numerous times, most recently an expanded 'anniversary' edition, published by the Feminist Press in 2009.

[7] Angus McLaren, *The Trials of Masculinity: Policing Sexual Boundaries, 1870–1930* (1997); Raewyn Connell, *Masculinities* (1995).

[8] McLaren (n. 7) 10 ff.

marital homicide spiked in the early to mid nineteenth century, which 'correlated with a shift in the balance of power between men and women and with changes in feelings and beliefs associated with marriage and romance'.[9] Ironically, improving conditions for women—greater access to education, law reform that preserved women's property in marriage, and temperance politics that raised marital cruelty into divorce statutes, coupled with increasing investment in the companionate model of marriage—led to higher rates of femicide in France and Britain as well as the U.S. Unrequited love and dashed hopes of heterosexual happiness inspired literature, art, and music in the romantic age, but men's anguish was also narrated in homicide trial transcripts. Men who killed their female partners or lovers were enraged at the changing configuration of gender relations in those countries, while in other parts of the world, where conservative masculine and feminine models held, the intimate femicide rate did not rise.

For historical actors, statistics tracking a rise in marital and intimate murders starting in the early nineteenth century did not convey such impressions: trials of inter-gender intimate violence did. Domestic homicides offer prime fodder for cultural production—confessions, love letters, lithographs and photographs, ballads, testimony, judgments—which confound the distinctions scholars sometimes draw between legal, political, and social dimensions of gender. By the mid-nineteenth century, murder in the family circle, when perpetrated by sons, husbands, and fathers, cast a shadow over the emergent sentimental ideal. Prosecutors urged jurors to punish transgressors of this ideal, the rare woman who killed a husband as well as the men increasingly expected to play their part in the domestic bargain. Karen Halttunen's brilliant analysis of men's storied intimate murders in nineteenth-century America points out that popular accounts allowed readers to 'have it both ways': an invitation to denounce 'outmoded patriarchy' and an opportunity to enjoy an 'illicit appeal to a cultural backlash against companionate marriage'.[10]

Masculinities, like femininities, change and shift in part through the crimes that come to law's attention, and historians agree that the late nineteenth and early twentieth century was a time of flux. But murder in the twentieth century tends to be the province of historical criminologists, rather than historians, whose work from the medieval period to the nineteenth century still forms the backbone of scholarship. Does this make a difference in questions, methods, or sources?

The legacy of masculinist criminology has been weightier than the traditions of 'men's' history, which social history productively undermined from the 1960s. Carol Smart, Frances Heidensohn, Nicole Hahn Rafter, and Elizabeth Stanko led the feminist attack on social scientists who wrote about homicide oblivious to the gender dynamics of lethal violence, yet fixated on race and class as explanatory

---

[9] Randolph Roth, *American Homicide* (2009) 251 ff.

[10] Karen Halttunen, *Murder Most Foul: The Killer and the American Gothic Imagination* (1998) 161–2 ff.

factors behind patterns of offending and punishment.[11] The power of numbers provides one explanation. Women across many jurisdictions have historically committed only about 10 per cent of murders, and a significant majority of men's murders have involved killings of other men. But cultural criminologists consider the very rarity of the female killer—the statistical outlier—and the men who killed spouses or girlfriends as subgroups that allow for comparisons to be made with the male-on-male murder norm. By the 1990s, criminologists, notably James W. Messerschmidt, pioneered the field of critical masculinity and crime studies, which focused on criminal offending as one of the ways in which men 'accomplish' masculinity, particularly, but not exclusively, marginalized men.[12]

In feminist research on women who kill, the opposite interpretation lingers in the image of the homicidal woman as 'doubly deviant'. This sociological term was used to describe moral and legal offending at large until the 1980s, when criminologists and other social scientists, including psychologists and women's studies scholars, began to apply it to define the female offender as transgressor of gender norms in addition to the criminal law. This adaptation is surprising, since the concept arguably reinforces Cesare Lombroso's description of the female offender as the criminal who defies her natural destiny as the nurturer of life.[13] The term has proven remarkably sticky. For instance, in the publisher's blurb for Lizzie Seal's 2010 study of female killers and their representations in twentieth-century England, we read that homicidal women 'rupture our assumptions about what a woman is'.[14]

Because references to double deviance still dot studies of women's lethal violence, not men's, two problems emerge. First, it supports Jones' politics of validating women's use of lethal violence as an antidote against sexism, especially compounded by racism, homophobia, and classism. The notoriety of female killers provides a rich source to analyse the criminal legal 'doing' of gender. This was the great contribution made in 1987 by sociologists West and Zimmerman, when they set an agenda for the study of gender's contestation and disruption, as well as its constitution in social interaction.[15] The subsequent call by Judith Butler to 'undo' gender may provide a way to imagine a future without sexed binaries, but it works poorly as an historian's cookie cutter on women's murders, stamping their lethal

---

[11] Carol Smart, *Women, Crime, and Criminology: A Feminist Critique* (1976); Frances Heidensohn, *Women and Crime* (1985); Nicole Hahn Rafter, Elizabeth Stanko (eds.), *Judge, Lawyer, Victim, Thief: Women, Gender Roles, and Criminal* Justice (1982).

[12] James W. Messerschmidt, *Masculinities and Crime: Critique and Reconceptualization of Theory* (1993).

[13] Shani D'Cruze, Sandra Walklate, Samantha Pegg (eds.), *Murder: Social and Historical Approaches to Understanding Murder and Murderers* (2006) 41 ff.

[14] Lizzie Seal, *Women, Murder and Femininity: Gender Representations of Women Who Kill* (2010). For the blurb, see: <http://www.palgrave.com/us/book/9780230222755> (accessed 12 June 2017).

[15] Candace West, Don H. Zimmerman, 'Doing Gender' (1987) 1 *Gender and Society* 125–51 ff.

violence (but not men's) as challenges to oppression.[16] Researchers who succumb to this temptation tread a murky moral path. Secondly, the deployment of the 'double' metaphor enervates inquiry into the multiple femininities that individual crimes can spin under distinct historical circumstances. Ironically, the legal history of women who kill is still playing catch-up to the most sophisticated histories of men's lethal violence, such as McLaren's. Multiple masculinities and femininities lurk in the commission, policing, prosecution, punishment, and representations of murder. It is our task, as historians, to ferret them out for the purpose of dissection.

IV. RAPE: MEN AS MONSTERS, WOMEN AS VICTIMS?

The first body of legal historical research on rape was constructed by lawyers working with black letter law. Internalist legal histories looked to case law, statutes, and law reports for evidence of authoritative pronouncements, which set standards of proof and sewed in pockets of defence.[17] Dry as they are, these works provided essential stepping stones that allowed historians to move beyond considering how law thinks, to question what has made law and what law has *made* in the realm of gender relations. Equally, they document what law disregarded as its subject at particular points in history. Consider the term 'rapist'. Historian Joanna Bourke notes that statutory definitions of rape date back centuries, while the perpetrator acquired this name only in the late nineteenth century, when the range of deviant sexual identities began to proliferate.[18] In 1894, a medical sage wrote: 'Society is no safer from the rapist, while capacity and will remain with him, than from the wild bull with his horns.'[19] Behind such a statement lie truths and lies that historians have picked apart by asking who fits the definition of 'the' rapist at different times and in different jurisdictions. If rape was a crime that endangered society, what accounts for large gaps between its penalties and the low likelihood of its enforcement? What factors led to the consideration of rape as a crime against the person, rather than an affront to male honour and an attack on

---

[16] Judith Butler, *Undoing Gender* (2004).

[17] The immunity of husbands was outlined by Chief Justice Matthew Hale in 1736 and upheld in England until the mid twentieth century. Matthew Hale, *Historia Placitorum Coronae: The History of the Pleas of the Crown, Volume I* (1736), 629 ff. See also Carolyn A. Conley, 'Sexual Violence in Historical Perspective', in Rosemary Gartner, Bill McCarthy (eds.), *The Oxford Handbook of Gender, Sex, and Crime* (2014) 207–24 ff.

[18] Joanna Bourke, *Rape: Sex, Violence, History* (2007) 11 ff.

[19] Charles Hamilton Hughes, *The Alienist and Neurologist* (1894) 178 ff.

patriarchal investment in female chastity? And how and why did men sometimes use criminal law to snare 'wild bulls'? Stories of persistence and change in masculinities and femininities lie in the answers to these questions.

In the 1970s the historiography of rape was hitched tightly to feminist activism, although it was overtaken by more rigorously academic studies of gender history by the 1980s. The germinal text in this field was Susan Brownmiller's, *Against Our Will: Men, Women, and Rape* (1975).[20] As much an irritant to historians as an inspiration, this radical feminist tome portrayed rape as a tool that has always been wielded for the patriarchal suppression of women. Only a minority of men raped, Brownmiller claimed, but every woman lives in fear of the crime and the sense she requires male protection and control. Historians inspired by the bestseller were almost as unfavourable as those who dismissed it as superficial and hysterical. Brownmiller failed to 'treat rape as a changing social force, as a dynamic in the social, sexual, and legal contexts of specific societies', the first generation of women's historians lamented, but her work produced attempts to give sexual coercion and violence a history that had erstwhile been 'ignored or trivialized'.[21]

Empirical studies soon qualified Brownmiller's claims, particularly the notion that rape is a consequence of male biological 'drives'. In 1986 the provocative question posed by historian Roy Porter—'Rape: Does It Have a Historical Meaning?'— brought out an army of researchers, who loaded themselves with records generated by police, prosecutors, courts, and prisons.[22] Newspapers and other forms of unofficial accounts further confirmed that rape's history has been coloured by shifting understandings of violence, harm, and consent, in addition to changing legal definitions and institutional responses to the crime. Like relations between the sexes more broadly, it is an offence with multiple historical meanings constructed less through statutes than through society and politics.

Scanning beyond the terrain of black letter law, feminist analysts of rape painted landscapes of law in action and law's inaction. This growing body of research outstripped histories of inter-gender murder by the 1980s, but its expansion responded to a distinct problem: historically low prosecution and conviction rates, and the unfathomable depths of unreported sexual assaults historians will never uncover. Large-scale anonymous surveys of female sexual experience, conducted in the 1980s onward by sociologists and criminologists, indicated that rates of assault and sexual abuse were undoubtedly far higher than statistics of documented complaints, and these findings cast further doubt on historic arrest and prosecution records as credible indices of rape's history.

[20] Susan Brownmiller, *Against Our Will: Men, Women, and Rape* (1975).

[21] Heidi I. Hartman, Ellen Ross, 'Comment on "On Writing the History of Rape"' (1978) 3 *Signs* 931–5, 932 ff. Shorter's 'On Writing the History of Rape' appeared in the same issue, 471–82 ff.

[22] Roy Porter, 'Rape: Does It Have a Historical Meaning?', in Sylvana Tomaselli, Roy Porter (eds.), *Rape: An Historical and Cultural Inquiry* (1986) 216–36 ff. For an early rejoinder, see Anna Clark, *Women's Silence, Men's Violence: Sexual Assault in England, 1770–1845* (1987) 2 ff.

Legal researchers continue to puzzle over the reasons for the shadowy history of sexual violence. Mary R. Block's sober observation puts the challenge of recording rape's history in perspective: the historical continuity is 'not knowing how many women are raped'.[23] Most historians and criminologists agree that victims' reluctance to report explains why prosecutions for rape are lower than the likely incidence of the crime. But how to prove this contention historically? Assertions that most women decided not to report assaults are necessarily inferential, since historians must move backwards from the exceptional cases, when women (or frequently their fathers, mothers, or husbands) did bring allegations of rape to the attention of magistrates and prosecutors. Where trial transcripts exist, they typically show that complainants who pressed charges were made to reveal evidence of bodily trauma, submit to examinations conducted by (mostly) male doctors, disposed to define all manner of physical damage as within the range of 'normal' intercourse. And finally, the complainant had to face withering attacks on her character and reputation in full court before neighbours, community members, and the press. The historian's surprise lies in finding cases that did not end in acquittals or lesser charges, such as attempted rape or indecent assault.

Did guilty verdicts, no matter how rare, give victims of sexual violence some confidence that their stories might stand up in court if they reported them? Historians of rape have been hesitant to ask this question directly for the sound reason that it cannot be answered definitely. Although trials that ended in convictions did give 'the rapist' a name and a face, the legal confirmation of 'outrages' perpetrated by a few men did not reduce respect for 'benchmark' men or provoke resistance to masculine hegemony until the 1970s. Nevertheless, every conviction record provides evidence that some male police agents, prosecutors, jurors, and judges were prepared to place some sexually violent men beyond the pale. Questioning why that readiness has varied, over time and between jurisdictions, is amenable to empirical research.

The penal frame of rape changed significantly from the eighteenth century, when it was a mandatory or optional capital crime in most Western jurisdictions, to the latter nineteenth century, when most jurisdictions in the Anglo-American sphere substituted less drastic penalties and produced more statutory subdivisions with an assortment of sanctions. In Victorian Britain, the reduction of rape from a capital to non-capital offence in 1841 was followed by an increase in the conviction rate. Historian Martin Wiener documented that approximately half of men prosecuted for rape between the 1840s and 1900 were convicted, whereas jurors in the early nineteenth century found fewer than 20 per cent of accused rapists guilty.[24] Did the

---

[23] Mary R. Block, 'Rape Law in 19th-Century America: Some Thoughts and Reflections on the State of the Field' (2009) 7 *History Compass* 5 1391–9, 1393 ff.

[24] Martin Wiener, *Men of Blood: Violence, Manliness and Criminal Justice in Victorian England* (2006) 147–8 ff.

women of the latter period, whose testimony led to the conviction of their alleged sexual attackers, feel a greater sense of justice than their earlier counterparts felt, after going through the process of laying complaints and testifying in trials that resulted in acquittals? It is difficult to imagine otherwise. But historians differ in their explanations of this shift. For Wiener, the 'civilizing offensive', manned by politicians and prosecutors determined to punish perpetrators, benefited women, so he deems it 'quite insufficient to simply characterize [the nineteenth century] as an age of "patriarchy"'.[25] Feminist historians disagreed and accused Wiener of tilting at the shadow Brownmiller cast, not the sophisticated histories she inspired. As Shani D'Cruze emphasizes, the growing number of 'men of blood' convicted in criminal courts cloaked 'everyday' sexual violence and more sharply defined the standards of sexual respectability expected of women deemed to be credible victims.[26] Despite these differences in interpretation, studies produced in the early 2000s increased scholars' awareness that the history of rape's criminal prosecution brings multiple masculinities into being, in the types of men accused of and sometimes convicted of rape and the men who policed, prosecuted, judged, punished, and treated perpetrators of sexual violence. Until the very recent past, both the dismissal of rape as a crime and its recognition as such have turned on men's judgment of men.

The early twentieth century saw new sources of authority emerge in the identification and diagnosis of sexual offenders, including 'the rapist'. Historical criminology and studies of sexology have shown that a treatment approach to sexual transgressors grew alongside changes in the criminal law.[27] Psychology and psychiatry added new categories of 'others', including sadists and psychopaths, branded as 'dangerous offenders', for whom especially long penal sentences and medical interventions, including castration, were prescribed. Early psychological writings turned bestial sexual aggressors and the monsters of the past into subjects of expert discourse. Beginning in the 1980s criminologists and historical sociologists incorporated the treatment of alleged rapists within incisive accounts of net-widening and the coercive power of deviant labelling.[28] Yet, subsequent studies have shown that expert interventions compounded persistent power imbalances, starting with but not ending with gender, which continued informally to authorize, encourage, facilitate, and cover up sexual assault, most notably rape committed in the context of marriage. Again, it was feminist agitation late in the twentieth century, not expertise on the part of 'psy' professionals, which brought this form of rape into the sphere of criminal law.[29]

---

[25] Ibid., 77 ff.

[26] Shani D'Cruze (ed.), *Everyday Violence in Britain, 1850–1950: Gender and Class* (2000) xi ff.

[27] Lucy Bland, Laura Doan (eds.), *Sexology in Culture: Labelling Bodies and Desires* (1998).

[28] David Rothman, *Conscience and Convenience: The Asylum and Its Alternatives in Progressive America* (1980).

[29] Clare McGlynn, Vanessa E. Munro (eds.), *Rethinking Rape Law: International and Comparative Perspectives* (2010).

Differences in the prosecution and punishment of sexual assault reaffirm that rape has a history, or more precisely, histories. This accords legal historical analysis an important role in combating both the tacit acceptance of sexual aggression's inevitability (rape is an evolutionary mechanism in human males, who like their animal counterparts, are driven to impregnate females of the species), and the stance that patriarchy is to blame, the dismantling of which will spell the end of rape. The first makes men dangerous automatons; the second holds out false hope. Even if we allow that the historical incidence of rape is likely much higher than the historical record can document, it has never been a ubiquitous male practice. Equally, rises and falls in prosecution and conviction rates have occurred without evidence of shifts in patriarchal institutions or social systems. Finally, higher conviction rates have not arisen from improvements in the status of women. Instead, they have included the criminalization of consensual heterosexuality; they have corresponded frequently with sweeps against other forms of prohibited sexuality, notably homosexual encounters, whether consensual or not; and the policing and punishment of rape has provided a vehicle for the stigmatization and terrorization of entire communities. Individual patriarchs, as well as the courts, have resorted to violence to punish rape, and culturally, socially, and politically entrenched patriarchy has coexisted comfortably with sexual assault, as long as only some sorts of offenders are convicted, typically strangers, youth, and men of the underclass.

The changing character and power of patriarchy play pivotal roles in rape's history, but historical analysis must always place it in an ensemble cast of contingency. The same imperative applies to the history of inter-gender homicide. In studying both of these offences, historians of the U.S. have asserted claims, implied and formal, of exceptionalism. The next section considers and questions those claims, pointing to the need for new questions and approaches.

V. AMERICAN EXCEPTIONALISM AND MURDER

The unique colonial and national history of the U.S. makes it an outlier in the history of murder and rape. In contrast to comparable liberal democracies of the modern era, the rate of murder has been high, particularly firearms-related homicides, and it has greatly exceeded the rate in other countries, at least since the American Civil War. The history of rape in the U.S. is also exceptional due to its linkage with slavery and the nature of racism that transformed, rather than attenuated, racial discrimination after emancipation. One benefit of this approach is the attention scholars of American history have brought to national and local cultures and to the unsettling association of violence and liberty embodied in American masculinities. In U.S. criminal justice scholarship, anti-racist politics in the 1980s exposed the inadequacy of exclusively gender-focused research, and researchers made a convincing case for an 'intersectional' approach to the study of violence and victimization.[30] However, American research paid less heed to convictions of men for intimate partner violence and the post-sentencing fate of convicted offenders, which is necessary to chart fully the changing relationship of gender and murder.[31] Did the means and frequency of inter-gender homicide in America produce nationally distinct femininities and masculinities? Macro-level studies that use 'the nation' as their frame may well turn out to obscure more than they disclose unless we design research to challenge what we think we know.

Certainty that homicide—American-style—has distinct features arises from the formally and informally acknowledged defences to murder in the nation's history.[32] The motives for inter-gender lethal violence, however, appear to have been widely shared across states and regions with varying levels of tolerance towards lethal aggression.[33] Over the nineteenth century, a man who faced a murder conviction for killing the paramour of his wife or lover stood a good chance of an acquittal or conviction on a lesser charge of manslaughter, even if he had stalked his victim. Most of the men who benefited from this allowance for masculine wounded pride were Anglo-Americans—middling sorts up to prominent figures. Despite the prejudices against Irish and, later, Southern European immigrants in the urban Northeast and Midwest, men who killed other men to protect their own or their family's honour could strike sympathetic hearts among the jurors who determined their fates. In the South, this culture of masculine honour defence in the wake of romantic disappointment or rivalry with a challenger was significantly more potent and enduring. Thus, the 'criminalisation of men' in the late-nineteenth century, which saw male jurors take a firmer stance against masculine violence in England, did not seize American jurors, despite concerted lobbying by first-wave feminists against men's use of violence to control women's behaviour. Nevertheless, Randolph Roth's research shows that in cases where jealous husbands and lovers killed wives and girlfriends, common factors appear to have been at play: the reputation of the couple; the standing of both in their communities; and the degree to which the alleged perpetrator could be seen as a

[30] Kimberlé Crenshaw, 'Mapping the Margins: Intersectionality, Identity Politics, and Violence against Women of Color' (1991) 43 *Stanford Law Review* 6 1241–79 ff.

[31] Carolyn B. Ramsey, 'Intimate Homicide: Gender and Crime Control, 1880–1920' (2006) 77 *University of Colorado Law Review* 101–93 ff.

[32] In 2006, to honour the work of historical criminologist Eric Monkkonen, the *American Historical Review* published a forum on the 'problem of American homicide'.

[33] Pieter Spierenburg, *A History of Murder: Personal Violence in Europe from the Middle Ages to the Present* (2008).

community member or outsider—factors evident in inter-gender murder across time and jurisdiction.[34]

The maxim of 'no duty to retreat', both historic and enduring in American criminal law, provides rich potential for the study of inter-gender homicide, but the stand-out study of the subject paid surprisingly little attention to masculinities and made no reference to femininities. Although Richard Maxwell Brown's 1992 classic framed the concept as one that reflected 'American history and society', women appear in this text only as what men fought over. Still, Brown was on the right track, helping to expose what that duty can tell us about gender, lethal violence, and the law in operation. In 1906, in an address before the American Bar Association, a Louisiana lawyer decried this form of American lawlessness, allowed by jurors and judges who believed men had the right to slay 'the seducer of a virgin' or the 'traducer of a woman unless he apologizes'.[35] The 1881 assassination of President James A. Garfield by Guiteau, a man whose defence lay in the assassin's alleged insanity, disinclined American juries (in contrast to European judges), to consider psychiatric readings of defendants' states of mind credible.[36] Yet they were more likely to turn to masculine readings of provocation and justification. The lawlessness that flared into mob violence in the Jim Crow era also doused the flames of criminal charges against men who stood their ground—but not just any men.

Race, as ever, mattered. In the time of slavery and the decades following emancipation, white supremacists dictated that African Americans had a duty to retreat, especially if they made any move against white men's interest in 'their own' women. But murder, everywhere, tends to occur within social groups, especially inter-gender homicides. Elizabeth Dale stresses that legal formalism was slow to solidify, even in major metropolises, such as Chicago and New York, as much as Black and immigrant groups might have wished that were the case.[37] Black men tried before white juries had much to fear from the strict application of law if they stood accused of killing women from their own communities. They also faced the greater prospect than their white counterparts of execution if convicted. Historians have begun to study evidence of high rates of spousal murder in oppressed groups. The statistics must be treated carefully but they cannot be ignored, lest we obscure the gender dynamics of murder within communities burdened by racism. In early twentieth-century New Orleans, for instance, Jeffrey Adler has connected extraordinarily high levels of intimate homicide to extreme poverty and exclusion from legal and political rights. Importantly, his work shows that class played a great role, since lethal conflicts over patriarchal household authority were lowest in Black

[34] Randolph Roth, *American Homicide* (2009) 257–9 ff.

[35] Richard M. Brown, *No Duty to Retreat: Violence and Values in American History and Society* (1992) 156 ff.

[36] Charles E. Rosenberg, *The Trial of the Assassin Guiteau: Psychiatry and Law in the Gilded Age* (1968).

[37] Elizabeth Dale, 'Getting Away with Murder' (2007) 111 *American Historical Review* 1 95–103 ff.

households where men earned higher incomes and attained greater security. By controlling for class, Adler found that in white homes, as well as those of African Americans, male rage over wives' infidelity, quarrelsomeness, or refusal to fulfil their duties frequently led to lethal violence.[38]

Women kill, too, and their male partners (along with infants) have been the prime targets of their wrath. Having already reviewed the pioneering work by Jones in this field, it is worth noting that few American historians draw attention to anything peculiar about the national character of women's inter-gender homicides outside the framework of race and sexual orientation.[39] There was no female 'duty to retreat', and masculine chivalry, rather than 'the unwritten law', is generally accepted as the cause for high levels of acquittal for women who killed abusive husbands. Closer attention to all cases in which women were convicted and executed for murdering their spouses will encompass the multiple femininities homicide prosecutions produced, without lapsing into the trope of double deviancy. The murder of William Druse, a white farmer in upstate New York, provides an example. In 1886 his wife, Roxalana, and his daughter, Mary, were charged with the crime. At the mother's trial and in the months following her conviction, numerous accounts of extreme marital cruelty circulated, but American suffragists split over the prospect of turning the case into support for their cause. Despite a protracted period of appeals, both legal and political, Mrs. Druse was hanged in 1887.[40] The crime and the penalty were American, but they occurred at a time when masculine chivalry towards the female killer was on the wane in other Anglo-American jurisdictions. By the early twentieth century the so-called 'domestic discount' lost its former value.[41]

The transnational campaign for woman suffrage, protest in favour of equal political personhood, and demands for legal equality had its downside in eroding patriarchal inclinations towards lenience. More comparative studies and transnational analysis, bridging from secondary studies in multiple jurisdictions, will allow us to test the impact of first-wave feminist rights-claiming on the willingness of male jurors to see female perpetrators as murderers, not murderesses. Studies of women's appearance as jurors in criminal trials involving intimate homicide, which occurred primarily in the early to mid twentieth century, will also help to test whether there is anything distinctive in American women's ways of judging the motives that led women to kill.

---

[38] Jeffrey S. Adler, '"I Wouldn't Be No Woman If I Wouldn't Hit Him": Race, Patriarchy, and Spousal Homicide in New Orleans, 1921–1945' (Fall 2015) 27 *Journal of Women's History* 3, 14–36 ff.

[39] Harry Greenlee, Shelia P. Greenlee, 'Women and the Death Penalty: Racial Disparities and Differences' (2008) 14 *William and Mary Journal of Women and the Law* 2, 319–35 ff.

[40] Carolyn Strange, 'The Domestic Empire under Threat in the Empire State: The Execution of Roxalana Druse, 1887', in Mark Finnane (ed.), *A Cultural History of Crime and Punishment in the Age of Empire* (forthcoming, 2018).

[41] David V. Baker, *Women and Capital Punishment in the United States: An Analytical History* (2016).

VI. RAPE: THE QUINTESSENTIAL AMERICAN CRIME?

If one consensus holds in the historiography of rape, it concerns America's unique rape problem, inseparable from the history of slavery and legacies of racism. The statistics are staggering and skewed by gender as well as race. Hodes found that two thirds of the men indicted for rape or related charges in the eighteenth century were Black, Indian, or transient foreigners; Block's study revealed that 80 per cent of the men executed for rape in early America were Black and 95 per cent of the accusers were white females.[42] Little changed by the twentieth century: 90 per cent of the men executed for rape in the U.S. between 1930 and 1964 were African American.[43] These disproportionate figures demand attention to the harm of racism, given deadly force through law's violence towards Black alleged rapists. And studies of extra-legal violence in the form of lynching document how accusations of rape authorized white terrorism.[44] However, the comprehension of gender in the history of rape will deepen as more historians explore the minority of cases in which African American men received fair trials and trials that show that some white complainants' low reputations mattered more to jurors than the colour of the accused's skin. Masculine bonds occasionally formed when jurors, judges, and governors regarded charges of rape as malicious or baseless. Statistical analysis is not equipped to explain such rarities. Indeed, it treats such cases as insignificant.

Close readings of individual trials indicate that the frequency of Black men's exoneration in rape cases has varied over time, which suggests that economic, social, and political modifications of gender and race are prone to change. When the value of enslaved males exceeded white men's concerns about threats to white womanhood, white masters frequently spoke on their behalf, paying for their defence and petitioning for pardons, as Vivienne Miller shows in her study of Florida during the Progressive Era.[45] The labour value of the Black male worker to propertied whites, who categorized them as investments, waned after emancipation, but the socially valued Black man did not disappear in the white-dominated economy. The good 'Negro', like the 'good native' in colonial contexts, could attract support from dominant men, particularly in cases involving

---

[42] Martha Hodes, *White Women, Black Men: Illicit Sex in the 19th-Century South* (1997) 1–6 ff; Sharon Block, *Rape and Sexual Power in Early America* (2005) 164 ff.

[43] John D'Emilio, Estelle B. Freedman, *Intimate Matters: A History of Sexuality in America* (2nd edn., 1998) 297 ff.

[44] Amy Louise Wood, *Lynching and Spectacle: Witnessing Racial Violence in America, 1890–1940* (2009).

[45] Vivienne M. L. Miller, *Crime, Sexual Violence, and Clemency: Florida's Pardon Board and Penal System in the Progressive Era* (2000).

complainants of dubious sexual reputation. In some jurisdictions, such as Virginia in the early twentieth century, historians have found that three quarters of Black men accused of rape were neither executed nor lynched.[46] Evidence of this nature needs to be woven into wider studies, to incorporate analysis of cases in which white jurors convicted white men of rape.[47]

Is the choice to emphasize race over gender, or gender over race, an intellectual or political one? The fractured and fraying politics of race relations in the U.S. suggests the latter. Yet, scholars of sexual violence are necessarily in the business of exhuming and examining uncomfortable truths. When we disclose evidence of fluctuating conviction rates over time or contrasts between states we must account for them, just as we needed to explore patriarchy's multiple dimensions, which have included the protection as well as oppression of women. Most recently, Estelle Freedman has grasped the nettle in her landmark study of sexual violence in U.S. history as a phenomenon that opens up broader questions concerning struggles over citizenship. Although she focuses on the late nineteenth and early twentieth centuries, when women's claims to citizenship and Jim Crow segregation and lynching terror coincided, her study demonstrates that for most of U.S. history, struggles for gender and racial justice have been divided, antagonistically so. Most significantly, Freedman underlines that African American women remain the least studied victims of rape, exceptionally vulnerable and exceptionally rare in the registers of criminal indictments.[48]

A. Where to from Here? Striking a Chord for Future Research

In 2013, when Freedman published her history of rape in the United States, she acknowledged the impact that Brownmiller's book made on her decision to tackle the subject anew. Similarly, Lizzie Seal's work on representations of women murderers in twentieth-century Britain acknowledges her debt to Hartman.[49] Four decades of feminist history, incorporating interdisciplinary scholarship on femininities and masculinities in and through criminal justice, has altered the historiographical landscape without losing site of its scholarly bedrock. Nevertheless, significant shifts have occurred. In the early 1990s, it was common for British and European

---

[46] Lisa Lindquist Dorr, *White Women, Rape, and the Power of Race in Virginia, 1900–1960* (2004) 22–4 ff.

[47] Carolyn A. Conley, 'Sexual Violence in Historical Perspective', in Rosemary Gartner, Bill McCarthy (eds.), *The Oxford Handbook of Gender, Sex and Crime* (2014) 207–24, 12 ff.

[48] Estelle B. Freedman, *Redefining Rape: Sexual Violence in the Era of Suffrage and Segregation* (2013) 27–8 ff.

[49] Seal (n. 14) 65 ff.

scholars to emphasize class in relation to norms of femininity in the historiography of women who kill, but ethnicity, race, sexual identity, and nationality have become the standard 'filters' the feminist legal researcher carries into the archive. Although the racialized rapist remains nationally distinct, the 'doubly' deviant murderess appears finally to be dead.

New possibilities for scholarship abound through the mass digitization of historical records, which has taken off since the Proceedings of the Old Bailey Online became searchable in the late twentieth century.[50] Thanks to genealogist-led campaigns to digitize newspapers, census records, and their preparedness to search for skeletons in family closets, new evidence emerges daily. Freedman, for instance, could not have conducted large-scale data analysis of trials involving adult males and under-age females until local newspapers across the U.S. became searchable online. Her systematic analysis confirmed that jurors were prepared to believe victims who had reached their mid-teens if they were white; however, jurors convicted men accused of sexually assaulting African American girls only if they were young children.[51] The researchers who first charted legal history research on gender and crime could not have posed the question behind Freedman's finding. What new questions await articulation? Data mining now allows us to probe subtle shifts in historical understandings of murder—over the course of a trial, appeals, and punishment, and over time, in the case of notorious murders, the significance of which can reverberate across decades. Using this approach, it is possible to produce fine-grained analysis of differences between the reportage and editorials that appear in newspapers, pamphlets, plays, and fictionalized accounts.[52] The quality of such studies continues to depend on vigilance against confirmation bias and openness to contradiction and complexity.

Research on topics as profound as rape and murder requires fearless and faithful study of the ways criminal justice processes made gender, and much else. To do so necessitates greater readiness to consider women who killed as culpable killers; to document cases in which women sexually assaulted males; to study cases in which men were falsely accused of rape; to incorporate the motivations of men ready to punish their fellow men, and embrace the rule of law over the unwritten script of masculine solidarity. More studies of the post-conviction disposition of criminal cases will also extend and deepen the field. In capital cases the pronouncement of a death sentence was a prelude, not a finale, to the process of criminal justice. The workings of the royal prerogative and administrative discretionary justice show how petitioners, freed from the rules of evidence, played freely with gender

---

[50] 'Old Bailey Online—About This Project—Central Criminal Court' (*Oldbaileyonline.org*, 2017) <https://www.oldbaileyonline.org/static/Project.jsp> (accessed 12 June 2017).

[51] Freedman (n. 48) 99–102 ff.

[52] Carolyn Strange, Daniel McNamara, Ian Wood, Joshua Wodak, 'Mining for the Meanings of a Murder: The Impact of OCR Quality on the Use of Digitized Historical Newspapers' (2014) 8 *Digital Humanities Quarterly* 1 ff.

tropes in anticipation of stirring the sympathies of decision makers.[53] Another promising line of research concerns rape in war, the study of which requires researchers to press beyond the confines of civilian criminal justice.[54] Scholarship in this field confirms that historians make their most significant contribution to public discourse when we demonstrate the historical variability of the seemingly intractable crimes of rape and murder. Some institutions, policies, and customs are conducive to their commission; others militate against their likelihood. Explicit or not, gender pervades these patterns.

Finally, the visual notion of gender's 'intersection' with demographic, social, and individual factors is due for a rethink as an analytical aid in criminal justice historical research. Kimberlé Crenshaw's influential methodological tool liberated the study of gender from the cul-de-sac of 'patriarchy', and it opened up space to consider multiple femininities and masculinities.[55] But every metaphor imposes its own rules of thought. To envision an intersection (of race, class, ethnicity, religion, age, etc.) with gender implies a main street; yet, which roads transect or widen? When we attempt to chart gender's intersectionality we act as post-hoc urban planners, describing this avenue of racism, that lane of class, and so forth. Furthermore, the tool is better suited to describe gridlock than to analyse change. What might researchers gain by substituting a sonic metaphor? As music theorist Jeremy S. Begbie explains, sounds, unlike visual entities, can occupy 'the same space while remaining audibly distinct'. Applying this understanding requires us to listen out for each crime's distinct chord and to the more complex chords associated with particular jurisdictions and periods. When themes and variations become apparent, the scope for comparative studies of gender and crime widens. Although high-profile cases make themselves heard above others in their own time, their recordings can be revisited and appreciated with new questions in mind. We need only consider the Jack the Ripper murders or the Lizzie Borden case to appreciate how some crimes and trials produce overtones that resonate long after historical events take place. Gender may or may not be the keynote to the interpretation of any crime, even in cases of rape and inter-gender violence, and the historian need not choose between gender and other factors. Again, by thinking sonically we acknowledge that simultaneous sounds do not 'cut each other off or obscure each other'; rather, they register '*through* each other'.[56] This, then, is the challenge for future criminal justice researchers: to analyse the historically dynamic 'interpenetration' of gender amidst changing timbres and accents of power.

---

[53] Peter King, *Crime, Justice, and Discretion in England 1740–1820* (2000).

[54] Carol Rittner, John K. Roth (eds.), *Rape: Weapon of War and Genocide* (2012).

[55] On the development and wider application of the metaphor, see <http://www.law.columbia.edu/news/2017/06/kimberle-crenshaw-intersectionality> (accessed 14 March 2018).

[56] Jeremy S. Begbie, *Theology, Music and Time* (2000) 24 ff (emphasis in original).

Bibliography

Mary R. Block, *Rape and Sexual Power in Early America* (University of North Carolina Press, 2005)

Mary R. Block, *Rape Law in 19th-Century America: Some Thoughts and Reflections on the State of the Field* (History Compass, 2009) 7: 1391–9

Joanna Bourke, *Rape: Sex, Violence, History* (Virago, 2007)

Anna Clark, *Women's Silence, Men's Violence: Sexual Assault in England, 1770–1845* (Pandora, 1987)

Carolyn A. Conley, 'Sexual Violence in Historical Perspective', pp. 207–24 in *The Oxford Handbook of Gender, Sex and Crime*, (eds.), R. Gartner, B. McCarthy (Oxford University Press, 2014)

Shani D'Cruze, S. Walklate, S. Pegg (eds.), *Murder: Social and Historical Approaches to Understanding Murder and Murderers* (Willan Publishing, 2006)

Estelle B. Freedman, *Redefining Rape: Sexual Violence in the Era of Suffrage and Segregation* (Harvard University Press, 2013)

Mary S. Hartman, *Victorian Murderesses* (Schocken Books, 1977)

Ann Jones, *Women Who Kill* (Holt, Rinehart and Winston, 1980)

Angus McClaren, *The Trials of Masculinity: Policing Sexual Boundaries, 1870–1930* (University of Chicago Press, 1997)

Carol Rittner, J. K. Roth (eds.), *Rape: Weapon of War and Genocide* (Paragon House, 2012)

Randolph Roth, *American Homicide* (Harvard University Press, 2009)

Joan Wallach Scott, 'Gender: A Useful Category of Historical Analysis' (The American Historical Review (1986) 91: 1053–75

Lizzie Seal, *Women, Murder and Femininity: Gender Representations of Women Who Kill* (Palgrave Macmillan, 2010)

Martin J. Wiener, *Men of Blood: Violence, Manliness and Criminal Justice in Victorian England* (Cambridge University Press, 2006)

CHAPTER 14

LEGAL HISTORY AS THE HISTORY OF LEGAL TEXTS

ANGELA FERNANDEZ*

THIS chapter provides an overview of legal archeology as (just one) example of legal history as the history of legal texts. The casebook case is the unit of analysis, the legal text in question. I argue that its history can and should be approached in a wide variety of ways, termed here 'internalist'. This is a form of legal history that places persons at the heart of its approach, creating a kind of prosopography of the common law of the law school curriculum.

When John T. Noonan wrote in the 1970s about persons in the law, he had in mind first and foremost the litigants. Their cases were the occasion for the production of legal doctrine but they disappeared as their dispute was translated into legal language, forms, and processes by the various professionals involved in the affair, the lawyers, and ultimately the judges. Noonan emphasized the way that professional legal roles risked becoming morally problematic masks, disguising the humanity that should be at the heart of the law.[1] Richard Danzig and Geoffrey Watson used the term 'capability

* Faculty of Law University of Toronto. This chapter benefited from presentation at the American Society of Legal History annual meeting in Toronto in 2016, specifically a commentary presented by R. W. Gordon. The author wishes to thank him and fellow panel participants, especially David Sandomierski for organizing the session and for his comments and suggestions. Thanks also to editors Markus Dubber and Christopher Tomlins for editorial direction and feedback on the piece, including at the small workshop co-organized with a handful of fellow contributors in May 2017 at the Centre for Ethics, University of Toronto. University of Toronto Faculty of Law research student Colin Romano provided excellent assistance with formatting footnotes and editing and substance suggestions.

[1] John T. Noonan, *Persons and Masks of the Law: Cardozo, Holmes, Jefferson, and Wythe as Makers of Masks* (1975).

problems' to describe the occlusion of what happened to the parties before, during, and after their case was heard and a report was produced for the legal system.[2] In law school and in legal practice the focus is typically on that report and the case as a precedent, i.e. what principle it has been taken to stand for and how that principle was used (e.g., rejected or modified) in later cases.

Linguistic anthropologist Elizabeth Mertz has described modern-day American in-classroom as one in which teacher and student approach legal cases as 'detachable chunks of discourse' from which supposedly legally irrelevant facts are ruthlessly excised in classroom discussion.[3] The student approaching a famous case for the first time will most likely find the same tendency in the assigned reading for that classroom discussion in his/her casebook. The law school casebook is a collection of (usually appellate level) case reports that has been abridged in order to neatly present their legal principles. The legally relevant would usually exclude who the litigants were, their background stories (e.g., why they were litigating the case), what happened to them after the case was decided or any information that did not make it into the formal court record. Legal treatise-writers, casebook compilers, and the authors of law journal articles generally follow these norms in treating the cases in a positivistic, asocial, and anti-contextual way. Justice was blind. It did not take such facts into consideration—even if it was clear that those facts were relevant or had subsequently become relevant.

Noonan's idea that it was important to tell the stories of the litigants in famous leading cases seemed to catch on. One thought that resonated with law teachers using legal discourse and the texts that animate discussion in the chunk-like way Mertz described is that it was important for law students to see where the principles they were being taught to parse, distinguish, and so on came from. From a pedagogical perspective, many law teachers share the belief that it is very important to show students that legal principles do not fall from the sky, fully-formed and timeless; they are products of their time and place and they might well have been expressed differently (or not at all) in different circumstances, and, perhaps most importantly, they might be expressed differently in the future.

For example, Mrs. Palsgraf and the seriousness of her injuries were rendered invisible by both Justices Cardozo and Andrews in the quest to turn her case into the example of the unforeseeable plaintiff in *Palsgraf v. Long Island Railway*.[4] Or consider Richard Danzig's article on *Hadley v. Baxendale*, which probably still stands as one of the best examples of this kind of legal historical research.[5] It enables students to see that

---

[2] Richard Danzig, Geoffrey R. Watson, (intro.) *The Capability Problem in Contract Law: Further Readings on Well-Known Cases* (1978) 1–2 ff.

[3] Elizabeth Mertz, *The Language of Law School: Learning to 'Think Like a Lawyer'* (2007) 45 ff.

[4] Noonan (n. 1) 112–14 ff.

[5] Richard Danzig, '*Hadley v. Baxendale*: A Study in the Industrialization of the Law' (1975) 4 *Journal of Legal Studies* 274 ff. It has been reprinted, in Douglas G. Baird (ed.), *Contracts Stories* (2006), where it appears as the first piece.

industrialization was crucial to understanding why the judges in 1854 England wanted a liability-limiting rule for common carries. Baron Alderson crafted the remoteness principle as a limit on recoverable damages in response to what were seen as excessive pro-plaintiff jury awards. This was a time when liability for the company's acts would fall personally on the director of the carrier company. Limited liability for railroads was one of the pre-eminent legal questions of the day. Despite their failure to mention either the importance of industrialization and railways to the national economy, it is unlikely that the judges in *Hadley v. Baxendale* did not see the railroad's importance as a carrier of the goods and people fuelling British industrialization.

Such legal historical work emphasized the importance of persons from at least two perspectives: first, that of the litigants, who like Mrs. Palsgraf often acted as the sacrificial lamb for the development of legal doctrine; and second, that of the judges, often motivated by concerns not included and addressed in their written reasons. For example, as Danzig details in *Hadley v. Baxendale*, the brother of one of the judges, Baron Parke, was the managing director of the carrier company Pickford's before Mr. Baxendale.[6] Surely, surmised Danzig, the financial implications of finding Baxendale personally responsible for the mill's lost profits were influencing his view of the appropriateness of finding Baxendale liable. Baron Parke also wrote the authoritative decision on the 1830 *Common Carrier Act*, which required a shipper to give notice of articles of great value or have their recovery limited to €10.[7] It stretches incredulity to believe that this hot issue of the day was not in his and the other judges' minds when Baron Alderson formulated the notification of the special circumstances branch of the foreseeability test in *Hadley v. Baxendale*. It is a puzzling aspect of the test and it created trouble on the facts of the case.[8] Danzig's suggestion is that the judges were following Parliament's lead on how to approach the touchy subject of common carrier liability.[9]

The special circumstances or notice branch of the foreseeability test was significantly watered down in a subsequent case about another mill part (lost this time rather than delayed): *B.C. Saw Mills*.[10] The judge who was so important to that determination? Sir James Shaw Willes, the lawyer who represented Pickford's in *Hadley*. Willes joined his opposing counsel in selecting *Hadley* for inclusion and comment in the widely used collection they co-edited, *Smith's Leading Cases*.[11] Danzig wrote that the rule in *Hadley v. Baxendale* was hardly an example of the common law 'working itself pure' in some apersonal way. The rule acquired 'substantial human assistance' from Willes, who was 'a central actor' in its 'importation, spread and interpretation [. . .] and he contributed toward these ends as an academic, a litigator and as an esteemed appellate judge'.[12]

---

[6] Ibid., 267 ff.   [7] Ibid. 264 ff.

[8] Baron Alderson proposed a very narrow characterization of what the carrier needed to be told in order to find that special notice was not given. Different reports and accounts say different things about what Pickford's clerk was or was not told. See ibid. 262–3, n. 53 ff.

[9] Ibid., 264 ff.   [10] *British Columbia Saw Mills v. Nettleship* (1868) 2 C.P. 499.

[11] Danzig (n. 5) 275–6 ff.   [12] Ibid., 276 ff.

Brian Simpson termed this type of legal historical research 'legal archaeology' and energetically contributed many studies of leading common law cases, some of which he published in a book called *Leading Cases in the Common Law* (1995). Simpson succeeded in showing that it was not only fun but interesting to learn more about cases that otherwise appeared to be like drab old furniture in common law legal education. The impressive duck decoys in *Keeble v. Hickeringill* (1707), the mysterious smoke ball in *Carlill v. Carbolic Smoke Ball Company* (1893), the utter obscureness of the rule against perpetuities in *Jee v. Audley* (1787), were all examples to which Simpson applied his partying touch.[13] Simpson also produced book-length studies on subjects like the famous cannibalism case *Dudley v. Stevens*.[14] Simpson's aim was more often than not to show the hypocrisy and nonsense (often bureaucratic and institutional) that underlay these decisions, an indirect challenge to the idea that the law was certain and scientific in some impersonal sense.[15]

Simpson also took the lead on bringing treatise-writers out of the shadows.[16] These scholars influenced the way that the law in reported cases was received, the uptake as it were, so the cases could operate as precedent in doctrinal understandings and circulate as such (whether warranted or unwarranted, as in the famous mistake and meeting of the minds case *Raffles v. Wichelhaus*).[17] Danzig was also interested in this alchemical process of uptake and influential circulation, tracing, for instance, the above ways that Sir James Shaw Willes helped *Hadley v. Baxendale* become 'a fixed star in the jurisprudential firmament', where it remains to this day.[18]

The use and reliance on casebooks and law review articles certainly informed the background understanding of famous leading cases as they developed over time, particularly into the twentieth century and the context of an academic law school using the case method of instruction. The case was (and still is) the primary unit of analysis. However, investigations of how cases came to be included in casebooks were few and far between. Why did some cases get included and others not? What were editors thinking when they dragged one of these specimens out of obscurity? Did the weight of past practice dictate their continued inclusion, or were other factors at play? Did they actually become useful in new ways to new generations of teachers and students, or was it just a strange kind of deference or inertia that kept them in the casebook where they continued to be read and discussed?

[13] A. W. Brian Simpson, *Leading Cases in the Common Law* (1995) 45–75 ff. (*Keeble v. Hickeringill*), 259–91 ff. (*Carlill v. Carbolic Smoke Ball Company*) 76–99 ff. (*Jee v. Audley*).

[14] A. W. Brian Simpson, *Cannibalism and the Common Law: The Story of the Tragic Last Voyage of the Mignonette and the Strange Legal Proceedings to which it Gave Rise* (1984). See also A. W. Brian Simpson, *In the Highest Degree Odious: Detention without Trial in Wartime Britain* (1992).

[15] See Robert W. Gordon, 'Simpson's Leading Cases' (1997) 95 *Michigan L.R.* 2044–54, 2053–4 ff.

[16] A. W. Brian Simpson, 'The Rise and Fall of the Legal Treatise: Legal Principles and the Forms of Legal Literature' (1981) 48 *University of Chicago L.R.* 632 ff.

[17] Simpson (n. 13) 135–62, 158–62 ff.

[18] Danzig (n. 5) 274 ff (quoting Grant Gilmore, *The Death of Contract* (1974) 49 ff).

I investigated these questions in a study on how *Leaf v. International Galleries*, a 1950 British mistake case about a John Constable painting, came to be included in the casebook most commonly used at my institution, the Faculty of Law at the University of Toronto.[19] The book was started by founding Dean Cecil Wright, but *Leaf* had been included by the person who became the institution's contracts teacher in 1950: James B. Milner. *Leaf* was not a famous or leading case. It is not generally taught in the United States. Digging around, I learned some interesting information about the pricing of Constables during and after the two World Wars. For example, Mr. Leaf could have thought he was purchasing a genuine Constable for £85 in 1944, and so it is not implausible that the purchase was a legitimate mistake. The study also led to some observations about Milner and his approach to teaching contracts. It provides one example of what the study of the casebook inclusion process might look like, for example examining the handover of the casebook from Wright to Milner, the views Milner expresses in its introduction, placement and use of the case over different editions, including another Canadian case from Newfoundland that it came to be paired with in teaching the doctrine of mistake to Canadian law students, and accompanying notes and questions to both cases.[20]

Rather than treating the casebook as a transparent indicator of what is and what is not important, such research problematizes the text. That problematization includes the book and the placement of the case in it, along with internal accompanying materials such as statute excerpts and pieces of legal scholarship or snapshots thereof. This tracing contextualizes what is an otherwise ruthlessly decontextualized artefact, and as Mertz would say 'recontextualizing' it and highlighting 'human agency to a greater degree, reminding us always that texts are created and recreated through people's actions and interpretations'.[21] As Mertz found, law school is an environment in which this bears emphasizing given the decontextualized way in which cases are generally approached. This decontextualization is exacerbated by the tendency of the casebooks to 'present "lines" of precedent using cases from disparate times and places [. . .] This approach collapses historical time and social context'.[22] Mertz writes that we need to take account of 'the continual process of extraction and recontextualization of the meaning of those written texts, a process wherein what appears to be the same text changes and takes on somewhat different meaning by virtue of new connections with novel contexts'.[23]

It is clear that legal scholars have become increasingly comfortable speaking about a 'canon' of cases and casebooks as the equivalent of the Norton anthologies of English or American literature: the anthologies of the law.[24] Also accepted

---

[19] *Leaf v. International Galleries* (1950) 2 K.B. 86. See Angela Fernandez, 'An Object Lesson in Speculation: Multiple Views of the Cathedral in *Leaf v. International Galleries*' (2008) 58 *University of Toronto L.J.* 481 ff.

[20] Ibid., 503–14 ff. For more on Milner, the casebook, and Milner's connections to Lon Fuller and Henry Hart from the time spent at Harvard Law School, see David Sandomierski, 'Tension and Reconciliation in Canadian Contract Law Casebooks' (2017) 54 *Osgoode Hall L.J* 1181 ff.

[21] Mertz (n. 3) 45 ff.   [22] Ibid., 63–4 ff.   [23] Ibid., 48 ff.

[24] J. M. Balkin, Sanford Levinson (eds.), Introduction to *Legal Canons* (2000); E. Allan Farnsworth, 'Contracts Scholarship in the Age of the Anthology' (1987) 85 *Michigan L.R.* 1406 ff.

is the idea that there is now an anti-canon, which figures infamous American constitutional law cases such as *Dred Scott* and *Plessy v. Ferguson*, alongside collusive cases such as *Buck v. Bell*, or notorious property cases like *Johnson v. M'Intosh*, or the particularly harsh contracts case *Peevyhouse v. Garland Coal*.[25]

My own work on the property law case *Pierson v. Post* includes focus on how the case was anthologized in American property casebooks in the twentieth century and approached in some of the over 700 law review articles that make reference to it, especially since the 1980s. It also traces the way that the case has been reproduced in different casebooks over subsequent editions and changes in placement (is it put at the beginning or deeper in the property casebook?), editing (is the dissent included? Are the lawyer arguments included? Is the Latin in the majority decision translated?), and the notes and questions accompanying the edited selection and in which directions they nudge or blatantly direct.[26]

The idea that there is an ideological perspective in the way that seemingly neutral legal rules like the capture rule in *Pierson* are presented in both the casebook and the law review literature seems too obvious to dispute. Such messaging echoes (and is echoed) in the rich history of other didactic or pedagogical forms of legal literature such as treatises (or Restatements), which bend heavily towards the normative while purporting to be merely descriptive. As Markus Dubber and I have written, it becomes 'impossible to view legal treatises as simply carriers of purportedly neutral, objective, rationalizing and systematizing principles. Their substance was deeply normative, while much of their authority was predicated precisely on their appearing not to be.'[27]

The focus on an extension of relevant 'persons' involved in and touching the great (or dreaded or even banal) pedagogical case, those involved in its uptake, deployment, and redeployment, is important because, as Simpson put it, 'common law rules enjoy whatever status they possess not because of the circumstances of their origin, but because of their continued reception.'[28] In other words, a community

[25] Stuart Banner, *How the Indians Lost their Land: Law and Power on the Frontier* (2005) 11 ff. (describing *Johnson v. M'Intosh* as having joined *Dred Scott* and 'a few others to form a small canon (or maybe an anti-canon) of famous cases law students are taught to criticize'); Balkin and Levinson, ibid., 13 (singling out *Plessy v. Ferguson* for legalizing Jim Crow and being used to teach students about legalized injustice). See also Judith Maute, '*Peevyhouse v. Garland Coal and Mining Co.* Revisited: The Ballad of Willie and Lucile', (1994–1995) 89 *Northwestern University Law Review* 1341–486 ff; Paul A. Lombardo, *Three Generations, No Imbeciles: Eugenics, the Supreme Court, and Buck v. Bell* (2008), both highlighted by Debora L. Threedy, 'Legal Archaeology: Excavating Cases, Reconstructing Context' (2006) 80 *Tulane L.R.* 1197 ff.

[26] See Angela Fernandez, *Pierson v. Post, The Hunt for the Fox: Law and Professionalization in American Legal Culture* (2018) ch. 7 ff.

[27] Angela Fernandez, Markus D. Dubber, 'Introduction', in Angela Fernandez, Markus D. Dubber (eds.), *Law Books in Action: Essays on the Anglo-American Legal Treatise* (2012) 5 ff.

[28] A. W. Brian Simpson, 'The Common Law and Legal Theory' in *Legal Theory and Legal History: Essays on the Common Law* (1987) 367–8 ff.

of meaning not only influences but in an important sense determines their meaning, and that meaning, like the meaning of any text, changes over time as the community of interpreters and their cares and concerns change.[29] In the situation of a legal case, without this continued reception, attention, and uptake, the case, however famous it once was, would become nothing or effectively nothing. This is important because it means that if, collectively, we stopped paying attention to the famous leading cases, they would actually lose their sway over us. These cases would cease to be the way scores of students are introduced to the concept of first possession (*Pierson v. Post*) or learn the concept of remoteness and foreseeability in tort and contract law (*Hadley v. Baxendale*).[30] Hence, like the emergence of the rules themselves from the cases, the reception and process of meaning-making that goes into a great case becoming great (or losing its status) is not transparent, self-evident, or naturally occurring and should not be treated (as it is usually implicitly treated) as such. It has, in other words, a history that we can and should reconstruct.

This form of legal history investigates and problematizes and, in that sense, pays attention to those who are paying the case attention. Why was it appealing to the legal scientists of its day or the treatise-writers or judges who looked back to it in a later period? How did that interest change over time and morph and bend? How did the case appear in different legal systems which have very different histories, as well as social and political contexts? This is internal history, yes, taking seriously the law's own forms and expressions, its own 'Mandarin materials,' as Bob Gordon would say.[31]

Crucially important is the fact that this internal approach to legal history is not committed to telling a Whiggish story of the common law working itself pure, getting better and better over time. It is an account of mixed and multifarious change. Indeed, more often than not the common law emerges looking like a muddler or a bumbler or a seriously inefficient rule-provider. The judges and lawyers making the decisions about where we go next are often steeped in institutional self-interest and hypocritical moralizing.[32] Where the externally-focused historian might tend to ignore or downplay what might well be the self-serving speech of legal professionals, the internalist starts by taking seriously what they say, their/our forms of expression. Start where they/we start, in a classroom casebook presentation or in a law review article setting out first principles. Take them/us at their/our word, as it were, and follow the train of thought. The inquiry will not stay internal. It will reach out using methods from intellectual and social history, without regard for how those styles often keep themselves separate, disciplining users to think only one or the other is an appropriate style of scholarship for them, the one they happen to be trained in.

---

[29] Stanley Fish, 'Working on the Chain Gang: Interpretation in Law and Literature', (1981–1982) 60 *Texas L.R.* 527 ff.

[30] *Pierson v. Post* (1805) 3 Cai. R. 175; *Hadley v. Baxendale* (1854) EWHC J70.

[31] Robert W. Gordon, 'Critical Legal Histories' (1984) 36 *Stanford L.R.* 122 ff.

[32] Gordon (n. 15) 2053–4 ff.

So, for instance, it would be a form of intellectual history to investigate how a treatise-writer treats (*traiter*) a topic and why or how certain ideas associated with a case are carried through a casebook and the interests of its editors. The methods of social history would be used to explore the life and background of the treatise-writer or investigate where a case happened, the backgrounds of the litigants and the lawyers and if jurors were involved, their economic backgrounds. The approach is ecumenical in that respect. You look at whatever you think is going to potentially shed light. However, there is a common starting point: taking something that the profession—the judges, the lawyers, the law teachers—have already decided is important, ask why and to what consequence. And perhaps ultimately whether that attention is deserved.

The internalist approach of case-in-context studies of common law cases tends to lay bare political or social issues more readily associated with public rather than private law, reminding us that private law cases too have their politics. Studies focusing on the common law have the virtue of being less American-specific in a way that is more relevant to those in countries outside of the United States.

Leading cases are common currency in a number of jurisdictions which employ the common law and trade in and refer to the same (often famous British or American) cases. This overlap derives from the widespread use of a case method of instruction in the law schools of other countries (e.g., Canada, Australia, Israel). Investigating the circumstances and origin of those common law cases and their uptake is an opportunity to explore how they fit into wider social and political forces. Taking this opportunity also leads to interesting questions of transplant and translation into the non-American legal culture, both in terms of the pedagogy and the legal profession of other different, particularized times and places.

What did *Pierson* mean to the Supreme Court of Canada when it was referred to in a late nineteenth-century fishing case involving international tensions about over-fishing between Canada and the United States and, in turn, relations between the United States and Great Britain? One of the judges in the case, *The Frederick Gerring*, reproduced most of the text of the majority decision in *Pierson*.[33] He was using the case to try and decide if the fish originally netted by the American boat outside the three-mile limit needed to be reduced to capture. Why? The boat had drifted into the three-mile limit while the men were still baling the fish, arguably in the eyes of the then-coastal patrol (and the Supreme Court of Canada agreed) 'fishing' in violation of the treaty between the United States and Great Britain, warranting seizure of the vessel.[34] This late nineteenth-century international, imperial, and nationalist Canadian context is very different than the tensions between rival ways

---

[33] *Frederick Gerring Jr. (The) v. R.*, (1897) 27 SCR 271, 305–7 (Girouard J.).

[34] Sedgwick J. defined 'fishing' as 'a continuous process beginning from the time when the preliminary preparations are being made for the taking of the fish and extending down to the moment when they are finally reduced to actual and certain possession.' Ibid., 281 ff.

of being wealthy in rural Long Island in the early nineteenth century that gave rise to the dispute over the fox between Pierson (from farming wealth) and Post (from mercantile wealth).[35]

The *Pierson* rule about possession established through violent occupation or capture has a different resonance when thinking about occupied territories in Israel and myths, for example, of how Tel Aviv rose out of the sand or in Australia in terms of tensions between white settlers and Aborigines.[36]

It would probably be fair to say that the legal-archaeological study of cases went mainstream in the 2000s. Foundation Press republished the Danzig and Watson collection in 2004 and they have a popular 'Law Stories' series.[37] The extent of historical work undertaken in these studies varies; however, it appears undisputed that there is an appetite for scholarship of this kind. Many law professors are willing to undertake the enormous amount of labour required to unearth and blow the dust off these cases, changing how they will be understood and interpreted in the future. These changes might bring the cases more in line with current concerns and interests, about which I will say more below. I do not see the work on the uptake of famous leading cases abating. Indeed, the pull to persons will likely increase. For example, University of British Columbia Press has inaugurated a 'Landmark Cases in Canadian Law' series, which promises to build a canon of importantly interesting case studies, bringing to prominence some cases that were not well-known or changing the understanding of their notoriety/fame.[38] In that sense, legal archaeology can be understood to be 'expanding the frame' in legal history.[39]

Witness the popularity of on-line research tools like ancestry.com used by genealogists, many of whom are amateurs looking into the history of their own family who become more and more professional about it (or at least intense) as their hobby grows (for many into something resembling an occupation). I believe

---

[35] Fernandez, *Hunt for the Fox* (n. 26) ch. 1 ff.

[36] I am thinking here about reactions to presentations on my *Pierson* work when I presented it in Israel at the Legal History Workshop at the Faculty of Law at Tel Aviv University in 2010 and at the Australia and New Zealand Law and History Society in Brisbane Australia in 2011. On Australia specifically, see Nancy E. Wright, A. R. Buck, 'Cross-cultural Conflict about Property Rights in Wild Animals in Australia: Law and Cinema', (2016) *Law, Culture and the Humanities* available at <http://journals.sagepub.com>.

[37] There are twenty to date. The first was edited by Robert L. Rabin, Stephen D. Sugarman's *Torts Stories* in 2003: <http://www.westacademic.com/Professors/ProductSearchResults.aspx?searchtypeas string=ADVANCED-SEARCH&tab=1&keywords=law+stories>. The University Press of Kansas also has book-length studies on a single case (as opposed to the Laws Stories edited collection approach) called 'Landmark Law Cases and American Society—Series', which started in the 1990s and really picked up steam in the 2000s with now over seventy-five titles: <https://kansaspress.ku.edu/series/landmark-law-cases-and-american-society.html?p=1 >.

[38] A book-length study on the Supreme Court of Canada fishing case *The Frederick Gerring* by Angela Fernandez, Bradley Miller, and Christopher Shorey will appear in this University of British Columbia Press series: *The Frederick Gerring, Canada's Pierson v. Post.*

[39] See Gordon (n. 15) 2051–2 ff.

that this behaviour reveals the inherent curiosity people have, not just about the past generally but *their* past specifically, a past that touches them in some direct and personal way (their family or the history of their house or where they live). The litigants, the lawyers, the judges, and the scholars who helped make a case famous and influenced how it was interpreted, the reporter (if it is an older case), the law teachers, who do not necessarily write scholarly articles or books about the case but who may help edit casebooks or teaching manuals, and who transmit their understanding of the case and its relevant principles orally in their classroom year-to-year over long careers. All of these characters, these persons, are like family members, ancestors, close and far, to law students and lawyers.

That is the sense in which what I call for here is a new kind of prosopography.[40] Older versions of such collective biographies would focus say on the leading lawyers and judges in a town or leaders of a church, uncritically celebrating them as heroes. I propose a critical approach to the material that is familiar and dear to lawyers and law students, one that historicizes and problematizes what internally exists using the tools of external social and intellectual history. Indeed, Simpson worked on a collective biography of leading common-law lawyers and judges, which took the form of short biographical entries, less in-depth than the *Dictionary of American Biography* or the *National American Biography* for the United States, neither of which were of course limited to lawyers and judges. It is, however, a handy little reference book, which shows he had something like this person-focused approach in mind, or at least thought there was something important about that dimension of things.[41] Simpson thought that the common law worked in a customary way and what he termed the 'gerontocratic' caste decided who and what were in and out.[42]

Once leading cases or teaching cases enter the 'jurisprudential firmament' or the canon, or however one wants to put it, they tend to stay. Treating them in an internalist way, not very differently from the way that a treatise or a textbook is typically used and understood, runs a risk of reinforcing rather than undermining their seemingly timeless quality. The internalist approach I advocate for here,

---

[40] I am indebted to Bob Gordon for suggesting the use of this term, which the *OED* defines in the following way: 'A study or description of an individual's life, career etc.; *esp.* a collection of such studies focusing on the public careers and relationships of a group in a particular period and place; a collective biography.' *Oxford English Dictionary*, available online at <http://www.oed.com>. For an example of such an approach in a work of literary legal history, see Jessica Winston, *Lawyers at Play: Literature, Law, and Politics at the Early Modern Inns of Court, 1558–1581* (2016) 49 ff. See also comment by Angela Fernandez, 'Literary Play at the Inns of Court and Early Modern Legal Professionalization', posted on Legal History JOTWELL (Journal of Things We Like (Lots)) Angela Fernandez, Literary Play at the Inns of Court and Early Modern Legal Professionalization, JOTWELL (May 31, 2018) (reviewing Jessica Winston, Lawyers at Play: Literature, Law, and Politics at the Early Modern Inns of Court, 1558–1581 (2016)), <https://legalhist.jotwell.com/literary-play-at-the-inns-of-court-and-early-modern-legal-professionalization/> (accessed 07 June 2018).

[41] A. W. Brian Simpson (ed.), *Biographical Dictionary of the Common Law* (1984).

[42] Simpson, 'Common Law and Legal Theory' (n. 28) 362 ff. ('the common law is best understood as a system of customary law, that is, a body of traditional ideas received within a caste of experts'),

however, problematizes, contextualizes, and refuses to take the timelessness at face value. There is probably some doubt among more externally-focused historians that sceptical distance can be maintained and that the internalist style of legal historical research will have a natural tendency towards conservatism and self-serving uncritical accounts, which credit change over time to books or ideas shorn of their political and social context.[43] However, that is not necessarily the direction in which an investigation will go. And if we eschew an internalist approach, we actually fail to appreciate how deeply conservative the legal profession is. Ignoring this history is in a very real sense ignoring our stuff, our legacies, good and bad: family members we love and those we should be more wary of.

My own hope is that these internalist histories will start moving in the direction of problematizations along the following lines: (i) looking at issues relating to race, gender, and class that have been a standard part of legal analysis since the 1980s, as well as newer social issues that post-humanism and the Anthropocene have pushed to the forefront of the minds of many relating to the environment and the position of nonhuman animals;[44] (ii) expanding the insights of law and literature and seeing legal texts as texts that change over time depending on how they are interpreted and recontextualized, again a law-as-narrative approach that has been popular for some time but has not really penetrated the consciousness of legal historians;[45] (iii) building on work in the tradition of the history of the book and the materiality of legal texts to expand beyond the material book trade and law book publishing world to electronic publishing and what that has done to the way that we encounter and consume legal texts (i.e., how do catch phrases like 'separate but equal' appear

376 ff. (Common law is customary law in the sense that 'it consists of a body of practices observed and ideas received by a caste of lawyers . . . These ideas and practices exists only in the sense that they are accepted and acted upon within the legal profession.') 377 ff. ('[t]he organization of the profession was gerontocratic . . . and promotion depended upon approval by the senior members of the profession.')

[43] See, e.g., Simpson's account of the influence of will theory, which he ties to the popularity of the English translation of Pothier's *Law of Obligations* in 1806 and a handful of other key texts. Simpson, A. W. B., 'Innovation in Nineteenth-Century Contract Law' in *Legal Theory and Legal History: Essays on the Common Law* (1987) 179–81 ff. Danzig points out that there must also have been a 'felt need' to turn to this concept of the strong autonomous individual who meets and comes into discrete exchange with another and their two wills meet. See Danzig (n. 5) 259 ff. Industrialization, increased anonymity in commercial exchange, and the rise of liberal individualism helps explain why the will theory in Pothier's book was so attractive to nineteenth-century contract law thinkers. See Patrick S. Atiyah, *The Rise and Fall of Freedom of Contract* (1979).

[44] For examples of legal environmental history, see Douglas C. Harris, *Fish, Law, and Colonialism: The Legal Capture of Salmon in British Columbia* (2001); Douglas C. Harris, *Landing Native Fisheries: Indian Reserves and Fishing Rights in British Columbia, 1849–1925* (2008); David Schorr, *The Colorado Doctrine: Water Rights, Corporations, and Distributive Justice on The American Frontier* (2012). Histories figuring nonhuman animals as an important historical force include Virginia DeJohn Anderson, *Creatures of Empire: How Domestic Animals Transformed Early America* (2004); Alan Mikhail, *The Animal in Ottoman Egypt* (2014).

[45] See Bernadette A. Meyler, 'Law, Literature, and History: The Love Triangle' (2015) 5 *U.C. Irvine L.R.* 365 ff.

on the Internet, e.g., on Wikipedia, and how does this play out in terms of citation and referencing practices).[46]

Noonan's call to bring out the persons so important to the legal process means moving beyond a view of legal texts as transparent and static *signifiers*. They are not bearers of a single meaning. Seeing the persons in the process moved us towards a greater awareness of the way in which what those texts are *signifying* is fluid. Those meanings are connected to audience and a wide range of persons who play a role in making that text 'great,' downgrading it, or assigning it a background workman-like role (e.g., as waystation to the current doctrinal situation). What is signifying and what is signified are then understood to be in a mutually reinforcing and ever changing relationship, the signified changing in response to the signifying and the signifying responding to what is now (temporarily at least) signified. The significance or meaning then is always changing and being influenced by legal actors who might purport to observe only, but whose observations and comment inevitably have an impact.[47]

As a general rule, concerns relating to race, class, and gender did not penetrate the work of legal historians like Simpson working on famous legal cases. It is as if they/we were inured to the overwhelmingly white, male, elite perspective of the judges whose words and social context they/we were struggling to understand. They/we ceased to notice or think it particularly problematic or just too obvious to warrant specific attention, or not something it was appropriate to fault them for.

Of course the twentieth-century rebellious and often progressive English judge Lord Denning was also often racist and sexist.[48] Of course the crusading women behind the challenge to female exclusion from the legal definition of persons in Canada supported eugenics and held other regressive views about race.[49] Of course the middle-class women who worked for the Toronto Police Court were moralizingly puritanical towards working class women.[50] Yet these unpleasant

---

[46] Thanks to David Minto for suggesting an inclusion on the materiality of legal texts and what that means for virtual legal texts. I agree with him that this is important future work. For more traditional approaches, see D. D. Hall, *Cultures of Print: Essays in the History of the Book* (1996); Michael Hoeflich, *Legal Publishing in Antebellum America* (2010).

[47] I am indebted to Chris Tomlins for suggesting using the signified/signifying distinction in this context. It is not exactly Ferdinand Saussure's theory of sign in semiotics but is within the range of ways that theory is routinely taken up and deployed by different scholars in different disciplines (e.g., the shift from Saussure's focus on speech to written text).

[48] Greig Henderson, *Creating Legal Worlds: Story and Style in a Culture of Argument* (2015) 53–5 ff. See also comment by Angela Fernandez, 'Law and Literature for Legal Historians', posted on Legal History JOTWELL (The Journal of Things We Like (Lots) (22 March 2016), available at <https://legalhist.jotwell.com/law-and-literature-for-legal-historians/> (accessed 3 May 2018).

[49] Robert Sharpe, Patricia McMahon, *The Persons Case: The Origins and Legacy of the Fight for Legal Personhood* (2007) 11 ff.

[50] See Amanda Glasbeek, *Feminized Justice: The Toronto Women's Court, 1913–1934* (2009); see also comment by Angela Fernandez, '*Feminized* not Feminist Justice at the Toronto Women's Court', posted on Legal History JOTWELL (The Journal of Things We Like (Lots)) (31 March 2011), available at <http://legalhist.jotwell.com/?s=feminized+justice> (accessed 3 May 2018).

truths are essential to the story that is there and that needs to be told. The inglorious aspects of a generally conservative legal profession is part of our stuff/legacy, an acknowledgement that does not necessarily trigger blame but is an important part of how things were and still are, features which need to cease being invisible if they are ever to change.

For example, do the regressive views of the 'famous five' behind the Canadian *Persons* case warrant our referral to them as the 'infamous five'? Despite their views, what they accomplished for equality in Canada was great. And the way that the case gave the Privy Council an opportunity to posit and expound upon the 'living tree' view of constitutional interpretation moves Canadian law away from the textualist/ referentialist approach that plagues American law. That approach is most obvious in the original intent approach to American constitutional law, which Canada has largely avoided given our 'living tree' doctrine developed by the Privy Council in the *Persons* case.[51]

I think a useful starting point is to ask ourselves what we meant and currently mean by greatness: who or what is credited with it and why? Is that deserved or undeserved? Where are the overlooked and under-acknowledged other forms of greatness?[52] Is there something about law and its authoritative coinage that ties it indelibly to greatness (or at least bindingness)? Can we ever get away from it? How do we get to the small-scale social or cultural history or microhistory/history from below/history of everyday life?

Law and Society has been committed to interrogating the gap between what Roscoe Pound called 'law in books' versus 'law in action' for a long time.[53] Classic works like Dirk Hartog's 'Pigs and Positivism' highlighted just how drastic that gap can be.[54] We now work knowing that this is how it will be, really having been taught to expect to see a gap. Yet it still feels like we have to choose which side of the aisle to be on: law or history. Working in a law school pushes those of us who do towards the 'law books' side, especially given the way that texts are the lifeblood of the law. Yet law is also an historically embedded social and cultural practice. Hence, the approach, it seems to me, should be to examine how those texts are deployed and redeployed, recontextualized as Mertz would say, by whom, and for what purposes. The basic point is that the 'law books' side need not be textualist or referentialist in its orientation or narrowly doctrinal. Recontextualizations can be thoughtful

---

[51] See Sharpe, McMahon (n. 49) 178–81 ff. (for an overview of the 'living tree' metaphor in the person's case).

[52] See Angela Fernandez, Beatrice Tice, 'Bertha Wilson's Practice Years (1958–1975): Establishing a Research Practice and Founding a Research Department in Canada', in Kim Brooks (ed.), *Justice Bertha Wilson: One Woman's Difference* (2009) 15–30 ff (for a focus on the contributions Wilson made as a lawyer working her way around gender barriers creating innovative legal research mechanisms rather than her usual fame as a judge).

[53] Roscoe Pound, 'Law in Books and Law in Action' (1910) 44 *American L.R.* 12 ff.

[54] Hendrik Hartog, 'Pigs and Positivism' (1985) *Wisconsin L.R.* 899 ff.

and nuanced and self-reflective.[55] Markus Dubber and I have described this as a scrambling of the distinction between 'law in books' and 'law in action': 'law books in action'.[56]

Questions like what is considered 'great' and whether it deserves to be inevitably pull the questioner into the process, making it difficult to maintain the historian's illusion of lofty, objective detachment. As illusion, it is probably better to face directly the truth that each of us will tell a story, including a legal historical story, differently. I found myself, for instance, emphasizing the gender, violence, and animal status in *Pierson*, along with slavery and colonialism.[57] This was not inevitable, but it was a combination of what I saw and what I believed others would be interested in hearing about in connection to the fox of the twenty-first century. This is internalist, yes, but moving outwards to other external and critical concerns. If we believe in the idea that there is only one way to do the history then we will be more likely I think to carry on and reproduce age-old blind spots in legal historical inquiry: when really it is the blind spots that should now most attract our attention.

Also important to my approach to *Pierson* was to emphasize the case as a literary text in order to appreciate the humour of the dissent, largely unappreciated by 200 years of our most serious legal scholars from James Kent, to Oliver Wendell Holmes Jr., to casebook editors and law journal authors in the twentieth century.[58] That humour, a specific style I call 'lawyerly solemn foolery', works to efface the problematic (e.g., anti-environmental) dimensions of the rule of capture as it came out of *Pierson*.[59] Having gotten stuck on the idea that James Kent was responsible for the elaborateness of the *Pierson* appeal, I came to realize that it was probably the lawyers and, crucially, the reporter who were most responsible for it taking the form it did.[60] The book has a chapter on the lawyers and a chapter on the reporter, George Caines.[61] Kent, the judge and the treatise-writer, was important for subsequent circulation of the serious rule; however, the other personnel were crucial and vital to the report taking the shape it did, particularly Justice Livingston for taking a humorous approach in the dissent in a way that has long captured the attention of its readers, law professors, and law students.

Once the legal historian deconstructs an important legal moment and shows the efforts of which legal professionals were responsible for its particular formulation or its uptake/reception, this does not leave everything as it was. It can, indeed, change it irrevocably. One of the basic points is to see that law is made in a wide variety

---

[55] See David Sandomierski, *Theory and Practice, Realism and Formalism, and Aspiration and Reality in Canadian Contract Law Teaching* (J. S. D. Dissertation, Faculty of Law, University of Toronto, 2017) (for a Mertz-inspired approach to Canadian contract law casebooks and interviews with Canadian contract law teachers).

[56] Fernandez, Dubber (n. 27) 5 ff.

[57] Fernandez, *Hunt for the Fox* (n. 26).   [58] Ibid., ch. 7 ff.   [59] Ibid., chs. 1 & 2 ff.

[60] Angela Fernandez, 'Pierson v. Post: A Great Debate, James Kent, and the Project of Building a Learned Law for New York State' (2009) 34 *Law and Social Inquiry* 301 ff.

[61] Fernandez, *Hunt for the Fox* (n. 26) chs. 4 & 6.

of ways, not just narrowly in the cases or in legislatures, or judges in their role as judges. Influence is exerted in the uptake, reception, and circulation of ideas amongst a wide range of actors. So, for instance, we may find out that a treatise-writer making a polite and deferential suggestion for a change in the law that was then taken up by a judge by the time of the next edition and reported there as if it had nothing to do with that treatise-writer.[62] Or Sir Frederick Pollock, both an influential treatise-writer and editor of the English law reports, had a tremendous influence on what cases the judges and lawyers of his day would be discussing and deciding were important or unimportant.[63] Tapping Reeve, proprietor of the Litchfield Law School, used the lectures at his school and the treatise he wrote from them, sometimes called the first American legal treatise, to convince students to make a change to the law allowing married women to make a will.[64]

The intervention might be of the above polite and scholarly kind. It might also involve a certain sort of destruction or loss. In my work on the *Pierson* case, I found an important record long thought to be lost—the original judgment role in the case. However, the process of extracting it from the archive resulted in its actual physical loss. It was either stolen as a result of my making its existence public or misplaced in all the hubbub. We learned more about the case due to its discovery.[65] It greatly assisted me in telling the story of the case in the way I thought it should be told. Yet the original is now gone.[66] Its discovery, in other words, turned out to be a mixed blessing. Would it have been better for it to have mouldered away without ever seeing the light of day? I think it was better that it was found. But it is also true that its discovery was its destruction. It is like bursting a bubble by reaching out to touch it, and it is a risk attendant in undertaking the examination, or excavation, as Simpson might say. Indeed, the archaeological metaphor is apt given the way that those diggers, however expert, must often end up unintentionally destroying what would have but for their intervention remained intact in the dirt, though never known to us.

In the situation of the excavation or archaeological exploration of a great leading case, what the investigator finds can certainly lead to a discrediting or questioning of the rightness of the decision. Consider two examples from the canon of Justice Benjamin Cardozo's New York Appellate Court decisions. Danzig and Watson's

---

[62] See Stephen Waddams, 'What Were the Principles of Nineteenth-Century Contract Law' in A. D. E. Lewis, Paul Brand, Paul Mitchell (eds.), *Law in the City: Proceedings of the Seventeenth British Legal History Conference, London, 2005* (2007) 308–10 ff.

[63] See Neil Duxbury, *Frederick Pollock and the English Juristic Tradition* (2004). The above example Stephen Waddams gives also involves Pollock.

[64] Angela Fernandez, 'Tapping Reeve, Coverture, and America's First Legal Treatise' in Angela Fernandez, Markus D. Dubber (eds.), *Law Books in Action: Essays on the Anglo-American Legal Treatise* (2012) 63 ff.

[65] See 'Forum, *Pierson v. Post*: Capturing New Facts about the Fox' (2009) 27 *Law and History Review* 145 ff.

[66] For an electronic posting of the photocopy I obtained in May 2007 and accompanying transcript of the description of my discovery and the document's loss, see <https://dataverse.scholarsportal.info/dataset.xhtml?persistentId=doi:10.5683/SP/3HJKJ7>.

additional materials on Cardozo's decision in *Jacob and Youngs v. Kent* tend to support his decision to characterize the deviation from the pipe specification at issue in the construction contract as inconsequential.[67] However, Cardozo's decision to imply a term, a reasonable or best efforts clause, in *Wood v. Lady Lucy-Duff Gordon* looks suspect given what has been discovered about other contracts Wood entered into at the time that did include a best efforts clause. One might have been intentionally omitted in Lady Lucy-Duff Gordon's case and if so, it seems problematic to read one in, as Cardozo did.[68]

Pace Law Review did a symposium on various aspects of the case and Lady Lucy Duff-Gordon's life.[69] One of the pieces highlighted Cardozo's trivialization of her as a fashion designer.[70] I now teach that case with this and other additional information, and it then becomes impossible not to see the issue, with students writing things in their exam answers like 'Cardozo was obviously biased against Lady Lucy Duff-Gordon'. However, it was not obvious to me in the earlier years I taught this case. Someone needs to point it out, and then it becomes obvious. And one is left to wonder if the case can or should be used as any kind of precedent today given the evidence that the presumption Cardozo made was problematic. Its pedagogical value certainly becomes something very different than it once was, or at least it can be.[71]

Like other cases after the onslaught of historical investigation, the case, if it is a pedagogical or teaching case, what I have called 'a common law in the law school curriculum',[72] the improperness of the case or its use by influential legal academics/ law teachers can (and indeed should) become part of the lesson. What will a judge do if/when he or she is presented with evidence that a case the other side is relying on as a precedent has been discredited or misinterpreted? Would he/she say that it does not matter because the case has been accepted as good law in their jurisdiction by whatever court binds them? Would he/she say that it's been relied on for too long by judges and commentators of too high a stature to be over-ruled or ignored? Or might they reject use of the case due to its problematic or confused/confusing

---

[67]   Danzig, Watson (n. 2) 95–118 ff.

[68]   Victor Goldberg, 'Reading *Wood v. Lucy, Lady Duff-Gordon* with Help from the Kewpie Dolls' in *Framing Contract Law: An Economic Perspective* (2006) 53 ff.

[69]   See 'Symposium: The Enduring Legacy of *Wood v. Lucy, Lady Duff-Gordon*' (2008) 28 Pace L.R. 161–454 ff.

[70]   Deborah Zalesne, 'Integrating Academic Skills into First Year Curricula: Using *Wood v. Lucy, Lady Duff-Gordon* to Teach the Role of Facts in Legal Reasoning' (2007–2008) 28 Pace L.R. 290–1 ff (noting that when Cardozo writes that Lady Lucy Duff-Gordon 'styles herself "a creator of fashions". Her favor helps a sale. Manufacturers of dresses, millinery, and like articles are glad to pay for a certificate of her approval. The things which she designs, fabrics, parasols, and what not, have a new value in the public mind when issued in her name'; this is 'not a neutral statement about her job, but a deeper implicit statement about her character').

[71]   See also Debora L. Threedy, 'A Fish Story: *Alaska Fish Packers Association v. Domenico*' (2000) Utah L.R. 346 ff. (for seriously problematic use of *Alaska Packers* as an example of 'economic duress' by legal scholars like Richard Posner.) Reprinted in Douglas G. Baird (ed.), *Contracts Stories* (2007) 335 ff.

[72]   Fernandez (n. 19) 518 ff.

inheritance and at the very least ask counsel to find them something else to rely on? Much, probably, would depend on the judge. It would be a significant moment, the practical demands of a precedent-based system in a particular jurisdiction meeting the academic legal historical enterprise, which tends to be more diffuse in terms of the relevance of jurisdictional boundaries and capacious in terms of time and attention that might be spent sorting through such matters. It would be interesting to get an account of that kind of conflict or encounter, where and in what ways it might already be happening (e.g., *Popov v. Hyashi* and the Barry Bonds record-breaking home-run baseball and the professors who weighed in on who owned the ball).[73] Do legal historians become legal experts in such proceedings?

The text of a legal case is a meaningful and living artefact, travelling through time assuming serial incarnations based on those who are handling it. Without them it would be inert matter that would quite likely be left to languish in the dustbin of history. Once we view a legal case in this way and acknowledge the role that a range of legal professionals play in the case becoming the thing that it is, this expansion of our notion of the relevant persons involved in its uptake raises many questions about the propriety of that influence.

It is easy to think that an invisible and impersonal process is at work. Once it is made visible and personal, we want to know if this was appropriate. For example: was it right for Tapping Reeve to have influenced his students to pass a statute empowering married women to make a will? We might like to see glimmers of a pseudo-progressiveness in the early nineteenth century, but how do we feel about a late-nineteenth-century treatise-writer using his book on state constitutional conventions to legalize and de-politicize those turbulent, eminently democratic eruptions, creating order from inherent disorder?[74] Much depends on our politics and beliefs, and reasonable people will disagree. Yet no conversation at all can happen until those processes are described in their historical detail, even if/when the historian tells it, he/she inevitably brings his/her own perspectives and experiences to the telling or re-telling of topics or cases that appear to us now in a different incarnation. It will be yet another incarnation rather than a final reckoning, but that is how it should be.

E. P. Thompson famously wrote that '[t]he greatest of all legal fictions is that the law evolves, from case to case, by its own impartial logic, true only to its own integrity, unswayed by expedient considerations.'[75] The 'expedient considerations' include politics and social context, which extend beyond what and who were originally involved in the case to those persons making choices and decisions relating to its 'uptake' and then its circulation. This uptake process is external in the sense that it is still linked to politics and social context, but it is also importantly internal in

---

[73] See *Popov v. Hayashi* (2002) WL 31833731 (Cal. Sup. Ct., San Francisco County).

[74] Roman J. Hoyos, 'A Province of Jurisprudence?: Invention of a Law of Constitutional Conventions', in *Law Books in Action: Essays on the Anglo-American Legal Treatise* (2012) 108 ff.

[75] E. P. Thompson, *Whigs and Hunters: The Origin of the Black Act* (1975) 250 ff.

a way that has a specific and special connection to the common law.[76] The idea then behind the 'internalist' person-based or collective biography/prosopography process I advocate for here is to expand what is subjected to historical scrutiny to blind spots relating to violence and injustice, combined with an awareness of the law as a text in the sense of being fluid and changing.[77] The legal historian and what he/she produces is next in a chain of interpreters that will go on inevitably interpreting as long as the law or the case remains of interest.[78]

The primary challenge then to this type of legal historical research is establishing what among all of the things that could be said should be emphasized or highlighted. What is relevant and what is just more detail?[79] Perhaps each generation works out for itself what is most relevant to it, keeping aspects of the older preoccupations and approaches, but adding new ones based on what they see around them as most important. Lawyers and judges in their most positivistic mode reassert singular meaning. However, what happens is not that one meaning wins and another loses, but it goes back and forth, creating a dialectic or dialogue about what is important and what is not.

It might be that the easy availability of electronic resources will lessen the role of persons in the law, such as the casebook editor or the treatise-writer, just as virtually automatic and widespread case reporting has dramatically decreased the discretion of the nineteenth-century law reporter.[80] However, I dare to say that law professors will be keen to adhere to their position as packagers and presenters of the law. If I am correct, there will always be packaging and presenting for legal historians to study in the form of persons in the legal process.

Bibliography

Richard Danzig, Geoffrey R. Watson, *The Capability Problem in Contract Law: Further Readings on Well-Known Cases* (Foundation Press, 1978; 2nd edn., 2004)

---

[76] See Gerald J. Postema, 'Classical Common Law Jurisprudence (Part I)' (2002) 2 *Oxford University Commonwealth L.J.* 155 ff; 'Classical Common Law Jurisprudence (Part II)' (2003) 3 *Oxford University Commonwealth L.J.* 1 ff. Postema uses ideas like what is practical or pragmatic, 'reasonable usage', and 'artificial reason' to get at what is specific and internal to the common law system.

[77] See Robert Weisberg and Guyora Binder, *Literary Criticisms of Law* (2000).

[78] Fish (n. 31).

[79] For two different versions of this question see Gordon (n. 15) 2045 ff. (framing the issue in terms of 'what's the point? Sometimes Simpson's method looks like legal realism run amok, the piling up of incidental particulars, *les faits pour les faits*, context for context's sake') and James E. Krier, 'Facts, Information, and the Newly Discovered Record in *'Pierson v. Post'* (2009) 29 *Law and History Review* 189–91 ff (drawing a distinction between facts and information).

[80] John H. Langbein, 'Chancellor Kent and the History of Legal Literature' (1993) 93 *Columbia L.R.* 577 ff.

Richard Danzig, '*Hadley v. Baxendale*: A Study in the Industrialization of the Law' (1975) 4 *Journal of Legal Studies* 249, reprinted in Douglas G. Baird (ed.), *Contracts Stories* (Foundation Press, 2006)

Angela Fernandez, 'An Object Lesson in Speculation: Multiple Views of the Cathedral in *Leaf v. International Galleries*' (2008) 58 *University of Toronto L.J.* 3

Angela Fernandez, Markus D. Dubber, (eds.), *Law Books in Action: Essays on the Anglo-American Legal Treatise* (Hart Publishing, 2012)

Angela Fernandez, *Pierson v. Post, The Hunt for the Fox: Law and Professionalization in American Legal Culture* (Cambridge University Press, 2018)

Robert W. Gordon, 'Simpson's Leading Cases [Review of *Leading Cases in the Common Law* by A. W. B. Simpson]' (1997) 95 *Michigan Law Review* 2044

Robert W. Gordon, 'Critical Legal Histories' (1984) 36 *Stanford Law Review* 57

Elizabeth Mertz, *The Language of Law School: 'Learning to "Think Like a Lawyer"'* (Oxford University Press, 2007)

John T. Noonan, *Persons and Masks of the Law: Cardozo, Holmes, Jefferson, and Wythe as Makers of Masks* (Farrar, Straus, and Giroux, 1975)

A. W. Brian Simpson, 'The Rise and Fall of the Legal Treatise: Legal Principles and the Forms of Legal Literature' (1981) 48 *University of Chicago L.R.* 632

A. W. Brian Simpson, (ed.), *Biographical Dictionary of the Common Law* (Butterworths, 1984)

A. W. Brian Simpson, *Legal Theory and Legal History: Essays on the Common Law* (Hambledon Press, 1987)

A. W. Brian Simpson, *Leading Cases in the Common Law* (Oxford University Press, 1995)

Debora L. Threedy, 'Legal Archaeology: Excavating Cases, Reconstructing Context' (2006) 80 *Tulane L.R.* 1197

....

CHAPTER 15

FROM EVOLUTIONARY FUNCTIONALISM TO CRITICAL TRANSNATIONALISM

COMPARATIVE LEGAL HISTORY, ARISTOTLE TO PRESENT

....

KATHARINA ISABEL SCHMIDT

I. INTRODUCTION

....

IN a 1995 lecture titled 'Comparative Legal History in North America: A Report', Charles Donahue delivered a bleak assessment of the field. 'The state of comparative legal history', he suggested, 'can be very briefly summarized. . . . As I understand the term, comparative legal history hardly exists any place in the western world today.'[1]

---

[1] Charles Donahue, 'Comparative Legal History in North America: A Report' (1997) 65 *Tijdschrift voor Rechtsgeschiedenis* 1 ff.

Just over twenty years ago Donahue all but rang the death knell for a discipline that had at several points in time seemed like a counterweight to legal history's most maligned qualities: its parochial outlook, disciplinary solipsism, and lack of critical perspectives.

Against the background of Donahue's statement this chapter proceeds in three steps. First, I explore practices of legal-historical comparison from their beginnings as an occasional element of ancient, medieval, and early-modern treatises to their institutionalization as a discipline at the turn of the twentieth century. Second, I make a case for 'critical transnationalism' as a way for legal-historical comparativists to produce works that are both timely and interesting. Third, I survey promising areas of and approaches to transnational legal research, all the while bearing in mind the particular challenge law poses to transnational history.

II. Historicizing Comparative Legal History

To be sure, Donahue's contention that 'comparative legal history hardly exists any place in the western world today' is problematic. If my task in this chapter is to carve out a vision of comparative legal history for the future, obituaries of this kind do not inspire much confidence. And yet, there may be much to gain from looking more closely at Donahue's observation and its context. It was thus, perhaps, not only the imminence of the new millennium and the deluge of stock-taking exercises it unleashed that gave Donahue reason for his 'report' in 1995. It may also have been the date's relative propinquity to the end of the Cold War, which made the topic of comparative legal history a particularly pertinent one for the late 1990s.

A. On the Uses and Abuses of Comparative Legal History in Modern Times

The century that was coming to an end had, after all, witnessed the use of comparative-historical arguments about law by authoritarians of every ilk, first and foremost the Nazis. Insights produced by the discipline had been integral to rhetoric on both sides of the Iron Curtain. They had also served as justifications for the forceful 'modernization' of 'Third World' countries around the globe. It was, in short, not only true but perhaps a good thing that Donahue could conclude when he did that comparative legal history was a thing of the past.

Going back further into the nineteenth century does not positively correct the discipline's severely tarnished reputation either. Comparative legal history had thus been mobilized to justify the colonization, subjugation, and annihilation of non-white, non-western, non-Christian populations. Over the course of the nineteenth century, comparative legal history had become a measuring rod for 'civilizational' progress, a crucial part of a pseudo-scientific process in which the laws and cultures of people outside western legal traditions could never compare favourably. With the end of the Cold War, as the putatively last vestige of the kinds of sentiments that had plunged the world into two gruesome global conflicts within the span of several decades, comparative legal history may have seemed to Donahue not only backwards but indeed beyond salvation.

It is important to remember that Donahue neglected a number of compelling works being written around the time he delivered his 'report'. Most prominently, I am thinking here of James Q. Whitman's comparative-historical treatments of shame sanctions, carceral punishment, dignity, privacy, church-state relations, consumer protection, and pre-modern criminal procedure.[2] Donahue's comments are instructive nevertheless. They hint at the problematic uses comparative legal history can be, and has been, put to. Before illustrating this point by reference to the history of the practice, however, another issue begs for clarification.

B. Comparative Legal History versus Historically Informed Comparative Law

In a recent piece, James Gordley suggested that comparative lawyers and legal historians are not only fellow travellers, but are in constant need of 'mutual support'.[3] What exactly, though, is comparative legal history and how, if at all, is it different from historically informed comparative law? 'Law', 'history', and 'comparison' are notoriously hard-to-pin-down concepts. Combining the three into what has,

---

[2] James Q. Whitman, 'What is Wrong with Inflicting Shame Sanctions?' (1998) 107 *Yale L.J.* 1055 ff; 'Enforcing Civility and Respect: Three Societies' (2000) 109 *Yale L.J.* 1279 ff; *Harsh Justice—Criminal Punishment and the Widening Divide between Europe and America* (2003); 'The Two Western Cultures of Privacy: Dignity versus Liberty' (2004) 113 *Yale L.J.* 1151 ff; 'Separating Church and State: The Atlantic Divide' (2008) 34 *Historical Reflections* 86 ff; 'Consumerism versus Producerism: A Study in Comparative Law' (2007) 117 *Yale L.J.* 340 ff; *The Origins of Reasonable Doubt—Theological Roots of the Criminal Trial* (2008). See also James Q. Whitman, 'A Letter from America' (2016) 132 *Zeitschrift der Savigny-Stiftung für Rechtsgeschichte (Germanistische Abteilung)* 441 ff.

[3] James Gordley, 'Comparative Law and Legal History', in Mathias Reimann, Reinhard Zimmermann (eds.), *Oxford Handbook of Comparative Law* (2006) 768 ff. See also Mathias Reimann, Alain Levasseur, 'Comparative Law and Legal History in the United States' (1998) 46 *A.J.C.L. (Supplement)* 1 ff.

at least in modern times, presented itself as an independent discipline only exacerbates the problem.

We cannot consistently distinguish comparative legal history and historically informed comparative law by reference to the working materials used by their respective practitioners. Law in its current configuration constitutes both the starting point and benchmark for comparative inquiries into history. Legal rules and principles presently in force cannot, in turn, be understood without recourse to the story of their historical coming-into-being.

Nor would a strict distinction based on the purpose of comparison be sustainable. Some comparativists, certainly, are more vocal than others about their reformist intentions. It would be naïve to think, however, that comparison ever constitutes a perfectly neutral practice.[4] Comparative legal historians, no less than comparative lawyers, are rarely ever interested only in explaining how law came to be what it is.

Neither is it possible to distinguish comparative legal history and historically informed comparative law based on their underlying assumption of law as either *explanans* or *explanandum*. We can certainly point to scholars who want to understand society and culture by reference to law's development over time; just like we can point to scholars who want to understand law by reference to the development of society and culture over time. The boundaries, however, blur.

There are easy cases, to be sure. A scholar comparing various European liability regimes with a view to legal harmonization, even when drawing on history extensively for this purpose, would to most of our minds be an historically-informed comparative lawyer. Conversely, we would think of a scholar comparing early-modern legal institutions for the purpose of explaining East-West economic divergence as a comparative legal historian—however relevant the topic to contemporary debates. The reason for these intuitions, though, may have to do with institutional affiliation more than anything else. I will come back to this.

For the purpose of my argument it is perhaps not necessary to distinguish sharply between comparative legal history and historically informed comparative law. Whatever lines we might want to draw between the two, their histories are entangled. My argument, in any case, about the pernicious uses to which legal-historical comparisons have been, and still can be, put applies to both.

A definitive account of either discipline remains to be written. The challenge of any such endeavour would be to avoid anachronistically grouping together practices of comparison that cohere only in hindsight. What I offer in the following are episodic glances into legal-historical comparisons over time with a view to setting up my case for a turn to what I call 'critical transnationalism'.

---

[4] See, e.g., Gerhard Dannemann, 'Comparative Law: Study of Similarities or Differences?' in Mathias Reimann, Reinhard Zimmermann (eds.), *Oxford Handbook of Comparative Law* (2006) 384 ff.

1. In the Beginning was Aristotle: Legal-Historical Comparison in Antiquity and the Early Middle Ages

In the *Politics*, written some time in the fourth century BC, Aristotle elaborated on how the organization of a political community could contribute to its citizens' realization of a life lived in virtue. In doing so, he made reference to the constitutional law and history of 158 Greek city-states. Of particular interest is Aristotle's construction of a relationship between constitutionalism and culture. I will have more to say about this below.

Skipping ahead more than half a millennium, late antique efforts to read Jewish alongside Roman and Christian texts are next. Church Fathers from Tertullian to Augustine engaged in polemic analyses of Jewish laws and customs, juxtaposing them with texts from early Christianity. The principal aim of this so-called *adversus-Judaeos*-literature was to demonstrate that Jewish failure to recognize Jesus as messiah disqualified them from the 'kingdom of god', leaving Christianity as the only 'true' religion.[5]

Another instance of Judeo-Christian comparison was the *Collatio Legum Mosaicarum et Romanarum*, written most probably some time in the fourth century. Dealing with a diverse range of subjects, the *Collatio* juxtaposed Latin excerpts from the Bible with statements from the jurists, Roman imperial laws, and contemporary codes. The *Collatio's* authorship and purpose are debated. One scholar recently suggested, however, that 'the most likely probability is that a Christian Collator attempted to draw pagan lawyers to Christianity through demonstrating the connections between the divine laws of Moses and the historic jurisprudence of the Romans.'[6]

Moving ahead to the fall of the West Roman Empire, what we encounter next are comparisons between Roman law and local custom. Beginning in the late fifth century, classical legal learning, in much of continental Europe, came gradually to be replaced by Germanic codes. The resulting normative pluralism and jurisdictional conflict inspired thinking about the relationship between different cultures and the development of their laws over time.

Importantly, this line of thought continued all the way into the eleventh- and twelfth-century Roman law revival, when medieval jurists became concerned with rehabilitating classical Roman texts vis-à-vis vulgar law and custom. Boncompagno da Signa's and Odofredus's denunciations of Lombard law, for one, exemplify the turn to legal-historical comparison for this purpose.[7]

---

[5] See generally Heinz Schreckenberg, *Die christlichen Adversus-Judaeos-Texte und ihr literarisches und historisches Umfeld (1.-11. Jh.)* (4th edn., 1999).

[6] Robert F. Frakes, *Compiling the Collatio Legum Mosaicarum et Romanarum in Late Antiquity* (2011) 151.

[7] See James Q. Whitman, 'The Lawyers Discover the Fall of Rome' (1991) 9 *Law and History Review* 191 ff.

More systematic efforts of this kind, however, did not see the light of day until after the rediscovery of Aristotle some time later. It is at this point that we witness something like a continuous practice of legal-historical comparison emerge.

2. *Legal-Historical Comparison and the Early Modern English Constitutionalist Tradition*

Early-modern English constitutionalists, in particular, were beginning to take a sustained interest in civil law-common law comparisons. They were motivated by larger concerns with socio-political difference and competition. Specifically, they sought to distinguish Anglo-Saxon liberties from continental despotism—an idea scholars have explored widely in the context of comparative criminal procedure.[8]

Faced with Henry VI's 'bastard feudalism', John Fortescue, for one, made a memorable case for justice over tyranny based on comparative evidence. His *In Praise of the Laws of England* (c. 1470) consisted of a master-student dialogue between Prince Edward, son of Henry VI, and his chancellor, in which the latter sought to convince the former of the value of English law and government. To this end, Fortescue contrasted English 'political and royal' kingship with the 'only royal' kingship of the French civil law tradition.[9] The laws of England were 'best', he argued, because they were uniquely suited to English conditions.

Importantly, Fortescue made his arguments against the civil law tradition by reference to Aristotelian method and thought. In addition to the work's question-answer structure, *In Praise of the Laws of England* restated Aristotelian arguments in favour of law as a moral institution. At a time of great anxiety about the status of the common law relative to competing normative orders as well as about the respective competences of church and crown, Thomas More, Christopher St. German, and Thomas Smith went on to expand on Fortescue's efforts.

More is almost never considered a legal-historical comparativist. His *Utopia* (1516), however, is full of law, and his approach to identifying social ideals through comparison resembles that of Aristotle.[10] More prefaced the description of his fictional island society with a passage in which the book's protagonist, Raphael Hythloday, recounts various conversations with continental scholars. These conversations provided More with an opportunity to showcase the advantages of trying to solve problems of law, policy, and government comparatively.

---

[8] See esp. John H. Langbein, *The Origins of Adversary Criminal Trial* (2003) 338 ff. For a general account of this idea see J. G. A. Pocock, *The Ancient Constitution and the Feudal Law—A Study of English Historical Thought in the Seventeenth Century* (1987).

[9] Shelley Lockwood (ed.), *Sir John Fortescue's On the Laws and Governance of England* (1997) xxiv ff.

[10] See generally George M. Logan, *The Meaning of More's Utopia* (1983). In this context attention should also be paid to those of More's texts that address questions of law more directly, first and foremost his *Debellation of Salem and Bizance* (1533).

Like Fortescue, St. German was a staunch opponent of clergy and papacy and like Fortescue, he emphasized the superiority of English common law over other legal traditions through the use of master-student dialectics.[11] St. German's *Doctor and Student* (1523) was thus specifically concerned with an exposition of the relationship between English common law and 'conscience', a foundational concept in the law of equity.

Despite, or because of, its rather one-sided account of the virtues of English as opposed to Roman and canon law, *Doctor and Student* remained a standard textbook well into the seventeenth century. While St. German's debt to Aristotle was mediated through Fortescue, Smith, as the last—and perhaps most interesting—of the English constitutionalists, stands for a more proactive engagement with Aristotelian thought.

Smith wrote his most well-known book, *A Discourse on the Commonwealth of England* (1565), while in France as an envoy of the English crown. In his friend Walter Hadden, he confided: 'And because in my absence [from England] I feel a yearning for our commonwealth I have put together three books here at Toulouse describing it.'[12] Smith went on to provide one of the most renowned surveys of Elizabethan government of his day, with an emphasis on its relative merit vis-à-vis continental systems.

In the *Discourse* he thus sought to clarify 'the principal points wherein [the English government] doth differ from the policy or government at this time used in France, Italy, Spain, Germany and all other countries which do follow the civil law of the Romans' and to illustrate 'points wherein the one differeth from the other, to see who hath taken the righter, truer, and more commodious way to govern the people'.

To Hadden, Smith explained further that he had given his comparative efforts 'the shape in which [he] imagined that Aristotle wrote of the many Greek commonwealth books which are no longer extant'. The *Discourse* thus begins with an explanation of the different 'kinds or fashions of government', which are clearly based on the tripartite typology Aristotle advanced in the *Politics*.

Smith was considerably more rigorous than Fortescue and St. German, whose comparisons were largely ornamental, if not desultory. While More showed an unprecedented willingness to engage in genuine comparison, Smith—out of all early modern English constitutionalists—exhibited the greatest proclivity for exploring both limits and opportunities of the comparative method in law and legal history.

Interestingly, Smith had been trained in both the civil and the common law tradition. In fact, he had spent some time in the early 1540s studying at the University of Padua, then hotbed of legal humanism. As a consequence, Smith

---

[11] See generally T. F. T. Plucknett, J. L. Barton, 'Introduction' in Plucknett, Barton (eds.), *St. German's Doctor and Student* (1974).

[12] L. Alston, 'Introduction' in Thomas Smith, *De Republica Anglorum* (L. Alston, ed., 1906) xiii (quoting Smith's letter) ff.

admired the Roman law tradition and, unlike Fortescue and St. German, took pride in his cosmopolitanism. Peter Stein went so far as to suggest that '[Smith's] civil law studies gave him a particular perspective, the ability to consider English institutions from the outside'.[13] Arguments of this kind will resurface as part of my discussion of the 'legal immersion'-debate below.

3. *Bodin and Renaissance 'Info-Lust'*

As important as Smith's reliance on Aristotle are the similarities between his ideas and those of Jean Bodin. Following the exhaustion of the glossatory method some time in the thirteenth century, late medieval jurists abandoned their scholasticism for a more pragmatic approach. The resulting *mos italicus* came to be criticized by sixteenth-century humanists for its alleged distortion of original sources. By way of alternative, the humanists turned to historical, philological, and systematic methods to restore the original meaning of Roman legal materials.

While mainstream humanists continued to uphold the *Corpus Iuris* as a source of universal legal truths, early sixteenth-century jurists associated with the *mos gallicus* sought to understand Roman law in its historical dimension. To the extent that Roman legal materials made reference to public law rules at all, they argued, those rules were wholly incompatible with the constitutional realities of sixteenth-century France. Against this background, Bodin moved in for the 'final consummation' of the break away from Roman law's exegetic authority.[14]

For one, Bodin attempted to create a kind of *jus gentium* out of those legal building blocks that were identical to every legal system. At the same time, he sought to identify the best possible solution to all other legal questions by means of critical comparison. In doing so he insisted on the need to go beyond Roman law.

In his *Methodus ad Facilem Historiarum Cognitionem* (1566), he famously wrote: 'I shall not mention the absurdity of wishing to draw conclusions about universal law from the laws of Rome. . . the only way to arrange the laws and govern the state is to collect all the laws of all or the most famous commonwealths, to compare them and derive the best variety'.

In his *Six Books of the Commonwealth* (1576), finally, Bodin formulated what Julian Franklin referred to as a 'theory of legal difference'. Bodin thus argued that in order to determine what kinds of legal rules would be most suitable for a particular society, attention should be paid to its natural environment and forms of political organization. 'The people . . . of the middle regions', Bodin suggested, 'have more force than they of the south and less policy: and more wit than they of the north,

---

[13] Peter Stein, 'Sir Thomas Smith: Renaissance Civilian', in Peter Stein (ed.), *The Character and Influence of the Roman Civil Law* (1988) 186 ff.

[14] Julian Franklin, *Jean Bodin and the Sixteenth Century Revolution in Methodology of Law and History* (1963) 2 ff. See also for translations of subsequent Bodin passages.

and less force; and they are more fit to command and govern commonwealths, and [are] more just in their actions.'

It is this last point in particular that illustrates the intellectual familiarity between Bodin and, once more, Aristotle. In the *Politics,* Aristotle had similarly drawn a distinction between Greeks, Asians, and Europeans in terms of skill, spirit, and thought in order to determine their respective predisposition for freedom or slavery. Bodin, like Smith, furthermore adapted Aristotle's typology of states. While Bodin rejected some of Aristotle's concepts for being based on elements only contingently present in Pericles's Athens, he pursued essentially the same questions, using similar categories and methods.

It would be wrong, however, to think of Bodin as a mere epigone of Aristotle. Indeed, Bodin significantly expanded on the comparative method of the *Politics,* reflecting both contributions and concerns of Renaissance humanism. For one, he could draw on both sources and critical textualism associated with the infamous forger Annius of Viterbo.[15] What is more, he had available to him works like Johannes Boemus's cosmography *The Manners, Laws, and Customs of All People* (1520), which provided him with a more expansive approach to comparison that included both legal and non-legal sources.[16]

In a recent book, Anne Blair suggested that '[w]hat was distinctive to the Renaissance was the large scale of accumulation of textual excerpts' fuelled by a 'newly invigorated info-lust that sought to gather and manage as much information as possible.'[17] It is this 'info-lust', arguably, that precipitated a change from pre-modern to modern legal-historical comparison. What distinguishes Smith and, especially, Bodin from Aristotle is thus the wealth and variety of their sources as well as the critical approach they used to 'manage' them.

And one more thing was new in the sixteenth century: the 'discovery' of the Americas. After 1492, the Spanish crown in particular began taking an interest in indigenous ways of life. Peter Martyr's *De Orbe Novo,* written between 1493 and 1525, thus set the course for further comparisons between 'civilized' European law and culture, on the one hand, and the 'primitive' customs of the colonized, on the other: '[The islanders of Hispaniola] go naked, they know neither weights nor measures, nor that source of all misfortunes, money; living in a golden age, without laws, without lying judges, without books . . . '.[18] Findings like these, as in other colonial contexts, soon came to

[15] See generally Anthony Grafton, *Defenders of the Text: The Traditions of Scholarship in an Age of Science, 1450–1800* (1991) 76 ff.

[16] See generally Anthony Grafton, *New Worlds, Ancient Texts* (1992) 99–101 ff.

[17] Anne Blair, *Too Much To Know—Managing Scholarly Information Before the Modern Age* (2010) 5 ff.

[18] Francis Augustus MacNutt, *De Orbe Novo, the Eight Decades of Peter Martyr d'Anghera; tr. from the Latin with Notes and Introduction* (1912) 79 ff.

determine questions about indigenous rights to land and, later, the capacity for self-determination.[19]

4. *Montesquieu and the Eighteenth-Century Rise of the 'Comparative Method'*

Only a handful of works produced during the two hundred years between Bodin and Montesquieu approached the quality and verve of the *Six Books of the Commonwealth*. None of them seem to have served as a stepping-stone for Montesquieu, however. Natural law scholars like Francis Bacon, Hugo Grotius, Gottfried Wilhelm Leibniz, Samuel Pufendorf, and Christian Wolff drew on foreign legal materials principally for the purpose of deductively illustrating their theories about law and justice.

Bacon, fittingly, likened scholars writing about law from the perspective of their own legal tradition to prisoners 'preaching from within shackles'.[20] His attempt to formulate strategies to transcend these shackles, however, provided little to go on. While Grotius's *On the Law of War and Peace* (1625) contained reference to an impressive range of legal materials, it is debatable whether he ever considered these to be independent sources of law. Leibniz, unfortunately, never made good on his call for a temporally and geographically comprehensive 'theatre of the legal world'.[21] As far as I can see, Pufendorf and Wolff never moved beyond illustrative uses of legal-historical comparison, either.

New impulses for legal-historical comparison in the two hundred years between Bodin and Montesquieu could perhaps have come from John Selden or Gianbattista Vico—two very different innovators in their own right. Selden's genuine comparative efforts in the *History of Tithes* (1618) and *De Synedris* (1650) were more sophisticated than much of what had come before. Vico's prescient historical method in *The New Science* (1725), in turn, set him apart from most of his contemporaries. Montesquieu, however, whose thinking had a revolutionary impact on mid-eighteenth-century European social and political thought, largely reverted back to Bodin.

In *The Spirit of the Laws* (1748) Montesquieu set out to examine the relationship between geographic and climatic conditions, forms of governance, and the 'spirit' of the law.[22] Like Bodin, Montesquieu was interested in similarity as well as difference. His proto-evolutionary determinism as well as his proto-liberal relativism

---

[19] See Thomas Duve, 'Indigenous Rights in Latin America: A Legal Historical Perspective' 2017-02 *Max Planck Institute for European Legal History Research Paper Series*.

[20] Francis Bacon, *De Dignitate et Augmentis Scientiarum* (1623) vol. III, 3 ff.

[21] See generally Gottfried Wilhelm Leibniz, *Nova Methodus Discendae Docendaeque Iuris Prudentiae* (1667).

[22] See, e.g., Robert Launay, 'Montesquieu: The Specter of Despotism and the Origins of Comparative Law', in Annelise Riles (ed.), *Rethinking the Masters of Comparative Law* (2001) 22 ff.

nevertheless made him look like a precursor of nineteenth-century comparativism. Importantly, the work was less specifically legal than a contribution to the nascent field of cultural, political, and religious comparison. As exemplified by the following non-exhaustive list, inductive comparativism had, by the mid-eighteenth century, become the method of choice for scholars across all fields of inquiry.[23]

In the tenth edition of his *Systema Naturae* (1758), natural scientist Carolus Linnaeus divided mankind into different racial 'varieties'. Around the turn of the nineteenth century George Cuvier began classifying animals based on the respective functioning of their organs. Friedrich Schlegel, Franz Bopp, and Jacob Grimm soon followed with their application of the comparative method to language and literature. Charles Lyell and Charles Darwin famously revolutionized geology and biology along similar lines. It is against this background that developments in nineteenth-century German legal science need to be read.

5. *Methodological Debates in Nineteenth-Century German Legal Science*

In his *Blick auf die deutsche Rechtswissenschaft* (1810), Paul Johann Anselm Feuerbach made a fervent case for legal-historical comparison: 'Why does the anatomist have his comparative anatomy? And why does the jurist not yet have his comparative jurisprudence? After all, comparison and combination are, in the empirical sciences, the richest source of all discoveries. It is only by considering all similarities and differences and the reasons behind them that we can comprehensively make sense of the singular essences and inner characteristics of every thing.'

The famous 1814 codification debate between Anton Friedrich Justus Thibaut and Friedrich Carl von Savigny equally touched on questions of comparison. Due to his identification of the nationally idiosyncratic *Volksgeist* as the source of all law, Savigny had little interest in foreign law. Thibaut criticized this sharply: 'Ten sophisticated lectures about the constitution of the Persians and the Chinese would awaken in our students more of a truly jurisprudential sense than a hundred lectures about the pathetic charlatanry underlying the law of intestate succession going from Augustus to Justinian.'[24]

Feuerbach's and Thibaut's statements highlight nineteenth-century jurists' commitment to comparison and history for the purpose of fashioning a legal science that reflected national culture and concerns. The gradual ascendance of teleological conceptions of history in this context heavily impacted legal scholarship. Following Georg Wilhelm Friedrich Hegel's notion of the *Weltgeist*, jurists started thinking of different kinds of law as tied to or indicative of different stages of history.

---

[23] For an overview, see e.g., Nils Jansen, 'Comparative Law and Comparative Knowledge', in Mathias Reimann, Reinhard Zimmermann (eds.), *Oxford Handbook of Comparative Law* (2006) 305 ff.

[24] Anton F.J. *Thibaut, Civilistische Abhandlungen* (1814) 433 ff.

The most famous—and certainly most interesting—scholar writing in this tradition was Eduard Gans.[25]

Reflecting his neo-Hegelian roots, Gans sharply criticized Savigny's 'micrology'. In the same breath, he made a powerful argument for a 'universal legal history', which he believed could uncover 'the spirit of the law as it has developed in Europe and exists today'. In keeping with his own ambitious demands, Gans subsequently dedicated himself to compiling what he called 'the law of inheritance in universal legal perspective', as part of which he compared Indian, Chinese, Mosaic-Talmudic, Islamic, Greek, and Roman inheritance laws. He planned further research on inheritance law in the German and Slavic Middle Ages as well as in modern times.

Gans's premature death prevented him from finishing his project. Mid-nineteenth-century German efforts in legal-historical comparison, however, continued on the shoulders of two no less prodigious scholars: Karl Marx and Karl Josef Anton Mittermaier. Marx's insights about property and capitalism were, as is well known, largely based on comparative-historical arguments about law. Mittermaier, in turn, drew on a wide variety of continental and Anglo-American sources in order to shed light on the nature of the criminal process and, in particular, the role of the jury within it.[26]

During the early 1840s the young Rudolf von Jhering engaged in a little-known attempt at writing a universal legal history of his own.[27] His interest in comparative-historical questions is evidenced also by his posthumously published work on the pre-history of Indo-European peoples.[28] Writing just a little later than Jhering was Josef Kohler, whose wide-ranging research included comparative law, universal legal history, and ethnological jurisprudence.[29] His analyses of colonial laws and customs, especially, stand out in this context.

6. *The Anglo-American Historical School*

Anglo-American legal scholarship in the second half of the twentieth century largely followed European trends. Influenced by German legal thought and with no small debt owed to contemporary social theory, Henry Maine famously argued

---

[25] See, e.g., Corrado Bertani, 'Das Erbrecht in weltgeschichtlicher Entwicklung (1824–1835) von Eduard Gans: Das erste Zeugnis vom Einfluss Hegels auf die Privatrechtsgeschichtsschreibung' (2007) 11 *Rechtsgeschichte* 110 ff; and Eduard Gans, *Naturrecht und Universalrechtsgeschichte* (2005).

[26] See, e.g., Markus Dubber, 'The German Jury and the Metaphysical *Volk*: From Romantic Idealism to Nazi Ideology' (1995) 43 *A.J.C.L.* 227 ff.

[27] Michael Kunze, 'Jherings Universalrechtsgeschichte: zu einer unveröffentlichten Handschrift des Privatdozenten Dr. Rudolf Jhering', in Heinz Monhaupt (ed.), *Rechtsgeschichte in den beiden deutschen Staaten (1988–1990): Beispiele, Parallelen, Positionen* (1991) 151 ff.

[28] See generally Rudolf von Jhering, *Prehistory of the Indo-Europeans* (1894).

[29] See Bernhard Grossfeld, Ingo Theusinger, 'Josef Kohler: Brückenbauer zwischen Jurisprudenz und Rechtsethnologie' (2000) 64 *RabelsZ* 696 ff.

that the movement of 'progressive' societies had been 'from status to contract'. Drawing on sources ranging from Roman and Hindu law to Biblical texts and Slavic, Germanic, and Irish legal materials, Maine's *Ancient Law* (1861) contained discussions on the early history of wills, property, contract, and criminal law with a view to illustrating the move from 'primitive' collectivism to 'modern' individualism.[30]

While Maine was particularly intent on justifying English colonial reforms of Indian customary law, his younger colleagues Frederic William Maitland and Frederick Pollock pursued, for the most part, less pragmatic aims. They nevertheless considered themselves to be writing in the same evolutionary-functionalist tradition. Maitland, for one, became famous for the dictum that '[h]istory involves comparison and the English lawyer who knew nothing and cared nothing for any system but his own hardly came in sight of the idea of legal history.'[31] Only through comparative-historical efforts was it possible to formulate a vision of law and society that reflected national concerns.

On the other side of the Atlantic, Oliver Wendell Holmes's *The Common Law* (1881) impressed its readers with sophisticated comparisons between the Anglo-American common and the Roman civil law tradition.[32] Similarly, scholars like Henry Adams, Melville Bigelow, James Bradley Thayer, and James Barr Ames were invested in tracing the Anglo-Saxon roots of American law. Much of their work was inspired by a desire to flesh out the nature of the American polity by reference to its legal history.

7. Twentieth-Century Developments

The year 1900 marks an important caesura in the entangled history of comparative legal history and historically informed comparative law. That summer, the first World Congress on Comparative Law took place in Paris. On this occasion, adherents of universal legal history, ethnological jurisprudence, and ancient law squared off against a younger generation of scholars concerned with strategic legislative reform based on comparisons of positive laws. The split that occurred famously traced Édouard Lambert's distinction between *histoire comparative* and *législation comparée*.[33]

In line with this, the study of comparative law and legislation established itself as part of the professional study of the positive law, to be undertaken by law professors

---

[30] See Katharina Isabel Schmidt, 'Henry Maine's "Modern Law": From Status to Contract and Back Again?' (2017) 65 *A.J.C.L.* 145 ff.

[31] Frederic William Maitland, *Why the History of English Law is Not Written* (1888) 11.

[32] See generally David Rabban, *Law's History—American Legal Thought and the Transatlantic Turn to History* (2012).

[33] See generally Stefan Vogenauer, 'Rechtsgeschichte und Rechtsvergleichumg um 1900—Die Geschichte einer anderen "Emanzipation durch Auseinanderdenken"' (2012) 76 RabelsZ 1122 ff.

and practitioners. What came to be known as comparative legal history, in turn, became more theoretical, allying itself with the humanities and the social sciences. It is based on this institutional separation—replete with diverging transdisciplinary connections—that a distinction between comparative legal history and historically informed comparative law seems most plausibly drawn.

Especially adherents of the nascent discipline of sociology became interested in legal-historical comparison as a source of knowledge about social life. Emile Durkheim, for one, had already drawn extensively on legal materials from both ancient and modern societies to formulate his distinction between mechanic and organic forms of social solidarity in *The Division of Labour* (1893). Law from various times and places similarly went on to play a crucial role as part of Max Weber's theories about the development of capitalism, religion, and the modern state, as expressed most famously in *Economy and Society* (1921–1922).

The Nazis, too, however, took an active interest in legal-historical comparison. Not only, as recently shown by Whitman, did they look to American race legislation as an inspiration for the Nuremberg Laws,[34] they also wanted to replace 'materialistic' and 'value-free' Roman law with 'idealistic' and 'value-laden' German(ic) law.[35] Drawing on the work of late nineteenth-century racial theorist Houston Stewart Chamberlain, Nazi jurists thus traced everything undesirable and 'un-Germanic' about Roman law to Jewish and other 'oriental' influences.

After the Second World War, interest in what had come to be defined as comparative law at Paris clearly outpaced interest in comparative legal history. That said, there were remnants of the idea that the development of a particular society's legal thought and practice over time allowed for some degree of insight into and evaluation of its culture. Scholars working during the Cold War—most famously René David, Konrad Zweigert, and Hein Kötz—operated on the assumption that it was possible to divide legal systems into 'families'.[36]

Problematically, this idea was subsequently picked up and inflated by the triumphalist 'legal origins'-literature of the 1990s, which was—perhaps—the last nail in the coffin of twentieth-century legal-historical comparison. In an effort to stimulate economic growth in underdeveloped regions of the world, a small group of American economists compared the performance of countries governed by the civil law tradition to that of countries governed by the common law tradition. Based on their finding that the latter group significantly outperformed the former, the

---

[34] James Q. Whitman, *Hitler's American Model—The United States and the Making of Nazi Race Law* (2017).

[35] See in particular Peter Landau, 'Römisches Recht und deutsches Gemeinrecht. Zur rechtspolitischen Zielsetzung im nationalsozialistischen Parteiprogramm', in Michael Stolleis, Dieter Simon (eds.), *Rechtsgeschichte im Nationalsozialismus—Beiträge zur Geschichte einer Disziplin* (1989) 11 ff.

[36] See René David, *Les Grands Systems de Droit Contemporains* (1964) and Konrad Zweigert, Hein Kötz, *Einführung in die Rechtsvergleichung* (1969).

World Bank issued recommendations for a range of policies reflecting common law regulatory principles.

One scholar discredited such ostentatiously facile empiricism through a humorous comparison of common and civil law countries regarding their respective performances in the FIFA World Cup. His caustic conclusion that 'especially French law . . . leads to good soccer' should not distract, however, from the seriousness of the matter.[37] By the turn of the millennium, practices of legal-historical comparison had amassed a rather ambivalent track record.

III. Towards Critical Transnationalism in History and Law

The pernicious uses to which legal-historical comparisons have been put certainly call for caution. They do not, however, suggest intellectual bankruptcy. Many disciplines were born out of the dubious alliance between academic knowledge-production and expansive state- and empire-building projects. Following years of soul-searching they have since recouped their integrity. In what follows I suggest that history's recent turn towards 'the transnational' should provide legal-historical comparativists with a source of both optimism and inspiration.

A. Discovering 'the Transnational' in History

Comparative history took off at the same time that comparative legal history, as it had crystallized at Paris, began disappearing into the quicksand of authoritarian ideology. In addition to Henri Pirenne and Otto Hintze, it was most famously Marc Bloch who made a case for historical comparison as a means of transcending the interwar's excessive nationalism. The nation, Bloch argued, was but one of several 'obsolete topographical compartments in which [historians] pretend[ed] to enclose social realities'. 'In each historical instant', Bloch argued, 'the appropriate geographical framework ha[d] to be found.'[38]

---

[37] Mark D. West, 'Legal Determinants of World Cup Success', *Michigan Law and Economics Research Paper No. 02-009*, available at: <https://papers.ssrn.com/sol3/papers2.cfm?abstract_id=318940> (accessed 30 April 2018).

[38] Marc Bloch, 'Pour une histoire comparée des sociétés européennes' (1928) 48 *Revue de Synthèse Historique* 15 ff.

Until the rediscovery of historical sociology in the post-war period, the comparative efforts of Pirenne, Hintze, and Bloch were either ignored or unfairly lumped together with the grand civilizational narratives of Oswald Spengler and Arnold Toynbee. Starting in the early 1960s, however, social scientists like Barrington Moore, Theda Skocpol, and Charles Tilly began using interdisciplinary methods to make comparative statements on the origins of dictatorships, revolutions, and changes in the structure of social organization generally. Comparative history, at least briefly, was on the way up.

With the rise of anti- and post-colonial studies in the late 1960s, however, this new comparative history, too, came under attack. Scholars of Latin America, Africa, and Asia identified resistance to European and American imperialism as a process that transcended national boundaries. Historians like C. L. R. James, Frantz Fanon, and Alejo Carpentier further called attention to the dialectic between colonialism and anti-colonialism in producing particularized forms of identity and meaning. The newly discovered variability of seemingly universal categories like race, class, and gender challenged both methodological nationalism and the comparative paradigm itself.

Michel Foucault's argument that power was ubiquitous, diffuse, and near impossible to pin down further detracted attention away from the nation state's real and analytic centrality. Comparative history, so the argument went, obscured rather than elucidated the insidious workings of power. It created the illusion of comparability, eradicating irreducible differences in the process. Clifford Geertz's argument about social scientific data as nothing but an externalist construction of those 'webs of significance [man] himself ha[d] spun' led to similar conclusions.[39]

Late twentieth-century works like Edward Saïd's *Orientalism* (1978) and Dipesh Chakrabarty's *Provincializing Europe* (2000) speak to the powerful influence the 'cultural turn' had exerted on historical scholarship. They also evidence a renewed concern with questions about the relationship between the 'self' and the 'other', the historian and her subject of study. In addition, Chakrabarty's work, in particular, reveals a growing interest in processes of globalization and their implication for the writing of history.

The end of the Cold War precipitated a move from Manichean bipolarity to global interconnectedness. The approaching millennium, as illustrated by Donahue's state-of-the-field report, heightened scholars' interest in contingency and crisis. Non-state actors made their presence felt in fields as diverse as human rights, terrorism, climate change, information technology, maritime piracy, and financial regulation. In response, 'new globalization' scholars turned to the study of heterarchical

---

[39] Clifford Geertz, *The Interpretation of Cultures* (1973) 5 ff.

and interdependent networks, further side-lining centralized and monolithic conceptions of power.

Institutional developments within the American historical profession further helped to put transnational history on the map. By the early 1990s, transnationalists David Thelen and Thomas Bender had been appointed to leading positions at the *Journal of American History* and the *American Historical Review*, respectively. Intent on toppling the prevalent 'American exceptionalism' paradigm, Thelen and Bender, aided by Australian historian Ian Tyrell, formalized what we now refer to as the 'transnational turn'. The publication of Daniel Rodgers's *Atlantic Crossings* (1998) subsequently popularized both term and approach beyond American academic circles.

The multiple genealogies of transnational history speak to both its timeliness and to the diverse range of approaches associated with it. That said, most transnationalists are principally concerned with denaturalizing the nation state as a foundational unit of historical analysis. The resulting focus on persons, objects, and ideas on the move has led to widespread rejections of depthless 'influence' and 'exchange' metaphors in favour of multi-dimensional 'translation-', 'hybridization-', and 'friction-'talk. In the absence of an Archimedean point from which to neutrally observe transnational processes, epistemological self-scrutiny constitutes an additional shared feature.

Rather than replacing the nation state's claims to hermeneutic pre-eminence with something else, transnational history constitutes 'a way of seeing'.[40] It forms part of a 'family of "relational approaches"' from which historians can pick and choose whenever their research presents them with questions that eschew national scales and categories.[41] My aim in the remainder of this chapter is to identify the 'transnational turn' in history as a robust starting point for thinking about the future of legal-historical comparison.

B. Discovering 'the Transnational' in Law

To this end, legal historians will be able to draw considerably on insights developed in other fields dedicated to the academic study of law. As I will show, the 'pluralism'-debate in legal sociology, anthropology, and theory, the 'transfer'-debate in comparative law, and the 'immersion'-debate in cultural legal studies dovetail neatly with the turn to 'the transnational' in history.

---

[40] C. A. Bayley et al., 'AHR Conversation on Transnational History' (2006) 5 *American Historical Review* 1454 ff.

[41] Michael Werner, Bénédicte Zimmerman, 'Beyond Comparison: *Histoire Croisée* and the Challenge of Reflexivity' (2006) 45 *History and Theory* 30 ff.

1. *Denaturalizing the Nation State: The 'Legal Pluralism'-Debate*

Like the move away from methodological nationalism, the move away from monistic conceptions of law has multiple genealogies. The idea of legal pluralism had lurked in the background of early anthropological works like Maine's *Ancient Law*. It was even more pronounced in the later works of Kohler, Albert Hermann Post, Bronisław Malinowski, E. Adamson Hoebel, and Karl Llewellyn. It, too, however, gained little traction until the rise of postcolonial studies.

In 1970, Franz von Benda-Beckmann popularized the term 'legal pluralism' with his analysis of the asymmetrical, yet complementary, nature of native and colonial law in Malawi. Together with his wife Keebet, Benda-Beckmann went on to found the *Journal for Legal Pluralism and Unofficial Law*, which placed inquiry into law's pluralistic nature at the centre of legal anthropology. While the term 'legal pluralism' has itself been subject to charges of ethnocentrism, it considerably broadened the concept of law to include 'customary', 'native', 'traditional', 'unofficial', and 'folk' law.

The same holds true for legal pluralism's sociological strand, commonly traced back to Eugen Ehrlich. Drawing on the experiences of his youth in the multi-ethnic (and multi-normative) Bukowina region, Ehrlich coined the phrase 'living law' to describe what Llewellyn later termed 'law in action'. 'The main source of legal evolution in our times, as in all times', Ehrlich argued, 'is to be found neither in the legislature, nor in legal science or the judiciary, but in society itself.'[42] State law, imposed from 'above', lacked both meaning and power compared to the people's own law from 'below'.

Following the law-and-society turn, post-war American scholars started exploring the existence of what Sally Falke Moore called 'semi-autonomous social fields' at home.[43] Emblematic for these efforts are Stewart Macaulay's analysis of contractual behaviour among Wisconsin businessmen, Robert C. Ellickson's examination of cattle disputes among Shasta County ranchers, Renée Rose Shields's description of the diamond trade among orthodox Jews in New York, and Lisa Bernstein's work on private ordering mechanisms in modern commercial law.

Bernstein's work especially bridges the gulf between classical legal pluralism and the 'new' global legal pluralism. At around the same time that historians turned to non-state actors and processes, legal theorists began exploring law's role as both object and subject of globalization. In 1987, Boaventura de Sousa Santos made a powerful case for what he called a 'postmodern' view of law: 'We live in a time of porous legality or of legal porosity, of multiple networks of legal orders forcing us to constant transitions and trespassing. Our legal life is constituted by an intersection of different legal orders, that is by *interlegality*.'[44] Legal pluralism was no longer an

---

[42] Eugen Ehrlich, 'Vorrede', in Eugen Ehrlich, *Grundlegung der Soziologie des Rechts* (1913).

[43] Sally Falke Moore, 'Law and Social Change: The Semi-Autonomous Social Field as an Appropriate Subject of Study' (1973) 7 *Law & Society Review* 719 ff.

[44] Boaventura de Sousa Santos, 'Law: A Map of Misreading—Towards a Postmodern Conception of Law' (1987) 14 *Journal of Law & Society* 398 ff.

experience limited to the colonized 'other' or the marginalized few within Western capitalist societies. Globalization had made law's plurality, too, a universal reality.

Drawing on Niklas Luhmann's theory of system and autopoesis, Gunther Teubner subsequently proposed a reinterpretation of legal pluralism as a debate not about groups and communities but about discourses and communicative networks. 'The social source of global law', he argued, 'is not the lifeworld of globalized personal networks, but the proto-law of specialized, organizational and functional networks, which are forming a global, but sharply limited identity'.[45] Scholars' attention thus turned increasingly to the question whether the new *lex mercatoria* and other instances of 'global law without a state' could be used to counteract state law deficits.

What anthropological, sociological, and theoretical accounts of legal pluralism have in common is their rejection of the nation state's exclusivity as a creator of valid and effective legal norms. For pluralists, '[l]egal centralism' is nothing but 'a myth, an ideal, a claim, an illusion'.[46] Though, to be sure, the fundamental question in this context, as succinctly put by Sally Engle Merry, is always '[w]here do we stop speaking of law and find ourselves simply describing social life?'[47] The 'legal transplant' debate connects to this.

2. *From 'Borrowings' to 'Irritants': The 'Legal Transplant'-Debate*

The term 'legal transplant' was popularized by Alan Watson, who, in his 1974 book by the same name, made the following two arguments: first, that 'legal transplants', also known as 'legal borrowings', constitute 'the most fertile source of legal development'; second, that such 'legal transplants' or 'legal borrowings' occurred 'without too great difficulty', because more often than not a particular legal rule exists independently of the society it had been made to govern.[48] After almost two decades of relatively silent reception, the book's second edition, published in 1993, provoked the ire of postmodern comparativists.

In an article, titled 'The Impossibility of "Legal Transplants"', Pierre Legrand not only rejected Watson's position as 'a most impoverished explanation of interactions across legal systems',[49] he also characterized it as 'the result of a particularly crude apprehension of what law is'. The meaning of a legal rule, Legrand argued, was not contained in the text but was 'constituted through the life of interpretive communities'. As rules moved from one interpretive community to another, they inevitably changed. Comparativists, Legrand argued, should consequently focus

---

[45] Gunther Teubner, 'Global Bukowina: Legal Pluralism in the World Society', in Gunther Teubner (ed.), *Global Law Without a State* (1997) 3 ff.

[46] John Griffiths, 'What is Legal Pluralism?' (1986) 24 *Journal of Legal Pluralism & Unofficial Law* 4 ff.

[47] Sally Engle Merry, 'Legal Pluralism' (1988) 22 *Law and Society Review* 869 ff.

[48] Alan Watson, *Legal Transplants—An Approach to Comparative Law* (1974).

[49] Pierre Legrand, 'The Impossibility of Legal Transplants' (1997) 4 *Maastricht Journal of European & Comparative Law* 111 ff.

on the 'lifeworlds' of interpretive communities, bearing in mind 'the situated, local properties of knowledge'.

More recent contributors to the 'legal transplant'-debate have situated themselves between Watson's textualism and Legrand's postmodernism. Teubner, for one, coined the term 'legal irritants' to characterize the complexity of convergence in European private law.[50] William Ewald, in turn, argued in favour of an intermediary position based neither on Watson's '*law in the books*' nor Legrand's '*law in action*', but on '*law in the minds*'.[51] Inga Markovits, finally, proposed a 'horticultural thought exercise' as part of which a particular rule's prognosis depends on a wide range of factors, including its self-contained nature or similarity to pre-existing norms within the target legal system.[52]

As we have seen, transnational historians have in recent times come to reject simplistic notions of 'influence' and 'exchange' in favour of metaphors that highlight both economic and emotional costs involved in boundary-crossing. Though still lacking in nuance, the 'legal transfer'-debate has moved comparative law scholarship into a similar direction. The even more recent 'legal immersion'-debate in cultural legal studies sheds further light on how to adequately conceptualize law and law-related phenomena on the move.

3. *Lost in Translation: The 'Legal Immersion'-Debate*

The question at the heart of the 'immersion'-debate concerned the proper role of the legal historian vis-à-vis her subject matter—a development that mirrors transnational historians' emphasis on epistemological self-scrutiny. Though less obviously aimed against Watson and other textualists, postmodern comparativists began drawing attention to the limits of cross-cultural analysis just before the new millennium. Rodolfo Sacco, for one, whose notion of 'cryptotypes' underscored the hidden nature of law's formative influences, remarked that '[i]t must be admitted that some expressions are untranslatable'.[53] Nevertheless, scholars of legal culture have formulated compelling arguments in favour of at least some degree of translatability.

Drawing on the work of Walter Benjamin, Homi K. Bhabha, and Chakrabarty, Lena Foljanty recently called attention to the originality of legal comparison.[54] In

---

[50] Gunther Teubner, 'Legal Irritants: Good Faith in British Law or How Unifying Law Ends up in New Divergences' (1998) 61 *The Modern L.R.* 11 ff.

[51] William Ewald, 'What Was It Like to Try a Rat?' (1995) 143 *University of Pennsylvania L.R.* 1889 ff.

[52] Inga Markovits, 'Exporting Law Reform: But Will It Travel?' (2004) 37 *Cornell International L.J.* 95 ff.

[53] Rodolfo Sacco, 'Legal Formants: A Dynamic Approach to Comparative Law' (1991) 39 *A.J.C.L.* 343 ff.

[54] Lena Foljanty, 'Legal Transfers as Processes of Cultural Translation: on the Consequences of a Metaphor' (2015) 2 *Kritische Vierteljahresschrift für Gesetzgebung und Rechtswissenschaft* 89 ff.

particular, she suggested 'cultural translation' as a new metaphor for emphasizing legal transfers' creative and procedural dimension. Despite the salience of this point, Foljanty's argument also raises new questions. In particular, it leaves open when 'cultural translation' is most likely to do justice to both original and target legal system.

As part of his 'holistic approach to legal cultures', Michele Graziadei argued that 'it is impossible to know what it is like to think like an American or an Italian lawyer unless that condition is experienced in the first person, that is to say, unless one actually becomes an American or an Italian lawyer'.[55] Similarly, Vivian Grossfeld Curran suggested that 'a valid examination of another legal culture requires immersion into [its] political, historical, economic, and linguistic context'.[56]

Curran made her case by reference to European émigré jurists to the United States whose work contributed to the rise of American comparative law during the early Cold War years. Émigré jurists, Curran argued, were 'uniquely well situated to engage in cultural immersion because they were. . . of at least two legal cultures; because they knew foreign languages . . . ; and because the breadth of their historico-cultural knowledge spanned many fields, making them interdisciplinarians *avant la lettre* . . .'[57]

One should not underestimate the difficulties European émigré jurists faced in the United States. They were thus perhaps not so much '*of* . . . two legal cultures' as merely *in* two legal cultures. Graziadei's and Curran's calls for holism and immersion, in any case, validly characterizes the epistemological commitment necessary for legal-historical comparativists to produce successful work. Indeed, it may be time for legal-historical comparativists to start thinking of their work in 'foreign' legal cultures as anthropological rather than strictly historical in nature.

c. From Evolutionary Functionalism to Critical Transnationalism

As we have seen, history's recent turn to 'the transnational' closely mirrors developments in the anthropological, sociological, theoretical, comparative, and cultural study of law. Scholars interested in legal-historical comparisons might thus benefit from combining the resulting insights into a workable approach of their own.

---

[55] Michele Graziadei, 'Comparative Law, Legal History, and the Holistic Approach to Legal Cultures' (1999) 7 *Zeitschrift für Europäisches Privatrecht* 538 ff.

[56] Vivian Grossfeld Curran, 'Cultural Immersion, Difference, and Categories in U.S. Comparative Law' (1998) 46 *A.J.C.L.* 43 ff.

[57] Ibid., p. 52.

Ideally, such an approach would speak to some of the objectives legal historians have in the past hailed as conducive to the advancement of their own discipline: a provision of critical perspectives on law and legal thought, a vindication of global legal history as well as a closer alignment between history, theory, and philosophy of law. What, then, might an approach to legal-historical comparison look like that takes seriously law's pluralistic nature, the complexity of transfers, as well as cultural translation's creative dimension?

The focus of the discipline, I would suggest, should be on movement, friction, and resistance rather than on a status quo perceived as inherently fixed or smooth. For one, inquiry should move from abstract geographical units of analysis to the people involved in creating legal meaning. Focusing on the way in which jurists— voluntarily or under pressure—moved between normative orders and how they thought about them promises to yield much-needed comparative insights into differences and similarities between legal cultures.

More often than not, reliance on foreign concepts and ideas helps jurists in one place to construct and reconstruct their legal identities, especially in times of jurisprudential contingency. Jurists use foreign concepts and ideas to provide national legal imaginations with innovative content on the one hand and to position these imaginations in opposition to such content on the other. Focusing on the way jurists understand, or perhaps even more importantly, *mis*-understand one another provides access to their jurisprudential mentality as well as, ultimately, our own.

At the same time, many paradoxes at the heart of legal-historical inquiry result from the unaccompanied percolation of ideas across real and epistemic frontiers. It would thus be interesting to analyse what ideas turn out to be more 'exportable' or 'on demand' than others, what ideas are forcefully pushed beyond national boundaries to garner transnational intellectual influence, or extracted from foreign legal systems for the purpose of strategic national enhancement. It would also be interesting to see how the channels through which ideas cross from one jurisprudential sphere to another affect what kind of lives they develop outside the context and place in which they were originally conceived.

IV. FIVE IMPULSES FOR FUTURE RESEARCH

The following five suggestions are meant to further move practices of legal-historical comparison into the direction of what I call 'critical transnationalism'. They are drawn from recent developments in both law and history.

A. Exploring the Origins of Absent Ideas

In a recent piece, Samuel Moyn highlighted that 'for every concept that does globalize, others do not do so'.[58] He further argued that a focus on those ideas that failed to transcend their own cultural and geographic boundaries and to take root elsewhere was 'a critical and necessary part of any plausible global intellectual history'. In line with this, I would suggest that legal historians, too, ought to pay attention to the 'non-globalization' of ideas about law.

In my own research I look at why realistic jurisprudence failed to take hold of early twentieth-century German legal science, all the while fundamentally changing American legal thought during the 1920s and 1930s.[59] Realism in law can be traced back to a small group of German-speaking scholars who referred to themselves as the Free Lawyers. Though somewhat prominent before the First World War, their Jewish backgrounds and left-leaning politics made them increasingly anathema during the Weimar period. Through American interest in German legal science as well as German-American encounters in exile, the German Free Law movement arguably served as an inspiration for the today infamous American Legal Realists.

To be sure, the picture of transatlantic legal realism becomes increasingly more complex when we take into account that law during Weimar and, especially, the Third Reich can in many ways be viewed as a peculiar variant of realistic jurisprudence in its own right. Using the 'non-globalization' of ideas as a new kind of legal-historical starting point, in any case, opens up new avenues for inquiring into the relationship between ideas and their contexts. It also promises to uncover similarities that an exclusive focus on 'successful' cross-boundary transmissions would leave hidden.

B. Pernicious Ideas and their Progeny

In addition to focusing on 'absent' ideas, legal-historical comparativists should also focus on ideas that are, for lack of a better word, 'bad'. In a recent article, Pierre-Yves Saunier diagnosed a 'prejudice against evil in the study of transnational civil society'.[60] Transnational historians' cosmopolitan worldview, he argued, had created a 'syllogistic knot' between boundary-crossing and 'positive moral

---

[58] Samuel Moyn, 'On the Nonglobalization of Ideas', in Samuel Moyn, Andrew Sartori (eds.), *Global Intellectual History* (2013) 187 ff.

[59] Katharina Isabel Schmidt, 'Law, Modernity, Crisis: German Free Lawyers, American Legal Realists, and the Transatlantic Turn to "Life", 1903–1933' (2016) 39 *German Studies Review* 121 ff.

[60] Pierre-Yves Saunier, 'Learning by Doing: Notes about the Making of the Palgrave Dictionary of Transnational History' (2009) 6 *Journal of Modern European History* 159 ff.

value'. The resulting historical blind spots exist also in the study of law and its history. While works on the transmission of human rights, the rule of law, and constitutional values abound, legal-historical comparativists could take more interest still in the movement of morally questionable ideas and institutions.

Recent works in the study of slavery and racism illustrate the timeliness of studying 'evil' transnationally and should be taken as models for future works in the same vein. Rebecca J. Scott's *Degrees of Freedom—Louisiana and Cuba after Slavery* (2005) as well as Alejandro de la Fuente and Ariela Gross's 2013 article 'Slaves, Free Blacks, and Race in the Legal Regimes of Cuba, Louisiana, Virginia: A Comparison' demonstrate that historians of race have for a long time thought comparatively and transnationally. Similarly, Whitman's *Hitler's American Model—The United States and the Making of Nazi Race Law* (2017) invites us to explore the dark historical underbelly of more contemporary legal systems.

c. Comparison as 'Historians' Category', Comparison as 'Actors' Category'

To the extent that there exists a 'syllogistic knot' not only between 'positive moral value' and transnationalism, but also between 'positive moral value' and law, legal-historical comparativists should contribute to its undoing. In this regard, they would benefit greatly from employing comparison not only as a 'historians' category', but also as an 'actors' category'. Micol Seigel recently made a compelling case for the proposition that, in certain circumstances, 'comparison serves as a better subject than method'.[61] In order to shed light on cross-cultural processes of communication, she argued, historians ought to focus on the comparative judgments of their actors rather than simply engage in comparisons themselves.

David Rabban's *Law's History—American Legal Thought and the Transatlantic Turn to History* (2012) constitutes a good example of the merits of Seigel's approach. As part of his investigation, Rabban hints at the possibility that American jurists misapplied Jhering's critique of German Pandecticism to nineteenth-century American classical legal thought. Through comparison between German and American jurists, he argues, Holmes, Roscoe Pound, and others—either wilfully or by accident—created a kind of transatlantic 'formalism myth' in opposition to which they could refashion American jurisprudence along proto-realist lines.

---

[61] Micol Seigel, 'Beyond Compare: Comparative Method after the Transnational Turn' (2005) 91 *Radical History Review* 62 ff.

D. Recognizing the Multidirectionality of Ideas

Given the additional layer of confusion that cloaks ideas with every new cross-cultural transfer, legal-historical comparativists should move beyond the unidirectional flow of legal and quasi-legal phenomena and pay attention to multidirectional and, especially, retrogressive flows. Looking at the extent to which ideas that are exported and subsequently reimported into a particular epistemic community are still legible to members of that community promises interesting insights about intellectual transfer processes. Udi Greenberg's *The Weimar Century—German Émigrés and the Ideological Foundations of the Cold War* (2014) exemplifies this point.

Greenberg tells the story of five German jurists who—due to their political commitment, their Jewish background, or both—left Germany for the United States in the early Nazi years. Educated in Weimarian constitutional thought, all five jurists went on to introduce liberal-democratic concepts into American Cold War politics and culture. Greenberg then looks at the re-importation of these ideas into postwar Germany, as his émigrés return from exile. The way Greenberg's ideas travel seems too smooth at times. His focus on ideological and jurisprudential 'homecomings' is nevertheless highly informative.

Greenberg could have paid more attention to those similarities between his protagonists that resulted from their shared experience as products of German legal science and education. In line with this, I would encourage legal-historical comparativists to seek inspirations from scholars dedicated to the conditions of knowledge production both inside and outside the academy, including, but not limited to, historians of science, professional sociologists, and anthropologists.

E. Contributing to a Global History of Knowledge

Jean-Louis Halperin recently mourned the absence of a robust tradition of 'historical sociology of law', calling for 'a renewed history of lawyers'.[62] 'What is called "the legal mind"', Halperin argued, 'is not something timeless and identical . . . but a variable combination of legal education, of the social backgrounds of jurists, and of the professional projects supported by mobilized groups.' Indeed, rigorous comparative study of the history of legal professions across times and cultures seems overdue. In addition, Jürgen Renn made a recent attempt to incorporate law into the burgeoning field of the transnational history of knowledge.

'[J]ust as the history of science has recently been widened to include a more encompassing history of knowledge', Renn argues, 'the history of law may also

---

[62] Jean-Louis Halperin, 'For a Renewed History of Lawyers' (2016) 56 *American Journal of Legal History* 53 ff.

be conceived of as part of a larger history of normativity.'[63] In the same way that historians of science moved from academic contexts to the production of knowledge in society, Renn argues, historians of law might in the future turn to 'the experiences that have shaped the fundamental precepts of normative thinking and practices'.

In line with this, it would be interesting indeed to focus on how lay communities subvert, resist, contest, shape, appropriate, and navigate foreign legal practices. More commonly employing comparative-historical perspectives, especially in the context of migration, would thus substantially enrich both the social and intellectual history of law.

v. Concluding Remarks: Law's Challenge to Transnational History

Questions remain about the challenges law poses to transnational history. The argument could be made that—pluralist and postmodernist critiques notwithstanding—law is inextricably intertwined with the nation state; that the state is constituted and, in turn, constitutes its subjects through law. While exigencies of time and space prevent me from exploring this argument as part of this chapter, I would suggest that transnational historians ultimately stand to profit from any of the challenges legal historians might in the future throw their way.

Bibliography

Laura Briggs et al., 'Transnationalism: A Category of Analysis' (2008) 60 *American Quarterly* 625 ff
Léontin-Jean Constantinesco, *Rechtsvergleichung* (Carl Heymanns Verlag, 1971)
Charles Donahue, 'Comparative Legal History in North America: A Report' (1997) 65 *Tijdschrift voor Rechtsgeschiedenis* 1 ff
William Ewald, 'What Was It Like to Try a Rat?' (1995) 143 *University of Pennsylvania L.R.* 1889 ff
James Gordley, 'Comparative Law and Legal History', in Mathias Reimann, Reinhard Zimmermann (eds.), *The Oxford Handbook of Comparative Law* (Oxford University Press, 2006) 768 ff

---

[63] Jürgen Renn, 'The Globalization of Knowledge in History and Its Normative Challenges' (2014) 22 *Rechtsgeschichte* 52 ff.

Walter Hug, 'The History of Comparative Law' (1932) 45 *Harvard L.R* 1027 ff

David Ibbetson, 'The Challenges of Comparative Legal History' (2012) 1 *Comparative Legal History* 1 ff

Andrew Lewis, 'On Not Expecting the Spanish Inquisition: The Uses of Comparative Legal History' (2004) 57 *Current Legal Problems* 57 ff

Daniel Rodgers, 'Introduction', in Daniel Rodgers et al. (eds.), *Cultures in Motion* (Princeton University Press, 2013)

Pierre-Yves Saunier, 'Learning by Doing: Notes about the Making of the Palgrave Dictionary of Transnational History' (2009) 6 *Journal of Modern European History* 159 ff

Micol Seigel, 'Beyond Compare: Comparative Method after the Transnational Turn' (2005) 91 *Radical History Review* 62 ff

Stefan Vogenauer, 'Rechtsgeschichte und Rechtsvergleichumg um 1900—Die Geschichte einer anderen "Emanzipation durch Auseinanderdenken"' (2012) 76 *RabelsZ* 1122 ff

Michael Werner, Bénédicte Zimmerman, 'Beyond Comparison: *Histoire Croisée* and the Challenge of Reflexivity' (2006) 45 *History and Theory* 30 ff

CHAPTER 16

ARCHIVAL LEGAL HISTORY

TOWARDS THE OCEAN AS ARCHIVE

RENISA MAWANI*

I. INTRODUCTION

The sea is history

Derek Walcott

The sea is slavery

Fred D'Aguiar

IN the early pages of *Lose Your Mother: A Journey Along the Atlantic Slave Route*, Saidiya Hartman introduces her readers to the elusive contours of slavery's

* Professor, Sociology, University of British Columbia. My deepest gratitude to Stefano Pantelone for the many conversations that helped to shape the ideas here, for sharing his unpublished work, and for his feedback on an earlier draft. Many thanks also to Chris Tomlins for his helpful commentary on a previous version of this chapter and especially for reminding me what I had forgotten.

archive: 'The archive contained what you would expect: the manifests of slavers; ledger books of trade goods; inventories of foodstuffs; bills of sale; itemized lists of bodies alive, infirm, and dead; captain's logs; planter's diaries.'[1] Slavery's archive, she maintains, is crowded with the documentation of commercial transactions and the (un)fitness of bodies commodified as cargo. Despite this voluminous production of texts, these records say little of the African men, women, and children who were captured from what was then the Gold Coast, transported in horrific conditions across the Atlantic, and enslaved in the Americas. 'I searched for the traces of the destroyed', Hartman writes of her own deeply personal journey to Ghana. 'In every line item, I saw a grave.'[2] Slavery's archive, despite its incompleteness, 'dictates what can be said about the past and the kinds of stories that can be told of persons catalogued'. Thus, to enter, she insists, 'is to enter a mortuary; it permits one final viewing and allows for a last glimpse of persons about to disappear into the slave hold'.[3] Searching the archive for the experiences of the enslaved is an exercise in futility, Hartman and others contend. It entails 'facing the void' and confronting 'absence, silence, negation, death, and perhaps even cultural genocide'.[4]

Hartman's reflections offer a powerful reminder of the absences and inadequacies of all official archives, particularly those of the transatlantic slave trade. She is not alone. For at least two decades, scholars of slavery have drawn attention to these gaps and omissions, how they influence what we know, or think we know, to be a history of transatlantic slavery.[5] More recently, slavery's archive has featured as a site of ethical, political, and methodological debate on what can be said of the horrors of slavery and what remains unspeakable.[6] Viewed from the fields of law and legal studies, these discussions raise additional questions on the limits and possibilities of archival legal history. The archive of slavery, Simon Gikandi observes, is filled with the sovereign claims of white slave owners. The ledgers, diaries, bills of sale, shipping registers, manifests, and the writings of captains and crews may offer invaluable insights into the institutions and operations of slavery, yet they provide little account of those captured, subjected, and killed. From the very start, law placed clear limits on slavery's archive. African captives confined in the ship's hold and bound to plantations were not permitted to write or represent themselves, even though some did.[7] Those who appeared before the law as victims, witnesses, and accuseds were prohibited from speaking and thus appear as silences in court books

---

[1] Saidiya Hartman, *Lose Your Mother: A Journey Along the Atlantic Slave Route* (2007) 17 ff.

[2] Ibid.   [3] Ibid.

[4] Vincent Brown, 'Mapping a Slave Revolt: Visualizing Spatial History through the Archive of Slavery' (2015) 33(4) *Social Text* 134 ff.

[5] Michel-Rolph Trouillot, *Silencing the Past: Power and the Production of History* (1995) 48 ff.

[6] See the special issue, 'The Question of Recovery: Slavery, Freedom, and the Archive' (2015) 33(4) *Social Text* 125 ff.

[7] Simon Gikandi, 'Rethinking the Archive of Enslavement' (2015) 50(1) *Early American Literature* 84 ff.

and transcripts.[8] As Gikandi describes it, 'record-keeping and the archiving gesture was a form of violent control . . . an attestation to the authority of natural history, the key to the ideology of white power . . . [where] the African could be reduced to the world of nature and the prehuman'.[9] If the archive is the commencement and commandment of law, as Derrida argues in *Archive Fever*, then to speak of slavery's archive is not only to speak of silence: it is to locate the force of law in white power.[10]

Critiques of slavery's archive, as compelling as they are, have not gone unchallenged. For some, the figure of the slave has always already haunted the archive, even in her conspicuous absence.[11] Others have argued, very persuasively, that hundreds of years of transatlantic slavery cannot be consigned to the past. Nor can it be reduced to one archive alone. Slavery's afterlives persist in many places. Responding to Hartman's comments on the presumed singularity of slavery's archive, David Kazanjian insists that slavery generated multiple archives that were penned and preserved in a myriad of European and indigenous languages. Reading beyond Anglo-American records, he suggests, might pluralize 'monolithic conceptions of slavery and *the* archive'.[12] For Kazanjian, drawing on alternative records and repositories is not merely an empiricist exercise in recuperation. Rather, a plurality of archives offers new methods, including modes of reading and writing. 'Before we theorize the archive of slavery as "a death sentence,"' he writes, 'we ought to consider how archives of slavery also teem with black lives whose languages and narrative forms might not be as familiar as the classic nineteenth-century Anglo-American slave narrative, but whose stories nonetheless have much to teach us not only about past slaveries, but also about the future of our own continuing struggles for freedom.'[13]

Christina Sharpe offers a resonant and equally forceful critique. 'Black scholars of slavery get wedged in the partial truths of the archives while trying to make sense of their silences, absences, and modes of dis/appearance', she writes. Yet, those 'methods most readily available to us sometimes, oftentimes, force us into positions that run counter to what we know'.[14] If Kazanjian encourages a search for additional archives that might problematize the hegemony of Anglo-American narratives of enslavement, Sharpe invites new analytic orientations through what she compellingly terms 'wake work'. This is a strategy of reading, writing, and thinking that generates

---

[8] Paul Finkelman, 'Slavery in the United States: Persons or Property?' in Jean Allain (ed.), *The Legal Understanding of Slavery: From the Historical to the Contemporary* (2012) 127 ff DOI:10.1093/acprof:oso/9780199660469.003.0007.

[9] Gikandi (n. 7) 93 ff.

[10] Jacques Derrida, *Archive Fever: A Freudian Impression*, trans. E. Prenowitz (1998) 1 ff.

[11] For a discussion of slavery and the archive in the context of American literature, see Toni Morrison, *Playing in the Dark: Whiteness and the Literary Imagination* (1992).

[12] David Kazanjian, 'Freedom's Surprise: Two Paths Through Slavery's Archive' (2016) 6(2) *History of the Present* 136 ff, my emphasis.

[13] Ibid., 139 ff.   [14] Christina Sharpe, *In the Wake: On Blackness and Being* (2016) 12 ff.

'new ways to live in the wake of slavery, in slavery's afterlives'.[15] Both Kazanjian and Sharpe insist on the ongoing now of slavery and its relevance to contemporary forms of black liberation and death. More importantly, for my purposes here, each suggests a (re)turn to the sea. Oceans, in their respective writings, emerge as productive sites of encounter. If Kazanjian proposes a spatial repositioning from the North Atlantic to the South, from Anglo America to Latin America, Sharpe summons a rethinking of slavery through the wake of the ship.[16] Together, they gesture to oceans as sites of multiple crossings that open new conceptual frames of reading archives as past, present, and future. Oceans, as I suggest below, may also be conceived in material and metaphorical terms as a legal archive. Commonly described as empty voids, and characterized in ways reminiscent of the archive of slavery, oceans, with their changing surfaces, variegated depths, and multiple temporalities carry fragments, sediments, and traces that invite other possibilities to write legal histories of slavery.

This chapter builds from my earlier work on 'law's archive'. There, I explore how law writes its authority and legitimacy through a double logic of violence: the violence of law and the violence of the archive.[17] In the remainder of this chapter I reconsider these dynamics of presence/absence and preservation/destruction through the ocean as legal archive. Although oceans cover more than seventy per cent of the earth's surface, they are regularly placed beyond the forces of law, politics, and history. But for writers of slavery, oceans are useful to think with. As Derek Walcott notes in the epigraph with which I begin, the sea is not an absence: 'The sea is history'. It is a vault filled with memories of racial violence that bears witness to the past, shapes the present, while generating imaginative possibilities for the future.[18] For Fred D'Aguiar, 'The sea is slavery'.[19] He and others insist that transatlantic slavery was a defining feature of modernity, one that remains central to our time.[20] The ocean, I argue here, is a legal archive filled with texts, objects, and artefacts. From the sixteenth century onwards, European efforts to know, map, and control the world's oceans produced an explosion of legal writing in the form of maps, ledgers, diaries, shipping lists, commercial documents, imperial decrees, and correspondence of various kinds. During the nineteenth and early twentieth centuries, virtually all commerce, communication, and migration were water borne,

---

[15] Ibid., 18 ff.

[16] Some of the most exciting work in the history of transatlantic slavery has focused on oceans, albeit not as archives. See, e.g., Ian Baucom, *Specters of the Atlantic: Finance Capital, Slavery, and the Philosophy of History* (2005); Brown (n. 4); Edouard Glissant, *Poetics of Relation*, trans. Betsy Wang (2010); M. NourbeSe Philip, *Zong!* (2008); Marcus Rediker, *The Slave Ship: A Human History* (2008); Sharpe (n. 14); Stephanie E. Smallwood, *Saltwater Slavery: Middle Passage from Africa to American Diaspora* (2008).

[17] Renisa Mawani, 'Law's Archive' (2012) 8 *Annual Review of Law and Social Science* 337–65 ff.

[18] Derek Walcott, 'The Sea is History' in *Derek Walcott: Collected Poems, 1948–1984* (1986) 364 ff.

[19] Fred D'Aguiar, *Feeding the Ghosts: A Novel* (1997).

[20] See also Baucom (n. 16). Here, Baucom argues that slavery was foundational to the emergence of finance capitalism. On the Atlantic as an archive of black counterculture see Paul Gilroy, *The Black Atlantic: Modernity and Double Consciousness* (1995).

oceanic, and riverine.[21] The sea has never been vacant. Through the movements of ships and in the writings of sovereigns, captains, merchants, subalterns, pirates, and fugitive/freed slaves, the world's oceans have long been juridical spaces marked by shared, overlapping, and competing legalities.[22] The sea is history. The sea is slavery. The sea is a legal archive of slavery.

Oceans offer a rich trove of legal, political, and financial writings that have featured prominently in genealogical and academic research. European contests over the Atlantic, to draw one example, were advanced through copious procedures of documentation that centred on navigation and commerce and were aimed at tracking the movements of ships, peoples, and cargos. By the eighteenth and nineteenth centuries, first in Britain and then the U.S., maritime control authorized regimes of racial discipline, surveillance, and legalized violence that expanded and intensified through the transatlantic slave trade. These regimes of terror circulated between sea and land, from ship to plantation, and continue to animate juridical forms today. The ship and the slave are deeply entangled in the concept of legal personhood, as I discuss in the final section below.

In its limitless undulations and ceaseless change, oceans expand law's archive from words and texts to objects, artefacts, spectres, and spirits. As an aqueous domain that materializes the tension between what can be known and unknown, the sea calls forth a productive mode of writing archival legal history, one that moves beyond the positivist orientation of retrieval and recovery. Though the ocean as legal archive may not fully recover the lost subjectivities of those enslaved, it draws our attention to the foundational role of slavery in the development of modern law and points to other imaginative possibilities in writing archival legal history.

II. OBJECTS, ARTEFACTS, AND ARCHIVES

> Bone soldered by coral to bone
> Mosaics
> Mantled by the benediction of the shark's shadow
>   Derek Walcott

[21] The riverine movements of people, commerce, and communications in the time of U.S. slavery is beautifully captured in Walter Johnson, *River of Dark Dreams: Slavery and Empire in the Cotton Kingdom* (2013).

[22] For a critique of oceans as empty see Philip E. Steinberg, *The Social Construction of the Ocean* (2001). For a discussion of oceans as competing sites of legality see Lauren Benton, *A Search for Sovereignty: Law and Geography in European Empires, 1400–1900* (2009), especially ch. 3. On oceans as juridical spaces produced through the movements of ships see Renisa Mawani, *Across Oceans of Law: The Komagata Maru and Jurisdiction in the Time of Empire* (forthcoming, 2018).

Michel Foucault's *Archaeology of Knowledge* may not be a text on law or history's archive. As a critical method and orientation, however, archaeology directs attention from textual *content* to *forms* of speech. 'The document', Foucault writes, 'is no longer for history an inert material through which it tries to reconstitute what men have done or said, the events of which only the trace remains.' Rather, 'history is now trying to define within the documentary material itself unities, totalities, series, relations'.[23] For Foucault, the archive is not 'the sum of all the texts that a culture has kept upon its person as documents attesting to its own past'. In his formulation, the 'archive is first the law of what can be said . . . it is that which differentiates discourses in their multiple existence and specifies them in their own duration'.[24] The archive is not a place, text, or record. It is a discursive structure that initiates, arranges, and enables systems of enunciability.

Foucault's reflections on the archive have generated a range of illuminating responses, mainly from historians and anthropologists, and less so from legal scholars. But there are notable exceptions. In her path-breaking book, *Files*, German media theorist Cornelia Vismann echoes Foucault's concerns of textual form over content. Law and legal studies, she argues, has had very little to say on the substance of law, including the textuality that underpins and informs it. 'Legal studies lack any reflection on their tools'. Lawyers may 'consult files to recapitulate past events. But they are of no interest in themselves, and they certainly do not turn into objects of scientific investigation.'[25] Legal scholars read and analyse records for their meanings, Vismann claims, but pay significantly less attention to the material structure, organization, and form of texts and documents. Describing files loosely and capaciously to include texts as wide-ranging as Roman columns, handwritten documents, and computer-generated data, Vismann is clear that 'law and files mutually determine each other'. Files provide a basis for law, giving it direction and directive, while fortifying its power. Significantly, 'files control the formalization and differentiation of the law . . . into authority and administration'.[26] As its material basis, files make law possible.

Over the past several years there has been a growing interest in both the discursive and material forms of law, including texts and archives. Many of these interventions have drawn varying degrees of inspiration from Vismann's history of files. My own work on 'Law's Archive', for instance, builds on Foucault, Derrida, and Vismann. In so doing, it aspires to move the conversation away from documents and files toward the outlines and effects of law's archive.

[23] Michel Foucault, *The Archaeology of Knowledge and the Discourse on Language* (1972) 7 ff.
[24] Ibid., 128–9 ff.
[25] Cornelia Vismann, *Files: Law and Media Technology*. Trans. Geoffrey Winthrop-Young (2008) 11 ff.
[26] Ibid., xii, xiii ff.

In Vismann's account, 'writing tools and rods are among the instruments of the law'.[27] Building from her insights, I contend that law's archive operates through a double logic of violence, the violence of law and the violence of the archive. This process of remembering and forgetting, protecting and erasing is what affords law its sovereignty and authority. Through the preservation and destruction of files and documents, law 'creates itself as a legitimate form of command'.[28] Law literally writes its own legitimacy and authority through textual production and self-referential procedures. Slightly revising Vismann's claims, I suggest that law both justifies and obscures the violence of the rod through the violence of legal writing. It generates its archive—and hence its authority—through a system of inscription and a set of citational practices. Law 'produces, expands, and destroys that which comprises its archive and in turn, that which constitutes law. . . . By referencing statutes and judgments that came before and by determining which are apposite, law cultivates its meanings and asserts its authority while at the same time concealing and sanctioning its originary and ongoing violence'.[29] Law's archive may be a dynamic site of struggle and contest, but in my earlier account it remains inherently textual. Like the melancholy archive of slavery described by Hartman and others, my own formulation holds few possibilities for counter-archives, including objects and artefacts.

In a recent essay on the court of the King's Bench, Paul Halliday pushes beyond conceptualizations of law as text, document, and/or record. Legal archives, he argues, have a history that is traceable to physical and material forms. What Halliday calls the 'stuff of law' cannot be captured in writing alone, he claims. The materiality of law includes 'physical objects and procedures for storing, using, and finding precedents to generate legal authority'.[30] Thus, the archive is not an aggregate of files alone. The proliferation of documents and documentation in the court of King's Bench, he observes, demanded new physical spaces, efficient methods of storage, and new forms of labour. This history of archives, Halliday insists, offers a different history of law. 'Law is made of words', he concedes, but 'law is also made of things'.[31] Legal precedents were not derived solely from the decision-making and reasoning of judges. As textual records and archival productions, precedents demanded the labour of court clerks who produced physical objects out of court sittings. These books and registries required offices and libraries, which in turn became the material foundations and the symbolic force of law. Moving from files to things, Halliday extends Vismann's arguments in interesting ways. 'Laws are founded on the legal force of writing (*ratio scripta*)', Vismann claims, 'but they are made public by a pre*face*, spoken by the *persona ficta* of the legislator'.[32] For Halliday, it was not the legislator or the judge that produced or recorded law, but

---

[27] Ibid., 29 ff.   [28] Mawani (n. 17) 351 ff.   [29] Mawani (n. 17) 341 ff.
[30] Paul D. Halliday, 'Authority in the Archives' (2014) 91(1) *Critical Analysis of Law* 110 ff.
[31] Ibid., 111 ff.   [32] Vismann, (n. 25) 21 ff emphasis in original.

the minor figure of the court clerk. By transforming statements into things, the clerk produced the physical and spatial materiality of archives as 'places, occupied by people doing work'.[33]

Writing of counter-archives and echoing arguments of legal form over content, several scholars have followed a materialist reading of law, albeit in other directions. Attentive to the genre and design of legal documents, Trish Luker suggests that archival sources must be read not solely for their content, as textual evidence, but also as artefacts that carry 'performative and productive capacity'.[34] For Luker, documents penned and preserved by colonial bureaucracies carry different meanings and consequences when they are interpreted in retrospect, through the political challenges of the contemporary colonial moment. Read out of time and context, these texts become objects that carry their own agentive liveliness and possibility. Documents retrieved from settler colonial archives, in this case Australia, may be 'a medium of communication'. But once they are stored and preserved in an archive, Luker contends, they become historical objects.[35] No longer tied to a colonial bureaucracy, these texts can operate as a counter-archive, one evoked by indigenous peoples to challenge the sovereignty and legitimacy of the settler state.[36] In this way, archives and counter-archives are not simply texts, documents, or files, but objects and artefacts with a power, potential, and wilfulness of their own. As Halliday puts it, law's 'obsessive attention to words causes us to miss something of vital importance', including its multiple material traces. If 'the law is also made up of things', as Halliday insists, then archival legal history must be open to alternative sites, substances, and imaginaries of what comprises law's archive.[37]

The archives of law and history have long been sites of contest over truth and justice. These struggles have only intensified as various communities recall memories and point to ongoing legacies of European colonialism, transatlantic slavery, and mass violence. To be sure, a growing recognition of the incompleteness of archives—whether history's archive, law's archive, or slavery's archive—has led to critical appraisals, as I discuss in the introduction to this chapter. At the same time, these limits have generated a search for other histories culled from alternative evidentiary forms. Since the mid-twentieth century, human bones have become important artefacts in recording, verifying, and documenting the violence of the past. Writing on the 'archive of bones', Antoinette Burton observes that the late twentieth century has witnessed a growing concern with the physical traces of war and destruction.[38] This search for material evidence, she notes, comes at a

---

[33] Halliday, (n. 30) 118 ff.

[34] Trish Luker, 'Animating the Archive: Artefacts of Law', in Stewart Motha, Honni van Rijswijk (eds.), *Law, Memory, Violence: Uncovering the Counter-Archive* (2016) 71 ff.

[35] Ibid., 71 ff.   [36] Ibid., 70 ff.   [37] Halliday, (n. 30) 113 ff.

[38] Antoinette Burton, 'Archive of Bones: Anil's Ghost and the Ends of History' (2003) 38(1) *Journal of Commonwealth Literature* 39 ff.

time when digitization has dramatically challenged and even altered how we think of histories and archives, including their veracity and authenticity. 'What is left in the wake of Auschwitz, Vietnam, Srebrenica, Ayodhya, Colombo, Basra, 9/11, and Tora Bora', Burton explains, is 'the detritus of history: fragments and shards, ashes and dust, rag and bone.' Drawing on these fragments, forensic scientists have sought to recuperate new truths, 'the kinds of testimony that living witnesses often cannot [provide], despite and of course because of the pathos of their memories'.[39] This physical evidence of the past has become central to claims for justice. With the development of new technologies, forensic scientists and archaeologists have searched other spaces—beneath the ground and at the bottom of the sea—for sedimentations and traces of the past. Like the archive of bones that gestures to the unthinkable and unspeakable conditions of mass violence, objects and artefacts retrieved from the sea have supplemented the gaps and silences of slavery's archive while producing other ways to imagine the resilience, creativity, and beauty of black life.[40]

The ocean as legal archive is material/figurative and human/nonhuman. The sea has many surfaces, layers, and dimensions that demonstrate the materiality of law and legal violence in productive ways.[41] From the sixteenth century onward, precisely because of the inherent difficulties in mapping, knowing, and navigating the seas, Atlantic crossings from the 'old world' to the 'new' produced novel and bountiful forms of legal writing. These included maps, ledgers, lists, ship manifests, registries, commercial transactions, diaries, and maritime fiction.[42] In the contemporary moment, these documents have featured prominently in family genealogies and increasingly in academic writing. But the ocean as legal archive is beyond text and file. At the same time that oceans have produced a proliferation of historical and legal documentation, its fury and ungovernability has generated other artefacts and objects. In the sea, everything is moving, living, and present, even if these forms of life are not fully visible. Traces emerge, re-emerge, surface, and submerge. A turn to the dynamic sea might displace and even disrupt the longstanding textual emphasis on archives as sites of death, destruction, and violence, while inviting new ways to imagine the past and history.

Oceans have long been competing sites of oppression and redemption, subjugation, and subversion, undulations that are vividly evident in histories of transatlantic slavery. Though not always apparent to the eye, traces of racial violence continue to mark the surfaces and depths of the sea as 'bone soldered by coral to bone'.[43]

---

[39] Ibid.

[40] See, e.g., Ayesha S. Hameed, 'Black Atlantis: Three Songs', in Forensic Architecture (eds.), *Forensis: The Architecture of Public Truth* (2014) 712–19 ff.

[41] On the Indian Ocean region see Stewart Motha, *Archiving Sovereignty* (forthcoming).

[42] On maritime fiction see Hester Blum, *The View from the Masthead: Maritime Imagination and Antebellum American Sea Narratives* (2008).

[43] Walcott (n. 18) 365 ff.

Marine archaeologists have successfully retrieved artefacts from shipwrecks and maritime disasters. These objects, recovered from ocean regions, have been used to date events and to establish specific rhythms, patterns, and resistances to transatlantic slavery.[44] As the detritus of an early global racial capitalism, maritime objects offer further insights into slavery's historical, contemporary, and ongoing effects. As Edouard Glissant explains, the ocean is a space that has no identifiable beginning or end: 'the entire ocean, the entire sea gently collapsing in the end into the pleasures of sand, make one vast beginning, but a beginning whose time is marked by these balls and chains gone green'.[45] Presenting alternative geographies and temporalities, the ocean invites a reimagining of law's archive in ways that underscore the foundational place of transatlantic slavery in the development of modern law. The ocean as legal archive presents objects and artefacts that push beyond the limits of slavery's archive, including its partial and uneven truths.

III. The Ocean as Legal Archive

> *. . . but the ocean kept turning blank pages looking for History*
> Derek Walcott

As an archive of law and history, oceans present a paradox. Both historically and in contemporary accounts, as I suggest above, the world's oceans and seas have been viewed as limitless, empty, and unknowable spaces. Unlike land, which has a legible history of law and politics, one that has been violently inscribed through territorial lines, borders, and divisions, the sea is perceived as an anti-archive, positioned outside the forces of legality and history. This negation of the sea has gained its meaning, most notably, against the elemental features of land. In *The* Nomos *of the Earth*, Carl Schmitt articulates the land/sea divide as both elemental and juridical: '[t]he earth is bound to law in three ways . . . as a reward of labour . . . as fixed boundaries . . . as a public sign of order'. Though the earth is primarily aqueous, Schmitt defines it terracentrically, through land alone. The ocean, he insists, is a fundamentally unique, elusive, and empty topography. 'The *sea* knows no such apparent unity of space and law, of order and orientation',

---

[44] See, e.g., the 'Slave Wrecks Project.' <https://slavewrecksproject.org/> (accessed 4 June 2017).
[45] Glissant (n. 16) 6 ff.

he claims. Vessels 'that sail across the sea leave no trace. "On the waves, there is nothing but waves".[46]

For some, the ocean as anti-archive offers a productive location from which to rethink the contours and coordinates of history as a discipline. 'What better locus to think about history, about the problematic of space, time and the historical object, than the sea', Alexis Wick asks. Drawing from Hegel and echoing Schmitt, Wick describes the sea to be 'a place that can host neither archive nor seminar, the two foundational features of the professional historical discipline'.[47] In his examination of the Red Sea, he argues that the sea has long been an object of historical and textual production. Though oceans and seas are historically constructed, through processes of mapping, navigation, shipping, and commerce, for Wick, the sea 'simply does not contain let alone produce an archive of its own'.[48] Reflecting on the opening verse of Walcott's 'The Sea is History', he questions and even challenges the objectives and aspirations of the oceanic turn. This poem, as Wick describes it, is regularly evoked 'to centralize maritime history'.[49] But for Walcott, in Wick's interpretation, the histories produced and contained in the sea remain obscure and not easily retrievable. Ultimately, in Wick's assessment, the sea cannot be an archive or a source of history. The sea 'dislocates, disperses, dissolves', and 'all that remains, all that washes up to the shore are fragments'.[50] It is precisely these fragments, in all their incompleteness, instability, and indeterminacy that present novelty, creativity, and possibility. The fluidity and mutability of oceans represent the instability and indeterminacy of history.

Over the past decade, the oceanic turn has invited additional sites, sources, and objects of historical analysis. To begin, the ocean features as a recurring metaphor in descriptions of archival and historical study. Researchers often characterize themselves as 'navigating archives' and sifting through a 'sea of information'. More recently, several scholars of global, transnational, and imperial history have turned to oceans as spaces of analytic novelty and historiographical possibility. For Burton, oceans invite new connections by pushing 'beyond the landlocked nation-state and beyond the terra firma that has been its presumptive ground'.[51] To be sure, the burgeoning field of maritime studies has encouraged a search for different archives and evidence, developments that are apparent in many fields, including studies of transatlantic slavery.[52] What I have termed 'oceans as method' offers alternative modes of reading, writing, and composing history, one that privileges movement

---

[46] Carl Schmitt, *The Nomos of the Earth: In the International Law of the Jus Publicum Europaenum*, trans. G. L. Ulmen (2003) 42–3 ff.

[47] Alexis Wick, *The Red Sea: In Search of Lost Space* (2016) 10 ff.   [48] Ibid., 188 ff.

[49] Ibid., 188 ff.   [50] Ibid., 188, 189 ff.

[51] Antoinette Burton, 'Sea Tracks and Trails: Indian Ocean Worlds as Method' (2013) 11(7) *History Compass* 497 ff.

[52] See, e.g., Sowande M. Mustakeem, *Slavery at Sea: Terror, Sex, and Sickness in the Middle Passage* (2016).

and mobility, while expanding beyond the constraints of land and territoriality.[53] Oceanic histories draw attention to circulations, interconnections, and overlaps across time and space and between colonial and imperial worlds.[54] If the sea, as I discuss below, opens a distinct set of itineraries and another philosophy of history, oceans carry serious implications for how we think of law's archive and of archival legal history beyond the presence/absence of texts, files, and documents.

Several scholars have mobilized the fluvial and aqueous properties of the sea to great effect, as a challenge to traditional historiography and the archives that inform it. In *Mediterranean Crossings*, Iain Chambers makes a compelling case for oceans as an ontology that changes how we write and represent the past. The sea 'promotes the adoption of a more fluid cartography', he contends, 'in which the presumed stability of the historical archive, together with its associated facts and interpretations, is set to float; susceptible to drift, unplanned contacts, even shipwreck. Sedimented in the sea are histories and cultures that are held in an inconclusive suspension.'[55] For Chambers, the metaphoricity of oceans invites new historical imaginaries: '[t]he metaphorical force of the sea, with its waves, winds, currents, tides, and storms, where the earth touches the sky in the infinity of a horizon that promotes a journey of navigation, dispersal, provides a more suitable frame for recognizing the unstable location of historical knowledge.'[56] The sea, like history and memory, is constantly moving. It exceeds geographical boundaries and temporal frames. Without a clear beginning or end, oceans cannot be easily periodized in terms of past, present, or future. These temporalities blend into and become one another. As a 'fluid cartography', the sea encourages new questions and approaches that escape conventional constraints of the archive. Indeed, some writers have turned to the sea in efforts to disrupt the linear chronology of slavery. 'Our entrance to the past is through memory' and salt water, M. NourbeSe Philip insists. Although 'the ocean appears to be the same . . . [it] is constantly in motion, affected by tidal movements', as are memory and history.[57]

For more than 400 years, transatlantic slavery has been 'a touchstone for the development of modern western economic, political, and legal systems', write the editors of a special issue on slavery and the archive.[58] Of all these institutions and structures, the role of slavery in modern finance has received sustained attention and documentation. In *Specters of the Atlantic*, Ian Baucom argues that transatlantic

---

[53] I develop this in my forthcoming book. See Mawani (n. 22).

[54] On the methodological potential of oceans see Burton, (n. 51); Isabel Hofmeyr, 'Complicating the Sea: The Indian Ocean as Method' (2012) 32(3) *Comparative Studies of South Asia, Africa, and the Middle East* 584–90 ff. See also Mawani, (n. 22); Renisa Mawani, Iza Hussin, 'The Travels of Law: Indian Ocean Itineraries' (2014) 32(4) *Law and History Review* 733–47 ff.

[55] Iain Chambers, *Mediterranean Crossings: The Politics of an Interrupted Modernity* (2008) 24 ff.

[56] Ibid., 27 ff.   [57] Philip (n. 16) 201 ff.

[58] Laura Helton, Justin Leroy, Max Mishler, Samantha Seeley, Shauna Sweeney, 'The Question of Recovery: An Introduction' (2015) 33(4) 125 *Social Text* 6 ff.

slavery was a foundational event in the development of financial capital, which continues to live on in the contemporary moment. Building on the insights and arguments of Walcott, Glissant, D'Aguiar, and others, Baucom describes his project as amassing a counter-archive of slavery, one that is firmly situated in the circum-Atlantic. Not engaging with debates on slavery's archive directly, and never discussing the ocean as an elemental, physical, and/or material space, Baucom presents a compelling reorientation, nonetheless. Through a creative reading of the silences of slavery's archive, he begins with the absent history of the *Zong*, an eighteenth-century British slave ship. The book commences with 'a gap in the archive', with an unacknowledged petition sent by Granville Sharp, a British abolitionist, to the Lord Commissioners of the Admiralty. Here, Sharp insists that the case of 132 slaves jettisoned from the *Zong* be formally investigated as murder.[59] Baucom uses this aperture with great skill. Through it, he weaves a riveting and conjoined history of transatlantic slavery, maritime insurance, and finance capital. This counter-archive of slavery 'constitutes more than an effective history of the event', Baucom insists. It is a history of the present, which carries 'the trace elements and perhaps also some of the secrets' of our own contemporary experience of history and the modern'.[60] For Baucom, slavery was foundational to the ascendancy of Britain's maritime prowess. Its imperial ambitions were realized through the invention of credit, which financed the protracted and dangerous voyages of slave ships, and through marine insurance, to which the slave as commodity was pivotal. The insurance contract, as Baucom describes it, is a 'paradigmatic document of the cultural, epistemological, and capital protocols' of the eighteenth and nineteenth centuries and an 'intensified repetition of that moment within our own exorbitantly financialized present'.[61] Through this counter-archive of the circum-Atlantic, Baucom traces a history of the present and an alternative philosophy of history.

The Atlantic, as it features in the work of Glissant, Walcott, and D'Aguiar disrupts the periodization of slavery as past and thereby over. For each of these writers, Baucom observes, a history of the Atlantic can only ever be an ongoing history of slavery, one that invites 'a responsible poetics of the modern' demanding we bear witness to slavery, a witnessing that challenges 'a post-Enlightenment understanding of the unfolding of historical time' and ultimately of progress.[62] Slavery is not history; slavery is now. Therefore, in Baucom's account, the Atlantic features not as the archive of times past but as an 'archive of the enduring'.[63] It is precisely through the 'enduring' that Baucom presents a philosophy of history in which the ocean features prominently. As an expansive and connective force, the Atlantic calls into question prevailing territorial divides and chronologies of history. In its multiple dimensions and changing temporalities, the Atlantic recasts

---

[59] Baucom (n. 16) see especially note one, 335 ff.   [60] Ibid., 4 ff.   [61] Ibid., 26 ff.
[62] Ibid., 312 ff.   [63] Ibid., 329 ff.

time and space, presenting novel ways to rethink the enduring mark of slavery in contemporary economic, political, and juridical forms.

Resonant with Baucom, Sharpe's 'wake work' also returns us to the Atlantic and to an 'archive of the enduring', one that continues to shape the present. Sharpe's focus rests not on the presence/absence of textual forms, but in the endurance of slavery in other elements and in other material forms. '[E]ven if those Africans who were in the holds, who left something of their prior selves in those rooms as a trace to be discovered, and who passed through the doors of no return did not survive the holding and the sea', Sharpe writes, 'they, like us, are alive in hydrogen, in oxygen; in carbon, in phosphorous, and iron; in sodium and chlorine.'[64] Those Africans who were 'thrown, jumped, dumped overboard in Middle passage' are not gone, 'they are with us still', Sharpe insists, 'in the time of the wake, known as residence time'.[65] The fluviality of the sea, as a moving and mutable force that disrupts the fixed coordinates of space and time, offers useful methodological insights into law's archive and archival legal history. By way of conclusion, the following section considers how the ocean as legal archive might help to foreground the foundational role of transatlantic slavery in the development of modern law. Specifically, I begin to trace its endurance in the conjoined juridical status of the ship and the slave as legal person, and in the metaphysical and magical processes by which law makes the inanimate animate and the animate inanimate.[66]

IV. THE SEA IS A LEGAL HISTORY
OF SLAVERY

. . . that was just Lamentations, it was not History

Derek Walcott

Oceans, as I argue throughout, are not empty. Nor are they sites of lawlessness, disorder, or anarchy. Rather, oceans are legally produced and arranged as distinct spaces: as territorial waters, contiguous zones, economic zones, and the high seas. The first three, depending on their proximity to territorial boundaries, fall within the jurisdiction of sovereign nation-states. The high seas, by contrast, cannot be controlled or occupied by any one sovereign power.[67] Although nation-states

---

[64] Sharpe (n. 14) 19 ff.   [65] Ibid.   [66] On law and magic, see Philip (n. 16) 196 ff.
[67] This was formalized in Hugo Grotius's *Mare Liberum*, published in 1609. See David Armitage (ed.), *The Free Sea: Hugo Grotius* (2004).

have jurisdiction over the ships that fly their flags and traverse ocean regions, as a legal domain, the high sea falls within the realm of international law. The spatial and legal distinctions imposed on ocean arenas have a long history that is rooted in the movement of European ships.[68] From the sixteenth century onward, as European vessels travelled farther and farther from shore in search of land, resources, and treasures, imperial polities raised pressing questions on the legal status of the sea.[69] The territorial lines that were eventually inscribed into ocean regions were initiated and expanded through imperial struggles over maritime commerce to which the transport of slaves proved crucial. One of the most significant contradictions in designating the high seas as a common space, Nicholas Mirzoeff argues, 'was the use of "free" oceanic trade to transport people as unfree property, or slaves'.[70] Maritime travel across the so-called 'free seas' encouraged unprecedented forms of racial violence that were deemed necessary to law's metaphysical processes of transforming people into property. The ocean as legal archive draws attention to modern maritime law and its significance to the governance of transatlantic slavery. Its circulations across land and sea serve as a persistent though forgotten reminder of slavery's ongoing relevance in the contemporary moment. Though there are many examples from which to draw, I focus briefly and suggestively on the concept of legal personhood.

If the archive is coterminous with the rise of the nation-state, as Vismann and Wick claim, then what is at stake in resituating the archive, law's archive, in the sea?[71] Moving beyond the constraints of terra firma, the ocean as legal archive invites an alternative and more expansive view of law. When viewed from the sea, law and legality are not static, fixed, or moored to national or territorial boundaries. Rather, law materializes as continuously moving and in transit. Legal idioms, ideas, and decrees travelled on ships and criss-crossed the seas in the writings and imaginaries of captains, colonial administrators, subalterns, and fugitive/freed slaves.[72] Legal exigencies and their proposed remedies were discussed, debated, and reconceived on protracted seaborne journeys amidst the fury of the sea. Refracted through shipboard conditions of solitude, boredom, and illness, laws were written, revised, and often transformed by the time they reached ports of call. The sea itself was never a smooth, contiguous, or uniform juridical space. Oceans were sites where indigenous, imperial, national, and international laws coincided, overlapped, and collided. British imperial laws, which sometimes recognized indigenous legalities, were layered atop of European ones, drawing direction and inspiration

---

[68] On the relationship between ships and space see Bernhard, Siegert, *Cultural Techniques: Grids, Filters, Doors, and other Articulations of the Real* (2015), esp. ch. 8 ff.

[69] See Armitage (n. 67).

[70] Nicholas Mirzoeff, 'The Sea and Land: Biopower and Visuality from Slavery to Katrina' (2009) 50(2) *Culture, Theory, and Critique* 293 ff.

[71] Vismann (n. 29) 117 ff; Wick (n. 47) 192 ff.

[72] Benton (n. 22) 3 ff. See also Mawani and Hussin (n. 54).

from existing legal practices and modes of governance already in circulation.[73] The Atlantic region offers a vivid case in point. As an international space that fell beyond the jurisdiction of the English common law, British and American jurists, as I discuss further below, governed the eighteenth- and nineteenth-century Atlantic unevenly and inconsistently through a composite of seafaring customs that would eventually become integral to modern maritime law. When the ocean is recast as a legal archive, it points to the mobile, mutable, and shared registers of Anglo law, their seaborne circulations, and the 'layered' sovereignties they engendered.[74] These overlapping jurisdictions are evident in British and American efforts to govern the transatlantic slave trade.

The land/sea divide that was so central to Schmitt's *Nomos* has now become a defining feature of the contemporary international legal order. This elemental distinction is not natural, neutral, or objective. It is the culmination of multiple and protracted histories of maritime transport, travel, and law. These distinctions between land and sea, which emerged from the transoceanic movements of ships, held significant implications for the capture, transport, and enslavement of Africans. Yet, curiously, the sea and the ocean-going vessels that crossed it have been given little attention in legal histories of slavery.[75] According to Paul Finkelman, slavery in the British Empire was 'governed by local laws, haphazardly passed by colonial legislatures or developed by colonial courts responding to specific events and cases'.[76] Though he says little of maritime law per se, he notes that the regulation of ships was crucial to the administration and governance of slavery. In Britain and subsequently the U.S., the development and expansion of maritime law was deeply entangled with the transport of captive Africans. The *British Navigation Acts*, which were intended to control the seas by targeting the ships that crossed them, became a key resource in ensuring Britain's imperial and maritime ascendancy through transatlantic slavery. To begin, these Acts required all plantation commodities, including slaves, be transported on British vessels. Second, they specified the legal status of slaves as property. According to the 1677 Act, 'negroes ought to be esteemed goods and commodities within the Acts of Trade and Navigation'.[77] The maritime standing of slaves as property also informed their legal status on land. Slaves were only regarded to be legal persons when they transgressed the law.[78]

---

[73] On the Indian Ocean region see Kerry Ward, *Networks of Empire: Forced Migration in the Dutch East India Company* (2009).

[74] On 'layered sovereignty' see Benton (n. 22) 123 ff.

[75] For notably exceptions see Baucom, (n. 16), Mustakeem, (n. 52), Rediker, (n. 16), and Smallwood, (n. 16).

[76] Finkelman (n. 8) 107 ff.

[77] V. C. D. Mtubani, 'African Slaves and English Law' (1981) 3(2) *Pula: Botswana Journal of African Studies* 71 ff.

[78] For a useful discussion of legal personhood and slavery see Colin Dayan, *The Law Is a White Dog* (2011).

On both sides of the Atlantic, laws governing the sea and those regulating slavery developed alongside each other and together. Before 1807, when Britain and the U.S. passed legislation to abolish the slave trade, many of the laws aimed at restricting transatlantic slavery targeted ships, seafarers, and maritime investors.[79] Legal and administrative practices aboard British and American vessels became vital to regulating the slave trade and to establishing the legal standing of those enslaved. Like Britain's *Navigation Acts*, ship ledgers and manifests played a significant role in transforming African captives from persons to property. If we read Vismann's insights oceanically, ship manifests and ledgers appear as early forms of legal writing. Administrative documents including lists, Vismann claims, were legal texts that preceded files. As law's 'point of departure', lists 'sort and engender circulation'.[80] As practices of enumeration, lists also classify, categorize, and abstract, often forcefully and violently. Historically, ship manifests operated as commercial, administrative, and legal documents that were central to maritime commerce. Manifests were required for all ships that entered foreign ports of call. These 'lists' did not simply catalogue persons and commodities. They determined their status as animate/ inanimate, legal/illegal, and free/unfree. Aboard slave ships, the captain's ledger, from which manifests were often compiled, was a clear symbol of sovereignty and authority. It set out the rules of the ship and recorded daily events, all in the interests of maximizing profits and maintaining order.[81] As expressions of legal power, manifests and ledgers were informed by and operated through changing registers of racial and legal violence. They reduced African captives 'to the basic common denominator', thus denying them a 'history, name or culture'.[82] Britain's *Navigation Acts* may have legally defined slaves as property, but it was through the mundane repetition of maritime law that African captives were denied their humanity.

The concept of legal personhood, which has become foundational to modern law as evidenced in the corporation, developed directly out of seaborne trade. Under British maritime customs, ships were regarded not as inanimate things, but as living persons. Captains, sailors, and seafarers commonly described their vessels in anthropomorphic terms and routinely personified them as women. Ships were believed to exhibit distinct moods, personalities, and dispositions that could either protect or imperil a captain and crew at sea.[83] By the 1800s, the personality of vessels under English maritime custom became an important doctrine in American law that continues to persist today. Under U.S. law, ships 'acquired the status of independent juridical persons, fictionally animate beings capable of contracting and committing offence, and by unique admiralty process subject to arrest, condemnation, and forfeiture for wrongdoing'.[84] It was through *in rem* proceedings, established under

---

[79] Finkelman (n. 8) 121 ff.   [80] Vismann (n. 29) 6 ff.   [81] D'Aguiar (n. 19) 128 ff.
[82] Philip (n. 16) 196 ff.
[83] Douglas Lind, 'Pragmatism and Anthropomorphism: Reconceiving the Doctrine of the Personality of the Ship' (2009–2010) 22(1) *U.S.F. Maritime Law Journal* 39–121 ff.
[84] Ibid., 39 ff.

admiralty law and used to secure maritime liens, that ships were transformed from inanimate things into legal persons. The vessel, not its owners, captain, or crew, was to be held responsible for wrongdoing, including debt. The personality of the ship proved crucial to regulating the movements of vessels along the high seas. The transformation of a ship from a thing into a legal person enabled U.S. courts to expand their jurisdiction across the seas by making decisions about vessels that flew an American flag but were anchored or detained in foreign waters.

The legal personhood of the ship, as it circulated in Atlantic worlds, would hold serious consequences for the transportation of slaves. In the first decades of the nineteenth century, the doctrine of legal personhood, as it applied to seaborne vessels, became an important feature of American jurisprudence. The concept of legal personhood has often been traced to U.S. Supreme Court judges Chief Justice John Marshall and Justice Joseph Story. Importantly, Marshall and Story also decided cases involving the legal status of slaves.[85] If efforts to govern the sea were deeply entangled with the transatlantic slave trade, as I am suggesting here, then the newfound status of the ship as legal person must be thought in relation to the denial of legal personhood for those enslaved. Just as moving ships in foreign waters generated a series of jurisdictional questions, so too did the itinerancy of fugitive slaves on land and sea. In 1842, more than four decades after the U.S. Supreme Court decided the ship to be a legal person, Justice Story reached a similar decision on the legal status of a slave. In *Prigg v. Pennsylvania*, Edward Prigg was accused of kidnapping a fugitive slave that he took with him to Maryland, thereby violating Pennsylvania's personal liberty law.[86] Justice Story—who in previous years made important judgments concerning the legal personhood of ships—defined a slave as property. If a slave was an inanimate thing and not a person, Story reasoned, slave owners could use *in rem* proceedings to recover runaway slaves. Drawing from maritime law, Story drew a clear relation between the ship and the slave.[87] If ships were legal persons that could be arrested and condemned, slaves were forms of moveable property that became legal persons only when they violated the law.[88]

The problem of runaway slaves was addressed directly through the *Fugitive Slave Act* of 1850. In an intriguing analysis that draws further associations between the laws of the sea, shipping, and the laws of slavery, Jonathan Gutoff compares the *Fugitive Slave Act* with the *Merchant Seaman's Act*, which preceded it by sixty years.[89] '[T]he provisions of the notorious Fugitive Slave Act, which required the rendition of runaway slaves and provided for the punishment of those who aided them', he writes, 'appear to have been modeled on provisions in the Merchant Seamen's

---

[85] Ibid., 52 ff.   [86] Finkelman (n. 8) 125 ff.

[87] For a discussion of *in rem* proceedings and fugitive slaves see Finkelman (n. 8) 126 ff.

[88] This point on slaves transgressing the law is made by Dayan (n. 78) 147 ff.

[89] Jonathan M. Gutoff, 'Fugitive Slaves and Ship-Jumping Sailors: The Enforcement and Survival of Coerced Labour' (2006) 9(1) *U. PA. Journal of Labor and Employment Law* 87–116 ff.

Act of 1790, which dealt with the problem of ship-jumping sailors.'[90] Gutoff offers convincing arguments on how the laws of land and sea were joined through slavery. Importantly, his intention is not to draw equivalences between the slave and the sailor. 'There is no denying that the legal regimes under which enslaved Africans and merchant seamen toiled were very different', he writes. 'The horrors suffered by Africans on the middle passage from Africa to North America and the subsequent sufferings they and their descendants endured in the fields, shops, and households of the eastern seaboard and the Caribbean were far greater than those inflicted on seamen.'[91] What Gutoff usefully underlines for his readers is how maritime law informed and shaped the *Fugitive Slave Act*, further concretizing the legal status of slaves as property. Under this Act, slaves had no right of appeal and no claims to *habeas corpus*. They were not permitted to testify on their own behalf.[92] Ultimately, their words, actions, and personhood were legally excluded from the archive of slavery and thereby lost to us today. To be sure, the ocean as legal archive may not recuperate the lost subjectivities of those enslaved. But the sea as a legal history of slavery unearths the ocean as legal archive. It reveals an afterlife of slavery that endures in juridical forms, including legal personhood, a legal history that remains forgotten and in need of retrieval.

In *Archive Fever*, Derrida reminds us that, '[t]he afterlife [survivance] no longer means death and the return of the specter, but the surviving of an excess of life which resists annihilation ("the survival of the most triumphant vital elements of the past").'[93] The ocean as legal archive points to the excesses of slavery that continue to endure and survive in the sea, through the legal status of the ship, the juridification of oceans, and in the 'residence time' that continues to animate the now.[94] The ocean as legal archive draws critical attention to a neglected aspect of slavery's archive, to objects, artefacts, and imaginaries that invite alternative ways to enter the 'archive of the enduring' and move us beyond the impasse of what can be said and what remains silenced in (legal) histories of transatlantic slavery.[95]

BIBLIOGRAPHY

Ian Baucom, *Specters of the Atlantic: Finance Capital, Slavery, and the Philosophy of History* (Duke University Press, 2005)

Fred D'Aguiar, *Feeding the Ghosts: A Novel* (HarperCollins, 1997)

Eduardo Glissant, *Poetics of Relation*, trans. Betsy Wang (University of Michigan Press, 2010)

Saidiya Hartman, *Lose Your Mother: A Journey Along the Atlantic Slave Route* (Farrar, Strauss, and Giroux, 2007)

[90] Ibid., 89 ff.   [91] Ibid., 89 ff.   [92] Finkelman (n. 8) 127 ff.
[93] Derrida (n. 10) 60 ff.   [94] Sharpe (n. 14) 19 ff.   [95] Baucom (n. 16) 329 ff.

Renisa Mawani, *Across Oceans of Law: The Komagata Maru and Jurisdiction in the Time of Empire* (Duke University Press, forthcoming, 2018)

Renisa Mawani, 'Law's Archive' *Annual Review of Law and Social Science* 8, 2012, 337–65

Stewart Motha, *Archiving Sovereignty* (University of Michigan Press, forthcoming, 2018)

M. NourbeSe Philip, *Zong!* (Wesleyan University Press, 2008)

Marcus Rediker, *The Slave Ship: A Human History* (Viking, 2007)

Carl Schmitt, *Land and Sea: A World-Historical Meditation* (Telos, 2015)

Carl Schmitt, *The* Nomos *of the Earth: In the International Law of the Jus Publicum Europeaeum*, trans. G. L. Ulmen (Telos Press, 2003)

Christina Sharpe, *In the Wake: On Blackness and Being* (Duke University Press, 2016)

Stephanie E. Smallwood, *Saltwater Slavery: A Middle Passage from Africa to American Diaspora* (Harvard University Press, 2008)

Cornelia Vismann, *Files: Law and Media Technology*, trans. Geoffrey Winthrop-Young (Stanford University Press, 2008)

Derek Walcott, 'The Sea is History' in *Derek Walcott: Collected Poems, 1948–1984* (Farrar, Strauss, and Giroux, 1986) 364–7

CHAPTER 17

···

SPELUNKING, OR, SOME MEDITATIONS ON THE NEW PRESENTISM

···

ELIZABETH DALE

IN 2017, the apparent dawn of a post-truth, alt-facts era, history has become the rage. Articles tell us that the age of Trump has made undergraduates seek history courses, while pundits debate the meaning of the Trump administration's embrace of Andrew Jackson.[1] This enthusiasm for the study of the past has had an understandable, if somewhat unexpected corollary—an increased interest in using the past to understand the present has marked the rise of what we might call the New Presentism.

I, too, am uncomfortable in what seems to be a world suddenly gone mad, in the literal sense of being irrational. And I rejoice at the possibility that undergraduates might want to study history (and its corollary that some graduate students in history might, therefore, find jobs teaching the subject). So I do not oppose the New Presentism. As I have noted in other contexts, I became a historian in order to use history to speak to and about the present.[2] And that is what I have tried to do

---

[1] DeNeen L. Brown, 'Trump called Andrew Jackson "a swashbuckler." The Cherokees called him "Indian Killer"' (2017) *Retropolis*, available at <https://www.washingtonpost.com/news/retropolis/wp/2017/11/28/andrew-jackson-was-calledindian-killer-trump-honorednavajos-in-front-of-his-portrait/?utm_term=.d93a54284a18> (accessed 22 April 2018).

[2] Elizabeth Dale, 'It Makes Nothing Happen: Reasons for Studying the History of Law' (2009) 5 *Journal of Law, Culture and the Humanities* 3 ff.

across my career. I have given impromptu lessons on the history of impeachment and the electoral college. I tossed out my lesson plan one day to teach about the O. J. Simpson verdict and spent several weeks at the end of fall semester 2000 helping my history students (and colleagues) understand the historical background of the issues in *Bush v. Gore*. I have been on panels about the Trayvon Martin tragedy. I wrote a history of the lost stories of police torture in Chicago in the years before Jon Burge and his crew tortured suspects on the south side Chicago.[3] I have written books that used history to make questions of law accessible to popular audiences.[4]

And yet, I think we need to approach the New Presentism with care. My concern is not the practice of presentism in and of itself. Rather, I wonder about what it says about how we view ourselves and our role in the world in which we find ourselves today.

I. PRESENTISM

For many years, the rule was simple: good historians rejected present-minded history.

That is the first lesson of undergraduate methods courses and a well-worn principle of graduate history seminars. Such a claim prompts the obvious question: what is this thing that historians must so carefully avoid? The works deploring the practice call it by any number of names: the 'Whig interpretation of history', 'law office history', 'present-minded history', 'progressive history', and 'applied history'. But while that variety of epithets suggests that presentism embraces a broad range of bad historical practices, as a practical matter the criticisms behind the titles share a common premise: if we use the past to help explain the present, our understanding of either, or sometimes both, will be distorted.

For all it is a truism, the rule against presentism is not a timeless verity. Many canonical works of early history were written with an eye towards their own times, as much as the events from the past that were their ostensible subject.[5] Still, a full-throated opposition to presentism has dominated historical study for nearly a century. When Alexander Butterfield attacked 'the Whig interpretation of history'

---

[3] Elizabeth Dale, *Robert Nixon and Police Torture in Chicago, 1871–1971* (Northern Illinois University Press, 2016).

[4] Elizabeth Dale, *Criminal Justice in the United States, 1789–1939* (Cambridge University Press, 2011); Elizabeth Dale, *The Chicago Trunk Murder: Law and Justice at the Turn of the Century* (Northern Illinois University Press, 2011).

[5] See, e.g., Thucydides, *The History of the Peloponnesian War*; William Bradford, *Of Plimouth Plantation*; Edward Gibbon, *The History of the Decline and Fall of the Roman Empire* (1734–1794).

in 1931, he wrote against historians who, he said, described the past as inexorably leading to a liberal constitutional present (or future). In 1970, in his book *Historians' Fallacies*, David Hackett Fischer deplored historians whose sense of 'American history is the steady progress of pragmatic liberalism from Jefferson to Jackson to Franklin Roosevelt.' At the start of the twenty-first century, Lynn Hunt railed against approaches to history that, in their crudest form, encouraged 'a kind of moral complacency and self-congratulation' and in their more nuanced versions led to history tied to contemporary events that 'might . . . be better approached via sociology, political science, or ethnic studies'.[6]

Historians of law have long voiced their own opposition to presentism, also known as law office history or, more recently, applied legal history. The former, as defined by Alfred Kelly in his famous article 'Clio and the Court', is history done by lawyers and judges to help support particular legal outcomes.[7] The latter is sketched in a more sympathetic debate over the practice between two contemporary historians, Karen Tani and Alfred Brophy, who worried that applied legal history, which deliberately looked at the history of contemporary problems, might too easily reduce history to 'the "usable" past'.[8]

As that summary suggests, specific political perspectives often drove the critics' concerns. Butterfield resisted the idea that the arc of history bent towards liberal parliamentary democracy, arguing that the idea of history-as-progress ignored the ambiguities of the past and the contingent nature of the present. Kelly condemned 'law office history' written 'to serve the interests of libertarian idealism'; while Fischer wrote against historians who used history to reveal the inexorable development of a particularly liberal style of government. Hunt worried that a presentist focus would inevitably reduce all history to the study of the twentieth century and the 'short-term history of various kinds of identity politics', and the Tani-Brophy debate reflected the fear that too much emphasis on historical study that had current applications might encourage neo-liberal efforts to reduce all scholarship to work that had practical application.

---

[6] David Hackett Fischer, *Historians' Fallacies: Toward of Logic of Historical Thought* (Harper and Row, Publishers, 1970); Herbert Butterfield, *The Whig Interpretation of History* (G. Bell and Sons, 1931); Lynn Hunt, 'Against Presentism' (2002) *Perspectives on History*, available online at <https://www.historians.org/publications-and-directories/perspectives-on-history/may-2002/against-presentism>.

[7] Alfred Kelly, 'Clio and the Court: An Illicit Love Affair' (1965) *Supreme Court Review* 119 ff.

[8] The discussion between Tani and Brophy took place across two academic blogs. For Tani's contributions see Karen Tani, 'What is Applied Legal History' (2012) *Legal History Blog*, available at <http://legalhistoryblog.blogspot.com/2012/07/what-is-applied-legal-history.html>; Karen Tani, 'More on Applied Legal History' (2012) *Legal History Blog*, available at <http://legalhistoryblog.blogspot.com/2012/07/more-on-applied-legal-history.html>.

For Brophy's contributions, see Alfred Brophy, 'What is Applied Legal History' (2012) *Faculty Lounge Blog*, available at <http://www.thefacultylounge.org/2012/07/what-is-applied-legal-history.html>; Alfred Brophy, 'Applied Legal History as Law Office History' (2012) *Faculty Lounge Blog*, available at <http://www.thefacultylounge.org/2012/07/applied-legal-history-vs-law-office-history.html>.

While it is tempting to conclude that at least some of the critics of presentism would have been satisfied by histories that were equally present-minded but supported different political agendas, that cynical focus ignores the problem many of those critics believed they were attacking. The concern, as they saw it, was not the point of view advanced itself: Butterfield, after all, argued that the answer to presentism was not to replace the faults of Whig bias with a Tory focus. For opponents of the practice, resistance to presentism reflected concerns about ethics and of scope. If history was written with an eye to advancing a particular cause, they feared it was more likely to disregard evidence that contradicted that goal. And if only history that was usable was written, then historical study deemed irrelevant to present day concerns would be ignored.

Alas, those problems transcend presentism. History departments often find themselves compelled to offer courses on subjects that students want; historians have been known to find it difficult to publish work that presses have deemed out of fashion. And even well-intentioned scholars may accidentally manipulate evidence or interpretation to support a thesis. The solution to those problems, aside from continuing to try to produce history that is unfashionable, is, as Butterfield admitted, for each generation to write and rewrite and rewrite history, to endlessly revise our understanding of the complicated nature of the past. That need not mean shutting out engagement with the past that is tied to contemporary concerns. Indeed, Hunt made precisely that point at the end of her essay on presentism, calling for historical exploration that kept the past and the present in creative tension by using the insights of the present to expand and reconfigure our inquiries into the past.

II. THE RISE OF THE NEW PRESENTISM

Hunt's remarks on presentism, given in 2002, marked a renewed interest in approaches that tied the study of history to the present. There were several reasons why this interest arose at the turn of the twenty-first century.

After years in which tenure-track jobs became harder to find, many members of the profession concluded that if history as a discipline was to be preserved and the training of future generations of historians continued, then historians and history departments had to find ways to show that historical inquiry was useful to the world outside the academy. The claim that to understand the present we must examine and try to understand the historical context that helped to give it shape became an increasingly popular professional response to both declining enrolments in history courses and diminishing employment opportunities for historians.[9]

Further support for presentism came from the many scholars who felt that arguments against usable history all too often were marshalled against efforts to make issues of sexuality, disability, or the lives of women or people of colour valid subjects of historical inquiry. Hunt conceded the point in her piece, where she pointedly noted that 'women's history, African American history, Latino history, gay and lesbian history, and the like have all made fundamentally important contributions to our understanding of history'. Unfortunately, opposition to the types of history Hunt listed was often framed in terms of presentism, precisely because attacking the method of the studies, rather than the subject, provided a neutral-seeming cover for efforts to erase some people from historical study. In response, some historians at the turn of the century embraced presentism because it allowed them to explore the history of the historiography that made those erasures possible.[10]

Others came to believe that those fortunate enough to be able to pursue careers in scholarship had a responsibility to use their positions for the greater good. Ibram Kendi, for example, argued that the training and relative leisure to think, explore, and reflect given to those of us who are paid to do scholarly research carried with it the obligation to put those privileges to good use by exposing the lies, erasures, and distortions of the past by governments or scholars. The idea that professional historians had a responsibility to use their platforms to engage popular debate made presentism a necessity, not just an option.[11]

In the first years of the twenty-first century, these discussions about presentism remained within the discipline, set out in scholarly journals, conferences, and the occasional public lecture. The presidential election of 2016 quickly pulled those conversation out into the world. On April 3, 2017 the *Washington Post* launched *Retropolis*, a blog 'aimed at connecting present-day news with its rich

---

[9] James Grossman, 'From the Executive Director: Everything Has a History' (2015) *Perspectives on History*, available at <https://www.historians.org/publications-and-directories/perspectives-on-history/december-2015/everything-has-a-history> (accessed 22 April 2018); Sidonie Smith, *Manifesto for the Humanities: Transforming Doctoral Education for Good Enough Times* (University of Michigan Digital Culture Books, 2015); Jo Gudi, David Armitage, *The History Manifesto* (Cambridge University Press, 2014).

[10] See, e.g., W. E. B. DuBois, *Black Reconstruction in America: An Essay Toward a History of the Part Which Black Folk Played to Reconstruct Democracy in America, 1860–1880* (1935; Free Press, 1998); Eric Foner, *Reconstruction: America's Unfinished Revolution, 1863–1877* (Harper Perennial Classic, 2011); Eric Foner, 'Why Reconstruction Matters' (2015) *New York Times*, available at <https://www.nytimes.com/2015/03/29/opinion/sunday/why-reconstruction-matters.html?_r=0>; Pamela Brandwein, *Reconstructing Reconstruction: The Supreme Court and the Production of Historical Truth* (Duke University Press, 1999).

[11] Ibram Kendi, 'Are You an Intellectual?', Graduate Commencement Address, University of Florida (2016), *UF News*, available at <http://news.ufl.edu/articles/2016/12/national-book-award-winner-addresses-uf-doctoral-grads.php>. See also Noam Chomsky, 'The Responsibility of the Intellectuals' (1967) 80 *New York Review of Books* 3 ff.

history.' Although written by the *Post*'s reporting staff, the paper promised the blog would be historically grounded, using material drawn from the paper's archives, in collaboration with Washington's many librarians, museum curators, and historians.[12] For all that its founding statement claimed that *Retropolis* was inspired by the notion that 'much of the news we cover today has echoes in the past', the histories published on the blog rarely offered much depth. It did not take long for historians, conceding the necessity of providing historical perspective, to raise the stakes. A few months after *Retropolis* was born, historian Moshik Temkin took to the pages of the *New York Times* to argue that historians (rather than journalists) should 'provide a critical, uncomfortable account of how we arrived at our seemingly incomprehensible current moment'. In other words, history had to be interpreted (by historians), not simply pulled out of an archive and dumped onto the web or into a news account. Although he did not refer to *Retropolis* specifically, Temkin's argument was clear: history had become too important to leave to amateurs, whether they were presidential advisors who prided themselves on reading Thucydides or newspaper reporters who drew on newspaper morgues to explain policy.[13] At roughly the same time, Keisha Bain and Ibram Kendi, whose commitment to publicly engaged history led them to create the history blog *Black Perspectives*, called on scholars to 'step out of the shadows of their libraries' in order to fight the onslaught of fake news and alternative facts.[14]

Thus, the New Presentism was born.

III. From Theory, to Practice

What does the New Presentism mean for legal historians? Contra Alfred Kelly, the proponents of the New Presentism do not argue, as did Justice Black in his appendix to *Adamson v. California*, that history can or should prove that those who wrote the Fourteenth Amendment intended to incorporate the entire Bill of Rights.[15]

---

[12] WashPostPR, 'The Washington Post launches Retropolis: A History Blog' (2017) *WashPostPR Blog*, available at <https://www.washingtonpost.com/pr/wp/2017/04/03/the-washington-post-launches-retropolis-a-history-blog/?utm_term=.143acc67599b>.

[13] Moshik Temkin, 'Historians Shouldn't Be Pundits' (2017) *New York Times*, available at <https://www.nytimes.com/2017/06/26/opinion/trump-nixon-history.html?_r=0>; Michael Crowley, 'Why the White House is Reading Greek History' (2017) *PoliticoMagazine*, available at <http://www.politico.com/magazine/story/2017/06/21/why-the-white-house-is-reading-greek-history-215287>.

[14] Keisha Bain, Ibram Kendi, 'How to Avoid a Post-Scholar America' (2017) *Chronicle of Higher Education*, available at <http://www.chronicle.com/article/How-to-Avoid-a-Post-Scholar/240352>. 'About', *Black Perspectives* at <http://www.aaihs.org/about-black-perspectives/>.

[15] *Adamson v. California* (1947) 332 U.S. 47, 92.

Nor, if I understand them correctly, do they believe that legal historians will be able to settle once and for all the question of what the scope of the Second Amendment truly is, regardless of what Justices Scalia and Stevens tried to assert in *Heller v. District of Columbia*.[16] Rather, their notion that historians have a responsibility to the public means that legal historians have a duty to help explain the context in which legal rules that are applied were adopted, and help uncover the experiences of people upon whom the laws have been enforced.

How, then, should we do it? To some extent we need only do what we have always done. In his overview of applied legal history, Alfred Brophy argued that we need only look around to see the various ways in which historical legal scholarship has always spoken to the present even as it struggled to add to our understanding of the past.[17] There is the example of legal historians who have testified as experts in cases involving election laws and voting rights,[18] or the example of scholars who waded into contemporary debates, writing on subjects like the Second Amendment. That work did not provide a final answer on what our gun laws should be, but over several decades, the work of historians across the political spectrum complicated and deepened that debate.[19] There is also the example of the legal historians who wrote the amicus brief that helped shape the rulings on same sex marriage.[20] Even works of traditional scholarship have played a role in shaping contemporary debates. Sally Hadden's *Slave Patrols*, which studied the ways in which Virginia and South Carolina policed their slave populations until the Civil War, might seem at first glance to have little to say to contemporary law or policy. Yet participants to debates over policing inspired by the Black Lives Matter movement have made arguments informed by her study and influenced by arguments advanced in her work.[21]

Much of that scholarship was ultimately published in the traditional formats of scholarly articles or books. But if we are writing history that is usable, Bain and Kendi argue that we also need to consider how to present our work in ways that are

---

[16] *Heller v. District of Columbia* (2008) 554 U.S. 570.

[17] Alfred Brophy, 'Introducing Applied Legal History' (2013) 31 *Law and History Review* 233 ff.

[18] Kritika Agarwal, 'Historians as Expert Witnesses: Can Scholars Help Us Save the Voting Rights Act?' (2017) *Perspectives on History*, available at <https://www.historians.org/publications-and-directories/perspectives-on-history/february-2017/historians-as-expert-witnesses-can-scholars-help-save-the-voting- rights-act>.

[19] 'Forum: Rethinking the Second Amendment' (2007) 25 *Law and History Review* 139 ff.

[20] Michael Grossberg, 'Friends of the Court: A New Role for Historians' (2010) *Perspectives on History*, available at <://www.historians.org/publications-and-directories/perspectives-on-history/november-2010/friends-of-the-court-a-new-role-for-historians>. See also, Rachel Hope Cleves, 'History from the Witness Stand: An Interview with George Chauncey' (2016) *Notches*, available at <http://notchesblog.com/2016/06/23/history-from-the-witness-stand-an-interview-with-george-chauncey/>.

[21] Sally E. Hadden, *Slave Patrols: Law and Violence in Virginia and the Carolinas* (Harvard University Press, 2003). For an example of activist literature relying on Hadden's work, see Adam Hudson, 'Beyond Homan Square: US History is Steeped in Torture', in Maya Schenwar, Joe Macaré, Alana Yu-lan Price (eds.), *Who Do You Serve, Who Do You Protect? A Truthout Collection* (Haymarket Books, 2016) 47 ff.

accessible to the people outside the academy who might make use of it.[22] And that means we need to think about presenting our work outside the confines of journals that are published behind paywalls and books that are priced for academic libraries. Publishing in open source journals is one way to do this. Working with museums, national parks, or institutions to translate academic scholarship into publicly accessible exhibits is another. Creating online exhibits, archives, and research reports is a third way of making historical scholarship both usable and accessible. Fortunately, we once again have a number of models. Tom Russell created an online archive about *Sweatt v. Painter*, the suit to integrate the University of Texas archive in the 1990s. That archive includes court papers, oral histories, and other resources for those who might wish to understand the impact of segregated education and the struggle to bring it to a close.[23] More recently, in 2015–2016, the Georgetown University Working Group on Slavery, Memory, and Reconciliation created a digital archive recording the history of that university's ownership of slaves. That website includes a report written by the committee, an archive of documents, and a timeline.[24] There are many other examples of online history blogs, written by scholars who want to bring scholarship to the public. In addition to the *Legal History Blog*, there are blogs that touch on law and history from specific perspectives, including *Black Perspectives: The Blog of the African American Intellectual Historical Society; Points: The Blog of the Alcohol & Drug History Society; Notches*, a history of sexuality blog; and the *Prison Public Memory Project*, a multimedia archive and blog that helps put incarceration into a larger context.[25] These sites offer a variety of models for how to do publicly engaged, and accessible, historical scholarship.

Nothing, of course, guarantees that this publicly engaged history will be used with nuance or even that good history will prevail over prejudice. We need only look at the duelling opinions in *Heller v. District of Columbia*, with their arguments about the true history of the Second Amendment, to see that historians, like authors, cannot control what their readers do with their work.[26] But the answer to that problem seems to me to be increased historical engagement with popular (or judicial) misuses of history, not withdrawal from the public sphere. Good history does not drive out bad history by virtue of its intrinsic merit. For the proponents of the New Presentism, history serves its purpose when it engages the public in discussion

---

[22] Bain, Kendi (n. 14).

[23] Thomas Russell, 'Sweatt v. Painter', *House of Russell*, available at <http://www.houseofrussell.com/legalhistory/sweatt/>.

[24] 'Report of the Working Group on Slavery, Memory, and Reconciliation', (2016) *Slavery, Memory, and Reconciliation Website*, available at <http://slavery.georgetown.edu/report/>.

[25] *The Legal History Blog*, available at <http://legalhistoryblog.blogspot.com>; *Black Perspective*, available at <http://www.aaihs.org/black-perspectives/>; *Points*, available at <https://pointsadhsblog.wordpress.com>; *Notches*, available at <http://notchesblog.com>; *Prison Public Memory Project*, available at <https://www.prisonpublicmemory.org>.

[26] *Heller* (n. 16).

about why particular claims rest on misplaced certainty or misunderstood history, and counters bad history with more nuanced and complicated alternatives.

iv. Into, Out of, or Round About the Cave?

New Presentism's idea that historians have an obligation to use their training to help society has an illustrious pedigree. It is, after all, the point of Plato's allegory of the cave, in book VII of *The Republic*.[27] There, those who were removed from their chains and brought out of the cave into the world of light were expected to return to the darkness of the cave to teach those left behind. Education, represented in the allegory by the chance to go out of the cave into the light, brought with it responsibility to share the knowledge gained from exposure to the reality behind the shadows.

Yet reflection on the allegory of the cave raises some cautions that we would do well to consider. The responsibility to return to the cave is, the allegory makes clear, a responsibility that carries with it serious costs. As Socrates and Glaucon agreed in the dialogue in the *Republic*, those who returned to the cave at the very least risked being mocked by the others and in some circumstances they ran the risk of being killed for their efforts.[28] The first months of 2017 suggest that pessimism is not misplaced. Ten states have passed laws allowing concealed carry of weapons on campus, while several others have considered it.[29] In June 2017, the National Rifle Association put out an ad called 'The Violence of Lies' which blamed a nameless 'they' who, among other things, 'use their schools' to incite demonstrators and violent protest.[30] And scholars who have 'gone too far' in engaging current events have faced death threats and other serious backlash.[31] That does not, of course, mean we should avoid trying to help our fellows. But it does, I think, mean that we need to spend some of our

[27] Plato, *Republic*, Book VII ff.   [28] Plato (n. 27) 517a ff.

[29] The states are Arkansas, Colorado, Georgia, Idaho, Kansas, Mississippi, Oregon, Texas, Utah, and Wisconsin. 'Guns on Campus: Overview', *National Conference of State Legislation*, available at <http://www.ncsl.org/research/education/guns-on-campus-overview.aspx>.

[30] Jonah Engle Bromwich, 'NRA Ad Condemning Protests Against Trump Raises Partisan Anger' (2017) *New York Times*, available at <https://www.nytimes.com/2017/06/29/us/nra-ad-trump-protests.html>.

[31] 'Professor Keanga-Yamahtta Taylor Cancels Speeches Amid Death Threats' (2017) *Democracy Now*, available at <https://www.democracynow.org/2017/6/2/headlines/professor_keeanga_yamahtta_taylor_cancels_speeches_amid_death_threats>.

thought and time reflecting on what we think of academic freedom and working to shore up its protections.

There are some other reasons for caution. In the *Republic*, Plato assumes (because it is consistent with his larger philosophical argument) that education functions as a complete break with the past. Thus, those who are exposed to the light are able to cast aside their old notions, absorb their new lessons completely, and take their fresh insights back into the cave, where they use their new understanding to reinterpret the shadows for their fellows trapped below.[32] It would be nice if this optimistic take on scholarly training were so and if it guaranteed that we were free from the delusions of the rest of society. But in *Racecraft*, Karen and Barbara Fields suggest that scholars are no more likely than other members of society to be able to escape from the mental terrain and belief (what they call racecraft) that makes racism possible.[33] Racism is, of course, a special problem all its own, but the point the Fields make about the difficulty of moving beyond racecraft can apply to our efforts to transcend other belief systems, such as the rule of law or the idea of democracy. At the very least, we need to beware of the possibility that our interpretations are influenced as much by the shadows of our society as by the light of day. That is true of any kind of scholarly study, of course, but when scholarship engages the public, it becomes more important since the pressure of the moment takes away our opportunity to wash our work clean through generations worth of revisions.

There is a final lesson from the allegory of the cave, one that Plato did not intend. Socrates' straight man, Glaucon, hints at it in the dialogue when he objects that making those who got to the surface go back into cave is a form of punishment, since it forces them give up the opportunity of living in light for darkness. But when Socrates reminds Glaucon that this is necessary given the larger goal of achieving the happiness of all, not just a few, Glaucon agrees that under those circumstances, those who escaped must return to the cave to help their fellows, and the dialogue moves forward.[34] That solves the problem for Plato, but it ignores the question implied by Glaucon's objection: why does helping society require working within the dark of the cave? Because we are not bound by Plato's overarching logic, we have alternatives. If we wish to help our fellows left behind in the cave we can, at the most extreme, try to bring the worlds of darkness and light together by destroying the cave. If revolution seems too extreme for prudent scholars, there is also the option of going back into the cave to explain what is keeping our fellows in their chains.

That last option would require us to offer a different sort of knowledge, flipping the premise of presentism on its head. Rather than starting with historical study and bringing it to bear to help explain the present, we would need to start with a careful study of the present, using our historical skills to interpret the world we

[32] Plato (n. 27) 518c ff.
[33] Karen Fields and Barbara Fields, *Racecraft: The Soul of Inequality in American Life* (Verso, 2012).
[34] Plato (n. 27) 519e ff.

find ourselves in today. Ultimately, as Marc Bloch's study of the French defeat in the Second World War, *L'Étrange Défaite*, demonstrates, that approach would require us to dig back into past.[35] But it would mean we had to first unpack the world we find ourselves in, to call into the question the darkness and the shadows in the cave, rather than accept them as a given.

BIBLIOGRAPHY

Keisha Blain, Ibram Kendi, 'How to Avoid a Post-Scholar America' (2017) vol. 62 *Chronicle of Higher Education*, issue 39

Marc Bloch, *L'Étrange Défaite* (Gallimard/Folio, 1990)

Alfred Brophy, 'What is Applied Legal History' (2012) *Faculty Lounge Blog*, available at <http://www.thefacultylounge.org/2012/07/applied-legal-history-vs-law-office-history.html>

Alfred Brophy, 'Applied Legal History as Law Office History' (2012) *Faculty Lounge Blog*, available at <http://www.thefacultylounge.org/2012/07/what-is-applied-legal-history.html>

Alfred L. Brophy, 'Introducing Applied Legal History' (2013) 31 *Law and History Review* 233

Herbert Butterfield, *The Whig Interpretation of History* (G. Bell and Sons, 1931)

Noam Chomsky, 'The Responsibility of Intellectuals' (1967) 80 *New York Review of Books* 3

Elizabeth Dale, 'It Makes Nothing Happen: Reasons for Studying the History of Law' (2009) 5 *Journal of Law, Culture and the Humanities* 3

Karen Fields, Barbara Fields, *Racecraft: The Soul of Inequality in American Life* (Verso, 2012)

David Hackett Fischer, *Historians' Fallacies: Toward a Logic of Historical Thought* (Harper & Row Publishers, 1970)

Jo Gudi, David Armitage, *The History Manifesto* (Cambridge University Press, 2014)

Lynn Hunt, 'From the President: Against Presentism' (2002) *Perspectives on History*, available at <https://www.historians.org/publications-and-directories/perspectives-on-history/may-2002>

Ibram Kendi, 'Commencement Address: Are You an Intellectual?' (2016) *UF News*, available at <https://www.aaihs.org/are-you-an-intellectual/>

Sidonie Smith, *Manifesto for the Humanities: Transforming Doctoral Education for Good Enough Times* (University of Michigan Digital Culture Books, 2015)

Karen Tani, 'More on Applied Legal History' (2012) *Legal History Blog*, available at http://legalhistoryblog.blogspot.com/2012/07/what-is-applied-legal-history.html>

Karen Tani, 'What is Applied Legal History' (2012) *Legal History Blog*, available at <http://legalhistoryblog.blogspot.com/2012/07/what-is-applied-legal-history.html>

---

[35] Marc Bloch, *L'Étrange Défaite* (Gallimard/Folio, 1990). The book is available in English, trans. Marc Bloch, *The Strange Defeat* (1999).

CHAPTER 18

LEGAL HISTORY

TAKING THE LONG VIEW

PAUL D. HALLIDAY

THERE is no view without a viewer. Jane Austen understood this. At a pivotal moment, readers of *Persuasion* join Austen's central characters in their first sight of the sea at Lyme.

After securing accommodations, and ordering a dinner at one of the inns, the next thing to be done was unquestionably to walk directly down to the sea. They were come too late in the year for any amusement or variety which Lyme, as a public place, might offer. The rooms were shut up, the lodgers almost all gone, scarcely any family but of the residents left; and, as there is nothing to admire in the buildings themselves, the remarkable situation of the town, the principal street almost hurrying into the water, the walk to the Cobb, skirting round the pleasant little bay, which, in the season, is animated with bathing machines and company; the Cobb itself, its old wonders and new improvements, with the very beautiful line of cliffs stretching out to the east of the town, are what the stranger's eye will seek; and a very strange stranger it must be, who does not see charms in the immediate environs of Lyme, to make him wish to know it better. The scenes in its neighbourhood, Charmouth, with its high grounds and extensive sweeps of country, and still more, its sweet, retired bay, backed by dark cliffs, where fragments of low rock among the sands, make it the happiest spot for watching the flow of the tide, for sitting in unwearied contemplation; the woody varieties of the cheerful village of Up Lyme; and, above all, Pinny, with its green chasms between romantic rocks, where the scattered forest trees and orchards of luxuriant growth, declare that many a generation must have passed away since the first partial falling of the cliff prepared the ground for such a state, where a scene so wonderful and so lovely is exhibited. (Jane Austen, *Persuasion*, chapter 11)

Only Austen's choices could make perspectives out of places—could make a bay 'sweet', a village 'cheerful', or low rocks among tidal sands 'the happiest spot' for contemplation. As they take in various views, Austen's viewers place Lyme and its people in three timescales. 'Many a generation must have passed away', as the tides flowed in and out. In summer, bathing machines lined the shore; in winter, only permanent residents remained. The sweep of natural time, cross-cut by annual social rhythms, was punctuated by ruptures brought about by unexpected natural actions—the collapse of a cliff face—and by human actions.

Austen's characters soon experienced such a rupture. Making sense of it meant thinking simultaneously in these three timescales: of enduring natural forces that 'prepared the ground' for human life; of yearly cycles of coming and going; and of contingent events, such as the one that would propel Austen's protagonists along paths none had foreseen. Only by putting the briefest instant in the longest possible view could Austen's characters make sense of it. Only in the long view could a young woman's fall from Lyme's cobb, with 'its old wonders and new improvements', be understood as a moment of revelation.

Austen demonstrates that the long view does not lie somewhere awaiting our gaze. It is a position we search out and decide to take, a position from which we might gain the kind of insights Austen provides at Lyme. It is a position where multiple timescales converge to reveal the meaning of an instant of human action. We find, as Austen's characters did, how meaning might be achieved by our decision to take a view of a particular kind; we find that only when we take the long view may we make sense of even the briefest moments.

1. The *Longue Durée* vs. the Long View

Artists and writers in Austen's England thought a lot about perspective and the picturesque: about what it means to choose one position instead of another from which to observe landscapes or human relationships, and thus about what it means to frame and thereby *take* a view.[1] A perspective that might enlighten or enliven, they argued, involved depth of field as much as it involved breadth or attention to detail. Our choice of position determines what we see and what we learn from what we see.

---

[1] Barbara Britton Wenner, *Prospect and Refuge in the Landscape of Jane Austen* (2006).

Taking the long view requires foremost that we find the place where we might mind the biblical observation that 'One generation passeth away, and another generation cometh: but the earth abideth for ever.' (Ecclesiastes 1:4) Seeing wide sweeps of time from a great distance entails humility: an acceptance of the limits of human agency, as individuals or in groups, to shape a world persistently driven by forces greater than ourselves. But taking the long view also involves examining enough human experience that we appreciate that the earth only *appears* to abide forever. Only in the long view, where we scan multiple generations, do we exercise the analytic patience that allows us to look past apparent persistence for the transformative moments that often lie hidden beneath. 'Is there *any* thing whereof it may be said, See, this *is* new?' (Ecclesiastes 1:10) Yes. We can only see what's new when we take the long view.

Taking a long view of law's pasts involves more than a broad survey. If length of time considered were the only requirement, then taking the long view would seem built into legal history, especially in its Anglophone varieties. Thinking through precedents looks like both a jurisprudential habit and a historical method as it often involves examining law's work across wide swathes of time.[2] But this is not the same as taking the long view. For thinking through precedents typically involves seeing law's pasts in the thinnest possible terms: as so many pearls of wisdom tied together in a string of judicial statements.

The common law imagination traditionally ordered ideas in genealogies: as so many begats beginning in mythical jurisprudential parents and projected forward into a redemptive future. Sir Edward Coke described law as a birthright, deploying a spiritually charged language by which past practices entailed future ones.[3] Henry Maine depicted developmental stages in sedimentary terms.[4] He and his predecessors scanned long spells and paradoxically united claims of changelessness to celebrations of legal improvement, summed up neatly in Maine's dictum, 'the movement of the progressive societies has hitherto been a movement *from Status to Contract*', in which contract was taken as a proxy for liberal political order.[5] Maine thus reduced his three-dimensional geological metaphor to a line with a point at one end. A linear, precedential view of the gathered wisdom of generations did not simply inform the future; it dictated the future.

---

[2] On the difference between thinking through precedents and thinking historically, see Paul D. Halliday, 'Authority in the Archives' (2014) 1 *Critical Analysis of Law* 113 ff.

[3] Paul D. Halliday, 'Birthrights and the Due Course of Law', in Lorna Hutson (ed.), *The Oxford Handbook of English Law and Literature, 1500–1700* (2017) 591 ff.

[4] Henry Sumner Maine, *Ancient Law: Its Connection with the Early History of Society, and its Relation to Modern Ideas* (1861) 3 ff.

[5] Ibid., 170 ff. Emphasis in original. On Maine and Frederic William Maitland's critique of Maine, see David M. Rabban, *Law's History: American Legal Thought and the Transatlantic Turn to Legal History* (2013), chapters 4 and 12 ff; Michael Lobban, 'The Varieties of Legal History' (2012) 5 *Clio@Themis: Revue électronique d'histoire du droit* 5 ff.

All these lawyer-historians recounted history as chronicle: 'first . . . , and then . . . , and then . . . , and finally'. But there is a difference between a chronicle of law over a long period—conceived in one dimension and pointed somewhere inescapable— and a history taken from the long view. Rather, a long view arises from our choices about the position we occupy as we take our view. We can take a long view when we search out a position from which we might discern relationships among what otherwise appear to be unrelated moments or phenomena scattered over multiple generations. We take a long view when we find the place where temporally disparate objects unite in a single analytic field, a place where seemingly contrary things might be drawn together into a synoptic vision revealing multiple trajectories entwined across time as it flows across human experience in all its dimensions. The long view suggests how the future will be determined by choices we make at any conjuncture of so many trajectories. The length of the view thus derives from the way it depends on and generates chronosthesia: the ability to see past, present, *and future* in an instant.

Legal historians might take the long view by mimicking the approach Austen adopted in her account of Lyme or, more prosaically, the one offered by Fernand Braudel. Like Austen, Braudel identified three temporal dimensions that had to be united to understand the world: geographical time, social time, and individual time. The first, he explained, 'unfolds slowly and is slow to alter . . . [and] tells the story of man's contact with the inanimate'. The second refers to the 'gentle rhythms, of groups and groupings', to social relations in states and societies. Last and least is the frame through which lawyer-historians like Coke or Maine cast their backward gaze: 'on the scale not so much of man in general as of men in particular . . . the history of events: a surface disturbance, the waves stirred up by the powerful movement of tides'.[6]

Like Austen, Braudel insisted that we must understand the tides if we are to make sense of surface disturbances. He asked us to accustom ourselves 'to a slower tempo, which sometimes almost borders on the motionless'. This is the *longue durée*. But we might only plumb the significance of *apparent* motionlessness by seeing it within the 'plurality of social time'. Braudel emphasized attention to that which 'borders on' the motionless to sharpen our ability to identify true ruptures.[7] Once we see time in long flows, we can begin to spot the moments that redirect it.

Braudel's account of the *longue durée* suggests the kind of work we must do. That said, there is a difference between the *longue durée* and taking the long view. It is the difference between object and observer. *Taking* the long view—emphasizing our actions rather than the things on which we act—calls to mind the position we decide to inhabit as we look upon a sweep of time and the fact that our choice of

[6] 'Time in History', *The Mediterranean and the Mediterranean World in the Age of Philip II* (1949), reprinted in Fernand Braudel, *On History*, trans. Sarah Matthews (1980) 3.

[7] Ibid., 33, 26.

position affects what we observe. Braudel was sensitive to this perspectival element of the *longue durée*; he was concerned with the observer's position as well as with the object of contemplation. By using the language of the long view, I mean to build upon rather than critique Braudel.

We can see the importance of taking the long view in legal history by returning to two further propositions from Braudel. First, there are, and should be, normative commitments enlivened by our work; there are problems we face now that only historical analysis can help us understand. If so, then we might shape our future based on what learn from the past—that what appears motionless may not be. Indeed, by our choices, we may affect the motion of that which only seems motionless. Second, taking the long view requires methodological pluralism. Let's consider each.

Braudel asked, '[i]s not history, the dialectic of time spans, in its own way an explanation of society in all its reality? and thus of contemporary society?' If the historical enterprise limits itself 'to the study of well-walled gardens', it will 'fail in one of its present tasks, of responding to the agonizing problems of the hour'.[8] Here, Braudel sharpened a point made by R. G. Collingwood.

[B]ecause the present contains the past in itself, the present is not determined by the past as something external to it, a cause of which it is the effect; the present is a free and living activity which embraces and sustains its own past by its own act.

History is something we do now. It is not performed upon some distant other, nor is the past of interest only as it constitutes any given now, even if the present unavoidably 'embraces and sustains its own past'. Rather, there is a dialectic of past with our now every time we attempt to rethink the thoughts of those who inhabited other ages. And this, according to Collingwood, is the purpose of history: to rethink thoughts.

Historical knowledge is the knowledge of what mind has done in the past, and at the same time it is the redoing of this, the perpetuation of past acts in the present . . . it is an activity of thought, which can be known only in so far as the knowing mind re-enacts it and knows itself as so doing . . . [The past is] not spectacles to be watched, but experiences to be lived.[9]

Collingwood, like Braudel, thus dismissed 'the false view of history as a story of successive events'. It is an activity, a thinking with and through past experiences.

[History] is not a passive surrender to the spell of another's mind; it is a labor of active and therefore critical thinking. The historian not only re-enacts past thought, he re-enacts it in the context of his own knowledge and therefore, in re-enacting it, criticizes it.[10]

The key is the historian's consciousness of the now she inhabits and the 'problems of the hour', in Braudel's words, that motivate critique of re-enacted thought.

---

[8] Ibid., 38, 4.
[9] R. G. Collingwood, *The Idea of History*, Jan Van Der Dussen (ed.) (1994), 187, 218.
[10] Ibid., 220, 215.

We flirt here with presentism, a word historians usually pronounce with a sneer. But presentism poses a problem only when we search the past for validation of our normative commitments rather than for all the others that lie out there. When we pursue the normative commitments of others, critique becomes reflexive: criticism of a re-enacted past provides the position for criticism of our now and thus for the construction of our future. Our analytic integrity faces no threat when contemporary concerns encourage us to seek positions for taking a long view, positions from which we might renew, refine, or reject our commitments as we see them afresh from the vantage others once held. Thus taking the long view involves an ethical commitment to discomfiting ourselves. The longer the view we take, the greater the distance from ourselves we see. The farther we see, the more we bring back to reconsidering the otherwise un-interrogated presuppositions that underlie the moral reasoning from which we make our future.[11]

Given this, taking the long view provides a jurisprudential as well as a historical method. It becomes a tool as we ask ourselves—prompted by thinking with the questions posed and values held by others long gone—to consider anew whether our laws serve the purposes we want them to serve.[12] As a form of jurisprudence, the long view reveals how persistent problems in realizing justice are only *seemingly* persistent: it helps us see what kinds of objects thrown by human choice into the flow of time might redirect it. Conversely, by seeing the objects created by our past legal authorities within the flows of human experience that generated them, we can think more clearly about how such objects—judicial dicta, treatises, a clutch of words uttered in a constitutional convention—might be read with greater probity and thereby revealed to have other properties than at first appear. As Collingwood put it, what the historian and the jurist does to 'so-called authorities is not to believe them but to criticize them'.[13]

The long view thus offers a retort to those varieties of jurisprudence gathered under the banner of originalism, most of which assert that words of a given instant might be understood only from within that instant in hopes that singular meaning might be attributed to them.[14] Collingwood might have called such an interpretive method 'scissors-and-paste' jurisprudence, in which we first decide what we want to know about—the meaning of a constitutional provision, perhaps—and then go 'in

---

[11] '[O]ne of the present values of the past is as a repository of values we no longer endorse, of questions we no longer ask.' Quentin Skinner, *Liberty Before Liberalism* (1998) 112.

[12] Markus Dubber calls for deploying history in the long view as a critical jurisprudential instrument: 'New Historical Jurisprudence: Legal History as Critical Analysis of Law' (2015) 2 *Critical Analysis of Law* 1 ff.

[13] Critique, Collingwood continued, would be performed by 're-enactment of past experience' in the mind of the historian—or the jurist. Collingwood (n. 9) 282.

[14] This is not the place to critique the many varieties of originalism. One useful approach, because it operates in the long view, is in Bernadette Meyler, 'Towards a Common Law Originalism' (2006–2007) 59 *Stanford L.R.* 551 ff.

search of statements about it'. Doing so assumes that a given text—e.g., Madison's notes—contains 'ready-made statements'. But a 'scientific' or critical history or jurisprudence 'contains no ready-made statements'. The critical jurist-historian,

does not treat statements as statements but as evidence: not as true or false accounts of the facts of which they profess to be accounts, but as other facts which, if he knows the right questions to ask about them, may throw light on those facts.[15]

Attending to 'other facts', the jurist-historian begins to find the place from which she may take a long view. Only from there—only situated in the flows of statements made over generations—can otherwise isolated statements be understood as containing ideas we might or must attend to because they contain the potential to transform human circumstances.

How shall we do this work? This leads to Braudel's second proposition: that we not only get out of our neatly periodized gardens, but that we leave our 'well-walled' disciplinary gardens, too. In part because he wrote as the economics profession became ascendant in public debate, Braudel emphasized analytic possibilities 'arising from a confrontation among the social sciences'.[16] We might go further, to provoke a confrontation among all disciplinary modes, from the social sciences, through the humanities, to law. We must pursue a kind of chronosthesia by which events, social cycles, and the *longue durée* unite in our present minds to provide us with ways of conceiving our possible futures. Doing this requires disciplinary ecumenism.

The long view, then, is not just a spell, however long that might be. It is not some large or distant object we gaze upon. Rather, it is a position we *take*, one where different kinds of convergence—temporal and disciplinary—might occur. Looking out from that position allows us to hold disparate things together and, in so doing, to see aspects of each of those things we might never see if we considered them in isolation.

11. WHERE SHALL WE TAKE THE LONG VIEW?

Where shall we find such places of convergence? How shall we do our work there?

Historical thinking is distinguished from other modes of social-cultural analysis by its engagement with specificity and by an attendant humility that counsels against over-generalization. As Collingwood put it,

---

[15] Collingwood (n. 9) 257, 274.

[16] Braudel (n. 6) 51. On the *longue durée* and its relevance as economics has captured the default position for participation in public debates, see Jo Guldi, David Armitage, *The History Manifesto* (2014), especially the introduction and chs. 1–2.

the things about which the historian reasons are not abstract but concrete, not universal but individual, not indifferent to space and time but having a where and a when of their own . . . History, therefore, cannot be made to square with theories according to which the object of knowledge is abstract and changeless.[17]

We come to a problem: the historian's obligation to specificity seems opposed to the long view's critical potential. Taking the long view threatens to involve us in analytic hubris. But the problem is more apparent than real; gaining the synoptic comprehension generated from the long view requires humility in the face of always-elusive evidence and careful attention to detail. As Austen reminds us, reading the meaning of a landscape or seascape means attending carefully to selected tidal pools, rocks, or structures.

Put another way, there is no opposition between micro-history and the long view. They require one another.[18] For Collingwood, an archaeologist, the problem was not that taking the long view meant foregoing attention to concrete things. Rather, it was where to position ourselves so that we might identify with equal clarity each of the concrete things in our field of vision and thereby comprehend them in a single, coherent view. Only in the long view do concrete things become legible as markers of continuity or rupture.

This positioning arises from an act of aesthetic and moral choosing about where to stand and how to draft an image of what we see from there. Hayden White calls this choice prefiguring, 'an essentially *poetic* act' by which the historian constitutes the field to be viewed.[19] Louis Mink called it comprehension, a 'kind of understanding which consists in thinking together in a single act, or in a cumulative series of acts, the complicated relationships of parts which can be experienced only *seriatim*'.[20]

One way to achieve such comprehension, David Armitage suggests, is through 'serial contextualism'. This yields a trans-temporal history that 'sets synchronic engagements within diachronic traditions that are centuries, in fact millennia, old'.[21] Diachronic traditions provide structures for putting what happened in serial form. This produces one kind of configuration by which disparate things might

---

[17] Collingwood (n. 9) 234.

[18] Jo Guldi and David Armitage have been criticized for overplaying a rift between micro- and macro-historical approaches. Deborah Cohen, Peter Mandler, 'The History Manifesto: A Critique' (2015) 120 *American Historical Review* 535 ff. But Guldi and Armitage call explicitly for micro-history's attendance to the archive and to otherwise lost aspects of human experience as a crucial aspect of work in the *longue durée*. Following Braudel, they are motivated to pursue a union of the two. Guldi, Armitage (n. 16) 119–21.

[19] Hayden White, *Metahistory: The Historical Imagination in Nineteenth-Century Europe* (1973) x.

[20] Louis O. Mink, 'History and Fiction as Modes of Comprehension', in Brian Fay, Eugene O. Golob, Richard T. Vann (eds.), *Historical Understanding* (1987) 50.

[21] David Armitage, 'What's the Big Idea? Intellectual History and the *Longue Durée*' (2012) 38 *History of European Ideas* 498 ff.

be comprehended together. Another name for this is narrative. As Mink put it, 'historical narrative does not demonstrate the necessity of events but makes them intelligible by unfolding the story which connects their significance'.[22]

Collingwood imagined narrative in musical terms. 'The time-beats of a symphony do not go on *ad infinitum* before the music begins and after it ends; they form an organization which exists only in the symphony itself.' It is only once we have heard the entire symphony, with all its parts,

so interpenetrating one another that each colours the rest and gives them their peculiar significance, that the rhythmical structure becomes intelligible and visibly necessary. Thus the parts of a symphony, though they are certainly played at different times, are seen as parts of the same symphony only when the listener overcomes this difference of time by being conscious of all the parts at once.

Having heard all the parts together, distinct objects cohere into a single configuration: 'What appears chronologically as a sequence must appear as a simultaneous whole in the historian's thought.'[23]

Narrative and music operate in the same way. What matters is not in telling, but in *having been told*, the story. '[I]n the configurational comprehension of a story which one *has followed*', as in the symphony one has heard,

the end is connected with the promise of the beginning as well as the beginning with the promise of the end, and the necessity of the backward references cancels out, so to speak, the contingency of the forward references. To comprehend temporal succession means to think of it in both directions at once, and then time is no longer the river which bears us along but the river in aerial view, upstream and downstream seen in a single survey.[24]

We might elaborate Collingwood's music image by imagining the effects of harmony and orchestration. What happens to notes 'played at different times' when they are also played simultaneously or by instruments of different timbres? After all, human experiences unfold in multiple series alongside one another. This is especially apparent when we see them in the long view. So it might be better to reconceive a linear series of notes—a bare melody—as a fugue: as a number of sounds or stories entwined, each modifying the others. In fugue, one plays a tune, then adds more atop the first. The original line persists, but it is constantly transformed by dissonances and resolutions one hears as the other lines play alongside. Thinking in fugue suggests that a better way to understand a diachronic tradition is not as a stream of experiences, but as a cluster of them.

[22] Mink (n. 20) 47.   [23] Collingwood (n. 9) 477 ff.
[24] Mink (n. 20) 56 ff. Emphasis in original.

This explains why Collingwood moved from one dimension into two when he suggested that the historian's work comes together into a 'web of imaginative construction'.[25] Like fictional narratives, historical narratives needn't be chronologically ordered, let alone concerned with causation, to serve their analytic purpose—to create a 'synoptic vision'. Similarly, Mink's river appears at first blush as a linear image, but it is the whole of the river seen at once that matters, not isolated bends or villages passed along the way. We come again to chronosthesia, realizing that we, like those whose thoughts we attempt to re-enact, are always trying to see the whole of Mink's river—past, present, future—at once.

Collingwood and Mink asked historians to take a view, to think in images rather than words. In taking up the metaphor of a constellation, Walter Benjamin conveyed the same need for a mental image that draws seemingly unrelated objects into what Mink called 'an individual act of seeing-things-together'.[26]

It isn't that the past casts its light on the present or the present casts its light on the past: rather, an image is that in which the past and the now flash into a constellation. In other words: image is dialectic at a standstill.[27]

By Benjamin's account, constellations not only unite distinct past objects into a single image in an instant of comprehension. They do so by making the position of *now* one of the objects in the constellation's flash. By putting herself into the field of objects observed, the beholder understands the view by understanding the position from which she takes that view.

Christopher Tomlins applies Benjamin's thinking to legal history. Doing so, we might realize Braudel's aim that any history, including histories of law, should respond to the problems of the hour. '[T]he critic/historian', Tomlins explains,

constructs constellations—that is, new historical objects or dialectical images that join together what may be quite distinct phenomena, whose significance can emerge only posthumously or retrospectively, in a relationship with the now that has apprehended their significance.[28]

Benjamin and Tomlins assert that we should attend to something quite different from the deep, contextualizing impulse of that explicitly 'critical' legal history associated with E. P. Thompson and Robert Gordon in the 1970s and 1980s. Their concern for the unavoidable complexity of context risks involution in the hands of the unwary historian. As Tomlins explains, '[t]he expertise of history sequesters

---

[25] Collingwood (n. 9) 244.

[26] Mink (n. 20) 55. Both Collingwood and Mink anticipated Hayden White's claim that the prefiguring work of the historian involves a choice that is 'ultimately aesthetic or moral rather than epistemological'. White (n. 19) xii.

[27] Walter Benjamin, 'N [Theoretics of Knowledge; Theory of Progress]' (1983) 15 *Philosophical Forum* 7.

[28] Christopher Tomlins, 'After Critical Legal History: Scope, Scale, Structure' (2012) 8 *Annual Review of Law and Social Science* 42.

past phenomena within a cage of context on the far side of a temporal frontier where they serve no particular purpose at all.' Instead, Benjamin's 'method of *montage* . . . turned convolution to constellation. Montage introduced a deliberately graphic, deliberately concrete, deliberately imagistic quality to Benjamin's representation of history as practice'.[29] Like a river or a symphony—only better because it pulls us into three dimensions—thinking in constellations allows us simultaneously to attend to all that is concrete in the stars, while leaving implicit the lines that connect them in our mind's eye. We can think big and long without having to provide an account of all the surrounding contextual space.

The bigger the constellation—the farther we are from all the other points surveyed—the better we are able to see our own presuppositions anew when they are also made into one of the objects in view. So there is more in considering constellations—or rivers and symphonies—than what may seem to be an unduly aestheticized account of historical explanation. We become conscious of an ethic that is most readily conceived in the full-bodied ways that metaphors like these convey. Let's think further about the content of such an ethics by examining the analytic surprises it can produce. For it is surprises that teach us most, and surprises that we will most readily see as the long view brings concrete things into combinations we can perceive by no other means.

III. Writing the Long View

A number of legal historians have for years written from the long view. Reviewing a few of their works demonstrates the possibilities. John Baker's account of Magna Carta during its first four centuries provides an excellent place to begin.[30] Older narratives operated on the assumption of a persistent appreciation of the charter's greatness from the moment it was produced. This assumption arose from and sustained a traditional liberal narrative about the origin of rights in the Anglophone world and their connection to legal practices. These rights manifested themselves in presumably consistent invocations of the charter, and especially its chapter 29, which required what later generations would call due process of law.

Baker tells a very different story by searching in a constellation of places: at the Inns of Court, in surviving manuscripts of judges and barristers, and in debates about personal liberty and the privileges of the church. Surprisingly, Baker finds little

[29] Christopher Tomlins, 'The Strait Gate: The Past, History, and Legal Scholarship' (2009) 5 *Law, Culture, and the Humanities* 31 and 19.

[30] J. H. Baker, *The Reinvention of Magna Carta, 1216–1616* (2017).

but silence—little but empty space—occasionally broken by narrow invocations of the charter from the fourteenth to the sixteenth centuries. This changed in 1581, when Robert Snagge gave a public lecture on chapter 29. Citations to that chapter increased in number and importance thereafter. Out of silence, chapter 29 suddenly became a linch-pin of the Englishman's peculiar liberty. Baker follows a new discourse linking liberty to the charter for the thirty-five years after Snagge's lecture, as Sir Edward Coke promoted views that would be carried forward in legal and political debate in the centuries following. By surveying centuries, Baker reveals the highly contingent ways in which a charter that languished in obscurity moved with surprising speed to the centre of the English legal imagination.

Consider a quite different book that yields equally surprising observations from the long view. While Baker concentrates on mandarin legal sources, Amy Louise Erickson studies sources of everyday life.[31] Erickson builds her sweeping account of women and property from the sixteenth century to the eighteenth around the stages of female life: as maids, wives, and widows. Even in a profoundly patriarchal world, Erickson finds, most men wanted the women in their lives to have independent command of property. By working in the archives of church courts and equity, Erickson finds possibilities for women that are hard to see when reading the printed prescriptive and doctrinal literature other scholars consult. Erickson also spends more time on non-litigation sources—testamentary records, bonds for separate estates—than on more commonly examined records concerned with litigation. Doing so, she reaches the astonishing conclusion that, 'coverture was—socially at least—a fiction'.[32] Nonetheless, women's circumstances did change over time: for instance, when late seventeenth-century statutes deprived women of advantages they once enjoyed by ecclesiastical law. By taking the long view, Erickson establishes a quite different account of long-standing experience against which a development like statutory changes to the law of probate takes on a surprising appearance.

Like Baker and Erickson, John Collins shows how we can only appreciate the meaning of short-term developments by taking the long view. Contrary to centuries of dicta that insisted that martial law operated outside of law, Collins finds that it was 'understood, debated, and practiced' as one of the many laws of England. By exploring from the late medieval period to the early eighteenth century, from England to Ireland, and the Caribbean to Africa and Asia, Collins shows martial law was 'dynamic but not arbitrary' and was deeply inflected with civil law norms.[33] A constant set of ideas varied in practice as empire spread and as parliamentary statutes regulated martial law's use at home and overseas.

[31] On the importance of 'mandarin' sources, see Robert W. Gordon, 'Critical Legal Histories' (1984) 36 *Stanford L.R.* 120.

[32] Amy Louise Erickson, *Women and Property in Early Modern England* (1993) 226.

[33] John M. Collins, *Martial Law and English Laws, c. 1500–c. 1700* (2016) 7 ff.

Collins demonstrates how taking the long view means following a feedback loop, in which questions about whether causation flows from ideas to action or the other way around are beside the point—idea and action constitute one another when seen in the long view. Andrew Fitzmaurice shows the same in his half-millennium account of ideas and practices concerned with occupation and sovereignty as a site of debate about the legitimacy of European empires. Just as Baker dramatically re-dates the onset of Magna Carta's importance, taking the long view allows Fitzmaurice to re-date the onset of the label *terra nullius*, which he finds was applied to colonial lands much later than we have supposed. Once we see that *terra nullius* was not a trans-historical concept, we get another surprise: that the language of *terra nullius* was used as much to critique imperial pretensions as to justify them.[34] As with martial law, this becomes easier to show when we see ideas in the hands of working lawyers and other imperialists as well as following them through the canonical texts on which most histories of legal ideas rely.

Collins and Fitzmaurice gain their insights by widening the map as well as deepening the temporal view. Lauren Benton puts geography at the heart of her five-century long analysis of European laws' global walkabout. Standing at a temporal-topographical junction, she charts law across multiple geographies—rivers, oceans, islands, and mountains. She uses these 'geographic tropes . . . to evoke particular patterns of the extension of law . . . ' from one epoch to the next. Doing so, she shows Westphalian sovereignty has always been an illusion. Seen from the long view, 'divided sovereignty appears less as a temporary concession to particular challenges of administering empire and more as a central premise of rule . . . '.[35]

For Collins, Fitzmaurice, and Benton, the long view becomes the means by which legal histories break out of their traditional borders. Temporal length inspires geographical breadth and awareness of law's plurality and mobility; it becomes harder and harder to contain law's history in national genealogies. Taking the long view—and seen in imperial or global perspective—even U.S. legal history yields new insights. Christopher Tomlins, by carrying the American experience at the intersection of law and labour back to Elizabethan servant laws, reveals how for centuries 'freedom and unfreedom [have] come together'. The revolution that formed a new nation means much less in light of the persistence of the fact that freedom and unfreedom have always been 'conditions of each other's existence' in American life.[36] Again, taking the long view shows that its chief benefit is the generation of surprises. In this case, surprises disturb the most traditional pretensions of sovereign isolation that still blinker so much legal historiography. Once the long view prompts

---

[34] Andrew Fitzmaurice, *Sovereignty, Property, and Empire, 1500–2000* (2014).

[35] Lauren Benton, *A Search for Sovereignty: Law and Geography in European Empires, 1400–1900* (2010) 296 ff.

[36] Christopher Tomlins, *Freedom Bound: Law, Labor, and Civic Identity in Colonizing English America, 1580–1865* (2010) 16.

us to look beyond national bounds, we open ourselves to see new concrete things—instances of longer, more geographically diffuse processes.[37]

All these historians have found the place from which it is possible to take the long view, a place where they could put apparently unrelated objects into an otherwise unseen constellation, thereby revealing the ways in which such objects were and are related. In doing so, they give us surprises. They give us insights we would not otherwise have, insights we might put to work in our now as we try to live at the place where law and national security collide; as we consider the ways certain practices in the law of property privilege some against others; or as we think anew about legal order as a problem in global relationships. Given the value of the long view, how shall we continue to do this work?

IV. THE LONG VIEW'S FUTURE

All the books discussed above are monographs by single authors who worked in isolation in the manner long practised by historians. There is no reason why individuals cannot continue to produce long view histories of particular phenomena—for instance, histories of law concerned with water or with the expropriation of property for the public good.[38] But working across multiple generations raises problems of scale: of the length of the flows we must chart to identify the critical objects that require explaining; of the number of such objects from across the centuries; and thus of the volume of sources we must consult.

The long view's future may now look very different from its past, for digitization gives us new solutions to these problems of scale. Digital archives put more objects into our view.[39] One possibility lies in making 'a single massive text object' out of many text objects of the same kind.[40] The makers of the *Old Bailey Proceedings* have produced spectacular results by gathering all reports of cases in the Old

---

[37] Oceanic perspectives have been especially helpful in this way: e.g., Mary Bilder, *The Transatlantic Constitution: Colonial Legal Culture and the Empire* (2004); Daniel J. Hulsebosch, *Constituting Empire: New York and the Transformation of Constitutionalism in the Atlantic World, 1664–1830* (2005); Stuart Banner, *Possessing the Pacific: Land, Settlers, and Indigenous People from Australia to Alaska* (2007).

[38] Joshua Getzler, *A History of Water Rights at Common Law* (2004); Susan Reynolds, *Before Eminent Domain: Toward a History of Expropriation of Land for the Common Good* (2010).

[39] For an especially vigorous promotion of the possibilities of digital tools applied to *longue durée* history, see Guldi, Armitage (n. 16) chapter 4.

[40] Tim Hitchcock, William J. Turkel, 'The *Old Bailey Proceedings, 1764–1913*: Text Mining for Evidence of Court Behavior' (2016) 34 *Law and History Review* 930.

Bailey—the court that heard most felony cases in London and Middlesex—from 1674 to 1913: 127,000,000 words covering nearly 200,000 trials. By making all those words into a searchable object, we see the long flow of practice against which it becomes possible to answer a number of questions about transformations in particular aspects of crime, criminality, and criminal law and to think about the relation of such transformations to other cultural, social, and political developments. Machine reading allows us to chart how the form and contents of a single source type changed over decades or centuries. Once we spot those changes, we can separate source effects from other changes occurring in criminality or the criminal law across long time scales and thereby spot significant yet otherwise imperceptible changes: for instance, the development of plea bargaining.[41]

Of course, 'no one has actually read' all the Old Bailey Sessions Papers, 'nor ever will'.[42] Fewer still will read all the *English Reports* or *Statutes of the Realm*. But this depends on what we mean by the word 'read'. Franco Moretti has shown through analysis of literary texts how computer-conducted 'distant reading' yields insights that no amount of close reading can. Distant reading involves a process whereby 'the reality of the text'—perhaps in extremely large quantities—'undergoes a process of deliberate reduction and abstraction'. This is the opposite of what students of literature and history have long been taught to do by drilling ever deeper into selected words or phrases. But this reduction of the text, as Moretti proposes, produces '*a specific form of knowledge*: fewer elements, hence a sharper sense of their overall interconnection. Shapes, relations, structures. Forms. Models.'[43] Moretti thus quotes Braudel approvingly: 'History is indeed 'a poor little conjectural science' when it selects individuals as its objects . . . but much more rational in its procedures and results, when it examines groups and repetitions.'[44] Like the historian taking the long view, Moretti puts seemingly unrelated events, in the form of words, in the same frame with medium-term cycles and longer-term structures to tease out surprising connections.

One might imagine reading the titles of statutes across centuries in the same way Moretti has used computing power to 'read' the titles of 7,000 novels. Doing so reveals otherwise imperceptible changes in the relationship of a literary genre to its marketplace as titles became shorter. Of course, full statutory texts might also be subjected to a similar exploration of 'quantitative stylistics'.[45] Indeed, this approach was taken in one of the first applications of a distant reading technique to legal texts: namely Douglas Hay and Paul Craven's creative analysis of hundreds

---

[41] Ibid., 933, 944.   [42] Ibid., 933.

[43] Franco Moretti, *Graphs, Maps, Trees: Abstract Models for a Literary History* (2007) 1. Emphasis in original.

[44] Ibid., 4, quoting Braudel, '*L'histoire, mesure du monde*', in *Les écrits de Fernand Braudel* (1997) vol. 2.

[45] Franco Moretti, 'Style, Inc.: Reflections on 7,000 Titles (British Novels, 1740–1850)', in *Distant Reading* (2013) 206.

of pieces of labour legislation from the sixteenth century to the nineteenth and from England across the empire to show paths of textual transmission and transformation.[46] Such an approach, which we can only undertake using digital tools, helps us think in new ways about how legal ideas and practices move globally, thereby revealing a key process in law's empire by which emulation and differentiation have occurred.

Self-curated corpora of treatises or cases from the sixteenth century to the twentieth would allow the rewriting of doctrinal history of particular concepts or areas of practice using text-mining and other digital strategies. Topic modelling, by which the semantic form and operation of texts might be explored in new ways, holds out promise for helping us see new questions we might ask of the past.[47] And the power of digital tools to turn textual matter into various quantifiable forms opens new opportunities for visualizing verbal relationships within and among a multitude of texts. Network analysis—e.g., examining the interconnection of individual lawyers or judges across large numbers of cases—might help us think about how personal relationships or the connections among certain expressions or ideas have prompted important developments in legal doctrines.[48] Exploring large bodies of geographically dispersed texts will help us literally map the incidence and movement of legal ideas. Visualization might even help us bring non-verbal sources into our analysis. With the help of archaeologists and architectural historians, virtual reconstructions of the spaces in which law works—for instance, prisons, courtrooms, and record offices—might prompt us to think seriously for the first time about the relationship of law to the physical world in which it operates.

But as virtually every serious scholar using digital tools admits, they have their limits.[49] Text-mining, topic modelling, and visualizations generally do more to prompt questions than to answer them. Answering them still requires plenty of close reading and other traditional forms of analysis.[50] The limits are more serious still. Some have argued that 'legal history is better positioned for a digital turn than most historical fields' owing to the relatively 'consistent forms of legal sources' which 'give structure to the information they contain. . . .'[51] But as the makers of the *Old Bailey Proceedings* warn, such consistencies are often more apparent than real.

[46] Douglas Hay, Paul Craven, 'Introduction', in Hay, Craven, (eds.), *Masters, Servants, and Magistrates in Britain and the Empire, 1562–1955* (2004).

[47] For a critique of topic modelling, see David Tanenhaus, Eric Nystrom, 'The Future of Digital Legal History: No Magic, No Silver Bullets' (2016) 56 *American Journal of Legal History* 157.

[48] For network analysis of one text, see Franco Moretti, 'Network Theory, Plot Analysis' (n. 45) 212 ff.

[49] A helpful set of principles for containing work done digitally is offered by Tanenhaus and Nystrom (n. 47) 156 ff.

[50] '[T]ext mining and statistical analysis of the trial accounts alone can point to precise moments of transition, and broader patterns of change, but need to be paired with close reading and archival research in order to fully explain the forces in play.' Hitchcock, Turkel (n. 40) 953.

[51] Stephen Robertson, 'Searching for Anglo-American Digital Legal History' (2016) 34 *Law and History Review* 1049.

And this is before we account for perhaps the most serious problem of all. All texts currently susceptible to machine reading share one characteristic: they first appeared in print. To work only with the kinds of printed texts that are most readily exposed to distant reading will shorten rather than lengthen our view. Indeed, it will obscure altogether the richest parts of our archives and obstruct our perspective on questions we cannot see. Ironically, doing big history by doing digital history ensures we might miss huge swathes of human experience. We might miss the flow of long, apparently motionless streams of legal experience found only in manuscript, and thus fail to observe the moments that mattered most.

One reason John Baker could transform our understanding of Magna Carta results from his career-long appreciation of the significance of learning found in manuscript sources. Manuscript persisted as the chief vessel for keeping and conveying legal knowledge for centuries after the advent of print.[52] Especially in light of the ease with which digital tools thrust print before our eyes, reading manuscripts, sometimes in large quantities across long periods, expresses a particular professional ethic: a commitment to search for other people's norms in the material forms in which they were most likely to express and store them. If epistemic humility is a central requirement of those who take the long view, then we must respect the *physical* properties of our sources and the demands they impose on us, even if that means we cannot use currently fashionable tools.

That said, even in the case of manuscript, there may be possibilities for digital work. Online repositories of images of manuscripts—for instance, the Anglo-American Legal Tradition (AALT)—are growing every day.[53] How to read them? The U.S. postal service sorts most mail using machines capable of optical recognition of handwriting. More ambitiously, a German project called *Transkribus* is applying machine learning to develop intelligent handwriting analysis. By first transcribing some text, then linking the transcription to an image of the manuscript of the text, the machine can learn to read a particular hand.[54] This is a remarkable enterprise, but such work will remain experimental for at least the foreseeable future. Working at scale, across large bodies of manuscript generated by different hands over years, let alone centuries, may be an insurmountable challenge. It is hard to imagine the many thousands of parchment membranes from the twelfth century to the nineteenth scanned by the AALT project being read by a machine. The work of thousands of clerks, each using highly varied forms of abbreviation, numeration, and non-alphabetic symbols might defeat even the most carefully taught machine. As we look upon the archive made by those clerks, we see that for all the help we might ask of our new technologies, only historians working in close can hope to

---

[52] John Baker, 'Why the History of English Law Has not Been Finished' (2000) 59 *Cambridge L.J.* 62 ff.

[53] See <http://aalt.law.uh.edu> (accessed 5 March 2018).

[54] See <https://transkribus.eu/Transkribus/> (accessed 5 March 2018).

produce meaningful conclusions from the long view. We still must work carefully on each star to understand a constellation.

Whether we or a machine does the gazing across the coherent bodies of court records kept in the same medium—on parchment rolls inscribed with iron gall ink—for half a millennium or more, we are reminded of a critical way in which law is distinguished from other realms of life: that it has, for generations, created unified runs of documents intended to inform and shape the ongoing conduct of its own work decades, even centuries, into the future. To a peculiar degree, law and its sources manifest chronosthesia, imagining past, present, and the possibilities of the future all at once. Like history taken from the long view, law reaches backward to project forward.

Given this, doing legal history by taking the long view matters. As John Baker and Andrew Fitzmaurice have shown, many notions we thought were of long duration arose later and by different means than we once believed. As we realize this, we begin to see those norms as the result of choices made in surprising moments rather than as inevitable consequences of processes no individuals might have shaped. One problem with the *longue durée* as Braudel understood it—as that 'which almost borders on the motionless'—is that it underscores forces against which no human choosing can prevail. By taking the long view, we see that forces that *appear* motionless weren't and aren't. By placing previously undetected or unconnected objects—events, texts—in long flows of time, we see when and how human choices redirected those flows. As we do, we appreciate how our law has been and remains a result of conscious efforts to articulate the good and to fashion practices for obtaining it. We watch as the normative commitments of others—some repellent to us, others surprisingly attractive upon close analysis—revealed themselves in the past. And we see what past commitments might do as we ponder those we mean to live by in the future.

BIBLIOGRAPHY

David Armitage, 'What's the Big Idea? Intellectual History and the *Longue Durée*' (2012) 38 *History of European Ideas* 493–507

Walter Benjamin, 'N [Theoretics of Knowledge; Theory of Progress]' (1983) 15 *Philosophical Forum* 1–40

Fernand Braudel, *On History*, trans. Sarah Matthews (University of Chicago Press, 1980)

R. G. Collingwood, *The Idea of History*, Jan Van Der Dussen (ed.), (Oxford University Press, 1994)

Markus Dubber, 'New Historical Jurisprudence: Legal History as Critical Analysis of Law' (2015) 2 *Critical Analysis of Law* 1–18

Jo Guldi, David Armitage, *The History Manifesto* (Cambridge University Press, 2014)

Louis O. Mink, *Historical Understanding*, Brian Fay, Eugene O. Golob, Richard T. Vann (eds.), (Cornell University Press, 1987)

Franco Moretti, *Graphs, Maps, Trees: Abstract Models for a Literary History* (Verso, 2007)

Franco Moretti, *Distant Reading* (Verso, 2013)

Christopher Tomlins, 'The Strait Gate: The Past, History, and Legal Scholarship' (2009) 5 *Law, Culture, and the Humanities* 11–42

Christopher Tomlins, 'After Critical Legal History: Scope, Scale, Structure' (2012) 8 *Annual Review of Law and Social Science* 31–68

CHAPTER 19

....

QUANTITATIVE LEGAL HISTORY

....

DANIEL KLERMAN*

QUANTITATIVE legal history is in a rather sorry state. Only about a quarter of recent works of legal history use even simple quantitative methods such as tables or graphs, and articles or books with more sophisticated methods, such as regression analysis, are extremely rare. The limited use of quantitative methods in legal history reflects, in part, the marginal place of numbers in scholarship produced by historians. On the other hand, given the increasing prominence of empirical work in law more generally, and given the emergence of new techniques for the quantitative analysis of texts, the infrequent use of statistical methods is surprising.

The infrequent use of quantitative techniques is also a missed opportunity. Scholars from other fields, including economics, sociology, and political science, are using statistics to analyse legal history. Such analysis is particularly helpful in understanding the effect of legal change and in analysing the influence of multiple factors on legislation, judicial decision-making, and citizen behaviour. While it is wonderful that people from other disciplines are using statistics to analyse legal history, legal historians might do it better, given their penchant for archival work and their superior knowledge of historical sources, context, and theory.

* The author thanks Scott Altman, Sam Erman, Bob Gordon, Ariela Gross, Philip Hoffman, Naomi Lamoreaux, Paul Mahoney, Chris Tomlins, and Gavin Wright for helpful comments and suggestions.

Legal historians could learn basic statistical analysis in graduate school or on their own. Or they could fruitfully collaborate with statisticians or social scientists with quantitative expertise. While co-authorship is relatively common in the social sciences, it is surprisingly rare in legal history. Collaboration between legal historians and quantitatively sophisticated social scientists presents a terrific opportunity for interdisciplinary work that could enrich the field.

This chapter first assesses quantitatively the use of quantitative methods in legal history (Section I). It then discusses a few examples of the successful use of numbers and statistics in recent books addressing legal historical topics (Section II). Section III discusses the future of quantitative legal history.

I. A Quantitative Analysis of the Use of Quantitative Methods in Legal History

As is fitting in a chapter on quantitative methods, this section attempts to document numerically the extent to which quantitative methods are, in fact, used in recent works of legal history. That is not a trivial task, because the field of legal history is not well defined, and the range of techniques that could be considered quantitative is vast. Table 19.1 below takes one approach, although, as with all quantitative analysis, other approaches are possible.

Table 19.1 examines four categories of scholarship: articles published in legal history journals in 2016, books reviewed in legal history journals in 2016, prize-winning articles, and prize-winning books. Even these four categories, of course, required further choices as to which journals and which prizes. The articles examined were those published in the main English-language legal history journals: *Law and History Review*, the *American Journal of Legal History*, the *Journal of Legal History*, and *Law and History*. The first two are published in the United States, the *Journal of Legal History* is published in England, and *Law and History* is the journal of the Australia and New Zealand Law and History Society. The books examined were those reviewed in these same four journals. The prizes are the Hurst Prize, awarded by the Law and Society Association for the best work in 'socio-legal' history, and five prizes awarded by the American Society for Legal History—the Surrency Prize (best article in *Law and History Review*), Sutherland Prize (best article on English legal history), the Cromwell Article Prize (best article in American legal history published by an early career scholar), the John Phillip Reid Prize (best monograph on Anglo-American legal history by a mid-career or

Table 19.1 Quantitative Analysis in Recent Works of Legal History*

	Articles published in 2016		Books reviewed in 2016		Prize-winning articles, 1988–2015		Prize-winning books, 1980–2016	
	Number	%	Number	%	Number	%	Number	%
Any quantitative tables or graphs	10	14%	14	26%	15	22%	20	38%
Two-way tables	3	4	14	26	13	19	15	28
Regressions	0	0	1	2	0	0	1	2
All (including books or articles without tables, graphs or regressions)	71		54		67		53	

* The author is also grateful to USC Law librarians for their assistance in locating and searching the large number of sources analysed in Table 19.1.

senior scholar), and the Cromwell Book Prize (best book in American legal history by a junior scholar).

About fourteen per cent of articles published in 2016 and twenty-six per cent of books reviewed in 2016 had quantitative tables or graphs. This could be seen as reasonably wide usage. The greater use of numbers in books may simply reflect their greater length, which allows more space for different types of analysis. Prize winning articles and books use tables and graphs at somewhat higher rates (twenty-two and thirty-eight per cent), which indicates that prize committees are receptive to quantitative work. It is also possible that the difference between prize-winning works and works reviewed or published in 2016 reflects greater use of quantitative methods before 2016. The prize data come from a longer period (1980–2016), and there is some evidence that earlier works were more likely to use statistics, although the number of works analysed here is insufficient to test that hypothesis rigorously. One particularly noteworthy early prize-winner was Lawrence Friedman and Robert Percival, *The Roots of Justice: Crime and Punishment in Alameda County, California, 1870–1910* (1981), which has sixty-eight quantitative tables.[1]

---

[1] The list of tables on pp. ix–xiii mentions seventy-one tables, but three of them were not quantitative, e.g., two of them displayed judges, their terms, and their dates of birth.

A much smaller percentage of works contain more sophisticated quantitative analysis. Only four per cent of articles published in 2016 contain two-way tables, and the use of two-way tables is lower for prize-winning books and articles as well. Two-way tables are tables that analyse a single outcome with two possibly explanatory factors. For example, while a one-way table might display the number of cases per year over ten years, a two-way table might display the number of cases per year over that same time period broken down by subject matter, region, or court. Such tables allow the researcher the see the way that two factors (e.g., year and court) affected the outcome variable (cases per year). It is also notable that most of the articles with two-way tables came from a single special issue of the *Law and History Review* devoted to digital humanities. If that issue were excluded, only a single article published in the four legal history journals in 2016 would have had a two-way table.

While tables can be used effectively to analyse the influence of two factors, they become more cumbersome when analysing three or more factors. Regression analysis is the standard way of exploring the effect of multiple factors. It was used only twice in the works analysed in Table 19.1. This is surprising and disappointing, because legal historians are often trying to tell complex stories about the effect of multiple factors, such as time, race, and gender. When quantitative data are available, regression analysis is an appropriate and powerful tool. It is notable that neither of the authors of the two works in Table 19.1 that used regression analysis have PhDs in history. One, Michele Landis Dauber, received her doctorate in sociology, and the other, Paul Mahoney, does not have a doctorate, although he is well known for his work in law and economics. As will be discussed in Section III, one reason there is so little quantitative analysis in legal history is that history graduate schools, which over the last few decades have trained the most prominent legal historians, do not generally teach quantitative methods and have relatively few faculty who use quantitative methods.

The next section discusses Dauber's and Mahoney's books (as well as Gavin Wright's *Sharing the Prize*) in some detail as examples of the way statistical analysis can enhance works of legal history.

II. Examples of Quantitative Legal History

While it is relatively rare for legal historians to use quantitative techniques, there are excellent examples. This section discussions three in depth.

A. Gavin Wright, *Sharing the Prize* (2013)

Gavin Wright's *Sharing the Prize* provides a compelling illustration of the way that relatively simple tables and graphs can be used to shed light on one of the central questions of modern legal history—whether the civil rights laws of the mid-1960s worked. He focuses on the South, arguing that the Civil Rights Act of 1964 and the Voting Rights Act of 1965 had their biggest impact on this region and that it is best to analyse their effects on a regional basis. Civil rights legislation, of course, also affected the North, but Wright argues that, given regional differences, it is helpful to focus on the South. Prior studies, he argues, which analysed the entire U.S., provide a less clear picture of the success of the civil rights revolution, because African-Americans started from a higher baseline in the North, and because controversies over busing and urban unrest led to different political and economic dynamics. Wright argues that if one focuses on the American South, the civil rights legislation of the mid-1960s, along with the litigation and civil and political mobilization it enabled, produced unambiguous economic gains for Southern blacks, without harming Southern whites.

Wright most often shows the effect of the civil rights legislation by using graphs and charts that compare some variable (e.g., per capita income or department store sales) over time. He can nearly always point to a significant positive improvement starting around 1965, shortly after the enactment of the Civil Rights Act of 1964 and the Voting Rights Act of 1965. Often those southern trends are compared to national trends, to show that while the whole country was doing well in the 1960s, the South was doing even better and that its divergence from national trends started around 1965. For example, in showing that public accommodations laws benefited the South, he shows not only that retail sales grew in the 1960s, but that retail sales in the South, as a percentage of total U.S. sales, were actually falling in the early 1960s, but started rising in 1965.[2] Similarly, Wright analyses median black male income by region. Black male income rose in all regions between 1955 and 2000, but black male median income in the 1950s was less than half of black median income in the Northeast and Midwest. By 2000, black median income in the South had risen so much that it was virtually identical to black male income in other regions.[3] Similarly, Southern male incomes for both whites and blacks grew between 1955 and 2000, but black Southern incomes were less than half of white male incomes in the 1950s. By 2000, the gap had narrowed dramatically, although it was still significant.[4]

Wright also skilfully uses net migration as a vivid indicator of economic change.[5] From 1900 to 1960, people, both white and black, left the South. For African Americans, this exodus is often called the 'Great Migration.' The net migration of whites during the same period, while smaller both in raw numbers and as a

---

[2] Gavin Wright, *Sharing the Prize* (2013), at 96.
[3] Ibid., at 146.   [4] Ibid., at 147.   [5] Ibid., at 143.

percentage of the Southern white population, is evidence that segregation, Jim Crow, and discrimination did not really benefit the white Southern population. Starting in the 1970s, migration patterns for African Americans reversed themselves, and hundreds of thousands of African Americans migrated to the South, where economic, political, and cultural conditions were perceived as more auspicious and welcoming. The reversal of migration flows shows that it was not just statistics that improved for Southern blacks, but that African Americans themselves perceived the change and altered their residential choices in response. Net white migration patterns also shifted, albeit a decade earlier. Wright argues that the fact that whites also found the South more attractive during and after the civil rights revolution shows that economic and political gains to African Americans did not come at the expense of whites, but instead whites and blacks 'shared the prize'.

Another particularly vivid and largely forgotten effect of the civil rights revolution was the swift desegregation of Southern hospitals. Threatened with loss of Medicare and other federal funding, Southern hospitals desegregated almost completely in a just a few months between July and December 1966.[6] The ensuing improvements in health outcomes were dramatic. Black infant mortality in the South, which, in the 1950s and early 1960s, was roughly double black infant mortality in the North, converged to Northern rates by 1975, with the most dramatic drops occurring in the late 1960s.[7] Although white infant mortality (both in the North and South) also declined, and black infant mortality in the North did as well, the improvements among Southern African Americans were much larger. Of course, these declines reflect not just better access to higher quality hospitals, but other changes, including improvements in education, nutrition, and sanitation. Nevertheless, these other changes also reflect the civil rights revolution, which desegregated schools, increased incomes (and thus access to food), and enhanced African American political power and thus helped ensure that public investments in sanitation benefited African Americans as well as whites.

Wright also addresses head on some of the 'downsides' of the civil rights revolution, including negative effects on black business districts, the persistence of poverty, and the 'possibility that the political and ideological legacy of Civil Rights era has served to impede further progress in recent decades'.[8] He is also careful to note that the landmark legislation of the 1960s did not, of itself, change conditions on the ground. Instead, litigation, local organizing, and individual courage were usually necessary to transform 'law on the books' into change 'on the ground'. Nevertheless, by using extensive quantitative evidence about business, employment, schools, and politics, Wright is able to persuasively illustrate the dramatic impact of civil rights legislation on the South, especially on African Americans living and choosing to migrate there.

Although Gavin Wright is aware of (and discusses) the extensive econometric literature on civil rights, the book eschews complex statistical analysis for

---

[6] Ibid., at 237–8.   [7] Ibid., at 239.   [8] Ibid., at 223.

easy-to-understand graphs and tables. In this way, Wright's work may serve as a model for many legal historians who neither know statistics nor have an inclination to learn it. Of course, the fact that Wright's graphs and tables are easy to understand does not mean that they were easy to create. In fact, like elegant narrative history, effective presentation of quantitative analysis takes many drafts, experimentation with alternative formats, and attention to reader feedback.

B. Paul Mahoney, *Wasting a Crisis: Why Securities Regulation Fails* (2015)

Paul Mahoney's *Wasting a Crisis* analyses the history of securities regulation with heavy reliance on regression analysis. In his view, prior historians have been bamboozled by the self-serving statements of legislators and regulators, who have touted their work as serving the public interest. In fact, Mahoney argues, much of securities regulation has benefited special interests—such as small banks or established high-end brokerages houses—at the expense of consumers. To reach these conclusions, Mahoney uses tools of political economy to analyse the political coalitions that lobbied for legislation and then uses the statistical tools of financial economics to explore the effects of regulation.

Mahoney starts by analysing blue sky laws, which were state laws enacted between 1911 and 1931, ostensibly to prevent fraud in securities markets. Mahoney finds that the states that enacted the most rigorous 'merit review' statutes were not those that had a greater incidence of securities fraud, but rather were states where small banks were common and stockbrokers were scarce. Small banks feared that potential depositors would invest in stocks rather than putting their money in savings accounts and CDs, so small banks sought regulation that would reduce securities offerings. Their concern, Mahoney argues, was market share not consumer protection. While larger banks in the pre-New Deal era could compete by entering the securities business themselves and so were not as threatened, small banks did not have the ability to compete in this way and thus sought legislation to hobble the securities industry, their competitor for savings and investment. In states where the securities industry was already well established, and thus where there were many stockbrokers, the securities industry could lobby effectively to prevent legislation. In states where the securities industry was weak, such as Kansas, Arizona, and North Dakota, small banks were more effective politically and could get the stringent regulation they sought. In contrast, where small banks were weak and the financial industry strong, such as New York, New Jersey, and Delaware, blue sky legislation was weaker (involving ex post litigation about fraud rather than pre-offering screening for merit or fraud), even though securities fraud was undoubtedly a larger problem in New York than in North

Dakota.[9] Mahoney also analyses the effect of blue sky laws and finds that the more stringent laws resulted in increases in bank profits, consistent with the idea that a key motivation for the legislation was the protection of banks.[10] Unfortunately, there is no good data on the incidence of securities fraud, so Mahoney cannot test whether blue sky laws reduced fraud and thus benefited consumers.

In his analysis of blue sky laws, Mahoney makes extensive use of regression analysis. While he uses tables to show that rural states with weak securities industries adopted the strongest regulation,[11] he rightly does not stop there, because many factors could affect the adoption of stringent legislation, including the incidence of securities fraud and the strength of small banks, the Democratic party, progressive politicians, and the securities industry. When analysing so many factors, tables become very cumbersome, and regression analysis is the most appropriate way to identify the important factors.

Later chapters address a variety of other issues in the history of securities law. Perhaps the most interesting is the analysis of whether the Securities Exchange Act of 1934 actually improved public disclosure. The 'market failure narrative' that Mahoney aims to debunk asserts that the public generally had very poor information about publicly traded securities before 1934 and that the Act's mandatory disclosure provisions provided valuable information to market participants. Mahoney (and a collaborator, Jianping Mei) test that theory using techniques from financial economics. If disclosures mandated by the Act aided traders, then prices would more accurately reflect the value of traded firms and likely future disclosures of profits and other information. As a result, the superior mandatory disclosures required by the Act should mean that when a firm later announces earnings, that announcement should have a smaller impact, because traders would previously have had better information with which to predict future earnings (p. 85). Thus, by comparing reactions to earnings announcements before and after the implementation of the Act's disclosure requirements, one can assess whether mandatory disclosures improved information to market participants. Mahoney finds they did not for a sample of 201 companies listed on the New York Stock Exchange. Nor is he surprised, because the SEC's disclosure requirements were modelled on the requirements already imposed by the New York Stock Exchange. While the SEC's requirements were somewhat different (and arguably more stringent), the differences were not large enough, Mahoney concludes, to measurably improve information available to the market.[12]

---

[9] Paul G. Mahoney, *Wasting a Crisis: Why Securities Regulation Fails* (2015), at 33.

[10] Ibid., at 35.   [11] Ibid., at 22.

[12] Nevertheless, because Mahoney's analysis was restricted, for data availability reasons, to firms listed on the New York Stock Exchange, it is possible that the SEC disclosure requirements improved information about firms listed on other exchanges that previously had more lax disclosure requirements. This public benefit may not, however, have outweighed the costs. As Mahoney points out, the effect of regulation is often to enforce 'best practices' on lower-cost firms and organizations, thus driving them

Mahoney's book should serve as a warning to legal historians, who often rely heavily on what historical actors themselves said. Mahoney argues that what legislators and regulators stated was often wrong or misleading. They made assertions that they thought were politically expedient, that they thought would be convincing to the public, and that would make their actions seem to be in the public interest. Nevertheless, Mahoney argues that quantitative analysis of what legislators and regulators actually did and of the effects of their actions provides superior insights into policymakers' motivation and whether policies actually benefited the public.

c. Michele Landis Dauber, *The Sympathetic State* (2013)

Michele Landis Dauber takes a very different approach. In Chapter 7 of her book, *The Sympathetic State*, she uses quantitative analysis of letters to Eleanor Roosevelt to uncover the 'moral economy' of public assistance. These letters usually asked Mrs. Roosevelt for material assistance and provided a narrative that the author hoped would convince Mrs. Roosevelt that he or she was deserving of aid. Like Mahoney, Dauber is sceptical of the veracity of what people wrote. By comparing the content of letters to census information, Dauber shows that the letters were often misleading—omitting important information and sometimes asserting facts that are likely to be flatly wrong. Nevertheless, Dauber thinks it very informative to analyse the letters, because their omissions and distortions reveal what their writers thought would be convincing.

Although Dauber skilfully discusses several illustrative letters, she notes that 'it is impossible to reliably detect systemic variation in a set of 529 letters simply by reading them'.[13] With so many letters, statistical analysis is necessary. Nearly any point could be 'proven' by quoting from one or two letters. Only by analysing the letters quantitatively and by controlling for multiple factors can reliable general conclusions be drawn. One of Dauber's findings is that the excuses in the letters did not vary much by gender, region, or indicia of social class.[14] From this Dauber infers that letter writers shared a common view of what counted as a valid excuse (or at least what they thought Mrs. Roosevelt would consider as such). In Dauber's words:

This practical imperative [to make a persuasive case for their own lack of fault] seems to have overwhelmed any systemic differences in the background of writers, producing more agreement on what constituted a good letter than would seem likely given the high degree

out of business and lessening competition. Indeed, about a quarter of exchanges went out of business within the first few years of the SEC's existence, and another quarter were acquired or scaled back their operations to avoid SEC regulation (p. 99). Whether the benefit of increased information outweighed the losses from less competition is an open question.

[13] Michele Landis Dauber, *The Sympathetic State* (2013), at 212.   [14] Ibid., at 213.

of regional, class, gender, and racial diversity among the writers. This agreement is a signal of the underlying moral economy in which these writers expected their letters to be read.[15]

Nevertheless, the letters were not uniform. Letters that requested assistance with unpaid debts tended to include more excuses, probably because debt 'raises the question whether the debt represents a flaw in the debtor's moral character. . . . willingness to spend beyond her means'.[16]

One of the strengths of Dauber's approach is that she embeds her statistical analysis in compelling narratives. She starts the chapter with summaries and quotations from several letters so that the reader gets a real feeling for the nature of her sources and the actual words used by the letter writers. Quantitative analysis need not be dry, and it does not need to displace the more traditional narrative and analytic methods used by legal historians. It can usefully supplement them, especially when historians are fortunate to possess large amounts of source material. In those situations, statistical analysis can allay suspicions that the historian is emphasizing unrepresentative pieces of evidence and can uncover patterns and factors that would otherwise be invisible.

D. Other Works

The three examples discussed in this section represent, of course, just a small sampling of legal historical works that use quantitative methods. Other scholars have used statistical analysis to address a wide range of issues, including the causes and effects of the nineteenth-century expansion of women's rights, the effect of the colonial imposition of common or civil law legal systems, the economic effects of the Glorious Revolution, the dynamics of medieval litigation, and the nature of slave captain contracts.[17] I chose to discuss in depth the books by Gavin Wright, Paul Mahoney, and Michele Landis Dauber because they illustrate the variety of ways quantitative methods can be use, and because they combine statistics with narrative and other methods in a way that legal historians are likely to find more persuasive. Some works of quantitative legal history emphasize the numbers so much and seem to abstract so much from context that legal historians (and others not committed to quantitative history) are unlikely to find them persuasive. But these three works show how statistics can be woven into a broader theoretical and narrative context to form a cohesive whole.

---

[15] Ibid., at 218.   [16] Ibid., at 213, 218.

[17] For works on all of these topics, see Daniel Klerman, 'Economics of Legal History' in Franceso Parisi (ed.), *Oxford Handbook of Law and Economics* (2017). For prior and related surveys, see Ron Harris, 'The Encounters of Economic History and Legal History' (2003) 21 *Law and History Review* 297 ff.; Daniel Klerman, 'Statistical and Economic Approaches to Legal History' (2002) *University of Illinois L.R.* 1167 ff.

iii. The Future of Quantitative Legal History

Sophisticated quantitative analysis is likely to remain marginal to legal history. A key reason is that legal historians are increasingly receiving their training as PhD students in history departments, where the faculty seldom use or teach quantitative methods.[18] Until the late 1970s, quantitative analysis and 'scientific history' more generally were important parts of historical studies.[19] Statistics were important to many kinds of historians, including Marxists, cliometricians (historians using modern non-Marxist economic models and large datasets), and followers of the *Annales* School. Nevertheless, in the late 1970s, many elite historians, including those mostly likely to train the next generation of scholars, turned away from social science and statistics towards more traditional narrative models. One of many reasons for this shift was the bitter debate over Fogel and Engerman's analysis of slavery in *Time on the Cross*. A consequence of the increasing statistical sophistication among cliometricians and of historians' turn to narrative is that quantitative historians are more likely to be found in economics departments than in history departments, and quantitative history is more likely to be published in economic journals.[20] For example, Gavin Wright is a member of the Stanford economics department, as is another distinguished economic historian, Avner Greif. There are, of course, notable exceptions. For example, Naomi Lamoreaux, although she is a member of the Yale economics department, is also chair of Yale's history department, where she has the opportunity to influence the large number of legal historians who receive their training at Yale.[21]

Economic history is also increasingly published in economics journals.[22] Similar trends can be found in legal history. As noted above, legal history journals and books

---

[18] On the aversion of most academic historians to social science and to the quantification that usually accompanies it, see Phillip T. Hoffman, 'Opening Our Eyes: History and the Social Sciences' (2006) 6 *Journal of the Historical Society* 93 ff; Jan de Vries, 'The Return from the Return to Narrative', Max Weber Lecture Series, European University Institute (2013). Both Hoffman and de Vries, of course, argue for greater use of social science by historians.

[19] Lawrence Stone, 'The Revival of Narrative: Reflections on a New Old History' (1979) 85 *Past & Present* 3 ff.

[20] Claudia Goldin, 'Cliometrics and the Nobel' (1995) 9 *Journal of Economic Perspectives* 191 ff.

[21] Her own distinguished work on the comparative history of legal business forms puts her in a good position to advise young legal historians. See, e.g., Naomi R. Lamoreaux, Jean-Laurent Rosenthal, 'Legal Regime and Contractual Flexibility: A Comparison of Business's Organizational Choices in France and the United States during the Era of Industrialization' (2005) 7 *American Law and Economics Review* 28 ff.

[22] Ran Abramitzky, 'Economics and the Modern Economic Historian' (2015) 75 *Journal of Economic History* 1240–51. On the paucity of economics and social science more generally in history journals, see works by Hoffman and de Vries above (n. 18).

considered of legal historical interest by the editors of those journals contain almost no sophisticated quantitative analysis. In contrast, economic and statistical analysis of legal history flourish in journals devoted to law and economics, economics, and political science.[23]

Of course, doctoral students in history can take courses in other departments and thus learn statistics and gain exposure to those in other departments who use quantitative methods for historical and other purposes. Similarly, those pursuing a doctorate in other fields can choose to focus on legal history topics. Nevertheless, as long as quantitative work remains so marginal to history departments, it is likely to be underused in legal history as well.

There is some reason to be optimistic that quantitative work may become more central to the field of history. Jean De Vries has even predicted a 'Return from the Return to Narrative' and thus an increased use of social scientific methods in history. If historians turn to the social sciences, they will they almost certainly use more statistics, because quantitative analysis is an integral part of most social science research.[24] Relatedly, here has been a recent upsurge in work on the history of capitalism, and that may presage greater interest in economic history and in quantitative work. On the other hand, much work in the history of capitalism eschews statistical analysis in favor of intellectual history or other approaches.

The emergence of digital humanities may also revive interest in quantitative approaches. Digital humanities uses new quantitative approaches designed particularly for the automated analysis of texts. Because legal historians so often deal with texts, digital humanities may prove an attractive approach. The fact that the *Law and History Review* recently devoted a special issue to 'digital legal history'[25] and that this Handbook includes a chapter on 'Legal History and Digital Humanities' is encouraging in this regard. On the other hand, legal historians may, at least for some time, prefer more traditional approaches to statistical analysis. Quantitative approaches have, until recently, relied primarily on the expertise of the researcher to convert legal sources into quantitative data. That is, the author generally must read the sources and 'code' them. Digital humanities approaches often reduce the human contribution to the analysis by having the computer 'read' and classify the sources. At the moment, computers are rather primitive readers, and it is yet to be seen whether analyses that rely heavily on textual comprehension software can provide genuine insight.

Legal historians might also be influenced by sub-fields of political science, such as American Political Development, where quantitative analysis is common.[26]

---

[23] See works cited in Daniel Klerman, 'Economics of Legal History' in Franceso Parisi (ed.), *Oxford Handbook of Law and Economics* (2017).

[24] de Vries (n. 18).   [25] (2016) 34 *Law and History Review* 831 ff.

[26] See, e.g., Daniel P. Carpenter, *The Forging of Bureaucratic Autonomy: Reputations, Networks, and Policy Innovation in Executive Agencies, 1862–1928* (2001).

Or, as Phillip Hoffman has pointed out, historians (including legal historians) could usefully employ tools from cognitive psychology and game theory, which already 'are revolutionizing fields such as law or political science'.[27] Because these tools are usually tested with statistical analysis of data, their use would almost inevitably lead to increased quantification. Similarly, techniques developed to analyse the effect of politics, institutions, and panel composition on modern judicial decision-making could be fruitfully applied to judges in the more distant past.[28] In this regard, it should be noted that the Supreme Court Database[29] has recently been updated to include information on Supreme Court cases and justices back to 1791, so much of the relevant data have already been coded. Of course, historians may want to focus on other courts and will thus need to code the data themselves. Even so, the Supreme Court Database and the many articles that analyse Supreme Court data can serve as useful models.

It is possible that legal historians will be inspired by this chapter or other works to learn and apply more quantitative techniques. They could do so by taking statistics and research methods courses offered by political science, economics, sociology, and other departments. Or they could teach themselves. A very useful resource for autodidacts could be Lee Epstein and Andrew D. Martin, *An Introduction to Empirical Legal Research*, a book specifically intended for legal scholars (although not necessarily legal historians) who have minimal quantitative training. Although it teaches some basics of statistical analysis, it also addresses important topics that statistics texts often ignore, such as research design, collecting and coding data, and persuasive presentation of results. Those who teach themselves quantitative methods (and indeed all who use them), would be well-advised to share ideas and drafts with social scientists in other departments. Those conversations can help the author avoid mistakes as well as spark more general conversations and interchange on methods as well as substance.

Perhaps the most promising avenue for quantitative legal history would be collaboration between legal historians and quantitative social scientists. Co-authorship is extremely common in the social sciences, but strangely rare in legal history. Collaboration provides a way to incorporate sophisticated methods without requiring independent mastery of those techniques by the legal historian. In collaborating, the legal historian is likely to learn considerably about statistics and quantitative research. Similarly, the legal historian can ensure that the quantitative analysis takes proper account of historical context and that narrative and other techniques are effectively used in the exposition.

---

[27] Hoffman (2006) 6 *Journal of the Historical Society* 94 ff.

[28] See, e.g., Lee Epstein, William M. Landes, Richard A. Posner, *The Behavior of Federal Judges: A Theoretical and Empirical Study of Rational Choice* (2013).

[29] See <http://supremecourtdatabase.org> or <http://scdb.wustl.edu/>.

IV. CONCLUSION

Although relatively few legal historians currently use quantitative techniques, there are some who do, and their work shows the potential power of statistics to disentangle the influence of multiple factors, to reveal the effect of legal change, and to uncover patterns in large quantities of text. The recent interest of historians in digital humanities and the history of capitalism may foreshadow increasing use of quantitative methods by historians, which may in turn influence the next generation of legal historians. Or current legal historians could benefit by educating themselves in quantitative methods or by collaborating with empiricists from other schools and departments.

BIBLIOGRAPHY

Ran Abramitzky, 'Economics and the Modern Economic Historian' (2015) 75 *Journal of Economic History* 1240–51

Daniel P. Carpenter, *The Forging of Bureaucratic Autonomy: Reputations, Networks, and Policy Innovation in Executive Agencies 1862–1928* (Princeton University Press, 2001)

Michele Landis Dauber, *The Sympathetic State* (University of Chicago Press, 2013)

Jan de Vries, 'The Return from the Return to Narrative' Max Weber Lecture Series (European University Institute, 2013)

Claudia Goldin, 'Cliometrics and the Nobel' (1995) 9 *Journal of Economic Perspectives* 191

Ron Harris, 'The Encounters of Economic History and Legal History' (2003) 21 *Law and History Review* 297

Phillip T. Hoffman, 'Opening Our Eyes: History and the Social Sciences' (2006) 6 *Journal of the Historical Society* 93

Lee Epstein, William M. Landes, Richard A. Posner, *The Behavior of Federal Judges: A Theoretical and Empirical Study of Rational Choice* (Harvard University Press, 2013)

Lee Epstein, Andrew D. Martin, *An Introduction to Empirical Legal Research* (Oxford University Press, 2014)

Daniel Klerman, 'Economics of Legal History' in Franceso Parisi (ed.), *Oxford Handbook of Law and Economics* (Oxford University Press, 2017)

Daniel Klerman, 'Statistical and Economic Approaches to Legal History' (2002) *University of Illinois L.R.* 1167

Naomi R. Lamoreaux, Jean-Laurent Rosenthal, 'Legal Regime and Contractual Flexibility: A Comparison of Business's Organizational Choices in France and the United States during the Era of Industrialization' (2005) 7 *American Law and Economics Review* 28

Paul G. Mahoney, *Wasting a Crisis: Why Securities Regulation Fails* (University of Chicago Press, 2015)

Lawrence Stone, 'The Revival of Narrative: Reflections on a New Old History' (1979) 85 *Past & Present* 3

Gavin Wright, *Sharing the Prize* (Harvard University Press, 2013)

PART III

PERSPECTIVES: LEGAL HISTORY IN MODERN LEGAL THOUGHT

CHAPTER 20

BLACKSTONE

JOHN V. ORTH

Sɪʀ William Blackstone (1723–1780) is the author of the single most important book in the history of the common law. Blackstone's four-volume *Commentaries on the Laws of England* (1765–1769), culminating a series of lectures he delivered at Oxford from 1753, changed the way lawyers thought about the law. Unlike all the other leading figures in the history of the common law, Blackstone made his contribution not as a judge or as a legislator, but as a scholar. Copies of his *Commentaries* spread rapidly throughout England's far-flung colonies, where they proved even more influential than in England itself, nowhere more so than in the ex-colonies that became the United States.

I. Biography

Blackstone's biography hardly prepares us for the scale of his scholarly achievement. The details of his life, devoted to university service and the law, are thoroughly documented in Wilfrid Prest's 2008 biography.[1] Despite a rather

---

[1] Wilfrid Prest, *William Blackstone: Law and Letters in the Eighteenth Century* (2008). See also Ian Doolittle, *William Blackstone: A Biography* (2001). Together these supplant David Lockmiller, *Sir William Blackstone* (1938) and L. C. Warden, *The Life of Blackstone* (1938).

difficult personality, Blackstone's undoubted mastery of the common law, demonstrated by his lecture series and subsequent book, eventually earned him a university professorship, a steady stream of legal clients, a seat in parliament (1761–1770), and finally a knighthood and judicial preferment (1770–1780). A man of many talents and wide-ranging interests—in architecture, poetry, Shakespeare criticism, prison reform—Blackstone would have deserved a place in any gallery of eighteenth-century English worthies. But without the *Commentaries*, it would have been a distinctly minor place. So exhaustive is Prest's research that little seemingly remains to be discovered about Blackstone's life, although Prest himself recommends further investigation into Blackstone's lectures, the regional and social characteristics of his clients, and his European contacts and correspondents.[2]

A. Law Professor

Like many other great books, the *Commentaries* began as university lectures—proof positive, if any were needed, of the intimate connection between teaching and scholarship. From their inception, Blackstone's lectures displayed a paradoxical aspect, a conservative project with radical implications. Before his lectures, the only law taught at the English universities was civil law, that is, the system of jurisprudence based on the *Corpus Juris Civilis*. Organized, rational, written in a learned language, Roman law was endowed with the prestige of classical civilization. The common law, by contrast, appeared uncouth and faintly barbaric, its basic vocabulary medieval Latin and a degenerate French, tainted with feudalism and the compromises of practice and the marketplace. Foreshadowing Paul Cezanne's later ambition to make Impressionism 'like the art of the museums',[3] Blackstone sought to make the common law fit for the universities. He began by offering his lectures as a private venture, open to fee-paying students—a precocious example of the marketplace of ideas. When a generous bequest by Charles Viner later permitted the establishment of the Vinerian Professorship of the Common Law, Blackstone became its first incumbent in 1758, but continued to offer his private course until 1766. Thereafter, his book made the lectures available to readers far beyond the confines of the university.

---

[2] Wilfrid Prest, 'Blackstone and Biography', in Wilfrid Prest (ed.), *Blackstone and His Commentaries: Biography, Law, History* (2009) 14 ff.

[3] See Joachim Gasquet, *Cezanne* (1921) 90 ('*J'ai voulu faire de l'impressionisme quelque chose de solide et de durable comme l'art de musées.*') ff.

No one can understand the *Commentaries* without first understanding the lectures from which they sprang. Advertising his course, Blackstone announced that he proposed 'to lay down a general and comprehensive plan of the laws of England; to deduce their history; to enforce and illustrate their leading rules and fundamental principles; and to compare them with the laws of nature and of other nations'—in other words, to cover the entire law school curriculum, including legal history, jurisprudence, and comparative law. Not intended for lawyers or even particularly for law students, but for undergraduates who were 'desirous to be in some degree acquainted with the constitution and polity of their own country', Blackstone announced that he would avoid the 'practical niceties, or the minute distinctions of particular cases'[4]—otherwise the characteristic concern of practicing lawyers. To aid students in the course, Blackstone prepared handouts, at first simple broadsheets, later a 200-page outline, *An Analysis of the Laws of England*, first published in 1756. So useful was the *Analysis* as an introduction to English law that it was soon in demand outside the university, even outside the common law world. Over the dozen years he offered his course, Blackstone periodically produced new editions of the *Analysis* until it was superseded by the *Commentaries*, the basic structure and contents of which were derived from it.

Like all lecture courses, Blackstone's evolved over the years. Student notes, several sets of which have survived, allow a reconstruction of Blackstone's steady refinement of the details of his 'general and comprehensive plan'. An example of what such sources can reveal is shown by Prest's comparison of student notes from successive series of lectures, documenting the growing significance that Blackstone accorded Magna Carta as he prepared a scholarly edition of 'The Great Charter' for publication in 1759.[5] A revised edition of 'The Great Charter', along with essays on collateral consanguinity, copyholders, and the law of inheritance, was published in two volumes in 1762 under the title *Law Tracts*.

Not only did Blackstone's lectures and ensuing book make English law available to a wider audience, the mere fact of the lectures initiated a reorientation of legal training, with momentous consequences. Learning law from lectures rather than from unsupervised reading and observation of working lawyers and judges—previously the only means of legal education—led to the slow divorce of legal study from legal practice. Thereafter, the common law was increasingly expressed as an organized statement of rules with a steadily growing role for the law professor, who together with the judge and the legislator came to form the trinity that made the modern common law.

---

[4] 12 William S. Holdsworth, *History of English Law* (1938) 745–6 (app. IV-1) ff.
[5] Wilfrid Prest, 'Blackstone's Magna Carta' (2016) 94 *N.C. L.R.* 1495, 1511–19 ff.

ii. The Commentaries

Although the *Commentaries* deserve the greatest scholarly attention, they also pose the greatest difficulty to researchers. Consistent with Blackstone's project to present the common law as intellectually respectable, his creative restatement of the law gave it a coherence it had hitherto lacked. Nor was Blackstone's 'plan of the laws of England' quite so comprehensive as he claimed. But before examining these issues, it is necessary to examine the text itself.

A. Text

In the last few decades a split has developed among scholars concerning which edition of the *Commentaries* to study. In 1979 the University of Chicago Press published a 'facsimile of the first edition of 1765–1769',[6] and this has become popular with Blackstone scholars, particularly historians. But just as the lectures evolved over twelve iterations, so the published text evolved over the eight editions published in Blackstone's lifetime. Posthumous editions were advertised as including 'the last corrections of the author' and began to include editor's notes devoted to later developments. Beginning with the twelfth edition (1793), prepared by Edward Christian, the text of the *Commentaries* achieved the status of a classic with standardized pagination indicated in the margin or inserted in the text.[7] Each subsequent edition indicated the standard pagination with an asterisk ('the star edition'). When the star page is cited, legal editorial practice dictates the omission of the date and edition, unless the citation is to material added by a particular editor.[8]

It should be emphasized that the first volume of the Chicago Blackstone is a facsimile of the edition published in 1765, which Blackstone corrected for a new edition of that volume in the following year, when he published the second volume. For purchasers of the 1765 edition, Blackstone prepared an eight-page Supplement, which is printed after the general index in volume four of the Chicago Blackstone.

---

[6] Although labelled a 'facsimile of the first edition of 1765–1769', the Chicago Blackstone is actually a facsimile of the first editions of each of the four volumes: volume one (1765), volume two (1766), volume three (1768), and volume four (1769). In 1766, a second edition of volume one was published; in 1768, a third edition. In 1767 a second edition of volume two was published; in 1768, a third edition. In 1769, when volumes three and four were published, the four volumes were issued as a set and labelled the 'fourth edition'.

[7] 1 William Blackstone, *Commentaries on the Laws of England* (Edward Christian, ed., 1793) ix note ff.

[8] *The Bluebook: A Uniform System of Citation* (12th edn., 2015) 15.8 ff. Hereafter in this article, citations to the *Commentaries*, abbreviated *Bl. Com.*, are to both the first editions of each of the four volumes and to the star edition.

As a consequence of the additions and corrections to volumes one and two, the index in volume four of the Chicago Blackstone, originally prepared in 1769 when the fourth volume was published, is not accurate in its references to the first volumes. Nor, for that matter, is Blackstone's index comprehensive in other regards, as Prest has shown with respect to references to Magna Carta.[9] It is also important to pay attention to the fact that over the two centuries after Blackstone's death, multiple editors included notes to update the *Commentaries*. Later lawyers and judges were often influenced by these notes as much as by Blackstone's text. Information on many of the American editors is provided by Michael Hoeflich.[10] Prest has pointed out that, in the absence of local Australian or New Zealand editions, Australasian lawyers used imported English, Irish, or even American editions.[11] Study of successive editors' notes provides periodic updates on legal developments, as well as insights into Blackstone's continuing relevance.

In 2016 Oxford University Press published a variorum edition of the *Commentaries*, allowing study of Blackstone's developing thought, as well as his responses to the political pressures to which he was exposed.[12] Shortly after the publication of volume one in 1765, for example, the adoption of the Stamp Act precipitated a confrontation with the American colonies. By then a member of parliament and loyal supporter of the Tory cause, Blackstone hastened to insert, first in the Supplement, thereafter in the text of later editions of volume one, significant qualifications on his earlier statements concerning the applicability of the common law in the colonies to emphasize colonial subordination to 'the imperial crown and parliament of Great Britain'.[13]

The most notorious example of Blackstone's revisions involves the seemingly technical question of eligibility for election to parliament, which unexpectedly became a major political issue in the case of the trouble-making John Wilkes. Speaking in the House of Commons in 1769 in support of the government's refusal to recognize Wilkes's re-election after expulsion, Blackstone was confounded when his book was quoted against him as he argued that expulsion disqualified a candidate for re-election.[14] While Wilkes' supporters exulted with the biblical figure of Job 'that mine adversary had written a book', Blackstone got an author's revenge by amending later editions of the *Commentaries*, beginning with the fourth in 1770.[15]

---

[9] Prest (n. 5) 1511, n. 95 (citing dozens of references to Magna Carta not included in the index).

[10] Michael Hoeflich, 'American Blackstones', in Prest (ed.), *Blackstone and His Commentaries* 171 ff.

[11] Wilfrid Prest, 'Antipodean Blackstone', in Prest (ed.), *Re-Interpreting Blackstone's Commentaries: A Seminal Text in National and International Context* (2014) 145, 153 ff.

[12] Oxford Edition of Blackstone (Wilfrid Prest, gen. ed., 2016). The only prior attempt at a variorum edition of the *Commentaries* was by William G. Hammond (1890), and its accuracy has been doubted.

[13] Supplement iii (correcting 1 *Bl. Com.* 105, line 30) ff; 1 *Bl. Com.* *109 ff.

[14] 1 *Bl. Com.* 170 ff.

[15] 1 *Bl. Com.* *176 ff. For the parliamentary context, see Prest, *Blackstone* 241–6 ff.

An example of an important revision, mainly of interest to property scholars, concerns the estate of tenancy by the entirety, the common law marital estate. Blackstone originally failed to include it in his discussion of concurrent estates in volume two on property, where lawyers would expect to find it.[16] Finally, in the ninth (posthumous) edition of 1783, prepared by Richard Burn and advertised as including Blackstone's autograph corrections on the eighth edition,[17] a sentence on the subject was awkwardly inserted in the discussion of joint tenancy.[18] Included thereafter in the canonical text, it was frequently cited by American courts.[19] On this fractured foundation much of the American law of tenancy by the entirety was built.[20] Quite possibly, the logical Blackstone had remained uncertain until his death how to accommodate the estate with two owners, which largely—but not completely—functioned as a sole estate, controlled by the husband.

Today the Chicago Blackstone remains useful for study of Blackstone's first thoughts on his various subjects, while the Oxford Blackstone allows study of Blackstone's second and subsequent thoughts, printing all the revisions ('varia') to the first editions of each volume, as well as expanding Blackstone's sometimes cryptic citations. For historians interested in the evolution of Blackstone's thought, the Oxford Blackstone is invaluable, but for legal historians interested in the *Commentaries'* impact on the later development of the common law, the star edition—the one cited by lawyers and judges for more than two centuries—remains essential.

It must be acknowledged how difficult it is to correlate the star edition with the Oxford Blackstone. One must first know that the star edition incorporates a revision, not something normally indicated; in addition, one must know on which page of the first edition of each volume the revision was inserted. For example, the revision made in response to the Stamp Act, which appears as page *109 in the star edition of volume one, was inserted in the first edition of volume one on page 105; in the Oxford Blackstone it appears among the varia on page 327 of volume one. The revision made in response to the controversy surrounding John Wilkes, concerning eligibility to re-election to parliament after expulsion, which appears on page *176 in the star edition of volume one, was inserted in the first edition of volume one on page 170; in the Oxford Blackstone it appears among the varia on page 339 of

---

[16] 2 *Bl. Com.* ch. 12 ('Of Estates in Severalty, Joint Tenancy, Coparcenary, and Common').

[17] 'ADVERTISEMENT concerning this ninth edition', 1 *Bl. Com.* (Richard Burn ed., 1783) xi ff. Hammond doubted that Burn had the 'self-restraint' to refrain from including his own revisions and based his variorum text on only the first eight editions. 1 *Bl. Com.* xvi (Hammond ed., 1890). While prominently noting Hammond's doubts, the general editor of the Oxford Blackstone nonetheless included the revisions in the ninth edition. 1 Oxford Blackstone xliii.

[18] 2 *Bl. Com.* *182 ff.

[19] For citations to 1890, see 2 *Bl. Com.* (Hammond ed., 1890), *182, n. g ff.

[20] See John V. Orth, 'Tenancy by the Entirety: The Strange Career of the Common Law Marital Estate' 1996 *B.Y.U. L.R.* 35, 35–40 ff.

volume one. And the key sentence on tenancy by the entirety, which appears on page *182 of volume two in the star edition, was inserted on the same page in the first edition of volume two; in the Oxford Blackstone it appears among the varia on page 379 of volume two.

B. *Sitz im Leben*

It is notorious that the *Commentaries* pay scant attention to contract and offer little of what today would be recognized as the law of tort, but in this regard they are largely reflective of existing law. The first book on the general principles of English contract law did not appear until the decade after Blackstone's death,[21] and the first treatise on modern tort law until the next century.[22] But even as a statement of the law of the third quarter of the eighteenth century, the *Commentaries* must be treated with caution. The book's structure had been set by the lecture course from 1753 to 1766. In four volumes reminiscent of the Institutes of the *Corpus Juris*, developed from lectures delivered over the four terms of the Oxford academic year, and devoted to four topics—rights of persons, rights of things, private wrongs, public wrongs—the *Commentaries* displayed the pleasing symmetry of Palladian architecture. Blackstone could not have anticipated the dramatic development of commercial law that was wrought by Lord Mansfield, chief justice of King's Bench in the three decades after 1756. To have incorporated these changes would have required a radical redesign of the *Commentaries*, as demonstrated fifty years later, when Chancellor James Kent composed his four-volume *Commentaries on American Law*.[23] To accommodate the new learning in the four canonical books, Kent dramatically restructured the text, omitting criminal law ('public wrongs') entirely and awkwardly running the greatly expanded coverage of contract and related commercial law topics over volumes two and three.

In addition, readers of the *Commentaries* would hardly guess at the significant role played by equity in contemporary legal practice; indeed, they would probably be misled by Blackstone's confusion of the law administered by the courts of equity (chancery) with the generalized meaning of equity as fairness in individual cases. The difficulty may be attributed to Blackstone's unease about discretionary justice. He was convinced that 'law, without equity, though hard and disagreeable, is much more desirable for the public good, than equity without law: which would make every judge a legislator, and introduce most infinite

---

[21] John Joseph Powell, *Essay upon the Law of Contracts and Agreements* (1790).

[22] Francis Hilliard, *The Law of Torts*, 2 vols. (1859).

[23] James Kent, *Commentaries on American Law*, 4 vols. (1826–1830). Kent was the first professor of law at Columbia College (now University) from 1794 to 1798 and again, after a break for judicial service, from 1824 to 1826.

confusion; as there would then be almost as many different rules of action laid down in our courts, as there are differences of capacity and sentiment in the human mind'[24]—an observation reminiscent of John Selden's classic quip that the measure of justice should not, like the length of the Chancellor's foot, vary from judge to judge.[25] As we will see, Blackstone's fear of judicial discretion and preference for hard-and-fast rules later influenced his most significant decisions as a judge.

By far the most important omission from Blackstone's text—and the one with the most far-reaching consequences—is the absence of an extended discussion of the writ system, then the nuts-and-bolts of English law. Before the *Commentaries*, legal literature was necessarily concerned with the intricacies of choosing the right cause of action. Substantive law was almost inseparable from procedure, but except in a few chapters, Blackstone essentially ignored the writs, thereby exposing legal rules to critical examination for the first time. Ironically, when on the bench, he showed himself more committed to maintaining the ancient distinctions than his fellow judges, but as a lecturer and the author of the *Commentaries*, he spared his audience many of these 'practical niceties', thereby allowing lawyers and non-lawyers alike an unobstructed view of the law's substance.

III. A Concordance of Discordant Canons

Blackstone's greatest contribution as a scholar was to provide a logical structure for his discussion of English law. Although he had predecessors in the attempt, they are largely unknown today except to experts. The common law itself, the product of centuries of decided cases, lacked any inherent order. Tennyson was not far wrong, although a little out of date, when he referred to 'the lawless science of our law / That codeless myriad of precedent / That wilderness of single instances'.[26] Blackstone's supreme achievement was to take the accumulated case law and synthesize it into a coherent intellectual whole. But his creative restatement of the law almost necessarily made it appear far more consistent than it was. He minimized legal contradictions and sought to rationalize even the strangest aspects of English law,

---

[24] 1 *Bl. Com.* 62 ff; 1 *Bl. Com.* *62 ff.

[25] John Selden, *Table Talk* (1689) (Frederick Pollock, ed., 1927) 43 ff.

[26] Alfred Lord Tennyson, 'Aylmer's Field 1793' (1864) ll. 432–9, in *The Poems of Tennyson* (Christopher Rick, ed., 1969) 1172 ff.

mainly by appeals to history—all in elegant prose that gained the admiration even of his critics.

The greatest challenge for modern researchers is to uncover Blackstone's intellectual moves as he organized his presentation, since he took pains to conceal them. For example, in presenting his rules for the construction of statutes in volume one, Blackstone confronted Sir Edward Coke's *dictum* (at least as commonly understood) that 'acts contrary to reason are void'.[27] This was, in effect, a claim that the common law can control statutes, a form of judicial review and a contradiction of the supremacy of parliament, hard won in the previous century in the English Civil War and Glorious Revolution. Unwilling to reject outright so high an authority as Coke, Blackstone restated the rule as 'acts of parliament that are impossible to be performed are of no validity', draining it of its subversive potential—and of any significant meaning. Then, in a sop to Coke, he added, but 'if there arise out of them collaterally any absurd consequences, manifestly contradictory to common reason, they are, with regard to those collateral consequences, void'.[28]

In a concession to changing sensibilities concerning marriage, Blackstone emphasized the legal fiction of the unity of persons and downplayed older justifications of the legal disabilities of married women based on scripture or the superior qualities of men. Not wholly absent from prior cases, marital unity was elevated by Blackstone into an organizing principle that rationalized a wide range of previously disparate rules. While giving a logical structure to the common law of marriage—and representing an advance on the earlier legal position of women— the fictional unity of husband and wife, sanctioned by the *Commentaries*, later hardened into a legal fact that long delayed recognition of the independent legal personality of married women.[29]

Still to be thoroughly explored by scholars is Blackstone's understanding of the relationship between law and economics. Writing before Adam Smith's *Wealth of Nations* (1776), Blackstone himself probably only dimly understood the connection, although it was slowly gaining recognition in the cases. For example, reconciling centuries of precedent with a smoothness that disguised the inherent conflicts, Blackstone expounded the law of nuisance as it applied to incorporeal hereditaments, that is, intangible property interests. Ancient authority held that 'if a ferry is erected on a river, so near another ancient ferry as to draw away its custom, it is a nuisance to the owner of the old one', meaning that the later entrant could be fined or enjoined. This, Blackstone explained, was because the owner of an ancient

---

[27] Dr. Bonham's Case, 8 Co. Rep. 107a, 77 *Eng. Rep.* 638 ('[W]hen an Act of Parliament is against common right and reason, or repugnant, or impossible to be performed, the common law will controul it, and adjudge such Act to be void.') ff.

[28] 1 *Bl. Com.* 91 ff; 1 *Bl. Com.* *91 ff. See also John V. Orth, 'Did Sir Edward Coke Mean What He Said?' (1999) 16 *Const. Comm.* 33 ff.

[29] See Tim Stretton, 'Coverture and Unity of Person in Blackstone's Commentaries', in Prest (ed.), *Blackstone and His Commentaries* 111 ff.

ferry became legally bound to keep it 'always in repair and readiness, for the ease of all the king's subjects'. The old ferry, in modern terms, had become a public utility. Consequently, it would be 'extremely hard, if a new ferry were suffered to share his profits, which does not share his burden'. But in the following sentence, after the piety that 'where the reason ceases, the law also ceases', he justified later cases holding that it is no nuisance to set up a mill, a school, or a trade 'in neighborhood and rivalship with another: for by such emulation the public are like to be gainers'. In this case, the profits lost by competition (emulation)—the 'creative destruction' celebrated by economists—he blandly dismissed with the Latin quip *'damnum absque injuria'*.[30]

IV. 'Everything-as-it-should-be Blackstone'

Bentham's epithet encapsulating his contempt for Blackstone as the complacent apologist of the status quo[31] has achieved such currency that it is difficult to see that the *Commentaries* actually contain significant criticisms of the law and serious proposals for its reform. Despite Blackstone's well-known suspicion of statutes, many of his complaints required legislative solutions. Albert Alschuler has catalogued some of Blackstone's proposals: 'creating a system for recording wills and deeds, expanding the right to counsel, restricting the death penalty, abolishing the doctrine that the bloodline of a felon is corrupted, and reforming England's game laws, inheritance laws, and poor laws'.[32] Undoubted master of the law of real property, Blackstone delved into the intricacies of the process for barring an entail, the estate that limited succession to direct descendants, usually male. With the goal of speeding up the process and rendering it 'less subject to niceties', he offered a short list of possible reforms, noticeably one that had been pioneered in the American colonies[33]—an early recognition of the way that influence could run from the periphery to the centre of the British Empire.

In the *Commentaries*, as later on the bench, Blackstone laid great stress on procedural protections for the accused. Clearly uncomfortable with the growing

---

[30] 3 *Bl. Com.* 219 ff; 3 *Bl. Com.* *219 ff.

[31] Jeremy Bentham, *A Fragment on Government* (1776) (J. H. Burns, H. L. A. Hart eds., 1988) 407 ff.

[32] Albert W. Alschuler, 'Rediscovering Blackstone' (1996) 145 *U. Pa. L.R.* 1, 40 (including citations) ff.

[33] 2 *Bl. Com.* 361 ff; 2 *Bl. Com.* *361 ff. See John V. Orth, 'Does the Fee Tail Exist in North Carolina?' (1988) 23 *Wake Forest L.R.* 767, 778–9 ff.

use of summary convictions, convictions by one or two justices of the peace after non-jury trials, he waspishly noted that the common law courts had at least 'thrown in one check upon them, by making it necessary to *summon* the party accused before he is condemned'.[34] Even while criticizing Blackstone for overestimating the safeguards against judicial abuse, John Langbein applauded him for 'identifying and recommending reform of the two worst features of the [trial] procedure of his day, the testimonial disqualification of the parties for interest, and the lack of pre-trial discovery for documents and certain forms of testimonial evidence'.[35]

But Blackstone was rarely strident, and his critical comments were usually couched in terms so emollient as almost to evade attention. Commenting on 'offenses against God and religion', for example, Blackstone was compelled to include the crime of witchcraft, 'of which our ancient books are full'. Piously noting that the possibility of witchcraft is attested 'in various passages both of the old and new testament' and adding in extenuation that it was punishable in the civil as well as in the common law, Blackstone tactfully observed that 'it seems to be the most eligible way to conclude, with an ingenious writer of our own, that in general there has been such a thing as witchcraft; though one cannot give credit to any particular modern instance of it'.[36] And he pointedly excluded the Jacobean statute on the subject from his list of the law's 'improvements'.[37]

Unlike Bentham, Blackstone's chosen role was to praise the common law, not to criticize it. '[O]ur lawyers . . . tell us', he said, 'that the law is the perfection of reason . . . and that what is not reason is not law'.[38] But Blackstone was too honest not to recognize the difficulty with this Panglossian formula, so he qualified it in a characteristic way: 'Not that the particular reason of every rule in the law can at this distance of time be always precisely assigned; but it is sufficient that there be nothing in the rule flatly contradictory to reason, and then the law will presume it to be well founded'.[39] The law is reasonable, in other words, because it presumes its own reasonableness; the burden of proving the contrary is on the critic. Legal history after Blackstone will be the story of the reversal of this presumption. In future, defenders of the status quo will bear the burden of proof.

---

[34] 4 *Bl. Com.* 279 ff; 4 *Bl. Com.* *282–3 (italics in original) ff. For a discussion of the use of summary convictions to suppress incipient trade unions, see John V. Orth, *Combination and Conspiracy: A Legal History of Trade Unionism, 1721–1906* (1991) 52–3 ff.

[35] John H. Langbein, 'Blackstone on Judging', in Prest (ed.), *Blackstone and His Commentaries* (citing 3 *Bl. Com.* 382–3) 65, 73 ff.

[36] 4 *Bl. Com.* 60 ff; 4 *Bl. Com.* *61 (citing 'Mr. Addison, Spect. No. 117') ff. See *Addison and Steele: Selections From the Tatler and the Spectator* (Robert J. Allen ed., 2nd edn., 1970) 285 ff.

[37] 4 *Bl. Com.* 429 ff; 4 *Bl. Com.* *436 ff.

[38] Cf. *Coke on Littleton* section 138 ('Reason is the life of the law; nay, the common law itself is nothing else but reason . . . , the Law, which is perfection of reason.') ff.

[39] 1 *Bl. Com.* 70 ff; 1 *Bl. Com.* *70 ff.

v. The Strange Career of
the Commentaries

Important as it is for scholars to uncover what went on behind the scenes as Blackstone prepared the lectures that became his great book, it is just as important, if not more so, for them to explain the remarkable staying power of the book. As England entered the age of reform in the 1830s, parliamentary legislation rendered so much of the *Commentaries* out of date that editor's notes seemed hardly adequate. In 1841 Henry John Stephen produced his four-volume *New Commentaries on the Laws of England*. Described as 'partly founded on Blackstone' and still in four volumes, the contents were strikingly rearranged to accommodate the new developments, compressing the coverage of tort and crime in order to find room for the greatly expanded coverage of contracts. Stephen's *New Commentaries* seemed to indicate that the old *Commentaries* would go the way of legal texts that survived in name only for years after the death of their authors, periodically rewritten by 'editors' to keep them topical, such as Burn's *Justice of the Peace*, first published in 1755 and still coming out in new editions almost a century later. In fact, Stephen's *New Commentaries* had even greater staying power and went through twenty subsequent editions down to 1950.

While conventional English legal history, following A. V. Dicey, gives Bentham and his disciples credit for many nineteenth-century legal reforms, Benthamism was much less influential in America. Blackstone's *Commentaries* had quickly put down deep roots at the end of the colonial period, providing a conveniently portable summary of the common law in a book-poor society. In an oft-quoted speech on the eve of the American Revolution, Edmund Burke reported that by then, Americans had bought nearly as many copies of the *Commentaries* as had the English themselves.[40] And despite Blackstone's opposition to Independence, his insistence on the 'absolute rights of individuals'[41] proved invaluable in the ideological struggle that preceded separation. Bentham's scoffing rejection of natural rights did not go down well with the revolutionary generation, which famously claimed for themselves 'certain inalienable rights'. Additionally, it is likely that many American apologists grounded their arguments on Blackstone's comments concerning the common law in the colonies that appeared in the first edition of volume one, which lacked the qualifications added to later editions.

Although Blackstone modestly described his *Commentaries* as rudimentary and addressed to students,[42] that almost certainly understated his ambition; nonetheless,

---

[40] Edmund Burke, 'Speech on Moving His Resolutions for Conciliation with the Colonies' (22 March 1775) in 3 *The Writings and Speeches of Edmund Burke*, P. L. Langford (ed.), (1996) 123 ff.
[41] 1 *Bl. Com.* chap. 1 ff.   [42] 4 *Bl. Com.* 399 ff; 4 *Bl. Com.* *406 ff.

he could hardly have anticipated that his book would be treated as definitive. Not surprisingly, in Westminster, rich in legal resources, it never was. In America, by contrast, the fortuitous timing of the *Commentaries,* the absence of other sources, and the book's accessible style, often made it the final word. Not simply a common law textbook, the *Commentaries* broadly appealed to the liberally educated elite, incorporating as it did many universal and natural law principles. In the debates over the Constitution, Blackstone was frequently invoked; his book literally in the hands of delegates at the important Virginia ratifying convention.[43]

Blackstone was a familiar presence in arguments in the U.S. Supreme Court during the first decades of its existence, before being displaced by indigenous authorities, themselves often inspired by the *Commentaries.* In the late twentieth and early twenty-first centuries, after decades of relative neglect, Blackstone reappeared in the Supreme Court, hailed as 'the preeminent authority on English law for the founding generation'.[44] Lost to sight was its origin in lectures to teenage undergraduates, many not destined for legal careers. Today, the numerous citations to the *Commentaries* actually exceed those from the earlier period.[45] To some extent, the Blackstone revival can be explained by the search for the 'original understanding' of the Constitution. But Jessie Allen has inquired whether the recent rise in Blackstone citations could also be part of 'a broader trend toward citing "classical" common law sources?' 'Is the Court becoming more academic in its analyses?'[46]

However valuable the study of Blackstone in the Supreme Court, there is also a need to study his influence in the several states. Once Independence was won, the federal structure of the new Republic meant that in America, unlike in England, there was no national legislature with authority to undertake wholesale legal reform. Each state was left to develop the law for itself, and state legislatures generally deferred to the courts, where Blackstone was accepted as unquestioned authority. In North Carolina, for example, aspiring lawyers reported reading Blackstone over and over again, especially volume two on the law of property ('rights of things'). A remarkable aid to memory for students, published in the state in 1838, depicts divisions and subdivisions of the *Commentaries* on the branches of a large tree, while making no reference to changes in the law since 1780, either in England or in America.[47] Beginning in 1849 and continuing

---

[43] Horst Dippel, 'Blackstone's Commentaries and the Origins of Modern Constitutionalism', in Prest (ed.), *Re-Interpreting Blackstone's Commentaries* 199, 201 ff.

[44] E.g., *Alden v. Maine* (1999) 527 U.S. 706, 715; *District of Columbia v. Heller* (2008) 554 U.S. 570, 593.

[45] Jessie Allen, 'Reading Blackstone in the Twenty-First Century and the Twenty-First Century Through Blackstone', in Prest (ed.), *Re-Interpreting Blackstone's Commentaries* 215, 217 ff.

[46] Ibid., 219, n. 6.

[47] Anonymous, *The Tree of Legal Knowledge, Designed as an Assistant to Students, In the Study of Law, In Which the Admirable System Laid Down by Blackstone, In His Commentaries, is Preserved* (1838), described in John V. Orth, 'Blackstone's Ghost: Law and Legal Education in North Carolina', in Prest (ed.), *Re-Interpreting Blackstone's Commentaries* 125, 127 and figs. 1–3 ff.

into the 1930s, the North Carolina Supreme Court required that candidates for admission to practice demonstrate familiarity with Blackstone, and instruction in the state's law schools remained largely based on textbooks heavily reliant on the *Commentaries*.[48] In the early twentieth century, a reforming chief justice blamed Blackstone for fostering the stand-pat conservatism of the state's lawyers and judges.[49] One of the dwindling number of states that still rely on the uncodified common law for the definition of major crimes (burglary, robbery, arson), North Carolina courts into the twenty-first century still quote Blackstone on the elements of these crimes.[50]

VI. AFTER THE COMMENTARIES

Blackstone's career after the *Commentaries* is something of an anti-climax. The consensus is that he was 'not a success at the Bar'[51] and that his parliamentary career was 'not distinguished'.[52] Perhaps, as Prest suggests, further research into Blackstone's clients would enhance his reputation, and Emily Kadens has demonstrated that Blackstone's opinions of counsel repay further examination,[53] but nothing can make him a leader to compare with Thomas Erskine or William Garrow. Similarly, although Prest has drawn attention to Blackstone's parliamentary contributions as a behind-the-scenes committeeman,[54] nothing can alter the fact that his political impact was negligible; his reticence to speak in debates was exceeded only by Edward Gibbon's total silence.[55] And it is unlikely that anything will alter Sir Lewis Namier's magisterial judgment: of the fourteen speeches Blackstone did deliver in the House, most were on subjects of 'secondary importance', and while 'very learned and original', they showed a lack of 'political common sense'.[56]

---

[48] See Orth, 'Blackstone's Ghost', in Prest (ed.), *Re-Interpreting Blackstone's Commentaries* 125, 129–37 (citing contemporary legal textbooks), 139 (app I) (citations to court lists of required reading) ff.

[49] John V. Orth, 'A Progressive Jurist Confronts Blackstone: "A Very Narrowing Effect Upon Our Profession"', in Wifrid Prest, Anthony Page (eds.), *Blackstone's Critics* ___ (2018).

[50] E.g., *State v. Watkins* (2012) 720 SE2d 844, 848 (quoting 4 *Bl. Com.* *226–7).

[51] Gareth H. Jones, *sub nom.*, in A. W. B. Simpson (ed.), *Biographical Dictionary of the Common Law* (1984), 58 ff.

[52] Ibid., 59 ff.

[53] Emily Kadens, 'Justice Blackstone's Common Law Orthodoxy', (2009) 103 *Nw. U. L.R.* 1553, 1571–4 ff.

[54] Prest, *Blackstone* 227–31 ff.

[55] Edward Gibbon, *Memoirs of my Life* (Betty Radice, ed., 1984) 159 ff.

[56] 2 Lewis Namier, John Brooke, *The House of Commons, 1754–1790* (1964) 96 ff.

Of Blackstone's later career, the most interesting is his judicial service. The law professor on the bench is rare, more so in England than in America; in his day Justice Blackstone was *sui generis*. Shortly after being named to the Court of Common Pleas in 1770, he accommodated a fellow judge by transferring to King's Bench, then dominated by the dynamic Lord Mansfield. Within months he seized the opportunity of a vacancy to return to Common Pleas, a relative backwater. As with his career as a barrister and as an MP, his judicial service is commonly dismissed as 'not distinguished'.[57] After a comprehensive review of the cases, Harold Hanbury, one of Blackstone's successors as Vinerian Professor, seconded the negative assessment while loyally tempering its harshness: 'If there were few diamonds in his judicial necklace, at least there were no gewgaws.'[58]

Oft-cited is the observation of Sir William Scott (later Lord Stowell) that 'more new trials were granted in causes which came before him on circuit, than were granted on the decisions of any other judge who sat at Westminster in his time', explaining that Blackstone was so 'extremely diffident of his opinion' that he failed to argue for it vigorously with his fellow judges.[59] In *Onslow v. Horne*, for example, a libel action in which Blackstone initially presided, he ruled that even the slightest variation between the defendant's statement and the plaintiff's evidence—quoting the date as '11' instead of '11th'—was a fatal variance, but later silently joined in the judgment of the full court to grant a new trial.[60]

It is notoriously difficult to determine a judge's personal opinions from his decisions on the bench, but a judicial philosophy does often appear—in Blackstone's case, insistence on strict rules to limit judicial discretion. Although collegiality was the norm, and dissents discouraged, Blackstone overcame his diffidence and refused to go along with a judgment that he thought blurred the distinction between actions in trespass and in case (technically, trespass on the case). The former was the means to remedy injuries that were the direct result of the defendant's act, while the latter was to remedy injuries in which the result was indirect. In *Scott v. Shepherd*, an action in trespass, the defendant had tossed a lighted firecracker ('squib') into a crowded market, where it was twice picked up and thrown again before exploding and injuring the plaintiff. Today the issue would be whether the defendant's action was the proximate cause of the plaintiff's injury. In Blackstone's day it was whether the plaintiff had chosen the proper form of action. While the majority of the judges were not inclined to look 'with eagle's eyes' at the distinction between the forms and gave judgment in

[57] Jones, in Simpson (ed.), *Biographical Dictionary* 59 ff.

[58] Harold Hanbury, 'Blackstone as a Judge' (1959) 3 *Am. J. Legal Hist.* 1, 27 ff.

[59] Quoted in James Prior, *Life of Edmond Malone, Editor of Shakespeare* (1860), 431–2 ff. Blackstone provided Malone with some astute textual criticism.

[60] *Onslow v. Horne* 2 Black W 750, 96 ER 439; 3 Wils 176, 95 ER 999 (CP 1770). For Blackstone's handling of the trial, see Simon Stern, 'William Blackstone: Courtroom Dramatist?', in Prest (ed.), *Re-Interpreting Blackstone's Commentaries* 21, 27–9 ff.

favour of the plaintiff, Blackstone disagreed, insisting that the proper cause of action was case; in his opinion the plaintiff needed to start over again.[61]

By far Blackstone's most momentous judicial utterance came in *Perrin v. Blake*, a landmark property case concerning the notorious Rule in *Shelley's Case*. Made famous by Sir Edward Coke's report of the sixteenth-century case of *Wolfe v. Shelley*, the Rule defies simple statement but was clearly implicated in the will at issue.[62] Lord Mansfield, conceding that the devise was 'within the letter of *Shelley's* case',[63] nonetheless refused to apply the Rule if it would defeat the testator's intention. Removed to the Exchequer Chamber, where judges from the other two common law courts reviewed the decision, Mansfield's judgment was overturned. In a thorough and ultimately persuasive opinion, Blackstone worried that allowing a testator's intention to prevail over a rule of law would mean that 'every man would make a law for himself'. Reminiscent of his fear of 'equity without law'—and perhaps informed by contemporary concerns that Mansfield was ignoring the distinction between the two—Blackstone warned against 'vague discretionary law'.[64]

Closely related to Blackstone the judge is Blackstone the law reporter. From the time of his call to the bar in 1746, he had compiled notes of decided cases. These only increased in number and extent after his appointment to the bench. From a modern perspective, law reporting at the time was in a primitive state. There were no official reports in the modern sense, and individual reporters—judges as well as barristers—supplemented their incomes by publishing reports in their own names (nominative reports). Blackstone's Reports in two volumes were published posthumously by James Clitherow, his son-in-law and executor, to raise money for the estate.[65] A similar pecuniary motive may have led to the separate sale and publication of his important judgment in *Perrin*.[66] Although printed 'at the direction in his will' and 'from his manuscript', the Reports are generally accepted to have diminished Blackstone's reputation. Hanbury obliquely agrees: 'It has been suggested that his reports are the least satisfactory part of his life's work.'[67] Scholars have often palliated the defects of Blackstone's Reports with the supposition that he had intended to revise them before publication, but Kadens pointed out that there is no evidence to support that. She argued that the text of the Reports as published

---

[61] *Scott v. Shepherd* 2 Black W 892, 96 ER 525; 3 Wils 403, 95 ER 1124 (CP 1773).

[62] For a fuller statement of the Rule, see John V. Orth, 'The Mystery of the Rule in Shelley's Case' (2003) 7 *Green Bag 2d* 145–53 ff. Coke's report of *Wolfe v. Shelley* is in 1 Co. Rep. 93b, 76 ER 206 (CP 1581).

[63] 1 *Collectanea Juridica, Consisting of Tracts, Relative to the Law and Constitution of England* (Francis Hargrave, ed., no date) 283, 321 ff. Partial reports in 1 Black W 672, 96 ER 392; 4 Burr 2579, 98 ER 355 (KB 1770).

[64] 1 *A Collection of Tracts Relative to the Law of England* (Francis Hargrave, ed., 1787) 489, 491, 496 ff.

[65] Both volumes of Blackstone's Reports, abbreviated Bl. W. or Black W., are reprinted in 96 ER. Clitherow included a brief biography of Blackstone as a preface to 1 Black W., which is not reprinted in the English Reports. Blackstone's nephew, Henry Blackstone, also published reports, Black H., reprinted in 126 ER.

[66] See editor's note, 1 *A Collection of Tracts* 487.   [67] Hanbury (n. 58) 26.

is 'the text Blackstone intended for us to see'.[68] If that is so, one is tempted to recall that even Homer nods.

With multiple reports of the same cases, law reporting was a competitive industry, and a connoisseurship of reports developed. Lord Mansfield was well known for 'doubting the report' if he disagreed with its reasoning or result. Possibly irked by Blackstone's rejection of his decision in *Perrin*, Mansfield later said, 'We must not always rely on the words of reports, though under great names: Mr. Justice Blackstone's Reports are not very accurate.'[69] John William Wallace, a nineteenth-century U.S. Supreme Court reporter, critically examined all the nominative reports and charitably concluded that '[t]he matter of Sir Wm [sic] Blackstone's accuracy is the less important, as most of the cases [he reported] in the King's Bench are reported in Burrow, and most of those in the Common Pleas by Wilson,—two of the very best of all English reporters.'[70] Reports of all three cases mentioned above— *Onslow, Scott*, and *Perrin*—exist in more than one version. Variations appear among them—for instance, Wilson gives more extended coverage to the arguments of counsel—but it is difficult to determine their significance.

VII. WHY BLACKSTONE MATTERS

Blackstone's *Commentaries* were read by more people, non-lawyers as well as lawyers, than any other English law book. Their influence is difficult to overstate, and extends into the twenty-first century. Almost as momentous was Blackstone's influence on legal education. The demonstration effect of his Oxford lectures was immediately obvious in America, where the world's second professorship devoted to the common law was established in Virginia in 1779. While gradual, the transfer of legal education from the law office and the courts to the university, which Blackstone pioneered, had an enormous impact on legal development, as law professors contributed to the formation of generations of lawyers and themselves came to play a significant role in legal development.

Today Blackstone's emphasis on rigid rules both in the *Commentaries* and in his judicial decisions can be dismissed as legalistic, exalting the letter over the spirit of the law. Certainly he seems sometimes to defend the indefensible. And his faith in legal rules, at least if rigorously enforced, to protect individuals from the abuse of

---

[68] Kadens (n. 53) 1579.   [69] *Devon v. Watts* 1 Dougl 86, 93, 99 ER 59, 64 (KB 1779).

[70] John William Wallace, *The Reporters Arranged and Characterized with Incidental Remarks* 444 (4th edn., 1882) (referring to the 5 volumes of James Burrow's Reports, in 97–8 ER and the 3 volumes of George Wilson's Reports, in 95 ER).

power may often seem naïve. But his warnings about discretionary justice, which would de-legitimate equitable resolutions by enlightened judges, sound more persuasive when judges are perceived to be oppressive or politicized.

Blackstone's lucid description of England's chartered liberties contributed directly to the development of a constitutionalist and rights-based jurisprudence, not just in America but throughout the world. His vision of law as grounded in the historical experience of a particular nation, rather than in rationalist principles, earned him condemnation as not 'scientific'.[71] But his anthropological approach has proved more effective in understanding the interaction of law and society than analytic jurisprudence. And his humane vision—for example, his belief that 'there is no man so indigent or wretched, but he may demand a supply sufficient for all the necessities of life, from the more opulent part of the community'[72]—was certainly more attractive than the philosophy of the utilitarian Gradgrinds who invented the fearsome poor houses and their modern successors. The uncritical tone of Blackstone's presentation, which attracted Bentham's derision, may have stabilized legal traditions, but at the same time, his limpid exposition of the law's fictions and artificiality opened it to inspection and criticism as never before, and in its own way contributed to the modernization of the common law.

BIBLIOGRAPHY

Albert Alschuler, 'Rediscovering Blackstone' (1996) 145 *U. Pa. L.R.* 1

Daniel J. Boorstin, *The Mysterious Science of the Law: An Essay on Blackstone's Commentaries Showing How Blackstone, Employing 18th Century Ideas of Science, Religion, History, Aesthetics, and Philosophy, Made of the Law at Once a Conservative and a Mysterious Science* (Harvard University Press, 1941)

Harold Hanbury, 'Blackstone as a Judge' (1959) 3 *Am. J. Legal Hist.* 1

Gareth H. Jones, 'Introduction', *The Sovereignty of the Law* (University Toronto Press, 1973)

Emily Kadens, 'Justice Blackstone's Common Law Orthodoxy' (2009) 103 *Nw. U. L.R.* 1553

Duncan Kennedy, 'The Structure of Blackstone's Commentaries' (1979) 28 *Buff. L.R.* 205

Ann Jordan Laeuchli (ed.), *A Bibliographical Catalog of William Blackstone* (Hein & Co., 2015)

Paul Lucas, 'Blackstone and the Reform of the Legal Profession' (1962) 77 *E.H.R.* 456

S. F. C. Milsom, 'The Nature of Blackstone's Achievement' (1981) 1 *Oxford J. Legal Studies* 1

Dennis R. Nolan, 'Sir William Blackstone and the New American Republic: A Study of Intellectual Impact' (1976) 51 *N.Y.U. L.R.* 731

Wilfrid Prest, *William Blackstone: Law and Letters in the Eighteenth Century* (Oxford University Press, 2008)

Wilfrid Prest (ed.), *Blackstone and His Commentaries: Biography, Law, History* (Hart Pub., 2009)

[71] See, e.g., *Encyclopedia Britannica* (11th edn., 1911) *sub nom.*

[72] 1 *Bl. Com.* 127, 1 *Bl. Com.* *131 (referring to the eighteenth-century Poor Laws) ff.

Wilfrid Prest, Anthony Page (eds.), *Blackstone's Critics* (Hart Pub., 2018)

Wilfrid Prest (ed.), *Re-interpreting Blackstone's Commentaries: A Seminal Text in National and International Contexts* (Hart Pub., 2014)

Alan Watson, 'The Structure of Blackstone's Commentaries' (1988) 97 *Yale L.J.* 795

CHAPTER 21

JEREMY BENTHAM (1748–1832)

PHILIP SCHOFIELD[*]

I.

SINCE the late 1960s Bentham scholarship has been driven by the appearance of volumes in the new authoritative edition of *The Collected Works of Jeremy Bentham*, prepared by the Bentham Project under the supervision of University College London's (UCL) Bentham Committee, and the successive General Editorships of J. H. Burns (1961–1979), J. R. Dinwiddy (1978–1983), F. Rosen (1983–2003), and the present author (1995 onwards). The thirty-third volume in the edition, entitled *Preparatory Principles*, was published in December 2016.[1] UCL possesses not only Bentham's physical remains in the form of his auto-icon, but also his literary remains in the form of around 60,000 folios of his manuscripts (a further 12,500 folios are deposited in the British Library). The earliest attempt at a major edition of Bentham's writings had been undertaken within a decade or so of his death by his literary executor John Bowring.[2] By the 1930s the Bowring edition was judged to be unsatisfactory as the basis for modern scholarship, and recognizing the role played in the foundation of the institution by Benthamite utilitarians and accepting

---

[*] Bentham Project, Faculty of Laws, University College London.
[1] Jeremy Bentham, *Preparatory Principles*, D. G. Long, Philip Schofield (eds.), (2016).
[2] *The Works of Jeremy Bentham*, John Bowring (ed.), 11 vols. (1838–1843).

its responsibility to do something with Bentham's papers (which Bowring had deposited in its Library), UCL established the first incarnation of the Bentham Committee with a view to producing an authoritative edition. Little progress had been made when the Second World War intervened, and the edition was abandoned. In the meantime Werner Stark, a Czech refugee working under the auspices of John Maynard Keynes, prepared a three-volume edition of Bentham's economic writings which was eventually published in the early 1950s.[3] With the encouragement of A. J. Ayer, the second and current incarnation of the Bentham Committee was established in 1959. Rejecting all previous editions of Bentham's writings, including that of Stark, the Committee made a fresh start, dividing the new edition into two main elements, the correspondence and the works, the latter based on works printed by Bentham himself, as well as the manuscripts. As the 'backbone' to the whole edition, priority was given to the correspondence, with the first two volumes being published in 1968, and the twelfth in 2006, thereby reproducing all known letters both from and to Bentham up to the end of June 1828. One more volume will complete the correspondence through to Bentham's death in 1832, though a further volume of indexes and supplementary letters—that is, those discovered after the appropriate volume had been published—will also be required. In the 'General Preface to the Collected Works', published in the first volume of Correspondence in 1968 and in An Introduction to the Principles of Morals and Legislation (hereafter I.P.M.L.), the first volume to appear in the works in 1970, it was cautiously estimated that the edition would run to thirty-eight volumes.[4] Having, as noted above, published the thirty-third volume, one might assume that the edition is close to completion. My conservative estimate, however, is that the edition will require not thirty-eight volumes, but eighty. Significant work has been undertaken on texts that will produce a dozen or so more volumes, namely Rationale of Judicial Evidence (5 volumes), Scotch Reform (2 or 3 volumes), Not Paul, but Jesus (2 volumes), and Logic and Language (1 volume). It is perhaps fair to say that in terms of work done as opposed to volumes published, we are about half-way through.

Why does the Bentham edition matter? The short answer is, because Bentham matters. The nineteenth-century utilitarian philosopher Henry Sidgwick claimed that Bentham was the pre-eminent representative of the Enlightenment and that Benthamism was 'the legacy left to the nineteenth century by the eighteenth', being the force against which the new 'philosophy of Restoration and Reaction has had to struggle continually with varying success'.[5] Richard Whatmore has pointed out to me that many of the leading figures of the eighteenth-century Enlightenment, by the

[3] Jeremy Bentham's Economic Writings, Werner Stark (ed.), 3 vols. (1952–1954).
[4] The Correspondence of Jeremy Bentham: Volume I, T. L. S. Sprigge (ed.), (1968) p. vii ff; Jeremy Bentham, An Introduction to the Principles of Morals and Legislation, J. H. Burns, H. L. A. Hart (eds.), (1970) p. vii ff.
[5] Henry Sidgwick, 'Bentham and Benthamism in Politics and Ethics', in Miscellaneous Essays and Addresses (1904) 136 ff.

time of their deaths around the turn of the nineteenth century, had come to believe that their revolutionary project for social reformation had failed and that their final works were beset with pessimism. From this perspective, the significance of Sidgwick's comment begins to emerge. The eighteenth-century Bentham, influenced by the radical Enlightenment of Helvétius, Voltaire, D'Alembert, and Diderot, seeing on the one hand the emergence of stable democracy in America, and on the other hand experiencing mistreatment at the hands of the British establishment over his panopticon prison scheme, developed into the politically radical Bentham of the nineteenth century, advocating at first 'democratic ascendancy' within the British Constitution and then a democratic republic, stripped of monarch, aristocracy, and established church. Bentham took the radical programme for parliamentary reform, with its demands for universal suffrage, secret ballot, equal electoral districts, and annual elections, and its traditional basis either in natural rights or the Anglo-Saxon constitution, and gave it a utilitarian justification, which paved the way, if not for the Great Reform Act of 1832, certainly for the People's Charter of 1848. As J. H. Burns expressed it, Bentham's career can be characterized as a move from 'Radical Enlightenment' to 'Philosophic Radicalism'.[6] The hopes of the Enlightenment for a rational basis for social organization, which seemed to have been dashed by the excesses of the French Revolution and the conservative reaction that followed, were kept alive and given systematic form, appropriate for a democratic, liberal age, by Bentham's programme for political, legal, and ecclesiastical reform, which, at the same time that it aimed to promote the interest of the community as a whole, did not threaten the security of property.

As well as its historical significance, Bentham's thought continues to be of philosophical importance. He was the founder of the doctrine of classical utilitarianism, which remains one of the main strands in liberal moral philosophy; his so-called felicific calculus is the basis for cost-benefit analysis in economics; he set the parameters for the modern discipline of jurisprudence by distinguishing law as it is from law as it ought to be, offering a profound critique of the natural law and the English Common Law, and proposing a whole range of legal reforms; his commentary on the French Declaration of Rights of 1789, with its memorable phrase 'nonsense upon stilts',[7] constitutes a devastating attack on the philosophy of natural rights, and hence on that of human rights; and he put forward perhaps the most radical vision of the democratic state ever devised. Furthermore, Bentham looms large in studies of surveillance thanks to Michel Foucault's account of the panopticon prison as a model for the modern state. Foucault went on to state that 'Bentham is more important for our society than Kant and Hegel'.[8] Prominent

---

[6] J. H. Burns, 'Jeremy Bentham: From Radical Enlightenment to Philosophical Radicalism' (1984) 8 *Bentham Newsletter* 4 ff.

[7] Jeremy Bentham, *Rights, Representation, and Reform: Nonsense upon Stilts and other Writings on the French Revolution*, P. Schofield, C. Pease-Watkin, C. Blamires (eds.), (2002) 317 ff.

[8] Michel Foucault, *Dits et écrits II. 1976–1988*, D. Defert, F. Ewald, J. Lagrange (eds.), (2004) 594.

scholars who have recently recognized Bentham's importance for their respective fields include Judith Resnik, Jon Elster, Faramarz Dabhoiwala, and David Armitage.[9] Over the years, while some have found Benthamism, and even Bentham himself, distasteful, few have dismissed him completely. If one accepts that Bentham deserves a place amongst the great thinkers, or merely the influential thinkers, the provision of authoritative texts is vital, not only for Bentham specialists, but for scholars from a wide variety of disciplines where Bentham's ideas have either been historically influential or have the potential to contribute to present and future debates.

If interest in Bentham is set to increase as more volumes appear in the *Collected Works*, the basis on which work is undertaken on the new edition should be a matter of interest to the scholarly community. The Bentham Committee originally envisaged that editorial work would be carried out on each volume by 'a scholar in the appropriate field',[10] but this model proved unsatisfactory, mainly because of the complexity of the tasks involved and the difficulty of maintaining a consistent approach. Hence, under Frederick Rosen's General Editorship, editorial work was brought 'in-house', with researchers, usually post-doctoral, appointed as editors, being supported by the General Editor. The employment of researchers depends upon the provision of financial resources. UCL's Faculty of Laws currently supports the full-time post of the General Editor, but otherwise the Bentham Project relies upon external funding. As General Editor, I have received generous support from the Economic and Social Research Council, the Arts and Humanities Research Council, and the Leverhulme Trust. I have also received significant grants from the Wellcome Trust, the Mellon Foundation, and the European Research Council, while the British Academy, which recognizes the Bentham Project as one of its sponsored research projects, provides a modest annual grant. I have adopted an opportunistic strategy towards fundraising, in that I attempt to match a particular volume or series of volumes with both the remit of a particular funding organization and the expertise of a member of my research staff. For research staff, a post-doctoral post is a useful stepping stone into a permanent academic position, and so their Benthamic expertise, built up over the course of a grant, is lost at that point to the Bentham Project, though in the meantime the researcher has to endure the anxiety that accompanies a time-limited post and the impending threat of redundancy. As things stand it is impossible to put any long-term strategy in place for progress in the edition because of the reliance on such external funding, which is, in relation to the overall length of time needed to complete the Bentham edition, extremely short-term, with grants being awarded for a maximum of five years and often only

---

[9] Judith Resnik, 'Bring Back Bentham: "Open Courts," "Terror Trials," and Public Spheres' (2011) 5 *Law and Ethics of Human Rights* Art. 1; Jon Elster, *Securities against Misrule: Juries, Assemblies, Elections* (2013); Faramerz Dabhoiwala, 'Lust and Liberty' (2010) 207 *Past and Present* 89 ff; David Armitage, 'Globalizing Jeremy Bentham' (2011) 32 *History of Political Thought* 63 ff.

[10] Bentham (n. 4 *Correspondence*) p. vii.

for two or three. Contrast this with the recently established Averroes edition at the University of Cologne, which has received funding for four research posts for twenty-five years each, with the intention of seeing the eighteen-volume programme through to completion. The most efficient and most beneficial means of producing the Bentham edition would have been to begin with a guaranteed endowment, thereby allowing work to proceed on a chronological basis (other strategies, such as to focus on the most famous works or on those that were attracting most attention at the time from Bentham specialists or scholars more generally, would not have been any less random than the current situation) and General Editors to concentrate on editing rather than on fundraising. The challenge of supporting long-term research projects is one that British academia has failed to meet.

II.

Returning to the relationship between the new edition and interpretive scholarship, the first volumes of works to appear were concerned with Bentham's early writings on law and legal philosophy, taking advantage of the fact that one of the scholars 'in an appropriate field' to take a serious interest in the editing of Bentham was the prominent Oxford legal philosopher H. L. A. Hart. Three volumes appeared under Hart's editorship or co-editorship with J. H. Burns: *I.P.M.L.* and *Of Laws in General*, both in 1970,[11] and *A Comment on the Commentaries and A Fragment on Government* in 1977.[12] These volumes contained material written between about 1775 and 1782 and were related to Bentham's attempt to draw up a penal code. Hart saw Bentham as the originator of the doctrine of legal positivism, of which he had himself given the standard account in *The Concept of Law* (1961). Over a course of years Hart produced a series of brilliant essays on Bentham, collected in *Essays on Bentham* (1982). Bentham specialists began to explore in detail the three newly edited volumes, and there followed a series of major books,[13] focusing on Bentham's legal philosophy and his critique of the Common Law. These authors also drew on Bentham's correspondence, supplemented where appropriate by texts drawn from the Bowring edition (some of which are English translations from Étienne Dumont's French recensions of Bentham's manuscripts—but that is another story). Much less attention has, on the whole, been paid to Bentham's later writings, though Rosen's

---

[11] Jeremy Bentham, *Of Laws in General*, H. L. A. Hart (ed.), (1970).

[12] Jeremy Bentham, *A Comment on the Commentaries and A Fragment on Government*, J. H. Burns, H. L. A. Hart (eds.), (1977).

[13] See the works by Harrison, Kelly, Lieberman, Lobban, Long, and Postema listed in the bibliography.

writings on the constitutional code are a notable exception, and to comparing Bentham's earlier and later writings, with Oren Ben-Dor's *Constitutional Limits and the Public Sphere* forming the exception here.[14]

No one was much inclined to dispute Hart's view of Bentham as a legal positivist, in that Bentham had distinguished clearly between law as it is and law as it ought to be, and in that this distinction appeared to map onto the twentieth-century distinction between fact and value (or description and prescription). In Hart's view, Bentham had developed a set of morally neutral terms in order to describe the nature of law (law as it is), as he himself had done in *The Concept of Law*, and had distinguished this exercise from that of assessing the goodness of the content of the law (law as it ought to be). I began to have doubts about Hart's approach when working on the manuscripts for Bentham's essay on 'Ontology' and then on Bentham's writings on logic more generally, of which the essay on 'Ontology' formed a part. Bentham's understanding of ontology and epistemology did not seem to be compatible with conceptual analysis, as it was understood by Hart and other twentieth-century philosophers. There was also the related question of the naturalistic fallacy. Many commentators sympathetic to Bentham tried to defend him from the charge that he had based his ethics on facts about the physical world, but it seemed plain to me that this was what he had explicitly done, since in his view there was no other meaningful basis. Given that Bentham argued that existence could only be predicated of physical matter, there seemed to be no space for any independent realm of ideas, or in other words for non-natural concepts. The whole enterprise of conceptual analysis would, I thought, have made no sense to Bentham.

Doubts were further raised in my mind by a paper given by the late Amanda Perreau-Saussine, who argued that Bentham was not a legal positivist in the Hartian sense.[15] It also came about that, with a view to producing a paperback edition of *Of Laws in General*, I began to check the accuracy of the transcription of the manuscripts that had been published in the original edition. Having discovered a number of transcription errors that had not been listed in the *Corrigenda* to that edition, I went on to find that serious mistakes had been made in the ordering of the material within some of the chapters. Perhaps understandably, given the disordered state of the manuscripts, the complexity of the subject-matter, the relative inexperience of the researchers who did much of the editorial work, and hence the lack of appreciation of Bentham's working methods, the volume presented a very misleading and confused version of the text. I embarked on the task of establishing a text that was faithful to Bentham's intentions. I discovered three major stages in the drafting of the text and presented the material in such a way that allows the reader to reconstruct them. When I presented these findings to the Bentham

---

[14]   See the works by Rosen and Ben-Dor listed in the bibliography.

[15]   Amanda Perreau-Saussine, 'Bentham and the Boot-Strappers of Jurisprudence: The Moral Commitments of a Rationalist Legal Positivist' (2004) 63 *Cambridge L.J.* 346 ff.

Committee, it was decided that the new text should not appear as a second edition of *Of Laws in General*, but should supersede that volume in the *Collected Works*, and appear under Bentham's original title, namely *Of the Limits of the Penal Branch of Jurisprudence*,[16] and thereby reassert its provenance as the seventeenth chapter of a proposed introduction to a penal code, of which the text published as *I.P.M.L.* composed the first sixteen chapters. I wonder whether Hart chose the title *Of Laws in General* (the phrase appears on a related manuscript, but was not intended by Bentham as a new title for *Limits*) because it seemed to link Bentham's work to his own theory of law by presenting it as an exercise in conceptual analysis? If that had been the case, it would have been akin to putting the cart before the horse, in that Hart would have allowed his own philosophical views to influence the way he had edited a historical text.

Having become concerned in the first place by the standard Hartian interpretation of Bentham as a legal positivist and then concerned that this interpretation had played some role in distorting the way in which Hart had approached the editing of *Of Laws in General*, I began to think about the relationship between Bentham's legal theory and more generally the principle of utility on the one hand, and his writings on logic and language (or more generally on ontology and epistemology) on the other hand.[17] I was also perplexed by the fact that the latter were generally referred to as Bentham's 'theory of fictions', a description which appears to have originated with Charles Kay Ogden, who republished Bowring's edition of the relevant manuscripts in the 1930s.[18] The assumption that 'fictions' and what Bentham termed 'fictitious entities' amount to the same thing has produced, and continues to produce, confusion in Bentham scholarship. A fiction, for Bentham, was a false statement of fact, while a fictitious entity was an abstraction, as I will explain below.

My confidence that it is appropriate to question Hart's interpretation of Bentham, and to emphasize Bentham's views on logic and language as the basis for this scepticism, has been strengthened by the work I have undertaken on *Preparatory Principles*. This volume had its genesis over forty years ago, when Douglas Long began the process of producing a pioneering, encoded transcript of the manuscripts, using a computer programme developed at the University of Western Ontario, which anticipated much of the work that is now standardly done in textual scholarship in the digital humanities. The material reproduced in *Preparatory Principles* does not form a traditional work, in the sense of a text divided into chapters and sections and following a coherent structure, but consists of a series of numbered passages, probably written over three or four years in the mid-1770s, in which Bentham noted ideas as and when they occurred to him. The work contains

[16] Jeremy Bentham, *Of the Limits of the Penal Branch of Jurisprudence*, Philip Schofield (ed.), 2010.

[17] Philip Schofield, 'Jeremy Bentham and HLA Hart's "Utilitarian Tradition in Jurisprudence"' (2010) 1 *Jurisprudence* 147 ff.

[18] Charles K. Ogden, *Bentham's Theory of Fictions* (1932).

multiple passages dealing with ontology and language, from which an illuminating account of Bentham's views can be pieced together, and the centrality of those views to his whole enterprise appreciated. It would have scarcely been possible to piece together such an account without the clarity that has been given to the material by its presentation in a *Collected Works* volume, including a table of contents, indexes, and a wealth of annotation. Bentham had developed a detailed account of his underlying philosophy of language, with its related notions of ontology and epistemology, by the mid-1770s (though that should be no surprise given Bentham's exposition of 'duty' in a well-known footnote in *A Fragment on Government*),[19] and that this gave rise to his distinctive philosophy of law. In short, it explains Bentham's originality. Once the centrality of Bentham's philosophy of language has been recognized, scholars will not only be able to reassess his writings on jurisprudence, but also to develop a more complete understanding of his voluminous later writings on codification in general, on the penal, civil, and constitutional codes in particular, on procedure and evidence, and everything else besides.

III.

One of the main themes in *Preparatory Principles* is what Bentham termed 'metaphysics', by which he meant the philosophy of language, and which was the subject-matter of universal jurisprudence. 'The business of Metaphysics', remarked Bentham, 'is . . . to examine what ideas we have belonging to the terms we use, and whether they are clear or no'. Every science had its 'leading terms', which were used in order to make other terms understood. The metaphysics of the science of law consisted 'in ascertaining the meaning, in fixing [the] ideas, belonging to the several terms of universal Jurisprudence, through the medium of which the technical terms of the particular Jurisprudence of any country are endeavoured to be explained'.[20] Bentham had in mind such terms as right, duty, and power, which, he claimed, could not be defined by the ordinary Aristotelian method *per genus et differentiam*. This in itself was an extraordinary insight, and we shall perhaps never know how Bentham arrived at it (though the answer may lie buried in some as yet untranscribed manuscript). The task of giving expositions of these terms belonged to the field of universal jurisprudence. What, then, was universal jurisprudence, and how were we to make sense of its key terms?

---

[19] Bentham (n. 12) 494 n. ff.   [20] Bentham (n. 1) 196 ff.

In the second section of *Limits*, Bentham distinguished three branches of jurisprudence. Censorial jurisprudence ascertained what the law 'ought to be'; (local) expository jurisprudence ascertained 'what the *law* is' in a particular nation or group of nations; and universal (expository) jurisprudence, which was relevant to 'all nations whatsoever', dealt with the words 'appropriated to the subject of law', which 'in all languages are pretty exactly correspondent to one another: which comes to the same thing nearly as if they were the same. Of this stamp, for example', continued Bentham, 'are those which correspond to the words *power, right, obligation, liberty*, and many others'. The subject-matter of universal jurisprudence was 'the import of words: to be, strictly speaking, universal, it must confine itself to terminology'.[21] Universal jurisprudence, as Bentham explained in the 'Preface' written for the publication of *I.P.M.L.* in 1789, was concerned with the '*form*' of the law, by which he meant

its method and terminology; including a view of the origination and connexion of the ideas expressed by the short list of terms, the exposition of which contains all that can be said with propriety to belong to the head of *universal jurisprudence*.

In a note, he added: 'Such as obligation, right, power, possession, title, exemption, immunity, franchise, privilege, nullity, validity, and the like.'[22] According to Bentham, each legal system had terms for entities that could be found in every legal system. The task of universal jurisprudence was to provide a sensible exposition for those terms.

I.P.M.L. and *Limits* were in effect exercises in universal jurisprudence, but while Bentham's philosophy of language constituted the ground, so to speak, on which these works were built, within them he gave no systematic exposition of his method. Such an exposition, as noted above, does exist in *Preparatory Principles*, where Bentham explained that the key to unlocking the mystery of legal discourse lay in demonstrating its relationship to the physical world. We grasped 'the signification of words, and [the] origination of the ideas which they signify' when 'the idea annext to any one word' was distinguished from 'the idea annext to any other', and when it had been shown 'how all the ideas we have that are complex, arise from, and are made up of, simple ones'.[23] Bentham explicitly followed John Locke in stating that ideas consisted of '[t]he several objects we are said to have in our mind when we are thinking'. Furthermore, he followed David Hume in distinguishing ideas into 'ideas properly so called' and 'impressions'. Taking sight, for instance, an impression of an object was present in the mind at the time that we perceived it, while an idea was a recollection of the object. Our ideas or impressions of, for instance, figure, extension, colour, smell, heat, hardness, space, and time were all derived

---

[21] Bentham (n. 16) 16 ff. [22] Bentham, *I.P.M.L.* (n. 4) 6 & n. ff.
[23] Bentham (n. 1) 265 ff.

from perception.[24] Bentham also accepted Locke's distinction between 'simple ideas' and 'mixed modes', to the extent that abstract terms ('mixed modes') could only be understood by reference to simple ideas, and that simple ideas were derived from bodies, that is physical objects, that had been perceived by our senses.[25] For Bentham, simple ideas consisted of 'events' and 'situations', both of which impressed 'sensible images on the mind', and both of which were dependent on 'bodies': events were bodies in motion, while situations were bodies at rest.[26] While matter and motion constituted everything that was perceived by 'our exterior senses', these were not 'two distinct things', because, 'The motion is not any thing that exists separately from matter'.[27] The single source of simple ideas, therefore, was matter, distributed into different bodies. It was linguistic usage that suggested that motion and rest existed separately from body: 'The body that moves, and the motion that it makes, may be spoken of . . . as two things: but in fact they are but one thing. The one thing that exists is the body itself that makes the motion'.[28] As well as sensations generated by external bodies in motion and at rest, simple ideas included internal sensations such as pain, pleasure, and volition, since these were simple ideas, which 'nobody defines, or if any one defines, nobody makes clearer by defining': indeed, they could not be defined, because only complex ideas could be defined.[29]

Bentham did not, however, accept Locke's view that all mixed modes could be explained by showing how they consisted of a combination of simple ideas, since certain abstract terms represented entities that could not be analysed in this way. Abstractions such as golden mountains and diamond billiard balls, for instance, were combinations of simple ideas put together by the imagination. This kind of abstract term represented entities that were quite different from the abstractions that were the subject-matter of universal jurisprudence.[30] Bentham's insight, as noted above, was that attempts to define abstract terms, such as 'Power, Possession, Property, &c. in Morals: Ratio, Part, Multiple, &c. in Mathematics', by means of 'the old method *per genus et differentiam*' were doomed to failure because the terms in question had no superior genus to which they could be referred. The terms characteristic of universal jurisprudence, such as power, duty, and right, had no superior genus by which they could be made known. If you heard the word cacalianthemum and were told that it was a sort of plant, you would gain some idea of the import of the word. A right or power, however, was not a sort of anything. The expositors who used 'the old method' nevertheless clung to their '*routine*', and attempted to find a higher genus: 'The consequence is they either take up such a definition as is useless, or give up altogether the task of finding one, as being either unnecessary or impracticable.'[31]

[24] Ibid., 382. See John Locke, *An Essay Concerning Human Understanding*, P. H. Nidditch (ed.), (1975) 47 ff., and David Hume, *A Treatise of Human Nature: A Critical Edition*, D. F. Norton, M. J. Norton (eds.), 3 vols. (2007) i. 7 ff.

[25] Bentham (n. 1) 95. See Locke (n. 24) 292.   [26] Ibid., 169.   [27] Ibid., 369.

[28] Ibid., 169.   [29] Ibid., 102.   [30] Ibid., 170 ff.   [31] Ibid., 97 ff., 111 ff.

The failure to explain the meaning of words by definition *per genus et differentiam* did not mean that the attempt to define such words was hopeless. There was, in fact, 'one way' that could be successful, though it was a method that 'never has been attempted yet'.[32]

Bentham explained that, in terms of language, both things with physical existence and abstractions were represented by noun substantives, which he divided into proper and improper, respectively: the former were the names of real entities, and the latter the names of fictitious entities. 'A proper substantive, the name of a real entity, is understood immediately and of itself it offers a certain image to the conception. An improper substantive offers no such image. Of itself it has no meaning. It means nothing till, with other words, it be compounded into some sentence. It then is seen to have a meaning, which is the clearer, the more clearly it is seen to be equivalent to some sentence the terms of which are names of real entities.'[33] Bentham's new method, then, was to produce 'a chain of Definitions', where the first definition consisted of 'words expressive of simple ideas'.[34] The chain of definitions had to begin with simple ideas, that is those images in the mind created by bodies that were immediately perceptible and were not themselves definable. Given that '[t]he ideas we have are *all* ultimately derived from substances; that is, from the *several natural bodies that surround us*', it followed that '*The origin of our ideas relative to Law can, therefore,* be sought for in no other source.'[35] Hence, it was only by relating the terms of universal jurisprudence to terms that signified simple ideas that the former would be understood: 'These [simple ideas] are the Capital we have to trade with. These, to speak with the Algebraists, are our known quantities, our a's, b's and c's. 'Tis by reference to these that we are to elicit the import of the x's, y's and z's, whose import there is occasion to make known.'[36]

Paraphrasis was the term that Bentham gave to the technique that he invented in order to expound the terminology of universal jurisprudence: 'To expound an improper substantive by Paraphrasis is to compleat it into a sentence, and for that sentence to find an equivalent sentence consisting of words significative of real entities'; and it is 'by Paraphrasis and Paraphrasis alone that fictitious entities, entities expressed by improper substantives, can be *expounded*'.[37] In order to understand what was meant by the word right, it had to be included in a sentence, and that sentence expounded 'by such another sentence as contains in it words that *are* capable of being defined'.[38] The word right was a noun substantive, but it did not signify a substance, neither a 'real concrete' substance nor a 'fictitious abstract' substance (that is, presumably, a fabulous entity), and hence was no more significant of itself than a preposition. In order to understand the word 'for', for instance, it was necessary to begin with a sentence in which the word appeared, and the same was true in relation to the word 'right'.[39] Take the notion of a legal power, which was not

[32] Ibid., 157. [33] Ibid., 401. [34] Ibid., 104. [35] Ibid., 200.
[36] Ibid., 103. [37] Ibid., 386. [38] Ibid., 247. [39] Ibid., 249.

the name of anything that existed and did not have a superior genus. In order to understand the idea, the term had to be placed in a sentence, or more precisely in a proposition: 'This proposition may be translated into another proposition that is equivalent: and that is composed of words which, taken separately, shall either be capable of a definition, or, what is still better, need none.' Hence, instead of saying that a power was a sort of some other thing, one might say that, 'To create a power in a person over a thing, or what is shorter and more familiar, to give a person a power over a thing, is to restrain another person from meddling with that thing, the first person being left unrestrained.'[40]

By the time that Bentham had finished adding to his 'Preparatory Principles' manuscripts, he had settled on the terminology that he would apply throughout the remainder of his career—noun substantives were used to signify entities that were fictitious, fabulous, and real. First, names of real entities represented bodies existing in the physical world: 'The only objects that really exist are *substances*: they are the only real entities.' The names of fictitious entities represented entities that did not actually exist in the physical world, but had to be spoken of as if they did exist.[41] Fabulous entities were the product of the imagination: 'such beings as, in the fables of the Poets, for example, have been represented and spoken of as really existing. Such as the Heathen Gods, the Chimæra, the Dragon, the Cockatrice &c.' Names of fabulous entities were words which represented 'assemblages of simple ideas which, though no where co-existing in any real subject, are manifest and determinate'.[42]

Bentham identified several benefits that would result from the creation of a science of universal jurisprudence. A first benefit was that there would be an end to disputes of law, as opposed to questions of fact. 'All Questions of Law are no more than questions concerning the import of words. Questions the solution of which depends upon skill in Metaphysics. As that master science, therefore, advances to it's perfection, this source of litigation will be contracted.'[43] A second benefit was that sensible communication would be established between jurists of different nations: 'By banishing as many as we can spare of the terms peculiar to our own local Jurisprudence, and giving a clear and steady exposition of such as we are obliged to retain in terms of universal jurisprudence, an easy and profitable intercourse may be kept up between the Jurists of the several nations, and an Englishman might read a comment upon his own laws in the languages of Spain or Sweden.'[44] A third benefit was that that, by giving 'paraphrases' of the various names of fictitious legal entities, Bentham would not only be able to use these terms in his own work, but would also clarify their meaning when used by other writers.[45]

Bentham was not involved in some form of conceptual analysis that would give rise to morally neutral legal terms, as Hart suggested. The obvious objection to this claim is that universal jurisprudence consisted in precisely such an enterprise, in

[40] Ibid., 380.   [41] Ibid., 424.   [42] Ibid., 386 ff.   [43] Ibid., 282.
[44] Ibid., 260.   [45] Ibid., 345.

that Bentham aimed to produce an exposition of legal terms (and of all abstract terms) that was true for all times and places, and as such was simply a matter of fact. This raises the difficult question of the notion of truth in Bentham's thought and its relationship to utility.[46] Suffice it to say that Bentham linked utility to truth in his argument that the correct (or true) exposition of legal terms, through universal jurisprudence, was a morally valuable endeavour. This point is supported by Bentham's theory of motivation, according to which there could be no morally neutral activity. All actions were motivated by a desire for pleasure and an aversion to pain, and therefore aimed (as far as the actor was concerned) at some morally desirable end. To say that an action was unmotivated was to talk nonsense. To say that something was morally neutral was, for Bentham, to say that it did not matter, because the only things that mattered were pleasure and pain. Whatever involved pleasure and pain involved moral value (whether positive or negative). A person would not embark on the enterprise of universal jurisprudence if they did not anticipate some value from the activity. To put it crudely, there was no point to moral neutrality.

IV.

Returning to *Limits*, the text, having expanded to the length of a book, was abandoned by Bentham. He later explained, in the 'Preface' to *I.P.M.L.*, that he had 'found himself unexpectedly entangled in an unsuspected corner of the metaphysical maze'.[47] While he did not state explicitly what the problem was that he had encountered, it was quite possibly that which he had set out to solve in *Limits*— namely that of explaining the distinction between penal and civil law. To make sense of this distinction in terms of universal jurisprudence, Bentham realized that he had to explain what was meant by a single and complete law. Instead of seeing the distinction as being, as in English law, between two different subject-matters of law, where the punishment for the penal or criminal offence was regarded as either more severe or more disreputable than that for the civil, Bentham came to recognize it as a logical distinction: every single and complete law had a penal and a civil element and, furthermore, a procedural element. Constitutional law was made up of a combination of civil and penal law and so fell into the overall pattern. Hence, a self-standing penal code, without the civil and procedural codes, would make no

---

[46] Philip Schofield, 'Jeremy Bentham on Utility and Truth' (2015) 41 *History of European Ideas* 1125 ff.
[47] Bentham, *I.P.M.L.* (n. 4) 1.

sense; nor would a self-standing civil code. Bentham seems to have spent a great deal of time reworking his ideas on these fundamental questions when visiting his brother Samuel in Russia in 1785–1788, when he had unfulfilled hopes of presenting a penal code to the Empress Catherine II. It was for this reason that Bentham wrote in French: his manuscripts survive under the headings of 'Projet Forme' and 'Projet Matière', that is form and matter, which appear to relate to universal and censorial jurisprudence, respectively. If we find that it was here that Bentham settled with himself the question of the relationship between the various branches of law, we will have a vital link between Bentham's early concern with the philosophy of law and his later schemes of codification, when his ambition was to write not a penal code only but a complete code, which he termed a 'pannomion'.

As a very brief example of Bentham's later views on codification, take his letter written in 1811 to James Madison, the President of the United States of America, where he noted that 'whatsoever features, whether of excellence or imperfection' were found in his codes would be related either to '*Matter*' or to '*Form*'. The excellence of the matter would be demonstrated in the rationale, which would consist of a '*perpetual Commentary of Reasons*' that would accompany the 'imperative or regulative matter', and show the connection between the provisions and '*the all-governing principle*, viz. *the principle of utility*'.[48] Here we have the link to censorial jurisprudence. The form of the law was concerned with not only the terminology of the law, but the arrangement of its matter in such a way as to be 'cognoscible' to those subject to it. Whatever 'practical good effect', noted Bentham, arose from the matter of the law, no matter how excellent in itself, would depend upon the law's 'cognoscibility'. The form of the law, the subject-matter of universal jurisprudence, included not only the proper exposition of key legal terms, but also the way in which the matter of the code would be presented to those subject to it. Hence, proposed securities for cognoscibility included the division of the pannomion into a general code and a series of particular codes; its division into matter of constant and matter of occasional concernment; and its division into main text and expository matter, the latter consisting of explanations of particular words which appeared in the main text. The penal code would be characterized by a distinction between each offence described in its '*ordinary* state', and matter which indicated 'the several causes of *justification*, *aggravation*, and *extenuation*, with the grounds of *exemption* from punishment, which apply to it'. Finally, Bentham recommended the use of 'promulgation papers', that is, standard forms for legal transactions such as conveyances and agreements, and instruments of judicial procedure.[49] Securities such as these were presented with modifications in various of Bentham's writings on codification in the final two decades of his life.

    [48] Jeremy Bentham, '*Legislator of the World*': *Writings on Codification, Law, and Education*, Philip Schofield, J. Harris (eds.) (1998) 7.
    [49] Ibid., 8 ff.

V.

While certain fundamental features appeared early and remained constant in Bentham's thought, such as his ontology and commitment to the principle of utility, there were developments and refinements over time, as he worked out the implications of these foundational principles in the light of changing circumstances. It is important to pay regard to the particular historical context in which Bentham was writing, and in particular to the provenance of, and intended audiences for, the particular writings that are under scrutiny. These factors made a difference to the way in which Bentham presented his arguments. Just to take one example: Bentham is well-known for his attack on the French Declaration of the Rights of Man of 1789,[50] and yet he advocated a similar document for Tripoli in 1822.[51] On the face of it, this appears to be inconsistent and needs explanation. Such things should also serve as a warning against presenting 'Bentham' as a timeless thought-system, and hence to ignore the circumstances in which he was writing and the fact that his views did change over time. If one thing can be said about Bentham, and indeed about anyone who takes utilitarianism seriously, it is that they will adapt their views to changing circumstances, as (hopefully) their knowledge increases and their judgement improves. The most obvious change in Bentham's perspective was his conversion to political radicalism in the first decade of the nineteenth century, through the emergence of the notion of sinister interest as a central feature of his thought. It is anachronistic to explain Bentham's thinking in the 1770s or 1780s by any reference to sinister interest, just as it is impossible to understand his thinking in the 1810s and 1820s without reference to it. Of course, it may be that the commentator wishes to develop the most coherent, complete, and consistent argument possible from Bentham's thought, or more loosely to find inspiration in aspects of his thought, whereupon the particular circumstances in which any particular work was written become less relevant. In that case, the commentator should not attribute his or her own adjusted conception or notion of the subject-matter in question to the historical Bentham.

There is much to be gained, both to historical and to philosophical disciplines, from appreciating Bentham's legal thought in its own context, and in particular by viewing it in relation to his own views on ontology and epistemology. One point of studying the past, and in particular such an original thinker as Bentham, is that such a study has the potential to offer us a critical perspective on our own current practices and beliefs. We understand better our present times through a

---

[50] Bentham (n. 7).

[51] See Jeremy Bentham, *Securities against Misrule and other Constitutional Writings for Tripoli and Greece*, Philip Schofield (ed.), (1990) 74 ff.

keener understanding of the past. History has a value in its own right, but history, in this case the history of thought, also offers a rich storehouse of materials for the contemporary philosopher. Once we adopt a historically-focused approach to Bentham, the questions will then revolve around the nature of utilitarian jurisprudence, rather than around the nature of legal positivism. This will allow us to look at how Bentham saw the relationship between form and content in his codes, and this approach can then be supplemented by work on the codes themselves. It may also provide new insights for legal philosophy in general.

Apart from the first volume of *Constitutional Code*,[52] none of Bentham's codes, in so far as they exist, have as yet been published in the *Collected Works*. There are thousands of pages of relevant manuscripts, as well as writings (published and unpublished) on other legal topics (I am not considering here writings on other topics such as political economy, panopticon, parliamentary reform, and religion), both from early and late in his career. Eventually this material—perhaps twenty volumes!—will be made available and will give us the most complete picture possible of the thought of arguably our greatest legal philosopher. At present, we have the four volumes from the late 1770s and early 1780s referred to above and a half-dozen or so volumes from the 1810s and 1820s which contribute significantly to our understanding of Bentham's legal theory and particularly his views on codification. The next batch of legal material I would like to see appear in the *Collected Works*, resources permitting, consists of 'Projet Forme' and 'Projet Matière'. Bentham scholarship is highly contingent and will remain so until many more volumes appear in the *Collected Works*. The appearance of the new edition of *Limits*, for instance, has started a process of the re-evaluation of Bentham's jurisprudence,[53] while the new edition of *Preparatory Principles* will fuel this process. When the 'Projet' materials are eventually published, there will be occasion for a further re-evaluation. And there is the promise of an amazing wealth of material still to come.

Bibliography

Oren Ben-Dor, *Constitutional Limits and the Public Sphere: A Critical Study of Bentham's Constitutionalism* (Hart, 2000)

E. De Champs, *Enlightenment and Utility: Bentham in French, Bentham in France* (Cambridge University Press, 2015)

R. Harrison, *Bentham* (Routledge & Kegan Paul, 1983)

H. L. A. Hart, *Essays on Bentham: Jurisprudence and Political Theory* (Clarendon Press, 1982)

---

[52] Jeremy Bentham, *Constitutional Code: Volume I*, F. Rosen, J. H. Burns (eds.), (1983).

[53] See G. Tusseau (ed.), *The Legal Philosophy of Jeremy Bentham: Essays on 'The Limits of the Penal Branch of Jurisprudence'* (2014).

P. J. Kelly, *Utilitarianism and Distributive Justice: Jeremy Bentham and the Civil Law* (Clarendon Press, 1990)

Michael Lobban, *The Common Law and English Jurisprudence 1760–1850* (Clarendon Press, 1991)

Douglas G. Long, *Bentham on Liberty: Jeremy Bentham's Idea of Liberty in Relation to his Utilitarianism* (University of Toronto Press, 1977)

G. J. Postema, *Bentham and the Common Law Tradition* (Clarendon Press, 1986)

Frederick Rosen, *Jeremy Bentham and Representative Democracy: A Study of the Constitutional Code* (Clarendon Press, 1983)

Philip Schofield, *Utility and Democracy: The Political Thought of Jeremy Bentham* (Oxford University Press, 2006)

W. Twining, *Theories of Evidence: Bentham and Wigmore* (Weidenfeld and Nicolson, 1985)

X. Zhai, M. Quinn, (eds.), *Bentham's Theory of Law and Public Opinion* (Cambridge University Press, 2014)

CHAPTER 22

HISTORICAL JURISPRUDENCE

MATHIAS REIMANN

I. INTRODUCTION: DEFINING THE TERRAIN

HISTORICAL jurisprudence treated law as inevitably a product of the past. Of course, jurists have long recognized that the law, like other social phenomena, has a history. But for historical jurisprudence, that history was not merely the background of the status quo; instead, it was an integral part of its present state. And of course, all legal historians have explored the law's past. But for historical jurisprudence, legal history was not an end in itself; instead, it was the principal means through which even present-day law must be understood. In short, the movement saw law as an *essentially* historical phenomenon which could be properly grasped *only* in light of its origins and genesis.

Historical jurisprudence was largely a nineteenth-century phenomenon. It must thus be seen in the context of the times, in at least three regards. First, it was part of that century's turn to history across most of the humanities; historical jurisprudence was the legal version of this broader trend. Second, it was based on the then-emerging modern concept of science which renounced philosophical speculation and deductive reasoning from absolutes and which required that knowledge be inductively derived from the observation of positive data; claiming to be a modern science, historical jurisprudence found such data in the law's past. Third, historical jurisprudence thus reacted against earlier and contemporary approaches which regarded law either as a timeless and logical system (natural law) or simply as a command of the sovereign (analytical jurisprudence); it defined itself not only by turning to historical research but also by turning against both the discussion of abstract logic and the search for legislative will.

Some precursors notwithstanding, historical jurisprudence first arose in the German romantic era in the early nineteenth century and lasted until it was gradually superseded by the sociological turn in legal thought around 1880–1920. Yet, this does not mean that it is merely of historical interest. As we will see in the Conclusion, historical jurisprudence raises lingering questions about the proper purpose of research and writing in legal history.

To lay the foundation, we will first take a look at historical jurisprudence in its various iterations; it was not only a German, but an international phenomenon (Section I). We will then be ready to describe the work done by its adherents, in particular their purposes, objects, and approaches (Section II). In addition, a proper understanding of historical jurisprudence requires recognition of its political implications (Section III). The Conclusion reflects upon the legitimacy of instrumentalizing legal history for current agendas.

II. Versions of Historical Jurisprudence: The Turn to History as a Transatlantic Phenomenon

Historical jurisprudence was not monolithic but came in a variety of forms. From its first appearance in Germany, it soon spread to other continental European countries, notably Austria, France, Hungary, Italy, and Russia.[1] In the late nineteenth century, the jurists' turn to history even became a transatlantic phenomenon.[2] We will focus here on the forms it took in Germany, England, and the United States. Even within these jurisdictions, it grew several, sometimes very distinct, branches.

---

[1] See the bibliography in Stephan Meder, *Rechtsgeschichte 383* (2014) 5th edn.

[2] David Rabban, *Law's History: American Legal Thought and the Transatlantic Turn to History* (2013); Mathias Reimann, *Historische Schule und Common Law* (1993).

A. The German Historical School: Variations on a Theme by Savigny

Since whole libraries have been written about the German Historical School,[3] a brief summary will suffice, focusing on the basic features that shaped the adherents' approach. These features were outlined by the School's founding father, Friedrich Carl von Savigny (1779–1861), in two of his earlier writings: his famous anti-codification tract *Vom Beruf unserer Zeit für Gesetzgebung und Rechtswissenschaft* (1814), and an introductory essay to a newly established legal periodical, *Ueber den Zweck dieser Zeitschrift*.[4] Its principal features are: the programme of a 'historical legal science', the view of law as custom, and the underlying concepts of organicism and, with some reservation, evolution.

It is important to note that Savigny's objective was *not* the pursuit of legal history as such but rather the establishment of a 'historical legal science' ('*geschichtliche Rechtswissenschaft*'). Largely in reaction against the eighteenth-century natural law tradition, which had relied on abstract reason and metaphysical speculation, Savigny pursued a *science of positive law based on a historical understanding*. Savigny's programme envisaged two basic steps: first, historical research must clarify which elements of our legal heritage are still viable and useful (casting the rest aside); second, these elements must be brought into a systematic order reflecting their internal coherence. Savigny's two monumental works exemplified these two basic steps in his field of specialty: he first produced a *history* of the Roman law (during the middle ages)[5] and then a *system* of (modern) Roman law.[6]

Savigny's program reflected a particular understanding of law: law was not a manifestation of abstract reason nor the product of human volition ('*Willkühr*') but rather—inevitably—the result of historical development. Since it manifested itself through habit and usage, at its core, it was a form of custom. And as custom, its development had a life of its own which lay largely beyond the control of individuals.

Savigny's notion of law as custom entailed the idea of an organic relationship between law and human life. He viewed law as an integral, indeed inseparable, part of a people's existence and tradition. It was organically linked to the surrounding culture because it emanated from the 'innermost character of the nation'[7] which

---

[3] The literature in German is vast; a masterfully written, and almost classic, though somewhat dated, overview is in Franz Wieacker, *Privatrechtsgeschichte der Neuzeit* (1967) 2nd edn., 348–430 (trans. Tony Weir, *A History of Private Law in Europe* (1995) 279–340). A more recent in-depth study is Hans-Peter Haferkamp, *Die Historische Rechtsschule* (2017). For overviews in English, see Rabban (n. 2) 92–106; Mathias Reimann, 'Nineteenth Century German Legal Science', *Boston College Law Review* 31 (1990) 837, 851–8; Peter Stein, *Legal Evolution* (1980) 51–65.

[4] Friedrich Carl von Savigny, 'Ueber den Zweck dieser Zeitschrift' (1815) 1 *Zeitschrift für geschichtliche Rechtswissenschaft* 1ff.

[5] Friedrich Carl von Savigny, *Geschichte des römischen Rechts im Mittalter* (1815–1831) Vol. 1-6.

[6] Friedrich Carl von Savigny, *System des heutigen römischen Rechts* (1840–1849) Vol. 1-8.

[7] Savigny, '*innerstes Wesen der Nation*' (n. 4) 6.

Savigny later famously called the 'spirit of the people' ('*Volksgeist*'). For Savigny, 'the people' was not, however, a sociological or ethnic, but rather a cultural, concept. Law thus had to be understood as a historical-cultural phenomenon.

Savigny's organicist conception of law and of its genesis is reminiscent of early nineteenth-century notions of evolution, be it in the realm of nature (Lamarck) or of the human spirit (Hegel). Yet, Savigny himself did not use the term evolution and he embraced the concept only in part. He did claim that law had developed from early popular forms to a state of professionalization so that today it lay no longer in the hands of the people as such, but was entrusted to the jurists. But he did not see law on a consistently progressive path. Some of his successors embraced an evolutionary understanding of law more openly, especially in the closing decades of the nineteenth century under the influence of Darwin.

The German Historical School as a fairly coherent movement lasted roughly from its inception in the early years to the middle of the nineteenth century. Yet, in a broader sense, most of nineteenth-century German legal science was Savigny's heritage. Savigny's disciples developed several variations on his basic theme. In particular, 'historical legal science' specialized along two dimensions. One was method: some jurists concentrated mainly on historical research while others engaged primarily in the law's systematization, although there was much overlap between these directions. The other dimension was substance: the (so-called) Romanists looked at the classical Roman sources while the (so-called) Germanists focused on indigenous law. In Section II, we will consider only the historical dimension, in both its Romanist and Germanist variety.

B. Historical Jurisprudence in England: From Maine to Maitland (and Beyond)

In England, historical jurisprudence began half-a-century later than in Germany. While the English movement was heavily influenced by the German model,[8] it differed in several respects. Most importantly, English historical jurisprudence was not based on a coherent theory of legal science. It rather followed the

---

[8] By 1860, Savigny's work was well-known in England. This was in part due to several translations, especially of his *System des heutigen römischen Rechts*, (n. 6), Elias Cathcart trans., *History of Roman Law During the Middle Ages* (1829); and of his *Vom Beruf unserer Zeit für Gesetzgebung und Rechtswissenschaft* (1814), Abraham Hayward trans., *On the Vocation of Our Age for Legislation and Jurisprudence* (1831); but also of his early treatise *Das Recht des Besitzes* (1803), (Sir) Erskine Perry trans., *Von Savigny's Treatise on Possession* (1848). In part, his ideas had also been introduced in law review articles, see, e.g., Anon., 'On the Schools of German Jurists' (1840) 6 *Monthly Law Magazine and Political Review* 77, 93–5.

particular inclinations of individual scholars. These scholars did not form a proper 'school.' They were connected simply by their interest in the historical dimension of law. In addition, they formed a much smaller group than in Germany. Never gaining mainstream status, they remained a distinct, though influential, minority in an environment dominated by the analytical school. English historical jurisprudence is thus best introduced by looking at some of its leading members.

The opening volley was fired by Henry Sumner Maine (1822–1888) with the publication of *Ancient Law* in 1861. Maine's objective was 'to indicate some of the earliest ideas of mankind, as they are reflected in ancient law, and to point out the relation of these ideas to modern thought'.[9] Maine essentially presented a history of various basic legal institutions, such as wills and succession, property, contract, delict and crime with an emphasis on their emergence in antiquity. There were many parallels with Savigny's work. Maine also reacted against abstract legal reasoning, in his case primarily the prevailing analytical jurisprudence based on ideas of Jeremy Bentham (1748–1832) and John Austin (1790–1859). Like Savigny, Maine proffered the alternative of a legal science grounded in historical data. Also like Savigny, he believed in organic development and in the continuity of cultural traditions, and he also focused mainly on Roman law. But there were differences as well. Unlike Savigny, Maine proceeded on a much higher level of generality with scant references to primary sources. And unlike Savigny, he emphasized progressive evolution from archaic (and collective) to civilized (and individualistic) conceptions of law, especially, in his most famous phrase, '*from Status to Contract*'.[10] Just as Darwin's *Origin of Species* had proffered a new approach to biology two years earlier,[11] *Ancient Law* opened a new perspective for Anglo-American jurisprudence. The book became hugely influential, especially in the United States. Maine subsequently published several other works written in a similar vein but dealing with more specific topics.

James Bryce (1838–1922) followed Maine's lead in important regards. Like Maine, he focused on antiquity and especially Roman law[12] and he wrote in a similarly broad-ranging, essayistic style. Yet, Bryce also provided more direct comparisons between 'the history and law of Rome and the history and law of England';[13] like many contemporaries, he saw strong parallels between the Roman and the British

[9] Henry Sumner Maine, *Ancient Law* (1861), Preface XV, references are to the Everyman's Library edn., New York (1917).

[10] Ibid., 100, italization and capitalization in the original.

[11] Charles Darwin, *The Origin of Species* (1859). Given the many similarities between these two books, it is tempting to assume that Maine was heavily influenced by Darwin. Yet, Maine had already begun to develop his ideas in earlier years, so Darwin's influence was probably not crucial.

[12] Bryce had studied Roman law with one of the leading authorities in the field, Adolph von Vangerow (1802–1880), in Heidelberg.

[13] James Bryce, *Studies in History and Jurisprudence* (1901, 2 vols.) Vol. 1, Preface, iii.

empires. And he was interested primarily in constitutional and political history, rather than in the institutions of private law.[14]

While Maine had founded, and Bryce had helped to establish, historical jurisprudence *in England*, neither provided an *English* historical jurisprudence in the sense of exploring the history of the common law. That was left to Frederic William Maitland (1850–1906) who finally turned to English legal history proper. Maitland left Maine's and Bryce's broadly generalizing, and somewhat amateurish, approaches behind. Under the influence of the Germanist scholars across the Channel, Maitland dug more deeply into the indigenous medieval sources than anyone before him. His magnum opus, *The History of English Law Before the Time of Edward I*, became the definitive work on the origins and development of medieval English law.[15] With Maitland, who left a vast oeuvre despite his early death, English legal historiography became fully professionalized and reached its zenith.

This is not to belittle the work of Maitland's principal successor, Paul Vinogradoff (1854–1925). Vinogradoff, who had studied in Berlin with Heinrich Brunner (1840–1915) and Theodor Mommsen (1817–1903), focused not only on the history and institutions of the common law, but also on the social conditions in medieval England.[16] His work carried English legal historiography into the twentieth century.

A distinct feature of this English tradition was its comparative dimension. In contrast to the mostly parochial German approach, which was rooted in Savigny's idea of a specific national '*Volksgeist*', the leading protagonists of English historical jurisprudence frequently considered legal systems more broadly and in comparison with each other. This tendency was most pronounced with Maine and Bryce who operated as jurists in a multicultural and multi-jurisdictional empire. Yet, even Maitland and Vinogradoff, who concentrated largely on indigenous legal history, frequently looked to across national boundaries.

c. United States: Henry Adams and His Disciples[17]

Leaving some precursors aside again, historical jurisprudence in the United States flowered in the closing decades of the nineteenth century (in part preceding

[14] In a similar vein, the work of Frederick Pollock (1845–1937) combined historical and comparative elements, see Frederick Pollock, 'English Opportunities in Historical and Comparative Jurisprudence', in F. Pollock, *Oxford Lectures and Other Discourses* (1890) 37.

[15] Sir Frederick Pollock and Frederic William Maitland, *The History of English Law Before the Time of Edward I* (1895, 2 vols., 2nd edn., 1898). Maitland is generally recognized as the principal author.

[16] Paul Vinogradoff, *Villainage in England* (1892); Paul Vinogradoff, *The Growth of the Manor* (1905); P. Vinogradoff, *English Society in the Eleventh Century* (1906).

[17] For a much more detailed account, see Rabban, (n. 2), 153–380; for the broader context, see Jürgen Herbst, *The German Historical School in American Scholarship* (1965).

Maitland). It combined elements of its German and English counterparts and thus occupied a middle ground between these two in four regards. First, American historical jurisprudence was also a reaction against an abstract and strictly logical approach; like Savigny's agenda, it was directed against continental European natural law (which had had a strong impact during the early Republic), and, like Maine's approach, it stood in opposition to English analytical jurisprudence (which became very influential later in the nineteenth century). Second, the American turn to history was triggered and influenced by Maine's *Ancient Law* but subsequently drew primarily on German research. Third, its theoretical foundation was German-inspired: it was also based on the notion that a true science of law must be based on historical facts, but its perspective was often closer to the English approach, especially where it contained comparative elements. Fourth, with about a dozen prominent adherents and several fellow travellers, American historical jurisprudence was still a small affair compared to its German side but a more powerful movement than in England; as such, it became a highly influential force in post-bellum legal thought.

As in Germany and England, historical jurisprudence in the United States was not monolithic. Its mainstream, however, shared an agenda which was narrower than in these other two countries. American scholars searched primarily for the roots of their own law and thus focused on the common law of medieval England; and since they mostly believed that the medieval common law's origins were Germanic, they looked mostly to the Anglo-Saxon past (see infra. II.1.) This, mainstream, American historical jurisprudence began with the publication of Henry Baxter Adams' seminal collection of *Essays in Anglo-Saxon Law* in 1876. Adams, who had studied in Germany, inspired a sizeable group of scholars in the newly established law schools on the East Coast. Of these scholars, Oliver Wendell Holmes acquired the most lasting fame, especially as the author of his (only) book, *The Common Law*. Published in 1881, it is still considered a classic of American jurisprudence—though like many classics, it is no longer read.

American historical jurisprudence also developed some distinctive features. One was a particularly strong emphasis on a combative concept of evolution. Many protagonists, like Holmes, saw legal development no longer as the quiet and peaceful process Savigny had envisaged, but rather as a struggle between competing interests—a conception reflecting the impact of Charles Darwin's biology, Herbert Spencer's (1820–1903) social theory, and eventually Rudolf von Jhering's (1818–1892) jurisprudence. In addition, there was a strong belief in progressivism, in part due to Maine's and Darwin's influence, in part perhaps simply as a result of the pervasive American infatuation with perpetual improvement. Yet, perhaps the most distinctive feature of American historical jurisprudence was its emphasis on law as custom, which in some instances took on a normative dimension with important political implications (infra. III.2.).

III. The Work of Historical Jurisprudence: Purposes, Objects, and Approaches

The work of the movement's members was so multifaceted that our analysis must greatly simplify if it wants to remain within the confines of this chapter. We can only provide an overview of the major directions. Up front, however, three general observations are in order.

First, while all members of the movement wrote about law from a historical perspective, not all actually engaged in serious historical research. Some, like James Coolidge Carter (1827–1905) did virtually none, while many others, among them Maine and Bryce, relied almost exclusively on the existing literature. The majority, however, did work, at least in part, from the original sources (infra. 3.), as was *de rigeur* in Germany, true for Maitland and Vinogradoff in England, and for Henry Adams and his disciples in the United States.

Second, scholars focused mainly on doctrinal and institutional aspects. They researched the development of substantive law (mainly private, but also constitutional and criminal law), procedure, courts, and sometimes centres of learning. Yet, the majority paid little or no attention to the law's social, political, and economic background or consequences. In short, their legal histories were internal, rather than social, some exceptions notwithstanding.[18]

Third, there was a great deal of cross-fertilization, with the German side mainly on the giving, the Anglo-American side on the receiving end.[19] German writing inspired the English scholars as well Adams and his disciples in the United States; Maine influenced the Americans, who in turn were later cited by Maitland. German, English, and American scholars corresponded about their work and reviewed each other's books.[20] Beginning in the 1870s, many tended to see themselves as parts of a common enterprise.

---

[18] A major (as well as famous) exception is Frederic Maitland, *Domesday Book and Beyond* (1887); this is also true for some of Paul Vinogradoff's work (n. 16).

[19] Savigny of course enjoyed quasi-iconic status even in the common law world. Among the Germanists, Heinrich Brunner (1840–1915) in particular had an enormous influence on Anglo-American scholarship, particularly on Maitland, see Johannes Liebrecht, *Brunners Wissenschaft* (2014) 39–42. Brunner, in turn, drew support for his views of the Germanic past from what he learned about English law, ibid., 235–6. Anglo-American scholars also relied on the work of Gierke, Nasse, Sohm, von Maurer, and many others; see the extensive bibliography in Henry Adams et al., *Essays in Anglo-Saxon Law* (1876) VII–XII.

[20] The most notable example is the close working-relationship between Brunner and Maitland (as well as Felix Liebermann), which was based on deep mutual respect, see ibid., 237–41.

A. Purposes: The Goals of Historical Research

Legal historical research pursued a variety of objectives. Although they often overlapped, it is helpful to distinguish three primary goals: a proper understanding of current doctrines and institutions; a comprehension of the law's evolution as a social phenomenon; and knowledge of the past for its own sake.

The most widely-shared, and thus most characteristic, purpose was to acquire a deep understanding of current doctrines and institutions. Since law was regarded mainly as a product of history, true mastery of the material could be acquired only by tracing its growth from the roots all the way to the present. Thus most scholars agreed that a historical understanding enabled lawyers to clarify and refine current doctrine. Beyond that, however, they held different views about the main practical benefits of this process. For some scholars, like Savigny, knowing law's history was important mainly because it enabled the present to maintain continuity with the past. To be sure, this did not mean blind adherence to historical relics; instead, jurists had to decide which legal elements bequeathed by the past were still useful and which should be abandoned. Still, since law was regarded as an organic whole, continuity was preferable. For others, however, like Holmes (and Maitland), the use of history was 'mainly negative and skeptical'.[21] Understanding the law's origins and growth allowed the present to liberate itself from the past and then to make its own choices.[22] From that point of view, tradition had little or no normative force.

A second major purpose of historical inquiry was to understand the evolution of law more broadly, i.e., as a social and cultural phenomenon. This kind of work aimed at unveiling the general features of legal development. For many, like Maine and Holmes, the principal characteristic of legal evolution was the progression from ancient and primitive to modern and developed forms of law.[23] This kind of scholarship was often broadly comparative.[24] Sometimes, it even veered in the direction of legal ethnology, especially in the work of German scholars Josef Kohler (1849–1919) and Albert Post (1839–1895). The resultant breadth of the approach could lead to superficiality and amateurism[25] which entailed the risk of distortion and error.

---

[21] Oliver Wendell Holmes, 'Law in Science and Science in Law', in Oliver W. Holmes, *Collected Legal Papers* (1920) 210, at 225.

[22] 'History sets us free and enables us to make up our own minds.' Oliver Wendell Holmes, *The Path of the Law*, 167, at 186–7.

[23] Maine (n. 9); A central thesis of Holmes' *The Common Law* (n. 21), was the development from internal (subjective) to external (objective) standards of liability.

[24] For an earlier example of a broadly comparative approach, pre-dating Maine by a generation, see Eduard Gans, *Das Erbrecht in weltgeschichtlicher Entwickelung* (4 vols. 1824–1835).

[25] E.g., Josef Kohler happily wrote about Chinese criminal law, Islamic and Babylonic law, the law of the Aztecs, ancient Indian law of procedure, etc.—all besides a full portfolio of scholarship on current German and international law.

Finally, in the closing decades of the nineteenth, and especially in the early twentieth, century historical research and writing increasingly sought to acquire knowledge (of the legal past) for its own sake. As such, it was no longer part of historical jurisprudence proper but turned into legal history as a discipline in its own right.[26] To be sure, the boundary between historical jurisprudence and pure legal history was often a matter of emphasis. Scholars like Savigny, Karl Friedrich Eichhorn (1781–1854), Pollock, and Holmes of course had a keen interest in the law's past, but their scholarship served primarily present-day purposes; they were still lawyers exploring history. By contrast, scholars like Theodor Mommsen (1817–1903), Heinrich Brunner (1840–1915), Maitland, and Melville Bigelow (1846–1921) were of course cognizant of their work's modern implications, but they were mainly writing legal history as such; they essentially became historians looking at law.

B. Objects: Roman and Germanic Law

The adherents of historical jurisprudence on both sides of the Atlantic saw the origins of their respective legal systems in either (ancient) Roman or (medieval) Germanic law. Interestingly, scholars paid much less, and in many instances no, attention to several other important heritages, especially the huge body of canon law, the law merchant in its many variations, and the natural law tradition of the early modern period.[27] As we will see (infra. III.1.), the respective contributions of Roman and Germanic sources to the modern law of Germany, England, and the United States were the subject of intense debates throughout the nineteenth century.

Roman law had a different status in the respective countries so that its study took different directions. In Germany, the reception of Roman law in the late middle ages had rendered it directly applicable by many courts and in the bureaucracies of the emerging modern state. For centuries, it had dominated legal education and practice as part of the *ius commune*. Thus, in the nineteenth century, Roman law was the core of Germany's legal system, especially in private law.[28] As a result, for most of the nineteenth century, Roman law was not considered part

[26] See Wieacker (n. 3), 'Entdeckung der Rechtsgeschichte' 416–30.

[27] There were some exceptions, e.g., Frederic William Maitland, 'Canon Law in England', in H. A. L. Fisher (ed.), *The Collected Papers of Frederic William Maitland* (1911) vol. 3 137.

[28] To be sure, the programme of Savigny's historical school was not the study of the early modern *ius commune* then in force; instead Savigny and his disciples returned to the writings of the Roman jurists in antiquity, i.e., to Roman law in its classical form. This agenda was boosted in 1816 when Barthold Georg Niebuhr (1776–1831) discovered, and Savigny quickly identified, the first (virtually) complete

of a by-gone past; its study was simply an integral element of current doctrinal work. As such, Roman law scholarship was pervasive, voluminous, and highly developed, although it was not properly historical. It was only towards the end of the nineteenth century, when modern legislation and eventually codification superseded the *Pandektenrecht*, that German scholars began to write about Roman law from a truly historical perspective,[29] as in the work of Theodor Mommsen (1817–1903), Otto Lenel (1849–1935), and Ludwig Mitteis (1859–1921). Thus, a genre of Roman legal history (*Römische Rechtsgeschichte*) was born. It flourished mainly in the twentieth century after the era of historical jurisprudence had come to an end.

In England, Roman law had played a limited but considerable practical role as *civil law* in various contexts since the high Middle Ages. It also had an academic home in the Regius Professorships which had existed at Oxford and Cambridge since 1540. Yet, in the second half of the nineteenth century it was no longer directly applicable in secular courts.[30] Nonetheless, English jurists paid a fair amount of attention to Roman law. In part, this was simply a manifestation of the generally high regard for classical studies. Yet, Roman law was also pursued for a variety of more specific purposes. Some, like Maine, studied it in search of clues about ancient law. Others, like Bryce, compared its development with that of English law.[31] Maitland was mainly interested in exploring the Roman law influence in England. Finally, towards the close of the century, the English study of Roman law increasingly liberated itself, as in Germany, from present-day concerns and developed into a specialty in its own right.[32]

In contrast to the situation in both Germany and England, Roman law never had any direct force in the United States, some civil law influence in the early Republic notwithstanding. Still, in the first half of the nineteenth century, Roman law enjoyed considerable attention among American gentlemen jurists—be it because they were intrigued by Niebuhr's and Savigny's discovery of Gaius' *Institutes* (1816),

---

copy of Gaius' *Institutes*, the most influential book of Roman law from the high classical period (second century AD). Savigny justified this return to antiquity *inter alia* by claiming, in his major historical work, *Geschichte des römischen Rechts im Mittelalter* (n. 5), that even in the Middle Ages (*c.* 500–1500 AD), the classical heritage had never been lost. For the German Romanists, the classical sources were also the most promising turf for training legal minds and thus of prime importance for legal education, see Haferkamp (n. 3) 31–110.

[29] See Franz Wieacker, *Römische Rechtsgeschichte* (Erster Abschnitt, 1988) 46–59.

[30] The situation was obviously different in Scotland as a mixed jurisdiction; there, elements of Roman law have remained in force until the present.

[31] Underneath this comparison lay an interest in the perceived parallels between the Roman and the British Empires, see, e.g., James Bryce, 'The Roman Empire and the British Empire in India', in James Bryce, *Studies in History and Jurisprudence* (1901) vol. I 1–84.

[32] See, e.g., Paul Vinogradoff, *Roman Law in Medieval Europe* (1909); Henry Roby, *Roman Private Law in the Times of Cicero and the Antonines* (1902).

because they operated in the classicist culture of the (slaveholding) Old South, or simply because they cultivated Roman law as a matter of higher learning.[33] After the American Civil War, however, that broader interest quickly waned. As American law matured, Roman law by and large lost its practical utility. And yet, some American historical jurists did keep a keen eye on it, as is perhaps most visible in the case of Holmes. They were not, however, focusing on Roman law (or its history) for its own sake. Instead, their interest was instrumental: like Maitland in England, they looked at Roman law mainly in order to gauge its role in their own legal tradition.

The other main field of the historical jurists' research and writing consisted of the mass of indigenous (i.e., non-Roman) law that had (at least allegedly) developed from the folk law of the early and high Middle Ages. It was variously called 'German', more often and more broadly 'Germanic' or even 'Teutonic'.

In Germany, the exploration of these Germanic sources was part of the historical school's original agenda. Thus, in the first half of the nineteenth century, many Germanists worked in the spirit of historical jurisprudence, i.e., guided by present-day purposes. Like their fellow Romanists, they aimed at building a scientific system, in their case of German Private Law.[34] Yet, many Germanists already looked at the past largely in and of itself, sometimes blending their approach with general historical as well as philological and linguistic studies, most famously in the case of Jacob Grimm (1785–1863). After the middle of the century, scholars increasingly turned to the history of German law for its own sake. They covered not only the earlier Frankish and later German heartlands but also the Nordic regions and, notably, Anglo-Saxon England, as in the work of Felix Liebermann (1851–1925). By the time when historical jurisprudence came into vogue in England and the United States, these German jurists had already produced a substantial body of sophisticated scholarship on their law's indigenous roots. This, as well as the originality and quality of their work, put them in a leading position vis-à-vis their common law colleagues—even with regard to medieval English law.

The other side of the Channel presented a completely different picture: well into the last third of the nineteenth century, English legal historiography was either rather superficial—or virtually non-existent. While Maine occasionally touched on it, he was by no means a historian of English law. As a result, Maitland famously lamented as late as 1888 that 'the history of English law [was] not written'.[35]

---

[33] Michael Hoeflich, *Roman Law and Civil Law and the Development of Anglo-American Jurisprudence in the Nineteenth Century* (1997) 50–73.

[34] See, e.g., Karl Friedrich Eichhorn, *Einleitung in das deutsche Privatrecht* (1823).

[35] Frederic William Maitland, 'Why the History of English Law is Not Written' (1888 inaugural lecture), in H. A. L. Fisher (ed.), *The Collected Papers of Frederic William Maitland* (1911) vol. I 480.

Indeed, for the time being, the writing of English legal history was largely left to the Germans and under their influence, since the mid-1870s, to the Americans. This began to change only in the 1880s—with Maitland himself.[36] In an outburst of scholarly production, this master of both doctrinal and socially contextualized legal history made up in about two short decades what generations before him had neglected. Maitland drew heavily on both German and U.S.-American scholarship but also delved deeply into the original sources himself. His two most important works, *The History of English Law Before the Time of Edward I* (1895) and *Domesday Book and Beyond* (1897), are widely regarded as the greatest books ever written on English legal history.[37] While a fair amount of Maitland's writing was related to present-day concerns, these two volumes are pure legal history and thus lie beyond historical jurisprudence proper. The same is true for the work of Maitland's main successor on the field of medieval legal history, Paul Vinogradoff.

In the United States, English legal history began to be written a decade before Maitland, i.e., in the 1870s. As mentioned, the signal event was the publication in 1876 by the young Henry Baxter Adams of a collection of *Essays in Anglo-Saxon Law*, written by himself and some of his students. Over the next three decades, about a dozen ultimately prominent American writers produced a substantial body of literature on the medieval origins and the genesis of the common law, often comparing it with other legal cultures, especially the Roman. Most of these scholars were interested in the past primarily in order better to understand and develop the law of the present; this is true, for example, for James Barr Ames (1846–1910), James Bradley Thayer (1831–1902), or John Norton Pomeroy (1828–1885). Some, however, pursued legal history mainly for its own sake, like Henry Adams (1850–1901) and Melville Bigelow (1846–1921), whose work then inspired Maitland.

Despite considerable diversity, the work done by the Germanists in Germany, by Maitland, Vinogradoff, and a few others in England, and by Adams and his followers in the United States can justly be regarded as a distinct transnational body of scholarship on early and medieval German(ic) and English law. This is true especially in light of the many academic relationships, influences, and references across national boundaries. By the beginning of the twentieth century, this body of scholarship was rich, mature, and, on the whole, of high quality. It constitutes the perhaps most enduring heritage of historical jurisprudence.

---

[36] Slightly before Maitland, James Fitzjames Stephen published *The History of the Criminal Law of England* (1883 3 vols.).

[37] John Hudson, *F. W. Maitland and the Englishness of English Law* (2007).

c. Method: Back to the Original Sources

As mentioned, historical jurisprudence saw itself as a form of 'science' based on the observation of concrete (in this case: historical) facts from which principles could be distilled by inductive reasoning. This approach mandated working with the original sources and studying them with careful attention to detail.

In Germany, Savigny took the lead by travelling far and wide to various archives and digging up original documents, especially for his *History of Roman Law in the Middle Ages*; among his successors, it became *de rigeur* to work from the sources themselves, both on the Romanist and the Germanist side. In the United States, Adams and his followers took after the Germans in the 1870s. Shortly thereafter, Maitland and Vinogradoff joined the bandwagon in England. Yet, the picture was not entirely uniform. To begin with, not everybody kept his nose that close to the ground; Maine or Bryce, for example, showed little interest in getting their hands dirty in dusty archives. Furthermore, while the mainstream Germans, under their influence the Americans, and in Britain especially Maitland were known for their 'exactness in detail',[38] Maine and Bryce in England, but also Kohler and Post in Germany painted with a much broader brush. Finally, some historical jurists, most notably Holmes, combined the study of the original sources with heavy reliance on secondary literature and mixed meticulous attention to detail with broad theorizing.

In addition to writing monographs and articles, many historical jurists made particularly lasting contributions by editing and publishing a multitude of original sources. Again, the Germans had already taken the lead in the early nineteenth century, e.g., with the ambitious project of the *Monumenta Germaniae Historica* (founded in 1819 and devoted to historical sources generally) and, among lawyers most famously, with the edition (by Johann Friedrich Ludwig Goeschen) of Gaius' *Institutes* (1820). The editions of original sources published in nineteenth-century Germany are too numerous to mention; they range from Jacob Grimm's *Deutsche Rechtsalterthümer* (1828) to Carl Gustav Homeyer's *Sachsenspiegel* (1842), and from Mommsen's *Digesta Iustiniani Augusti* (1868–1870) to Otto Lenel's *Edictum Perpetuum* (1883). In the 1870s, the common lawyers began to follow suit; English historian William Stubbs published his *Select Charters and other Illustrations of English Constitutional History* (1870), and American legal scholar Melville Bigelow produced a much noted edition of *Placita Anglo-Normannica* (1879). Most importantly, however, in 1887, Maitland founded the *Selden Society* under whose auspices he subsequently edited and published a significant number of original sources. Like the *Monumenta Germaniae Historica*, the *Selden Society* has continued to operate all the way to the present.

---

[38] Oliver Wendell Holmes, Review of Adams et al., 'Essays in Anglo-Saxon Law', *American Law Review* (1877) 11, 327.

iv. POLITICAL IMPLICATIONS: LEGAL TRADITIONS, LAWMAKING, AND LAISSEZ FAIRE

Historical jurisprudence was not a purely academic matter, but also had considerable political implications. In particular, its adherents fought about the identity of their legal traditions, worried about the distribution of lawmaking power, and with their evolutionary view of law, often supported laissez faire politics.

A. Identity: The Struggle for the Soul of the Law

For most of the nineteenth century, jurists in the three countries considered here struggled with an identity crisis: they worried about the essential character of their respective legal traditions as either indigenous or Roman. While the debates revolved about a common core, they played out somewhat differently on both sides of the Atlantic.

In Germany, the issue was not *whether* the Roman law had had a significant influence, because that was entirely beyond cavil. Instead, the struggle concerned two questions beyond that. One was the *exact extent* of that influence. Surely in the area of private law, the Roman component's predominance was undeniable. The Germanists, however, sought to show that important elements of present-day law had medieval German roots, for example in the area of corporations, banking, and negotiable instruments. The second question was the *desirability* of Roman influence. After a period of harmonious cooperation in the early years of the historical school, the Germanists felt increasingly marginalized and eventually began to oppose the reign of Roman law altogether. They pointed out that its reception had put the law into the hands of learned jurists, thus alienating it from the people. Primarily for that reason, Georg Beseler (1809–1888) famously denounced the reception of the Roman law as a 'national disaster'.[39]

The German debate thus took an openly political turn. The conflict between the Romanists and Germanists became particularly pronounced during the 1848/9 revolution because the former were associated with the ruling monarchies and their oppressive bureaucracies, while the latter sided with the calls for a modern constitution, if not for a republican government. The tension between the Roman and German sides resurfaced later in the century when the German Civil Code (*Bürgerliches Gesetzbuch* (BGB)) was being drafted. Leading Germanists like Otto von

---

[39] Georg Beseler, *Volksrecht und Juristenrecht* (1843) 42 ('*Nationalunglück*').

Gierke (1841–1921) accused the Code's first draft (1887) of embodying the excessive individualism of Roman law and of lacking the greater social and collective elements of the indigenous German tradition.[40]

In the Anglo-American orbit, the main issue was more fundamental, i.e., whether the common law was significantly shaped by Roman influence at all—or whether it was essentially cut from indigenous, i.e., Anglo-Saxon, cloth.[41] In the earlier and mid-nineteenth century, many scholars in both England and the United States advocated the former position, claiming Roman origins for core common law concepts, such as the trust. Beginning in the 1870s the tide began to turn. Now, the Americans lead the charge against a Romanist view of the common law, most prominently among them Holmes. In *The Common Law*, he broadly canvassed the roots of the Anglo-American tradition to conclude that they were Germanic (or 'Teutonic'), rather than Roman. Soon, this became the majority view among the American historical jurists. A decade later, Thomas Scrutton also assessed the Roman law influence in England as sporadic and limited.[42] Maitland essentially agreed and explained why no full-scale reception continental-style had occurred in England.[43] For Maitland, this did not mean, however, that English law was therefore 'Teutonic;' instead, it had absorbed various foreign influences and then developed in its own peculiar institutions and character.[44]

As on the continent, the Anglo-American debate had political dimensions, although they were not as prominently displayed. In England, the assertion of the common law's Teutonic origins was also an affirmation of the broader culture's true Englishness which was routinely associated with political liberty. This implied a decidedly negative view of the medieval Norman invasion and reign which were associated with political oppression.[45] In the United States, the Teutonic roots of the Anglo-American tradition were invoked to reassert local (grassroots) decision making in reaction against increasing concentration of political power at the state and federal levels. In a much popularized and heavily romanticized view of history, a straight line was drawn from the freemen councils in the Teutonic forests

---

[40] Otto von Gierke, *Der Entwurf eines bürgerlichen Gesetzbuches und das deutsche Recht* (1889).

[41] Michele Graziadei, 'Changing Images of the Law in XIX Century English Legal Thought', in Mathias Reimann (ed.), *The Reception of Continental Ideas in the Common Law World 1820–1920* (1993) 115ff.

[42] Thomas Scrutton, *The Influence of the Roman Law and the Law of England* (1885). Scrutton of course recognized the importance of the civil law in the ecclesiastical and the admiralty courts; on that aspect, see Daniel Coquillette, *The Civilian Writers at Doctor's Commons, London* (1988).

[43] Frederic William Maitland, *English Law and the Renaissance* (1901).

[44] See Graziadei, (n. 41), 158–63. Maitland's views are best summarized in Pollock and Maitland (n. 15) Introduction, xxii–xlviii.

[45] This theme was lavishly captured, as well as popularized, by one of the most widely read nineteenth-century English novels, i.e., Walter Scott, *Ivanhoe* (1820). Even Pollock and Maitland, who maintained a more balanced view of the Norman influence, spoke of the invasion as a 'catastrophe', Pollock, Maitland (n. 15) 86.

to the New England township meetings.[46] In addition, the affirmation of English roots sometimes had racial implications. Especially in the United States, it was in part a reaction by the Anglophone elite against the perceived threat by waves of immigration from non-Germanic regions, especially from Eastern Europe and the Mediterranean.[47]

B. Lawmaking: Legislation v. Legal Science

Historical jurisprudence invited opposition to legislation. If the essential nature of law was not, as the analytical jurists had postulated, the command of the sovereign but rather the product of *longue durée* historical evolution, the law lay largely beyond the ad hoc will, and arguably even beyond the power, of the legislator. Thus the historical jurists tended to be sceptical, or even hostile, towards statutory lawmaking, albeit to varying degrees.

This hostility was most visible in the respective debates about codification. Just as Savigny famously (and for the time being, successfully) argued against a German civil code in the early nineteenth century, so James Coolidge Carter campaigned (also successfully) against the project of a New York Civil Code in its closing decades. Like many of their contemporaries, both rejected codification as fundamentally at odds with the essentially historical nature of law. In their views, a code certainly should not, and in fact could not, really *change* the law; but even a mere codification of the status quo was harmful because it would stunt the law's natural growth.[48]

Many historical jurists were hostile to piecemeal legislation as well. To be sure, their hostility was not necessarily all-encompassing. They were opposed mainly to legislation in private (rather than criminal or other public) law, and they made exceptions in particular circumstances. Still, most of them rejected statutes as a routine vehicle of lawmaking in the traditional areas of the civil and the common law.

This anti-legislative attitude had two main roots which can be labelled jurisprudential and professional. Its jurisprudential root was their view of law as essentially a form of custom. Since this custom naturally emanated from the habits of the people, it quasi-automatically reflected the true needs of society. Legislative interference with this process was thus likely to do more harm than good. In addition, many historical jurists conceived of the law as an integrated

---

[46] Mathias Reimann, 'In such forests, liberty was nurtured.' 'Von den germanischen Wurzeln der angloamerikanischen Freiheit', in Gerhard Köbler, Hermann Nehlsen, *Wirkungen europäischer Rechtskultur* (1997) 933ff.

[47] On the discussion of racial ideas among the historical jurists, see Rabban (n. 2) 329–34.

[48] Mathias Reimann, 'The Historical School against Codification: Savigny, Carter, and the Defeat of the New York Civil Code' (1989) 37 *American Journal of Comparative Law* 95ff.; Lewis Grossman, 'Langdell Upside-Down, James Coolidge Carter and the Anti-Classical Jurisprudence of Anticodification' (2007) 19 *Yale J. of Law and the Humanities* 149ff.

and harmonious ('organic', 'seamless', etc.) whole which should not be disturbed by legislation. The professional root was the historical jurists' claim to leadership. Since law was a product of history, its exploration, cultivation, and development was a matter of legal science—and thus belonged in the hands of legal scientists. In the continental legal tradition, these were the academically trained jurists, in particular the law professors.[49] In the common law orbit, the trained experts had long been the members of the bench and bar, though legal academics played an increasingly important role as well. By contrast, legislators were not scientifically qualified but rather chosen politically—and thus unfit for the job. In other words, the development the law was too delicate a task to be left to the politicians.

c. Conservatism and Liberalism: A Laissez-Faire Preference

The historical jurists' hostility towards legislation was also fuelled by their general dislike of radical change and their aversion to state regulation of private affairs.

Historical jurisprudence was inherently conservative in the sense of preferring slow evolution over abrupt change. Savigny's historical school emphasized continuity with the past and flirted with Romanticism, and the common lawyers' practice of reasoning from past decisions rather than future agendas rendered their mode of thought conservative as well. Yet, again, there were exceptions: some historical jurists, like Holmes and Maitland, were quite open to legal change.

In addition, historical jurisprudence often went in hand-in-glove with classical (nineteenth-century) liberalism. Many of its adherents were highly sceptical towards state interference with private rights. At the dawn of the movement, Savigny, reacting against the paternalistic tradition of continental Europe's enlightened monarchies, denied 'that the world can be fundamentally helped by regulation and government' and bemoaned the 'rage to govern'.[50] At the end of the movement, Carter, reacting against the regulatory agendas of his own time, riled against the state as a *schoolmaster* with the whole of society as its pupils'.[51] Especially in the Anglo-American orbit, many historical jurists believed that legal systems, left unto themselves, would automatically develop towards a liberal order, in Maine's famous words, '*from Status to Contract*'.[52]

Where the penchant for preserving the status quo combined with the rejection of regulatory interference, the result was a laissez faire attitude towards society and

[49] See James Whitman, *The Legacy of Roman Law in the German Romantic Era* (1990).
[50] Friedrich Carl von Savigny, 'Stimmen für und wider neue Gesetzbücher', *Zeitschrift für geschichtliche Rechtswissenschaft* 1 (1816) 1, 44.
[51] James Coolidge Carter, *Law, Its Origin, Growth and Function* (1907) 225.
[52] Maine (n. 9) 100 (emphasis in the original).

economy. Building on classical Roman law, the German Romanists created the framework for a free market society,[53] just as the Anglo-American jurists presented their common law as the appropriate regime for a capitalist economy with strong property rights, extensive freedom of contract, and restricted tort liability, particularly for industrial accidents. Especially for many historical jurists in the United States, society and the market were best guided not by the state but by Adam Smith's 'invisible hand.' To be sure, the picture was not completely uniform. As mentioned, the Germanists critiqued the draft *BGB* for its excessive individualism and advocated more social rights and obligations. And even in the United States, the adherents of historical jurisprudence were not as blind to the excesses of capitalism and not as broadly committed to laissez faire politics as Roscoe Pound later claimed.[54]

v. Conclusion: The Instrumentalization of Legal History

Historical jurisprudence petered out between the 1880s and the First World War. There were some notable publications even after 1914, but they were an aftermath, mostly collecting or reprinting earlier work.[55] By 1920, historical jurisprudence was legal history.

The movement's decline and fall had several reasons. Some were country-specific. In Germany, Rudolf von Jhering launched a devastating critique against the historical school and pushed jurisprudence towards a sociological approach; and in 1900, the enactment of the *BGB* cut private law largely off from the past. In England, Maitland's death in 1906 marked the beginning of the erstwhile decline of historical scholarship, as neither he nor Paul Vinogradoff had trained successors who could continue their work. In the United States, legal thought turned towards pragmatism and, under the leadership of Roscoe Pound (himself influenced by Jhering), embraced sociological jurisprudence. In addition, the First World War ended the cooperation between German and Anglo-American legal scholars. But there were also two deeper reasons for the movement's demise which were common to all three countries. With its backward looking conception of law, historical

---

[53] Franz Wieacker, 'Pandektenwissenschaft und industrielle Revolution', in F. Wieacker, *Industriegesellschaft und Privatrechtsordnung* (1974) 55 ff.

[54] See Rabban (n. 2), especially 3, 430–42.

[55] Association of American Law Schools, *The Continental Legal History Series* (11 volumes, 1914–1928); Paul Vinogradoff, *Outlines of Historical Jurisprudence* (2 vols., 1920–1922). See also John Wigmore (ed.), *Select Essays in Anglo-American Legal History* (3 vols. 1907).

jurisprudence was fundamentally at odds with the forward looking reform agendas of the twentieth-century regulatory state; legal history simply did not provide solutions for the problems of industrialization, labour-conflict, and urbanization (and legal historians, turning more purely historical, stopped trying). And with its claim that law as a science belonged in the hands of trained legal experts, historical jurisprudence was essentially un-democratic; this rendered it incompatible with a lawmaking process in which legislatures, not legal scientists, ultimately call the shots.

What has survived is legal historiography in its own right, having gradually divorced itself from historical jurisprudence. For the last century, legal historians have thus pursued knowledge of the past for its own sake, not in aid of current agendas. More historians than lawyers, their goals have been academic, not practical. They have recognized that the pursuit of practical goals tends to taint historical research. Indeed, the work of many historical jurists, perhaps most notably Maine, Holmes, and Carter, provides tell-tale evidence of selective bias and distorted interpretation. In recognition, Maitland warned his contemporaries that '[i]f we try to make legal history the handmaid of dogma she will soon cease to be history.'[56]

Still, looking at historical jurisprudence raises the question of whether the instrumentalization of historical work for present practical purposes is really illegitimate per se. The question presented itself squarely once again in the debate about a common private law for Europe in the 1990s. When a group of scholars led by Reinhard Zimmermann suggested building a European private law on the heritage of the early modern *ius commune*, more traditional legal historians vigorously protested such an instrumentalization of their discipline. The former essentially endeavoured to revive the tradition of historical jurisprudence; the latter insisted on a purist approach to legal historiography.[57] Can the conflict between an instrumental and a purist approach be resolved?

It is interesting to note that in common law world today, legal history pursued for its own sake has *not* eliminated legal history serving current practice. The reason is that in contrast to their civil law colleagues, common lawyers still often think about present-day law in historical terms: the law is the product not only of present legislative or judicial will, but also of a long tradition. For a common lawyer, therefore, the past is not merely background to, but often an integral part of, current law. In this sense, engaging legal history for practical purposes is inevitable, and it simply sits side-by-side with legal history as a purely academic pursuit.

There is no reason why this should not be possible in the civil law orbit as well. It is imperative to recognize, of course, that these two forms of legal history are very different enterprises which must be carefully separated. Maitland saw that clearly over a century ago. He warned that in doing historical work, we must not 'mix two different logics, the logic of authority, and the logic of evidence. What the lawyer

[56] Maitland (n. 35) 492.
[57] Gerhard Dilcher, Pio Caroni (eds.), *Norm und Tradition. Fra norma e tradizione* (1998).

wants is authority [for his position]; what the historian wants is evidence [of past realities].[58] Maitland intimated that much of historical jurisprudence can be faulted for having mixed that up. But he also indicated that if this mistake is avoided, an instrumentalized approach *à la* historical jurisprudence can peacefully coexist with a purist approach unconcerned with practical utility.

Whether, to what extent, and how even a purely academic legal history can contribute to present day lawmaking and legal practice is of course an entirely different question. It lies beyond the scope of this chapter.

BIBLIOGRAPHY

1. Works of Historical Jurisprudence

Association of American Law Schools, *Continental Legal History Series* (Little, Brown, and Co., 11 vols. 1914–1928)

Henry Adams, *Essays in Anglo-Saxon Law* (Little, Brown, and Co., 1876)

James Barr Ames, *Lectures on Legal History* (Harvard University Press, 1913)

Oliver Wendell Holmes, *The Common Law* (Little, Brown, and Co., 1881)

Henry Sumner Maine, *Ancient Law* (J. Murray, 1861)

Sir Frederick Pollock, Frederic William Maitland, *The History of English Law before the Time of Edward I* (Cambridge University Press, 1895, 2nd edn., 1898)

Friedrich Carl von Savigny, 'Ueber den Zweck dieser Zeitschrift', *Zeitschrift für geschichtliche Rechtswissenschaft* 1 ff (Mohr und Zimmer, 1815) 1–17

Friedrich Carl von Savigny, *Vom Beruf unserer Zeit für Gesetzgebung und Rechtswissenschaft* (1814) (trans. Abraham Hayward as *The Vocation of Our Age for Legislation and Jurisprudence*, 1831)

John Henry Wigmore, *Select Essays in Anglo-American Legal History* (Little, Brown, and Co., 3 vols. 1907).

2. Writings about Historical Jurisprudence

Hans-Peter Haferkamp, *Die Historische Rechtsschule* (Vittorio Klostermann, 2017)

Michael Hoeflich, *Roman Law and Civil Law and the Development of Anglo-American Jurisprudence in the Nineteenth Century* (University of Georgia Press, 1997)

David Rabban, *Law's History: American Legal Thought and the Transatlantic Turn to History* (Cambridge University Press, 2013)

Mathias Reimann, *Historische Schule und Common Law* (Duncker & Humblot, 1993)

Mathias Reimann, 'Nineteenth Century German Legal Science', *Boston College Law Review* 31 (1990) 837ff.

---

[58] Maitland (n. 35) 491.

CHAPTER 23

LEGAL FORMALISM

MICHAEL LOBBAN

THE era of 'legal formalism' is usually taken to refer to the period in American legal thought between the 1860s and the 1920s, when a new generation of post-bellum treatise-writers and legal academics sought to discover the underlying principles of common law cases and put them into a rational order. This period is sometimes also referred to as the era of 'classical legal thought', a phrase which takes in not only the perceived methodology of the jurists, but a broader *Weltanschauung* shared by the judiciary, which favoured laissez-faire and individualism.[1] In contemporary jurisprudence, the term 'formalism' refers to a specific approach to adjudication and constitutional interpretation, which has its defenders as well as its critics.[2] However, in the era under study, it was neither a term which jurists used to describe themselves, nor one which their critics used to describe them.

'Formalism' was in many ways defined by the anti-formalist critiques of the later generation of 'Realist' thinkers.[3] In the view of the Realists, 'formalists' treated law as a system of abstract concepts, which could be applied by deduction to the facts of any particular case. They were blind to the policy choices and social purposes, which had shaped the content of law. They saw law as an adjudicative system in which

---

[1] Duncan Kennedy, *The Rise and Fall of Classical Legal Thought* (2006; 1st written 1975); William M. Wiecek, *The Lost World of Classical Legal Thought: Law and Ideology in America 1886–1937* (1998); Grant Gilmore, *The Ages of American Law* (1977); Morton J. Horwitz, *The Transformation of American Law, 1870–1960* (1992).

[2] See, esp., Frederick Schauer, 'Formalism' (1988) 97 *Yale L.J.* 509–48 ff; Frederick Schauer, *Playing by the Rules: A Philosophical Examination of Rule-Based Decision-Making in Law and in Life* (1991).

[3] See Anthony J. Sebok, *Legal Positivism in American Jurisprudence* (1998) 49, 57 ff: 'As a theory of law, it exists only as a reflection of scholars like Holmes, Pound, Llewellyn and Frank.'

judges neutrally resolved disputes between autonomous individuals, rather than one in which legislation played a critical role; and consequently, they privileged private law and marginalized public law.[4] It generated (in Roscoe Pound's famous critique) a 'mechanical' form of jurisprudence in which rules and doctrines were judged 'by their conformity to a supposed science and not by the results to which they lead'.[5] Recent scholarship has questioned this image of the legal thinkers of the 'Gilded Age'. The range of opinions within 'orthodox' legal thought in this era has been shown to have been rather larger than the Realist caricature suggested, with many jurists developing theories in which moral reasoning and historical investigation played major roles.[6] As shall be seen in this chapter, the 'formalist' jurists were not simply narrow logicians who had imbibed the learning of analytical jurisprudence. They were scholars bred in the common law tradition, who sought to make sense of it for a new age, by incorporating the methods of the latest jurisprudential learning, both historical and analytical.

I.

If 'formalism' was to be defined by its critics, the *locus classicus* of that critique is generally agreed to be Oliver Wendell Holmes's 1880 review of Christopher Columbus Langdell's *Summary of the Law of Contracts*. For Holmes, Langdell was 'the greatest living legal theologian . . . so entirely is he interested in the formal connection of things, or logic, as distinguished from the feelings which made the content of logic, and which have actually shaped the substance of the law'.[7] Langdell came to be seen as the intellectual progenitor of an entire 'tradition' of scholars devoted to the taxonomy of legal concepts. He had famously revolutionized law teaching at Harvard by introducing the case method. For Langdell, law, 'considered as a science, consists of certain principles or doctrines', which the student had to master so well as 'to be able to apply them with constant facility and certainty to the ever-tangled skein of human affairs'. If the volume of case law was massive,

---

[4] See Karl Llewellyn's description of the 'Formal Style' in *The Common Law Tradition: Deciding Appeals* (1960) 38.

[5] Roscoe Pound, 'Mechanical Jurisprudence' (1908) 8 *Columbia L.R.* 605, 606–8.

[6] See Bruce A. Kimball, *The Inception of Modern Professional Education: C.C. Langdell, 1826–1906* (2009); David Rabban, *Law's History: American Legal Thought and the Transatlantic Turn to History* (2013); Stephen A. Siegel, 'Francis Wharton's Orthodoxy: God, Historical Jurisprudence, and Classical Legal Thought' (2004) 46 *American Journal of Legal History* 422; Stephen A. Siegel, 'Joel Bishop's Orthodoxy' (1995) 13 *Law and History Review* 215.

[7] Book Review, (1880) 14 *American L.R.* 233–5, 234.

fundamental legal doctrines could be teased out of a much smaller number of leading cases.[8] By a correct classification and arrangement of the material found in the cases, the major categories of law could be identified, the basic principles which underpinned them elaborated, and the rules relating to particular categories put into a rational order.

As Dean of the Harvard Law School, Langdell assembled a group of scholars who applied his method to a range of topics. It included men like James Barr Ames and William A. Keener, who developed his method of case teaching, as well as other colleagues such as John Chipman Gray, Joseph A. Beale, and Samuel Williston. Their doctrinal works were replete with comments which suggested a vision of law as a closed system of rational rules. For instance, having figured out the Rule against Perpetuities from case law stretching back to the Middle Ages, Gray announced that '[i]f the answer to a problem does not square with the multiplication table one may call it wrong, although it be the work of Sir Isaac Newton; and so if a decision conflicts with the Rule against Perpetuities, one may call it wrong, however learned and able the court that has pronounced it.'[9] William Keener also appeared to share this mechanical vision of science. Explaining the case-method pioneered by Langdell, he stated that '[t]he facts of the case correspond to the specimen, and the opinion of the court, announcing the principles of law to be applied to the facts, correspond to the memoir of the discoverer of a great scientific truth.'[10] For Keener, the misclassification of legal topics was 'not only unscientific, and therefore theoretically wrong', but also 'destructive of clear thinking, and therefore vicious in practice'.[11] For many Realists, the 'legal fundamentalism' of this kind of scholarship was most clearly encapsulated in Beale's *Treatise on the Conflict of Laws*.[12] In this treatise, Beale stated that law was 'not a mere collection of arbitrary rules, but a body of scientific principle'. The general body of law—*ius* as opposed to *lex*—was 'a branch of practical philosophy; by which, through the use of reason and experience, legal generalisations may be made'. Purity of doctrine could be lost through wrong decisions, 'thus warping legal principle by bad precedent', and the 'application of general principles may be inhibited by legislation'. Indeed, bad decisions and legislative changes led to the 'peculiar local law of any jurisdiction' deviating from 'the general doctrine of the prevailing legal system'.[13]

---

[8]   Christopher C. Langdell, *A Selection of Cases on the Law of Contracts* (2nd edn., 1879) ix–x.

[9]   J. C. Gray, *The Rule against Perpetuities* (1886) v. On this work as an example of formalism, see Stephen Siegel, 'John Chipman Gray, Legal Formalism and the Transformation of Perpetuities Law' (1982) 36 *University of Miami L.R.* 439.

[10]   He added 'the facts of the case correspond to the apple which suggested to Sir Isaac Newton the law of gravitation.' William A. Keener, 'The Inductive Method in Legal Education' (1894) 28 *American L.R.* 709, 713, 718.

[11]   William A. Keener, *A Treatise on the Law of Quasi-Contracts* (1893) 3 ff.

[12]   Jerome Frank dubbed this approach 'Bealism': *Law and the Modern Mind* (1949) 55 (1st edn., 1930).

[13]   Joseph H. Beale, *A Treatise on the Conflict of Laws* (1916) 135.

Such comments did not, however, amount to a theory of law. Langdellian 'formalism' did not generate a theory, beyond the occasional statement of method found in prefaces or interleaved in the text. The underlying theory was often inferred by critics, who wished to use it as a foil for their own ideas. Realists who were sceptical about the autonomy of legal doctrine drew their inspiration from Holmes's aphorism—included in his review of Langdell—that the 'life of the law has not been logic: it has been experience'. Those who were sceptical about its centrality in determining legal outcomes were inspired by Holmes's later comment that '[t]he prophecies of what the courts will do in fact, and nothing more pretentious, are what I mean by the law'.[14] But in fact, such comments were not out of step with the views expressed by a number of scholars who were tarred with the brush of 'formalism'. Having spent most of his career writing on property law, Gray only turned to jurisprudence in 1909, when he published *The Nature and Sources of the Law*. In this work, he argued that law was the set of rules applied by the courts in any state: nothing was law which the judges did not apply as such.[15] In Gray's opinion, courts were constantly making *ex post facto* law, and it was entirely open for the court in one common law jurisdiction to decide a novel case differently from a court in the neighbouring jurisdiction. Judges were not investigators uncovering truth, like Newton: if Newton was wrong, the universe remained unmoved; but if judges went awry, their bad decisions remained law.[16] Even Beale argued for the need to study law with a view to its 'readjustment and reform'. Invoking the new 'sociological jurisprudence' of Pound, he said that 'we must examine the law objectively to learn its social purpose and to see how far that purpose is being accomplished'.[17]

In fact, the 'formalist' project of attempting to put the common law into a rational order and to seek underlying principles was one which was engaged in by a large number of scholars on both sides of the Atlantic, who did not think of law as a whole as a closed system of reasoning and would not have seen themselves as Langdellian 'disciples'. They included Holmes himself, as well as such scholars as James Bradley Thayer, John Henry Wigmore, and Melville Madison Bigelow in the United States and Frederick Pollock and William Anson in England. The idea that the scholar could seek to put the body of the law into a rational form was not seen as requiring him to adhere to a theory of law which treated it as a closed system. For instance, Bigelow, whose highly 'formalist' *Law of Torts* commenced with an analytical chapter on 'General Theory and Doctrine', and followed with chapters on specific torts beginning with a 'statement of the duty' involved in each one, told his students that '[t]he limitations of logic, in the presence of social change—the dangers of it— should be plainly taught'.[18] In his view, 'a scientific school of law' should study all

---

[14] Oliver W. Holmes, 'The Path of the Law' (1897) 10 *Harvard L.R.* 457, 461.

[15] J. C. Gray, *The Nature and Sources of the Law* (1909) 82.   [16] Gray (n. 15) 97, 99.

[17] Joseph H. Beale, 'The Necessity for a Study of Legal System' 1914 *A.A.L.S. Proceedings* 31, 39. Quoted in Brian Z. Tamanaha, *Beyond the Formalist-Realist Divide: The Role of Politics in Judging* (2010) 16.

[18] Melville M. Bigelow, *Centralization and the Law: Scientific Legal Education* (1906) 183.

the 'sources when the law is to be declared'—not only precedents and historical doctrines, but also 'the direct and indirect immediate sub-legal sources—business and pursuit generally, and the other less tangible influences which go up to make the sum total—the political, economic, psychological, and personal influences'.[19] In another lecture, he said 'the law is continuous only in time. In point of substance it is broken up into periods of the ascendancy of certain social and economic forces . . . the books do not contain, either in development or in germ, all the law'.[20]

II.

When it came to their doctrinal writing, these writers were following in the footsteps of several generations of legal scholars, who had sought to digest and make sense of the increasingly large volume of case law. Ever since the publication of Blackstone's *Commentaries,* Anglo-American jurists had searched for principles within the common law and to set them out in logically ordered treatises which commenced with the more general matters and descended to particulars. Nor was the language of scientific inquiry new to Langdell. His Harvard predecessor, Simon Greenleaf, said in 1838 that '[a]djudged cases, are, to the philosophical student of the law, what facts are to the student of natural science. They are the elements from which, by the process of induction, his mind ascends to the higher regions of the science, scans it boldest outlines, and familiarises itself with its great and leading principles'.[21] What made the literature of the later nineteenth century appear innovative was its greater rigour than many earlier treatises, which were often digests of cases on fragmented topics, put together by young lawyers seeking to make their name.

There were practical reasons why jurists began to attempt more systematic treatises. With the abolition of the forms of action on both sides of the Atlantic in the third quarter of the nineteenth century, a framework of classification long used by lawyers and law students was removed; and jurists were led to look for substantive principles to make sense of the broader classifications of 'contract' and 'tort'. In this era of reform, it was increasingly evident that a different kind of textbook was needed. In the first treatise on torts, published in Boston in 1859, Francis Hilliard commented that hitherto, this area of the law had always been discussed in books relating to procedure, evidence, or the courts. 'By a singular process of inversion', he wrote, '*remedies* have been substituted for *wrongs*'. This was

---

[19] Ibid., 203.   [20] Bigelow, 'Notes' (1907) 23 *L.Q.R.* (1907) 1–4, 2.

[21] 'Cambridge Law School: Notes of Professor Greenleaf's Introductory Lecture, at the Present Term' (1838–1839) 1 *Law Reporter* 217, 218.

'to reverse the natural order of things; to give a false view of the law as a system of forms rather than principles; to elevate the positive and conventional above the absolute and permanent'. By rethinking this approach, Hilliard hoped to have 'evolved a series of principles, far less fragmentary and disconnected' than were to be found in the forms of action.[22] It was this ambition which was shared by the jurists of the Gilded Age.

Three intellectual influences which came together to shape the approach of this new generation of treatise writers. The first was that of common law forensic reasoning. There was a well-established tradition in common law thought that the law was composed of principles and doctrines which had a life outside their expression in particular cases. The common law was conceived of as a body, not as a collection of fragments. This law was not to be found in the verbal formulation of a rule embodied in any particular decision, but in the wider reasoning which explained the case. It was made up of the *rationes decidendi*, the principles derived from a body of cases. This meant that when a judge had to decide any case, he began with his '*principle* for a guide' (as Justice J. T. Coleridge put it), and only then looked to other decisions to see how the principle had been applied in them.[23] This was a vision which continued to appeal to many jurists. Joel Bishop, who has been described as 'a seminal classical legal scholar' for his methodology, which suggested that broad principles could be induced from case law and then applied deductively to new cases,[24] saw the law as system of principles and spoke of particular decisions as being 'evidence of the law'.[25] He described a legal system made up of legal 'points'—particular rules which could be identified and enumerated—which could be 'practically reduced to, or merged in, *principles*', which were 'universal, applying in all cases where its particular nature renders it applicable'.[26]

A similar fidelity to the common law tradition can be seen in the approach both of Holmes and Langdell. In 1870, Holmes explained that 'it is the merit of the common law that it decides the case first and determines the principle afterwards'. Judgments were not made as a matter of logic, with decisions made on the basis of syllogistic deductions from major premises. Rather, the *ratio decidendi* or principle was worked out later: 'It is only after a series of determinations on the same subject matter, that it becomes necessary to "reconcile the cases", as it is called, that is by a true induction to state the principle which until then has been obscurely felt'.[27]

---

[22] Francis Hilliard, *The Law of Torts or Private Wrongs* (2nd edn., 1861) vi–vii (1st edn., 1859).

[23] 'Copies of the Lord Chancellor's Letters to the Judges, and of their Answers, respecting the Criminal Law Bills of the Last Session', in *Parliamentary Papers* 1854 (303) LIII 389, 12. Quoted in Michael Lobban, 'Legal Theory and Judge-Made Law in England, 1850–1920' (2011) 40 *Quaderni Fiorentini* 553, 565.

[24] Siegel 'Joel Bishop's Orthodoxy' (n. 6) 216, 228.

[25] Joel Prentiss Bishop, *The First Book of the Law* (1868) §§ 61, 65–6.

[26] Ibid., §§ 185, 191. Principles could be used to overrule erroneous decisions, for 'authority does not consist of *cases* but of *principles*' (ibid., § 98).

[27] Oliver W. Holmes, 'Codes and the Arrangement of Law' (1870) 5 *American L.R.* 1.

This was also the approach of Langdell's casebook, which asked students to tease out the wider principle from a collection of cases which were set out in order of their historical development.[28] They both accepted what was a commonplace by the later nineteenth century: that the common law was a growing and developing system of law, whose flexibility and growth might be stunted by codification.

The second influence was that of Austinian jurisprudence. In his lectures—posthumously published in 1863—Austin aimed to 'analyse certain notions which meet us at every step, as we travel through the science of law'[29] and to abstract the 'necessary principles, notions and distinctions' to be found in all advanced legal systems. Having defined his legal concepts, Austin sought to map out a system of the different kinds of rights and duties which might exist. Although his definition of law as the command of sovereign came in for much criticism, even his critics saw value in the analytical exercise of defining legal concepts and categories. While Austin also favoured codification, his lectures on jurisprudence served to provide a toolkit for those working in the common law tradition, who did not seek a definitive code. The mass of materials lying in case law would be put into a better and more rational order, if the jurist applied clearer concepts to them. By the second half of the nineteenth century, when the forms of action were being abolished on both sides of the Atlantic, these tools were of increasing importance to jurists seeking a new way of organizing law.[30]

The third influence was that given by the rival approach of historical jurisprudence. Where Austin's jurisprudence was timeless and static, Sir Henry Maine's *Ancient Law* (1861) stressed the contingent and changing nature of law. He had argued that in progressive societies, social necessities always ran ahead of law. Three devices—legal fictions, equity, and legislation—had been developed in order to ensure that law would keep up. Legal fictions were associated with the common lawyers' predilection for pretending that all remained unchanged, even as they were changing the law. Maine showed that modern conceptions of property and contract were not timeless categories, but had evolved over time, as progressive societies evolved from being based on status to being based on contract.[31] Maine's work was extremely popular and widely read. His approach to legal questions might have held out the promise of a more sociological jurisprudence, encouraging jurists to relate changes in law to changes in the wider society, and to use law as a vehicle through

---

[28] See Thomas C. Grey, 'Langdell's Orthodoxy' (1983) 45 *University of Pittsburgh L.R.* 1, 28–32.

[29] J. Austin, *Lectures on Jurisprudence, or the Philosophy of Positive Law* (1873) 4th edn., (ed. R. Campbell) 34.

[30] The treatise writers who were said to have been the first to put the law into a principled form drew heavily both on Austin's analytical jurisprudence and on the German Pandectist literature which had also inspired him. See for instance S. M. Leake, *The Elements of the Law of Contracts* (1867).

[31] See further Raymond Cocks, *Sir Henry Maine: A Study in Victorian Jurisprudence* (1988), and Michael Lobban, *A History of the Philosophy of Law in the Common Law World* (2007) 189–204.

which to trace and explain changes in social structure.[32] It might have encouraged jurists to abandon the jurisprudence of concepts and to look for a jurisprudence of purposes, as Jhering's attack on *Begriffsjurisprudenz* sought to do. However, Maine did not absolutely reject the Austinian vision: indeed, he endorsed it as the best conceptual apparatus with which to explain modern law. Austin's work and Maine's were reviewed together, and many reviewers regarded the works as complementary. Many readers of Maine did not feel compelled to relate doctrinal changes to wider social developments; but they did draw the lesson that to understand the shape and purpose of modern legal doctrine, it was necessary to trace the history of the doctrine.

In taking this historical approach to doctrine, they were not influenced only by Maine's version, but also looked to the German historical school and in particular the example of Savigny. Although Savigny felt that law was at base the custom of the people—and manifested its spirit or *Volksgeist*—and that it developed organically over time, he argued that as society specialized, so that part of the *Volksgeist* was articulated through the voices of jurists, who had the task both of developing the law and of giving it systematic unity.[33] For Savigny, the task of the legal historian was to uncover leading principles and notions, which could then be systematized—as Savigny himself did in his *System des heutigen römischen Rechts*. Savigny—and the Pandectist school which provided the very model for mid nineteenth-century reformers of legal education—united a historical and an analytical approach. As he put it, the essence of the systematic method was to set out the connections, which wove together individual concepts and rules into a coherent whole.[34]

III.

Later critics sometimes accused the 'formalists' of inhabiting that very 'heaven of legal concepts' which had been so mocked by Rudolf von Jhering.[35] They also associated formalism with Austinian analytical jurisprudence, in which (in Pound's

---

[32] See, e.g., Frederic Harrison, 'Maine on Ancient Law' (1861) 19 (n.s.) *Westminster Review* 457–77, 465.

[33] F. C. von Savigny, *System des heutigen römischen Rechts*, vol. 1 (1840) 45, §14 ff. See also Mathias Reimann, 'Nineteenth Century German Legal Science' (1990) 31 *Boston College L.R.* 837, 852–3.

[34] Savigny (n. 33) xxxvi.

[35] Rudolf von Jhering, 'In the Heaven of Legal Concepts: a Fantasy', trans. Charlotte L. Levy (1985) 58 *Temple L.Q.* 799. See Felix S. Cohen, 'Transcendental Nonsense and the Functional Approach' (1935) 35 *Columbia L.R.* 809–49.

phrase) 'new situations were always to be met by deductions from traditional fixed conceptions'.[36] However, while it is clear that this generation of jurists was very influenced by Austinian analytical toolbox of concepts, they did not think that these conceptual tools could themselves determine the content of the law, or generate answers to new legal questions. Instead, they were to be used better to arrange the materials of historical case law.

The importance of analytical jurisprudence is perhaps best seen by its use by scholars who were sceptical about Austin. Frederick Pollock—who proclaimed that 'the philosophy of the English or "analytical" school is not mine'[37]—nonetheless engaged in the Austinian enterprise of seeking accurate definitions for the purposes of classification. In his *First Book of Jurisprudence*, he explained that '[i]n order to have any real working acquaintance with a system of law we must inquire, not only what duties and rights are recognised, but how rights are acquired and lost; what rights are capable of transfer, and how; by what acts and events duties are imposed; how far and in what ways duties can be transmitted; and how they are discharged'.[38] He explained that the classifications and divisions made by lawyers were 'formal' ways of 'reducing the world of human action to manageable items'.[39] One such classification was the classical distinction between the duties and rights owed to particular individuals (*in personam*)—such as contractual duties—and those owed to the world at large (*in rem*).[40] Pollock's treatment was clearly influenced by Austin's discussion. Thus, he defended the method of distinguishing the 'general part' from the 'special part', since it was convenient for purposes of exposition that 'those principles and rules which are found in all or most portions of the subject . . . are disposed of before the several branches are entered upon'.[41] Elsewhere, he argued that comparative study could disclose 'typical conceptions which are common to all legal systems' and that the jurist could deduce some necessary 'general ideas of law', including duty, intent, negligence, ownership and possession from a study of such systems.[42]

In his early publications, Holmes also sought to devise an analytical a system of classification, based on different kinds of duties. Taking a critical view of Austin's method, he argued that any arrangement of law had to be made on the basis of duties, not rights, since duties preceded rights both 'logically and chronologically'.[43] For Holmes, the purpose of classification was to make the law knowable: this was

---

[36] Quoted in Sebok (n. 3) 45.

[37] Frederick Pollock, *A First Book of Jurisprudence for Students of the Common Law* (1896) vii.

[38] Ibid., 73.   [39] Ibid., 80.

[40] Ibid., 81. Pollock also noted the distinction between 'Substantive and Adjective law', ibid., 97.

[41] Ibid., 102.

[42] Frederick Pollock, 'The Methods of Jurisprudence', in *Oxford Lectures and Other Discourses* (1890) 10.

[43] Holmes, 'Codes' (1870) 5 *American L.R.* 1, 3. See also Oliver W. Holmes, 'The Arrangement of the Law: Privity' (1872) 7 *American L.R.* 46.

best done by proceeding 'from the most general conception to the most specific proposition or exception in the order of logical subordination'.[44] In his first article setting out his system of classification on the basis of duties, Holmes criticized Austin's definition of law as the command of the sovereign, making the point that 'by whom a duty is imposed must be of less importance than the definiteness of its expression and the certainty of its being enforced'.[45] If this seemed to prefigure some of Holmes's later suggestions that law was to be found in what courts actually did, the point he was making here was that international law—in which the rules were so definite that they could be digested in case books and where violations were in fact punished—was a proper subject for a law book, and was something to be included in a comprehensive classification. Consequently, his classification began with the duties of sovereign powers to each other, before turning to the duties owed to the sovereign by citizens, and the various categories of duties citizens might owe each other. These duties were tabulated in a series of articles which followed. Holmes was here attempting to improve upon Austin's method of classification, not to abandon its ambition.

Langdell himself had read Austin, and was clearly influenced by his method of analysis and classification.[46] Although few of the systematic treatise-writers of the late nineteenth century wrote extensively about the analytical method, they accepted the notion that a taxonomy of legal concepts could be made, which distinguished between the major categories of law, and which helped clarify the meaning of notions such as right and duty, which were to be found in all advanced legal systems. However, it did not follow that once the jurist had uncovered the structure of legal concepts, he would be able to deduce the content of the rules as a matter of logic.[47] The late nineteenth-century jurists used the tools of Austinian analysis to classify and distinguish areas of doctrine found in the common law cases. They remained part of a common law tradition of juridical thought insofar as they did not—except in the most formal sense—see law in terms of the commands of a sovereign legislator and his subordinates, but as a body of principles and rules which developed with the community and was found in its case law. At the same time, they drew the lesson of Maine, that legal doctrines and even legal concepts were not timeless, but were often contingent, that their development had to be traced by a careful study of the sources, and that this might lead the jurist to re-evaluate the doctrine. This explains why so many of

---

[44] Holmes, 'Privity' (1872) 7 *American L.R.* 47. Cf. Oliver W. Holmes, 'Possession' (1878) 12 *American L.R.* 688, 702.

[45] Holmes, 'Codes' (1870) 5 *American L.R.* 1 at 4.

[46] See Christopher C. Langdell, 'A Brief Survey of Equity Jurisdiction' (1887) 1 *Harvard L.R.* 55–8 and 'Classification of Rights and Wrongs' (1900) 13 *Harvard L.R.* 537–56 and 659–78.

[47] Nor had this been Austin's argument: if the clarification of concepts would make it easier for the judge to understand the legal question which was being posed, he was still a subordinate legislator who was expected to decide novel cases on the basis of utility.

these jurists—including Langdell, Holmes, Ames, and Bigelow—spent so much time exploring the history of legal doctrines, tracing the evolution of ideas from the medieval Year Books onwards.[48]

The centrality of historical, rather than purely logical, analysis to these scholars' explanation of doctrines can be seen particularly clearly in the late nineteenth century debates over the nature and function of consideration in contract. If Langdell's discussion of offer and acceptance seemed to have a tinge of scholastic logic about it (inviting Holmes's barb), his treatment of consideration—that quirk of common law contract doctrine, which held that an informal contract was only binding if there had been a benefit given to the promisor or a detriment suffered by the promisee—was rooted in historical argumentation. Langdell explained that there were two kinds of consideration, which were respectively enforced by the actions of debt (the more ancient form) and of *assumpsit* (which was of more recent growth).[49] They were different in nature: the essence of consideration in debt cases was the benefit conferred on the debtor, while in *assumpsit*, it was the detriment suffered by the promisee. In a very compressed discussion, Langdell explained how the rise of the action of *assumpsit* had modified as well as relaxed the old consideration. It was not a necessary development, for it would have been perfectly rational for the courts to require no consideration in *assumpsit* cases; '[b]ut whatever may have been the merits of the question originally, it was long since conclusively settled.'[50] If Langdell's ultimate conclusion seemed dogmatically definitional—that detriment was the essential feature of consideration in *assumpsit*—it was a dogma derived from historical analysis. Holmes in turn expanded on the topic in *The Common Law*, where he argued that it was necessary to know something about the ancient action of debt 'to understand the enlightened rules which make up the law of contract at the present time'.[51] He dug deeper than Langdell, giving a speculative history of the procedural origins of the requirement for a *quid pro quo* in cases of debt, and arguing that it was by a process of accident and analogy that a doctrine of consideration identified with detriment came to be applied in *assumpsit*.[52] However, neither his conclusions nor his method were particularly out of line with Langdell's. Rather than being driven by the nature of the thing—as a matter of logical reasoning—both of these scholars saw the doctrine of consideration as being given shape by its history. At the same time, the need to account for the doctrine of consideration led both of these men to reject the—logical—will theory of contract, which had been favoured by European jurists such as Savigny, and instead to develop a 'bargain'

[48] On this, see Rabban (n. 6) 153–309.
[49] Christopher C. Landell, *Summary of the Law of Contracts* (2nd edn., 1880) 58.   [50] Ibid., 61.
[51] Oliver W. Holmes, *The Common Law* (1881) 251 ff. In Mainite vein, he added that 'whenever we trace a leading doctrine of substantive law far enough back, we are very likely to find some forgotten circumstance of procedure at its source' (253).
[52] Holmes (n. 51) 258, 285. Cf. Oliver W. Holmes, 'Early English Equity' (1885) 1 *L.Q.R.* 162, 171.

theory.[53] Moreover, this theory was the end-point of their explanation, rather than a starting point for further deductions.

A careful exploration of the history of legal doctrine could also raise questions about its nature and function, and its suitability for the modern age. Ames, who praised Langdell's focus on detriment as the key notion for consideration in developing his own history,[54] noted that the definition still left a crucial question unanswered: what was to be understood by 'detriment'?[55] His historical examination of the topic revealed that courts had changed their approach over time: whereas an older stand of cases suggested that forbearance to prosecute an invalid claim was not regarded as a detriment, the more modern authorities took a different view, and one which 'accords well with the views of business men'.[56] A close study of the older cases also revealed that some modern views of consideration which disappointed the reasonable expectations of businessmen (such as the modern notion that part payment could not satisfy a larger debt) rested on misunderstandings of the historical material. Ames's conclusion from a study of the case law was that 'any act or forbearance given in exchange for a promise'—however minimal—could constitute the detriment required for consideration to be present. In his view, this meant that the mere act of uttering a promise could be consideration for a counter promise.[57] Although Ames claimed that this made for 'logical simplicity in the law' and was 'a just deduction from the decided cases', it was also designed specifically to achieve a result which was desired by business.[58] The debate over the nature of consideration continued to rage, and Ames's view remained a controversial one.[59] What is significant for our purposes is that these scholars regarded the best interpretation of the doctrine which was to be found in the historical case law to be open to contestation and

[53] For Langdell, 'as every consideration is in theory equal to the promise in value, so it is in theory the promisor's sole inducement to make the promise' Langdell (n. 49) 78. For Holmes, 'the promise must be made and accepted as the conventional motive or inducement for furnishing the consideration': Holmes (n. 51) 293.

[54] Ames argued that the two aspects of consideration did not derive from the same root, but had different sources: the 'benefit' side derived from the action of debt, whereas the 'detriment' side derived from the action on the case for deceit, whence it migrated into the action of *assumpsit* for nonfeasance: J. B. Ames, 'The History of Assumpsit: I—Express Assumpsit' (1888) *Harvard L.R.* 1, 14.

[55] J. B. Ames, 'Two Theories of Consideration: 1. Unilateral Contracts' (1899) 12 *Harvard L.R.* 515.

[56] Ibid., 518.

[57] Ames, 'Two Theories of Consideration. II. Bilateral Contracts' (1899) 13 *Harvard L.R.* 29, 32: 'the giving of the promise is not only an act, but an act that neither was under any obligation to give'.

[58] Ames (n. 55) at 531.

[59] Holmes's view that a more significant act was required derived from his theoretical understanding of the function of consideration as 'the conventional inducement of the counter promise'—it was 'not a *promise* to pay damages or, etc, but an act imposing a liability to damages *nisi*.' He went on, 'You commit a tort & are liable. You commit a contract and are liable *unless* the event agreed upon, over which you may have no, and never have absolute, control, comes to pass.' M. DeWolfe Howe, *The Holmes-Pollock Letters: The Correspondence of Mr Justice Holmes and Sir Frederick Pollock* (1961) vol. I 177.

discussion, and were not loath to suggest interpretations which best fitted the needs of modern society.

In dealing with topics such as contract—what Maine had seen as the *terminus ad quem* of the development of western societies—the jurists at the end of the nineteenth century were discussing what they regarded as largely settled topics. Their aim was to interpret the case law and rules inherited from the past, rather than to point to ways in which the law should develop in the future. When Langdell discussed the rule to be adopted for contracts made by the post, it may have been a matter which (in his view) had not yet been settled definitely by the courts, but it was one for which he felt the rationale of the common law rules on offer and acceptance generated a clear answer. Policy considerations were, in this area, 'irrelevant' for the common lawyer, since the question could be settled by doctrinal reasoning (though as has been shown, Langdell also considered broader aspects of convenience in his discussion).[60] In dealing with topics such as contract law, these treatise-writers sought to set down the 'general part', the general rules in the common law which determined how contracts were to be made, interpreted, and dissolved. It was not part of their purpose to deal with particular different kinds of contracts, and the various policies which related to them: indeed, their very jurisprudential project was to get away from the fragmented works which had featured so prominently in the earlier literature. Nor were they concerned with the broader policy question of which contracts should be enforced, and which regulated, beyond (in some cases) the limited treatment offered in chapters on unlawful agreements. These were matters for legislation. In the law of contract, the 'formal' or 'general' part could be separated from the more 'substantive' questions or 'special' part which dealt with what kinds of contractual agreements should be maintained.[61]

IV.

It was no coincidence that the most 'logical' common law treatises were to be found in the law of contract, for it was in this area of private law that jurists—whether Anglo-Saxon or continental—were most able to tease out rules in a largely abstract

---

[60] See Bruce A. Kimball, 'Langdell on Contracts and Legal Reasoning: Correcting the Holmesian Caricature' (2007) 25 *Law and History Review* 345, 373–82.

[61] Although the 'classical' school is often associated with an ideology of freedom of contract, the doctrine set out in the general treatises was not incompatible with detailed regulatory regimes for particular kinds of contract: see, e.g., J. B. Matthews, *The Law of Money Lending Past and Present* (1906); Alan Leslie, *The Law of Transport by Railway* (1920).

way. The law of torts, which was in flux in the later nineteenth century, presented a different kind of challenge to those who wanted to elucidate its principles: for if it was possible to define the elements of a contract without addressing the question of which kinds of contracts were to be enforced, it was much harder to define the elements of tort without considering which kinds of wrongs were to be redressed. When Holmes chided Langdell's striving for *elegentia juris* or *logical* integrity of the system as a system' in his review of the *Summary*, it was in part because of his awareness—at a time when he was developing his own ideas of tort—that the common law of torts could not be set out in this way. In the year before the review, in an article on tort, Holmes had already pointed to 'the failure of all theories which consider the law only from its formal side', since they failed to see that law was 'for ever adopting new principles from life at one end' while retaining 'old ones from history . . . which have not yet been absorbed or sloughed off'. In this article, he argued that the 'secret root' of the law was the 'considerations of what is expedient for the community' which were 'traceable to public policy in the last analysis'.[62] Nonetheless, if Holmes was sceptical about the purely logical method, it was his ambition at this time to look for the general principles in the common law governing liability in torts. Moreover, it was part of his own aim to develop 'a connected scheme to analyze the fundamental conceptions of the law'.[63] Although Holmes came to be seen as the first major critic of 'formalism', his own efforts to explain the law of torts stood at the centre of the project of explaining common law doctrines and coherent bodies of law based on identifiable principles, which stood at the heart of the project of the private law treatise writers at the end of the nineteenth century.

The principles governing tort could not be figured out as a matter of a priori definition, at least not unless the view was taken that all actors should be held strictly liable in tort for harms caused by their acts. However, this was not a theory which could explain the common law, which had seen a recent expansion of the doctrine of negligence. Nor, in Holmes's view, was it a theory which made logical sense, given the potentially infinite chain of causation for any event which resulted in harm.[64] Rather than being purely logical, a theory of tort had to explain the developing doctrine of the common law in the best way. In common law style, Holmes sought to derive a theory which would both explain the principle behind the doctrine, and show how it served the needs of the present society. Part of this project entailed looking at the history of the common law to explain the ambit of certain doctrines, which might (as with the case of consideration) call into question present understandings which were based on a flawed reading of history. Holmes did this in his article of 1879 on 'Common Carriers', which ended with a statement of his famous 'paradox of form and substance'.[65] Holmes's aim in the

---

[62] Oliver W. Holmes, 'Common Carriers and the Common Law' (1879) 13 *American L.R.* 609, 631.
[63] Oliver W. Holmes, 'Trespass and Negligence' (1880) 14 *American L.R.* 1, 1n.   [64] Ibid., 9–10.
[65] Holmes, 'Common Carriers' (1879) 13 *American L.R.* 609, 631.

article was to show the incoherence of the modern rule that common carriers were held strictly liable for damage to goods carried by them. A detailed discussion of legal history showed how the ancient law of bailments, which had held all bailees strictly liable for the loss of bailed goods (for which they had a remedy over against the thief) had been remodelled in the early modern era (in part because of the rise of *assumpsit*) to make common carriers strictly liable for any damage done to them (even though they had no remedy over). It was a doctrinal development which 'made the carrier's burden heavier than it was in the time of the Year Books'.[66] Holmes's history aimed to show that one could only understand 'to what extent the old common law of bailment still survives' by 'enumerating the decisions in which the old law is applied'; but he added that if this were done, the scholar would 'find it hard to bring them together under a general principle'.[67] The point of Holmes's article was to show that '[i]f there is a sound rule of public policy which ought to impose a special responsibility upon common carriers, as those words are now understood, it has never yet been stated'; for the policy which shaped the early modern developments had been 'part of a protective system which has passed away'. Without being placed on such firm foundations, the doctrine of strict liability was like the 'clavicle in the cat', surviving after its use had been forgotten, and resulting in 'failure and confusion from the merely logical point of view'.[68] In Holmes's view, doctrine had to be tested by asking what function it fulfilled, and whether it fulfilled it in a coherent fashion.

Holmes went on to develop his own theory of torts, which sought to marginalize strict liability. In 'Trespass and Negligence', he argued that 'the principle of our law is that loss from accident must lie where it falls', even where the instrument of misfortune was another person, unless that person could have foreseen and avoided the harm. This argument was based in part on logic—or arguments from 'consistency', as Holmes put it. It also relied on an examination of historical authorities, for he claimed that the common law had 'never known' a rule of strict liability.[69] Holmes also invoked 'policy' once again, though the policy in question— that it was no more just to make a man liable for unforeseen harms done to another than to require him to insure that person against being struck by lightning—might as well be described as a moral or philosophical argument. It was in this article that Holmes developed his idea that the standard of care imposed was an objective one, not a subjective one. This theory was based in part on Holmes's 'policy' arguments about how societies could best be made to function, and in part on his interpretation of past common law cases. It was a theory which explicitly linked the development of the rules of the common law—in determining which acts were to be held as

---

[66] Ibid., 625–6.   [67] Ibid., 628.   [68] Ibid., 630.

[69] Holmes, 'Trespass and Negligence' (1880) 14 *American L.R.* 1, 7 ('unless in that period of dry precedent which is so often to be found midway between a creative epoch and a period of solvent philosophical reaction').

blameworthy—with the values of the community as expressed by a jury. According to his theory, people were to be punished for falling short of the standard which was regarded as morally blameworthy by the community. The legal standard was set by the jury, and then formulated into rules of law by courts over time. As he put it, '[a] judge who has sat at *nisi prius* ought gradually to acquire a fund of experience which enables him to represent the common sense of the community in ordinary instances far better than an average jury.'[70]

When seeking the principles of the law of tort, it was much more necessary to develop a theory about the content of that law—which harms were to be compensated and how far—than was the case with contract law, where the jurist could much more easily define what a contract was, without having to discuss which contracts should be enforced. To that degree, Holmes's disagreement with Langdell may have reflected the fact that their main preoccupations at this time were on different areas of law. At the same time, Holmes's own work on tort suggests that he thought it possible to work out a theory of torts which would be able to guide the judge and jurist in making sense of the inherited case law and in guiding its future development. Holmes's project was ambitious: having in 1870 wondered whether that 'Torts is not a proper subject for a law book',[71] he set out to uncover an underlying theory which could explain the area. While he repeatedly spoke of the scholar needing to look for 'policy', it was the 'policy of the law' which he here had in mind, for it was the jurist who was to develop the law rather than 'the man of statistics or the master of economics'.[72]

Holmes's approach to developing his theory of tort was entirely consistent with the wider aims of the late nineteenth-century treatise-writers. Indeed, it proved a model for other writers seeking a generalized theory of tort. They included Frederick Pollock, who declared in 1887 that 'the purpose of this book is to show that there really is a Law of Torts, not merely a number of rules of law about various kinds of torts—that this is a true living branch of the Common Law, not a collection of heterogeneous instances.[73] There were 'elements of coherence' to be found in the cases, which showed that 'the law of torts is a body of law capable of being expressed in a systematic form under appropriate general principles'.[74] Pollock said he had tried in the book 'to turn to practical account the lessons of what I saw and heard' at Harvard Law School, and noted that it had been 'put into shape after, or concurrently with, free oral exposition and discussion of the leading cases'.[75] Like Holmes, Pollock sought to tease a general principle out of heterogeneous case law, teasing 'authentic general principles' from a mass of particular remedies, general propositions for which there was no direct authority, but which best explained the underlying law. In the event, it proved very difficult

[70] Ibid., 33.   [71] Book Review (1871) 5 *American L.R.* 340.
[72] The phrase is from Holmes's 'Path' (1897) 10 *Harvard L.R.* 457, 469.
[73] Frederick Pollock, *The Law of Torts* (1887) vi.   [74] Ibid., 5.   [75] Ibid., vi.

for tort scholars to devise a coherent theory to explain the law of tort, and point to principles which could explain its trajectory of development. In the view of some scholars, Holmes himself had lost faith in the enterprise by the 1890s,[76] although Pollock did not. Throughout the twentieth century, tort scholars like Pollock and his followers struggled to develop a theory which accurately reflected the doctrine it purported to explain: but they remained committed to the 'formalist' project of seeking coherence in the case law.

V.

In one respect, the Realist critique was correct. The treatise-writers of the Gilded Age did not see judges (or jurists) as subordinate legislators, who were to be educated in how best to decide cases to make it fit present policy needs. They rather saw the common law as a system of adjudication between litigants. They assumed that a careful historical investigation of the existing case law, informed by a developed toolbox of analytical concepts, would help clarify the law, and help judges to make more consistent decisions. As Gray explained, if it was the judge who made the law in each individual case, there was great value in the judge being guided by settled *sources* of law, since it would avoid the need for everything to be worked out *de novo* in any case. If matters were not regarded as settled by authority, he argued, 'an army of judges would not suffice to keep a society moving'.[77] For men like Gray, careful scholarship could contribute further, by explaining the rationale of common law rules in a way which would ensure that legislators did not throw the law into confusion—and generating high litigation costs—by enacting careless legislation.[78]

In common with many generations of jurists before them, the thinkers often misnamed 'legal formalists' assumed that the law applied by the common law courts was coherent, and could be classified into distinct, broad categories. However, they did not think these categories were closed, nor that they were timeless, or unchanging, or unrelated to social needs. They saw the common law as a developing body, which served the needs of its community; but they sought to make better sense of it, by using the latest tools offered by analytical and historical jurisprudence.

---

[76] Whether Holmes adhered to his earlier views by the late 1890s is a matter of debate: see Daniel R. Ernst, 'The Critical Tradition of Writing American Legal History' (1993) 102 *Yale L.J.* 1019.

[77] Gray (n. 15) 252.   [78] Gray (n. 9) v, 439–44.

Bibliography

Neil Duxbury, *Patterns of American Jurisprudence* (Oxford University Press, 1995)

Grant Gilmore, *The Ages of American Law* (Yale University Press, 1977)

Thomas C. Grey, 'Langdell's Orthodoxy' (1983) 45 *University of Pittsburgh L.R.* 1, 28–32 ff

Morton J. Horwitz, *The Transformation of American Law, 1870–1960* (Oxford University Press, 1992)

Duncan Kennedy, *The Rise and Fall of Classical Legal Thought* (Beard Books, 2006)

Bruce A. Kimball, *The Inception of Modern Professional Education: C. C. Langdell, 1826–1906* (University of North Carolina Press, 2009)

William P. LaPiana, *Logic and Experience: The Origin of Modern American Legal Education* (Oxford University Press, 1994)

David Rabban, *Law's History: American Legal Thought and the Transatlantic Turn to History* (Cambridge University Press, 2013)

Anthony J. Sebok, *Legal Positivism in American Jurisprudence* (Cambridge University Press, 1998)

Stephen A. Siegel, 'Joel Bishop's Orthodoxy' (1995) 13 *Law and History Review* 215 ff

Robert Stevens, *Law School: Legal Education in America from the 1850s to the 1980s* (University of North Carolina Press, 1983)

Brian Z. Tamanaha, *Beyond the Formalist-Realist Divide: the Role of Politics in Judging* (Princeton University Press, 2010)

G. Edward White, *Tort Law in America: An Intellectual History*, (Oxford University Press, expanded edn., 2003)

William M. Wiecek, *The Lost World of Classical Legal Thought: Law and Ideology in America, 1886–1937* (Oxford University Press, 1998)

CHAPTER 24

....

SOCIOLOGICAL JURISPRUDENCE AND THE SPIRIT OF THE COMMON LAW

....

NOGA MORAG-LEVINE[*]

....

I. INTRODUCTION

....

In the midst of the constitutional tumults of the Lochner era, Roscoe Pound published two essays in the legal periodical *Green Bag* offering his interpretation of the legal crisis of the time and outlining a course of response. The first was titled 'The Spirit of the Common Law', the second 'The Need of a Sociological Jurisprudence', and together they summed up the key precepts of the project that would launch Pound's career during the decade preceding the First World War and forge the lens through which early twentieth-century American legal history would come to be viewed going forward.[1]

---

[*] Daryl Thompson provided excellent editorial assistance in the preparation of this manuscript. I likewise thank for their comments Malcolm Feeley, Nicola Giocoli, Jonathan Levine, Chris Tomlins, and participants in the Tel Aviv University workshop on chapters in this handbook.
[1] Roscoe Pound, 'The Spirit of the Common Law' (1906) 18 *The Green Bag* 17 ff; Roscoe Pound, 'The Need of a Sociological Jurisprudence' (1907) 19 *The Green Bag* 607 ff.

'The Spirit of the Common Law' began and ended with an ode to the centuries-long resilience of common law institutions against competition from rival systems, key to which was the common law's ability to adapt in response to the changing demands of the time. The current age required such an adaptation, Pound argued, in this instance through diminished emphasis on the rights of individuals relative to those of society at large. Notwithstanding this call for reform, the article concluded with the prediction that 'this same obstinate individualism of the common law, which makes it fit so ill in many a modern niche, may yet prove a necessary bulwark against an exaggerated and enfeebling collectivism'.[2] Whereas legal history was the starting and ending point in the 'Spirit of the Common Law', in 'The Need of a Sociological Jurisprudence' Pound called for a new model of legal research that—putting Blackstone's commentaries as well as historical legal science behind—aimed at 'scientific apprehension of the relations of law to society and of the needs and interests and opinions of society of to-day'.[3]

Like these two essays, most of Pound's writing during this period exhibits tensions and contradictions, so that it is possible, at different times, to read his project as aimed at divergent objectives: one directed at the preservation of common law institutions and principles in the face of growing public disrespect, and the other geared towards the promotion of legal reforms in the service of progressive principles of social justice. It was as the latter, for the most part, that sociological jurisprudence came to be understood, beginning with Pound's progressive contemporaries. Within this story, sociological jurisprudence is credited with at least three fundamental contributions to legal scholarship and American judicial politics. The first, and most important, is the displacement of legal formalism and its attendant laissez-faire constitutionalism. The second, in part a product of the Brandeis Brief, is the belief in the transformative potential of properly motivated and informed courts and hence litigation as tool of social change. And the third is the understanding, transmitted from Pound through the Legal Realists to Law and Society scholars, of the gap between the 'law in the books' and the 'law in action' as the definitive research agenda fusing law and social science.[4]

Notwithstanding these accolades, the meaning and significance of sociological jurisprudence's actual contribution have long been subject to debate, beginning with Pound himself who by 1921 termed the approach the 'fashion of the time' and added that it was possible to 'overrate' its value.[5] Karl Llewellyn reached much the same conclusion, though for different reasons, when in 1930 he said of sociological

---

[2] Pound (n. 1) 'The Spirit of the Common Law', 25 ff.

[3] Pound (n. 1) 'The Need of a Sociological Jurisprudence', 610 ff.

[4] See Edwin W. Patterson, 'Some Reflections on Sociological Jurisprudence' (1958) 44 *Virginia L.R.* 395 ff.; Susan S. Silbey, 'Law and Society Movement', in Herbert M. Kritzer (ed.), *Legal Systems of the World* (2002) 860 ff.

[5] Pound (n. 1) 'The Spirit of the Common Law', 10 ff; Silbey (n. 4) 860 ff.

jurisprudence that it 'remains bare of most that is significant in sociology', leaving one 'embarrassed by the constant indeterminacy of the level of [its] discourse'.[6] Multiple later writers variously expressed the view that sociological jurisprudence achieved its status, despite, or perhaps because of its meagre content.[7] Perhaps most importantly, a growing body of scholarship has questioned the accuracy of the formalist narrative that sociological jurisprudence helped superimpose on the Lochner era.[8]

Making better sense of sociological jurisprudence requires, at the start, greater emphasis on the source and meaning of Pound's anxiety over the future of the common law in America: the rising influence of continental legal and administrative ideas during an era of growing transatlantic exchange.[9] Primary in this connection was the threat that the legal profession, legal education, and common law institutions as such confronted from German-educated social reformers and social scientists bent on replicating continental legislative and administrative models in the United States. Longstanding tensions within the American polity between common law and civil law-based conceptions of regulatory authority subsequently came to a head in pitted controversies over codification, the creation of boards and commissions, and judicial review of social legislation. The fundamental question on the table was the future of judicial supremacy over both administration and legislation within the American constitutional order. Within this context, Roscoe Pound selectively drew on European social legal theory with the goal of saving the common law from itself.

Pound himself was explicit on the inspiration that his sociological jurisprudence derived from contemporary continental theoretical developments, most importantly Rudolf von Jhering's biting critique of the German historical school's 'Jurisprudence of Conceptions'.[10] Likewise, subsequent writings on sociological jurisprudence have often highlighted the various ways in which Pound kept step with Jhering.

This chapter, by contrast, finds the difference between core aspects of Jhering's and Pound's intellectual projects more instructive on the meaning of sociological jurisprudence: Jhering thought of law—meaning private Roman law—as the product of force and the end result of a struggle between self-serving interests. Law, in other words, was devoid of a priori value or entitlement to respect from the state. Pound, by contrast, held profound admiration for the common law tradition and saw it as based in deep-seated historical custom, rather than force. Pound, who changed his mind on so much else, never wavered on this point. The history

---

[6] Karl Llewellyn, 'A Realistic Jurisprudence—The Next Step' (1930) 30 *Columbia L.R.* 435 ff.

[7] William P. LaPiana, *Logic and Experience* (1994) 156 ff.

[8] E.g., Brian Tamanaha, *Beyond the Formalist-Realist Divide* (2010); David M. Rabban, *Law's History* (2013) 472 ff.

[9] Daniel Rodgers, *Atlantic Crossings: Social Politics in a Progressive Age* (1998).

[10] Roscoe Pound, 'Mechanical Jurisprudence' (1908) 8 *Columbia L.R.* 610 ff.

of Roman Law, for Jhering, served to unmask the materialist interests behind ostensibly neutral legal rights, and hence destabilize them, whereas it was with the opposite goal, that of preserving and strengthening the common law, that Pound examined its history.

What sociological jurisprudence offered in addition—though Pound was less explicit on this—was an answer to the challenge that growing competition from social sciences presented to the legal profession and the law schools. The turn to sociological jurisprudence meant in practice an injection of social-scientific content into legal pedagogy and legal research, a move whose benefits included both the preparation of law graduates for the new demands of legislative and administrative work and the bringing of better resources and reputation to American law schools, many of which still lagged behind other departments in the larger university environment. Created in the process was a socio-legal paradigm that both rescued law from the danger of insular irrelevance and ensured its continued existence as an academic discipline apart from the social sciences. Transported into legal historical research, this paradigm has had the dual effect of both lowering the barriers separating law from society and countering an alternative unified model where law and society might have existed as an integrated, barrier-free field.[11]

II. American Law and Politics in the Shadow of Germany

Beginning with a trickle in the mid-1870s and reaching a flood by the 1890s, American students headed to Germany for post-graduate education, often in economics. The experience, during a time of growing German revolt against laissez faire and a newly unified German state, shaped the world-view of these young intellectuals who, upon their return to America, left the marks of their German encounter across a broad spectrum of social-political endeavours.[12] This was a development with potentially portentous implications for the future of legal education, legal profession, and common law institutions—most importantly judicial supremacy.

---

[11] Christopher Tomlins, 'Foreword: "Law as . . ." II, History as Interface for the Interdisciplinary Study of Law' (2014) 4 *University of California Irvine L.R.* 1 ff.

[12] Rodgers (n. 9) 77 ff.

A. Legal Science and Social Science

By contrast with the situation in continental Europe, where law served as a pillar of university training going back to medieval Bologna, legal education was a new and uncertain entrant into American universities during the nineteenth century. Whether under the auspices of the English Inns of Court, or apprenticeship with members of the bar, the education of common lawyers was long the purview of the legal profession and its more practically oriented mindset. This tradition presented a dual challenge before the effort, starting in Harvard at 1816, to introduce common law teaching and scholarship into American universities. One was the need to persuade aspiring lawyers, and the legal bar more generally, of the professional benefits of university legal education. The other, somewhat in tension with the former, followed from the pressure to establish the law as a theoretical and scientific discipline equal to those around which American universities were building their standing during the second half of the nineteenth century.

Within this context, and consistent with the larger pattern of German academic influence, American law schools looked to the jurisprudential theories broadly known in Germany during the nineteenth century as legal science (*Rechtswissenschaft*). As Christopher Columbus Langdell, who as dean of Harvard Law School led this movement, would later explain, if law was to become a respectable academic discipline, it was essential to establish that 'law is a science', since 'If law be not a science, a university will consult its own dignity in declining to teach it.'[13] A legal-scientific approach to law provided the means for elevating the status of American law schools to a position comparable to that 'occupied by the law faculties in the universities of continental Europe'.[14]

The theories falling under the broad umbrella of German legal science were varied and complex but revolved around the understanding of law as a formal, systemic, and autonomous enterprise. Known as pandectism (after the German term for Justinian's *Corpus Juris*), this system was built from private law concepts and principles drawn from historical Roman law sources. With these principles identified, legal history completed its purpose, and the subsequent development of the law depended on a rational process of deductive extrapolation. The organization of law, as Georg Friedrich Puchta, the most influential scholar associated with this approach during the second half of the nineteenth century described it, could be likened to a pyramid in which higher-order abstract principles dictated more concrete sub-principles and applications. Seen through this lens, law was a closed, self-contained system that functioned in isolation of

---

[13] Christopher C. Langdell, 'Teaching Law as a Science' (1887) 21 *American L.R.* 123 ff.
[14] Ibid.

the political and social world. The legitimacy of a legal rule depended instead upon its 'systematic correctness and logical truth'.[15]

In the hands of Langdell and other classical legal scholars, legal science meant a common law-based method in which court cases, rather than the writings of Roman law scholars, served as the texts out of which abstract principles of law were to be extracted. The pedagogical practice that followed from this, known as the 'case method', was directed at the discovery of the principles hidden within judicial opinions via a 'Socratic' dialogue between students and their professors. In the process, legal science consequently transformed from a deductive method, based in Roman law texts, to an inductive process geared at the extraction of legal principles from appellate judicial decisions.[16]

By the 1870s, when American legal education first embarked on this project, deductive legal science was subject to growing criticism in Germany, with Rudolf Jhering leading the charge. A pandectist during his early career, Jhering later experienced a profound change of heart. In a complete turnaround, upending the legal-theoretical premises of his time, Jhering provocatively wrote in 1866:

The desire for logic that turns jurisprudence into legal mathematics is an error and arises from misunderstanding of law. Life does not exist for the sake of concepts but concepts for the sake of life. It is not logic that is entitled to exist but what is claimed by life, by social relations, by the sense of justice—and logical necessity, or logical impossibility, is immaterial.[17]

With this statement Jhering launched a new legal movement later known as the 'Jurisprudence of Interests' (*Intressenjurisprudenz*), defined in opposition to the 'Jurisprudence of Conceptions' (*Begriffsjurisprudenz*), a term that came to serve for Jhering as a derogatory reference to the abstract aspirations of German legal science.

Jhering's ideas first entered American legal discourse through the writings of Oliver Wendell Holmes. Holmes's famous aphorism, 'The life of the law has not been logic: it has been experience', and his warning against treating the legal process 'as if it contained only the axioms and corollaries of a book of mathematics', read like a near-paraphrase of Jhering's words above.[18] Whereas Jhering directed his critique at the conceptual methods of German legal science, Holmes's target, it has long been understood, was Christopher Columbus Langdell, the man who as the first Dean of Harvard Law School set out to organize American legal education along legal-scientific lines.[19]

---

[15] Franz Wieacker, *A History of Private Law in Europe with Particular Reference to Germany* (1995) 317 ff.

[16] Josef Redlich, *The Common Law and the Case Method in American University Law Schools* (1914) 15 ff.

[17] Translated and cited in Peter Stein, *The Character and Influence of the Roman Civil Law* (1988) 37 ff.

[18] Oliver Wendell Holmes, *The Common Law* (1881) 1 ff.

[19] 'Book Notices' (1880) 14 *American L.R.* 232 ff (reviewing Christopher C. Langdell, *A Selection of Cases on the Law of Contracts*).

While the treatment of law as a self-contained scientific enterprise—that was therefore insulated from other academic disciplines—was a defining element of Langdellian legal pedagogy, by the 1880s the trend in Germany and elsewhere in Europe was towards increased integration between the teaching of law and the social sciences, economics most importantly.[20] Following this lead, in a speech he delivered before law students in Boston University in 1897, later famously published as 'The Path of the Law', Holmes bemoaned 'The present divorce between the schools of political economy and law', and encouraged 'every lawyer to seek an understanding of economics' so as to better understand the 'ends sought to be attained and the reasons for desiring them'. He likewise blamed the emphasis on 'analogy, discrimination, and deduction' within legal education for blinding lawyers to the fact that 'they were taking sides upon debatable and often burning questions'.[21]

B. German Administration as a Threat to Legal Hegemony and the Common Law

The legal profession dominated most aspects of American public life during the nineteenth century, as Tocqueville famously observed, but German academic influences threatened the hegemony of American lawyers in this respect. In Germany the primary academic degree leading to careers in all branches of the state bureaucracy and politics was *Staatswissenschaft* (meaning state or political science). Generally understood as training in administration and rooted in cameralist sciences, *Staatswissenschaft* was inherently interdisciplinary (in today's terminology) in its approach, linking economics, statistics, and law. The emphasis, within this approach, was on the role of legal and political institutions in the satisfaction of human needs.[22] During the height of the German-American university connection, *Staatswissenschaft* closely aligned with emergent critiques of laissez faire economics, under the leadership of what came to be known as the German Historical School. Motivated by the growing urgency of social inequalities, labour disputes, urban dislocation, and related consequences of rapid industrialization, the German historical school promoted social reform based in empirical understanding of the origins and scope of the crisis.

[20] Max Rümelin, trans. M. Magdalena Schoch, 'Developments in Legal Theory and Teaching during my Lifetime', in M. Magdalena Schoch (ed.), *The Jurisprudence of Interests* (1948) 26 ff.; Charles Gide, 'The Economic Schools and the Teaching of Political Economy in France' (1890) 5 *Political Science Quarterly* 603 ff.

[21] Oliver Wendell Holmes, 'The Path of the Law' (1897) 10 *Harvard L.R.* 465, 468 ff.

[22] Erik Grimmer-Solem, *The Rise of Historical Economics and Social Reform in Germany 1864–1894* (2003) 42 ff.

In the United States, the impact of the *Staatswissenschaft* tradition was evident, among other ways, in the creation of new political science departments geared at the education of future civil servants. The emphasis within these programs was on comparative study of institutions, administrative primarily, with the ultimate goal of adapting European models to the United States. As Frank Goodnow, the first president of the American Political Science Association, wrote in 1893 in the preface to a book on *Comparative Administrative Law*, the knowledge to address 'Our modern complex social conditions' could 'be obtained only by study, and by comparison of our own with foreign administrative methods.'[23] Explaining the rationale behind the teaching of administration as a specialized subject under the umbrella of political science, Woodrow Wilson identified the need to adapt scientific theories of administration 'developed by German and French professors' so that they can help in solving 'our own problems of administration in town, city, county, State, and nation'.[24] That the proper models to be followed were continental, rather than English, was an often explicit message.

Graduate training in political science and administration emerged in this context as an alternative to law for those seeking a career in public service, whether as legislators or administrators. In lieu of traditional common law training, new forms of expertise came to be seen as the requisite for climbing up the government career ladder, whether in the administrative or the legislative branch. Well beyond the threat it posed to the professional interests of lawyers and legal educators, the growing influence of the new social scientific and legal theories arriving from Europe cast a serious shadow over the future of core common law principles of judicial supremacy.

In Germany and elsewhere on the continent, the existence of legislative prerogative and administrative discretion were long-recognized elements of police, or the regulatory authority of the state. Within this framework, administrative and policy sciences informed the exercise of regulatory discretion with new forms of expertise, together with the encouragement of greater state intervention in economic relations relative to an earlier era of laissez faire. In the continental context there existed as a consequence inherent compatibility between the new social scientific turn and the core premises of public law. Within the American common law world, by contrast, the emergence of new social-scientific claims for legislative and administrative expertise presented a far-deeper challenge.

The community of social scientists who sought to build new administrative institutions under a German-inspired vision of the social state, or 'liberal

---

[23] Frank J. Goodnow, *Comparative Administrative Law I* (1893) iv ff.

[24] Woodrow Wilson, 'Three Essays on Administration', in *Papers of Woodrow Wilson* vol. 5 (1885) 49, 52 as cited and discussed in Robert Adcock, *Liberalism and the Emergence of American Political Science: A Transatlantic Tale* (2014) 215 ff.

positivism' in Michael Lacey's terms, imported into American administrative discourse a view of sociology and related social sciences as an alternative legal paradigm.[25] What social science offered, over traditional legal learning, were tools for establishing 'a new system of governance' founded on 'the existence of reliable ways of publicly monitoring the actual effects of incentives in achieving social purposes'.[26] For this reason, as the sociologist Lester Ward put it in 1893, 'Before progressive legislation can become a success, every legislature must become, as it were, a polytechnic school, a laboratory of philosophical research into the laws of society and of human nature.'[27]

The consequence was unprecedented escalation of longstanding tensions between progressive proponents of the German administrative paradigm and defenders of court-centred, common law-based governance. Though these tensions had been part of American life from the start, the emergence of Germany, rather than England, as a viable administrative model presented the common law with a qualitatively different threat. The argument from the common law side variously insisted on judicial supremacy as a core element of the American constitutional order. Where administrative law was concerned, the claim, most closely associated with the writings of the English V. A. Dicey, posited an inherent discordancy between continental administrative law and common law principles of the rule of law. On the constitutional side, the view that made its way from the writings of Thomas Cooley to Justice Fields' dissent in the *Slaughterhouse Cases*, and Christopher Tiedeman's influential treatise on the police power, read the Constitution to require that judges be given a veto over the circumstances justifying legislative interventions through the police power. The countervailing argument, put forth by various continental-inspired progressives, viewed administrative law as compatible with the constitution and expected judges to uphold the legislative facts underpinning social legislation under a presumption of constitutionality.

The Supreme Court first ruled on the all-important question of the constitutionality of work-hour limits in 1898 when it upheld hour restrictions for miners and smelters in *Holden v. Hardy*, a case that progressives celebrated as an ultimate victory for the presumptive constitutionality of social legislation. By 1905, *Lochner v. New York* would turn things around. In the wake of the case, built-up anger against the courts fuelled a growing list of initiatives aimed at controlling the exercise of judicial powers including proposals aimed at the recall of judges, and constitutional amendments that would have curtailed judicial review.

---

[25] Michael J. Lacey, 'The World of the Bureaus: Government and the Positivist Project in the Late Nineteenth Century', in Michael J. Lacey, M. O. Furner (eds.), *The State and Social Investigation in Britain and the United States* (1993) 150 ff.

[26] Ibid., 152 ff.   [27] Lester Frank Ward, *Dynamic Sociology* (2nd edn., 1897) 37 ff.

III. ROSCOE POUND
AND SOCIOLOGICAL JURISPRUDENCE

Pound first attempted a systematic analysis of the meaning of and reasons behind the surrounding legal crisis in a speech he delivered in 1906 before the American Bar Association under the title 'The Causes of Popular Dissatisfaction with the Administration of Justice'. A more accurate title, more faithful to the fear evident at the heart of the speech, might have substituted 'Judicial Review', or 'Supremacy of Law', for the more antiseptic 'Administration of Justice'. 'Dissatisfaction with the administration of justice is as old as law', Pound conceded in the opening sentence of his speech. What distinguished the crisis at hand was its direct and powerful challenge to 'the common law doctrine of supremacy of law' and the traditional subordination of administration to 'common law liabilities and judicial review'. 'Courts are distrusted, and executive boards and commissions with summary and plenary powers' have largely been freed 'from judicial review'.[28] The core problem, in other words, was the growing presence of continental-styled institutions of administrative law in the United States. From this problem definition, Pound then looked to German social theories of law as means of regaining popular trust in the courts. At the same time, Pound offered sociological jurisprudence as an answer to the legal-professional and legal-academic dislocations the German university connection has helped bring about.

A. Sociological Jurisprudence and the Law Schools

It was from his post as Dean of the University of Nebraska Law College, an appointment he held between 1903 and 1907, that Pound launched the sociological jurisprudence project. Made part of the University in 1891, the Nebraska Law College was a relative newcomer and a stepchild of sorts on a campus whose mission and funding prioritized agriculture, the natural sciences, and the 'useful' arts.[29] Throughout his time as Dean in Nebraska, Pound was concerned with the financial resources of the Law College and its seemingly inferior status within the land grant institution.

---

[28] Roscoe Pound, 'The Causes of Popular Dissatisfaction with the Administration of Justice' (1906) 14 *The American Lawyer* 445 ff.

[29] Robert E. Knoll, *Prairie University: A History of the University of Nebraska* (1995) 1 ff.

Pound devoted much of his 1903 inaugural speech as dean to the need for law schools to update their curriculum, moving beyond the traditional 'dogmatic instruction' typical of the 'large and older schools', meaning Harvard. The reforms he envisioned at that point consisted of the addition of 'collateral studies', specifically history of law, jurisprudence, philosophy, and roman Law. In justification he offered, in part, the rationale that lawyers had to acquire a broader store of knowledge if they were to protect their traditional role as legislators.[30] The implicit reference was to the threat the social sciences posed in this respect, but notably Pound's list of suggested courses excluded any drawn from new policy sciences. Likewise absent from the speech was any attempt to link legal curricular reform with the surrounding political and legal crisis.

The first time Pound articulated such a connection was in 1905 in an article he published in the *Columbia Law Review* under the title 'Do We Need a Philosophy of Law?' The problem, as Pound framed it, was rapidly declining support for the common law, meaning judicial supremacy, in the face of overly individualist doctrines and repeated judicial invalidation of labour laws. The fault was not with the judges, Pound was careful to point out, since the decisions '[a]s the law stands . . . were rightly determined'.[31] The source of the problem was the excessive individualism of the law itself and the need for it to 'hold a more even balance between individualism and socialism'.[32] The correct answer to the problem was not to be found, however, in the recall of judges or packing the courts. 'To my mind', Pound offered instead, 'the remedy is in our law schools. It is in training the rising generation of lawyers in a social, political and legal philosophy abreast of our time'.[33] He ended the article with a rhetorical question: '[M]ust not a philosophy of law founded on a sound knowledge of the elements of the social and political science of to-day form part—and a necessary part—of the equipment of the trained lawyer?'[34]

Once again, in the 'Need of a Sociological Jurisprudence', Pound attributed the law's weakening 'hold upon the American people' to 'the manner in which law is taught and expounded'.[35] Here, for the first time, Pound directed his pedagogical criticism at 'legal science' and the 'sterility' it imparted to legal thought, though the exact contribution of legal science to the surrounding legal crisis was left unspecified. Pound's prescription was for law instructors to engage, in a critical fashion, with the legal and political controversies of the time. Contrary to the view that law existed as a politically neutral science, and should be taught as such, Pound called upon law professors to bring into the classroom, in tandem with their teaching of doctrine,

---

[30] Roscoe Pound, *The Evolution of Legal Education: An Inaugural Lecture* (1903) 14 ff.
[31] Roscoe Pound, 'Do We Need a New Philosophy of Law?' (1905) 5 *Columbia L.R.* 345 ff.
[32] Ibid., 352 ff.   [33] Ibid.   [34] Ibid., 353 ff.
[35] Pound, (n. 1) 'The Need of a Sociological Jurisprudence'.

perspectives drawn from contemporary political, economics, and sociological theories, even if that meant taking issue with governing legal authorities on the 'nature of justice and rights'.[36]

However, in contrast to Holmes's argument in the 'Path of the Law' and the emergent continental practice on which it drew, Pound opposed the addition of separate social science courses, such as economics, to the curriculum. To him the proper method for introducing law students to social ideas and critiques was through 'concrete legal problems' and 'actual decisions', rather than 'abstract courses'.[37] This approach ensured that lawyers, rather than social scientists, would stay in charge and that legal doctrine would remain the central pillar of legal education.

Pound made no secret of the synergy between his sociological jurisprudence and the interests of the legal academy. At least twice in 'The Need of a Sociological Jurisprudence' he alluded to this point. The first was when he warned that absent pedagogical adaptation, lawyers risked 'giving up their legitimate hegemony in legislation and politics to engineers and naturalists and economists'.[38] The second such instance pertained to legal research, rather than teaching, and the ability of social science to funnel more money into the law schools and hence their capacity to compete for resources within the larger university. Whereas 'Research of almost every other sort has been endowed' and 'Laboratories are set up to investigate every other human interest', the law schools have been left behind, there being 'no endowments for juridical research'.[39] To change this it was necessary for the law schools to produce more socially relevant, and hence fundable, research, such as the production of statistics on the operation of judicial administration. 'Law teachers ought to be making clear to the public what law is and why law is and what law does and why it does it', Pound wrote.[40]

In 1910, his project by then well under way, Pound famously crystallized the research agenda of sociological jurisprudence as bridging the gap between the 'law in the books' and 'law in action'. Here again, similar to his preferred approach to legal pedagogy, Pound made legal expertise essential to carrying out the requisite research. Pound's message to the lawyers was to make use of the lessons of economics, sociology, and philosophy, and 'cease to assume that jurisprudence is self-sufficient'. At the same time, and of at least equal importance, however, Pound's message to the rival ambitions of the social scientists, as Christopher Tomlins put it, was that the task of aligning the law in the books with the law in action was 'work that only lawyers could do'.[41]

---

[36] Ibid., 611 ff.   [37] Ibid., 611 ff.   [38] Ibid., 612 ff.
[39] Ibid., 608 ff.   [40] Ibid., 608 ff.
[41] Christopher Tomlins, 'How Autonomous Is Law?' (2007) 3 *Annual Review of Law and Social Science* 61 ff.

B. Jhering, Pound, and Legal History

In choosing 'The Spirit of the Common Law' as the title of his 1905 article, Pound gestured to Jhering, whose early scholarly reputation was based on an ambitious, multi-volume project: 'The Spirit of Roman Law through the Stages of its Development' (*Der Geist des römischen Rechts auf den Stufen seiner Entwicklung*). In keeping with the precepts of the research tradition to which he belonged at the time, the project was geared towards the discovery of the constitutive universal principles of Roman law, a plan that Jhering ultimately left unfinished after he lost faith in pandectism.[42] Already in *Der Geist*, however, and in departure from leading pandectists such as Puchta, Jhering had argued for the separation of the methodology of legal science from the substance of classical Roman law. Jurists, he wrote, had to face the fact that 'the times of Ulpian and Paulus are gone forever and will not return despite all efforts. To wish to retrieve them one would have to forget that every age should be an original, and not the copy of another.'[43] The spirit of the law as such transcended substantive doctrines, rooted in the differing circumstances of each age and different stages of the law's development.

Echoing Jhering, Pound organized his own article around the possibility of decoupling historical substantive principles, most importantly a priori commitment to the rights of individuals, from the spirit of the common law as such by asking: 'Is this common law respect for the individual inherent and fundamental? Does it represent a sixteenth and seventeenth century color, then acquired, or is it deeper-seated and intrinsic?'[44] It was a question to which the article ended up giving two, ultimately contradictory, answers. One encouraged lawyers to 'hold a more even balance between individualism and collectivism' and warned against mistaking 'seventeenth century dogmas, in which temporary phases of its individualist bent were formulated, for fundamental tenets of the common law'.[45] The other, a page later and 180 degrees apart, disputed the current economical and sociological view of individualism as a 'relic of the past' and offered that the 'obstinate conservatism' of the lawyers, 'may yet save for us a valuable—nay an indispensable—element in our institutions'.[46]

Pound's ambivalence regarding the implications of Jhering's early work for common law history was all the more acute when it came to the positivist and instrumentalist legal theories of Jhering's later life, as developed in his two most influential books: *The Struggle for Law* (*Der Kampf um's Recht*) (1872) and

[42] Hasso Hofmann, 'From Jhering to Radbruch: On the Logic of Traditional Legal Concepts to the Social Theories of Law to the Renewal of Legal Idealism', in Damiano Canale, Paolo Grossi, Hasso Hofmann (eds.), *A History of the Philosophy of Law in the Civil Law World, 1600–1900* (2005) 302 ff.

[43] Mathias Reimann, '*Nineteenth Century German Legal Science*' (1990) 31 *Boston College L.R.* 862, citing and translating R. von Jhering, 1 *Vom Geist des Römischen Rechts aufden verschiedenen Stufen seiner Entwicklung* (9th edn., 1907) 47 ff.

[44] Pound (n. 1) 'The Spirit of the Common Law' 22 ff.   [45] Ibid., 24 ff.   [46] Ibid., 25 ff.

The Purpose of Law, better known in English as *Law as a Means to an End* (*Der Zweck im Recht*) (vol. I, 1877; vol. II 1883). The origins of law, as Jhering came to see it, were rooted in the ability of the powerful to monopolize force on behalf of selfish interests, making the survival of law forever contingent on the state's willingness to back it up with force. It was, as such, the prerogative of the state, 'the only source of law', to determine which interests are deserving of protection and, where necessary, sacrifice law so as to protect the collective life. The key insight to be derived from the understanding of law as purpose grounded in force was that rather than an end in itself, law existed as a 'means to an end, the final end being the existence of society'.[47]

In his 'Law in Books and Law in Action', Pound, sounding very much like the later Jhering, said of the 'history of juristic thought' that 'it tells us nothing unless we know the social forces that lay behind it'.[48] Elsewhere, however, Pound was open regarding his discomfort with key aspects of Jhering's approach. In 'The Scope and Purpose of Sociological Jurisprudence', published in 1912, Pound openly distanced himself from Jhering's view of legal history and the purpose of law. '[I]t must be conceded', Pound wrote there, 'that Jhering ignores an important element in the development of law.' Contrary to Jhering's reading of law as the product of force, 'Legal history shows clearly enough that ideals of justice and of morals have been controlling factors in all periods of growth.'[49] The abdication of law in favour of administration was the danger lurking when we equate law with welfare of society.

If Jhering's work nonetheless held 'enduring value for sociological jurisprudence', Pound argued, it was due to its thorough debunking of the formalist methodology of conceptual jurisprudence and the lessons to be derived regarding the similar methodological deficiencies responsible for the laissez-faire orientation of the courts. 'The jurists of whom Jhering made fun, translated to a heaven of juristic conceptions . . . have their counterpart in American judges who insist upon a legal theory of equality of rights and liberty of contract in the face of notorious social and economic facts.' The lesson to be taken from the 'conception of law as a means towards social ends', in marked dilution of Jhering's subordination of law to life, was a requirement that jurists 'keep in touch with life'.[50] For Pound, at the end of the day, law, meaning common law, was not a means, but an end.

---

[47] Neil Duxbury, 'Jhering's Philosophy of Authority' (2007) 27 *Oxford Journal of Legal Studies* 38 ff.

[48] Roscoe Pound, 'Law in Books and Law in Action' (1910) 44 *American L.R.* 34 ff.

[49] Roscoe Pound, 'The Scope and Purpose of Sociological Jurisprudence II' (1911) 25 *Harvard L.R.* 145 ff.

[50] Ibid., 146 ff.

c. Sociological Jurisprudence and the Invention of Formalism

In posing sociological jurisprudence as antithetical to formalism Pound built on a foundation that Holmes, in various earlier writings, had left in place. Holmes's most important, though arguably unintended, contribution in this respect was the following words in his legendary, if ambiguous, *Lochner* dissent: 'General propositions do not decide concrete cases. The decision will depend on a judgment or intuition more subtle than any articulate major premise.'[51] Standing alone, these words appear to suggest that the Court's majority was guilty of the same fault Holmes's earlier critique attributed to Langdell—blind belief in logic to the exclusion of judicial intuitions and other elements of social experience as a determinant of legal reasoning. Holmes's warning on the limits of deduction from 'general propositions' was, however, seemingly not intended as a critique of Justice Peckham's opinion in the case, as Thomas Grey has noted. Instead, as is evident when read in the context of the entire paragraph, the statement served to qualify Holmes's own, earlier declaration that 'a constitution is not intended to embody a particular economic theory, whether of paternalism and the organic relation of the citizen to the State or of laissez faire.'[52] The qualification served to acknowledge that notwithstanding the constitution's neutrality on the choice among economic theories, there could be other grounds, such as personal liberty, for viewing freedom of contract as a protected constitutional right. But this qualification aside, Holmes, as he emphasized later on, believed that his own earlier proposition was indeed capable of shedding significant light on the source of the majority's error. In other words, contrary to the meaning and significance it acquired over time, Holmes's language in *Lochner* on the limits of deductive reasoning amounted to a tangential cautionary note directed at readers of his own argument.[53]

Holmes's actual complaint against the majority was instead over its failure to defer to the judgment of the democratically elected New York legislature under the circumstances at hand. In his view, a correct reading of the 14th Amendment required the Court to uphold legislation except where 'a rational and fair man necessarily would admit that the statute proposed would infringe fundamental principles as they have been understood by the traditions of our people and our law'. Applying this test to the bakers law, Holmes concluded that the fact that 'A reasonable man might think it a proper measure on the score of health' sufficed to establish the constitutionality of the law.[54] Where the majority fell short, in other words, was in its insistence that it was independently entitled to evaluate the

---

[51] *Lochner v. New York* (1905) 198 US 76 (Holmes J, dissenting).
[52] *Lochner v. New York* (1905) 198 U.S. 75.
[53] Thomas C. Grey, *Formalism and Pragmatism in American Law* (2014) 139 ff.
[54] *Lochner v. New York* (1905) 198 U.S. 76.

pertinent facts. Nevertheless, it is as a statement expressing the opposite sentiment, meaning criticism of the Court's insulation from facts, that Holmes's dissent and through it the entire decision would come to be read through the lens of Pound's sociological jurisprudence.

The process began with the inclusion of the following words in Pound's 1908 article, 'Mechanical Jurisprudence': 'The manner in which the Fourteenth Amendment is applied affords a striking instance of the workings to-day of a jurisprudence of conceptions ... The conception of freedom of contract is made the basis of a logical deduction.'[55] He followed up with a flurry of writings and speeches delivered in the decade following *Lochner* in which he tied the legal and constitutional crisis at hand to the unwillingness or inability of judges to give up on 'predetermined conceptions' and engage with the fact.[56]

Pound's reading of Holmes's dissent may well have been mistaken, as discussed above. Furthermore, contemporary progressive critiques of *Lochner* had little to do with conceptualism or deductive logic. As Ernst Freund put it in 1910 in reference to recent labour cases, including *Lochner*, 'No other construction can be placed upon these decisions than that the courts assume the power to look into the question of fact.'[57] Notwithstanding, the formalist problem definition soon took hold, partially thanks to the success of the National Consumers League (NCL) litigation strategy in *Muller v. Oregon*, famously known thereafter as the Brandeis Brief.

The brief, which the NCL submitted in that case, departed from the prevailing practice by stressing socio-medical evidence on the health risks associated with long work hours for women laundry workers, evidence aimed at establishing the constitutionality of an Oregon statute that limited women's work hours in that industry. When the Supreme Court upheld the Oregon statute less than three years after *Lochner*, the credit went to the Brief. The success of the remedy that the Brandeis Brief administered retrospectively confirmed the view that the initial deficiency in the *Lochner* Court's reasoning was its formalist insulation from real-world facts. But contrary to the narrative that soon took hold, it was not formalist conservative judges but progressive defenders of social legislation who long sought to exclude proof regarding the alleged health and other benefits of legislation from judicial review. The progressive perspective on social legislation was that it was entitled to a presumption of constitutionality, independent of any scientific proof of underlying injury to health or any other predetermined rationale. The exclusion of extra-legal evidence fit with that agenda, whereas it was inconsistent with the conservative view regarding the subordination of social and economic legislation

---

[55] Pound (n. 10) 615 ff.   [56] Roscoe Pound, 'Liberty of Contract' (1908) 18 *Yale L.J.* 462 ff.
[57] Ernst Freund, 'Constitutional Labor Legislation' (1910) 4 *Illinois L.R.* 620, as quoted and discussed in Brian Z. Tamanaha, *Beyond the Formalist-Realist Divide: The Role of Politics in Judging* (2010) 36 ff.

to rigorous judicial oversight. The conventional historiography on the Brandeis Brief has seemingly gotten this story turned on its head.[58]

Though Pound's sociological jurisprudence seemingly had little if anything to do with the Brandeis Brief at the start, its role in the subsequent transformation of the Brief's meaning was profound. To begin with, there existed a surface similarity between the sociological call for empirical investigations of the actual workings of law, bridging the gap between 'the law in the books and the law in action', in Pound's famous phrase, and the Brandeis Brief's introduction of medical and social scientific evidence into the courts.[59] Pound himself contributed in this regard when, in 1912, he offered the Brief as evidence of 'a new tendency to take more account of the social facts involved in the application of legal rules'.[60] For a long time afterward, the Brandeis Brief stood as 'the first example of sociological jurisprudence in action, the instantiation of Pound's call for informing legal judgment with the data of the social sciences'.[61] That the Brandeis Brief began as a concession on the part of progressives to conservative insistence on judicial scrutiny largely disappeared from legal history.

The speed and thoroughness with which sociological jurisprudence's formalist problem definition took hold followed from the degree to which many progressives, particularly the lawyers among them, shared Pound's discomfort with proposals for radical reforms of the courts.[62] Providing a key example, Louis Brandeis told a gathering of the Chicago Bar Association in 1916: 'What we need is not to displace the courts, but to make them efficient instruments of justice; not to displace the lawyer, but to fit him for his official or judicial task.'[63] What formalism offered progressives such as Brandeis was a compromise formula aimed at improving, rather than abandoning, the oversight function of courts. In the United States it would take until close to the end of the century for the formalist thesis to be subject to serious doubt. Well before that, and probably not by chance, foreign critics of the *Lochner* Court's attitude towards social legislation saw nothing formalist in the constitutional doctrines of the era, with the 'instruments of judicial supremacy', and the 'humble stature of legislation in common law America' instead taking the blame.[64]

---

[58] See generally Noga Morag-Levine, 'Facts, Formalism, and the Brandeis Brief: The Origins of a Myth' (2013) *University of Illinois L.R.* 59 ff.

[59] Roscoe Pound, 'Law in the Books and Law in Action' (1910) 44 *American L.R.* 22 ff.

[60] Roscoe Pound, 'The Scope and Purpose of Sociological Jurisprudence' (1912) 25 *Harvard L.R.* 513 ff.

[61] William Wiecek, *The Lost World of Classical Legal Thought: Law and Ideology in America, 1886–1937* (1998) 195 ff.

[62] William G. Ross, *A Muted Fury: Populists, Progressives, and Labor Unions Confront the Courts, 1890–1937* (1994) 15 ff.

[63] Louis D. Brandeis, 'The Living Law' (1916) 10 *Illinois L.R.* 468 ff.

[64] Jacco Bomhoff, *Balancing Constitutional Rights: The Origins and Meanings of Postwar Legal Discourse* (2013) 54 ff.

In Germany, the perceived connection between formalism, or legal science, and laissez-faire followed from the former's contribution to the creation of an ostensibly autonomous sphere of private law, a sphere with which the state's public law institutions were not to interfere. The sole function of the state, as Puchta saw it, was 'the preservation of a lawful order of freedom that stood above all party interest'. In denigrating Puchta's school of thought as conceptualist, or formalist, Jhering and the broader movement with which he was associated sought to unmask the law's politically neutral pretences. It was not conceptual hair-splitting, but a battle, at times violent, between competing political interests that gave rise to law, and it was as such in reference to the interests of society at large that the utility of economic rights such as freedom of contract ought to be judged. Delivered in Germany against the backdrop of a rising tide of socialism, this critique carried a transformative, even subversive, bite. Transposed via sociological jurisprudence into turn-of-the-twentieth-century American progressive politics, anti-formalism, leaving its continental radical connotations behind, transformed into an instrument of liberal legalism.

VI. Conclusion

Borrowing from contemporary German legal theory, Pound turned in the early twentieth century to the 'new creed' of sociological jurisprudence as an antidote to transatlantic-inspired threats to the long-term survival of the common law.[65] Most directly at issue was the rise of social science as an alternative, civil-law-affiliated, administrative paradigm that simultaneously threatened the academic interests of the law schools, the professional concerns of the bar, and the core constitutional principles of judicial supremacy. To all of these, sociological jurisprudence offered essentially the same corrective—a more empirical, fact-sensitive approach to law, whether in legal research and pedagogy or the adjudication of constitutional disputes. Pound outlined the precepts of this project in a long list of articles and planned its culmination with a future book.

Rather quickly, however, Pound appeared to have lost interest in this ambitious agenda. The promised book on sociological jurisprudence never materialized.

[65] Roscoe Pound, 'The Scope and Purpose of Sociological Jurisprudence' (1911) 24 *Harvard L.R.* 594 ff.

Instead, borrowing from his 1906 essay, Pound published a book titled *The Spirit of the Common Law* in 1921. Sociological jurisprudence received only a cursory, and ultimately sceptical, treatment, coupled with a warning against a reductionist economic approach to legal history devoid of recognition of the all-important role of logic and analogy in law.[66]

Pound's change of heart seemingly responded to the worry that in the hands of the emergent Realist movement, a theory he thought of as offering a lifeline to the common law was at risk of co-optation in the service of the administrative state whose ascendance Pound intended his sociological jurisprudence to forestall. Notwithstanding Pound's desertion, the project lived on with the legal realists, and later the Law and Society movement, each in turn offering their own versions of court-centred models of interdisciplinary legal inquiry.

Late-nineteenth-century German social science and attendant theories of the state posited an integrated field linking legal, political, social, and economic theories. Within this model the social science disciplines, rather than the law, emerged as the proper academic homes for research on constitutional, legislative, administrative, and related public law subjects. Countering this challenge, the various 'law and . . ' versions of socio-legal analysis collectively offered a formula that, while opening the law-schools' doors to empirical social-scientific perspectives, also protected the status of law as a separate and distinct 'juridical sphere'. Consistent with this, the treatment of legal development as a phenomenon related to but still different in kind from political and social history became the mark of American legal historical research going forward.[67]

Equally important was the impact of sociological jurisprudence on legal history's construction of the Lochner era: the implantation of the erroneous formalist conception of the Court, a conception that long survived sociological jurisprudence itself, at least in its original formulation. Largely hidden as a consequence was the extent to which the constitutional battle lines of the early twentieth century were drawn between rival, common law- and civil-law-based paradigms of administrative governance, a point that Pound understood well. The ease with which formalist constructions of the Lochner Court took hold—even as the Lochner justices themselves insisted on reviewing the underlying legislative facts—is difficult to explain, other than through the widely shared common-law sensibilities of progressive-era lawyers, well beyond Pound. In this, sociological jurisprudence seemingly offers legal historians one more lesson on the ways in which historical narratives that are consonant with the values of legal elites are liable to gain purchase, facts, or no facts.

---

[66] Pound (n. 5) 10 ff.

[67] Catherine L. Fisk and Robert W. Gordon, Foreword: '"Law as . . .": Theory and Method in Legal History' (2011) *University of California Irvine L.R.* 519 ff.

Bibliography

Neil Duxbury, 'Jhering's Philosophy of Authority' (2007) 27 *Oxford Journal of Legal Studies* 38

Thomas C. Grey, *Formalism and Pragmatism in American Law* (Brill, 2014)

N. E. H. Hull, *Roscoe Pound and Karl Llewellyn: Searching for an American Jurisprudence* (University of Chicago Press, 1998)

Laura Kalman, *Legal Realism at Yale, 1927–1960* (University of North Carolina Press, 1986)

William P. LaPiana, *Logic and Experience: The Origin of Modern American Legal Education* (Oxford University Press, 1994)

Roscoe Pound, *The Spirit of the Common Law* (Marshall Jones, 1921)

David M. Rabban, *Law's History: American Legal Thought and the Transatlantic Turn to History* (Cambridge University Press, 2013)

William G. Ross, *A Muted Fury: Populists, Progressives, and Labor Unions Confront the Courts, 1890–1937* (Princeton University Press, 1994)

Brian Z. Tamanaha, *Beyond the Formalist-Realist Divide* (Princeton University Press, 2009)

Christopher Tomlins, 'Framing the Field of Law's Disciplinary Encounters: A Historical Narrative' (2000) 34 *Law and Society Review* 911

David Wigdor, *Roscoe Pound, Philosopher of Law* (Greenwood, 1974)

John Fabian Witt, *Patriots and Cosmopolitans* (Harvard University Press, 2007)

CHAPTER 25

THE RETURN OF LEGAL REALISM

DAN PRIEL*

I. THE MYTHOLOGY OF LEGAL REALISM

LIKE nations, academic disciplines are imagined communities. Like nations they have their histories of emancipation, not from foreign forces but from oppressive ideas. Like nations they have their founding fathers, who lived in selfless pursuit of independence. In disciplines' foundation narratives, these semi-mythical heroes fought to bring to the rest of humanity the gift of fire while others—driven by a combination of self-interest, stupidity, and inertia—stood in the way. Like in national narratives, the heroes end up overpowering the villains, thereby reassuring us that eventually, although only after a bitter fight, right triumphs over wrong. And like national narratives, these founding stories often have only a tenuous relation with the truth.

The founding narrative of American lawyers has the formalists as its villains. These benighted figures believed that legal decision-making involved mechanical deduction from legal principles that existed throughout waiting to be discovered; that morals, politics, history, sociology, and psychology were all irrelevant to the law; that law was an objective science. Then along came a group of young and

* Osgoode Hall Law School. I thank the volume editors and workshop participants at the University of Toronto for their suggestions on an earlier draft of this chapter.

valiant rebels, the Legal Realists,[1] who challenged the formalists on all that. At first, the world mocked them: they were compared to the Nazis,[2] and their ideas were described as a 'jurisprudence of despair'.[3] A generation later their thought was rejected by scholars adamant on bringing order back to the law. In the end, however, light prevailed over darkness: the Realists' ideas were widely accepted and their names have been forever etched in the American (Academic) Lawyers' Hall of Fame.

As law has always been a geographically bound discipline, this story is not just one about disciplinary emancipation, it is also a national one. For the Legal Realists were *American* Legal Realists, whose ideas were a mix of that distinctly American philosophy of pragmatism,[4] coupled with a peculiarly American obsession with extending the domain of science to human affairs. By displacing the distinctively European formalism, the Realists' work marked the coming of age of American law and jurisprudence as an independent, self-sufficient, legal system. Look at American law and legal scholarship from the pre-Realist period and it is full of references to non-American sources, and not just English cases. American judges and scholars frequently cited sources in German, French, even Italian. After Legal Realism, American lawyers were happy to export their views and ideas, but no longer seemed to think others had much to offer them. It is a narrative marked by a vision of the Realists' 'extraordinary optimism'.[5]

This, with some poetic license, is the story of legal realism as many have come to know (and teach). To those familiar with the Realist creation myth, it is surprising to discover how recent it is. Writing in 1961, Grant Gilmore spoke of legal realism entirely in the past tense. In his characteristically blunt style, Gilmore described legal realism as a symptom of, and a response to, a crisis. It had a role to play at a particular historical moment. With the changing of times, a confident and prosperous America no longer needed it.[6] This is not just how younger law professors, engaged in the well-known academic ritual of generational parricide,

---

[1] In what follows 'Legal Realism' and 'Legal Realists' refers to the group of individuals (Karl Llewellyn, Jerome Frank, Walter Wheeler Cook, Max Radin, and so on) who are active around the 1930s and who are typically considered the members of this intellectual group. By contrast 'legal realism' refers more broadly to the loose set of ideas (law in its social context, the indeterminacy of legal language, an emphasis on empirical research) that are now associated with the Legal Realists.

[2] See, e.g., Walter B. Kennedy, 'My Philosophy of Law', in *My Philosophy of Law: Credos of Sixteen American Scholars* (1941) 147, 151–2.

[3] See Philip Mechem, 'The Jurisprudence of Despair' (1936) 21 *Iowa L.R.* 669.

[4] See Max Fisch, 'Justice Holmes, The Prediction Theory and Pragmatism' (1942) 39 *J. of Philosophy* 85, 85–6 *passim*.

[5] Bruce Ackerman, '*Law and the Modern Mind* by Jerome Frank' (1974) 103 *Dædalus* 119, 122; see also Hanoch Dagan, *Reconstructing American Legal Realism & Rethinking Private Law Theory* (2013) 64, 74, 153.

[6] Grant Gilmore, 'Legal Realism: Its Causes and Cure' (1961) 70 *Yale L.J.* 1037; cf. Brainerd Currie, 'The Materials of Law Study' (1955) 8 *J. of Legal Education* 1, 4. Gilmore echoed here some of the Legal Realists' contemporary critics. See Mechem (n. 3).

spoke of legal realism. At about the same time, Thurman Arnold, Hessel Yntema, and Karl Llewellyn, three of Legal Realism's founding fathers, offered their retrospective assessments, and they had much in common with Gilmore's verdict. Arnold, for instance, wrote that '[r]ealistic jurisprudence is a good medicine for a sick and troubled society. The America of the early 1930's was such a society. But realism, despite its liberating virtues, is not sustaining food for a stable civilization.'[7] This view of realism, as a phenomenon with a limited shelf life, now long past, persisted for quite some afterwards. 'As a coherent intellectual force in American legal thought', wrote Jack Schlegel in 1980, 'American Legal Realism simply ran itself into the sand.'[8] As late as 1995 Neil Duxbury considered the death of legal realism a done deal. There are 'here and there', he said, those 'who claim to be "legal realists" [but t]hey are . . . a very rare breed'.[9]

Yet in the very same year Gilmore was offering his post-mortem we also find the beginning of what would become the slogan of the new narrative of legal realism. In a short review of Llewellyn's *Common Law Tradition* Walter Gellhorn is quoted saying that 'we are all realists now'.[10] In the context of the previous assessments, these words could be read to mean that the ideas advanced by the legal realists were now incorporated into legal knowledge and therefore that interest in the realists could be laid to rest. But in due course, these words have acquired a different meaning, roughly that no matter what are one's other convictions, there is a fundamental insight that everyone *now* accepts, and it is an insight 'we' all owe to legal realism. If in the other narrative legal realism was seen as a jurisprudence of crisis, one that waxes in times of discord (the 1930s, 1970s) and wanes in times of prosperity (the 1950s, 1980s), in the new narrative legal realism was perceived as a jurisprudential fundamental, almost a universal truth about law.

A few notable exceptions aside, suddenly everyone wanted in on the realist bandwagon. What was in that bandwagon was less clear, so everyone had a version of legal realism in their own image: the realists were legal positivists; or they rejected legal positivism; or they were natural lawyers.[11] They were early adopters of efficiency as normative standard for law and promoters of ideas

---

[7] Thurman Arnold, 'Jerome Frank' (1957) 24 *University of Chicago L.R.* 633, 635; Hessel E. Yntema, 'American Legal Realism in Retrospect' (1960) 14 *Vanderbilt L.R.* 317, 325 (by 1960 'the movement of American legal realism lost the momentum that energies elsewhere spent should have sustained, and never since has been in position to realize its full possibilities'); Karl N. Llewellyn, *The Common Law Tradition: Deciding Appeals* (1960) 508.

[8] John Henry Schlegel, 'American Legal Realism and Empirical Social Science: The Singular Case of Underhill Moore' (1980) 29 *Buffalo L.R.* 195, 195.

[9] Neil Duxbury, *Patterns of American Jurisprudence* (1995) 158 (footnote omitted).

[10] Beryl Harold Levy, Book Review (1961) 109 *University of Pennsylvania L.R.* 1045, 1047. This is the earliest reference I found of this phrase in relation to legal realism.

[11] Contrast Brian Leiter, *Naturalizing Jurisprudence* (2007) 79–80, 134–5 with Dagan (n. 5) 59–60, 129 and Harry W. Jones, 'Law and Morality in the Perspective of Legal Realism' (1962) 61 *Columbia L.R.* 799, 808.

of market regulation; or they were critics of such ideas.[12] They were pioneers of a social-scientific approach to law; or their work represented the 'humanistic bent of Historicism'.[13] Their ideas were an early incarnation of critical legal studies; or they were fundamentally different from, even opposed to, them.[14]

Beyond this, the realists have been described as modernists, instrumentalists, pragmatists, sceptics; in some sense all plausible attributions, but all so vague they hardly help in articulating a coherent view. To make matters even more confusing, in addition to the old legal realism we now have a burgeoning 'new legal realism'. Its adherents see themselves as descendants of, but also different from, the old legal realists. Inevitably, it already comes in different flavours.[15]

This state of affairs gives rise to what I will call 'the realist puzzle': How can scholars who otherwise agree on very little all see themselves as legal realists? As I see it, there are four possible explanations, not mutually exclusive: (a) that the Realists' ideas were banal and obvious; (b) that they identified something fundamental that—despite all other differences—all contemporary legal scholars now accept; (c) that different people simply identified in the realists whatever they had already believed; and finally (d) that the Realists were less consistent than people commonly assume. Though there is little direct discussion of the realist puzzle in writings on legal realism, I think it is a useful framework for considering some current trends in scholarship on legal realism, in a way that I hope helps put some recent discussions in a new light.

The first response rejects the realist creation myth. What the realists said was banal, obvious, and largely unoriginal, so no wonder people holding such different views could all accept their claims. In fact, what the Realists said was already familiar when they said it. Something like this thesis has been put forward recently by Brian Tamanaha.[16] Tamanaha's main strategy for this conclusion is historical: going over neglected writings from the generations before the rise of Legal Realism, in the supposed heyday of formalism, he unearthed numerous quotations with a distinctly legal-realist ring to them. The upshot of his argument is that Legal Realism is not just obvious to all of us today, it has always been uncontroversial. Look beyond the realists' self-aggrandizing claims to originality, he suggests, and you find virtually

---

[12] Contrast Alan Schwartz, 'Karl Llewellyn and the Origins of Contract Theory', in Jody S. Kraus and Steven D. Walt (eds.), *The Jurisprudential Foundations of Corporate and Commercial Law* (2000) 12, 15, 16 with Joseph William Singer, 'Legal Realism Now' (1988) 76 *California L.R.* 465, 477.

[13] Contrast Herbert M. Kritzer, 'Empirical Legal Studies before 1940: A Bibliographic Essay' (2009) 6 *J. of Empirical Legal Studies* 925, 926 with William J. Novak, 'Legal Realism and Human Rights' (2011) 37 *History of European Ideas* 168, 171.

[14] Contrast Singer (n. 12) 475, 482–95, 532–3 with Wouter de Been, *Legal Realism Regained* (2008).

[15] See Stewart Macaulay, 'The New Versus the Old Legal Realism: "Things Ain't What They Used to Be"' (2005) *Wisconsin L.R.* 365; Victoria Nourse and Gregory Shaffer, 'Varieties of New Legal Realism: Can a New World Order Prompt a New Legal Theory?' (2009) 95 *Cornell L.R.* 61.

[16] Brian Z. Tamanaha, *Beyond the Formalist–Realist Divide* (2010) 68.

nothing new. We are all realists now, if you wish, because we have always been realists.

There is no doubt that some of the claims to originality attributed to the Legal Realists are partly based on caricaturizing the views they attacked, instead of a serious attempt at examining the pre-Realist scholarship. To sustain the realist creation myth it was necessary to exaggerate the views of those who came before them, thereby making the Realists' achievement appear more significant. In looking up the work of many now-forgotten scholars Tamanaha helped contribute to our understanding of the intellectual background in which the Legal Realists emerged, as well as cut them down to size.

Nevertheless, there are reasons to be doubtful of a strong version of this view. One reason to doubt the claim that all the Realists gave us were platitudes that more-or-less everyone—including everyone in their day—already accepted, emerges from examining contemporary reactions to their ideas. If Tamanaha's thesis were right, we would expect to see the Realists being challenged by their contemporaries for the banality of their ideas. Instead, many of their critics berated them for seeking to dismantle much of the familiar order.[17] This is difficult to reconcile with the claim that everything they said was old hat. Put slightly differently, one may reject the realist creation myth but still hold that the Realists have made an important, even if not earth-shattering, contribution. And when looked more closely, something like this may be precisely how the Realists themselves understood their insights. In possibly the single best-known Realist article, after listing several realist themes, Llewellyn said that '[n]one of the[se] ideas . . . is new'.[18] What was new, he said, was their combination into a single package, and with that their pursuit 'consistently, persistently, insistently to carry them through'.[19] Sometimes this is all it takes for intellectual posterity.

Another reason to doubt Tamanaha's strong conclusion is that by focusing on the American intellectual scene, it is difficult to see who they were arguing against. In the present context, when American scholars rarely look beyond American scholarship, let alone consider legal theory from civil-law countries, it is easy to forget that a century ago things looked very different. Much of the rejection of formalism was not only directed at its perennial bugbears Christopher Columbus Langdell and Joseph Beale, but at German conceptualism.[20] I believe we cannot

---

[17] See Gilmore (n. 6) 1037 (realism 'violently engaged men's minds'). For these early critiques see Neil Duxbury, 'The Reinvention of Legal Realism' (1992) 12 *Legal Studies* 137.

[18] Karl N. Llewellyn, 'Some Realism about Realism—Responding to Dean Pound' (1931) 44 *Harvard L.R.* 1222, 1238.

[19] Ibid., (emphasis omitted).

[20] This was clearly one target of Roscoe Pound, 'Mechanical Jurisprudence' (1908) 8 *Columbia L.R.* 605, 610, as it was of Holmes's early writings. On this see Mathias W. Reimann, 'Holmes's *Common Law* and German Legal Science', in Robert W. Gordon (ed.), *The Legacy of Oliver Wendell Holmes, Jr.* (1992) 72. Whether Langdell and Beale fit that German mould remains contested to this day.

understand the Realists' ideas unless we put them within a broader historical and geographical context. Against this broader picture, I think it is an exaggeration to say that the distinction between realism and formalism is, as Tamanaha argues, 'empty of independent meaning'.[21]

The distinction between realism and formalism is the key to the second response to the realist puzzle. Whatever disagreements we find among legal theorists working today, according to this response, it exists over a foundation of tacit agreement, namely the rejection of formalism. We are all realists now, if you wish, because (whatever else we are) we are not formalists.

Just as with realism, it is not always entirely clear what formalism is. As Brian Simpson once remarked, at times 'formalism' is 'little more than a loosely employed term of abuse',[22] but I think we can sharpen both terms and make sense of the distinction between the two. I will focus here on a single idea, that of the autonomy of law and especially the separation of law from politics. Formalists claim that law has its own distinctive modes (or 'forms') of thought, and a largely self-contained body of coherent concepts and ideas that can and should be used to answer legal questions; realists deny this. The reason to focus on this single idea of law's autonomy is because to this day self-styled formalists embrace it,[23] and because many other ideas associated with formalism and realism can be explained in terms of their relationship to law's autonomy.

I understand the autonomy of law not as a conceptual claim but as a normative one, an ideal, variably realized in real-world legal specimens. For the formalist, law is only a distinct intellectual discipline, with its distinctive set of concepts and forms of reasoning, when it is autonomous. The more law becomes entangled with other normative systems and other disciplines it becomes an empty shell, a cover for something else that is, by definition, not law. Realism, before anything else, is the rejection of formalism in this sense: law does not depend for its existence, significance, or intellectual livelihood, on being autonomous.

Although the rejection of formalism as a unifying idea that 'we' can all accept helps explain the current popularity of legal realism, it still leaves out an important piece of the puzzle. Rejecting formalism is a negative thesis; it is thus *consistent* with many different views. To the extent that they all reject legal formalism, different scholars can even claim legal realism as a theoretical foundation or and the Realists' work as inspiration. However, this falls short of any positive claim that contemporary scholars could identify as their own. Much of the scholarship on legal realism has attempted to articulate more positive ideas, and it is here that we encounter the wide

---

[21] Tamanaha (n. 16) 162.

[22] Brian Simpson, 'Legal Iconoclasts and Legal Ideals' (1990) 58 *University of Cincinnati L.R.* 819, 834.

[23] The *locus classicus* of modern formalism is Ernest J. Weinrib, *The Idea of Private Law* (1995), especially chs. 1, 2, and 8. A somewhat different formalist approach is found in the works of Peter Birks, for example, *An Introduction to the Law of Restitution* (rev edn., 1989) 1–22.

proliferation of views on realism. It is here that we encounter the third response to the realist puzzle: Different scholars picked and chose whatever they liked from the writings of the Legal Realists, interpreting it in their own image.

This response to the puzzle of the prevalence of realism can be presented by way of a familiar realist theme about adjudication, transposed to the domain of legal scholarship. One reason for the indeterminacy of adjudication associated with legal realism is that legal materials contain such a vast body of conflicting rules, concepts, principles, policies, and propositions, that any competent lawyer can reconstruct from them a plausible legal argument for virtually any desired conclusion. A similar argument can be made with regard to legal realism itself. There were many Legal Realists, who wrote many different things. They never sat together to hammer out a manifesto, and (as we shall shortly see) it is doubtful they would have succeeded in coming up with one if they did. Furthermore, as there is no perfect agreement on who belonged to the ranks of the realists (was Benjamin Cardozo a realist? Was Jerome Frank a central or marginal realist?), different scholars have ample source material to reconstruct legal realism in their own image.

In saying this I do not suggest any deception on the part of any scholar, only the familiar point that we read texts through the lens of our prior convictions. In this respect, the ideas of the Legal Realists are no different from other past thinkers who have been subjected to widely divergent readings; except, perhaps, that given the number of Legal Realists, the range of plausible interpretations in their case is probably even wider. Once the Realists were canonized as revolutionaries of (American) law, it was almost inevitable that whatever one happened to find important had to be traced back to the Realists.

Unfortunately, as an answer to the realist puzzle, and as an attempt to understand their historical significance, this is hardly a response. Rather than identifying a distinct realist theme, it turns legal realism into an empty vessel into which anyone can project their own views, views that can be (and may have been) arrived at completely independently of the work of Legal Realists. If legal realism means whatever one wants it to mean, it means nothing.

Of course, this is not how the different interpreters of realism see things. For each modern interpreter, their reading of legal realism is the correct one. The result is a small industry of studies, each identifying the essence of legal realism and challenging competing accounts.[24] This response to the realist puzzle is continuous with the previous one in that its proponents do not deny that there are differences, at times significant ones, among the Legal Realists; yet these scholars insist that underneath these differences one can identify a kernel of an important, coherent,

---

[24] For a sample see Dagan (n. 5); Leiter (n. 11); Singer (n. 12); Michael Steven Green, 'Legal Realism as Theory of Law' (2005) 46 *William and Mary L.R.* 1915. William Twining, 'Talk about Realism' (1985) 60 *New York University L.R.* 329; William Twining, *Karl Llewellyn and the Realist Movement* (2nd edn., 2012) 418–35, contain a judicious discussion of various interpretations of legal realism.

and original set of ideas. We are all realists now, if you wish, because realism is what I do (said by everyone).

It is perhaps against this diversity of opinion that one sympathizes with Duxbury's conclusion that legal realism was an intellectual 'mood' more than a clearly defined ideology.[25] Notably, however, both those who identified a certain idea as the core of legal realism and those who denied it assumed that for legal realism to be a meaningful category it had to be explicable in terms of a small set of ideas that all Realists shared. It is this assumption—that there is a *positive* idea that goes beyond rejecting the autonomy of law—that I seek to challenge. I think Llewellyn was right when he said that the realists were united only in their negations, scepticisms, and curiosities.[26] When we move to more positive ideas, we must distinguish between two very different legal realisms. Each makes for a reasonably internally coherent ideological package, but the two are at odds with each other. These two camps' respective ideas differ not on detail, tactic, or emphasis; they reflect two sets of views that on a series of fundamental issues were deeply opposed to each other.

It is this idea that I will pursue in the rest of this chapter. I aim to show how on several central issues Realists belonging to the two different camps held opposite views. The success of the realist brand today rests, at least in part, on this difference, and perhaps also on the fact that the differences between these two legal realisms have not been adequately acknowledged.

II. Two Legal Realisms

So far I have identified legal realism in negative terms, as the opposition to formalism and more specifically to the idea of the autonomy of law. To understand this idea more clearly, it will be useful to break it down into two elements.[27] One is the techniques of legal reasoning such as identifying the ratio of a case, distinguishing, and so on. The other is the articulation of the premises themselves. The idea of the

[25] Duxbury (n. 9) 65. In a similar vein Horwitz complained about 'the obvious contradictions within Realism'. Morton J. Horwitz, *The Transformation of American Law 1870–1960: The Crisis of Legal Orthodoxy* (1992) 170.

[26] Llewellyn (n. 18) 1234.

[27] My argument in this section builds on Dan Priel, 'Legal Realisms' (unpublished manuscript), where it is developed at greater detail. Certain nuances in the argument had to be ignored for the sake of brevity.

autonomy of law is that both of those elements—the process of reasoning and the substantive premises on which legal conclusions rely—can be learned from legal materials themselves. Law was thus perceived as aspiring to the status of a rigorous science, whose laboratory is the law library.

The Realist attack on formalism focused much more on the question of the premises than on an attack on the reasoning process. Here, Holmes's 'Path of the Law' proved a rallying cry for the Realists, for one of its messages was that the premises of legal argument were not internal to the law, but depended on the prevailing social attitudes of a particular time and place. He insisted that these attitudes were essential to the formulation of the premises of legal argument, including those that seem most entrenched, most purely legal: 'We do not realize', said Holmes in that famous address, 'how large a part of our law is open to reconsideration upon a slight change in the habit of the public mind.'[28] Notice that for Holmes the problem was *not* so much with the syllogism itself: Holmes insisted that logic is essential to thinking rationally, and that whatever escapes rational thought lies 'outside the law of cause and effect, and as such transcends our power of thought'. The formalist error was thinking that it was merely legal materials that we plug into the syllogism. 'Behind the logical form lies a judgment as to the relative worth and importance of competing legislative grounds.' That judgment is 'often inarticulate . . . yet [it is] the very root and nerve of the whole proceeding. You can give any conclusion a logical form'.[29]

If the premises used in legal argument cannot be wholly derived from 'within' the law, where do they—and where should they—come from? It is here that we can begin to identify two distinct realist camps. One camp, in effect, has argued that the source of reliable premises for legal analysis should be the source used in all other domains of human knowledge, namely empirical science. To Realists of this type, law will continue to be a backward science so long as its premises continue to be based on unquestioned common sense and prevailing opinion that dominates the common law. Improvement of the law, and the progress of society, will be achieved by abandoning unscientific methods and unreliable ideas and replacing them with the data and methods of the natural sciences. Felix Cohen complained that '[i]t is still the fashion, in the law, to refer to conscience as the final source of moral knowledge', even though that conscience is largely the product of culture and socialization.[30] Just as common-sense perception is of limited value in physics, what appears right and wrong needs to be subjected to the methods of science: 'Modern ethics', he wrote, 'seeks to attain moral knowledge through the methods of science', and this

[28] Oliver W. Holmes, 'The Path of the Law' (1897) 10 *Harvard L.R.* 457, 466.

[29] Ibid., 465, 466. Attacks on logic as itself biased and indeterminate are a feature of C.L.S. works from the 1970s and 1980s. They are virtually non-existent in the writings of the writings of the legal realists.

[30] Felix S. Cohen, 'Modern Ethics and the Law' (1933) 4 *Brooklyn L.R.* 33, 45–6.

approach 'may serve as a challenge to entrenched moral dogmas that enslave the law'.[31] I call the legal realists who accepted this view 'scientific legal realists'.

Like these scientific legal realists, the other realist camp rejected the idea of law's autonomy. However, these realists were also sceptical of the view that the methods or findings of the natural sciences could or should be the source for alternative premises for legal argument. Instead, these realists believed that law is ultimately a reflection of the values of the people, and it is in the probing of these values that lawyers will find the right answers to legal questions. This perspective has led these realists to a much more sympathetic view of lawyers and their methods, and—contrary to the popular image of the Realists—to a generally favourable view of the common law and its determinacy. The error they sought to correct was the image of law as a pure science to which an exalted elite is inducted in law school. Instead, they wanted to reshape the understanding of law into a results-oriented, problem-solving practice, informed by community norms and values. Karl Llewellyn, the best-known of these Realists, did not think the law needed to be replaced by science. The common law functioned by seeking a solution to a wide-ranging problems through the analysis of a 'concrete controversy', which was open for 're-examination' when later controversies arose. Rather than dismiss the methods of the lawyer as a sham, he stated that lawyers' methods such as 'distinguishing' and 'limiting' past cases 'serve[] at once to test and refresh rules of law by recurrent earthy contact with new experience'.[32] This technique was justified precisely because it was unscientific. When relying on it, '[t]he court voices . . . as an official organ, not only The Law, but, in its sizing up of the situation and the controversy . . . also the residual *non-expert* horse-sense of the community'.[33] The legal realists who adopted this stance thought the law was fairly determinate, that judges were not free to decide cases any way they wanted, and when legal materials are properly analysed, they reveal the law. Because this strand of legal realism sought continuity with the common law tradition, and because of its conservative streak, tying the law and its authority to the values of the community, I call the legal realists who belonged in this group 'traditional legal realists'.[34]

---

[31] Ibid., 42, 46. Other statements of scientific legal realism are found (among others) in Felix S. Cohen, 'Transcendental Nonsense and the Functional Approach' (1935) 35 *Columbia L.R.* 809; Edward S. Robinson, 'Law—An Unscientific Science' (1934) 44 *Yale L.J.* 235; Hessel E. Yntema, 'The Implications of Legal Science' (1933) 10 *New York University L.Q.R.* 279; Walter Wheeler Cook, 'My Philosophy of Law', in *My Philosophy of Law* (1941) 51.

[32] Karl N. Llewellyn, 'American Common Law Tradition and American Democracy' (1942) 1 *J. of Legal and Political Sociology* 14, 30.

[33] Ibid., 31.

[34] In addition to the works of Llewellyn, which fairly consistently reflect traditional realism, other examples of realist works that reflect this view are found in (among others) Leon Green, 'The Duty Problem in Negligence Cases' (part 1) (1928) 28 *Columbia L.R.* 1014; Arthur L. Corbin, 'The Law and the Judges' (1914) 3 *Yale R.* (n.s.) 234; Max Radin, 'Legal Realism' (1931) 31 *Columbia L.R.* 824. On most issues Jerome Frank was aligned with these realists.

The sceptical reader may counter that I make too much of this distinction, but I believe it has important ramifications to a series of issues on all of which Realists from these two camps held very different views. It is an accepted truism that the Realists attacked the formalists for their belief in the determinacy of law. This is often true of scientific legal realists. Felix Cohen, for instance, famously derided much of it as circular reasoning that rested on 'transcendental nonsense'.[35] However, this view stands in sharp contrast to that of traditional legal realists. To understand their position, it is necessary to distinguish between legal doctrine and legal reasoning, what we call 'the lawyer's trade craft', and the law. Traditional legal realists insisted that mastery of the lawyer's tradecraft was essential skill for lawyers, but they were not sufficient for explaining the determinacy of law.

Llewellyn, for instance, insisted that older casebooks adopting 'more traditional approaches have hold of a something that must not be lost: doctrinal clarity, conceptual precision, sharpness of legal thought'.[36] Such statements may sound odd to those used to the familiar story of legal realism. But while acknowledging that legal materials contained conflicting ideas, the scope of precedent in past cases could be read broadly or narrowly, the words found in statutes were often vague and open to different interpretation, Llewellyn insisted that this 'do[es] not of course mean that judges are free'.[37] Frank's view on the matter was not very different. He had a life-long obsession with the indeterminacy of fact finding, but when the parties agreed on the facts, he conceded that 'the judicial response . . . is completely or almost completely predictable'.[38] The key to explaining this apparent contradiction is by recognizing that for traditional realists *law was more than legal doctrine and lawyer's craft*. While legal materials alone were easily manipulated by any well-trained lawyer, this did not mean that *law* was indeterminate, because the stabilizing force of law came from factors beyond the doctrinal elements of law. (This point is further explained below.)

A similar surprise awaits those who examine traditional realists' scholarship, as well as their views on scholarship. Legal realists are today often taken to be pioneers of the interdisciplinary study of law, and especially of empirical legal research. This is a fairly accurate description of the scientific Legal Realists, most notably Underhill Moore. Other scientific realists (such as Walter Wheeler Cook and Yntema) argued for the need for such studies and for greater receptiveness for the scientific spirit in legal studies. By contrast, the attitude of the more traditional legal realists was far more critical about such approaches. Llewellyn described some of the empirical studies conducted by the scientific Legal Realists, the

[35] Cohen (n. 31); see also Yntema (n. 31) 301–3.
[36] Karl N. Llewellyn, 'On the Problem of Teaching "Private" Law' (1941) 54 *Harvard L.R.* 775, 779.
[37] Karl N. Llewellyn, 'Legal Tradition and Social Science Method—A Realist's Critique', in W. F. G. Swan and Leverett S. Lyon (eds.), *Essays on Research in the Social Sciences* (Washington: Brookings Institutions, 1932) 89, 108 n. 8.
[38] Jerome Frank, 'What Courts Do in Fact' (pt. 2) (1932) 26 *Illinois L.R.* 761, 762.

'nadir of idiocy' and spoke of the 'not-yet-social science'.[39] Frank warned of the false certainties of the 'dehumanized religion of science'.[40] These Realists were at most willing to accept that other disciplines could provide useful information that might be relevant to lawyers, but they were apprehensive of the idea that was so central to the scientific legal realists, that law itself should be turned into a science. Law, they insisted, was an art or a craft, based on instinct and judgment. To the extent that traditional realists looked beyond legal materials, they were much more likely to turn to history (Radin), to philosophy, religion, and music (Frank), or to cultural anthropology (Llewellyn) than to the natural sciences.

It is not just in their jurisprudential writings that traditional legal realists expressed sympathy to legal doctrine. More than any theoretical statement, it is in their writings on particular areas of law that one finds the true attitude of traditional legal realists to law and adjudication. By today's standards, the writings of traditional legal realists appear highly doctrinal. They relied heavily on the analysis and critique of hundreds of cases and the detailed exposition of legal doctrine. For Llewellyn, Arthur Corbin, the author of a mammoth treatise on contract, was an intellectual hero and his scholarship a model of legal realism.

These differences recur in the two Realist groups' views on legal education. Traditional legal realists maintained that legal education was an education geared towards training practicing lawyers. Llewellyn's introduction to law, *The Bramble Bush*, is at times a bit eccentric, but much of it is dedicated to instructing students in the traditional arts of reading a case, identifying its holding, and developing a feel for a legal area.[41] A running theme in the writings of traditional realists on legal education was not that it was too doctrinal, but that it was too removed from the needs of the legal practitioner. For Frank this was a cause he turned and returned numerous times over the years. His proposed solutions to the problems of law school—or 'lawyer school', in his telling suggested renaming—were greater emphasis on clinical education (especially trial advocacy), the hiring of faculty with legal practice experience, and the elimination of appellate decisions as a central teaching tool even in basic courses.[42]

The scientific realists also found much to dislike with the legal education of their day, but for altogether different reasons. In their mind, the problem with legal education was that it was still so divorced from scientific method. Yntema and Oliphant looked to medical schools as a model for law schools to imitate. Oliphant argued that medical schools used to teach their subject in isolation

[39] Karl N. Llewellyn, 'On What Makes Legal Research Worthwhile' (1956) 8 *J. of Legal Education* 399, 401; Karl N. Llewellyn, 'McDougal and Lasswell Plan for Legal Education' (1943) 43 *Columbia L.R.* 476, 482; see generally K.N. Llewellyn, 'The Theory of Legal "Science"' (1941) 20 *North Carolina L.R.* 1.

[40] Jerome Frank, *Fate and Freedom: A Philosophy for Free Americans* (1945) 134.

[41] Karl N. Llewellyn, *The Bramble Bush* (1930), chs. 2–4. See also the discussion in Karl N. Llewellyn, *The Case Law System in America* (Michael Ansaldi trans., 1989 [1933]) 12–16.

[42] Jerome Frank, 'A Plea for Lawyer-Schools' (1947) 56 *Yale L.J.* 1303.

from other sciences (such as physics and biology) with a focus on the teaching of medicine by way of apprenticeship. The 'revolution' in medical education and practice, he said, came when 'blood tests and scientific diagnosis . . . replace[d] tongue gazing and guess'. He argued that law schools would benefit from a similar revolution.[43]

III. THE LURE OF FORMALISM

The views of scientific legal realists may not be very surprising, as they fit the image of the legal realists as proponents of radical change in the law. The views of traditional legal realists, by contrast, seem to call into question their claims to challenging the legal formalists. If, as I argued, traditional legal realists were sympathetic to legal doctrine, the common law, and legal determinacy, in what way where they opposed to formalism?

The key to answering this question is avoiding two common tendencies in the scholarship on legal realism. One is inattention to the fundamental difference between the two Realist groups; the other is a similar tendency to confuse an attack on one very particular view of legal doctrine for a global criticism of legal doctrine. Traditionalists rejected the idea that language and logic *alone* could constrain judges. It does not follow that the law is necessarily indeterminate. For traditional realists, this meant paying more attention to real-world legal practice. Doing so, they thought, could explain how law was determinate, even if language was not.

To understand this last point it is necessary to understand the historical context in which the legal realists worked, and the view of law—formalism—that they saw themselves challenging. Partly thanks to the realists, formalism is often presented a patently implausible view, so much so that demolishing it requires no effort. While I think formalism is indeed indefensible, it is important to give it its best hearing, to try and explain why its basic tenets are attractive and why it poses an important challenge to alternative views.

I think formalism is best explained by way of two related ideas, one epistemological, the other political, both explicable in terms of the particular historical moment in

---

[43] Herman Oliphant, 'Parallels in the Development of Legal and Medical Education' (1933) 167 *Annals of the Academy of Political and Social Science* 156, 160; Yntema (n. 31) 281–2 n. 5, 293–4. Frank too compared medical schools to law schools, but for him the main pedagogical idea to take from them was the need for more clinical education. See Jerome Frank, 'Why Not a Clinical Lawyer-School?' (1933) 81 *University of Pennsylvania L.R.* 907, 915–16.

which formalism came to prominence. Formalism is related to the emergence of the modern research university, a German invention that was later copied in the English-speaking world. The teaching of a professional trade like law in university, and especially a research-oriented university, was not obvious. One of the means for justifying it was showing how what had hitherto been an unintellectual practice, often learned by apprenticeship, could be turned into a respectable science. Formalism thus appears, from a historical perspective, not (as it is sometimes presented by its current defenders) as reflecting what law has always been before lawyers were seduced by the false charms of interdisciplinarity. It is the product of a particular time, and was developed as a response to the rise of the research university and the need to justify the study of law ('as a science') in it. Within such a conception of knowledge, law could 'exist' as a respectable discipline only if it could be shown to be intellectually self-sufficient.[44]

A second explanation for the attraction of formalism is political. Formalism was not just a claim about the nature of legal concepts, it was also a view about the authority of law. Law had authority, and *could only have legitimate authority*, if it was rationalized and thereby kept apart from politics. The gist of the idea is that law can be legitimate only if it is objective and apolitical, only if anyone presented with a legal question (no matter their political persuasion or social background) could agree on what the law requires. The core of the formalist ideology is that *only* if law satisfies this condition can it have legitimate authority. On this view, to maintain the legitimacy of law, it is formalism or bust.

The epistemological and the political considerations are closely connected. The suggestion that underlying the messiness and apparent disorder of law, especially the common law, it can be shown to be coherent and rational meant that law could be the subject for study and research in a university. Like the biologist who identifies order on the seeming disorder of the natural world, the academic lawyer's task is to identify order on the apparent disorder of the common law. By doing so, law can be seen as a worthy subject for academic study, no less scientific than the work of the botanist who classified plants. Importantly, this order also provided a justification for putting the coercive power of the state behind that law. If law's objective order is identified, we have a justification for giving unelected judges the power to issue decisions.

This is, at bottom, the challenge formalism poses, and it is a formidable one. For all the derision directed at it, the idea of law's autonomy remains a staple of both academic and popular discussions on law. It is reflected, for example, in those incantations made by judicial appointees on the importance of following

---

[44] 'Every science is a system in its own right; and it is not sufficient that in it we construct according to principles, and so proceed technically, but we must also set to work architectonically with it as a separate and independent building.' Immanuel Kant, *Critique of Judgment* (James Creed Meredith trans., 2007 [1790]) 209.

and keeping their politics and personal convictions out of the law. As much as we would like to dismiss these as pro forma remarks that no-one really believes, the fact remains that it is *these* empty phrases they repeat. And as much as we know that judges cannot entirely extricate themselves from their background, opinions, and values, this view remains an ideal that legal systems strive for. For this reason, to answer the formalist challenge it was not enough to point out to the realities of legal practice or to exciting discoveries from the sciences; it was also necessary to provide an alternative account of the authority of law. To challenge the formalist *ideal* it was necessary to show that the formalist explanation of the authority of law was not the only possible one. Put differently, if one thinks that the formalist picture is as a matter of unattainable *and* that no alternative account of law's authority could be provided, the inevitable implication is that law and the power it exerts are illegitimate.

The two versions of legal realism had the idea of the autonomy of law as their target, but they had two very different responses to the formalist conception of law.[45] As I described it the formalist combines a conception of law that has two components: it sees law *as a science* that takes the study of *legal materials* as its object. Traditional legal realists wanted to make the study of law and legal education more in line with legal practice, to turn it away from theoretical abstractions and back to realities of its everyday practice. Their objection to formalism was fundamentally an objection to the idea of law as an abstract science of legal concepts. Realism for them meant recognizing that law was a pragmatic, results-driven practice that was constantly changing in response to the needs of the community it was serving.

Contrary to popular perceptions of legal realism, however, this did not mean lawyers should pay less attention to the cases; it meant the opposite. For the formalist, legal reality consisted of principles that were *exemplified* in the cases. For traditional realists one had to look in the mass of cases and identify the fine-grained legal doctrine found in it. These traditional legal materials are valuable as a repository of practitioners' practical solutions to problems. These solutions are local, contingent, and messy; they may not result in a coherent structure, but they work. To insist on organizing them, to overintellectualize them, is thus to give us a less accurate picture of the law.

The problem with this characterization of law is that it only heightens the concern that law is illegitimate, for it suggests that law could no longer be seen as 'objective' in the right sense as to legitimize it. If there was no independent way of validating the soundness of legal decisions, it is no longer obvious how judges could justify or criticize them. The response of traditional realists was that certainty in the law

---

[45] What I say in the text here is a bit misleading as the idea of autonomy manifests itself in two quite different ways. There are, in a way, two distinct versions of formalism. See Dan Priel, 'Conceptions of Authority and the Anglo-American Common Law Divide' (2018) 65 *American J. of Comparative L.* 609.

comes from keeping it tethered to the values and norms of the community. An early essay by Arthur Corbin, one that Llewellyn later hailed as one of the earliest examples of legal realism, made this point abundantly clear. To the 'heresy' that the legal profession ought to 'seek the law elsewhere than in statutes and decisions' because that would imply judges merely decide according to their personal whims, Corbin replied:

[T]he certainty of law will remain where it has always been; and when a judge is a law unto himself, we shall criticise and recall and impeach and even hang him. Wherever the moral law and custom of the people and the business and customs of commerce are uniform and certain, there the law is certain. Where they are unsettled or merely forming, there the law is uncertain, and uncertain in must remain.[46]

This point helps explain these Realists' response to formalism. By confining themselves to law libraries formalists gave a mistaken view of law as consisting only of legal materials, which they then analysed using the tools of the lawyer's tradecraft. Inevitably, the formalists were forced to the conclusion that whatever stability and certainty there was in the law, it *had* to come from these sources. This in turn implied that through the sheer force of intellect one had to make legal doctrine coherent, and thereby certain and stable. Most people take the realist challenge to the determinacy of legal materials as leading to the conclusion that law is indeterminate. But to hold this view is to accept the formalists' view that the determinacy of law comes from legal materials alone. By contrast, traditional realists accepted the formalists' conclusion that law was fairly determinate, but rejected the premise that law consisted exclusively of materials found in the law library. Once that premise was rejected, it was possible for them to argue, as Corbin did, that the stability of law came from the *combination* of legal materials and societal influences.

This is why traditional legal realists were generally sympathetic to the common law, far more so than scientific realists. The common law made it obvious to anyone who cared to take it seriously that law was not *just* rules. Legal doctrine is essential for 'stabilizing the litigation process and in guarding it against *ad hoc* improvising'.[47] But doctrine alone was not sufficient: Certainty in the law was the product of the legal practitioner's 'fruitfully marr[ying] a knowledge of decision making's "normative" side to the insights acquired from legal sociology'.[48] In this way traditional realists flip the formalist's view of law. For the formalist the ideal

---

[46] Corbin (n. 34) 242–3. As this passage makes clear traditional legal realists (more so than their scientific counterparts) did not think of uncertainty as an unmitigated evil. In fact, many of them saw it as a necessary corollary of the idea that law reflects the values of the community and some even embraced it as a valuable means for allowing the law to adapt itself to changing circumstances.

[47] Leon Green, 'The Thrust of Tort Law: Part II: Judicial Law Making' (1962) 64 *West Virginia L.R.* 115, 126.

[48] Llewellyn (1989) (n. 41) 82, 90.

of law as an autonomous science was the guarantee that law could be certain and determinate. Traditional realists' demonstration of the indeterminacy of legal materials alone was meant to expose the error in this view, but it did not imply that law itself was indeterminate. This is because exactly what the formalists wanted to keep out of the law was the key to its certainty. It was the fact that in addition to '*rule*-stuff', the word-clad and word-limited authoritative formulas', the law also consisted of a 'body of ideals and idealizations which the law men often use without putting or seeing them in words at all',[49] that gave law its stability. In short, traditional realists attacked what they perceived as unrealistic *interpretations* of legal doctrine, but they did not mean such criticisms to undermine the value of legal doctrine itself.

The common law did not just make all this evident, when properly used (i.e., not in the way formalists did), it encouraged the incorporation of these additional elements that provided law with its certainty.[50] And this, as Llewellyn and others made clear, was not just a response to the problem of uncertainty, not just an alternative description of how law works. It was also the basis for providing an alternative explanation for law's legitimacy. It was through its conformity with constantly changing community values that law maintained its legitimacy, one that turned the abstract ideal of self-government to reality. This explains how law could be legitimate even though it does not enjoy math-like universal objective validity. Law could be different in different times and places, law could be constantly in flux, law could even be controversial, without any of this undermining its legitimacy.[51]

I described formalism as a *science* of *legal materials*. Traditional realists rejected the former and (with important changes) accepted the latter; scientific realists made the opposite move. These realists wanted to maintain the scientific aspirations for the law, but not in the form of the closed, autonomous legal science. For these legal realists, true legal science had to be continuous with the natural sciences. And as lawyers' methods for finding legal answers were so different from the scientists', it was no surprise that the law was often a mess.

Once again, this was not just an epistemological concern. For some scientific realists, over-reliance on lawyers' method was not merely insufficiently scientific, it was fundamentally immoral. The closed science of law meant that, essentially

[49] See Karl N. Llewellyn, *The Theory of Rules* (Frederick Schauer ed., 2011 [1938–1940]) 50. Llewellyn's famous essay on the canons of statutory interpretation, 'Remarks on the Theory of Appellate Decision and the Rules or Canons about How Statutes Are to Be Construed' (1950) 3 *Vanderbilt L.R.* 395 is often read as a devastating attack on legal determinacy. Careful reading reveals a rather different message. See especially ibid., 398–9.

[50] See, e.g., Leon Green, 'The Development of Doctrine of Stare Decisis and the Extent to Which It Should Be Applied' (1946) 40 *Illinois L.R.* 303, 321 (stare decisis 'has kept open the way for the continuous growth of the law in obedience to pressure outside the law').

[51] See Max Radin, *Stability in Law* (1945) 21, 23; Green (n. 47) 127.

the only standard against which we can measure law is internal coherence ('logic'). But, scientific realists complained, there is little point in getting the law to be perfectly logical and internally coherent, if what is so coherently demanded is morally wrong.[52] Importantly, the traditional realist approach was not much better, for the community values it celebrated were nothing more than personal convictions, imprecise and vague, and as such at best resembled science at a primitive stage of its development.

To attain certainty on these foundational questions of value, lawyers had to turn the same source that provided certainty to other aspects of life. Question of value, Cohen explicitly said, were question of fact,[53] and as such they were in principle answerable using the same methods employed for answering other questions of fact. More concretely, this meant, as it often does, some version of consequentialism. It was scientific realists, and only scientific realists, who spoke of 'studying and teaching law as an *implement* of social well-being' and sought to reconceive of lawyers as 'social engineers'.[54] Those who hold this view typically then further advance the idea that the authority of law is grounded in the greater expertise of the law-makers. This is a justification that ties political authority with epistemic authority: Law is an instrument for improving the lives of people, and its legitimacy depends on epistemic authority, on its ability to *actually* achieve that task. The turn to the sciences is thus a turn to a method that proved itself capable of generating superior understanding of the world and greater control over it. Law understood as a science in this sense had a place in the university not by isolating itself from other disciplines, but by incorporating their insights.

At bottom, then, these two versions of legal realism rest on two competing views of legal and political authority, and perhaps also, at further remove, of human nature. Any attempt to summarize these views in a sentence inevitably leaves out much nuance. Still, one can summarize traditional realism as premised on the view that law is a natural outgrowth of the particular society it exists in, whereas the scientific realists thought of law as a contrivance. If

---

[52] See Felix Cohen, 'The Ethical Basis of Legal Criticism' (1931) 41 *Yale L.J.* 201. Coherence remains to this day a central normative tenet of formalism. See Weinrib (n. 23) 29–36.

[53] Felix S. Cohen, 'The Subject Matter of Ethical Science' (1932) 42 *International J. of Ethics* 397, 399; see also Robinson (n. 31) 263–4. Oliphant took a somewhat different stance. He also wanted to rid legal analysis (and social sciences more generally) of what he called 'speculative thinking, unfettered by the exhausting labor and disturbing concreteness of empirical effort'. He suggested that if lawyers engaged in concrete questions, they could provide scientifically valid solutions to them without having to worry about value questions. See Herman Oliphant, 'Facts, Opinions, and Value-Judgments' (1932) 10 *Texas L.R.* 127, 136, 138.

[54] Oliphant (n. 53) 162 (emphasis added); Robinson (n. 31) 236. Frank dedicated an entire chapter, revealingly entitled, ' "Legal Science" and "Legal Engineering" ', to a critique of such ideas. See Jerome Frank, *Courts on Trial* (1949) ch. 14.

labels are needed, then traditional legal realism is 'organic' whereas scientific legal realism is 'mechanistic'.

IV. Solving the Puzzle

If the account presented in this chapter is correct, we have an answer to the realist puzzle. The immediate impetus for legal realism was a conception of law that emerged at a particular time and in response to the challenge of teaching law at a university. In this respect, legal realism was a reaction to a specific concern of its time, and as such should be of limited interest for us today. But in another sense, realist thinking reflects attempts to explain the authority of law in the modern state; understood in this broader sense both the problems the Realists were grappling with and their answers are still relevant.

I have said little in this chapter on ideas typically thought of as the most important tenets of legal realism: adjudication and the prediction theory. This omission is intentional. I believe focusing on adjudication gives it an outsize significance in relation to its actual place in the Legal Realist oeuvre. Even to the extent that the realists did discuss adjudication, it was part of a larger theoretical picture, and it is this picture that needs to be better understood in order to understand the Realists' views on adjudication.

It is this picture that I therefore attempted to highlight. The Realists attacked a view of law that they thought was not connected to reality; hence, their call for 'realism'. But different Realists meant something quite different by this word. For one group of Realists, this meant the felt experience of real-world law by judges, lawyers, and even laypeople, along with their semi-articulate values. For another group, the realities that lawyers (practitioners included) were missing were those that came from the natural sciences, the most reliable source for a realistic understanding of the world. This difference manifested itself in the two groups' thinking about the path to law's improvement. For realists of the first camp, it was the needs, desires, and values of real-world people that should be the driving force behind legal reform; for realists of the second type, these needs had to be channelled through the lens of information now provided by science.

The way I presented the two Realist camps, and their different responses to the formalist idea of law's autonomy, help explain realism's continuing relevance. It is difficult to generalize over the extraordinarily diverse legal scholarship of the subsequent decades, but in different ways it reflects competing attempts to solve the problem of reliable premises that give way to legitimate law in ways that resemble the two versions of legal realism. Law-and-economics is the epitome of the attempt to turn to science as a source for reliable premises; more recent forays into cognitive psychology, evolutionary biology, and neuroscience reflect newer manifestations of this approach. The assumption underlying all of them is that the true knowledge provided by science is the key to making law do a better job in regulating human affairs, 'better' often understood in a broadly consequentialist manner. On the other hand, sociological and cultural approaches to law are descendants of the second realist approach. Such approaches are far more inclined to blur the distinction between law and other normative orders (what is now called 'legal pluralism'), and by extension, the boundaries between law and society. Real law grows naturally out of the society in which it is found, and it loses its legitimacy when it loses touch with that society. That is why 'we are all realists now' rings true; not because we are all the same, but because the fundamental rift on this question found in Legal Realists' writings is central to contemporary debates about law. In more or less conspicuous ways this divide is found in debates in such diverse areas as tort, evidence, and the regulation of environmental risks, as well as many others. These are not just differences of technique, two paths to the same endpoint. They reflect philosophical differences on the authority of law. In a democratic society, the choice between them is unlikely to go away.

BIBLIOGRAPHY

Works by Legal Realists

Felix S. Cohen, *Ethical Systems and Legal Ideals* (Falcon Press, 1933)

Jerome Frank, *Courts on Trial: Myth and Reality in American Justice* (Princeton University Press, 1949)

Jerome Frank, *Law and the Modern Mind* (Bretano's, 1930). A 1949 reprint includes a new preface by Frank Leon Green, *Judge and Jury* (Vernon Law Books, 1930)

Karl N. Llewellyn, *The Bramble Bush: Some Lectures on Law and Its Study* (Oceana, 2nd edn., 1951; 1930). Most recently reprinted as *The Bramble Bush: The Classic Lectures on the Law and Law School* (Oxford University Press, 2008)

Karl N. Llewellyn, *The Case Law System in America*, Michael Ansaldi trans., (University of Chicago Press, 1989), translation of *Präjudizienrecht und Rechtsprechung in Amerika* (Th. Weicher, 1933)

Karl N. Llewellyn, *Jurisprudence: Realism in Theory and Practice* (University of Chicago Press, 1962) (a collection of previously published articles)

Edward S. Robinson, *Law and the Lawyers* (Macmillan, 1935)

Interpretations of Legal Realism

Hanoch Dagan, *Reconstructing American Legal Realism & Rethinking Private Law Theory* (Oxford University Press, 2013)

Neil Duxbury, *Patterns of American Jurisprudence* (Oxford University Press, 1995) ch. 2

Morton J. Horwitz, *The Transformation of American Law 1870–1960: The Crisis of Legal Orthodoxy* (Harvard University Press, 1992) chs. 4–8

Laura Kalman, *Legal Realism at Yale, 1927–1960* (University of North Carolina Press, 1986)

Brian Leiter, *Naturalizing Jurisprudence: Essays on American Legal Realism and Naturalism in Legal Philosophy* (Oxford University Press, 2007) chs. 1–4

John Henry Schlegel, *American Legal Realism and Empirical Legal Science* (University of North Carolina Press, 1995)

Brian Z. Tamanaha, *Beyond the Formalist–Realist Divide: The Role of Politics in Judging* (Princeton University Press, 2010)

William Twining, *Karl Llewellyn and the Realist Movement* (Cambridge University Press, 2nd edn., 2012)

CHAPTER 26

....

&: LAW _ SOCIETY IN HISTORICAL LEGAL RESEARCH

....

CATHERINE L. FISK

I. INTRODUCTION: THE ORIGINS OF THE AMPERSAND

....

LAW & society vis-à-vis historical legal research means at least two distinct, though interrelated, things. First, the law & society movement, as the 1960s descendant of Legal Realism, was for a generation almost synonymous with the interdisciplinary study of law in the United States. Legal history was a branch of law & society, at least when the history was more than what historians deride as 'law office histories' (simplified tales of doctrinal origins and evolution written by or for a court[1]). Second, law & society was an approach to legal history associated in particular with the pioneering work of James Willard Hurst beginning in the 1940s, when Hurst urged legal historians to 'examine law not in terms of doctrinal classification, but in terms of a given economic or cultural function or activity'.[2] In both of these senses, law & society has been so significant that almost

....

[1] See, e.g., Stephen A. Siegel, 'How Many Critiques Must Historians Write?' (2011) 45 *Tulsa L.R.* 823 ff.
[2] J. Willard Hurst, 'Legal History: A Research Program' (1942) *Wisconsin L.R.* 323, 329 ff.

no sophisticated work of legal history published in the last quarter century has escaped its influence.

The fields of study encompassed by the society half of the law & society dyad grew tremendously in the late twentieth century and the early twenty-first. The growth of socio-legal history occurred at the same time that many disciplines had late-century turns to history (historical sociology, history of political institutions, historicism in literary studies). A turn to history in socio-legal studies was, in some respects, part of the late twentieth-century wave of historicism across the social sciences and humanities. At the same time, legal scholars moved away from the lawyerly focus on legal doctrine that had, with the exception of the Legal Realists, characterized legal scholarship in the first half of the twentieth century. The rise of empirical legal studies, law & economics, and the growth in the number of law professors with PhDs in sociology, anthropology, American studies, political science, and economics, along with history, all contributed to the growth of socio-legal history. In short, the society part of law & society enjoyed robust growth that could not but affect the way that legal history was done.

At the same time, the law side of the law & society dyad expanded, too. The rise of legal pluralism in the 1980s and 1990s expanded scholars' conception of law and, therefore, exploded the possible subjects of legal study. When Hurst prescribed his research program for legal history in 1942, he acknowledged the possibly all-encompassing nature of both the law and the society halves of the dyad. But Hurst narrowed the object of the legal historian's study to what he called 'legal' controls and sanctions, which he defined by reference to the 'law-man's peculiar expertness' in dealing with 'primary sources'.[3] He urged legal historians to focus on the arena of social life to do with those 'who employ the power and act in the name of the politically organized community'[4] and on economic problems, 'on the hypothesis that this will be the focus of the dominant problems in the law of our time'.[5] But pluralism and the turn to history demanded a much broader lens than Hurst's focus on formal law and on 'economic problems'.

The expansion of both halves of the law & society dyad inevitably raised questions about the conjunctive metaphor. If anything can count as law (as legal pluralists would have it), and if the society half of the dyad encompasses almost everything (as law & society scholars would have it), then the ampersand becomes problematic. At the very least, its meaning becomes murky. For the most part, law & society scholars, channelling Felix Cohen's Legal Realist aura, rejected as 'nonsense'[6] the notion that somehow law exists separate from society.

The concept of the ampersand might instead be thought of as a manifesto for socio-legal studies generally and socio-legal history in particular. Legal historians,

---

[3] Ibid., 328 ff.   [4] Ibid., 325 ff.   [5] Ibid., 331.

[6] Felix S. Cohen, 'Transcendental Nonsense and the Functional Approach' (1935) 35 *Columbia L.R.* 809 ff.

like scholars generally, ought not to study just treatises, statutes, and cases, nor seek to find logic or meaning just in the reasoning articulated by judges and lawyers. Rather, they should set their sights more widely on how legal systems are used to pursue particular ends,[7] what contracting parties do,[8] the social, political, and cultural landscape of criminal courts[9] or property disputes[10] or debtors' prisons,[11] or how family members talk about and seek power using legal claims.[12]

After a brief survey of different interdisciplinary approaches to historical study of law, this chapter explores the growth of both halves of the law & society dyad. Then the chapter explains how that growth put pressure on the conjunctive metaphor that has long been used to describe the relationship between law and that which stands outside law, whether it be society, economy, polity, or something else. I suggest that the nature of law & society approaches to history has a great deal to do with what practitioners of the historical study of law conceptualize as being required by the ampersand, or by whatever other metaphor one might put in its place.

II. A BRIEF INTERDISCIPLINARY HISTORY OF INTERDISCIPLINARITY IN THE HISTORICAL STUDY OF LAW

Law & society as a field of study and an approach to the study of law had its seeds in Roscoe Pound's contrast between law in the books and law in action.[13] Its first heyday was in the 1920s and 1930s, when, as Robert Gordon quipped, 'much of the Columbia faculty dreamed that every course might be partly one in sociology'.[14]

---

[7] Lawrence M. Friedman, 'The Usury Laws of Wisconsin: A Study in Legal and Social History' (1963) *Wisconsin L.R.* 515, 515 ('The legal system of any particular jurisdiction pursues specific economic and social goals') ff.

[8] Stewart Macaulay, 'An Empirical View of Contract' (1985) *Wisconsin L.R.* 465 ff.

[9] Michael Willrich, *City of Courts: Socializing Justice in Progressive Era Chicago* (2003).

[10] Dylan C. Penningroth, *The Claims of Kinfolk: African American Property and Community in the Nineteenth-Century South* (2003).

[11] Bruce H. Mann, *Republic of Debtors: Bankruptcy in the Age of American Independence* (2009).

[12] Hendrik Hartog, *Man and Wife in America: A History* (2000); John W. Wertheimer, 'Gloria's Story: Adulterous Concubinage and the Law in Twentieth-Century Guatemala' (2006) 24 *Law & History R.* 375 ff.

[13] David Rabban offers a lucid account of Pound's jurisprudence from the standpoint of the intellectual history of law and legal history and citations to the relevant literature in chapter 13 of his book, *Law's History: American Legal Thought and the Transatlantic Turn to History* (2013).

[14] Robert W. Gordon, 'Historicism in Legal Scholarship' (1981) 90 *Yale L.J.* 1017, 1051 ff.

Though law faculties did not widely or enduringly embrace empiricism then,[15] around 1960, sociologists, political scientists, and anthropologists embraced socio-legal studies with gusto, founding the Center for the Study of Law and Society at the University of California at Berkeley in 1961 and the Law and Society Association (LSA) in 1964. The LSA held its first meeting at the annual meeting of the American Sociological Association in 1964 and then met at the American Political Science Association, the American Anthropological Association, and the Association of American Law Schools in 1965. Over time, scholars in the humanities joined colleagues in law schools and the social sciences in seeking in the LSA a community of like-minded *confreres* united mainly by the desire to study law from some perspective other than the analysis and synthesis of legal doctrine as taught in most American law schools.

Law & society vis-à-vis the historical study of law means that history is a methodology for study of law and, more importantly, that legal history should not merely describe the evolution (or stasis) of legal doctrine or legal institutions over time. Rather, legal historians must be guided in their work by the mantra that the meaning and function of law cannot be understood without close attention to social, economic, and political context.

Within legal history, the distinct law & society emphasis on context when studying the history of law was pioneered by J. Willard Hurst at the University of Wisconsin.[16] The law & society approach to legal history as practiced by Hurst was, as Gordon famously said, evolutionary functionalism.[17] Legal history was deeply influenced by a belief that law was an instrument of public policy that was used deliberately to achieve particular economic goals and that it could be studied using the historical version of social science empirical methods.[18] Thus, scholars produced meticulous studies of how contract law, or economic regulation by some branch of government, was shaped, used, and produced by the efforts of railroads, canal companies, or business corporations.[19]

Once law & society scholars convinced substantial numbers of faculty in American law schools that the study of law should encompass more than the

[15] Ibid.; Laura Kalman, *Yale Law School in the Sixties* (2005); John Schlegel, 'American Legal Realism and Empirical Social Science: From the Yale Experience' (1979) 18 *Buffalo L.R.* 459 ff.

[16] J. Willard Hurst, *Law and Economic Growth: A Legal History of the Lumber Industry in Wisconsin, 1836–1915* (1964); J. Willard Hurst, *Law and the Conditions of Freedom in the Nineteenth-Century United States* (1956).

[17] Both the term 'evolutionary functionalism' and its application to the law & society approach to legal history are Bob Gordon's. Robert W. Gordon, 'Critical Legal Histories' (1984) 36 *Stanford L.R.* 57, 59 ff.

[18] See Michael Grossberg, 'Social History Update: "Fighting Faiths" and the Challenges of Legal History' (1991) 25 *J. Social History* 191 ff.

[19] See Susanna L. Blumenthal, 'Of Mandarins, Legal Consciousness, and the Cultural Turn in US Legal History' (2012) 37 *Law & Social Inquiry* 167, 171 ff.

analysis and synthesis of doctrine, legal historians became important members of faculties in many law schools. So, too, did economists, sociologists, political scientists, philosophers, and critical theorists. Theory, empirical studies, and law & economics became even more influential in legal scholarship in the 1990s than legal history. The number of law schools hiring faculty with a PhD as well as (or even in lieu of) a JD exploded in the 1990s and 2000s.[20] Predictably, the professional and disciplinary controversies that occur within disciplines and that define the boundaries between disciplines found their way into the law & society field. In legal history, as in other arenas of scholarly debate, 'any field that historians had well trampled was a tremendous battleground of specialized professional controversy'.[21] The importation of professional controversy from the humanities and social sciences into law schools enlarged methodological debates among law faculties. Differences of opinion about empirical methods, theories, and proper objects of inquiry left their marks in law & society scholarship generally, and in the subset that examined history.

The early growth of socio-legal history in law schools in the late 1970s and early 1980s coincided with the creation of one of the most significant cauldrons of intellectual ferment about law: Critical Legal Studies (CLS or Crits). CLS deeply influenced legal history as scholars turned to history to gain a critical foothold on contemporary doctrine and correlated doctrinal change that favoured the interests of the wealthy and powerful to economic and political changes that did so similarly.[22] CLS, especially a path-breaking article by Robert Gordon, challenged the evolutionary functionalism of the sort practised by Willard Hurst.[23] Gordon's insight, which is now taken for granted but was a quite radical departure from law and society scholarship at the time, was that law matters, as Hendrik Hartog put it in an essay on the contribution of Gordon's seminal article to legal historiography.[24] Gordon asserted that law & society approaches to legal history, which focused mainly on how 'society' influenced law, neglected to consider how law influenced society or, more specifically, how law itself *was* society, how law produces as it reflects legal consciousness.[25] In Gordon's terms, one task of critical legal history was to 'bring[] home to mainstream lawyers the historicity and ideological nature of those lawyers' ordinary ways of thinking'.[26]

---

[20] See Steven Wilf, 'Law/Text/Context' (2011) 1 *U.C. Irvine L.R.* 543, 552 ('In 1960, there were only five legal historians operating in elite law schools while today legal historians are considered an essential part of the infield of any major law school.'); Brian Z. Tamanaha, *Failing Law Schools* (2012) 58 ff.

[21] Gordon (n. 14) 1052 ff.

[22] Morton J. Horwitz, *The Transformation of American Law, 1780–1860* (1977).

[23] Gordon (n. 17) 57, 110–12 ff.

[24] Hendrik Hartog, 'Introduction to Symposium on "Critical Legal Histories"' (2012) 37 *Law & Social Inquiry* 147, 152 ff.

[25] Gordon (n. 17) 57 ff.   [26] Ibid., at 122.

Along with or just after the Crits came feminist,[27] Critical Race Theory,[28] and Queer Theory[29] strands of legal historical scholarship. All of them, in one way or another, build on the notion that the 'personal is political' and all are necessarily socio-legal. The feminist statement that 'the personal is political'[30] illuminates the way in which the growth of women's, gender, LGBTQ, and sexuality studies expanded the range of ways in which law can be studied historically. Such work *requires* a *socio*-legal approach, as a study focusing on state law, or law on the books, will never capture the ways in which law operates on bodies. All these forms of critical inquiry rest on a capacious notion of what law is and where law operates that rejects the binary connoted by the ampersand. As Michelle McKinley explained of Latin American legal studies, 'those studying gender-based and *campesino*- or identity-based mobilizations have de-centred the state as the legitimate object of analysis in an effort to account for the complex negotiations that less powerfully situated actors engaged in through legal action'.[31]

At the same time that legal history as practised in law schools and history departments was being transformed by critical studies and pluralism, in the social sciences and humanities scholars began to embrace historical methods to understand whatever phenomena was under study. The 'historical turn' in sociology and politics was especially important in expanding the range of topics, methods, and practitioners of historical analysis of law, for law is a crucial object of inquiry in much sociological and political science work. Political theorists produced histories of law and governance and of the people and institutions in which theories developed.[32] American Political Development scholars and new institutionalists in political science and sociology studied constitutional history, of course,[33] but also the

[27] On the evolution of theory in feminist legal history, see Mariana Valverde, 'The Rescaling of Feminist Analyses of Law and State Power: From (Domestic) Subjectivity to (Transnational) Governance Networks' (2014) 4 *U.C. Irvine L.R.* 325 ff.

[28] See, e.g., Angela Onwuachi-Willig, *According to Our Hearts:* Rhinelander v. Rhinelander *and the Law of the Multiracial Family* (2013).

[29] See, e.g., Katherine Franke, *Wedlocked: The Perils of Marriage Equality* (2015).

[30] On the origins of the phrase, see Dale M. Smith, *Poets Beyond the Barricade: Rhetoric, Citizenship, and Dissent* chapter 2, n. 41 (2012), who notes the phrase had been used by civil rights activists in the 1960s but that it became popularly associated with feminism when Carol Hanisch published an essay entitled "The Personal Is Political" in a 1969 pamphlet edited by Shulamith Firestone and Anne Koedt called *Notes from the Second Year: Women's Liberation: Major Writings of the Radical Feminists*.

[31] Michelle A. McKinley, *Fractional Freedoms: Slavery, Intimacy, and Legal Mobilization in Colonial Lima, 1600–1700* (2016) 11 ff.

[32] Jennifer Nedelsky, *Private Property and the Limits of American Constitutionalism: Madisonian Framework and Its Legacy* (1994); Louis Menand, *The Metaphysical Club: A Story of Ideas in America* (2002).

[33] See, e.g., Howard Gillman, *The Constitution Besieged: The Rise and Demise of Lochner Era Police Powers Jurisprudence* (1993). Of course, the study of constitutional history as a branch of political science is not a new phenomenon. See, e.g., Alpheus Thomas Mason, *The Supreme Court from Taft to Warren* (1958).

history of race and civil rights,[34] the welfare state,[35] labour,[36] and the administrative state.[37] Sociologists and political scientists published books on periods of time further in the past than legal historians writing on the same topic.[38] The historical turn expanded the methodologies of law and society scholarship on history and the number of practitioners.

Law and humanities also grew as a field from the 1970s onwards, both as legal scholars discovered and embraced post-structuralist theory and as scholars in departments of literature and English began to write about law, not only as it appears in novels, poems, and plays, but as a series of texts in its own right.[39] Law— its texts and its contexts—became a fertile field of literary study.[40] A special issue of *English Language Notes* on 'Juris-Dictions' punned on a legal term to highlight the linguistic (diction) essence of law. In literature departments and in law schools, scholars approached the legal text as its own context.[41] Law and literature (which has its own problems of the conjunctive metaphor) caught on in law schools and in literature and English departments at the same time that the 'New Historicism' grew as a movement or method in literary studies.[42] This confluence of interest in history, text, and context in literary studies of law created what Bernadette Meyler called a love triangle between law, literature, and history.[43]

[34] Paul Frymer, *Black and Blue: African Americans, the Labor Movement, and the Decline of the Democratic Party* (2008); John David Skrentny, *The Ironies of Affirmative Action: Politics, Culture, and Justice in America* (1996).

[35] Theda Skocpol, *Protecting Soldiers and Mothers: The Political Origins of Social Policy in the United States* (1992).

[36] Karen Orren, *Belated Feudalism: Labor, the Law, and Liberal Development in the United States* (1991); Victoria Hattam, *Labor Visions and State Power: The Origins of Business Unionism in the United States* (1991).

[37] Compare Daniel Ernst, *Tocqueville's Nightmare: the Administrative State Emerges in America, 1900–1940* (2014); Nicholas R. Parrillo, *Against the Profit Motive: The Salary Revolution in American Government, 1780–1940* (2013); Stephen Skowrownek, *Building a New American State: The Expansion of National Administrative Capacities, 1877–1920* (1982); Morton Keller, *Affairs of State: Public Life in Nineteenth Century America* (1977); William Novak, *The People's Welfare: Law and Regulation in Nineteenth-Century America* (1996).

[38] Compare Skocpol (n. 35); Felicia A. Kornbluh, *The Battle for Welfare Rights: Politics and Poverty in Modern America* (2007); Karen M. Tani, *States of Dependency: Welfare, Rights, and American Governance, 1935–1972* (2016); Daniel J. Walkowitz, *Working With Class: Social Workers and the Politics of Middle-Class Identity* (1999).

[39] See, e.g., Jane B. Baron, 'Law, Literature, and the Problems of Interdisciplinarity' (1999) 108 *Yale L.J.* 1059 ff; James B. White, *The Legal Imagination* (1973).

[40] Paul K. Saint-Amour, *The Copyrights: Intellectual Property and the Literary Imagination* (2003); Nan Goodman, *Banished: Common Law and the Rhetoric of Social Exclusion in Early New England* (2012); Peter Goodrich, *Law in the Courts of Love: Literature and Other Minor Jurisprudences* (1996); Peter Goodrich, *Legal Discourse: Studies in Linguistics, Rhetoric, and Legal Analysis* (1987).

[41] 'Juris-Dictions' (2010) 48 *English Language Notes* no. 2 (special issue ed., Nan Goodman).

[42] See, e.g., Elliott Visconsi, *Lines of Equity: Literature and the Origins of Law in Later Stuart England* (2008).

[43] Bernadette Meyler, 'Law, Literature, and History: The Love Triangle' (2015) 5 *U.C. Irvine L.R.* 365 ff; Julie Stone Peters, 'Law, Literature, and the Vanishing Real: On the Future of an Interdisciplinary Illusion', in Austin Sarat et al., *Teaching Law and Literature* (2011) 71, 83–4 ff.

Finally, law & society approaches to legal history were enthusiastically embraced in the growing field of colonial and post-colonial studies. These, too, invite historical methodologies and studies on law in part because the process by which a migration of people becomes a conquest and then a colony takes time, as does the process by which a colony ceases to be a colony and becomes post-colonial. Thus, although legal anthropologist Sally Engle Merry began her ethnography of colonial law in Hawai'i by examining sixty years of local court records, just as she had done in New England courts, she found herself constantly expanding the context she considered. Her legal anthropology thus became a legal history as she sought to explain 'the economic and social transformations of the region . . . and the conceptions of race and difference that underlay the plantation system', and, ultimately, how the legal system under study came to Hawai'i and how it differed from the Native Hawai'ian legal system that it replaced.[44] Colonial and postcolonial studies also challenge American or western notions of law by inviting study of the overlapping laws of the colonizer and the colonized, the colonizer's manipulation of heterogeneous and overlapping systems of religious, customary, state, and international laws to govern colonies and post-colonial places,[45] and what Lauren Benton called the 'accommodation, advocacy within the system, subtle de-legitimation, and outright rebellion' that constitute the ways conquered or colonized groups sought to respond to the imposition of law.[46]

III. THE EXPANSION OF 'LAW'; THE EXPANSION OF 'SOCIETY'

If the origins of socio-legal history in multiple fields as recounted above are a narrative of expansion, so, too, is its evolution, to which I now turn. More scholars! More disciplines! More methods! More subjects of study! Both halves of the law & society dyad grew dramatically from the 1970s onward, even as the methodological pluralism that has been the defining feature of law & society work continued to be the only thing holding the whole enterprise together.

---

[44] Sally Engle Merry, *Colonizing Hawai'i: The Cultural Power of Law* (2000) 10 ff.

[45] Iza R. Hussin, *The Politics of Islamic Law: Local Elites, Colonial Authority, and the Making of the Muslim State* (2016); Mitra Sharafi, *Law and Identity in Colonial South Asia: Parsi Legal Culture, 1772–1947* (2014).

[46] Lauren Benton, *Law and Colonial Cultures: Legal Regimes in World History, 1400–1900* (2000) 3 ff.

On the law side of the dyad, the expansion came from several quarters and took many forms. For several decades, scholars of legal pluralism debated the definition of law, never ultimately reaching a consensus.[47] All definitions of law in legal pluralism are quite capacious, allowing for the law side of the dyad to encompass a very broad range of social relations indeed.[48] Legal historians embraced a much wider range of things that one might study to understand law. In an especially influential and felicitously titled article, 'Pigs and Positivism', Hendrik Hartog explored disputes over the right of nineteenth-century New Yorkers to keep pigs in the street as a way of doing the legal history of social and political practice.[49] In short, the expansion of what law means and how to study it in history transformed the theory and method of legal history. As I explain more fully below, the continued expansion of the meaning of law has been the most significant feature of legal history in the past half-century.

On the other side of the ampersand, the range of social fields in which something like law can be studied historically expanded correspondingly. Studies of religious law have long invited an expansive notion of law, but as American law schools have expanded their focus from canon law and gained interest in Islam, the Western European division between state law and religious law blurred.[50] The influential social histories of the 1960s, 1970s, and 1980s inspired historians of law or law-inflected topics to do bottom up studies.[51] Expansion in the historiography of social history had an especially marked impact on labour law history. Bottom-up social histories of labour, histories of institutions of labour governance, and histories of government repression of labour expanded the range of legal history.[52]

---

[47] Brian Z. Tamanaha, 'Understanding Legal Pluralism: Past to Present, Local to Global' (2008) 30 *Sydney Law Review* 375 ff.

[48] John Griffiths, 'What is Legal Pluralism?' (1986) 24 *J. Leg. Pluralism* 1 ff; John Griffiths, 'The Idea of Sociology of Law and its Relation to Law and to Sociology' (2005) 8 *Current Legal Issues* 49 ff.

[49] Hendrik Hartog, 'Pigs and Positivism' (1985) *Wisconsin L.R.* 899 ff.

[50] See, e.g., Intisar A. Rabb, *Doubt in Islamic Law: A History of Legal Maxims, Interpretation, and Islamic Criminal Law* (2015).

[51] Among the many examples one might consider are Robert L. Tsai, *America's Forgotten Constitutions: Defiant Visions of Power and Community* (2014); Erika Lee, *At America's Gates: Chinese Immigration During the Exclusion Era, 1882–1943* (2003); Daniel Lord Smail, *The Consumption of Justice: Emotions, Publicity, and Legal Culture in Marseille, 1264–1423* (2003). An early example of this kind of work is Lawrence Friedman and Robert Percival, *The Roots of Justice: Crime and Punishment in Alameda County, California, 1870–1910* (1981).

[52] Even social histories of labour typically include consideration of the negotiation and operation of collective bargaining agreements and mechanisms of union self-governance. See, e.g., Vicki L. Ruiz, *Cannery Women Cannery Lives: Mexican Women, Unionization, and the California Food Processing Industry, 1930–1950* (1987). The story of American labour is so deeply intertwined with government repression of labour activism that legal history suffuses the field. See, e.g., Laura Weinrib, *The Taming of Free Speech* (2016); Reuel Schiller, *Forging Rivals: Race, Class, Law, and the Collapse of Postwar Liberalism* (2015); Christopher L. Tomlins, *The State and the Unions: Labor Relations, Law,*

Studies of race, slavery, and migrations of peoples and colonization, which, along with work discussed already, have been among the most significant work of socio-legal history in the past half-century and have dramatically expanded the realm of law & society work in history. Slavery was, of course, a legal institution as well as a totalizing cultural and political phenomenon. It thus invites a broad conception of law and how law operates. Historians need a correspondingly broad 'lens', Rebecca Scott said in her work on post-emancipation Cuba and Louisiana, 'in order to seek out patterns of individual behaviour without losing sight of the ways in which these are framed by a broader economy and polity'.[53] American history from the first English settlement on the North American continent to the American Civil War, Christopher Tomlins argued, was a 'formative conjunction of law and colonizing' in which labour practices loomed large in law's colonizing project.[54] Michelle McKinley illustrates the enormous possibilities of an expansive notion of where law operates in *Fractional Freedoms: Slavery, Intimacy, and Legal Mobilization in Colonial Lima, 1600–1700*, which explores 'that fertile space between law on the books and the law in action' to understand the ways in which enslaved women in colonial Lima 'could exploit that gap or breach' to advance their claims to rights as spouses, mothers, and workers.[55] Even traditional legal concepts like property were complicated by research showing that property ownership was widespread among slaves in the antebellum American south even though there was no legal framework to recognize or protect slaves' property rights.[56]

An expansive notion of law and an equally expansive notion of society opened new fields of inquiry. It also allowed scholars to throw their efforts into lifting up subaltern groups through serious study of people and places that an older generation of scholars would have considered beneath their notice. This was heady stuff for scholars who wanted to believe that their ivory tower labours were contributing to progressive social change. Methodological pluralism—the notion that almost anything goes in the space of the ampersand so long as it is rigorous or persuasive or at least plausible—allowed scholars to ignore disciplinary controversy and just get on with their work.

There are, however, some historiographic drawbacks to a very capacious understanding of law and society. If anything can count as law and anything can count as society, and a scholar can tie the two together using any method (sociology, cultural studies, anthropology, literary studies, etc.), law & society becomes so capacious a field that it stretches the notion of field almost to the breaking point.

---

and the Organized Labor Movement in America, 1880–1960 (1985); Daniel R. Ernst, *Lawyers Against Labor: From Individual Rights to Corporate Liberalism* (1995); Josiah Bartlett Lambert, '*If the Workers Took a Notion': The Right to Strike and American Political Development* (2005).

[53] Rebecca J. Scott, *Degrees of Freedom: Louisiana and Cuba After Slavery* (2005) 5 ff.

[54] Christopher L. Tomlins, *Freedom Bound: Law, Labor, and Civic Identity in Colonizing English America, 1580–1865* (2010) 525 ff.

[55] McKinley (n. 31) 241 ff.   [56] Penningroth (n. 10).

In the end, one cannot entirely neglect consideration of the kinds of claims that can be made about the connection between the two halves of the dyad. What kinds of causal claims *can* be made about the role of society in law or the role of law in society? Is it wrong to imagine them as a dyad? Does the ampersand reinforce the idea that law is ever separate from society? If so, does that constrain our imagination about what law is? History as a discipline, unlike quantitative fields like economics and sociology, does not have a consensus view about the kinds of methods that make causal claims convincing (other than rigorous research and careful reading). Historians especially struggle, therefore, with the question of whether law is autonomous and with the causal relationship between law and whatever lies outside of law. It is to the debate over how law and society relate to each other that this essay now turns.

IV. In, And, As: Relationships and Causal Claims

The growth in law and society scholarship in the 1970s produced a huge increase in functional and empirical claims about law and legal change. It was no longer intellectually respectable for elite legal scholars to write articles recounting doctrinal change without considering the social context that produced the change. Doctrine could no longer be imagined as an entirely autonomous system. At the same time, the growth in critical theory produced a trenchant critique of the functional and empirical account of law/society relations on which the 'law and' framework rests. Although Hurst's program for socio-legal history had declared that 'we should study the causal interaction of legal and non-legal institutions in the control of affairs',[57] Crits destabilized the accepted verities about the origins, functions, and evolution of law, skewering the 'just so' stories that dominated doctrinal legal scholarship and early law & economics scholarship, too. Critical theory, Ritu Birla explained, invited legal history as critical practice to 'confront the problem of the autonomous subject exercising intentioned agency'.[58] But if the existence of subjects exercising intentional agency is up for grabs, historical inquiry in law is in trouble. Alas, critical theory produced no replacement for the problematic 'law and' theory it had undermined.

The 'law & __' framework survived, in part by default and in part because of the capaciousness of the conjunctive metaphor. It allowed all manner of claims about

---

[57] Hurst (n. 2) 323 ff.

[58] Ritu Birla, 'Law as Economy: Convention, Corporation, Currency' (2011) 1 *U.C. Irvine L.R.* 1015, 1036 ff.

the natures of law and history and about the insights one might gain from studying law as part of other domains of human activity. The ampersand enabled scholars to paper over carefully hedged claims of causation and obscure vagueness or ambiguity of claims about the relation between law and whatever stood outside law or whatever followed the ampersand. So historians of law could say that law 'shaped' or 'influenced' society,[59] or vice versa, or that they were mutually constitutive.[60] Causal claims became either impossible or so vague that it was tiresome to debate them and perhaps more intellectually productive to just move on.

The big and, by now, tedious theoretical problem that vexed so much legal history for a generation after Critical Legal Studies—is law ideological superstructure or is it foundational? Is it something mostly determined by external social forces or is it itself a cause?—has now been dismissed. Law constitutes society and society constitutes law; law is *embedded* in much of human existence and human existence is embedded in law.[61] So, too, have socio-legal historians moved beyond the empirical social science problem of causation. Legal history as practised today does not aim to identify a series of variables and use the past as an experiment to prove that one or two variables produce particular effects. Teleological theories are out, but so too are theories that insist all is irreducibly particular, contingent, and complex. Contingency and complexity remain, but are pushed aside enough to tell a story with a narrative arc. Narrative creativity is admired for itself.[62] Critical theory has left a crucial legacy that a critical stance, with occasional aspirations to the redemptive possibilities of critical history, is a shared commitment, even if its theoretical underpinnings are a bit creaky.

The difficulty of making big or even small causal claims might have prompted legal historians to abandon them entirely. But the temporal nature of history seems to insist upon some kind of argument about a relationship between what happened first and what happened next. And the need for such an argument is even more acute in socio-legal history which is, by definition, an examination of law in some sort of context.

It has been taken for granted for over thirty years that law and society are not two distinct realms of human activity and that each is constitutive of the other. What, then, is the significance of the persistence of the ampersand? Apart from habit, it reflects the difficulty of reorienting the project of socio-legal history to thinking about law as society rather than law as distinct from it.

The word that follows the ampersand states a claim about how one thinks about law and how one goes about studying it, in the present or in the past. A legal historian trained in or influenced by economics approaches socio-legal history quite differently than one trained in or influenced by another discipline, even

---

[59] William A. Forbath, *Law and the Shaping of the American Labor Movement* (1991).
[60] See Ariela Gross, *What Blood Won't Tell: A History of Race on Trial in America* (2008) 13 ff.
[61] Birla, (n. 58) 1015, 1020 ff.   [62] James Goodman, *Stories of Scottsboro* (1994).

when both are studying the same field of law. An economic historian's study of the history of intellectual property law makes claims about the aggregate effect of patent and copyright law on American economic development because economists are trained to work with lots of numbers and to think about aggregates.[63] But a study of the same intellectual property topic in the same era by scholars trained in history or theory approaches the problem of causation quite differently. They make more qualified and more multi-factored causal claims about the relationship between law and that which is outside law, or resist straightforward causal claims entirely, or examine intellectual and social origins rather than economic effects.[64] Indeed, the differences go beyond whatever causal claims are connoted by the ampersand. Again, taking the subject of intellectual property and technical or cultural innovation and their history, an encompassing vision of the nature of law permits the finding of law in norms of attribution and in ethnographies of how people involved in creating texts, images, and technologies make claims about their relationship to their work[65] or political struggles over mobility of people and innovative technologies.[66]

The persistence of the dyad reflects as it perpetuates lawyers' and law professors' investment in law's autonomy and in the authority that their expertise gives them. Indeed, the questions of authority, responsibility, and expertise of the lawyer doing legal history were the questions that most seemed to trouble Hurst in his seminal 1942 essay that announced the research program for law & society work in legal history.[67] That aspect of legal consciousness—that *the law* is something distinct, or at least meaningfully separable from simple exercises of power by powerful government officials and those who work with them—endures because liberal legalism is better than the alternative systems of governance that advanced economies have tried in the history of human endeavour. When John Roberts testified before the United States Senate in the hearing on his nomination to be Chief Justice of the United States, most scholars and lawyers scoffed at his statement that a Supreme Court justice is just an umpire who calls balls and strikes without regard to the justice's own values. And, yet, no one really wants to abandon the idea that law is a set of principles that constrain state and private power. Those trained to take law seriously

---

[63] B. Zorina Khan, *The Democratization of Invention: Patents and Copyrights in American Economic Development* (2005).

[64] Catherine L. Fisk, *Working Knowledge: Employee Innovation and the Rise of Corporate Intellectual Property, 1800–1930* (2009); Oren Bracha, *Owning Ideas: The Intellectual Origins of American Intellectual Property, 1790–1909* (2016); Steven Wilf, 'Copyright and Social Movements in Late Nineteenth-Century America' (2011) 12 *Theoretical Inquiries in Law* 123 ff; Steven Wilf, 'The Making of the Post-War Paradigm in American Intellectual Property Law' (2008) 31 *Columbia J.L. & Arts* 139 ff.

[65] Catherine L. Fisk, *Writing for Hire: Unions, Hollywood, and Madison Avenue* (2016); Jessica Silbey, *The Eureka Myth: Creators, Innovators, and Everyday Intellectual Property* (2015).

[66] Doron S. Ben-Atar, *Trade Secrets: Intellectual Piracy and the Origins of American Industrial Power* (2004).

[67] Hurst (n. 2) 323 ff.

as law find it depressing to think of it as merely congealed politics or a fig leaf covering the naked exercise of power.

Although it may be neither desirable nor possible for legal history to free itself from the law & society paradigm, efforts to explore the operation of the conjunctive metaphor provoked many new approaches to legal history. One of the most sustained recent published efforts to promote new thinking about the law & society framework in legal history was a series of three symposia published in the *U.C. Irvine Law Review* under the title 'Law As . . .'[68] The goal of the symposia was, as the convener Christopher Tomlins explained, 'to deploy history as an interpretive practice . . . with which to engage law; and simultaneously to offer history as a substantive arena in which other interpretive practices from across the broad spectrum of the humanities and social sciences can undertake their own engagement with law'.[69] The remainder of this chapter surveys some of the alternative conceptions of the law/society relation in recent socio-legal history.

One of the most influential ways of conceptualizing law in the past generation has been as a form of discourse, sometimes referred to as rights talk, sometimes as speech acts, and sometimes (as noted above) through plays on the term juris-diction, with an emphasis on the diction. Marianne Constable argues that '[i]n the context of legal history's reliance on textual materials (both law and history rely largely on written texts and their authority), a revitalized and explicitly rhetorically informed legal history hastens the death throes of the law-in-action/law-on-the-books distinction' because law is both a series of speech acts by officials, as philosophers have observed, and also by those who criticize law.[70]

Tomiko Brown-Nagin, Risa Goluboff, and Christopher Schmidt all consider the civil rights movement, and especially the challenge that local activists, student sit-ins, and radical civil rights groups made to the litigation strategy of the NAACP, to illuminate the various conceptions of law.[71] As Schmidt points out, different participants in the civil rights struggle, and different scholars studying it and other social movements since, have conceptualized law narrowly (as just the work of lawyers and courts, or just statutes and judicial decisions) and broadly (as consciousness, as claiming, as rights talk) for various reasons particular to their

---

[68] '"Law As . . .": Theory and Method in Legal History' (2011) 1 *UC Irvine L.R.* 519 ff; '"Law As . . ." II, History As Interface for the Interdisciplinary Study of Law' (2014) *U.C. Irvine L.R.* 1 ff; '"Law As . . ." III—*Glossolalia*: Toward a Minor Historical Jurisprudence' (2015) *U.C. Irvine L.R.* 239 ff.

[69] Christopher Tomlins, 'Foreword: "Law As . . ." III—*Glossolalia*: Toward a Minor (Historical) Jurisprudence' (2015) *U.C. Irvine L.R.* 239, 239 ff.

[70] Marianne Constable, 'Law as Claim to Justice: Legal History and Legal Speech Acts' (2011) 1 *U.C. Irvine L.R.* 631, 632–3, 636 ff. See also Marianne Constable, *Our Word is Our Bond: How Legal Speech Acts* (2014).

[71] Tomiko Brown-Nagin, *Courage to Dissent: Atlanta and the Long History of the Civil Rights Movement* (2011); Risa L. Goluboff, *The Lost Promise of Civil Rights* (2007); Christopher Schmidt, 'Conceptions of Law in the Civil Rights Movement' (2011) 1 *U.C. Irvine L.R.* 641 ff.

ambition, their position, and their critique of the work of others.[72] The notion of law as a form of consciousness is sometimes more sociological or anthropological, as when it reflects the way in which people think of themselves as having or not having certain rights or responsibilities. At other times, especially in the work of scholars well read in psychoanalytic theory, the notion of law as consciousness becomes a theoretical frame about the nature of law and the nature of the psyche that are quite abstract.[73]

As noted above in the discussion of colonial and postcolonial studies, a substantial amount of legal historical scholarship conceptualizes law as a modality of rule and as an expression of sovereignty.[74] This broader conception of law is an apt way of studying colonization, for law is crucial to the colonizing project.[75] Law is a method by which the colonizer asserts its authority and the legitimacy of its authority over the colonized people and the territory in which they live. And colonial regimes are especially fertile grounds for study of overlapping forms of law, as the colonizing people must negotiate the relationship between their law and the laws of the people who are colonized.[76]

Law has also been studied as a technology, what Chris Tomlins called 'a means of doing and making do', and also as knowledge or a form of science.[77] In this conception, law is characterized as an organized system (a technology) for making things happen, just like other technologies are thought to be human-contrived devices or systems for accomplishing things—the telephone, radio, television, or Internet for communication, the computer for data storage and analysis, the automobile for transport, or money as a medium of economic exchange.[78] This conception of the relationship between law and society emphasizes, obviously, the instrumental function of law and also its nature as a human-devised system. But thinking of law

---

[72] Schmidt (2011) 1 *U.C. Irvine L.R.* 641, 667–76 (discussing a broad range of scholarship on the civil rights movement and social movements) ff.

[73] Norman W. Spaulding, 'The Historical Consciousness of the Resistant Subject' (2011) 1 *U.C. Irvine L.R.* 677, 689, begins his analysis with a description of what he calls the 'first scene' of an execution and concludes with the statement that 'law must be detached from the desire for order and studied as a site of resistance'. In between he says: 'Law as memory, as oral, unwritten, folklore; law driven beyond history by memory; modern history arriving, with resistant subjects, at the first scene.'

[74] Mariana Valverde, '"The Honor of the Crown is at Stake": Aboriginal Land Claims Litigation and the Epistemology of Sovereignty' (2011) 1 *U.C. Irvine L.R.* 955 ff.

[75] Paul Frymer, 'Building an American Empire: Territorial Expansion in the Antebellum Era' (2011) 1 *U.C. Irvine L.R.* 913 ff; Paul Frymer, *Building an American Empire: The Era of Territorial and Political Expansion* (2017).

[76] Benton (n. 46).

[77] Christopher L. Tomlins, *Freedom Bound: Law, Labor, and Civic Identity in Colonizing English America, 1580–1865* (2010) 5. On law as knowledge or science as law, see Barbara Shapiro, *Probability and Certainty in Seventeenth-Century England: A Study of the Relationships Between Natural Science, Religion, History, Law and Literature* (1983).

[78] See, e.g., Roy Kreitner, 'Money in the 1890s: The Circulation of Politics, Economics, and Law' (2011) 1 *U.C. Irvine L.R.* 975; Sarah Seo, *Policing Everyman: How Cars Transformed American Freedom* (forthcoming, 2018).

as a technology, especially since the various industrial and computer revolutions have made technological control over humans (rather than human control of the world through technology) a staple of science fiction or dystopian nightmare, also emphasizes the ways in which the causal arrow between law and society moves in both directions. Except here, law is the tool of humans even as humans become the tool of law.

Law can also be conceptualized in ways more or less diffuse as social relations. One version of this, as noted above, was Hendrik Hartog's early effort to turn the attention of American legal historians to local custom.[79] Another is Laura Edwards' examination of local order, what her sources called the peace, in the antebellum South as law.[80] In this conception, household relations and neighbourhood customs,[81] norms about attribution,[82] or corporate practices[83] are all conceived of as law, though they may exist without formal state-created law, or with only a tenuous relation to it, or even in contravention of it.[84]

The list of ways in which law might be imagined and studied could go on at length and will be out of date as soon as it is in print, for innovation is the desideratum of most contemporary scholars. This summary is, to quote Robert Gordon once again, merely a *Pocket Guide to the Common and Exotic Varieties of the Social/Legal Histories of North America*.[85] (Except this one has a good deal less analytic insight and will probably have much less staying power than his.)

V. CONCLUSION: THE INEVITABILITY OF THE AMPERSAND?

Law & society was originally a type of legal history associated with J. Willard Hurst, but now it is practised in one form or another by almost every academic at an Anglophone university who claims to be a legal historian. Law & society has

---

[79] Hartog (n. 49) 899 ff.

[80] Laura F. Edwards, 'The Peace: The Meaning and Production of Law in the Post-Revolutionary United States' (2011) 1 *U.C. Irvine L.R.* 565 ff.

[81] Jill Elaine Hasday, *Family Law Reimagined* (2014); Hendrik Hartog, *Man and Wife in America: A History* (2000); Robert Ellickson, *Order Without Law: How Neighbors Settle Disputes* (1991); Robert Ellickson, *The Household: Informal Order Around the Hearth* (2008)

[82] Fisk (n. 65).

[83] Lauren Edelman, *Working Law: Courts, Corporations, and Civil Rights* (2017).

[84] Sarah Barringer Gordon, *The Mormon Question: Polygamy and Constitutional Conflict in Nineteenth-Century America* (2002).

[85] Gordon (1984) 36 *Stanford L.R.* 57, 58 ff.

been good for legal history as a discipline. As a dominant form of interdisciplinary legal scholarship, law & society dramatically transformed American law schools. Opening the doors of law school teaching to legal historians enabled the field of legal history to benefit from the tremendous expansion of law faculties in the 1980 to 2008 period. Law students no longer had to find the university's history department in order to study law's history as something other than the evolution of doctrine or to understand the history of the profession itself.[86] Law & society has promoted a huge variety of types of legal historical work. It has kept legal historians in conversation with a wide range of scholars.

It is not too much to say that for those who believe that history can ever tell the truth about the past, the idea that law must be studied in context to be understood in its true nature has been essential. Without it, most legal historians would doubt that the work we do has a shot at approaching some version of the truth. So, whatever the ampersand means, at least it means that we should be thinking about the nature of law and its relationship to whatever other aspects of human endeavour are relevant to our topic.

It would be unfair to leave the impression that the conjunctive metaphor that has been so crucial to socio-legal history for nearly a century has been a constraint that should be transcended or abandoned rather than an enormously empowering way to imagine what law is and was and how it should be studied. Rather, by proposing that the ampersand itself be an object of study, and by cataloguing some of the ways in which it has become so, this essay means to suggest simply that the field of socio-legal history is broad and perhaps growing broader. And that is a good thing for those who like either to read or to write about law, about history, and about whatever it may be that unites them with the rest of human experience.

Bibliography

Lauren Benton, *Law and Colonial Cultures: Legal Regimes in World History, 1400–1900* (Cambridge University Press, 2000)

Tomiko Brown-Nagin, *Courage to Dissent: Atlanta and the Long History of the Civil Rights Movement* (Oxford University Press, 2011)

Robert W. Gordon, 'Critical Legal Histories' (1984) 36 *Stanford L.R.* 57

Robert W. Gordon, 'Historicism in Legal Scholarship' (1981) 90 *Yale L.J.* 1015 ff.

---

[86] See, e.g., Kenneth Mack, *Representing the Race: The Creation of the Civil Rights Lawyer* (2012); James A. Brundage, *The Medieval Origins of the Legal Profession: Canonists, Civilians, and Courts* (2008); Robert W. Gordon, 'The American Legal Profession, 1870–2000', in Michael Grossberg and Christopher Tomlins (eds.), *The Cambridge History of Law in America vol. III* (2008); Robert B. Stevens, *Law School: Legal Education in America from the 1850s to the 1980s* (1983); Peter H. Irons, *The New Deal Lawyers* (1982).

Ariela J. Gross, *What Blood Won't Tell: A History of Race on Trial in America* (Harvard University Press, 2008)

Hendrik Hartog, *Man and Wife in America: A History* (Harvard University Press, 2000)

Hendrik Hartog, 'Pigs and Positivism', 1985 *Wisconsin LR* 899 ff

Morton J. Horwitz, *The Transformation of American Law, 1780–1860* (Harvard University Press, 1977)

J. Willard Hurst, *Law and the Conditions of Freedom in the Nineteenth-Century United States* (University of Wisconsin Press, 1956)

'"Law As . . .": Theory and Method in Legal History' Symposium, 1 *U.C. Irvine Law Review* 539 ff

Michelle A. McKinley, *Fractional Freedoms: Slavery, Intimacy, and Legal Mobilization in Colonial Lima, 1600–1700* (Cambridge University Press, 2016)

'Symposium on "Critical Legal Histories"' (2012) 37 *Law & Social Inquiry* 147 ff

Christopher L. Tomlins, *Law, Labor, and Ideology in the Early American Republic* (Cambridge University Press, 1993)

Christopher L. Tomlins, *Freedom Bound: Law, Labor, and Civic Identity in Colonizing English America, 1580–1865* (Cambridge University Press, 2010)

CHAPTER 27

LEGAL HISTORY AND THE MATERIAL TURN

TOM JOHNSON

I.

THIS chapter considers the implications of the 'material turn' in the humanities and social sciences for the study and writing of legal history. The material turn here refers to the recent surge of scholarship which has turned a critical gaze on both physical objects and materiality; on the one hand, this entails a focus on the constitutive role of material things in human society and culture, and on the other, an interrogation of 'material' as a category of analysis, with a particular emphasis on deconstructing this category. Legal scholars in several different disciplines have themselves contributed to this turn, have begun to explore where such lines of inquiry might lead when applied to the study of law, and allied concepts such as government, punishment, and sovereignty. Although relatively few legal historians have incorporated these kinds of ideas into their work, the material turn may yet have significant implications for the way that we think about and write the history of law.

What follows, therefore, lays out some potential intersections at which these two fields could converge. In the first place, as the few exploratory forays in this area have shown, legal historians will certainly enrich their analyses by considering the role of things more carefully; furthermore, in the more radically theoretical approaches to materiality itself, there is an exciting opportunity to rethink the very phenomenon of law in past societies. In the second place, a legal historical perspective—with its emphasis on change over time and its well-developed capacity for technical analysis in relation to historical evidence—will help to enrich the ongoing material turn in legal studies. By bringing legal history into conversation with the literature on materiality, then, the intention is also to produce a mutual critique; this, hopefully, will point to some new avenues of research.

This chapter proceeds initially by tracing the genealogies of some of the broader intellectual trajectories that led to a sharper, identifiable 'turn' towards the concept of materiality in the late twentieth and early twenty-first centuries. Subsequently, I suggest three paths forward by which legal historians might incorporate these insights into their research. I have labelled these approaches 'categorizing', 'materializing', and 'filing'. The first, 'categorizing' refers to the possibility of redrawing ontological categories—between, for example, object and human—which could open up new ways of understanding law in the past. The second, 'materializing', looks at an analytical approach in which law is understood as a phenomenon composed of the material things it draws into itself. The third path, 'filing', looks at the materiality of legal systems, both through their processes of record creation and their performative praxis, focusing attention on the co-constitutive nature of law and its material-bureaucratic apparatus.

These approaches, and the monikers which I have accorded them, are certainly not identifiable 'schools of thought', but rather reflect various emphases within theoretical approaches to materiality. Each has a different relevance to the way that we might use the insights of the material turn to inflect the way that we write legal history. Discussing each of these approaches respectively, I suggest some illustrative historical examples—often drawn from my own field of expertise in the law and society of medieval England—in order to elucidate what are still, at this stage, largely theoretical frameworks derived from studies of the modern world. The radical claims made by such studies mean that we ought to proceed with some caution, and so with each I have tried to offer a critique that is at once thorough while remaining sensitive to the aims of its particular approach, rather than attempt a procrustean critique of the material turn as a whole. The conclusion provides a short summary of the analytical benefits to be gained by pursuing these avenues.

II.

The material turn in the humanities seems to fit with broader trends in contemporary society: its focus on the power of the material world seems highly fitting in an era of burgeoning environmental destruction; its terminology of networks and flows seems apposite for the information age; its deconstruction of the categorical division between humans and objects mirrors the breaking-down of these boundaries in bioengineering. If such explanations seem too glib, it is also worth emphasizing that within the discipline of History, there is a more obvious explanation for the new focus on materiality, now that we have fully rounded the earlier 'cultural' turn.[1] The possibilities suggested by New Cultural History, with its focus on texts, meanings, culture, and, above all, discourse—mirrored in legal studies by Critical Legal History and the proliferation of Law and Society histories—have faded with familiarity and become routine. The material world seems to offer something much more tangible as a focal point for analysis; and it is noteworthy that other recent historiographical trends, such as the history of the body and the history of emotions, have also sought to move beyond 'discourse' as the main object of historical concern.

Of course, the material turn owes a good deal more to these antecedents than this caricature would suggest, and it ought also to be seen as part of a longer trajectory of evolving post-structuralist critique. To take an example, New Cultural Historians might point out that a phenomenon such as 'madness' could be a cultural and historical construct; but while this is no longer surprising, a simplified materialist perspective would extend the thought further, perhaps to say that the idea of a discrete mind suffering from 'madness' is just as much a construct as the disease itself (why is the brain conceptually separate from, say, the nervous system, the skull, or indeed the rest of the body?). And in fact, post-structuralist ideas, such as the Foucauldian notion of 'the body' as a subject of historical analysis, or the Bourdieusian emphasis on performative praxis, have remained important, and indeed evolved, across both 'turns'. If the strength of the current focus on materiality is certainly new, then, it has developed, nonetheless, from two main sources.[2]

In the first place, various strands in Michel Foucault's thought can be traced through to present concerns with materiality.[3] The most important is the founding notion of 'biopolitics', a concept that he brought to fruition in lectures given at the *Collège de France* in 1978–1980.[4] Like many of Foucault's ideas, biopolitics is founded upon a historical thesis. He posits that the seventeenth and eighteenth centuries saw the erasure of traditional political sovereignty exercised by rulers over subjects. Over

---

[1] Caroline Bynum, 'Perspectives, Connections & Objects: What's Happening in History Now?' (2009) 138:1 *Daedalus* 73–4 ff.

[2] Some important works nonetheless sit in rather different intellectual traditions: e.g., the essays in Arjun Appadurai (ed.), *The Social Life of Things: Commodities in Cultural Perspective* (1986).

[3] See Peter Miller, Nikolas Rose, 'Introduction: Governing Economic and Social Life', in P. Miller, N. Rose (eds.), *Governing the Present: Administering Economic, Social and Personal Life* (2008) 1–25 ff.

[4] Michel Foucault, *The Birth of Biopolitics: Lectures at the Collège de France, 1978–1979*, Michel Senellart (ed.), trans. Graham Burchell (2008).

this period, with the emergence of political economy (*raison d'état*), governments increasingly attempt to define, measure, and ultimately manage 'phenomena characteristic of a set of living beings forming a population: health, hygiene, birthrate, life expectancy, race . . . '.[5] For many thinkers, this move to understand the way modern states govern life itself has had radical implications for the way we think about sovereignty, politics, and the foundations of modern liberalism.[6]

But at a more granular level, Foucault's thesis has also prompted new ways of understanding government. Unlike the straightforward coercive power of pre-modern rulers over their subjects, the power of the measuring the modern state is diffused in the subject population itself. Government is constituted by a series of techniques—public health policies, housing projects, transport systems—that attempt to forge certain characteristics in the population it intends to command; government thus becomes a recursive exercise, creating political subjects who are moulded to be governed. Parsed as 'governmentality', scholars using these ideas have shown how phenomena as diverse as auditing, the lighting of city streets, and the development of cubicles in public bathrooms, have helped to create trustworthy, visible, modest, sanitized workers, subtly administered and unwittingly obedient to these regimes of conduct.[7]

In this focus on the physical infrastructure of governance, governmentality is closely and sometimes explicitly linked to a mode of materialist thought that emerges from a rather different intellectual tradition, following the thought of Bruno Latour.[8] This field evolved out of a quintessentially post-structuralist project, to investigate the creation of scientific knowledge, and show that such knowledge was—and is—produced, rather than revealed, and thus highly contingent on its historical and social circumstances. It was the genius of Latour to see that this indeterminacy made it necessary to redraw the boundaries of sociology: 'yes, scientific facts are indeed constructed, but they cannot be reduced to the social dimension because this dimension is populated by objects mobilized to construct it . . . [which] cannot be reduced to the reality "out there" invented by the philosophers of science'.[9] That is to say, we are stuck explaining the material world as a social construct, while continuing to explain society in terms of the material world.

---

[5] Ibid., 317 ff.

[6] Most recently, in the influential work by Giorgio Agamben, *Homo Sacer: Sovereign Power and Bare Life*, trans. Daniel Heller-Roazen (1998).

[7] Respectively, Michael Power, *The Audit Society: Rituals of Verification* (1994); Chris Otter, *Victorian Eye: A Political History of Light and Vision in Britain, 1800–1910* (2008); Tom Crook, 'Power, Privacy and Pleasure: Liberalism and the Modern Cubicle' (2007) 21:4/5 *Cultural Studies* 549–69 ff.

[8] For this association, see Tony Bennett, Patrick Joyce, 'Introduction', in Tony Bennett, Patrick Joyce (eds.), *Material Powers: Cultural Studies, History and the Material Turn* (2010) 5–10.

[9] Bruno Latour, *We Have Never Been Modern*, trans. Catherine Porter (1993) 6.

Latour attempts to cut this Gordian knot by destroying the distinction between natural and social objects—that is, between the material world and we humans who inhabit it. In place of the idea of human subjects moving around a world of objects, he sets out a 'sociology of associations' in which both human and nonhuman things—or 'actors', as both exercise agency, insofar as they contribute to caused effects—are combined into assemblages or networks (hence the appellation 'Actor Network Theory'). This is a radical position, but it has two major advantages. First, it draws our attention to the dense imbrication of the relationships between people and things, within which power and agency are much more complexly dispersed than we tend to acknowledge. Second, the critical starting point that there is no pre-existing 'society' is hugely liberating: it makes the task of scholars to focus more on how and why different actors are assembled together into entities that resemble solid wholes.[10]

In the thinking of Latour, materialist approaches emerging from a diverse range of disciplines have coalesced. The philosophical movement known as Speculative Realism, for example, folds him into a genealogy encompassing Heidegger, Merleau-Ponty, and Deleuze; Jane Bennett's influential interpretation of his ideas has drawn out their implications into a compelling 'political ecology of things'.[11] For archaeologists, working in a discipline with such a focus on the material world, Latour offers a series of new ways to think about human-nonhuman relationships. And for literary scholars in particular those who, like historians, had become disenchanted with discourse—Latourian critique represents an opportunity to escape the world of pure texts and re-examine the nature of representation.[12] Together with Foucault, his critical standpoint informs many of the questions that the material turn raises. Now, we turn to see how they might apply to legal history.

III.

It is hopefully uncontroversial to state that law is intimately related to its categories: as the great medieval legal historian S. F. C. Milsom remarked, 'the categories into

---

[10] Bruno Latour, *Reassembling the Social: An Introduction to Actor-Network-Theory* (2005) 84 ff.
[11] Jane Bennett, *Vibrant Matter: A Political Ecology of Things* (2010).
[12] Bill Brown, 'Thing Theory' (2001) 28 *Critical Inquiry* 1, 1–22 ff.

which lawyers classify life [exist] ... even in a customary system'.[13] The interrogation of these categories, both in terms of the ways in which they have been formulated in different historical societies, and the specific reasons why they were formulated in such ways—why this conceptual boundary between was drawn *here*—must be a central task of legal history. This kind of analysis, therefore, is not necessarily new, but a critique of legal categories can be extended so that it pushes up against some of our most entrenched ontological boundaries, such as those which separate people and animals, or artificial and natural objects. 'Categorizing' as a mode of legal historical analysis can thus help us to understand how law has been used to construct or police these boundaries in past societies.

To begin with, it may be useful to consider a historical example in which the links between legal and more philosophical distinctions are made extremely explicit. The work we call *Bracton*, a thirteenth-century treatise that attempted to squeeze English law into Roman categories, stated that it was possible to distinguish 'things' (*res*) in three ways: first, on the basis of whether a thing may be owned or not; second, whether a thing is corporeal or incorporeal; and third, on the basis of a thing's use, whether it was common to all, used by a community (*universitas*), or by an individual. As soon as legal writers begin to chop up the world in this way they also create categories that intersect with the material. 'The corporeal', claims *Bracton*, 'is that which can be touched'.[14] This works very well for the writer's contrast between a corporeal animal and the incorporeal right to drive it over a piece of land: straightforwardly, you cannot slap the flanks of a right. But it is less useful when the writer comes to consider problem cases: 'smoke and air are also corporeal, for air is one of the four elements of which all bodies are composed and created. It is that which is inhaled and exhaled from the body as wind and breath'.[15] What apparently began as categories of legal discourse thus quickly melt away into scientific ideas about the composition of the world.

Searching out such distinctions can help to situate past legal discourses in their wider intellectual context. But vice versa, such categorizations also have consequences for the way that law may apprehend the material. A useful example here is property. If property is, roughly, a relationship between persons with respect to a thing, then analyses have tended to focus on the former half of that definition. But how ought we to understand the relation between person and thing? Kevin Gray has looked at this problem by thinking about 'what' can and cannot be property. His solution revolves around 'excludability': whether a particular resource can be effectively separated off from common use, whether by legal, moral, or physical

---

[13] S. F. C. Milsom, 'Introduction', to Sir Frederick Pollock and Frederic William Maitland, *The History of English Law Before the Time of Edward I* (2nd edn., 1968) vol. 1, lv ff.

[14] 'Corporales vero quae tangi possunt': *Bracton on the Laws and Customs of England*, ed., George E. Woodbine, trans., with revisions and notes, by Samuel E. Thorne (1968–1977) vol. 2, 39 ff.

[15] Ibid., 48 ff.

criteria. For example, a lighthouse can be property, because it can be closed off from other people, by (conceptual) property boundaries and (actual) physical fences; the beam of light thrown out by its beacon cannot be property, because it is impossible to restrict third party use of the resource.[16]

Historically, it is important to think about how such legal, moral, and physical criteria of excludability work in co-ordination. A good example of this is the status of tombs in classical Roman law, which were deliberately placed outside of the property regime; as *res religiosae* (things of religious law), sepulchres could never be heritable, sold, used as a guarantee, seized as a security, nor subject to a servitude. Of course, this prohibition created problems for those who claimed interests in the remains of the dead, the land in which they were buried, or the monuments which marked their burial. It was thus the physical tomb, rather than the body, which was accorded specially protected status. As Yan Thomas points out in his subtle analysis of this phenomenon, 'the law thereby sanctuarised the tomb rather than the deceased. It protected a thing which in turn contained another thing . . . The institutional form was based on the prohibition of access to a thing through which one gained access to another thing'.[17] Tombs were excluded from law because they themselves excluded.

Perhaps the most tantalizing opportunity for this kind of analysis lies in those historical moments where the indeterminacy of material categorization becomes clear, and where its bite is sharpest. Defining the ontological status of slaves in the nineteenth-century Caribbean and United States, for example, presented a significant problem for contemporary jurists: were they persons, or things? As Colin Dayan has argued, judges of the antebellum South found it much more convenient not to treat slaves as animate *things*, but as circumscribed *persons*. For example, slaves were sometimes said to have undergone 'civil death' (a notion later applied to incarcerated prisoners), whereby their legal person was unrecognized by law and their physical bodies could be completely controlled; another legal avenue, intersecting with racialized hierarchies of intelligence, denied black slaves the possession of reason, volition, or morality in relation to other classes of chattel, such as animals. Indeed, these boundaries between person, animal, and object were constantly shifting in legal discourse; 'the very incommensurability of persons and things was necessary to underpin the institution of slavery'.[18] Part of the violence of the law, here, was its refusal to allow slaves one status or the other.

Finally, the way that past legal discourses categorized materials did not just have consequences for the treatment of those materials at law, but also for the ontological status of law itself. Consider *Bracton*'s return to the discussion of corporeality: while

---

[16] Kevin Gray, 'Property in Thin Air' (1991) 50 *Cambridge L.J.* 295 ff.

[17] Yan Thomas, '*Res Religiosae*: On the Categories of Religion and Commerce in Roman Law', in Alain Pottage and Martha Mundy (eds.), *Law, Anthropology and the Constitution of the Social: Making Persons and Things* (2004) 66 ff.

[18] Colin Dayan, *The Law Is a White Dog: How Legal Rituals Make and Unmake Persons* (2011) 139 ff.

law does deal with some incorporeal things, such as rights and servitudes, there are other things 'which do not exist in contemplation of law, as . . . good and evil spirits, the soul of the world and the souls of men'.[19] The larger metaphysical architecture that supports claims about the corporeality of certain *res* is thus also linked to the very scope of law itself and where it is segmented off from the spiritual realm. Deciding what can be touched, then, is linked intimately to what law may touch. And vice versa, the capacity of law to categorize the material in certain ways serves to place law itself outside of such considerations, to exclude law itself from the material; a conceptual move that would seem to be foundational to the very idea of law.[20] Untangling the way that this exclusion has been achieved, and through which intellectual means, is thus an important task for historians.

For all the potential of this mode of investigating past legal discourses, it is precisely this focus on discursive categories that seems to undermine it, for two reasons. In the first place, retaining a focus on discourse seems to go against the spirit of the material turn. As important as it may be to work out how jurists and judges attempted to categorize the material world, such an analysis excludes any critical scrutiny of materiality itself and in its place proffers only a lukewarm inquiry into representations. In the second place, if we remain at the level of discourse, if law is merely a means of categorizing the material world, then we have failed to properly scrutinize its claim to be able to categorize, and in turn, its ontological status as discourse. Therefore, law is a priori excluded from the material. As Nick Blomley pointed out in a ground-breaking work of 1996, this exclusion is a profoundly ideological move with many consequences for the way that law is understood: following his analysis, legal historians need to consider under what circumstances law is 'dematerialized' in this way, how this move is justified, and to what ends.[21] When we begin to see 'law' as part of the material world which it seeks to delineate, then we can begin to perform other kinds of legal-historical analysis altogether.

IV.

This leads us straight to the second avenue of inquiry here, which I have dubbed 'materializing'. This mode of analysis has a genealogy distinct from those discussed

---

[19] Here as elsewhere in the treatise, this is taken from the famous civilian jurist Azo: *Bracton* (n. 14) 48, n. 8 ff.

[20] David Delaney, *Law and Nature* (2003) 23 ff.

[21] Nicholas K. Blomley, *Law, Space, and the Geographies of Power* (1994).

in the introduction above, and which is worth briefly mentioning; it developed largely from the earlier 'spatial turn' in the humanities of the 1990s (spurred, among other things, by the English publication of Lefebvre's *The Production of Space* in 1991).[22] Initially, scholars began to think about all the ways in which law was complicated by its relationship to space.[23] For example, in a 1999 article Richard Ford examined the 'compelling and hopelessly arbitrary' boundaries that lie behind the 'legal paradox' of territorial jurisdiction, work that has been followed up by historians interested in the development of sanctuary—as a space conditionally exempt from secular criminal jurisdiction—in the western Middle Ages.[24] But beyond this preliminary conversation, some scholars saw the possibility of reshaping analyses of both law and space through a more sustained critical engagement between the two traditions. Thus a whole new sub-discipline, Legal Geography, emerged to interrogate both how law 'takes place' in space, and conversely how spatial ideas are co-opted into law through concepts such as scale, topography, boundaries, and so forth.

From the very inception of this field, Legal Geographers perceived in this critique the opportunity to reconceptualize law: '"doing law" in geography helps our understanding of how law shapes physical conditions and legitimates spatiality, and makes clear that law has a physical presence, or even many presences'.[25] This idea needs some unpacking, because it provides the basis of a new interpretative framework. To begin with, it solves the riddle posed by an analysis which focuses on law's 'categorizing' of the material world, noted just above, by refusing to grant legal discourse a separate ontological status, above and apart from the world it categorizes. And indeed for legal historians, this insight represents an important opportunity to think about the kinds of societies, cultures, and states (like our own) which imagine law as immaterial, a floating discourse uncompromised by material reality. For an understanding of how weird this is, historically, we might look to early complex polities—such as the Classic-period Maya and the kingdom of Urartu—which, in the compelling analysis of Adam T. Smith, seem to have imagined authority and sovereignty as fundamentally spatial, as opposed to discursive, phenomena.[26]

---

[22] The work had been published in French in 1974: Henri Lefebvre, *The Production of Space*, trans. Donald Nicholson-Smith (1991). Also important was Edward W. Soja, *Postmodern Geographies: The Reassertion of Space in Critical Social Theory* (1989).

[23] See, e.g., Theodore Steinberg, *Slide Mountain, or the Folly of Owning Nature* (1995).

[24] Richard Ford, 'Law's Territory (A History of Jurisdiction)' (1999) 97 *Michigan L.R.* 4 850ff. A useful introduction to sanctuary is Karl Shoemaker, *Sanctuary and Crime in the Middle Ages, 400–1500* (2011).

[25] Jane Holder, Carolyn Harrison, 'Connecting Law and Geography', in J. Holder, C. Harrison (eds.), *Law and Geography* (2002) 5 ff.

[26] Adam T. Smith, *The Political Landscape: Constellations of Authority in Early Complex Polities* (2003).

Beyond this conceptual reorientation, however, there are more concrete modes of analysis that this model offers. If we propose that law has a physical presence, then we quickly come to the question of what physical forms it might take. One option is to think about law's materiality in a holistic way. Though law, as it is conventionally understood, cannot be touched, it touches nearly everything. Law shapes the material form and functions of the cars we drive, through environmental directives and intellectual property regimes; it excludes us and our cars from moving into certain places, through property law; it prevents us from (or penalizes us for) particular spatial actions, such as driving too fast, through traffic codes. In short, law has effects in the world—and might be said to be constituted by those effects. A legal geographer named David Delaney has coined the term 'nomosphere' to describe this pervasive spatiality of law.[27]

To take one example of how this might work in legal-historical analysis: the enclosure movement of the sixteenth and seventeenth centuries was a major shift in English agrarian history, as common fields and wastes—heaths, copses, pastures—customarily used communally by tenants were claimed, closed off, and parcelled up into separate fields (often for pasture) by manorial landlords. As has long been recognized, this process was closely entwined with the law, as new legal interpretations of seigneurial property rights in these marginal lands undergirded and justified their seizure. But it was not neat interpretations which kept tenants out of their commons; as Nick Blomley has pointed out, this work was accomplished in practice by the construction of hedges. Understood by contemporaries as a symbol of enclosure, the hedge was what actually enabled pieces of private property to be carved out of land that was previously open and communal.[28] Hedges in early-modern rural England carried through the threat of law and made the lords' legal claims real. This kind of focus on law enables us to see how it has been entangled in the material environments and lived realities of past societies.

In some ways, this entanglement becomes clearer when it is challenged or undone; thus we speak of the law being 'broken' (a metaphor common to many European languages), an image of physical destruction. Indeed, it is precisely law's material presence that makes it vulnerable to challenge. The enclosure hedges of the seventeenth century were not erected unopposed: they were dug up, burned, and even buried by furious tenants. But without hedges to mark the newly-imposed

[27] David Delaney, *The Spatial, the Legal and the Pragmatics of World-Making: Nomospheric Investigations* (2010).

[28] Nicholas Blomley, 'Making Private Property: Enclosure, Common Right and the Work of Hedges' (2007) 18 *Rural History* 1, 5 ff.

boundaries, can the law be said to have been 'in force'? Some tenants went further still, and conducted 'mass ploughings', which aimed to restore the open fields to their original arable state.[29] These actions reveal an understanding of property rights that was deeply connected to the physical environment itself and, moreover, a willingness to challenge the law through material means. At this crucial juncture in the history of real property in England, we may thus understand the debates taking place 'on the ground' as *part of* legal discourse.

Another option within this 'nomospheric' approach to legal history is to place more emphasis on the experiential dimensions of a materialized law. A legal history of sound could tell us rather a lot about the development of the category of nuisance. The current municipal law codes for the city of New York operate on the general rule that it is illegal to make 'unreasonable noise'; this limit is more specifically defined in relation to nightclubs (amplified sound may not be more than 7dB at 15-ft distance from the property) and dogs, which may not bark for more than ten minutes in the daytime (or five minutes at night).[30] A sensory legal history could tell us about the conjunction of emotional, embodied responses to irritation or disgust with the legal categories and means of enforcement that developed alongside them. From the barbed wire laid around private property to the pepper spray and electric shocks administered by the police on disorderly or suspected offenders, the time is ripe for a proprioceptive history of the law, tracing its sanctioned violence through the bodies of those it touches.

We might also explore the ways law has been materialized through its absorption of particular objects. I have begun to explore this avenue in my own research into the medieval English law of shipwreck; dealing with the ownerless items that washed ashore, local courts in the fourteenth century used a series of procedures to establish them as 'property', a process which I argued was at once legal and ontological.[31] Indeed, classical, medieval, and pre-modern European law offer a number of legal objects that are good to think with, from the law of treasure trove to 'bane' and deodand, the objects which were held responsible for homicide. Before these are dismissed as medieval obscurities, it is worth noting that the deodand—the object whose movement 'caused' an individual's accidental death—was abolished by statute only in 1846 and was still regularly collected in the late eighteenth century; as Paul Schiff Berman has argued, this idea underlies

---

[29] Briony McDonaugh, 'Making and Breaking Property: Negotiating Enclosure and Common Rights in Sixteenth-Century England' (2013) 76 *History Workshop Journal* 48–9 ff.

[30] Mariana Valverde, 'Seeing Like a City: The Dialectic of Modern and Premodern Ways of Seeing in Urban Governance' (2011) 45 *Law & Society Review* 2, 305–6 ff.

[31] Tom Johnson, 'Medieval Law and Materiality: Shipwrecks, Finders, and Property on the Suffolk Coast, *c.* 1380–1410' (2015) 120 *American Historical Review* 2 407–32 ff.

the practice of civil forfeiture in modern common law jurisdictions.[32] Law can thus be materialized through strange legal objects of its own creation, which develop highly distinctive conceptual trajectories.

For all the possibilities offered by histories of a materialized law, however, there are two major problems with this kind of approach. The first is theoretical. As Tim Ingold has pointed out in a series of bracing articles, in naming 'materiality' or 'the material world' as a domain for analysis, we are performing precisely the kind of ontological partition—between an 'out-there' and an 'in-here' (that is, in our heads)—that we are purporting to refute.[33] To put this another way, it is possible to be sceptical about whether there is a material world independent of its conceptualization by humans; it does not, after all, explain itself. These concerns do not, at least in my view, necessarily abrogate the value of this 'materialist' approach, which lies, I think, in highlighting aspects of law—in particular the consequences of its universalizing claims—that otherwise tend to remain shadowy. But, these philosophical issues can act as useful brakes on tendentiousness: we must always ask whether declaring the law to be 'material' is expedient for the exploration of a particular legal history. What works for enclosure and deodands may not add much that is useful to the history of trusts.

The second problem with this kind of analysis is that its claims about the all-encompassing reach of law over the material world—or in Ingold's iteration, through its surfaces, mediums, and materials—may, contrariwise, make it more difficult to establish its power. If law is always-already-there, then how does it achieve its purchase? This question is not an objection, perhaps, so much as an invitation for further research. But it does signal that the general emphasis of the 'materializing' approach is on law as a means, on its effects in the world, and its debt to a longer tradition of 'law and society' histories; it thus suffers from the same problem that Chris Tomlins has identified in differentiating law from its context, 'too protean to be demarcated', an analysis of law that locates it everywhere begins to suffer from 'categorical collapse'.[34] This is a consequence of the focus here on effects: a 'materialized' law takes us closer to power, authority, and promulgation and thus away from rules, procedure, and administration. In the next section, we turn to see how these focal points can be brought closer together through a different approach to the materiality of law.

---

[32] Teresa Sutton, 'The Deodand and Responsibility for Death' (1997) 18 *The Journal of Legal History* 3, 44–55 ff; Paul Schiff Berman, 'An Anthropological Approach to Modern Forfeiture Law: The Symbolic Function of Legal Actions Against Objects' (1999) 11 *Yale Journal of Law & the Humanities* 1, 1–45 ff.

[33] Tim Ingold, 'Materials against Materiality' (2007) 14 *Archaeological Dialogues* 1, 1–16 ff; Tim Ingold, 'Toward an Ecology of Materials' (2012) 41 *Annual Review of Anthropology* 427–42 ff.

[34] Chris Tomlins, 'Historicism and Materiality in Legal Theory', in Maksymilian Del Mar, Michael Lobban (eds.), *Law in Theory and History: New Essays on a Neglected Dialogue* (2016) 67 ff. A similar point is made in Alain Pottage, 'The Materiality of What?' (2012) 39 *Journal of Law and Society* 1, 167–83 ff.

V.

The third avenue of inquiry explored here, 'filing', is also the most heterogeneous. It draws together, in a rather artificial manner, a disparate body of scholarship which focuses upon the 'paperwork'—quite literally, the work done by paper—in the making of law. These scholars come from diverse traditions and disciplines, and no attempt will be made here to draw out a conceptual genealogy for what is, even in a novel field, probably the newest approach to understanding the relationship between law and materiality. I will focus on the shared concerns that have emerged: an attention to the physical composition of physical texts, such as files, documents, and reports, their movements and actions within legal systems, and the way that these actions relate to forms of law and legal thought. In short, these approaches represent an attempt to understand how actors derive a phenomenon called 'law' from so much paperwork: how law is assembled from this mass of written material.

The strength of this 'filing' approach, as opposed to those surveyed just above, is that it offers what we could call an 'ethnographic' account of law's materiality, focusing on the role of physical things within domains that social actors understand as 'legal'. In the first place, then, it manages to overcome the problem with 'categorizing'. It does not accord legal discourse any prior ontological status; rather, in a mode that owes much to Latour's 'Actor-Network Theory', law is epiphenomenal, emerging from the mass of intricate human and documentary movements in and around the landscape of courts.[35] In the second place, precisely because it relies on the accounts of actors, it can also skirt from the bolder—and more complicated—claims about the physical presence of law in the world made in the 'materializing' approach, without suffering from 'categorical collapse': a legal document seems a much purer material fragment of the law, than, say, a piece of barbed wire, a hedge, or a piece of shipwreck. By looking at the way that law has been physically performed, it is thus possible to explore law's materiality from inside itself, on its own terms.

To begin with, such an approach can add a critical edge to more traditional descriptions of legal practice in past societies. The history of courtrooms, for example, is of more than antiquarian interest. The question, indeed, of when and why courts begin to take place in specially designated rooms is a good place to start here. Contrast the thirteenth-century English common law courts with their contemporary ecclesiastical relations: on the one hand, a small group of men sitting around a room in Westminster Hall, speaking to one another in specialized Anglo-Norman French; on the other hand, episcopal consistories held in porches or vestibules of cathedrals (among other places), often noisy, public spaces where

---

[35] Bruno Latour, *The Making of Law: An Ethnography of the Conseil d'État*, trans. Marina Brilman and Alain Pottage (2010).

brawls might break out during proceedings.[36] In the latter, indeed, the court space was understood to govern a particular set of postures: Bonaguida of Arezzo (fl. 1250) wrote that advocates to the court ought not to bob their heads, wave their hands, or shuffle their feet, in order to appear humble and agreeable. From their physical features to the affective regimes they have conditioned, there is much more to be written about the way that courts have produced law through this spatial performance of embodied expertise.

Yet there is more to this than just a theorization of formalist analysis. Cornelia Vismann's remarkable monograph on the media technology of law signals more ambitious paths forward. Among the first of its many insights is the point that files, in seeming to have condensed 'acts' into writing, have decisively shaped the positivist tendencies of the discipline of academic History (not to mention Legal History) throughout the nineteenth and twentieth centuries.[37] But beyond such historiographical refinement, Vismann traces in different historical contexts the ways that the cultural logic of files and filing has shaped the form of law; from the connections between copying and cancelling documents in the emergence of the Chancery (Latin: *cancellaria*) as an institution in late Antiquity, to the development of public archives in the early nineteenth century in the formation of the nation-state, we can begin to see the multiple ways in which law and legal systems are materialized through writing and shape the world they occupy. The medieval legal proverb, *Quod non est in actis non est in mundo* ('what is not in documents is not in the world'), could be rephrased without the double negative: 'the real world is found in files'.[38]

A more specific example that may help to illuminate the value of this approach is the development of 'copyhold', a form of property tenure in English common law. Most peasants in medieval England held their land by insecure tenure 'at the will of the lord', and according to local custom, as administered through the local manorial court. Copyhold emerged in the peculiar socio-economic conditions after the Black Death, when the scarcity of tenants meant that they were more easily able to negotiate the duration and condition of their tenure; many thus began to demand a copy of the court roll which recorded their entry into some land, as a record of their advantageous terms. As tenants took physical possession of their copies, so rolls that had remained hitherto closed off in seigneurial archives came to be widely dispersed. A practice that had begun as an attempt to fix the terms of tenure thus made written legal documents the foundation of customary tenure, and in the creation of written evidence, fundamentally changed the nature of that

---

[36] Paul Brand, 'Inside the Courtroom: Lawyers, Litigants and Justices in England in the Later Middle Ages', in Peter Coss (ed.), *The Moral World of the Law* (2000) 91–133 ff; James A. Brundage, *The Origins of the Legal Profession: Canonists, Civilians, and Courts* (2008) 421–30 ff.

[37] Cornelia Vismann, *Files: Law and Media Technology*, trans. G. Winthrop-Young (2008) 8–11 ff.

[38] Ibid., 56 ff.

tenure: copyhold was established as an estate in common law in the middle of the sixteenth century.[39] The materiality of a particular documentary form, then, generates its own legal historical trajectories.

This kind of approach does not just explain 'law and society', however, but can also be deployed to explain intellectual developments within law and jurisprudence, as Alain Pottage and Brad Sherman have shown in their vivid history of modern patent law. They start from the wider intellectual climate in the eighteenth century which fostered the possibility of ideas for machines possessing a reality independent of the material forms in which they were expressed. The proliferation of the 'model' as the form of claims of intellectual property, and the kinds of 'common sense' legal arguments that it encouraged, in turn, came to exert a crucial bearing on the development of patent law itself. As they put it: '. . . nineteenth century patent models were jurisprudential engines, or in which, figuratively, patent law itself was machine made'.[40] While patent law clearly has a distinct valence when it comes to the relationship between form and function (or matter and idea), their approach is suggestive of the ways that legal thought can become bound up in metaphors which assume a materiality of their own.

In sum, this group of related approaches to the relationship between law and materiality which I have called 'filing' offers perhaps the most promising avenue for further research. Even at its most straightforward level, it offers a way for legal historians to foreground the physical and performative aspects of law, the way in which it has been produced in highly particular places through the enlisting of certain kinds of behaviours, speech, and regimes of affect; in its more complex instantiations it can show how the interface between law and its substantiation can form a central dynamic in both is intellectual development and its role in society. Future histories of medical law, of crime and forensics, not to mention other areas mentioned above, such as property and environmental law, must consider this relationship closely. But as well as assisting in the understanding of these more technical (or technological) areas of legal history, an intense focus on the materiality of legal documentation would seem to contain the possibility of reconfiguring much wider areas of law, from contracts to testaments—both are popularly imagined as, above all, authoritative pieces of paper.

Nonetheless, it is also worth sounding a couple of notes of caution. In the first place, the line between critical analyses of the performance of law and merely descriptive accounts of past practice might prove too thin; histories of gavels, wigs, and robes would have to show how they were fragments of an apparatus of 'law' that exercised a bearing on legal proceedings or legal development. In the second

---

[39] On the common law of copyhold, see J. H. Baker, *An Introduction to English Legal History* (4th edn., 2002) 307–9 ff. A masterful analysis of the current state of research can be found in Mark Bailey, *The Decline of Serfdom in Late Medieval England: From Bondage to Freedom* (2014) 20–36 ff.

[40] Alain Pottage, Brad Sherman, *Figures of Invention: A History of Modern Patent Law* (2010) 106 ff.

place, the problem with straining to make law out of an assembly of material things is that it cannot help but prematurely reify 'law'—falling into the same trap as 'categorizing'—and thus, as a theory, does not explain anything 'extra'. As Pottage writes, the radical potential of this theory lies in 'its capacity to rediscover or reconstruct law in circumstances in which it might seem to have disappeared'; and both he and Chris Tomlins have seen in Foucault's *dispositifs*—enunciations that emerge in their composition from disparate elements—the possibility of an approach that postpones law in the analysis while working carefully towards it.[41] Here, perhaps, are the beginnings of a new avenue for legal historical research.

VI.

....

To recap: the material turn, at its core, has two main insights to offer legal historians. The first is that 'the material' is a construct, a realm of action that humans have invented; it is therefore possible to subject this construct—and for our purposes, the way it has been imagined by or interacted with law—to critique. The second insight is that the historical phenomenon of law itself has been constituted by material things. Depending on how far we cast our analytical net, these things may just include those that we consider to be 'legal', or they may stretch to include the whole of the physical world. The different kinds of tactics pursued here, in 'categorizing', 'materializing', and 'filing' represent the ways that legal scholars and theorists (and in a few cases, historians) have begun to address these insights, but there are undoubtedly other ways forward; at least one of these, hopefully, will emerge from the development of *dispositifs* as a practical tool, refiguring 'law' as a temporary condition created by certain assemblages, rather than an analytic object in historical analysis.

The 'material turn' as a theoretical apparatus is no longer in its infancy, but as is the way so often with scholarly trends, the initial shock of its dramatic assertions has receded to leave a productive space in which second-order studies—using the theory to arrive somewhere else, analytically—can flourish. For my part, I see in the critical study of materiality an opportunity to 'stress test' some of our operating assumptions about what law is and what it has been in past societies. It may be that asking radically naïve questions about the nature of the physical world and the composition of law does not yield new answers, but I would be surprised if it does not at least lead us to ask new questions. Ultimately, the material turn will be judged on whether it creates something beyond itself. I think it has the potential to do this,

[41] Pottage, (n. 34) 1, 180 ff.

and in bending so fissile an object as law, we will soon find cracks and fractures that open up new materials for research.

Bibliography

Nicholas K. Blomley, *Law, Space, and the Geographies of Power* (The Guilford Press, 1994)

Irus Braverman, 'Hidden in Plain View: Legal Geography from a Visual Perspective' (2010) 7 *Law, Culture and the Humanities* 2 173–86

Colin Dayan, *The Law Is a White Dog: How Legal Rituals Make and Unmake Persons* (Princeton University Press, 2011)

David Delaney, *Law and Nature* (Cambridge University Press, 2003)

Richard Ford, 'Law's Territory (A History of Jurisdiction)' (1999) 97 *Michigan L.R.* 4, 843–930

Kevin Gray, 'Property in Thin Air' (1991) *Cambridge L.J.* 50, 252–307

Jane Holder, Carolyn Harrison (eds.), *Law and Geography* (Oxford University Press, 2002)

Tom Johnson, 'Medieval Law and Materiality: Shipwrecks, Finders, and Property on the Suffolk Coast, c. 1380–1410' (2015) 120:2 *American Historical Review* 407–32

Bruno Latour, *The Making of Law: An Ethnography of the Conseil d'État*, trans. Marina Brilman and Alain Pottage (Polity, 2010)

Javier Lezaun, 'The Pragmatic Sanction of Materials: Notes for an Ethnography of Legal Substances' (2012) 39:1 *Journal of Law and Society* 20–38

Alain Pottage, Brad Sherman, *Figures of Invention: A History of Modern Patent Law* (Oxford University Press, 2010)

Christopher Tomlins, 'Historicism and Materiality in Legal Theory', in Maksymilian Del Mar, Michael Lobban (eds.), *Law in Theory and History: New Essays on a Neglected Dialogue* (Hart, 2016)

Cornelia Vismann, *Files: Law and Media Technology*, trans. G. Winthrop-Young (Stanford University Press, 2008)

CHAPTER 28

MARXIST LEGAL HISTORY

CHRISTOPHER TOMLINS

'MARXISM', wrote the American legal historian William E. Nelson in 1985, 'is not about to disappear as an attractive ideology or as a powerful political force in the world.'[1] Even on its face, Nelson's prediction was rash: the Marxism dutifully regurgitated as political orthodoxy by the communist parties of the socialist bloc was anything but an attractive ideology or a powerful force (in any intellectually defensible sense) in the world of the mid-1980s. Quite apart from its own internal ideological scleroses, by the time Nelson wrote, the bloc's inability to recover from the early 1980s world recession—combined with Soviet entrapment in war in Afghanistan—had already turned the historical conjuncture decisively against Soviet and Eastern European socialism.

But perhaps Nelson meant the academic world. There, Susan Easton argues, Marxism in its new 'Western' garb had indeed reached something of a high point 'in the 1970s and early 1980s'. Still, as the centre of orientation had 'shifted from radical movements . . . to the academy' Western Marxism had become ever more 'rigid and scholastic'—less and less attractive, less and less powerful, enmeshed in its own deepening theoretical crisis.[2] In the United Kingdom, the Althusserian fault-line established by the mid-1970s created more than a decade of savage division. Barry

---

[1] William E. Nelson, 'Standards of Criticism', in William E. Nelson, John Phillip Reid, *The Literature of American Legal History* (1985) 309 ff.
[2] Susan Easton, *Marx and Law* (2008) xi ff.

Hindess and Paul Hirst's assault on the 'sterility of modern Marxist economic theory', which they blamed on uncritical loyalty to *Capital*, was but one more deep fracture in a community they had already roiled with their highly theoreticist *Pre-Capitalist Modes of Production* (1975). But English Marxism had in any case long since been soured by the bitter *New Left Review*-centred cleavage between the prominent Marxist historians E. P. Thompson and Perry Anderson. Each would pause in their own dispute during the 1970s only (separately) to disparage Hindess and Hirst. In the United States, meanwhile, the spectacular collapse in 1980 of Eugene Genovese's professedly pluralist and well-heeled *Marxist Perspectives* after only ten issues offered clear warning of deep fissures in the North American academic Marxist community.[3]

So all was not well in the world of mid-1980s Anglophone Marxism. By then, in both the United States and the United Kingdom, the Western Marxism that had seemed so full of promise in the early 1970s was fully embarked on 'its passage to post-Marxism and beyond'.[4]

Unaware of any of this, Nelson added an even stranger coda to his strange prediction. 'I expect neo-Marxist legal history to continue to flourish.'[5] The coda was puzzling because there was no *in situ* flourishing 'neo-Marxist' school of legal history. There were occasional, isolated, histories that might wear the label: Mark Tushnet described his *American Law of Slavery* (1981) as explicitly reliant on 'Marxist theoretical constructs', but Tushnet had abandoned Marxism and its intractable crisis by the time Nelson wrote. My own *The State and the Unions* (1985) would gesture in the direction of relative autonomy theory, but it had not been published in time for Nelson's assessment. Inspired by Antonio Gramsci, Genovese had devoted all of 24 pages (of 800) in *Roll, Jordan, Roll* (1974) to 'The Hegemonic Function of the Law'. Thompson's *Whigs and Hunters* (and the Thompson-inspired *Albion's Fatal Tree*) might also be thought of as neo-Marxist legal history. Were these what Nelson meant? They were both published in 1975, shortly after Anderson's *Passages from Antiquity to Feudalism* and his *Lineages of the Absolutist State* (both 1974). Nelson's coda was a decade out of date.

An extended exchange between Nelson and Robert W. Gordon proved enlightening. It established that by 'neo-Marxist legal history' Nelson actually meant the genus of legal-historical scholarship that he associated with the U.S. Critical Legal Studies (CLS) movement. Nelson was not enamoured of the work of critical

---

[3] Eugene D. Genovese, Warren I. Susman, 'A Note to Our Readers' (1978) 1 *Marxist Perspectives* 3 ff.; 'Marxist Journal Ceases after 10 Issues', *New York Times* (1 February 1981).

[4] Ellen Meiksins Wood, *Democracy Against Capitalism: Renewing Historical Materialism* (2016) 8 ff. One obstinate North American bright spot was Catherine McKinnon's determined development during the 1980s of a sophisticated feminist theory of law and the state in dialog with Marx. See Catherine McKinnon, 'Femininsm, Marxism, Method and the State: An Agenda for Theory' (1982) 7 *Signs* 515 ff.; 'Feminism, Marxism, Method and the state: Toward Feminist Jurisprudence' (1983) 8 *Signs* 635 ff.; and *Towards a Feminist Theory of the State* (1989).

[5] Nelson (n. 1) 309 ff.

legal studies historians. He thought its value as historical scholarship trivial—mere dreary repetition of a well-trodden 'realist/instrumentalist' contention 'that power, not law, determines the outcomes that legal institutions will produce', that 'legal institutions adopt rules which serve the dominant interest groups in society'. That, apparently, was what made it neo-Marxist. That, and 'its challenge to law', which he thought 'potentially subversive'.[6]

Gordon's response dissociated CLS history both from Nelson's 'realist/instrumentalist' canard and from Marxism. 'What is fascinating to me about this basic misapprehension of yours with respect to CLS work is that you are hardly alone in it, but share it with many other critics of CLS. The reasoning process seems to be something like this: CLS people identify themselves as on the Left; Left means Marxism; Marxism means a vulgar-instrumentalist view of law.' Gordon noted in passing that few Marxists were any longer vulgar instrumentalists, but defending Marxism (or neo-Marxism) was not his purpose. CLS had little or nothing to do with Marxism. Most CLS historians were 'extremely critical of orthodox Marxist historiography'. The one CLS historian whom Nelson had actually named as a Marxist (Tushnet) had actually drawn 'more on structuralist' than Marxist 'traditions of explanation'. CLS historians wrote 'careful, thorough, almost lovingly detailed, histories of the development of legal ideas and practices'. They did so in an attempt 'to discover the sunken codes of shared inarticulate assumptions that underlie apparently neutral decision systems'. They claimed no particular genius; they were producing no more than 'a tiny fraction of the good history that's coming out'. Nevertheless, to contend that nothing worthwhile could be learned from CLS history seemed 'ungenerous in the extreme'.[7]

The exchange between Nelson and Gordon reprised a contest that had occurred ten years before to define Morton Horwitz's *Transformation of American Law* (1977). That contest was triangular rather than bilateral, in that it actually included a Marxist corner as well as anti- and post-Marxist views. The Marxist corner, though not uncritical of the book, was overall celebratory. Without agreeing that *Transformation* was itself Marxist scholarship, Marxist historians took its main arguments to indicate that a sophisticated Marxist legal historiography was approaching its moment of realization. The anti-Marxist corner was, of course, condemnatory. It denounced *Transformation*'s 'conspiratorial materialism'. The post-Marxist corner, favourably disposed to the book, found claims that *Transformation* embodied or foreshadowed a Marxist legal historiography equally nonsensical. Post-Marxists believed the Marxist moment had passed, its analytic possibilities overwhelmed by unresolvable conceptual contradictions. Of the two corners in the contest competing *for* the book—and for its author—the post-Marxist corner won. Certainly *Transformation*'s

---

[6] 'An Exchange on Critical Legal Studies between Robert W. Gordon and William Nelson' (1988) 6 *Law and History Review* 162 ff.

[7] Ibid.

author was convinced. It is unclear whether Horwitz considered *Transformation* a Marxist work at the time he wrote it (judging the question on the basis of the book itself it seems to me very unlikely). But by the early 1980s he had clearly repudiated 'covering law' theorizations of social change of any stripe.[8]

Then in the 'take-off' stage of what would prove to be thirty years of extraordinary growth, in which critical legal historians would play an essential, sustained, and constantly stimulating role, Anglophone legal history as practiced in the United States lacked any clear Marxist component. Nor, in the wake of the 1970s, was there any obvious U.K.-based or continental European school.[9] Critical legal history pointed instead in the direction of 'the intellectual history of the rise and fall of paradigm structures of legal thought'. Or it advocated 'field-level' research into vernacular legal consciousness. Considerable latent tension existed between these two possibilities. The former's structuralist quest for order underlying variation in accounts of legal thought was not compatible with historicist descriptions of law as immanently 'plural, contested, constructed'. The tension would eventuate in declarations of victory for the latter variant. Critical doctrinal history was assimilated to post-structural multiplicity in the huge wave of historicist inquiry into 'the study of law at the vernacular level' that marked the apogee of legal history's growth curve.[10] But neither in conception nor execution could either alternative be described as Marxist. In the era of rapid expansion in legal-historical study, no Marxist legal history was forthcoming.

This brief history of the maturation of legal history in the Anglophone academy, then, is in part the history of an absence. To a degree the absence is attributable to the intellectual ambitions of CLS as a movement—its desire to underscore its own radical difference, its superior criticality. As Akbar Rasulov writes, 'In the broader symbolic economy of the CLS project, the part that was most commonly allocated to Marxism was that of an essentially talentless but unfailingly big-headed distant relative in a second-rate Victorian novel, a supporting character whose sole reason

---

[8] Robert W. Gordon, 'Critical Legal Histories' (1984) 36 *Stanford L.R.* 57 ff.; Wythe Holt, 'Morton Horwitz and the Transformation of American Legal History' (1982) 23 *William & Mary L.R.* 663 ff.; John Phillip Reid, 'A Plot Too Doctrinaire' (1977) 55 *Texas L.R.* 1307 ff.; Morton J. Horwitz, 'Mark Tushnet, Legal Historian' (2001) 90 *Georgetown L.J.* 134 ff. (noting that between 1977 and 1983, CLS came to the position that there was nothing 'left to save in Marxism as methodology').

[9] On the U.K., see Costas Douzinas, 'A Short History of the British Critical Legal Conference or, the Responsibility of the Critic' (2014) 25 *Law and Critique* 187 ff.; Tim Murphy, 'BritCrits: Subversion and Submission, Past, Present and Future' (1999) 10 *Law and Critique* 237 ff. On continental Europe, see Emilios Christodoulidis and Johan van der Walt, 'Critical Legal Studies: Europe', (this volume). On the absence of any 'attempt to develop a specifically Marxist form of historical reflection' in France, Germany, and Scandinavia, see William H. Sewell, Jr., *Logics of History: Social Theory and Social Transformation* (2005) 37–8 ff.

[10] Gordon (n. 8) 57 ff.; Robert W. Gordon, 'The Past as Authority and as Social Critic: Stabilizing and Destabilizing Functions of History in Legal Argument', in Terrence J. McDonald, ed., *The Historic Turn in the Human Sciences* (1996); Robert W. Gordon, ' "Critical Legal Histories Revisited": A Response' (2012) 37 *Law & Social Inquiry* 200 ff.

for being introduced into the story was to help the reader perceive more efficiently the inherent moral superiority of the main protagonist.'[11] In part, however, the absence was Marxism's own doing. The possibility for a Marxist historiography of law alongside the critical project disintegrated in the early 1980s for the same reasons that academic Marxism disintegrated: an inability to fashion a satisfactory resolution to the base/superstructure problem, hence an inability to locate law vis-à-vis the essential components of a Marxist theory of history.

Forty years after the 1975–1985 decade of socialism's macro-political crisis, and of Western Marxism's metastasizing theoretical crisis and eventual dispersal, we are in the grip of a new fast-forming historical conjuncture. Both globally and within its historic Anglophone heartlands, capital is at war with itself. It is liberalism's turn (in both traditional and neo embodiments) to feel the cold pinch of disintegration. In such times, comparatively sheltered in our own neck of the woods, yet recognizing the presence of the present in every historical investigation, recognizing (more acutely) that the lines of perspective that construct an object of historical investigation create it contemporaneous with ourselves because they 'converge in our own historical experience',[12] *at this moment* what opportunities exist for renewing the attempt to create a Marxist legal historiography? What responsibilities attend that effort?

1. The Requisite Prolegomenon:
Marx and Engels on Law

Without exception, every account of the place of law in the work of Marx and Engels affirms that nowhere in their work was law made a direct object of study. Precisely because no guiding determinative text exists, developing a Marxist 'theory' of law is necessarily a work of extrapolation and interpretation undertaken post hoc using fragmentary sources within an extensive corpus of writings that are not consistent with one another.

This notwithstanding, certain texts loom larger than others in the process of construction. In the spirit of a conjunctural *ridurre ai principia* let us visit just two of them—one extremely prominent, and one relatively obscure.

---

[11] Akbar Rasulov, 'CLS and Marxism: The History of an Affair' (2014) 5 *Transnational Legal Theory* 622 ff.

[12] Walter Benjamin to Theodor Adorno (9 December 1938) in Howard Eiland, Michael W. Jennings (eds.), *Walter Benjamin: Selected Writings, Volume 4, 1938–1940* (2006) 108 ff.

A.   Preface to *A Contribution to the Critique of Political Economy* (1859)

First comes the best known,[13] the perennially analysed, the most 'austerely structural',[14] the text that G. A. Cohen identifies as Marxism's ur-text,[15] in which Marx summarizes the essential conclusions he has reached in 'the course of my study of political economy' in the matter of social determination of human existence and consciousness.

In the social production of their existence, men inevitably enter into definite relations, which are independent of their will, namely relations of production appropriate to a given stage in the development of their material forces of production. The totality of these relations of production constitutes the economic structure of society, the real foundation, on which arises a legal and political superstructure and to which correspond definite forms of social consciousness. The mode of production of material life conditions the general process of social, political and intellectual life. It is not the consciousness of men that determines their existence, but their social existence that determines their consciousness. At a certain stage of development, the material productive forces of society come into conflict with the existing relations of production or—this merely expresses the same thing in legal terms—with the property relations within the framework of which they have operated hitherto. From forms of development of the productive forces these relations turn into their fetters. Then begins an era of social revolution. The changes in the economic foundation lead sooner or later to the transformation of the whole immense superstructure.
   In studying such transformations it is always necessary to distinguish between the material transformation of the economic conditions of production, which can be determined with the precision of natural science, and the legal, political, religious, artistic or philosophic—in short, ideological forms in which men become conscious of this conflict and fight it out. Just as one does not judge an individual by what he thinks about himself, so one cannot judge such a period of transformation by its consciousness, but, on the contrary, this consciousness must be explained from the contradictions of material life, from the conflict existing between the social forces of production and the relations of production. No social order is ever destroyed before all the productive forces for which it is sufficient have been developed, and new superior relations of production never replace older ones before the material conditions for their existence have matured within the framework of the old society.

'The tenor of the passage is unmistakeable' writes Paul Phillips. 'The material forces of production are primary and any change in the superstructure merely reflects a previous change in the base.'[16] Is this indeed so?

---

[13] Karl Marx, *A Contribution to the Critique of Political Economy* (1977), available at <https://www.marxists.org/archive/marx/works/1859/critique-pol-economy/preface.htm>. For a slightly different translation, see Karl Marx, 'Preface to *A Contribution to the Critique of Political Economy*,' in *Karl Marx and Friedrich Engels: Selected Works* (1970) 180 ff.

[14] Alex Callinicos, *Making History: Agency, Structure, and Change in Social Theory* (2nd edn., 2006) ix ff.

[15] G. A. Cohen, *Karl Marx's Theory of History: A Defence* (2000) vii ff.

[16] Paul Phillips, *Marx and Engels on Law and Laws* (1980) 197 ff.

Let us elaborate. At any 'given stage in the development of the material forces of production', the 'economic structure of society' is constituted by the totality of relations of production. In turn, relations of production operate within a definite legal framework, which is determinative of those relations of production to such an extent that conflict (or harmony) between material productive forces and relations of production is 'the same thing' as conflict (or harmony) between material productive forces and legal (property) relations. The one is the other. Thus we may conclude that Marx would not disagree with the proposition that legal (property) relations constitute 'the economic structure of society, the real foundation'. Entry into these relations is involuntary, which is to say they are not subject to individual determination. Rather they are socially determined. Social consciousness, hence social determination, ordinarily corresponds to prevailing production relations because 'the mode of production of material life'—that is, of human existence as such—'conditions' (it does not *determine*) 'the general process of social, political and intellectual life'. Marx has described an equilibrium built on a foundation of prevailing property relations.

But the equilibrium is not static. Material productive forces (tools, raw materials, population characteristics) *develop*. 'At a certain stage of development, the material productive forces of society come into conflict with the existing relations of production'—that is ('the same thing') they come into conflict with the prevailing framework of property relations. The disequilibrium between material productive forces and prevailing property relations registers—as one would expect—in the 'legal and political superstructure' erected on the real foundation of society's economic structure in the form of a disturbance in prevailing property relations. 'Then begins an era of social revolution' that is 'fought out' in the superstructure, where it gains idiosyncratic[17] expression in all of the various 'ideological forms' ('legal, political, religious, artistic or philosophic') 'in which men become conscious of th[e] conflict' between material productive forces and prevailing property relations.

Marx carefully distinguishes 'the material transformation of the *economic conditions* of production', which we can assume is a constant (i.e., dynamic) from the actual conflict which that transformation engenders between the social forces of production and the relations of production at the point where the latter cease to facilitate the further development of the former and instead constrict ('fetter') that development. It is that conflict, fought out in the superstructure, that will work the transformation of the economic structure by generating 'new superior relations of production' i.e., a new framework of property relations. The 'economic conditions of production' are simply a material substrate whose continuing transformation

---

[17] Men's consciousness of the conflict arises 'from the contradictions of material life'. But consciousness per se is not a good guide to the true nature of the transformation that gives rise to the conflict.

(autonomous development) *below* the economic foundation—'which can be determined with the precision of natural science' (e.g., plate tectonics)—is the clock that ticks towards the moment when the relations of production cease to accommodate the social forces of production and disequilibrium begins.[18] This moment is protracted: 'No social order is ever destroyed before all the productive forces for which it is sufficient have been developed, and never replace older ones before the material conditions for their existence have matured within the framework of the old society.'

Marx explains that in formulating the position embraced in the preface he had been led *from* jurisprudence *to* the study of political economy by the incapacity of his jurisprudential training alone to explain the course of legal and political debates that his position as editor of the *Rheinische Zeitung* (1842–1843) had required he address. 'I . . . found myself in the embarrassing position of having to discuss what is known as material interests'.

My inquiry led me to the conclusion that neither legal relations nor political forms could be comprehended whether by themselves or on the basis of a so-called general development of the human mind, but that on the contrary they originate in the material conditions of life, the totality of which Hegel, following the example of English and French thinkers of the eighteenth century, embraces within the term 'civil society'; that the anatomy of this civil society, however, has to be sought in political economy.[19]

By 'material conditions of life' we might understand Marx to be referring to 'the economic conditions of production'—the autonomous material substrate of geography, demography, and technology below the economic structure susceptible to precise scientific investigation. But Marx identifies the totality of the material conditions of life with civil society, the anatomy of which is to be sought in political economy. Here is the material life whose mode of production conditions the general process of social, political, and intellectual life—the legal relations and political forms that constitute the relations of production. And the operative term here is 'conditions.' *Origination in* is not the same thing as *determination by*.

The effect of this reading is a radical attenuation of the distance and causal directionality that orthodox Marxism posited between economic structure and legal and political superstructure. Marx's materialist conception of history remains

---

[18] Cohen (n. 15) 30 ff. argues 'the productive forces occur *below* the economic foundation' where they 'strongly determine the character of the economic structure, while forming no part of it.' My terminology is somewhat different, because 'productive forces' can be ambiguous. In addition, my reading of the 'Preface' differs from Cohen's. I agree that the material conditions of production are the basis of all social organization, including the economic structure. In other words 'all social organization' means *one* interactive structure, outside of which 'economic conditions' are situated. I *disagree* that those material conditions are strongly determinative. I argue rather that they are a limit condition on human existence.

[19] Marx (n. 13).

very much in evidence, in the form of the economic conditions of production—the autonomous substrate—that furnish the ineluctable limit-conditions of human existence. Rather than a determining base and a determined superstructure, however, we encounter dynamic interaction between distinct components (the economic, the legal, and political) of the same structure.[20]

B. Friedrich Engels to Walther Borgius (25 January 1894)

In this letter,[21] written near the end of his life, Engels responds to a request from the German economist (and individualist anarchist) Walther Borgius for an explanation of what Marx and he meant in using the term 'economic conditions'. Engels' response is broad, and basic, and also discriminating, in the fashion suggested by my reading of the 1859 Preface.

What we understand by the economic conditions, which we regard as the determining basis of the history of society, are the methods by which human beings in a given society produce their means of subsistence and exchange the products among themselves (in so far as division of labour exists). Thus the *entire technique* of production and transport is here included. According to our conception this technique also determines the method of exchange and, further, the division of products, and with it, after the dissolution of tribal society, the division into classes also and hence the relations of lordship and servitude and with them the state, politics, law, etc. Under economic conditions are further included the geographical basis on which they operate and those remnants of earlier stages of economic development which have actually been transmitted and have survived—often only through tradition or the force of inertia; also of course the external milieu which surrounds this form of society.

We can pause to note that 'the economic conditions' as described here are the determining basis of 'the history of society' at large, not of the actuality of a given society. They encompass 'the production and reproduction of real life'[22] (i.e., demography), the 'entire technique of production and transport' (technology), and 'the geographical basis' (physical factor endowments) characterizing, from the range of historical examples cited (tribal, feudal, bourgeois, inertial remnants of earlier stages), *any* given society at *any* stage of development. The economic conditions are descriptive, not determinative. Indeed, for good measure Engels adds in 'the external milieu'—a word with no determinative capacity at all. Here once again, in

---

[20] Christopher Tomlins, 'Organic Poise? Capitalism as Law' (2016) 64 *Buffalo L.R.* 61 ff.

[21] Friedrich Engels to Walther Borgius (25 January 1894), available at <https://www.marxists.org/archive/marx/works/1894/letters/94_01_25.htm>. For a slightly different translation, see *Selected Works* (n. 13), 693–6 ff.

[22] See Friedrich Engels to letter to Joseph Bloch (21 September 1890), available at <https://www.marxists.org/archive/marx/works/1890/letters/90_09_21.htm>. See also *Selected Works* (n. 13) 682–3 ff.

other words, is the autonomous material substrate that exists *beneath* (and above, and all around) everything that is 'structural.'

Engels continues.

Political, juridical, philosophical, religious, literary, artistic, etc., development is based on economic development. But all these react upon one another and also upon the economic base. It is not that the economic position is the cause and alone active, while everything else only has a passive effect. There is, rather, interaction.

While emphasizing interaction Engels also engages in 'last instance' reasoning, asserting that 'the economic relations, however much they may be influenced by the other political and ideological ones, are still ultimately the decisive ones.' But this is a comment on how to understand 'historical development' as such. Again, therefore, rather than a determining base and a determined superstructure, we encounter dynamic interaction between distinct components of the same structure.[23]

II. ON THE SINGULARITIES OF THE ENGLISH

The most famous legal-historical statement about law written by any purported Anglophone Marxist belongs to the late Edward Palmer Thompson, to wit:

the notion of the regulation and reconciliation of conflicts through the rule of law—and the elaboration of rules and procedures which, on occasion, made some approximate approach towards the ideal—seems to me a cultural achievement of universal significance . . . We ought to expose the shams and inequities which may be concealed beneath this law. But the rule of law itself, the imposing of effective inhibitions upon power and the defence of the citizen from power's all-intrusive claims, seems to me to be an unqualified human good.[24]

Thompson's pronouncement has had a long shelf life, the subject of considerable debate in the late 1970s and early 1980s, revived for re-inspection periodically by critics and defenders ever since. For my purposes here the question is whether the claim itself, offered as the conclusion to one of the few Anglophone legal histories written by a self-identifying Marxist, offers a point of purchase for Marxist legal history.

Judged by what he wrote in 1980, Perry Anderson seems to think it does, calling Thompson's conclusion to *Whigs and Hunters*, rather extravagantly, 'the most remarkable exploration of the multiple meanings and functions of law ever written

---

[23] Ibid.
[24] E. P. Thompson, *Whigs and Hunters: The Origin of the Black Act* (1977) 265–6 ff.

by a Marxist or any other historian', an account 'of exemplary subtlety and insight' that 'should be accepted by every Marxist'.[25] Amongst Thompson's liberal defenders, on the other hand, the answer has been that it does not. For Martin Krygier, for example, who fervently desires and welcomes the diminution of Marxist historical exploration of law (or for that matter of anything) 'A liberal's only complaint might be that it took Thompson so long to get there'.[26] Once Thompson did get there he became useful primarily as a club with which to belabour other Marxists less willing than he to climb aboard the rule of law bandwagon.

For Marxist critics of Thompson, the answer has also been, by and large, that it does not.[27] For my purposes here that criticism is much more important than liberal rapture because it exposes aspects of Thompson's position to which liberals are insensitive, or indifferent.[28]

What was at issue? In its empirical detail, Thompson's book, *Whigs and Hunters*, quite unambiguously cohered with the general contention that law was anything but autonomous relative to economy and society—'It is astonishing the wealth that can be extracted from territories of the poor, during the phase of capital accumulation, provided that the predatory élite are limited in number, and provided that the state and the law smooth the way of exploitation', for example; and 'The greatest of all legal fictions is that the law evolves, from case to case, by its own impartial logic, true only to its own integrity, unswayed by expedient considerations.'[29] Having written the book, Thompson became disturbed by what he had written and added a supplementary conclusion so violently orthogonal to his book's substance as virtually to disown it.[30] The change of tack arose not from a last-minute anxiety that his own 'sour' account of the eighteenth-century's legal system was wrong (Thompson did not repudiate one word of the book's substance) but from fear his book might be read to lend support to those within the broad range of Western Marxist thought against whom he aligned himself, specifically adherents of 'a sophisticated, but

---

[25] Perry Anderson, *Arguments within English Marxism* (1980) 70, 198 ff. But see *infra*, text at n. 46.

[26] Martin Krygier, 'Marxism and the Rule of Law: Reflections after the Collapse of Communism' (1990) 15 *Law & Social Inquiry* 646 n. 36 ff.

[27] See, e.g., Adrian Merritt, 'The Nature and Function of Law: A Criticism of E. P. Thompson's "Whigs and Hunters"' (1980) 7 *British Journal of Law and Society* 194 ff.

[28] My account here relies on Christopher Tomlins, 'How Autonomous is Law?' (2007) 3 *Annual Review of Law and Social Science* 45 ff. Thompson himself professed to see no contradiction between his embrace of 'the rule of law' and his idea of Marxism, a feat he managed by qualifying the unqualified. 'If I have argued elsewhere that the rule of law is an "unqualified human good" I have done so as a historian and a materialist. The rule of law, in this sense, must always be historically, culturally, and, in general, nationally specific. It concerns the conduct of social life, and the regulation of conflicts, according to rules of law which are exactly defined and have palpable and material evidences—which rules attain towards consensual assent and are subject to interrogation and reform.' E. P. Thompson, *Writing by Candlelight* (1980) 230–1 ff.

[29] Thompson (n. 24) 245, 250 ff.

[30] Daniel Cole calls it 'an epiphanic conversion'. See Daniel H. Cole, '"An Unqualified Human Good": E. P. Thompson and the Rue of Law' (2001) 28 *Journal of Law and Society* 183 ff.

(ultimately) highly schematic Marxism'—Althusserian structuralism—that, as he (mistakenly) understood it, treated law as no more than an expression of infrastructural productive forces and relations, 'an instrument of the de facto ruling class' that defined and defended 'rulers' claims upon resources and labor-power' and mediated class relations in such a way as to 'confirm and consolidate existing class power'. In the body of the book Thompson had described in considerable detail the rise of an oligarchy—'Hanoverian Whigs of the 1720s and 1730s . . . a hard lot of men [who] remind us that stability, no less than revolution, may have its own kind of Terror'—that had indeed 'employed the law, both instrumentally and ideologically, very much as a modern structural Marxist should expect it to'. But, Thompson's conclusion insisted, the law as such transcended its uses. Certainly, courts, judges, and lawyers might fight to assimilate law to particular class interests; certainly, in the form of 'particular rules and sanctions' (ideology), law stood 'in a definite and active relationship' to the social. But in a distinct instantiation that Thompson denoted 'simply . . . law', which he expounded definitionally as 'its own logic, rules and procedures', the law could not be assimilated to particular interests, nor did it appear to stand in any detectable relation to the social. In this instantiation 'simply . . . law' was possessed of 'its own characteristics, its own independent history and logic of evolution'. It stood on its own as the rule of law—'a genuine forum' within which social and class conflicts might be fought. 'Simply . . . law', then, was law's essence, transcendently autonomous. And as such, it was also, transcendently, 'an unqualified human good'.[31]

Such was Thompson's desire to refute structural Marxism that he ended up caricaturing the target the better to deride it. The European Marxists whose structuralism Thompson disparaged—Louis Althusser, Nicos Poulantzas— were hardly the reductionists Thompson made them out to be. Althusser's account of law stressed its 'relative autonomy'—relative, that is, to demands emanating from the social. In a series of crucial texts first published between 1965 and 1975, Althusser fundamentally revised orthodox (Third International) Marxist conceptions of base and superstructure in a fashion that conclusively destroyed orthodoxy's economic determinism.[32] As Bob Jessop has summarized it, Althusserian structuralism held that a mode of production (a society) was 'a complex structured whole' comprising 'several relatively autonomous regions' (the economic, the juridico-political, the ideological) that conditioned each other. Relations of production must be reproduced if the structured whole is to continue overall, but how those relations are actually reproduced at any given moment in any actually existing social formation—any actually existing capitalism—depends

[31] Thompson (n. 24) 16, 258–67 ff.

[32] Louis Althusser, *For Marx* (1969); *Essays in Self-Criticism* (1976). Louis Althusser et al., *Reading Capital: The Complete Edition* (2015).

upon practices within the several relatively autonomous regions, none of them per se dominant, and on the relationships persisting among them. Thus, 'the Althusserian approach tends to be perfunctory in its treatment of economic determination . . . and to focus on the specific properties of the several regions as if they were autonomous'.[33] Althusser theorized non-economic components of the structured whole as a diverse assemblage of state apparatuses, some repressive (police, prisons, army), others persuasive (schools, churches, media, law). Althusser's ideological state apparatuses were dispersed and differentiated; they did not secure particular class interests but rather were sites of struggle between classes for control.

The implications of the Althusserian approach for law were clarified in the work of Nicos Poulantzas, whose focus was 'the autonomization and effectivity of law and the dominance of juridical ideology in bourgeois societies'.[34] It was Poulantzas more than any other Althusserian theorist who developed most fully the relative autonomy critique of reductionist Marxist theories of the state. These were the theorists that Thompson baldly represented as incapable of distinguishing between 'arbitrary power and the rule of law'. In fact, Thompson's polemic obscured how closely, on certain points, his own formulations reproduced Althusserian formulations. Thompson claimed as his own the insight that 'the rules and categories of law penetrate every level of society', that law contributes to self-definition and identity. 'Productive relations themselves' he observed 'are, in part, only meaningful in terms of their definitions at law'.[35] But this departs in no real particular from Poulantzas's insistence upon understanding the specific place and function of law in the reproduction of specific modes of production, or from his Althusserian identification of ideology as an autonomous region in which relations of production were reproduced and in which law interpellated agents of production in isolation, on its own terms, forming their social relations.[36] Thompson rejected structuralist theory as 'a desperate error of intellectual abstraction', but his own words in defense of empirical historical description were themselves at least as desperately imprecise (in the sentence quoted above, for example, what exactly is the measure of 'in part'?) and contradictory. For although Thompson posed as impassioned defender of empirical history, when his own history showed ('again and again', as he noted) that 'the actuality of the law's operation in class-divided

---

[33] Bob Jessop, 'On Recent Marxist Theories of Law, the State, and Juridico-Political Ideology' (1980) 8 *International Journal of the Sociology of Law* 339 ff.

[34] Ibid. 342 ff. See Nicos Poulantzas, *Political Power and Social Classes* (1973); *State, Power, Socialism* (1978).

[35] Thompson (n. 24) 266, 267 ff.

[36] Jessop (n. 33) 352 ff. That is, law addresses itself, peremptorily, to a subject to whom, in the act of interpellation, it ascribes certain powers and capacities, thus producing and reproducing the subject as an effect of itself.

societies' belied its rhetoric, he rejected that too. Having lambasted relative autonomy as reductionism in disguise, the only place he had left to himself was the normative romance of good and evil. The Black Act was 'a bad law, drawn by bad legislators, and enlarged by the interpretations of bad judges'. The rule of law was 'an unqualified good'.[37]

Ostensibly Thompson's polemical ire was directed outward, and as his sense of grievance festered he indulged his latent xenophobia—'A cloud no bigger than a man's hand crosses the English Channel from Paris, and then, in an instant, the trees, the orchard, the hedgerows, the field of wheat, are black with locusts.'[38] But the debate over the rule of law, and over Thompson's rubbishing of Althusserian Marxism, was as much an incident in a larger 'argument within English Marxism' that had begun ten years before. The argument was at first generational, conducted between Marxist historians (history was the only site of any sustained and original Marxist intellectual work in the English Marxist tradition), principally Thompson and Perry Anderson. Its primary frame of reference was provided by developments in Western Marxism since the 1920s, notably the 'novel and labile Marxism' of Antonio Gramsci (1891–1937) whose 'theory of the superstructures' gave rise to the concept of class hegemony, over which Anderson and Thompson warred.[39] The argument widened in the 1970s when it was joined by the younger Marxist socio-political theorists Barry Hindess and Paul Hirst.

The argument began in a contest for editorial direction of the *New Left Review* in the early 1960s, and accelerated in polemical exchanges over the historical nature and contemporary direction of Marxism in England. The exchanges did Thompson no credit. As he would a decade later when flailing at Althusser in 'The Poverty of Theory', Thompson equated virtually any attempts at generalizable theoretical restatement of empirical historical circumstance as reductionist and 'Stalinist'. His 'Peculiarities of the English', written in reply to Anderson's 'Origins of the Present Crisis' and other essays by Anderson and Tom Nairn, was particularly patronizing, ignorant, and Blimpish. 'Anderson and Nairn are very sadly mistaken if they think that, in these latter days, they are going to overthrow "empiricism" in the name of a self-sufficient Marxist system, even if this system has been tarted-up with some Sartreian neologisms . . . England is unlikely to capitulate before a Marxism which cannot at least engage in a dialogue in the English idiom.'[40] Thompson directed much the same sentiment a decade later at Hindess and Hirst, whose *Pre-Capitalist Modes of Production* and *Mode of Production and Social Formation* symbolized both

[37] Thompson (n. 24) 266, 267 ff.

[38] E. P. Thompson, 'The Poverty of Theory or an Orrery of Errors', in *The Poverty of Theory and Other Essays* (1978) 166–7 ff.

[39] Perry Anderson, 'Socialism and Pseudo-Empiricism' (1966) 1/35 *New Left Review* 2 ff.

[40] E. P. Thompson, 'The Peculiarities of the English' (1965) 2 *Socialist Register* 337 ff. On matters of ignorance, see Anderson (n. 39) 27–8, discussing Thompson on Gramsci.

a major importation of Althusserian structuralism into English Marxism and an attempt to move beyond it in certain crucial respects that emphasized the value of theoretical abstraction at the expense of history, and the centrality of class struggle and political practice to the proper object of Marxist analysis, which was always 'the current situation'.[41] For Hindess and Hirst, 'Marxism as a theoretical and a political practice, gains nothing from its association with historical writing and historical research. The study of history is not only scientifically but also politically valueless'.[42] Thompson wrote back with laboured irony:

I am told that, just beyond the horizon, new forms of working-class power are about to arise which, being founded upon egalitarian productive relations, will require no inhibition and can dispense with the negative restrictions of bourgeois legalism. A historian is unqualified to pronounce on such utopian projections. All that he knows is that he can bring in support of them no historical evidence whatsoever. His advice might be: watch this new power for a century or two before you cut your hedges down.[43]

Were one inclined to be generous to Thompson, to see the many contradictions of *Whigs and Hunters* as a struggle within Thompson's own Marxism, one might decide that its conclusion was an attempt to dilute the instrumentalist message of its substance with a discussion of 'the hegemonic function of the law'.[44] Like *Albion's Fatal Tree*, the development of which it accompanied, *Whigs and Hunters* might thus be thought of as a Gramscian book – not in any sense a surprising assessment given the ascendancy Gramsci had enjoyed in the 1970s turn of Anglophone Marxism towards the study of law and the state.[45] The difficulty with generosity is, first, that Thompson showed little inclination to be generous himself, far too fond of *ad hominem* 'police actions' against enemies on the left of the type of which he groundlessly accused Althusser. Second, no Marxism can stretch to encompass the bourgeois legality of Thompson's 'generic and hypostatized construct, "the rule of law"'.[46] In this move, as Martin Krygier rightly observes ('what took him so long?') Thompson, self-professed materialist notwithstanding, began his exit from Marxism. The Squire of Empirica Parva[47] fashioned himself anew, as Richard Oastler.

[41] Barry Hindess and Paul Hirst, *Pre-Capitalist Modes of Production* (1975), and *Mode of Production and Social Formation: An Auto-Critique of Pre-Capitalist Modes of Production* (1977).

[42] Hindess and Hirst (n. 41) 1975 312, and generally 308–23 ff.

[43] Thompson (n. 24) 266 ff. In 'Poverty of Theory' (n. 38) Thompson derided Hindess and Hurst as 'bourgeois *lumpen-intelligentsia*; aspirant intellectuals, whose amateurish intellectual preparation disarms them before manifest absurdities and elementary philosophical blunders, and whose innocence in intellectual practice leaves them paralysed in the first web of scholastic argument which they encounter.'

[44] This is Genovese's formulation in *Roll, Jordan, Roll*.

[45] See Sol Picciotto, 'The Theory of the State, Class Struggle, and the Rule of Law', in Bob Fine et al. (eds.), *Capitalism and the Rule of Law: From Deviancy Theory to Marxism* (1979) 164 ff.

[46] Anderson (n. 25) 200 ff.   [47] Paul Q. Hirst, *Marxism and Historical Writing* (1985) 59 ff.

III. THE THREE COMINGS
OF EVGENY PASHUKANIS

Edward Thompson did not bother to elaborate his scornful reference to 'new forms of working-class power . . . founded upon egalitarian productive relations' obviating any necessity for 'the negative restrictions of bourgeois legalism'.[48] It was just one more laugh line in his blunderbuss assault on Althusserianism. But it coincided, roughly, with the second major event in mid-1970s Western Marxism, which was—alongside the efflorescence of Althusserian Marxism—the recovery from relative obscurity of the commodity-form theory of law first developed in the 1920s by Evgeny Pashukanis.

Evgeny Pashukanis (1891–1937) was an early Soviet jurist, a participant in the 'rich, open-ended, and diverse' Soviet debates of the 1920s over the theory of law and the state, and the author of a number of important works in Marxist philosophy of law, amongst which *The General Theory of Law and Marxism* ensured his pre-eminence in his field. For thirteen years the single most important figure in Soviet legal life, in 1937 Pashukanis was denounced by Andrei Vyshinsky as a counter-revolutionary and shot. 'His writings displayed the potential for a profound theoretical development of the Marxist view of law and the state' Michael Head observes. 'But this potential was strangled by the needs of Stalin's regime . . . limitations and flaws that can be found in his theorising reflected the requirements of the rising bureaucratic caste'.[49]

Pashukanis was by no means unknown outside the Soviet Union, acknowledged by Western jurists and commentators both during his life and after as 'an imaginative Marxist, the most imaginative to appear among Soviet lawyers'.[50] But this first wave of recognition was essentially a professional assessment of Pashukanis for his impact on Soviet legal thought. It included no one with any desire actively to employ Pashukanis as a theorist of law. Anglophone Marxist scholars did not 'discover' Pashukanis until the mid-1970s, when, as we have seen, the influence first of Gramsci and then of Althusser on Western Marxism had already stimulated widespread interest in ideology, the state, and law.

This second wave of recognition was led, separately and more or less simultaneously, by Chris Arthur in the United Kingdom and Isaac Balbus in the United States. Working from the only (deficient) translation of *The General Theory* then available, Arthur described the main components of commodity-form theory

---

[48] Thompson (n. 24) 266 ff.

[49] Michael Head, *Evgeny Pashukanis: A Critical Reappraisal* (2008) 168 ff.

[50] John N. Hazard, 'Foreword', in Piers Beirne, Robert Sharlet (eds.), *Pashukanis: Selected Writings on Marxism and Law* (1980) xi ff.

in a 1977 essay entitled 'Toward a Materialist Theory of Law' published in *Critique*. The essay identified Pashukanis, 'a little known Russian', as the only real and original contributor to a materialist philosophy of law', and outlined his three fundamental emphases: law was 'an historic form which achieves fullest expression in the bourgeois epoch'; law was tied 'to the commodity economy' in that a necessary condition of commodity exchange was the participation of legal subjects routinely endowed with rights to possess and exchange its objects; and bourgeois law had no proletarian afterlife. The third point (which Thompson had scorned) followed of necessity from the first two, for the very form 'law' corresponded in structure to the form of bourgeois commodity exchange that proletarian revolution would end.[51] To the extent that a socialist society required regulation, its form would be purely technical (the equivalent of a railway timetable).[52] Throughout his essay, Arthur quoted *The General Theory* extensively (amending the Babb translation where appropriate).

From a legal point of view, the capacity to perfect commodity exchange is merely one of the concrete manifestations of the general attribute of legal capacity and capacity to act. Historically, however, it is precisely commodity exchange which furnished the idea of a subject as the abstract bearer of all possible legal claims. It is only in the conditions of commodity production that the abstract legal form is generated—that is to say, it is only there that the capacity to have a right in general is distinguished from specific legal claims and privileges. It is only the constant transfer of rights taking place in the market which creates the idea of an immobile bearer of those rights. In the market, the obligee is himself obligated at the same time . . The possibility of being abstracted from the specific differences between subjects of rights and of bringing them within a single generic concept is thus created.[53]

Arthur followed up in 1978 with a new edition of *The General Theory* ably translated by Barbara Einhorn.[54]

In the United States Isaac Balbus also published a commentary on *The General Theory* in 1977. In his case Balbus had been led to *The General Theory* in the course of his own attempts to develop a Marxist theory of law out of dissatisfaction

[51] C. J. Arthur, 'Towards a Materialist Theory of Law' (1977) 7 *Critique* 31 ff. At that time the only English translation of the *General Theory* was by Hugh W. Babb, published in *Soviet Legal Philosophy* (1951) 111 ff.

[52] See Evgeny Pashukanis, *The General Theory of Law and Marxism*, Barbara Einhorn trans. (2002) 79 ff.

[53] Arthur (n. 51) 37 ff. The passage illustrates Pashukanis's concentration on exchange relations, for which he is criticized by those who emphasize that Marx prioritized relations of production. But as Marx makes quite clear, without 'the sale and purchase of labour-power' in the market, that 'very Eden' of 'freedom, Equality, Property and Bentham', there will be no 'hidden abode' of capitalist relations of production to start with. See Karl Marx, *Capital: A Critique of Political Economy* (1967), I, 167 ff.

[54] Evgeny Pashukanis, *Law and Marxism: A General Theory*, C. J. Arthur (ed.), Barbara Einhorn trans. (1978).

with instrumentalist/reductionist arguments. 'Only after "working out" the homology between the commodity form and the legal form did I discover that Pashukanis had developed essentially the same analysis roughly fifty years ago!' Notwithstanding its subtitle—'An Essay on the "Relative Autonomy" of the Law'—Balbus's essay was bare of any engagement with Althusser. Nor did it address Gramsci. It simply wrote off everything intervening between *The General Theory* and 1977: 'Almost all . . . Marxist work on the law is, unfortunately, a regression from the standard established by Pashukanis's pioneering effort.'[55] Appearing in the mainstream socio-legal journal *Law & Society Review*, the most significant effect of Balbus's essay, perhaps, was to restate Pashukanis in terms that established both a point of contact and terms of distinction between the emerging Marxist theory of the legal form and concurrent U.S. debates, whether in orthodox liberal jurisprudence that had traditionally canvassed the opposition between law's self-determination (formalism) and other-determination (instrumentalism),[56] or in CLS (itself then just emerging) personified in Balbus's *Law & Society Review* interlocutor, David Trubek, a Weberian-influenced sceptic of orthodox (instrumentalist) Marxism who was at the time loosely affiliated with CLS.[57]

Whether you were a formalist *or* an instrumentalist, Balbus argued, you embraced the same logic, a logic that the Marxist theory of the legal form was able to overcome and refute. Both the formalist and the instrumentalist held that analysis of law's relation to society under capitalism could be advanced by empirical inquiry into whether law was a creature (instrument) of the will of powerful social actors. Instrumentalist hypotheses would be satisfied by evidence of law's responsiveness to the will of the socially powerful; formalist hypotheses would be satisfied by evidence of law's lack of responsiveness, its exhibition of tendencies to develop in response to its own internal dynamics. If one accepted the instrumentalist-formalist continuum, the scholar's only option was to approach the autonomy question as a broker, establishing some empirically determinable point of compromise or balance between formalist autonomy and instrumentalist non-autonomy. But law's autonomy from the preferences of particular social actors could *never* establish law's systemic autonomy.

The formulation that *to the degree that the law does not respond directly to the demands of powerful social actors it is autonomous, in the sense that it functions and develops according to its own internal dynamics* omits the possibility that the law is not autonomous

---

[55] Isaac D. Balbus, 'Commodity Form and Legal Form: An Essay on the "Relative Autonomy" of the Law' (1977) 11 *Law and Society Review* 571 ff.

[56] For a summary, see Tomlins (n. 28) 46–9 ff.

[57] David M. Trubek, 'Complexity and Contradiction in the Legal Order: Balbus and the Challenge of Critical Social Thought about Law' (1977) 11 *Law and Society Review* 529 ff.

from, but rather articulates with and must be explained by, the systemic requirements of capitalism precisely because it does not respond directly to the demands of these actors.[58]

Balbus proposed that the latter possibility was demonstrable once one transcended the 'common conceptual terrain' of the instrumentalist-formalist continuum for the 'wholly different theoretical terrain' of Marx's 'logic of the commodity form'. The relationship between law and capitalism was conceptually systemic: the very form of law (exchange of people) was homologous with the form of capitalism (exchange of commodities). The homology of legal form and commodity form lay in their reproduction of the same logic of equivalence: 'in a capitalist mode of production, products take on the form of individual commodities'; in the legal form that corresponds to a capitalist mode of production, human beings 'take on the form of individual citizens'.[59] Commodities and citizens obeyed the same productive logic: in each case, they had been abstracted from specific, real substances (products, persons) and rendered what, in fact, they could not be—equals. In each case, the attribution of equality rendered the commodity, the citizen, exchangeable with its equivalents—other commodities, other citizens—through the operation of dedicated transactional media: markets and law.

In Balbus's rendition, then, the 'relativity' of relative autonomy was not structuralist, in the Althusserian sense, but essentialist. It was an expression of correspondent logics of capital and law.

The homology between the legal form and the commodity form guarantees both that the legal form, like the commodity form, functions and develops autonomously from the preferences of social actors *and* that it does *not* function and develop autonomously from the system in which these social actors participate. Stated otherwise, the autonomy of the Law from the preferences of even the most powerful social actors (the members of the capitalist class) is not an obstacle to, but rather a prerequisite for, the capacity of the Law to contribute to the reproduction of the overall conditions that make capitalism possible, and thus its capacity to serve the interests of capital as a *class*.[60]

Although unacknowledged, there were hints here of Genovese's version of law's 'hegemonic function' and so the possibility of a link to historical research. Indeed Balbus declared somewhat cryptically that his goal was reunification of structure (in the sense of synchronic homology evident at a given historical moment) with history (the conditions of homology's existence and repetition).[61] But little

---

[58] Balbus (n. 55) 572 (emphasis in original) ff.
[59] Ibid., 575 ff.   [60] Ibid., 585 (emphasis in original) ff.
[61] Ibid., 587 ff. Balbus noted, self-critically, that the relevance of his theorization (and hence, implicitly, that of Pashukanis) to the current moment was questionable, given that the historical moment of competitive capitalism that informed it was over.

historical pick-up actually occurred, nor did Balbus have any obvious interest in Marxist legal history. Indeed, his primary conclusion steered Pashukanis in a very different direction. 'The foregoing analysis has important implications for a theory of the "legitimation" and/or "de-legitimation" of the legal form, *and thus, of the capitalist state*.'[62] This confirmed the lodgement of commodity-form legal theory in the camp of what was known as 'capital logic' Marxism, by which Balbus was clearly influenced.[63] This school, primarily German in origin, had also appropriated Pashukanis during the 1970s. Its 'principal concern' was defined in 1980 for Anglophone audiences by Bob Jessop as 'to derive the *form* of the capitalist state from the nature of capital and/or to establish those *functional prerequisites* of accumulation whose satisfaction must be mediated through state activity'.[64] As China Miéville has argued, capital logic is indeed 'theoretically fecund', but its appropriation of the commodity form to its state theory program resulted in an elision of commodity-form theory's potential to explain the legal form.[65]

In the four years following 1977, Pashukanis attracted considerable attention from Anglophone Marxists attempting to develop a Marxist theory of law. This second wave of recognition peaked in 1981 without the emergence of a clear theorization of the legal form, however, and then fell off almost as rapidly as it had arisen, coinciding with the deepening theoretical crisis of Marxist explanation in general. In the world of the linguistic turn, 'structural determination' fell before a world that seemed 'irreducibly contingent'.[66] Cohen's enterprising defence of the materialist conception of history apart, Analytic Marxism proved a barren and rather unappealing waystation.[67] '[D]iscursive construction . . . replaced material production as the constitutive practice of social life.' New identity-based social movements captured ever more attention. Marxism was suddenly so old-fashioned. 'And then came the collapse of Communism.'[68] By the end of the 1980s the few who were left found themselves wandering amid rubble.

But there was to be a third coming for Evgeny Pashukanis, and with it a new chance for a Marxist legal history.

[62] Ibid., 581 (emphasis added) ff.

[63] Through the work of, e.g., Claus Offe.

[64] Jessop (n. 33) 343 ff. Compare Bob Jessop, 'Recent Theories of the Capitalist State' (1977) 1 *Cambridge Journal of Economics* 353 ff, which also surveys capital logic Marxism (361–4) but makes no mention of its appropriation of Pashukanis.

[65] China Miéville, *Between Equal Rights: A Marxist Theory of International Law* (2006) 122 ff.

[66] Wood, *Democracy Against Capitalism*, 8 ff. And see Joyce Appleby, 'One Good Turn Deserves Another: Moving beyond the Linguistic; A Response to David Harlan' (1989) 94 *American Historical Review* 5 1326–32 ff.

[67] For a taste, see Jon Elster, *Making Sense of Marx* (1985). For analysis of the analysts, see Marcus Roberts, *Analytical Marxism: A Critique* (1996).

[68] Wood (n. 4) 8 ff.

iv. Of the Current Conjuncture

We live in deeply uncertain times. The open rightwing rupture with neo-liberalism in the United States and parts of Western Europe is a rupture within capital that pits 'old' sectors (durable manufacturing, fossil energy, agribusiness, construction) against 'new' (tech, information, renewable energy, social media). The rupture has mobilized bilious neo-mercantilist revanchist nationalism against neo-liberalism's fanatic maximization of global 'free' market competition in the movement of commodities, capital, and people. At its extremes, capital's civil war offers us a choice between anarcho-capitalism and the possibility of resurgent fascism.

One mark of the times has also been a slow, almost imperceptible, accretion of attempts to renew Marxist theorizing, which in our particular neck of the woods is manifest in renewed discussion of Marxism and law. It was said of the 'immense proliferation of theory' that characterized Western Marxism in the 1960s and 1970s that 'whenever theory multiplies it is the surest sign that something has gone badly wrong'.[69] Whatever the truth of that observation, current circumstance does not suggest another immense proliferation so much as careful reappraisal of what the original proliferation actually wrought, and as a means of responding not to another crisis of Marxism but to the crisis ongoing elsewhere—the crisis of global capital. It is a reappraisal being undertaken in the form of practice—that is, application. And the character of that practice gives one cause for optimism. After thirty years of wilderness there are no old loyalties left to be defended. The old loyalists are dead or departed; their game is not worth our candle. Marxists can be non-sectarian, experimental, even pragmatic in the positions we build and adopt. The most serious problem of the moment is not intellectual but political, not lack of imagination or rigour, but lack of 'an active working-class movement' that can both inform and discipline the theoretical and empirical work of a Marxist intelligentsia. This defect is particularly acute in the United States, but it is hardly a problem unique to North America.[70]

It is telling, then, that for those interested in writing legal history informed by a Marxist theory of law, the most promising developments, responding to definite movements, are to be found in what is currently the most cosmopolitan of settings. The primordial landscape of Western Marxism is being rejuvenated by work in international law. There is considerable irony here. One of E. P. Thompson's prefatory observations to *The Making of the English Working Class* bade 'the greater part of the world . . . still undergoing problems of industrialization' to pay attention to

---

[69] Costas Douzinas, Ronnie Warrington, 'Domination, Exploitation, and Suffering: Marxism and the Opening of Closed Systems' (1986) 1986 *American Bar Foundation Research Journal* 803 ff.

[70] The observation is Tushnet's, albeit from a different era. See Mark Tushnet, 'Review Essay' (1980) 7 *British Journal of Law and Society* 123 ff.

English experience. 'Causes which were lost in England might, in Asia or Africa, yet be won.'[71] The answer from, for example, B. S. Chimni, invites us to reverse the flow of information and learning, the polarity of experience.[72]

The plurality of current Marxist thought in international law of relevance to the project of a Marxist legal history is on display in *International Law on the Left: Re-examining Marxist Legacies*, edited by Susan Marks.[73] The collection includes revised versions of a number of germinal articles on Marxism and international law originally published in the *Leiden Journal of International Law* alongside new work. Marks herself is a figure of considerable importance in the upswing for her own scholarship, not least her enviable essay 'False Contingency', which neatly turns the tables on Roberto Unger's conflation of determination with fatalism in *False Necessity* and in the process liberates Marxism from some of CLS's most strident critiques.[74] So is Robert Knox.[75] But the single most impressive study to emerge so far from among Marxist international law scholars—one that Marxist-inclined legal historians will find particularly helpful in their own engagements—is China Miéville's *Between Equal Rights: A Marxist Theory of International Law* (2005).[76] Framed by the violence of the Iraq War, Miéville's book combines in equal measure (1) a detailed critique of 'mainstream' theory of international law; an assessment of then-existing 'radical' (Marxist) and 'critical' (CLS) modes of critique of the mainstream; and a cogent evaluation of Evgeny Pashukanis's commodity-form theory of the legal form that, notwithstanding his own critique of Pashukanis, Miéville identifies as by far the most promising of available Marxist approaches to international law (hence the 'third coming' of Evgeny Pashukanis to which I alluded in the previous section), with (2) a substantial, though not exhaustive history of half a millennium of international law, from the fifteenth century to the present, the purpose of which is to demonstrate the applicability of commodity-form theory, *but with a crucial additive*, which Miéville derives from his critique of Pashukanis, as follows:

'Coercion', [Pashukanis] writes, 'as the imperative addressed by one person to another, and backed up by force, contradicts the fundamental precondition for dealings between the owners of commodities'. This is *absolutely untrue* . . . sometimes Pashukanis's excessive formalism leads him to neglect the 'succulence' of dialectical contradictions inherent in seemingly stable categories.[77]

---

[71]   E. P. Thompson, *The Making of the English Working Class* (1966) 13 ff.

[72]   B. S. Chimni, 'Marxism and International Law: A Contemporary Analysis' *Economic and Political Weekly* (6 February 1999) 337 ff; B. S. Chimni, 'Third World Approaches to International Law: A Manifesto' (2006) 8 *International Community Law Review* 3 ff.

[73]   Susan Marks (ed.), *International Law on the Left: Re-examining Marxist Legacies* (2008).

[74]   Susan Marks, 'False Contingency' (2009) 62 *Current Legal Problems* 1 ff.

[75]   See Robert Knox, 'Marxism, International Law, and Political Strategy' (2009) 22 *Leiden Journal of International Law* 413 ff; Robert Knox, 'Marxist Approaches to International Law,' in Ann Orford, Florian Hoffmann (eds.), *The Oxford Handbook of the Theory of International Law* (2016) 306 ff.

[76]   See Miéville (n. 65).   [77]   Ibid., 126 ff.

The 'logic' of the commodity form theory of the legal form so appeals to Pashukanis's formalism, says Miéville, that he represents it as sufficient of itself as an explanation of the legal form. He forgets his own observation, earlier in the *General Theory*, that historically 'it is *dispute*, conflict of interest, which begins the legal form, the legal superstructure . . . law begins with dispute'.[78] The apparent absence of coercion from the heart of Pashukanis's theory of the legal form is what permits Miéville to embrace its applicability to bourgeois international law, the voluntarisic character of which is derived from the (elaborately bemoaned) absence of a global agency of enforcement. But in both locales (the theoretical, the actual) the absence is only apparent. First, 'violence and coercion are immanent in the commodity relationship itself'. Whether formalized by fists or by law, property relations are relations of *exclusion*. Second, 'in legal systems without superordinate authorities', as in international law, 'the coercive violence of the legal subjects themselves regulates the legal relation.' Hence Miéville's conclusion (entitled 'Against the Rule of Law'): 'The chaotic and bloody world around us *is the rule of law*.'[79]

V. CONCLUSION

Marxism has never had more than a fringe presence in legal history. Since the early 1980s, legal historians who consider themselves Marxists, or who at least contemplate Marxism as a rich and stimulating source of inspiration, have been particularly scarce on the ground. During this era, legal history—like cognate disciplines—has been inclined, in Ellen Wood's words, to favour 'contingency, fragmentation and heterogeneity'. It has been indifferent to 'totality, system, structure, process, and "grand narratives"', given instead to the study of the 'alternative "discourses", activities and identities' that inhabit the 'interstices' of a capitalism that in its very ubiquity has simply faded into the boring background.[80] All this is the post-structural truth of the 'critical legal history' that has reigned in our 'post-Marxist' times.

But we have seen that in the current conjuncture there is a certain restlessness in the air. Scholarship in International Law, which stirred first, promises much, and across a wide front.[81] In the moment of its (most recent) crisis, American historians

[78] Pashukanis (n. 52) 93 (emphasis added) ff.

[79] For critiques of Miéville, see Knox (n. 75); Mike MacNair, 'Law and State as Holes in Marxist Theory' (2006) 43 *Critique*, 230–1 ff. The latter borders on sectarian.

[80] Wood, *Democracy against Capitalism*, 1 ff.

[81] See, e.g., Rose Sydney Parfitt, *The Process of International Legal Reproduction: Subjectivity, Historiography, Law, Violence* (2018). The possibilities in international law are not narrowly defined. See, e.g., the work of the participants in the following collections on neo-liberalism: Honor Brabazon

have rediscovered capitalism, with a vengeance.[82] These stirrings and rediscoveries prime legal historians to follow, to participate.[83] Doing so, they will discover allies they didn't know they had.[84] They will also discover a remarkable array of Marxist theoretical concepts lying ready and waiting for use, powerful tools gleaming in a new day's morning light, still heavy with the grease that has preserved them within their crates.[85]

The primary responsibility of this moment is to avoid repeating old errors. Legal historians need to discover that what makes Marxist legal history useful and attractive is less that it is a particular way of doing legal history that produces specific outcomes than that it is an explicitly *historical* method.[86] In the service of fresh thinking let us open our minds to the risk of new mistakes with abandon. Let us shun the four horsemen—dogma, sectarianism, excessive abstraction, and political correctness. Let us be generous, plural, imaginative. And as we give ourselves once more to 'the nameless rapture of the struggle'[87] let us remember to give thanks for William E. Nelson, with whom I began. For on 27 September 2008, literally the morning after global finance capital had teetered on the edge of a final cataclysmic plunge as U.S. House Republicans rebelled against the $700bn emergency bank bailout and Treasury Secretary Henry Paulson on bended knee begged Democratic House Speaker Nancy Pelosi not to do the same, Bill Nelson informed an audience

---

(ed.), *Neoliberal Legality: Understanding the Role of Law in the Neoliberal Project* (2017); Ben Golder, Daniel McLoughlin (eds.), *The Politics of Legality in a Neoliberal Age* (2017). See generally Grietje Baars, '"Reform of Revolution"? Polyanian versus Marxian Perspectives on the Regulation of the Economic' (2011) 62 *Northern Ireland Law Quarterly* 415 ff.

[82] See, e.g., Michael Zakim, Gary J. Kornblith (eds.), *Capitalism Takes Command: The Social Transformation of Nineteenth Century America* (2012); Christine Desan, Sven Beckert (eds.), *American Capitalism: New Histories* (2018).

[83] See, e.g., Nate Holdren, *Blood Money: Law, Commodification, and the Human Truths of Injury in the Long Gilded Age* (forthcoming); Marc W. Steinberg, *England's Great Transformation: Law, Labor and the Industrial Revolution* (2016). See also Steinberg's earlier articles, 'Marx, Formal Subsumption and the Law' (2010) 39 *Theory and Society* 173 ff; and 'Capitalist Development, the Labor Process and the Law: The Case of the Victorian English Pottery Industry' (2003) 109 *American Journal of Sociology* 445 ff.

[84] See, e.g., Brian Leiter, 'Marxism and the Continuing Irrelevance of Normative Theory' (2002) 54 *Stanford Law Review* 1129 ff.; Brian Leiter, 'Why Marxism Still Does Not Need Normative Theory' (2015) 37 *Analyse & Kritik* 23 ff.

[85] For what one might think of as useful texts that help to bridge the 'post-Marxist' gulf that yawns between 1985 and roughly 2005, see, e.g., Tony Smith, *Dialectical Social Theory and its Critics: From Hegel to Analytical Marxism and Postmodernism* (1993); Andrew Levine, *A Future for Marxism? Althusser, the Analytical Turn, and the Revival of Socialist Theory* (2003). For a recent example of what's fresh in Marxist scholarship at the junction of political theory and history, see William Clare Roberts, *Marx's Inferno: The Political Theory of Capital* (2017).

[86] On which see Christopher Tomlins, 'Of Origin: Toward a History of Contemporary Legal Thought', in Justin Desautels-Stein, Christopher Tomlins (eds.), *Searching for Contemporary Legal Thought* (2017) 23 ff.

[87] Akbar Rasulov, 'The Nameless Rapture of the Struggle': Towards a Marxist Class-Theoretic Approach to International Law' (2008) *Finnish Yearbook of International Law* 19 243–94 ff.

gathered at Harvard Law School to wish Morton Horwitz a happy retirement that 'we need to know' once and for all 'that Marxian materialism, even in elegantly restated forms, no longer has significant political force'.[88] What more could possibly guarantee *revival* at this moment than another of Bill's effable predictions?

BIBLIOGRAPHY

'An Exchange on Critical Legal Studies between Robert W. Gordon and William Nelson' (1988) 6 *Law and History Review* 162 ff

Perry Anderson, *Arguments within English Marxism* (Verso, 1980)

Isaac D. Balbus, 'Commodity Form and Legal Form: an Essay on the "Reliative Autonomy" of the Law' (1977) 11 *Law and Society Review* 571 ff

Susan Easton (ed.), *Marx and Law* (Ashgate Publishing, 2008)

G. A. Cohen, *Karl Marx's Theory of History: A Defence* (Princeton University Press, expanded edn., 2000)

Michael Head, *Evgeny Pashukanis: A Critical Reappraisal* (Routledge-Cavendish, 2008)

Paul Q. Hirst, *Marxism and Historical Writing* (Routledge & Kegan Paul, 1985)

Catherine McKinnon, *Towards a Feminist Theory of the State* (Harvard University Press, 1989)

Susan Marks (ed.), *International Law on the Left: Re-examining Marxist Legacies* (Cambridge University Press, 2008)

Susan Marks, 'False Contingency' (2009) 62 *Current Legal Problems* 1 ff

China Miéville, *Between Equal Rights: A Marxist Theory of International Law* (Brill, 2006)

Evgeny Pashukanis, *The General Theory of Law and Marxism*, Dragan Milovanovic intro., Barbara Einhorn trans. (Transaction Publishers, 2002)

E. P. Thompson, *Whigs and Hunters: The Origin of the Black Act* (Penguin Books, 1977)

E. P. Thompson, *The Poverty of Theory and Other Essays* (The Merlin Press, 1978)

Christopher Tomlins, 'Of Origin: Toward a History of Contemporary Legal Thought', in Justin Desautels-Stein, Christopher Tomlins (eds.), *Searching for Contemporary Legal Thought* (Cambridge University Press, 2017) 23 ff

Christopher Tomlins, 'Organic Poise? Capitalism as Law' (2016) 64 *Buffalo L.R.* 61 ff

Mark Tushnet, 'A Marxist Analysis of American Law' (1978) 1 *Marxist Perspectives* 96 ff

---

[88] William E. Nelson, 'Horwitz and the Direction of Legal Thought,' in Hamilton, Brophy (eds.), *American Legal History* 500–3, 502 ff.

CHAPTER 29

STRUCTURALIST AND POST-STRUCTURALIST LEGAL HISTORY

JUSTIN DESAUTELS-STEIN

THIS short depiction of historical method in the registers of structuralist and post-structuralist theory begins with postmodernism. Of course, what postmodernism was, or whether it was, may remain forever contested. Nevertheless, my sense is that at least in the structuralist and post-structuralist contexts of legal historiography, a postmodern sensibility provides certain points of orientation, a set of landmarks. The argument is this: if we imagine postmodernism as a family of suggestions for historicizing the legal world, we can also imagine post-structuralism and structuralism as two historical postures, two ways of practising the postmodern. The post-structuralist posture, as I sketch it through the medium of the genealogy, embraces certain postmodern anxieties and runs with them. The structuralist posture, as I sketch it through the medium of archaeology, is similarly receptive to the postmodern. But rather than let postmodernism run riot in a flattened and hybridized present, the structuralist posture performs rather differently. The structuralist experiences the dizzying vertigo of the genealogy and, in the midst of the free-fall, erects grand, totalizing structures of legal thought.

It is in this sense that the labels are misleading, since I take structuralist legal history to really be a kind of *post*-post-structuralism. Because of this sense of passage, I begin with a discussion of postmodernism and its suggestive gestures.

I then turn to the post-structuralist posture of legal history, and conclude with a summary of its structuralist rival.

I. Postmodern Suggestions

Let us begin with a roster of postmodern suggestions, or a postmodern sensibility, about how to think of the relation(s) between history and social reality.[1] A first sign of our encounter with this sensibility is the presence of a heavy scepticism about the availability of apodictic stories marching through time. If we want to name it, we can say that postmoderns are anxious about 'grand', 'master', or 'meta' narratives, historical explanations and periodizations reaching across space and time. The postmodern suggestion that we worry about meta-explanations is broader than the typical concern about progress narratives as developed by, let's say, a Walt Whitman Rostow.[2] Just as much on the hook is Giovanni Arrighi's leftist story of capitalism: a story of capitalism and its historical modes of material production as the central drivers in the history of what might be called modernism and the turn to the postmodern, and an idea that seems to posit a fundamental anchor in the centre of 500 years or more of Western history.[3] Like Rostow's manifesto, this is a history of continuities and consistencies, though instead of a history of victories we see a history of exploitation and domination. When we encounter deep explanations such as these, we know we're in postmodern territory if we sense a heavy weight in the air, a sense that the articulation of a homogenizing grand narrative of capital, whether in its conservative or emancipatory registers, is simply naïve. Where totalizing continuities once were, the postmodern suggests breaks, ruptures, gaps.

A similar but distinct postmodern suggestion is that we worry about 'totality.' The 'war on totality',[4] as Fredric Jameson says, is about a number of interrelated concerns. Chief among them is the work of Friedrich Nietzsche's 'knights of totality'

---

[1] In the pages that follow, many readers will wonder at certain absences, among them that of Jacque Derrida, along with so many others. These absences are generally strategic and due to the limits of space more than anything else. For a recent overview, see Brian McHale, *The Cambridge Introduction to Postmodernism* (2015). See also, Perry Anderson, *The Origins of Postmodernity* (1999); in subsequent footnotes: Anderson (n. 1); Terry Eagleton, *The Illusions of Postmodernism* (1996). For an example, see George Butterick, 'Charles Olson's The Kingfishers and the Poetics of Change' (1989) 6 *American Poetry* 28 ff.

[2] W. W. Rostow, *The Stages of Economic Growth: A Non-Communist Manifesto* (1991).

[3] Giovanni Arrighi, *The Long Twentieth Century: Money, Power, and the Origins of Our Times* (2010). See also, Immanuel Wallerstein, *Historical Capitalism with Capitalist Civilization* (2011).

[4] Fredric Jameson, *Postmodernism, or the Cultural Logic of Late Capitalism* (1992) 400 ff.

and their ostensible production of integrated, coherent, and unified concepts aimed to pass beyond the bounds of immediate experience and trace the contours of the universal and the true.[5] True, the postmodern assault initially took these Knights to be Marxists, and it was the Marxist usage of totality that came under fire.[6] But liberal totalities are just as vulnerable, and to take a quintessential illustration, postmoderns have worried much about the totality of the autonomous, independent, intentional subject. The suggestion is that we regard the totality of the individual as myth. As Judith Butler has recently put it:

[W]hen we speak about subject formation, we invariably presume a threshold of susceptibility or impressionability that may be said to precede the formation of a conscious and deliberate 'I.' That means only that this creature that I am is affected by something outside of itself, understood as prior, that activates and informs the subject that I am. When I make use of the first-person pronoun in this context, I am not exactly telling you about myself.[7]

What we are dealing with here, instead of the so-called sovereign individual, is an infinite play of interpretative possibilities and language games,[8] a schizophrenia of desire rather than a fixed order of the personal.[9]

A third postmodern suggestion underscores hostility towards philosophical realism, flowing over Descartes, Bacon, Locke, Hume, Kant, and the analytic tradition and into continental modes as well.[10] The problem, in every case, is the problem in motivating empirical and/or naturalizing claims about how the world really is. Instead, postmoderns suggest a world of radical indeterminacy, endless heterogeneity and plurality, wanton randomness, multiple multiples, simulacra, copies without originals. As Maurice Merleau-Ponty suggested, in step with the Cartesian tradition was the fantasy of 'Objective Thought', which in its various ways 'build[s] up all knowledge out of determinate qualities, offers us objects purged of all ambiguity, pure and absolute, the ideal rather than the real themes of knowledge'.[11] This purging and the belief in the freestanding object was 'based on the foreshadowing of an imminent order which is about to spring upon us a reply to questions merely latent in the landscape'.[12] But Objective Thought was mistaken in its presentation of a world awaiting rational analysis, a world kept distant from the perceiving subject. To move away from this representational view of knowledge and enter the chiasm of consciousness in world and world in consciousness, was therefore to accept 'the indeterminate as a positive phenomenon'.[13] Standing against

---

[5] Martin Jay, *Marxism and Totality: The Adventures of a Concept from Lukacs to Habermas* (1986) 12–13 ff.

[6] Jay (n. 5), at 512–13 ff.   [7] Judith Butler, *Senses of the Subject* (2015) 1 ff.

[8] See, e.g., Jean-Francois Lyotard, *The Postmodern Condition: A Report on Knowledge* (1984) 33 ff.

[9] See, e.g., Gilles Deleuze, Felix Guattari, *Anti-Oedipus: Capitalism and Schizophrenia* (2009).

[10] See, e.g., Richard Rorty, *Philosophy and the Mirror of Nature* (1981).

[11] Maurice Merleau-Ponty, *Phenomenology of Perception* (1962) 11 ff.

[12] Ibid., at 17 ff.   [13] Ibid., at 320 ff.

this understanding of an empirical pursuit of an objective world was therefore a prioritization of experience with radical indeterminacy, a 'post-empiricism'. 'The world', said Merleau-Ponty, 'does not hold for us a set of outlines which some consciousness within us binds together into a unity'.[14]

These three postmodern suggestions (concerns about meta-explanations, totalities, and objectivism or realism) are all, in a sense, bottomed out on a view of time. Though it is certainly a view predating the postmoderns, it became something of an unstated orthodoxy. This view concerns the 'reality of time'. It is a simple if radical view: time is real, and if time is real, everything changes sooner or later. Belief in the reality of time therefore undermines belief in permanent structures, immutable laws, totalities that might exist outside of time. If time is for real, and transformations are inevitable, there can be no permanent structures in the world. Believing in the reality of time is therefore suggestive of what we ought *not* to do in our attempts to write legal history.

The next two suggestions, in contrast, are more positive, giving the postmodern historian something of a plan of action. And so, a fourth postmodern suggestion is that we see the past as a scattered intermixture of legal hybrids.[15] If postmodern concerns about the erosion of disciplinary boundaries and the relentless free play of the *social* is right, Bruno Latour and his associates have suggested that the implications are all for the good. The modern proclivity for separating out the human world of culture from the nonhuman world of nature never *really* took place, and at least one sort of 'postmodernism' assists in getting at this final, porous, truth.[16] As Latour has explained:

Our intellectual life is out of kilter. Epistemology, the social sciences, the science of texts—all have their privileged vantage point, provided they remain separate. If the creatures [i.e., hybrids] we are pursuing cross all three spaces, we are no longer understood. Offer the established disciplines some fine sociotechnical network, some lovely translations, and the first group will extract our concepts and pull out the roots that might connect them to society or to rhetoric; the second group will erase social and political dimensions, and purify our network of any object; the third group, finally, will retain our discourse and rhetoric but purge our work of any undue adherence to reality—*horresco referens*—or to power plays . . . That a delicate shuttle should have woven together the heavens, industry, texts, souls, and moral law—this remains uncanny, unthinkable, unseemly.[17]

A second and far less favourable suggestion about how to view the world is Jameson's argument about the postmodern pastiche.[18] A spectacle with its climax

---

[14] Ibid., at 328–9 ff.

[15] See, e.g., Pierre Schlag, 'The Dedifferentiation Problem' (2009) 42 *Cont. Phil. R.* 35 ff; Bruno Latour, *The Making of Law: An Ethnography of the Conseil d'État* (2009).

[16] For a recent take, see Bruno Latour, *An Inquiry into Modes of Existence: An Anthropology of the Moderns* (2013). Of course, Latour himself has adamantly opposed what he takes to be postmodernism. Bruno Latour, *We Have Never Been Modern* (1993).

[17] Latour (n. 16) at 5 ff.   [18] Jameson (n. 4) at 9 ff.

in the United States of the 1970s,[19] and in which, to blend the terms of Guy Debord and Perry Anderson, the presence of pastiche reflects a society in which its every pore has been saturated 'in the serum of capital'.[20] Postmodern pastiche offers up a 'new kind of flatlessness or depthlessness, a new kind of superficiality in the most literal sense, perhaps the supreme formal feature of all the postmodernisms . . .'[21] For Jameson, this surface sensibility is a by-product of postmodern anxiety, for its first three suggestions yield a situation in which we are forever divorced from everything with depth: history, individuality, reality.[22] Pastiche, as a result, involves a blank and blind 'imitation of dead styles, speech through all the masks and voices stored up in the imaginary museum of a now global culture'.[23] It is a practice, once more, 'which randomly and without principle but with gusto cannibalizes . . . styles of the past and combines them in overstimulating ensembles'.[24]

If these suggestions about hybridity and pastiche indicate an arrival in the land of the postmoderns, what I want to explore next is less of a cognitive mapping of that territory and more of a diagnostic of two historical postures that each, in their own way, find motivation in these postmodern indicia. The first posture is post-structuralist historicism, and I take the idea of the 'legal genealogy' to be a helpful illustration of that posture. The second posture is structuralist legal history. Similarly inclined towards these postmodern cues, the structuralist posture is nevertheless distinct from its post-structuralist sibling. One might wonder if it wouldn't be better to reverse the order here, since structuralism must by definition come prior to *post*-structuralism. But as I suggested above, for whatever worth a particular chronology might have here, structuralist legal history requires of the historian a passage *through* post-structuralism, yielding an elaboration of structural insights minus the structural dogma.

II. Post-Structuralist Genealogy

Between the postmodern gate and these two passageways stands Michel Foucault. In his work we see the gestures of both post-structuralist genealogy and structuralist archaeology, and as we peer down the post-structuralist passage, Foucault's *Nietzsche, Genealogy, History* greets the gaze.[25] Hostility to grand narratives, historical totalities, and positivist devotion to objective reality: these are all on

---

[19] Anderson (n. 1) at 84–5 ff.   [20] Ibid., at 55 ff.   [21] Jameson (n. 4) at 9 ff.

[22] Ibid., at 185, 250 ff.   [23] Ibid., at 18 ff.   [24] Ibid., at 19 ff.

[25] Michel Foucault, 'Nietzsche, Genealogy, History', in Paul Rabinow (ed.), *The Foucault Reader* (1984).

abundant display. In the essay's opening lines, Foucault makes it clear just how aggressive a genealogical history ought to be, for it opposes the key questions of conventional historical research: why did this happen? What is the original basis for what has since developed? As Foucault explained, 'The traditional devices for constructing a comprehensive view of history and for retracing the past as a patient and continuous development must be systematically dismantled.'[26] Why? The answers are familiar. There is not in history an essence of things to be discovered through careful research, nothing 'already there' in some cognizable past, only a false metaphysics of universality. Weaning ourselves from these childish delights, Foucault recommends we instead bear gleeful witness to the discontinuity of trace events. With careful, plodding patience, the genealogist finds 'not a timeless and essential secret, but the secret that they have no essence or that their essence was fabricated in piecemeal fashion from alien forms.'[27]

In a genealogy, we find no historical foundations but only fragments, bits and pieces here and there of what was naively assumed a unity. Rather than continuities, the genealogist discovers 'the heterogeneity of what was imagined consistent with itself'.[28] Drenched in humility, a genealogy finds at the beginning of things no noble beginnings, but only and always the detritus of some other, some often awful thing, 'episodes in a series of subjugations.'[29] What the genealogist uncovers and aims to reveal is the 'hazardous play of dominations.'[30] As a kind of historical training in good character, genealogy is also an exercise in maturity. For rather than indulge in the adolescent hopes for a historical point at which 'the truth of things corresponded to a truthful discourse', the genealogist is wise enough to see that 'truth is undoubtedly the sort of error that that cannot be refuted because it was hardened into an unalterable form in the long baking process of history.'[31] Humble and battle-hardened, the genealogist is brave to boot, brave enough to wield a knowledge not made for mere understanding, but a knowledge for cutting.[32] Hence Foucault's announcement of the genealogist's mission:

[Genealogy] will cultivate the details and accidents that accompany every beginning; it will be scrupulously attentive to their petty malice; it will await their emergence, once unmasked, as the face of the other. Wherever it is made to go, it will not be reticent—in 'excavating the depths', in allowing time for these elements to escape from a labyrinth where no truth has ever detained them. The genealogist needs history to dispel the chimeras of the origin, somewhat in the manner of the pious philosopher who needs a doctor to exorcise the shadows of his soul . . . History is the concrete body of a development, with its moments of intensity, its lapses, its extended periods of feverish agitation, its fainting spells; and only a metaphysician would seek its soul in the distant ideality of the origin.[33]

---

[26] Ibid., at 88 ff.   [27] Ibid., at 78 ff.   [28] Ibid., at 82 ff.   [29] Ibid., at 83 ff.

[30] Ibid.   [31] Ibid., at 79 ff.

[32] Ibid., at 88 ff. For further discussion of this aspect of what Mark Poster has dubbed Foucault's 'theoretical asceticism', see Mark Poster, *Critical Theory and Poststructuralism* (1989) 73 ff.

[33] Foucault (n. 25) at 80 ff.

As we transition towards legal history, genealogies of law have become increasingly prevalent, some strongly influenced by Foucault's original mandate, others genealogical only in name.[34] Peter Goodrich's *Oedipus Lex* is helpfully representative of the former.[35] In this study of law's 'rhetorical unconscious', Goodrich insisted on the Foucauldian production of 'histories of the present', histories inevitably caught up in the now as much as the then. Goodrich explained, 'The past can only be deciphered, and the only reason for that decipherment is the interest, pleasure, crisis, or peril of the contemporary . . . Retrospection is a kind of sorcery that imagines, invents, and reinvents those losses that mark survival or that constitute, in its most ancient sense, the image of contemporary identity as person, institution, collectivity, or law.'[36] This much was as true of law as for anything else, in which a legal genealogy turns 'to the multiple images of the broken mirror, to a past that is both fecund and fluid',[37] and provides 'a gently uncomprehending account of the multiple forms of the past'.[38] These historical shards are, as the imagery suggests, plural, complex, contingent, disorderly, dangerous: the broken mirror 'tears apart so as to set one past against another'.[39]

And which pasts? Law's official history, its authentic, traditional life? Nope. 'The genealogical method looks to the plurality of institutional histories and not only to its legitimate forms. Either as supplement or as excess, genealogical method traces equally the various unconscious forms of institutional transmission. It provides a reading of custody and succession, permutation and repetition through the symbols, the icons, idols and failures, the deaths and survivals, the singularities and the repetitions embedded in the *longue durée* of all institutional forms.'[40] As Foucault might have advised, legal genealogies care nothing for origins or continuities of descent. They crave 'the study of the dispersed traditions of common law, its disparate sources and its several languages, its forms of delirium, its imaginary objects. There is, in other words, no real object of legal science but only the phantasm of unity necessary for the maintenance of the profession itself.'[41] And what's more, said Goodrich, legal genealogies, like all genealogies, are made for upending our received understandings; they are made for cutting: 'To analyze the unconscious of law is to read the institution against itself, to read it paradoxically or against its common sense . . . To read the institution against itself is to read the history of institutional repression as a history of incorporations, a pathology of failures, exclusions, losses, traumas, and their symbolic recollection.'[42]

In this deeply postmodern posture, post-structuralist genealogy suggests a history of law that is endlessly dedifferentiated, its boundaries with economics,

---

[34] For discussion, see Ben Golder, 'Contemporary Legal Genealogies', in Justin Desautels-Stein, Christopher Tomlins (eds.), *Searching for Contemporary Legal Thought* (2017).

[35] Peter Goodrich, *Oedipus Lex* (1995).

[36] Ibid., at 20–1 ff.   [37] Ibid., at 25 ff.   [38] Ibid., at 28 ff.   [39] Ibid., at 35 ff.

[40] Ibid., at 25 ff.   [41] Ibid., at 27 ff.   [42] Ibid., at 29–30 ff.

culture, and politics ultimately indiscernible. As Pierre Schlag has remarked, and recalling Latour, the legal world is a world of hybrids. But these hybrids 'are not merely mixed identities. They are identities mixed in such a manner that their different social and legal aspects are inextricably intertwined—both conceptually and ontologically… Not only are the eggs broken, but the omelet has been cooked.'[43] The legal genealogy, as a result, is history of omelettes upon omelettes, a history in which the currents of law and society and economy and culture intermix and interlace.

The historical intermixture of the legal hybrid suggests a revolt against traditional intellectual legal history, and indeed, a work like *Oedipus Lex* is designed for precisely that purpose. The genealogical revolt, however, went only so far.[44] If we consider the dominant mode of American legal historiography in the twentieth century— functionalist historicism—the rebellion seems now to have largely mellowed out. In the main, functionalist historians sought to understand legal change in response to the basic conditions of material life by identifying the essential 'needs' of society and the powerful interests that had a hand in shaping those needs.[45] Functionalist historicism consequently understood law as a sometimes-faithful servant of society. It is only sometimes-faithful in the sense that, when law is functioning properly, it will have identified a relevant basket of social needs or interests, and hence fashioned itself so as to satisfy those needs and interests. When this happens, law in action and law in the books are happily harmonized. But law seems to have a mind of its own, remaining fascinated with rules that have fallen out of step with the real world, the social world law it is meant to serve. In this functionalist historicist version of the law and society perspective, or if you like, a 'law and . . .' sensibility, the role of jurists, including legal historians, was to set law in its proper social context. By the 1980s, functionalist historicism was under assault. In the register of the legal genealogy, functionalist historians were accused of mistaking society's real needs and interests for unavoidably particularized and local preferences about those needs and interests. It was just wrong to think that we could use positivist social science as a means for figuring out law's social ends and the right social contexts in which those ends might be realized.[46]

This postmodern critique was, in many ways, right on target. At the same time, rather than having displaced the 'law and . . .' sensibility of functionalist historicism with a radical alternative, post-structuralist genealogy ended up deepening that sensibility's basic assumptions. The functionalists were keen to explain law's

---

[43] Schlag (n. 15) at 45 ff.

[44] See generally, Christopher Tomlins, 'Historicism and Materiality in Legal Theory', in Maksymillian Del Mar, Michael Lobban (eds.), *Law in Theory and History: New Essays on a Neglected Dialogue* (2016).

[45] See, e.g., Lauren Benton, *Law and Colonial Cultures: Legal Regimes in World History, 1400–1900* (2002).

[46] Peter Gordon, 'Contextualism and Criticism in the History of Ideas', in Darrin McMahon, Samuel Moyn (eds.), *Rethinking Modern European Intellectual History* (2014).

development by way of a context in which law fulfilled some given political or economic function. The post-structuralists countered that these contexts were too hazy, too slippery, that the causal arrows moved in too many conflicting directions to generate anything like a 'true' account of why law did what it did. At the same time, post-structuralists didn't give up on the idea of constructing social contexts for law. It was rather that they now wanted to multiply the contexts, maybe forever, exploring the ultimately unknowable textures and traces of law's dedifferentiated presence. The historical project remained the setting of law in social context, but now in a hybridized context, split in pieces, shattered. Legal genealogies, like functionalist histories, were still in the 'law and . . .' paradigm. Only instead of 'law and . . . society', the mantra became 'law and . . . everything, always already'.

III. STRUCTURALIST LEGAL HISTORY

As functionalist historicism continued to develop in the general atmosphere of post-structuralist genealogy, the future of legal history looked certain. The important questions were now about getting as many contexts as possible into the conversation: an intensely plural, very complex conversation, to be sure. What also seemed certain at the turn of the twenty-first century was that, for whatever legal genealogies might become, they would sympathize with both the postmodern penchant for ground-level hybridity and the postmodern anxiety about deep structure. After all, thinkers like Goodrich and Schlag identified themselves—sometimes at any rate—as *post*-structuralists. Indeed, as the new century rolled in, the idea of structuralist legal history was bearing an especially unwelcome albatross.[47] Legal structuralism seemed out of step with postmodernism altogether, with its apparent inclination for totalizing and universally transcendent explanations for an autonomous *Law*. And to be sure, structuralism didn't seem interested in explaining law's history with reference to particular contexts, such as the lumber industry, the sex industry, or any other that might come to mind. Structuralist history seemed obsessed instead with doctrine, and to that end smacked of an embarrassing kind of history that wasn't really history at all: 'law office history'.[48] What's more, these legal structures seemed to move through time, rising above the fray of human desire and domination. As a result, structuralist legal history appeared to reflect everything

---

[47] For a summary of the story, see Justin Desautels-Stein, *The Jurisprudence of Style: A Structuralist History of American Pragmatism and Liberal Legal Thought* (2018).

[48] For discussion of law office history, see Laura Kalman, 'Border Patrol: Reflections on the Turn to History in Legal Scholarship' (1997) *Fordham L.R.* 87 ff.

that sickened the postmoderns: deep structures, overarching totalities, failures to account for hybrids, true accounts of the real.

The irony is that structuralist historiography is every bit as receptive to the postmodern sensibility as legal genealogy. As I will suggest, structuralist legal history is arguably even *more* receptive. A key difference is one of orientation. For rather than sing along with the siren song of hybrid pastiche, smashing the shards of history into smaller and smaller fragments, structuralist legal history takes these postmodern dissonances and composes a tune of another sort.

As we peer into this second passageway—that of structuralist legal history— once again we find Michel Foucault as a designated greeter. Rather than genealogy, however, the way here is paved with Foucault's less fashionable archaeology.[49] Having taken the pre-given unity of a discipline as a provisional starting point, what happens once we divest the object of its 'natural totality'?[50] Say that the object in question is a so-called discipline, that of political economy. Foucault explained that in performing an archaeological interrogation of that object-discipline, one must characterize in political economy 'the coexistence of these dispersed and heterogeneous statements; the system that governs their division, the degree to which they depend upon one another, the way in which they interlock or exclude one another, the transformation they undergo, and the play of their location, arrangement, and replacement'.[51] In the encounter with these dispersed statements, we look for regularities—what Foucault called a 'discursive formation'—which were themselves conditioned by deep rules formed in a 'preconceptual field'.[52] 'A discursive formation will be individualized if one can define the system of formation of the different strategies that are deployed in it; in other words, if one can show how they all derive (in spite of their sometimes extreme diversity, and in spite of their dispersion in time) from the same set of relations.'[53] But how will these statements and strategies *derive*?

Certain groups of statements put these rules into operation in their most general and most widely applicable form; using them as a starting point, one can see how other objects, other concepts, other enunciative modalities, or other strategic choices may be formed on the basis of rules that are less general and whose domain of application is more specified. One can thus describe a tree of enunciative derivation: at its base are the statements that put into operation rules of formation in their most extended form, at its summit, and after a number of branchings, are the statements that put into operation the same regularity, but one more delicately articulated, more clearly delimited and localized in its extension. Archaeology—and this is one of its principal themes—may thus constitute the tree of derivation of a discourse.[54] Further, 'The conditions to which the elements of this division are subjected we shall call the rules of formation. The rules of formation

---

[49] Michel Foucault, *The Archaeology of Knowledge and the Discourse on Language* (1972).
[50] Michel Foucault, *The Order of Things* (1994) xx ff.   [51] Foucault (n. 49) at 34 ff.
[52] Ibid., at 63 ff.   [53] Ibid., at 68 ff.   [54] Ibid., at 147–8 ff.

are conditions of existence . . . in a given discursive division.'[55] The point is not to demolish 'political economy' merely in order to see if it could be replicated, in order to vindicate empirical presumptions; the question is whether a given unity might be destroyed and then reassembled in order to discover whether there were rules governing what *could* be said in that discipline, and whether and when these rules had been operative.[56] These linguistic rules were hiding in the spaces between statements, the 'what has been said', in the relations that thread them together.[57] 'It is these rules of formation, which were never formulated in their own right, but are to be found only in widely differing theories, concepts, and objects of study, that I have tried to reveal, by isolating, as their specific locus, a level that I have called, somewhat arbitrarily perhaps, archaeological.'[58]

It is these linguistic patterns and regularities that 'make possible the formation of a whole group of various objects . . . One might say, then, that a discursive formation is defined . . . if one can establish such a group; if one can show how any particular object of discourse finds in it its place and law of emergence . . .'[59] The object, Foucault instructs, is instituted through linguistic practices, though not in such a way that they construct the object from the inside out, but rather in such a way that the rules *enable the object to appear*: 'The object does not await in limbo the order that will free it and enable it to become embodied in a visible and prolix objectivity; it does not preexist itself, held back by some obstacle at the first edges of light. It exists under the positive conditions of a complex group of relations.'[60] And finally:

The dispersion itself . . . can be described in its uniqueness if one is able to determine the specific rules in accordance with which its objects, statements, concepts and theoretical options have been formed: if there really is a unity, it does not lie in the visible, horizontal coherence of the elements formed; it resides, well anterior to their formation, in the system that makes possible and governs that formation.[61]

As we transition from Foucault's general archaeology to legal history, we do not see as precise a transposition here as we did with Goodrich and the approach of post-structuralist genealogy. In the initial wave of 1970s and 1980s work produced by structuralists like Roberto Unger, Duncan Kennedy, Gerald Frug, and David Kennedy, Foucault's writings were far less influential than, say, those of Claude Levi-Strauss.[62] Nevertheless, I see Foucault's archaeology as the more useful platform with which to understand the launch of a structuralist legal history. To get it off the ground, let me begin by contrasting the structuralist approach to the problem of context with that of the genealogist. Perhaps surprisingly, structuralist legal history

---

[55] Ibid., at 38 ff.   [56] Ibid., at 48 ff.   [57] Ibid., at 68–9 ff.

[58] Foucault (n. 50) xi ff.   [59] Foucault (n. 49) 44 ff.   [60] Ibid., at 45 ff.

[61] Ibid., at 72 ff.

[62] For a more recent example, see Duncan Kennedy, 'Three Globalizations of Law and Legal Thought', in David Trubek, Alvaro Santos (eds.), *The New Law and Development: A Critical Appraisal* (2006).

is as interested in context as any legal genealogy. However, the context sought out by the structuralists is quite different than Latour and Schlag's dedifferentiated hybrids and much closer to Foucault's discursive formations. What's more, it is not just a different kind of context, it is also that legal structuralists use context for a different purpose. As Robert Gordon explained the goal of post-structualist history:

A strong antifunctionalist, antideterminist critique tends to dissolve the history of any social phenomenon into simply thick description, skeptical alike of grand narratives and indeed any accounts of causation. It is all very contingent, all very complicated. To the extent this does happen, it is a mixed blessing. It is the job of history—is it not?—to mess up and complicate the generalizing social sciences' models of how the world works with evidence that in one place or another actual developments skipped a stage in a model or went through the stages in reverse or bypassed the stages altogether.[63]

And as Goodrich has suggested in a different register, 'The ornaments, symbols, and images of law, in this instance the figures of the legal text, indicate those slips or unconscious motives that allow for the reconstruction of an "other scene" of legal judgement. That other scene is that of the unconscious, of repressed desires and internalized prohibitions, of the affects and identifications that constitute reason and institute law, as visibility, as affect, as text.'[64] What Gordon and Goodrich together are suggesting is that in the post-structuralist posture, a legal historian's job is to crawl the world over, pulling on those threads that have conventionally united our mythological visions of law's place in society, pulling on those threads, wherever they lead, until we just can't pull any longer.

Which brings us to the contrasting image of the structuralist's preferred context for situating law. That context is a *legal* context. That's right, the structuralist seeks to understand 'law' in a 'legal context'. This odd locution might seem to implicate one of two possibilities, but neither is what I have in mind. The first wrong turn is towards so-called doctrinal history. This is a history in search of the evolution of legal rules, paying attention to how those rules have changed over time. A second unintended possibility for 'legal context' would look for something like a traditional 'philosophy of history', wherein the historian seeks out basic questions about the nature of law and how that nature was conceived differently at various moments in time. For the structuralist, and following Foucault's archaeological gestures, the identification of a legal context entails the identification of a particular mode of legal thought.[65] Legal thought refers to the language of legal argument—the moves, techniques, and styles jurists use in the process of putting legal rules into action,

---

[63] Robert Gordon, 'Critical Legal Histories Revisited: A Response' (2012) *Law and Social Inquiry* 200, 212 ff.

[64] Goodrich (n. 35) at 220 ff.

[65] As I have suggested at length elsewhere, I think that the best understanding of structuralist legal history involves a discussion of Foucault, but requires more. We also need sizable doses of Duncan Kennedy, Roberto Unger, Ferdinand de Saussure, Maurice Merleau-Ponty, and Roland Barthes, among other things. See Desautels-Stein (n. 47).

giving the rules momentum, and when done successfully, giving the rules a gloss of necessity. To put the point another way, when the structuralist historian constructs a mode of legal thought, she is (re)constructing a legal grammar, a layer in the legal structure that is operationally distinct from law's 'rules'. The realm of doctrine, of course, is relevant to legal thought. But rather than focus solely on the content of rules, the structuralist historian's attention to legal thought directs us to the ways in which jurists put the rules into legal arguments.

Understanding legal thought as an elaborate and complex legal context reflects a powerful historiographic shift. Legal thought refers to the grammatical structure of background practices that constitute a legal language. It refers to the mechanics of legal style: the patterns of argumentative practice. It refers to the lexical terrain of technical knowledge immanent in legal concepts, what we might otherwise call rules or 'doctrines'. The legal context of legal thought is about all of this: the structure's basic grammar, its argumentative style, and its lexicon. Consequently, while a structuralist history of legal thought *is* about legal concepts (the language's lexicon), a concept's rules are not the end but only the beginning of the story. Rather than focus solely on the content of rules, or on the settled state of those rules as the aim of the pursuit, structuralist legal history uses the legal concept as an open invitation for exploring the history of legal thought. Thus, while the structuralist places doctrine in context, she doesn't put them in anything that looks like a familiar historical context: political, economic, cultural, etc. She puts doctrine in the historical context of legal thought.

If we follow Foucault's example of political economy, a structuralist legal history of political economy begins with political economy's legal context, and the search for legal context begins with a lexicon, the terrain of legal concepts.[66] But which concept? In the context of liberal legal thought, for example, we know to consider property and contract as provisional starting points. Saying as much, however, doesn't get us very far, as these so-called 'bodies of law' are disciplinary fields that need demolishing. As the demolition begins, what comes into view is a veritable sea of legal concepts, pieces of technical knowledge strewn about in a litter of rules. Now, it hardly makes sense to assume that every legal field will present its lexicon in the same way; at least there is no reason to assume as much. But when we come to the lexical sea of 'property law', with its concepts of trespass, nuisance, estates, trusts, servitudes, and so on, we confront a list of open-ended choices, and very little in the way of 'settled' doctrines. For most of us, an encounter with an open-ended list of contrasting technical rules is a little (or a lot) unpleasant. The experience, we might say, is one of dissonance. Presented as a series of technical choices emphasizing tension without resolution, fragmentation without harmony, with few markers of

---

[66] Reinhart Koselleck's conceptual history is helpful example for how to think about legal concepts as an open-ended lexicon of technical knowledge. Reinhart Koselleck, *The Practice of Conceptual History* (2002).

majority and minority rule, and little sense of a settled terrain, legal concepts seem muddled, confused, and demanding coherence.

Most of the time, a collection of rules in the context of some legal concept aims at reconciliation and the *settling* of the law in terms of predictable expectations. This want, certainly seductive, is the want of the shortcut. This is the want of a *settled* law, not a legal concept so split down the middle that we're forced to choose between competing justifications, any of which might be supportable in an appropriate context. This unsettled feeling, as experienced in the exemplary case of servitudes, as some commentators have suggested, 'is a little like diving into a swamp at night, swimming and floundering in terror, and emerging quite fortuitously on some unknown shore in the morning. When it is all over you're sorry that it happened, you don't understand anything you saw but you know that you didn't like it, and you are extremely grateful that you blundered out'.[67] My suspicion is that our sorry experiences with legal concepts like that of servitude has much to do with our unfulfilled desires for reification and shortcuts. That is, the reason we experience the concept as a 'mess' has everything to do with what we think a legal concept is supposed to look like—settled, coherent, predictable. What we want is a rule of law ideal that functions independently of judicial discretion, and not an open invitation for judges to simply choose between competing justifications. What's worse, so this line of reasoning goes, we can promulgate lists of conflicting rule-pairs for many legal concepts, perhaps a majority of them, and so while the rules of servitudes might appear especially swampish, once we start looking closely we find the swamp to cover a great deal of American law. In the end, we should avoid this road altogether, since what we find at its end is the uncomfortable conclusion that law is simply politics by another name. In order to stave off such nihilism, the argument is to look as best we can for coherence and predictability, for the settling of a harmonious law.

I think that these points are mistaken. It is a mistake, first, to think that a confrontation with the tensions immanent in a legal concept must yield to the postmodern conclusion that law is just politics, a predetermined and dedifferentiated hybrid. But it is also a mistake to think that the way to immunize the legal profession from nihilism is to search out for reifications and shortcuts in order to generate the impression of settled law. And so, one might wonder, if the structuralist emphasis on the indeterminacy of legal concepts isn't intended to illuminate the politics of law—as the genealogy aims to do—what is its purpose? Rather than on the one hand attempt to settle the law and make the rules cohere is some 'reasonable' way, or on the other hand bask in the hybridization of law and politics and everything else, the structuralist historian focuses on the way judges, lawyers, and legal academics *use* those conflicting rules. Forget for the moment about trying to reconcile the

[67] Sheldon Kurtz and Herbert Hovenkamp, *Cases and Materials on American Property Law* (1987) 608 ff.

rules or multiplying the contexts. Ask instead: are there patterns of argument in the professional practice of the jurist? Is there a deep structure governing the formal aspects of our styles of practice?

As the structuralist looks closer, she finds that the sense in which a given legal concept appears to a jurist depends on that jurist's training. Coming back to the example of the servitude for a moment, many jurists are likely amateurs in the context of building arguments out of its lexicon. And if the jurist is an amateur, the law of servitudes appears as a menu of indeterminate and technical rules. The business of concluding for one rule over another, and fashioning that conclusion in way that looks legally necessitated, will be challenging. If, on the other hand, the jurist is a master, the lexicon manifests quite differently. Rather than flinch in the bracing dissonance, the experienced jurist moves fluidly, flowing from background practice oh-so-easily into a neutral and natural conclusion. Certain elements in the lexicon will draw the jurist, others recede. Certain choices will sing out as majority rules, others will fall away as exceptions. And as the master jurist, that jurist trained in the rituals and techniques of legal argument, finds a source of momentum carrying him from the facts, into the technical space of the concept, and out into a conclusion, he practices a certain *style*.[68]

This master jurist is the real target of structuralist legal history.[69] The master jurist's practice of legal argument comes so naturally that a great deal of the conceptual indeterminacy—the raw fact of ideological choice—very rarely comes into conscious view. It is not that this master jurist is unthinking, a simpleton on autopilot. It is rather that, in his juridical expertise he has become so utterly familiar with the lexicon that the lexicon draws him in certain directions just as the 'lines of force' operating on a soccer field draw the player through the game.[70] For the master jurist, in other words, a substantial amount of the argumentative work is in the background. Only when there is a glitch, a novel legal question requiring unfamiliar answers, does the argument enter a rational foreground, surfacing the conceptual dissonance.[71]

This is the point at which structuralist legal history comes, interrogating the jurist's background practices and asking whether, when, and why these practices recur. If they do, perhaps we have happened upon a legal style, and perhaps in turn we compose a legal grammar that figures in from the background. Structuralist legal history is therefore an orchestration of the various styles manifested by

---

[68] The history of legal style has something in common with what Hayden White calls the 'tropics of discourse', the figures, tropes, and grooves in a language-system's terrain, 'linking' *langue* and *parole*. See Hayden White, *Tropics of Discourse: Essays in Cultural Criticism* (1978) 72 ff.

[69] And it is here that the structuralist turns to case law, not for statements of the rule but for examples of argumentative practice. See, e.g., *Neponsit Property Owners Association v. Emigrant Industrial Savings Bank* (1938) 278 N.Y. 248; *Eagle Enterprises v. Gross*, (1976) 349 N.E. 2d 816.

[70] Maurice Merleau-Ponty, *The Structure of Behavior* (1963) 168–9 ff.

[71] For discussion, see Hubert Dreyfus and Charles Taylor, *Retrieving Realism* (2015) 52 ff.

different jurists at different moments in time. It is not a composition of the rules, situated in some non-legal context. It is a composition of the rules situated in the legal context of legal thought, or, if you like, the context of what it means to think like a lawyer. And, as it turns out, these styles change over time. Structuralist legal history explores the historical structure of these styles, in their basic grammar and lexical comportment, and how they transform in the lexical context of various legal concepts.

If this blend of semiotics and phenomenology is suggestive of the structuralist approach to legal historiography, what is especially postmodern about it? And why, as I suggested, must the structuralist pass through a *post-structuralist* experience along the way? As suggested in the review of Foucault's writings, structuralist legal history works out accounts of the past in the language of totality and the grand narrative, rejecting the postmodern predilection for a plurality of contexts, revelling in the pastiche and the hybrid. But if the structuralist's account of legal thought, with its grammars, lexicons, and styles, seems out of step with the postmodern pastiche, how can it at the same time be a postmodern sensibility?

The trick is to separate out postmodernism's negative orientations from its positive directions.[72] Post-structuralist genealogy, for example, heeds the post-modern anxiety about essentializing a historical narrative or a conceptual totality, and rightly so. It is a mistake to see in these narratives and totalities a fixed set of arrangements existing outside of time. If we place our faith in a select set of historical arrangements and believe that, for better or worse, they enslave the social world, we have made the mistake of mystification, of reification, of naturalization, or in a word, of underestimating the reality of time. For if time is for real, everything changes, including those narratives and totalities that may seem to endure through time and space. The spirit of postmodernism accepts this view of real time, rejecting totalities and narratives because of their seemingly a-historical character. Contingency, complexity, particularity, plurality—these are the call-signs of a postmodernism out to undermine the view that the world might *really* be governed by permanent structures marching through history. The past cannot control the future, if everything truly transforms sooner or later. Post-structuralist genealogy takes these cues and runs with them. And as they run, they find themselves with a view of history as hybrid and pastiche, and a role for historians as wrecking-crew.

Structuralist historians believe that the genealogists give us one way of making good on the postmodern understanding of contingent time. But they also believe that it isn't the only way; maybe not even the 'best' way. The reason for this parting, this splitting between a postmodern sensibility about the reality of time—which the structuralist shares—and a post-structuralist direction for historiography—which

---

[72] The remainder of the discussion draws heavily on Roberto Unger, *The Self Awakened: Pragmatism Unbound* (2009); Roberto Unger and Lee Smolin, *The Singular Universe and the Reality of Time: A Proposal in Natural Philosophy* (2014).

the structuralist rejects—is that structuralist historians view hybrids and the pastiche of the present as invitations for structural combination, constellation, and composition, not ends in themselves.[73] What's more, structuralists understand this inclination to explore the depths of structure and the climes of higher-order proposals as entirely in line with the postmodern understanding of time. If time is for real, meaning, if the reality of time demands a recognition that everything changes, discontinuously and at various speeds, then it is a mistake to reject structural explanations. The discovery of contingency and plurality and hybrids and all the rest does not lead to the conclusion that the only way to think about history is as a flat and depthless stream of indeterminate figures in an everlasting present. In fact, this conclusion flies in the face of the postmodern worry about time. If time is for real, then there can never be an 'only way' to think about history. It is to absorb the postmodern concern *incompletely*, if we believe a genealogy to be the only way of making good on contingency and complexity. If time is truly contingent, really *real*, then structural explanations can prove as edifying as anything else. Perhaps even more.

Nevertheless, structuralist legal history faces a danger, and that is making the mistake of past social theory: identifying deep social structures that embody a closed set of permanent arrangements for politics, society, and the economy; a set of arrangements that while socially constructed are conceived as indivisible systems beyond our ability to transform them. What structuralist legal history learns from genealogy is the terror of confusing deep structure and higher-order proposals with essentialized manifestations of the true. In order to avoid these mistaken theories of structure, structuralist legal history must experience the terror first-hand. It's no joke: the realization that time is for real and that everything changes, must inoculate the structuralist from mistaking her structural composition for a statement of facts, standing outside of time. This is the way in which we can gain structuralist insight and avoid structural dogma; seek out the grammars and styles in the history of legal thought, all the while very much alive to the mantra that time is for real and that there can be nothing natural, neutral, or necessary about these structures of legal thought.

Structuralist legal history parts from post-structuralist genealogy in another, related way. As we have seen, legal genealogies often follow Foucault's framing of a 'history of the present'.[74] Once again, the focus on the present might seem like a logical corollary of the postmodern view of time. If we find ourselves eternally sceptical about historical totalities and grand narratives, both past and future

---

[73] For further discussion, see Justin Desautels-Stein and Christopher Tomlins, 'Afterword', in Justin Desautels-Stein and Christopher Tomlins, *Searching for Contemporary Legal Thought* (2017).

[74] For a recent attempt to situate a preoccupation with the historical present as against the postmodern, see Ranjan Gosh, Ethan Kleinberg (eds.), *Presence: Philosophy, History, and Cultural Theory for the Twenty-First Century* (2013).

seem ready to collapse in an interminable now. It is always, on this view, *now*. It is real, and it is complicated, and it is everywhere. But structuralist legal history takes the postmodern view of time in a different direction. In structuralist legal history, the composition of legal thought forms around a more committed view of the reality of time. In this view, a fixation on the present mystifies both the process in which structures transform, and the powers of individuals to participate in structural transformation. For the structuralist historian, time never languishes in an everlasting present, but rather flows in a fluid stream of cessation to becoming. Or, in other words, to understand a structure of legal thought we must see it in time; we must see what it is ceasing to be and what it might become, we must see its social discontinuities in the continuity of real time. The genealogist's *now* fails to capture and understand this process of ceasing to be and coming into being. If we fail to understand the structure in its grammar, its style, and its lexicon, both what it has ceased to be, and what it has not yet become, then we do not yet have an image of the structure in the reality of time. If we fail to understand how a structure transforms, from what it was into what it might be, we have failed the postmodern criterion of temporal contingency. It is for this reason that Roberto Unger ends his book *What Should Legal Analysis Become?* with the following:

Our interests and ideals remain nailed to the cross of our arrangements. We cannot realize our interests and ideals more fully, nor redefine them more deeply, until we have learned to remake and reimagine our arrangements more freely. History will not give us this freedom. We must win it in the here and now of legal detail, economic constraint, and deadening preconception. We shall not win it if we continue to profess a science of society reducing the possible to the actual and a discourse about law anointing power with piety. *It is true that we cannot become visionaries until we become realists. It is also true that to become realists we must make ourselves into visionaries.*[75]

To sum up, both post-structuralist genealogy and structuralist legal history are receptive to the postmodern suggestions I outlined at the first. But whereas post-structuralist historicism understands the postmodern view of time in a hybridized legal world of pastiche and presence, structuralist legal history understands the 'reality of time' differently. Rather than reject the elaboration of structural orchestration outright as a sacrilege, structuralism constructs historical totalities and narratives right in the middle of genealogical carnage. It is in the carnage that the structuralist develops structural insight, higher order proposals for social transformation, and totalities and narratives that edify our experience while escaping the accusation of dogma. It protects itself from the danger of dogma by hewing close to the postmodern view of the reality of time: everything changes, always. Structures never reflect sets of institutional arrangements that might exist outside of time, ways in which society just *is* or just *has to be*. Structures always exist

---

[75] Roberto Unger, *What Should Legal Analysis Become?* (1996) 189–90 ff.

in a temporal naturalism, rendering them contingent, always changing. Of course, the pace of change depends on much—sometimes structural transformation is very slow. How can we speed it up? How can structural transformation accelerate? A beginning is to look for and understand the grammars and styles of legal thought, what they have been, and what they might become. For if we cannot see what the structure of practice might come to be, if these imaginative possibilities remain mystified, structural transformation remains ever more difficult, and our present circumstances ever more frozen.

Bibliography

Roland Barthes, *Critical Essays* (Northwestern University Press, 1972)

Justin Desautels-Stein, *The Jurisprudence of Style: A Structuralist History of American Pragmatism and Liberal Legal Thought* (Cambridge University Press, 2018)

Hubert Dreyfus, Charles Taylor, *Retrieving Realism* (Harvard University Press, 2015)

Michel Foucault, *The Order of Things* (Routledge, 1994)

Michel Foucault, *Archaeology of Knowledge* (Pantheon, 1972)

Michel Foucault, 'Nietzsche, Genealogy, History', in Paul Rabinow (ed.), *The Foucault Reader* (Pantheon, 1984)

Fredric Jameson, *Postmodernism, or, the Cultural Logic of Late Capitalism* (Duke University Press, 1992)

Colin Koopman, *Genealogy as Critique: Foucault and the Problems of Modernity* (Indiana University Press, 2013)

Duncan Kennedy, *Legal Reasoning: Collected Essays* (Davies Group, 2008)

Duncan Kennedy, 'Three Globalizations in Law and Legal Thought', in David Trubek, Alvaro Santos, (eds.), *The New Law and Development: A Critical Appraisal* (Cambridge University Press, 2006)

Philip Lewis, 'The Post-Structuralist Condition' (1982) 12 *Diacritics* 2

Christopher Tomlins, 'Towards a Materialist Jurisprudence', in Daniel Hamilton, Alfred Brophy (eds.), *Transformations in American Legal History II: Law, Ideology, and Methods—Essays in Honor of Morton J. Horwitz* (Harvard Law School, 2011)

Roberto Unger, *What Should Legal Analysis Become?* (Verso, 1996)

Roberto Unger, *The Self Awakened: Pragmatism Unbound* (Harvard University Press, 2009)

Roberto Unger, *The Critical Legal Studies Movement: Another Time, A Greater Task* (Verso, 2015)

Roberto Unger, Lee Smolin, *The Singular Universe and the Reality of Time: A Proposal in Natural Philosophy* (Cambridge University Press, 2014)

CHAPTER 30

....

SEZ WHO? CRITICAL LEGAL HISTORY WITHOUT A PRIVILEGED POSITION

....

JOHN HENRY SCHLEGEL*

> No more than they can we suppress
> The universal wish to guess
> Or slip out of our own position
> Into an unconcerned condition.
> *Law Like Love*
>
> W. H. Auden

BACK around the turn of this century when Chris Tomlins was working on the British colonization of North America, I happened to read a draft of some part of this wonderful work dealing with the language used by and about the colonizers. After reading Chris' critique all of the talk about helping the savages by bringing them Christianity and denigrating them for their uncivilized behaviour, I emailed him with a question something like, 'Can you name a conquering civilization that lamented its colonization, and so destruction, of a more advanced, more noble civilization?' Trick question, I suppose. He shot back a not-quite-so brusque version

* Thanks to Michael, Barry, Dan, Laura, and Fred for their help and my friends at the University of Virginia Law School's legal history colloquium for reading and commenting on an earlier draft.

of, 'No.' To which I immediately replied to the effect of, 'If such behaviour is so ordinary, then why are you being so hard on this group of colonizers?' His response was typical in its directness. He stated something along the lines of, 'But, if I have to accept the ordinariness of this attitude, then I can't make my argument!'

Sensibly, Chris ignored my criticism, and we are all better for his having done so, since his argument was a good one—that the bedrock of the American experience was violence towards others and not the oft-trumpeted search for freedom.[1] Still, this brief exchange has haunted me ever since, for it pointed at a problem that at the time I only inchoately perceived about the work of my friends, the scholars involved in Critical Legal Studies (CLS), a problem with the way that we treated our critiques as complete when we finished, as the last thing that could be said on the subject. Now the odd thing about this problem was that the targets of our critique seemed to agree with us. They acted as if disproving our assertions was the only way to deal with our critique. It seldom seemed that in response they considered mounting a critique of our own set of foundational assumptions. This too was puzzling.

Now it is important here to remember that Chris is a partisan of critique, but in no sense a member, or even a fellow traveller, of Critical Legal Studies. So, I tell this little story because it clearly and cleanly sets up a problem with CLS history, however fine such work is, and it is fine. How was it not a problem for us that we did not critique our own set of assumptions as best as we could? How could it not be the case that we too owned and suppressed a set of debatable groundings on which we based our argument? How was it that we claimed a position outside of history and interest at the same time that we were objecting to the assumption of such a position on the part of others? It is this question that I wish to examine.

Of course, like so many things, it all started with Willard Hurst. When he strongly asserted the functionalism of law there were bound to be objectors somewhere. Whether Hurst meant 'necessarily' functional I rather doubt. His notion of the 'bastard pragmatism' that he saw at the root of much law, suggests that he saw functionalism as tied to reason in some way that distinguished it from narrow interest. One might put his understanding as something along the line that law is functional in the same way that, in the absence of a hammer, a crescent wrench will do to pound a nail into soft pine. This may be a way to get the job done, but in the end not a very good way, as anyone who has examined my attempts at home repairs would conclude.

CLS is one place where the objectors appeared; Bob Gordon,[2] Morty Horwitz,[3] and Mark Tushnet[4] led the affray. In some ways Willard was a strange target. He was anything but a consensus historian.[5] And he too objected to the Vietnam War,

---

[1] *Freedom Bound: Law, Labor, and Civic Identity in Colonizing English America, 1580–1865* (2010).

[2] 'James Willard Hurst and the Common Law Tradition in American Legal Historiography' (1975) 10 *Law and Society R.* 9 ff.

[3] Or at least so I remember, though I admit I cannot find an appropriate citation.

[4] 'Lumber and the Legal Process' 1972 *Wisconsin L.R.* 124 ff.

[5] Avi Soifer makes this as clear as possible: 'Willard Hurst, Consensus History and the Growth of American Law' (1992) 20 *Reviews in American History* 124 ff.

the truncation of Civil Rights achievements, the crippling of organized labour, objections that for the most part were common to CLS partisans. But he was a partisan of the Brandeisian Progressive, New Dealer type, and we were not. He had faith in reason and in the ability of facts to shape its use, but an abhorrence of the ordinary uses of reason to justify private interest. While we shared his abhorrence, we did not share either of his faiths, or at least sort of did not. In the end the fight over functionalism amounted to nothing, but what it spawned was important. Critique, even Roberto Unger's 'Total Critique', in Webster's words 'the examination . . . of a thing or situation . . . with a view to determining its nature or limitations', was to be the major intellectual approach for CLS scholars, even the historians.

In the academic world of the North Atlantic, the invocation of critique ties any activity to Kant's Critiques, and on the left to the work of the Frankfurt School, but more importantly to the idea of reason as a standing aside from the object of critique, a standing in a (privileged) place, distanced from the object, setting it apart so as to permit seeing the object in its true nature. This is, of course, also the position of the liberal narrative of law that was the object of the CLS critique (and of Tomlins's critique as well). For CLS scholars, the claim of 'liberal legalism' that while small bits of law might need fixing, the great structure was fundamentally sound, was shot through with unexamined preferences for some citizens and not others, in particular preferences that established the otherness of these persons—non-whites, women, labourers. Such preferences betrayed the falsity of the cognate claim that our liberal democracy was founded on the equality of its citizens.

The CLS critique of law was extremely effective in the 1980s, so effective that it brought forth more than a bit of moral panic on the part of liberal legalist scholars, particularly those of a more politically conservative stripe. Still, as the 1980s turned into the 1990s the relevant question turned from the nature of liberal legalism to what had happened to CLS: why had it faded away? Feminist Jurisprudence and Critical Race Theory took centre stage with their separate, but parallel, assertions that personal experience grounded their critiques, maybe even supplanted reason as a grounding for critique. By then almost no one remembered the scholarship of Art Leff. His devastating takedowns of both Richard Posner[6] and Roberto Unger[7] were mostly forgotten, as was his assertion that there can be no such a thing as a grounding for law or morals other than one based on a belief in God.[8] Indeed, by then it was becoming clear that in the case of International Human Rights, a pure, even primitive, positivism provided a sufficient grounding for legal action.

At the same time that these events were taking place, the American reception of the great theoretical hubbub, often emanating from France, that began with Thomas

---

[6] Arthur Leff, 'Economic Analysis of the Law: Some Realism about Nominalism' (1974) 60 *Virginia L.R.* 451 ff.

[7] Arthur Leff, 'Book Review: Knowledge and Politics' (1977) 29 *Stanford L.R.* 879 ff.

[8] Arthur Leff, 'Law and Technology: On Shoring Up a Void' (1976) *Ottawa L.R.* 536 ff; Arthur Leff, 'Unspeakable Ethics, Unnatural Law' 1979 *Duke L.J.* 1229 ff.

Kuhn's *The Structure of Scientific Revolutions*[9] and Paul Feyerabend's *Against Method*,[10] the rediscovery of Ludwig Wittgenstein's *Philosophical Investigations*,[11] and then Richard Rorty's *Philosophy and the Mirror of Nature*,[12] quieted down. Seemingly forgotten was work by Gramsci, Lukcas, and Althusser, among the various Marxisms; the Structuralism of Levi-Strauss, Saussure, and Barthes; the Deconstruction of Derrida; the Post-Structuralism of Foucault and Deleuze; a good dose of Literary Theory from the likes Eagleton and Fish; the Critical Theory of the Frankfurt School and Habermas; remnants of the Existentialism of Kierkegaard, Sartre, Buber, and Heidegger; Merleau-Ponty's Phenomenology; Clifford Geertz's anthropology of 'thick description', and especially for the historians, E. P. Thompson's *The Making of the English Working Class*[13] and *Whigs and Hunters: The Origin of the Black Act*,[14] as well as the essays in *Albion's Fatal Tree*.[15] Much of this work, though clearly not that of the historians, suggested, as had Leff, that the grounding of reason was, if not impossible, at least very, very hard.

In retrospect, the surprising thing about this 1990s' quietude is not the fact itself; academia fashion changes, though usually less frequently than couturier fashion, but rather that the theoretical hubbub going on while CLS was in its heyday seemed to have had little impact on CLS scholarship. We never questioned the grounding of our own work, which often littered its star footnote with citations to, or at least wave-of-the-hand mentions of, this heterogeneous body of once fashionable work. As best as I can remember, we believed that by adopting critique and turning that method on its liberal legalist practitioners, we did not have to confront the question of grounding, in retrospect a confusion of method—lever—with grounding—a place to stand—in our attempt to move legal scholarship and teaching, a proper Archimedean understanding of our job.

Which is not to say the fancy academic theorists questioned their own work either. Most everyone seemed to go along unself-reflexively, secure in his or her understanding that at least his or her scholarship was securely grounded, even if everyone else's wasn't. Such is, of course, a preposterous position, for much of the relevant fancy academic or CLS scholarship implicitly, and often explicitly, asserted that the thought and action that was the subject of critique was not just suffering from ignorance of the true facts, but rather that it all but intentionally hid the truth, or at the very best constructed an argument that obscured the politically loaded valence of the thought or action in question, and so elided the truth, a truth known, not empirically, but by the exercise of reason.

Thirty years ago, in the waning days of CLS, it seemed to me that the implicit problem of the grounding of truth could be solved locutionarily. In an essay review of a fine piece of intellectual history,[16] I reasoned as follows:

---

[9] (1970).   [10] (1975).   [11] (1968).   [12] (1979).   [13] (1963).
[14] (1975).   [15] (1975).   [16] Laura Kalman, *Legal Realism at Yale* (1986).

If there is no epistemologically privileged position, then I cannot know that intellectual history is better written in the fullness of such social context as one can muster. But by the same token, I am not limited to mere belief, as the notion of belief is parasitic on the notion of knowledge. Well, if I cannot know and am not limited to belief, then I guess that I am sure that I am right. At least I have given my best arguments. If you are not persuaded, try some arguments of your own. In the alternative, there is always thumb wrestling.[17]

As I look back, this reasoning was for me, generally a pessimist, a surprisingly optimistic assessment, as well as notably self-contradictory, for it invoked both a post-modern legal scholarship that mostly never happened in law and a modern legal scholarship that ignored the problem of grounding, of privileging a position, except when it revelled in occupying such. In such a circumstance, giving one's best arguments simply will not do. One needs to put those arguments under serious pressure, not wait for someone else to do the job. CLS historical work almost never put its arguments under any pressure. However, it seems to me that to the extent that our work can survive serious pressure, that work will be strengthened. What follows is a modest attempt to begin to undertake such a task, if only in a narrow area.

It would be easy to make my point by focusing on other than the best work. However, doing so would undermine my own argument by producing a cognate of the kind of work I am criticizing. Instead, I have chosen to look at the labour history written by CLS scholars because it is both the largest body of CLS historical work— and work of an especially high quality. Moreover, friends and acquaintances have written much of this work. They have taught me most of what I know about labour history and in many cases have helped me with the corresponding industrial history that is more central to my interests. Their work is worthy of my efforts. Indeed, sensible people might suggest that I am fatally overmatched.

I wish to start with a piece by Karl Klare about the work of the Supreme Court in the late 1930s, *Judicial Deradicalization of the Wagner Act and the Origins of Modern Legal Consciousness, 1937–1941*.[18] The piece began with the altogether defensible assertion that the Wagner or National Labor Relations Act's often vague language allowed for multiple possible interpretations of its provisions. It then turned to several Supreme Court decisions that contributed significantly to the tone of post-war labour law. These decisions emphasized the centrality of labour peace such as would ensure continuing industrial production by instituting a contractual regime that would channel worker grievances into a labour-management structure that focused bargaining on wages, hours, and benefits and so preserved management prerogatives over the organization of the production process. Throughout, the piece contrasted this understanding of the Act with one that might have treated democratic participation in the production process as central, an understanding that might have reduced, if not eliminated, the alienation of workers from their

---

[17] (1989) 'The Ten Thousand Dollar Question' 41 *Stanford L.R.* 435, 467 ff.
[18] (1978) 62 *Minnesota L.R.* 265 ff.

work by de-emphasizing the importance of the contractual agreement between union and management.

A CLS detractor might explain all of these decisions by pointing out that the sit down strikes in the pursuit of union goals that occurred in these years created a reasonable fear of union disruption of production. But given the amount of management disruption of workers' lives over the previous 150 years, such an explanation is hardly worth a mention, even if accompanied by the modestly rational fear of communist infiltration in the union movement. Another possible justification of these decisions, founded on the necessity for a clean demarcation of the working class from the management class, is equally unsatisfactory for similar reasons. After all, the owners and managers of industrial enterprises regularly unsettled the lives of labourers over the same period of time. Disruption of a status quo simply won't cut it. Nor is there any reason to believe that the union movement so respected chief Justice Hughes that anything he would have written for the Court would have been a sufficient justification for these decisions. However, there is a possible, if ultimately limited, justification in the nature of the American economy in the early twentieth century that surely deserved to be taken into account by CLS scholars. Still, to understand what that justification is would require knowing some of the history of that economy at least back to the Gilded Age, if not earlier.

Start with a basic truism. Real competition sucks! Operating at the point where marginal cost (including the marginal cost of capital) equals marginal revenue is damn scary. Bankruptcy is uncomfortably close. The same is even clearer for labour. The place where the last ounce of effort equals the last cent in wages puts abject poverty, if not starvation, uncomfortably close. Now, of course, as consumers, labour prefers goods sold at marginal cost and as consumers, capital prefers wages set at marginal cost, but that is not to say that the structural similarity of these positions with respect to competition suggests a real-world similarity of situations. Corporate bankruptcy does not imply the starvation that may follow from the loss of a job; after all, resource endowments of capital and labour are radically different, otherwise labour would, or at least might, draw on resources and simply reinvest, as capital has done. Still, neither capital nor labour likes living in a competitive market; both have every reason to wish to escape it. They have long tried to do so.

Before the First World War big capital attempted to overcome competition by the merger of competitors to the point that the market sway of one participant was such as to create an effective monopoly, or at least to protect all of the other participants in the dominant firm's shadow. Eventually the Supreme Court made this difficult. Labour tried unionization. Here, even after securing legislation in its favour, the lower federal courts similarly managed to make unionization difficult by enjoining strikes on various grounds. Neither capital nor labour was happy with the result. Still, even more unhappy was small and medium-sized capital, the far more numerous local retailers, wholesalers, and manufacturers, who were finding that their relative, transportation-cost-based insulation from local competition was being eroded by the growth of big capital.

For a brief time during the Great War, The National War Labor Board tried to impose a set of policies that bore an astonishing resemblance to what became the Wagner Act—policies that clearly reflected a distaste for competition. After that war was over big capital seems to have started trying to limit competition through oligopolistic structures, though it was still extraordinarily worried about the possibility that unionized labour would upset such fragile structures. Medium and small capital, generally more dispersed geographically, tried to create similar structures through the mechanism of establishing business associations, such as the Maple Flooring Manufacturers Association, but retailers and wholesalers still felt left out.

These actions seem to have taken place in tandem with the ideas of a group of economists, called Institutionalists, who started writing before the Great War. They believed that economic instability was the result of excess production of goods and services, coupled with relentless downward pressure on producer prices caused by 'chisellers' who reduced prices and otherwise 'cut corners' for temporary personal advantage. These economists argued that downward pressure on prices could be resisted if producers banded together into groups that would work both to 'coordinate' production (i.e., manage reduction and expansion) and to isolate and vilify chisellers, so as to enforce good—and thereby suppress 'unfair'—trade practices. Their ideas coalesced into a theory called Associationalism.

This theory was essentially a Main Street, though not therefore a small town, theory. It hoped to maintain high wages through the high prices that would support small, local retail or wholesale businesses. It was not *laissez-faire* in a different guise, for it assumed some level of governmental involvement in the economy to remedy insufficient demand in poor times by increasing, not decreasing, employment and by providing social insurance so as to maintain the disposable income of wage earners faced with unemployment or retirement. Which is not to say that as a general matter either capital or labour supported the whole package, but it was a package that attracted some progressives in the years after the First World War and that obviously informed much New Deal legislation, both that found constitutional and that found unconstitutional.

It is also true that these ideas are redolent of Spanish, Italian, and German corporatism that turned Fascist in the mid-1930s. However, at the same time it is possible that such ideas were attractive on their own as a way of mediating between the claims of capital and labour, granting capital some protection from sudden bankruptcy and labour some protection from declining income. It is not hard to see Associationalism as implying exactly what happened, a law that recognized the centrality of labour peace such as would ensure continuing industrial production under a contractual regime that would channel worker grievances into a labour-management structure that focused bargaining on wages, hours, and benefits and so preserve management prerogatives over the organization of the production process.

In order to effectively criticize this regime it is not enough to say that from the perspective of radical labour it denied workers their rights to self-determination in structuring their employment and the production process, any more than it is enough to say that from the perspective of radical capital it would be sufficient to criticize this regime for failing to allow capital to exclude labour from any role in structuring the terms and conditions of employment. One would at least need to recognize that in these years competition had been experienced as sufficiently inimical to the interests of both capital and labour so that both had reason to dampen it.[19] The desire to limit competition might well explain the choices that the Supreme Court made in the early years of interpreting the Wagner Act.

Next consider a piece about a much earlier period in American labour history, Wythe Holt's *Labor Conspiracy Cases in the United States, 1805–1842: Bias and Legitimation in Common Law Adjudication*.[20] The piece examined all the reported early nineteenth-century cases in which unions of journeymen were charged with common law criminal conspiracy for evidence of anti-union bias. These years experienced a continuing breakdown of the once traditional relationship of the irregular, but shared, work schedule of masters and journeymen in urban areas in both the clothing and shoemaking trades and its replacement with the growth of more regular, but no longer shared, work schedule punctuated with layoffs of indefinite duration—an early approximation of factory employment. The journeymen objected to these changes and in response they formed unions to fight for better wages and terms of employment. Masters responded by bringing charges that these unions were engaged in a criminal conspiracy. The journeymen's arguments in defence of their unions centred on the loss of worker independence, self-esteem, and local communal estimate of worth, all of which were related to the changes in working conditions.

The varying reports of these cases quite clearly illustrated the claim of bias against the journeymen on the part of the various judges who ruled for employers in these cases. However, the piece did not stop there, but also identified the causes of the change in working conditions in significant detail—urbanization, expansion of urban markets, growth of an Atlantic market economy subject to periodic disruption followed by reinvigorated competition, and in-migration of both domestic farm workers and foreign labourers. Still, in this piece these causes seem to be related to, and justify the actions of, the journeymen alone. This is strange.

---

[19] Both Holmes—*Vegelahn v. Gunther* (1896) 167 Mass. 92, 108–9 and *Plant v. Woods* (1900, dissent) 176 Mass. 492, 505—and Brandeis—*Hichman Coal & Coke Co. v. Mitchell* (1917, dissent) 245 U.S. 229, 271 —understood this point, though not in precisely the same way.

[20] (1984) 22 *Osgoode Hall L.J.* 591 ff.

If competition sucks, change in the circumstances of competition sucks even more. The stability of the master-journeyman-apprentice relationship was pretty much dependent on limited or even absent local competition. Competition was limited by the combination of the geographic structure of the local area and the cost of transportation. Limited competition allowed for informal constraints on price by producers, as well as local social constraints on avarice, and so allowed marginal revenue at least modestly to exceed marginal cost. Absent competition abetted the maintenance of social relations between the three statuses, often in a combination with shared residence and working space.

Significant urban growth and a reduction of transportation costs both increased competition; together they were even worse. The piece recognized that the increase in the size of port cities, in part by in-migration from surrounding rural areas and Northern Europe, and in part by the expansion of the Atlantic market, both littoral and oceanic, significantly changed the terms of competition among the masters. This change thus threatened both the economic and social position of what it meant to be a master. Possible responses to this change were several. Some older masters could effectively retire; others might concentrate on up-market niches where price was less important. However, for most masters the major alternative to the slow descent into bankruptcy was to abandon the master-journeyman-apprentice model of the trade to a greater or lesser extent. Whether choosing to cut back on the enrolment of apprentices or to move into real factory production and so expand the number of employees who would formerly have been treated as apprentices, or even to try developing a model of something in between, the strategy of economic and social survival chosen by most masters was that of reducing the cost of labour. Process innovation was unlikely to reduce costs significantly, and even if it did, the advantage it provided was likely the same—reducing the cost of labour.

Thus, it was anything but surprising that it was the journeymen who felt squeezed by the alteration in the terms of competition and for whom unionization was an obvious response. Nor was the response of the masters to unionization surprising, as they were being squeezed, too. Both parties were finding that their economic and social status was under assault. Both were fighting to maintain that status in a world where urbanization, in-migration, and changes in transportation were fraying the social bonds on which the apprentice-journeyman-master system depended for its maintenance. Neither group was acting implausibly. In a world where, economically speaking, sunk costs are sunk and so should be ignored by each group, the sunk human capital that was under threat of being rendered less valuable was a life. Lives are not as easily dispensed with as might be an outmoded lathe or a no longer needed hand tool. Indeed, the capital recovery period for a life is probably longer than that life itself, extending forward at least until one's children are well settled.

Here then the choice that law made in this time of economic disruption was not just between labour and management, as this piece asserts and as is plainly the case, but also a choice between two groups that were seeing their settled lives upended, just as was the case with the Wagner Act in the 1930s. One group chose to attempt to organize collectively and the other appeared not to, though, of course, it would have been much easier for the masters to hide their cartel, if there were one, than for the journeymen to hide their union.[21] And so facially the courts were doing exactly what they said—holding both groups to the identical competitive standard, while at the same time ignoring the difference in the resources that each could bring to address the change in economic and social circumstances that threatened both groups' lives. And so, it is less the obvious class bias in the courts of law that the piece so clearly documents that is troubling. After all, such is a constant in the history of law. Rather, it is the difference in response to similar threats to the social and economic position of both groups in this time of economic turmoil on the part of judges.

Dianne Avery dealt with the years in between Klare's piece and Holt's: *Images of Violence in Labor Jurisprudence: The Regulation of Picketing and Boycotts, 1894–1921*[22] focused on opinions in litigation, primarily in the federal courts and of Supreme Court Justices, most of whom were active during the heydays of the *laissez-faire* Gilded Age. In great detail it first derived and then traced out the impact of the judicial understanding that workers were irrational and easily prone to violence, especially when under the influence of 'outsiders', persons not part of an individual factory's workforce. For these judges such a propensity to violence meant that any resort to more confrontational economic weapons than the strike (a passive unwillingness to work), weapons such as picketing and boycotts, needed to be very carefully policed lest they interfere with employer's rights of property.

The piece made it clear that it was not just labour that could be described as being prone to violence. As Brandeis and Holmes recognized, the idea of a somehow uncoercive economic warfare was implausible.[23] The economic warfare between producers that was part of legally approved competition was just as coercive, just as threatening to the rights of property, as anything that workers might do. Still, the failure of judges to see this equivalence made it clear that when limiting labour action to activities that were not coercive, judges in fact preferred one of the parties in a labour dispute.

At several points *Images of Violence* noted the economic disruption that characterized the *laissez-faire* years. The combination of the final build-out of the rail transportation system, the great growth of metal bending technology, and the growth in immigration from Southern and Eastern Europe significantly increased the level of competition both between manufacturers and between workers. The adoption of the Sherman Anti-Trust Act showed how quickly manufacturers saw merger, and so growth of geographic scope, as a possible way to regain a modest

---

[21] This point was made some years ago by a man named Adam Smith: *The Wealth of Nations* (1789, 5th edn.) Bk. 1, chap. 8, paras. 11, 12, 13 ff.

[22] (1988) 37 *Buffalo L.R.* 1 ff.   [23] See (n. 19).

control over pricing that market expansion had reduced. Similarly, the adoption of the Interstate Commerce Act showed how quickly both farmers and rural manufacturers became dependent on rail transport to build market access and the degree to which freight rates impacted such access, even for business that were on railroad mainlines. Perhaps, equally importantly, the American Civil War was understood as a lesson in the economic importance of unimpeded railroad transport for the economy as a whole.

In competitive circumstances such as these, smaller producers felt an intense production-related cost pressure. Larger producers who had generally engaged in various financial shenanigans to reach such size found that similar pressures were magnified by the fiscal discipline of the debt repayment schedule that regularly accompanied such expansion. All of these pressures were augmented by the seeming necessity of ever increasing expenditures for capital goods that accompanied technological change. For firms of either size the major cost that could be controlled when competition brought price pressure was wages, or so it seemed to management. For labour such cost control through wage reduction, head-count reduction, skilled labour reduction, the dreaded speedup, or often a combination of all four, amounted to a decrease in economic and social status/security. For management a possible inability to control costs also amounted to a similar decrease in economic and social status/security.

This last statement with the introduction of the word 'management' shows the degree to which the years that this piece explored were different from the years before the American Civil War. The masters were management and owners as well. The possibility of shifting language from 'master' to 'management' indicates the degree to which the separation of ownership and control, so firmly attached to scholarship of the late 1920s, was already in full swing in the Gilded Age 1890s. Andrew Carnegie may have 'owned' Carnegie Steel, but the fact that his ownership was so noteworthy indicates how unusual such a circumstance already was. One may identify John D. Rockefeller with Standard Oil, but he was not that firm's owner in the sense that Carnegie owned Carnegie Steel; Henry Ford did not secure both ownership and control until he brought out the Dodge brothers in 1919.

Owners, so-called stockholders, often had different concerns than managers, and large stockholder managers more different still. For a manager the threat of economic failure was in some real sense the same as such failure was to a worker—job loss, diminished income, a lower standard of living, and a concomitant decline in social status, unless job search quickly resulted in securing equivalent employment—a pretty iffy possibility, though of a different magnitude for workers than managers. Stockholders faced a loss of income, often substantial given that the stockholder with a well-diversified portfolio didn't appear on the economic scene until after the Second World War. But in most cases an even modestly diversified stockholder had wealth concentrated in only a few equity positions and so the loss of one such position might mean a significant decline in the value of one's estate.

While there is little reason to cry over such a relevantly large loss—destitution was unlikely to be the result—smaller losses might be thought of differently given that corporate debt and even preferred stock was owned in small amounts, often as part of a sort of do-it-yourself retirement plan, by the much larger group of families who qualified in some sense as middle class. Yet, even these supposedly more secure investments had a bad habit of becoming valueless at the same time that the issuer declared bankruptcy, at least in the case of manufacturing companies. For such middle class owners a decline in social and economic status was also likely, and new jobs hard to find.

Owner stockholders, so-called controlling persons, were in these years primarily family and friends of the founders of the original business. In many cases these people were leeches on the tits of capitalism, more concerned about maintaining social status and lifestyle than about any particular investment. But not always; often they were unwittingly friends of the workers, especially when out of sentiment for the founders they pushed to keep the business alive far longer than a heartless capitalism would dictate based on the notion that sunk costs are sunk.

Again, I am not arguing for the moral equivalence of capital and labour, any more than I argued for such equivalence in the Early Republic or the 1930s. Capital always has more options for recovery from an economic setback than labour and thus is more able to be generous. But, what I am arguing is that it is not surprising that when trying to understand behaviour at a time when the species of capitalism that the law confronted was about as close to dog-eat-dog as sensible people might wish, one needs to understand why capital might have felt itself to be as much under siege as did labour.

Capital's response to labour in the Gilded Age and thereafter was not just a reflexive ideological defence of itself, though there was quite a bit of that, but also it was a response to the same forces that made labour's lot so awful. And equally important, capital was not an undifferentiated 'it.' Capital represented groups of people in many situations with many different concerns, only some of which I have identified. A stronger argument for the inappropriateness of the consistent understanding of labour violence that the courts peddled in these years would have recognized the degree to which that understanding responded only to what some capitalists experienced, individuals whose response came from a place closer to that of labour than anyone was willing to admit.

The Development of the Employment at Will Rule,[24] by Jay Feinman, helps to bring my point about the differential similarity of capitalism's creative destruction home once again. This piece reviewed the slow alteration of the American version of the traditional English rule that a hiring for other than a specified duration is presumed to be for one year. As in the years before the American Civil War the most

---

[24] (1976) 20 *American Journal of Legal History* 118 ff.

common hirings slowly changed from agricultural and domestic to commercial and manufacturing, doctrinal confusion seemed to increase, both in the cases and on the part of the treatise writers. After that war, bargain theory of contract entrenched itself at the same time that litigation slowly shifted to claims made by middle managers whose employment opportunities increased as businesses grew in size. Most of these cases thus turned on questions of the intent of the parties. After a series of contradictory cases in New York, the major commercial jurisdiction in the United States, all of which involved middle managers, in 1895 the matter was finally settled by the New York Court of Appeals with the explicit adoption of the employment at will rule, a rule that quickly spread throughout the land.

It is fitting that this bit of law should solidify in the high Gilded Age and right after the great Panic of 1893. Middle management was the last part of economic life that had a claim to being something other than either owners or workers, neither capital nor labour. It was a precarious status at a time when competition was so cut-throat. In such an era everyone was expendable. Not surprisingly, middle management was not again treated well until after the New Deal and wartime destruction overseas reduced competition to an oligopolistic minimum, but even then 'at will' survived, whatever might have been the then middle manager's expectation of future employment.

Little understanding can be found in the CLS literature of the circumstances of fired middle managers. Workers, yes; management, no; much less owners of various kinds whose businesses became bankrupt. And yet, all of these people have families, suffer loss, surely not the same loss, but loss nevertheless. In this way CLS history suffers from the problem that we regularly asserted was inherent in the work of in our liberal legalist opponents—the belief that our perspective was timeless, privileged, true even. But critique, whether based on class, ethnicity, gender, or sexuality, is no more privileged than that of the object of critique. Neither research nor personal experience establishes the truth of an interpretation of events. The high ground is to be found with the recognition that there is no such thing . . . for nobody.

That history is part of a world in which one cannot know, but is not therefore limited to belief, as I wrote earlier, does not mean that one cannot say anything with an appropriate level of assurance, a politics even. In our writing we choose who are the winners, who are the losers, and sometimes even who are the also-rans. But no matter what our choice is, the question remains: with what degree of assurance may we speak? Who sez? Here I would argue that assurance is greater when one recognizes and accounts for those whose understanding of the events in question does not square with one's own. Such an understanding is appropriate not because it is fairer—that proposition is silly—but because it is more human—compromised, fallen even, self-centred, and best understood in a lived context that for each of us combines both the comfort of present circumstance and the fear of change that may threaten social and economic position in scary ways. This is even true when telling stories in which we believe that 'the good guys' won, not everything—law is always trumped by culture to a greater or lesser degree—but something. No matter how important the achievement may be, there will always have been losers, at least from their perspective, people who believe that their social and economic position has been diminished. It is by recognizing their loss that we strengthen our win by validation of their, and thus our, common humanity.

Consider the Tomlins's work I spoke of at the outset. It seems relatively obvious that the explorers and colonists that he speaks about were pretty scared in this world that was new to them, despite the vast difference in weaponry between themselves and the people already settled in North America. It seems fairly common, ordinary even, that people who find themselves in what they take to be scary places make up stories that justify their behaviour in these places. Such stories appear in the news every week with respect to white people in black neighbourhoods. Recognizing this likelihood would not diminish the power of Tomlins's story, rather, by taking these peoples' fears (on both sides) seriously and accounting for both those real fears and the brutal reactions they brought, his story would be strengthened, just as would be the case with CLS historians writing about the workers, managers, and masters/owners faced with economic change in CLS stories about labour history.

Now, none of this criticism should be taken to suggest that the CLS labour historians should be faulted for the history that they actually wrote. There really was no other choice. They, like Tomlins, told stories that cried out for the telling since they had never before figured prominently in the tale of law in America. Thus the fault, if there be fault, as opposed to another of the endless list of examples of historians 'doin' what comes naturally', was on the part of the liberal legalist historians who should have included the stories of American workers, indeed of democracy's losers of all kinds, in their telling of the story of the triumph of American law and legal culture. Their scholarship, like ours, would have been made stronger had they recognized loss as they wrote of what they saw as gain. Having not done so, the temptation to highlight their error was simply too tasty to pass up. CLS historians enjoyed the feast.

I hope that what I have said is not interpreted to mean that I believe in the possibility of writing 'objective' history. Auden captures the human desire to 'slip out of our own position', but he also recognizes the impossibility of doing so, except as a boast. Yes, dates and places and texts can be known in the way that astronomers know that that big, yellow-orange ball that appears in the sky with some regularity is a star around which our planet orbits, but as soon as an historian tries to give shape, and so meaning, to what in the words of William James is that 'blooming, buzzing confusion' of particularities by including and excluding, emphasizing or de-emphasizing things, any plausible claim to objectivity goes out the window.

Historians live in the world that Peter Novick so trenchantly described as *That Noble Dream*.[25] We are always trapped by our past and our present, by our race

---

[25] (1988).

and ethnicity, our gender and sexual orientation, our education and class position, our toilet training and other rebellions. All of these things preclude us from ever acquiring either an 'unconcerned' or a privileged position. But being trapped does not mean that we have no obligation to do our very best to understand the many worlds of the people in our various stories about the past. We need to understand, and not in caricature, simultaneously both the workers and the capitalists, the feminists and the misogynists, the racists and the objects of their vilification, the urbanists and suburbanists and ruralists, the adherents of various religions and those without such beliefs.[26] This is not because their beliefs and actions are of equal value—our writing ultimately discloses how we value them, as it should—but because they are all humans, all trapped in their past and present just as we historians are, and so our efforts to understand them tells us something about the world that our species instantiates. And, after all, that is the point of studies in the humanities and social sciences, studies that history is a part of.

After reading a less fleshed-out version of this piece, Barry Cushman impishly asked, 'Can you name a successful critical reform movement that devoted a lot of effort to analyzing and critiquing its own animating foundational assumptions?' And so I am pleased to return to where I started, but with a more modest answer this time, though not obviously Chris Tomlins's answer. I know that the answer to Barry's question is 'no', but as an intellectual utopian—my fifty years of attempting to identify and sell a less awful curriculum for the first year of law school ought to be sufficient evidence—that 'no' does mean that we of the party of the left should not try. As a utopian I believe that when not in a Maoist mode, self-criticism would more fully reflect the position that scholars, especially the historians whose work I know and love, are in when and whatever they write. And I hope that such more capacious reflection on the limitations of positionality just might allow our critique to be effective for more than the statutory fifteen minutes of Warholian fame. If you disagree, stop by for some thumb wrestling.

Bibliography

James B. Atleson, *Values and Assumptions in American Labor Law* (University of Massachusetts Press, 1983)

Craig Becker, 'Property in the Workplace: Labor, Capital and Crime in the Eighteenth-Century British Woolen and Worsted Industry' (1983) 69 *Virginia L.R.* 1487 ff

[26] Dan Ernst reminds me that such will not be easy, for when he made a similar assertion in presenting the chapter on the Danbury Hatters Case from his book *Lawyers Against Labor: From Industrial Rights to Corporate Liberalism* (1995) at the labour history meetings, the great labour historian David Montgomery protested, 'I'm supposed to feel sorry for a capitalist?' Had I been there, I hope that I would have had sufficient courage to have spoken in Dan's defence and answered, 'No, for a human.'

Louis Galambos, 'The U.S. Economy in the Twentieth Century', in Stanley L. Engerman, Robert E. Gallman (eds.), 2 *The Cambridge Economic History of the United States* (Cambridge University Press, 2000) 969 ff

Colin Gordon, 'Workers Organizing Capitalists: Regulatory Capitalism in American Industry, 1920–1932', in Colin Gordon, *New Deals: Business, Labor and Politics in America, 1920–1935* (Cambridge University Press, 1994) 87 ff

Alfred S. Konefsky, 'As Best To Subserve Their Own Interests': Lemuel Shaw, Labor Conspiracy, and Fellow Servants' (1989) 7 *Law and History R.* 219 ff

Naomi Lamoreaux, 'Entrepreneurship, Business Organizations and Economic Concentration', in Stanley L. Engerman, Robert E. Gallman (eds.), 2 *The Cambridge Economic History of the United States* (Cambridge University Press, 2000) 403 ff

Jonathan Levy, *Freaks of Fortune: The Emerging World of Capitalism and Risk in America* (Harvard University Press, 2012)

D. W. Meinig, *The Shaping of America: Transcontinental America, 1850–1915* (Yale University Press, 1998)

D. W. Meinig, *The Shaping of America: Global America: 1915–2000* (Yale University Press, 2004)

Pierre Schlag, *The Enchantment of Reason* (Duke University Press, 1998)

John Henry Schlegel, 'Notes Toward an Intimate, Affectionate and Opinionated History of the Conference on Critical Legal Studies' (1984) 36 *Stanford L.R.* 391 ff

Philip Scranton, *Proprietary Capitalism: The Textile Manufacture at Philadelphia, 1800–1885* (Cambridge University Press, 1983)

Martin J. Sklar, *The Corporate Reconstruction of American Capitalism, 1890–1916: The Market, the Law and Politics* (Cambridge University Press, 1988)

Robert Steinfeld, *The Invention of Free Labor: The Employment Relation in English and American Law and Culture, 1350–1870* (University of North Carolina Press, 1991)

CHAPTER 31

....

CRITICAL LEGAL STUDIES

EUROPE

....

EMILIOS CHRISTODOULIDIS
AND JOHAN VAN DER WALT

I. CRITICAL THEORY: EUROPEAN TRAJECTORIES

....

IN this chapter we trace the tradition of Critical Theory in Europe in the way it has informed and framed legal thought. A key, and distinctive, element of this legal tradition is that it characteristically connects to the *state* as constitutive reference; in other words it understands the institution of law as that which organizes and mediates the relation of the state to civil society. The other constitutive reference is *political economy*, a reference that typically grounds this tradition of thinking about the law in the materiality of the practices of social production and reproduction. It is in these connections, of the institution of law to the domains of the state and of the political economy, that critical legal theory locates the function of law, and the emancipatory potential it affords on the one hand, and the obstacles to emancipation it imposes, on the other.

Given the centrality of the state, as form of political organization and integration, in the next section (II) we take Hegel—as pioneering theorist of the dialectic relation between state and civil society—as the historical point of departure of the tradition of critical theory in general and of critical legal theory in particular. It is to Hegel that one may usefully trace back the variety of trajectories of European critical legal thought, and relate to him the wide range of its instantiations, with special emphasis on their reciprocal influences, overlaps, and differences.

The approach we take in this chapter is thematic, and it is against the background of the Hegelian/Marxist legacy that we visit and relate a number of theorists who have contributed most decisively to the European tradition of critical theory. While not all were centrally concerned with the institution of law, important insights can be drawn from them in the direction of critical legal theory. We will look at the work of the important Hegelian Marxist Georg Lukács. We will visit the tradition of critical theory of the *Frankfurt School* as it emerges from the legal theory of the Weimar Republic when the Institute for Social research was set up in Frankfurt and brought within its ambit important thinkers like Erich Fromm, Herbert Marcuse, Walter Benjamin, Otto Kirscheimer, Franz Neumann, Hugo Sinzheimer, and others, under the directorship of Theodor Adorno and Max Horkheimer. Distinctive of the work of the legal theorists among these scholars is the way that they conceptualized the integration of state and civil society; notable here was Neumann's distinctive take on state theory, as well as Sinzheimer's left-wing economic constitutionalism. After the war, some of the protagonists returned from exile to the Institute, and their thinking took a 'negative' turn away from the notion that the dialectic might deliver emancipation. Adorno would—after Auschwitz—largely surrender political critique to the 'aesthetic turn', while for Horkheimer the collaboration of men in society will be left contradiction-laden 'with all its waste of work-power and human life, and with its wars and its senseless wretchedness',[1] unless social actors act on the deficit that is experienced by them *as alienation*, a prospect increasingly remote in the face of the instrumental logic of bourgeois constitutionalism. The 'communicative turn' of the later generation of the Frankfurt school around the key figure of Jürgen Habermas, will redirect critical theory by taking recourse to the exigencies of communicative reason or ethics. In the process, however, it would give up the tradition's Marxist legacy, arguably divesting it of much of the more radical thinking that marked the work of Horkheimer and Adorno. The effect of this 'communicative turn' in Critical Theory was to transform critique into a concern with the 'positive dialectic' (as opposed to Adorno's 'negative dialectic') at work in the 'co-originality' of democracy and rights or public and private autonomy.

Running alongside the trajectory of critical theory in Germany, there emerges out of the École Normale Supérieure in Paris, and around the leading figure of Louis Althusser, a Marxist (and Marxian) current of critical thought. Of particular importance here is the largely forgotten work of Nicos Poulantzas, the writings of Étienne Balibar and Alain Badiou, and the recently much celebrated work of Jacques Rancière. The work of Foucault at the ENS would develop largely in dialogue with that tradition.

---

[1] Max Horkheimer, 'Traditional and Critical Theory', in The Continuum Publishing Company (eds.), *Critical Theory: Selected Essays* (1976) 204 ff.

A parallel strand of critical legal theory, drawing in part from Gramsci's theory of hegemony, finds expression in the theorists of the 'material Constitution' of the Italian Left. The emphasis here is on the production of *political unity* as the latter proceeds through processes of 'condensation' and 'distension' of social forces and the mobilization of *collective subjects* which provide the 'efficient cause' of the development of the material constitution, as developed in the work of the leftists of the *Operaismo* and *Autonomia* movements that emerged out of the syndicalist movement, key amongst whom was Antonio Negri. Negri's materialist understanding of the constitution drove him to focus on movement, rather than origins. Constitutional development is for Negri the result of continuous formation and re-formation of social forces, as dictated by class struggles that forge the collective subjectivity of the revolutionary class.

A comprehensive picture of the spectrum of the strands of critical legal theory must include also the somewhat *sui generis* strand of its development in Britain. Key to understanding its particular trajectory is an emphasis on both its Marxist beginnings, its decisive break with Marxist thinking in the 1980s, its subsequent 'turns'—'ethical', 'aesthetic', and 'political'—of the last few decades, and its alignments (and misalignments) with feminism and critical race theory. All these developments are traceable to the 'peripatetic' Critical Legal Conference that since the 1980s has formed its main vehicle and institutional expression.

Like its continental-European counterpart, the 'Britcrits'[2] emerge as a distinct radicalized academic tradition in the mid-1970s, initially by drawing selectively on Louis Althusser and Eugeny Pashukanis, and with a passing interest in Nicos Poulantzas (especially his exchange with Ralph Miliband)[3] and Bernard Edelman.[4] Althusser's theory of the interpellation of the subject (of law) has had a lasting influence beyond that early phase, and his theory of the 'relative autonomy of law' allowed the early critical theorists to distance themselves from the more reductive ('economistic') analyses and to focus more decisively on legal *ideology*.[5] An important difference with the U.S. movement was the clear emphasis of the British CLC on *collective* frames of explanation of identity and action, in contrast to the more individualist forms of critique developed by its U.S. counterparts. This difference is attributable to the proximity of the former to the traditions of political trade unionism in Britain. This period sees also a productive alignment

---

[2] Tim Murphy, 'BritCrits: Subversion and Submission, Past, Present and Future' (1999) 10 *Law and Critique* 3, 237 ff.

[3] See the useful account of the debate in Elizabeth Nash, William Rich, 'The Specificity of the Political: The Poulantzas-Miliband Debate' (1975) 4.1 *Economy and Society* 87 ff; see also Nicos Poulantzas, *State, Power, Socialism* (1978) trans. Patrick Camiller 110 ff.

[4] Bernard Edelman, *Ownership of the Image: Elements of a Marxist Theory of Law* (1980).

[5] See in particular Paul H. Hirst, *On Law and I* (1979); Barry Hindess, Paul Q. Hirst, *Pre-Capitalist Modes of Production* Vol. 2 (1975); John Holloway, Sol Picciotto, *State and Capital: A Marxist Debate* (1979).

with feminist theory.[6] Another important affinity (given also the Lacanian turn in Althusser's thought) was with Freudian and Lacanian themes and *problématiques*, an orientation that has run alongside the critical project in Britain ever since.

It might be argued that the distinctive voice of the Critical Legal Conference only emerges with their postmodern turn[7], which coincides with their break with Marxism, and the translation into English of certain key works of Foucault and Derrida, in particular the latter's essay 'Force of Law'.[8] 'The reception of Derrida,' says Tim Murphy, 'encouraged critique as etymology, as word-play and as symptomatology';[9] and while in the U.S. CLS strand the deconstructive turn primarily takes the form of 'trashing' or 'deviationist doctrine', in the British variant, with its reluctant engagement with substantive law, it is largely played out as a critique of legal form and as 'fractious hostility to legal rules'.[10]

Out of these distinct histories and trajectories come diverse critical understandings of the role of law. What they have in common is an understanding of law as emerging from, or overlaying, a contradiction between Capitalism and Democracy that is operative in Western democracies under the aegis of constitutionalism. That constitutionalism is fraught with paradox (between constituent and constituted power)[11] is a clear indication of the depth of the contradiction, which also finds expression, inter alia, in the difficulty of navigating the boundary between public and private law. Of concern, here, is the difficulty or impossibility of reconciling the notion of a collective *common* good and the pursuit of *private* interests and fortunes under capitalist conditions. The tensions are recurrent and ineradicable, and it is here that questions that *animate* critical legal theory take shape. The tensions relate to the contradictory elements of modern Western and/or Westernized societies, be this in the form of the constitutional state as *both* organizer of oppression (the Capitalist State) *and* of solidarity (the Social State), those that abound between capitalist proprietary interests, on the one hand, and social rights, on the other, as well as those that arise from different modes of government, notably technocracy (with its emphasis on economic expertise and 'output' legitimacy) on the one hand, and popular sovereignty (with its emphasis on democratic self-government and 'input' legitimacy), on the other.

The responses of critical legal theory to these tensions range widely: (i) from radical Marxian strategies of 'immanent critique' and the critique of liberal rights

---

[6] See in particular Annette Kuhn, AnnMarie Wolpe, *Feminism and Materialism: Women and Modes of Production* Vol. 7 (2012).

[7] See Ronnie Warrington, Costas Douzinas, with Shaun McVeigh, *Postmodern Jurisprudence: The Law of Text in Texts of Law* (1991).

[8] Jacques Derrida, *Force of Law: The 'Mystical Foundation of Authority'* (2002).

[9] Murphy (n. 2) 255 ff.

[10] Peter Goodrich, 'The Critic's Love of the Law: Intimate Observations on an Insular Jurisdiction' (1999) 10.3 *Law and Critique*, 345 ff. Goodrich characterizes it as a 'critique of law that is to all appearances steadfastly indifferent to substantive law and does not engage with doctrine', 349 ff.

[11] See Martin Loughlin, Neil Walker, *The Paradox of Constitutionalism: Constituent Power and Constitutional Form* (2007).

and bourgeois parliamentarism from the point of view of industrial democracy; (ii) to the various forms of accommodation articulated in the 'communicative turn' of the current phase of the Frankfurt School (Habermas, Wellmer, Honneth, etc.); (iii) to the development of a post-modern form of critical thinking initially connected to the work of Lyotard, then Derrida, and then taken up by the U.S. 'Crits'; (iv) to the articulation of forms of post-state critical thought in the forms of 'constitutionalism from below' associated with the global South; (v) to the forms of critical thinking associated and articulating on a global scale in the struggles against 'Empire' (as per the influential work of Hardt and Negri), etc. The above inventory of *current* manifestations is only indicative and, in any case, incidental to a volume committed to exploring the interrelation between legal history and jurisprudence with its emphasis on historical inquiry. We will contend that it is towards the junctures between these different critical theoretical responses that critical historical inquiry will need to elucidate new insights that may come to inform and revitalize the tradition of critical legal thought and theory, while remaining attentive to its self-understanding as *intervention* and conscious of the ineradicably political dimension of its undertaking.

II. The State and the Critique of Domination: Hegel's Legacy

History is the dissimilating journey of the Absolute through time, and this journey arrives at its destination with the consolidation of modern statehood, contended Hegel.[12] The journey is 'dissimulating' because of the way it presents the Absolute as a series of finitudes and partial truths. However, throughout this journey, the Absolute *remains* the Absolute, and finitude is not to be considered its facade, but its reality, for the word 'façade' does not belong to the vocabulary of the Absolute.[13] The task of philosophy, Hegel thought, is to comprehend the relation between the eternal reality of the Absolute and its dissimulation in time as a series of finitudes.

---

[12] Georg Wilhelm Friedrich Hegel, *Philosophie der Geschichte*, in Hegel, *Werke in zwanzig Bänden 12* (1970) 57 ff: 'Der Staat ist die göttliche Idee, wie sie auf Erden vorhanden ist'; *Philosophie des Rechts*, in Hegel, *Werke 7* (1970) 398 ff (par 257): 'Der Staat ist die Wirklichkeit der sittlichen Idee.'

[13] Hegel rejected Platonist and Kantian conceptions of the phenomenal world as 'mere appearance', that is, as a mere façade behind which the essence of things remained hidden. Appearance— *Erscheinung*—is for him the manifestation of essence. See the whole 'second section' on Erscheinung, *Wissenschaft der Logik II*, in Hegel, *Werke 6* (1969), which is encapsulated in the phrase 'essence must appear'—'[das] Wesen muss erscheinen' 124 ff.

The history of critique—be it philosophical or social—is a history of refusals to give up this Hegelian 'mythologeme'. This is true also of Marxian critiques (critiques that insist on 'turning it on its head.') For if critique forever tracks a distorted relation between the Absolute and its finite appearance, no critique would be possible if its language would not sustain a relation—however strained—between what is and what ought to be. Critique that would sever *what ought to be* completely from *what is* would not command the comprehension it requires to figure *as* critique. This incomprehensibility or incomprehension is the flaw, Hegel insisted, that renders Kant's conception of critique pointless. For him, Kant's categorical severance of *what is* (*Sein*) from *what ought to be* (*Sollen*) terminates meaningful assessment. The incurable hermeneutic deficit—the incorrigible incomprehension—that looms large here is evident. What can duty (*Pflicht/Sollen*) mean for us if it bears no plausible link with any response to finite circumstances? It should be evident that the notion of critique simply evaporates when no instance of concrete existence can meaningfully bear the burden of an imperative. The Marxian notion of immanent critique pivots on this key insight that emerged from Hegel's critique of Kant.

Our concern with the history of critique keeps the Hegelian mythologeme in place and retains the emphasis on its centrepiece, the modern state. It traces a number of its key mutations in the course of the twentieth century and it reflects on what it might mean for critique to give up on Hegel's magnificent ruse.

A. The Significance of the State in the History of Critique

Critique, as we know it, always occurs in the context of, and takes its opportunity from, a long history of theological, ontological, and sociological divisions. Engagement with this history begins with the faltering of the 'Eusebian myth' that considered the Roman Emperor the incarnation of divine providence. This myth was written all over the simultaneous *association* (*quod principi placuit legis vigorem habet*) and *dissociation* (*princeps legibus solutus est*) of law and the will of the Emperor in Roman law.[14] A similar association and dissociation of law and sovereignty was already evident in the separation of *potestas* and *auctoritas* during the time of the Roman Republic.[15] These two maxims—both authored by the Ulpian—reflect an early attempt to sustain some kind of division between the finite and infinite within the organization of power and law. One might go further and conceive the Eusebian myth as emerging in the Roman legal imagination in order to host a series of new myths regarding the division of finite and infinite power, the first of which was

---

[14] Joseph Canning, *A History of Medieval Political Thought* (2014) 1300–1450 ff.

[15] For an instructive discussion, see Giorgio Agamben, *State of Exception*, trans. Kevin Attell (2005).

the doctrine of the Two Swords through which the medieval Christian imagination sought to settle a long history of battles between Emperor and Clergy (or later, King and Clergy) for a single overarching title that would comprise both finite power and infinite authority.[16]

Not many centuries passed before a critical imagination wedged into the body of the King so as to split it into two, thereby producing the symbolism of the King's two bodies, his terrestrial body, on the one hand, and his celestial body, on the other.[17] But splitting or doubling the King's body was as good as knifing him. The myth of divine royalty was evidently approaching total exhaustion by the time half of the King—the crucial half representing the infinite continuation of his reign ('the King is dead, long live the King')—was all too evidently nothing but an effigy. The modern state was on its way and it soon either just got rid of the King or reduced him to a cultural relic (a living effigy) that all too evidently no longer commanded any force that was remotely worthy of a dialectic between the finite and the infinite. The time of the myth of transcendence was over. The modern state had no option but to internalize this dialectic and this internalization became the birth scene of the social critiques associated with the Modernity and with Hegel and Marx, in particular.

B. Hegel and the Internalization of Critique in the Context of the Modern State

The key feature of the modern state remains its concern with a constitutive division or split. Niklas Luhmann writes:

The necessity to provide foundations—of which the profound rootedness in the division between thought and existence cannot be discussed here—splits social reality with cleaving force into a sphere of the state and a sphere of society. The state has to justify itself to and in society. (Hegel's conception, which takes over this principle of division but inverses the foundational relation, never received a real following.)[18]

---

[16] The doctrine of the Two Swords gave way in turn to a late medieval restatement of the Eusebian conviction of the unity of divine and secular power. This restatement of the Eusebian myth emerged with the doctrine of the Divine Right of Kings, which once again endowed the King with both secular power and religious authority. Once more the finite and the infinite appeared reconciled in the corridors of earthly government, but this reconciliation was also not to last long. See John Neville Figgis, *The Theory of the Divine Right of Kings* (1922).

[17] Ernst Kantorowicz, *The King's Two Bodies: A Study in Medieval Political Theology* (1957).

[18] Niklas Luhmann, *Grundrechte als Institution* (1965) 27 ff.

[Es ist] die Notwendigkeit der Begründung, deren tiefe Wurzeln in der Scheidung von Sein und Denken hier nicht freigelegt werdern können, die mit bohrender Kraft die soziale Wirklichkeit aufspaltet in eine Sphäre des Staates und eine Sphäre der Gesellschaft. Der Staat hat sich in der

Our concern with this key passage from Luhmann's early work does not only pertain to his acute observation regarding 'the cleaving force' (*bohrende Kraft*) through which the modern state founds itself by means of a division between civil society and the state (proper), but also and especially to the throwaway parenthesized sentence with which it ends: 'Hegel's conception, which takes over this principle of division but inverses the foundational relation, never received a real following.' To be sure, Luhmann is not suggesting here, at odds with overwhelming evidence, that Hegel received no following. He is only referring to the fact that Hegel's invocation of the state as the author and civil society as the object of justification never received a following. The history of nineteenth century law and politics in Germany (but surely also in the United States and France) was certainly one in which the conservative patrimonial interests of a bourgeois civil society gained the upper hand in the organization of the state, thereby entrenching the power of civil society to demand justification from the state instead of having to justify itself to the state.

Hegel's philosophy of law and the state indeed pivoted on the observation that an unleashed civil society will eventually destroy the conditions for individual autonomy on which itself was based. Three passages from the *Grundlinien des Philosophie des Rechts* describe civil society dramatically as the monstrous power that ultimately consumes all of human existence, impoverishes and excludes the working class from whatever benefits it promises, and heaps disproportionate wealth on a small number of individuals:

Civil society is rather the monstrous power which draws men into itself and claims from them that they work for it, owe everything to it, and do everything by its means.[19]

When civil society is in a state of unimpeded activity, it is engaged in expanding internally in population and industry. The amassing of wealth is intensified by generalising (a) the linkage of men by their needs, and (b) the methods of preparing and distributing the means to satisfy these needs, because it is from this double process of generalisation that the largest profits are derived. That is one side of the picture. The other side is the subdivision and restriction of particular jobs. This results in the dependence and distress of the class tied to work of that sort, and these again entail inability to feel and enjoy the broader freedoms and especially the intellectual benefits of civil society.[20]

When the standard of living of a large mass of people falls below a certain subsistence level—a level regulated automatically as the one necessary for a member of the society— and when there is a consequent loss of the sense of right and wrong, of honesty and the self-respect which makes a man insist on maintaining himself by his own work and effort, the result is the creation of a rabble of paupers. At the same time this brings with it, at

---

Gesellschaft und an der Gesellschaft zu rechtfertigen. (Die Auffassung Hegels, die das Trennschema übernimmt, aber das Begründungsverhältnis umkehrt, blieb ohne reale Folgen.)

[19] Hegel, *Grundlinien der Philosophie des Rechts,* in Hegel, *Werke 7* (1970) 386 ff (par 238). The English translation of Knox (1821) quoted in the text above is slightly amended.

[20] Hegel (n.19) 389 ff (par 243).

the other end of the social scale, conditions which greatly facilitate the concentration of disproportionate wealth in a few hands.[21]

The proximity of Hegel's to Marx's critique of bourgeois society speaks for itself from these passages. The difference between them only commences with the opposite paths of critique on which they embarked. Marx viewed the state as fundamentally implicated in the class struggle and, at least in Engels' account of it, ultimately little more than an instrument with which the bourgeoisie protected its interests, hence also Engels' normative prediction that the state will disappear when the class struggle comes to an end. The observation that the nineteenth century state ultimately became little more than a placeholder for bourgeois interests was sociologically correct. Hegel, however, still held on to the belief that the state was the only plausible guarantor for the universal moral autonomy that Kant's practical philosophy articulated and which the French Revolution sought to make a concrete reality. His thinking still contemplated an early revolutionary generation that consider the state as the source of liberty and not a threat to it.[22]

Nineteenth-century private law jurisprudence was a conspicuous pillar among those from which Hegel 'never received a following,' as Luhmann puts it. One of the most celebrated twentieth-century historians of private law, Franz Wieacker, would observe with regard to nineteenth-century private law jurisprudence that the potential of Hegel's philosophy to reconcile concept and history made no impression on German private law theory.[23] However, it did make an impression on German public law theory. One of the most eminent and influential examples in this regard would be the work of Rudolf Smend. Smend expressly relied on a Hegelian conception of the dialectic between the finite and infinite to articulate a theory of the state as an integrating force that constantly articulates or rearticulates itself in history, thereby reconciling its eternal normative core with whatever vicissitudes of historical contingency may come to befall it.[24]

Of course, the side of Hegel that was at work in Smend's thinking was not the revolutionary Hegel who consistently toasted Bastille day as long as he lived[25]— the one whom Wieacker evidently considered as a critical alternative to the private law jurisprudence of the Historical School that ended up serving the Restoration

---

[21] Hegel (n. 19) 389 ff (par 244). For an instructive discussion, see Joachim Ritter, 'Hegel und die französische Revolution' in *Metaphysik und Politik* (2003) 183–255 ff; 'Hegel and the French Revolution' (1984).

[22] See Walter Leisner, *Grundrechte und Privatrecht* (1960) 22 ff.

[23] Franz Wieacker, *Privatrechtsgeschichte der Neuzeit* (1967) Göttingen: Vandenhoeck & Ruprecht 415 ff.

[24] As he put it in a key passage: 'The constitution is the legal order of the state, more specifically, of the life in which the state has its living reality, that is, its process of integration. The meaning of this process is the perennial renewal of the living totality of the state and the constitution is the statutory articulation of norms with which some aspects of this integration must comply.' Trans. Rudolf Smend, 'Verfassung und Verfassungsrecht', *Staatsrechtliche Abhandelungen und andere Aufsätze* (1994) 189 ff.

[25] See Ritter (n. 21) 196 ff.

movement—but a Hegel who could be employed in a conservative cultural restoration movement not unlike and quite likely historically related to both the Historical School and the Restoration.[26] For the conservative Smend,[27] the task of cultural historical interpretation, which could integrate Germany and the German people, was to be conferred to a judiciary that was widely perceived from the side of socialist and workers movements as partial to the old status quo of the German Empire; hence the insistence of these movements that courts should have no revisionary powers vis-à-vis the legislation of the new Republic.

This was precisely the message of the progressive constitutional theorists of the time, notable among whom were Franz Neumann and Hermann Heller. Both Neumann and Heller would place their faith in parliament, positive legislation, and positive law. They were legal positivists and their positivism was motivated by a concern with social-democracy that for them evidently outweighed all concerns with German cultural identity. Later, post-Radbruch, generations of 'progressive' legal theorists for whom legal positivism would become a swear word, conveniently remained ignorant of this progressive political motivation of the Weimar positivists. The Weimar Left, however, knew that a conservative judiciary with interpretive powers could easily undo the social-democratic revolution in Germany by reading their own cultural values into the general principles of the Weimar Constitution. It should be noted that another major constitutional theorist of the time, Hans Kelsen, whom later generations—and especially one famous contemporary—would deride for his lifeless positivism and normativism, also disqualified the judiciary from interpreting the broad principles of the Constitution.[28] The 'famous contemporary' noted here was Carl Schmitt, the constitutionalist theorist who eventually completely unleashed the interpretive powers of judges by turning every clause of law into an open clause of law.[29]

Schmitt's unleashing of judicial powers of interpretation in 1933—for purposes of making sure that the fundamental tenets of the National Socialist movement permeated every aspect of German society—stands in clear contrast to Neumann's critical assessment of the transformation of private law that was taking place at the

[26] Smend was an exponent of the *cultural-historical integration movement* during Weimar Germany that considered General Von Hindenburg the personal embodiment of German cultural-historical identity and therefore the only political force that could integrate Germany and the German people. Moreover, Smend also conferred the task of cultural historical interpretation, through which the state was to perform its task of integrated German society, to a judiciary that was widely perceived, especially from the side of the social and workers' movements, as partial to the old status quo of the German Empire; hence the insistence of these movements that courts should have no revisionary powers vis-à-vis the legislation of the new Republic.

[27] See Smend (n. 24) 145 ff. See also Peter C. Caldwell, 'Is a 'Social Rechtsstaat' Possible? The Weimar Roots of a Bonn Controversy' in Caldwell, Scheuermann (eds.), *From Liberal Democracy to Fascism: Legal and Political Thought in the Weimar Republic* (2000) 143 ff.

[28] Hans Kelsen, 'Wesen und Entwicklung der Staatsgerichtbarkeit', in Robert Christian Van Ooyen (ed.), *Wer soll der Hüter der Verfassung sein?* (2008) 39 ff.

[29] Carl Schmitt, *Staat, Bewegung, Volk* (1933).

hands of the Weimar judges. The open principles of private law such as 'good faith' and 'good morals' (*gute Sitten/boni mores*) became general principles of private law jurisprudence with regard to which even clearly applicable statutory rules of law could be re-assessed and re-interpreted by the courts. The liberal application of the general principles of law thus became an effective instrument with which democratic legislation could be circumvented. In 1933, Julius Hedemann published a small book in which he cautioned against the general flight into the general clauses of law (*Flucht in die Generalklauseln*).[30] Schmitt responded to Hedemann by arguing that every rule of law had become a general clause of Nationalist Socialist rule that judges had to employ programmatically to promote the dynamic ideals of the movement.[31] Neumann described the general development of concern here, in detail in his 1937 essay '*Der Funktionswandel des Gesetzes im Recht der bürgerlichen Gesellschaft*.'[32] It began, he shows, with the Weimar judiciary's remarkable appropriation of the power to review parliamentary legislation—something that was unheard of in the jurisprudence of the *Reichskammergericht* and other supreme or high courts of Europe since the French Revolution—in view of the demands of reasonableness and good faith. The main aim of these newly adopted review powers was to counteract the social security and anti-trust legislation of the new social democratic republic. And their cumulative effect was to establish an institutional concept of law that ultimately reduced the relations between autonomous legal subjects to the demands of an imperative communal fidelity (*Gemeinschaftstreue*) that shielded the naked social reality of an authoritarian state serving the concerns of a handful of private monopolies.

The Hegelian idea of the state safeguarding its citizens against the monstrous consumption of moral autonomy by civil society had evidently collapsed into an antithesis from which dialectic escape was no longer a realistic prospect. Far from a powerful state with the sovereign power to protect its citizens, the National Socialist state was ultimately a weak societal construction that fell prey to the demands of powerful private social actors.[33] The National Socialist movement itself attached no more than expedient importance to the state. It was an incidental form with which the dynamism of the movement was prepared to compromise as long as it served its purposes.[34] However, the lasting legacy of the movement was to cast an enduring shadow over the idea of the state as the source of liberty. Later generations that increasingly failed to distinguish between the National Socialist movement and state would accordingly also commence to view the state as a threat instead of a

---

[30] Justus Wilhelm Hedemann, *Die flucht in die generalklauseln: Eine Gefahr für Recht und Staat* (1933).

[31] Schmitt (n. 29) 43–4 ff.

[32] Franz Neumann, 'Die Funktionwandel des Gesetzes im Recht der bürgerlichen Gesellschaft', *Zeitschrift für Sozialforschung* (1937) 542–96 ff.

[33] See Chris Thornhill, *A Sociology of Constitutions: Constitutions and State Legitimacy in Historical-Sociological Perspective* (2011) 321–6.

[34] Neumann (n. 32) 591 ff.

source of liberty. This would indeed then also become one of the main features of the most significant post-war political developments in Europe, namely, the series of treaties that would lead to the formation of the European Union. It is not an exaggeration to suggest that distrust of national states was a driving force of this development. Neither is it an exaggeration to suggest that this development itself contributed much to the further demise of the idea of the state as an emancipatory force. And this is how one of the key normative ideals of Modernity unravelled in the course of the second half of the twentieth century to the extent that percipient observers of this development would invoke in this regard the return of feudalism.[35]

A crucial ambivalence remains evident in critical theory when it comes to its attitude towards the state. As was mentioned already, for the Marxist Left the state remained harnessed to the interests of the capitalist class, even though the precise nature of that alignment was hotly debated. Amongst the most insightful approaches and certainly one of the most complex was that of Nicos Poulantzas, who argued that the state was the 'material condensation' of the relations of social power as these find contradictory expression within the ambit of the state itself, which thus ceases to be a monolithic bloc, as Engels arguably still suggested, but instead harbours antagonisms that lend themselves to the strategic action of political actors.[36] At the other, *post*-Marxist end of critical theory, Habermas will argue for a continuity between legislative and executive political functions. In an argument that stresses the 'co-originality' of democracy and rights, he envisages a form of political organisation under which popular sovereignty—as exercised through legislative channels of will-formation—is transferred to the state for implementation so long as it remains sufficiently undistorted by the systemic logics of money and bureaucracy. Relying on Husserl, Habermas refers to this distortion of popular sovereignty by the systemic logics of money and bureaucracy as 'the colonisation of the lifeworld'.

Across the varieties of critical theory, then, an undeniable contradiction would continue to complicate this increasing marginalization of the idea of the state as the main emancipatory force in modern societal organization. The state has remained the only power with real capacity to coerce. Military and police capabilities have not been transferred to other social actors, despite the pervasive trans-nationalization and globalization of economic, societal, cultural, and even governmental arrangements. This has led one prominent observer to contend that state sovereignty still underpins the whole movement towards transnational 'social constitutions' that marks the world order of the late twentieth/early twenty-first century.[37] The

---

[35] Alain Supiot, 'The Grandeur and Misery of the Social State: Inaugural Lecture Delivered on Thursday 29 November 2012' (Collège de France 2013) 82 [2013] *N.L.R.* 99; Supiot, *L'Esprit de Philadelphie* (Paris: Seuil 2010) 103–8; Supiot 'The Public–Private Relation in the Context of Today's Refeudalization' *International Journal of Constitutional Law* 11, 1 (1 January 2013) 129–45.

[36] Crucial in this regard is the recognition of the material rootedness of ideology in the social processes through which social relations are reproduced. See Poulantzas (n. 3).

[37] Dieter Grimm, *Die Zukunft der Verfassung II* (2012) 312 ff.

question that beckons in this regard concerns the way this contradiction will be resolved or processed in the course of the twenty-first century. Will sovereign statehood reassert itself as an emancipatory form of social organization, or will it all too evidently become reduced to a useful obfuscation of social forces that have no concern with the emancipatory ideals of Modernity?

III. Critical Theory as Ideology-Critique

If the return to Hegel allowed us to recover the critical vein of Marxism from the standpoint of its own philosophical foundation, and to focus it on the critique of domination (*Herrschaftskritik*), another vein can be shown to take its cue from Hegel's *dialectical method* for purposes of articulating a critique of ideology (*Ideologiekritik*).

A. Immanent Critique

For this we turn, with Marx, to the processes of production and social reproduction to identify the *locus* of critique. Basic categories of the operation of the economy and the material reproduction of society are expressions of capitalist relations. They are constitutively mediated through the basic categories of private law that give expression to them as acts of freedom and autonomous agency. Key features of material organization of society are thereby distorted, misrepresented, eclipsed, or elided in the very process that supposedly gives expression to them. By tracking, fastening onto, and 'exploiting' the contradictions that the imaginary constitution of society therefore inevitably incurs, the critical method is able to engage actors normatively in forms of contestation of the reality of their situation. The critical element appears both at the level of the experience of meaning (or sense) and of structure/agency. The first, semiotic route, takes us to the processes of meaning construction; the second leads us to questions of structure and agency and the way in which speaking positions—rather than what is spoken *about*—are formed.

There is much to develop at this juncture of meaning-construction and agency, and we can begin with the notion of *immanent critique* to capture the idea of theory as practical, engaged activity. A useful instantiation here is Max Horkheimer's famous essay 'Traditional and Critical Theory' and the way he describes the lived experience of meaning-creation, and of its deprivation. The primary transcendental move of critical thought, says Horkheimer, referring to Kant's transcendental condition of knowledge, must presuppose the existence of its object. It must reflect on the a priori that conditions the very possibility of the object. For the Hegelian that he is, 'the tension between the concept and being is inevitable and ceaseless'. Critical theory installs itself in the instituting gap between the two and articulates them in dialectical terms. What drives the dialectic, according to Horkheimer (who repeats Marx's insight here), is not some speculative commitment to coherence, but a deficit that is experienced by social actors *as alienation*. 'The critical theorist', he says, 'finds himself *confronted* with the real experience of disharmony or alienation.' Much of Horkheimer's critical enterprise is directed to tracking the 'productive' tension between processes he deems 'objective' and the 'subjective' experience they generate in those who find themselves subjected to them. There arises a discrepancy between what law promises—freedom, equality, self-determination—and what it delivers. Note how crucial for 'immanent critique' is the embeddedness in actual experience: it means that the representation of that discrepancy, and contradiction, is not merely an *expression* of historical reality but a force of *change* within it because it attaches to the experience of social actors who are striving to make sense of their experience. 'Immanence', in other words, always-already implicates the historically poised, necessarily unfinished nature of human engagement, which suggests that the engagement is not something subjects can stand back from, but one that comes upon them with the 'force of present distress' which they need to 'make rational'.[38] For critical theory, the awareness of its own partiality, the rational falling short of the categories of thought, is what drives them to transcend current forms of their finitude. A certain incomprehensibility of suffering as such calls forth a response by the subject, whether it takes the form of de-mystifying the capitalist surface forms of equality, or the critique of domination through culture, or ideology critique. The inaugural gesture of critical thought is reflexivity over its own partiality.

B. The Dialectic of Subjectivity

The history and theory of the subject, that is, of an agency that is actively engaged in the formation of the social world, is central to the conceptual development of critique and critical theory that would come to the fore in the dialectic thought of Hegel and Marx. We take here a brief look at two key moments of what might be called the Hegelian-Marxian narrative of the dialectic of subjectivity, namely, the revitalization of the dialectic of subjectivity in the thought of Georg Lukács and its undoing in the work of Theodor Adorno. They represent key moments in the trajectory of European critical thought.

The central concern of Lukács' epochal revision of Marxist thinking was the rehabilitation of the dialectic between subject and object and the reinstating of

---

[38] Horkheimer (n. 1) 215 ff.

the revolutionary subject. Lukács considered both these elements—the dialectic between subject and object and the agency of the revolutionary subject—to have disappeared from the late phase of Marx's work (largely as a result of the influence of the thought of Engels). Central to Lukács' revision of Marxist thinking was the endeavour to replace what had become the objective dialectic of categories (later also associated with scientific historical materialism) with a revolutionary dialectic in which the proletariat would again assume the role of revolutionary subject.[39] The revolutionary agency of the proletariat that Lukács sought to rehabilitate in Marxist critique consisted, according to him, of destroying the false objectivity that resulted from capitalist commodity fetishism and the resulting *reification of social relations*.[40] For purpose of this rehabilitation he considered it necessary to return to the key concern of subjective agency in Hegel's dialectic, stressing in this regard the important influence of Fichte's emphasis on the primacy of action and praxis on Hegel's conception of the dialectic.[41]

The discovery of the revolutionary subject or agent of history in German Idealism nevertheless gave way to—as Lukács put it—the mystification of Spirit in Hegel's thought, a mystification that Marx duly demystified by turning the history of Spirit into the history of matter, and historical Idealism into historical materialism, before historical materialism, too, lost its concern with material historical agency in the conceptualism of the late Marx. It is this conceptualism that Lukács sought to replace with real historical and subjective agency, and for purposes of which he turned to the revolutionary potential of the proletariat, only to discover that the proletariat itself is already so implicated in the reification of social relations— concerned with its own immediate class interests instead of the emancipatory ideal of the classless society—that it no longer offers the promise of historical agency, in any case, not without guidance that will alert it to its true historical interests. It is for this guidance that Lukács turned to the leadership of the Communist Party.[42]

Lukács thus articulated and published in 1923 what may be considered the last major aspirational conception of relatively orthodox Marxism to invoke the utopian potential embodied in the discontent of the proletariat and the epistemological leadership of the Communist Party, before the disaster of the Stalin-Hitler Pact derailed this current of Marxist thinking for good in 1939, at least as far as Western Marxism is concerned. One of the most pertinent responses to this disaster would come from two social theorists of the Frankfurt School: Max Horkheimer and Theodor Adorno. Their legacy would be to place the very notions of historical subjectivity and the idea of an emancipatory dialectic between subject and object in question. Their co-authored essay on *The Dialectic of Enlightenment* (1944) already commenced with an equation of subject-formation and reification. The subject itself is as such a product of reification and dominance and can therefore not be

---

[39] See Georg Lukács, *History of Class Consciousness* (1971) 1–5 ff.   [40] Ibid., 83 ff.
[41] Ibid., 121–31 ff.   [42] Ibid., 314–39 ff.

invoked for purposes of contemplating a revolutionary de-reification of social relations, they argued. Adorno would articulate this thought further in a way that directly challenged Lukács' view of the subject as an agent of emancipation. One can consider the following key passage from his *Negative Dialectics* (1966) one of the crucial statements of critical theory's despairing withdrawal from the philosophy of the subject and the whole legacy of German Idealism:

The human mind is both true and a mirage: it is true because nothing is exempt from the dominance which has brought it into pure form; it is untrue because, interlocked with dominance, it is anything but the mind it believes and claims to be. Enlightenment thus transcends its traditional self-understanding: It is demythologization—no longer as a *reductio ad hominem*, but the other way round, as a *reductio hominis*, an insight into the delusion of the subject that will style itself an absolute. The subject is the late form of the myth, and yet the equal of its oldest form.[43]

It is obvious that the subject, considered by Adorno the very product and vehicle of dominance, can no longer be expected to enter into an emancipatory dialectic with the object. The thing, the object, that figured for Lukács as the product of reification and commodification becomes the abode of a non-identity that critical theory should shield against the domination of subjectivity, as another key passage from *Negative Dialectics* makes clear:

If a man looks upon thingness as a radical evil, if he would like to dinamize all entity into pure actuality, he tends to be hostile to otherness, . . . to that nonidentity which would be the deliverance, not of consciousness alone, but of reconciled mankind. Absolute dynamics, on the other hand, would be that absolute action whose violent satisfaction lies in itself, the action in which nonidentity is abused as a mere occasion.[44]

The work *Negative Dialectics* is itself an attempt to resist conceptual grasping of the object (the key concern of German Idealism). It considers conceptual thinking as such as a suppression of objectivity and endeavours to transcend the concept trough the concept—*über den Begriff durch den begriff hinauszugelangen*[45]—by developing a method of conceptual constellations that 'circled' the object instead of grasping it directly.[46] However, the distrust of conceptual thought as irredeemably bound to annihilate nonidentity ultimately moved Adorno to shift his concern with a reconciliation between subject and object premised on the non-identity between them, to art. Art (especially or at least Avant-Garde art), he argued, concerns a mimetic approach to the object that respects non-identity by portraying, exactly, the lack of reconciliation between subject and object.[47] With these thoughts Adorno took leave of the pursuit of a *dialectic* reconciliation between subject and object that was still central to Lukács' work. He pursued, instead, a *negative dialectic* that stressed the recognition of non-identity and lack of reconciliation between subject and object as

---

[43] Theodor Adorno, *Negative Dialectics* (1973) 186 ff.   [44] Ibid., 191 ff.   [45] Ibid., 27 ff.
[46] Ibid., 163 ff.   [47] Ibid., 26 ff; See also Theodor Adorno, *Ästhetische Theorie* (1980) 251 ff.

the last resort for the promise of a 'reconciled mankind.' One might contribute the dilemma in which his thinking ended up, in the final analysis, to a failure or refusal to let go of the subject-object relation—the essential legacy of German Idealism—as the key organizational premise of his thinking, notwithstanding his attempt to think this relation negatively. A different line of critique would be opened by a thinking that duly began to take leave of this relation, or rather, commenced to contemplate a release from it by shifting its focus to the possibility of *an event* that precedes the constellation of subject and object and sets the scene for their appearance. Adorno already mentioned—almost in passing—the *incidence* of artistic intuitions in *Negative Dialektik* that hits the work of the artist like flashes of lightning—'[a]uch in die künstlerische Arbeit schlagen sie . . . als Blitze von oben ein.'[48] This thought, however, did not detain him. It would, however, become the arresting thought in the work of Jean-Francois Lyotard, which we will visit briefly later.

c. From the History of the Subject to the Future of the Event

If the transformation of the critical project can be seen as a move from the dialectic of the subject to a focus on the event, it is because the unfolding of subjectivity in history could not guarantee that it would resist the reification that the history of Capitalism relentlessly imposed on it. This is what the story of the Negative Dialectic tells, and it is also clearly expressed in the emphatically anti-Hegelian currents of Marxism associated with the rise of structuralist thought. Amongst the most important here are the theories that emanated from the Ecole Normale Superieure in Paris around the key figure of Louis Althusser, perhaps the most typical exponent of the anti-Hegelian, *structuralist* current of Marxism, with its emphasis on the structural determination of subject positions and possibilities of action *without* dialectical overcoming. Reading *Capital* closely, Althusser takes from Marx the notion that the fetish phenomenon—the commodity form—on which is based capitalist exchange, arises as co-original with what may be envisaged as the possibilities of human association under capitalist conditions. It is impossible to step back from it, or to put it in question dialectically. In one of his most quoted essays, on the function of 'ideological state apparatuses', Althusser distinguishes between forms of capitalist state repression (police, prison service, military) and ideological forms that operate behind the backs of agents, as it were, in calling them forth ('*interpellating*' them is his term) under specific descriptions to occupy subject positions that reproduce the relations of production according to the logic and the exigencies of capitalism. The subject of these relations is not in a position to step behind the ideological

---

[48] Adorno (n. 43) 26 ff.

forms and to question them, because they inform constitutively what it means to be a 'free' subject and what it means to exercise those freedoms. The constitutional imaginary of bourgeois democracy cannot be put to question by actors who rely on its semiosis of freedom, subjecthood, and self-determination to make sense of their social experience. To contest bourgeois democracy demands a complete transcendence of its terms, and of the juridical condition that determined the construction of sense. Only revolution can comply with this demand for exhaustive transcendence.

A similar impasse relating to the subject position is posed by the tradition of revolutionary syndicalism in Italy and the post-Gramscian currents of the autonomist syndicalist movements. If 'to speak of constituent power is to speak of democracy,' as Antonio Negri puts it in the opening sentence of his early work on the concept (*Il potere constituente*), the fact that it appears as constitutional, that is, comes always-already implicated with constitutional form, means that democracy is already straitjacketed to the conditions and limitations of capitalist legality. To be valid, popular will must be imputed to the constitution that establishes the conditions under which the popular will can be expressed *as* sovereign. Law and democracy are reconciled only via the suppression of a paradox that impacts on constitution-making as never, inevitably, fully democratic, if democracy, *ex hypothesi* must remain sovereign to contest and determine the conditions of its exercise. The tradition of revolutionary thought—a tradition that also informs Negri's work—in the variety of its instantiations typically returned to the promise of *constituent power* to face up to precisely that reflexive question. 'What is constituent power from the perspective of juridical theory?' asks Negri, whose priority of course lies with constituent power as an expression of the potentiality *to break with* the logic of capitalist reproduction.

Here is Negri of the earlier work:

[The constituent] is the source of production of constitutional norms – that is, the power to make a constitution . . . in other words the power to establish a new juridical arrangement . . . This is an extremely paradoxical definition: . . . Never as clearly as in the case of constituent power has juridical theory been caught in the game of affirming and denying, absolutising and limiting that is characteristic of its logic (as Marx continually affirms.)[49]

Negri tracks a sequence of reductions, inflicted by juridical reason in the context of its 'taming' and instrumentalizing the constituent, and in the process inflicting 'every type of distortion'.

Constituent power must itself be reduced to the norm of the production of law; it must be incorporated into the established power. Its expansiveness is only shown as an interpretative norm, as a form of control of the State's constitutionality, as an activity of constitutional revision. . . . In this the juridical 'covers over and alters the nature of constituent power.' . . .

---

[49] Antonio Negri, *Insurgencies: Constituent Power and the Modern State* (1999) 2 ff.

'This is how the juridical theory of constituent power solves the allegedly vicious circle of the reality of constituent power. But isn't closing political power within representation nothing but the negation of the reality of constituent power?[50]

The 'interpreters of law' are at pains to maintain the 'vitality' of the system, while navigating that vitality away from any kind of dangerous democratic excess.[51] Amongst the jurists it is only Schmitt, for Negri, that posed the question of constituent power 'with extraordinary intensity'.[52] The 'constituent' is preserved in Schmitt in the logic of the decision, that is never purely of the order of the 'constituted'. But in tying it to the logic of the exception, Schmitt 'capitulates to the force of an attraction that is by now devoid of principles'.[53]

In the much celebrated later work *Empire*, the emphasis shifts away from the state, but the key problematic remains: how can the subject claim a truly revolutionary speaking position that is not already contaminated by the system of capitalist social reproduction. For Negri, the (collective) revolutionary subject, as wielder of constituent power, must remain under-determined and resist subsumption under the dominant symbolic order. To pick up the thread for this incongruent representation, we will need to go back to a certain Italian current of Marxism out of which Negri's work grew: the 'operaismo' movement of the 1960s that formed the springboard for the later 'autonomist' current of Italian Marxism in the 1970s, in which Negri was a leading figure. What is distinctive about the autonomist movement is the centrality it gives to a project of working class self-valorization that crucially, resists the hegemonic representational orders of Capitalism and refuses to define the movement through those vocabularies. This entailed the rather paradoxical insistence not to identify the revolutionary-subject-to-be—the working class—through work. The system of work, they argued, provides a context within which the self-identification of the proletariat as potential revolutionary subject is always-already undercut. That is because, to put it in the terms Marx used in the Manifesto, 'a class of labourers, live only so long as they find work, and find work only so long as their labour increases capital'. Thus, practically, political action for the Autonomia was undertaken in terms of refusal to work, wildcat strikes, spontaneous slow downs, acts of sabotage, and bad-faith reformism (the political programme of demanding more from management than management could possibly deliver, etc.).

---

[50] Ibid., 3–4 ff.

[51] Three traditions of constitutional interpretations undertake this 'labor of constitutional interpretation: there are advocates of transcendental solutions, advocates of immanent solutions, and synthesisers who integrate constituent power as 'coextensive and synchronic' into 'the positive constitutional system.' See Negri (n. 49) 2. Kelsen is typical of the first position and Schmitt of the second; and although not mentioned by Negri, Habermas, with his achievement of the synthesis or co-implication of constituent and constituted power, might be the most celebrated of the 'synthesisers' of the third approach.

[52] Ibid., 24.   [53] Ibid., 21.

At the conceptual level, the possibility for self-identification of the working class is cancelled in this undertaking. Negri can only call upon a 'project of destruction'. At stake, for him, is to undo the symbolic grip that capitalism exerts on the proletariat with its control—at the very point of the recovery of meaning—of the vocabularies and representational orders within which self-valorization is otherwise doomed to take place. The injunction of Operaismo and then Autonomia to undertake political praxis 'dal punto di vista operaio' becomes tragically both urgent and impossible because that point of view forever slips back to existing schemata and makes alternatives visible only in terms of dislocations it marks rather than any consistent programme of 'self-valorization'. 'We find ourselves', protests Negri, 'with a revolutionary tradition that has pulled the flags of the bourgeoisie out of the mud.'[54] Like the Marx of *The 18th Brumaire*, his call is to 'let the dead bury the dead'. And yet, despite its tragic contradiction, for Negri it is of paramount importance to remain with the project of self-valorization.

It is this project that takes a positive turn in *Empire*.[55] By transferring a distinction between *potentia* (force) and *potestas* (authority, command) that he borrows from Spinoza, into politics, Negri considers it is possible to subordinate the concept of sovereignty/*potestas* to its continuing actualization in *potentia*. And *potentia* becomes the term for constituent power. The constituent power of the multitude remains inalienable and does not freeze into entrenched representations ('the people's autonomy lives before its formalisation', he says). In *Insurgencies* he wrote of 'an irresistible provocation to imbalance, restlessness and historical rupture'; ceaseless self renewal. In continuity with this earlier work, the main thrust of *Empire* is a call to resist the (by now) familiar problem of representation: that every moment of self-constitution—and the revolutionary moment as ultimate self-constitution— must yield to a pre-constituted order. We have already discussed the problem that without this yielding, praxis would find no leverage and identity no register. The difficulty is that the yielding is at once a necessary condition, because without it there is no representational space, and yet cancels out the new in the very act of accommodating it in pre-existing schemata. In all of this, the idea of constitutional self-government comes with the 'self' over-determined. The collective self of this self-government is a self significantly pre-determined in the past, always-already encumbered with its limitations.

If the problem is put like this: 'how can the multitude—the first-person plural— initiate an action if it is the action itself, its undertaking and acceleration, that positions the subject?', then the answer must be that the subject of constituent power is only ever the insurgent subject, the emergent property of an action, not its instigator or agent. Could it be then that in linking the two questions and answers together Negri allows 'dialectic' to do more that he initially envisaged?

---

[54] Negri, *The Savage Anomaly: The Power of Spinoza's Metaphysics and Politics* (1991).
[55] Antonio Negri, Michael Hardt, *Empire* (2000).

By producing incommunicable resistances to its practices as totalizing context and target of resistance, 'Empire' allows a growing coincidence, a certain accumulation of struggles, even an 'over-determination of contradictions' as Althusser would have it. In the process of this accumulation, the emergence of the anti-capitalist movement as universal subject becomes a real possibility.

The operation of 'Empire' as a system of global capitalism depends on a totalizing inclusion, whereby all conflict is replicated as crisis. Conflicts are played out as fragmentary and local, and thus not only innocuous but actually instrumental to the reproduction of Empire. But, as production comes increasingly to coincide with communication (in that it is 'communication' that has displaced all other commodities), what guarantee, asks Negri, is it possible for the system to give that this condition (this internalization) will continue? What guarantee can it give that contingencies will not become subversive to the system, instead of remaining nothing but fully internalised as opportunities to instigate responses through which the system re-entrenches itself as sole and total context? What assurance can it have that its unprecedented subsumption of the social to capital will just continue? There is no meta-guarantee (and ideology can no longer provide the reproduction of meanings at a meta-level) that social production, living labour, desire, and all that dynamism, will be harnessed to reproduce the given framework of relations and will not instead erupt asymmetrically and break with the pressures of homology. And what is crucial here is that 'Empire' in a sense makes available the space of resistance, and sustains its opening and opportunity, by the very fact that it has been so spectacularly successful in subsuming society to capital in the first place.

D. Theorizing the Event

What remains to be thought in view of the moments of critique traced above is its transformation from a concern with subjectivity to a concern with the event; and more specifically, from a concern with subjectivity as irreducibly determined by its history, to the event as inception of an undetermined and unprecedented future. For purposes of contemplating this transformation, we situate Negri's concern, above, with an *always insurgent subjectivity* that resists the reduction of constituent to constituted power (and the *accomplishment* of subjectivity that this reduction implies) within the development of critical theory from Lukács to Adorno, on the one hand, and the emergence of a concern with *the event*, on the other, in a host of late twentieth-century thinkers of whom the work of Alain Badiou and Jean-Francois Lyotard can be selected as representative. From the perspective offered by the thinking of the event, we shall pose the question whether the insurgent subjectivity contemplated by Negri does not, in fact, concern the sheer insurgence of the event that predates whatever (restorative) subjectivity may come to be announced in its wake. If this question is to be answered positively, one would have to ask whether this turn from a concern with the revolutionary subject that is predetermined by its own history to a concern with an unprecedented event that inaugurates an as-yet-undetermined future does not also announce an exploration of critique that breaks with the tradition of dialectics and seeks to solicit moments of rupture that refuse dialectic incorporation.

Lyotard's engagement with avant-garde art thematized the anxious concern of the artist with the irreducible uncertainty and unpredictability of the *event*, the irreducible uncertainty of whether something will come; the irreducible unpredictability of the *there is*, the *il y a*.[56] His endeavour in *Le Différend*, in his own words, would be nothing but addressing the question whether something could be *happening—[e]n écrivant ce livre, [j'ai] eu le sentiment de n'avoir pour destinaire que le Arrive-t-il?* And the thinking of the event concerned for him the ultimate resistance to the instrumental use of time—*l'ultime résistance que l'événement peut opposer à l'usage comptable du temps*.[57] It is here that contemporary critical theory finds its most forceful impetus, that is, in a radical non-identity thinking that no longer takes the relation between subject and object as its point of departure, but simply thinks in terms of an incommensurable emergence of new possibilities of political action and the aporetic regard for ways in which this emergence may be solicited without returning to the philosophy of the subject. It is exactly this impetus that one discerns in Negri's concern with constituent power that refrains from subject formations that are nothing but the continuation or repetition of already available histories.

For an other, different, theorization of the event one must turn to Alain Badiou, another of the Marxist theorists that emerged from Althusser's circle.[58] At one level at least, Badiou's argument contests Negri's frontally. For Badiou the 'reach' into that which Negri assumes to be an underdetermined *multiplicity* is always and can only be directed by, and thus contained within, what he calls *the situation*, 'contained' as past memory, present options and future scope. And while structures are indeed re-embedded and renewed in time, the renewal proceeds along given pathways, and it is always the situation that shapes and delimits the 'encounter' with whatever may be outside it, establishing in the process the very meaning of encounter, of *what* is situated and against what it is situated, establishing, that is, reference to self and other. Evidently dismissing the 'situation-transformative' claims of the tradition of dialectic thinking, Badiou insists that the historically engaged subject envisaged by this tradition remains trapped in the situation. For Badiou, for the engaged—situated—subject there is *nothing* beyond the situation.

Thus Badiou's account of the 'situation', to begin with, presents us with closure that is totalizing. In terms of semiosis, for Badiou the closure of situations is *condition*

---

[56] Jean François Lyotard, *L'inhumain, Causeries sur le temps* (1988) 101–18.

[57] Lyotard, *Le différend* (1988) 15 ff.

[58] Though in Badiou's case, the relationship with his teacher was fraught, to say the least. For a fascinating account of the tensions see Dominique Lecourt, *The Mediocracy: French Philosophy since the Mid-1970s* (2002).

of signification, of the creation of meaning, of something counting-as *x*. And that is why resistance is caught up in a double bind here. While *negation* is crucial for breaking *out of* the confinement of the situation, it cannot avoid playing a functional role *within* the situation. The problem for critique here is that as a value in the dyad of exclusive alternatives, negation *confirms* the situation as much as affirmation does. Normative orders at this point exploit negation as a means of immunising themselves from challenge. Negating the situation by operating within its own semiotic universe thus forever slips back into affirming it, not transcending it.

And yet, for all the totalizing hold of the situation, Badiou attaches the possibility of critique, and therefore of resistance, to the idea of the *event*. The event cannot be inferred from the situation. 'As something that cannot be recognized as one in the situation, an event is the presentation of inconsistency in the situation.'[59] 'From within the situation the existence of the event cannot be proved, it can only be asserted. An event is something that can only be said to exist in so far as it somehow inspires subjects to wager on its existence.'[60] What does it mean to 'assert' what is denied presence?

We do not for present purposes need to follow Badiou in the critical-theorization of how the new breaks into the 'situation' as an 'event'. Suffice it so say that for him the event remains 'unpresented and unpresentable' and its belonging to a situation is undecidable from within the situation itself.[61] Instead the appearance of the event follows a certain logic of *rupture*, an emergence that could not be counted-for from within the situation, and an opportunity that arises paradoxically *in spite of* the opportunity-structure available.

IV. CONCLUSION

The critical concern with the event and the emergence of radical utopian possibilities of action that is at stake in the contemplation of *constituent* power (in terms of itself, and not in terms of something else) is irreconcilable with the critical concern with the normative framework of the state and the whole gamut of *constituted* power implied by this normative framework. It is nevertheless the task of critical theory not to neglect either of these possibilities of critique. The critical project on which,

---

[59] Peter Hallward, *Badiou: A Subject to Truth* (2003) 115 ff. See also Peter Hallward, 'Order and Event' (2008) 53 *New Left Review* 97–122 ff.

[60] Alain Badiou, *Being and Event* (1988) trans. Oliver Feltham (2008) 214 ff.

[61] Badiou (n. 60) (2008) 199 ff et 202 ff.

for instance, Neumann embarked unfolded squarely within the parameters of existing conceptions of constituted power. Its critical thrust, however, is not in the least blunted today in a time that executive judiciaries are again (or still) the secret agents of the emaciation of the state and the reduction of the normative framework of Modernity to the logic of the market. This critical project, however, must remain accompanied by the thinking of unheard possibilities of political action, were it not ultimately to collapse into a complacent endorsement of the compromised justice that known forms of political organization offer. It is for this reason that critical theory must continue to think, with Negri, the aporetic thought of a constituent power that can only be understood in terms of itself and not at all in terms of constituted power. Caught between these two irreconcilable and opposite trajectories, critical theory faces the difficult and awkward task of constantly articulating and rearticulating its own in/coherence.

Let us finish by *reiterating* some of the fundamentals of Critical Theory as captured variously by our thinkers, and with special emphasis on the critique of juridical reason and its critical deployment.

The first thing to note is that critique begins in the context of the articulation of specific constellations of meaning, where the creation of meaning occurs in terms of specific imaginaries, with their vocabularies and rules of signification. It also occurs in the context of specific sets of social relations, institutional arrangements and processes of social reproduction. In both senses it is always *in media res.*

In the second place, critique involves the acquisition of distance from the conceptual forms that determine identity and action. This 'distance' cannot and does not assume or imply fully fledged reflexivity. But it does allow for the introduction of contingency where necessity was assumed. This is both key to critical thinking and one of its steepest requirements, one that Althusser for one, as we saw, thought impossible in relation to the fundamentals of capitalist relations. Marx's analysis of the fetish phenomenon is, as we saw, a case in point: for Marx too the commodification of social relations occurs *ab initio.* Stepping behind this commodification in order to recover 'non-alienated' social relations is therefore not possible. Where founding assumptions carry a certain self-evidence into the imaginary constitution of society, as inscribed in language and as mobilizing specific systems of signification and material support, critical theory demands the recognition of the contingency of those foundations.

The reflexive move is emphatically *not* a stepping *outside* of the context that might afford an objective (as opposed to class-inflected) view. It is always defined by the partiality of contextually situated and historically conditioned perspectives.

And yet the critical perspective is one that fastens onto contradiction, a term under which we can here subsume also fundamental inconsistencies, silences, and exclusions, discrepancies between what the system promises and what it is *capable* of delivering. Capable is an important word here; unlike 'likely' it carries a structural limitation. For example a capitalist labour market cannot deliver on the promise of full employment because a market—in order that it be able to optimize supply and demand—requires a structural element of unemployment to maintain itself *as a market*. In this respect critique distinguishes itself from mere criticism. It is not just aimed at the rectification of inconsistencies. In contrast, the object of critique is to expose contradiction and offers neither rectification nor reconciliation.

Where contradictions have been tracked, ideology critique aims to expose them as the *systematic* expression of dominant interests—irrespective of whether these are class interests, or whether they pertain to gender, race, or underlie other forms of oppression. Ideology critique approximates the critique of domination most clearly when these particular interests combine in hegemonic constellations.

CHAPTER 32

FEMINIST HISTORIOGRAPHY OF LAW

AN EXPOSITION AND PROPOSITION

MARIA DRAKOPOULOU

I. INTRODUCTION, OR WHAT'S IN A NAME?

> 'What did this mean for women?'
>
> Mary Linton Shanley[1]

WITH this simple question Shanley delimited the parameters of a nascent form of historical scholarship emerging in the U.S. Academy: that of women's legal history. The individual studies deemed to belong to this new field shared neither a common ideology nor a common theoretical approach or methodology. They were united

---

[1] Mary Shanley, 'Suffrage, Protective Labor Legislation, and Married Women's Property Laws in England' (1986) 12 *SIGNS* 63 ff.

by the orientation of their legal-historical inquiry, with its core focus directed at addressing Shanley's essential concerns, namely: why, how, and in what ways does law, in all its historical instantiations, matter for women?

In defining their scholarship as one positing women and women's conditions at the heart of their historical interrogations of law, these feminist legal scholars demonstrated a keen interest in reckoning their discipline's nature, place, and function in the Academy. Next to the numerous formal academic texts their studies generated, they often wrote accounts of their scholarly engagement; seeking to explicate, debate, define, and redefine the key themes and issues concerning the field, its activities and utility, as well as its allies and adversaries.

From the outset feminist legal historians in the USA openly declared their alliance to two major disciplinary developments that had taken place in the 1970s, those of 'critical legal history' and 'women's history'. In so doing, they shared in the critical spirit that underpinned the desire of the former to unsettle mainstream histories of law, and adopted the mantle of the latter, to correct the historical narrative by instituting women firmly within it. Yet, they also pointed out significant differences marking the emphasis of their own inquiry. Whilst critical legal history, they argued, showed little if any real interest in women, women's history tended to touch upon law in superficial and peripheral ways, treating it as something of a digression. So, although both these established strands of intellectual inquiry that had preceded the 'birth' of women's legal history helped create a fertile ground for its development, its affiliations with them were by no means fixed. Of the two, the bond between feminist legal history and women's history was the closer and the more varied in form, both in terms of its institutional and conceptual nature.

The emergence of feminist legal history as an academic subject had been particularly facilitated by the institutional gains feminist historians had made in the 1970s. So when the first symposium devoted to feminist legal history was held at the Akron Law School, Ohio, in October 2007, it was against the background of a supportive and co-operative intellectual milieu provided by numerous meetings and conferences of feminist historians held over the previous twenty years. Moreover, this association also yielded significant intellectual fruit, with feminist legal historians drawing upon conceptual rationales, theoretical insights, and methodologies developed by feminist historians, and using them to transform and progress the theoretical and critical edge of their own field. This was perhaps most evident in borrowings from the work of Joan Scott; in particular, her methodological innovation of employing gender as a category of historical analysis; an innovation which shifted the focus of legal-historical inquiry from women to gender and subsequently impacted upon the field's very name.

Feminist legal historians did not merely account for their own coming into being and for the present state of this new field. In employing the collective term 'new women's legal history' they simultaneously acknowledged the existence of a past body of literature to which they were heirs and unequivocally differentiated between this past and their present. Their received legacy comprised historical writings that included descriptions, and occasionally analyses, of the relationship of women and law. For instance, reference was often made to wider histories such as Richard Morris' 1959 *Studies in the History of American Law*, which included an overview of women's rights in early American law. Similarly, Mary Beard's 1946 pioneering study *Woman as Force in History* was frequently cited; a work which, though not wholly focussed on the legal, analysed the relationship between women's property rights and the equity courts, as well as what she considered to be the civilizing influence of the female sex on general matters of justice. The 'new' women's legal history embraced and built upon these older studies, fully centring women as the subject of its concern. But the term 'new' did not only signify a reformulation of its relationship to the past. It also revealed its position in respect to the present and to the future. Positioning itself in the present as another genre of feminist legal scholarship, whilst also acknowledging its intellectual bond to feminist history, it extended its reach well beyond its 'natural environment', that of the Law School, thereby admitting to a complex institutional and intellectual identity.

In conceding to the existence of a past, whilst claiming a distinct interdisciplinary and present identity, feminist legal history not only authorized its own singularity, but also simultaneously embedded itself firmly within a specific academic tradition, thus securing its claim to its own future. Most significantly however, by being so attentive to presenting and differentiating its own being, and delimiting its own past, present, and future, feminist legal history demonstrated an awareness of its own positionality; of its own identity and place, whether in institutional, professional or intellectual terms. So, that which in 1980s USA had been heralded as the 'new women's legal history', and by 2000 had come to be interchangeably referred to as 'gender and legal history' or 'feminist legal history', now boasted a growing body of historical knowledge about the relationship of women and law, together with a consciousness of itself as situated knowledge.

This concern with the situatedness of the field was not met with the same fervour on the other side of the Atlantic. In the English Academy there was neither a clearly designated institutional space of enunciation, nor a group of scholars openly claiming identity as 'feminist legal historians'. More specifically, in contrast to North America, in English women's history conferences there have been practically no contributions devoted to feminist legal history or women's legal history; with the same holding true for the biannual British Legal History Conference. Similarly, with the exception of just two papers, there has been no such presence in *The Journal of Legal History* since it was first published 1979.[2] In fact, it was only in October

---

[2] Rosemary Auchmuty, 'Early Women Law Students at Cambridge' (2008) 29 *Journal of Legal History* 63 ff.; Cynthia Neville, 'Women's Charters and Land Ownership in Scotland 1150–1350' (2005) 26 *Journal of Legal History* 25 ff.

2016 that UK feminist legal scholars, in collaboration with the Women's History Network, first organized a national academic event explicitly devoted to feminist legal history, a one-day conference entitled 'Doing Women's Legal History'.

The virtual absence of feminist legal historians in the UK can be largely accounted for by the manner in which the feminist project in law was conceived. Firmly locating itself within the legal academy, from its inception it allied itself to 'socio-legal' and 'critical legal studies', sharing an interest in law's social context with the former, and a focus on the interrelationship between theory and practice, with the latter. It also adopted a particular critical spirit (often of Marxist orientation) alongside an understanding of modern law as a structure of power. The modern feminist legal interventions in England were therefore principally shaped by: an analytical concern with the power of law, whether conceived of in sociological, Marxist, or Foucauldian terms; a critical interrogation of the myriad ways in which contemporary law affects women's social being; and, in honouring its links with feminist activism, a wish to respond to its own critiques by correcting law's wrongs towards women, and hence a desire for a politics of legal change.

Through its explicit commitment to contemporary law and legal changes directed at improving women's lot, this emphasis on law's power, and the most effective means of combating this power, served to valorize the present and posit legal arrangements affecting living women as those most worthy of consideration. An overarching concern with questions of how things are and how they can be bettered tended to marginalize and displace the need for historical inquiry. This is not to argue that the feminist legal scholar has lacked a historical consciousness, or that she has been hostile to historical understanding. Nor is it to imply that there has been an absence of historical writings about women and law in England. Rather, it is to point out that this historical inquiry has not been integral to, or a condition of, clearly demarcated theoretical, critical, and political objectives. As a result, English feminist legal history developed almost exclusively outside the Law School, with virtually all the appreciable volume of historical knowledge on women and law being the work of feminist historians rather than scholars of law, and a concomitant absence of any assertion that this history belongs to the genre 'feminist legal history'.

Although this discussion of women's legal history has been limited to its development in the USA and England, the justification for doing so is driven neither by a wish to attribute special significance to these jurisdictions, nor an interest in studying them comparatively. They have been prioritized because they comprise two fundamentally different modalities through which the field has developed. The former, thriving in the institutional and professional awareness of the feminist legal historian enjoys an independent life filled with confidence in its present, and productive optimism for its future. The latter, with its overtly political orientation towards legal changes that benefit women, in nurturing indifference to historical inquiry, effectively assigns such inquiry to history rather than law.

These two modalities can be thought of as occupying opposite ends of a spectrum of possible variations along which other jurisdictions of the English-speaking world can be positioned. For example, in Australia, in a manner akin to that of England, the history of women and law is neither constituted as a distinct field, nor 'resides' within the Law School. Here, with the exception of a few legal scholars, the writing of the history of women and law resides in history departments, where its practice is left to feminist historians.[3] Yet in Canada, though not enjoying anywhere near the same richness of outputs, level of persistence, or intensity of self-reflexivity as in the USA, historical studies of women and law have nevertheless secured institutional and intellectual recognition as an independent field of legal inquiry.

The presence of distinct modalities shaping the appearance of feminist legal history raises questions as to how we might best think of it as a unified field, define its boundaries, and decide what to include or exclude. And what criteria might we use in doing so? Should these merely be formal ones, the disciplinary *locus* of production, or should the author's formal declaration of herself as a feminist legal historian take precedence? Alternatively, could the substantive content of the study, the historical orientation of an account of women and law, suffice as a definition?

Clearly, such questions are highly pertinent in the context of this chapter. Yet what follows neither engages directly with such normative issues, nor seeks to offer a blueprint as to how the field should be delimited. The intention is not to be prescriptive, but in discussing the field's 'fortunes' it is necessary to consider how it is conceived of as a unified field of study. In the first instance, the paper adopts Shanley's view that the category 'women's legal history' or 'feminist legal history' embraces all those studies which, whilst employing a historical perspective, interrogate the different ways in which women and law relate to each other. This allows a greater latitude of inclusivity and scope in terms of its substantive content because posing the dyad 'women and law' together with historical inquiry as the definitive components emphasizes substantive similarities and brings together studies irrespective of formal differences, such as national context, the author's traits, or the discipline of which they were products.

In adopting this approach the following text is divided into two parts. The first surveys the current state of the field, and, by setting aside national borders and disciplinary origins, pays attention to the broader themes, topics, and issues feminist legal history has chosen to privilege. The second, building upon this presentation of the field, offers a critical understanding of what exists by drawing attention, not only to the thematics of feminist legal history, but also to the process of its production; in particular, the implications of its interdisciplinary nature. Finally, the second part, in pursuing a critical account of the work produced, briefly considers possibilities for otherwise thinking of and 'doing' feminist legal history.

---

[3] These legal scholars include Larissa Behrendt, Ann Genovese, Judith Grbich, Kim Rubenstein, and Nicole Watson.

II. *MNEMOSYNE* OR THE WRITING
OF WOMEN'S LEGAL HISTORIES

'The men being the Historians they seldom condescend to record
the Great and Good Actions of Women'

Mary Astell[4]

Writing women in the history of law was, and still is, the feminist legal historian's original and most significant pledge. By capturing women's past encounters with law, she can dispel the *lethe* of the legal record, recover that which had been obliterated, and correct the distortions and omissions made by the dominant, male memory. In pursuit of this goal, a plethora of studies emanated from law schools, history schools, and women's studies departments alike. But irrespective of their *locus* of production, each can be assigned to one of two major thematic categories. The first is directed at a close scrutiny of law broadly conceived and its treatment of women in different historical periods. The second, posing women rather than law as its starting point, is focussed on women's attitudes to law, their thoughts and activities with reference to law, and their contributions to the legal sphere.

In the context of the first theme the feminist legal historian's attention is turned to those legal structures, practices, and institutions that mark women's existence and experience. Not surprisingly, in the early years of the field's development, inquiry primarily addressed that which had come to be regarded as 'a woman's place', namely the so-called 'private sphere'; the realm most closely associated with women's confinement and oppression. A creative arena for new narrative forms was thereby opened in which stories about law and women's affective and personal existence could be told. Here, domestic life, family, marriage, divorce, parental rights, and property constituted the core topics, with numerous histories specifically addressing the doctrine of coverture, dower, the married women's property acts, the rules of inheritance, and the custody of children. Yet despite this concerted focus on branches of law regulating the private domain, the law governing women's public standing was not neglected. Many such histories on this topic emphasized the distinctive female experience in the public realm and highlighted the severe limitations law imposed on their capacity to be recognized as persons and as free agents in this sphere.

During the early development of feminist legal history the juxtaposition of the private/public dichotomy provided an important analytical framework within which to explore the relationship between law and the place and role of women and men in society. However, debate over whether female experiences should be

---

[4] Mary Astell, 'Christian Religion', in Bridget Hill (ed.), *The First English Feminist* (1986) 201.

understood in such contrasting terms, a debate that had first sprung up amongst feminist historians, soon spilt over into feminist legal history. It was argued that the apparent elevation of the private/public framework to the status of a near-natural, and hence 'inevitable' conceptual category reflecting essential differences in the sexes, might serve to obscure rather than reveal the past and prove as much a hindrance as a help. This was seen to be particularly true of important topics, such as sexuality, reproduction, and motherhood, which were not easily characterized as either public or private; for instance, because their regulation was a matter of public policy and concern. Similarly, categorizing key legal arrangements, such as the marriage contract, dower or the rules of inheritance, as private affairs obscured the fact they remained part of a wider regulatory legal framework that effected material and gendered consequences in both domains. This inadequacy of the notion of separate spheres was perhaps most apparent in those histories engaged with women's work, property, and inheritance rules. These revealed how the relevant discourses were closely interconnected and how they contributed to the formation of an ideology of separate spheres for the sexes. Similarly, histories of the patterns of women's property holding exposed the significant effects these private arrangements had had on the structure of the economy in different historical periods.

As the field of women's legal history continued to grow it encompassed an ever-widening range of subjects. No aspect of women's lives, whether at home or in the market as factory worker, labourer, or independent entrepreneur, escaped examination. The implications of their specific contacts with legal structures were also carefully scrutinized, whether in regards to the judicial and penal systems, the state, or the welfare system. Nor did feminist legal historians limit themselves to traditional conceptions of what constitutes law. They interrogated a variety of legal texts and firmly grounded their inquiries in primary sources, legal archives, legislative and parliamentary records, and court records and proceedings. In so doing, they carefully related their findings to relevant jurisprudential debates, legal doctrine and theory, and to judicial interpretations and reasoning. Furthermore, through acknowledging that law does not exist in a vacuum, but reflects social, cultural, and political norms, at the same time they cross-referenced and correlated this material with key political, economic and cultural discourses, with popular culture and with broader feminist discourses of the time.

Feminist legal historians did not just innovate by producing new agendas of historical research in regards to the nature and breadth of the legal materials they employed and the manner in which they used them. Neither was their handling of the private/public dichotomy their only insightful theoretical contribution. Following in the steps of their 'sisters' in the fields of history and law, they also introduced significant methodological departures into their own engagements. Their initial reliance on the belief that in any given historical period all women experience law in essentially the same way, a belief that had allowed the positing of a unitary subject of historical analysis, was fatally compromised by debates raging in other domains of feminist scholarship. The recognition of differences within the category of 'Woman', differences registering a considerable diversity of conditions and experience, had rapidly gained ascendancy. The effect was to shift the focus of inquiry onto the way in which law contributes to and/or constitutes and legitimizes these differences, as well as the implications such differences might have for women's legal status and experience of law. As a result, legal histories that had first spoken of and spoken to a unified subject were now displaced, giving way to histories of difference, whether this be of race, class, religion, sexual orientation, or some other category.

This methodological shift from sameness to difference as a guiding principle for feminist legal historians was further complemented by the institution of an important new concept, that of gender. Introduced to legal historical inquiry, gender became— and for many still is—the preferred term of reference in regards to women's legal history because it testifies to female and male identities as cultural constructs instead of biologically given. Rooted in culture and history, rather than nature, gender identity was conceived as a social institution: a system of social organization of differences that establishes a series of societal expectations and behaviours coded as male or female. In doing so it not only orders the social life of individuals, but also sustains, reinforces and reproduces hierarchical relationships between men and women. The appreciation of gender as a constitutive element of social relationships and, in particular, as a signifier of power differentials, led the feminist legal historian to revisit the analytic framework of her historical practice. So, in addition to all her other tasks, she now had to unravel the role of law in forming and informing the precise meanings of femininity and masculinity and explore law's role in the evolution of these meanings in order to understand how they are produced, circulated, and legitimized by law across time.

Acknowledging gender as a site of power allowed feminist legal historians to study and employ it as a tool for locating women's experience of law whilst arguing that all legal experience is gendered. For example, it had become increasingly obvious that certain legal rules or doctrines, such as coverture, hitherto thought of as only affecting women, had far reaching implications for both genders. By enforcing such doctrines, law was seen as producing two distinct legal frameworks, one for men and one for women, and to thereby maintain and reproduce the power differentials between the two.

This engendering of women's legal history also resulted in the production of broader legal histories of gender relations and the creation of a new field of legal history, that of masculinity and men's studies. In addition, the acceptance of gender, together with the notion of difference as legitimate grounds of historical analysis, precipitated an array of studies exploring its interrelationship with other forms of difference, such as race and class, and conclusions about how these interact to create and reinforce other distinct forms of power relationships.[5]

---

[5] See Felice Batlan, 'Engendering Feminist Legal History' (2005) 30 *Law and Social Inquiry* 823 ff.

The first theme of feminist legal history brought forth an impressive body of historical material and numerous women's legal histories whose primary purpose was to demonstrate law's authority to control women's lives, allow or restrain their activities, and withhold or grant them rights. Whereas this theme investigated the relationship of women and law by positing law and its effects on women's lives as its object of inquiry, the second explored the nature of this relationship from the opposite direction, from the perspective of women. This drive was fuelled by a desire to counter-balance the representations of women that pervaded the historical considerations of law's conduct towards them. Whether in discussions of coverture, of women being denied personhood, their inability to hold property, their exclusion from the public sphere, or of their lack of civil rights, existing texts had consistently yielded a somewhat bleak understanding of womanhood. It seemed that the place of women could only be one of an object of regulation, a passive subject, or a victim, and hence, devoid of any capacity to resist.

Establishing a venerable line of foremothers actively engaged with law, feminist legal historians roundly dismissed this picture as wholly inaccurate. Through recovering previously lost or overlooked evidence of women's activities in respect to law, they revealed numerous examples of conflict and resistance where women had opposed or circumscribed law using opportunity, invention, cunning, and wit, whilst often exercising considerable courage in the process. They showed women to have been important 'movers and shakers' throughout law's history and argued vociferously that they be granted their rightful place in the legal history books. What is more, this recaptured past, which retold 'her-story' as one of women's deeds, was not just intended as an 'innocuous supplement' filling in missing parts of existing narratives. In revealing a shared existence of women past and present, it established a continuity across time and provided evidence of a common identity; an identity which would allow for women's self-recognition, both as legitimate subjects of historical analysis and as legal subjects.

Integrating women into law's history challenged the very contours of traditional legal history and its representations of womanhood. A profusion of positive histories followed, which detailed women's past resistance to law's oppression and their contributions to the development of law and legal institutions. Understandably, the earliest texts to emerge from this reorientation were stories of women's courage and bravery in the face of law; stories that evidenced the steadfast denial of many to accept their legal 'fate' and to instead speak out and engage in acts of resistance. Initially they dealt with the more obvious examples: the struggles for suffrage and civil rights, and efforts to reform particularly onerous legal rules, such as those regulating women's property, the custody of children, and the fight to gain self-ownership by repealing the law of coverture. Yet resistance was not only conceived of in terms of collective struggle; for individual women also had frequently used existing law and the courts to their advantage. They had regularly brought specific grievances before the law in the form of petitions, divorce suits or charges of rape, and had tried to bypass the stringent limitations law imposed upon them. In so doing, they had demonstrated considerable intelligence and creativity, whether through exploiting loopholes or gaps in the letter of the law, or in exposing and using contradictions and inconsistencies they discovered in judicial interpretations and reasoning. One well-documented example was the considerable variance found in the enforcement of coverture, which in part was the result of the many and highly imaginative ways in which women had been able to manipulate legal devices and use legal stratagems to obviate their status as *fem covert*. Similarly, histories were written of women who stood forth as litigants using the courts and legal instruments to sue for a range of actions: including cruelty, slander, inheritance, and debts; whilst others even told of women criminals who through their crimes were seen as having asserted themselves on behalf of the female sex.

Histories detailing women's struggles for legal change therefore did not only evidence a spirit of resistance or a commitment to equality through a politics of legal change. They also narrated a rich historical vein of inventive argument, compelling reasoning, and sophisticated critiques of law and rights. They revealed the complex political and legal debates women had become embroiled in, and how these had been articulated in open political arenas and corridors of power, often through the exercise of personal connections and status in support of the issue in question. For example, those nineteenth-century New York women who, in supporting the claim that wives be paid for domestic work, evoked what Siegel calls 'the earning statutes'. Also, the host of others, many of high social rank, who justified the need for their presence in public life by detailing the benefits they would bring from qualities associated with motherhood and other familial roles. The scope of these histories even extended to include the, often heated, contestations and controversies that had taken place within the feminist camps, such as those concerning suffrage, the abolition of laws protecting women's labour, prostitution, the repeal of the contagious diseases acts, and the nature of love and the institution of marriage.

The special significance feminist legal historians accorded the nineteenth-century politics generated a particular interest in the phenomenon of legal reform. Traditionally regarded as a somewhat 'neutral' activity associated with the normal progress of society, legal reform is seen as an essentially 'natural' process in the evolution of law. As such, it commanded little interest in conventional histories of law, with the sparse body of literature that existed being largely of a descriptive nature; essentially accounting for the facts and arguments employed during major changes to law at specific historical moments. Feminist legal historians pioneered an innovative engagement with this phenomenon by bringing it under their analytical lens and stepping beyond the reporting and analysis of arguments in support of particular reforms. They generated a small, but growing, number of studies offering detailed explorations of the major feminist legal reform campaigns of the nineteenth century; for example, studies that offered analysis of differences between the sexes in modes of thinking and acting in regards to changing law, or accounts of the conditions of possibility of campaigns that had sought to do so.

Finally, the integration of women into the history of law could not be complete without sharing histories of the main protagonists in women's battles with law; those who devoted so much of their thoughts and lives to effecting improvements in the conditions of women. These heroic individuals—radicals, fighters, and champions of specific causes—dared to dream and strive to achieve what many must have thought close to impossible. In paying due respect to these their fore-mothers, who notably included the first female students and servants of law in the legal professions, feminist legal historians carefully crafted biographies that honoured and respected their subjects' ideas and ideologies, as well as any differences according to race, class, religion or other qualification.

III. Forgetfulness, or the Paradox of Feminist Legal Historiography

> I am trying . . . to go back through all those places where I was exiled-enclosed so he could constitute his there. To read his text to try to take back from it what he took from me irrecoverably . . . I am trying to re-discover the possibility of a relation to air. Don't I need one, well before starting to speak?
>
> Lucy Irigaray[6]

The preceding review offered an exposition of the field in terms of its substantive content as a history of the relationship between women and law. Paying attention to the modes in which this relationship was conceived, examined, and concluded, it arranged the histories according to two major themes, namely law's treatment of women and women's attitude to law. The critical approach adopted in this section requires a closer and different kind of scrutiny, with attention shifting to the thematics of the field. An account of the modality of the two major constitutive themes, the intellectual and political alignments that have shaped their identity, together with their directional form, allows a critical appreciation of their efficacy, as well as their sense of achievement in and contribution to furthering the topics of their inquiries.

---

[6] Lucy Irigaray, *The Forgetting of Air* (1999) 171.

Situated between law and history, particularly the feminist permutations thereof, feminist legal history occupies no fixed abode. Yet despite this ambivalence of location and belonging, it boasts a unique identity whilst maintaining strong links with both fields; although each link is of an essentially different nature. To law it is indebted for the substantive content and the object of its inquiry: the same centring of 'women and law', which, driven by a deep-seated belief that law fundamentally affects women's social being, has been the primary locus of modernity's feminist project in law. To history, it turns for its modes of inquiry: the methodological and conceptual apparatus of historical practice, along with many of the analytical categories it uses, such as patriarchy, sex, gender, and periodization. Feminist legal history has denied neither its 'natural' affinity to law and history, nor the debt it owes to both. But it has not simply received. It has also bestowed its own gifts upon these 'sister' fields; a reciprocity testified to by the manner in which its two thematic categories are articulated, the resolutions each arrives at, and the nature of the historical outcomes each produces.

The histories presented under the first major theme, the scrutiny of law and its treatment of women, in sharing essential qualities with feminist legal scholarship, necessarily lean in its direction. Law, broadly conceived, constitutes the object of interrogation, whilst women's experiences and lives generate the criteria according to which feminist judgment delivers its verdicts. The extent of the feminist project, however, is hardly exhausted by exposure and denunciation. It is not enough for the feminist gaze to scrutinize law and identify normative patterns injurious to women. Its critical and political credibility is unequivocally associated with the desire to effect change by offering reconstructive propositions as to how best right that which is wrong and secure real, practical benefits for women. In contrast, the critical and political task of the feminist legal historian is less transparent. Whilst the feminist legal scholar engaging in a politics of legal change in the present is invariably looking ahead and imagining a different and brighter future, the feminist legal historian's enterprise is directed at the past. This difference in temporal orientation shadows existing similarities and, in furnishing a clear demarcation between the fields, allows for an easier appreciation of feminist legal history's efficacy.

Writing women into law's history lifts the veil of silence and cures the amnesia of the historical record. Accumulating a wide-ranging knowledge, it shows that the relationship between women and law is not immutable, but contingent upon historical conditions. Although highly significant and valuable in themselves, such offerings furnish few if any conspicuous gains in the fundamental understanding of the relationship between women and law. The exercise of historical memory does, however, involve an ordering of past events in relation to each other and to those of the present. And it is here, within this hermeneutical synthesis constituting the feminist legal historian's creative task, where the critical and political gravity of the contribution of the histories of the first theme is to be found.

The first lesson told of this past is that there has been a degree of continuity and consistency in law's conduct towards women. Despite varying considerably in nature and intensity, law has continued to operate in ways that constrain, discriminate against, disadvantage, or disempower women. Feminist legal historians do not posit the past as the radical 'other' of the present; they treat the two as merging in a 'continuum of oppression'. This continuity, in justifying knowledge claims about the nature of law as patriarchal or sexist, affirms, reinforces and energizes feminist challenges to modern law's claims to autonomy, neutrality, and objectivity. Feminist legal scholarship is thus gifted with a deeply textured past replete with detailed instances of law's function as bearer and enforcer of norms that oppress women. These exemplify, clarify, illuminate, and supplement present understandings of law's power to affect women's lives at both the symbolic and material level. So notwithstanding the temporal disjunction marking the horizon of their respective inquiries, conceptions of law articulated by feminist legal history and feminist legal scholarship concur. Historicizing law's conduct may add no major political or critical novelties to feminist legal scholarship's agenda, but it does serve to strengthen the modern diagnoses and arguments about the nature and power of law.

The second lesson also concerns the nature of law, but seeks to nuance the conclusions of the first by painting a more accurate picture through the study of women's interventions in law. Lending a careful ear to the rhythms of the feminist politics of legal reform and an observant eye to the detail of their conditions and processes, these types of history have sought to transmit past wisdom and experiences of attempts to 'feminize' law and thereby enrich, embolden, or even warn against the current politics of legal reform.[7] Some narrate the past as directly relevant to the present and claim political and critical credentials by communicating the lessons of the past to guide feminist strategies for legal policy and reform today.[8] Others, offering a less optimistic appreciation of the politics of legal reform, dismiss this notion of a 'usable past' and caution against an instrumental use of law that places unswerving confidence in its capacity to deliver long-given, yet unfulfilled, promises to fully recognize women's humanity; their autonomy, freedom, and equality.[9]

The legal histories hitherto discussed aver their efficacy and their political and critical contributions not from their study of the past per se, but from its validity for the present and future concerns of feminist legal scholarship. Thus, despite the distinct temporal planes they occupy, there is more synergy between the two

---

[7] Most of these histories have been produced in the U.S.A., e.g., see the significant work of Reva Siegel and Felice Batlan in this area.

[8] This type of history is what some historians refer to as 'applied legal history'. See the discussion in Tracy A. Thomas, 'The New Face of Women's Legal History' (2008) 41 *Akron Law Review* 697 ff.

[9] Warnings against legal reform have mainly been produced in U.K. See, e.g., Maria Drakopoulou, 'Feminism, Governmentality and the Politics of Legal Reform' (2008) 17 *Griffith Law Review* 330 ff; Carole Smart, *Feminism and the Power of Law* (1989) 160 ff.

than meets the eye. This is not the case with feminist legal histories written in the context of the other major theme: women's attitudes to law. The core lesson of the past provided in these histories stems from their recovering women as subjects before the law and as agents in the making of its history. The writing of micro-histories, whether of individual actors, or women's collectives handling their own or others' legal affairs, together with grand narratives of women's battles to effect legal change, serve both objectives. The former prove women's determination to stand and face law as litigants, or highlight contributions by women judges and lawyers in re-conceptualizing and expanding the limits of the legal system. The latter recognize women as forces of change and progress, as makers of their own history, and as protagonists of history for all women to come. Both provide ample evidence of the 'feminization' of law: the considerable part that women, guided by their own visions and sense of justice, have played in the transformation of law.[10]

This 'enchantment' with women's agency is not peculiar to feminist legal history. In taking their first steps in the 1970's, feminist historians had espoused the self-same promise to engraft women as subjects of history and as history makers. Positing women as subjects and active agents in respect to law has therefore also defined feminist legal history's position as a 'sister' field to feminist history. Weaving women's deeds and contributions into the tapestry of legal history mirrors feminist history's practice of writing 'compensatory histories' or histories of 'women worthies': histories whose purpose it is to excavate women's past and re-institute it in the historical process. However, feminist legal history's rationales and methodological choices were not the only testimony to the ties binding the two fields together. Their directional form and functional orientation, along with their claims of efficacy and contribution, attested to the same. More specifically, although these histories were produced as means of writing women into the history of law, they could just as well be seen as histories of writing law into the history of women. This is not to suggest they have not been invaluable in engendering new modes of thinking about female subjectivity and identity with reference to law. Instead, it is to emphasize the theoretical and political 'symbiosis' of the two fields, whose rich and bountiful offerings are enjoyed rather more by feminist history than by law. This is perhaps most evident in the way these histories portray law. Since their purpose is to establish female agency, a focus on law itself is seen to be of little immediate relevance. In effect, emphasizing women's conduct towards law displaces it as an object of historical analysis in its own right. It is instead apprehended and utilized as a depository of valuable material facilitating the historian's work; a structure bearing special importance as a reliable source of evidence in support of narratives of women's active historical presence.

[10] See Tracy A. Thomas, Tracey Jean Boisseau, 'Introduction Law History and Feminism', in Tracy A. Thomas, Tracey Jean Boisseau (eds.), *Feminist Legal History* (2011) 15 ff.

This examination has revealed a paradox in feminist legal history's self-representation. This paradox becomes apparent once the definition of the field, as the history of the relationship between women and law, is juxtaposed to the field's substantive content, as 'translated' into the historical narrations of the field's products. The very act of naming clearly demarcates the field's territory as a distinct form of scholarship occupying a separate intellectual space and possessing a unified object of inquiry. Already at its inception feminist legal history endeavoured to situate itself by accounting of its own province. By carefully separating its 'territory' from that of its two principle neighbours, history and law, it authorized the recognition of its own autonomy and singular identity as an academic field. Yet, when attention moves from the field's delimitation to its accomplishments, and, in particular, to the theoretical and methodological exchanges that have shaped them and their effects, the field's identity is exposed as being rather more fragile than it would perhaps care to admit. The paradox marking feminist legal history lies precisely in this peculiar combination of the institutional autonomy to which feminist legal history's definition points, and the intellectual dependency upon its 'sister fields', demonstrated by the many studies it has nurtured.

This paradox however, cannot easily be dismissed simply as a 'casualty' of the field's interdisciplinary nature. Its presence is both a symptom of the limitations of the field's legal and historical imagination, as well as its critical efficacy, and at the same time a register of traces which lead to other possibilities of analysis and understanding of the past relationship between women and law. The unquestionable rootedness in and fidelity to the dyad of 'women and law' that feminist historical inquiry bears implies that whatever form and direction its analysis takes, it will eventually return to this, the field's originary *locus*. Here, feminist engagement with the history of law must entail reference to empirical women, even if it formally refers to gender, because it is empirical women who stand at the receiving end: it being against women's lives with and experiences of law that the oppressive function of law is to be measured and apprehended. As a result, law is precluded from standing alone as an object of inquiry worthy of historical feminist engagement in its own right.

The practice of feminist legal history need not necessarily remain walled in this way. Law's nature and form of power can be thought of in other ways than operating solely on the social terrain where it affects women; for it is not only the relationship of law and women that has a history, but law as a distinct body of knowledge has its own history, too. Interrogation of the constellation of texts, symbols, clusters of images, and practices, and the modes in which they are received, presented, modified, and transmitted afresh from past to past, and from past to the present, invites a different understanding of law's nature and power. Engaging feminist historical analysis with law's language, reason, and practice, as manifested in the handing down of law's tradition, shifts focus away from the oppressive power exercised on women's social being towards a creative one. Located in the apprehension of social life in law's imaging and imagining mind, this power is a life-giving and life-defining one, cohering structures of human existence and engendering modes of social life within and beyond the realm of law. Analysis of this power reveals law's logic of divisions and its role in the creation and maintenance of difference, thereby raising questions pertinent to the feminist legal historian's analysis and critique of law. She can, for instance, ask how sexual difference is inscribed into its tradition, in what ways it constitutes a systemic element of the canonical production of legal knowledge, or, how sexual difference shapes and founds law's relationship to the social world; ultimately, what is the sexual economy of law's power? Employing an analytics of sexual difference to re-read law's tradition in this way also constitutes an act of remembering and recovering of the past; that is, the past of law. Establishing connections across time and exploring, in diachronic inquiry, the modes and intensity of law's reliance upon sexual difference reveals the conditions of possibility of law's power without collapsing what is transient into what is permanent in the manifestation of this power. Positing law's life and history as an object of analysis with a view to exposing their fundamental reliance upon sexual difference, not only offers a more comprehensive view of the nature and power of law, it also involves an exploration of the relationship between women and law, albeit not in terms of effects, but in terms of the forms of women's belonging to law; of what it means to live with law rather than under law.

Framing the relationship of women and law in terms of belonging displaces concern with the normative constraints of law. It concentrates on women's forms of social life, which, captivated and structured by law's spatial and temporal orders, become visible at the junctures of the social and the legal that law's power authorizes. Questions of belonging, however, do not only address those historical forms of women's social being that law engenders. They create a discursive space wherein alternative accounts of conduct and agency may arise.

Feminist legal history hitherto has accounted for its situatedness as a field in institutional terms only. Questions of positionality that engage the subject position and identity of the scholar, such as: 'who speaks', 'how', 'why', and 'from where'—questions that reference her reflective spirit and awareness of her own place and function in the production of knowledge—have been largely neglected. In raising these questions the feminist legal historian asks whether or how she can partake in the event of law's tradition and its process of transmission. In other words, with what right, and from what standpoint, can she, with no obvious filiation to the many generations of male makers, teachers, interpreters, custodians, and receivers of law's tradition, intervene in law, and what form her intervention should take? These are questions not only of conduct, role, and responsibility of the feminist legal historian in the performance of her tasks. They also invite reflection on her filiation to female and 'feminist' juristic traditions reminding her thus of her obliviousness to her own past. They call for the excavation and recovery of suppressed or lost female genealogies in law as well as feminist textual traditions critical of law, thus constantly mediating past and present in what can be seen as an alternative understanding of what a history of the process of 'feminization' of law may be.[11]

The close alliance between sexual difference, history, and law I have set out in this chapter opens a discursive space wherein a novel way of conducting feminist legal history can flourish. Here, feminist legal history need not operate as a methodological stance adding a historical dimension to feminist legal scholarship's diagnoses and concerns about the present relationship of women and law. Neither is it to be appreciated for its corrective function or its use of law as an evidentiary structure offering proof of women's agency and brave deeds. Nor does it have to present its contributions and accomplishments as offerings in aid of the desired ends of another field.

This 'otherwise feminist' history, although continuing to remain faithful to interdisciplinarity, is able to clearly distinguish its own direction of historical research from that of its 'sister' fields. It can thus adapt any intellectual borrowings to its own independent theoretical and methodological concerns, whilst the contributions of the histories it narrates, offerings of a new way of thinking critically about law, sexual difference, and belonging, together with a self-reflective practice of feminist legal history, are both worthy accomplishments in their own right and yet complementary to that which already exists.

Bibliography

Felice Batlan, *Women and Justice for the Poor: A History of Legal Aid, 1863–1945* (Cambridge University Press, 2015)

Felice Batlan, 'Law and the Fabric of the Everyday: The Settlement Houses, Sociological Jurisprudence and the Gendering of Urban Legal Culture' (2006) 15 *Southern California Interdisciplinary Law Journal* 235 ff

Constance Backhouse, *Carnal Crimes: Sexual Assault in Canada, 1900–1975* (Irwin Law, 2008)

Constance Backhouse, *Petticoats and Prejudice: Women and Law in Nineteenth-Century Canada* (Women's Press/Osgood Society, 1991)

Leonore Davidoff, Catherine Hall, *Family Fortunes: Men and Women of the English Middle Class 1780–1850* (Routledge, 1987)

Frances Dolan, *Dangerous Familiars: Representations of Domestic Crime in England 1550–1700* (Cornell University Press, 2016)

Frances Dolan, *Marriage and Violence The Early Modern Legacy* (Philadelphia: University of Pennsylvania Press, 2008)

Ann Genovese, 'On Australian Feminist Tradition: Three Notes on Conduct Inheritance and the Relation of Historiography and Jurisprudence' (2014) 38 *Journal of Australian Studies* 430 ff

Peter Goodrich, *Law in the Courts of Love* (Routledge, 1996)

---

[11] Scholarly commitment to such an 'otherwise feminist' legal history has already been made by legal scholars. See, e.g., the work by Ann Genovese and Peter Goodrich.

Peter Goodrich, 'Gynaetopia Feminine Genealogies of Common Law' in Oedipus Lex: Psychoanalysis, History, Law (University of California Press, 1996) 144 ff

Barbara Hanawalt, The Wealth of Wives: Women Law and Economy in Late Medieval London (Oxford University Press, 2007)

Bronach Kane, Fiona Williamson (eds.), Women, Agency and the Law 1300–1700 (Routledge, 2015)

Serena Mayeri, Reasoning from Race: Feminism, Law and the Civil Rights Revolution (Harvard University Press, 2011)

Mary Joan Mossman, The First Women Lawyers A Comparative Study of Gender, Law, and the Legal Professions (Hart Publishing, 2006)

Amy Stanley, From Bondage to Contract: Wage Labour, Marriage, and the Market in the Age of Slave Emancipation (Cambridge University Press, 1999)

Reva Siegel, 'The Right's Reasons: Constitutional Conflict and the Spread of Woman-Protective Anti-Abortion Argument' (2008) 57 Duke L.J. 1688 ff

Reva Siegel, 'Home as Work: The First Woman's Rights Claims Concerning Wives' Household Labor, 1850–1880' (1994) 103 Yale L.J. 1073 ff

Tracy A. Thomas, Tracey Jean Boisseeau (eds.), Feminist Legal History Essays in Women and Law (New York University Press, 2011)

Margaret Thornton and Ann Genovese, 'On the Liberal Promise: A Conversation' (2015) 41 Australian Feminist Law Journal 3 ff

Tim Stretton (ed.), Marital Litigation in the Court of Requests 1542–1642 (Cambridge University Press, 2008)

Tim Stretton, Women Waging Law in Elizabethan England (Cambridge University Press, 1998)

Tim Stretton, Krista J. Kesselring (eds.), Married Women and the Law: Coverture in England and the Common Law World (McGill-University Press, 2014)

Rachel Sturman, The Government of Social Life in Colonial India: Liberalism, Religious Rights and Women's Rights (Cambridge University Press, 2012)

Barbara Young Welke, Law and the Borders of Belonging in the Long Nineteenth Century United States (Cambridge University Press, 2010)

Barbara Young Welke, Recasting American Liberty: Gender, Race, Law and the Railroad Revolution, 1865–1900 (Cambridge University Press, 2001)

CHAPTER 33

CRITICAL RACE THEORY AND THE POLITICAL USES OF LEGAL HISTORY

H. TIMOTHY LOVELACE, JR.

IN 1976, Derrick Bell shocked the civil rights community. Bell, a former lawyer for the NAACP Legal Defense and Educational Fund (LDF), authored a deeply controversial article entitled, 'Serving Two Masters: Integration Ideals and Client Interests in School Desegregation Litigation'. Bell analysed school desegregation litigation in Boston, Detroit, and Atlanta and argued that lawyers often failed to fully comprehend the intricacies of the client-lawyer relationship in school desegregation cases. 'How should the term "client" be defined in school desegregation cases that are litigated for decades, determine critically important constitutional rights for thousands of minority children, and usually involve major restructuring of a public school system?' Bell asked. 'How should civil rights attorneys represent the often diverse interests of clients and class in school suits?' For Bell, the national NAACP and the LDF's lawyer-centred approach to legal transformation did not necessarily benefit or properly represent the needs of the campaign's intended beneficiaries.

Bell also highlighted the inability of modern civil rights litigation to advance real racial justice. He declared that racial balancing should not be the sole goal of the desegregation movement. Bell noted that NAACP founder and towering scholar, W. E. B. DuBois, had wrestled with this question in a 1935 article published in the *Journal of Negro Education*. In 'Does the Negro Need Separate Schools?' DuBois proclaimed, 'The Negro needs neither segregated schools nor mixed schools. What he needs is education.' Bell wholeheartedly agreed with DuBois's conclusion. Simply desegregating public schools pursuant to *Brown v. Board of Education*, Bell contended, had not and would not end racial inequalities in education. The national NAACP and LDF needed to direct more attention to unequal and inadequate school resources and help more black parents participate meaningfully in school policymaking. These piercing criticisms of the NAACP's strategy reflected Bell's deep frustration with legal liberalism, the left's misplaced hope in racial balancing remedies, and growing racial retrenchment across the nation. Bell's willingness to dissent from civil rights orthodoxy would radically reshape the study of race, law, and history.[1] The result would lead to the creation of critical race theory.

This chapter opens by examining the role of historical analysis in the development of critical race theory. Section II explores how legal historians of the civil rights movement, in turn, imported insights from critical race theory to develop three decades of movement scholarship. Section III charts new scholarly directions for both critical race theorists and legal historians. The chapter concludes with reflections on how legal history and critical race theory have influenced contemporary struggles for racial justice.

I. THE ROLE OF LEGAL HISTORY IN CRITICAL RACE THEORY

Four years after Bell published 'Serving Two Masters', he shocked the civil rights establishment again. In '*Brown v. Board of Education* and the Interest Convergence Dilemma', Bell argued that *Brown* was not the product of the Court's commitment to legal formalism or simple morality alone. Bell maintained that *Brown* could best be understood through a 'consideration of the decision's value to whites'. He pointed to three potential motivations for the Court's decision: the U.S.'s struggle with communist countries; assurances to veterans of the Second World War who fought for freedom and equality abroad yet were denied it at home; and that the South could

---

[1] Derrick Bell, Jr., 'Serving Two Masters: Integration Ideals and Client Interests in School Desegregation Litigation' (1976) 85 *Yale L.J.* 470 ff.

not make the transition from the plantation to the Sunbelt until state-sponsored segregation ended. Here, Bell, most notably, highlighted the U.S. government's brief in *Brown*, which called for the Court to view the case within the 'context of the present world struggle between freedom and tyranny . . . .' For Bell, racial 'progress' only occurred when civil rights leaders' interests coincided with elite whites' interests. This idea of the 'interest convergence dilemma' became a staple of critical race theory. From its inception, critical race theory self-consciously engaged legal history to criticize liberal legal reform and to develop coherent frameworks for ending racial subordination.[2]

Other key themes emerged in critical race theory's foundational texts. These themes similarly derived from historically grounded analyses. Neil Gotanda's 'A Critique of "Our Constitution is Color-Blind"' mobilized particular visions of the past to argue that justice was not colour-blind and had never been colour-blind. Gotanda declared that colour-blindness was a euphemism for white racial domination, and this potent idea became a premise of critical race scholarship.[3] Alan Freeman's 'Legitimizing Racial Discrimination through Anti-Discrimination Law: A Critical Review of Supreme Court Doctrine' explored the Court's civil rights jurisprudence from *Brown* through the present. In this magisterial work, he urged readers to consider civil rights cases from the perspective of victims and not perpetrators.[4] The anti-subordination perspective soon became a core principle in critical race theory. Kimberlé Crenshaw coined the term 'intersectionality' in her brilliant 1989 essay, 'Demarginalizing the Intersection of Race and Sex: A Black Feminist Critique of Antidiscrimination Doctrine, Feminist Theory and Antiracist Politics'. In the essay, Crenshaw drew upon the historical experiences of black women like Sojourner Truth and Anna Julia Cooper to challenge single-axis analyses of modern racism. While liberals praised contemporary anti-discrimination law, Crenshaw found that anti-discrimination law did not effectively protect black women. Traditional legal examinations of discrimination fostered the notion that 'all the women were white and all the blacks were men'. Critical race theorists extended Crenshaw's methodological approach to consider race's intersections with other identity categories, such as class, religion, and sexual orientation.[5] Richard Delgado's 'Storytelling for Oppositionists and Others: A Plea for Narrative' recognized that legal scholarship was a site for the

---

[2] Derrick Bell, Jr., '*Brown v. Board of Education* and the Interest-Convergence Dilemma' (1980) 93 *Harvard L.R.* 518 ff.

[3] Neil Gotanda, 'A Critique of "Our Constitution is Colorblind"' (1991) 44 *Stanford L.R.* 1 ff.

[4] Alan Freeman, 'Legitimizing Racial Discrimination through Anti-Discrimination Law: A Critical Review of Supreme Court Doctrine' (1978) 62 *Minnesota L.R.* 1049 ff.

[5] Kimberlé Crenshaw, 'Demarginalizing the Intersection of Race and Sex: A Black Feminist Critique of Antidiscrimination Doctrine, Feminist Politics and Antiracist Politics' (1989) 1989 *University of Chicago Legal Forum* 139 ff.

production of racial power. Delgado's approach offered innovative ways to retell legal stories and thus re-invited history into critical race theory.[6] Conventional liberal discourse held that racism was a deviation from core American values. Critical race theorists broke from this belief. The evolution of white supremacy in this country had been instructive. Racism, they proclaimed, was quintessentially American.

Critical race theory found favour with cohorts of scholars seeking to expand the 'outsider' legal scholarship. Legal scholarship on the experiences of Latinx, Asian American, Middle Eastern, and South Asian, American Indian, and LGBTQ communities followed the creation of critical race theory. These bodies of literature, like critical race theory's foundational texts, relied heavily on historical methods. Scholars frequently located current forms of subordination in historical discrimination, and they attempted to provide their own interpretations of important political struggles, court opinions, and legislative debates.[7]

Critical race theorists produced more conventional works of legal history, such as Kendall Thomas's path-breaking article, *Rouge et Noir Reread: A Popular Constitutional History of the Angelo Herndon Case*. Herndon was a black labour organizer convicted of insurrection for attempting to create coalitions between black and white workers in Georgia. In 1937, the U.S. Supreme Court overturned Herndon's conviction in *Herndon v. Lowry*. The decision was a watershed civil liberties victory. Thomas's gripping account of *Herndon* deviated from traditional accounts of the case. For Thomas, legal historians frequently submerged the voices of clients in their narratives, privileging courts, lawyers, and doctrine. Thomas sought to reconstruct history 'from the bottom up'. He took law, lawyers, and legal institutions seriously, but he also relied on archival sources to allow the 'subaltern' to speak for themselves. He fused social and cultural history to legal history, and in the process, he laid a clear road map for legal historians of the civil rights movement to follow.[8]

Most critical race theorists, however, employed legal history instrumentally. They primarily revisited the past as a strategy to frame their claims on contemporary discrimination, avoid past mistakes, and demand reparation for old and continuing harms. These scholars, in the words of Kimberlé Crenshaw, 'look[ed] back to move forward'.[9]

---

[6] Richard Delgado, 'Storytelling for Oppositionists and Others: A Plea for Narrative' (1989) 87 *Michigan L.R.* 2411 ff.

[7] Richard Delgado, Jean Stefancic (eds.), *Critical Race Theory: An Introduction* (2017) 3 ff.

[8] Kendall Thomas, 'Rouge et Noir Reread: A Popular Constitutional History of the Angelo Herndon Case' (1992) 65 *Southern California L.R.* 2599 ff.

[9] Kimberlé Crenshaw, 'Twenty Years of Critical Race Theory: Looking Back to Look Forward' (2011) 43 *Connecticut L.R.* 1253 ff.

II. The Role of Critical Race Theory in Legal History

By the 1990s, critical race theory had become embedded in legal history. Civil rights historians, including those who did not identify as critical race theorists, increasingly embraced some of Bell's criticisms of *Brown* and legal liberalism. In *The Hollow Hope*, Gerald Rosenberg argued that although *Brown* was celebrated as the most important Court decision of the twentieth century, *Brown* left African-Americans with little more than an empty guarantee of racial equality. *Brown* did not immediately desegregate most schools in the former Confederacy, Rosenberg properly asserts. In fact, *Brown* spurred Massive Resistance. Rosenberg maintained that school desegregation did not begin in earnest in the South until the passage of the Civil Rights Act of 1964 when Congress and the President joined the Court in the fight for desegregation. He concluded that contrary to the triumphal reading of legal liberalism in the traditional *Brown* narrative, politics proved to be a more strategic vehicle for social change than courts. Rosenberg powerfully declared, 'The celebration of *Brown* serves an ideological function of assuring Americans that they have lived up to their constitutional principles without actually requiring them to do so.'[10]

Rosenberg's criticisms of *Brown* resonated with Michael Klarman, author of '*Brown*, Racial Change, and the Civil Rights Movement'. Klarman, too, emphasized the limitations of the NAACP's court-centred strategy in *Brown*. For Klarman, racial progress was occurring in the U.S. before *Brown*. Klarman, following Bell's scholarship, showed that the Second World War, the Cold War, and the Great Migration gave blacks new-found political power. Nonetheless, *Brown* undermined those gains in the short-run, Klarman asserted, because the ruling was a counter-majoritarian decision in the South. *Brown* sparked an incredible backlash and stymied civil rights progress. It polarized Southern politics and led to the extremist politics of men like Bull Connor, George Wallace, and Orval Faubus. Klarman's scholarship offered a cautionary and helpful tale to those interested in achieving racial progress through courts. Litigation might be a tool in the social movement repertoire, but as history has aptly demonstrated, litigation is a slow, expensive, and conservative method for social and legal change. We might add that heavy reliance on litigation might thwart popular participation in the struggle for racial equality.[11]

---

[10] Gerald Rosenberg, *The Hollow Hope: Can Courts Bring about Social Change?* (1991).

[11] Michael Klarman, '*Brown*, Racial Change, and the Civil Rights Movement' (1994) 80 *Virginia L.R.* 7 ff.

Rosenberg and Klarman's investment in depicting *Brown* as a failure, however, yielded several sweeping and inaccurate conclusions. For example, in *The Hollow Hope*, Rosenberg sought to diminish *Brown's* legacy by arguing that *Brown* was uninfluential with those involved in the movement's direct action campaigns. Klarman once echoed this bold assertion, but he has since slowly backed away from it.[12] In *The Hollow Hope*, Rosenberg asked, 'Was [Martin Luther] King motivated to act by the [*Brown*] Court? From an examination of King's thinking, the answer appears to be no.' Rosenberg continued, 'King rooted his beliefs in Christian theology and Gandhian non-violence, not constitutional doctrine. His attitude to the Court, far from a source of inspiration was one of strategic disfavor.'[13] Such a spurious claim epitomizes one of the major epistemological problems that frustrated critical race scholars and historians like Kendall Thomas. Too frequently, *The Hollow Hope* rendered black activists as objects and not subjects and overlooked readily available sources on black life in the post-*Brown* years.

In fact, King had wrapped himself in *Brown's* mantle very early in his career. Several months after the start of the Montgomery Bus Boycott, King proclaimed that his role in the boycott had changed. He was no longer simply leading a local campaign to end racial insults on buses and add more black bus drivers; he was now also leading black Montgomerians' fight to export *Brown* into intrastate transportation. In the 1950s, although King was not a lawyer or a national NAACP official, he interjected himself into the organization's fiercest school desegregation battles, often in unexpected ways. In 1957, for example, as Thurgood Marshall relied on federal litigation to desegregate Little Rock's public schools, King taught the Little Rock Nine spiritual strategies they could use to implement *Brown* in the halls of Central High School. For King, his approach did not conflict with the work of the NAACP's lawyers. Christian love and Gandhian non-violence were simply means that students could use to give *Brown* life. King toured the country throughout this period christening '[t]he May 17 decision . . . a New Emancipation', calling 'for an immediate start toward the implementation of the May 17 U.S. Supreme Court decision banning the segregated school system', and praising *Brown* for helping to create the 'new Negro . . . which we see all over the South and all over the nation today'. In fact, the first major event the Southern Christian Leadership Conference (SCLC) ever held and Dr. King's largest live audience until the 1963 March on Washington—the Prayer Pilgrimage for Freedom—was an outdoor civil rights rally commemorating *Brown's* third anniversary. If *Brown's* 'success' is to be measured through such linear, causal chains leading to the end of segregated schools, then scholars like Professor Rosenberg might be right that the Court's decision was ultimately a failure. However, if scholars measure *Brown's* 'success' in

---

[12] Michael Klarman, *From Jim Crow to Civil Rights: The Supreme Court and the Struggle for Racial Equality* (2004).

[13] Rosenberg (n. 10) 139 ff.

the same way that Dr. King measured 'success' during this period, we might come to different conclusions.[14]

A new wave of civil rights scholarship emerged, as legal historians more thoughtfully employed the theoretical advances of critical race theory. Mary Dudziak's *Cold War Civil Rights: Race and the Image of American Democracy* built from Derrick Bell's reading of the ties between the Cold War and the civil rights movement. Dudziak expanded Bell's work by relying on extensive domestic and foreign research to illustrate how the fight for the hearts and minds of the Third World influenced U.S. law and policy. Years before the U.S. government submitted its brief in *Brown* to improve America's image abroad, the U.S. submitted briefs in cases like *Shelley v. Kraemer, McLaurin v. Oklahoma State Regents*, and *Sweatt v. Painter* to promote U.S. Cold War interests. After *Brown*, Cold War politics remained an engine for the civil rights movement. During the Little Rock Crisis, President Dwight Eisenhower federalized troops to ensure that the Little Rock Nine were able to attend Central High School. Eisenhower was no strong supporter of school desegregation, Dudziak persuasively shows, but his decision was driven, in part, by how the Little Rock crisis was tarnishing the U.S.'s international reputation. *Cold War Civil Rights* is a significant addition to civil rights and critical race scholarship, as it provides ample historical evidence to confirm Bell's assertions about mid-century civil rights reform. Civil rights progress was not simply a moral issue; it was also a foreign policy issue.[15]

Risa Goluboff's *The Lost Promise of Civil Rights* is also a substantial contribution to the critical race and civil rights literatures. Goluboff revisits the world of civil rights before *Brown* and discovers that civil rights lawyers were not narrowly focused on ending racial discrimination in education. Here, she takes the complaints of black workers to the Department of Justice in the 1940s as the starting point for her analysis. Given the Great Depression and the subsequent expansion of the wartime industries, the national NAACP, an organization she argues that had not been profoundly committed to labour organizing, became more interested in addressing the labour issues confronting black workers. Goluboff contends that labour-based litigation was a viable means to pursue racial equality in the period before *Brown*. She offers masterful readings of the Court's labour jurisprudence and draws attention to points of contingency in the development of civil rights strategy and doctrine. Nonetheless, due to rampant red-baiting during the early Cold War and the success of the *Brown* litigation, the NAACP marginalized its constitutional litigation around issues of labour, Goluboff states. The normative implications of *The Lost Promise of Civil Rights* are evident—and very much in line with critical race theory. In the book's early pages, Goluboff declares, '[B]y uncovering the

---

[14] H. Timothy Lovelace, Jr., 'King Making: *Brown v. Board* and the Rise of a Racial Savior' (2017) 57 *A.J.L.H.* 393 ff.

[15] Mary Dudziak, *Cold War Civil Rights: Race and the Image of American Democracy* (2000).

historical alternatives to the civil rights law we know as our own, we can broaden the imagination about the possibilities for addressing the remnants of Jim Crow still facing the nation today.' Goluboff's scholarship is a clarion call to those interested in pursuing economic equality.[16]

In *Courage to Dissent: Atlanta and the Long Civil Rights Movement*, Tomiko Brown-Nagin offers a theoretically sophisticated and deeply researched account of racial politics in the capital of the U.S. South. Brown-Nagin's community-based study allows her to develop themes in Derrick Bell's 'Serving Two Masters.' Brown-Nagin demonstrates that the city's black leaders differed with the national NAACP during the NAACP's school desegregation campaigns. Brown-Nagin's attention to the interiority and diversity in black politics is remarkable. There was never a singular black community unified over the desegregation process, and many black educators often were deeply ambivalent over the value and meaning of immediate desegregation. Atlanta's civil rights establishment resisted the national NAACP's push towards immediate desegregation and instead favoured a gradual implementation process. Moreover, Brown-Nagin illuminates how black student frustration with *Brown* and legal liberalism drove many black student activists to air their grievances in the streets rather than in courtrooms. She analyses the students' readings of law, explaining how protesters made constitutional claims with their bodies in city streets. Atlanta, once known as the 'the city too busy to hate', witnessed violent clashes over the future of American constitutional law—the meaning of equal protection, the scope of private property rights, and the potential uses of the commerce power. And although these students were vocal about some elders' disdain for direct action, Brown-Nagin deftly highlights how Atlanta's student activists frequently turned to NAACP-affiliated lawyers for legal defence, bail funds, and advice. These lawyers provided students with the legal resources necessary to keep them involved in their demonstrations. Such a 'volatile marriage' between Atlanta's students and civil rights lawyers, Brown-Nagin compellingly argues, helped to create the political context for the enactment of the Civil Rights Act of 1964.[17]

Kenneth Mack's *Representing the Race: The Creation of the Civil Rights Lawyer* demonstrates the possibilities and the limitations of identity politics by engaging critical race theory's insights on identity performance. Throughout the book, Mack gracefully uses biographical accounts to propel his analysis of intra-racial tensions within the black bar. He examines the lives of biracial and fair-skinned lawyers, including John Mercer Langston, to explore colourism. He reveals how Sadie Alexander and Pauli Murray navigated the intersectional obstacles of sexism and heterosexism. He probes the words and actions of militant black lawyers, like

---

[16] Risa Goluboff, *The Lost Promise of Civil Rights* (2007).

[17] Tomiko Brown-Nagin, *Courage to Dissent: Atlanta and the Long History of the Civil Rights Movement* (2011).

Cecil Moore, to discuss generational divides. Each of these facets of identity, Mack persuasively argues, were obstacles that leading black lawyers had to navigate successfully to become and maintain their statuses as 'representatives of the race.' Mack then uses this textured reading of racial identity within the bar and, more specifically, within the white-dominated, public space of a courtroom, to advance a powerful claim: that success in the profession required civil rights lawyers to perform like white men. Lawyers, like Charles Hamilton Houston, Thurgood Marshall, and Sadie Alexander, Mack demonstrates, won great respect from the white bar and black communities by acting 'authentically' black while personifying the norms of their most successful white counterparts. These lawyers were able to cross the colour line and join the legal fraternity, Mack asserts, through their skills of racial presentation. Mack leaves readers with a wonderfully rich conclusion. He situates the election of President Barack Obama in this genealogy of fair-skinned blacks able to successfully transcend racial barriers and represent the race.[18]

III. Legal History and the Race to the Future

Critical race theory developed, in part, from a sharp appraisal of the civil rights bar. This section suggests additional areas of inquiry for scholars interested in revising the civil rights and critical race historiographies. This first part of this section returns to enduring conceptions of NAACP lawyering. Early critical race theorists problematized NAACP lawyers' construction of racial leadership. This part asks an even more fundamental question about the creation of movement leadership: how did Southern NAACP lawyers and chapters replace existing black leadership and assume the race's vanguard? The second part of this section discusses the growth of the black bench. Critical race theorists, sociologists, and political scientists have long documented the statistical relationships between race, gender, and judicial decision-making. Legal historians might expand the scholarship here by returning to the archival record and describing how distinguished black lawyers leveraged their racial leadership to join the judiciary. The final part of this section examines arguably the most misunderstood social movement in the post-civil rights era: black power. Now more than a half century after Stokely Carmichael's cry for black power in rural Mississippi, the movement remains a taboo topic in much of the academy. This portion of the chapter, nonetheless, urges legal historians to explore how black

---

[18] Kenneth Mack, *Representing the Race: The Creation of the Civil Rights Lawyer* (2013).

power influenced the black bar, transformed the legal academy, and continues to structure contemporary discussions of racial justice under law.

A. NAACP Lawyers and the Creation of Constituents

In 'Serving Two Masters', Derrick Bell noted that his concerns over lawyer-client relationships in the NAACP's school desegregation litigation were not novel criticisms. Bell cited *NAACP v. Button* to make his point. In 1956, the Virginia General Assembly amended its criminal statutes regulating the solicitation of legal business to chill the activism of the NAACP's Virginia State Conference. State legislators charged that NAACP lawyers were engaging in unethical conduct by stirring up litigation and pursuing the NAACP's interests rather than black litigants' interests. The U.S. Supreme Court invalidated the Virginia law. The Court held that the NAACP's litigation was 'a form of political expression' protected by the First Amendment. Bell condemned Massive Resistance, but he also took the question of conflicts of interest in the NAACP's litigation seriously. He emphasized the potential tensions between the national NAACP, its Virginia lawyers, black plaintiffs, and the black communities that civil rights lawyers purported to represent.[19]

Revisiting the civil rights movement in Virginia invites new questions for legal historians and critical race theorists. If the legal staff of the Virginia State Conference often subordinated the desires of its clients and did not actually represent 'community' interests (whatever the simplified conception of those interests might be), how did it become the largest civil rights organization in the state? How did the Virginia State Conference construct an organizational model that allowed it to consolidate its power and position itself and its leadership at forefront the Virginia's freedom struggle? And how did the Virginia State Conference's organizational model attempt to remake mid-century civil rights lawyering?

Although the NAACP is the largest and oldest civil rights organization in the country, curiously, NAACP state conferences and their affiliated attorneys have all but escaped book-length study. Much of the extant scholarship on NAACP lawyers has instead focused on nationally recognized lawyers, ignoring how the NAACP's federated structure facilitated democratic experimentation at the local and state levels. Many scholars have lambasted NAACP lawyers for being too accommodationist, too far from the 'masses', and unconcerned with issues of social welfare. Yet the NAACP, unlike most other civil rights organizations, was a mass membership organization. Legal historians are well-positioned to reconsider NAACP lawyers, a group whose history is filled with misconception, by analysing

---

[19] Bell (n. 1) 493 ff.

how the State Conference's legal staff became vital to building and sustaining a popular movement.

During the civil rights movement, the Virginia State Conference was arguably the most successful and best organized state conference of the NAACP. African-American lawyers were central to this success. Richmond-born and Roanoke-reared attorney Oliver Hill was a founding member of the State Conference, and in its early days, the organization routinely relied on the legal and political strategies of esteemed lawyers like Hill, Spottswood Robinson, and Samuel Tucker. The Virginia State Conference boasted the largest number of local branches in the nation, and the state's legal team, mainly comprised of top-flight, Howard Law graduates, was hailed as being a 'credit to the race' for being at the cutting edge of civil rights lawyering. In the 1940s, national NAACP officials chose the Virginia State Conference to help lead the attack on segregated education due to the Virginia staff's sterling legal reputation and impressive fundraising abilities. NAACP lawyers from other states often journeyed to the Commonwealth to watch the State Conference's social engineers litigate its school desegregation cases. These visiting attorneys returned to their home states and attempted to adapt the Virginia lawyers' arguments to their own state's conditions. Virginia's legal staff also ventured to branches outside of the state. They used their experiences in Virginia to counsel NAACP attorneys in other states on how to manage lawyer-client relationships, mobilize local communities, use litigation and non-litigation strategies, and mediate conflicts with competing civil rights lawyers and organizations. Virginia's NAACP lawyers were masters of tactical and organizational innovation. How they were able to construct a large organizational base remains a topic that deserves far greater attention.[20]

Re-examining the Virginia State Conference's origins would be critical to the intellectual project. Most considerations of the NAACP's activity in Virginia begin with *Alston v. School Board of Norfolk*.[21] A fresh study might begin with an exploration of black lawyers' Depression-era, criminal litigation. Years before the State Conference began its assault on the Virginia's segregated educational system, men like Hill won acclaim through criminal litigation. After Hill helped to found the State Conference, the State Conference's lawyers and officials devoted great attention to criminal justice reform. They travelled the Commonwealth advocating for prisoners' rights, protesting police brutality and mob violence, and representing indigent, black Virginians facing capital punishment. Several questions follow. How were 'respectable' lawyers and State Conference officials able to organize around people and causes often deemed 'unworthy'? Why did the idea of expanding a mass membership organization appeal to cash-strapped lawyers? How did the

[20] Larissa Smith, 'A Civil Rights Vanguard: Black Attorneys and the NAACP in Virginia', in Peter Lau (ed.), *From the Grassroots to the Supreme Court: Brown v. Board of Education and American Democracy* (2004) 129 ff.

[21] *Alston v. School Board of Norfolk*, 112 F. 2d 992 (4th Cir. 1940).

lessons these attorneys learned in criminal practice—canvassing rural Virginia communities during criminal investigations, litigating in Jim Crow courtrooms, and using media to dramatize the failings of the Southern justice system—shape the future of civil rights lawyering and organizing?

The Virginia State Conference's legal staff also created new conceptions of rights and political possibilities. For example, in a world with no landmark federal or state statutes targeting environmental degradation and before a thriving U.S. environmental rights movement, the Virginia State Conference boldly confronted environmental racism. During the late 1950s and early 1960s, NAACP attorneys challenged the siting of landfills in black neighbourhoods by fusing their deep ecological concerns to common law remedies and extra-legal activism. For the attorneys and their communities, environmental rights were civil rights. Accordingly, the Virginia NAACP's mid-century environmental activism forces environmental and civil rights scholars to reconceptualize the historical relationship between both social movements. Similarly, legal historians might explore how the NAACP's structure encouraged local branches to experiment in the fight against discrimination in other under-studied areas, including wages, public housing, military contracting, hospital administration, nursing home care, and mental health treatment. While the national NAACP had its imperatives, local branches were able to supplement the national agenda with programmes tailored to local and regional needs. Branches welcomed the lawyers' expertise in structuring their legal and political programmes. Moreover, given the dearth of practising lawyers in the Jim Crow South, hosting civil rights lawyers at community events raised the lawyers' and the organization's profiles. This ability to collaborate both horizontally and vertically within a mass membership organization helped branches develop more sophisticated and relevant agendas, offered a mechanism for cultivating business and membership, and gave branch leadership and conference lawyers greater prestige in the state.

Finally, some critical race theorists and legal historians have used moments in the movement, such as the 1960 sit-ins, to demonstrate how NAACP lawyers threatened to de-radicalize grassroots civil rights activism. According to the conventional story, NAACP lawyers initially repudiated the direct action. Thurgood Marshall's proclamation that 'he was not going to represent a bunch of crazy colored kids who violated the sacred property rights of white folks' has often operated as the evidence of the inherent conservatism of NAACP lawyers.[22] The master narrative emphasizes great generational and class divides in movement activism. In the standard account, the student campaign was the real voice of the grassroots. The older, NAACP lawyers, on the other hand, were insufficiently militant and elitist. This narrative distances NAACP lawyers from the community organizing tradition

---

[22] Mark Tushnet, *Making Civil Rights Law: Thurgood Marshall and the Supreme Court, 1936–1961* (1994) 310 ff.

and renders student activists, not NAACP lawyers, as the true engines for radical legal and social change.[23]

The story of the Virginia State Conference offers a powerful counter-narrative to the received wisdom. In 1939, Samuel Tucker organized a sit-in in a segregated public library in Alexandria, Virginia. Tucker's ideas about civil disobedience drew inspiration from Mohandas Gandhi's passive resistance campaigns and United Auto Workers' strikes in Flint, Michigan. More than two decades after Tucker's first sit-in, students from Virginia Union University contacted the Virginia State Conference's legal staff about conducting their own sit-ins in February 1960. The NAACP lawyers advised the students on the applicable law and policing practices, raised bail money for students, and provided the students' legal defence. The lawyers' actions encouraged the student demonstrations that swept across the former capital of the Confederacy. The State Conference helped to usher another phase of the movement. Student leaders, like Charles Sherrod, soon took starring roles in the decades' gripping civil rights battles, building on the experiences and instruction of the Virginia State Conference's leadership. The NAACP lawyers' longstanding appreciation of direct action fundamentally informed a new generation of civil rights activism.

B. Blacks on the Bench

While the historical scholarship on black lawyers is generally underdeveloped, the historical scholarship on black judges is woefully inadequate. The black bench's larger-than-life personalities—men like Thurgood Marshall—dominate the genre. Many black jurists who achieved celebrity status in their own right—A. Leon Higginbotham, Jr., Wade McCree, Jr., and Ernest 'Dutch' Morial, to name a few—do not even have book-length biographies. The careers of other pioneering black judges remain in relative obscurity despite the proliferation of civil rights scholarship.

During the civil rights movement and shortly thereafter, presidents appointed select blacks to the federal judiciary not simply for achieving 'traditional' markers of legal distinction; in many cases, these lawyers also needed to be well-known, race men and, on rare occasion, race women. Judges Spottswood Robinson, Constance Baker Motley, and Robert Carter rose to prominence as eminent NAACP litigators. Judge Damon Keith co-chaired the Michigan Civil Rights Commission during the turbulent 1960s and was nominated to the Eastern District of Michigan just two months after his efforts to quell Detroit race riots in 1967. That year President Lyndon Johnson defended his decision to appoint Thurgood Marshall to the U.S. Supreme Court rather than another black judge by pointing to Marshall's perceived

---

[23] Mack (n. 18) 4 ff.

racial 'authenticity.' 'Son, when I appoint a nigger to the court', Johnson reportedly told one aide, 'I want everyone to know he's a nigger.'[24]

Other renowned black lawyers trickled into the federal judiciary on the heels of these groundbreaking appointments. Their racial credentials were striking. Perhaps, more interestingly, most had deep ties to the NAACP. Gabrielle McDonald built her national reputation after the enactment of the Civil Rights Act of 1964 as an LDF attorney litigating early employment discrimination cases. Nathaniel Jones won widespread acclaim as the Executive Director of the Fair Employment Practices Commission, Assistant General Counsel of the Kerner Commission, and General Counsel of the NAACP. Years after Horace Ward unsuccessfully attempted to desegregate the University of Georgia as a law student, he returned to the state as a lawyer and worked with Constance Baker Motley and Donald Hollowell to open the institution's doors. Legal historians might provide more synthetic accounts of the connection between racial leadership and federal judgeships. Moreover, such an exploration might shine light on topics such as the evolution of the term 'judicial activism'.

President Jimmy Carter was central to the demographic shift in the federal judiciary. Early in his presidency, the Georgia native pledged to grow the black bench, but he faced stiff opposition from Southern U.S. Senators, like Harry Byrd, Jr. of Virginia. Nonetheless, in a four-year span, Carter appointed more blacks to the federal bench than all of his predecessors combined.[25] Scholars might provide thicker accounts of these nomination and confirmation processes, the racial impact of the Omnibus Judgeship Act, competing conceptions of judicial merit during the Carter administration, and how blacks' efforts to diversify the bench eventually extended to other minority groups.

Most African-American judges during this period, however, presided over state and local courts. Some policymakers appointed blacks to the bench as direct concessions to spirited extra-judicial activism. Returning to this history might, too, focus attention to the concept of 'judicial activism.' Others might detail the promise of judicial reform in the wake of major Supreme Court and Congressional victories. For example, the Court's 'one person, one vote' cases and the Voting Rights Act of 1965 ostensibly gave blacks greater chances of electing black judges. Newly elected black judges might then provide judicial solutions to illegal searches and seizures, unreasonable bail, selective prosecutions, ineffective counsel, and unfair court judgments. Studies could trace how activists and lawyers attempted to democratize judicial elections. Furthermore, scholars might explain how early black judicial candidates fundraised for their campaigns, framed their jurisprudential philosophies, and mobilized citizens around and between elections.

---

[24] Robert Dallek, *Lone Star Rising: Lyndon Johnson and His Times, 1908–1960* (1991) 519 ff.

[25] Elliot Slotnick, 'Lowering the Bench or Raising it Higher?: Affirmative Action and Judicial Selection During the Carter Administration' (1982) 1 *Yale L. & Policy R.* 270 ff.

Some former civil rights lawyers did not end their activism when they entered the U.S. judiciary. These judges spread their visions for justice abroad after joining the bench. Judge Higginbotham helped to design South Africa's Constitutional Court after the fall of apartheid and served as an international mediator at the request of Nelson Mandela. Judge Jones travelled throughout Africa, participating in rule of law initiatives in Nigeria, Egypt, Uganda, Tanzania, South Africa, Namibia, and Somalia. After Judge McDonald stepped down from the federal bench, she served as a judge and then president of the International Criminal Tribunal for the Former Yugoslavia. Judge McDonald was subsequently appointed as an arbitrator on the Iran-United States Claims Tribunal. The work of these jurists offers fruitful sites to explore themes ranging from the global legacies of the U.S. civil rights movement to the efficacy of legal transplantation.

Lastly, legal historians might probe the careers of black non-lawyers who were actually able to assume judicial and quasi-judicial roles. Most notably, Charles Evers, a former NAACP field secretary and brother of civil rights martyr, Medgar Evers, was elected mayor of Fayette, Mississippi in 1969. Charles Evers had no formal legal training, but in his role as mayor, Evers presided over the city's police court. Juanita Stout, the first black woman elected to any U.S. judgeship, travelled from Pennsylvania to Mississippi to teach Evers courtroom procedure. Other black judges, like George Crockett, Jr., volunteered the former activist their assistance as well. Such a unique judicial position might offer a prism to understand racial solidarity in the legal profession and chart the hopes, challenges, and disappointments of judicial politics.

c. Black Power and the Legal Profession

In 1968, Algernon Johnson Cooper founded the Black American Law Student Association (BALSA). From its earliest days, the organization's national leadership identified 'Malcolm X and Stokely Carmichael as inspirations' and conceived of itself as a 'logical outgrowth' of the era's assertions of 'self-determination and blackness.' The students organized spirited panel discussions on topics such as affirmative action, access to justice, reparations, discrimination against black women, *Brown*'s legacy, and the future of black law schools. In its first three years of existence, black law students had established nearly 100 chapters of the organization. BALSA students were part of a generation that brought black power to college campuses across America.[26]

---

[26] Robert Pickett, 'Black American Law Student Association: Alive and (Doing) Well' (1971) 1 *National Black L.J.* 285 ff.

Practitioners also established all-black organizations during the black power movement. In 1969, more than 100 black lawyers launched the National Conference of Black Lawyers (NCBL), self-described as 'the legal arm of the black liberation movement'. The group named Robert Carter and Floyd McKissick, National Director of the Congress of Racial Equality, as co-chairmen. Carter's leadership in the organization is historiographically significant. His appointment represents the popularity of black power and upsets the overly simplistic renderings of the NAACP's 'conservative' leadership. Other prominent black lawyers who are typically associated with civil rights and not black power were founding NCBL members: Fred Gray, attorney for Rosa Parks and Martin Luther King, Jr. during the Montgomery Bus Boycott, Vernon Jordan, the former director of the Voter Education Project, and Eleanor Holmes Norton, the current Congresswoman for the District of Columbia. NCBL-affiliated lawyers assisted in the defence of Angela Davis, the Attica Brothers, and Assata Shakur. The organization expanded its efforts abroad, collaborating with activist organizations in Cuba, Guyana, Palestine, and Southern Africa.[27]

Even black judges—a group roundly described as paragons of black respectability, for better or worse—embraced tenets of black power. In 1971, the National Bar Association (NBA), with assistance of the Ford Foundation, established the NBA's Judicial Council. Judge George Crockett, Jr. served as the Judicial Council's first chair. Black power meant producing more black judges, and its founding meeting, the Judicial Council pledged to increase black representation in federal and state judiciaries. The Judicial Council also sought to 'eradicate[e] of racial and class bias from every aspect of the judicial and the law enforcement process'. The Judicial Council's logo reflected the cultural nationalism of this period. Founders redrew Lady Justice as an urban black woman with an Afro. The newly reconstituted figure held the scales of justice in her left hand and was lifting her blinders with her right hand. The Judicial Council's logo read, 'Let us remove the blindfold from the eyes of American justice. Too long has it obscured the unequal treatment accorded to poor people and black people under our law.' The Judicial Council's logo highlighted the unresolved and inherent flaws in the U.S. justice system. Furthermore, this portrayal boldly challenged the notion of judicial neutrality. Appeals to impartiality, according to the nation's first and only association of black judges, actually impeded America's quest for equal justice under law. This insight later became a cornerstone of critical race theory.[28]

Many legal historians have been reluctant to devote sustained attention to the relationship between black power organizations and the transformation of the legal

---

[27] 'National Conference of Black Lawyers' (1971) 1 *National Black L.J.* 286 ff.

[28] Judith Resnik, Dennis Curtis, *Representing Justice: Invention, Controversy, and Rights in City-States and Democratic Courtrooms* (2011) 103 ff.

institutions. The black power movement is conventionally portrayed as violent, anti-white, and anti-rule of law. Remembering the roots of black bar associations founded in the late 1960s and early 1970s might provide a decidedly different view of black power. Black law students, lawyers, and judges attempted to use black power to desegregate the legal profession and increase the race's faith in the U.S. justice system.

One might easily argue that the silences in the legal historiography over black power are not accidental. The production of knowledge is deeply political. Moreover, the task of legal historians becomes more difficult when discussing an unpopular topic. When legendary lawyers, like Fred Gray, are associated with black power, they may become, in the words of Vincent Harding, 'inconvenient heroes'.[29]

Finally, scholars might consider how black power reshaped the legal academy. There were relatively few black law students at most U.S. law schools before the black power movement. Black power activism led many institutions to adopt affirmative action in admissions. And as Justice Lewis Powell's opinion in *Regents of California v. Bakke* illustrates, even after the end of the movement, black power continued to inform debates over affirmative action.[30] Legal historians might re-examine the origins of the diversity rationale in light of Powell's views on black power. Legal historians might also detail the black power movement's profound impact on legal education. Derrick Bell—an NCBL founding member and speaker at the NBA Judicial Council's founding meeting—opened his casebook, *Race, Racism, and American Law*, with the iconic photograph of Tommie Smith and John Carlos. Smith and Carlos were the 1968 U.S. Olympic medallists who raised their fists in a black power salute during the playing of 'The Star-Spangled Banner'. Kimberlé Crenshaw, a former student of Bell's, once described the impact of her encounter with the casebook's opening photograph and Bell's scholarship. 'To those of us who were then law students and beginning law teachers, Bell's inclusion of the Smith-Carlos photograph as a visual introduction to his law school casebook', Crenshaw recalled, 'suggested a link between his work and the black power movements that most of us "really" identified with, whose political insights and aspirations went far beyond what could be articulated in the reigning language of the legal profession and the legal studies we were pursuing.' Over the next decade, these legal scholars hosted critical race conferences, established new courses, and created organizations to articulate their visions of freedom. Their sustained engagement with activism, legal theory, and history have helped to define race scholarship ever since.[31]

---

[29] Vincent Harding, *Martin Luther King: The Inconvenient Hero* (1996).
[30] *Regents of California v. Bakke* 438 U.S. 265 (1978).
[31] Kimberlé Crenshaw, 'Introduction', in Kimberlé Crenshaw, Neil Gotanda, Gary Peller, Kendall Thomas (eds.), *Critical Race Theory: The Key Writings that Formed the Movement* (1995) xx ff.

CONCLUSION

The Black Lives Matter movement has been an incredible and successful force in the current struggle for racial justice. Its activists are in clear conversation with the scholarship on the civil rights movement, black power movement, and critical race theory. They have stressed the importance of group-centred leadership and community organizing. They have encouraged citizens to put their bodies on the line to challenge racism in the criminal justice system. They have skilfully used media to mobilize local people and reach international audiences. They have even pushed past the politics of respectability to demand full human dignity.

Lawyers have played instrumental roles in the Black Lives Matter movement. Attorneys from groups ranging from the National Lawyers Guild to the Arch City Defenders have supervised protests and represented countless activists in court. Lawyers and legal scholars have teamed with activists to popularize and interrogate powerful historical metaphors, like 'the new Jim Crow', 'the new peonage', and 'debtors' prison'. Critical race theorist Justin Hansford travelled with the family of Michael Brown to testify before the United Nations Committee against Torture. The 'Ferguson to Geneva' strategy was inspired by older black activists who declared that racism was not simply a civil rights issue but also as a human rights issue. Kimberlé Crenshaw helped to coin the #SayHerName campaign, which built from her pioneering scholarship on intersectionality. This hashtag reflects the idea that racial violence is not only a problem affecting black men. Crenshaw underscored that there are gender-specific ways that violence harms black women, including queer and transwomen. The movement's unabashed embrace of all black lives has been a much needed intervention in an era once heralded as post-racial.

Yet, Black Lives Matter still faces many of the institutional issues its forerunners confronted. What organizational models best allow activists to expand their popular constituencies while facilitating leader accountability and avoiding the pitfalls of brokerage politics? What organizational models best sustain participants' energies and commitments over time? And how might diverse activists, scholars, policymakers, and practitioners maintain radical, consensus-building spaces that possess the ability to address pressing issues of law and policy? If Black Lives Matter is to remain vibrant and reach its emancipatory potential, it must tackle these deep structural and ideological questions. I am confident the movement will.

BIBLIOGRAPHY

Derrick Bell, *Race, Racism and American Law* (Little, Brown, 1980)
Kimberlé Crenshaw, Neil Gotanda, Gary Peller, Kendall Thomas (eds.), *Critical Race Theory: The Key Writings that Formed the Movement* (The New Press, 1995)

Mary Dudziak, *Cold War Civil Rights: Race and the Image of American Democracy* (Princeton University Press, 2000)

Francisco Valdes, Jerome Culp, Angela Harris (eds.), *Crossroads, Directions, and a New Critical Race Theory* (Temple University Press, 2002)

Ian Haney López, *Racism on Trial: The Chicano Fight for Justice* (Harvard University Press, 2003)

Adrien Wing, (ed.), *Critical Race Feminism: A Reader* (New York University Press, 2003)

Angela Harris, 'From Stonewall to the Suburbs?' (2006) 14 *William and Mary Bill of Rights J.* 1539 ff

Risa Goluboff, *The Lost Promise of Civil Rights* (Harvard University Press, 2007)

Tomiko Brown-Nagin, *Courage to Dissent: Atlanta and the Long History of the Civil Rights Movement* (Oxford University Press, 2011)

Devon Carbado, Mitu Gulati, *Acting White: Rethinking Race in 'Post-Racial' America* (Oxford University Press, 2013)

Kenneth Mack, *Representing the Race: The Creation of the Civil Rights Lawyer* (Harvard University Press, 2013)

Keeanga-Yamahtta Taylor, *From #BlackLivesMatter to Black Liberation* (Haymarket Books, 2016)

Richard Delgado, Jean Stefancic (eds.), *Critical Race Theory: An Introduction* (New York University Press, 2012)

CHAPTER 34

QUEERING LAW'S EMPIRE

DOMINATION AND DOMAIN IN THE SEXING UP OF LEGAL HISTORY

DAVID MINTO

'To what class of offences shall we refer these irregularities of the venereal appetite which are stiled unnatural?' So opened Jeremy Bentham's late eighteenth-century essay on 'Offences Against One's Self'—a titular formulation that offered its own queer answer, with implications for not only the 'offenders' in question, but also the concept of law.[1]

Responding in part to William Blackstone's contention in his *Commentaries on the Laws of England* that 'the infamous *crime against nature*' amounted to a felonious offence against 'the persons of individuals', Bentham rejoined that it was unclear quite whose security was at stake.[2] For Blackstone, the *crime against nature*

---

[1] Jeremy Bentham, Louis Crompton, 'Offences Against One's Self: Paederasty (Part 1)' (1978) 3:4 *Journal of Homosexuality* 389 ff; Jeremy Bentham, Louis Crompton, 'Jeremy Bentham's Essay on 'Paederasty' (Part 2)' (1978) 4:1 *Journal of Homosexuality* 91 ff.

[2] William Blackstone, *Commentaries on the Laws of England* (1765–1769) vol. 4, 215 ff.

represented a 'deeper malignity' than rape and its very mention was 'a disgrace to human nature', with death the punishment mandated by reason and the express law of God. Bentham's atheism, however, did not recognize the latter authority, while his objection to Blackstone's conflation of consensual and violent acts precipitated a different conclusion regarding sexual 'irregularities'. This he apparently reached despite himself. 'I have been tormenting myself for years', Bentham attested, 'to find if possible a sufficient ground for treating them with the severity with which they are treated at this time of day by all European nations'. But then of course came the punch line: 'upon the principle of utility I can find none'. Same-sex sex acts (which Bentham conceived of primarily as pederastic relations between willing men and youths) presented a tough case for his pleasure-aggregating philosophy and drew from him frequent oaths signalling his disgust. Yet as the author wrestled with the operations of his own 'prejudice', the topic also offered a powerful illustration of the radical departures of Bentham's positivist jurisprudence—perhaps especially of the paradigmatic challenge this take on the crime against nature presented to natural law.[3]

Given the relative youth of queer legal history as a recognized subfield, it is worth underlining the forceful presence of queer sex in the writing of two legal thinkers who are so canonical that this section of the *Oxford Handbook* opens with separate chapters on them. Of course, neither writer would have anticipated the development of a whole subfield of legal scholarship that determindly communes with those Blackstone condemned or that might exploit this particular brief encounter of their legal minds. Nevertheless, since its rise during the early years of the U.S. AIDS crisis, queer studies has made a virtue of co-opting terms of offence in the most grievous of circumstances, and there need be no exception here. Both writers indeed announce certain themes that should be of keen interest to today's queer legal historians.

Here, Blackstone's violent taciturnity may be as revealing as Bentham's more prolix reflections on sex and law. For one thing, when the author of the *Commentaries* reassured his readers that he would not dwell on this 'offence of so dark a nature', he pointed, curiously, to 'the delicacy of our English law' that actually had the power to put such offenders to death. This expression justified the euphemistic conventions of Blackstone's resort to Latin phrasing and his speed at drawing a line under the subject. It also, however, implied the challenge queerness posed to law's very ability to maintain and describe itself.[4]

That queer machinations may inhabit euphemism, silences, and secrecy is also indicated by Bentham's productions; although his interest in 'offences against one's self' was barely recognized before the late 1970s, Bentham, in the privacy of his manuscripts, returned to the provocative case study at multiple times in his career. Freed from obscurity, some of his thoughts might appear close to a strange kind of

---

[3] Bentham, Crompton, 'Offences Against One's Self: Paederasty (Part 1) (n. 1) 389 ff.

[4] Blackstone (n. 2) 215 ff. See also Lee Edelman, Homographesis: Essays in Gay Literary and Cultural Theory (1994) 5 ff.

prescience. The early essay, for instance, touched on themes linking sex and law to religion, publicity, emotion, demography, domesticity, and discipline that anticipate many useful queer legal angles in the present.[5] Meanwhile, Bentham's reaction to a paucity of data also tangentially suggested the benefits of comparative sightlines across time and space, referencing the discussions of an international republic of letters and case studies from ancient Rome to contemporary Tahiti. There is much that a new generation of legal historians could queerly turn out from all this.

While queer legal history remains a fluid field, scholarly interest in the power law wields over sexual subjectivities, subcultures, identities, bodies, and lives has been perhaps the most prominent theme at its centre. In addition, there has been significant legal scholarship advancing a queer critique of law, demonstrating how law's operations serve dominant interests related to normative gender and sexuality (often labelled as 'heteronormativity'), and this work has on occasion delved into the historical background to develop its point.[6] Such approaches to queer legal scholarship might be expected from theorist David Halperin's influential assertion that: '[q]ueer is by definition whatever is at odds with the normal, the legitimate, the dominant'—with law, of course, easily made to stand for the contrasting elements.[7] Many of these individual works offer models of scholarship that deservedly continue to inspire offshoots.

But by instead skipping back a couple of centuries to Blackstone and Bentham's conflicting takes as its starting point, this chapter will suggest two broad and distinctive directions that could benefit the field if developed in addition. The first direction relates to the historical circumstances in which queerness presented a 'hard case' for those charged with making or enforcing law, sometimes strengthening their existing understandings of law and the legal system, but in other instances provoking a crisis of administration and adjudication or even a jurisprudential paradigm shift.[8] This first direction, in other words, probes the ways in which queerness challenged the law of police officers, politicians, advocates, judges, and legal theorists, beyond law simply disciplining queerness. The second direction, meanwhile, points to the profound gaps in queer legal history when it comes to thinking comparatively between different jurisdictions or transnationally across their bounds. Here, I intend to flag up how queerness in legal history might usefully be taken, and take us, beyond jurisdictional domains.

---

[5] See, e.g., his essays written in the mid-1810s that have recently been published in Philip Schofield, Catherine Pease-Watkin, Michael Quinn (eds.), *Of Sexual Irregularities, and Other Writings on Sexual Morality* (*Collected Works of Jeremy Bentham*) (2014).

[6] For a definition of 'heteronormativity' see Lauren Berlant, Michael Warner, 'Sex in Public' (1998) 24:2 *Critical Inquiry* 548 ff.

[7] David Halperin, *Saint Foucault: Towards a Gay Hagiography* (1995) 62 ff. Through this framing, Halperin also contended that the 'queer' was not necessarily linked to sexual or gender identity.

[8] The jurisprudential usefulness of 'hard cases', in which the result of judicial decision making is not clearly dictated by statute or precedent, is of course associated with Ronald Dworkin, also the author of *Law's Empire* (1986).

It would be misleading to claim a complete absence of work in these areas. And yet, in scholarly bids to contest naïve popular accounts of ever advancing national legal progress, the tendency to stress law's disciplinary domination of queer lives has arguably curtailed analysis of a wider range of power dynamics at play and limited the focus, by and large, to the locus of power found in the nation state.

Of course, given well-documented histories of legal discrimination and violence, scholars can find strong justifications for continuing to prioritize the critique of law's disciplinary force within jurisdictions. Furthermore, while law's overtly hostile treatment of certain gay men and lesbians in some countries may have lessened in recent decades, the very expansion of their citizenship and legal rights can be argued to brighten the lines excluding others. That dynamic is likely to be especially pertinent for queer legal history where sexual difference intersects with animus along lines of class, race, religion, disability, gender identity, and so on—an important topic to investigate in itself.[9]

But this chapter does not seek to bookend Blackstone and Bentham with the final word. The themes and examples it presents—prompted mainly by my own research on gay 'homophile' activism in the West, pursued oftentimes by middle-class white men—don't mean to deny the necessity of other approaches and certainly can't claim to represent the full diversity of queerness. Likewise, references and recommended readings are drawn primarily from U.S. scholarship (which has played such a strong role in instigating queer interventions), although the chapter encourages readers to look beyond it. The directions I offer then are floated in a spirit of intellectual curiosity before a field that is at its best in defying the anointment of orthodoxies. That will include any inadvertently suggested in the below.

1. Queerness, Law, and the Making of Strange Bedfellows

There are many ways in which to interpret the 'queer' prefix of queer legal history. It might simply indicate work centred on gay, trans, or LGBTQ people,

[9] The notion of intersectionality now prominent in feminist, gender, and queer studies extends from law professor and critical race theorist Kimberlé Crenshaw's foundational elaboration of the theory. See Kimberlé Crenshaw, 'Mapping the Margins: Intersectionality, Identity Politics, and Violence against Women of Color' (1991) 43:6 *Stanford L.R.* 1241 ff. For a U.S. movement history highlighting the significance of post-1960s queer divides along race and class lines with regard to law and order policing and quality-of-life laws, see Christina Hanhardt, *Safe Space: Gay Neighborhood History and the Politics of Violence* (2003).

adding queer to a menu of legible identity categories or advancing queer as an umbrella term covering them all. Equally, however, queer can oppose the fixity and coherence of identitarian terms, signalling among other things an appeal to post-structuralism, attention to the playful and performative, a critique of normativity, and a determination to bridge scholarly and political practice. The mutually exclusive multitudes the term contains are surely part of its charm, with queer studies perhaps better thought of as an eclectic and sometimes contradictory corpus rather than as a coherent philosophy or programme. Still, a brief and partial take on how the queer and the legal have previously come together will help to clarify the potential for additional approaches.

Law indeed was present at the moment queer studies firmly established itself in the United States during a critical watershed transpiring between the 1980s and 1990s. Scholars from a variety of disciplines who contributed to this queer turn tended to emphasize the performative aspects of gender and sexuality, wilfully addressing the structuring force of sexual categories in the West and self-consciously seeking to advance radical approaches to sexual politics, with Gloria Anzaldúa, Gayle Rubin, Michael Warner, and Teresa de Lauretis among them.[10] But for queer legal history, the distinctive bearing of law on two iconic texts from 1990 may be particularly instructive. On the one hand, there is the opening of Judith Butler's *Gender Trouble*, which confronts the reader with Michel Foucault's claim that 'juridical systems of power *produce* the subjects they subsequently come to represent'. On the other, there is Eve Sedgwick's *Epistemology of the Closet*, whose introduction alerts readers that it was written in the traumatic wake of the 1986 US Supreme Court decision in *Bowers v. Hardwick* that found state sodomy prohibitions to be constitutional.[11] As Bruno Perreau notes, Butler and Sedgwick ultimately shared an interest in 'deconstructing the performative power of categories of gender and sexuality', and in doing so 'undertook a critique of the hegemony of heterosexual representations of society and its impact on subjectivity, the body, and the naming of self'.[12] But the invocations of law at the beginning of their most famous texts are suggestive of different legal dynamics. With a bit of squinting (and without wishing to reduce the broader complex books), the two examples evoke alternate and perhaps conflicting visions of law as either producing or repressing queer lives. Both analytic takes on law—as productive or repressive— have proved useful for thinking about the historical legal regulation of sex and gender. Both emphasize the stakes of law's domination over queer lives, even as they suggest the importance of resistance and lapses.

[10] For a helpful synopsis, see Bruno Perreau, *Queer Theory: The French Response* (2016) 78 ff.

[11] Judith Butler, *Gender Trouble: Feminism and the Subversion of Identity* (1990) 2 ff; Eve Kosofsky Sedgwick, *Epistemology of the Closet* (1990) 6 ff.

[12] Perreau (n. 10) 80 ff.

Beyond those scholars most closely associated with the queer turn, however, historians of sexuality of a variety of stripes have drawn heavily on legal sources. Indeed, decades before the first generation of professional scholars of gay and lesbian history in the United States, Donald Webster Cory's 1951 work *The Homosexual in America* included a chapter on 'A World of Law-Abiding Villains', where Cory delved into the history of criminalization in the United States and recent patterns of arrests in New York City, while elsewhere in the book remarking on the discriminatory effects of broader regulation that included firings from government employment and exclusions from GI Bill benefits.[13] Subsequent scholarly histories of sexuality produced in the United States from the 1980s started to go beyond chronicling regulation in order to critique it, instead mining legal paper-trails as one of the most significant source bases for interpreting cultures of sexuality in the past. Official state and judicial records (such as those produced by military enquiries, police surveillance, liquor authorities, and court cases) and quasi-official ones (such as those produced by vice societies monitoring compliance with law) provided an uncommonly rich cache of evidence for the U.S. field. During the nineteenth and twentieth centuries, queer lives and subcultures were targeted by a range of repressive laws extending well beyond sodomy statutes, including laws on cross-dressing, solicitation, vagrancy, obscenity, and public order, which in themselves produced extensive if disturbing archives. Put simply, the legal material generated might be read not only to gauge the motivations, mechanisms, and effects of regulation over time, but also to recover something of the lives of those coming within regulation's grasp.

An exemplary account of the importance of such trails can be found at the end of George Chauncey's *Gay New York*, where a note on sources begins by stating that the 'records of the public and private agencies that policed sociability and sexual life . . . were particularly useful', going on to highlight the papers of district attorneys, magistrates' courts, licensing agencies, investigative commissions, and so on. Still, one aspect to bear in mind when it comes to law's relation to queer lives and subcultures is Chauncey's cautionary stress that such records sometimes provided 'more evidence about the preconceptions of the police than the people they were policing'. Oral histories proved crucial to accessing the experience of the latter. Indeed, Chauncey forcefully used these to puncture, among other things, the assumption that gay men uncritically internalized dominant culture's view of them.[14]

Whatever their biases and limitations, legal sources clearly played an important role in establishing the history of sexuality as a field as such. Recently, however,

---

[13] Donald Webster Cory, *The Homosexual in America: A Subjective Approach* (1951) 49 ff. Cory was the pseudonym of sociologist Edward Sagarin.

[14] George Chauncey, *Gay New York: Gender, Urban Culture, and the Making of the Gay Male World* (1994) 365 ff.

some scholars have sensed that a more specialist iteration of queer legal history has acquired a critical mass and distinction to make it more its own entity, at least in the United States. Felicia Kornbluh's insightful 2011 review essay, for instance, identified 'an emerging canon of queer legal history' of 'enormous significance', constituting indeed a 'third generation of histories of sexuality of the United States' after the social movement and community studies of previous decades. Noting that this new wave also developed from women's history scholars who had elucidated truncated forms of female citizenship in arenas such as marriage and welfare, Kornbluh concluded that queer legal historiography had gone on amply to substantiate the operation of a 'gay exception' to the dominant formal doctrines of twentieth-century US law. '[W]hen appellate courts upheld the rights claims of diverse Americans', Kornbluh summarized, 'suspected homosexuals were disallowed from entering the country, exiled to the margins of the welfare state, silenced about their intimate lives, disgraced, and defamed.'[15]

The past decade alone has indeed seen a number of standout U.S. works that either inspired or have made good on the promise of queer legal history that Kornbluh saw. Margot Canaday's *The Straight State* put front and centre the U.S. federal state's elaboration over the twentieth century of a legal category of homosexuality through sources relating to immigration, welfare, and military service, and demonstrated the accretion of a regulatory regime favouring heterosexual citizenship that coincided with the development of the U.S. state. Marc Stein's *Sexual Injustice* advanced a re-interpretation of 1960s and 1970s Supreme Court decisions on sexual and reproductive rights, emphasizing a legal and cultural conservatism that contrasted with the liberal spin of many other commentators. Regina Kunzel's *Criminal Intimacy* brought together the history of sexuality with the rise of the carceral state to expose the unevenness of sexual taxonomies and identities during the U.S. twentieth century and uncover strikingly wide-ranging disciplinary flows of penitential power through and beyond prison walls. Nayan Shah's *Stranger Intimacy* foregrounded the racial and class dynamics of sexual citizenship by exploring the intimate worlds of twentieth-century South Asian migrant labourers in the U.S. Pacific Northwest as they came into contact with the police, courts, and other regulatory agents. And Clare Sears's *Arresting Dress* examined the operation of anti-cross dressing laws in San Francisco from the mid-nineteenth century on, bringing together municipal court records with cultural exposés to argue that law actively produced new definitions of gender normality and abnormality.[16]

---

[15] Felicia Kornbluh, 'Queer Legal History: A Field Grows Up and Comes Out' (2011) 36:2 *Law & Social Inquiry* 537 ff.

[16] Margot Canaday, *The Straight State: Sexuality and Citizenship in Twentieth-Century America* (2009); Marc Stein, *Sexual Injustice: Supreme Court Decisions from Griswold to Roe* (2010); Regina Kunzel, *Criminal Intimacy: Prison and the Uneven History of Modern American Sexuality* (2008); Nayan Shah, *Stranger Intimacy: Contesting Race, Sexuality, and the Law in American North West*

Any of these works would provide a compelling model or a starting point for further research in queer legal history. Yet, of course, they also suggest further scholarship along paths not taken, including with regard to domination and domain.

II. DOMINATION

Despite the diversity of substantive interests among queer legal historians, a fairly clear connecting theme has been the ways in which law dominates queer subjects, whether to produce or repress them. Kornbluh, reflecting on administrative and judicial state power as described by Canaday and Stein, detected exciting departures in their work from a 'field that has been saturated with narratives of sex and power derived from the early writing of Michel Foucault', but also saw indebtedness to that model.[17] Early- to mid-Foucault foregrounded the diffuse but disciplinary reach of penology, psychiatry, and sexology over both inner and outer lives, famously casting the nineteenth-century emergence of the homosexual as one result.[18] Canaday's book insisted that the homosexual—in the United States, at least—also came into being as a legal category, albeit subject to a more uneven taxonomy than Foucault's theories of speciation implied, as an anaemic U.S. federal state expanded during the twentieth century and 'increasingly developed conceptual mastery over what it sought to regulate'.[19] Given such renewed scholarly interest in institutional power exercised through bureaucracies and courts, Kornbluh concluded: 'Queer legal history now turns toward understanding the exercise of conventional forms of power over and against sexual minorities'.[20] Domination has remained the dominant frame, even as scholars have nuanced their vision of law's disciplinary powers by showing how legal capacity could fail or was resisted.

In this section, I seek less to undermine any of these particular readings of power (which have yielded important and generative insights), than to probe what domination may obscure if taken as the delimiting perspective of queer legal history. Recently, in the adjacent field of surveillance studies, some scholars have begun to push back against Foucault-inspired models that fail to consider 'any notion of personal autonomy'—the possibility that, in the words of David Rosen and Aaron

(2011); Clare Sears, *Arresting Dress: Cross-Dressing, Law, and Fascination in Nineteenth-Century San Francisco* (2015).

[17] Kornbluh (n. 15) 555 ff.

[18] Michel Foucault, *The History of Sexuality*, vol. 1, *An Introduction*, trans. Robert Hurley (1976; 1990) 43 ff.

[19] Canaday (n. 16) 3 ff.   [20] Kornbluh (n. 15) 555 ff.

Santesso, 'at least a kernel of personality, that a freedom of thought and action, might survive the onslaught of State or social discourses'. Queer legal history rarely presents quite so extreme a vision directly; Canaday's groundbreaking work, for instance, also addressed aspects of state incapacity, and the sophistication of its analysis does much to inspire the conversation I would like to have. But atmospherically, at least, the claim that law essentially works 'over and against' queer subjects is by this point an orthodox perspective for queer legal history. While the insinuation of law's domination remains tempting for the political purchase it provides, it comes at the cost of diminishing not only the agency of self-fashioning queer lives, but also reverse currents of queerness that may challenge, redirect, or even exploit law. Even more simply, the attraction to domination as a frame forecloses consideration of potentially more benign aspects of relation between queer lives and law.

Again, scholars can and do offer compelling justifications for an approach that emphasizes queer critique of law itself, especially given contemporary popular commentary seduced by straightforward narratives of legal progress. There is certainly a legitimate argument to be made that, fundamentally, queer legal studies stands to gain most coherence and purchase by adapting the kind of dominance model Catherine MacKinnon has developed for feminist legal theory. Meanwhile, interventions such as Dean Spade's exposure of legal equality frameworks that leave trans and gender non-conforming folks especially vulnerable to what Spade terms administrative violence suggests the nefarious practices law can allow. Critiquing this, unfortunately, remains urgent and necessary work. Yet to the extent that law's dominating and disciplining qualities now provide the paradigm for queer legal history, there may be benefits to also engaging these terms as a question.[21]

Returning to Bentham offers one tantalizing thread to pull at, given that his early argument against sodomy prohibitions implicitly raised questions as to the power law possessed. Notably, a key strand in his essay on 'Offences Against One's Self' considered whether legal punishment might in fact aggravate the problem in its sights and produce a negative result, at least through the lens of utility. On the one hand, Bentham cast doubt on the notion that punishment would advertise the practice of sodomy more than it repressed it, since '[i]n former time, when it was not punished, it prevailed to a very great degree; in modern times in the very same countries since it has been punished it has prevailed in a much less degree.' But on the other hand, Bentham suggested that punishment encouraged resentment, a kind of subcultural formation, and perhaps even a political problem. It was both 'the severity with which it is now treated by the laws and the contempt and abhorrence with which it is regarded by the generality of the people', Bentham charged, that had 'the effect of rendering those persons who are the objects of it more attached

---

[21] David Rosen, Aaron Santesso, *The Watchman in Pieces: Surveillance, Literature, and Liberal Personhood* (2013) 9 ff; Catherine MacKinnon, *Toward a Feminist Theory of the State* (1989); Dean Spade, *Normal Life: Administrative Violence, Critical Trans Politics, and the Limits of Law* (2011).

than they would otherwise be to the practice it proscribes'. There is a glimmer of the proto-Foucauldian here, but Bentham's stress lay on how this 'persecution' was counterproductive in terms of utility, with the law causing more 'mischief' than the offence. Much as law might attempt to dominate, from Bentham's utilitarian perspective it ran the risk of backfiring 'in point of experience'.[22]

Over a century and a half later, Cory's 1951 book also considered the limits of the law's power and reach, this time avowing the 'subjective approach' of a homosexual outlook. His chapter titled 'A World of Law-Abiding Felons' opened by insisting that the popular impression that 'the homosexual is in constant conflict with the law' was correct only in a 'narrow sense', given Cory's assessment that 'few are arrested or convicted of crimes'. That of course is a position for historians to examine rather than trust, especially given differentials by race, class, and location. Cory did perceive that the 'homosexual is, unfortunately, in a position before the law where he cannot effectively fight back' and held that this had affective consequences; '[h]ow degrading', he wrote 'to have to play the comedy of the courts and pretend to share the world's contempt for that which one secretly aspires to defend'. The threat of law's capricious draconianism certainly shaped homosexual subcultures and could wreck individual lives. Yet the court's world was one of 'comedy' and the absurdity of sexual statutes 'makes law itself a laughing stock in the eyes of any intelligent person'. And while of course it was desirable to secure the 'repeal of the antiquated laws against homosexuality, with their frequent denial of civil and constitutional rights', Cory insisted that such an event would be only 'one small step' when it came to 'the communal rehabilitation of the homosexual'. Social opprobrium, Cory predicted, would remain, so that the 'pariah can take but small satisfaction from the fact that he is no longer a law-breaker'.

There is, I am trying to suggest, some scope for queer legal history to take such a remark more seriously. It is counter-intuitive for any disciplinary approach to begin by de-emphasizing the potential import or influence of the main thing that it studies. Doing so, however, need not leave the law immune to political critique and would help to open up complex and far-reaching questions about its interpolation with other factors bearing on queer politics, social life, and identity formation.[23]

Cory's notion that a significant effect of sexual statutes was to make the law into a laughing stock among thinking people starkly raises an alternative research question reversing the power dynamics implied by a queer critique of law's domination, instead asking how homosexuality has posed a problem for law. While a strong contemporary strand of queer studies is interested in 'pink-washing' (through state and corporate exploitation of gay rights), queerness may also have had bearing on the law in ways more likely to disturb the legal system than to be harnessed by elites for political gain. Given the massive shifts in the social formations and cultural presence of gender and sexuality over the twentieth

---

[22] Bentham and Crompton (n. 1) 389 ff.   [23] Cory (n. 13) 49 ff.

century in the United States and elsewhere, we might expect queerness to have had a variety of relations to patterns of jurisprudence and legal practice over that same period. Given that queerness could press on imaginations even at times of discursive taboo, its implications for the operations and underpinnings of the legal system itself remain under-explored.

Some of my own research aims to rectify that by probing the role homosexual offences played in post-Second World War Anglo-American debates about the relationship between morality and the criminal law, which in turn connected to broader jurisprudential divides between natural law theorists and positivists. In both Britain and the United States in the 1950s, gay sex between men remained criminalized, while a wide variety of behaviours that transgressed gender or sexual norms left the perpetrator vulnerable to legal sanction. That, however, does not mean that the punishment of such transgressions enjoyed automatic legitimation, even among those responsible for the regulation. Furthermore, Sedgwick and other queer theorists have indicated the potential strength of queerness's symbolic import even amidst the operation of strong taboos, with *Epistemology of the Closet* advancing that the critical analysis of a chronic crisis of homo/heterosexual definition is key to understanding 'virtually any aspect of modern Western culture'.[24] Could the spectre of the crime against nature, then, have helped to raise doubts in legal minds about the efficacy of natural law or a necessary relation between morality and law?

In thinking about the cultural import of homosexuality on Anglo-American legal imaginations and the signals of changing visions of legal thought, I have been struck by the queerness of U.S. judicial references to constitutional penumbras as a place to dig in. A number of legal scholars have of course previously pointed to penumbras (those spaces of partial illumination between perfect light and perfect shadow) as an important if controversial metaphor in U.S. jurisprudence since at least the early twentieth century; Oliver Wendell Holmes referenced penumbras as far back as 1873. In U.S. constitutional law, the term has come to signify rights not explicitly stated by the constitution but that may be inferred from those that are, lurking in the penumbras of the explicit.[25] In a looser way, however, the content, dimensions, and operations of penumbras are bound also to resonate with queer studies scholars, who have long probed the dependencies between secrecy and disclosure, the boundaries between the implied and the blatant, and the significance of the marginal and the latent. Given their association with the partial shadow of an

[24] Sedgwick (n. 11) 1 ff. Although sceptical of this claim, David Alan Sklansky has already indicated how useful legal scholars may find Sedgwick in a bracing article arguing that 1960s policing of homosexuals had a subtextual impact on the constitutionality of U.S. criminal procedure: ' "One Train May Hide Another": *Katz*, Stonewall, and the Secret Subtext of Criminal Procedure' (2008) 41:3 *U.C. Davis L.R.*

[25] Holmes quoted in Burr Henly, ' "Penumbra": The Roots of a Legal Metaphor' (1987) 15:81 *Hastings Constitutional Law Quarterly* 81 ff.

eclipse, penumbras are not simply a matter of judicial side-eye, but evoke celestial shifts. Queerness indeed may on occasion have provided a stimulant for judicial penumbral recalibration, with implications for law itself that went beyond having to deal with the dawning recognition of a legal category of homosexuality.[26]

Judges of course represent only part of a legal system that contacts with queerness affected in ways deserving of greater attention, which some up and coming scholars are already taking on. Looking back to a post-Second World War U.S. context of anti-gay policing that included bar raids enforcing state liquor regulations, plain-clothes decoys spurring solicitation arrests, and secret surveillance of public bathrooms, it might be tempting to see vice squads as unconstrained repressive agents and find little more to say. Yet a recent dissertation by Anna Lvovsky that focuses on the three aforementioned sites forcefully shows how much there is to address, tracking striking shifts in policies and practices and offering an especially fine-grained account of the police's often startlingly paradoxical relation to changing social scientific expertise. Among other things, Lvovsky advances a bold conceptual vision of police officers as 'epistemic agents' shaping public perceptions of a gay world that became increasingly prominent in the U.S. mass media, while in effect having to deny that same expertise in court to secure convictions. The emphasis on police 'mastery' over queer lives (drawing on Foucault and others to contest gay liberation narratives that conflate publicity and progress) of course weighs somewhat against the questioning of legal domination this chapter would like to open up. Still, even on that narrow point, Lvovsky's sophisticated dissection of the public/private status of gay bodies and acts detected by the law also indicates the extent to which the legal system's different parts could come into conflict as they approached queerness. More importantly, it promises a significant book. A preview has recently arrived in the form of an arresting article on clandestine police surveillance, ending on the compelling point that the efficiency of such anti-homosexual policing 'depended on not the spread of cultural knowledge within the state, but rather on its selective distribution among state actors, creating knowledge gaps that weakened potential checks on police power on the ground'.[27]

Other scholars, meanwhile, have moved to suggest sources of change and even of queer resistance in the broad machinery of the U.S. legal system. Marie-Amelie George's recent account of a transformation in LGBT rights over the second half of the twentieth century, for instance, argues that whereas in the early postwar decades 'the administrative state served as a powerful engine of discrimination against homosexuals', by the mid-1980s many bureaucrats 'had become allies, subverting

---

[26] See David Minto, 'Perversion by Penumbras: Wolfenden, *Griswold*, and the Transatlantic Trajectory of Sexual Privacy', *American Historical Review*, forthcoming.

[27] Anna Lvovsky, 'Queer Expertise: Urban Policing and the Construction of Public Knowledge About Homosexuality 1920–1970', PhD dissertation (2015); Anna Lvovsky, 'Cruising in Plain View: Clandestine Surveillance and the Unique Insights of Antihomosexual Policing' (2017) *Journal of Urban History* (online) 16 ff.

statutory bans on gay and lesbian foster and adoptive parenting and promoting gay-inclusive curricula in public schools'. Taking explicit aim at Foucault's theories of governmentality, George explains the move towards 'bureaucratic agency' through scientific developments that influenced those working within the administrative state, with both scientists and bureaucrats serving 'as a source of liberation, rather than unmitigated repression'.[28]

And to bring us back again to classic terrain of this *Handbook*'s section on 'modern legal thought', a further productive place from which to push may lie where queerness intersects the broad operations of the legal system not simply as the object to be regulated but more obviously as an agent contributing to law. When Sedgwick invoked *Bowers* in *Epistemology of the Closet,* she raised such a possibility by conveying contemporary rumours that a closeted gay law clerk or justice had shaped the decision.[29] But recent work has probed other queer interventions in law. Scholars such as Brittney C. Cooper and Rosalind Rosenberg, for instance, now challenge us to reckon with the life and legal legacy of the African-American civil rights lawyer Pauli Murray, who had a complex relationship to gender identity, sometimes retrospectively described as trans, and whose co-authored 1965 piece 'Jane Crow and the Law' influenced the thought and advocacy of Ruth Bader Ginsburg among others.[30]

To pick an example close to my own research, a quick glance into the life and thought of the English legal philosopher H. L. A. Hart stands to illuminate. Indeed, Hart is a useful figure to consider here because he not only became a canonical legal philosopher in the postwar Anglo-American legal world, but also had some kind of personal relationship to queerness. This we can glean from an impressive intellectual biography of him by Nicola Lacey that is anxious to pre-empt concern about intruding into Hart's private life in its first few pages. Lacey writes that while 'some readers may feel that I have been too generous in my use of the personal material—particularly that relating to his feelings about his sexuality and his marriage—my judgment was that it was essential to any interpretation of him as a whole person'. For Lacey, the 'rule of thumb' was to include reference to personal material—including Hart's confessed homoerotic urges—when it 'sheds light on the development of his ideas and the course of his career'. At least one reviewer strongly questioned the value of its inclusion, holding that 'it is hard to see how the

---

[28] Marie-Amelie George, 'Bureaucratic Agency: Administering the Transformation of LGBT Rights' (2017) 36 *Yale Law & Policy Review* ff.

[29] Sedgwick (n. 11) 74 ff.

[30] Pauli Murray, Mary O. Eastwood, 'Jane Crow and the Law: Sex Discrimination and Title VII' (1965) 34:2 *George Washington L.R.* 232 ff; Brittney C. Cooper, 'Queering Jane Crow: Pauli Murray's Quest for an Unhyphenated Identity' in Brittney C. Cooper, *Beyond Respectability: The Intellectual Thought of Race Women* (2017); Rosalind Rosenberg, *Jane Crow: The Life of Pauli Murray* (2017). Other scholars recently addressing Murray's life and legacy include Serena Mayeri, Sarah Azaransky, and Dayo Gore.

domestic and sexual dynamics of the Hart household' could meet that standard. The same reviewer, however, also noted an 'authorized' quality to the biography (despite Lacey's own rejection of that term), given the author's dependence on and intimacy with Hart's wife, Jenifer, and his children and friends.[31]

Any biographical endeavour involves ethical decisions as to what to reveal, which may prove fraught for queer subjects who actively concealed aspects of their life. In her portrayal of Hart, however, there is a plausible case that Lacey's own rule of thumb justified greater attention to queerness, rather than less of it. It is surely not too much of a stretch to imagine that Hart's experiences of intimacy and sexuality met at points with, for instance, his sustained philosophical interest in the relationship between morality and law. The queerness of his biography can be argued to have direct bearing on an arresting moment at the end of the first chapter of his 1963 book *Law, Liberty, and Morality* when he referred to the 'infliction of a special form of suffering—often very acute—on those whose desires are frustrated by fear of punishment', affecting 'the development or balance of the individual's emotional life, happiness, and personality'. Yet beyond this, associative connections might even be drawn to Hart's more abstract discussions of rules and obligations or to the notion of 'recognition' so important to his 1961 opus *The Concept of Law*. Of course, there are dangers of being reductive or essentializing, and there is a risk too of tacking close to those insults historically levelled at queer public figures in order to dismiss them. But at such a moment as when Hart describes how an external observer of a group not only may be able to predict whether deviation 'from normal behavior will meet with hostile reaction', but also might be able 'to live among them without unpleasant consequences', the question is begged as to whether there is something queer to unpack about Hart's jurisprudence itself.[32]

III. DOMAIN

An alluring but as yet barely touched area for queer disturbances in law can be found in human rights—or what Bentham might have called 'nonsense upon stilts'. Following interventions by Samuel Moyn and others, a significant strand in the consolidating field of human rights history identifies an important turning point as taking place in the 1970s, when among lawyers and others an understanding of human rights as claims proceeding from international law against nation states

---

[31] Nicola Lacey, *A Life of H. L. A. Hart: The Nightmare and the Noble Dream* (2004) xix ff; G. Edward White, 'Book Review' (2005) 29 *Melbourne University L.R.* 29 317 ff.

[32] H. L. A. Hart, *Law, Liberty, and Morality* (1963) 23 ff; H. L. A. Hart, *The Concept of Law* (1961) 89 ff.

achieved new prominence.[33] Here, I want to suggest, a simultaneous rise in LGBT activism and rights claims—made at local, national, and international levels in and beyond the West—offers an intriguing corollary to the apparent paradigm shift in the legibility of human rights demanding enforcement against sovereign states.

'Human rights', of course, have been invoked in a variety of ways along spectrums of rhetorical and legal meaning, so that quite what is referred to may shift markedly by place and time. Diverse and inconsistent usage, however, might usefully produce more lines of enquiry as to the intersection with queerness rather than fewer. In the case of Michigan college town Ann Arbor, for instance, it was a local Human Rights Party that successfully agitated for a pioneering 1972 ordinance banning discrimination on the basis of race, national origin, sex, age, and religion, which was extended to sexual orientation later that year. There is a genealogical case for delving into the long and distinctive history of the term *Menschenrecht* in German queer organizing and subcultures, while the postwar geopolitical legal scene surely had some relation to a 1951 telegram from a consolidating transnational homophile movement urging the United Nations to grant 'human, social and legal equality to homosexual minorities throughout the world'.[34] Beyond unpacking particular sites of queer human rights claims, there is the question of what queer studies may have to say about expanding or contracting legal visions of humanity and the aspects of intimate life not easily articulated through civil rights traditions. Dramatic historical shifts in the cultural presence of queer social formations suggests again both a potential stimulus of and a diagnostic for what Mark Philip Bradley has described as *The World Reimagined* in regard to U.S. relations to human rights.[35] At the same time, leftist critique of human rights as a stalking horse for imperial intervention and the rollout of neo-liberalism may be galvanized further by queer studies scholars who express well-grounded suspicion of rights appealing to concepts of dignity in tension with queerness and of formal sexual equality that ignores economic justice.[36]

The implication of queerness in the global frame of human rights represents just one aspect of a second major pursuit in queer legal history this chapter would like to push: remedying the continued lack of work thinking comparatively between jurisdictions or transnationally across their bounds. Perhaps most straightforward

---

[33] Jan Eckel, Samuel Moyn (eds.), *The Breakthrough: Human Rights in the 1970s* (2014).

[34] *Blätter für Menschenrecht*, for instance, was one of the most popular queer publications of Weimar Germany; see Robert Beachy, *Gay Berlin: Birthplace of a Modern Identity* (2014) 231 ff. For a reproduction of the 1951 telegram, see Leila J. Rupp, 'The Persistence of Transnational Organizing: The Case of the Homophile Movement' (2011) 116:4 *American Historical Review* 1016 ff.

[35] Mark Philip Bradley, *The World Reimagined: Americans and Human Rights in the Twentieth Century* (2016).

[36] See, e.g., Lisa Duggan, *The Twilight of Equality? Neoliberalism, Cultural Politics, and the Attack on Democracy* (2003); Lucinda Grinnell, '"Intolerable Subjects": Moralizing Politics, Economic Austerity, and Lesbian and Gay Activism in Mexico City, 1982–1985' (2012) 112 *Radical History Review* 89 ff.

here are questions about what political scientists call 'diffusion' that would give us a better picture of how particular laws regulating sexuality and gender have circulated. But while parts of this picture (such as the inheritance of colonial sodomy statutes by U.S. states) may be relatively clear, much is left to unpack about the intricacies of circulatory mechanisms, translations, and adaptations, and what these reveal about the legal systems they helped to constitute or transgress.[37] Again, queerness has potential here to shine analytic light on transnational legal systems themselves. After all, historians of sexuality who have thought about the field's relation to a transnational turn have pointed out that 'interconnection' is a central analytic uniting the two areas, while 'exchange' and 'encounter' are among the keywords they share.[38]

Of course, as has also been observed since historians paid concerted attention to the possibilities of transnational approaches back in the 1990s, the complexity of thinking about 'nations within nations' or following questions across borders to wherever they go means that speculative discussion proves easier than pursuit. There is little reason to suppose queer transnational legal history would be an exception, although some historiographic threads do already exist to weave together. Dagmar Herzog's twentieth-century history of *Sexuality in Europe*, for instance, makes ready comparative use of legal material to quickly cover a wide range of topics over a large canvas. Further work comparing or tracking laws on age of consent, indecency, sodomy, rape, prostitution, marriage, child protection, and sex trafficking stands not only to sharpen claims about particular jurisdictions, but also to raise questions about sexuality's relation to different political and legal systems. A seemingly straightforward question concerning the bearing of judicial review on sexual politics opens up vistas of nuanced and complex permutations when thought about across time and place.[39]

Complexity may be especially pronounced, and especially treacherous, when legal historians of sex, gender, and intimate relations in the West attempt to move beyond the skews of academic attention and resources. The role of law, criminalization, Islamic jurisprudence, and legal medicine in a book such as Afsaneh Najmabadi's *Professing Selves* on transsexuality and same-sex desire in Iran suggests some of the departures from prominent Western narratives a more global queer legal history would present. That the Islamic Republic of Iran not only rules homosexuality to be punishable by death (in a way that is well advertised in the West), but also permits and partially subsidizes sex reassignment surgery (enabling some kinds of non-normative living less legible to Western eyes) indicates the necessity for queer legal historians to acquire deep knowledge of the locations they traverse. Queer studies is

---

[37] For an example of a possible approach, see Jennifer M. Spear, 'Colonial Intimacies: Legislating Sex in French Louisiana' (2003) 60:1 *The William & Mary Quarterly* 75 ff.

[38] See Margot Canaday, 'Thinking Sex in the Transnational Turn: An Introduction' (2009) 114:5 *American Historical Review* 1250 ff, quoting Joanne Meyerowitz in the same issue.

[39] Dagmar Herzog, *Sexuality in Europe: A Twentieth Century History* (2011).

not the only field, of course, that would benefit from increasing scholarship coming from the Global South and from transnational collaboration.[40]

Which is also to say that transnational queer legal history must be wary of universalizing any claims it makes about law's relationship to gender and sexuality, or to assuming that a national legal story will look the same in an international context. Indeed, one burgeoning area of analysis in contemporary work on queer studies has elaborated a critique of what it terms 'homonationalism', emphasizing among other things how liberal states can co-opt gay rights at home for less than liberal ends abroad. While some of the most prominent examples of writing in this genre have now generated critiques of their own, the broad relations between shifting sexual regulation and geopolitics continue to present an area of investigation that can reframe how we think of both.[41] Historians have of course already written significant histories on such topics as the imperial regulation of venereal disease, prostitution, and miscegenation, while theoretically engaged scholars have shown ways in which the regulation of sex and intimacy was constitutive of imperial power.[42] Queer legal historians are as well placed as any to explore this tricky terrain.

IV. CONCLUSION

If there is one salient feature of the emergence of queer legal history across the intersections of sex, gender, law, and the past, it is surely that as a field it is predisposed to defy orthodoxy. This, of course, includes any agenda I am tempted to advance here.

The basic indeterminacy of what 'queer' signifies can indeed support varied and even contradictory agendas; for the United States alone, recent titles thinking about the regulation of sexuality have alternately declared *Victory* in one case and identified a new *War on Sex* in another. While the former viewpoint might appeal to the passage of marriage equality, the latter volume examines how decades of progress in areas of gay and reproductive rights co-exists with an intensification of punitive

---

[40] Afsaneh Najmabadi, *Professing Selves: Transsexuality and Same-Sex Desire in Contemporary Iran* (2013).

[41] See, e.g., Perreau (n. 10) 121 ff, critiquing the discussion of the 2003 U.S. Supreme Court case *Lawrence and Garner v. Texas* in Jasbir K. Puar, *Terrorist Assemblages: Homonationalism in Queer Times* (2007).

[42] See, e.g., Philippa Levine, *Prostitution, Race and Politics: Policing Venereal Disease in the British Empire* (2003); Stephen Legg, *Prostitution and the Ends of Empire: Scale, Governmentalities, and Interwar India* (2014); Ann Laura Stoler, *Carnal Knowledge and Imperial Power: Race and the Intimate in Colonial Rule* (2010).

and often pernicious sex offender registries, HIV criminalization, and the targeting of sex work.[43] And then, of course, while we now have a number of insider and outsider accounts about the path to U.S. marriage equality, we also have innovative and provocative legal scholarship that points to its strategic, ideological, and indeed legal perils, with Katherine Franke's *Wedlocked* drawing some cautionary tales through comparisons to what marriage rights brought to Africa-Americans freed from slavery in the 1860s.[44]

There is something to be said for those who demand 'queer' maintain political as well as intellectual valence when applied to legal history, which would honour the particular activist and scholarly elaborations of the term in the United States. And yet, if we are to expand and complicate the geographies of how we queer law's empire, the permeability of queerness and its openness to further change is one of its most valuable aspects. Keeping alive the question of law's sometimes assumed powers over and against sexual minorities provides one possible way forward—one that does not have to lose the bite of political critique. Deepening the comparative and transnational perspective of queer legal history, meanwhile, would be an especially welcome step.

BIBLIOGRAPHY

Margot Canaday, *The Straight State: Sexuality and Citizenship in Twentieth-Century America* (Princeton University Press, 2009)

George Chauncey, 'How History Mattered: Sodomy Law and Marriage Reform in the United States' (2008) 20:1 *Public Culture*, 27–38

Brittney C. Cooper, 'Queering Jane Crow: Pauli Murray's Quest for an Unhyphenated Identity' in Brittney C. Cooper, *Beyond Respectability: The Intellectual Thought of Race Women* (University of Illinois Press, 2017) 87–114

William N. Eskridge, *Gaylaw: Challenging the Apartheid of the Closet* (Harvard University Press, 1999)

Katherine Franke, *Wedlocked: The Perils of Marriage Equality* (New York University Press, 2015)

Marie-Amelie George, 'Bureaucratic Agency: Administering the Transformation of LGBT Rights' (2017) 36 *Yale Law & Policy Review*, 83–154

David M. Halperin, Trevor Hoppe (eds.), *The War on Sex* (Duke University Press, 2017)

Felicia Kornbluh, 'Queer Legal History: A Field Grows Up and Comes Out' (2011) 36:2 *Law & Social Inquiry*, 537-59

Regina Kunzel, *Criminal Intimacy: Prison and the Uneven History of Modern American Sexuality* (Chicago University Press, 2008)

---

[43] Linda Hirschman, *Victory: The Triumphant Gay Revolution* (2012); David M. Halperin, Trevor Hoppe (eds.), *The War on Sex* (2017).

[44] Katherine Franke, *Wedlocked: The Perils of Marriage Equality* (2015).

Eithne Luibhéid, *Entry Denied: Controlling Sexuality at the Border* (University of Minnesota Press, 2002)

Anna Lvovsky, 'Cruising in Plain View: Clandestine Surveillance and the Unique Insights of Antihomosexual Policing' (2017) *Journal of Urban History* (online)

Clare Sears, *Arresting Dress: Cross-Dressing, Law, and Fascination in Nineteenth-Century San Francisco* (Duke University Press, 2015)

Nayan Shah, *Stranger Intimacy: Contesting Race, Sexuality, and the Law in the North American West* (University of California Press, 2011)

David Alan Sklansky, ' "One Train May Hide Another": *Katz*, Stonewall, and the Secret Subtext of Criminal Procedure' (2008) 41:3 *U.C. Davis L.R.*, 875–934

Marc Stein, *Sexual Injustice: Supreme Court Decisions from* Griswold *to* Roe (University of North Carolina Press, 2010)

Timothy Stewart-Winter, 'Queer Law and Order: Sex, Criminality, and Policing in the Late Twentieth-Century United States' (2015) 102:1 *The Journal of American History*, 61–72

PART IV

TRADITIONS:
TRACING LEGAL
HISTORY

CHAPTER 35

ROMAN LAW

CLIFFORD ANDO*

I. INTRODUCTION

ROMAN law[1] as an academic field is flourishing today.[2] It does so in conditions of unprecedented diversity as regards linguistic, disciplinary, and national context. Its present condition and future trajectories will to a large extent be determined by intellectual developments exogenous to Roman legal history as such, as the questions, methods, and concerns of other fields inflect the practice of jurists and historians in the Roman tradition. But the present and future of Roman legal history will also be shaped by that tradition. By this, I gesture at the fact that Roman law

* David B. and Clara E. Stern Professor; Professor of Classics, History and Law and in the College, University of Chicago; Research Fellow, Department of Biblical and Ancient Studies, University of South Africa.

[1] Roman legal sources are cited according to the following abbreviations: *Dig.* = *Digesta*, whose Latin text is available with English translation in Alan Watson (ed.), *The Digest of Justinian* (1985). Lenel = Otto Lenel, *Palingenesia Iuris Civilis* (1889). *C.J.* = Paul Krueger (ed.), *Codex Justinianus* (1954). Bruns-Gradenwitz = Karl Bruns, Otto Gradenwitz (eds.), *Fontes Iuris Romani Antiqui* (7th edn., 1909); FIRA = Salvator Riccobono (ed.), *Fontes Iuris Romani Antejustiniani* (1968), 3 vols. *Roman Statutes* = Michael Crawford (ed.), *Roman Statutes* (1996) 2 vols.

[2] Recent essays surveying the state of the field and its recent past include Ari Bryen, 'Law in Many Pieces' (2014) 109 *Classical Philology* 346–65; Laurens Winkel, 'Roman Law and its Intellectual Context', in David Johnston (ed.), *The Cambridge Companion to Roman Law* (2015) 9–22; Ulrike Babusiaux, 'The Future of Legal History: Roman Law' (2016) 56 *American Journal of Legal History* 6–11; and Janne Pölönen, 'Framing "Law and Society" in the Roman World', in Paul du Plessis, Clifford Ando, Kaius Tuori (eds.), *The Oxford Handbook of Roman Law and Society* (2016) 8–20. See also Paul J. du Plessis, Clifford Ando, Kaius Tuori, 'A Word from the Editors', in Du Plessis, Ando, Tuori (eds.) (2016) 3–7.

has been a system of practice and field of academic study for some 2,400 years. The contours of contemporary study are inevitably the product of complex and imbricated historical factors: the non-codification by the Romans of the classical period of their own public law; solutions taken in the classical period and later to resolve conflicts among sources of law of very different antiquity; the codification in late antiquity of academic jurisprudence regarding private law; the on-going prestige of Roman civil law in medieval and late medieval Europe, which made it a resource for analogical argumentation in both public and international law; and much else besides. In what follows, I seek to evaluate the contribution made by some of these factors to Roman legal history as a contemporary endeavour, with an eye to (but without prediction regarding) its future.

II. Historical Self-Consciousness in the Roman Legal Tradition

The Roman legal system was already felt to be old by insider participants and theorists of the first century BC. In part this resulted from their own awareness of linguistic change: the Romans believed that their law had first been codified in the mid-fifth century BC—in the so-called Twelve Tables—and by the dawn of classical jurisprudence and Roman philosophy in the age of Cicero (BC 106–43) the language of the Twelve Tables was already archaic.[3] Not for naught do we owe a considerable number of the surviving quotations from that codification to the lexicographical tradition. That is to say, much of what we know about the actual wording of the oldest codification of Roman law derives from those who mined it for examples of archaic language. What is more, even those who cited it as an historical source, whether for early Roman history generally or the history of positive law more narrowly, could only get access to that knowledge via a text that confronted readers even of the first century BC with the deep pastness of their past.

By the time Roman jurisprudential texts begin to survive in bulk, which is to say, by the later first century AD, this ferment of awareness and reflection had given rise to an historical self-consciousness on the part of Roman lawyers of significance to this inquiry in various ways.[4] For one thing, the Romans came to understand language,

---

[3] There have been many attempts to reconstruct the content and wording of the Twelve Tables. Notable twentieth-century editions include Bruns-Gradenwitz (n. 2) 15–40; E. H. Warmington (ed.), *Remains of Old Latin* vol. 3 (1938) 424–515; FIRA (n. 2) 1:21–75; and *Roman Statutes* (n. 2) 2:555–721.

[4] The writings of the earliest jurists are probably still most easily accessed in Ph. Eduard Huschke, Emil Seckel, Bernhard Kübler (eds.), *Iurisprudentiae anteiustinianae reliquiae* (1908); see also Franz

customs, and norms to be subject to interrelated forces of historical change. As regards the Twelve Tables, for example, the jurist Sextus Caecilius Africanus, whose floruit falls in the first half of the second century AD, wrote that those who found its content hard to understand or appreciate were to be excused: 'For long lapse of time has rendered old words and customs obsolete, and it is in light of those words and customs that the sense of the law is to be understood' (Gellius, *Attic Nights* 20.1.6, trans. Rolfe). What is more, on this understanding legal change was properly motivated by multiple forms of historical change: demographic, social, cultural, technological, and so forth. So, for example, the first-century AD jurist Pomponius ascribed some historical changes in procedure and public law (not least as regards sources of law) to demographic change; others he ascribed to historical contingencies.[5] By the time of the great jurists of the early third century AD, the problem could be theorized as one inherent to considerations of the rule of law and modes of legal change: it lies in the nature of things, wrote Ulpian, that there is more stuff in the world than there are words (Ulpian, *Ad Sabinum* bk. 30 fr. 2747 Lenel = *Dig.* 19.5.4). The resulting pressure drove both the development of conventional modes of statutory interpretation and related understandings of legal language—of metonymy, metaphor, analogy, and so forth—and also the writing of new law. That these needs were complexly correlated is explicit in the claims advanced by the emperor Justinian in the sixth century AD about the relationship between statutory interpretation and the sovereign power of law-making. 'Social life is always hastening to bring forth new forms'; hence God himself had assigned to the emperor the task of correcting, settling, and regulating 'all those things that happen in an innovative way' (*Constitutio Tanta* §18, 21). By contrast, where the relationship of new forms to old was simply analogical, 'judges were to know that imperial decisions were to be applied not simply to the cases for which they were produced, but to all similar ones'.[6]

This entire problematic found expression in two further features of the Roman legal tradition that have had profound impact on how Roman legal science (and Roman legal history) developed in the late medieval and modern periods. Here it is crucial to know that many Roman statutes remained in force for hundreds of years.

Peter Bremer (ed.), *Iurisprudentia antehadriana* (1898), 2 vols. By far the best survey of its period (AD 117–284) is that offered by Detlef Liebs in part III, 'Jurisprudence', in Reinhart Herzog, Peter Lebrecht Schmidt (eds.), *Nouvelle Histoire de la Littérature Latine*, vol. 4 (2000) 92–248. Alas, vol. 3 of that series has never been published. Dario Mantovani, 'More than Codes: Roman Ways of Organising and Giving Access to Legal Information', in du Plessis, Ando, Tuori (eds.) (n. 2) 42, offer the richest brief survey available of Roman attempts to organize legal knowledge.

[5] Pomponius, *Encheiridion* fr. 178 Lenel = *Dig.* 1.2.2.*pr.*, 7, 11. For some reflection on the distinctiveness and importance of this aspect of Roman legal thought see Clifford Ando, *Roman Social Imaginaries* (2015) 58–72.

[6] *C.J.* 1.14.12.*pr.* On analogical argument in Roman law see Ando, *Imaginaries* (n. 5) and Ando, '*Exemplum*, Analogy and Precedent in Roman Law', in Michèle Lowrie, Susanne Lüdemann (eds.), *Between Exemplarity and Singularity: Literature, Philosophy, Law* (2015) 111–22.

Laws passed by the Roman people between the fifth and first centuries BC were cited, debated, and interpreted by jurists not for their evocation of a long-lost past, but because in a terribly meaningful way they continued to regulate contemporary social conduct. That said, one could not simply apply a clause of the Twelve Tables from fifth-century BC Rome to sixth-century AD Constantinople. What is more, no Roman lawyer thought that one could. Beyond the development of modes of statutory interpretation and rules of precedent (on which more below), varied forms of legal innovation intervened to establish new procedures for adjudication. Despite this necessary openness of the system to change at a practical level, it is important to stress that on ideological and theoretical planes, improvization and innovation were nearly always understood to operate in such a way as to respect not simply earlier statute, but in particular the source of law of that earlier statute. This ideological need appears to have motivated or, perhaps, found expression in the invention of some of the earliest Roman legal fictions.[7]

Another feature of the Roman legal tradition that is properly regarded as an expression of their historical self-awareness is their attachment to the lemmatic commentary as a genre of literary production.[8] By this means, the historicism at the heart of statutory construal in the Roman tradition was enacted through the consistent and precise measuring of the distance between earlier contexts of application and the context of production of new jurisprudential literature. In the first instance, this occurred in academic jurisprudence via the writing of commentaries on statute: how were its words and language to be interpreted, so as to keep them relevant to some new context of application? But as the context of production of statute receded into the past, what was required was not some new assessment of the language of the Aquilian law (for example) in relation to the present, but of the range of conventional and accepted interpretations of Aquilian law of the immediately prior generation. In other words, Pomponius would not write a commentary on the *lex Aquilia*, but a commentary on Labeo's commentary on the *lex Aquilia*, and Ulpian would write a commentary on Pomponius's commentary on Labeo's commentary on the *lex Aquilia*. In this way, the very contemporaneity and comprehensiveness of juristic writing paradoxically led to the gradual elision from their texts of the words upon which they notionally commented. As each new generation of jurists wrote commentaries on earlier commentaries on statute law, they gradually ceased to quote the original words of the statute, which receded ever farther into the past. Those words were clearly understood to remain in some way dispositive—indeed, the genre of the lemmatic

---

[7] On procedural fictions that operated so as to respect earlier sources of law see Gaius, *Institutes* 4.10-32 (with the caveat that the text has not been perfectly transmitted and its interpretation is difficult). On the problem of conflicts among sources of law at Rome see Clifford Ando, *Law, Language and Empire in the Roman Tradition* (2011) 1–36.

[8] Ando, *Roman Social Imaginaries* (n. 5), 66; see also Ulrike Babusiaux, 'Der Kommentar als Haupttext', in Nils Jansen, David Kästle (eds.), *Kommentare in Recht und Religion* (2014) 15–55.

commentary might be said to genuflect before the power of the original wording—but the power of those words could only be accessed via acts of interpretation that enabled their language to map present-day social conduct, which had itself been oriented around the requirements of law as then understood.

To write in this way is to wrestle with a puzzle to which Bruce Frier gave enduring formulation a generation ago. Frier focused on the content of Roman legal argument rather than the genres of legal writing (as above), but the problem remains the same: a great deal of surviving Roman jurisprudence lacks argumentation altogether but simply declares the law; if jurists refer to anything, it is to each other rather than case law or metrics of social change exogenous to the law; for all that they propounded social-historical theories of legal change and situated theories of legal legitimacy, their historical reflections were often dogmatic in orientation.[9] After a fashion, this feature of Roman jurisprudential literature may be at least partially explained by the form of autonomy claimed and sustained by the jurists in the early classical period, whose origins are charted in Frier's subsequent monograph.[10] On his understanding, jurists won their independence—they established their social and institutional autonomy—via the performance of disinterest and a kind of rationalized mastery: doctrinalist modes of argumentation enacted a kind of disavowal of attention to, and therefore influence from, social and political conditions, while judgment on mastery was made via patterns of recognition enacted solely (and circularly) by others in the guild.[11] In short, the autonomy of legal reasoning was enacted and inscribed in juristic literary production via both its forms (responses to and commentary upon each other's works) and content (forms of argumentation that insist upon apparent disinterest and radical decontextualization).[12]

[9] Bruce W. Frier, *Landlords and Tenants in Imperial Rome* (1980) 197.

[10] Bruce W. Frier, *The Rise of the Roman Jurists: Studies in Cicero's Pro Caecina* (1985); see also Aldo Schiavone, *The Invention of Law in the West*, trans. Jeremy Carden, Antony Shugaar (2012) 131–225. An older, ideational-philosophical mode of tracing this history is visible in Fritz Schulz, *History of Roman Legal Science* (1953 [1946]) 38–86.

[11] For an analysis of Frier's work in this domain see Clifford Ando, 'Afterword', in Dennis Kehoe, Thomas A. J. McGinn (eds.), *Ancient Law, Ancient Society: Studies in Honor of Bruce W. Frier* (2017) 183–91.

[12] On these features of Roman legal writing see Ari Z. Bryen, 'When Law Goes off the Rails, Or, *Aggadah* among the *Iurisprudentes*' (2016) 3.1 *Critical Analysis of Law* 9–29; see also Liebs (n. 4) and Ulrike Babusiaux, 'Legal Writing and Legal Reasoning', in du Plessis, Ando, Tuori (eds.) (n. 2) 176–87. On the intellectual and historical contexts of these developments see Claudia Moatti, *The Birth of Critical Thinking in Republican Rome*, trans. Janet Lloyd (2015 [1997]); on the evolving social position of jurists and other intellectuals in the passage from democratic republic to republican monarchy, see Andrew Wallace-Hadrill, '*Mutatio morum*: The Idea of a Cultural Revolution', Thomas Habinek, Alessandro Schiesaro (eds.), *The Roman Cultural Revolution* (1997) 3–22. Not everyone shares this view of the deficiencies of legal argument in surviving excerpts of Roman jurisprudence. For a rather more optimistic effort to assess the situation see Dario Mantovani (ed.), *Per la storia del pensiero giuridico romano: da Augusto agli Antonini: atti del seminario di S. Marino, 12–14 gennaio 1995* (1996).

This review of historical questions is useful, perhaps, insofar as it draws on recent scholarship on the legal profession, the autonomy of law, and the genres of jurisprudential writing in classical Rome. It is by contrast essential to the conduct of historical legal research, because the forces and traditions that delivered to us the evidence of the Roman legal tradition establish the preconditions of scholarship. Further conditions were set by the editorial work performed in the great codifications of late antiquity (and perforce at other times as well) and the elaboration and use of Roman legal texts in the late medieval and early modern periods. To these topics I will shortly turn. For the moment, allow me to point out that no other legal tradition of the ancient Mediterranean—save in complex respects Jewish law in the Roman period[13]—develops any remotely similar practices that we might denominate a theory of autonomous law, or traditions of statutory interpretation, or rules of precedent, or institutions of legal education and practices of jurisprudence.[14]

The tendencies thus far invoked—that inclining jurists towards formalist and dogmatic argumentation and those responding to deep-seated impulses towards historicism and contextualism—find specific conjuncture in the codifications performed in the fifth and sixth century, which resulted in, first, the *Codex Theodosianus* and the body of material that Gothofredus named the *Corpus Iuris Civilis*. It perhaps cannot be stated firmly or often enough that it is moderns who seek to reconstruct classical Roman law from these texts—who employ them as sourcebooks for the contexts whence the late antique editors draw their material. The scholars who produced the late ancient codifications, by contrast, had no normative interest in knowledge of the past for its own sake: their object was the preservation of knowledge of law relevant to the regulation of social action going forward. (The narrowness of 'our' interest in classical Roman law has issued in a similar deficit of attention to the landscape of the law and, in particular, the nature and transmission of what we might denominate academic legal literatures between the end of classical jurisprudence in the early third century AD and the age

---

[13] For merely a taste of contemporary scholarship on Rabbinic literature as legal literature see Barry Scott Wimpfheimer, *Narrating the Law: A Poetics of Talmudic Legal Stories* (2011); Natalie Dohrmann, 'Law and Imperial Idioms: Rabbinic Legalism in a Roman World', in Natalie Dorhmann, Annette Yoshiko Reed (eds.), *Jews, Christians, and the Roman Empire: The Poetics of Power in Late Antiquity* (2013) 63–78; Natalie Dohrmann, 'Means and End(ing)s: Nomos versus Narrative in Early Rabbinic Exegesis' (2016), 3.1 *Critical Analysis of Law* 30.

[14] For recent surveys, analysis, and bibliography on law in the ancient Near East and Greece see Raymond Westbrook (ed.), *A History of Ancient Near Eastern Law* (2003) 2 vols.; Seth Richardson, 'Before Things Worked: A "Low-Power" Model of Early Mesopotamia', in Clifford Ando, Seth Richards (eds.), *Ancient States and Infrastructural Power: Europe, Asia and America* (2017) 17–62; Michael Gagarin, David Cohen (eds.), *The Cambridge Companion to Ancient Greek Law* (2005); Mark Sundahl, David Mirhady, Ilias Arnaoutoglou (eds.), *A New Working Bibliography of Ancient Greek Law (7th–4th Centuries BC)* (2011).

of Justinian.[15]) There is in addition the problem that the codifications of imperial constitutions in particular required the late ancient editors to extract from complex documents—which had in their totality spoken to issues of justification, relevance, and positive law—statements of legal principle wholly abstracted from the cases and contexts that generated them.[16] It is only rarely that the autonomous transmission of textual material allows us to compare the as-it-were legal content of the excerpts in the *Codes* from the 'superfluity of words' that the original texts were deemed to contain. Alas, it was precisely those words that described the first-order problem that the imperial authorities sought to solve and connected an understanding of it to the legal principle that remains available to us. Similar problems and others attend efforts to reconstruct either classical law or even classical modes of legal argument from the excerpts of jurisprudence selected for inclusion in the sixth-century AD *Digest*. It is not simply that some material is systematically omitted—for example, that dealing with the pluralist landscape of the empire prior to the universalization of citizenship in 212 AD. In addition, it is clear that the late ancient editors privileged certain kinds of literature, and certain forms of argument: for example, there *was* a literature elaborating the challenges presented by particular cases, but excerpts from it are preserved very rarely and nearly exclusively when the emperor himself was a participant to deliberation.[17]

As with the history of legal thought and education between the end of classical jurisprudence and the reign of Justinian, so the history of the Roman tradition between the sixth century and the so-called rediscovery of classical Roman law in the high middle ages has not figured prominently in historical legal study of Roman law.[18] (Even more shocking, but arising from different ideological causes, has been the neglect of Spanish Roman law and the *Siete Partidas* in favour of attention to

[15] That many histories of 'Roman law' end with the close of Roman jurisprudence scarcely needs demonstration: see, e.g., Schiavone (n. 10). Important exceptions surveying legal thought and literature include Schultz (n. 10), 262–329; H. F. Jolowicz, Barry Nicholas, *Historical Introduction to the Study of Roman Law* (3rd edn., 1972), 469–515; Liebs (n. 4); and Detlef Liebs, 'Droit et littérature juridique', in Reinhart Herzog, Peter Lebrecht Schmidt (eds.), *Nouvelle Histoire de la Littérature Latine*, vol. 5 (1993) 61–82, on the years 284–374 AD. Max Kaser, *Das Römische Privatrecht*, part 2: *Die Nachklassischen Entwicklungen* (1975 [1959]) remains the best, indeed indispensable, survey.

[16] On the nature of the editorial work performed by those responsible for the late ancient codifications of imperial constitutions see John Matthews, *Laying Down the Law: A Study of the Theodosian Code* (2000); Serena Connolly, *Lives Behind the Laws: the World of the Codex Hermogenianus* (2010); and Simon Corcoran, 'The Codex of Justinian: The Life of a Text through 1,500 Years', in Bruce Frier (ed.), *The Codex of Justinian* (2016) 1:xcvii-clxxxi.

[17] On the surviving accounts of jurists as advisors to emperors in legal deliberation see Michael Peachin, 'Jurists and the Law in the early Roman Empire', in Lukas de Blois (ed.), *Administration, Prosopography and Appointment Policies in the Roman Empire* (2001) 109–35, whose general reflections on shifts in the genres of imperial law-making in the high Roman empire deserve sustained attention. See also Ando, 'Exemplum' (n. 6); and Bryen, 'When Law Goes off the Rails' (n. 12).

[18] Peter Stein's very elegant and careful study, *Roman Law in European History* (1999), devotes a scant five pages to the period (38–43).

Italian and French institutions and scholars between the eleventh and thirteenth centuries.) The point is obviously not that the history of law, legal institutions, legal education and so forth from the eleventh century on has been neglected in itself. It is rather that each age of scholarship constructs its understanding of ancient law on the foundations laid by prior ones, and while medieval legal history frequently understands its objects of study as developments on Roman legal traditions, modern historians of ancient law have been far less assiduous in conducting archaeologies of the archetypal concepts and narratives that they have received.[19] No scholar has done more to demonstrate the value of work in this vein than Yan Thomas; the neglect of his work in Anglophone scholarship will hopefully be remedied by ongoing translation projects.[20]

The study of the Roman legal tradition between the eleventh century and the writing of the Code Napoléon—to choose two broad bookends—offers two further dividends. One is an obvious corollary to the notion that we cannot view the Roman past except through the landscape of intervening centuries, namely, that the modern civilian tradition—the modern law of Europe and its post-colonial epigones—cannot be understood as formed in some unmediated fashion from 'Roman law'. This is so in spite of the fantasy advanced by nineteenth-century historicists—many of whom contributed substantively or ideologically to the writing of national codes—that it was possible via supreme acts of scholarship and ratiocination to strip away the accumulation of centuries and come to know classical Roman law in something approaching its original form.[21] Rather, even doctrinally-oriented historical scholarship must trace the Roman roots of modern law down through its imbricated receptions and revisions.[22]

The second dividend paid to modern scholars of ancient law by attending to the history of the Roman legal tradition between the recuperation of manuscripts of the late ancient codifications and the early nineteenth century is as follows. The encounter of high and late medieval scholars with texts of the Justinianic codifications impelled several developments in historical and linguistic thought, which can for present purposes be regarded under the banner of humanist philology. As with the scholarship of figures like Petrarch, Valla, and even Vico, but with wider and

---

[19] Recent medieval legal scholarship notable for its historical self-consciousness includes Marta Madero, *Tabula Picta: Painting and Writing in Medieval Law*, trans. Monique Dascha Inciarte, Roland David Valyre (2010 [2004]); Emanuele Conte, *Diritto comune: storia e storiografie di un sistema dinamico* (2009); Emanuele Conte, Massimo Miglio (eds.), *Il diritto per la storia: gli studi storico giuridici nella ricerca medievistica* (2010); and Marta Madero, *La loi de la chair: le droit au corps du conjoint dans l'oeuvre des canonistes (XIIe–XVe siècle)* (2015).

[20] See for now Yan Thomas, *Les opérations du droit*, Marie-Angèle Hermitte, Paolo Napoli (eds.), (2011); the failure of this volume to include a bibliography of Thomas' publications is hard to explain.

[21] James Q. Whitman, *The Legacy of Roman Law in the German Romantic Era* (1990); Stein (n. 18) 104–23; Frederick C. Beiser, *The German Historicist Tradition* (2011) 214–52.

[22] The great monument of modern scholarship in this vein is Reinhard Zimmermann, *The Law of Obligations. Roman Foundations of the Civilian Tradition* (1990).

more significant effects, what was at issue was the perception of historical distance between the classical world and the present, along many axes, including those of language, culture, and norms. Thus, whatever the pretensions of contemporaneous classicisms or ideologies of kingship, which is to say, however they imagined themselves as continuous with the classical past, not only could one not read or write classical Latin (or classical sources) except through artifice, so the new science of philology—which told us, as it were, what classical languages had meant—also became a pre-eminent tool in the historical archaeology of what had henceforth to be deemed past societies.[23] These conditions not only shaped the scholarly practice and genres of production of readers of classical legal texts, but guided and shaped their habits as regards the abstraction of rules and principles from those texts; the development of practices of analogical argumentation; and so forth.[24] This much is of course well known, even if modern historians of ancient law fancy themselves unobliged to regard this as the past of their own practice. What I want to stress is the further aspect, that the problems generated by historical change in respect of language in and of itself; of fit between the language of statute and contemporary conceptualizations and vernaculars; and that between substantive law and the situations it seeks to regulate, with which lawyers wrestled between the eleventh and seventeenth centuries—these all exist in a relation of homeomorphy with problems that the Roman jurists, too, had confronted. That this is little recognized is due, in part, to the existence in late antiquity and late medieval Europe of structurally similar pressures towards reading Roman legal literatures in pursuit of rules[25]—this was how classical Roman law might be codified and read so as to be the law of the future in Justinianic Constantinople; and the editorial work performed in that age established the conditions of possibility for similar approaches to Roman law after the eleventh century. Intelligent reading of the late medieval tradition might therefore spark more imaginative readings of classical sources, with an eye towards an enriched understanding of their theories of law, language, and social change.[26]

[23] Donald R. Kelley, *Foundations of Modern Historical Scholarship. Language, Law and History in the French Renaissance* (1970); H. E. Troje, *Graece leguntur. Die Aneignung des byzantinsichen Rechts und die Entstehung eines humanistischen Corpus Iuris Civilis in der Jurisprudenz des 16. Jahrhunderts* (1970); Ian Maclean, *Interpretation and Meaning in the Renaissance; The Case of Law* (1992); J. G. A. Pocock, 'Classical and Civil History: The Transformation of Humanism' (1996) 1 *Cromohs* 1–34 (http://www.fupress.net/index.php/cromohs/article/view/15758/14654); Donald R. Kelley, *Faces of History: Historical Inquiry from Herodotus to Herder* (1998) 130–61.

[24] For a brief overview of the Roman legal tradition in this period see Stein (n. 18) 38–70; Laurent Mayali, 'The Legacy of Roman Law', in Johnston (ed.), (n. 2) 374–95; and R. H. Helmholz, 'Canon Law and Roman Law', in Johnston (ed.), (n. 2) 396–422. At greater length, see Paul Vinogradoff, *Roman Law in Medieval Europe* (1929 [1909]), or O. F. Robinson, T. D. Fergus, W. M. Gordon, *European Legal History* (2005 [1985]).

[25] Peter Stein, *Regulae Iuris: From Juristic Rules to Legal Maxims* (1966); see also Peter Stein, *The Character and Influence of the Roman Civil Law* (1988) 53–100.

[26] One benefit might exactly be a more deeply historicized understanding of the emergence of the concept of the 'principle of law' (*regula iuris*), kindred to notions of the 'force' or 'meaning' of

The historical self-consciousness of ancient legal history as a discipline is far better served where the nineteenth century is concerned. By far the best known development in historical legal research in this period is the emergence of the German historicist school. The influence of its leading figures—Friedrich Carl von Savigny, Bernhard Windscheid, and Rudolf von Jhering—in fields far from Roman law (including, of course, the writing of the German civil code) would be impossible to overestimate.[27] But the prestige value of Roman law, not least in legal education but also in legal theory and comparative law, was such that Roman legal scholarship played an essential role in many arenas, and some aspects of this history are now being expertly charted.[28] For historians of Roman law, an essential correlate to investigations of this kind will be efforts to understand not simply how Roman law was studied and used, but how those contexts of study and use affected even notionally disinterested forms of scholarship.[29]

III. Modern Trends

The focus thus far has been on a set of deeply interrelated issues. The form of autonomy won by the jurists in the first century BC impelled developments in the genres of legal writing and forms of jurisprudential argument that favoured

a statute (*vis legis*). For all its intelligence and learning, the extant literature is simply a-historical in its explanatory ambitions and methods. Sustained reflection on the late medieval reception of the notion of the 'rule' might have proved salutary. See Stein (n. 25); Bruno Schmidlin, *Die römischen Rechtsregeln. Versuch einer Typologie* (1970).

[27] Reinhard Zimmermann, *Roman Law, Contemporary Law, European Law; The Civilian Tradition Today* (2001), offers historical and normative perspectives on the legacy of German historicism of remarkable sweep. See also Whitman (n. 21); Stefan Friesenfeld, 'The Influence of German Legal Theory on American Law: The Heritage of Savigny and his Disciples' (1989) 37 *The American Journal of Comparative Law* 1–7; Michael H. Hoeflich, 'Savigny and his Anglo-American Disciples' (1989) 37 *The American Journal of Comparative Law* 17–37; Joachim Rückert, *Savigny-Studien* (2011).

[28] Luigi Capogrossi Colognesi, *Dalla storia di Roma alle origini della società civile. Un dibattito ottocentesco* (2008); Kaius Tuori, *Lawyers and Savages: Ancient History and Legal Realism in the Making of Legal Anthropology* (2015); see also Stein (n. 25), 151–552; Alan Diamond (ed.), *The Victorian Achievement of Sir Henry Maine: A Centennial Reappraisal* (1991); David S. Clark, 'Development of Comparative Law in the United States', in Mathias Reimann, Reinhard Zimmerman (eds.), *The Oxford Handbook of Comparative Law* (2006) DOI: 10.1093/oxfordhb/9780199296064.013.0006 (accessed 4 October 2016); and Clifford Ando, 'Il diritto romano e i giuristi romani nella cultura giuridica americana', in Aldo Schiavone (ed.), *Giuristi Romani e Storiografia Moderna dalla Palingenesia iuris civilis agli Scriptores iuris Romani* (2018) 99–111.

[29] See, e.g., Kaius Tuori, *Ancient Roman Lawyers and Modern Legal Ideals: Studies on the Impact of Contemporary Concerns in the Interpretation of Ancient Roman Legal History* (2007); Zimmermann (n. 27).

decontextualized, internalist, and hyper-rationalized forms of reasoning. The sheer antiquity of the materials of Roman law, processes of historical change, and the increasing diversity of the world that Roman legal institutions were called upon to regulate—by virtue, that is, of the expanding empire—likewise drove the jurists to craft modes of statutory interpretation, forms of analogical reasoning, and theories of language and practices of abstraction that sustained norms of legal legitimacy while allowing laws drafted in highly particularized linguistic, ecological, and social contexts to be applied in situations scarcely imaginable in the context of the law's production. (Herein lies something of the affinity between Roman law as a system of imperial law and Rabbinic law as the law of a diaspora.) Finally, the codification of Roman law in late antiquity, especially that undertaken in the sixth century AD, had normative rather than historical ambitions: the editors were charged to abstract from the massive legacies of classical textual material resources in the form of norms, arguments, and justification that would be useful in regulation forms of action in the future, including novel forms of social action yet to be devised. We have likewise seen that many similar pressures were operative in the European contexts where classical Roman legal texts—in the form of manuscripts of the Justinianic collections—were received and mobilized as a prestige body of norms and source for analogical elaboration. It should thus be apparent that the traditional modes of legal historical scholarship in the Roman law tradition, namely, analytic jurisprudence and dogmatic historiography, had both epistemic and political affinities with the interests that delivered the textual source materials of Roman law to medieval and modern Europe. For this reason, the ongoing pursuit of dogmatic historiography, which is to say, notionally historical rational reconstructions of Roman doctrine, without consideration for social and historical context or attention to cognitive-linguistic and conceptual-historical problems, is simply a dead end. It is simply a form of naïve collaboration with the ideological and imaginative horizons established by insiders.

That said, many kinds of legal material were not codified or subject to commentary in classical antiquity, nor were they edited and their excerpts preserved in the later Roman empire. These include official documents issued by statal authorities: statutes, colonial charters, boundary stones, and cadastral records, and legal instruments such as treaties and military discharge papers. They also include copies belonging to individuals of documents arising in the course of civil litigation or interaction with state authorities or institutions of dispute resolution: summons, petitions for redress, personal copies of census returns, witness statements, wills, divorce records, and so on. These were written in antiquity on the full range of media exploited for the transmission of texts: on tablets of bronze or pieces of stone, on wax tablets or wooden boards, sheets of papyrus and fragments of pottery. The discovery, recuperation, editing, and understanding of these texts—including their assembly in corpora, so that they can be studied in aggregate—have constituted one of the most significant advances in the knowledge of antiquity on the part of late medieval and modern historical scholarship. Many of the most characteristic forms of modern ancient legal history are consequent upon the gradual discovery and elucidation of these materials.[30] To that work I now turn.

iv. Public law

One of the curiosities of the Roman legal tradition is the powerful unwillingness of the Romans to codify their own public law.[31] Few are the modern states without written constitutions—the United Kingdom and Israel are probably the most prominent cases. The historical study of the operations of public power in Rome therefore requires specific forms of imagination. The Roman case further resembles that of the UK in another crucial respect: the Romans did have a robust tradition of writing charters both for their own colonial foundations and for non-Roman towns that were reorganized as Roman communities as a matter of public law.[32] That is to say, the Romans were willing to write constitutions for others; they simply

[30] Surveys of epigraphic and papyrological discovery as relevant to legal history may be found in James G. Keenan, J. G. Manning, Uri Yiftach-Firanko (eds.), *Law and Legal Practice in Egypt from Alexander to the Arab Conquest: A Selection of Papyrological Sources in Translation, with Introductions and Commentary* (2014); Gregory Rowe, 'The Roman State: Laws, Lawmaking and Legal Documents', in Christer Bruun, Jonathan Edmondson (eds.), *The Oxford Handbook of Roman Epigraphy* (2015) 299–318; Tommaso Beggio, 'Epigraphy', du Plessis, Ando, Tuori (n. 2) 43–55; José Luis Alonso, 'Juristic Papyrology and Roman Law', du Plessis, Ando, Tuori (n. 2), 56–69. For a survey of the evidence provided by surviving wax tablets see Joseph Georg Wolf, 'Documents in Roman Practice', in Johnston (n. 2), 61–84. A useful overview of the use of documents in Roman private law is Elizabeth A. Meyer, 'Writing in Roman Legal Contexts', in Johnston (n. 2) 85–96. Still valuable as a notionally comprehensive view (in its day) is Leopold Wenger, *Die Quellen des römischen Rechts* (1953).

[31] An observation along these lines commences nearly every modern handbook survey of Roman public law: for bibliography, see Clifford Ando, 'The Origins and Import of Republican Constitutionalism' (2013) 34 *Cardozo Law Review* 917–35 at 919 n. 7. See also T. Corey Brennan, 'Power and Process under the Republican "Constitution"', in Harriet I. Flower, *The Cambridge Companion to the Roman Republic* (2014 [2006]) 19–53; and Francisco Pina Polo, 'SPQR: Institutions and Popular Participation in the Roman Republic', in du Plessis, Ando, Tuori (n. 2) 85–97.

[32] The fullest extant Roman colonial charter is that for the Roman colony at Urso. English text and translation in Crawford (n. 1), 1:393–454; see also Antonio Caballos Rufino, *El Nuevo Bronce de Osuna y la Política Colonizadora Romana* (2006). The easiest way to access a reconstruction of a Roman municipal charter is via Javier González, 'The *Lex Irnitana*: A New Flavian Municipal Law', (1986) 76 *Journal of Roman Studies* 147–243. Saskia Roselaar, 'Local Administration', in du Plessis, Ando, Tuori (n. 2) 124–36 provides an excellent survey of the material.

chose not to impose one on themselves. Despite the paucity of source material consequent upon this ancient ideological tradition, interest in Roman public law has been intense and continues unabated, and may be understood within a number of frameworks.

To begin with, it is essential to understand that Roman public law has long been cited and continues to be discussed in normative argument, for reasons of history, prestige, and its nearly unique status as a democratic republic that became a long-lived republican monarchy. This tradition commences at the latest in the twelfth century, when figures like Portius Azo unfolded particular understandings of Roman terms like *imperium* (magisterial power of command) so as to shape contemporary debate on the relationship of imperial to local sovereignty.[33] A moment characteristic in its aetiology, if wholly unusual in its historical influence, was the discovery, display, and citation of the so-called *Lex de imperio Vespasiani* ('Law on the public power of [the emperor] Vespasian'), by Cola di Rienzo, the self-declared 'tribune of the people' of Rome, who used the text not simply to undergird historical-normative claims about the tribunate, but about the ontology of the residual sovereignty that inhered in the Roman people, in the first century AD, and in his own day.[34] Arguments of this kind have continued to be advanced in the twentieth and twenty-first centuries by figures such as Carl Schmitt (and Georgio Agamben), for whom Roman history offered essential case studies in the nature and dangers of emergency powers, as well as Benjamin Straumann, who understands something like properly 'constitutional' thought to have developed at Rome in response to the inability of traditional norms in the late Republic to constrain magistrates in office, on the one hand, and in particular the people in its desire to create extraordinary magistracies, on the other.[35]

Recent inquiry into Roman public law as an historical matter can also be understood as wrestling with important questions of method. For one thing, the Romans report many titles of statutes that regulated public law matters, but relatively few of these survive even in fragments.[36] Roman legal historians were

---

[33] Myron Piper Gilmore, *Argument from Roman Law in Political Thought 1200–1600* (1941); Ando (n. 7) 81–114; Daniel Lee, 'Hobbes and the Civil Law: The Use of Roman Law in Hobbes' Civil Science', in David Dyzenhaus, Thomas Poole (eds.), *Hobbes and the Law* (2012) 210–35; Magnus Ryan, 'Political Thought', in Johnston (n. 2) 423–51.

[34] *Lex de imperio Vespasiani*: a text and transation may be found in Crawford (n. 1) 549–53. The bibliography is immense.

[35] Kaius Tuori, 'Schmitt and the Sovereignty of Roman Dictators: From the Actualization of the Past to the Recycling of Symbols' (2016) 42 *History of European Ideas* 95–106; Benjamin Straumann, *Crisis and Constitutionalism: Roman Political Thought from the Fall of the Republic to the Age of Revolution* (2016); Alexander Yacobson, 'Cicero, the Constitution, and the Roman People' (2015 [published 2016]) 29 *Ancient History Bulletin* 157–77.

[36] Giovanni Rotondi, *Leges Publicae Populi Romani* (1912) provides a catalogue of attested Roman statutes. Several provisional attempts to update his catalogue have been commenced.

therefore forced in the nineteenth century to adopt relatively capacious notions of what legislative or constitutional history might look like, and likewise of what a legal 'source' might be. A recent trend has been to accept that the Romans long operated without explicit statutory enactments regarding the powers of magistrates, and therefore that histories of magistracies and public powers should be written ostensively, by compiling and mapping attested actions by magistrates, both those that were treated as routine and those that were contested.[37] Where histories of the early and middle Republic are concerned, a number of questions of interpretation and method intervene: how reliable are later Roman sources for these early centuries? To what extent do they retroject the institutional conditions of later Roman history to the early Republic? Can Roman claims of continuity of certain religious sanctions and customary norms as conditioning the exercise of statal power be trusted, and on what grounds? What political, sociological, and demographic conditions—connected with imperial expansion, the political economy of slavery, and vast internal and horizontal social mobility—should be understood to have affected the operation of public institutions, and how might be these be detected in light of the representational commitments of ancient narrative?[38]

In all this, it might paradoxically be said that there has been relative neglect of the statutes of public law from the late Republic that do survive, even in fragments.[39] This is particularly true if one's concerns are not narrowly the substance of any given clause (regarding procedure in cases of debt for a specific sum of money where the debtor admits the obligation but fails to give satisfaction via stipulation, say), but rather underlying principles of jurisdiction; the scope of popular sovereignty; the nature and status of legal language; the historical self-consciousness of legislative authorities; problems of knowledge of law in conditions of low literacy; and so on.

[37] See Hans Beck, Antonio Duplá, Martin Jehne, Francisco Pina Polo (eds.), *Consuls and* Res *Publica: Holding High Office in the Roman Republic* (2011); Francisco Pina Polo, *The Consul at Rome: The Civil Functions of the Consuls in the Roman Republic* (2011); an inquiry with kindred ambitions but different method is T. Corey Brennan, *The Praetorship in the Roman Republic* (2000), 2 vols.

[38] Three recent interventions in this field are Frederik J. Vervaet, *The High Command in the Roman Republic: The Principle of the 'summum imperium auspiciumque' from 509 to 19 BCE* (2014); Fred K. Drogula, *Commanders and Command in the Roman Republic and Early Empire* (2015); Alejandro Díaz Fernández, *Provincia et Imperium: El mando provincial en la República Romana (227–44 AD)* (2015). A perspective from a very different tradition is Wolfgang Kunkel, Roland Wittmann, *Staatsordnung und Staatspraxis der römischen Republik*, part 2: *Die Magistratur* (1995).

[39] The most important exception is Jean-Louis Ferrary (ed.), *Leges Publicae: La legge nell'esperienza giuridica romana* (2012).

V. LAW AND SOCIETY SCHOLARSHIP

Janne Pölönen has recently invoked a distinction between lawyers' histories and historians' histories operative in Roman historical legal scholarship.[40] He makes reference to public law and cites works that assumed the salience, indeed, the monopoly power of state institutions in the organization of private life: formal legal institutions, backed by the power of the state, extended their authority uniformly throughout the territory that the state claimed as its own, and down through its population. He traces the dominance of these assumptions to the aspirations of legislators and theorists of the state, who declared positive law pre-eminent above all other sources of norms and whose ideal codification would provide a gapless, rationalized, and hypostasized system of rules. (This chapter has suggested that ideological forces and scholarly practices in the Roman tradition drove the production of a similar theoretical self-understanding on the part of Roman jurists from a very early date.) On his view, the form of legal history—and many aspects of legal education—practised among Romanists housed in law schools in many civil-law countries continues to actualize such an understanding of the nature of law.[41]

Historians' histories—and, one might add, ancient legal history in Anglophone countries *tout court*—now proceed on very different principles. In part this is consequent upon the gradual publication of the documentary records of case law that have been deciphered and published since the late nineteenth century; in part it follows on the politics of empire studies and the practices of scholarship that these impelled; and in part it partakes of broader movement in legal sociology and law-and-society scholarship in the field of legal history. As will be apparent, these categories overlap in many important ways. Nonetheless, they can also be disaggregated in the interests of analysis. In what follows I take them in turn.

The recovery and elucidation of ephemeral documents on papyrus, which matured as a technical-scientific enterprise at the end of the nineteenth century, rapidly transformed the study of ancient law. The range of genres of legal material suddenly exploded. It scarcely exaggerates to say that prior to 1890, the source material exploited for the history of Roman private law was restricted nearly wholly to academic jurisprudence, quotations and paraphrases of statute, and imperial constitutions of one kind or another. Already by 1902, it was clear that the world had changed, and by 1912 the first sourcebook and overview had been published.[42] Some of the most exciting work in contemporary ancient legal history exploits this material, not, as in the past, asking in a narrowly dogmatic way how

[40] Pölönen (n. 2).   [41] See also Zimmermann (n. 27) 1–52.

[42] Leopold Wenger, *Papyrusforschung und Rechtsgeschichte* (1903); Ludwig Mitteis, Ulrich Wilcken, *Grundzüge und Chrestomathie der Papyruskunde*, vol. 2:2: *Juristischer Teil* (1912).

Roman was the law of Roman Egypt, but what we can say about legal culture, access to legal institutions, the coexistence of statal and non-statal mechanisms of dispute resolution, and so forth, in the single best-attested context of law in the world before AD 1000.[43]

Egypt was, of course, subjected to waves of imperial conquest: from Achaemenian Persia, to Alexander the Great, to Rome, to Sasanian Iran, and back to Rome, before the Islamic conquest in AD 639/40. The imbrication of legal cultures and language groups and the ways in which successive conquerors continued, contained, and grandfathered the legal systems that they nominally succeeded can be studied in Egypt as nowhere else in the ancient Mediterranean world. Unfortunately, the attention of papyrology as a science has not focused uniformly on all attested languages: Demotic Egyptian and Greek (and the small number of surviving Latin papyri) have received greatly more attention than Coptic, Pahlavi, or Arabic texts. Coptic began receiving sustained attention from a small cadre of scholars in the second quarter of the twentieth century, and Arabic texts are now faring somewhat better (though in no relation to their surviving number).[44] These fields look to yield rich material for harvest in years to come. The questions posed of Egypt as a colonial legal system can, of course, be addressed to other contexts, and occasionally sustained detective work has yielded exciting results.[45] Again, the ongoing exploitation of new epigraphic discoveries is likely to prove essential.

Finally, whereas at one time one might have traced the origins of self-consciously socio-legal history and law-and-society scholarship on the ancient world to the work of a small handful of scholars—above all, perhaps, John Crook and Bruce Frier[46]—today the variety of theoretical commitments on display mirrors that of the wider field of historical legal research.[47] Returning for a moment to the history

---

[43] The bibliographies in Keenan, Manning, Yiftach-Firanko, (n. 30), and Alonso (n. 30) provide convenient starting points. Allow me to single out Traianos Gagos, Peter van Minnen, *Settling a Dispute: Towards a Legal Anthropology of Late Antique Egypt* (1994); Ben Kelly, *Petitions, Litigation, and Social Control in Roman Egypt* (2011); and Ari Z. Bryen, *Violence in Roman Egypt: A Study in Legal Interpretation* (2013).

[44] Joseph Mélèze Modrzejewski, *Loi et Coutume dans l'Égypte grecque et romaine* (2014) is a milestone in the study of the law of Egypt across imperial regimes. It revises a thesis completed in 1970 that circulated in tiny numbers. See also Andrew Monson, *From the Ptolemies to the Romans: Political and Economic Change in Egypt* (2012), and Petra Sijpesteijn, 'The Arab Conquest of Egypt and the Beginning of Muslim Rule', in Roger Bagnall (ed.), *The Oxford Handbook of Papyrology* (2007) 437–59.

[45] See, e.g., Georgy Kantor, 'Knowledge of Law in Roman Asia Minor', in Rudolf Haensch (ed.), *Selbstdarstellung und Kommunikation: die Veröffentlichung staatlicher Urkunden auf Stein und Bronze in der römischer Zeit* (2009) 249–65; Julien Fournier, *Entre tutelle romaine et autonomie civique. L'administration judiciaire dans les provinces hellénophones de l'Empire romain (129 av. J.-C.—235 apr. J.-C.)* (2010); Ari Z. Bryen, 'Judging Empire: Courts and Culture in Rome's Eastern Provinces' (2012) 30 *Law and History Review* 771–811; Georgy Kantor, 'Law in Roman Phrygia: Rules and Jurisdictions', in Peter Thonemann (ed.), *Roman Phrygia: Culture and Society* (2013) 143–67.

[46] J. A. Crook, *Law and Life at Rome* (1967); Frier (n. 9); Frier (n. 10).

[47] Here I can not do better than point to the bibliographies in Bryen (n. 2); Winkel (n. 2); and du Plessis, Ando, Tuori (n. 2).

of scholarship on documentary evidence for Roman law, it once focused—necessarily—on problems of philology, the reconstruction of the texts, and situating them in context. Some of this work displays a particularism that resists historical understanding; in other instances, it issues in catalogues and lists: what Roman legal actions are attested as having been conducted among aliens, and when and where did this occur? Here one must remember that the context of Roman law was the Roman empire. The context for the study of Roman law is one of remarkable advances in historical understanding of Roman society in virtually every respect, not least as regards its political economy, its culture of knowledge, and its status as an empire. If one source of inspiration to historical legal study of Roman law more recently and going forward is the advances in socio-legal scholarship more generally, another should be the empirical and theoretical richness of ancient studies. The future of ancient legal history is bright.

Bibliography

Adolf Berger, *Encyclopedic Dictionary of Roman Law* (American Philosophical Society, 1953)

Ari Z. Bryen, *Violence in Roman Egypt: A Study in Legal Interpretation* (University of Pennsylvania Press, 2013)

Paul du Plessis, Clifford Ando, Kaius Tuori (eds.), *The Oxford Handbook of Roman Law and Society* (Oxford University Press, 2016)

Bruce W. Frier, Dennis P. Kehoe, 'Law and Economic Institutions', in Walter Scheidel, Ian Morris, Richard Saller (eds.), *The Cambridge Economic History of the Greco-Roman World* (Cambridge University Press, 2007) 113–43

Bruce W. Frier, *The Rise of the Roman Jurists: Studies in Cicero's Pro Caecina* (Princeton University Press, 1985)

Max Kaser, *Das römische Privatrecht*, part 2: *Das altrömische, das vorklassische und klassische Recht* (C.H. Beck, 1971 [1955])

Max Kaser, *Das Römische Privatrecht*, part 2: *Die Nachklassischen Entwicklungen* (C.H. Beck, 1975 [1959])

Max Kaser, *Das römische Zivilprozessrecht*, (C.H. Beck, 2nd edn., Karl Hackl, 1996)

Yan Thomas, *Les opérations du droit*, Marie-Angèle Hermitte, Paolo Napoli (eds.) (Seuil, 2011)

CHAPTER 36

....

MEDIEVAL CANON LAW

....

KARL SHOEMAKER*

1. INTRODUCTION

....

THE term canon law refers to the body of law developed by the Catholic Church
to govern the body of Christ on earth. Derived from the Greek *kanón* (a reed or
stick used as a measure or ruler; cf. the English 'cane'), the word came first into
Christian usage to name the various discrete regulations governing life in early
monastic communities. In time—for we should recognize that what would develop
into medieval canon law was neither coeval with the birth of Christianity nor an
ineluctable feature of it—canon law came to designate the totality of laws, legislation,
judicial processes, and institutions promulgated by the Church and enforced by its
officers upon Christians, and sometimes non-Christians. In its own terms, medieval
canon law encompassed both doctrine and discipline and was drawn from 'the
Law and the Gospels'—as well as select portions of patristic theology, conciliar
pronouncements, synods, and papal decrees.[1] In its most capacious formulation,
theorized but never actualized, canon law was the body of laws administered by the
Church, whose Pope stood as the *iudex ordinarius*—that is, a judge whose office holds
inherent rather than delegated jurisdiction—of every soul in the world. Canonists
held that canon law was superior to secular law because of its primary concern with

---

* Professor of History and Law, University of Wisconsin, Madison.

[1] *Decretum,* D.1 *dicta Gratiani ante* c.1. An English translation of this portion of the *Decretum* is
available in *Gratian: The Treatise on the Laws,* trans. Augustine Thompson and James Gordley (1993) 3.

salvation and the care of souls, though canon law conceded to secular authorities' prerogatives over certain matters, particularly those that might result in corporal or capital punishment 'so that ... human temerity can be controlled'.[2] Although canon law conceded spheres of autonomy to secular power, determination of the actual boundaries and hierarchies between secular and ecclesiastical authorities sometimes gave rise to the most contentious and historically momentous disputes of the medieval era.

The chronological parameters of 'medieval canon law' are malleable. That is, they are arbitrary in the same general way that the term 'medieval' is a contingent periodization harbouring a range of unspoken cultural judgments about the meaning of Rome, Europe, Christianity, and the rest of the world. Most scholarly accounts of medieval canon law begin with some notice of the monastic rules of earliest Christian communities, then discuss the growing role of regional episcopal councils in the sixth through ninth centuries, and conclude with canon law's 'classical age.' Here, 'classical age' typically designates the period from the twelfth through fifteenth centuries. In that period, the lawmaking activities of the Church became increasingly identified with the promulgation of papal legislation, and canonists produced voluminous commentaries and glosses on those decrees. In terms of the quantity and quality of juristic output, as well as in terms of institutional and social reach, this period is generally regarded as the most important epoch of canon law. It is in this period that canon law came to frame European social and spiritual life with increasing vigour and capacity. The legal machinery for defining, exposing, and punishing heresy, the development of just war doctrines, the institutional means to define and discipline sexual deviancy, the reform and development of criminal law processes and doctrines, increased judicial oversight of marriage, and increased legal control of entry into religious life—these are just a few of the more prominent areas in which canon law made major reforms between the twelfth and fifteenth centuries. Most discussions of medieval canon law conclude around the time of the Reformation when the Catholic Church lost its claim to pan-European jurisdiction. But the unavoidable arbitrariness involved in the term 'medieval canon law' is highlighted perhaps by the fact that the textual foundation of canon law's classical age remained authoritative in Catholic ecclesiastical jurisdictions until the reissue and reform of the *Corpus Iuris Canonici* in 1917. Indeed, systems of canon law continue to operate today among many communities of faith, including Roman Catholics, Orthodox Christians, and Anglicans, though the binding authority of such legal decisions as are issued under such regimes today are largely dependent on the consent of the members.[3] In the Middle Ages, conversely, the Church could generally, though not always, rely on civil authorities to enforce its judicial rulings, as well as to recognize papal interdicts and excommunications pronounced

---

[2] *Decretum* (n. 1) D.4, c.1 12.
[3] James A. Brundage, *The Medieval Canon Law* (1995) 187–8.

by authorized ecclesiastical officers. This basic relationship was not abrogated in many parts of Europe until the eighteenth century, or even later. Nonetheless, the conventional chronology honoured by historical scholarship on canon law tends to focus on its heyday and the ascendancy of the medieval Church's state-like attributes.

Medieval canon lawyers, however, had a rather different understanding of law's periodization and of the place of their law within human history. In his commentary on the canons of the Fourth Lateran Council, Henry of Segusio, better known as Cardinal Hostiensis and one of the most prominent canon lawyers of the thirteenth century, posited three distinct ages of law. The first age, which spanned from creation until the giving of the Ten Commandments to Moses, he termed a 'time before law'. In that first age, mankind was ruled only by the *lex naturale*, which Hostiensis articulated as containing 'two precepts ...: what you want to be done to you, do to me. What you do not want done to you, will not [to do to me].' Far from Hobbes' wolfish state of nature, Hostiensis attributed a modicum of sociability to the *lex naturale*. The second age, which Hostiensis defined as 'under law', spanned from the moment God gave Moses the Ten Commandments on Mount Sinai until the Advent. In this age, the law acted as a kind of tutor, preparing for the arrival of Christianity and the Advent of the third age. This third and last age, which Hostiensis termed the 'age of grace', is the current age. It began 'when the Son of God' fulfilled the Old Testament law and 'taught us the Gospels, by which we are ruled today'.[4] This current age will conclude with the Last Judgment—an event whose character as a juridical act was not lost upon medieval canonists.

The ages of law deployed by Hostienses were not novel. The '*ante legem, sub lege, sub gratia*' formulation clearly reproduced a formulation that had been offered by Augustine and which was well known to medieval theologians and exegetes.[5] It belonged to a well-developed Christian theological discourse in which the European Jews who still observed the Old Testament law were considered as 'living letters of the law'—embodied object lessons for Christians who, as the theologians would have it, should now know better than to slavishly observe the old law and should instead live the grace promised by the Gospels.[6]

Christianity never embraced the radical anti-nomialism hinted at in this opposition between the old law and the new age of grace. To the contrary, medieval

[4] Gl. ord. ad X 1.1.1 *iuxta ordinatissimam*, 'Hec fuit dispositio: quia tria tempora: tempus ante legem, et tempus sub lege, et tempus gratie. In tempore ante legem habebant homines ius naturale, quo regebantur, quod consistebat in his duobus preceptis contentis his versibus: Quod tibi vis fieri, mihi fac: quod non tibi, noli / Sic potes in terris vivere iure poli. Dist. 1 in principio. In tempore sub lege regebantur decalogo Moysi dato a Deo: et tunc contingebat omnia in figura, que completa fuerunt tempore gratie, quondo Dei filius nos docuit precepta evangelica, quibus hodie regimur.' *Corpus juris canonici emendatum et notis illustratum*, 4 vols. (Rome: 1582), vol. 2, col. 9. See, e.g., Knut Wolfgang Nörr, 'Recht und Religion: über drei Schnittstellen im Recht der mittelalterlichen Kirche' (1993) 79 *Zeitschrift der Savigny-Stiftung für Rechtsgeschichte (KA)* 1–15.

[5] *Enchiridion*, cap. 18, *Corpus Christianorum* 46, 112–13.

[6] Jeremy Cohen, *Living Letter of the Law: Ideas of the Jew in Medieval Christianity* (1999).

Christianity developed a robust legal tradition with legislation, courts, and elaborate legal processes. Despite the ambivalence expressed towards the Mosaic Law, the Gospels presented Christ as the fulfilment of the law, not the destruction of the law. Crucially, though, early Christianity came to hold that observance of the Old Testament law was not essential to salvation.[7] After some initial doctrinal controversies, the dietary restrictions of the old law were abandoned. Jettisoned as well was the requirement for male circumcision, thereby reducing a significant barrier of entry to the new and growing religion. Still, early on, Christian communities found it necessary to establish the rules and processes to govern themselves. Such rules were as yet nothing like the immense body of law and commentary that canon law would become in the later Middle Ages, but the age of grace turned out to also be an age of law.

Of course, medieval canonists would have seen no contradiction here. First, medieval canon lawyers did not understand their discipline to be bounded by the three ages of law Hostienses delineated—rather they came to teach that canon law transcended all three ages. For just as human history would end in the Last Judgment, Christian theology also taught that human history began with a crime and a legal process. In fact, it was in the Garden of Eden, not the Advent, that medieval canonists located the inception of their own discipline. According to Stephen of Tournai, the passage of Genesis that told how Adam was charged with disobedience by God for eating the forbidden fruit was describing a legal process. Adam had in fact attempted to claim an '*exceptio*' by laying a criminal countercharge against Eve. 'The woman that you gave to me as a companion deceived me and I ate.' Adam thus became a legal actor invoking a legal form of process. 'And thus', Stephen of Tournai explained, 'litigating, or what we commonly call the form of pleading, appears to have arisen in Paradise.'[8] Tournai lifted this account from the glossator Paucapalea, who leaves us the earliest surviving glosses on Gratian's *Decretum*. Finding canon law in the Garden of Eden was a commonplace of the classical era of medieval canon law. But there was much at stake in the claim that canon law already existed at the moment God confronted Adam for his sin. By finding the origins of canon law processes in sacred history, canonists vested canon law with two foundational attributes. First, canonists could claim for canon law a historical priority that competed with theology in the rank of

---

[7] See James Brundage, *Medieval Canon Law* (1995) 5.

[8] Johann Friedrich von Schulte (ed.), *Die Summa des Stephanus Tornacensis* (Giessen: Emil Roth, 1891): 'Cum enim Adam de inobedientia argueretur a domino, quasi actioni exceptionem obiiciens relationem criminis in coniugem, immo in coniugis actorem convertit dicens; "Mulier, quam dedisti mihi sociam, ipsa me decepit et comedi." Sicque litigandi, vel, ut vulgariter dicamus placitandi forma in ipso paradiso videtur exorta.' Cf. Paucapalea's *summa* has been printed in J. F. von Schulte (ed.), *Summa über des Decretum Gratiani*, (Giessen: Emil Roth, 1890) 1–2; See also, Ken Pennington, 'Law, Criminal Procedure', *Dictionary of the Middle Ages: Supplement 1* (New York: Charles Scribner's Sons-Thompson-Gale, 2004) 309–20.

scientiae.[9] Second, it could be claimed that canon law stood above the three historical ages of law, encompassing, according to Hostiensis, both 'the new law and the three ages of law'.[10] In this view, canon law was not the creation of human actors, but rather a subdivision of divinely revealed law and coeval with the foundation of the world. Without a source in some secular enactment, canon law could claim supremacy over the laws made by kings.

II. HARMONY

In its own terms and that of the scholarly tradition, the classical age of canon law was characterized by harmony, or at least a harmonizing impulse. Gratian's *Decretum*, produced sometime in the first half of the twelfth century, sought to harmonize a discordant mass of legal texts into a coherent body—a task announced in its long title '*A Concordance of Discordant Canons*'. According to Stephan Kuttner's famous thesis, twelfth-century canonists confronted dissonance throughout the textual tradition inherited from the Church fathers and the first millennia of episcopal councils. In response, they sought to harmonize legal sources, ecclesiastical institutions, and the mystical body.[11] At the head of these efforts was an obscure figure named Gratian.[12] Possibly a monk, it seems likely that he was teaching law at the university in Bologna during the first decades of the twelfth century.[13] If he was not himself a law teacher, his text was very popular with law teachers who quickly adopted it. Some claim Gratian was a bishop but the evidence is not satisfying.[14] Many portions of the *Decretum* seem suited to classroom exercises if only because the hypotheticals seem so outlandish—perfectly tailored to raise issues a law professor might wish to

---

[9] See, e.g., E. James Long, 'Utrum iurista vel theologus plus proficiat ad regimen ecclesiae: A *Questio Disputata* of Francis *Caraccioli*' (1968) *Mediaeval Studies* 30:134–62.

[10] Hostiensis, *Summa Aurea, Proemium*, num. 41 (Lyon: 1537).

[11] Stephan Kuttner, *Harmony from Dissonance: An Interpretation of Medieval Canon Law* (1961).

[12] See, John T. Noonan, 'Gratian Slept Here: The Changing Identity of the Father of the Systematic Study of Canon Law' (1979) *Traditio* 35: 145–72; Peter Landau, 'Gratian' in *Theologische Realenzyklopädie* XIV (1985); Peter Landau, 'Quellen und Bedeutung des gratianische *Dekrets*' in (1986) *Studia et documenta historiae et iuris* 52: 220; Stephan Kuttner, 'Gratien' in *Dictionaire d'histoire et de géographie ecclésiastiques* XXI (1986) 1236; Anders Winroth, *The Making of Gratian's* Decretum (2000) 5–8.

[13] But compare R. W. Souther, who claims Gratian was a lawyer and not a teacher, *Scholastic Humanism and the Unification of Europe* (1995) 303–5.

[14] Noonan, 'Gratian Slept Here' 153–4.

discuss, but not representative of the sorts of cases that might ordinarily require adjudication. The *Decretum* takes on the task of introducing students to both a complex and sometimes conflicting welter of authoritative texts and a method for resolving such conflicts as might arise between the texts. Moreover, the *Decretum* is likely the work of more than one person. The form we have received it in is quite certainly the result of at least two and possibly more recensions. As Anders Winroth has shown, the second recension contains significantly more Roman law material than the first.[15]

The *Decretum* is curious as a law book. For one thing, it is not a compendium of statutes. It contains very little that looks like legislation. None of it looked like the core texts of the Roman law that were also being studied anew in Europe's emerging universities. The body of materials deployed in the *Decretum* ranged from Scripture passages to the enactments of contemporary ecclesiastical councils. It included snippets of patristic writings, papal letters, and synodal pronouncements taken from all the corners of Christendom over the previous 1,000 years. These snippets number over 3,800 in all. The first part of the *Decretum*, known as the *Distinctions*, is separated into 101 sections. The first twenty are comprised of didactic material, offering definitions of natural law, secular law, custom, and canon law, among others. The remaining *Distinctions* deal with general matters of Church discipline and the administration of orders. The second part of the *Decretum* is comprised of thirty-six *causae*, hypothetical cases constructed for the purpose of establishing legal propositions and reconciling discordant sources. The *causae* have the distinctive smell of the classroom. The third part, added soon after the first recension, is called *De Consecratione* and deals with sacraments and worship. The intellectual method deployed was strongly influenced by the kind of things Peter Abelard had done with theology in his controversial *Sic et Non*, though Gratian rarely left discordant authorities open-ended in the way Abelard had. Romanists at Bologna were similarly attempting to reconcile Roman law texts with one another, though they had the advantage of a self-contained and relatively homogenous source base. Surveying a mass of different textual genres, authorities, and sources, Gratian occasionally offered *dicta* laying out preferred readings and reconciling contradictory sources. The *Decretum* was not the first compilation of canonical sources. In fact, Gratian worked from the texts of a relatively small number of compilers that had preceded him: Anselm of Lucca, Ivo of Chartres, Alger of Lièges, and (though possibly through an intermediary source) Isidore of Seville. With the exception of Isidore of Seville, the other canonists Gratian relied upon were active in the late eleventh or early twelfth centuries. But Gratian's was by far the most ambitious attempt to compile sources, deal with inconsistencies, and establish a priority between canons issued by episcopal councils and decrees

[15] See on this the pathbreaking work of Anders Winroth, *The Making of Gratian's* Decretum (2000).

issued by the papacy. Gratian offered what was essentially a papalist vision of canon law. Episcopal councils mattered, but only insofar as they had been 'received' by the Roman Church.

Prior to the eleventh century, there had been little will to produce a canonical collection of the size and scope of the *Decretum*. There had of course been earlier production of canon law texts. Since the Roman Empire first recognized and endorsed Christianity, episcopal councils had gathered to address issues facing Christian communities. In doing so, they sometimes issued rules. The earliest of these often were concerned with defining correct doctrine as well as with defining the proper scope of pastoral care, particularly in regard to orphans, widows, and the imprisoned. This included the production of penitential handbooks, whose purpose was to guide priests in the administration of penance and absolution upon sinners.[16] But as bishops had increasingly stepped into the urban political role that had previously been filled by Roman aristocrats, these councils also sometimes turned to broader issues of governing a Christian polity.[17]

In the Carolingian era, Charlemagne's Christian-imperial vision had stimulated interest in producing canonical source collections, the most prominent of which was the *Dacheriana*. The *Dacheriana*, relying in part on a chronologically arranged collection that Pope Hadrian had created sometime before 774, presented materials taken from Frankish and Iberian ecclesiastical councils. Similarly, high-pitched controversies over episcopal power generated canon law treatises and canon law collections. One of the most widely circulated of these collections, the *Pseudo-Isidorian Decretals*, mixed cleverly forged papal decrees with authentic materials. As an intervention into controversies over episcopal power in Francia, the *Pseudo-Isidorian* forgeries were an important source of material for regulating episcopal power in the centuries that followed. Only in the early modern period did Protestant scholars definitely show the forged character of these decretals. But these pre-eleventh-century collections, whether forged or otherwise, tended to enjoy only regional circulation and limited audiences. The picture is one of diversity and pluralism, not centralized textual authority.

A dispute that erupted in Tours around 800 or 801 provides an interesting window into this early period of canon law. The dispute concerned whether a criminous clerk was eligible to claim sanctuary before having performed penance for his crime. Charlemagne, who appears to have taken a personal interest in

---

[16] See, Cyrille Vogel, Allen Frantzen, *Les 'libri paenitentiales'* 2 vols. (1978–1985).

[17] On the earliest centuries of canon law see Antonio Garcia y Garcia, *Historia del derecho canonico, vol. 1: El primer milenio* (1967); On the political dimensions of this development, see Claudia Rapp, *Holy Bishops in Late Antiquity: The Nature of Christian Leadership in a Time of Transition* (2005).

the case, thought that sanctuary seekers should have to perform penance before receiving sanctuary for a crime. Alcuin, the abbot at Tours where the clerk had fled, argued to the contrary. Alcuin's response is preserved in a letter: 'How can it be said that a guilty sinner should not be received by the Church?' 'If sinners cannot enter the church, perhaps there may not be found a priest who can say mass in it.'[18] Alcuin's cheeky response provoked Bishop Theodulf of Orléans to respond in writing. Theodulf wielded passages of the Theodosian Code, Irish and Frankish canon-law collections, and Visigothic and Salic royal law to argue that sanctuary protections should be more limited and required penance before admission. That Alcuin's position was more fully supported by the canonical authorities is less important than how the incident highlights the lack of any unified textual basis in canon law to settle such questions in the ninth century.

Gratian's *Decretum* prepared the ground for a different form of engagement with canonical authorities. Unlike the ad hoc use of textual authorities that had characterized the earlier age, the *Decretum* offered not so much textual authority as a method for marshalling the massive source base into coherent legal arguments. This dramatic transformation in canon law that began in the twelfth century should be understood as part of the broader intellectual currents sometimes called the renaissance of the twelfth century. Situated within other currents—the growth of the medieval universities, the resurgence of Roman law as a tool of urban and royal administration in Europe, and reliance on the written record as a tool of governance—the development of canon law shows the hallmarks of the great transformations in state building in late medieval Europe. Brian Tierney offered a measure of canon law accomplished in this period: 'To sketch in outline the growth of the *Corpus iuris canonici* from the appearance of Gratian's *Decretum* to the outbreak of the Great Schism, is, in effect, to record the process by which the Church became a body politic, subject to one head and manifesting an external unity of organization.'[19]

---

[18] *Epistolae* 245 (MGH, *Epistolae* 394). For a detailed account of the circumstances that gave rise to the dispute between Alcuin and Charlemagne and a discussion of the letters that record the dispute, see Luitpold Wallach, *Alcuin and Charlemagne: Studies in Carolingian History and Literature* (1959) 109; and also Wallach's 'A Manuscript of Tours with an Alcuinian Incipit' (1948) *Harvard Theological Review* 51 258. Rob Meens, 'Tumult in Tours: Alcuin en Theodulf van Orleans in Conflict over Een Asielzoeker' (2003) *Madoc* 17:104–13; Rob Meens, 'Sanctuary, Penance, and Dispute Settlement under Charlemagne: The Conflict between Alcuin and Theodulf of Orléans over a Sinful Cleric' (2007) *Speculum* 82:277–300; and Sam Collins, *Domus Domini patet figura mysterii: Architectural Imagination and the Politics of Place in the Carolingian Ninth Century* (PhD diss. U.C. Berkeley, 2005); Sam Collins, *The Carolingian Debate over Sacred Space* (2012).

[19] Brian Tierney, *Foundations of Conciliar Theory: The Contribution of the Medieval Canonists from Gratian to the Great Schism* (1955) 13–14.

III. DISHARMONY

As scholars have long noticed, the 'harmonious' successes of the canonists in consolidating their text base and laying the ground for an increasing profess-ionalization of the discipline contributed to dissonances as well. One such site of dissonance arose in professional competition between canonists and theologians. It emerged in part out of a divide between those who understood the Church as a pastoral institution and those who understood it as rigorously hierarchical administrative entity. In a famous passage of *De consideratione*, composed around 1148 and perhaps within a decade after the appearance of the *Decretum*, Bernard of Clairvaux asked his former student, Bernard of Pisa, who by then had been elected Pope Eugene III (1145–1153):

Therefore, when do we pray? When do we teach the people? When do we edify the Church? When do we meditate on the Law? However, everyday in the [papal] palace they make such a noise of the laws, but of Justinian, not of the Lord.[20]

Bernard of Clairvaux's remarks put in sharp contrast the pious understanding of 'Law' claimed by twelfth-century theologians and pastors and the crass understanding of 'laws' attributed to canon lawyers. In Bernard's view, the '*Lex domini immaculata*' was concerned with the conversion and nurturing of souls, while the *leges* preferred by canonists caused 'strife and scoffing, [and] subverted judgment'.[21] Bernard wondered how the pope, 'a pastor and bishop of souls', could tolerate the litigious prattle that beset him daily.[22] This awful litany—litigious prattle, increased reliance on Roman law sources, decreased reliance on scripture, and the seeming abandonment of pastoral care—might be understood as one gauge of the relative ascendancy of canon lawyers within the administrative hierarchy of the medieval Papacy. Bernard lamented a world that he could see fading. Before the middle of the twelfth century, any parish priest making pilgrimage to Rome from any European backwater could reasonably expect the opportunity to make oral confession to the pope. By the early thirteenth century, the papal penitentiary had developed to such a size that the incoming petitions and outgoing penances and absolutions, which numbered in the tens of thousands per year at that point, were almost entirely submitted and

[20] *De consideratione* 1.4 in *Opera*, (eds.), J. Leclercq, H. M. Rochais (Rome, 1963), vol. 3, 399 [PL 182:732–3] 'Denique quando oramus? quando docemus populos? quando aedificamus Ecclesiam? quando meditamur in lege? Et quidem quotidie perstrepunt in palatio leges, sed Justiniani, non Domini....Nam certe lex Domini immaculata, convertens animas. Hae autem non tam leges, quam lites sunt et cavillationes, subvertentes judicium. Tu ergo pastor et episcopus animarum, qua mente, obsecro, sustines coram te semper silere illam, garrire istas?'

[21] Ibid. The phrase 'lex Domini immaculate' is a reference to Psalms 18:8.

[22] Ibid. 'Tu ergo, pastor et episcopus animarum, qua mente, obsecro, sustines coram tu semper silere illam, garrire istas?'

responded to in writing. The personal audience and pastoral care had given way to a massive bureaucratic enterprise, and men trained in law were needed to run it.

Bernard's criticisms were echoed by others. Some of the greatest theologians of the Middle Ages weighed in to make disparaging remarks about canonists and their perceived legalism. Albert the Great, in the midst of doctrinal disputes concerning the sacraments, remarked that canonists do not know how to solve objections; they only know how to make them.[23] The claim that canon law distracted from spiritual matters was oft-repeated. Aquinas chastised professors of theology who scoured the 'little glosses of the jurists' for authority when they ought to turn their attention to divine rather than human judgment.[24] Later, Dante followed Aquinas when he lamented that study of the Gospels and the great doctors suffered while the margins of the decretals were full of scribbles.[25]

Tension between theology and canon law seems to have emerged simultaneously with the development of the new universities, which, by the thirteenth century, had dedicated faculties to the study of canon law. As scholars have noticed, this led to intellectual autonomy for both canon law and theology that only grew more pronounced in the later Middle Ages.[26] No longer considered a branch of theology, as it had been before the twelfth century, canon law could claim to be a self-standing discipline by the late twelfth century. Canon law's autonomy contributed to increasing professionalization and fuelled rivalries between canonists and theologians. Competition for preferments, which increasingly tipped in favour of the lawyers by the fourteenth century, also aggravated rifts between theologians and canonists. The division between the two sciences can be characterized as one of at least 'partial opposition' from the thirteenth century and thereafter.[27] The opposition scholars have noted is in part indicated by the decreasing number of students who took degrees in both canon law and theology. While several important canon lawyers held theological degrees, the professionalization and specialization that marked canon law in the fourteenth century coincided with fewer men who trained in both sciences.

---

[23] *Commentarium in libros Sententiarum IV*, d. 27, 21; G. de Lagarde, *La naissance de l'esprit laïque au déclin du moyen age*, 2 (Paris, 1958) 333 n. 84.

[24] *Questiones quodlibetales*, IX, a.9: 'Inconsum et deresibile videtur, quad sacrae doctrinae professores iuristarum glossulas in auctoritatem inducunt vel de eis disceptent, cum plus sit assentiendum divino iudicio quam humano.'

[25] The Divine Comedy of Dante Alighierri, (ed. and trans.), J. D. Sinclair, 3 vols. (rev. edn., 1948), Paradiso, canto ix, ln. 133–5 (138). See also, canto xii, lns. 82–5 where the juridical labours of Hostiensis are equated with love of this world.

[26] 'Un témoignage de désaccords entre cononistes et théologiens', in *Études d'histoire du droit canonique: dédiées à Gabriel le Bras*, 2 vols. (1965) 861–4; Joseph de Ghellinck, 'Magister Vacarius; Un jurists théologien peu aimable pour le canonists' (1943) *R.H.E.* 44: 173–8.

[27] *Die Geschichte der Katholischen Theologie seit dem Ausgang der Väterzeit* (1933) 34–5.

It is possible, of course, to exaggerate the conflict between theologians and canonists. Even theologians who severely criticized canon lawyers maintained respect for canon law itself. Much of their criticism was aimed at perceived careerism and legalism among canonists and can be understood, at least in part, as a consequence of the success canonists increasingly enjoyed in obtaining positions within the Church. Still, a high degree of intellectual cross-fertilization between canonists and theologians is evident. Theologians and canonists read and responded to each other on questions regarding marriage, the sacraments, the *credo*, legal personhood, whether canonists or theologians were better suited to rule within the Church, and many other matters. Whether canonists themselves were responsible for the increasing litigiousness of the late Middle Ages is doubtful. As medieval legal historians have shown, a range of feuding and disputing practices that had long flourished in Europe were increasingly channelled into legal processes.[28] What canon lawyers can be credited with is erecting the architecture by which many of these various forms of disputing, from violent self-help to ad hoc forms of negotiation and arbitration, were brought within an increasingly consistent form. Canon law relied heavily on the work of the Roman lawyers, who in the twelfth and thirteenth century had laboured mightily to reinstate the legal process of the learned Roman law and to get rid of the old modes of proof that were still relied upon in many courts in Europe.

IV. NEW PROCESSES

The old mode of proof that most vexed Roman and canon lawyers was the divine ordeal. At its core, the divine ordeal was a physical proof, by which accused would have to prove her innocence by being submerged into a body of blessed water (which would not receive a guilty person), or taking up a red-hot bar of iron his hands (festering burns would reveal the hidden guilt).[29] These ordeals are among

---

[28] See, e.g., Daniel Lord Smail, *The Consumption of Justice: Emotions, Publicity, and Legal Culture in Marseille, 1264–1423* (2002).

[29] John Baldwin, 'The Intellectual Preparation for the Canon of 1215 against Ordeals', *Speculum* (1961) 36:613–36; Rebecca Coleman, 'Reason and Unreason in Early Medieval Law' (1974) *Journal of Interdisciplinary History* 4:571–91; Peter Brown, 'Society and the Supernatural: A Medieval Change' (1975) *Daedalus* 104:133–51; Paul Hyams, 'Trial by Ordeal: The Key to Proof in the Early Common Law' in *On the Laws and Customs of England: Essays in Honor of Samuel E. Thorne*, Morris Arnold et al. (eds.), (1981) 90–126; Robert Bartlett, *Trial by Fire and Water: The Medieval Judicial Ordeal* (1986); Richard Fraher, 'IV Lateran's Revolution in Criminal Procedure: The Birth of Inquisitio, the End of the Ordeals, and Innocent III's Vision of Ecclesiastical Politics' in *Studia in Honorem Eminentissimi Cardinalis Alphonsi M. Stickler* (ed.), R. I. Castillo Lara, (1992), 97–111; Finnbar McCauley, 'Canon

the most recognizably alien features of the medieval legal tradition. They were employed in many parts of Europe from roughly the early ninth century until the early thirteenth century. They were wildly unpopular among the learned elites at places like the University of Paris and the University of Bologna. Nonetheless, they were still practised routinely under the auspices of royal law in many parts of Europe, including England, the German lands, and France.

In 1215, under the strong leadership of Pope Innocent III at the Fourth Lateran Council, a canon was issued forbidding priests from participating in the ordeal. Clergy could no longer bless the water or the iron used in the ordeal, effectively ending the practice across Europe. The same council had provided directions for replacing it. For example, in Canon 8 the papacy tried to find a delicate balance between insulating clerics against false accusations of wrongdoing (which might be brought from spite or jealousy, and which the ordeal practice facilitated) and simultaneously increasing the Church's capacity for clerical discipline through legal processes. The solution was a hierarchical arrangement in which ecclesiastics of superior rank could discipline clerics of a lower rank, yet were themselves insulated from accusations made by inferiors or by laypersons. Canon 38 placed important checks on judges in these cases by requiring them to employ 'a notary or two competent men' to record the judicial process. The aim was for judicial accountability. The prescribed process required that a judge would 'oversee all the acts of the inquiry, namely, citations and delays, refusals and exceptions, petitions and replies, interrogations and confessions, the depositions of witnesses and presentation of documents, interlocutions, appeals, renunciations, decisions, and other acts which take place'.[30] All these steps in the inquiry were to 'be written down in convenient order, the time, places, and persons to be designated'.[31] This inquisitorial mode of trial would be at the forefront of the scaffolding they erected and would last for 500 years until legal reforms of the eighteenth century were implemented.

The stated purpose of Canon 38 was to provide a record in cases where someone claimed they were subject to a 'dishonest or imprudent' judge.[32] But it did much more than this. It mandated the conditions under which all ecclesiastical litigation would be recorded and, here was the rub, amenable to review by superior judges within the ecclesiastical hierarchy, culminating, in principle, with the pope who was the *iudex ordinarius* of everyone. Judges failing to comply with the requirement that their proceedings be recorded were liable to punishment. Taken together, these two canons represented canon law's response to the end of the divine ordeal. Judicial

---

Law and the End of the Ordeal' (2006) *Oxford Journal of Legal Studies* 26:473–513. My own somewhat polemical contribution to the debates is 'Criminal Procedure in Medieval European Law' in (1999) *Zeitschrift der Savigny-Stiftung für Rechtsgeschichte* 116:174–201.

[30] C. 38. *Constitutiones Concilii quarti Lateranensis una cum Commentariis glossatorum* (MIC, Series A: Corpus Glossatorum 2; Vatican City, 1981) 1–172.

[31] Ibid.   [32] Ibid.

inquiries were to follow a prescribed order—including allegations, responses, interlocutory appeals, depositions, etc.—and put into a written dossier that could be transmitted through a judicial hierarchy. The obligations of pastoral care were taking on an increasingly juridical character. This so-called 'inquisitorial model' of litigation depended upon active judges, increasingly with university degrees in law, who were invested with broad powers to initiate criminal and civil proceedings, examine witnesses, even under torture, and to act (in principle, at least) as a brake on the adversarial tendencies of earlier medieval legal traditions.

The inquisitorial procedures established at the Fourth Lateran Council to replace the ordeal were the work of an episcopal council, even if Innocent III exercised a strong hand throughout the entire proceeding. But papal lawmaking was becoming an ever more important feature of canon law. In the 1190s Bernard of Pavia gathered nearly 1,000 papal decrees into five books.[33] Bernard's was just the first of five more decretal collections. The growth of decretal material presented a huge challenge. Counterfeit decretals were a growing problem, and the papal curia was becoming increasingly anxious to defend against a growing market for forged decretals. In 1234, when Pope Gregory IX authorized the promulgation of the *Gregorian Decretals* (known colloquially as the *Liber extra*), he was recognizing an important shift in how canon law was made and secured by the Church. The *Liber extra* contained over 2,000 papal decrees. Papal legislation, more than recourse to the sources Gratian had laboured to harmonize, was the focus of canon lawyers going forwards. Over the course of the thirteenth century, five more decretal collections would be promulgated. The early fourteenth century saw two more major collections issued, though they were not nearly as large as the *Liber extra*.

v. CONCLUSION

The classical era of medieval canon law witnessed several important historical transformations. Canon lawyers may have understood their profession to have been already present in the Garden of Eden, but the abandonment of the ordeal and the reliance on inquisitorial modes of trial represented a monumental change in how law was practised and how judgments were made not just within canon law, but within the Western legal tradition. Similarly, like the secular states around it, the medieval papacy operated increasingly in state-like ways. Popes issued

[33] Charles Duggan, *Twelfth-Century Decretal Collections and Their Importance in English History* (1963).

legislation. Ecclesiastical courts applied it. Lawyers, who by the late twelfth century could professionalize in canon law, represented the growing throngs of litigants who sought legal decisions in Church courts. The textual and methodological tools canon lawyers deployed were products of the great intellectual transformations of the twelfth and thirteenth centuries, and they honed them with exquisite precision in the following centuries. It may have been an age of grace, but it was also an age of lawyers and of law.

BIBLIOGRAPHY

Uta-Renate Blumenthal, *The Investiture Controversy: Church and Monarchy from the Ninth to the Twelfth Century* (University of Pennsylvania Press, 1988)

James Brundage, *Medieval Canon Law* (Routledge, 1995)

Charles Donahue, Law, *Marriage, and Society in the Later Middle Ages* (Cambridge University Press, 2008)

Paul Fournier, Gabriel Le Bras, *Histoire des collections canoniques en Occident puis les fausses décétales jusqu'au Décret de Gratian*, 2 vols. (Sirey, 1931–1932; repr. Aalen, 1972)

Linda Fowler-Magerl, *Ordo iudiciorum vel ordo iudiciarius: Begriff und Literaturgattung* (Vittorio Klostermann, 1984)

Antonio Garcia y Garcia, *Historia del derecho canonico, vol 1: El primer milenio* (Instituto de Historia de la Teologia Española, 1967)

Jean Gaudemet, *L'église dans l'empire romain (IVe–Ve sèicles)* (2nd edn., Sirey, 1989)

Richard Helmholz, *The Spirit of Classical Canon Law* (University of Georgia Press, 1996)

Stephan Kuttner, *Harmony from Dissonance: An Interpretation of Medieval Canon Law* (Archabbey Press, 1960)

Stephan Kuttner, Gratian and the Schools of Law, *1140–234* (Variorum Reprints, 1983)

Kenneth Pennington, *Pope and Bishops: The Papal Monarchy in the Twelfth and Thirteenth Centuries* (The University of Pennsylvania Press, 1988)

Kenneth Pennington, 'Learned Law, Droit Savant, Gelehrtes Recht: The Tyranny of a Concept' (1994) *Rivista internazionale di dirrito commune* 5:197–209

Kenneth Pennington, Wilfried Hartmann (eds.), *History of Medieval Canon Law* (Catholic University Press, 1999)

Brian Tierney, *Foundations of Counciliar Theory: The Contribution of the Medieval Canonists from Gratian to the Great Schism* (Cambridge University Press, 1955)

Walter Ullmann, *The Growth of Papal Government in the Middle Ages: A Study in the Ideological Relation of Clerical to Lay Power* (2nd edn., Methuen and Company, 1962)

Anders Winroth, *The Making of Gratian's* Decretum (Cambridge University Press, 2000)

CHAPTER 37

THE TRANSFORMATION OF THE COMMON LAW

MODERNISM, HISTORY, AND THE TURN TO PROCESS

KUNAL M. PARKER*

I. INTRODUCTION

IN 1921, the Carter Professor of Jurisprudence at the Harvard Law School, Roscoe Pound, made a curious statement: 'We have come to believe in conscious lawmaking—perhaps, indeed, to have too much faith in what may be achieved thereby.'[1] What did Pound mean by 'conscious' law-making? Was 'conscious' lawmaking opposed to 'unconscious' lawmaking? Pound hints at a historic shift from 'unconscious' to 'conscious' lawmaking. He also strikes a note of caution: it is possible to have 'too much faith' in the latter.

* Professor of Law, University of Miami School of Law. I would like to thank audiences at Columbia Law School, Cornell Law School, and the Florida International University School of Law for their reactions to an earlier version of this chapter.
[1] Roscoe Pound, *The Spirit of the Common Law* (1921) 175 ff.

This chapter traces the transformation of American common law thinking between the nineteenth and twentieth centuries. Pound's statement is typical of early twentieth-century legal attitudes. For many at the time, the common law was a kind of 'unconscious' lawmaking that had to be repudiated in favour of legislative and administrative 'conscious' lawmaking. This bespoke a massive change in the ways in which American legal thinkers would conceive of the place of the common law (indeed, law itself) in the American polity. But even after the common law underwent this change, it is by no means clear that lawmaking would become entirely 'conscious' or, in other words, that all elements of 'unconsciousness' in lawmaking would be eradicated. Pound's fear that Americans might have 'too much' faith in 'conscious' lawmaking might have been exaggerated: the 'unconscious' never quite went away.

In order to proceed, it is important to draw attention to the nature of the profound intellectual shift that brought about the transformation in thinking about the common law. Beginning in the late nineteenth century, a far-reaching intellectual transformation often dubbed 'modernism' spread across the Euro-American world. Modernism took different forms depending on national, linguistic, and disciplinary contexts. Nevertheless, its impact was transformative in fields ranging from science to painting, mathematics to music, law to literature. For our purposes, a convenient point of departure might be the historian Peter Gay's working definition. Conceding that modernism was 'far easier to exemplify than to define', Gay identified as twin features of modernism, 'the lure of heresy', on the one hand, and 'a commitment to a principled self-scrutiny', on the other.[2] Both these features of modernism were instantiated, I want to suggest, through a turn to a new conception of history.

Where history for much of the nineteenth century and earlier had been foundational and teleological, modernist history in its strictest form neither contained meaning nor offered direction. Instead, it functioned to chip away at the pretended supra-historical foundations of phenomena, whether God, reason, logic, morality, transcendent aesthetic rules, or historical teleologies themselves, by showing those phenomena to exist only in historical time. In their use of history, in other words, modernists were iconoclasts. This is what Gay has in mind when he speaks of the 'lure of heresy'. Modernists' anti-foundational use of history led to what Gay calls 'principled self-scrutiny'. For once the supra-historical foundations of phenomena were undermined, ground was cleared. Modernists would have to ask themselves, with full 'consciousness', what they wanted the present and future to be.

In the United States, the spread of the modernist historical sensibility bore two crucial consequences. *First*, as the modernist historical sensibility eroded

---

[2] Peter Gay, *Modernism: The Lure of Heresy from Baudelaire to Beckett and Beyond* (2008) 1, 3–4 ff.

the putative a-historical foundations of phenomena, what had previously been taken as firm constraints upon individual and democratic self-making loosened. The consequence was an expansion of what was rendered subject to deliberation as a matter of democratic politics. *Second*, the erosion of a-historical foundations affected how knowledge claims would henceforth be made. The modernist historical sensibility undercut 'knowledge that', or substantive knowledge, by eroding its foundations. But the knowledges of the present and future, i.e. those which modernists would themselves create, would also have to be subjected to the test of modernist history. Henceforth, knowledge would have to be less sure of itself, more aware of its tentativeness. This resulted in an intense preoccupation with the means and processes through which knowledge was produced. Modernist thinkers were thus highly self-conscious about *how* they created knowledge. Under such conditions, 'knowledge that' gave way, as it were, to 'knowledge how'.[3]

The foregoing discussion of the modernist sensibility is critical to understanding the argument of this chapter about the transformation of the common law. From the American Revolution until the end of the nineteenth century, at a time when the American state was relatively undeveloped, the common law played a critical role in the American polity. It comprised substance and method: common law judges declared law for the community through step-by-step, gradualist lawmaking that balanced continuity and change. Giving common law judges such a significant role in lawmaking was not considered inconsistent with the democratic project. In a world replete with foundational and teleological thinking ('knowledge that'), the constraint of judge-made common law on democratic self-making was one constraint among many.

The emergence of a modernist sensibility in the late nineteenth century, combined with the growth of the post-Civil War state, changed this. Operating with an anti-foundational, distinctly modernist historical consciousness, legal thinkers such as Oliver Wendell Holmes, Jr. began to chip away at the long-accepted foundations of the common law. Mere 'unconscious' repetition of precedent, they argued, was insufficient to deal with the issues facing the country's increasingly complex industrial economy. What was needed was 'conscious' lawmaking of the kind Pound referred to.

As the locus of 'conscious' lawmaking shifted to legislatures and administrative agencies, the common law ceased to be a kind of 'knowledge that' and increasingly became a kind of 'knowledge how'. Legal thinkers surrendered the specification of ends to legislatures and administrative agencies and began to see their own job as the specification of ways, means, processes, and procedures. As the law's ontology shifted to being a means, however, a modernist confrontation with the limits of

---

[3] I derive the terminology of 'knowledge that' versus 'knowledge how' from Gilbert Ryle, *The Concept of Mind* (1949). Ryle uses the terms in very different ways.

'consciousness' combined with older common law vocabularies such that judges and legal thinkers continued to resist the impulse to entirely account for—i.e., render fully 'conscious'—their decision-making. This is most clearly seen in the judicial career of Felix Frankfurter and in the academic career of the constitutional theorist (and Frankfurter's law clerk), Alexander Bickel.

This chapter is organized as follows. Section II traces the career of the common law until the end of the nineteenth century. Section III examines the common law's transformation into means and explores the persistence of older common law vocabularies. Section IV offers conclusions as to the career of the common law after its transformation into means.[4]

II. The Common Law before the Twentieth Century: Means and Ends

Drawing upon Renaissance philological techniques, sixteenth-century Western European legal thinkers began to realize that the corpus of Roman law they had once considered an unchanging whole was in fact a messy amalgam of original text and subsequent annotation that had arisen in chronological time. This was a discovery with explosive consequences. If law had arisen in chronological time, did this not imply that law could be *made* in chronological time? Europe's would-be absolutist monarchs were quick to seize this opportunity. If law could be made, who better to make it than the monarch himself?

In response to royal arrogation of control over law-making, early seventeenth-century English common law thinkers came up with an authoritative formulation of the common law. It consisted of the following interrelated ideas: (a) conjoined notions of legal temporality and substance; (b) ideas about the division of roles between sovereign, legislature, and judge; and (c) claims associated with the freedoms of the people and England's 'ancient constitution'.

---

[4] This chapter is drawn from a larger ongoing study of the impact of modernism on political and legal thought in mid-twentieth century America. It is a companion piece to 'Law and Regime Change: The Common Law, Knowledge Regimes, and Democracy Between the Nineteenth and Twentieth Centuries' (2016) 3 Critical Analysis of Law ff, with which it overlaps in argument, structure, and some text. It also draws upon the following previously published essays and chapters: 'Modernist Forms and Their Critics: A Review Essay' (2016) 51 *Tulsa L.R.* ff; 'Writing Legal History Then and Now: A Brief Reflection' (2016) 56 *American Journal of Legal History* ff; and 'How Law Should Avoid Mistakes: Alexander Bickel's Modernist Jurisprudence of Mood', in Austin Sarat et al. (eds.), *Law's Mistakes* (2016). In addition, the discussion in Section II is drawn from Kunal M. Parker, *Common Law, History, and Democracy in America, 1790–1900: Legal Thought Before Modernism* (2011). There

First, as they moved away from medieval ideas of law as timeless and universal, early seventeenth-century English common lawyers attributed a special non-historical temporality to the common law that effectively immunized it from historicization. The common law did not reflect universal principles, common lawyers argued, but consisted of the 'immemorial' customs of the English. Referring to a time beyond the 'memory of man', 'immemoriality' defied one's ability to identify the point at which the common law had arisen. It also implied that the common law comprised the collective wisdom of multiple generations, which made it superior to other arrangements. No single individual—not even the monarch—could exceed the accumulated wisdom reflected in the pronouncements of the common law judge.

Second, and following upon this, common lawyers insisted that only the common law judge possessed the necessary qualifications to articulate what they called the 'reason' of the common law. Sir Edward Coke, the thinker who did more than any other to restate the common law in the early modern period, extolled the common law as an 'artificiall perfection of reason, gotten by long study, observation, and of experience, and not of every man's natural reason ... '.[5] The common law judge's arrogation of the right to declare law limited monarchical encroachment *and* legislative tampering. In *Bonham's Case* (1610), Coke suggested that the common law might go so far as to limit the reach of parliamentary statutes: '[W]hen an Act of Parliament is against common right and reason, or repugnant, or impossible to be performed, the common law will controul it, and adjudge such Act to be void.'[6]

Third, the common law's strongest claim to legitimacy was that it embodied the 'immemorial' *customs* of the English. *Qua* custom, the common law was deemed to arise spontaneously and to crystallize by dint of repetition over time. Because the common law judge merely declared what was already there, the common law was freer and better suited to the people than acts of kings and legislatures. In his *Irish Reports* dedicated to Lord Chancellor Ellesmere in 1612, Sir John Davies, then attorney general for Ireland, equated the common law with 'the *Common Custome of the Realm*' and continued: 'And this *Customary Law* the most perfect and most excellent, and without comparison the best, to make and preserve a Commonwealth. For the *written Laws* which are made either by the Edicts of Princes, or by Councils of Estates are imposed upon the Subject before any Triall or Probation made .... But a *Custome* doth never become a Law to bind the people, until it hath been tried and approved time out of mind ... '.[7]

(and hence here), discussion draws heavily from J. G. A. Pocock, *The Ancient Constitution and the Feudal Law* (1957).

[5]   Sir Edward Coke, *The First Part of the Institutes of the Laws of England; or A Commentary Upon Littleton* (2 vols.) (1979) Vol. I L.2.C.6.Sec.138 ff.

[6]   *Bonham's Case* (1610) 77 ER 646, 652.

[7]   Unpaginated preface dedicatory to *Irish Reports* (*Les Reports des Cases & Matters en Ley, Resolves & Adjudges en les Courts del Roy en Ireland. Collect & digest per Sir John Davis Chivaler, Atturney Generall del Roy en cest Realm*) (London: E. Flesher, J. Steater, H. Twyford, 1674).

Thus, early seventeenth-century common law thinking brought together (a) the temporality of 'immemoriality'; (b) the role of the common law judge as declarant of the law; and (c) the association of the common law with custom and freedom. Understandings of the 'common law' operated at many different scales, ranging from England's 'ancient constitution' to doctrines that governed relations between private individuals and between individuals and the state.

Early seventeenth-century common law thinkers such as Coke had insisted that the common law of their day had come down to them unaltered from Anglo-Saxon times. By the end of the seventeenth century, however, such a view had become unsustainable. The work of antiquarians was beginning to prove that what had been considered an 'immemorial' common law—especially the law of real property and political structure—was a result of the Norman Conquest. Late seventeenth-century common law thinkers had to confront the fact that the common law was a legacy of feudalism.

In response to the assertion that the common law had changed in chronological time, common lawyers created an enduring language to characterize not the common law's substance, but rather its method. Accepting the fact of change, they maintained that the common law nevertheless changed 'insensibly', so slowly, gradually, and incrementally that its movement went unnoticed by those it touched and dissolved into continuity. Thus, Sir Matthew Hale, in his *History of the Common Law of England*, observed in a well-known passage: 'But tho' those particular Variations and Accessions have happened in the Laws, yet *they being only partial and successive*, we may with just Reason say, that They are the same English Laws now, that they were 600 Years since in the general. As the Argonauts Ship was the same when it returned home, as it was when it went out, tho' in that long Voyage it has successive Amendments, and scarce came back with any of its former Materials ... .'[8] By virtue of its method, in other words, the common law would join identity and difference, both changing perpetually and never changing.

In the eighteenth century, following Parliament's victory over the monarch, common lawyers switched from worrying about the law-giving powers of British monarchs to worrying about the law-giving skills of Parliament. The incremental method of common lawyers calibrated continuity and change better, they insisted, than episodic legislative acts. Sir William Blackstone's mid-eighteenth-century *Commentaries on the Laws of England*, unquestionably the most influential single text in the common law tradition, hailed common law judges as 'living oracles' who were 'long personally accustomed to the judicial decisions of their predecessors.' Blackstone pressed on parliamentarians a common law sensibility, urging them 'to watch, to check, and to avert every dangerous innovation, to propose, to adopt, and to cherish any solid and well-weighed improvement; [and

---

[8] Matthew Hale, *The History of the Common Law of England* (1971) Charles M. Gray (ed.), 39–40 ff.

to be] bound ... to transmit that constitution and those laws to their posterity, amended if possible, at least without any derogation.'[9]

By the mid-eighteenth century, when Blackstone wrote, 'history' had ceased to be a mere matter of chronological dating. Instead, it had come to possess a powerful meaning and direction (the phrase 'philosophy of history' comes to us, after all, from the eighteenth century). Consistent with this meaning and direction, certain socio-political formations were increasingly understood as belonging to an outmoded past, while others were heralded as markers of the future. In the English-speaking world, the most famous exemplar of this thinking was the Scottish Enlightenment feudalism-to-commerce narrative. This was a historical trajectory that corresponded with what many eighteenth-century Britons thought they were living through: the withering away of feudal land tenures, the expansion of commerce and finance, the growth of empire.

Blackstone's *Commentaries* were the work of an orthodox common lawyer focused far more on the law of real property than on the emerging law of commerce. Nevertheless, sensing the forces of 'history' impinging upon the common law, Blackstone chose to celebrate the eighteenth-century 'commercialization' of the common law as an instance of the success of the common law method. Describing how common lawyers had incorporated commercial doctrines into the common law imperceptibly and without seeking legislative assistance, Blackstone likened the common law to an inherited feudal castle fitted out for modern living: '[We] inherit an old Gothic castle, erected in the days of chivalry, but fitted up for a modern inhabitant. The moated ramparts, the embattled towers, and the trophied halls, are magnificent and venerable, but useless and therefore neglected. The inferior apartments, now accommodated to daily use, are cheerful and commodious, though their approaches may be winding and difficult.'[10] Notwithstanding the pressure of history, and as a consequence of the common law method, Blackstone tells us, the eighteenth-century Englishman is still at home in the feudal castle of the common law.

The American Revolution was inspired by many different intellectual currents: republican thought, Lockean natural rights ideas, Scottish historical concepts, Protestant millenarian notions, and, to be sure, common law ideas. However, the more radical revolutionary voices saw the overthrow of British power as an opportunity to wipe the slate clean. In *Common Sense* (1776), Thomas Paine put it jubilantly: 'We have it in our power to begin the world over again.... . The birthday of a new world is at hand.'[11] This call for a radical break with the past, made in the name of the right of a free people to give itself its own

---

[9] William Blackstone, *Commentaries on the Laws of England: A Facsimile of the First Edition of 1765–1769* (1979) 1, 69, 9 ff.

[10] Ibid., 3, 268 ff.

[11] Thomas Paine, 'Common Sense', in *Basic Writings of Thomas Paine* (1942) 65 ff.

laws in the here and now, could not have been more at odds with common law sensibilities.

Paine's call to break completely with the past was not shared by all Americans of the revolutionary era. Indeed, from the perspective of Paine's critics on both sides of the Atlantic, his ideas found dramatic and terrifying instantiation in the French Revolution. In the most famous common lawyerly response to the French Revolution's radical break with the past in the name of abstract principles and rights, Edmund Burke's *Reflections on the Revolution in France* (1790) defended the British constitutional order as 'a sort of immortality through all transmigrations'.[12] While this phrase captures something of the temporality of the common law, Burke went even further, arguing that the British political system 'is never old, or middle-aged, or young, but in a condition of unchangeable constancy, moves on through the varied tenour of perpetual decay, fall, renovation, and progression.... [In] what we improve, we are never wholly new; in what we retain, we are never wholly obsolete....'[13]

Burkean common lawyerly commitment to continuity with the past also found support in the independent United States. In a series of lectures delivered at the College of Philadelphia between 1790 and 1792, U.S. Supreme Court Justice James Wilson assured his audience that 'with regard to ... many ... subjects, we have renewed, in our governments, the principles and the practice of the ancient Saxons'.[14] Far from breaking with the old common law, the new American constitutions were a vindication of the old. Most American legal thinkers at the time would likely have concluded that it was impossible to make sense of the 'written' U.S. Constitution in isolation from its 'unwritten' common law background.

Throughout the nineteenth century, but especially in the Early Republic and Jacksonian Era, the common law was vigorously attacked for its British, monarchical, and feudal origins; on the ground that it was the shadow cast by the past over the democratic majority of the present; and because it was administered by unelected judges. Despite some successful attempts at codification, however, the common law not only survived in the United States, but enjoyed considerable prestige. Why?

Notwithstanding the institution of political democracy, nineteenth-century America was a society that understood the world to have 'given' foundations. Nineteenth-century Americans regularly turned to the Bible to affirm or interrogate the logics, rationalities, and hierarchies of nature and society. When they turned to more secular knowledges such as 'history', that 'history' strikingly resembled the Christian eschatology it replaced insofar as it allowed its adherents to believe that polity and society were possessed of meaning and direction. This holds for all the

---

[12] Edmund Burke, *Reflections on the Revolution in France* in *Two Classics of the French Revolution* (1989) 34 ff.
[13] Ibid., 46 ff.   [14] *The Works of James Wilson* (1896) 2, 278 ff.

major secular historical sensibilities of the nineteenth century, from those of Hegel to those of Sir Henry Maine. The same holds for all the affiliated knowledges, from anthropology to economics to political science, that developed over the nineteenth century.

To understand the world in terms of 'given' foundations—God, history, nature, or something else—was to insist that individual and democratic self-making was bounded. Nineteenth-century knowledges suggested that there were limits to human thought and action, that a great deal simply lay beyond the power of human beings to change.

It was widely accepted, for example, that there were limits to individual self-making. While this was true for all, these limits were especially pronounced for those subordinated in terms of the 'natural' hierarchies of class, gender, and race. For example, in *Bradwell v. The State* (1872), the U.S. Supreme Court was asked to rule upon whether the recently ratified Fourteenth Amendment would render invalid an Illinois law barring women from the practice of law. The Court refused to extend the Fourteenth Amendment this way. Justice Bradley's concurring opinion shows how the 'laws' of 'nature' and the 'Creator' could be used to squelch a woman's demand for self-making: '[T]he civil law, as well as nature herself, has always recognized a wide difference in the respective spheres and destinies of man and woman. ... The paramount destiny and mission of woman are to fulfill the noble and benign offices of wife and mother. This is the law of the Creator. ... In the nature of things it is not every citizen of every age, sex, and condition that is qualified for every calling and position.'[15]

What was true for individuals was true for agglomerations of individuals. Many believed that there were firm limits to what political democracies could accomplish. Thomas Carlyle, a mid-nineteenth-century conservative writer with a wide following in Great Britain and the United States, expressed this sense of democracy's limits by comparing political democracy to a ship. Would the establishment of political democracy among the ship's crew enable the ship to round Cape Horn? Carlyle answered in the negative: 'Your ship cannot double Cape Horn by its excellent plans of voting. ... Ships accordingly do not use the ballot-box at all; ... [Democracy] is a very extraordinary method of navigating, whether in the Straits of Magellan or the undiscovered Sea of Time.'[16]

In a world in which myriad foundational knowledges constrained self-making by individuals and democracies, the common law functioned as one constraint among many. For much of the nineteenth century, the American state was relatively undeveloped. With the help of a burgeoning number of legal treatises and an active bar, American common law judges filled the regulatory vacuum created

[15] *Bradwell v. The State* (1872) 83 U.S. 130, 141–2 ff (Bradley, J., concurring).
[16] Thomas Carlyle, *Latter-Day Pamphlets* (1901) (1850) 15–16 ff.

by the state by reformulating contract, property, and tort law so as to enable the transformation of the United States' agrarian economy into a commercial and industrial powerhouse. Far from being a 'problem' for American democracy, the judge-made common law was lauded for its substance and its gradualist method, for its ability to bind past, present, and future together while it directed the United States through a massive transformation. This is clear from any number of nineteenth-century American treatments of the common law. For example, James Walker's *The Theory of the Common Law* (1852) maintained: '[T]he Common Law presents for our investigation a continuity of doctrine, which binds the present to the past,—a chain of rules unbroken by revolutions, not blurred by codification,— in short, a body of original facts. ... It is stable, because its principles are founded upon truth; it is capable of amelioration, because that is of the nature of humanity.'[17] In Walker's rendering, the common law is important for its substance (it is founded upon 'truth') and for its method (it represents 'a continuity of doctrine' while being 'capable of amelioration'). Many nineteenth-century lawyers expressed similar views. Furthermore, they regularly joined common law temporalities to historical ones, insisting that the common law, with its incrementalist method, was better able to instantiate the logic of history than legislatures were.

As the nineteenth century drew to an end, however, the understandings of democracy, law, and history that together had created a particular place for the common law in the American polity were beginning to unravel. It is to an account of that erosion, and to the reimagining of the place of the common law in the American polity, that we now turn.

III. The Common Law as Means: The Twentieth Century

The modernist historical sensibility was brought to bear in important ways on law in general, and on the common law in particular. The late nineteenth-century writings of Oliver Wendell Holmes, Jr., the foremost American legal thinker of the period, reveal this with breathtaking clarity.

Holmes' now little read masterpiece *The Common Law* (1881) was a model of the modernist historical method. It opened with lines that are now a celebrated rendering of how law's claim to embody formal logic foundered at the touch of history: 'The life of the law has not been logic; it has been experience. The felt necessities of the

---

[17] James M. Walker, *The Theory of the Common Law* (1995) (1852) 11–12 ff.

time, the prevalent moral and political theories, intuitions of public policy, avowed or unconscious, even the prejudices which judges share with their fellow-men, have had a good deal more to do than the syllogism in determining the rules by which men should be governed.'[18] *The Common Law* built on these opening lines by demonstrating that common law doctrines that were widely believed to rest on supra-historical foundations such as logic, reason, and morality were in fact nothing more than an agglomeration of historical errors, clumsy switches of substance and procedure or long-forgotten transpositions from one context to another. This was modernist history at its best: history used to tear down, rather than to point in any particular direction.

Over the next two decades, Holmes' critique of the common law intensified. In 'The Path of the Law' (1897), he launched an assault on antiquity and continuity, two hallowed bases of the common law: 'It is revolting to have no better reason for a rule of law than that so it was laid down in the time of Henry IV. It is still more revolting if the grounds upon which it was laid down have vanished long since, and the rule simply persists from blind imitation of the past.'[19] This attack on the common law's foundations became a call for reflection in the here and now about what law was to be. In 'Privilege, Malice, and Intent' (1894), Holmes argued: 'The time has gone by when law is only an unconscious embodiment of the common will. It has become a conscious reaction upon itself of organized society knowingly seeking to determine its own destinies.'[20] Here we discern the modernist preference for 'conscious' lawmaking and a questioning of the common law as an 'unconscious embodiment of the common will' (undoubtedly a reference to the common law judge's claim to declare the custom of the community).

Holmes' critique of the common law struck a chord. As the nineteenth century gave way to the twentieth, the United States was engulfed by a massive socio-economic transformation resulting from urbanization, industrialization, and immigration. Common law courts that had made law for much of the nineteenth century were deemed unfit to handle these challenges because their solutions were individual-centred, fault-based, private law doctrines. Diverse groups—farmers, labour unions, urban reformers, and others—pressed for legislative and administrative solutions that were truly social in scale.

However, common lawyerly federal courts all too often stymied federal and state attempts to modify laissez faire. For reformers, the doctrine of 'substantive due process' was the most troubling instance of how the federal courts joined the common law to the Constitution. In the late nineteenth century, the U.S. Supreme Court declared that the Due Process Clauses of the Fifth and Fourteenth Amendments

[18] Oliver Wendell Holmes, Jr., *The Common Law* (1881) 1 ff.

[19] Oliver Wendell Holmes, Jr., 'The Path of the Law' (1897), in Sheldon Novick (ed.), *The Collected Works of Justice Holmes: Complete Public Writings and Selected Judicial Opinions of Oliver Wendell Holmes* (1995) 3, 399 ff.

[20] Oliver Wendell Holmes, Jr., 'Privilege, Malice, and Intent' (1894), in (n. 19) 3, 377 ff.

to the U.S. Constitution protected 'liberty of contract'; federal and state legislation therefore could not unduly abridge the freedoms of employers and employees to contract.[21] The decision effectively constitutionalized common law contract rights and immunized them from governmental efforts to regulate capital-labor relations. In *Lochner v. New York* (1905), the case that came to symbolize early twentieth-century judicial overreaching, the U.S. Supreme Court struck down a New York law that regulated the length of the work day in bakeries on the ground that the law interfered with workers' and employers' 'liberty of contract'.[22] Overall, from the late nineteenth century through the mid-1930s, the U.S. Supreme Court struck down state legislation in approximately 400 cases; more than half of these were decided on the basis of the Fourteenth Amendment.[23]

Unsurprisingly, Progressive-era critics of decisions such as *Lochner* seized eagerly upon the Holmesian critique of the common law. If, as Holmes had shown, the common law could not be accounted for in terms of supra-historical foundations such as logic, reason, and morality, but was instead 'merely' historical, did this not imply that judge-made law was 'political'? Did this not, furthermore, suggest that unelected common lawyerly federal judges were usurping the place of democratic majorities (and the administrative agencies they created) when it came to making law? In the early twentieth century, prominent common law judges such as Benjamin Cardozo were themselves repudiating the old idea of the common law judge as declaring a preexisting law. When one looked into how judges came up with rules, especially in hard cases, Cardozo argued, there was not a great deal of difference between judge and legislator: 'No doubt the limits for the judge are narrower. ... None the less, within the confine of these open spaces and those of precedent and tradition, choice moves with a freedom which stamps its action as creative. The law which is the resulting product is not found, but made. The process, being legislative, demands the legislator's wisdom.'[24] With common law judges themselves openly likening what they did with what legislators did, something unthinkable in the long tradition of the common law, it is easy to see how far the distinction between 'law' and 'politics' had eroded by the 1920s.

Progressive-era legal thinkers labored to come up with an appropriate role for law in relation to democracy after law's supra-historical foundations were shown to be spurious. There were multiple non-mutually exclusive responses, of which I shall discuss three.

First, especially in the realm of constitutional law, one response to the collapse of the 'law'-'politics' distinction brought about by the rise of modernist thinking was to argue for ever more deferential standards of constitutional review. Substantive common law doctrines could no longer so easily be joined to the constitutional text on the ground that they represented 'truth.' In his *Lochner* dissent, Holmes, appointed

---

[21] *Allgeyer v. Louisiana* (1897) 165 U.S. 578.   [22] *Lochner v. New York* (1905) 198 U.S. 45.

[23] Mark Silverstein, *Constitutional Faiths: Felix Frankfurter, Hugo Black, and the Process of Judicial Decision Making* (1984) 37 ff.

[24] Benjamin N. Cardozo, *The Nature of the Judicial Process* (1921) 113–15 ff.

to the U.S. Supreme Court in 1900, articulated this position when he accused the majority of conflating its subjective conception of truth with constitutionality: '[A] constitution is not intended to embody a particular economic theory, whether of paternalism and the organic relation of the citizen to the State, or of *laissez faire*. It is made for people of fundamentally differing views, and the accident of our finding certain opinions natural and familiar or novel and even shocking ought not to conclude our judgment upon the question whether statutes embodying them conflict with the Constitution of the United States.'[25] The statement illustrates brilliantly the modernist rejection of 'knowledge that'. The fact that we might hold certain opinions is an 'accident'; it does not go to any final truth and therefore must be disassociated from the question of a law's constitutionality. Democratic majorities must be given greater leeway to make their own choices. But Holmes did not suggest that the word 'liberty' in the Fourteenth Amendment constituted no check at all. His proposed standard of constitutional review in the case—'that a rational and fair man necessarily would admit that the statute proposed would infringe fundamental principles as they have been understood by the traditions of our people and our law'[26]—is more deferential to legislatures, but is every bit as susceptible to manipulation as the *Lochner* majority's legal test.

Second, in the early twentieth century, various schools of legal thought with names like Sociological Jurisprudence and Legal Realism attempted to situate law in 'social context' to get away from the excesses of legal formalism and conceptualism. The most consequential effect of placing law in social context would be the loss of the distinctively lawyerly. Viewed thus, the common law would simply vanish into 'society'. Some early twentieth-century legal scholars adopted just such a position as they turned from law other disciplines, whether economics, political science, psychology, or sociology. Law would be re-made along the lines set out by this or that discipline. Political democracy, and the expert-run administrative agencies it created, would dislodge common law judges.

Third, and coming to the focus of this chapter, legal thinkers re-imagined the role of law in relationship to political democracy in ways that were far more transformative. Just as modernists in various realms of endeavour were shifting from 'knowledge that' to 'knowledge how', early twentieth-century legal thinkers insisted that legal knowledge cease to check democratic legislatures on substantive grounds and increasingly focus on the specification of ways, means, methods, processes, procedures, and protocols for arriving at substantive decisions. In the new dispensation, *this* was what would distinguish 'law' from 'politics'. As the Legal Realist Karl Llewellyn put it in 1931: 'For while we may properly proclaim that general propositions do not decide concrete cases [a reference to Holmes' *Lochner* dissent], we none the less must recognize that *ways* of deciding, *ways* of thinking,

---

[25] See (n. 22) 198 US 75–6.   [26] Ibid., 76.

ways of sizing up facts ... are distinctly enough marked in our courts so that we can know a lawman, by his judging reactions, from a layman.'[27] In the 1940s, Llewellyn was even clearer, arguing that the key to law was not so much 'what courts have decided', but 'how they go about deciding cases, and *how* they use the authorities *with* which they work, and how and why those authorities themselves came into existence'.[28]

This same shift is discernible in legal thinkers' understanding of the common law. For Pound, writing in 1921, the common law was 'essentially a *mode* of judicial and juristic thinking, a *mode* of treating legal problems rather than a fixed body of definite rules ... '.[29] Substantive law could be repackaged as a means. Thus, Pound insisted that the common law provided substantive resources for mitigating the excessive individualism animating decisions such as *Lochner*. The common law had differed sharply from its rival, the Roman law. According to Pound, '[t]he central idea in the developed Roman system is to secure and effectuate the will. All things are deduced from or referred to the will of the actor'.[30] However, the common law tradition focused not on the will of the individual actor, but rather on the feudal legal relation—master-servant, landlord-tenant, bailor-bailee, principal-agent— thereby giving the law much greater leeway for shaping rights, duties, warranties, and the like (*Lochner*, for Pound, was more Roman law-like than common law-like). But Pound was interested not in the content of any particular set of relations, but in the relation as *technique*. Substance had become means: the relation was 'a fundamental mode of thought, a mode of dealing with legal situations and with legal problems which gives wholly different results, a mode of thought which has always tempered the individualism of our law ... '.[31]

Pound's rendering of the common law as a means was not just an acceptance of the modernist critique of law's 'truth'. Like many common lawyers of his day who worried about the rise of the administrative state, Pound felt that the supremacy of law was being threatened by 'the rise of executive justice, the tendency to commit everything to boards and commissions which proceed extra-judicially and are expected to be law unto themselves ... '.[32] His version of the common law as means was advanced as an alternative to administrative ways of proceeding. But perhaps Pound need not have worried too much. During the early decades of the twentieth century, the confrontation between American common lawyers and government by commission and agency took the form of the former's insisting that the latter incorporate common law procedures.[33]

---

[27]   Karl N. Llewellyn, 'Frank's Law and the Modern Mind' (1931) in *Jurisprudence: Realism in Theory and Practice* (1962) 107 ff (emphasis in original).

[28]   Llewellyn, 'The Crafts of Law Re-Valued' (1942) in (fn 28) 318 ff (emphasis in original).

[29]   Pound (n. 1) 1 ff (emphasis added).   [30]   Ibid., 21 ff.   [31]   Ibid., 15 ff.

[32]   Ibid., 7 ff.

[33]   Daniel Ernst, *Tocqueville's Nightmare: The Administrative State Emerges in America 1900–1940* (2014).

Enterprising lawyers in the early twentieth century were quick to recognize that the infiltration of the administrative state by common law procedures was an opportunity. Towards the end of his career, the archetypical Progressive (and later New Dealer) Felix Frankfurter recalled a note he had penned in the summer of 1913. In Frankfurter's note to himself, we see an adumbration of the new understanding of the means-like, procedural, processual role of law in the new state: 'In the synthesis of thinking that must shape the Great State, the lawyer is in many ways the coordinator, the mediator, between the various social sciences.'[34] As the social sciences that would dominate the new administrative agencies claimed more and more territory from law, Frankfurter observed, the lawyer would become 'the coordinator, the mediator ...'.

Perhaps the high point of the pre-Second World War emphasis on law as means, coeval with the triumph of the New Deal and the U.S. Supreme Court's 'retreat' from *Lochner*, was the Court's declaration that constitutional review would henceforth intervene in the affairs of democracy only upon failure of the democratic *process*. In the celebrated footnote 4 of *United States v. Carolene Products* (1938), Justice Stone suggested that, now that it had given up on 'substantive due process' of the *Lochner* variety, the Court might begin to subject to 'more exacting judicial scrutiny' under the Fourteenth Amendment 'legislation which restricts those political processes which can ordinarily be expected to bring about repeal of undesirable legislation'; similarly exacting scrutiny might be extended to statutes grounded in 'prejudice against discrete and insular minorities ..., which tends seriously to curtail the operation of those political processes ordinarily to be relied upon to protect minorities ... '.[35] If *Lochner* read a substantive socio-economic philosophy ('knowledge that') into the Due Process Clauses of the Constitution, the *Carolene Products* footnote talks of invoking the very same Due Process Clauses only when political processes malfunction ('knowledge how'). Constitutional law's role is the policing of processes.

In the pre-Second World War period, legal thinkers had conceived of the turn to process and procedure as part of the Progressive socio-economic agenda. However, faced with the horrors of Nazism and Stalinism and searching for defensible legal limits to state power, mid-twentieth-century American legal thinkers began to conceive of process and procedure as something important in and of itself. But law's retreat from designating ends towards specifying means neither solved the problem posed by the collapse of the 'law'-'politics' distinction, nor spelled the disappearance of traditional common law vocabularies. This is clearly illustrated by the judicial career of Felix Frankfurter after his elevation to the U.S. Supreme Court in 1939.

[34] Felix Frankfurter, *Felix Frankfurter Reminisces; Recorded in Talks with Dr. Harlan B. Phillips* (1960) 81 ff.

[35] *United States v. Carolene Products* (1938) 304 U.S. 144.

For Frankfurter, constitutional review of legislative action was supposed to be deferential and proceduralist. For example, in *Driscoll v. Edison Light & Power Co.* (1939), Frankfurter argued that the U.S. Supreme Court should not interfere in the substantive rate-setting work of commissions—something federal courts had been doing regularly—because rate setting did not involve 'questions of an essentially legal nature in the sense that legal education and lawyer's learning afford peculiar competence for their adjustment'.[36] Only when questions 'of an essentially legal nature' came up—and what was more 'essentially legal' than procedure?—should courts intervene.

In 1949, the legal scholar Louis Jaffe described Frankfurter on the Court as 'forever disposing of issues by assigning their disposition to some other sphere of competence. His world is the urban world of the division of labor, of the specialist, the expert. He is the craftsman conscious and proud of the illusive niceties germane to his own skill and, in consequence, scrupulous in his regard for the integrity of impinging spheres of competence.'[37] But Frankfurter's modernist world was highly attuned to that which lay *beyond* 'conscious' determination. An appreciation of the imprecise, the vague, the non-rational—in short, the limits of the 'conscious'—pervades Frankfurter's writings. Thus, in his reminiscences, he states: 'You damned sociologists, you historians who want to get it all nice and fine on paper, you haven't learned how much in this world is determined by non-syllogistic reasoning, or without conscious exploration of a problem with a view to reaching a logical conclusion.'[38] We might read Frankfurter's acute sensitivity to the limits of 'conscious exploration of a problem' as being akin to Cardozo's exploration of the judicial method, a modernist stance in which the ultimate form of 'consciousness' gestures towards its own limits. However, Frankfurter's sense of the limits of 'consciousness' also fused effortlessly with the 'unconscious' languages of the common law. For even as he championed the administrative state, Frankfurter never repudiated the common law, proclaiming proudly: 'I'm bred in the law. I'm a common lawyer.'[39]

Frankfurter's sense of the difficulty of wielding law to check democracy thus emerged not only from being a committed Progressive/New Dealer opposed to the regime of *Lochner*, but also from a very strong common lawyerly sense of the difference between the work of courts and the work of legislatures, between an enduring Constitution ('law') and episodic legislation ('politics'). Thus, Frankfurter insisted: 'For judges at least it is important to remember that continuity with the past is not only a necessity but even a duty.'[40] At the same time, however, Frankfurter maintained that the Constitution not be fixed in time, that it 'was made for an

---

[36] *Driscoll v. Edison Light & Power Co.* (1939) 307 U.S. 104, 122 (Frankfurter, J., concurring).
[37] Louis L. Jaffe, 'The Judicial Universe of Mr. Justice Frankfurter' (1949) 62 *Harvard L.R.* 359 ff.
[38] Frankfurter (n. 34) 10 ff.   [39] Ibid., 248 ff.
[40] Felix Frankfurter, 'Some Reflections on the Reading of Statutes' (1947) 47 *Columbia L.R.* 535.

undefined and expanding future ... '.[41] Thus, the Constitution should both change and not change, exactly as the common law had always done. Frankfurter had long praised the common law's temporality of 'insensibility'. In 1939, he had written that 'the Court's influence has been achieved undramatically and imperceptibly, like the gradual growth of a coral reef, as the cumulative product of hundreds of cases, individually unexciting and seemingly even unimportant, but in their total effect powerfully telling in the pulls and pressures of society'.[42]

This common law temporality of 'insensibility', could be achieved through an intense focus on means, procedure, and process. Procedure secured freedom by securing individuals against state power. Furthermore, procedure—relative to substance—was relatively stable across time. But procedure also acted as a buffer against substantive constitutional change because it allowed for a repeated deflection of substantive questions. In 1934, Frankfurter had written approvingly: 'The Court has ... evolved elaborate and often technical doctrines for postponing if not avoiding constitutional adjudication.'[43] Once on the Court, he offered the memorable formulation: '[T]he most fundamental principle of constitutional adjudication is not to face constitutional questions but to avoid them, if at all possible.'[44]

Frankfurter argued that procedure, much like Coke's 'artificial reason', was not accessible to everyone: 'Some of these rules may well appear over-refined or evasive to the laity. But they have the support not only of the profoundest wisdom. They have been vindicated, in conspicuous instances of disregard, by the most painful lessons of our constitutional history.'[45] The same sense of common lawyerly monopoly of knowledge appears repeatedly in Frankfurter's approach to the Due Process Clause of the Fourteenth Amendment. Resisting the effort of Justice Black and others to fix the meaning of the Due Process Clause as incorporating the Bill of Rights, Frankfurter insisted upon the 'wisdom [of] our predecessors in refusing to give a rigid scope to this phrase'.[46] Due Process was a real, but nevertheless blurry, concept that was a matter of judgment: 'These standards of justice [incorporated in the concept of Due Process] are not authoritatively formulated anywhere as though they were prescriptions in a pharmacopoeia. But neither does the application of the Due Process Clause imply that judges are wholly at large.'[47]

Judging, for Frankfurter, was an activity that resisted complete representation: this was yet another place where his modernist and common lawyerly sensibilities fused. As he put it: '[J]udgment is not drawn out of the void but is based on the

---

[41] *Baumgartner v. United States* (1944) 322 U.S. 665, 673 (quoting *Hurtado v. California* (1884) 110 U.S. 516).

[42] Felix Frankfurter, *Mr. Justice Holmes and the Supreme Court* (1939) 3–4 ff.

[43] Felix Frankfurter, 'The Supreme Court of the United States', in Archibald MacLeish, E. F. Pritchard, Jr. (eds.), *Law and Politics: Occasional Papers of Felix Frankfurter, 1918–1938* (1939) 25 ff.

[44] *United States v. Lovett* 1946 328 U.S. 303, 320 (Frankfurter, J., concurring).   [45] Ibid.

[46] *Malinski v. New York* (1945) 342 U.S. 401, 414 ff (Frankfurter, J., concurring).

[47] Ibid., 417 ff (Frankfurter, J., concurring).

correlation of imponderables all of which need not, because they cannot, be made explicit.'[48] Indeed, the judge had to be something of an artist: '[J]udges ... must have something of the creative artist in them; they must have antennae registering feeling and judgment beyond logical, let alone quantitative, proof.'[49] Thus, when it came to deciding what was a 'case or controversy'—a threshold constitutional limitation on the jurisdiction of the federal courts—Frankfurter insisted that only the 'expert feel of lawyers' could resolve the issue.[50] Due Process was also a 'feeling'. Frankfurter once characterized it as 'respect enforced by law for that feeling of just treatment which has been evolved through centuries of Anglo-American constitutional history and civilization...'.[51] The British Constitution, which Frankfurter admired greatly, consisted also of a 'feeling which has the support of the country expressed through a firm majority of the House of Commons'.[52] Some years before his appointment to the bench, Frankfurter had written of the U.S. Supreme Court: 'What is decisive is the Court's feeling for the integrity of the judicial process.'[53]

In judging on the basis of 'feeling', however, Frankfurter also spoke very much like a traditional common law judge who claimed to speak 'for' the community. In *Haley v. Ohio* (1948), Frankfurter joined the Court in finding that the police had extorted a confession from a fifteen-year old African American boy in violation of the Due Process Clause. Deciding whether a confession was voluntary or coerced, Frankfurter argued, invited a 'psychological judgement that reflects deep, even if inarticulate, feelings of our society. Judges must divine that feeling as best they can from all the relevant evidence and light which they can bring to bear for a confident judgment of such an issue ... .'[54] As judges 'divined' the feelings of the community, in a 'gradual process of judicial inclusion and exclusion, as the cases presented for decision shall require', the Due Process Clause would acquire meaning.[55]

Nothing illustrates the fusion of mid-century modernist legal thinking with pre-modern common law sensibilities better than Frankfurter's faith in this ability to 'divine' his way through the legal dilemmas of Due Process. The ability to 'divine' was also, for him, the highest praise he could bestow on a judge. As he put it in his adulatory book on Holmes: 'Other great judges have been guided by the wisdom distilled

---

[48] Frankfurter (1947), 47 *Columbia L.R.* 532 ff.

[49] Felix Frankfurter, 'The Judicial Process and the Supreme Court' (1954), in Philip Elman (ed.), *Of Law and Men: Papers and Addresses of Felix Frankfurter, 1939–1956* (1956) 39 ff.

[50] *Joint Anti-Fascist Refugee Committee v. McGrath* (1951) 341 U.S. 123, 150 (Frankfurter, J., concurring).

[51] Ibid., 162 ff.   [52] Frankfurter (n. 42) 68 ff.

[53] Felix Frankfurter, James Landis, 'The Business of the Supreme Court at October Term, 1932' (1933) 47 *Harvard L.R.* 277 ff.

[54] *Haley v. Ohio*, (1948) 332 U.S. 596, 603 (Frankfurter, J., concurring). Indeed, Frankfurter maintained: 'Our Constitutional system makes it the Court's duty to interpret those feelings of society to which the Due Process Clause gives legal protection.' Ibid., 605 ff.

[55] *State of Louisiana ex. Rel. Francis v. Resweber*, (1947) 329 U.S. 459, 471 (Frankfurter, J., concurring).

from an active life; Mr. Justice Holmes was led by the divination of the philosopher and the imagination of the poet.'[56]

The new understanding of law as means, process, and procedure reached an apogee in the post-Second World War period with the rise of the Legal Process School. Many of the major exponents of the Legal Process School—Alexander Bickel, Paul Freund, Louis Jaffe, Edward H. Levi, Henry Hart, Albert Sacks, Herbert Wechsler, Harry Wellington—were affiliated in one way or another with Frankfurter. In the Harvard Law School of the late 1950s, the capital of Legal Process thinking, a student reminisced, 'Felix Frankfurter was God'.[57]

The views of the Legal Process school are set forth most clearly in Henry Hart's and Albert Sacks' *The Legal Process*, a set of teaching materials widely used in American law schools in the 1950s. Hart and Sacks conjured up something they called 'the principle of institutional settlement', pursuant to which the principal function of law was to demarcate the boundaries that separated the different components (legislatures, courts, agencies, and individuals) of the modern state.[58] Once decisions had been made by the right authority on the basis of the right procedure, inquiry was at an end.

For Hart and Sacks, procedure was a crucial bulwark against 'disintegrating resort to violence'.[59] In a legal world in which substantive knowledge had been turned over to non-lawyer experts, furthermore, procedure was still knowable by lawyers. It is not surprising, then, that Hart and Sacks elevated procedure over substance: 'In the long run, these procedures and their accompanying doctrines and practices will come to be seen *as the most significant and enduring part of the whole legal system because they are the matrix of everything else*.'[60]

But Frankfurter's emphasis on procedure found by far its most conservative and common lawyerly rendering in the writings of his law clerk and protégé, the Legal Process scholar Alexander Bickel, arguably the most celebrated constitutional theorist of the post-Second World War period. Bickel endorsed 'the exquisite balance' between adhering to a legal 'principle' and also keeping that 'principle' in suspension through recourse to common lawyerly, procedural devices.[61] Doing so, he believed, was the 'secret of the [Court's] ability to maintain itself in the tension between principle and expediency'.[62] As he put it: 'A sound judicial instinct will generally favor deflecting the problem in one or more initial cases, for there is much to be gained

---

[56] Frankfurter (n. 42) 24–5 ff.

[57] Quoted in William M. Wiecek, 'American Jurisprudence After the War: "Reason Called Law"' (2001) 37 *Tulsa L.R.* 862 ff.

[58] Henry M. Hart, Jr., Albert M. Sacks, William N. Eskridge, Philip B. Frickey (eds.), *The Legal Process: Basic Problems in the Making and Application of Law* (1994) (tent. edn., 1958) 4 ff.

[59] Ibid.   [60] Ibid., 6 ff (emphasis added).

[61] Alexander M. Bickel, *The Least Dangerous Branch: The Supreme Court at the Bar of Politics* (1962) 155 ff.

[62] Ibid., 69 ff.

from letting it simmer, so that a mounting number of incidents exemplifying it may have a cumulative effect on the judicial mind as well as on public and professional opinion.'[63] This was Frankfurter speaking through Bickel, to be sure, but also a much longer line of common law jurists making themselves heard through him.

From the mid-1960s until his death, Bickel grew increasingly conservative. In important part, his ire focused on the jurisprudence of the later years of the Warren Court. The road forged by the Warren Court, he railed, was too determined, too clear: too much 'knowledge that' and not enough 'knowledge how'. In *The Supreme Court and the Idea of Progress* (1970), Bickel attacked the Court for pushing egalitarianism relentlessly 'in the belief that progress, called history, would validate their course, and that another generation, remembering its own future, would imagine them favorably'.[64] From Bickel's increasingly Burkean perspective, the Court seemed, like the French Revolutionaries, always to be taken up with 'some luxuriant outburst of theory', the long-standing enemy of the common lawyerly disposition.[65]

Bickel accused the Warren Court of lacking a common lawyerly measure of imprecision in its application of legal 'principles'. He complained that the Court was shedding 'a wise suspense in forming opinions, wise reserve in expressing them, and wise tardiness in trying to realize them'.[66] Bickel's Burkean, common lawyerly impulse to decelerate the rate of change meshed with the Legal Process understanding of the ontology of law as process, procedure, and method, because nothing afforded better protection against heedless and dangerous change than a commitment to procedure. In *The Morality of Consent* (1975), Bickel hailed the 'hard-core of procedural provisions, found chiefly in the Bill of Rights' that possessed a 'relative definiteness of terms' and 'definiteness of history'.[67] The Warren Court had congratulated itself on 'cutting through legal technicalities, in piercing through procedure to get to substance. But legal technicalities are the stuff of law, and piercing through a particular substance to get to procedures suitable to many substances is in fact what the task of law most often is.'[68]

But Bickel may have exaggerated the Warren Court's willingness to ignore process and procedure. Writing in 1974, just after the Warren Court era had ended, Bruce Ackerman wrote that, '[w]hile it is far too soon to comprehend fully how this emphasis on process will ultimately affect the law in practice, there can be little doubt that its impact has already been profound.'[69] Ackerman cited the various efforts of the Warren Court that were directed, precisely, at the correction of defective legal and political processes. As he put it: 'the political process, the criminal process, and, more recently, the processes of civil and administrative litigation have been

[63] Ibid., 176 ff.
[64] Alexander M. Bickel, *The Supreme Court and the Idea of Progress* (1978) 13–14 ff.
[65] Alexander M. Bickel, *The Morality of Consent* (1975) 24 ff.   [66] Bickel (n. 64) 31 ff.
[67] Bickel (n. 65) 29 ff. (quoting Felix Frankfurter, *Law and Politics* 10, 12)
[68] Bickel (n. 65) 121 ff.
[69] Bruce A. Ackerman, ' "Law and the Modern Mind" by Jerome Frank' (1974) 103 *Daedalus* 123 ff.

revolutionized to assure at least some access for all citizens'.[70] With the Burger Court, this emphasis on process continued, albeit in a more conservative Bickel-like vein. William Eskridge and Philip Frickey have identified the Burger Court's emphasis on standing, mootness, and ripeness as 'procedural techniques to postpone or deflect hard substantive issues'.[71] The Legal Process school extended its influence well into the 1970s and beyond, John Hart Ely's *Democracy and Distrust* (1980) being the grand synthesis of U.S. constitutional law as a filling out of the 'process'-like logic of the *Carolene Products* case.[72]

IV. CONCLUSION

The emergence of modernism and the erosion of foundations that it entailed was key to the transformation of the common law as the nineteenth century gave way to the twentieth. As modernists shifted from 'knowledge that' to 'knowledge how', law in general (and the common law in particular) increasingly surrendered its claims to check democracy in substantive ways, and became instead means, ways, processes, and procedures. But it is not clear that law, even in its new 'procedural' role, was able to become a fully 'conscious' kind of lawmaking. In the thought of Felix Frankfurter and Alexander Bickel, one sees a modernist vocabulary pushing at the limits of the 'conscious' come together with an older pre-modern common lawyerly languages as legal thinkers sought to rethink the procedures of the modern state.

From a contemporary standpoint, the shift from 'knowledge that' to 'knowledge how' looks like a period piece. The tortured sensibilities of Felix Frankfurter and Alexander Bickel, so intensely aware of the tottering of the old foundations and the urgency of coming up with a language to account for the place of law *after* the loss of foundations, seem to have little counterpart in the serene complacency of those convinced of the truths of religion, or tradition, or the free market. For those convinced of such truths, the common law has also been invaluable. A more comprehensive account of the common law in twentieth-century America would tell the story of how it intersected with libertarianism, with law-and-economics, and with Christian conservatism.[73]

---

[70] Ibid., 124 ff.

[71] See Eskridge and Frickey, 'Historical and Critical Introduction', in Hart, Sacks (n. 58) cxvi ff.

[72] John Hart Ely, *Democracy and Distrust: A Theory of Judicial Review* (1980).

[73] For an attempt to canvass some of these developments, see Ken Kersch, 'Constitutive Stories About the Common Law in Modern American Conservatism', in Sanford Levinson et al. (eds.), *American Conservatism* (2016).

That story has not been told here. But what *has* been told here could connect up with what has not been insofar as it underscores the protean character of the common law. The perplexing marriage of scepticism and mystification, modernist historical sensibilities and pre-modern temporalities through which the common law made a career in twentieth-century America gestures to the way it has functioned in other fields, other disciplines, other ways of knowing.

BIBLIOGRAPHY

Alexander M. Bickel, *The Least Dangerous Branch: The Supreme Court at the Bar of Politics* (Bobbs-Merrill, 1962)

Alexander M. Bickel, *The Morality of Consent* (Yale University Press, 1975)

Alexander M. Bickel, *The Supreme Court and the Idea of Progress* (Harper & Row, 1978)

William Blackstone, *Commentaries on the Laws of England: A Facsimile of the First Edition of 1765–1769* (University of Chicago Press, 1979)

Edmund Burke, *Reflections on the Revolution in France* (Stanford University Press, 2001) (1790)

Benjamin N. Cardozo, *The Nature of the Judicial Process* (Yale University Press, 1921)

Neil Duxbury, *Patterns of American Jurisprudence* (Oxford University Press, 1995)

Daniel Ernst, *Tocqueville's Nightmare: The Administrative State Emerges in America, 1900–1940* (Oxford University Press, 2014)

John Hart Ely, *Democracy and Distrust: A Theory of Judicial Review* (Harvard University Press, 1980)

Henry M. Hart, Jr., Albert M. Sacks, William N. Eskridge, Philip B. Frickey (eds.), *The Legal Process: Basic Problems in the Making and Application of Law* (Foundation Press, 1994) (tent. edn., 1958)

Oliver Wendell Holmes, Jr., *The Common Law* (Little, Brown, 1881)

Morton Horwitz, *The Transformation of American Law, 1780–1860* (Harvard University Press, 1977)

Morton Horwitz, *The Transformation of American Law, 1870–1960: The Crisis of Legal Orthodoxy* (Oxford University Press, 1992)

Sheldon Novick (ed.), *The Collected Works of Justice Holmes: Complete Public Writings and Selected Judicial Opinions of Oliver Wendell Holmes* (University of Chicago Press, 1995)

Kunal Parker, *Common Law, History, and Democracy in America, 1790–1900: Legal Thought Before Modernism* (Cambridge University Press, 2011)

J. G. A. Pocock, *The Ancient Constitution and the Feudal Law: A Study of English Historical Thought in the Seventeenth Century* (Cambridge University Press, 1957)

Roscoe Pound, *The Spirit of the Common Law* (Marshall Jones Co., 1931) (1921)

G. Edward White, *Patterns of American Legal Thought* (Bobbs-Merrill, 1978)

G. Edward White, *The Constitution and the New Deal* (Harvard University Press, 2000)

CHAPTER 38

TRACING LEGAL HISTORY IN CONTINENTAL CIVIL LAW

HEIKKI PIHLAJAMÄKI

I. INTRODUCTION

THE German sociologist Hartmut Rosa discusses a 'detemporalization of history' in late modernity. According to Rosa, 'what has been lost are the [...] "metatemporal" plans of history, life, and daily activities that determined the temporal qualities of events and actions beforehand and made the time of [...] history susceptible to planning and allowed them to appear *directed*'.[1] Not by accident, history as a scientific discipline was born in the nineteenth century to provide such metatemporal stories. This lost world of history was also the period of the classical, Weberian concept of modernity of the nineteenth and twentieth centuries, carrying with it an Enlightenment belief in social progress. In the 1960s and 1970s this all changed, and social theoreticians or historians rarely believe in progress or any similar grand stories any more.

The history of continental legal history reflects these changes. Legal history is a product of nineteenth-century modernity. My examples of historical research in

---

[1] Hartmut Rosa, *Social Acceleration: A New Theory of Modernity* (2013) 168 ff.

law from the pre-modern era (thus, pre-nineteenth century) show that although methodologically, premodern legal historians were no less able scholars, their scholarly interests were different. They were concerned with certain elements of the past only, such as the legal sources of ancient Rome or such, which could help to create a glorious past for their country.

In the nineteenth century this changed, as legal history became, first, the instrument which helped to distinguish the best parts of the legal heritage in order for them to be developed further and to serve as building blocks of the new systematic legal order. In the second—positivist—phase, when the legal system started to be developed without being detached from history, legal history was left on its own. It now evolved into a device which served as legitimation for the existing legal orders. In late modernity (the 1970s, to be more precise), then, legal history increasingly became a device of critical theory or an independent discipline.

When did jurists or legal scholars become aware of their discipline's history? And why? When did they become interested in legal history for its own sake— not intimately linked to their activities as contemporary lawyers? Historical considerations in continental law have a history of their own. Commonplace claims often heard today such as 'current law cannot be understood apart from its history' have been far from self-evident when one observes civil law in a long perspective. Some exceptions notwithstanding, legal history has played a minor role in law and legal scholarship. When we look at legal history written by legal scholars, as this chapter explains, legal history's importance as an academic discipline has largely depended on its significance in legal reasoning. When legal reasoning has depended on historical arguments, the value of legal history has increased. When legal reasoning has been less interested in historical points of view, the significance of legal history has decreased. Nevertheless, to some extent, history has always been present in continental civil law. Besides legal reasoning, the fluctuations and changes in historical scholarship have greatly influenced legal history.

This chapter proceeds chronologically. Section II starts with a short introductory note on the role of legal history in ancient Roman law and the legal scholarship of medieval glossators and commentators. However, the section mainly discusses 'the first legal historians', the sixteenth-century humanists. The humanists were the first to study legal history for the mere sake of being interested in history, although their historical interests should also be viewed in the context of the contemporary interests of rising absolutist states. Section II then turns to the dominant schools of continental legal scholarship in the seventeenth and eighteenth centuries, the 'Neo-Bartolists' and the *usus modernus pandectarum*. Although these schools gave in considerably to a pressing need to accommodate modern legislation with the inherited *ius commune*, legal history still contributed to a great extent to their work. Section III concentrates on the rise of the Historical School in Germany and the corresponding movements elsewhere in continental Europe. Methodologically, the representatives of the Historical School were the first professional legal historians in the modern sense of the term. However, their method was intimately linked to the emerging 'science of law' (*Rechtswissenschaft*) and was not an independent discipline, as legal history is today. The independence of legal history, as Section V explains, was a paradoxical consequence of its marginalization within legal scholarship. Towards the end of the nineteenth century, law increasingly turned into a positivist branch of scholarship. In law, positivism meant the dominance of statutory law that left little space for legal history in argumentation. Legal history now turned, more than anything, into a national discipline and a back-up science for the natural scholarship of positive law. Section VI briefly retells the story of the rise of European legal history in the post-war period and the recent trends towards a creation of global legal histories. It will be shown that, once again, legal history's turns have in many ways followed from not only legal scholarship in general, but also from developments in historical science and global politics. In our rapidly changing legal universe, this may be legal history's best chance to survive—and its only hope.

II. Legal Humanism and Legal History

The legal humanists of the sixteenth century were the first legal scholars specifically interested in the history of law. Ancient Roman jurists were too practical-minded to care for legal history. Medieval glossators and commentators, although they relied on a historical source, Justinian's *Corpus iuris civilis*, were notoriously disinterested in the historical veracity of their interpretations. For the glossators, it was important to be able interpret the *Corpus iuris* as a self-consistent body of rules. For the commentators, the practical functioning of the text (and often even more the Gloss to it) mattered as well. These interests left no space or need for historical ponderings. Late-medieval humanists specialized in letters were already criticizing medieval jurists for their lack of interest in history, and the representatives of *jurisprudentia elegantior*—later to be called legal humanism—frowned upon them even more.

The history of legal humanism begins with Lorenzo Valla and Maffeo Vegio, whose main target of criticism was the corrupt Latin of medieval commentators. Valla's *Elegantiae linguae Latinae* praised ancient Roman jurists, whose texts had been included in the Digest, and condemned Tribonian and the medieval jurists such as Accursius, Bartolus, and others for mistreating the original Latin in the Digest. Vegio's *De verborum significatione* pointed out that if Tribonian had not already mutilated the original text, Bartolus would have had no need for his baffling commentaries.[2]

Guillaume Budé, Ulrich Zasius, and Andrea Alciato are usually considered as the first to have systematically practised the humanist method on legal sources. Budé's *Annotationes in Pandectas* (1508) was a commentary on books 1–24 of the Digest. Less an actual work on law (Budé was not a jurist), the *Annotationes* was an explanation of defective texts and difficult terms. Concentrating on linguistic differences, Budé had little interest in the cultural circumstances in which concepts had developed and were used, and neither did he care much for the legal-dogmatic implications of his findings.[3] Zasius's *Lucubrationes* (1518) was already a true legal work to which the humanistic method was applied. Andreas Alciatus, in turn, wrote three important works, in which he used the new humanist methodology. With Alciatus, the centre of legal humanism moved to France in the sixteenth century—first to Avignon and then to Bourges, which soon established itself as the centre of legal humanism. The greatest of Alciatus's followers, the *Alciatei*, in Bourges were Jacques Cujas, François Hotman, François Douaren, and Hugues Doneau.[4]

Even though the significance of legal humanism for the development of legal scholarship is beyond doubt, in practical legal life their importance always remained minimal. As Peter Stein put it: 'The scholar could be a humanist, but the practitioner had to be a Bartolist'.[5] Even if legal humanism had little to offer to practical legal life, it significantly influenced legal scholarship. Humanist legal thought was closely intertwined with the Renaissance admiration of all things antique, and at the same time, humanists were deeply suspicious of medieval legal thought. The main object of study was the same as that of the medieval jurists, the *Corpus iuris civilis*, but the humanist approach to Justinian's compilation was radically different. According to Douglas Osler's definition, '[l]egal humanism [...] signifies the investigation of Roman law, using philological and historical methods, as part of the historical study of antiquity, and may be contrasted with the pragmatic, unhistorical application of Roman law to the conditions of contemporary Europe'.[6] Taking advantage of the latest developments in philology, humanists took to correcting what they considered to be mistakes made by the medieval commentators. Reconstructing the original text of the *Corpus iuris* from later interpolations and understanding the original text was crucial for humanists. But they did not stop here: it was equally

---

[2] Peter Stein, 'Legal Humanism and Legal Science' (1986) 54 *Tijdschrift voor Rechtsgeschiedenis* 297–306 ff (hereafter Stein, 'Legal Humanism').

[3] See Michael Monheit, 'Guillaume Budé, Andrea Alciato, Pierre de l'Estoile: Renaissance Interpreters of Roman Law' (1997) 58 *Journal of the History of Ideas* 21–40, 27 ff.

[4] On legal humanism, see the many articles of Douglas J. Osler, for instance, 'Images of Legal Humanism' (2001) 9 *Surfaces* 101–6 ff; and 'Legal Humanism', at <https://www.rg.mpg.de/research/legal-humanism> (hereafter Osler, 'Legal Humanism').

[5] Stein, 'Legal Humanism' (n. 2) 304 ff.   [6] Osler, 'Legal Humanism' (n. 4).

important for humanist legal scholars to identify and correct interpolations made by Justinian's main editor, Tribonian, and his crew.

The first wave of legal humanists were 'true' legal historians in that they were primarily interested in finding out the true wording of the ancient authoritative texts and in cleansing out later 'false' interpretations. But at the same time, this first wave of legal humanists were traditional and conservative in that they used the new philological and historical methods precisely to uphold the sanctity of the Digest. The second wave of legal humanists no longer admired Roman law. As Donald Kelley has noted, many of them did not stop short of establishing the interpolations of scholastics and Justinian's law-drafters. Humanists like Baudouin concluded that it was also indispensable to chart the tradition of Roman law before and after Justinian. They wanted to understand the law in the first two centuries, now identified as the classical period of Roman law. Some applied the new method even to a reconstruction of the Twelve Tables. Instead of wanting to save Roman law in its pure form, some of the later humanists emphasized its poor suitability to their own world and used their historical insights to argue political points in their own time. Many of them Protestants, the later humanists considered all Roman influences as vile and worth purging. François Hotman is a good example of this. Hotman attempted to show, in his main work *Francogallia* (1573), that besides being a corrupt combination of classical and Justinian ingredients, Roman law had pushed out of its way Frankish constitutions and customary law, which would have suited the French society much more naturally.[7] According to Hotman, a French lawyer equipped with Roman rules of property and succession (and disregarding the feudal law on land holding) would be equally as lost as if he had arrived among American savages.[8]

Although humanists had disdained canon and feudal law, the wish to establish longer perspectives on the tradition of Roman law led them to cast a critical eye on the history of these bodies of law as well.[9] Just as they did with classical Roman law, humanists worked with philological methods, producing critical editions of central texts. The most important of these was Gratian's *Decretum*. Lorenzo Valla, who had discovered the falsity of the Donation of Constantine, was the first to attack the *Decretum*. Neither Valla nor Erasmus, also aware of the historical deficiencies of the *Decretum*, ever came to produce a critical version of the authoritative work on canon law. This was done instead by Antoine de Mouchy (1547) and the official *correctores* of the Roman Church (1582). Similarly, humanists engaged from early on in historical debates on whether feudalism was of Roman imperial pedigree.

[7] Ralph E. Giesey, 'When and Why Did Hotman write *Francogallia*?' (1967) 3 *Bibliothèque d'Humanisme et Renaissance* 81–611 ff.

[8] Stein, 'Legal Humanism' (n. 2) 303 ff.

[9] Donald R. Kelley, 'The Rise of Legal History in the Renaissance' (1970) 9 *History and Theory* 2, 174–94 ff.

Some of them indeed reinforced the widespread contemporary assumption that feudal law derived from ancient Rome, whereas others argued that feudal law was modern in origin. The decisive blow to the assumption that feudal law had imperial Roman origins came from Charles Dumoulin, who in his commentary on the Parisian *coutume* (1539) asserted that the vocabulary of feudal law was modern and that much of Europe, France included, were politically not successors of the Roman Empire. *Libri feudorum*, the standard twelfth-century collection of imperial statutes and customs of northern Italy, was shown not to represent French or German customs. Jacques Cujas, in his critical edition of *Libri feudorum* (1566), then confirmed all this.

Although not directly useful in practical legal argumentation, legal humanism undermined the authority of the *Corpus iuris civilis* and its most influential part, the Digest. After sixteenth-century legal humanists had nailed down their theses, the law of Justinian was increasingly looked upon as a historical artefact only and subject to rational critique. For the proponents of developing absolutism this was beneficial, as space was created for the rising royal law. It is no wonder that it was François Hotman, a legal humanist, who decisively contributed to replacing the Digest's order of presenting legal materials with a new ordering principle, inspired by the French humanist philosopher Pierre de la Ramée (Petrus Ramus). Legal history, once invented, immediately showed its revolutionary potential.

III. Legal History in *Mos Italicus* and *Usus Modernus Pandectarum*

Although French legal humanism had little impact on legal practice and waned as a distinguishable school of scholarship after the sixteenth century, historical interests remained an integral part of legal scholarship. This is the reason why legal historians today are careful in not distinguishing too neatly between humanism or *mos gallicus*, on the one hand, and *mos italicus* or *usus modernus pandectarum*, on the other. Even though *mos gallicus* in its 'purest' form as textual criticism did not survive, the results of humanist learning could not be ignored. Legal history, already in the texts of the sixteenth-century humanists, proved to be not only a politically innocent method in the service of antiquarian interests but at times it could also be true social and legal dynamite.

If the birth of French and indeed continental legal history in its humanist form can be dated to sixteenth-century legal humanism, other European regions followed suit in the seventeenth and eighteenth centuries. Then humanist research interests already coalesced with practical concerns. All over continental Europe, early modern jurists developed ways of combining Roman law, although selectively and no longer as a strictly authoritative source, with local legal sources, and many of the *mos italicus* or *usus modernus* scholars at the same time also wrote historical works or used historical arguments.

In Spain, for instance, the *mos gallicus*, or French legal humanism, is usually associated with Francisco Ramos del Manzano (1604–1683), professor at Salamanca. Ramos del Manzano and his many followers, although they adopted the historical methods of French humanists, at the same time continued their everyday legal reasoning in the spirit of *mos italicus* or 'neo-Bartolism', which until then had been the dominating school of legal thinking.[10]

A good example of how historical methods were introduced and used in German legal scholarship is the work of Hermann Conring (1606–1681), the 'father of German legal history'. Conring is known as the author of *De origine iuris germanici* (1643). In this work Conring showed how Roman law had not been introduced in Germany, contrary to what was believed, in the Constitution of Lothair III (r. 1134–1137) in 1135, but instead had already existed in the works of fifteenth-century academic scholars.[11] The Dutch Elegant School, or Dutch legal humanism, of the seventeenth and eighteenth centuries is a prime example of how early modern legal scholars combined the humanist way of using Roman law, without its medieval binding *auctoritas*, with practical insights and local sources.[12] An Italian scholar active in England, Alberico Gentili's work illustrates the same point.[13]

Although Roman law and historical concerns did not disappear with legal humanism, national legal scholarship gained ground in the seventeenth and eighteenth centuries. Note incidentally, many of the 'fathers' of national legal histories were also seventeenth-century scholars, followers of *usus modernus* with a historical taint. Besides Ramos del Manzano, Conring, and John Selden (1584–1654) the father of English legal history, the 'father of Swedish legal history', Johan Stiernhöök (1596–1675), lived and work in the same century. His main historical work, *De jure sveonum et gothorum vetusto* (1674), was an investigation of the medieval Swedish provincial laws. The historiographical value of his work has

---

[10] On Ramos del Manzano and other Spanish humanists, see Mariano Peset and Pascual Marzal, 'Humanismo jurídico y tardío en Salamanca' (2009) 14 *Studia Historica* 63–83 ff.

[11] On Conring, see Constantin Fasolt, 'Hermann Conring and the History of European Law' in Christopher Ocker, Michael Printy, Peter Starenko, Peter Wallace (eds.), *Politics and Reformations— Histories and Reformations: Essays in Honor of Thomas A. Brady, Jr.* (2007) 113–34 ff.

[12] Govaert C. J. J. van den Bergh, *Die holländische elegante Schule: ein Beitrag zur Geschichte von Humanismus und Rechtswissenschaft in den Niederlanden 1500–1800* (2002).

[13] See Alain Wijffels, '*Antiqui et recentiores*: Alberico Gentili: Beyond *mos italicus* and Legal Humanism' in Paul J. du Plessis, John W. Cairns (eds.), *Reassessing Legal Humanism and its Claims: Petere Fontes?* (2016) 11–40 ff.

been much discussed in older Swedish research: some see *De jure* as a masterpiece, some as belonging to antiquarian nationalistic history writing, and yet others have praised the book in nationalistic tones.[14]

Stiernhöök's main historical work should be observed within the context of contemporary European scholarship, particularly that of Grotius and Conring. Both of them had close ties with Sweden.[15] Stiernhöök's *De jure*, indeed, is in methodological debt to Conring's *De origine*. Both authors approach the history of domestic law as a subject in itself, but in clearly political contexts. This kind of approach was, in Conring's case, an obvious consequence of his refutation of the Lothairian Legend: if Roman law was not in force as imperial legislation but rather as legal practice, then national statutory and customary law were at least as important as Roman law as legal sources and worthy of a history of their own.[16] Conring's legal history, then, had practical contemporary aims as well.

Stiernhöök, as a Swedish legal historian, had no authoritarian conception of Roman law to combat. *Ius commune* had only started to make its headway into Sweden, first slowly in the sixteenth century and somewhat more forcefully in the seventeenth century. When the learned law arrived in Sweden, early modern humanism had already demolished or at least diminished the authority of Roman law. Humanists had relegated Roman law to the position of a legal source which was used, not because of its status of imperial law, but because of its continued *usus* or because of the *ratio iuris* it represented. The nascent Swedish legal scholarship of the seventeenth century could conveniently receive whatever Roman law it did as part of this *usus modernus pandectarum* notion of legal reasoning.

Stiernhöök's situation also differed in another sense from that of Conring. Because Roman law was clearly present in seventeenth-century Germany, both in scholarship and in judicial practice, Conring needed to find an explanation for this phenomenon. Since imperial command was not the explanation for him, he needed to show how Roman law had come down to his times in legal practice. Stiernhöök, in turn, had no need for this kind of explanation and could therefore concentrate on the Swedish medieval laws only.

Stiernhöök accepted Roman law as a source, but only when Swedish laws and customs did not provide the norms necessary to solve a legal problem. Legal history

---

[14] Kjell Åke Modéer, 'Historia, juridik och politik: en skiss till en vetenskaplig Stiernhöök-biografi' in Kjell Åke Modéer (ed.), *Johan Olofsson Stiernhöök: Biografi och studier 1596–1996* (1996) 97–104 ff (hereafter Modéer, 'Historia, juridik och politik'):

[15] Grotius was the Swedish ambassador to Paris, and his works were well known in Sweden. Conring exchanged letters with the Swedish Chancellor of the Realm, Axel Oxentierna, and sent his *De origine* to the Chancellor. As one of the consequences of the Peace of Westphalia, Conring counselled the Swedish crown regarding the jurisdiction of Bremen. In addition, he was married to the daughter of Johan Stucke, Sweden's Chancellor at Bremen-Verden. See Modéer, 'Historia, juridik och politik' (n. 14) 101 ff, and the references therein.

[16] See Klaus Luig, 'Conring, das deutsche Recht und die Rechtsgeschichte' in Michael Stolleis (ed.), *Hermann Conring (1606–1681): Beiträge zu Leben und Werk* (1981) 355–98 ff.

served no direct purpose in Stiernhöök's legal dogmatics. However, the fact that legal history was isolated from Stiernhöök's legal argumentation did not mean that legal history was meaningless, or of academic value only for him. At the very least, legal history served for him as a tool to legitimize contemporary national law, in much the same way as the seventeenth-century 'polyhistors' took to creating glorious national pasts. An obvious example is Olaus Rudbeck (1630–1702), who constructed a primeval 'Gothic' Sweden, which he identified with Plato's Atlantis.

Conring and Stiernhöök share a conception of historical legal research as providing a historical legitimacy to law. Here, they continued a centuries-old practice of building on tradition as a legitimation: things were good precisely because they were ancient.[17] As an example, one need only mention medieval canonists, who preferred always to justify their standpoints, no matter how innovative they were, by referring to the Church Fathers; or the widespread use of documents such as the Donation of Constantine or the Pseudo-Isidorian Decretals.

Let us sum up so far. Legal humanism caused a revolution in legal scholarship. It destroyed the authoritative basis of Roman law such as it had come down from the late Middle Ages. Legal humanists not only directed their attention to the 'true' contents of classical Roman law. Some of them also took to explaining the tradition of Roman law through the centuries to their own time. In this process, humanists increasingly understood Roman law as a historical phenomenon, one that changed in time. Space—and the need—for national legal histories emerged. Combining Roman law and local sources of law, *usus modernus pandectarum*, as practical jurisprudence continued the work of the most practical-minded legal humanists.

IV. NINETEENTH CENTURY: THE HISTORICAL SCHOOL

Legal history's next *Blütezeit* began as a result of the nineteenth-century cultural Romanticism. A Prussian aristocrat and professor of the University of Berlin, Friedrich Carl von Savigny, emerged as the main progenitor of the new school of jurisprudence. One can hardly understand Savigny's *Historische Schule* without its surrounding cultural and political climate. After the final demise of the Holy Roman Empire in 1804, Germany no longer formed a political entity. The French Revolution had exerted great influence on German intellectual circles, causing many of them to turn conservative. Culturally, this was the period of Romanticism and

[17] See António Hespanha, 'Legal History and Legal Education' (2004) 4 *Rechtsgeschichte* 41–56, 42 ff.

nationalism at the same time. From the legal point of view, many experts thought that something ought to be done about the large numbers of legal sources inherited from the previous centuries, a corpus which was indeed becoming difficult even for jurists to handle. Whether the solution was codification in French or Austrian style became a hotly debated issue.

Savigny's famous programme appeared in his pamphlet *Vom Beruf unserer Zeit für Gesetzgebung und Rechtswissenschaft* (1814). Savigny compared law with poetry and language: all of them developed freely in the consciousness of the *Volk*. Legal historical investigations were needed to find out how law had developed into the present and which of its parts and institutions were the most endurable and worth preserving. Savigny's own answer was paradoxical: it was the Roman law, such as it had developed through the centuries, which represented the best part of the German legal heritage. The jurists were the carriers of this legal past, and they best knew how to interpret the *Volksgeist* when it came to law. Because law developed organically, codification was not a good idea—at least not in the present state of German law. For Savigny, as it had been for his predecessors in earlier centuries, the strength of legal history lay in its power as tradition: law was good because (or if) it had endured.

Legal history for Savigny did not exist as an approach in itself, but was intimately linked with his view on jurisprudence. In this way, Savigny continued in the vein of the more practical-minded humanists and *usus modernus* scholars. The legal institutions charted out with the help of legal history were to be organized into a coherent 'system', which Savigny wanted to explain in detail in his *System des heutigen römischen Rechts*, left unfinished. The system of Savigny's *Rechtswissenschaft* or 'legal science' was further elaborated by the so-called Pandectists, of which Georg Friedrich von Puchta and Bernhard Windscheid are the best known. The scholarship of the Pandectists functionally replaced the lacking codification by providing Germany with a common framework of private law. Eventually, the Pandectist legal scholarship provided the basis for the German Civil Code of 1900.

The teachings of the Historical School were effectively transmitted to future generations of lawyers. In the Law Faculty of the University of Berlin in 1844, roughly a third of all teaching was devoted to legal history (Roman law and German Legal History). Savigny and his followers otherwise dominated the first half of the nineteenth century (1810–1849) as well. About two thirds of the legal dissertations and *Habilitationsschriften* were historical, and a clear majority of the teachers can also be counted as Savigny's followers.[18] A modern method of legal history based on source criticism developed. In Germany, the link between legal history and positive law remained close until the end of the nineteenth century and the promulgation of the Civil Code in 1900. This is why the discipline still did

---

[18] Rainer Schröder, 'Rechtswissenschaft, Rechtsstudium, Rechtspraxis' in Heinz-Elmar Tenorth (ed.), *Geschichte der Universität Unter den Linden 1810–2010 4: Genese der Disziplinen, Die Konstitution der Universität* (2010) 123–47, 139, 142, 145 ff.

not become institutionalized as an independent discipline in law faculties until the years 1870–1930, paradoxically because legal history lost its immediate significance for contemporary law.[19]

Legal history, as a modern academic subject, grew from the basis of the Germanist branch of the Historical School. The division between Romanists and Germanists was then reproduced all over the Western world as part of the reception of the German way of organizing universities and law schools. Continuing the Romanist tradition, chairs of Roman law were established in most Western universities. Chairs of 'legal history'—often accompanied with a national epithet ('Spanish', 'Swedish', or 'French')—were founded to continue the Germanist line of research. In this way, the Historical School came to play a decisive role in the formation of legal history as an academic subject everywhere in the Continent, although the ways in which this interest converted into an independent discipline varied.

France came first. From early on, legal historians' primary task was to create a national legal history on the basis of the Napoleonic codes and the reorganization of the State after the Revolution.[20] To take another example from further north, in Sweden, most legal scholarship was influenced by the Savigny School throughout the nineteenth century. The first actual chair of legal history in the University of Uppsala was founded in 1835, although the experiment only lasted two years. From 1866 onwards, a chair of Roman law, legal history, and legal encyclopaedia came to cover both the Romanist and Germanist orientations.[21] In Hungary's main university, the Eötvös Loránd in Budapest, the first chair specializing in legal history ('History of Law and State') was established in 1855, and the first chair in Hungarian legal history in 1872.[22] In Spain, national legal history was a creation of late nineteenth and early twentieth centuries. In 1887, Eduardo de Hinojosa published the first part of the *Historia general del Derecho español*, but was never able to continue the work. The true beginning of Spanish legal history is, then, usually connected to other aspects of de Hinojosa's endeavours, the establishment of the *Centro de Estudios Históricos* in 1910 and the founding of the journal *Anuario del Derecho Español* in 1924.[23] In the Baltic Provinces of the Russian Empire, the influence of the Historical School was felt as well. Legal historians produced their scholarship as professors of 'private law and Roman law' or 'provincial laws', and the chairs of legal history as an independent subject had to wait until the twentieth century.[24]

---

[19] Johannes Liebrecht, 'Rechtsgeschichte' in *Handwörterbuch des europäischen Privatrecht* <http://hwb-eup2009.mpipriv.de/index.php/Rechtsgeschichte> (accessed 27 May 2018).

[20] Jean Hilaire, 'L'approche historique d'un système juridique: L'enjeu français' (1994) 62 *Tijdschrift voor Rechtsgeschiedenis* 1, 35–45, 45 ff.

[21] Carl Frängsmyr, *Uppsala universitet 1852–1916* (2010) 435 ff.

[22] <http://majt.elte.hu/Tanszekek/Majt/International/Deutsch.htm> (accessed 27 May 2018).

[23] Santos M. Coronas González, *Manual de Historia del Derecho Español* (1996) 29–31 ff.

[24] In Estonia's national university at Tarto, the Chair of Estonian legal History was founded in 1927: see Toomas Hiio and Helmut Piirimäe, *Universitas Tartuensis 1632–2007* (2007) 348–59 ff.

In many cases, the impact of the Historical School fell well short of what Savigny probably would have wished. Friedrich Carl von Bunge, the towering figure in Baltic legal scholarship in the nineteenth century, for instance, was Savigny's follower— at least in principle. In practice, he did not quite follow Savigny's programme so slavishly as to construct new rules on the basis of those established as enduring through historical investigation. In fact, Bunge constructed his famed Baltic Civil Code on the basis of empirical studies on contemporary judicial practice.[25] Much the same can be said of most other continental countries as well: Savigny's intended ties between history and norms began to loosen in the second half of the nineteenth century, if they had ever even existed. The heritage of the Historical School nevertheless persisted in the continental law faculty curricula: history was—and has been ever since—considered essential for the self-understanding of an educated jurist.

The emancipation of legal history also meant that its *raison d'être* changed. No longer could legal history base its existence on providing an overall, ancient legitimation, or concrete sources for contemporary law. Historically interested *usus modernus* scholars had done the former, and the Historical School had done both. The late nineteenth and early twentieth centuries, however, were radically changing the political system of the European continent and the Western countries culturally close to it. Democratization was well on its way and was closely linked to the supremacy of parliamentary statutes as a legal source.[26]

The nineteenth century was also the decisive period of legal modernization, which is closely linked to what Max Weber called the 'rationalization' of Western law. For Gerhard Dilcher, the Historical School fundamentally represented the trend towards rationalization. For Savignyan Romanists or 'Pandectists', legal history per se was not central; instead, it served to provide materials for systematizing the law in the nineteenth century. Unlike the representatives of the *usus modernus*, and not interested in building a direct historical continuum with them, the Romanists built directly on ancient law. The 'Romanticism' of the Historical School was less typical for Romanists than for the Germanist branch of the Historical School, the representatives of which, because of the nature of their enterprise, needed to build their teaching on a more heterogeneous array of mostly medieval law.

Accelerating social change was the order of the day, and law needed to follow suit. Despite the large impact of German legal scholarship, Germany's dispersed political structure protracted statutory development which could only start after

---

[25] The Code was to endure from 1865 until the end of the Second World War in 1945. On the relationship of Bunge's scholarship to the Historical School, see Marju Luts, *Juhuslik ja isamaaline: F. G. v. Bunge provintsiaalõigusteadus* (2001).

[26] Since this chapter does not deal with the common law world, it will not dwell on common law any longer. Suffice it to say that an analogous movement towards legal positivism emerged there too: American formalism, the rise of the statute-based administrative law, and the American codification movement are examples of this.

the unification in 1871. Legal history, therefore, remained in the service of legal science longer than in many other parts of the continent. The Civil Code started the process in France: in 1807, Napoleon founded a professorial chair on 'the history of legislation', which was to be in responsible for presenting 'a tableau of various civil and criminal codes, political institutions, and public law adopted successively by other people down to the Napoleonic Code'.[27] Towards the end of the century, new fields of law, such as administrative law and labour law, emerged in Europe to meet the needs of the new social state, and even codes were not considered to be perpetual any more. In this intellectual climate, the best legal history could do was to accommodate. It could present the contemporary statutory legal system as the culmination of a historical development. The method of legal history evolved into 'histories of legal dogmatics', *Dogmengeschichte*, which concentrated on showing the development of law as an evolution of legal constructions and institutions, statutory texts, and theories about them. Archival studies or cultural contexts of law were less important. Legal history, concentrating on written laws and legal theories, now exposed the different phases through which legal history had passed in order to reach the present. This was the legal history of the modern nation-state *par excellence*, based on an evolutionary, historicist idea of law as something which was culturally and socially contingent.[28]

Although national histories and legal histories dominated the nineteenth century, this is not the full story. Following Hegel's philosophy of history, Eduard Gans was the first to publish a work on 'universal' legal history.[29] Joseph Unger's book on the universal history of marriage law[30] followed Gans' model. The idea of universal legal history was, to some extent, revived in the early twentieth century,[31] not least due to the impact of Oswald Spengler[32] and Arnold Toynbee's universalizing history writing. None of these, however, posed a great threat to the prevailing paradigm of national legal history.[33] Universalism was, however, barely reflected in legal history at that point: a curious exception is William Seagle's *Quest for Law* (1941, translated into German as *Weltgeschichte des Rechts* in 1951).

[27] Cited in Donald Kelley, *Historians and the Law in Postrevolutionary France* (1984) 49 ff.

[28] On Enlightenment-inspired, historicist historical writing, see F. R. Ankersmit, 'Historicism: An Attempt at Synthesis' (1995) 34 *History and Theory* 3, 143–61 ff.

[29] *Das Erbrecht in Weltgeschichtlicher Entwickelung* [History of the Law of Inheritance in the Development of World History, 1834]. To be sure, attempts at universal history had begun much earlier. On universal history writing in sixteenth-century France (François Hotman, La Popelinière, Nicolas Vignier, and Estienne Pasquier), see Zachary Sayre Schiffman, 'An Anatomy of the Historical Revolution in Renaissance France' (1989) 42 *Renaissance Quarterly* 3, 507–33 ff.

[30] *Die Ehe in ihrer weltgeschichtlicher Entwicklung* (1850).

[31] See Josef Kohler, 'Rechtsphilosophie und Universalrechtsgeschichte' in Franz von Holzendorf, Josef Kohler (eds.), *Enzyklopädie der Rechtswissenschaft* (1904) 1–69 ff.

[32] See e.g., Oswald Spengler, *Der Untergang des Abendlandes: Umrisse einer Morphologie der Weltgeschichte* (1918, 1922); and Arnold Toynbee, *A Study of History* (1934–1961).

[33] See Johann Braun's foreword to his edition of Eduard Gans, *Naturrecht und Universalrechtsgeschichte: Vorlesungen nach G. W. H. Hegel* (2005) XLIX–L ff.

v. The Present and the Future
of Legal History

After the Second World War, new methodological alternatives started to appear on the scene of continental legal history. Three tendencies, simultaneous in part, characterize post-Second World War legal history. First, the prevailing paradigm of national positivism was starting to appear less and less satisfactory, and the national boundaries were no longer the most obvious framework of study. This was surely connected to the post-war critique against legal positivism in general. Transnational legal history gained momentum soon after the Second World War as European legal history, or as a history of *ius commune*, in the works of the Italian Francesco Calasso and the Germans Paul Koschaker, Franz Wieacker, and Helmut Coing.[34] In the background of their efforts, it is often noted, was the wish to do something to repair the European unity, badly torn apart by the world wars, by showing how much Europeans had in common. This led to the foundation of the Max Planck Institute for European Legal History in Frankfurt in 1964. A major research centre in the field, the Institute produced a series of remarkable works on the history of European private law in the 1970s and 1980s.[35] A similar line of research has been continued ever since, not least by Reinhard Zimmermann, whose *Law of Obligations* (1992), and Manlio Bellomo's *The Common Legal Past of Europe, 1000–1800* (1995), are the most recent grand monuments of the school.

European legal history was a remarkable leap out of the national framework, but it was by no means the final word on the internationalization of legal history. European legal history has been criticized for defining Europe narrowly and for only concentrating on the continent's heartlands. Since the master narrative of European legal history is constructed on the basis of learned law or *ius commune*, it is essentially a story, which begins in medieval Italy with its glossators and commentators, continues to the sixteenth-century France and the Humanist School, and then proceeds to the Netherlands with its Elegant School of the seventeenth and eighteenth centuries, only to land safely in nineteenth-century Germany and the Pandectist School, the culmination of European legal history.[36] Because this story is

---

[34] It may be added, however, that transnational legal history had already appeared in the 1920s, when the history of Spanish colonial law (*Derecho indiano*) emerged in the works of the Argentinian historian Ricardo Levene. *Derecho indiano* then came to form an important part of the common understanding of Latin American legal historians. On the creation of *Derecho indiano* as a discipline, see Thomas Duve and Heikki Pihlajamäki, 'Introduction: New Horizons of *Derecho Indiano*' in Thomas Duve, Heikki Pihlajamäki (eds.), *New Horizons of Spanish Colonial Law: Contributions to Transnational Early Modern Legal History* (2015) 1–8 ff.

[35] See in particular Helmut Coing (ed.), *Handbuch der Quellen und Literatur der neueren europäischen Privatrechtsgeschichte I–III* (C. H. Beck 1973–1988).

[36] See Douglas Osler, 'The Myth of European Legal History' (1997) 16 *Rechtshistorisches Journal* 393–410 ff.

based on innovations of legal scholarship, European legal history in its traditional *ius commune* form leaves little space for national variations or legal practice. For this reason, large tracts of the Continent—such as the Nordic countries, Eastern Europe, or even the Iberian Peninsula—do not appear in standard text books of European legal history. Lately, the Europe of legal history has remarkably expanded.[37] Perhaps not surprisingly, the expansion of European legal history roughly follows that of Europe as a political entity.

Moreover, the temporal emphases of legal history changed. Even in the nineteenth century, legal historians still followed the German models and were primarily interested in ancient Rome (if they were Romanistically oriented) or medieval law (if they were of a more Germanist bent). From the 1950s onwards, competing interests clearly began to move from the margins to the centre. Franz Wieacker's 'private law of the modern period' was an early example of moving the temporal interest to newer times and adding a cultural approach to the *Dogmengeschichte*.[38] Similarly in Sweden, Stig Jägerskiöld published studies on seventeenth-century national legal history, basing his work on archival studies on court records.[39] In Germany, the National Socialist past came under scrutiny and the sub-discipline of contemporary legal history (*juristische Zeitgeschichte*) emerged.[40]

Politics, as well, had an impact on legal history. The 1960s—and especially 1968—was one of the great turning points, with tremendous social upheavals and political protests across the globe. In the social and historical sciences, different versions of leftist social, cultural, and economic views emerged. In the 1970s, legal history also opened itself up to new methodologies which challenged the *Dogmengeschichte* even more and could now be converted into a tool of critique.

German legal history had soon regained its pre-war leading position in continental legal history, and many of the leading continental scholars in the 1970s and 1980s were Germans. Students of Sten Gagnér, of Swedish origin and the legal history professor at the University of München, played a prominent role in the methodological reform of German legal history: suffice it to mention Michael Stolleis (history of public law and the law of National Socialist Germany) and Joachim Rückert (Savigny and the Historical School, contemporary legal history). German scholars were, however, no longer the only ones exerting influence on other continental scholarly circles. Parallel to the German discussions, the American

---

[37] As a recent example, see Serge Dauchy, Georges Martyn, Anthony Musson, Heikki Pihlajamäki, Alain Wijffels (eds.), *The Formation and Transmission of Western Legal Tradition: 150 Books that Made the Law in the Age of Printing* (2016).

[38] Franz Wieacker, *Privatrechtsgeschichte der Neuzeit* (1952).

[39] Stig Jägerskiöld, *Studier rörande receptionen av främmande rätt i Sverige under den yngre landslagens tid* (1963).

[40] For an excellent overview, see Joachim Rückert, 'Zeitgeschichte des Rechts: Aufgaben und Leistungen zwischen Geschichte, Rechtswissenschaft, Sozialwissenschaften und Soziologie' (1998) 115 *Zeitschrift für Savigny-Stiftung, Germanistische Abteilung* 1–85 ff.

Critical Legal Studies movement was closely followed in many parts of continental Europe, particularly in Scandinavia. Many of the most prominent CLS scholars were legal historians, people such as Morton J. Horwitz and Robert Gordon. New areas of research entered the scene, such as the history of public and criminal law. Theoretical debates on the role and methods of legal history ensued. Even though politically the most critical voices on the European continent were not legal historians, but rather legal theorists, the methods of legal history changed as well. Archival studies and social science methods spread fast, and even comparative methods were making inroads into legal history. As to the latter, Raoul van Caenegem (Belgium) should be given particular mention, and for legal historians approaching methods of social science, one could mention, for instance, Francisco de Tomás y Valiente (Spain), António Hespanha (Portugal), Bernhard Schnapper (France), Ditlev Tamm (Denmark), Kjell Åke Modéer (Sverige), and Heikki Ylikangas (Finland).

The changes of the 1970s and 1980s, however, did not amount to a new common approach or a methodological revolution anywhere on the continent. Instead, the loss of faith in master narratives resulted in a variety of methodologies, amongst which the most conservative ones also still figured.[41] In many countries the main stream of legal history remained in very much the same positivist mode in which it had been since the late nineteenth century. The *Dogmengeschichte* is still alive and well. In addition, a new demand for national legal histories arose in nations which were previously behind the Iron Curtain.

During the twenty-first century, the newest trends have been towards comparative, global, and transnational legal histories. Despite important exceptions (some mentioned above), it seems that the methodological reforms have advanced more rapidly in small countries (such as Belgium, the Netherlands, and the Nordic countries) than in the large ones. Comparative legal history is a good example of this. In its classical nineteenth-century form, comparative law first emerged to meet the needs of national law-drafters. It did not make sense for each and every law-maker to invent every wheel anew; instead, it was better to look systematically into what colleagues abroad had done. Comparative law was the tool with which to do this. At the end of the nineteenth century and beginning of the twentieth, comparative law was institutionalized in the form of academic chairs, societies, and journals.[42] In legal history, as explained above, national orientation remained mainstream for much longer, and the regional legal histories of Europe and Spanish America did not seriously threaten national legal histories until the 1990s. After the fall of the Berlin Wall, the end of the Cold War, and the expansion of the European Union, a clear break with the national orientation in legal history came under high

---

[41] See Thomas Duve, 'German Legal History: National Traditions and Transnational Perspectives' (2014) 22 *Rechtsgeschichte* 16–48, 24–5 ff.

[42] On the history of comparative law, see the articles in Mathias Reimann, Reinhard Zimmermann (eds.), *The Oxford Handbook of Comparative Law* (2006).

demand. Again, this was not only a phenomenon of law but seen across the field of social sciences. Legal historians, however, quickly picked up the trend. Comparative anthologies of different subjects began to appear—even works in which different legal orders were systematically compared from the historical point of view. During the 1990s and 2000s, comparative legal history became institutionalized. Chairs of comparative legal history were established, and an international society (The European Society of Comparative Legal History), together with a journal (*Comparative Legal History*), were founded in 2010 and 2013, respectively.

As was previously noted, the nineteenth and early twentieth centuries had already produced universal histories. Universal and global histories have been an influential strand of research again during the past few decades. The modern giants, Immanuel Wallerstein and Ferdinand Braudel as the biggest names, however, have very little left of the earlier universal historians' developmental optimism. The period after Europe's crazy year of 1989, then, has been a tremendous boost to universal, or global, history writing.[43]

Unsurprisingly, globalization theories have necessarily affected legal history as well, and European legal history no longer suffices for ambitious legal historians. Global legal history can, however, mean different things.[44] First, it can point to an aspiration to create one grand narrative of global law. Although no single authoritative work on global legal history has yet appeared, many scholars have begun to prepare the ground. Theoretical contributions to the theme already exist, and text books have started to appear. Whether the authors of these works themselves actually believe in the possibility of writing one grand narrative is another thing. It is difficult to see why such a global history would be impossible, if we are able to write national or European legal histories. Second, global legal history can mean concentrating on globalizing tendencies in law, of the kind which can readily be found in the fields of mercantile law, constitutional law, procedural law, and human rights. Little exists, so far, in this category—at least if we look for a truly global, not just a European or 'Western', coverage. Third, in practice global legal history often means simply breaking away from a Eurocentric world view. Growing amounts of scholarship appear nowadays on themes such as Chinese legal history, African legal history, and different colonial legal histories.[45] Some fields of law have aggressively expanding histories which no longer limit themselves to national or European playing fields. Ever since Martti Koskenniemi's ground-breaking *Gentle Civilizer of Nations* (1996), international law has been practically dominated by

---

[43] See, e.g., Jürgen Osterhammel, *The Transformation of the World: A Global History of the Nineteenth Century* (2014).

[44] See, e.g., Thomas Duve, 'Global Legal History: A Methodological Approach' in *Oxford Handbooks Online—Law*, January 2017, DOI: 10.1093/oxfordhb/9780199935352.013.25; and Ditlev Tamm, *Retshistorie: Danmark—Europa—Globale perspektiver* (Jurist- og Økonomforbundets Forlag 2005).

[45] See, e.g., Teemu Ruskola, *Legal Orientalism: China, The United States, and Modern Law* (2013).

the historical approach, and historians of commercial law also have adopted the global law approach.

How do comparative, European, global, and transnational legal histories relate to each other? European and global approaches are not problematic at all, as they are simply geographical definitions. Comparative legal history, then, is much more vexing as a concept, and in fact the term is beginning to seem increasingly outdated. In its classical form, that is, systematic comparisons of national laws A and B, comparative law and comparative legal history are reactions or corrections to the legal paradigm of the nation state. Understood in this way, comparative scholarship depends on the national paradigm of the nineteenth century.

Classical comparisons are nevertheless sometimes needed. If, however, it is defined only in terms of classical comparison, comparative legal history hardly meets modern demands. The classical comparisons simply do not capture but a small fraction of all such non-national phenomena which merit studying, such as legal transfers, transnational rules, and global influences. They are better caught in the net of what could be called transnational legal history, in which national and regional legal phenomena are observed in international and transnational contexts. Transnational legal history would not, of course, exclude national frameworks altogether (any more than it would dismiss European or global legal histories). On the contrary, national legal histories ought to remain high on the agenda of legal historians—after all, national states have been prime producers of normative material since the early modern period. Nevertheless, even national legal histories need to be understood in larger transnational contexts. Writing a history of legal codification of any country without referring to the transnational context of the codification movement would today not only be inadequate, it would be misleading and false. Thus, dividing legal history into 'regular' and 'comparative' is beginning to seem forced, and it may be more fruitful to think that all legal history should be fundamentally transnational. And if all legal history is transnational, why not simply call it legal history? Profound changes in methodology do not all need to be incorporated into the names of the disciplines.

In today's legal history, all epochs and world regions seem to be present at the same time. This reminds one once again of Rosa's modernization theory, based on the idea of social acceleration. Since legal history had become an object of knowledge in its own right, the research interests of legal historians have multiplied at an accelerating pace. To legal humanism's ancient interests, medieval legal history was added in the seventeenth and eighteenth centuries. When legal history as an academic discipline emerged in the late nineteenth and early twentieth centuries, scholars all but abandoned these themes. New ones, however, kept popping up. Regional histories, such as Spanish colonial law and European legal history; nineteenth- and soon twentieth-century national legal histories; all the way up to contemporary legal history, which brings the past practically to the present. As a legacy of the nineteenth century, most of the continental legal history until the early twentieth century was the history of private law and the history of ancient private law at that. After the Second World War, all possible lacunae have been filled, and we have the history of all sorts of public, international, criminal, and procedural law. As methods go, the late nineteenth-century *Dogmengeschichte* and the history of statutory law still exist, but they have been complemented with precious archival work. In addition to them, legal historians have adopted all other possible methods from neighbouring sciences: the critical legal histories of the early 1970s are doing well in all of their forms, and the different ways of conceiving law's transnational nature are thriving. All epochs, all subjects, all geographical areas are present at the same time, while a huge synthesis still awaits its author.

Does legal history gain in importance as the pace of legal change accelerates? It is simple to answer this question affirmatively. Modern legal history, more than anything, is about explaining legal change in its cultural, political, social, and transnational contexts. If those changes multiply, the need for scholarly explanations increases as well.

BIBLIOGRAPHY

Govaert C. J. J. van den Bergh, *Die holländische elegante Schule: ein Beitrag zur Geschichte von Humanismus und Rechtswissenschaft in den Niederlanden 1500–1800* (Vittorio Klostermann, 2002)

Helmut Coing, *Handbuch der Quellen und Literatur der neueren europäischen Privatrechtsgeschichte I–III* (C. H. Beck, 1973–1988)

Thomas Duve, 'Global Legal History: A Methodological Approach' in *Oxford Handbooks Online—Law*, January 2017, DOI: 10.1093/oxfordhb/9780199935352.013.25

Paul J. du Plessis, John W. Cairns (eds.), *Reassessing Legal Humanism and its Claims: Petere Fontes?* (Edinburgh University Press, 2016)

António Hespanha, 'Legal History and Legal Education' (2004) 4 *Rechtsgeschichte* 41–56, 42

Donald R. Kelley, 'The Rise of Legal History in the Renaissance' (1970) 9 *History and Theory* 2, 174–94

Donald R. Kelley, *Historians and the Law in Postrevolutionary France* (Princeton University Press, 1984)

Paul Koschaker, *Europa und das römische Recht* (Biederstein, 1947)

Douglas J. Osler, 'The Myth of European Legal History' (1997) 16 *Rechtshistorisches Journal* 393–410

Joachim Rückert, 'Zeitgeschichte des Rechts: Aufgaben und Leistungen zwischen Geschichte, echtswissenschaft, Sozialwissenschaften und Soziologie' (1998) 115 *Zeitschrift für Savigny-Stiftung, Germanistische Abteilung* 1–85

Michael Stolleis, (ed.), *Hermann Conring (1606–1681): Beiträge zu Leben und Werk* (Duncker & Humblot, 1981)

Franz Wieacker, *Privatrechtsgeschichte der Neuzeit* (Vandenhoeck & Ruprecht, 1952)

CHAPTER 39

JEWISH LAW

STEVEN WILF*

JEWISH law is often considered a law without an army or a navy. It fits within the vexed category of what has been called 'law without nations' where there is no coercive apparatus to enforce norms. Robert Cover's *Nomos and Narrative* famously celebrates the absence of coercion through prison and corporal punishment in diasporic Jewish law and instead—in his romantic reading of the past—claimed that social cohesion created its normative sinews.[1] In contrast, proponents of deploying Jewish law as the grounding for a modern Jewish state, such as the late Israel Supreme Court Justice Menachem Elon, have argued that throughout the diaspora until the eighteenth-century Jewish courts with significant policing power operated in Christian and Islamic lands. While these two historiographic narratives are clearly at odds, they share one fundamental presumption. Jewish law is identified as autonomous.

This chapter takes the opposite approach. It argues that Jewish law's distinctive nature is constructed from the ancient to the modern period in the midst of a complex, competing world of plural legalism. It will examine how Jewish law appropriated, resisted, and oddly conserved, sometimes while claiming as its own, other forms of legalism—such as Roman or modern law—to create the impression of being a legal *other*. Jewish law is a complex legal system, spanning millennia

* Anthony J. Smits Professor of Global Commerce, Law School, University of Connecticut.

[1] Robert Cover, 'Nomos and Narrative' in Martha Minow, Michael Ryan, Austin Sarat (eds.), *Narrative, Violence and the Law: The Essays of Robert Cover* (1992) 95–172 ff. Menachem Elon, *Jewish Law: History, Sources, Principles*, trans. Bernard Auerbach, Melvin J. Sykes 4 vols. (1994) I: 1–46 ff.

from its Biblical origins to the present, emerging from creative centres across the globe, punctuated by a vast *corpus juris* including monumental compilations and codes, and including over 300,000 known *responsa* (legal decisions). It is nearly impossible to characterize such a diverse legal tradition.[2]

One constant for over two thousand years has been interaction with other legalities that contributed to Jewish law's vitality through appropriation. How was this accomplished? Such influences are not always clear. Residing next to other, more powerful forms of legalism, ironically, has led to obscuring external contributions to Judaic legal culture. Law, in general, often assumes a conservative guise. But minorities operating in scattered diasporic communities must be particularly vigilant about guarding its distinctiveness. Jewish law, not surprisingly, rendered veiled and even expressly denied appropriating as part of a broader strategy for claiming authenticity. Rabbinic figures—for these were the architects of Jewish legalism through the millennia prior to the modern period—policed the boundaries of Jewish law by relying almost exclusively on internal precedent and carefully scrutinizing attempts to transplant norms from outside the traditional corpus of Jewish law. Concerned about substantive law, they proved much less circumspect about adopting external forms for the legible embodiment of law.

How should Jewish law be constructed? Was it primarily oral or written, case law or codes, directed towards judgments or flexible, somewhat abstract principles? And does the genre of legal writing ultimately matter? Jewish law's denial of importing substantive law is intimately connected to its radical mutation into multiple borrowed material forms. This chapter's major focus, then, is tracing the shape-shifting, chimeric legal embodiment of Jewish law because—as is argued here—materiality arrayed for caching legal norms fundamentally shapes its very essence. The question of what *is* Jewish law continues to our own time. I conclude with two contemporary trends in Jewish law: the stalled—perhaps even failed—attempt to deploy Jewish law as a foundational legal system for the modern Israeli state and, secondly, the project of mining traditional religious Jewish law for its non-parochial, broadly conceptual jurisprudential principles.

Prior to embarking on a remarkably brief survey of a long and complex legal history, a few preliminary points about scope are in order. This chapter cannot aspire to being comprehensive, and indeed it remains almost impossible to follow Jewish law's historical arc for the past 2,000 years from the seedtime of Talmudic reasoning in late antiquity until the present. Jewish law is notable for its claims to a continuous tradition lasting millennia and its broad scope—including civil, criminal, family, and ceremonial law. As befits a volume about the significance

---

[2] On Jewish law generally, see N. S Hecht, B. S. Jackson, et al. (eds.), *An Introduction to the History and Sources of Jewish Law* (1996); Ephraim E. Urbach (ed.), trans. Raphael Posner, *The Halakhah: Its Sources and Development* (1986); Christine Hayes (ed.), *The Cambridge Companion to Judaism and Law* (2017); Elon (n. 1).

of historical analysis, it is directed in particular to non-specialists in the field who are intrigued by the legal structures of a jurisprudential system that had its beginnings outside of Western legal culture even though much of its own past has been intimately entangled with Western law. But to begin, a few caveats.

First, much of Jewish legal history remains directed towards intellectual history, with only a few studies addressing the operation of Jewish courts and law as a functioning system of law in its social settings. The focus of this chapter therefore will be about the development of the *interpretive* power of Jewish law and how that discourse has been shaped by its historical context. Jewish law, or *halacha*, as it is known in Hebrew, has been seen by its practitioners as a seamless conversation spanning generations and geographic locations. But its interpretive clout has been rooted in sharp debates and competing schools of legal analysis, including antinomian elements rejecting normative authority.

The chapter, secondly, begins only with the rise of rabbinic legal discourse at the beginning of the Common Era. Of course, Jewish law is rooted in Biblical law. Its statutes apply not only to communities in the broad Biblical period from the emergence of the Patriarchs through the establishment of a monarchy in the Land of Israel, but also are seen as exercising binding authority in contemporary *halacha* as a kind of foundational higher law. Nevertheless, Biblical laws are often apodictic (absolute mandatory injunctions such as the commandments of the Decalogue) or casuistic (case law that is conditioned upon a set of circumstances such as goring an ox). In both of these instances, legal norms are rarely justified. As one scholar explains, Biblical law 'does not seem to have been a highly developed autonomous field or a "system" in any real sense of the word'. Our inquiry thus begins with the rabbinic turn to interpretation.

Christine Hayes identified Jewish law as constitutive.[3] But constitutive of what? In the eleventh century, the preeminent legal authority Saadia Gaon famously remarked that Jews are 'a people by virtue of its laws (*shara'i*)'. *Halacha* is constitutive of national identity, of local communities, of individuals engaged in a plethora of legal practices from religious ceremonies to economic relations in the sphere of property and markets. For Jews, law has been a cultural centrepiece. Twentieth-century theologian Abraham Joshua Heschel referred to the 'pan-halachacism' of Jewish law as a unifying force. But the geographic metaphor for this chapter is not law as an island. It is law as a borderland—porous, a site of appropriation and exchange, a liminal space positioned between one culture and another, and a boundary policed by those who seek to identify practices that stand in opposition to core Jewish legal norms. In sum, it is the locus of legal pluralism. And the shifting of this interpretive frontier is the particular narrative of Jewish law that this essay seeks to articulate.

---

[3] Ibid., 2–3 ff.

I. A LAW OF SIGNIFICANT CONTENTION

Towards the end of the Second Temple period (roughly 530 BC to AD 70), Jewish law emerged as a counterpoint to a Roman imperium which often relied upon local provincial elites for governance of a vast empire. As Hayim Lapin has shown, the rabbinic elite fashioned an alternative form of dispute resolution through courts grounded by indigenous legal traditions. Jews, moreover, employed law to stake a claim to antiquity in order to establish status in a Greco-Roman world that understood the age of a civilization as a mark of distinction. Philo of Alexandria (25 BC to AD 50) described Moses as a foundational legislator (νομοθέτης) like Plato or Solon. According to Philo, Mosaic Law is in harmony with nature, preserved through the reverence of Jews, and unique insofar as it preceded the formation of a state rather than being created in the midst of ordinary political governance. The valorization of law as a centrepiece of Jewish culture emerges in the midst of jostling over the role of the Jews as a subject people. Legitimizing claims to sovereignty are ever present.

The acrimonious legal debates of the first century AD must be seen in this context. On one side was the paradigm of the Republic of Zeno, the Stoic ideal that law was universal and lived according to basic common precepts of nature that fostered virtue. The Pharisees, a political and religious movement appearing in this period, argued that Jewish law embodied moral principles derived from its divine origins while remaining flexible and capable of responding to social change. The cornerstone of this approach was their radical claim that the oral law was an authoritative legal tradition parallel to the Written Law contained in scripture. Sadducees and the followers of the Qumran (Dead Sea) sect denied the authority of unwritten sources.[4] Nevertheless, the Pharisees insisted oral law could be traced to the revelation at Sinai and transmitted from Moses to rabbinic figures as an unbroken chain. Taught by masters who emulated Moses, it demanded that students serve teachers and form associations in order to memorize legal teachings. The emphasis upon oral law reflected Greek notions that non-written law was superior to its written counterpart because it was a living law, more flexible and reflecting practical wisdom (*phronesis*).[5]

Drawing upon the cultural heartland of the Greco-Roman world, Pharisees and their rabbinic heirs in late antiquity often adopted the tropes of Greek law. Their

---

[4] Aharon Shemesh, *Halakhah in the Making: The Development of Jewish Law from Qumran to the Rabbis* (2009).

[5] Christine Hayes, *What's Divine about Divine Law: Early Perspectives* (2015) 66–70 ff. On the role of oral law in rabbinic thinking, see Elizabeth Shanks Alexander, 'Orality of Rabbinic Writing', in Charlotte Elisheva Fonrobert, Martin S. Jaffee (eds.), *The Cambridge Companion to The Talmud and Rabbinic Literature* (2007) 38–57 ff.

judges wrapped themselves in the Jewish *tallit*, a cloak with ritual fringes serving as a mnemonic device for the commandments, much as Roman philosophers imitated the Greeks by donning the *pallium*. Legal discourse might take place at meals resembling the *symposium*. And the focus upon oratory, so significant for Greek legal culture, was matched by a Jewish predilection to integrative narratives, often of the rabbis themselves, interlaced with strictly legal content. Oral law as an equal to *lex scripta* was a radical assertion of authority. It was a kind of rewritten scripture in much the same way as Deuteronomy was a second Torah or the Book of Jubilees might be seen as a second edition of part of the existing Biblical canon. In this sense, Jewish law is a series of second acts.

Perhaps no second act is as impressive the Mishnah, whose name itself means a repetition of the law. Although a century and a half intervened between the destruction of Judaism's central cultic center at Jerusalem in AD 70 and the compilation of the Mishnah, the dispossession of Palestinian Jewry must be seen as the backdrop for the making of the Mishnah—the first formal code created to summarize existing *halacha*.[6] This period was marked by the Great Revolt (AD 66–73), the War of Quietus (c. AD 115) against the Emperor Trajan which had devastating consequences for diaspora Jewry, and the Bar Kokhba Rebellion (AD 132–135) resulting in the long-term unravelling of a Jewish presence in the land of Israel. The rabbinic tradition that three thousand laws disappeared in the period of mourning for Moses (B. Temurah 16a) reflects their own sense that law was elusive, fragile, and needed to be reconstructed in a disenchanted world distant from direct revelation.[7]

The Mishnah (*c.* AD 200) was a redaction of oral legal traditions which might be lost in this time of crisis. While the text of the Mishnah contains numerous mnemonic devices attesting to earlier strata of remembered law, it shifted Judaism's terrain from a Greek memorized oral law to a Roman written codified law. This revolutionary act by Judah Ha-Nasi, the Mishnah's redactor, transgressed the prohibition against committing oral *halacha* to writing. It was only justified by virtue of the fear that the law would be forgotten. As the very end of the Mishnah's first tractate, *Berakhot*, states 'they made void your Law [making the oral written] because it was a time to work for the Lord'. By this definition, the Mishnah was an emergency code (*Ausnahmezustand*).

The Mishnah simply may have been intended to provide a working text for didactic purposes. But it soon emerged as a full-fledged authoritative code. It provided a systematic ordering of norms into six major categories dealing with subjects as disparate as agricultural laws, holidays, family law, torts, and ritual law.

---

[6] Dov Zlotnick, *The Iron Pillar: Mishnah—Redaction, Form, and Intent* (1988).

[7] On the importance of trauma as a feature of Jewish law, see David Weiss Halivni, *Revelation Restored: Divine Writ and Critical Responses* (1997); Steven Wilf, *The Law before the Law* (2008); William Kolbrener, *The Last Rabbi: Joseph Soloveitchik and the Talmudic Tradition* (2016) 109–11 ff.

Codification reflected a deeply logical structure that supplanted the Torah—whose narrative was determined by a divine lawgiver—with a collection of clearly defined areas of law. Centuries later, Maimonides, in his commentary to the Mishnah, would state that the beauty of the language, its organization, and succinct presentation would ensure the Mishnah's primacy at the core of Jewish legal discourse. But what does that say about the rupture emerging between the written law and a newly written oral law? In every way, this determination to provide order reflected a sense of dislocation, disenchantment—the loss of the divine voice of prophecy and a determination to establish a mooring for legal norms in a deeply disordered political landscape. Although the Mishnah was compiled in the land of Israel, it may still be considered a diasporic legal document since it materialized after the dislocations of the Jewish War, the rebellions under Trajan, and the destruction of the scribal center of Jerusalem. It was composed in the Galilean hinterland of Jewish culture.

While the Mishnah became the canonical text for a new legalism emerging in the beginning of the third century, oral law was similarly embedded in institutions. During the period of the Pharisees and the early rabbinic movement, transmission often cantered in households. It took place through the personal relationship between master and disciple or within the framework of conviviality among legal scholars. Yet the presence of a new *lex scripta* in the form of the Mishnah may have provided the impetus for the appearance of academies—and with academies arose competing schools of legal analysis. The preeminence of the academy is embodied in the Talmudic phrase 'the Torah is only acquired in a group' (B. Berakhot 63b). In the third generation of rabbinic scholars, for example, R. Ishmael and R. Akiva, whose legal pedagogy was so influential that they were called 'the fathers of the world' (B. Shekalim 8a) were identified with competing approaches: the former preferred the plain reading of the Mishnaic statute while the latter embraced wide-ranging, even vertiginous, creative meanings.

The great nineteenth-century German legal historian Rudolf von Jhering famously stated that Rome conquered the world with law by transforming it into science. In many ways, the legalism of the rabbinic movement did not have to become the cornerstone of a religious association. But the originally marginal, somewhat loosely connected, and fractured *equipe* of Jewish legal scholars conquered Judaism with law by turning law into a matter of contention. The Talmud (completed *c.* 500 AD) was a commentary on the Mishnah and followed its basic structure of the division into six orders depending upon subjects such as agriculture or torts. Yet the Talmud is much more than an explanation of the written Mishnah text. Later generations would call it 'the sea of Talmud', which captures both its vastness and its tempests. The Talmud is composed of sixty-three tractates spread out over what today comprises over 6,000 folio pages. But it is telling that the unit most familiar to students is the *sugya*—the legal argument which is set off by the debate itself without any sort of signposting, such as a section heading. The unending debates of the Talmud—the constant squalls roiling the Talmudic sea—identified competing positions as if the final prescriptive norm was less significant than the legal reasoning. The scholar Resh Lakish, for example, was admiringly said to be able to raise twenty-four objections to every law issued by his close associate and brother-in-law R. Yoḥanan (B. Bava Metzia 84a). Certainly the deeply associative text of the Talmud, intent upon capturing and identifying the differences among rabbinic law teachers, seems more like a pedagogic work than strictly a legal code.[8]

The Talmud, written in the *lingua franca* of Aramaic, therefore retained a sense of orality through its debates as juxtaposed to the more elegant and terse codified text of the Mishnah that was composed in Hebrew. In a sense, then, the Talmud's orality reinforced the notion of the Mishnah's increasing function as a *lex scripta*. The academies of the Talmudic scholars were seen as a successor to the Sanhedrin—the high court of the Second Temple period.[9] Before the destruction of Jerusalem (AD 70), this court of seventy members met in the Temple's Chamber of Hewn Stones. Its authority rested upon this unique location and was paralleled by the written law embodied in the Temple's preservation of a Torah scroll intended to serve as the ultimate arbiter where there might be disputes among scribes over the exact form of the text.

After the destruction of Jerusalem and the Bar Kokhba Revolt, the Sanhedrin migrated to the Galilee and began a circuit of shifting locations in Galilean towns. The Sanhedrin's authority waned even as academies emerged with their teachers claiming a similar status to judges. The failure in 363 of a project under the Emperor Julian to rebuild the Temple—and return the Sanhedrin to the site that was the foundation of its authority—and the subsequent imperial suppression of the court under Julian's successors rendered the Sanhedrin an irrelevant institution. The academies did not simply preserve existing law, they undertook a rule-making function. Rabbinic power rested upon their role as the authoritative interpreter of Jewish law. The legal scholar—not the priest, not the prophet, nor the landed aristocracy—was accorded cultural primacy. In the Talmudic period, various legal scholars developed hermeneutic methods such as deploying *a fortiori* logic, looking at surplusage in the original Biblical texts, and analogous rules for similar cases. Hillel developed seven hermeneutic rules, and R. Ishmael thirteen rules. In many ways, these techniques resemble dynamic statutory interpretation with Biblical passages serving as the core statutory texts.

These forms of analysis were a hallmark of Talmudic legalism. They merged with those employed in exegesis—and therefore legal and non-legal methods

---

[8] See Jeffrey L. Rubenstein, *The Culture of the Babylonian Talmud* (2003) 147–51 on the Talmudic legacy of debate. Steven D. Fraade discusses rabbinic multi-vocal approaches in 'Rabbinic Polysemy and Pluralism Revisited: Between Praxis and Thematization' (2007) 31 *Association for Jewish Studies* 31–27 ff.

[9] The use of a highly procedural and performative depiction of capital punishment reflects a rabbinic assertion of judicial powers, see Beth A. Berkowitz, *Execution and Invention: Death Penalty Discourses in Early Rabbinic and Christian Cultures* (2006) 17–19 ff.

for interrogating Biblical texts were part of the same cultural project. For the purposes of *halacha*, the written law was composed solely of the initial five books of the Bible—not the entire Biblical corpus—and these were considered the sole indisputable source for legal precedent. One more rabbinic technique, appropriating a Biblical passage purely for rhetorical purposes even when it was commonly agreed that the law was a novel invention of Talmudic scholars (*asmakhta*), highlights the relationship of the oral law to its written law moorings. On one hand, *lex scripta* was a touchstone of legitimacy and a disciplining limitation for constructing new norms. On the other hand, hermeneutic and rhetorical devices permitted creative, often strikingly innovative departures from precedent. Codification further bolstered rabbinic claims to legitimacy. Insufficient scholarly attention has been directed towards comparing the mechanisms of Jewish and Roman law codification. Yet the Talmud materialized in the shadow of two major Roman law codifications promoted by emperors situated in Constantinople: the Codex Theodosius (AD 438) and what would later come to be known as the Justinian *Corpus Iuris Civilis* (AD 534). The Roman legal codes, like the Talmud, included a variety of texts and moral rhetoric that suggested their roles as a sort of legal archive preserving precedent.

Halacha as a hegemonic legalism emerged, I have argued, alongside an unquestionably legitimate, self-assured Roman law. By contrast, Jewish law's uneasy relationship with centralizing institutions often led to competing claims to authority. During the Geonic period (589–1034) there was an attempt to reconstruct legal authority around Babylonian academies located in the prosperous lands located between the Tigris and Euphrates rivers in what is now modern day Iraq. The Geonim relied upon their inheritance of the Babylonian Talmud for authority. Yet a second Talmud, the Talmud of the Land of Israel, compiled about a century earlier, was composed of strands from a variety of Galilean sources. It incorporated more material on agricultural laws than its Babylonian counterpart. What is important, however, is to consider how Geonim needed to respond to a counterclaim to authority launched by the scholars of the Land of Israel with Tiberias on the Sea of Galilee as their cultural epicentre. Tiberias was the home of the Masoretic tradition—which sought to ensure that the written text of the Torah was preserved in its most perfect state and to standardize its pronunciation. At the same time—much as the oral and written laws rubbed shoulders in pre-destruction Jerusalem—an animated visual culture emerged in late antiquity which included synagogue art, midrash—or literary exegetical, non-legal material, and evocative and eidetic poetry (*piyyutim*). This luxurious cultural constellation developing in Tiberias rested upon images at least as much as upon nomos.

Tiberias had the further advantages of being situated in the Land of Israel. Its citizens could assert the legacy of once having served as the home to the major academy of R. Yoḥanan and Resh Lakish (*c.* AD 250) (B. Bava Metzia 117a). The Geonic turn to the primacy of legal analysis bolstered their power in response to the Tiberian tradition. Two new major academies, Sura and Pumbedita, cemented the link between the legalism of the Babylonian Talmud and a flourishing seat of authority for the Geonim. In about 890, Hai Gaon directed the relocation of Pumbedita to Baghdad as Babylonian Jewry became increasingly urbanized. Since the Abbasids moved the Muslim caliphate's capital to Baghdad in AD 762, the nearby academies found themselves in the heartland of an Islamic empire stretching across the Middle East through North Africa and extending into the Iberian Peninsula. Under Muslim rule, communications became more efficient. Such an improvement, combined with claims of preeminent legal authority, led to the formation of a new robust and varied literature of responsa as Geonic authorities responded to inquiries from across the diaspora.

Two important legal genres emerged during the Geonic period: responsa and halachic digests. Responsa were replies to legal queries from the entire Jewish diaspora. Examples of legal decisions rendered in particular cases through written texts might be found throughout the Talmud. Yet it was under the Geonim that a full-fledged responsa literature fully developed. The Geonim envisioned themselves as a central authority in matters of law. While they operated within the context of academies, it was critical to extend their influence through a vast communicative network. Responsa were often terse, addressing specific cases, and pragmatic. But it was also the sort of epistolary jurisprudence that was deployed by Muslims through the *fatwa*. As evidenced by the Cairo Geniza, Cairo was the place where responsa were disseminated to scattered communities in the West. We can imagine medieval merchants carrying missives tucked alongside goods as they crossed borders, making their way through shipping lanes in the Mediterranean Sea as they disseminated law forged in the sophisticated metropole of the Caliphate.

The halachic digest was an innovation of the Geonic period. This new genre was akin to the modern legal treatise. More importantly, it resembled the contemporary Islamic *mukhtaṣar* of abridged legal manuals.[10] It was a departure from the Talmudic model by eschewing associative reasoning for focus on a particular legal topic such as the law of succession, bailments, or torts. Unlike the Mishnah, it was not a collective work. Individual authorship was highlighted by an introduction.[11] While the Babylonian Talmud was granted preeminence within the great Geonic academies, Saadia Gaon (died AD 942), perhaps the most famous of the Geonim, began to draw upon the Talmud of the Land of Israel as well—thereby uniting a variety legal traditions as the Geonim asserted its claim to legal pre-eminence.[12]

Saadia's legalism was shaped by religious disputes. The emergence and rapid growth of the Karaite movement challenged the authority of the oral law. Reawakening

---

[10] Lena Salaymeh, *The Beginnings of Islamic Law: Late Antique Islamicate Legal Traditions* (2016) 160–1 ff.

[11] Robert Brody, *Saʿadyah Gaon* (2013) 123–32 ff.

[12] For some examples of Geonic legal innovation, see Robert Brody, *The Geonim of Babylonia and the Shaping of Medieval Jewish Culture* (1998) 62–4 ff.

old legal controversies from the first century AD, the Karaites argued that the very notion of oral law implied that the divine written law was imperfect. Moreover, the late formation of oral law, the variation in its forms, and its contentious debates over legal issues demonstrated to the Karaites that rabbinic legalism was unsound. Saadia responded by asserting that the written law is incomprehensible on its own terms without an explanation. Divine revelation at Sinai, he argued, had to simultaneously reveal dual forms of Torah, written and oral, at the same moment.

The controversy between Karaite and Rabbinic Jews shared remarkable similarity to the contemporary *fiqh* debates in Muslim law over whether the precedential material of law—such as the Qur'an in Islam or, if we were to apply this to rabbinic Jews, the Pentateuch—can be separated from the theoretical and methodological means of deriving legal rules. Law needed reason. Yet this claim led Saadia to a parallel problem: what are reason's limits? Saadia distinguished between rational and auditory laws—those statutes only obeyed because they are pronounced by a creator. Revelation, Saadia suggests, is necessary to guide reason as it seeks precision. Everyone might agree through reason that homicide is a crime. Yet what punishment, for example, should be meted out for violating this norm? Laws of Sabbath and festivals—ceremonial laws—may be reasonable even if not based purely upon *ratio*. Both revealed law and reasoned law need to assist each other. Saadia blurred the boundaries between philosophy and law, between the written and unwritten Torah, and between what constitutes precedent and the power of the human mind in constructing a natural law.[13] In this regard, he might be considered as taking the initial steps toward the sophisticated Jewish jurisprudence that would flourish in the Middle Ages.

II. CODIFICATION AND LOCALISM

Following in Saadia's footsteps, Iberian Jewish Aristotelian philosopher and apologetic historian David Ibn Dawud in 1161 completed *Sefer Ha-Qabbalah*, a work responding to the Karaite critique by tracing an unbroken chain of legal tradition from Moses to his own day. Towards the end of the book there is a remarkable story about four Geonic scholars who journeyed by ship in the Mediterranean on their way to a convocation for Torah study. The four were captured by Muslim raiders and ransomed to communities along the coast. While the ultimate fate of one of the legal scholars remains unknown, the other three ended up settling

---

[13] Jonathan Jacobs, *Law, Reason, and Morality in Medieval Jewish Philosophy* (2010) 187 ff.

in Alexandria, Maghreb, and Córdoba. Each founded an academy of their own. The Córdoba scholar, significantly called R. Moses as if even his name suggested a role as progenitor of law, married into a prominent local family, raised many disciples, and turned Córdoba into a major centre for legal study.[14] Putting aside the question of the historicity of the Tale of the Four Captives, this story captures with photographic precision the decisive moment when Jewish law was wrestled from the centralizing control of the Babylonian Geonim and spread throughout the western Mediterranean. By the end of the tenth century, Córdoba was already on its way to becoming an autonomous Islamic cultural capital—separated from caliphate control from the east—and to beginning a remarkable culture renaissance. Not surprisingly, Jewish law paralleled this development by declaring its independence from the Geonic academies.

Legal codes and customary law are often considered antipodes. Codes are systematic, ordered into discrete subsections of law, generally succinct, and constructed with architectural sensibilities by lawgivers. Local customs are discursive, poorly defined, ambiguous and uncertain, and rest on nothing more than a vague sense of *consensus omnium*. Yet both codes and custom were instruments to pry away legal authority from the Geonim. Beyond the need for regional autonomy, the legal literature of the Geonim itself demanded codification. Digests covered only limited areas of law and left numerous lacunae. Responsa were scattered, directed towards an immediate problem, and not always collected for use by posterity.

The challenge of codification was assumed by R. Isaac Alfasi (1013–1103), who headed an Iberian academy in Lucena. His code—or as we shall see really a quasi-code—*Sefer Ha-Halakhot*, is organized precisely in the order of the Talmudic tractates and begins each section with the relevant Talmudic passages. Alfasi's code was considered an abridged form of the Talmud—a kind of pedagogic outline of existing Talmudic law. It included a pastiche of narrative material alongside discussions of law. Clearly, *Sefer Ha-Halakhot* as a genre stands halfway between a compendium of earlier legal documents and a full-fledged code. Grounding Jewish law in its Talmudic sources provided authority beyond Geonic texts, but it also ignored the broader philosophical issues raised by Saadia.

If Iberian Jewry was simply seeking familiarity with basic legal norms without having to wade through the immense expanse of Talmud, then Alfasi's code might have been sufficient. But Jewish law was in competition with philosophical thinking. Aristotelian and neo-Platonic systems imported from Arabic texts had made the Iberian Peninsula a hothouse of intellectual speculation. Indeed, as this essay argues, Jewish law's evolution was perched precariously between two forms of *otherness*. First, there was the model of different genres and conceptions of legalism such as Greek orality, Roman codes, and Islamic responsa. But, secondly, there were

---

[14] Abraham ibn Daud, *Sefer Ha-Qabbalah: The Book of Tradition*, trans. Gerson D. Cohen (1967) 63–5 ff.

competing claims to authority within the Jewish tradition. Sometimes these rivals were alternative geographic centres, sometimes different interpretive schools as seen during the Talmudic period, sometimes Jewish groups like the Sadducees or the Karaites who valorized written law as opposed to oral law, and—as we shall see in later periods—sometimes even those embracing Jewish antinomian traditions. In the case of Iberian Jewry, Alfasi's fairly black letter legal treatise must have seemed inadequate against the elegant clarity of philosophy.

Moses Maimonides (1135–1204) agreed that Alfasi's work was not quite a code. In a comment explaining why he would compose what would become perhaps the most important code of Jewish law, he asserted that his people are 'lacking a true and comprehensive book of its laws'.[15] Maimonides described how historical 'vicissitudes' have placed legal knowledge at risk. Partly, Maimonides is drawing upon the precedent of Judah Ha-Nasi, who wrote the Mishnah because so much learning was being forgotten. He called his own code *Mishneh Torah*, perhaps as a gesture to the composition of the Mishnah. Yet it also reflected Maimonides fashioning of his own biography. Religiously zealous Berber invaders from North Africa, the Almohads, conquered Córdoba in 1148. The Almohads effectively ended Córdoba's golden age and threatened religious minorities. Maimonides fled to southern Spain, then to Fez in North Africa. Finally, he settled in Fustat, Egypt. Maimonides is known as a legalist, a physician who wrote a number of medical treatises, a political leader of the Egyptian community, the creator of a lucid Hebrew writing style, and a polymath. But he was also a refugee. His first act as a public figure was to redeem captives who had been seized by Crusaders. Maimonidean codification is a response to the imperfection of historical contingency—his 'vicissitudes'—that threatened to break a chain of oral tradition. It created a code composed in beautifully unadorned Mishnaic Hebrew and followed subject matter categories independent of the underlying Talmudic texts. Intended to serve Jews regardless of locality, the Maimonidean code sought a more perfect embodiment of law.[16]

Maimonides ensured that the God of the philosophers might also be the God of the lawyers. In one decisive code, he swept away the clutter of Talmudic discursive and associative readings. Maimonides ambitiously outlined his codification project: 'In brief, a person will not need to have recourse to any other work to ascertain any of the laws of Israel. This work is intended as a compendium of the entire oral law, including the enactments, customs, and decrees instituted from the days of Moses, our teacher until the redaction of the Talmud as expounded for us by the Geonim in all the works composed by them since the completion of the Talmud (Mishneh Torah, Introduction).' Maimonides used his editorial perch to

---

[15] Moshe Halbertal, *Maimonides: Life and Thought* (2014) 89 ff.
[16] Isadore Twersky, *Introduction to the Code of Maimonides* (*Mishneh Torah*) (1980) 1–96 ff. David Gillis, *Reading Maimonides' Mishneh Torah* (2015) 12–79 ff.

select dispositive laws and ignored minority or contradictory approaches. Geonic opinions were sometimes cast aside. On occasion the code even deviates from an accepted Talmudic norm. Most strikingly, unlike the Mishnah, all law was presented anonymously. In contrast to both the Mishnah and the Talmud, where scholars were readily named and—perhaps as a remnant of a disciple tradition—served as the object of narratives, there was only the single nameless voice of a unified Jewish law. Such novel innovations prompted Moshe Halbertal to ask whether the *Mishneh Torah* is a *summa* of existing law or whether it serves a more radical task of creating a new *halacha*.[17]

Maimonides envisioned a Jewish law liberated from contention. Yet almost as soon as it was published the code's claim to absolute authority became a matter of controversy. A number of fierce critics launched attacks, most notably R. Abraham ben David of Posquières. In defense of positions taken in the *Mishnah Torah*, a collection of medieval commentators called the armour bearers (*nosei keilim*) were written that are now published surrounding the Maimonidean text. No matter how much he sought to do so, Maimonides could not escape the traditional contention of Jewish law. Maimonides may have had an inkling of the polemic literature his code would spawn, for he begins with a list of 613 precepts from the written law that form the foundation for the oral law.[18]

This introduction is based on a passage in the Talmud (B. Makkot 23b), which states that there are 613 Biblical commandments. The 365 negative precepts correspond to the number of days in the year, while the 248 positive laws reflect the number of limbs and organs in the body. It is unclear to what extent this enumeration was accepted in the Talmud as a normative principle, and indeed it was seen by some later commentators as simply a rhetorical embellishment. Nevertheless, the idea of being able to calculate and order the number of laws proved to be a powerful organizing tool for framing a broad, often discursive legal system. Throughout the Middle Ages, a number of scholars, most notably Maimonides, but also Saadia Gaon, Moses ben Jacob of Coucy, and Isaac of Corbeil, whose list was a poetic enumeration of laws in verse, created their own accounting of laws. These often differed from each other—the critique of Nachmanides' critique of Maimonides' enumeration is particularly significant. What was intended as a widely accepted outline soon itself became a matter of contention.

The ordering of 613 precepts has the making of a proto-code. In modern times codification has often been regarded as an enterprise that settles law. Attempting to construct a definitive list of Biblical legislation meant posing a number of difficult questions. Were these laws as stated intended for future generations or were they merely immediate commands? Aaron of Barcelona followed closely Maimonides's enumeration. Nevertheless, he adds additional explanations intended to identify

---

[17] M. Halbertal (n. 15) 164–96 ff.
[18] Yitzḥak Heinemann, *Ta'amei HaMitzvot beSifrut Yisrael* (1953).

the rationale behind each law. For example, the law forbidding a husband from travelling away from his wife during the first year of marriage is based on the rational reason that 'he has to appropriate her image and all her activity into the heart until every act of another woman and everything about her will become for one's nature something alien' (*Sefer Ha-Chinuch*, 582). Placing law in the philosophical skein of natural reason portrayed legal rules as rational—but also prompted a larger debate about law's fundamental purpose.

If Iberian Jewry chose the path of codification with a philosophical bent, then Ashkenazi Jewry in the Rhine valley might be said to have turned towards customary, local law. 'Custom trumps legislation' was a phrase deployed by Ashkenazi Jews rather than their Spanish counterparts. Moreover, Ashkenazi Jews did not seek codes as substitutes for the untidy discursive logic of the Talmud, but instead sought to augment the Talmud with commentaries such as those of Rashi (Shlomo Yitzhak of Troyes, 1040–1105), and two generations of medieval commentators from the twelfth century to the middle of the fifteenth century called the Tosafot. These works often deployed dialectics and—when rendering legal decisions—commonly included opposing opinions.[19] Tosafot legal literary culture might be considered a river culture—extending all the way from York in England through the river ways of France, the Rhine valley, and Regensburg on the Danube, to as far east as Prague. Perhaps the close association with merchants contributed to its favouring customary, deeply contextual local legalism. Trade routes provided a means for circulating manuscripts and ideas—replacing the Mediterranean hinterland of the Geonim.[20]

We do not know enough about manuscript production in medieval Jewry. There were no Jewish scribes like those in Christendom supported by wealthy monastic lands and funded through bequests from a landed aristocracy. Periodic dislocation through exile or war and the destruction of manuscripts such as occurred during the 1242 Paris burning of the Talmud must have taken a toll on the diffusion of legal knowledge. Twentieth-century scholar Marc-Alain Ouaknin brilliantly argued that the burnings of the Talmud returned the work to the status of an oral text.[21] But the Tosafists already followed traditions of a more fluid legal discourse through what was essentially a glossator tradition. Just as their Christian contemporaries produced terse canon and Roman commentaries as marginalia so did Jewish scholars of the Talmud. Yet while the *dissensiones*, as they were called by medieval Roman lawyers, sought to bridge contradictions, clashing Tosafists often highlighted their own disagreements with Rashi and with each other.

---

[19] Ephraim Kanarfogel, *Peering through the Lattices: Mystical, Magical, and Pietistic Dimensions in the Tosafot Period* (2000) 118–22 ff.

[20] On community localism, see Joseph Isaac Lifshitz, *Rabbi Meir of Rothenburg and the Foundation of Jewish Political Thought* (2016) 54–82 ff. On manuscript culture, see Talya Fishman, *Becoming the People of the Talmud: Oral Torah as Written Tradition in Medieval Jewish Cultures* (2011) 176–88 ff.

[21] Marc-Alain Ouaknin, *Le Livre brûlé* (1984) 23–45 ff.

iii. Modernity and the Jewish Return to Legal History

With the expulsion of Iberian Jewry from Spain (1492) and the forced conversion of the Jews of Portugal (1497), a new set of vicissitudes—to return to Maimonides' phrase—disrupted legal transmission. Iberian Jews were in diverse lands, largely in Italy, North Africa, Turkey, and the Near East. Competing cultural frameworks were deployed in the midst of this crisis. Jewish mysticism—which would become a cornerstone of sixteenth-century Safed, philosophical, and historical understandings of the meaning of exile such as expounded in the works of Ibn Verga (c. 1520), and a return to pious individual behaviour as proposed by Jacob ibn Ḥabib's En Yaaqov, suggested alternative approaches to traditional legalism. In the midst of this cultural struggle,[22] Joseph Karo, a Spanish exile who lived first in Salonika and later in Safed, published a new code, the Shulchan Arukh (1522) with a rationale stated in his introduction similar to that used by Judah ha-Nasi and Maimonides to justify committing to writing a largely oral law: the wisdom of the wise might perish. In many ways, the Shulchan Arukh was a work of synthesis. In fact, Karo's work was even more wedded to written legalism than earlier works for it was published at the beginning of print technology. To derive legal rules, it convened an imaginary court composed of Alfasi, Jacob ben Asher (born 1269) who wrote the Arba'ah Turim, a Spanish commentary, and the Maimonidean code. Envisioning this invented three judge panel as casting a ballot on every normative issue, Karo decided simply to follow the majority. Perhaps as a way of synthesizing Ashkenazi customary law and Sephardic codified law, the Shulchan Arukh permits a greater latitude for custom. A major set of emendations were made to the original by R. Moses Isserles (1520–1572) from Cracow. This turned the code into a source for both Sephardi and Ashkenazi Jewry. If Maimonides sought to create a unitary legal text, Karo instead fashioned a more pluralistic code around which different sorts of legal actors could coalesce.[23]

Unlike the Maimonidean code, the Shulchan Arukh only included religious, family (which in the early modern period was still largely a confessional domain), and ceremonial law—and ignored the rich legal traditions in torts, contracts, property, and criminal law. Behind the unification was hidden a major split: increasingly, as early nineteenth-century German Jewish philosopher

---

[22] For a sense of competing Jewish ideologies among sixteenth-century Sephardi exiles, see Jeremy Cohen, *Solomon Ibn Verga, Shevet Yehudah, and the Jewish-Christian Encounter* (2017) 150–82 ff; and Marjorie Lehman, *The En Yaaqov: Jacob ibn Ḥabib's Search for Faith in the Talmudic Corpus* (2012) 1–15 ff.

[23] Isadore Twersky, *Studies in Jewish Law and Philosophy* (1982) 130–47 ff; R. J. Z. Werblowsky, *Joseph Karo: Lawyer and Mystic* (1962) 6–7 ff.

Moses Mendelssohn suggested, law belonged largely to the state. Religion, as a confessional framework, should address a personal relationship to the divine, not outward performance of norms. Mendelssohn's thinking became the kernel of the Reform movement's antinomianism. A second strand of German philosophical analysis identified Jews with the corporeal, the historically contingent, and the archaic.[24] In particular, law was the object of this critique. Abraham Geiger, a founder of *Wissenschaft des Judentums*, the movement for an academic study of Judaism, sought to show that law's imperfections arose from the fact that it was an historical artifact.

Ironically, nineteenth-century Orthodox Jewish legalists adopted the German distaste for historical contingency and commonly argued that Jewish Law was a meta-historical construction, eternal, and deeply logical. It was not just German antipathy to a corporeal legal corpus with a bricolage of archaic rules, but the German philosophical technology of dialecticism that inspired the turn towards jurisprudence. In what must be one of the most unlikely of all Jewish legal appropriations, Hegelian dialectics from Berlin permeated traditional provincial yeshivas in the cultural hinterland of Eastern Europe. In the late nineteenth century, various schools emerged, including in particular the Brisk school at the leading yeshiva of Volozhin, which embarked upon the project of constructing an analytic jurisprudence of *halacha*. For Brisk, Jewish law was dialectic—a series of conceptual constructs that are often broken down into binaries such as those laws where obligations are *in personam* and others where they apply *in rem*. The Brisk approach presumed the existence of a collection of meta-legal principles that explain the underlying reasons why early authorities might take opposing positions. For example, some early jurists considered whether ripened grain ready for harvest should be categorized as immovable property since in a formal sense the stalks were tied to the land while others saw the grain as produce within the context of a harvest and therefore moveable property. Brisk scholars constructed such legal set pieces as classic illustrations of the difference between the meta-principles of formalism and contextualism.[25]

The intellectual ferment in Eastern Europe prompted a demand for legal decisions rendered through abstract analysis rather than relying on custom as embodied by the decision of a local authority. Moreover, print culture provided a vehicle to provide guidance to the religious Jewish circles beyond elite academies.

---

[24] Michael Mack, *German Idealism and the Jew: The Inner Anti-Semitism of Philosophy and German-Jewish Responses* (2003) 23–41 ff; and Jonathan M. Hess, *Germans, Jews, and the Claims of Modernity* (2002) 1–23 ff; Leora Batnitzky, Yonatan Brafman, *Jewish Legal Theories: Writing on State, Religion, and Morality* (forthcoming) provides primary texts from all facets of modern Jewish legal theory.

[25] Yitzhak Adler, *Iyun be-Lomdut: Biurim ve-Hidushim be-Sugyot ve-Shas u-be-Divrei ha-Rishonim* (1989) 113–23 ff. Shai Akiva Wozner, 'Avi Derech he-Limud ha-Yeshivatit: R. Hayyim HaLevi Solovietchik me-Brisk', in Benyamin Brown, Nisim Leon (eds.), *Ha-Gedolim: Ishim she-Azivu et penei ha-Yahadut he-Haredit ve-Yisrael* (2017) 152–75 ff.

To address this need, R. Israel Meir Kagan published in 1902 the *Mishnah Brurah*. This code had a much narrower compass than that of Maimonides—and was only directed towards addressing ceremonial or ritual matters.[26] But its most notable feature was the embrace of analytic jurisprudence. If the Orthodox religious milieu was largely envisioning a law tailored fairly strictly to religious dictates, Jewish nationalists, influenced by the nineteenth-century German writings of Friedrich Karl von Savigny, believed that every nation must have its own laws that encompassed its spirit. In 1918, an organization for the revival of Jewish law was founded in Moscow. During the 1920s and 1930s, *Mishpat Ivri*, as the movement came to be known, increasingly directed its efforts to constructing a civil law version of Jewish law updated for modern circumstances, systematically organized, and, most importantly, stripped of its religious elements.

Mishpat Ivri was a utopian movement—part of a broader movement of national rebirth united under Zionism. Was its new attempted codification still part of Jewish law? As Assaf Likhovski writes, distilling legal rules 'from the mass of indigenous social norms, ordering them according to Western categories, codifying them, uprooting them from their social context, and replacing their previous sources of authority with the authority of Western courts were bound, even with the best of intentions, to create something new'.[27] Jewish law was seen as a decolonizing measure. Nevertheless, it took longer for an idealized conception of Jewish law to take root in the new state of Israel founded in 1948 than other aspects of the national rebirth, such as the shaping of the modern Hebrew language.

In 1980, the Knesset enacted the Foundations of Law statute revoking Article 46 from the time of the British Mandate, which required recourse to English law to address any lacunae in Israeli law. Instead, when there is a gap, courts should decide a case 'in light of the principles of freedom, justice, equity, and peace of Israel's heritage'. Jewish governance was much easier as a utopian ideal than as a matter of everyday politics. The *Realpolitik* of a complex security situation and the absorption of a diverse population coming as refugees from post-Holocaust Europe, Muslim countries in the Middle East as these newly post-colonial lands were increasingly inhospitable to those perceived as outsiders, and, eventually, post-Soviet countries made it difficult to establish a coherent, unifying legal regime. Supreme Court justices Aharon Barak and Menachem Elon, a leading proponent of *Mishpat Ivri*, sharply disagreed about the nature of the Foundations of Law statute. Barak's position ultimately proved victorious. Israeli law was interpreted as demanding broad universal principles be applied—and hence encouraged the

---

[26] Michael J. Broyde, Ira Bedzow, *The Codification of Jewish Law and an Introduction to the Jurisprudence of the Mishna Brura* (2014); Haym Soloveitchik, 'Rupture and Reconstruction: The Transformation of Contemporary Orthodoxy' (1994) 28 *Tradition* 64–131 ff.

[27] Assaf Likhovski, *Law and Identity in Mandate Palestine* (2006) 132–48 ff. For an example of codification at work, see Isaac Herzog, *The Main Institutions of Jewish Law*, 2 vols. (1936).

importation of global legal norms—only calling for the reliance on Jewish law as a matter of last resort.[28]

The late twentieth century created a split between two sorts of Jewish law. On one side stood a set of norms possessed by Orthodox Jews with only informal mechanisms for sanctions, largely emphasizing everyday religious life and preoccupied with complex dialectics—the essence of contention. On the other side, *Mishpat Ivri* was intended as official law backed by a state's power, stripped of religious elements and seeking codification to tidy up the muddled corners of a Jewish law that has developed over millennia. Any ordinary observer of these two movements in the middle of the century would have pointed to *Mishpat Ivri* as having the better chance of success. Yet *Mishpat Ivri* was an historical failure. The jurisprudence of *halacha* has proved firmer ground for a renaissance in Jewish legal thinking. The return to Israel did create dense traditional communities which demanded grappling with broad issues of economic law. Diaspora Jews who encountered a rapidly shifting modernity found themselves trying to adapt Jewish law to second generation feminism, gender fluidity, heightened social interaction with non-Jewish neighbours, new technologies, pluralism, and democratic norms of governance.[29] Much of recent Jewish law scholarship has fixated upon the conceptual *legerdemain* of Jewish law and its constant creative reinvention when faced with adaptations to radically different contexts. In this regard, the Brisk traditional jurisprudential legacy oddly has proved much more influential than the codification impulse of Jerusalem's *Mishpat Ivri*. Moreover, the turn to jurisprudence has led to a growing conception of Jewish law *as* law—often with reference in the United States to similarities and difference with American law.

IV. LEGALISM—BECOMING LAW

The presumption for contextual legal historians is that their task is to trace how law responds to social, economic, and political challenges. Sometimes Jewish law is more autonomous (as Cover and Elon have asserted), sometimes more open, permeable, and appropriating (as argued in this chapter). Law is so central to Jewish culture, from the Biblical commandments carted down from Mount Sinai to medieval commentators filling the margins of parchment manuscripts by the rivers of northern Europe, to utopian dreamers who hoped to perform the ultimate

---

[28] Menachem Mautner, *Law and Culture in Israel* (2011) 32–44 ff.
[29] See, e.g., Tamar Ross, *Expanding the Palace of the Torah: Orthodoxy and Feminism* (2004).

act of cultural alchemy in transmuting an ancient religious law into the mode of governance for a modern state, that it has been taken for granted as a persistent and pervasive cornerstone.

Yet this chapter has tried to show that Jewish law is, in fact, a shape-shifter. It constantly changes its form. In one period it might be a list of apodictic laws. In others, however, law can turn into the archetype of a legal master imitated by disciples. It might be expressed by a court like the Sanhedrin. Or it assumes the guise of an inscribed scroll, a comprehensive code and its sharp-elbowed commentaries, the quarrels of the rabbinic academy, an epistolary legalism, philosophical reasons for commandments, or local customs operating against formal norms. In our own times, we have seen Jewish law both as a reworked civil code serving as a Constitutional benchmark for secular Israeli law and the pronouncement of a charismatic religious legal scholars unknowingly influenced by analytic legal philosophy.

The significance of such a list—and it could be much more extensive—is not simply that law changes. Every legal historian knows, as Bernhard Schlink reminds us, that law's progress is a traveller's tale across time where being capsized or captured like Odysseus is more likely than a peaceful journey home. What is important is that Jewish law is always trying to *become* law. It wants to be a first-cousin of Greek law-in-the-heart. It wants to be as settled as a Roman code, as influential to distant brethren as a Muslim *fatwa*, as rational as medieval notions of natural law, as much a part of a tradition as a glossator's notes, as useful as the French *Code Civil*, and as jurisprudentially clever as the Rube Goldberg constructions of a German or American legal academic. Jewish law, in short, is above all about wanting to be law.

The pluralism of legal embodiment—all the different genres smuggled from just beyond its borders for expressing legal thinking—created another kind of pluralism. It made for a *lieu désaccord*, a space of fractured authority where disagreements might occur. Indeed, the one constant thread weaving through the history of Jewish law is contention. And does not every difference render legible Jewish law as it might be (*lex ferenda*), rather than simply what it is?

Bibliography

Shalom Albeck, *Introduction to Jewish Law in Talmudic Times* (Bar Ilan University Press, 2013)

Leora Batnitzky, Yonatan Brafman, *Jewish Legal Theories: Writings on State, Religion, and Morality* (Brandeis University Press, 2018)

Boaz Cohen, *Jewish and Roman Law: A Comparative Study*, 2 vols. (Jewish Theological Seminary Press, 1966)

Robert Cover, 'Nomos and Narrative' in Martha Minow, Michael Ryan, Austin Sarat (eds.), *Narrative, Violence and the Law: The Essays of Robert Cover* (University of Michigan Press, 1992)

David Daube, *Talmudic Law* (Robbins Collection—University of California, Berkeley, 1992)

Menachem Elon, *Jewish Law: History, Sources, Principles*, trans. Auerbach Bernard, Melvin J. Sykes, 4 vols. (Jewish Publication Society, 1994)

Moshe Halbertal, *Maimonides: Life and Thought* (Princeton University Press, 2014)

David Weiss Halivni, *Revelation Restored: Divine Writ and Critical Responses* (Westview Press, 1997)

Christine Hayes, *What's Divine about Divine Law: Early Perspectives* (Princeton University Press, 2015)

Christine Hayes (ed.), *The Cambridge Companion to Judaism and Law* (Cambridge University Press, 2017)

N. S. Hecht, B. S. Jackson, et, al. (eds.), *An Introduction to the History and Sources of Jewish Law* (Oxford University Press, 1996)

Isaac Herzog, *The Main Institutions of Jewish Law*, 2 vols. (Soncino Press, 1936)

Jonathan Jacobs, *Law, Reason, and Morality in Medieval Jewish Philosophy* (Oxford University Press, 2010)

Jacob Katz, *Exclusiveness and Tolerance: Studies in Jewish-Gentile Relations in Medieval and Modern Times* (Oxford University Press, 1961)

Jacob Katz, *Tradition and Crisis: Jewish Society at the End of the Middle Ages* (Oxford University Press, 1993)

Assaf Likhovski, *Law and Identity in Mandate Palestine* (University of North Carolina Press, 2006)

David Novak, *Natural Law in Judaism* (Cambridge University Press, 1998)

Aharon Shemesh, *Halakhah in the Making: The Development of Jewish Law from Qumran to the Rabbis* (University of California Press, 2009)

Haym Soloveitchik, 'Rupture and Reconstruction: The Transformation of Contemporary Orthodoxy' 28 *Tradition* 64–131 (1994)

Isadore Twersky, *Introduction to the Code of Maimonides* (*Mishneh Torah*) (Yale University Press, 1980)

Ephraim Urbach, (ed.), trans. Raphael Posner, *The Halakhah: Its Sources and Development* (Yad le-Talmud, 1986)

Michael Walzer, Menachem Lorberbaum, et al., *The Jewish Political Tradition*, 3 vols. (Princeton University Press, 2003, 2006, and 2018)

Steven Wilf, *The Law before the Law* (Rowman & Littlefield Publishers, 2008)

CHAPTER 40

HISTORICAL RESEARCH ON ISLAMIC LAW

LENA SALAYMEH[*]

I. INTRODUCTION

ISLAMIC law is not a self-evident category of analysis. Defining and understanding the category is a subject of both academic and popular debates. These debates reflect the long history (more than 1400 years), broad geographical expanse, and extensive demographic diversity of the Islamic legal tradition. Muslims (numbering approximately 1.6 billion today) have understood and produced Islamic law in dissimilar and changing ways throughout history. Nevertheless, there is a conventional presumption that Islamic law is the result of Islamic legal hermeneutics anchored in canonical Islamic scriptural texts. There is an additional, less common, presumption that Islamic law is generated by an 'Islamic state', even when the state does not rely on Islamic legal hermeneutics.[1] Historical

* Associate Professor, Tel Aviv Law. For responding to my informal survey about historical research on Islamic law, I thank Guy Burak, Amr Osman, David Powers, SherAli Tareen, and Luke Yarbrough. For comments on this piece, I thank Guy Burak, Rhiannon Graybill, Amr Osman, SherAli Tareen, and the participants in a Tel Aviv Law workshop dedicated to this volume.

[1] I have differentiated between Islamic jurisprudence and Muslim legalities, defining the latter as legal hermeneutics anchored in a state or other legal system that may or may not be Islamic and with a population that may or may not be majority Muslim. Lena Salaymeh, 'Commodifying "Islamic Law" in the U.S. Legal Academy' (2014) 63 *Journal of Legal Education* 640 ff.

research on Islamic law inevitably confronts these (and other) challenges of defining Islamic law, by including and excluding historical evidence in ways that construct meanings for 'Islamic law'. In this chapter, I suggest some ways in which the subjects and the methods of historical research on Islamic law contribute to defining Islamic law today.

This chapter centres on historical research about Islamic law in the Western academy, which has increased significantly in recent years. I concentrate on contemporary scholarship in English, although I also relied on (somewhat outdated) surveys of scholarship in German and Spanish.[2] The dynamics motivating historical legal research on Islamic law in the Muslim world are beyond the scope of this chapter.[3] Although this survey of recent historical research on Islamic law is broad, I emphasize some of the key political questions and methodological conundrums that frame this body of scholarship. Moreover, this chapter is not comprehensive: scholarship on the early modern and modern histories of Islamic law and scholarship on Islamic legal history outside the Arab world are under-represented.

II. POLITICAL DYNAMICS

While there are multiple motivations for historical research on Islamic law in the Western academy, political dynamics deserve particular attention. Undoubtedly, contemporary geo-politics—principally the prevalent and incorrect presumption that Westerners are in a civilizational conflict with Muslims—provokes much scholarly (and non-scholarly) interest in the history of Islamic law. In addition, because anti-Muslim propaganda exploits the mythology of 'sharia law' (sic), Islamophobia influences—directly and indirectly—much scholarship on Islamic law.[4] These circumstances (the 'green threat' and Islamophobia) operate in both

---

[2] See Hilmar Kruger, 'The Study of Islamic Law in Germany: A Review of Recent Nooks on Islamic law' (2000–2001) 15 *Journal of Law and Religion* 303 ff; Delfina Serrano Ruano, 'Spanish Research on Islamic Law, 1990–1999' (2000) 15 *Journal of Law and Religion* 331 ff. A useful, though outdated, bibliography is Laila Al-Zwaini and Rudolph Peters, *A Bibliography of Islamic Law, 1980–1993* (1994).

[3] For an overview of a bit of this scholarship, see Chibli Mallat, 'Islamic Law Research in the Twentieth-Century Middle East (1998) 8 *Asian Research Trends* 109 ff.

[4] I distinguish between the propaganda terms 'sharia' or 'sharia law' and the Arabic terms 'sharī'ah' (divine law) and 'fiqh' (juristic interpretations of divine law). Islamic law is a category that includes fiqh. On these terminological distinctions, see Salaymeh (n. 1); Lena Salaymeh, 'Propaganda, Politics, and Profiteering: Islamic Law in the Contemporary U.S.' (2014) *Jadaliyya*, <http://www.jadaliyya.com/Details/31276/Propaganda,-Politics,-and-Profiteering-Islamic-Law-in-the-Contemporary-United-States> (accessed 1 March 2018).

the background and the foreground of Islamic legal studies, as scholars react to and against these contemporary dynamics in their historical research. Just as Western colonialism shaped nineteenth- and twentieth-century scholarship on Islamic law, so too does Western neo-imperialism shape contemporary Islamic legal studies.[5] This is why critiques of Orientalism, which extend beyond the work of Edward Said into other theoretical approaches (including subaltern and critical secularism theory), remain productive bases for analysing historical research on Islamic law.[6] Notably, critiques of Orientalist scholarship are not directed at scholars, but rather at scholarly methods.[7] As opposed to identity, it is the power dynamics and methods of Western scholarship and Islamic objects of study that significantly shape historical research on Islamic law.

Since Islam plays a unique role in Western self-conceptualizations and mythologies, historical research on Islamic law reflects the broad, dialogical process by which the West defines itself as the opposite of its ultimate Other, Islam.[8] Historical research on Islamic law has the tendency to characterize Western law and Islamic law as opposing ideal-types. Conventional assumptions presume that Western law is liberal, democratic, restrained by the rule of law, facilitative of capitalism, and secular. Correspondingly, conventional assumptions misconstrue Islamic law as conservative, despotic, irrational, limiting of economic growth, and 'religious'.

First, because Westerners celebrate liberalism as a 'superior' ideology, identifying or negating the presumed illiberalism of Islamic law is a common preoccupation of historical scholarship. Accordingly, contemporary Islamic law scholarship anachronistically investigates modern, liberal notions, including freedom, rights, and equality; much of the historical scholarship on the Islamic legal status of non-Muslims, women, and slaves falls under this category.[9] In other words, Islamic legal

---

[5] Léon Buskens, Baudouin Dupret, 'The Invention of Islamic Law: A History of Western Studies of Islamic Normativity and Their Spread in the Orient', in François Pouillon, Jean-Claude Vatin (eds.), *After Orientalism: Critical Perspectives on Western Agency and Eastern Re-appropriations* (2015) 31–47 ff.; Wael B. Hallaq, 'The Quest for Origins or Doctrine? Islamic Legal Studies as Colonialist Discourse' (2002) 2 *U.C.L.A. Journal of Islamic and Near Eastern Law* 1 ff.; David S. Powers, 'Orientalism, Colonialism, and Legal History: The Attack on Muslim Family Endowments in Algeria and India' (1989) 31 *Comparative Studies in Society and History* 535 ff.; John Strawson, 'Encountering Islamic Law', in *Critical Legal Conference Held in New College* (1993), <http://www.iium.edu.my/deed/lawbase/jsrps.html> (accessed 1 March 2018); John Strawson, 'Islamic law and English texts' (1995) 6 *Law and Critique* 21 ff.

[6] On subaltern theory, see Ranajit Guha (ed.), *A Subaltern Studies Reader, 1986–1995* (1997). On critical secularism theory, see Talal Asad, *Genealogies of Religion* (1993); David Scott, Charles Hirschkind (eds.), *Powers of the Secular Modern* (2006).

[7] Lena Salaymeh, 'Imperialism, not Imperialists: The 'Good Orientalist' and Nineteenth-Century German Orientalism' (forthcoming).

[8] Said made this point in Edward Said, *Orientalism* (1978). For a recent engagement with liberalism's construction of Islam as the Other, see Joseph A. Massad, *Islam in Liberalism* (2015).

[9] On liberal assumptions about women and Islamic law, see Lena Salaymeh, 'Imperialist Feminism and Islamic Law', *Hawwa* (forthcoming).

historiography often imposes modern socio-legal concepts, particularly modern rights discourse (human, animal, environmental, gender, minority, and LGBTIQ+). Second, because Westerners celebrate the modern nation-state and liberal democracies as the ideal forms of government, important themes of historical research are Islamic governance and codification (or 'modernization') of Islamic law. Here again, the prevailing assumption is that premodern Islamic states could not have developed or nurtured modern, liberal nation-states.

Third, because Westerners perceive the 'rule of law' as limiting violence, much contemporary scholarship on Islamic law scrutinizes ostensibly 'harsh' criminal or warfare laws. The historical normativity of Islamic law is effaced by the implicit tendency to compare Islamic legal history with idealized notions about contemporary Western law. Fourth, because Western capitalism is presumed to explain the West's ascendance, many studies of Islamic legal history investigate property relations (especially trusts) and some commercial laws, which are presumed to have limited capital development in the Muslim world.[10] Fifth, because Western law is understood uncritically as secular, much scholarship on Islamic legal history emphasizes its 'religious' dimensions, despite the anachronism of applying the notion of religion to premodern history.[11] Religion is not a transhistorical category, but rather the modern construct of secularism; religion has no clear or consistent meaning. Misinterpreting the Islamic legal tradition as 'religious' has far-reaching limitations on Islamic legal historiography.

The interrelated and broad contemporary notions of liberalism, democracy, the rule of law, capitalism, and secularism often skew historical legal research on Islamic law by projecting anachronistic concepts. Since it is not possible to find these contemporary concepts in the historical record, much scholarship contributes to the widespread misconception that Islamic law is deficient or that it is always and already historical, such that it is incompatible with modernity. Put differently, because anachronistic notions dominate historical research on Islamic law, Islamic law tends to be perceived as a historical artefact.

---

[10] On Islamic laws related to trusts (*awqāf*), see Peter C. Hennigan, *The Birth of a Legal Institution: The Formation of the Waqf in Third-Century A.H. Ḥanafī Legal Discourse* (2004); Baber Johansen, *The Islamic Law on Land Tax and Rent: The Peasants' Loss of Property Rights as Interpreted in the Hanafite Legal Literature of the Mamluk and Ottoman Periods* (1988); Powers (n. 5); Richard van Leeuwen, *Waqfs and Urban Structures: The Case of Ottoman Damascus* (1999); Farhat J. Ziadeh, 'Property Rights in the Middle East: From Traditional Law to Modern Codes' (1993) 8 *Arab Law Quarterly* 3 ff. On the problematic claim that Islamic law prevented capitalism, see Timur Kuran, *The Long Divergence: How Islamic Law Held Back the Middle East* (2013).

[11] On the limitations of applying 'religion' to non-Western traditions and premodern history, see Asad (n. 6). On the anachronism of the category of 'religion' in Islamic legal historiography, see Lena Salaymeh, 'Taxing Citizens: Socio-Legal Constructions of Late Antique Muslim Identity' (2016) 23 *Islamic Law and Society* 333 ff.

III. Overview of Contemporary Historical Research

Although Islamic law is commonly viewed as a historical relic, the predominant methods for researching Islamic law are not historical. For the most part, research on Islamic legal history is conducted from the perspectives of textual studies (typically, Near Eastern studies), social history, anthropology, or political science, depending on the period of study. Generally, textual studies dominate late antique and medieval historiography, social history dominates early modern historiography, and anthropology and political science dominate modern historiography. The prominence of particular disciplines within each historical period reflects that scholars who specialize in each period usually receive dissimilar disciplinary trainings in the Western academy. In turn, the prevalence of certain disciplines within specific periods of historical research tends to frame each historical period within a limited set of questions. By way of example, the dominance of textual studies confines historical inquiry to close textual questions; similarly, the dominance of social history confines scholarship to social, rather than jurisprudential questions. Moreover, because history departments rarely hire (or train) historians of premodern Islam and law schools rarely hire (or train) specialists in Islamic law, historical research on Islamic law is at the margins of historical studies and of legal studies.[12]

While these broad disciplinary boundaries frame historical research on Islamic law, the particularities of historical sources influence how each historical period is studied. In what follows, I offer a rough, brief, and chronological overview of Islamic legal history and corresponding scholarship.[13]

A. Late Antique (610 to 800)

Late antique Islamic law encompasses the beginning of the Islamic movement up to approximately the beginning of the ninth century. The Prophet and his legal and political successors administered Islamic law, simultaneously drawing upon customary, regional traditions and articulating new legal perspectives. Muslim legal actors fused pre-Islamic legal traditions with Islamic ones. Jurists used historical

---

[12] Scholars of late antique or medieval Islamic history or Islamic law typically teach in Near Eastern Studies or Religious Studies departments. On how law schools in the United States influence Islamic law scholarship, see Salaymeh (n. 1).

[13] For an encyclopaedic overview of Islamic legal history, see Lena Salaymeh, 'Islamic law', in James D. Wright (ed.), *The International Encyclopedia of Social and Behavioral Sciences* (2015).

research to determine the legal value of events during the Prophet's life because these events have precedential value. Jurists generally adopted one or a combination of two approaches: the rationalist approach anchored jurisprudence in logical thinking, and the traditionist approach anchored jurisprudence in sacred, textual sources. Law was developed and taught in legal circles, networks, and eventually, formal legal schools. This period was legally heterodox, as a wide variety of approaches to Islamic law coexisted.

Late antique Islamic legal historiography has expanded significantly in recent years as several scholars have dedicated monographs to the first centuries of Islamic legal history.[14] Much of this scholarship attempts to trace the 'origins' of Islamic law and to identify the legal actors who laid the 'foundations' for Islamic law. The emphasis on 'origins' reflects the methodological dominance of philology, especially source-criticism.[15] Source-criticism consists of comparing surviving textual sources and, based on a set of allegedly neutral principles, determining which source is older or more authentic. While source-criticism may provide a means of arranging several manuscript variants, it is not a basis for the writing of history. Because source-criticism is an influential method in the field, discovering the date and true 'origins' of Islamic law in pre-Islamic legal traditions remains a problematic objective in Islamic legal historiography.[16] Islamic law, however, does not have a date of birth because it simply began when the Islamic movement began. In addition, Islamic law does not have an authentic or true 'origin' because the Islamic legal tradition, like all legal traditions, is hybrid. Indeed, the Islamic legal tradition recycles pre-Islamic and Islamic laws in ways that are immeasurable and often indiscernible. Put differently, Islamic law does not have an 'origin' because, in late antiquity, non-Islamic and Islamic laws were enmeshed in a shared 'Near Eastern' legal culture.

Source-criticism inculcates a broad approach to sources that emphasizes not only searching for origins, but also reporting the contents of textual sources, rather than analysing them theoretically or historically. This is why much of the scholarship in late antique Islamic legal studies synthesizes the contents of legal texts (whether documentary or narrative) with little, if any, analysis.[17] The philological

---

[14] Patricia Crone, *Roman, Provincial and Islamic Law: The Origins of the Islamic Patronate* (2002); Yasin Dutton, *The Origins of Islamic Law: The Qur'an, the Muwatta' and Madinan 'amal* (1999); Wael B. Hallaq, *The Origins and Evolution of Islamic Law* (2005); Steven C. Judd, *Religious Scholars and the Umayyads: Piety-Minded Supporters of the Marwanid Caliphate* (2014); Harald Motzki, *The Origins of Islamic Jurisprudence: Meccan fiqh Before the Classical Schools* [Die Anfänge der islamischen Jurisprudenz: Ihre Entwicklung in Mekka bis zur Mitte des 2./8. Jahrhunderts (1991)] (Marion H. Katz trans. 2002).

[15] Lena Salaymeh, '"Comparing" Jewish and Islamic Legal Traditions: Between Disciplinarity and Critical Historical Jurisprudence' (2015) 2 *Critical Analysis of Law* 153 ff.

[16] I elaborated on the connection between the search for Islamic 'origins' and methodological limitations, as well as alternative frameworks for Islamic legal historiography in *The Beginnings of Islamic Law: Late Antique Islamicate Legal Traditions* (2016).

[17] Kruger (n. 2) 309.

method emphasizes micro-textual translation and summary, rather than macro-contextual and relational analysis. Some scholars have debated and considered the implications of philology's dominance in the study of late antique (and medieval) Islamic legal historiography.[18] However, few scholars have engaged alternative methods for exploring late antique Islamic legal history. One important exception is Hocine Benkheira, who implements a historical-anthropological approach to late antique Islamic legal historiography.[19] Interdisciplinary methods are crucial to facilitate a shift from micro-textual questions to macro-historical questions in late antique Islamic legal historiography. A significant subject area of potential research is integrating a wide array of narrative and documentary sources in order to scrutinize the reciprocal relationship between late antique Islamic legal practice and juridical scholarship. By way of example, we know little about how Umayyad judicial practices shaped jurisprudential activity and texts.[20] In short, late antique historiography should focus on Islamic law beyond texts and should read texts more critically and contextually.

B. Medieval (800 to 1500)

In the medieval era, Muslim jurists became professionalized, paralleling the 'Abbāsid empire's development of an increasingly more complex bureaucratic system. Muslim jurists debated the role of oral law—the orally transmitted traditions about the legal practices of the earliest generations of Muslims—in Islamic jurisprudence. A combination of challenges to the authority of oral reports and increasing availability and accessibility of materials for writing (particularly paper) led to the intensifying importance of recorded (written) tradition-reports (*aḥadīth*) and other textual sources in Islamic jurisprudence. In turn, the growing reliance on textual sources shifted Islamic jurisprudence away from the reconstruction of social-historical precedents and towards textual interpretation. Muslim scholars gradually differentiated historical and legal genres as the juristic

---

[18] See, e.g., the debate between Hallaq and Powers: Wael B. Hallaq. 'Groundwork of the Moral Law: A New Look at the Qur'ān and the Genesis of sharīʿa' (2009) 16 *Islamic Law and Society* 239 ff.; David S. Powers, 'Wael B. Hallaq on the Origins of Islamic Law: A Review Essay' (2010) 17 *Islamic Law and Society* 126 ff.

[19] See Mohammed Hocine Benkheira, 'Un libre peut-il épouser une esclave? Esquisse d'histoire d'un débat, des origines à al-Shāfiʿī (m.204/820)' (2008) 84 *Der Islam* 246 ff; 'Jouir sans enfanter? Concubines, filiation et coït interrompu au debut de l'Islam', (2013) 90 *Der Islam* 245 ff; 'L'impuissance sexuelle, motif légal de rupture du lien matrimonial' (2014) 21 *Islamic Law and Society* 1 ff.

[20] On Umayyad judges and jurists, see Judd (n. 14). On the significance of using Umayyad judicial activity to understand contemporaneous jurisprudence, see Muhammad Khalid Masud et al. 'Qāḍis and Their Courts: An Historical Survey', in Muhammad Khalid Masud et al. (eds.), *Dispensing Justice in Islam: Qadis and Their Judgements* (2006) 11 ff.

profession became more specialized. Hundreds of legal schools of thought consolidated or disappeared, leaving several orthodox legal schools, each of which articulated slightly distinct jurisprudential principles. Thus, canonization of legal texts coincided with consolidation of legal orthodoxy, which was reinforced in the tradition of legal commentaries. Legal education occurred in and outside of formal, endowed colleges, which were centres of education and political activity. During the medieval period, Islamic legal orthodoxy coalesced.

Whereas late antique historiography generally focuses on the 'origins' of Islamic law, medieval historiography is concerned with the 'origins' of the orthodox Islamic jurisprudential methodology (*uṣūl al-fiqh*), which are associated with 'foundational' texts or scholars.[21] Just as Islamic law does not have 'origins', orthodox Islamic jurisprudence does not have 'origins'. Here again, textual studies directs scholarship towards close readings that are dislocated from their socio-political and historical surroundings. Consequently, medieval legal histories that situate Islamic law within its various socio-political surroundings are relatively rare.[22] Many aspects of orthodox Islamic jurisprudence are the result of socio-political and historical conditions in the medieval era that were common to Islamic and non-Islamic (particularly Jewish) legal traditions. Medieval Islamic law operated within and reflected Islamicate legal culture, encompassing both Muslims and non-Muslims.[23] Historically situated comparisons with medieval, non-Islamic legal traditions would be very productive. While some scholars have integrated discursive and legal theoretical approaches to the study of medieval Islamic law, interdisciplinary approaches remain infrequent.[24]

Many studies of early medieval Islamic law have revealed significant details and nuances about legal education[25] and the consolidation of orthodox legal schools.[26]

---

[21] Wael B. Hallaq, *A History of Islamic Legal Theories: An Introduction to Sunni usul al-fiqh* (1997); *Authority, Continuity and Change in Islamic Law* (2001); Christopher Melchert, *The Formation of the Sunni Schools of Law, 9th–10th Centuries C.E.* (1997); 'Traditionist-Jurisprudents and the Framing of Islamic Law' (2001) 8 *Islamic Law and Society* 383 ff.

[22] David Stephan Powers, *Law, Society, and Culture in the Maghrib, 1300–1500* (2002); David S. Powers, 'Four Cases Relating to Women and Divorce in Al-Andalus and the Maghrib, 1100–1500' in Masud, *Dispensing Justice* (n. 20) 383–409 ff.; Maya Shatzmiller, 'Women and Wage Labour in the Medieval Islamic West: Legal Issues in an Economic Context' (1997) 40 *Journal of the Economic and Social History of the Orient* 174 ff; *Her Day in Court: Women's Property Rights in Fifteenth-Century Granada* (2007).

[23] These ideas are explored in detail in Salaymeh (n. 16).

[24] Sherman A. Jackson, 'From Prophetic Actions to Constitutional Theory: A Novel Chapter in Medieval Muslim Jurisprudence' (1993) 25 *International Journal of Middle East Studies* 71 ff; Baber Johansen, *Contingency in a Sacred Law: Legal and Ethical Norms in the Muslim fiqh* (1999).

[25] George Makdisi, *Religion, Law and Learning in Classical Islam* (2002); Joseph E. Lowry et al. (eds.), *Law and Education in Medieval Islam: Studies in Memory of Professor George Makdisi* (2004).

[26] Peri Bearman et al., *The Islamic School of Law: Evolution, Devolution, and Progress* (2006); Nimrod Hurvitz, 'Schools of Law and Historical Context: Re-examining the Formation of the Ḥanbalī *madhhab*' (2000) 7 *Islamic Law and Society* 37 ff; Nurit Tsafrir, *The History of an Islamic School of Law: The Early Spread of Hanafism* (2004).

While this is an important and rich area of scholarship, it has the unintended consequence of minimizing non-orthodox legal schools (or heterodox legal activity) and the role of the state.[27] (An exception is the Ẓāhirī legal school, which has received significant scholarly attention.[28] This scholarly interest may reflect the significance of contemporary textual-literalist approaches to Islamic law.) That is, the orthodox legal schools were not the only loci of legal activity. For example, as Farḥāt Ziyādah noted, much scholarship neglects the procedural rules that were essential to upholding justice.[29] Similarly, texts of juristic disagreement (*ikhtilāf*) have not been thoroughly researched, particularly as to how this genre contributed to the consolidation of legal orthodoxy and identification of legal heresy. Several important studies have been dedicated to Mamluk legal history, but this area remains under-researched.[30] In addition, the geographic range of medieval Islamic legal historiography remains quite limited.

c. Early Modern (*c.* 1500 to 1800)

State practices and bureaucracies both expanded and unified the dominance of Islamic law in the early modern era. Whereas previous empires permitted multiple legal schools to coexist in many localities, Ottoman courts became the primary venue for litigation throughout the Ottoman Empire. The Ottoman state became intimately involved in every aspect of judicial activity—from training jurists and court personnel, to selecting judges, to promulgating legal codes.[31] Similarly, Awrangzīb, Mughal Emperor of India, ordered the compilation of an Islamic law compendium based on the most authoritative legal opinions of the Ḥanafī school; the result is known as al-Fatāwá al-ʿĀlamgīrīyah (compiled between 1664–1672), and the text was an important reference work throughout South Asia and beyond for generations. The Ottomans designated the Ḥanafī legal school as the empire's official school, appointed a chief jurist, and established law schools in the areas they conquered; as a result, law students began to migrate away from other Islamic legal schools as a step towards a career in the Ottoman bureaucracy.

---

[27] Sherman A. Jackson, *Islamic Law and the State: The Constitutional Jurisprudence of Shihab al-Din al-Qarafi* (1996); Muhammad Qasim Zaman, 'The Caliphs, the ʿulamāʾ, and the Law: Defining the Role and Function of the Caliph in the Early ʿAbbāsid Period' (1997) 4 *Islamic Law and Society* 1 ff.

[28] Camilla Adang et al., *Ibn Ḥazm of Cordoba: The Life and Works of a Controversial Thinker* (2013); Amr Osman, *The Ẓāhirī Madhhab (3rd/9th-10th/16th century): a textualist theory of Islamic law*. Studies in Islamic law and society (2014).

[29] Abī Bakr Aḥmad ibn ʿAmr ibn Muhayr al-Shaybānī al-Khaṣṣāf (d. 874; Iraq) and Abī Bakr Aḥmad ibn ʿAlī al-Rāzī al-Jaṣṣāṣ (d. 982; Iraq), *Kitāb adab al-qāḍī* (Farḥāt Ziyādah ed., 1978).

[30] Yossef Rapoport, *Marriage, Money and Divorce in Medieval Islamic Society* (2008) 1.

[31] Baki Tezcan, *The Second Ottoman Empire: Political and Social Transformation in the Early Modern World* (2010).

Early modern Islamic legal historiography is dominated by studies based on Ottoman court records.[32] Islamic legal history under the Mughal Empire (1526–1540, 1555–1857) and the Safavid dynasty (1501–1736) are understudied.[33] Ottoman legal historiography is rarely comparative and, therefore, infrequently situates Ottoman law within global legal trends. Expanding the geographical coverage of early modern Islamic legal historiography would likely alter prevalent understandings of this period. Ottoman legal historiography is also overly focused on Ottoman archival records (especially courts records), which are often used for social (rather than legal) history.[34] A potentially important source for research is the legal decrees of Ottoman jurists, which have been understudied.[35] In addition, jurisprudential texts and juristic networks have not been explored fully. Nevertheless, Ottoman historiography has made important contributions to Islamic legal historiography by refuting stereotypes about Islamic law and by highlighting the role of the state and non-state groups in shaping Islamic law.

Ottoman legal historiography has been instrumental in refuting Max Weber's stereotype of *Kadijustiz*, which caricatures Islamic law as an irrational, arbitrary legal system, the antithesis of liberal and predictable, modern (secular) law.[36] Recent scholarship has used Ottoman court records to illustrate that Ottoman judges followed well-known procedural and substantive rules. Indeed, Ottoman judges were bureaucrats and their method of adjudication was as systematized as other Ottoman administrative acts.[37] Ottoman legal historiography has also overturned the stereotype that the Ottoman state was despotic. Numerous studies demonstrate that a combination of tradition and bureaucracy prevented a sultan from indiscriminately using his power.[38] For example, Sultan Süleyman (1465–1520), known as 'the Lawgiver', acquired a reputation for justice by punishing Ottoman administrators who had abused their power. By delineating the role of the

---

[32] Notable works include James E. Baldwin, *Islamic Law and Empire in Ottoman Cairo* (2017); Boğaç A. Ergene, *Local Court, Provincial Society, and Justice in the Ottoman Empire: Legal Practice and Dispute Resolution in Çankiri and Kastamonu (1652–1744)* (2003); Ahmed Fekry Ibrahim, *Pragmatism in Islamic Law: A Social and Intellectual History* (2017); Başak Tuğ, *Politics of Honor in Ottoman Anatolia: Sexual Violence and Socio-Legal Surveillance in the Eighteenth Century* (2017).

[33] On Mughal law, see .e.g., Muhammad J. Akbar, *The Administration of Justice by the Mughals* (1948); M. L. Bhatia, *The Ulama, Islamic Ethics and Courts Under the Mughals: Aurangzeb Revisited* (2006).

[34] See Dror Ze'evi, 'The Use of Ottoman Shari'a Court Records as a Source for Middle Eastern Social History: A Reappraisal' (1998) 5 *Islamic Law and Society* 35 ff. A notable exception to the early modern focus on social history is Guy Burak, *The Second Formation of Islamic Law: The Ḥanafi School in the Early Modern Ottoman Empire* (2015).

[35] Colin Imber, *Ebu's-su'ud: The Islamic Legal Tradition* (2008).

[36] Max Weber, *Economy and Society: An Outline of Interpretive Sociology* (1978).

[37] Haim Gerber, *State, Society, and Law in Islam: Ottoman Law in Comparative Perspective* (1994).

[38] See Ramazan Acun, Fatma Acun 'Demand for Justice and Response of the Sultan: Decision Making in the Ottoman Empire in the Early 16th Century' (2007) 2 *Balkan Studies* 125 ff.; Feridun M. Emecen, 'The Ottoman Legal System in the Reign of Sultan Süleyman the Magnificent', in Tülây Duran (ed.), *The Ottoman Empire in the Reign of Süleyman the Magnificent* (1988) 111–26 ff.

Ottoman state in shaping Islamic law, Ottoman legal historiography has contributed significantly to complicating the oversimplification that Islamic law is 'jurists' law'.

D. Modern (1800 to 1950)

In the modern era, the transition from empires to nation-states transformed Islamic law. The Ottoman Empire initiated reforms (*Tanẓīmāt*, reorganization) in the nineteenth century. The Gülhane Rescript (1839) confirmed the civil and economic rights of all Ottoman subjects, while endorsing Islamic law as the source of Ottoman law. The Ottomans promulgated multiple legal codes that were implemented by state courts (*niẓāmiyyah*). After 1869, the Ottoman Empire followed a civil code known as the *Mecelle-i Ahkam-i Adliye* (the Ottoman civil code); structured like the French civil code, the Ottoman civil code integrated both Islamic legal principles and a variety of Islamic substantive and procedural laws. Under the Sykes-Picot agreement, the British and the French enacted a post-First World War division of the Ottoman Empire into colonies. Throughout the nineteenth century, colonial administrators composed handbooks (or legal guides) about Islamic law that had long-lasting influences. Post-colonial, Muslim-majority states established hybrid legal systems, largely based on colonial law.

Modern historiographies of Islamic law concentrate on how the Ottoman legal reform movement, colonialism, and codifications transformed Islamic law.[39] This scholarship illustrates that legal changes that began during the Ottoman Empire intensified after its disintegration, the establishment of colonial regimes, and the later founding of quasi-independent nation-states. There is significantly less scholarship on legal transformations in the Mughal Empire. Colonial officers/scholars played a key role in promoting the notion that Islamic legal texts differed from Islamic legal practices.[40] Consequently, scholars often project these colonial assumptions of a 'gap' between theory and practice onto historical texts. This has resulted in relatively less scholarly attention to Islamic law beyond the modern nation-state. For example, there was significant scholarly discussion, commentary on, and explanation of the codification of Islamic law by contemporaneous jurists; yet, modern legal historiography in the West has rarely investigated these local responses to codification processes. More specifically, scholars have analysed the work and legacy of Egyptian jurist 'Abd al-Razzāq al-Sanhūrī without fully

---

[39] Iza R. Hussin, *The Politics of Islamic Law: Local Elites, Colonial Authority, and the Making of the Muslim State* (2016); Powers (n. 5); Scott Alan Kugle, 'Framed, Blamed and Renamed: The Recasting of Islamic Jurisprudence in Colonial South Asia' (2001) 35 *Modern Asian Studies* 257 ff.

[40] See Buskens, Dupret (n. 5) 33 (observing that 'the relationship between theory and practice, which has since become central in the Western study of Islamic law, originated in these scholarly and political debates of the nineteenth century').

investigating resistance to his codification projects.[41] Similarly, much modern legal historiography focuses on top-down codifications and legal reforms of Islamic law within particular states, without exploring the bottom-up production of Islamic legal thought in those areas. The legal changes of the modern era primarily resulted in the emulation of the legal systems of European states, in terms of juristic training, court procedures, and legal doctrines. Modern historiography would benefit from more explicitly comparative and contextual studies that place Islamic legal practices within regional socio-economic transformations.[42] Doing so would clarify the complex and diverse processes of how legal discourses and practices were transformed in the transition from early modern empires into modern nation-states.

IV. An Agenda for Future Scholarship

In briefly summarizing Islamic legal history and legal historiography, the previous section sought to illustrate that there are two primary challenges for historical research on Islamic law: avoiding anachronistic historical questions and adopting a broader range of methods in order to ask different kinds of historical questions. Because Islamic legal historiography tends to be insular and overly technical, it is important for future scholarship to engage with theoretical debates in law, history, religious studies, and critical theory. In what follows, I offer some suggestions for future historical research on Islamic law. (These suggestions do not encompass the temporal and geographic breadth of Islamic legal studies.)

A. Terms and Concepts

A primary challenge for historical research on Islamic law is applying terms and concepts that are historically (or contextually) appropriate; this is a challenge for all historical research, but it is compounded in this case because contemporary political questions so often provoke Islamic legal-historical research. Within the field, discrepancies in the use of the terms 'Islamic law', 'sharīʿah' (divine law), and 'fiqh' (juristic interpretations of divine law) are the result of deep conceptual variations,

---

[41] On the Sanhūrī code, see Guy Bechor, *The Sanhuri Code, and the Emergence of Modern Arab Civil Law (1932 to 1949)* (2007).

[42] Fahad A. Bishara, *Sea of Debt: Law and Economic Life in the Western Indian Ocean 1780–1950* (2017).

inflected by contemporary issues in the understanding of law. Yet historical research on Islamic law is only implicitly involved in debates about the meaning of 'law'. How to define 'law' underlies the late antique historiographic debate on Islamic law's beginning, since scholars often project narrow or inaccurate definitions of law on the historical record. Likewise, the debate in medieval historiography on when, how, and who initiated orthodox Islamic jurisprudence (*uṣūl al-fiqh*) revolves around what constitutes a jurisprudential text. Early modern legal historiography is often preoccupied with defining Ottoman law in relation, or in opposition, to Islamic law. Modern legal historiography seems either to question the existence of Islamic law in the modern world or to presume its omnipresence.[43] Many of these historiographic fixations could be avoided if scholars adopted explicit and rigorous definitions of law and of Islamic law that are transhistorical. By way of example, when Buskens and Dupret claim that colonial administrators and scholars invented the concept of 'Islamic law', it is because they define law as positive law.[44] However, not all law is positive law; moreover, Islamic law encompasses positive law and other forms of law. In other words, Islamic law is a normative legal praxis and not a legal code.[45]

A related conceptual challenge within the field concerns the role of the state in Islamic legal history; while Islamic law is often described as jurists' law, the state played a significant role in shaping the legal tradition, particularly through the patronage of particular legal schools.[46] The role of the state in Islamic legal history is understudied in the late antique period, as compared to the medieval, early modern, and modern periods, for which scholarship ascribes increasing significance to the state. Although in recent years there have been more studies of the relationship between Islamic law and Islamic states across historical periods, this area needs more scrutiny.[47] For instance, it is important to interrogate why scholars tend to use the categories of Islamic law and Ottoman law, but not Umayyad law, 'Abbāsid law, Fāṭimid law, or Mamluk law. The subcategory of Ottoman law reflects the significance of the Ottoman archives in differentiating the Ottoman legal tradition. Nevertheless, we should reconsider the *substantive* reasons for why we use some state-based legal categories and not others. Relatedly, the analytic category of Islamic administrative law has been underexplored. In general, research on Islamic law and governance indicates the urgency with which scholars have taken up the

[43] On the absence of Islamic law, see Wael B. Hallaq, 'Can the Shari'a Be Restored?', in Yvonne Yazbeck Haddad, Barbara Freyer Stowasser (eds.), *Islamic Law and the Challenges of Modernity* (2004) 21–54 ff. The perspective of omnipresence is present in contemporary propaganda about Islamic law.

[44] See Buskens, Dupret (n. 5) 31 (arguing that 'the phenomenon of normativity in Muslim societies existed before and was independent of the introduction of the concept of Islamic law by colonial administrators and scholars').

[45] Put differently, Islamic law is not a set of legal doctrines. It is a legal tradition in which doctrines are generated through recourse to Islamic sacred texts.

[46] See, e.g., Tsafrir (n. 26); Burak (n. 34).

[47] Zaman (n. 27); Benjamin Jokisch, *Islamic Imperial Law: Harun Al-Rashid's Codification Project* (2007); Jackson (n. 27); Hussin (n. 39); Gerber (n. 37).

contemporary question of Islamic statehood, but this research would benefit from more engagement with Islamic political thought and political theory.[48]

When historical research on Islamic law confronts the meaning of 'law' or the role of the state, it inevitably grapples with the false question of how to fit Islam within the modern category of religion.[49] In general, historical research on Islamic law is conducted without sufficient attention to the relevance of law and irrelevance of religion as categories of historical analysis. Too much historical scholarship on Islamic law begins with the false presumption that religion is a separate sphere (usually separate from the secular, or the state). Integrating critical secularism theory would prevent secular assumptions from clouding historical research on Islamic law. Recent scholarship in critical secularism theory demonstrates that secularism is not the neutral or objective opposite of religion; instead, secularism constructs the category of religion in various ways depending on the specific location and subject. In particular, exploring how modern, secular nation-states define, transform, and obscure Islamic law to suit their purposes is an important topic of research that depends on historical understanding.[50] That is, to perceive how the modern nation-state constructs Islamic law as 'religious law', it is necessary to contrast this secular construction with historical Islamic legal traditions.

B. Global and Regional Legal Histories

Historical research on Islamic law is implicated so deeply in contemporary, rather than historical, concerns that it is often decontextualized and disconnected from global or regional historical dynamics. An important potential area of research is situating Islamic law in global historical trends. By correlating Islamic legal practices to corresponding practices in global legal traditions, we might observe patterns or historical shifts that would otherwise be indiscernible. In addition, there are specific areas of Islamic law that would benefit from more historically situated analysis of global practices. For instance, historical research on Islamic slavery laws would profit from comparative engagement with recent scholarship on the Atlantic slave trade. Islamic laws of slavery appear, on the one hand, to reflect regional, customary practices and, on the other hand, to have been applied selectively.[51]

---

[48] Wael B. Hallaq, *The Impossible State: Islam, Politics, and Modernity's Moral Predicament* (2013).

[49] Examples include Fred McGraw Donner, *Muhammad and the Believers: At the Origins of Islam* (2012); Shahab Ahmed, *What Is Islam?: The Importance of Being Islamic* (2016).

[50] See Hussein A. Agrama, 'Sovereign Power and Secular Indeterminacy: Is Egypt a Secular or a Religious State?', in Mateo Taussig-Rubbo et al. (eds.), *After Secular Law* (2011) 503 ff (observing that 'the state is always drawing a line between the religious and the secular, and reserving its sole authority to do so').

[51] On slavery, see Kecia Ali, *Marriage and Slavery in Early Islam* (2010); Jonathan E. Brockopp, *Early Mālikī Law: Ibn ʿAbd al-Ḥakam and His Major Compendium of Jurisprudence* (2000).

Furthermore, regional legal history would enrich Islamic legal historiography by situating Islamic law within local trends. Some scholarship on the late antique and medieval eras has examined the relationships between Byzantine, Sasanian, rabbinic Jewish, and Islamic legal traditions; however, much of this scholarship has focused on derivative, linear connections. Horizontal analyses are less frequent, yet would be more illuminating. Three potentially significant areas of historical intersection between Islamic and regional non-Islamic legal traditions are the relationship between oral and written legal traditions, the systematization of jurisprudence, and the canonization of legal texts. For the early modern and modern eras, it would be especially beneficial to situate Ottoman law in relationship to Mughal and Safavid law. Collaborative scholarship would be a highly productive means of exploring the interrelationships between regional legal traditions of a specific period. Relatedly, global and regional legal historiographies may contribute to the necessary task of decentring the Arab world from Islamic legal historiography. Too much Islamic legal historiography ignores Islamic law in geographic areas that are presumed to be 'peripheral'. For instance, Islamic legal history in places like Indonesia or parts of sub-Saharan Africa have not been thoroughly investigated.

c. Materiality and Book History

While traditional papyrology and numismatics have contributed to Islamic legal historiography, they have also advanced a problematic dichotomization between documentary and narrative sources.[52] By moving beyond this dichotomy and the assumptions embedded within it, recent scholarship in textual studies would greatly benefit historical research on Islamic law. Specifically, critical philology, critical bibliography, and book history integrate close textual analysis with an anti-positivist orientation and with theoretical engagement; this approach greatly improves many of the deficiencies in conventional philological approaches. Moreover, existing narratives of Islamic legal history do not integrate fully factors related to materiality, including the production of manuscripts, introduction of paper, changes in the cost of scribal work, and implications of printing (especially its relationship to codification).[53] Brinkley Messick's historical ethnography of legal textual authority offers a productive model for scholars.[54] Combining critical theory and historical anthropology, Messick uses the materiality of texts to explore

---

[52] On papyrology in Islamic legal historiography, see Salaymeh (n. 16) ch. 1.

[53] On materiality in the Islamic world, see George N. Atiyeh, *The Book in the Islamic World: The Written Word and Communication in the Middle East* (1995); Adam Gacek, *The Arabic Manuscript Tradition* (2012).

[54] Brinkley M. Messick, *The Calligraphic State: Textual Domination and History in a Muslim Society* (1993).

questions of authority in Yemen from the nineteenth century to the late twentieth century. In addition, some recent scholarship has examined the canonization of specific Islamic legal literature.[55] However, in general, historical research on Islamic law should incorporate critical insights from materiality and book history more thoroughly into both macro- and micro-narratives of Islamic legal history.

D. Specialization, Multi-Disciplinarity, and Theory

Some scholars of Islamic legal history specialize in particular areas of law (such as criminal law or family law). Nevertheless, deeper specialization, coupled with methodological variety and theoretical engagement, would enhance scholarship in the field. For instance, scholars specializing in medieval Islamic international law should not only investigate comparative international legal history, but also legal theory and political theory. Similarly, scholarship on Islamic trusts would be enriched by more in-depth study of legal and economic theory, as well as comparative analyses. Likewise, historical research in Islamic legal ethics, particularly bioethics, would yield interesting results if it incorporated comparative and theoretical work.[56] Sustained engagement with theoretical literature has yielded promising results in, by way of example, late antique legal studies. A growing number of scholars of late antiquity are pursuing historical research on late antique law that integrates multiple historical sources, interdisciplinary approaches, and legal theory. In a recent symposium issue on ancient legal historiography, the diverse contributions shared an engagement with modern legal theory and moderate use of close textual analysis.[57] Dislocating the close reading of texts from its dominant position in research on Islamic law would open up possibilities for Islamic law to be a site for investigating historical and theoretical questions of importance outside the field of Islamic legal studies.

An acutely important area of historical research on Islamic law that has been under-historicized and under-theorized is gender and sexuality. Although a growing area of research, studies of women, sexuality, and Islamic legal history are usually not comparative or theoretically engaged.[58] By focusing on the global and regional situations of women—not only Muslim women—in particular

---

[55] Ahmed El Shamsy, *The Canonization of Islamic Law: A Social and Intellectual History* (2013); Jonathan Brown, *The Canonization of al-Bukhari and Muslim: The Formation and Function of the Sunni hadith Canon* (2011).

[56] Abdulaziz Abdulhussein Sachedina, *Islamic Biomedical Ethics: Principles and Application* (2009).

[57] Clifford Ando, 'The Varieties of Ancient Legal History Today' (2016) 3 *Critical Analysis of Law* 1 ff; Caroline Humfress (ed.), *Cambridge Comparative History of Ancient Law* (forthcoming).

[58] Khaled Abou El Fadl, *Speaking in God's Name: Islamic Law, Authority, and Women* (2001); Ali (n. 51); Hina Azam, *Sexual Violation in Islamic Law: Substance, Evidence, and Procedure* (2015); Scott Alan

historical periods, scholars can avoid perpetuating problematic stereotypes. Much of the literature on the status of women in Islamic legal history is not only a-historical and decontextualized, it is theoretically unsophisticated and thereby contributes, often unintentionally, to problematic ideological projects, especially imperialism.[59] Some historical research on Islamic law incorrectly presumes that the category of 'woman' is universal or transhistorical. By recognizing the nuances and varieties of women's experiences, critical feminist theory and queer theory would greatly enhance historical research on Islamic law and women, as well as other disempowered groups.

E. Interrogating Orthodox Narratives of Islamic Legal History

Prevalent methodologies in Islamic studies oriented the study of Islamic legal history around the falsification of Islamic historical sources. Consequently, scholars tended to treat Islamic historical sources as objects of technical dissection: they evaluated the chains of transmission and the texts of tradition-reports in order to determine authenticity or reliability. Few scholars have analysed how these sources narrate their own histories. In other words, how did medieval scholars narrate late antique Islamic legal history? And how did early modern scholars narrate late antique and medieval Islamic legal history? Put differently, how Islamic sources *composed* Islamic legal history has not been the subject of critical scrutiny. In writing the history of Islamic law, orthodox Muslim scholars not only proposed narratives about the past, they constructed boundaries for orthodoxy using the past as the template for authority and legitimacy. The stories that Muslim scholars told about the past of the Islamic legal tradition deserves more detailed scrutiny and critical engagement. Sociology of religion and critical theory would provide important tools for investigating these histories.

6. Islamic Legal History in Contemporary Controversies

A potentially productive avenue of future research concerns exploring how distinct actors use Islamic legal history in present controversies, particularly as an ideological tool. By way of example, during the Arab uprisings of 2010/2011, a variety of figures

---

Kugle, *Homosexuality in Islam: Critical Reflection on Gay, Lesbian and Transgender Muslims* (2013); Judith E. Tucker, *Women, Family, and Gender in Islamic Law* (2008).

[59] For an overview, see Salaymeh (n. 9).

used Islamic legal history either to justify or to delegitimize popular uprisings. In their legal decrees or more extensive legal writings, contemporary jurists, pseudo-jurists, and activists pointed to Islamic history as offering precedents for or against overthrowing authoritarian regimes.[60] How did these various contemporary Muslim actors and activists fashion Islamic legal history? Anti-imperial and anti-colonial movements across the Muslim world mine Islamic legal history for precedents and for justifications of their activities. Similarly, both state and non-state actors turn to Islamic legal precedents to condemn or to justify the use of violence. Contemporary Islamic legal opinions on the use of violence in war or in rebellion are engaged directly with Islamic legal history in ways that have not been fully explored. In short, how contemporary Muslim movements and actors employ Islamic legal history is a promising area of future research.

v. Conclusion

This chapter provides a partial sketch of recent Islamic legal historiography in the West, with modest suggestions for future research. Historical research on Islamic law is a burgeoning field facing many of the political and normative challenges of scholarship in Islamic studies more generally. It would behoove this field to confront these challenges more directly both by acknowledging them and by recognizing how they influence the contemporary writing of historiography. In turn, it is important to resist allowing contemporary politics to dictate the borders and content of historical research on Islamic law. With a wide array of sources and questions that have not yet been investigated thoroughly, historical research on Islamic law is a field that will continue to grow and transform in unpredictable ways. Adopting more interdisciplinary methods and integrating more comparative and theoretical approaches will greatly enrich the field.

Recommended Reading

Late Antique (610–800)

Wael B. Hallaq, 'Groundwork of the Moral Law: A New Look at the Qur'ān and the Genesis of Sharīʿa' (2009) 16 *Islamic Law and Society* 239 ff

---

[60] On the use of Islamic history in the Egyptian coup of 2013, see Amr Osman, 'Past contradictions, contemporary dilemmas: Egypt's 2013 coup and early Islamic history'. (2015) 24:2 *Digest of Middle East Studies* 303–26.

Harald Motzki, *The Origins of Islamic Jurisprudence: Meccan fiqh Before the Classical Schools* [Die Anfänge der islamischen Jurisprudenz: Ihre Entwicklung in Mekka bis zur Mitte des 2./8. Jahrhunderts (1991)] Islamic History and Civilization. Studies and Texts, Vol. 41. (trans. Marion H. Katz, Brill, 2002)

Medieval (800–1500)

Ahmed El Shamsy, *The Canonization of Islamic Law: A Social and Intellectual History* (Cambridge University Press, 2013)

Yossef Rapoport, *Marriage, Money and Divorce in Medieval Islamic Society* (Cambridge University Press, 2008)

Muhammad Qasim Zaman, *Religion and Politics Under the Early ʿAbbāsids: The Emergence of the Proto-Sunnī Elite* (Brill, 1997)

Early Modern (c. 1500–1800)

Guy Burak, *The Second Formation of Islamic Law: The Ḥanafī School in the Early Modern Ottoman Empire* (Cambridge University Press, 2015)

Boğaç A. Ergene, *Local Court, Provincial Society, and Justice in the Ottoman Empire: Legal Practice and Dispute Resolution in Çankiri and Kastamonu (1652–1744)* (Brill, 2003)

Haim Gerber, *State, Society, and Law in Islam: Ottoman Law in Comparative Perspective* (State University of New York Press, 1994)

Modern (1800–1950)

Iza R. Hussin, *The Politics of Islamic Law: Local Elites, Colonial Authority, and the Making of the Muslim State* (University of Chicago Press, 2016)

Scott Alan Kugle, 'Framed, Blamed and Renamed: The Recasting of Islamic Jurisprudence in Colonial South Asia' (2001) 35 *Modern Asian Studies* 257 ff

Brinkley M. Messick, *The Calligraphic State: Textual Domination and History in a Muslim Society* (University of California Press, 1993)

David S. Powers, 'Orientalism, Colonialism, and Legal History: The Attack on Muslim Family Endowments in Algeria and India' (1989) 31 *Comparative Studies in Society and History* 535 ff

CHAPTER 41

'BY THE LIGHT OF THE MOON': LOOKING FOR CHINA'S RICH LEGAL TRADITION

TAHIRIH V. LEE[*]

THE field of Chinese legal history is beset by nearly insuperable obstacles. How to decode ancient and pre-modern texts, when even modern texts until the 1940s used a literary language that differed from spoken Chinese? How to access primary sources when they are locked away in rooms that are barred not just to non-Chinese scholars, but to Chinese scholars as well? How to recognize 'law' when China's government, intelligentsia, and its wider population have debated the law's very definition, its very utility? An old Chinese saying evokes a widespread cynicism about even the existence of a rule of law in China: 'Chinese law is like the light of the moon; it is different at the beginning of the month than in the middle of the month.' In other words, the moon's shape constantly changes, suggesting that in China law means whatever the ruler is content at present to say that it means. In another way,

* Associate Professor of Law, Florida State University. The author thanks William Alford, Nancy Park, Mary Szto, Chang Wejen, and Margaret Woo for their encouragement, instruction, and inspiration at crucial moments.

too, this saying is relevant to our historiographical purpose here; the moon's light serves as a metaphor for the less than ideal conditions under which Chinese legal historians have operated. Its light is a secondary light, illuminating the landscape imperfectly.

As difficult as it is, doing Chinese legal history provides crucially useful information. Pronouncements about China's basic predispositions must be tested. We do not yet know whether the rule of law, that is, law that bound the lawmaker and served the public, has ever taken hold in China. We do not know the extent to which substantive law reached the population at large and affected the lives of those in this, the world's most populous society. We do not understand the sources of authority of the law and its officers and the level of respect for them held by the population. Regional variations in a legal landscape that has stretched over nearly four million square miles have not yet come into view.

Because many unanswered questions beckon from this significant part of the world, the obstacles have not prevented a body of research from developing. Taiwanese historian T'ung-tsu Ch'ü and social anthropologist Sybille Van Der Sprenkel, a European who was born and raised in China and who taught in London, used a broad swathe of contemporary legal digests from the Qing-period (1644–1911), producing two classic books in 1962[1] that are still useful and seem fresh in their approach. They looked quite straightforwardly at the way the district magistrates were supposed to apply law and, in some instances, how they actually did. Ch'ü seemed primarily concerned with dispelling a longstanding stereotype of corrupt local-level courts in late imperial China. He argued that personal relationships between the magistrate and his staff did not lead to inefficiency but to its opposite. He even explained the illegitimate behaviour of 'runners', the translated term used for those staff of the magistrate who delivered and enforced his orders, and who notoriously extracted bribes from the local population, as understandable given their low social status. He brought the local gentry into the picture by showing their role as intermediaries between magistrates and the people and briefly touched on local custom by noting that the magistrate had to follow it, at least as far as the people demanded it. Throughout, Ch'ü aimed to build a uniform picture of judicial work in Qing China and may have gone too far in glossing over details that contradicted that picture, as when he concluded about the staff who drafted documents for the magistrate and kept his records, '[t]he government was fully aware of the consequences of the clerks' corruption.'[2]

Van Der Sprenkel was sensitive to the difficulty of defining law and distinguishing what is legal from what is not. She was interested in getting at the implementation of law at the ground level. So she assembled information about the customary,

---

[1] Ch'ü T'ung-Tsu, *Local Government in China Under the Ch'ing* (1962); Sybille Van Der Sprenkel, *Legal Institutions in Manchu China* (1962).

[2] Ch'ü (n. 1) 197–8 ff.

local institutions of the *dibao* village elder, the *baojia* system of organizing neighbourhoods, the family, and guilds and treated them as 'subsidiaries of the official courts', which delegated powers to them and allowed their participants to enjoy an efficiency and a freedom from corruption that she said was endemic to the magistrates' courts. She wisely probed the problem of tension between local custom and the magistrate sent by the emperor from far away. Her anthropological training was on display when she used the concept of 'structure' to analyse the Qing bureaucracy and when she recognized that the concept of face was a means to exercise social control.[3] In so doing, she barely touched on the futile problem of litigiousness, namely, how quick people were to use the courts. Her scrupulous attention to detail and high scholastic standards moved her to look for double sourcing to confirm her findings.

Taiwanese legal historian Chang Wejen has since then continued this grand scale of study and should soon publish the closest we will have to a definitive work on Qing judicial institutions. Steeped in the classics of Chinese philosophy as well as in the various languages of its legal documents produced over two and a half millennia, Chang is in a preeminent position to synthesize reams of archival material. Chang has in the meantime mentored numerous other Chinese legal historians. He thus occupies a unique place in the field that future scholars will have trouble filling.

The Qing dynasty has drawn most of the attention of legal historians. Van Der Sprenkel focused on the Qing because its institutions were a 'culmination' of all previous eras (2). A few years later, Chang Chen Fu-Mei and John Watt each wrote significant studies on the judicial work of the Qing district magistrates.[4] No doubt, the survival and availability of documents has played a part in this choice. Dutch linguist Anthony Hulsewé was a rare exception, producing a much-referenced work on Han dynasty (206 BC to AD 220) law[5] as well as working on the Qin (221–206 BC) and the Tang (AD 618–907). His rival in Germany, Karl Bücker, focused on the Tang.[6] Kung-chuan Hsiao attempted a sweep of thousands of years and in the process indulged in some broad generalizations and simplistic reasoning, such as 'The system constructed by [the ruler] Shang Yang was extremely uniform because it was based on the definite meanings of words. Due to the authoritative principle and the definite titles of the law, both officials and people understood their rights and duties and committed to them.'[7] Despite their limitations, all of these mid-twentieth-century authors, regardless of the time periods they chose, provided support for an appreciation of the sophistication of China's experience with law over a lengthy and unbroken span of time.[8]

[3] Van Der Sprenkel, *Institutions* 1, 47, 80–96, 99–101 ff.
[4] Chen, Fu-mei Chang. 'On Analogy in Ch'ing Law' 30 *Harvard J. of Asiatic Studies* (1970) 212 ff; John Robertson Watt, *The District Magistrate in Late Imperial China* (1972).
[5] A. F. P. Hulsewé, *Remnants of Han Law* (1955).
[6] Karl Bücker, *Quellen zur Rechtsgeschichte der T'ang-Zeit* (1946).
[7] Kung-chuan Hsiao, *A History of Chinese Political Thought* (1978) 87 ff.   [8] Ibid., 177.

During the twentieth century, scholars in Europe and the United States published useful translations of the dynastic legal codes. From Paul Rachnevsky's translation into French of the *Zhi Yuan Xinge*, which had introduced Mongolian customary law into the dynastic codes of China in 1291,[9] to Jiang Yonglin's translation into English of the *Da Ming Lü*,[10] to William Jones's translation into English of the *Da Qing Lü Li*, these valuable primary sources became available to scholars who do not sufficiently read Chinese and, at least in the case of Jones's, vastly improved upon past translations. The importance of these codes may have been exaggerated by legal historians who had little access to other primary sources of law in dynastic China, but their importance should nonetheless not be ignored. In 400 BC, the earliest known promulgated code in China appeared.[11] The last dynastic code continued to have effect for several years after the fall of the last dynasty in 1911. During that nearly 2,500 years, rarely more than a few years passed without some law code officially being in force over vast stretches of what is now the People's Republic of China. The form and content of the central code remained largely stable for half that time, undergoing substantial revisions only twice between 737 AD and 1911.

To further expand access to primary materials on Chinese legal history, translators should turn their gifts to case records from courts throughout China's three-thousand-year experience with them. Dirk Bodde and Clarence Morris led the way fifty years ago with flawed translations of and annotations on 190 Qing dynasty cases selected from a series of compilations created by officials from the Board of Punishments.[12] More recently, Brian McKnight and James Liu contributed a book-length translation of judgments from the Song dynasty (AD 960–1279).[13] This collection shows, if nothing else, the high level of intelligence and detail involved in Chinese judicial work during the first millennium, an important corrective to assertions that China lacked a sophisticated legal tradition.

Having completed this brief overview of the foundations of the field of Chinese legal history, let us now delve into questions of methodology and approach. Three such questions face the field now and in the near future. First, historians, law scholars, and anthropologists with their different training and bases of knowledge, ask different questions about law, and I would like to explore how these three approaches have shaped the field and offer potential for contributions to come. Using

---

[9] Lien Sung, Paul Ratchnevsky, *Un Code Des Yuan* (trans. Paul Ratchnevsky) (1937).

[10] *The Great Ming Code: Da Ming Lü* (Yonglin Jiang, trans., 2005).

[11] Sung, Ratchnevsky (n. 9) xv ff.

[12] Derk Bodde, Clarence Morris, Jingqing Zhu, *Law in Imperial China: Exemplified by 190 Ch'ing Dynasty cases* (1967) (trans. Dirk Bodde). For details on the flaws, see the superb Fu-Mei Chang Chen 'Review: Law in Imperial China by Hsing-an hui-lan' 29 *Harvard J. Asiatic Studies* (1969) 247 ff. The title of the book is misprinted in this publication; the Hsing-an hui-lan was a name given to the series of compilations of cases.

[13] *The Enlightened Judgments: Ch'ing-ming Chi, The Sung Dynasty Collection* (Brian McKnight, James Liu, trans.).

all of these approaches helps us to better probe the sources of authority of the law and of its officers and the level of respect for them held by the population. Second, comparative law inextricably intertwines with Chinese legal history, and its use and abuse needs to be examined and its lessons learned. Proper use of a comparative approach may, in particular, further our understanding about whether the rule of law, that is, law that bound the lawmaker and served the public, has ever taken hold in China. Third, given the sophistication for centuries of Chinese rulers' efforts to propagate official lines about the law, it has been exceedingly difficult for scholars to pierce through it to see what was actually happening on the ground. We will have to succeed better at this if we want to understand the extent to which substantive law reached the population during different periods of China's history. Something like a law-and-society approach, where law's distinctiveness from society is treated more as myth than reality, may help in this endeavour.

I. Methodological Balance: Historians, Lawyers, and Anthropologists

For the last two decades, the field of Chinese legal history has begun to reap the benefits of archival work in China and Taiwan. Outstanding research has been done by historians trained in the history departments of American, Chinese, and European universities. For the most part, they have lacked law degrees. It may not be a coincidence that these studies tend to use court cases as lenses onto Chinese society rather than into China's legal system itself. The training provided by historians of China in the United States over the past generation has emphasized linguistics and interpretation of text and broad political and social developments. The rigour of this training and the heroic dedication required to acquire those skills should not be underestimated, and each of these historians deserves our admiration. Missing from their purview, however, is a technical understanding of law, which would make them alert to various uses of positive law and of procedure to arrive at judicial decisions, to solve problems, and to strengthen the control of government officials over the affairs of others.

Historians Xu Xiaoqun, Feng Shaoting, Man Bun Kwan, Mark Allee, and Thomas Buoye have each separately gathered and analysed thousands of court records involving land and buildings produced in the nineteenth century and, in some cases, early twentieth. Their principal conclusions revolve around trends in demography, population density, commercial practices, and violence, and only secondarily do they trace developments in the law or in judicial treatment of disputes.

For Buoye, for example, lawsuits are windows onto the violence associated with disputes over landed property. In order to understand the resort to violence he focuses upon disputes in eighteenth-century Guangdong, Sichuan, and Shandong Provinces in which litigants murdered or maimed their opponents after judgment: 'Disputes that ended in lethal violence despite efforts at official adjudication revealed the depth of the social tensions in the eighteenth century and offer insights into why many people resorted to violence.'[14] A lawyer would wonder about the effects of the magistrate's procedures and reasoning upon the litigants' respect for the ruling. Such disputes might not gauge the depth of pre-litigation tensions as clearly if the magistrate were aggravating the tensions during the litigation. Buoye rules out the magistrates' conduct as a variable by concluding simply that magistrates were uniformly 'efficient'[15] and conscientious because they always examined the title deed and ordered a survey of the land's boundaries, but he does not lay bare to us much in the case records that supports this. Lawyers are trained to advocate for opposing points of view, a skill that requires them to recognize and combat self-serving arguments. They thus would want to know more about a possible bias in the records upon which Buoye relies. These records appear to have been created by the magistrates themselves to report on their work to their superiors, as was required within the hierarchy of China's government. Why would they allow traces of inefficiency to creep into documents that were undoubtedly used to evaluate their performance?

To make the point that magistrates tried all means at their disposal to resolve land disputes, Buoye highlights cases in which the magistrate departed from the terms of the written agreement when ordering extra payments to be made as part of an effort to settle a later disagreement.[16] A lawyer would consider the possibility that departing from the terms of the agreement was not efficient and that such a practice undermined the authority of the magistrate's decision, perhaps smacking of favouritism or seeming to lack any principled basis.

Buoye asserts that 'economic conditions'—meaning the need for more agricultural land to feed a rapidly growing population—'provided incentives to alter property rights', and does not consider that the law itself—here, the customary practice of the *dian*—made it easy for people to assert claims to land. When land was transferred under the aegis of a *dian*, it was sold with a right of repurchase. As he explains,

---

[14] Thomas M. Buoye, 'Litigation, Legitimacy, and Lethal Violence', in Zelin, Ocko, Gardella (eds.), *Contract and Property in Early Modern China* (2004) 97 ff. The sane quest for information about China's social and economic arrangements motivated Buoye's larger study *Manslaughter, Markets, and Moral Economy Violent: Disputes over Property Rights in Eighteenth-Century China* (2000). In its final chapter, he 'explore(s) the implications of this study for our understanding of the social and economic history of late imperial China' (p.15)

[15] Ibid., 99 ff., and Buoye 'Manslaughter' (n. 14) 206.   [16] Ibid., 109–11 ff.

this practice appears to have grown up out of respect for ancestral land and the community's desire to keep it in descendants' hands. Buoye helpfully describes the efforts of the Yongzheng Emperor, who was possibly the Qing dynasty's most powerful ruler, to clarify and limit the use of the *dian*. But when Buoye counts these new laws as evidence of changes to society in their time (1736–1756)—'reforming the laws on conditional sale was related to large-scale economic changes … .'[17]—he is leaving aside the possibility that the legal mechanism of the *dian* was simply poison to Chinese society, that it was a faulty law that needed correction in order to stem its ill effects. Weaknesses in the laws or in legal mechanisms are well-known to the scholar with legal training, perhaps mainly because we have run across so many of them.

In Buoye's search for explanations for violence, he concludes that the inadequacy of the resources available to the magistrate led to a lack of enforcement of his decisions, and that this explains the violent recriminations that followed some of them.[18] Buoye may be alluding to a need for higher salaries for the magistrate's staff that might have kept them from taking bribes in exchange for not enforcing the decisions. But might he equally mean that if more police delivered the judicial order or kept watch over the litigants that violence would have been reduced? Whether more police in a community reduces violence is a controversial proposition; one could just as plausibly argue that they increase violence, especially if they are armed and use their arms. Add to that the reputation of the runners, those judicial assistants who carried out the orders of the magistrate, for corruption, and the argument about inadequate resources is further weakened. The more corrupt personnel in a community, the more violent it would become. A lawyer would take the argument further; surely a police state is not the only way to ensure the enforcement of judicial decisions. Consensus as to peaceful values, respect for authority, strong community ties—all these come to the mind of the legal scholar as alternative possibilities.

A desire to combat the stereotype of the corrupt Qing magistrate motivates the work of these historians, and others, notably Madeleine Zelin and Bradly Reed. As such, they have taken up the mantle of T'ung-tsu Ch'ü, who, during the mid-twentieth century, sought to defend the magistrates and their staff, by showing a more complex picture of their work. The negative view arose centuries ago. As opium addiction spread during the nineteenth century, it weakened familial structures and economic productivity, leading to desperate poverty and hopelessness for many. The population surge two hundred years earlier that Buoye highlighted accelerated by the nineteenth century, while the number of magistrates did not grow as fast, overwhelming them and undermining their ability to enforce the law. Foreign officials eager to find excuses for establishing their own local governments and courts in China played up the ineffectiveness of the magistrates and the harshness

---

[17] Ibid., 101, 105–6 ff.   [18] Ibid., 112 ff.

of their legal proceedings.[19] The Chinese Communist Party intelligently took up the cry against imperial Chinese officials in order to justify the Party's efforts to depose those then in power. So, a nefarious image of the district magistrate, long a figure of popular lore,[20] was appropriated for various political purposes for over a hundred years.

Milking the negative image of the magistrate does not foreclose the possibility, however, that magistrates were actually venal. This is a question that must be carefully addressed in research, in a way that allows for wide variation in the conduct of these officials, as well as for the possibility that they engaged in widespread malfeasance. Bradly Reed dug up significant material on the staff employed by the district magistrates in Sichuan Province during the Qing period. His sophisticated approach refuses to dichotomize the state and society, which would relegate the magistrate's staffs to one side or the other, but instead sees China as full of 'nests of socially differentiated institutions, practices, and resources ....'[21] His rubrics come from political science, as in Samuel Huntington and Joseph Nye, who help him deconstruct, or relativize, the concept of corruption, to look beyond it to the efficiencies gained by the work of these personnel. Even after such an exhaustive study of the workings of the district magistrate's *yamen*, we cannot assume the clerks and runners to be permanently rehabilitated. Nancy Park's work on the administrative regulations that bound the magistrates into a vast bureaucracy during the Qing period promises to reveal a deeply rooted dysfunction that made litigation a scary place for litigants.

Connecting the details of the archival materials to the bigger picture is difficult. Xu Xiaoqun ambitiously tackled the concept of modernity in order to illuminate legal reforms from about 1900 to the 1940s. He made admirable use of archives in China and painstakingly pieced together a picture of the Guomindang government's courts in Jiangsu Province. The conceptual construct of modernity, whose meaning is malleable and depends on historical and social context, however, needs to be fleshed out beyond a mere inference that it is an 'external pressure to conform to Western-defined international standards ...'[22] He more clearly gauged 'the reach of the state',[23] a phrase from political scientist Vivienne Shue that has exerted a widespread impact on the field of Chinese law and legal history.[24]

---

[19] See Tahirih V. Lee, *Courts and Local Autonomy: The International Mixed Court of Shanghai*, PhD dissertation (1990).

[20] Fictional court cases comprised a literary genre by the late Ming dynasty. See the stories entitled 'One Hundred Court Cases' discussed in James St. Andre's 'Reading Court Cases from the Song and the Ming', in Robert E. Hegel, Katherine Carlitz (eds.), *Writing and Law in Late Imperial China* (2007) 193 ff.

[21] Bradly W. Reed, *Talons and Teeth, County Clerks, and Runners in the Qing Dynasty* (2000) 5 ff.

[22] Xu Xiaoqun, *Trial of Modernity* (2008) 334 ff.   [23] Ibid., 7 ff.

[24] Vivienne Shue, *The Reach of the State: Sketches of the Chinese Body Politic* (1988).

The prolific Philip Huang used Qing China to critique Max Weber's typology that relegated non-western legal systems to a category marked by 'instrumentalism and irrationality'.[25] It is a critique well worth doing, even with a narrow range of case records and quick thinking about the text of codified law from that era. He portrayed Qing law as a counter-example of Weber's categorization in that its stable and massive body of statutory law acted as a bulwark against arbitrary decisions by the emperor. This conclusion remains little more than conjecture, however, without a more detailed examination of the implementation of that statutory law. Another counter-characteristic, according to Huang, lay in the Qing code, which was meant to offer practical and consistent guides for the resolution of real problems and disputes. It is true that the code is comprised almost exclusively of instructions to magistrates about how to weigh evidence and how and when to impose corporal punishment and, in a smaller number of provisions, fines.

Madeleine Zelin's work on the fiscal side of the administration of justice in Qing China stands as a paragon of intelligent yet prudent extrapolation from archival records in the service of important questions.[26] Training her sights on the reach of China's government and its sophistication during the Qing period, she concludes that the archival records from Qing district magistrates' yamen unearthed by herself and others debunk the previous view 'that the state was of marginal importance in the process of establishing property rights'.[27]

If law schools in the United States begin to produce more Chinese legal history scholars, including those who also have PhDs in Chinese history, a course correction will be possible. Scholarship would likely begin to emphasize procedure and the strategic use of law towards personal ends. We could then learn more about how courts were used by the imperial government and its subjects, and the republican governments and their subjects thereafter, why statutory law remained so stable over a millennium, and the durability and variety of local customs.

In an era of diminishing budgets, however, American law schools are more likely than not to continue to marginalize both legal history and Asian law, relegating their teaching and research to the fringes of the legal academy's mission. In a similar way, institutional conditions in China and in Europe have stymied the contributions of Chinese legal historians. Law schools in all parts of the world may wake up, however, to the forces that are driving China into the centre of the global economy and therefore beef up support for research into the millennia-long developmental arc of Chinese law. China's own archives, newly opened in the late 1980s to scholars as a part of the *Gaige kaifang* policy begun by Deng Xiaoping, are more closed now than they were twenty years ago. May this trend reverse as well.

---

[25] Philip Huang, *Civil Justice in China: Representation and Practice in the Qing* (1996) 225–6 ff.

[26] Madeleine Zelin, *The Magistrate's Tael* (1984).

[27] Madeleine Zelin, 'A Critique of Property Rights in Prewar China', in Zelin, Ocko, Gardella (eds.), *Contract and Property in Early Modern China* (2004) 18 ff.

What can come from anthropology? The field work on courts and dispute resolution in Tibet by Rebecca French, a law scholar and an anthropologist,[28] stands as a landmark achievement in the field of Chinese law. Although she aimed for the anthropologist's goal of taking a snapshot of society and therefore washed out chronology and development, hers was in some respects an historical inquiry because the institutions and methods she described had been in use for generations. We need to mimic her appreciation for visual detail, as in her reconstruction of the layout of various types of courtrooms. We need to deploy the anthropologist's eye to note the importance, say, of litigants' posture when writing legal documents. At least for more recent periods, we need to resort more often to interviews of participants and those who can give second-hand accounts, as French does. These tools in the anthropological toolkit will help us delve beyond the official line about law, into local custom and the daily realm of norms and values and the other sources of the authority of law. These tools also help us to broaden our notions of where law is; she saw judicial and legal proceedings taking place in a variety of settings, including the disciplinary hearings in monasteries and in rules committee meetings. The anthropologist's perspective can also help broaden the legal historian's conception of the goals and characteristics of law. In contrast to Anglo-American Common Law lawyers and judges, the Tibetans whom French interviewed, for example, did not see consistency in outcomes as desirable, because they believed every person and matter to be unique.

II. A COMPARATIVE APPROACH: REWARDS AND PITFALLS

If legal historians of China grounded themselves in Comparative Law, it might help keep culturally-embedded assumptions about law from creeping into their analysis. Comparative Law is where we get the useful ideas of 'sources of law' and 'legal institutions', both more neutral than their corresponding terms 'statutes', 'case law', and 'constitutions', with respect to the former, and 'courts', with respect to the latter. Madeleine Zelin's frequent contact with comparative law scholars may have helped her develop neutral phrasing such as 'security of property rights', 'the costs of transactions', and 'limitations imposed by custom on private agreements' that avoid describing Qing China using constructs from the Anglo-American legal world.[29]

For decades, William Alford's path-breaking work on China's cultural support for copying intellectual achievements was the strongest statement from within

---

[28] Rebecca French, *The Golden Yoke* (1995) 145, 148–9, 155 ff.   [29] Zelin (n. 27) 26 ff.

the legal academy for the need to understand China's legal culture on its own terms, a legal tradition unique and particular to China, before any comparative analysis or foreign legal transplants be attempted there, including the notions of intellectual property that had developed in the United States and Europe.[30] He identified in China a strongly rooted reverence for classical art works and texts and a longstanding predilection for mimicry of them. Imitation was tantamount to respect and made China inhospitable to laws that would make intellectual products into a property whose use could be monopolized. At the same time, his was one of the clearest voices advocating for a comparative approach to the study of Chinese law. From Alford's teaching and research it is clear that comparing legal traditions is the other side of the coin that values the unique characteristics of each. Karen Turner advanced a similar argument, maintaining that research by an outsider into Chinese law is inherently comparative.[31]

Comparative research on Chinese history holds promise, particularly where the counterpoint is chosen for reasons related to the scholarship rather than the scholar. I hope we will see more well-crafted comparisons between law in China's past and contemporaneous law elsewhere, like that of Par Cassel, who chose to compare China to Japan in the late nineteenth century in order to learn why Japan strengthened more quickly on the international stage in the twentieth century than did China.[32] By concluding that China's centralizing revolution came too late to save it from the worst humiliations of this 'system of Extraterritoriality', while Japan's, through the centralizing regime of the Meiji Restoration, came just in time, Cassel deftly avoided overgeneralizing the experiences of these two distinctly different Asian nations. He gave proper due to indigenous responses and developments, thus surmounting any crabbed view that all the important actions were taken by the western invaders. China's own history possessed antecedents to extraterritoriality, Cassel discovered. The Manchu empire contained different legal orders with varying degrees of central supervision. In disputes between the majority Han and the ruling minority Manchus, Manchus were given a kind of immunity or extra procedural review.

While Cassel briefly falls into the trap of depicting foreign activity in China as penetration,[33] which cannot but imply that China was passive and weak, Li Chen corrects that distorted picture with a history of diplomatic relations between China's government and several others during the century before the system of Extraterritoriality. The record uncovered by Chen contains multiple examples of China's officials' shows of strength and of foreigners' impotence.[34] Chen's, Cassel's, and Alford's studies exemplify the principle that legal history and comparative law aid one another. Tracing the journey of legal ideas and influences across geography,

---

[30] William P. Alford, *To Steal a Book is an Elegant Offense* (1999) 9–29 ff.
[31] Karen Turner, 'Rule of Law Ideals in Early China' 6 *J. of Chinese L.* (1992) 1 ff.
[32] Par Cassel, *Grounds of Judgment* (2011) 26, 33–8 ff.   [33] Ibid., 11 ff.
[34] Li Chen, *Chinese Law in Imperial Eyes: Sovereignty, Justice, and Transnational Politics* (2015).

which is what comparative law scholarship does, without a time-sensitive inquiry, however, leads to distortions, such as laments about a gulf between China's 'legal tradition' and that of 'the West'. This analysis takes us down a well-trod path towards a view of both China and those 'Western' places that demeans China and vaunts the other places. Thomas Stephens' dichotomy between 'East' and 'West' in *Order and Discipline in China: The Shanghai Mixed Court 1911–1927* typifies this approach. What seems to depict two independent and internally cohesive legal cultures instead measures a stereotype of one of them (the 'East') against an idealized version of the other (the 'West') and finds the former falling short.

William Alford itemized China's legal achievements in a stern rebuttal to the notion that it lacked any experience with the rule of law.[35] In a similar vein, Chang Wejen's and Susan Weld's work on Zhou dynasty law reveal that law codes and courts were part of China's government for centuries longer than any present European government. Chang recently published a masterful treatment of Chinese legal philosophy and its impact on China's government over the past 2,500 years. With painstaking care he methodically laid out no less than nine different points of view about law advocated by various philosophers and statesmen over those millennia, thereby revealing some of the richness of China's experience with law. His elucidation of the three types of law in the Zhou dynasty provides strong support for the inventiveness of Chinese legal culture. These were the *li*, translated as 'rites', something like a cross between religious ritual and social mores, which came from the gods and were performed for the gods, yet were discernible by the human heart after cultivating it with contemplation of key works of literature; the *zongli*, which were rules applied within clans and were decidedly man-made; and the *fa*, or punishments, whose nature stirred the greatest controversy and were said to originate with the Miao people, a group considered distinct from the Chinese Han.[36]

Chang's conclusion takes him to a slightly different place from William Alford's staunch defence of China's experience with the rule of law. Law consistently was used to support a concentration of power, not to restrain it, Chang concludes (481). After Chang's exhaustive survey, no one could dispute this, but we must somehow fit into this bleak picture the glimpses we have of law used for the public good. The Yongzheng Emperor attempted to clarify and limit the *dian* for no other apparent reason, it seems from Buoye's account,[37] than to stem the confusion over property rights and the resulting violence from its abuse. This appears to be an instance of the central ruler protecting his people, and therefore, even if the emperor did not consider himself bound by it, because he had no need to sell or buy land, he used law in a way that may be consistent with the rule of law.

---

[35] William P. Alford, 'The Inscrutable Occidental?' 64 *Texas L. R.* (1986) 915 ff.
[36] Wejen Chang, *In Search of the Way: Legal Philosophy of the Classic Chinese Thinkers* (2016) 5 ff.
[37] Buoye (n. 14) 105 ff, relying on Yang Guozhen (1988).

After Matthew Sommer's masterful research, it is more difficult to detect benevolent motives in the same emperor's regulation of sexual practices and prohibitions on the sale of women using the *dian*. The Qing Code contains other examples of law whose ostensible purpose was to promote the public good. Provisions that prescribe lashing with a bamboo pole for men who prostituted their wives or forced women into bigamous marriages may have satisfied a certain desire to keep women virtuous, a desire that had more to do with aesthetics than the public welfare, but how could it not also promote the welfare of women? Sommer examined thousands of official records about cases involving the sale of wives and produced two books concerned with understanding the social dynamics of family relationships and sexual mores and the intentions of the government in regulating prostitution.[38] Sommer sees such laws as a means to exert more control over the population as a whole. Sommer's inspiration for this view came in part from Michel Foucault, whose analysis of the regimes within prisons and monasteries depicts their limits on sexual practices as power plays. This sounds more like 'rule by law' than the 'rule of law' and jibes more with Yu Xingzhong's view of law in China as perennially instrumental rather than with Chen Shouyi's faith in periodic appearances of the rule of law, as is described in the next section.

Chang Wejen documents with care the first publication of a law in China, and in so doing, he illustrates how vitally important cultural context is to understanding the implications of any law. In 536 BC, the Zheng state's code of punishments was carved on a bronze vessel and placed in open spaces where people could gather to discuss them. The purpose was to restore order, maintains Chang, and publication accomplished this because it filled a void: 'There was no social authority to create a new set of moral rules that people could readily agree to and accept.'[39] Chang reveals here that he believes that societies need a unified set of rules imposed by a ruler. I wonder, though, if the act of publishing these punishments was not more akin to a threat, as in, if you behave in this way, be forewarned that you will be punished. If so, then the issue of law's transparency is surely culturally conditioned. Whereas in the Anglo-American world, where codes did not come into being until the nineteenth century, and where the law resided in the spoken word in courtrooms, legal transparency has been identified with individual rights and curbs on governmental power. But from this example in China, legal transparency was paired with an exercise of state power. Edward Farmer's work on the Ming Emperor Zhu Yuanzhang provides further examples of this pairing.[40]

---

[38] Matthew Sommer, *Sex, Law, and Society in Late Imperial China* (1994); *Polyandry and Wife-Selling in Qing Dynasty China: Survival Strategies and Judicial Interventions* (2015).

[39] Chang (n. 36) 14–15 ff.

[40] Edward L. Farmer, *Zhu Yuanzhang and Early Ming Legislation: The Reordering of Chinese Society Following the Era of Mongol Rule* (1995).

There is yet another beneficial direction towards which a comparative approach could steer the field of Chinese legal history, that involving a mature treatment of globalization. Chinese investment now influences the governance of parts of Africa and of Latin America; it is only a matter of time before its laws will shape those legal systems and others. There is therefore no more important time to research precedents for an extraterritorial impact of Chinese law. Past episodes of the international influence of Chinese law include the transplantation of the Tang Code into Korea and Japan. Foreign incursions into China during the sixteenth through nineteenth centuries have been carefully and engagingly treated by Jonathan Spence, John Fairbank, Arthur Waley, and R. Randle Edwards, and more recently by Alison Conner, Christian Henriot, Frederic Wakeman, Jr., and Barak Kushner. According to my research, municipal councils were introduced from France into several coastal cities of China in the mid-nineteenth century. Christian Henriot researched the internal workings of the Municipal Council of Shanghai and showed it to promote sanitation and urban infrastructure even as it imposed foreign rule upon hundreds of thousands of Chinese.[41]

The influence of China on Europe, on the other hand, during that era remains underexplored. Napoleon's Civil Code of 1804 famously borrowed its structure and the content of some provisions from the late Roman emperor Justin's *Corpus Juris Civilis*. And yet, European diplomats with experience in China today speak of evidence that Napoleon admired the vast bureaucracy run by China's emperor and looked to it when constructing his own bureaucracy. Why, then, when centralizing France's governance into his person as emperor, would he not have looked to the world's oldest code-based legal system still in force, to its then law code which had been in force for over a century and a half at that time? That code contained provisions for punishment of district magistrates when they did not properly apply the code. Similarly, Napoleon's Civil Code's 'Preliminary Part' contains a provision that threatens criminal punishment of judges who refuse to judge cases on the basis that no code provision covered them.[42] Even if the roughly equivalent Roman legal maxim '*Judex qui litem suam fecit*' [Judge who made his suit] provided inspiration for that French provision, could not have the Qing code provisions as well?

There is another reason to learn more about past efforts by China to export its law. My research in archives in China and places outside to where consular records were spirited away during the Chinese Communist Party's consolidation of its rule shows that foreigners exercised vast powers over Chinese subjects in Shanghai during the late nineteenth and early twentieth century and used law in a variety of ways—as a guise, as a weapon, as a shield—to accomplish this feat. The Chinese who were subjected to this law adapted and cleverly seized opportunities afforded them under this patchwork of multiple foreign legal regimes.[43] Nonetheless, the century-long experience by Chinese with foreign rule, in Shanghai and elsewhere in China,

---

[41] Christian Henriot, *Shanghai 1927–1937: Municipal Power, Locality, and Modernization* (1993).
[42] *Code civile*, Art. 4.   [43] Lee (n. 19).

must have left in its wake legions of souls seething at the injustice of it. Mao Zedong well understood this reaction and brilliantly used it to win enough public support for the Chinese Communist Party, against great odds, to steer it into the position of central ruler in 1949.

Carol Tan has helped illuminate the complexities of foreign courts on Chinese soil by uncovering the attempts of British Consular judges to stem a wave of Chinese female suicides in Weihaiwei in the early twentieth century. British statute created a court in this tiny piece of Shandong Province in northeast China that was to mimic 'as far as circumstances admit' courts in England,[44] including their being bound by 'the Statute Law and other law for the time being in force in England ….' Despite the statute's charge, the judges, when dealing with a wave of both suicides and kidnappings of Chinese women, complied with the law and custom of the area, and to some extent cultivated an appearance, locally, of compliance and reinforcement of them.

III. PENETRATION OF LAW INTO SOCIETY

Piercing the official line, which usually gives the impression that law is self-enforcing and is evenly and equally enforced across the entire territory subject to the law, is of the utmost importance if we are to understand the degree to which law penetrated into Chinese society before today's Chinese Communist Party brought its rule deep into everyday life. In a sense, this is political scientist Vivienne Shue's 'reach of the state', except that as law scholars we are concerned specifically about law's role. As noted earlier, anthropological methods help us to see through official versions of a legal system, because they allow us to examine the record closely and from an ordinary person's perspective. The Law and Society approach, where we dispense with the myth that law operated autonomously from society, should help with this endeavour. It corrects the exaggerated self-importance that official stances about law naturally give to it. Scholarship open to a multiplicity of perspectives helps us stand in people's shoes, appreciate the strategic uses of law deployed by subjects of the law as well as lawmakers, and understand ways in which law presented opportunities for advancement and survival unintended by the lawmakers.

Finding sources untainted by the official line is an exceedingly difficult and sensitive project. The contrasting conclusions of two mainland law scholars, Yu

---

[44] Carol G. S. Tan, ' "Hurry No Man's Cattle": British Rule and Suicide in China' 26 *J. Legal History* (2005) 281 ff.

Xingzhong and Chen Shouyi, illustrate this. Training their sights on the 1950s through the 1980s, Yu saw continuity in the government's approach to law, while Chen, who served as Dean of Peking University's Law School, saw discontinuity and an abrupt about-face. An instrumental approach to policy choices continued unabated throughout those several decades, argued Yu,[45] while Chen attributed nothing less than the institution of the rule of law to the government's moves in the late 1970s and 1980s.[46] While neither view diverged completely from the official line in the 1990s that the rule of law was resurrected by the Chinese Communist Party beginning in 1978 to encourage economic growth and foreign investment, Chen's depiction resonates more closely with that story, because it suggests that the rule of law had actually taken root in that short span of time. Yu's view was more sanguine, more willing to allow for some distance between policy pronouncements and reality.

To avoid glib and counterproductive conclusions, future scholarship on Chinese legal history would do well to include more sensitivity to China's uniqueness. Chinese law on its own terms, not implicitly compared to the law of the author, may work a corrective to condescension and fictitious yardsticks. Fei Chengkang's work on clan codes reveals a rich vein of statutory codes and courts that for centuries were based entirely within families.[47] Mary Szto's research into religious ritual shows an integral relationship between government courts and their spiritual counterparts which were overseen by Taoist and Buddhist priests, guilds, and families. Priests wrote petitions and filed them in underworld courts and wrote contracts that protected their signatories from suit in the afterlife. Priests also described these 'spirit courts', to warn the living about the hellish punishments meted out in them. Even the living were subject to suit there. And the courts offered hope for justice in the afterlife where it could not be attained on earth.[48]

With their detail drawn from a variety of written sources not typically considered legal in European or American legal history, such studies shed light while leaving to others the task of finding analogues elsewhere in the world. In Jiang Yonglin's second book,[49] he draws upon a lifetime of research into law during the Ming dynasty and finds important connections between it and religious beliefs. This study, and those of Fei and Szto, uncover multiple sources of legitimacy of law in China and alternatives to brute force for its enforcement, such as shame, shunning, and fear of divine retribution. At the same time, these studies help us to broaden definitions of legal rubrics, such as 'rule of law', in ways that are more universal, that capture a more diverse human experience.

---

[45] Yu Xingzhong, 'Legal Pragmatism in the People's Republic of China' 3 *J. Chin. L.* (1989) 29 ff.

[46] Chen Shouyi, 'A Review of Thirty Years of Legal Studies in New China' 2 *J. Chin. L.* (1988) 181 ff.

[47] Fei Chengkang, *Zhongguo de jia fa zu gui [Family and Clan Regulations in China]* (1998).

[48] Mary Szto, 'Strengthening the Rule of Virtue and Finding Chinese Law in 'Other' Places: Gods, Kin, Guilds, and Gifts' 35 *Suffolk Transnational L. R.* (2012) 1 ff.

[49] Yonglin Jiang, *The Mandate of Heaven and the Great Ming Code* (2011).

The development of law in China can be seen as a story of law's penetration into society. And so, it is useful here to approach the subject of historiography by starting with the source of law that was most limited in its reach—the dynastic codes and imperial edicts—and then to move from there to examine sources of law that allowed for progressively greater effect on the population. These codes never existed in an institutional vacuum, and we can learn what they evince about the institutional framework around the emperor who enacted them. The codes contain within themselves important clues about their reach, and so textual analysis provides a fruitful avenue for inquiry. The contents of the *Da Qing Lü Li* make clear that it was written not for the general public but for the district magistrates. It is full of sentencing guidelines and default rules for processing evidence, which are instructions for judges rather than prescriptions for the general public. Far from evincing law's distance from the population, the procedural nature of the code reveals an intense concern by China's rulers in the implementation of its policies.

Moving outward from the central codes of China's legal system we come to the governmental institutions that implemented them. We need to know more about the Board of Punishments, the officials in Beijing who stood above the district magistrates in a vast bureaucracy and whether and to what extent they were followed. Biographical research into who wrote the supplementary statutes and the provisions that were periodically added to the *Da Qing Lü Li*, of the kind Betsey Bartlett produced in her study of the Grand Council, would help illuminate the motives of these men. During various periods the emperor's top administrators deployed a myriad of other mechanisms that used administrative-style regulations to ensure that the magistrates were enforcing the laws in a way that did less harm than good. Brian McKnight used official writings and case records from the Song period to depict the implementation of law as a means for social control.[50] Nancy Park's study of these rules for Qing magistrates and their superiors promises to reveal the great extent to which hierarchy marked that bureaucracy and its approach to making decisions. Chang Wejen's imminent monumental publication on the entire Qing judicial system will no doubt fill in large pieces of the picture for us and answer longstanding questions, such as how much discretion the district magistrate exercised.

Disregard for judicial decisions, the lack of their enforcement, the lack of consensus as to peaceful values, minimal respect for the authority, weak community ties—all these come to the mind of the legal scholar as supplementary explanations for the violence surrounding land rights. Future scholarship on these aspects of the social fabric will help to explain the blatant disregard for judicial decisions shown by some of the litigants in eighteenth-century Guangdong, Sichuan, and Shandong Provinces that Thomas Buoye studied. Buoye hints at

---

[50] Brian E. McKnight, *Law and Order in Sung China* (1992).

the possibility of this when he writes that an 'erosion of shared ethical norms regarding property rights created uncertainty and weakened the persuasive power of the local magistrate'.[51]

Further afield lie provincial and district governments, those whose jurisdiction spanned sub-units of China and who were in a position to carry law into the lives of their subjects to a greater extent than the dynastic codes aimed to do. How did the *Daotai*, often translated as 'Prefect', exercise his authority and to what extent was he bound by the same rules that bound the subjects of his locality? Other local institutions exerted power by the late Qing and should not be ignored. Maura Dykstra looks at the control over local commercial matters that the lawmakers in Beijing exercised in the eighteenth through early twentieth centuries. Her method involves looking first at a central legal initiative, such as a new national bankruptcy statute, and then surveying contemporary court cases in one large and commercially robust city. She does not stop at the words of the case records, but pursues concurrent activities in local institutions such as chambers of commerce to gauge the effects of the law.[52]

The more we learn about how these institutions functioned, the more flux we will surely see. In Bradly Reed's exhaustive treatment of the clerks and runners who carried out the commands of the district magistrates and who were paid out of the magistrates' own salaries, localities became increasingly adept at organizing their own affairs and fending off intrusion from the statutory regime of Beijing. Change is equally apparent in Matthew Sommer's extensive material on the regulation of sexual mores during those same two and a half centuries, but his material shows an increasingly aggressive use of national law to control the population.

Finally, documents that reflect private ordering hold significant potential for shedding light on the zones of autonomy from central rule, and the effectiveness of government efforts to regulate economic affairs. This is an issue to which Madeleine Zelin has recently turned her perceptive gaze. From her study of property litigation during the Qing, she concludes that 'the rights of property were well defined'.[53] And yet, Feng Shaoting read hundreds of documents pertaining to the sale of buildings in Shanghai in the nineteenth and early twentieth centuries and found evidence of frequent reworking of the promises in such documents long after they had been signed and dated.[54] We get a taste of the malleability of promises in the contracts he gathered when he describes contracting parties asking for more supplemental

---

[51] Buoye (n. 14) 103 ff.

[52] Maura Dykstra, 'Beyond the Shadow of the Law: Firm Insolvency, State Building, and the New Policy Bankruptcy Reform in Late Qing Chongqing' 8 *Frontiers of History of China* (2013) 406 ff.

[53] Zelin (n. 27) 19 ff.

[54] Feng Shaoting, 'Supplemental Payment in Urban Property Contracts in Mid to Late Qing Shanghai', in Zelin, Ocko, Gardella (eds.), *Contract and Property in Early Modern China* (2004) 160–1, 209 ff.

payments than was agreed to in the contract or in the customary law that provided for one supplemental payment outside of the terms of a contract. Would the violence attending the property disputes studied by Buoye have roiled if property rights had been clear? Zelin sees some involvement by the government in defining the rights of property and in enforcing them, but she also acknowledges an 'increasing use of self-enforcing mechanisms, like deposits', which she links to a growing 'political instability'(25) and describes that involvement as limited only by what is necessary 'to protect the greater good' (23).[55]

Care must be taken not to project American or European conceptions of these private legal tools upon the artefacts examined in China. How do you prove that a jade tablet carved with the boundaries of a tract of land, a price, and the names of buyer and seller is not simply a memorial of a transaction, like a receipt, rather than a promise to do something that parties to the transaction agree will be enforceable by a third-party neutral? We know relatively little about the use of contracts, commercial paper, and land title documents during any period of Chinese history. Hugh Scogin bravely made inroads into a period two thousand years ago.[56] In a pioneering work, Valerie Hansen read and analysed from multiple perspectives a cache of about 500 documents from the city of Dunhuang in the northwestern province of Gansu and from the city of Turfan in the southwestern province of Xinjiang from the 700s AD to the 900s AD. From these hubs of the Silk Road she concluded that contracts were ubiquitous in China from the seventh to the fifteenth century, a broad conclusion that may be substantiated after more documents from more locations in China are plumbed.[57] Zelin and Hansen agree that contract forms were standardized at this time, the significance of which is important for understanding the freedom of people to reach agreements and the degree to which the language of the contract actually reflected the intentions of the contracting parties.

Documentation of transactions provide glimpses at the zones of autonomy in which they operated. Did participants invoke law in their routine or important affairs? Did they expect others to invoke it? What did people dare to do without permission of government or without consulting the law? Could they strategize with the help of legal experts? Looking broadly at people's choices within the constraints set by law will reveal more than will asking how litigious they were. If Melissa Macauley's research on pettifoggers in Qing China does not prove that there was a strong demand for litigation, it shows at least that scribes who

[55] Zelin (n. 27) 23, 25 ff.

[56] Hugh Scogin, 'Between Heaven and Man: Contract and the State in Han Dynasty China' 63 *Southern California L. R.* 1325 ff.

[57] Valerie Hansen, *Negotiating Daily Life in Traditional China: How Ordinary People Used Contracts, 600–1400* (1995).

specialized in writing petitions to the district magistrate to assist litigants were important figures, inspiring public commentary and occupying a place in the popular imagination.[58]

Personal connections, known in China as *guanxi,* form relationships built on shared interests and a foundation of trust. Such relationships obviate the need for contracts, which are necessary only for 'arms-length' transactions where the parties do not trust each other to keep their promises, where they are willing to treat each other as if there is no prior relationship that generates its own, more complex set of demands. If each person's loyalties are fixed by a web of personal relationships, neither contracts nor law can be enforced upon them, because law is an objective, external standard that has no place within the subjective realm of personal relationships and the claims they make upon the individual. Similarly, litigation provides relief where personal relationships do not exist or have broken down. How important were personal connections during various periods of China's past?

Even partial and imperfect answers to these questions will illuminate our under-standing of the reach of law in China in eras before our own. Private documents may not reveal how sophisticated China was, how highly developed its legal system was, or how litigious its people were, as the dyadic East-West 'rule of law' scholars would have it. Instead, they reveal how much freedom there was in China to order one's affairs. If Chang Wejen's observation that law throughout the past 2,500 years in China was used exclusively by rulers to centralize their control, never as a means for granting or protecting rights to the populace,[59] we must consider all the more carefully the reach of that law.

Of course, what counts as law? Mark Allee sets out some examples of what he calls 'customary law' related to land ownership and control in Taiwan and Sichuan.[60] The term 'customary law' glides over the question of whether custom is law, but we need to pay attention to this definitional problem in China's past in order to measure the freedom people enjoyed to order their affairs. In a preliminary study, Ramon Myers and Fu-Mei Chan Chen found evidence of widespread customary practices that they believed held the status of law and exerted positive effects on the economy.[61] Philip Huang endeavoured to compare law and custom during the Qing and Republican eras.[62] The description of local customary rules in their rich diversity across China throughout its past remains to be done.

[58] Melissa Macauley, *Social Power and Legal Culture: Litigation Masters in Late Imperial China* (1998).
[59] Chang (n. 36) 481 ff.
[60] Mark A. Allee, 'The Status of Contracts in 19th Century Chinese Courts' in Zelin, Ocko, and Gardella (eds.), *Contract and Property in Early Modern China* (2004) 160 ff.
[61] Ramon Myers and Fu-Mei Chan Chen, 'Customary Law and the Economic Growth of China during the Ch'ing Period' 3 *Ch'ing-shi wen-t'i* (1976) 1 ff.
[62] Philip C. C. Huang, *Code, Custom, and Legal Practice in China* (2001).

IV. CONCLUSION

The field of Chinese legal history is buffeted by many of the same headwinds facing other areas of legal history, such as those associated with trends in academia that seek a facile relevance and a monetizable scholarship, and that expect quick and clear answers. The linguistic and logistical challenges that must be surmounted in order to read archival material in Chinese, however, set this field apart and in some way helps explain why the field is thought to be still in its infancy.

Can we find another salient characteristic of the field of Chinese legal history by considering the rise of China in the twenty-first century? Surely we can, and we must. That characteristic might be expressed with the words 'central', or 'pivotal' words that run contrary to perceptions in many quarters that the study of China is 'boutique-y' or otherwise on the periphery of the world's concern. Not since AD 700, when the law code of Empress Wu Zitian's Tang dynasty spread to Korea and Japan and its armies reestablished the Silk Road and came within a hair's breadth of Europe, has it been as urgent for the world to understand China's vast experience with law. The great longevity of China's law codes and the millennia of its formalized rules for trying disputes and meting out punishments which were prescribed in law put Chinese legal history in a class by itself, deserving of study for its own sake, for the sake of better understanding a significant piece of the human experience with law.

Continuing to build on the language training and knowledge about Chinese society that has produced many important works, we must extend the legal historian of China's training to include a technical understanding of law and anthropological tools, such as interviewing and attention to the body and visual cues, and sensitivity to a broad array of moments where law takes effect. Legal historians of China would do well also to become sophisticated about the comparative significance and potential of their work. European legal historian Matthew Dyson believes that legal history is 'the study of the causation in historically and legal relevant events'.[63] Proving causation is nearly impossible, but comparative legal history will help us go in this bold direction, a direction that scholars of other places' legal histories are going. Happily, there seems to be a trend among the current generation of historians who read imperial-era court cases to develop effective means to probe beyond the official version of law and into the effects of law on everyday life. May such work continue to enrich our appreciation of the challenges and the ingenuity of Chinese experiences of law.

---

[63] Matthew Dyson, 'If the Present Were the Past' 56 *American J. Legal History* (2016) 41 ff.

BIBLIOGRAPHY

Thomas M. Buoye, *Manslaughter, Markets, and Moral Economy: Violent Disputes over Property Rights in Eighteenth Century China* (Cambridge University Press, 2000)

Par K. Cassel, *Grounds of Judgment: Extraterritoriality and Imperial Power in Nineteenth-Century China and Japan* (Oxford University Press, 2012)

Wejen Chang, *In Search of the Way: Legal Philosophy of the Classic Chinese Thinkers* (University of Edinburgh Press, 2016)

Li Chen, *Chinese Law in Imperial Eyes: Sovereignty, Justice, and Transcultural Politics* (Columbia University Press, 2015)

T'ung-tzu Ch'ü, *Local Government in China Under the Ch'ing* (Stanford University Press, 1962)

Chengkang Fei 费成康, *Zhongguo de jia fa zu gui* 中国的家法族规 *[Family and Clan Regulations in China]* (Shanghai she hui ke xue yuan chu ban she 上海社會科學院出版社 [Shanghai Academy of Social Sciences], 1998)

Valerie Hansen, *Negotiating Daily Life in Traditional China: How Ordinary People Used Contracts, 600–1400* (Yale University Press, 1995)

Yonglin Jiang, *The Mandate of Heaven and the Great Ming Code* (University of Washington Press, 2011)

Melissa A. Macauley, *Social Power and Legal Culture: Litigation Masters in Late Imperial China* (Stanford University Press, 1998)

Bradly W. Reed, *Talons and Teeth, County Clerks, and Runners in the Qing Dynasty* (Stanford University Press, 2000)

Matthew H. Sommer, *Sex, Law, and Society in Late Imperial China* (Stanford University Press, 2000)

Sybille Van Der Sprenkel, *Legal Institutions in Manchu China* (London School of Economics, 1962)

Guozhen Yang, 杨国桢 Ming Qing tu di qi yue wen shu yan jiu 明清土地契究 /Research on Ming and Qing Land Sales Documents] (Renmin chubanshe 人民出版社 [People's Press], 2009 rev edn)

CHAPTER 42

TRADITIONS

TRACING LEGAL HISTORY, ABORIGINAL/INDIGENOUS LAW (AUSTRALIA/NEW ZEALAND)

SHAUNNAGH DORSETT

I. INTRODUCTION

STORIES of encounters between Indigenous peoples in both Australia and New Zealand and the British Empire have been told many times and from many perspectives.[1] They are still being told. Stories of *legal* encounters and of the legal relations between Indigenous peoples, the Empire, the succeeding nation-states, and those who arrived under their auspices have also been told. Like more general histories, consideration of the history of legal relations between Indigenous peoples, the state, and settlers has been wrapped up with the history of dispossession and is now often tied to questions of legal consequences under current law. Land, the taking of it, and the results of this have, in the latter part of the twentieth century

---

[1] Ann Curthoys, 'Indigenous Subjects' in *Australia's Empire*, D. M. Schreuder, S. Ward (eds.), (2008) 78 ff.

and early twenty first century, become central to how we think not just about the shape of current relations between Indigenous peoples and the settler state, but to how we think about the histories of those relations. In law, this is particularly acute, as these histories have become inextricably part of attempts to find legal forms through which to acknowledge and deal with that dispossession. Less talked about, though equally important, is another form of dispossession (or perhaps better displacement): that of law itself. The sheer scale of the taking of land in Australia, and of the processes by which land was converted into Western legal interests in New Zealand, has tended to obscure the fact that it was not just land that was taken, but that indigenous laws (*tikanga* Māori in Aotearoa/New Zealand) struggled to survive the onslaught of settler law and even now are dismissed by many as 'not law', or as being mere remnants, or simply as having not survived. In both places, historians and lawyers alike have struggled with how to think about these displacements, with how to deal with their consequences in modern law, and with how to find a place for the histories of these displacements in modern legal processes.

There are obvious commonalities between colonies: they share common legal heritage and traditions. Moreover, Indigenous peoples in both were subjected to the forces of rapid settlement and were governed through combinations of Christianization, civilization, military and settler violence, and the criminal law. These forces, however, played out rather differently in the different colonies and resulted in particular histories. Timing, local circumstance (vastly different geographies and climate), and the ways in which the local indigenous populations were viewed by colonial authorities all contributed to different trajectories. Thus, despite the commonalities, the divergences have meant that discussion of these matters has rarely been brought into a common field(s). While both nations struggle with how to think about their pasts and how to live with those pasts in the (legal) present, these struggles have rarely been brought into conversation. The subjects of these dispossessions themselves see the common concerns. However, outside this, histories have almost exclusively remained tied to one or the other.[2] Comparative or transnational accounts are rare. In many areas of scholarly endeavour, not the least this one, 'trans-Tasman history' never really got going. In some ways this is a product of very different legal starting points for the colonies of Australia and New Zealand, at least as regards their indigenous inhabitants. This in turn was a product of the different ways in which British authorities regarded Indigenous Australians and Māori. One group was considered low on the scale of civilization, had little discernible by way of law,

---

[2] One of the few exceptions is the work of Damen Ward. See, in particular, 'The Politics of Jurisdiction: "British" Law, Indigenous Peoples and Colonial Government in South Australia and New Zealand, c. 1834–60', DPhil thesis, Oxford University, 2003 ff.

had a relationship with land that the British did not understand, and offered little in the way of trade. The other had a more recognizable attachment to land, had norms that the British recognized as laws (albeit ones considered uncivilized compared to those of the settlers), and had goods to trade and labour that was vital to the survival of the colony. These different beginnings grew into different legal processes and institutions though which Indigenous peoples and their laws came into relation with (or did not come into relation with) the settler state. How then did and do the laws of indigenous Australians and Māori come into relation with the national laws of these states?

Seeking to think about multiple laws from various places in the same chapter—let alone in the same field—always poses challenges. This is particularly so when considering the way the common law has encountered the laws of indigenous Australians and of Māori. From similar common traditions and heritages there have been varied trajectories. These divergences generally have consequences for how we might think about doing (or whether we want to do) comparative or transnational histories, as well as particular consequences for writing a chapter such as this. To what extent does an exercise such as this flatten particularity? Is the gain of looking at continuities and divergences enough to warrant the exercise? And what might be lost in so doing? These matters are returned to briefly in the concluding comments. Whether or not the gain is worth the loss, inevitably choices must be made as to when, and with respect to what, the points of contact between the two are located. This chapter, therefore, considers one often used, but increasingly maligned, source of historical material—court decisions—in order to suggest two contact points between jurisdictions through which to think about indigenous laws and settler laws. It also pays attention to only two (rather conventional) times of contact: the colonial and the present. In many ways this choice reproduces ongoing gaps in tracing and thinking about legal encounters with Aboriginal law in Australia and, to a lesser extent, in New Zealand. Scholarship on legal encounter has tended to be centred on the colonial period to the detriment of the later nineteenth century and much of the twentieth century.[3] Finally, it should be emphasized that this chapter looks at the ways in which colonial and modern law engaged/s with aboriginal law from the perspective of the colonizer, not the colonized. The traditions are those of Western law, not the First Peoples of either nation.

---

[3] For exceptions see Heather Douglas and Mark Finnane, *Indigenous Crime and Settler Law: Sovereignty after Empire* (2012), and the work of Amanda Nettelbeck, for example, '"We are Sure of your Sympathy": Aboriginal Uses of the Politics of Protection in 19th Century Australia and Canada' in Penny Edmonds, Anna Johnston (eds.), 'Empire, Humanitarianism and Violence in the Colonies' (2016) 17 *Journal of Colonialism and Colonial History* DOI: 10.1353/cch.2016.0009 ff.

II. Dispossession and Displacement: Immediate Contexts and Obvious Differences

There has, as noted at the outset, been little work on legal encounter which has crossed all Australasian colonies. There are obvious reasons for this, reasons which are common to almost any endeavour to think comparatively or transnationally with law and/or history and which do not need recitation here. We might simply point to the problems of accessing materials; the difficulty for non-New Zealanders of understanding Māori concepts and language, which pervade primary and secondary sources; and the relatively small cadre of scholars in both Australia and New Zealand when compared, for example, to North America. Recent digital innovations, such as the provision of colonial newspapers on-line, in Australia *Trove*, and in New Zealand *Papers Past*, has played a role in making more material available to scholars.[4] While this has lead to a quantitative increase in scholarship, it has not all been to positive effect. Context is vital in any comparative endeavour, and here is no different. In the main, however, scholars from each place are aware of the different beginnings and attitudes in the Australasian colonies and in New Zealand and are respectful of divergences. Nevertheless, the relatively small body of literature makes it difficult to bridge the divide. Moreover, there is still so much work to be done in each place—and even between the former Australian colonies—that understanding those differences and bringing matters together may take some time.

Even before considering the two small points of contact between jurisdictions chosen for this chapter, therefore, some context is required. Much of how we have thought about, and continue to think about, Indigenous Australians and their laws, for example, draws on a deep history of denial—denial of any legally recognizable relationship between Indigenous Australians and their country, and denial that Indigenous Australians had laws recognizable as such. In 1788 Indigenous Australians had lived on the Australian continent and surrounding islands for over 50,000 years. They were self-governing peoples with complex laws relating to all facets of life: family and land, life and law. Tribes and clans entered into agreements with each other to govern boundaries, trade, and rituals. There was diversity between people across the continent, but also similarities forged in shared bonds to country, the Dreamtime, art, and ritual. Yet little of this was visible or understandable to the British and others who followed in their wake. What were settlers to make of these

---

[4] *Trove* and *Papers Past* are digitised newspaper collections available for the National Library of Australia and the National Library of New Zealand, respectively. See <http://trove.nla.gov.au/newspaper/> and <https://paperspast.natlib.govt.nz>.

people whose culture was so alien and laws so unrecognizable? Initial opinions and views as to the nature of indigenous law and the ownership of land were, in fact, more mixed than is often thought. However, for many decades Australia's national narrative was dominated by a view of history which began with European settlement and which relied on an erasure of any time in which indigenous Australians were recognized as the First Peoples. As Attwood reminds us, the anthropologist W. E. H. Stanner once famously referred to this as a 'culture of forgetfulness'.[5]

By the 1840s, and the time of New Zealand's formal settlement, the idea that Aboriginal Australians had neither law nor rights to land had taken hold. Moreover, the idea that Aboriginal Australians were dying out, inevitably doomed to extinction, had also begun to take hold.[6] It is impossible to collapse a complex early history of encounter into a few short sentences, but it might suffice here to note that by the late nineteenth century any early ideas of plurality had largely been forgotten, while wide-scale dispossession in many parts of Australia had had drastic effects on Aboriginal peoples, their land, and their culture. Things, however, were somewhat different in New Zealand, formally annexed some fifty years after New South Wales. Timing was crucial. A distinct reluctance to take sovereignty over New Zealand meant that by the time the British determined to do this, different policies, different intellectual views, and different understandings of Indigenous peoples and their place in the Empire held sway.

While the status of Māori law in the 1840s is still the subject of some debate, there seems little doubt that colonial administrators viewed the status of Māori and their laws quite differently from the way in which they viewed the same matters in the Australian colonies. While the colonizing British Government asserted sovereignty over the islands of New Zealand, they understood that this assertion of sovereignty hardly meant that the common law had become the legitimate or even effective law of the land. It had been acknowledged prior to colonization that Māori were sovereign (although whether for the British that meant quite the same sovereignty as enjoyed by European nations was debatable) and that they had their own laws, however brutal or sometimes 'uncivilized' they appeared to European eyes. After the acquisition of sovereignty, all British subjects in New Zealand were formally subject to British law, and this included Māori, who were declared 'subjects' by Art. III of the Treaty of Waitangi. Despite this, the British, at the outset at least, did not intend Māori to be subject to British law in all circumstances. In particular, there was no assumption that Māori would necessarily be amenable to British law with respect to many *intra*-Māori matters. Outside the small, isolated, and vulnerable British settlements, most Māori, and many out-settlers, lived according to *tikanga*

---

[5] W. E. H. Stanner, *After the Dreaming* (Sydney, 1969) in Bain Attwood, 'The Past as Future: Aborigines, Australia and the (dis)course of History', (1996) *Australian Humanities Review*, <http://www.australianhumanitiesreview.org/1996/04/01/the-past-as-future-aborigines-australia-and-the-discourse-of-history/> (accessed 30 April 2018).

[6] Curthoys (n. 1) 91 ff.

Māori, and the authorities—both local and metropolitan—were painfully aware that British legal authority was largely unenforceable. The question was not so much whether Māori had law, it was one of which parts of it could or should be recognized and enforced at common law, and of how Māori could be encouraged to take up British law.[7]

Despite this, settlement nevertheless took place by dispossession. Across the nineteenth century land and resources were increasingly transferred from Māori to the Crown.[8] However, dispossession took place by somewhat different means from those which had prevailed in the Australian colonies. Crown purchase (under the Crown's right of pre-emption), *raupatu* (confiscation), particularly during military conflict between Māori and Crown forces, and the operation of the *Native Land Acts*, by means of which customary title was to be transformed into freely alienable fee simple title, meant that by the end of the nineteenth century little customary land remained,[9] although this is not to say that no land remained in Māori hands. Rather, the form of title had changed. The purchase, confiscation, and conversion are, however, one explanation for why New Zealand has not experienced the phenomenon of common law claims to native or aboriginal title which have been so prominent in Australia and Canada from the late twentieth century. These processes have meant that it would be extremely difficult for Māori to fit within the confines of the doctrines of aboriginal or native title with its emphasis on continuity and uninterrupted connection.[10] From these somewhat divergent beginnings there were different trajectories. In particular, a plethora of institutions, from early land commissions, to the Native Land Court, to the modern Waitangi Tribunal, resulted in a quite different fora through which to engage with the Crown than those which characterized Australian Indigenous-Crown relations. The point is not so much that these all had positive outcomes for Māori (far from it), but that a history of engagement developed that could be drawn upon in modern processes, from claims before the Waitangi Tribunal to the modern treaty process.

By the late 1960s in both jurisdictions (and more broadly across the Anglophone world) indigenous activists had begun to agitate for redress for the loss of land and for justice for devastating imperial and colonial practices.[11] These culminated in two quite different judicial processes. In New Zealand, the Waitangi Tribunal,

---

[7] See Shaunnagh Dorsett, *Juridical Encounters: Māori and the Colonial Courts, 1840–1852* (2017) 2–3 ff.

[8] Ian Pool, *Colonization and Development between 1769 and 1900: The Seeds of Rangiatea* (2015).

[9] Native Lands Act 1862 (NZ); Native Land Act 1865 (NZ); R. P. Boast, 'Buying the Land, Selling the Land: Governments and Māori Land in the North Island 1865–1921 (2008); Richard P. Boast, Richard S. Hill (eds.), *Raupatu: The Confiscation of Māori Land* (Wellington, 2009).

[10] See Carwyn Jones, *New Treaty, New Tradition: Reconciling New Zealand and Māori Law* (2016).

[11] See Miranda Johnson, *The Land is our History: Indigeneity, Law and the Settler State* (2016).

a permanent commission of inquiry, is tasked with making recommendations to the Crown based on 'acts or omissions' of the Crown relating to breaches of 'the principles of the Treaty of Waitangi'.[12] As part of its remit the Tribunal has undertaken a number of inquiries into historic claims, in particular with respect to confiscation and land transactions in the nineteenth century. In Australia, by contrast, questions of redress were left to the regular courts, to be determined at common law, according to the doctrine of native title.[13] Much of the legal attention over the last decades has been on these two processes. There are of course others. The legal landscape is too complex to unpack for present purposes: New Zealand's modern treaty process; statutory land rights regimes in Australia; redress for the 'stolen generations'. The list is long. What has, however, received comparatively less attention is the legal relations of indigenous law and *tikanga* Māori (outside of issues of redress for land) to the national polity in general, and to the common law in particular.

Physical dispossession was more obvious to those who chose to look than was the loss of law. In Australia, the latter, after all, required some initial assumption that Aboriginal peoples had recognizable laws that should be respected and enforced at all. In New Zealand it was accepted that Māori retained some law, but questions as to what extent it was recognized and whether it should be recognized as such in the modern era are still being addressed. The institutional emphasis on dispossession of land and the histories of the dispossession—by force and by law—have outstripped histories which seek to understand more broadly how the common law met indigenous law and how this might impact on how we understand the relations between the two in the modern era. Moreover, with the exception perhaps of the work of Damen Ward and Lisa Ford, what histories have emerged have remained tied to particular jurisdictions. Lack of sources, the small cadre of scholars engaged in this activity, and the need to find points of entry into comparisons and contrasts have all contributed to this matter.[14]

---

[12] *Treaty of Waitangi Act* 1975 (NZ), as amended by *Treaty of Waitangi Amendment Act* 1985 (NZ). See R. P. Boast, 'The Waitangi Tribunal: "Conscience of the Nation" or Just Another Court' (1993) 16 *U.N.S.W.L.J.* 223 ff. For a history of the rise of the tribunal see Belgrave, *Historical Frictions: Māori Claims and Reinvented Histories* (2006). For reports see <https://www.waitangitribunal. govt.nz>.

[13] *Mabo v. State of Queensland (No. 2)* (1992) 175 CLR 1; Paul G. McHugh, *Aboriginal Title: The Modern Jurisprudence of Tribal Land Rights* (2011); Sean Brennan, Megan Davis, Brendan Edgeworth, Leon Terrill (eds.), *Native Title from Mabo to Akiba: A Vehicle for Change and Empowerment?* (2015).

[14] Lisa Ford, *Settler Sovereignty: Jurisdiction and Indigenous People in America and Australia, 1788–1836* (2010); Damen Ward, 'Constructing British Authority in Australasia: Charles Cooper and the Legal Status of Aborigines in the South Australian Supreme Court, c. 1840–1860' (2006) 34 *Journal of Imperial and Commonwealth History* 483 ff.

III: Legal Encounters: Traditions and Techniques, Common Law Jurisdiction

So where are the points of comparison? And where we should direct our attention? Work over the recent decades in both Australia and New Zealand on colonial legal encounters has centred on questions of sovereignty and jurisdiction over the new Indigenous inhabitants of the Australasian colonies. While this has largely been confined to examinations of single colonies, Damen Ward's work shows that working through the lens of jurisdiction can be productive in drawing out commonalities between colonies and their approaches.[15] This work draws on common inherited legal traditions. An emphasis on legal technique, rather than substance, can illuminate similar issues across time and place. Rather than focusing on divergences—for example the existence or not of a treaty—it looks to the technologies and techniques of the common law.[16]

In Australia, investigations into common law jurisdiction and the amenability of indigenous Australians to settler law owe much to the work of Bruce Kercher and his colonial case recovery project, begun in the 1990s and still, albeit rather scaled back, on-going. Kercher's 'discovery' of early decisions of the New South Wales Supreme Court disrupted the dominant narrative of an early colonial period legally characterized by blanket refusal to consider that Indigenous Australians had laws which could be recognized as such. Admittedly the breach in this narrative was not strong—at least in terms of precedent. Finding cases in which the New South Wales Supreme Court had been more equivocal about the status of Aboriginal peoples and their laws did not lead to any re-thinking of these matters in the modern period. If not precedent, however, Kercher's new cases were significant historical sources, sources which started, and have continued to contribute to, much broader conceptual and contextual analyses of the legal relations between the laws of the settlers and of the colonized in colonial New South Wales. While early work focused on New South Wales, this began to spread to include other colonies, such as South Australia and Western Australia.[17] Moreover, thinking with jurisdiction has allowed some much needed comparative work. Ford's examination of jurisdiction and the formation of settler sovereignty in New South Wales and Georgia stands out, as does Damen Ward's examination

---

[15] Ward (n. 2).   [16] Shaunnagh Dorsett, Shaun McVeigh, *Jurisdiction* (2012) ch. 3 ff.

[17] Ward, (2006) 34 *Journal of Imperial and Commonwealth History* 483 ff; Ann Hunter, 'The Boundaries of Colonial Criminal Law in Relation to Inter-Aboriginal Conflict ('Inter Se Offences') in Western Australia in the 1830s–1840s' (2004) 8 *Australian Journal of Legal History* 215 ff; Amanda Nettelbeck, '"Equals of the White Man": Prosecution of Settlers for Violence against Aboriginal Subjects of the Crown, Colonial Western Australia' (2013) 31 *Law & History Review* 355; Douglas and Finnane (n. 3).

of constructing jurisdiction over indigenous peoples in South Australia and New Zealand.

In New Zealand, similar case recovery efforts also led to new historical sources. Understandings of the legal relations between British law and *tikanga* Māori had been of interest for much longer. Despite this, work of a similar nature to that in Australia still did not appear until the 2000s. While in the 1970s scholars such as Alan Ward produced detailed accounts of British policy and law as applied to Māori, questions as to exactly how that law was viewed (as *law*?) have remained a live issue.[18] Moreover, considerable new material, mostly relating to cases, did not emerge until the late 2000s. As will be noted later, unlike in Australia, some of these court decisions have gone on to have later lives as precedent. Overall, however, they have also acted as a catalyst for better and more nuanced conceptual and contextual histories of early legal encounters. While historians of all ilks have begun to draw on these new sources, their impact has perhaps been most noticeable in legal histories of encounter.[19]

The scale of this scholarship should not, however, be exaggerated. It still remains the domain of a small number of scholars and the potential for comparative work—or even for bringing investigations into similar fields—largely remains untapped. What is most interesting, it is suggested, in thinking about law and legal relations, is not so much the substance of early cases, although that in itself has been important. Rather, it is the tracing of legal technique. This approach takes thinking with and through legal traditions seriously, here those specifically of the common law. How have encounters been legally structured, and how do they continue to be legally structured? What kinds of legal techniques have been, and are, employed by the common law in its encounters with new laws in new colonies? Thinking this way has obvious ramifications for understanding of (if not necessarily sorting out of) the problems faced by modern courts in articulating the relationship between indigenous laws and the laws of the nation-state. While the use of such historical legal sources to examine colonial encounters and the place of Indigenous laws in the new colony have become more common, using them to think through the place of those same laws in modern law is less so. We are comfortable in modern law with using cases as precedent. We are less comfortable with examining them as relics and reminders of legal technique, and as historical rather than strictly legal sources.

All of this is rather abstract and requires some context and further explanation. In the late 1990s and late 2000s, respectively, new cases emerged in both Australia and New Zealand which shone light on early attempts to argue that the common law did not apply to relevant indigenous defendants. In each of these cases

---

[18] Alan Ward, *A Show of Justice: Racial 'Amalgamation' in Nineteenth Century New Zealand* (1973).

[19] Shaunnagh Dorsett, '"Sworn on the Dirt of Graves": Sovereignty, Jurisdiction and the Judicial Abrogation of "Barbarous" Customs in New Zealand in the 1840s' (2009) 30 *The Journal of Legal History* 175 ff.

the same question was asked: did the common law have jurisdiction over the defendant where the matter was *inter se*; in other words, where it did not involve the persons or property of a settler? For those versed in the history of the common law this approach was hardly surprising. The technology of jurisdiction has been traditionally used by the common law as a technique for regulating relations with other laws: ecclesiastical law; manorial law; equity. So one might expect the common law courts, the institutions through which the law speaks, to consider its relation to indigenous laws in the same way. Of course, to ask this question at all assumes that there might be another law. In 1829 in *R v. Ballard*, Forbes CJ was faced with questions of the amenability of an Aborigine to the common law for the murder of Borrondire, or Dirty Dick, near Sydney. He declined to assert jurisdiction and noted that the British had never intervened in such matters, characterizing local indigenous law as just that—law—albeit law which was 'shocking ... to our notions of humanity and justice'. Nevertheless, he noted that the Aborigines 'make laws for themselves, which are preserved inviolate, & are rigidly acted upon'.[20]

Some almost twenty years later the New Zealand Supreme Court was also faced with questions of its own jurisdiction, this time for the murder of Kopereme by Rangitapiripiri.[21] The same question was asked: Did the court have jurisdiction? And a slightly different answer was given. Yes, said the court, but not over all matters *inter se*, just with respect to those which were unacceptable as against the laws of humanity. Murder was such a one. Again, the very question assumes another law, but here the stark differences in how settlers and colonial officials viewed Māori, and their relative place on the 'scale of civilization', led to a rather different conclusion. However, the underlying common law technique was the same.

Both *Ballard* and *Rangitapiripiri* were lost from view. As precedent, the decision in *Ballard* lasted less than seven years. In 1836 the same court changed its mind, declaring it had jurisdiction over all indigenous matters *inter se*. Effectively there was no indigenous law recognizable as such.[22] This later case was reported, and so it lived on in historical and judicial memory, while early approaches conveniently fell by the wayside. *Rangitapiripiri* was also lost. It was not, however, overturned. Rather, its loss was part of a general forgetting—or perhaps better refusal—of a time when *tikanga* Māori was taken seriously as law. As across the later nineteenth century in

[20] *R. v. Ballard*, unreported decision of the Supreme Court of New South Wales, 13 June 1829, Forbes C.J. and Dowling J. A transcript of the notebook of Dowling J. has been provided by Kercher: 'R. v. Ballard, R. v. Murrell, R. v. Bonjon' (1998) 3 *Australian Indigenous Law Reporter* 412 ff. The quote is at 413. To a similar effect see *R. v. Boatman or Jackass and Bulleye*, Dowling J., 23 February 1832, Proceedings of the Supreme, Court of New South Wales, Vol. 64, Archives Office of New South Wales, 2/3247.

[21] *R v. Rangitapiripiri*, unreported decision of the Supreme Court of New Zealand, 1 December 1847, Chapman J., reported in the *New Zealand Gazette and Cook's Strait Guardian*, 4 December 1847, 2–3 ff; 'Notebook entitled 'Criminal trials No.5', 1847–1849 MS-0411/013 Hocken Library, Dunedin 23–6 ff.

[22] *R v. Jack Congo Murrell* (1836) 1 Legge 72. Later recovery of material relating to *Murrell* shows that the Reported version of the case was not quite accurate, see Ford (n. 14).

Anglophone colonies generally, the laws of indigenous peoples were, to the extent they were recognized at all, repositioned as something less—custom—subordinated to the common law as the new national law of the colony, now nation. By the late twentieth century much of the history of plurality had been erased. Indigenous law and *tikanga* Māori were considered not to have survived, recognized only as customary remnants secreted in the interstices of the common law, more often than not denied the force of *law*. Dispossession, the consequent sundering of law from land, depopulation, and other consequences of colonization had inevitably impacted on indigenous laws. Moana Jackson, a noted Māori leader, has recently characterized the problem in these terms: much damage, he stated, had been done since 1840 to the practical effectiveness of *tikanga* as a legal process. However, he stated, 'attempts to rebuild [*tikanga* Māori] are being hamstrung when we are told so often that there is no such thing, or its been extinguished or it has no validity ... '.[23]

So what does thinking with cases from the 1840s tell us about the shape of the relations of laws in modern New Zealand, for example? In 2012 a case came before the courts in which the rights of an executor at common law were placed squarely against the rights of the deceased's family under relevant *tikanga* Māori to determine the place of burial.[24] Thus, at issue directly was the relation of common law to Māori law. The facts were simple. After Mr Takamore's death his family had taken his body and buried it, without the consent of his executrix Ms Clarke, in a family *urapa* (burial ground) in accordance with Tūhoe custom. Ms Clarke wished Mr Takamore to be buried in Christchurch. Should the matter of who has the right to determine disposal of the body have been accorded to the common law, and therefore resided in Ms Clarke, or should the common law have given effect to Tūhoe custom?

Both the Court of Appeal and the Supreme Court attempted to articulate ways in which the relevant Tūhoe 'custom' could be given some value or force within the common law. The Court of Appeal considered whether the relevant Tūhoe custom could be recognized as common law custom, applying the traditional criteria of recognition since time immemorial, reasonableness, certainty, continuity, and non-extinguishment. The Court determined that it could not.[25] Despite this inquiry, in the end that court elected to take a more 'modern approach', in which custom would be integrated into the common law where possible (perhaps not clearly acknowledging that the first approach was also one of integration).[26] The New Zealand Supreme Court unanimously determined that Mr Takamore's body should be returned to his executrix for reburial at a place of her choosing. While the majority and the two minority judgments disagreed as to whether the 'executor ruler' was part of the law of New Zealand, and hence as to the primacy of the rights to be accorded the personal representative, all members of the court agreed that in

---

[23] Expert evidence of Moana Jackson in *R v. Tamati Mason* [2012] NZHC 1361, Heath J. (HCNZ) [48].
[24] *Takamore v. Clarke* [2012] 1 NZLR 573 (NZCA); *Takamore v. Clarke* [2012] NZSC 116 (NZSC).
[25] *Takamore v. Clarke* (NZCA), [121]–[175], [162]–[165].   [26] Ibid., [255] ff.

determining how a person was to be buried, *tikanga* was a relevant consideration—a matter to be given weight and value—although they differed considerably as to how relevant a consideration it should be.[27]

The decision in *Takamore* was cautiously welcomed by some as providing some prospect for the inclusion of Māori values in decision-making. However, the parameters of the decision are far from clear. What kinds of decision-making? How will relevant considerations be identified? More concerning is the impoverished nature of the relations between common law and *tikanga* Māori as articulated by both courts. There is no recognition of the innate legal force of *tikanga*. It is relegated to a 'relevant consideration', and it is a consideration whose relevance is determined not by Māori, but by common law judges.[28] Problematically, the law (and the courts) have lost any language through which to articulate legal relations between laws. What was *law* is now *custom*. We remember substance but not technique. To look back at early cases, such as *Rangitapiripiri*, is not to say that suddenly national law will make way for, or give equal status to, *tikanga*. But these cases do remind us of how the common law ordered relations in another time and place. More to the point, they remind us that there is a legal language through which these relations could be articulated and understood. *Rangitapiripiri* reminds us of the legal traditions which were inherited, which underpinned, and which continue (unseen) to underpin how indigenous law comes into relation with the modern legal system. Thinking about jurisdiction does not provide an immediate practical response to the question of (re)framing relations between laws. But an understanding of how these matters were considered at the outset of the colony and how they might be understood now can help to refute the idea that *tikanga* Māori has no force or validity.

IV. Institutions and Cases: Displacing Laws

A second way of thinking of cases as historical materials which can help us trace indigenous laws and their encounters with settler law is through investigation of colonial curial institutions. English courts, sometimes by way of other places in the Empire, arrived in both Australia and New Zealand, to be transplanted and

---

[27] *Takamore v. Clarke* (NZSC), Elias C.J. [94]; Tipping, McGrath, Blanchard J.J. [164], William Young J. [213]; see Dorsett (n. 7) Conclusion.

[28] And see Justice Joseph Williams, 'The Harkness Henry Lecture—Lex Aotearoa: An Heroic Attempt to Map the Māori Dimension in Modern New Zealand Law' (2013) 21 *Waikato Law Review* 1, 33, as to the difficulties experienced by some judges in understanding key concepts of Māori law ff.

domesticated in new environs. We know little of how Aboriginal Australians or Māori interacted with these new settler courts. Recovery projects, such as those outlined above, have given us much information about superior courts. There have also been individual studies of indigenous interaction (most commonly in the context of criminal law) with those courts.[29] However, while cases in superior jurisdictions, such as *R v. Ballard* or *R v. Rangitapiripiri*, can tell us much about matters such as the shape of sovereignty or the legal techniques of encounter, they can tell us almost nothing of the quotidian interactions of Indigenous peoples with settler law. Much of that occurred in lower courts, many of which are yet to receive any scholarly attention. This is a fertile site for investigation of the encounters of laws in both Australia and Aotearoa/New Zealand.

In both the Australian colonies and Aotearoa/New Zealand one site of engagement for indigenous peoples with settler law was the new courts of the colonizers. In all jurisdictions, magistrates courts, staffed primarily by lay persons (often ex-military), dispensed justice in both towns and remote parts of the colonies. From King George Sound in Western Australia to Nelson in New Zealand, magistrates adjudicated not just criminal matters (the traditional fare of English magistrates courts), but also increasingly, as the nineteenth century wore on, civil matters. We still have very little idea of the extent to which indigenous peoples engaged with these lower courts. The hundreds of small encounters in lower courts hardly have precedential value. Lay magistrates often did not have a particularly nuanced understanding of the law and in any case they were generally 'equity and good conscience' jurisdictions. Hence, decisions were made on that basis. However, as in the first example, the value of these decisions does not lie in their precedential value. Moreover, in many cases there is no real record of proceedings which is extant—other than that the relevant parties came to court, broadly what they came to court for, and a brief noting of the outcome. What is interesting for historians, however, is that they came to court at all. And what little material we have for the various Australasian jurisdictions suggests very different patterns and motivations for attendance in the Australian colonies to those of Māori in Aotearoa/New Zealand. How then might these encounters tell us something about indigenous laws and their encounters with British law in the new colonies? What might it tell us about legal relations between indigenous peoples and the laws of the nation state now? While superior court decisions such as *Rangitapiripiri* or *Murrell* might have set the 'formal framework' for recognition (or not) of indigenous laws, that tells us little of how these decisions were understood and implemented (or not) at the interface of indigenous and settler law on the frontier.

In colonial New South Wales and South Australia, for example, Aboriginal engagement with lower courts was far more likely to be through involuntary

---

[29] For South Australia in the nineteenth century, e.g., see Amanda Nettelbeck, Russell Smandych, Louis Knafla, Robert Foster, *Fragile Settlements: Aboriginal Peoples, Law and Resistance in South-West Australia and Prairie Canada, 1830–1914* (2016).

subjection to the law, in particular the criminal law. While it may be that new data will show a more extensive proactive use of courts by Aboriginal Australians later in the century, current material suggests a more expected pattern of the imposition of criminal law as a form of colonial governance. Recent work by Nettelbeck, for example, has begun to explore indigenous interaction with resident magistrates in the context of protective governance measures in one area of colonial South Australia, as well as later in the century.[30] As yet, however, we are a long way from a comprehensive view of the nature and extent of aboriginal interaction with lower courts in the various Australian colonies. Moreover, in the Australian context, Douglas and Finnane's work tells us that *Murrell* was not quite the watershed that it might seem to modern eyes. Extensive use of later materials has shown that in some cases, courts, superior and inferior, were still hesitant to take jurisdiction and that room was made for 'customary law' (and sometimes still is) in other ways, for example in imposing sentences in criminal matters. The imposition of criminal law, particularly with respect to *intra* indigenous violence was, and is, piecemeal, uneven, and imperfect.[31] At heart of the encounters of criminal and customary law that they investigate is the same problem of the failure of settler law to acknowledge and accommodate another law.

In the context of Aotearoa/New Zealand, specifically, we know that Māori were active users of both the criminal and civil jurisdictions of the new Resident Magistrates Courts. While Māori were also undoubtedly subjected to the law, in particular the criminal law, data shows that from the outset of the colony Māori also laid criminal information both against settlers and each other. As the first decade of colonization wore on, aided by the creation of the civil jurisdiction of the Resident Magistrates Court, they also increasingly sued settlers, and on occasion each other, for unpaid wages, for debts for unpaid goods, for trespass on cultivations, and a raft of miscellaneous civil matters.[32] In themselves, each of these small encounters cannot tell us much. The kinds of records that remain list only the barest of information. What is of interest, however, is the fact of engagement itself: the voluntary engagement with settler curial institutions. Undoubtedly the colonial authorities promoted the use of the new courts. Policies and incentives were provided, and jurisdictions crafted, in order to encourage Māori to bring their disputes to British law. The hope was that this voluntary uptake would result in the withering of indigenous law and its institutions as fora for adjudication.

This material is interesting in its own right. Knowing more about the kinds of matters that brought Indigenous peoples in the Australasian jurisdictions to court would help us build a richer picture of the encounter of laws on the frontier and the

---

[30] E.g., Amanda Nettelbeck, '"Keep the Magistrates Straight": Magistrates and Aboriginal 'Management' on Australia's North-West Frontiers, 1833–1905' (2014) 38 *Aboriginal History* 19 ff.

[31] Douglas, Finnane (n. 3).

[32] For a full examination of this in the Crown colony period (1840–1852) see Dorsett (n. 7).

nature of the changes in those encounters over time. We are only at the beginning of this process. However, these small encounters can tell us more. They might provide another way of thinking about how Aboriginal law was displaced in the colonial period and the complex nature of how the displacement of laws happened. They tell us something of the changing *structure* of encounter. In New Zealand, a history of proactive uptake of the new courts by Māori was, for example, one important element leading to the eventual displacement of *tikanga* Māori through a 'forum shift', from traditional adjudicatory fora to those of the new institutions of the settlers. In the Australian colonies such a voluntary coming to law is less obvious. Nevertheless, the failure to recognize, and consequent displacement of, indigenous law had the same effect.

Again, an example may aid in thinking about this. Again, that example comes from New Zealand. There has simply been less judicial investigation of 'custom' in Australia (outside of the immediate context of native title). In 2013 Tamati Mason was charged with one count of murder and one of attempted murder. Before the trial commenced he applied for a ruling from the court that the matter should be dealt with according to *tikanga* Māori. This was a plea to the jurisdiction of the court, in the same way as pleas to jurisdiction were made in the early period. Counsel for Mason framed the question as one of whether 'some form of parallel or alternative criminal jurisdiction based on Maori custom is available to Maori and, in this particular case, to Mr Mason so that the serious allegations made against him can be tried in that forum'.[33] Sykes contended that *tikanga* Māori 'existed and continues to operate as a source of law in its own right'.[34] Such an argument required two propositions to be accepted. First, in the colonial period there was a 'developed Māori legal system (the customary system) that could investigate and impose sanctions for serious criminal conduct'; second, that that customary system 'continues in force today and represents a parallel system of justice'.[35]

Such an argument raised, yet again, questions of how to craft the relations between *tikanga* Māori and national law. The idea that there was such a law in 1840 was easily accepted by the court. However, the court also concluded that the relevant customary system had since been extinguished by the *Crimes Act*. That Act was, the judge concluded, effectively a code, and its jurisdictional provisions made it clear that the Act applied to all acts done or omitted in New Zealand.[36] Had the court not concluded this, however, another problem would have arisen. Counsel for Mason had argued that the existence of another jurisdiction would have allowed the allegations against him to be tried 'in that forum'. But what was that forum? From where did *tikanga* speak? Who would adjudicate and where? Jurisdiction (of indigenous and non-indigenous laws alike) assumes that laws speak from a place. On appeal, the Court of Appeal noted that the trial judge 'was correct to find that

---

[33] *R v. Tamati Mason*, [2012] NZHC 136 (HCNZ), Heath J [6].   [34] Ibid., [7].
[35] Ibid., [10].   [36] Ibid., [37].

there is no room for another institution or body to try an individual for murder or for attempted murder whether brought against Māori or Pākehā or someone of another ethnicity'.[37] Problematically, the turn to new courts from the 1840s, and the consequent forum shift, has left questions as to the location of indigenous laws (not just in New Zealand) and a consequent problem of finding a place from which those laws can speak. Those places may still exist, but from the perspective of the common law they are difficult to discern.

V. CONCLUDING COMMENTS

So what are the prospects for (legal) histories and thinking in the future about the past in these two places? As noted at the outset, despite the push towards comparative, and latterly, transnational, history in the context of indigenous peoples and their laws in Australia and Aotearoa/New Zealand this field has remained remarkably vacant. This raises questions about to what extent we might want to try to think more about law and history in these two places in a comparative or transnational way and what might be gained or lost by doing so?

It is now almost axiomatic that as historians we should be undertaking not just comparative, but transnational, work. Once a creature of the margins, transnational history is now mainstream.[38] Historians, however, know the costs and difficulties of doing genuinely transnational (or even multi-jurisdictional) work. The problems of cost and access have already been mentioned. Where such work can be done well, it clearly has the power to become more than the sum of its parts; comparison can often reveal details of national histories that might otherwise remain hidden. But chapters such as this show some of the difficulties of doing such work. It is not intended here to launch into a critique of transnational and comparative history, except to note that in some ways this chapter has itself been an instantiation of the problems of doing comparative history or bringing diverse contexts into relation. Where are the points of contact to be located? How much context is enough? While, if done carefully, bringing indigenous laws in Australia and New Zealand into conversation could be revealing, such a comparison also has the potential to flatten description, sheer away particularity, and drain the political. The trajectories of Aotearoa/New Zealand and the Australian colonies have been in many ways quite

---

[37] *Tamati Mason v. R* [2013] NZCA 310, Ellen France, Stephens, Miller J.J. (NZCA) [24].

[38] Alecia P. Simmonds, Anne Rees, Anna Clark, 'Testing the boundaries: Reflections on transnationalism in Australian history' in Anna Clark, Anne Rees, Alecia P. Simmonds, (eds.), *Transnationalism, Nationalism and Australian History* (2017) 1–14.

different, not least, as already briefly alluded to, the different institutions which have developed through which the respective First Peoples have engaged with the settler state. Care has to be taken. There is also so much work still to be done at the national level. The dictates of publishers and universities, for example, should not deter historians from undertaking such work.

Nevertheless, there are spaces in which work across jurisdictions might fruitfully be undertaken. There are commonalities that derive from imperial laws (e.g., status of colonies), inherited laws (e.g., English land law), and common intellectual frameworks (e.g., protective governance). Much still needs to be done to trace how these may have played out in the different locations: the continuities and the disruptions. The examples given in this chapter are only one way of doing that. Moreover, the common imperial and intellectual frameworks mean that there are common historical materials upon which to draw and to which local responses can be tracked. There is little doubt, however, that this is an easier task to undertake if one compares the early period, rather than the later. As the colonies progressed, ways of engaging with settler law and the emerging nation state diverged. Different legal frameworks emerged and so did different mechanisms through which the laws of Indigenous peoples came into relation with those of the relevant colony/nation state. Here the inherent difficulties attendant with doing comparative or transnational histories become more obvious.

Recent moves by Māori to move beyond the Tribunal and make claims at common law (at least where still possible) bring with them the other possibilities. One way to compare might be to look at legal traditions and techniques. Another might be to examine how history is used by the courts (and the Waitangi Tribunal) in these contexts. All draw on similar historical materials, although perhaps the weight given and the way they are viewed varies between countries.[39] Colonial office policy, official despatches, formal instructions, historic legislation, letters, diaries, and newspapers all are now routinely drawn upon, not just as they always have been in academy, but also by courts and tribunals.[40] This of course, raises attendant questions as to how historians and lawyers/judges view and use these materials and how commensurate (or not) law and history are as disciplines.[41] Perhaps most importantly, however, is the emphasis now given, particularly by the Waitangi Tribunal, on oral histories as evidence, coeval with documentary sources.[42]

---

[39] See ch. 55 in this volume.

[40] For a example from the native title arena in Australia see *Members of the Yorta Yorta Aboriginal Community v. Victoria* (2002) 214 CLR 422. For a very recent New Zealand example, in the context of the Crown's fiduciary duty to Māori, and an extensive use of historic materials by the court, see *Proprietors of Wakatu and Ors v. Attorney-General* [2017] NZSC 17.

[41] Curthoys et al. is arguably the most important work produced in Australia on these questions.

[42] See, e.g., the Waitangi Tribunal, *He Whakaputanga me te Tiriti: The Report on Stage One of the Te Paparahi o Te Raki Inquiry*, WAI 1040 (Lower Hutt: Legislation Direct 2014).

The approach taken in this chapter to try to use one type of material, the traditional 'case', as a general source through which to think about the relations of indigenous to modern law in two countries is only one example of work we might do. Such an approach will not point the way to a means through which we might structure the encounter of indigenous and national law in the twenty-first century. However, an understanding of what these legal relations may have looked like historically reminds us that in both countries indigenous laws live on in the interstices of the new legal system and its new institutions. The challenge is to uncover the historical materials that will help us locate those interstices and provide a richer picture not just of displacement of law, but of its survival.

Bibliography

Paul Carter, *The Road to Botany Bay: An Exploration of Landscape and History* (1987)

Ann Curthoys, 'Indigenous Subjects' in *Australia's Empire*, D. M. Schreuder, S. Ward (eds.), (University of Minnesota Press, 2008) 78 ff

Ann Curthoys, Ann Genovese, Alex Reilly, *Rights and Redemption: History, Law and Indigenous Peoples* (UNSW Press, 2008)

Shaunnagh Dorsett, *Juridical Encounters: Māori and the Colonial Courts, 1840–1852* (University of Auckland Press, 2017)

Shaunnagh Dorsett, Shaun McVeigh *Jurisdiction* (Routledge, 2012)

Heather Douglas, Mark Finnane, *Indigenous Crime and Settler Law: Sovereignty after Empire* (Palgrave MacMillan, 2012)

Lisa Ford, *Settler Sovereignty: Jurisdiction and Indigenous People in America and Australia, 1788–1836* (Harvard University Press, 2010)

Mark Hickford, *Lords of All the Land: Indigenous Property Rights and the Jurisprudence of Empire* (Oxford University Press, 2011)

Miranda Johnson, *The Land Is Our History: Indigeneity, Law and the Settler State* (Oxford University Press, 2016)

Carwyn Jones, *New Treaty, New Tradition: Reconciling New Zealand and Māori Law* (UBC Press, 2016)

Paul G. McHugh, *Aboriginal Title: The Modern Jurisprudence of Tribal Land Rights* (Oxford University Press, 2011)

Ani Mikaere, 'Tikanga as the First Law of Aotearoa' (1997) 10 *Yearbook of New Zealand Jurisprudence* 24

Amanda Nettelbeck, Russell Smandych, Louis Knafla, Robert Foster, *Fragile Settlements: Aboriginal Peoples, Law and Resistance in South-West Australia and Prarie Canada, 1830–1914* (UBC Press, 2016)

Damen Ward, 'The Politics of Jurisdiction: "British" Law, Indigenous Peoples and Colonial Government in South Australia and New Zealand c. 1834–1860', DPhil thesis (Oxford University, 2003)

Irene Watson, 'Sovereign Space, Caring for Country, and the Homeless Position of Aboriginal Peoples' (2009) 180 *South Atlantic Quarterly* 27

CHAPTER 43

INDIGENOUS RIGHTS

LATIN AMERICA

THOMAS DUVE

ACCORDING to international and national constitutional law, indigenous peoples in most Latin American countries have the right to maintain and strengthen their distinct political, legal, economic, social, and cultural institutions. As a consequence of a long process of recognition of their (limited) legal autonomy, many indigenous peoples now practise their own laws, cultural traditions, and customs. In doing so, they draw on history, reconstructing their legal pasts, recreating—or even creating—their identities, a process intensely related to what is sometimes called 'ethnogenesis'. At the same time, historical research has increasingly pointed out the intense interaction between indigenous peoples and European invaders during the colonial period. Thus, it has become clear that many of the so-called 'indigenous' or 'colonial' legal traditions are more properly seen as hybridizations of indigenous and colonial laws and legal practices. What does this mean for the current debate on the rights of indigenous peoples?

The aim of this chapter is to introduce this historiography and its relevance to law and to present some methodological challenges in writing the history of indigenous rights in Latin America resulting from this fairly recent shift in (legal) historiography. It starts with a short introduction to the recognition of indigenous rights in the present and the past (Section I). Second, it surveys the legal historiography of indigenous rights in Latin America, emphasizing the changing context of historiography, the new interpretation of the indigenous peoples' histories, especially in the overall colonial period, and recent research on the history of the rights of the indigenous peoples in Latin America (Section II). Finally, it addresses some methodological problems of doing research on the legal history and the rights of indigenous peoples (Section III).

i. The Recognition of Indigenous Rights in the Present and the Past

According to Art. 5 of the UN Declaration on the Rights of Indigenous Peoples from 2007 (A/RES/61/295), indigenous peoples have the right to maintain and strengthen their distinct political, legal, economic, social, and cultural institutions, while retaining their right to participate fully, if they so choose, in the political, economic, social, and cultural life of the state. This UN Declaration is the culmination of a long process of a growing recognition of indigenous peoples' rights on an international level as well as on the level of many national constitutions.[1] As a consequence, many indigenous peoples of Latin America are now claiming and exercising their right to self-determination. They are practising their own laws, their own cultural traditions and customs.

In going about such practices, many indigenous peoples look back to millenary legal traditions that originated centuries before European invasion. However, these legal traditions have evolved in continuous processes of translation of previous beliefs and practices into the present. Due to migration and the imperial expansion of some indigenous peoples, like the Inca, in the pre-conquest period, there were processes of hybridization even before European invasion.[2] After the so-called 'conquest', the development and exercise of indigenous rights was generally determined by colonial conditions. European invaders imposed their cultural systems and, simultaneously, their law on the conquered. Yet there were important differences. Some regions have been less affected by the European presence, in some cases there was intense co-operation and thus a certain respect for indigenous peoples' political and juridical systems, and in others the European invaders simply eradicated what they had found. The Spanish and Portuguese crowns pursued

---

[1] For this process, see S. James Anaya, *Los pueblos indígenas en el derecho internacional (trans. of 2nd edn. by Rodríguez-Piñero Royo, Luís)* (2005); José Bengoa, *La emergenica indígena en América Latina* (2nd edn., 2007). A good introduction to indigenous peoples in international law in: Alexandra Tomaselli, *Indigenous Peoples and their Right to Political Participation* (2016) 31–59 ff.

[2] See, e.g., Christian Duverger, *El primer mestizaje. La clave para entender el pasado mesoamericano* (2007) and the various contributions in *The Cambridge History of the Native People*, Vol. 2, 3 ff.

distinct colonial policies, though there might have been more commonalities than traditionally believed.[3]

Colonial legal systems were not homogenous and closed. On the contrary, they were structurally open. European *ius commune*, shaped by a multinormative past and, until at least the eighteenth century, characterized by overlapping jurisdictions, provided an intellectual and institutional framework for the integration of different legal traditions. Moreover, the Castilian and the Portuguese crowns were not only shaped by this tradition, but had developed their own practices of making *convivencia* possible over the preceding centuries on the Iberian peninsula,[4] with a mixture of what some modern observers call 'tolerance' with oppression and violence.[5] These experiences contributed to a process of hybridization of indigenous legal traditions with those the conquerors had brought to Latin America. The structural openness soon found expression in concrete legislation. The first known decree on these matters dates from 1530, ordering crown officials to collect information about the 'order and way of living' of the indigenous peoples of New Spain, recognizing their right to live according to their 'good practices and customs as long as they were not against our Christian religion'.[6] In a later royal decree dating from 1555, Spanish King Charles V stated that antecedent indigenous laws as well as those newly enacted would be respected. Some decades later, reforms of the colonial administration, like Viceroy Toledo's Peruvian ordinances, granted judicial autonomy to members of indigenous communities in their respective settlements. Another century later, some of these particular decisions, like Charles V's royal decree of 1555, were collected in the *Recopilación de Indias* (2.1.4), referring to the '*laws and good customs*' of the pre-conquest period and the '*usages and customs which had been observed*' afterwards.

Even if this respect has been classified as an example of a (weak) legal pluralism, there were important limits to the autonomy granted to the indigenous peoples: a repugnancy clause explicitly excepted those usages and customs that violated the principles of Christianity or royal legislation. However, as a result of these concessions and some previous royal laws and decrees dating from as early as 1500 and 1512 (*Leyes de Burgos*) that qualified the indigenous people as rational persons, later papal documents (*Sublimis Deus*) and intense debates on the status of the indigenous peoples, which affirmed their condition as human

---

[3] Tamar Herzog, *Frontiers of Possession: Spain and Portugal in Europe and the Americas* (2015).

[4] See, on this complex topic, the survey by Maya Soifer, 'Beyond Convivencia: Critical Reflections on the Historiography of Interfaith Relations in Christian Spain' (2009) 1 *Journal of Medieval Iberian Studies* ff.

[5] On the legal tradition of dealing with *infideles* see James Muldoon, *Popes, Lawyers, and Infidels* (1979).

[6] See on this Ricardo Zorraquín Becú, 'Los derechos indígenas' (1986) 14 *Revista de Historia del Derecho* ff.

beings and free vassals of the crown, the members of indigenous communities were subject to the normativities of at least two worlds: the general legal regime in the colonial territory as well as to their own (very heterogeneous) laws. They were integrated asymmetrically into a colonial legal system that was itself based on difference.

This legal regime changed considerably under the conditions of modern constitutionalism following the independence movements in the nineteenth century. To many indigenous peoples, the political reforms carried out in this period, especially the aggressive modernizing policies of the nineteenth and early twentieth centuries, represented existential threats.[7] Like other special rights and privileges, those of the indigenous peoples were expunged from the official legal landscapes. Seemingly liberal constitutions were enacted and established in the centre of national legal orders. In theory, all citizens were made equal, and there was little or no space for differences to be recognized in law, and even less so for those the encroaching immigrant societies saw as part of a backward, uncivilized past. If inequality persisted not only in practice, but also in law, apportioning rights of political participation unequally, it was to favour powerful groups in the Creole elite and Euro-American society. Indigenous peoples were the big losers in the process of eradicating a jurisdiction-centred justice system with provisions for limited autonomy. State-building processes, land registration, new property laws, territorial expansion, and resettlement policies left only limited margins of autonomy to the indigenous peoples. Nonetheless, indigenous rights persisted through practice and often unwritten transmission. They shaped—or at least influenced—daily life in many places. Today, as a consequence of the substantial changes in international and national regulations as well as in cultural perceptions, some Latin American states officially recognize indigenous rights and grant judicial autonomy to indigenous peoples. As in earlier colonial times, members of indigenous communities are subject to general as well as special legal regimes in modern constitutional legal systems that are trying to respond to the growing demand for recognition of ethnic, social, and cultural diversity. As a consequence, indigenous legal institutions and indigenous practices of administering justice have gained purchase in much of Latin America. Vernacular languages have been readmitted in some courts, and some judicial sentences are being published in indigenous languages.

In this fairly recent process of restituting legal autonomy, history has become an important argument.[8] In Bolivia—the most significant experiment in putting

---

[7] See on this Bartolomé Clavero, *Derecho indígena y cultura constitucional en América* (1994); Bartolomé Clavero, *Freedom's Law And Indigenous Rights* (2005).

[8] See for an overview over the definition of indigenous peoples as communities 'having a historical continuity with pre-invasion and pre-colonial societies' (Commission on Human Rights, Sub-Commission on Prevention of Discrimination and Protection of Minorities, 1983), or the application

political claims of autonomy and pluralism into constitutional practice by far—returning to indigenous traditions predating the colonial period has been the central legitimation for the transformation of the political system. Indeed, article 30 of the 2009 Bolivian constitution defines the 'rural native indigenous people and nationality' as those human collectives that share a 'cultural identity, language, historic tradition, institutions, territory and worldview, whose existence predates the Spanish colonial invasion'. Also in other countries, the general tendency is to base legal recognition of indigenous peoples on successful claims of ancestral traditions, or at least on their ability to prove certain practices' historical roots in their communities' lives. Collective and individual property rights are protected whenever the claims can be historically justified. In many specific contexts of current legal life, self-identification based on tradition and, concomitantly, the history of these traditions—in a word, legal history—plays a major role. History has become a constitutive element of constructing modern legal pluralism.

II. THE LEGAL HISTORIOGRAPHY OF INDIGENOUS RIGHTS

In spite of its importance, the legal historiography of indigenous rights in Latin America has only recently been given its due. For a long time, (legal) historians have paid only limited attention to the fact that indigenous peoples have vivid legal traditions beyond the limits recognized by official law and were not simply practising outdated customs that were bound to disappear. Not least due to the domination of Euro-American academic traditions and practices in Latin American academia during large parts of twentieth century, indigenous peoples' rights have remained a blind spot of the discipline. They seemed to be merely a case for anthropology, not for legal history. This has changed dramatically in recent decades.

of ILO 169 to 'tribal peoples ... whose status is regulated wholly or partially by their own custom or traditions ...' and to 'peoples ... who are regarded as indigenous on account of their descent from the populations which inhabited the country' and further criteria developed during the preparation of the UN Declaration; Tomaselli (n. 1) 32–9 ff. On the importance of self-identification and the role of tradition in the case of Bolivia see Andrew Canessa, 'Who Is Indigenous? Self-Identification, Indigeneity, and Claims to Justice in Contemporary Bolivia' (2007) 36 *Urban Anthropology and Studies of Cultural Systems and World Economic Development* ff.

A. Changing Contexts of Historiography

To understand the current debates, it is important to look at least briefly at some aspects of the changing contexts of historiography. Since the 1980s, most Latin American countries have experienced an intense process of re-democratization and a wave of new constitutions.[9] Many of these constitutions incorporated the transcendent reforms in international law regarding the protection of indigenous rights that took place in the same period. An important step in this process was the International Labour Organization's adoption of Convention 169, 'Indigenous and Tribal Peoples Convention' (ILO 169) in 1989, which was ratified by many Latin American countries. ILO 169 made history a central argument in claiming the status and the attendant legal privileges of being recognized as 'indigenous people' because it applies to 'tribal peoples in independent countries whose social, cultural and economic conditions distinguish them from other sections of the national community and whose status is regulated wholly or partially by their own customs or traditions or by special laws or regulations' and to 'peoples in independent countries who are regarded as indigenous on account of their descent from the populations which inhabited the country […] at the time of conquest or colonisation or the establishment of present state boundaries and who, irrespective of their legal status, retain some or all of their own social, economic, cultural and political institutions'. Similarly, the UN General Assembly adopted the UN Declaration on the Rights of Indigenous Peoples in 2007 (A/RES/61/295), which elevated a group's self-identification, traditions, and historical identity formation to the level of a fundamental consideration in determining its status. All this was possible due to the emergence of a transnational indigenous rights movement, among other factors, which raised local conflicts to the international level.

Political decolonization and intensifying globalization, however, not only created fertile conditions for the transnational indigenous rights movement and thus empowered many local actors. It also catalysed some mortal threats to indigenous peoples. Since the late 1980s, many Latin American countries witnessed a period of economic growth, stronger integration into the world economy, and deregulation, adopting development models labelled today as 'new extractivism', which rely heavily on the extraction of natural resources.[10] In consequence, many rural areas that had been difficult or impossible to access—often the homelands of indigenous peoples—have been subjected to increasing extractivist activities since the 1980s. Even in countries like Bolivia, this has led to worsening conflicts between political and economic development models, legally speaking between ethnic rights and

---

[9] On the 'New Constitutionalism' see Detlef Nolte, Almut Schilling-Vacaflor (eds.), *New Constitutionalism in Latin America: Promises and Practices* (2012); for a general picture of the development of law in Latin America in this period, see César Rodríguez-Garavito (ed.), *Law and Society in Latin America: A New Map* (2015).

[10] Henry Veltmeyer, James Petras (eds.), *The New Extractivism: A Post-Neoliberal Development Model or Imperialism of the Twenty-First Century?* (2014).

class-based rights.[11] One decade after the UN Declaration, it seems as if the growing legal recognition of indigenous peoples has deepened complex processes of re-indigenizaton and an important strengthening of indigenous peoples' interests in the public discourse. It has also aggravated conflicts, not least because most states have failed to provide a juridical framework to realize these rights and resolve the resulting conflicts. Thus, despite progress in some areas, recent decades have seen often violent conflicts between state authorities and indigenous peoples claiming their rights, mostly regarding the possession of land.[12]

In addition to these political developments, historical theory and methodology have shifted, too, which has profoundly affected the historiography on indigenous peoples and their rights, especially during colonial period. Subaltern history and postcolonial studies have reached even the mainstream of professional academia. Due to the increasing influence of Anglo-American academia and its intellectual preferences, race, ethnicity, and identity formation, among other factors, have become key topics of historical research in regard to Latin America. Ethno-historiographical methods have been refined and increasingly integrated into historical accounts. As a consequence, historiography has been sensitized to the 'invention of traditions', of identities, and the complex process of ethnic definition ('ethnogenesis'). Since the late 1970s, legal anthropology has devoted its attention to analysing situations of legal pluralism and the integration of diversity into unitary systems,[13] emphasizing the importance of law, which has long been seen as a mere epiphenomenon of social structure. In line with this trend, the rise of global history has—after some delay—finally spread to Latin America.[14] Given that global history promotes decentralising historical narratives, argues for equal opportunities to interpret history and, especially, discarding the reductionist interpretations and stereotypes in colonial perspectives, like passivity, isolation, and the undifferentiated marginalization of indigenous peoples in colonial empires, this is a weighty shift. Another priority of such global (legal) history is to use analytical frames derived from indigenous regional logics, rather than from European historiography,[15] respecting indigenous or non-European or North-American epistemologies.[16]

[11] Rickard Lalander, 'Ethnic rights and the dilemma of extractive development in plurinational Bolivia', (2016) *The International Journal of Human Rights* <https://doi.org/10.1080/13642987.2016.1179 869> ff (accessed 24 April 2018).

[12] On this development, see the case study on the Mapuche in José Bengoa, *Mapuche, colonos y el Estado Nacional* (2014).

[13] Willem Assies, Gemma van der Haar, André J. Hoekema (eds.), *The Challenge of Diversity, Indigenous Peoples Multicultural Interlegality and Reform of the State in Latin America* (2000).

[14] Serge Gruzinski, *Les quatre parties du monde. Histoire d'une mondialisation* (2004); Marcello Carmagnani, *El otro occidente. América Latina desde la invasión europea hasta la globalización* (2nd edn., 2011); Matthew Brown, 'The global history of Latin America' (2015) <https://doi.org/10.1017/ S1740022815000182> ff (accessed 24 April 2018).

[15] Boaventura de Sousa Santos, *Epistemologies of the South: Justice against Epistemicide* (2014).

[16] Bartolomé Clavero, *Derecho global. Por una historia verosímil de los derechos humanos* (2014); Sebastian Conrad, *What is Global History?* (2016); Thomas Duve, 'Global Legal History: Methodological

The emergence of indigeneity as a global identity during the Cold War along with new communications technologies and greater sensitivity to the value of biological and cultural diversity have provided indigenous peoples with new opportunities to generate and respond to public attention.[17] The various forms of *indigenismos*[18] and (re-)indigenization processes in Latin America have their own histories, rooted even in earlier periods,[19] but are nonetheless facets of a global phenomenon,[20] which is inseparably bound to a global trend of addressing past injustices and the underlying global regimes of memory.[21]

B. Indigenous Peoples' Histories

The shifts in policy and in general scholarly discourse since the 1980s and their impact on the historiography of indigenous peoples and their rights have been catalysed by two momentous events. The first, in 1992, was the 500th anniversary of the arrival of Europeans in America, and the second is the wave of celebrations that has been sweeping across Spanish America since 2010 in remembrance of two centuries of so-called 'independence' from Spain. These two events have brought to light very different views on the history of indigenous peoples in the wake of European expansion and from the advent of the nation-state until today. It was not least a confrontation between traditional national historiographical communities and those who advocated for a renovation of perspectives.

The picture that has emerged from this evolution has substantially modified our vision of indigenous peoples' histories, especially with regards to Hispanic America. Whereas early general historiography and more specialized writings on the relation between indigenous peoples and the Spaniards[22] or the Portuguese[23] focused on the

Approach', *Oxford Handbooks Online* (2017) <https://doi.org/10.1093/oxfordhb/9780199935352.013.25> ff (accessed 24 April 2018).

[17] On the performance of indigeneity, see Laura R. Graham, H. Glenn Penny (eds.), *Performing Indigeneity: Global Histories and Contemporary Experiences* (2014).

[18] Estelle Tarica, 'Indigenismo', in William Beezley, Lauren Derby (eds.), *Oxford Research Encyclopedia of Latin American History* (2016) <https://doi.org/10.1093/acrefore/9780199366439.013.68> ff (accessed 24 April 2018).

[19] See, e.g., Rebecca Earle, *The Return of the Native: Indians and Myth-Making in Spanish America, 1810–1930* (2007), Marisol de la Cadena, *Indigenous Mestizos: The Politics of Race and Culture in Cuzco, Peru, 1919–1991* (2nd edn., 2003).

[20] On the USA, see, e.g., David E. Wilkins, *Hollow Justice: A History of Indigenous Claims in the United States* (2013).

[21] James Clifford, *Returns: Becoming Indigenous in the Twenty-First Century* (2013); Henry Rousso, 'Hacia una globalización de la memoria' (2015) *Nuevo Mundo Mundos Nuevos* <https://doi.org/10.4000/nuevomundo.68429> ff (accessed 24 April 2018).

[22] E.g., Charles Gibson, *The Aztecs under the Spanish Rule: A History of the Indians of the Valley of México, 1519–1810* (1992 [1964]).

[23] E.g., John Hemming, *Red Gold: The Conquest of the Brazilian Indians, 1500–1760* (1978); John Hemming, *Amazon Frontier: The Defeat of the Brazilian Indian* (1987).

Europeans' role, be it heroic or iniquitous, and viewed indigenous peoples merely as an object of an economic, political, or spiritual conquest, attention has shifted since the 1960s to how indigenous peoples experienced conquest and colonization. Miguel Leon-Portilla's 'Visión de los vencidos' (1959), as well as his later works and those that build on them, shows to what degree this traditional depiction relies on a biased sample of sources. A history of the vanquished, which itself was criticized as inadequate for its perpetuation of colonial frames and interpretations, was to replace the history of the victors.[24] In legal history, the teachings of the School of Salamanca, for a long time considered as an expression of *The Spanish Struggle for Justice in the Conquest of America*,[25] now seemed just *Another Face of Empire*.[26]

Recent scholarship followed up on these developments. Increasing cross-fertilization between archaeology, philology, anthropology, and historical research on indigenous peoples has fostered the progressive emancipation from European periodization and analytical frames springing from Europe and North America.[27] In some recent attempts, European conquest and colonization are represented not as the fateful dawn of history, but as an episode in a longer story of imperial rule on the American continent, especially in the form of the Incan and Aztec empires.[28] This entails problematizing stereotypes like the 'conquest', the encounter between 'the Castilians' or 'the Portuguese' and 'the natives' in favour of reconstructing

[24] For a useful survey on Hispanic America, see James Lockhart, *The Nahuas After the Conquest: A Social and Cultural History of the Indians of Central Mexico, Sixteenth Through Eighteenth Centuries* (1992); James Lockhart, Lisa Sousa, and Stephanie Wood, *Sources and Methods for the Study of Postconquest Mesoamerican Ethnohistory* (2007).

[25] Lewis Hanke, Susan Scafadi, and Peter Bakewell, *The Spanish Struggle for Justice in the Conquest of America* (2002).

[26] Daniel Castro, *Another Face of Empire: Bartolomé de Las Casas, Indigenous Rights, and Ecclesiastical Imperialism* (2007).

[27] See the contributions to the seminal *Cambridge History of the Native Peoples of the Americas* (1999) ff, especially the surveys by Sabine MacCormack, 'Ethnography in South America: The First Two Hundred Years', in Frank Salomon, Stuart B. Schwartz (eds.), *The Cambridge History of the Native Peoples of the Americas* (1999), vol 3: South America, Part 1, <https:// doi.org/10.1017/ CHOL9780521630757.004> ff; Karen Spalding, 'The Crisis and Transformations of Invaded Societies: Andean Area (1500–1580)', in ibid., <https://doi.org/10.1017/CHOL9780521630757.014> ff; Murdo J. MacLeod, 'Mesoamerica Since the Spanish Invasion: an Overview', in Richard E. W. Adams, Murdo J. MacLeod (eds.), *The Cambridge History of the Native Peoples of the Americas* (2000), vol 2: Mesoamerica, Part 2, <https://doi.org/10.1017/CHOL9780521630757> ff; as well as John Monteiro, 'The Crisis and Transformations of Invaded Societies: Coastal Brazil in the Sixteenth Century', in Frank Salomon, Stuart B. Schwartz (eds.), *The Cambridge History of the Native Peoples of the Americas* (1999), vol 3: South America, Part 1, <https://doi.org/10.1017/CHOL9780521630757.015> ff; Robin Wright and Manuela Carneiro de Cunha, 'Destruction, Resistance, and Transformation— Southern, Coastal, and Northern Brazil (1580–1890)', in ibid., <https://doi.org/10.1017/ CHOL9780521630764.007> (all accessed 24 April 2018) ff; Manuela Carneiro de Cunha and Mauro Almeida, 'Indigenous People, Traditional People and Conservation in the Amazon' (2000) 129 *Daedalus, Journal of the American Academy of Sciences* on Portuguese America ff.

[28] Matthew Restall, 'The Americas in the Age of Indigenous Empires', in Jerry H. Bentley, Sanjay Subrahmanyam, Merry Wiesner-Hanks (eds.), *The Cambridge World History* (2015) ff.

complex multi-ethnic relations of competition and co-operation between various European, indigenous, and other actors.[29]

Obviously, this shift of perspective in no way negates the devastation caused by disease, war, subjugation to foreign cultural systems, and economic exploitation. The integration of the American continent into the world economic system caused an immense and asymmetric transfer of resources from America to Europe and other world areas. It transformed the political and legal system. Spanish imperial politics instituted power structures that maintained supremacy by conferring limited authority to various subsidiary bodies. In many cases, superior ruling elites of indigenous societies were disempowered, while at the same time hereditary lords and local elites (*caciques, kurakas*) served as mediators, collected tribute, and organized coercive labour of the common people (*macehuales, runa*). Some indigenous societies were transformed into less stratified systems, hierarchically reorganized, and physically resettled. Thus, Latin American indigenous peoples became part of the Spanish and Portuguese empires and were subjected to their imperial rule—a system of governance that consisted of overlapping jurisdictions, leaving margins of autonomy and comprising zones of more or less intense penetration by colonial authorities and culture.

However, it is precisely due to this intense reorganization of societies and the underlying legal practices that it is often difficult to delineate the indigenous and non-indigenous worlds. The European invaders based their power simultaneously on brutal extermination and submission, but also on recognition and the limited empowerment of indigenous peoples. The alliances and interactions between the conquerors and the conquered were malleable. Some regions were subjected to aggressive transformation, while others seem to have maintained more autonomy. There were zones of intense contact and exchange. Many recent studies have illuminated how intergroup communication employed multilingual practices in secular and church life.[30] The so-called '*indios ladinos*', referring to Catholic and literate members of indigenous communities,[31] and *mestizos*, as the most numerous segment of society, who were yet extremely ambiguous in their practices

---

[29] See, e.g., Laura E. Matthew, Michel R. Oudijk (eds.), *Indian Conquistadors: Indigenous Allies in the Conquest of Mesoamerica* (2007); Kevin Terraciano, 'Indigenous Peoples in Colonial Spanish America', in Thomas Holloway (ed.), *A Companion to Latin American History* (2008) ff; Susan Kellogg, 'The Colonial Mosaic of Indigenous New Spain, 1519–1821', in William Beezley, Lauren Derby (eds.), *Oxford Research Encyclopedia of Latin American History* (2016) <https://doi.org/10.1093/acrefore/9780199366439.013.29> ff (accessed 24 April 2018); Robert C. Schwaller, *Géneros de Gente in Early Colonial Mexico* (2016).

[30] For New Spain see, e.g., Martin Nesvig, 'Spanish Men, Indigenous Language, and Informal Interpreters in Postcontact Mexico' (2012) 59 *Ethnohistory* ff; John F. Schwaller, 'The Expansion of Nahuatl as a Lingua Franca among Priests in Sixteenth-Century Mexico' (2012) 59 *Ethnohistory* ff.

[31] Kenneth J. Andrien, Rolena Adorno (eds.), *Transatlantic Encounters: Europeans and Andeans in the Sixteenth Century* (1991); John Charles, *Allies at Odds: The Andean Church and Its Indigenous Agents, 1583–1671* (2010).

of belonging,[32] attract increasing interest. These groups sometimes combined the binary categories of a *república de indios* and a *república de españoles*, a 'useful fiction'[33] that has long shaped politics as well as historiography. Whereas for a long time, the concept of 'blood purity' (*limpieza de sangre*) was seen as a tool of exclusion, it has become clearer that this concept was also used against elites and served for racial passing.[34] Research on the continuity of indigenous rule, which has persisted over centuries in some instances, and on its changing institutions and practices is now more refined, aided by improved mapping of (often spatially limited) colonial power.[35] In fact, many regions that were especially prone to conflict, like that of the Mapuche, are now seen as zones of autonomy that were tolerated, if not legally sanctioned, until well into the nineteenth century.[36] After independence, some indigenous peoples even considered themselves completely independent from the new nation-states—just as is the case today, when indigenous peoples claim their status as 'people' in terms of legal autonomy.

In addition to this discovery of porous boundaries and parallel lives, it is becoming clearer to what extent indigenous community councils (*cabildos indígenas*), which had long been ignored due to a paucity of written records, have been acting with considerable margins of independence.[37] Similarly, there is also growing appreciation for the degree to which social and political rule built on and instrumentalized precolonial structures, as was the case, for instance, in the same spatial reorganization which was meant to break previous power structures,[38] the economic organization of labour services, and tribute collection. Recent attention to indigenous agency, especially the role of cultural brokers and translators,[39] indigenous elites,[40] their extensive networks and economic activities,[41] in addition to

[32] See, e.g., Joanne Rappaport, *The Disappearing Mestizo: Configuring Difference in the Colonial New Kingdom of Granada* (2014).

[33] Karen Graubart, 'Competing Spanish and Indigenous Jurisdictions in Early Colonial Lima', *Oxford Research Encyclopedia of Latin American History* (2016) <https://doi.org/10.1093/acrefore/9780199366439.013.365> 3 ff (accessed 24 April 2018).

[34] Nikolaus Böttcher, Bernd Hausberger, Max S. Hering Torres (eds.), *El peso de la sangre: limpios, mestizos, y nobles en el mundo hispano* (2011).

[35] On the 'myth of completion', see Matthew Restall, *Seven Myths of the Spanish Conquest* (2003) 64–76 ff.

[36] Bengoa (n. 12).

[37] See Graubart (n. 33); Yanna Yannakakis, Martina Schrader-Kniffki, 'Between the "Old Law" and the New: Christian Translation, Indian Jurisdiction, and Criminal Justice in Colonial Oaxaca' (2016) 96 *Hispanic American Historical Review* ff.

[38] E.g., Jeremy Ravi Mumford, *Vertical Empire: The General Resettlement of Indians in the Colonial Andes* (2012).

[39] Alcira Dueñas, 'The Lima Indian "Letrados": Remaking the "República de Indios" in the Bourbon Andes' (2015) 72 *The Americas* ff.

[40] Gabriela Ramos, Yanna Yannakakis (eds.), *Indigenous Intellectuals: Knowledge, Power, and Colonial Culture in Mexico and the Andes* (2014).

[41] Luis Miguel Glave Testino, *Trajinantes: caminos indígenas en la sociedad colonial, siglos XVI/XVII* (1989); Daniel K. Richter, Troy L. Thompson, 'Severed Connections: American Indigenous Peoples and the Atlantic World in an Era of Imperial Transformation', in Nicholas Canny, Philip Morgan (eds.), *The*

many investigations of cultural translation and the hybridization of cultural systems, has shaken the image of a small group of Europeans indiscriminately dominating huge populations only by force.[42] The field of relevant actors now includes previously ignored groups, like the descendants of slaves trafficked from Africa,[43] indigenous women,[44] and indigenous individuals who left their communities behind to live as vagabonds or *forasteros* in urban contexts.[45] Current historiography depicts processes of negotiation, translation, and learning in societies characterized by ethnic discrimination as a part of a broader system of inequality, but also by stark variation in their regional and historical contours. In the end, they were all Imperial subjects.[46] The legal system is increasingly seen as an arena of encounter, and it has consequently been studied more intensely since the 1980s,[47] not least as a source for ethno-historical research.[48] Generally speaking, historians emphasize the significance of the legal system as an arena of negotiation as well as a source of power and cohesion in the Spanish Empire.[49]

The drive in historical scholarship to revalorize indigenous actors and to overcome enduring stereotypes has also shed new light on the independence movements and the emergence of the nation-state and its structures in the nineteenth and twentieth centuries. It has become clear that, already by the end of Spanish rule in Hispanic America, the room for indigenous elites to manoeuvre had shrunk considerably. The Bourbon Reforms, upward social and economic mobility of creoles, abortive mass rebellions, like that of Tupac Amaru (1780–1783)

Oxford Handbook of the Atlantic World: 1450–1850 (2011) <https://doi.org/10.1093/oxfordhb/978019921 0879.013.0029> (accessed 24 April 2018).

[42] For the early Andean region, see Juan Carlos Estenssoro Fuchs, *Del Paganismo a la santidad. La incorporación de los indios del Perú al catolicismo, 1532–1750* (1998); Gonzalo Lamana, *Domination without Dominance: Inca-Spanish Encounters in Early Colonial Peru* (2008); W. George Lovell, Christopher H. Lutz, Wendy Kramer, William R. Swezey, *'Strange Lands and Different Peoples': Spaniards and Indians in Colonial Guatemala* (2013); Alcira Dueñas, 'Introduction. Andean Articulating Colonial Worlds' (2015) 72 *The Americas* ff.

[43] Rachel O'Toole, *Bound Lives: Africans, Indians, and the Making of Race in Colonial Peru* (2012); Michelle McKinley, *Fractional Freedoms: Slavery, Intimacy, and Legal Mobilization in Colonial Lima* (2016).

[44] Karen Graubart, *With Our Labor and Sweat: Indigenous Women and the Formation of Colonial Society in Peru, 1550–1700* (2007).

[45] Ann M. Wightman, *Indigenous Migration and Social Change: The Forasteros of Cuzco, 1570–1720* (1990).

[46] Andrew B. Fisher, Matthew D. O'Hara (eds.), *Imperial Subjects: Race and Identity in Colonial Latin America* (2009).

[47] For the Andean region as an important starting point, see Steve J. Stern, *Peru's Indian Peoples and the Challenge of Spanish Conquest* (1982); for New Spain, see Woodrow Borah, 'The Spanish and Indian Law: New Spain', in George A. Collier, Renato I. Rosaldo, John D. Wirth (eds.), *The Inca and Aztec States, 1400–1800* (1982).

[48] Susan Kellogg, *Law and the Transformation of Aztec Culture, 1500–1700* (1995).

[49] Ethelia Ruiz Medrano, Susan Kellogg (eds.), *Negotiation within Domination: New Spain's Indian Pueblos Confront the Spanish State* (2010).

with its roughly 100,000 casualties, and the political transformations that followed independence and constitutionalization gravely compromised the autonomy of indigenous peoples. The sometimes-catastrophic effects on indigenous peoples wrought by constitutionalism, nation-building, and the first wave of economic globalization in the second half of the nineteenth century are becoming ever clearer.[50] The growth of the institutions attendant to the nation-state, especially the production of ideological and infrastructural conditions amenable to the centralization of rule, only reinforced this process. Many indigenous freedoms in law or in fact ended with the integration of vast regions that had remained outside state control. National citizenship, new technologies of rule, like surveying and the introduction of cadastres, immigration policies, racist and social Darwinist ideology, and the creation and selective implementation of legal orders based on abstraction, uniformity, and the protection of liberal property rights in the nineteenth and early twentieth centuries have been analysed, among other perspectives, in terms of their impact on indigenous peoples. The history of indigenous peoples' suffering due to forms of totalitarianism and (state) terrorism, with some regional variation, and the history of the 'emergence of the indigenous' in twentieth century has just begun to be written.[51]

c. The History of Indigenous Laws and Indigenous People's Rights

The traditional discipline of legal history as practised at law schools in Latin America has only partially adopted these more recent views of general historiography and integrated them into its analytical framework, both in the case of the more traditional research on colonial Spanish America, often referred to as *derecho indiano*, as well as in the case of Brazilian legal history.[52] Since their beginnings in the early (or for Brazil, later) twentieth century, both legal historiographic communities were more

---

[50] See the survey in Hill Jonathan Hill, 'Indigenous Peoples and the Rise of Independent Nation-States in Lowland South America', in Frank Salomon, Stuart B. Schwartz (eds.), *The Cambridge History of the Native Peoples of the Americas* (1999), vol 3: South America, Part 2, <https://doi.org/10.1017/CHOL9780521630764.012> ff (accessed 24 April 2018); Brooke Larson, *Trials of Nation Making: Liberalism, Race, and Ethnicity in the Andes, 1810–1910* (2004); Alicia Mayer González, Miguel León-Portilla (eds.), *Los indígenas en la Independencia y en la Revolución mexicana* (2010); Florencia Mallon, 'Indigenous Peoples and the Nation-States in Spanish America, 1780–2000', in José C. Moya (ed.), *The Oxford Handbook of Latin American History* (2011) ff; for Brazil, see Tracy Devine Guzmán, *Native and National in Brazil: Indigeneity after Independence* (2013).

[51] Bengoa (n. 12).

[52] On the research tradition of the *derecho indiano*, see Víctor Tau Anzoátegui, *Nuevos horizontes en el estudio histórico del derecho indiano* (1997); Thomas Duve, Heikki Pihlajamäki (eds.), *New Horizons in Spanish Colonial Law. Contributions to Transnational Early Modern Legal History* (2015) <https://doi.org/10.12946/gplh3> (accessed 24 April 2018).

interested in writing the prehistory of the various national legal systems that had emanated from independence than in their indigenous pasts.[53] When looking at the rights of indigenous peoples, legal history focused on aspects like their legal status, royal legislation to protect them, and the adaptation of Castilian institutions to the particularities of the New World.[54] This state-centred perspective is even visible in authors like Miguel Bonifacio, a Bolivian legal historian who devoted much of his scholarly activity to indigenous rights. Studies treating processes of legal mestization and hybridization remained in the minority,[55] partly because researchers relied almost exclusively on the colonial archives, in particular on the Spanish-language records they contained. In the same vein, there was little attention to the widespread dispossession and legal marginalization of indigenous peoples in nineteenth- and twentieth-century constitutionalism.

In the last three decades, history of indigenous rights and indigenous law has become a lively field of research, not least because of the aforementioned transformations in the general context and the converging interest of general historians and legal historians, but also due to seminal and provocative studies of Spanish legal historian Bartolomé Clavero.[56] Since then, many studies have shown the complexity of the juridical operations which were used to determine the legal status of indigenous peoples. Privileges like those which *ius commune* had developed for the so-called *miserabiles personae*[57] or categories like being native[58] could be applied to indigenous people as well as to those from Iberian origin, blurring accepted boundaries between the allegedly separate worlds of colonized and colonizers. Moreover, research has shown to what extent indigenous elites made use of royal

---

[53] See, for a legal historical perspective on the problems of writing the history of indigenous law, Fernando de Trazegníes Granda, 'El derecho prehispánico. Una aproximación al estudio de la historia del derecho en las culturas sin derecho' (2002) 30 *Revista de Historia del Derecho* ff.

[54] Juan Manzano Manzano, 'Las leyes y costumbres indígenas en el orden de prelación de fuentes del Derecho Indiano', *Instituto Internacional de Historia del Derecho Indiano, Primer Congreso, Buenos Aires 1966* (*Publicación de las Actas*, 1967) ff; Zorraquín Becú (n. 6); Margarita Menegus Bornemann, 'La costumbre indígena den el Derecho Indiano, 1529–1550' (1992) 4 *Anuario Mexicano de Historia de Derecho* ff; Fernando de Trazegníes Granda, 'La nobleza incaica en el Derecho Indiano' (2010) 22 *Revista Chilena de Historia del Derecho* ff; Mauricio Novoa, *The Protectors of Indians in the Royal Audience of Lima. History, Careers and Legal Culture, 1575–1775* (2016).

[55] Miguel Angel González de San Segundo Sombra, *Un mestizaje jurídico: El derecho indiano de los indígenas* (1995).

[56] E.g., Clavero (n. 7).

[57] Thomas Duve, *Sonderrecht in der Frühen Neuzeit. Studien zum ius singulare und den privilegia miserabilium personarum, senum und indorum in Alter und Neuer Welt* (2008); Thomas Duve, 'La jurisdicción eclesiástica sobre los indígenas y el trasfondo del Derecho Canónico universal', in Ana de Zaballa Beascoechea (ed.), *Los indios, el Derecho Canónico y la justicia eclesiástica en la América virreinal* (2011).

[58] Tamar Herzog, 'The Appropriation of Native Status: Forming and Reforming Insiders and Outsiders in the Spanish Colonial World' (2014) 22 *Rechtsgeschichte—Legal History*, <https://dx.doi.org/10.12946/rg22/140-149> ff (accessed 24 April 2018); Tamar Herzog, *Defining Nations: Immigrants and Citizens in Early Modern Spain and Spanish America* (2003).

courts to defend themselves both against the abuses of local colonial authorities and against other indigenous groups.[59] It has become clear in several cases that the use of judicial institutions throughout the colonial period was not restricted to elites, but was rather open to larger parts of the indigenous population.[60] This corresponds to general findings on indigenous literacy, which have expanded the notion of the 'lettered city' far beyond the limited supposition of colonial elites.[61] Recent research has also drawn attention to the fact that even marginalized groups, like slaves of African descent, made use of ecclesiastical courts,[62] as did indigenous people.[63] There were even cases of notaries from African descent.[64] Interestingly, the strategic use of colonial courts also implied the use of indigenous materials as evidence, which in turn were produced and reproduced in pragmatic judicial contexts.[65]

One aspect of these findings seems especially noteworthy in the context of this chapter: indigenous peoples' use of royal and ecclesiastical courts and the introduction of indigenous law in these claims were not without consequences for the indigenous legal traditions themselves. When trying to argue their claims, indigenous actors had to translate their own legal regimes, like their concept of what the Christian tradition calls 'property', for instance, into the language and logics of the colonizing society.[66] This translation led to the counterintuitive result,

[59]   For early New Spain, see the pioneering work of Woodrow Borah, *Justice by Insurance: The General Indian Court of Colonial Mexico and the Legal Aides of the Half-Real* (1983); Kellogg (n. 48); Brian Philip Owensby, *Empire of Law and Indian Justice in Colonial Mexico* (2008); Yanna Yannakakis, *The Art of Being In-Between: Native Intermediaries, Indian Identity, and Local Rule in Colonial Oaxaca* (2008); for Andean regions, e.g., see Stern (n. 47); Jeremy Ravi Mumford, 'Litigation as Ethnography in Sixteenth-Century Peru: Polo de Ondegardo and the Mitimaes' (2008) 88 *Hispanic American Historical Review* ff; José Carlos de la Puente Luna, Renzo Honores, 'That Which Belongs to All: Khipus, Community, and Indigenous Legal Activism in the Early Colonial Andes' (2015) 72 *The Amercias* ff; Dueñas (n. 39); for a comparative survey, see Yanna Yannakakis, 'Comparative Indigenous History of the Americas', in Trevor Burnard (ed.), *Oxford Bibliographies in Atlantic History* (2013) <https://doi.org/10.1093/obo/9780199730414-0173> ff (accessed 24 April 2018).

[60]   Owensby (n. 59); Ramos/Yannakakis 2014 (n. 40).

[61]   Alcira Dueñas, *Indians and Mestizos in the 'Lettered City': Reshaping Justice, Social Hierarchy, and Political Culture in Colonial Peru* (2010); Joanne Rappaport, Tom Cummins, *Beyond the Lettered City: Indigenous Literacies in the Andes* (2012); Ramos/Yannakakis (n. 40).

[62]   De la Fuente Alejandro de la Fuente, 'Slaves and the Creation of Legal Rights in Cuba: Coartación and Papel' (2007) 87 *Hispanic American Historical Review* ff. Michelle McKinley, 'Fractional Freedoms: Slavery, Legal Activism, and Ecclesiastical Courts in Colonial Lima, 1593–1689' (2010) 28 *Law and History Review* <http://www.jstor.org/stable/25701148> ff (accessed 24 April 2018).

[63]   Jorge E. Traslosheros, Ana de Zaballa (eds.), *Los indios ante los foros de justicia religiosa en la hispanoamérica virreinal* (2010); Ana de Zaballa Beascoechea (ed.), *Los indios, el Derecho Canónico y la justicia eclesiástica en la América virreinal* (2011).

[64]   Silvia Espelt-Bombin, 'Notaries of Color in Colonial Panama. Limpieza de Sangre, Legislation, and Imperial Practices in the Administration of the Spanish Empire' (2014) 71 *The Americas* ff.

[65]   Ethelia Ruiz Medrano, *Mexico's Indigenous Communities. Their Lands and Histories, 1500–2010* (trans. Russ Davidson, 2010).

[66]   Karen Graubart, 'Shifting landscapes: Heterogeneous Conceptions of Land Use and Tenure in the Lima Valley' (2017) 26 *Colonial Latin American Review* ff.

as Tamar Herzog has emphasized, that it was precisely the respect for native rights that brought about a major reorganization of these rights and contributed to their transformation. Similarly, Spaniards defending themselves against indigenous claims sometimes cited pre-conquest law, and resettled communities were granted land rights according to Spanish legal concepts, thereafter adopting these concepts as their own.[67] With the passage of time, indigenous claimants could often draw upon early translations of indigenous rights that were adopted and used by indigenous peoples as their own, despite having transformed indigenous traditions as, for example, in the case of the *Relación de Michoacán*.[68] In other words, indigenous actors' use of secular and ecclesiastical courts led to a certain blending of traditions—a typical situation that legal anthropologists have proposed calling 'interlegality'.[69]

Yet indigenous peoples acted not only as litigants at crown courts and ecclesiastical tribunals, but also administered justice in lower courts. Administrative reforms, like Francisco de Toledo's ordinances, explicitly granted indigenous communities and their *cabildos* in his realm, the Viceroyalty of Peru, the right to hear all civil litigation on claims of minor economic value and other conflicts, like land use. They also granted jurisdiction over their subjects' labour to indigenous leaders.[70] In this jurisdictional activity, indigenous authorities drew on both indigenous and colonial laws, appropriating semantics, concepts, and practices from both orders.[71] For New Spain, recent studies have emphasized the vernacularization of Spanish and Christian legal thought and the blending of traditions in the local administration of indigenous justice. At least in some seventeenth and eighteenth-century cases, indigenous authorities even defended the existing colonial legal order against what they called the 'old law': the pre-conquest indigenous law.[72] In some cases, it has also been shown how authorities from indigenous councils communicated with local and peninsular authorities, participating actively in the process of normative production.[73] Representatives of influential groups of mestizos, often at least closely related to authorities in indigenous communities, used early church councils, like

---

[67] Tamar Herzog, 'Did European Law Turn American? Territory, Property and Rights in an Atlantic World', in Thomas Duve, Heikki Pihlajamäki (eds.), *New Horizons in Spanish Colonial Law: Contributions to Transnational Early Modern Legal History* (2015); Tamar Herzog, 'Colonial Law and "Native Customs": Indigenous Land Rights in Colonial Spanish Amerika' (2013) 63 *The Americas* ff.

[68] On these processes, see Barbara E. Mundy, *The Mapping of New Spain. Indigenous Cartography and the Maps of the Relaciones Geográficas* (2000).

[69] André J. Hoekema, 'European Legal Encounters Between Minority and Majority Culture: Cases of Interlegality' (2005) 37 *The Journal of Legal Pluralism and Unofficial Law* <http://commission-on-legal-pluralism.com/volumes/51/hoekema-art.pdf> ff (accessed 24 April 2018).

[70] See Karen Graubart, 'Learning From the Qadi: The Jurisdiction of Local Rule in the Early Colonial Andes' (2015) 95 *Hispanic American Historical Review* ff; Graubart (n. 33).

[71] Puente Luna and Honores (2015) 72 *The Amercias* (n. 59).

[72] Yannakakis, Schrader-Kniffki (2016) 96 *Hispanic American Historical Review* (n. 37) ff.

[73] Dueñas (2015) 72 *The Americas* (n. 39) ff.

the Third Provincial Council in Lima 1582–1583, to lobby for their interests, achieving favourable changes in ecclesiastical and royal legislation.[74]

Of course, these studies are necessarily tied to specific local contexts and periods. They do not admit generalization. However, taken together with the apparently frequent processes of 'racial passing' and flexible ascriptions to different ethnic groups, these complex patterns of 'consumption of justice' clearly indicate porous boundaries and a considerable dynamic of exchange and hybridization between indigenous and non-indigenous justice systems.

D. Methodological Challenges

These developments call for some remarks on key challenges for future research in legal history, especially regarding method. To the extent that legal historiography is not only dedicated to the legal past, specializing in the different modes of law and their historical functions, but also tries to connect its findings with problems and questions in current juridical scholarship, three aspects seem especially noteworthy, and they are closely related to general methodological problems of global legal history as part of legal scholarship.[75]

III. Multi-normativity

The first aspect that requires more intense study for the sake of more nuanced historiography and for a better conceptual purchase on current legal issues is how to analyse situations commonly referred to as 'legal pluralism'.

The concept of 'legal pluralism' is popular, but not unproblematic. It has succeeded in destabilizing state-centred perspectives on the past and other legal regimes, which tend to be legalistic, sometimes anachronistic, and Eurocentric, beyond mere Western modernity. However, the case of indigenous peoples' laws in the colonial period shows that it might also lead to a misunderstanding of the complex and profoundly different ways of administering justice. The often-cited practice of 'forum-shopping', well-known to modern jurists, seems to indicate that the choice

---

[74] Thomas Duve, 'El Concilio como instancia de autorización. La ordenación sacerdotal de mestizos ante el Tercer Concilio Limense (1582/83) y la comunicación sobre el Derecho en la monarquía española' (2010) 40 *Revista de Historia del Derecho* ff.

[75] Duve (n. 16) ff.

of courts implies a choice of law, but this only obtains to a very limited extent. When indigenous communities claimed their property rights, they might have used the colonial legal order, but this legal order recognized indigenous law and accepted indigenous forms of proof and translation of indigenous concepts. By the same token, judges in indigenous courts might not restrict themselves to 'indigenous law'. They might even oppose the traditional indigenous rights as the 'old law' and favour a normativity that had emerged in a long process of blending cultural traditions by (cultural) translation. Can such hybrid normativity be adequately represented by the concept of legal pluralism? A concept like interlegality, which André Hoekema[76] developed precisely to address the interpenetration of different legal orders, might be more helpful, despite its framing in European terms of majority/minority, which are inapplicable to Latin American cases.

But even after replacing 'plural' with 'inter', the problem of 'legal' and 'legality' remains. Focusing on the 'legal' aspect privileges state-centred perspectives and tends to create a semantic difference between different layers of normativity, granting the quality of 'law' to some and denying it to others, like custom. Already this bias might seem sufficient to abstain from its use. Moreover, it falls short when the goal is to understand the importance of normative spheres that are not law in a state-centred sense, or not even part of the usual 'non-law', like custom, but that might be considered religious normativity, including rites, religious obligations, or even consensus about what should be done and avoided. They are seen as simply different to what the Western tradition habitually calls 'law' and perhaps not even part of the classical canon of 'non-law'. While such distinctions between written law, custom, and moral, might apply to the Western legal past (although even this is doubtful), they do definitely not fit indigenous normativities. Neither does the concept of 'legal pluralism' leave a space to integrate the normativities that emerge from a praxeological perspective on human action: implicit knowledges that underlie practices, are contingent but not random, and might have decisive effects on how normative options are translated into concrete cases. How, for example, can we explain practices of not applying prescriptions, sometimes without any explicit rule, that seem to fit and have been applied in other cases? How do the aesthetic and material dimensions, the presence of certain objects or conditions and their perceptions, which seem to be so important for indigenous administration of justice, enter into the analysis? Research on indigenous laws needs analytical tools that grasp the underlying assumptions about consensual—and accordingly stable—normativities that affect all sorts of cultural reproduction as well as the cultural translation of concepts into different times and languages. Some of these phenomena have been addressed by the recent French sociology of conventions.[77]

---

[76] Hoekema (n. 69).

[77] Rainer Diaz-Bone, Claude Didry, Robert Salais, 'Conventionalist's Perspectives on the Political Economy of Law: An Introduction' (2015) 40 *Historical Social Research* <https://doi.org/10.12759/hsr.40.2015.1.7-22> ff (accessed 24 April 2018).

Here, conventions are understood as interpretative frames that coordinate operative situations. Such conventions develop out of concrete situations and can be stabilized network structures. They are related to specific forms of cognition and are applied with a normative intention.

The combination of these two perspectives—the norm-theoretical approach of 'normative and jurisdictional pluralism' or interlegality, along with the more action-theoretical approach of the sociology of conventions—helps to describe the complexity of normative orders as well as the process of normative appropriation. Yet, even together they fail to grasp the dynamics leading to normativity's continuous (re)production, especially in diverse epistemic settings. Above all, even when combined, they do not escape the danger of essentializing normative orders, treating these as if they were stable. Cultural studies, social science, and recent historiography on indigenous peoples, by contrast, have shown that the production of normativity by groups can only be understood dynamically, situationally, and relationally. Thus, any analysis of these normative spheres is incomplete without reflection on the dynamics of producing normativity in an internally diverse setting. Any representation of indigenous peoples' normative orders under colonial rule must consider the mechanisms of ethnicity construction. To understand complex societies and how their regulatory regimes reproduce themselves, legal history needs to draw upon social scientific scholarship on such dynamics as, for example, ongoing debates about ethnic boundary-making and conviviality.[78] An open concept like multi-normativity, which is designed to analyse situations of translating normativities in diverse epistemic settings, might help to reconstruct this complexity.[79]

IV. FREEZING DIFFERENCES

Another specific danger of the current re-indigenization by juridification is intimately related to historical discourse: the fallacy of essentializing the identities, traditions, and practices of groups that have succeeded in establishing themselves as relevant actors. Since indigenous peoples are usually identified genealogically, the conservation of their social practices, customs, traditions and their self-identification as, for example, in ILO 169, bears a certain danger

---

[78] Andreas Wimmer, *Ethnic Boundary Making: Institutions, Power, Networks* (2013); Steven Vertovec, 'Introduction: Formulating Diversity Studies', in Steven Vertovec (ed.), *Routledge International Handbook of Diversity Studies* (2015) ff.

[79] Duve (n. 16).

of 'freezing differences'[80] in the sense of creating seemingly stable historical identities through law.[81] Another reason for concern is that in order to obtain recognition as indigenous peoples, cultural stereotypes and preferences often prevail that romanticize and exoticize their referents or perpetuate and privilege other cultural patterns.[82] On the one hand, indigenous peoples run the risk of becoming trapped in their own traditions without the opportunity to develop them productively. On the other hand, other groups demanding autonomy then run the risk that their demands be ignored or that their protests could even be criminalized. At the risk of sounding indelicate, it might be the case that, in many cases, the driving force behind the process of recognizing indigenous peoples' rights is not so much the desire to restore historical tradition but simply the political calculation to grant more autonomy to certain groups that succeeded in asserting their claims in the political debate. In the long run, it might be inevitable to admit this.

v. Nothing Pure

Another provocative question of major significance to legal history is related to the continuous transformation of legal traditions, to the flexibility of collective ascriptions that constitute and reconstitute themselves, and the inevitable interrelatedness of their normative orders: is there even such a thing as 'indigenous rights'? They obviously exist—at least in a conceptual sense—as is evidenced by actors invoking them in their claims and arguing about their content. Moreover, it should be clear that there are no 'pure' traditions, especially not in legal spaces that were, like most of Latin America, in at least intermittent contact with other normative systems. The problem lies in the fiction of purity and historical stability, even if actors do not claim, as does the Bolivian constitution, traditions 'whose existence predates the Spanish colonial invasion'.

How do we deal with this, however, given that national and international law presuppose the existence of these 'indigenous laws' and trigger related processes of ethnogenesis and tradition-building? Legal history would do well to draw attention to the fundamental conceptual problems that arise from this kind of use

---

[80] Sérgio Costa, 'Freezing Differences: Politics, Law, and the Invention of Cultural Diversity in Latin America', in Aldo Mascareño, Kathya Araujo (eds.), *Legitimization in World Society* (2012).

[81] Adam Kuper, 'The Return of the Native' (2003) 44 *Current Anthropology* ff.

[82] For a survey of the debate and its problems relating to Brazil, see Carneiro de Cunha and Almeida (2000) 129 *Daedalus, Journal of the American Academy of Sciences* ff.

of history in judicial contexts.[83] This entails fostering debates about how different epistemic traditions clash in court, not only from a theoretical perspective,[84] but also considering the pragmatics of judicial contexts. It might, therefore, be necessary to reflect more deeply on what is variously referred to as 'forensic legal history': a methodological reflection on the use of legal history in court.[85]

BIBLIOGRAPHY

José Bengoa, *La emergenica indígena en América Latina* (2nd edn., Fondo de Cultura Económica Chile, 2007)

Karen Graubart, 'Competing Spanish and Indigenous Jurisdictions in Early Colonial Lima', *Oxford Research Encyclopedia of Latin American History* (Oxford University Press, 2016) <https://doi.org/10.1093/acrefore/9780199366439.013.365>

Tamar Herzog, 'Colonial Law and 'Native Customs': Indigenous Land Rights in Colonial Spanish Amerika' (2013) 63 *The Americas* 303–21

Susan Kellogg, 'The Colonial Mosaic of Indigenous New Spain, 1519–1821' *Oxford Research Encyclopedia of Latin American History* (Oxford University Press, 2016) <https://doi.org/10.1093/acrefore/9780199366439.013.29>

Florencia Mallon, 'Indigenous Peoples and the Nation-States in Spanish America, 1780–2000', in José C. Moya (ed.), *The Oxford Handbook of Latin American History* (Oxford University Press, 2011) 281–308

Detlef Nolte, Almut Schilling-Vacaflor (eds.), *New Constitutionalism in Latin America: Promises and Practices* (Ashgate, 2012)

Brian Philip Owensby, *Empire of Law and Indian Justice in Colonial Mexico* (Stanford University Press, 2008)

Ethelia Ruiz Medrano, *Mexico's Indigenous Communities. Their Lands and Histories, 1500-2010* (2010)

Robin Wright and Manuela Carneiro de Cunha, 'Destruction, Resistance, and Transformation—Southern, Coastal, and Northern Brazil (1580–1890)', in Frank Salomon, Stuart B. Schwartz (eds.), *The Cambridge History of the Native Peoples of the Americas* (Cambridge University Press, 1999) vol 3: South America, Part 1, <https://doi.org/10.1017/CHOL9780521630764.007>

Ricardo Zorraquín Becú, 'Los derechos indígenas' (1986) 14 *Revista de Historia del Derecho* 427–51

---

[83] See on the problem of claim-oriented research in a different context Arthur J. Ray, *Aboriginal Rights Claims and the Making and Remaking of History* (2016).

[84] Margaret Kovach, *Indigenous Methodologies: Characteristics, Conversations, and Contexts* (2009) 2009; Sousa Santos (n. 15).

[85] Ramses Delafontaine, *Historians as Expert Judicial Witnesses in Tobacco Litigation: A Controversial Legal Practice* (2015).

CHAPTER 44

INDIAN LAW

MITRA SHARAFI[*]

WHAT does the future hold for the field of Indian legal history, which has burgeoned since the late 1990s? This chapter explores opportunities for methodological innovation through digital history, oral history, and collaboration between scholars. These approaches promise to counterbalance certain patterns that have developed to date, particularly the heavy reliance on written English-language records from the colonial period.

I. THE LONG SHADOW OF COLONIALISM

Within the field of Indian legal history, the colonial period dominates. The focus has been on British India from the late eighteenth century until independence in 1947, and on the history of religion and gender in India's various personal law

* At the University of Wisconsin Law School, the author thanks members of the South Asia Legal Studies Working Group (particularly Cynthia Farid, Arpita Gupta, James Jaffe, Elizabeth Lhost, Marc Galanter, Sunil Rao, and Mark Sidel) and her writing group (Tonya Brito, Gwendolyn Leachman, and David S. Schwartz) for their comments. The author is also grateful to Nicholas J. Abbott, Rohit De, Leigh Denault, and Tushna Thapliyal for their thoughts. AIR SC stands for the All India Reporter Supreme Court. This chapter was written in 2017.

systems.[1] Why have scholars been so fixated on the colonial era, compared to the periods before and after? The answer lies in the colonial archive: it is voluminous, comparatively well preserved, and relatively accessible in Britain and India (although preservation efforts are still needed). As the study of Indian legal history has become increasingly populated by historians since the 1990s, archival features have shaped the field more than during the second half of the twentieth century, when scholars tended to be academic lawyers less focused on archival research.[2]

A second explanation relates to language: does a preference for English or a lack of fluency in other Indian languages push many scholars towards the study of British India? This possibility intersects with the problems of limited access to and comparatively poor preservation of non-English-language sources; it may be impossible to separate language preference from the source issue. However, relying on non-English primary sources would allow scholars to better explore a host of themes and venues, including non- and quasi-state religious law; legal consciousness reflected in popular songs, films, and street plays; and the legal culture of princely states.[3] Stepping away from sources in English (along with Persian and Sanskrit, for that matter) would also enable scholars to trade a pan-India framing for a focus on regional and community-specific legal cultures.

One could protest that legal history is by definition state-centric, and that if one wants to study law in modern Indian history, the core texts will be in English. This explanation may hold for the case law of apex courts and all-India legislation. But it becomes less and less compelling as one moves from the colonial to princely state courts (pre-1947), from the all-India to the local level, and from state to non-state law.

Finally, it may be that colonial legal history dominates because of academia's self-replicating mechanics. Faculty members who specialize in the colonial period have attracted graduate students interested in the same era or have steered students in this direction, given the advisors' own expertise. In addition, language skills for the less commonly taught South Asian languages (meaning all languages other than Hindi, Urdu, Sanskrit, or Persian) are often hard to acquire at universities outside of India. Together, these factors may have funnelled scholars, particularly those outside of India and of non-Indian background, into the study of British India.

---

[1] For an overview of the field, see Mitra Sharafi, 'South Asian Legal History' (2015) 11 *Ann. Rev. of Law and Soc. Sci.* 309 ff. Although most areas of Indian law since the colonial era have been governed by a single body of law for all (territorial law), Indian family law consists of separate bodies of religious law (personal law) applied by the state's mainstream civil courts—and by judges who are not necessarily members of the religious communities in question.

[2] Academic lawyers like J. D. M. Derrett, Marc Galanter, Upendra Baxi, and Rajeev Dhavan produced most scholarship on Indian legal history during the second half of the twentieth century. See Sharafi (n. 1).

[3] E.g., see Elizabeth Lhost, 'Between Community and Qānūn: Documenting Islamic Legal Practice in Nineteenth-Century British India' (PhD dissertation, University of Chicago, 2017); and C. Creekmur, M. Sidel (eds.), *Cinema, Law, and the State in Asia* (2007).

Within the historiography of India's colonial legal history, two questions stand out. The first is the 'who won?' question; the second is the colonial continuities debate. *Who won* when colonized people won cases in the colonial courts? This question is a version of one of the most important questions in legal history among scholars of England and the U.S.: were courts rigged in favour of elites, as Marxist scholars suggested in the 1970s?[4] Or did they provide an arena of struggle where non-elites could find their voice and protect their interests, as Hendrik Hartog and others have argued?[5] Could there be another, equally compelling way to understand the experience of litigation?

For British India, it could be most productive to ask, *who won in what ways?* Did Indian litigants (particularly non-elites) win by occasionally winning a case against the state or British parties? Or did the state win by forcing litigants to fight out these conflicts within the state's own system? Did even victorious Indian litigants win the battle but lose the war by winning their cases on the state's terms? Did the colonial courts act like a pressure-valve system in which other forms of anti-colonial resistance and conflict were diffused (for some time) by allowing occasional victories to Indian litigants? Put more broadly: what did it mean for Indian litigants to win cases in the context of colonial rule? How did this change in independent India—or did it? Racial difference became a less prominent theme in the independent period, but communalism, casteism, and colourism did not.[6] The question persisted: did non-elites have the possibility of experiencing their day in court in any meaningful way? What of India's post-1950 era with a written constitution, when non-elites like sex trade workers and Muslim butchers asserted their constitutional rights?[7] And how should we understand the rise of public interest litigation in the wake of India's temporary slide into authoritarianism during Indira Gandhi's Emergency (1975–1977)?[8]

If the courts were open arenas for conflict, then the gateway question of access to the courts becomes all-important. Scholarly histories of legal aid and pro bono work in India are important projects that scholars have only begun to explore.[9]

---

[4] E.g., see Douglas Hay, Peter Linebaugh, John G. Rule, E. P. Thompson, Cal Winslow (eds.), *Albion's Fatal Tree: Crime and Society in Eighteenth-Century England* (1975).

[5] See Barbara Young Welke and Hendrik Hartog, ' "Glimmers of Life": A Conversation with Hendrik Hartog' (2009) 27 *Law Hist. Rev.* 643.

[6] In the South Asian context, communalism refers to conflict between ethno-religious (e.g., Hindu, Muslim) communities.

[7] See Rohit De, *A People's Constitution: The Everyday Life of Law in the Indian Republic* (2019).

[8] See Upendra Baxi, 'Taking Suffering Seriously: Social Action Litigation in the Supreme Court of India' (1985) 4 *Third World Legal Studies* 107 ff.; Oliver Mendelsohn, 'The Supreme Court as the Most Trusted Public Institution in India' in O. Mendelsohn, *Law and Social Transformation in India* (2014) 245 ff.; and Anuj Bhuwania, *Courting the People: Public Interest Litigation in post-Emergency India* (2017).

[9] See N. R. Madhava Menon, 'Legal Aid and Justice for the Poor', in Upendra Baxi (ed.), *Law and Poverty: Critical Essays* (1988) 341 ff.; Marc Galanter and Jayanth K. Krishnan, ' "Bread for the

The role of non-governmental organizations are also part of India's access-to-justice history, as are public interest litigation and legal pluralism.[10] Socio-legal scholars have declared a 'renaissance' in the study of access to justice in the USA.[11] Legal historians might pursue this topic further for India, not least of all to better contextualize Indian case law.

The 'colonial continuities' debate also begins with the colonial period, although from the vantage point of the post-colonial. How should we regard colonial-era law in independent India? What role have colonial institutions and values continued to play in the post-colonial legal system? Is all or only some colonial-era law in force today tainted by the perceived exigencies of colonial rule? Does the fact that certain cases and legislation in force today were produced by the colonial system mean that they should be rejected and replaced whenever possible? The pre-colonial is relevant to this debate, too. Early modernists can tell us whether concepts like anti-sodomy prohibitions, *thuggee* or dacoity (highway robbery associated with particular 'criminal tribes'), and even the caste system and Hinduism as unified entities, for instance, were as distinct to the colonial period as colonial historians suggest.[12]

The colonial continuities debate has also spilled beyond the bounds of academia. It figures into assessments of sedition and anti-terrorism laws in India today. Most prominently, it has played a central role in struggles over gay rights in the Indian courts. In 2009, the Delhi High Court found the 'unnatural offences' provision of the Indian Penal Code (section 377) to be unconstitutional.[13] Four years later, the decision was overruled by the Indian Supreme Court.[14] Critics of section 377 (including the Delhi High Court) asserted that the criminalization of same-sex intercourse was a British import and that it was suspect because it was a colonial-era law. Conservative defenders of section 377 argued that on the contrary, it was the concept of gay *rights* that was foreign and a form of cultural neo-imperialism. The accusation of being under Western influence, in other words, is a rhetorical weapon used by both sides. Is homophobia as enshrined in the criminal law an instance of cultural imperialism that lives on in post-colonial India? Or are LGBTQ rights a set of outside values being imposed on Indian

---

Poor": Access to Justice and the Rights of the Needy in India' (2003–2004) 55 *Hastings L.J.* 789 ff.; and A. Gupta, 'Pro Bono and the Corporate Legal Sector in India', in D. B. Wilkins, V. S. Khanna, D. M. Trubek (eds.), *The Indian Legal Profession in the Age of Globalization* (2017) 275 ff.

[10] On public interest litigation, see Bhuwania (n. 8).

[11] Catherine R. Albiston, Rebecca L. Sandefur, 'Expanding the Empirical Study of Access to Justice' (2013) *Wisc. L.R.* 101 ff.

[12] See Bernard Cohn, 'The Census, Social Structure and Objectification in South Asia', in Bernard Cohn, *An Anthropologist among the Historians and other Essays* (1987) 224 ff.; and Romila Thapar, 'Imagined Religious Communities? Ancient History and the Modern Search for a Hindu Identity', in Romila Thapar, *Interpreting Early India* (1992) 60 ff.

[13] *Naz Foundation v. Government of NCT and others* 2010 Crim. L.J. 94 (India).

[14] *Suresh Kumar Koushal and another v. Naz Foundation and others* AIR 2014 SC 563.

society in neo-colonial fashion? Neither side seems willing to admit that Western influence may have played a major role both in IPC section 377 *and* in its potential invalidation.

The colonial continuities debate plays out in complex ways at several levels. While its participants argue over which perspective is more tainted by Western influence, the discussion itself replicates a pattern established during the colonial period. Then, as now, debates over legal reform were particularly fierce when they pertained to sexual practices, echoing Partha Chatterjee's idea of an inner sphere of family (and sex) being aspirationally beyond the reach of government regulation.[15] In other words, the section 377 debate is the latest in a line of contentious reform debates since the colonial period over sex and sexuality, including debates over the age of consent (focused on child marriage) and Hindu widow remarriage (aimed at ending its prohibition). There is also the relationship between criminalization and the formation of same-sex identity. In many parts of the world, the criminalization of sodomy was a catalyst for the rise of homosexual identity, particularly among men. If the Indian story is similar, then LGBTQ opponents of the anti-sodomy law may find colonialism to be not only the source of their oppression, but also of their sexual orientation-based identity.

Anil Kalhan, Arudra Burra, Kalyani Ramnath, Rohit De, and others have addressed the colonial continuities debate directly.[16] Another body of work also comes at many of the same issues obliquely. This is the scholarship on the vernacularization (here meaning Indianization) of colonial law.[17] The argument goes that over time, key features of colonial law—like the English language itself—became Indian.[18] Complex bundles of ideas from the rule of law and constitutionalism to women's rights travelled from the metropole to the colony under British rule. However, these soon became reshaped, melded, and 'braided' together with South Asian languages, value systems, institutional cultures, and models of governance, along with customary and religious systems of norms and dispute resolution.[19] For instance, Indian

---

[15] Partha Chatterjee, *The Nation and its Fragments: Colonial and Postcolonial Histories* (1993) 116 ff.

[16] See Anil Kalhan, Gerald P. Conroy, Mamta Kaushal, Sam Scott Miller, Jed S. Rakoff, 'Colonial Continuities: Human Rights, Terrorism, and Security Laws in India' (2006) 20 *Col. J. Asian Law*, 125 ff.; Arudra Burra, 'The Cobwebs of Imperial Rule' (2010) 615 *Seminar* 79 ff.; Rohit De, 'Rebellion, Dacoity, and Equality: The Emergence of the Constitutional Field in Postcolonial India' (2014) 34 *Comp. Stud. S. Asia Afr. Middle East* 260 ff.; and symposium issue of (2016) 31 *Am. U. Int. L.R.*, particularly Arudra Burra, 'What is 'Colonial' about Colonial Laws?' 137 ff. and Kalyani Ramnath, '*ADM Jabalpur's* Antecedents: Political Emergencies, Civil Liberties, and Arguments from Colonial Continuities in India' 209 ff.

[17] For a leading study of vernacularization in the context of international law, see Sally Engle Merry, *Human Rights and Gender Violence: Translating International Law into Local Justice* (2006).

[18] See the related concepts of transculturation, circulation, and flow in anthropology and comparative literature, e.g., David Damrosch, *What Is World Literature?* (2003); and Stuart Alexander Rockefeller, 'Flow' (2011) 52 *Current Anthropology* 557 ff.

[19] The braiding terminology is borrowed from Projit B. Mukharji, *Doctoring Traditions: Ayurveda, Small Technologies, and Braided Sciences* (2016).

petitioning cultures and adjudicatory bodies like *panchayats* (caste or community councils) shaped the evolution of the colonial legal system.[20]

In fact, both the 'who won?' and colonial continuities debates may overstate the divide between colonial and non-colonial. The colonial and the non-colonial represented the far ends of a spectrum, rather than a closed or binary set of options. Legal historians at their best have recognized that most of what they examine comes from the concoction in the middle. Some of the field's richest work has explored the points of fusion and repurposing of Anglo institutions that took on new life in India, along with Indian concepts that adapted to new conditions under colonial rule.

Despite the attention already paid to colonial India, there remain further issues to explore. We need more research on local and specialty courts (like the salt courts and railway courts), the lower levels of the legal profession, women in the legal profession, and law and the military during the colonial period—all areas where access to primary-source materials may be challenging. The intersection between legal history and a number of other sub-fields within history are also ripe for research. These include the place where the history of law meets: the history of the book and print culture; the history of the administrative state; environmental history; the history of science, technology, and medicine (including disaster and sound studies and the history of intoxicating substances); the history of material culture (including legal dress, furniture, and other 'law props' and symbols); and the history of architecture, the city, and space (including legal geography).[21]

Historians of colonial Indian law should also cultivate a greater awareness of socio-legal studies, an interdisciplinary body of scholarship produced by academic lawyers and social scientists.[22] Despite a rich scholarship fostered by the Commission on Legal Pluralism and the *Journal of Legal Pluralism and Unofficial Law* since the 1970s and 1980s, historians of India only discovered the concept of legal pluralism once it was shepherded into the discipline of history by Lauren Benton in 2002.[23] Other concepts developed by socio-legal scholars are waiting to be put to better use by legal historians. These include the study of legal consciousness (how do people decide they have a legal rather than a social problem?) and the social reception of legal outcomes, including those mediated through social movements.[24]

---

[20] See Bhavani Raman, *Document Raj: Writing and Scribes in Early Colonial South India* (2012); James A. Jaffe, *Ironies of Colonial Governance: Law, Custom, and Justice in Colonial India* (2015); and introduction by Rohit De and Robert Travers to 'Petitioning and Political Cultures in South Asia', *Mod. Asian Stud.* special issue (2019).

[21] For work that combines the history of law, materiality, and spatiality, see Paul Halliday, 'The Stuff of Law: Some Material Considerations from Britain and its Empire, ca. 1450–1850' (presented at the University of Wisconsin Law School, 18 April 2017).

[22] Many socio-legal scholars are affiliated with the Law and Society Association.

[23] Lauren Benton, *Law and Colonial Cultures: Legal Regimes in World History, 1400–1900* (2002).

[24] On legal consciousness, see Mitra Sharafi, *Law and Identity in Colonial South Asia: Parsi Legal Culture, 1772–1947* (2014) 58–71.

Many of these same themes are equally under-explored for the post-colonial period, such that scholars may avoid the traditional periodization of working either pre- or post-1947. Not only has 1947 traditionally acted as a divider between historical periods of study, it has also functioned as a disciplinary boundary segregating historians from political scientists. Increasingly, though, historians since the new millennium are working on both sides of Indian independence, carving out periods that make more sense for their subject of study than the political 'full stop'—and start—of 15 August 1947.

II. THE FUTURE OF INDIAN LEGAL HISTORY

A. Early Modern India and Digital Humanities

How should Indian legal history move beyond the bulge of colonial historiography? The legal history of early modern India is a much less populated era of study than its colonial counterpart. Equally, scholarship on the legal history of the Mughal empire, the dominant power in early modern India, is a much smaller body of work than the legal history of other Asian empires of the same period, particularly the Ottoman and Qing. This pattern partly reflects the availability of primary sources. Mughal legal history lacks the richness of records for Ottoman legal history, with its *kadi* court records, or late imperial China, with its Qing dynasty legal code— perhaps because the Mughal legal system was less centralized. That said, even the sources that do exist are under-used.[25] This pattern may reflect the challenges of gaining access to them when they are housed, largely uncatalogued, in regional Indian archives.

Digital humanities tools are especially useful here.[26] Network analysis may illuminate connections between individuals and families appearing in early modern legal sources, including merchants, religious figures, courtiers, judges, and others involved in using or structuring law.[27] A hub of early modern sources from the same locale could form the basis for a digital mapping project that would reconstruct

[25] For exceptions, see Farhat Hasan, *State and Locality in Mughal India: Power Relations in Western India, c. 1572–1730* (2004); and Nandini Chatterjee, 'Reflections on Religious Difference and Permissive Inclusion in Mughal Law' (2014) 29:3 *J. of Law and Religion* 396 ff.

[26] See generally Lara Putnam, 'The Transnational and the Text-Searchable: Digitized Sources and the Shadows They Cast' (2016) 121(2) *Am. Hist. Rev.*, 377 ff. and the (2016) 34 *Law and History Review* special issue on digital legal history.

[27] For a model drawn from U.S. digital legal history, see 'O Say Can You See: Early Washington, D.C., Law & Family': <http://earlywashingtondc.org/> (accessed 1 March 2017).

aspects of socio-spatial life—with the ability to highlight environmental, residential, commercial, or religious sites, for instance. Such a project could also show how these geographies changed over time, using a map with a sliding timeline.[28] Both network analysis and mapping should be of special interest to scholars wanting to use legal sources to write about social history, in other words. For those more interested in the development of law and legal culture, text analysis can illuminate the migration and permutation of legal terms and concepts across time and territory.[29] Digital tools should not be ends in themselves. Rather, they are means of generating insights and arguments that would not be otherwise evident.

Even the simple digitization of manuscript sources is of great value. Fields like the medieval history of China and Europe, as well as Ottoman history, have been invigorated by online access to materials that formerly lay buried in Eurasian archives. The volume of sources is smaller and older for early modern India than for the colonial period, making digitization both a better defined task and perhaps a more pressing one for the early modern period. The Rajasthan and Andhra Pradesh State Archives are making great efforts to digitize their early modern collections. Aparna Balachandran and Rochelle Pinto noted in 2011, however, that while many regional archives in India have digitization schemes, there is little talk of making the end products accessible via the Internet.[30] In some cases, digital versions of sources are only available from a limited number of computer terminals in the archive's reading room, for instance.[31] The reasons for this approach may be varied and complex, including fear of losing in-person visitors and of posting online material deemed politically volatile. Taking one more step back, even having a computer-searchable catalogue of holdings (available online) is relatively new at the time of writing for the National Archives of India and does not yet exist for many regional archives in India. In other words, digitization for Indian legal history means not just the kind of text and network analysis one typically associates with digital humanities projects. Before that, it means digitizing the sources themselves. And even before that, it means converting paper catalogues into computerized ones.

As with digital history in general, it is important to recognize that the selection biases inherent in the paper archive are replicated and amplified through digital approaches. Because digitization only makes more accessible documents already selected for preservation in the physical archive, the priorities and interests of those initial selection processes necessarily reproduce themselves in the digital

---

[28] For a U.S. model, see 'Digital Harlem: Everyday Life 1915–1930': <http://digitalharlem.org/> (accessed 1 March 2017).

[29] For an American model, see Kellen Funk and Lincoln Mullen's work on the Field Code's proliferation across American states: <http://kellenfunk.org/field-code/> (accessed 1 March 2017).

[30] Aparna Balachandran, Rochelle Pinto, *Archives and Access* [2011] 73.

[31] See Aparna Balachandran, 'The Delhi State Archives' (14 September 2009), available at <https://cis-india.org/raw/histories-of-the-internet/blogs/the-cyborgs/the-delhi-state-archives> (accessed 05 May 2018).

forum.[32] For instance, officials decided that certain types of documents were worth preserving, while others were destroyed to make space.[33] The categorization of records as classified or the case-by-case decisions by archivists that documents are too politically sensitive for viewing are further examples of filters that play a powerful role in the shape of the paper archive.[34] Digital history projects can only work with the products of these earlier processes. Inevitably, they also introduce their own added layer of selection—in deciding what documents to digitize and make available first, or at all. In medieval European history, the most visually spectacular manuscripts (namely those with colour illumination) tended to be digitized first, taking priority over humbler manuscripts.[35] Balachandran and Pinto note that private papers have not been prioritized in digitization efforts at one South Indian archive because of the legal ambiguity surrounding the archives' relationship with donor families.[36]

One critique of digital humanities initiatives in Western academia is that they privilege existing Euro-American sources and archives. Digitizing early modern Indian legal sources is itself one step towards redressing the balance. In India, digitization efforts for the colonial and post-colonial period are already evident through state-funded platforms. These include the Digital Library of India (rare published sources) and the Bombay High Court's Virtual Museum (which includes some unpublished case records).[37] There may also be other potential sources of support, too. The British Library's Endangered Archives Program, for instance, is available to preserve pre-modern collections of archival materials.[38] UNESCO's Memory of the World program recognizes primary sources of world historical significance that are at risk of being lost.

The need to better preserve Indian archives is of course a larger and more general issue, applying to documents from all periods. Despite the laudable digitization efforts already noted, India's vast documentary collections are on balance deteriorating at an alarming rate. Dinyar Patel has assessed the state of Indian

[32] See Balachandran, Pinto (n. 30) 50–81.

[33] On the destruction of Bombay High Court records to make space in 1923–1924, see Mitra Sharafi, 'Two Lives in Law: The Reminiscences of A. J. C. Mistry and Sir Norman Macleod, 1884–1926', in D. Y. Chandrachud et al. (eds.), *A Heritage of Judging: the Bombay High Court through 150 Years* (2012) 279–80.

[34] On the refusal to share maps of disputed regions and documents that 'may incite communal disharmony' at the Indian National Archives in Delhi, see Balachandran, Pinto (n. 30) 28, 77.

[35] The author thanks Samantha Kahn Herrick for this observation.

[36] Balachandran, Pinto (n. 30) 67 (on the Tamil Nadu State Archives in Chennai, India).

[37] See <https://ndl.iitkgp.ac.in/> (accessed 5 May 2018) and http://bombayhighcourt.nic.in (accessed 1 March 2017).

[38] Project 636 (2013) led to the creation of a digital archive of Indian Christian manuscripts (particularly from Goa) in Konkani, Marathi, Portuguese, Latin, and English. The British Library has also launched its 'Two Centuries of Indian Print: 1713–1914' project, which will digitize 4,000 rare or early printed Bengali-language books in its collections. See Maja Kominko (ed.), *From Dust to Digital: Ten Years of the Endangered Archives Programme* (2015).

archives explicitly.[39] A greater investment needs to be made in the preservation of India's documentary past. The question is: *by whom*? Indian governments (state and federal) are the obvious candidates, despite competing financial demands that many would consider to take priority. International and non-state entities like the British Library or the Ford Foundation are other options. On the one hand, their involvement may raise questions of India's sovereignty and control over its own cultural heritage. Such concerns are raw given the colonial past. On the other hand, the needs are so great and time-sensitive that arguably the preservation of the documents should be paramount. S. R. Mehrotra and Dinyar Patel assert that international funding is necessary for the digitization of the vast Dadabhai Naoroji collection, for instance.[40]

There are also non-state groups in India that may be able to help. Continuing with the cause of Mehrotra and Patel, a funding source within the Parsi community could perhaps help fund the digitization of the Naoroji papers, for instance. Dadabhai Naoroji (1825–1917) was arguably the most important nationalist figure before M. K. Gandhi, and he was a member of the Parsi or Zoroastrian community that has sponsored preservationist projects of many kinds. Corporate sponsors are another possibility. This option seems particularly interesting since the introduction of the world's first corporate giving requirement in 2014. Under Indian company law, businesses with annual revenues over ten billion rupees ($150 million) must now give two per cent of their net profits to charity. This new rule only creates another reason for Parsi-founded corporate giants like Tata or Godrej to consider funding the digitization of the Naoroji papers. Both companies host corporate archives of their own. In short, the need to preserve and digitize legal historical sources from the early modern period onward is an urgent one whose potential funders ought to include entities beyond the state in India. The Naoroji papers are a prime example because of their association with the Parsi community, which has a long history of philanthropy. However, the greater age and fragility of early modern sources makes their digitization perhaps even more pressing.

B. Independent India and Oral History

The legal history of independent India is a better populated and more active field than its early modern counterpart, perhaps because not only historians and lawyers, but also political scientists, anthropologists, and sociologists write about this later

---

[39] By Dinyar Patel, see 'In India, History Literally Rots Away', 'Repairing the Damage at India's National Archives', 'India's Archives: How Did Things Get This Bad?', and 'The Parsis, Once India's Curators, Now Shrug as History Rots' all in *New York Times* (20–22 March 2012). See also the 'Archives and Access' blog at <https://publicarchives.wordpress.com/> (accessed 19 March 2017).

[40] S. R. Mehrotra, Dinyar Patel (eds.), *Dadabhai Naoroji: Selected Private Papers* (2016) xlv.

period. Here, too, there are exciting methodological possibilities for future research. In particular, oral history is underused and offers a new way into the lived experience of law, particularly for periods of history too recent or sensitive to be well documented or accessible in the written archives.

Despite oral history's ascendance since the 1970s and its new world of tools and platforms created by the digital revolution, very little oral history has been done by legal historians of India. They remain focused on written sources. Through their disciplinary training and culture, many historians retain a vague discomfort with oral primary sources, grounded perhaps in an awareness of the mutability and fallibility of memory. However, written sources also contain factual inaccuracies. Like many oral history interviews, they may be put into writing many years after the episodes they describe. And whether written or oral, primary sources are framed in ways that reflect their authors' agenda and biases. These shared features aside, the choice is often not between oral and written sources, but between oral and *no* sources. Oral history interviews recover narratives that may otherwise be unavailable in any other format, in other words. As such, the conservative historian's impulse to confirm claims made in oral interviews with written sources is not always possible. An alternative approach is to evaluate oral narratives on their own terms—to use them to reflect upon the creation of identity, memories, nostalgia, and memorialization. This means not trying to extract some kind of factual accuracy from an interview, but instead focusing on the meaning a narrative creates for its speaker or for the speaker's community.[41] In short, learning from oral historians (as well as qualitative social scientists) will help legal historians gain access to a rich parallel universe of primary materials while grappling with the methodological challenges of interviews.[42]

The traditional way to start would be to record interviews with legal professionals, particularly senior legal luminaries willing to reflect upon their careers and times.[43] Scholars of South Asian legal studies have carried out interviews of this type.[44] It would be worth fine-tuning their approach by adopting the protocols and best practices of oral historians for conducting, preserving, and disseminating interviews.[45]

[41] E.g., see Richard White, *Remembering Ahanagran: A History of Stories* (1998) 4–6, 302–3.

[42] See Alastair Thomson, 'Four Paradigm Transformations in Oral History' (2007) 34 *Oral Hist. Rev.* 34:1 49 ff.

[43] See video interviews with Iqbal Chagla and others at <www.mylaw.net> (accessed 7 July 2017). For a UK model, see 'National Life Stories: Legal Lives' at <http://www.bl.uk/projects/national-life-stories-legal-lives>(accessed 8 March 2017).

[44] See Jayanth Krishnan, 'Professor Kingsfield Goes to Delhi: American Academics, the Ford Foundation, and the Development of Legal Education in India' (2004) 46 *Am. J. of Leg. Hist.* 447 ff; George H. Gadbois, Jr., *Judges of the Supreme Court of India, 1950–1989* (2012); and Marc Galanter, Nick Robinson, 'Grand Advocates: The Traditional Elite Lawyers', in Wilkins, Khanna, and Trubek (n. 9) 455 ff.

[45] See the Oral History Association's 'Principles and Best Practices for Oral History' (2009) <http://www.oralhistory.org/about/principles-and-practices/>; and 'Oral History in the Digital Age' <http://ohda.matrix.msu.edu/best-practices/> (accessed 7 March 2017).

The most obvious project of this kind would focus on leading lawyers and judges during and in the aftermath of Indira Gandhi's Emergency, an experience that mobilized a generation of lawyers to defend the rule of law and constitutionalism in its wake. Another idea would be to interview legal professionals and officials in order to reconstruct institutional histories. India has a variety of specialty courts, for instance, like motor accident courts (the Motor Accident Claims Tribunal, est. 1959) and consumer courts (the National Consumer Disputes Redressal Commission, est. 1986). Oral history interviews could illuminate the history of these court systems, which have received less attention than they deserve.

A broader approach would consist of oral history interviews of litigants and social movement actors, as well as legal professionals. For instance, one could interview former princely families on the famous Privy Purse case of 1971. This lawsuit challenged the government's failure to honour agreements made with the formerly independent princely rulers who gave up power and allowed their polities to become part of independent India after 1947.[46] One could interview victims and non-profit organizations involved in the Bhopal disaster of 1984, the world's worst industrial accident to date. A complex transnational trail of litigation followed, for which an extensive digital archive is now available.[47] Equally, oral histories relating to sex-selective abortion or transnational surrogacy could create a rich body of primary sources on legal consciousness, legal consultation, the side-stepping of legal prohibitions, and the interaction between changing social views and legal regimes.[48]

Oral history and legal history exist as relatively discrete sub-fields within history and move along their own conference circuits. There has been little overlap or contact between these two scholarly communities for Indian history. But there should be more, and the relatively new Oral History Association of India is encouraging scholars to explore the intersection between oral narratives and legal studies. Historians of the 1947 partition and independence of India, the Commonwealth, and South Asian diaspora have done extensive and impressive work with oral history, including as digital humanities initiatives.[49]

---

[46] *H. H. Maharajadhiraja Madhav Rao Jivaji Rao Scindia Bahadur of Gwalior and others v. Union of India and another*, AIR 1971 SC 530.

[47] See Marc Galanter's collection of papers in 'Bhopal: Law, Accidents, and Disasters in India' at <http://repository.law.wisc.edu/bhopal-collection> (accessed 05 May 2018).

[48] The surrogacy industry was legal and largely unregulated by Indian law from 2002 until 2016. See Amrita Pande, *Wombs in Labor: Transnational Commercial Surrogacy in India* (2014); and Prabha Kotiswaran, 'Do Feminists Need an Economic Sociology of Law?' (2003) 40(1) *J. Law Soc.* 115 ff. at 132–5. On sex-selective abortion, see Sital Kalantry, *Women's Human Rights and Migration: Sex-Selective Abortion Laws in the United States and India* (2017).

[49] E.g., see Ritu Menon, *Borders & Boundaries: Women in India's Partition* (1998); and Devika Chawla, *Home, Uprooted: Oral Histories of India's Partition* (2014). For online oral history archives, see the 1947 Archive <http://www.1947partitionarchive.org/>; the Cambridge Centre of South Asian Studies audio archive <http://www.s-asian.cam.ac.uk/archive/audio/>; Commonwealth Oral Histories <http://www.commonwealthoralhistories.org/>; and the Houston Asian American Archives oral histories <https://scholarship.rice.edu/handle/1911/79695> (accessed 7 March 2017).

Admittedly, there are institutional challenges to doing oral legal history. Graduate students in history departments do not usually receive training in oral history. The exceptions are those scholars working in fields like the history of indigenous peoples and African history.[50] Short courses on oral history do exist. The Columbia Oral History program and Science History Institute offer such training in the USA, as do the Oral History Society and the British Library's National Life Stories in the UK. However, these opportunities are generally rare.

It is important for those using oral history methods to adhere to ethical standards in the field. For academics in many countries, these standards take the form of principles agreed upon within the sub-disciplinary community of oral historians. For scholars based in the USA, there has been the added requirement of obtaining human subjects research approval from their home university's Institutional Review Board (IRB) prior to doing interviews. The American IRB system arose to prevent the type of abuse of human subjects by researchers that occurred during the Holocaust. For decades, the rules developed for research in medical and other scientific fields also applied to oral history research. At many American universities, getting IRB approval to do oral history could be a confusing, time-consuming, and challenging process. It has no doubt discouraged many historians who work with written sources from attempting to acquire new skills for oral history. As of 2018, however, oral history may soon be exempted from the IRB approval process.[51] For legal historians of India based in the USA, this change would make oral history less logistically challenging.

c. Law's Reach

The history of Indian case law has burgeoned as legal historians have begun using courts as archives over the past decade. Scholars have unearthed case files buried in the records rooms, storage warehouses or *godowns*, and functioning courtrooms of Indian courts themselves, including the Supreme Court of India and the High Courts of Bombay, Madras, and Allahabad.[52] Scholars have also (re-)discovered the

---

[50] See Jan Vansina, *Oral Tradition as History* (1985), and Luise White, Stephen Miescher, David William Cohen (eds.), *African Words, African Voices: Critical Practices in Oral History* (2001). The author thanks Neil Kodesh for these references.

[51] See the U.S. Federal Policy for the Protection of Human Subjects: <https://www.federalregister.gov/documents/2017/01/19/2017-01058/federal-policy-for-the-protection-of-human-subjects> (accessed 1 February 2017).

[52] See De (n.7) (Supreme Court of India), Sharafi (n. 24) (Bombay High Court), Alastair McClure, 'Violence, Sovereignty, and the Making of Colonial Criminal Law in India, 1857–1914' (PhD dissertation, University of Cambridge, 2017) (Allahabad High Court), and Kalyani Ramnath, 'Boats in a Storm: Law, Politics, and Jurisdiction in Postwar South Asia' (PhD dissertation, Princeton University, 2018) (Madras High Court).

records of the Judicial Committee of the Privy Council, the highest court of appeal for the British Empire. While American legal history has long relied heavily on appellate case files and the stories they allow scholars to tell, this development is relatively recent for Indian legal history.

Indian court archives are neither easy to access nor well preserved.[53] Even so, they offer incredibly rich primary-source material to those who persevere and are interested in a broad swathe of court records rather than the papers from a single case or two. Scholars with the stamina for this type of research should also be aware of some of the uneven patterns it can produce. One potential criticism is that this type of work privileges the rare and rarefied experience of appellate litigation over the everyday work of the lower courts. The latter captured the experience of a far larger number of people moving through the legal system. Some work has been done on the history of local courts in India, particularly by scholars based in India, and other should follow.[54]

It is also easy to forget when using appellate court records that law is about more than just courts. It is also about legal culture and consciousness, legislation, regulation, policing, and punishment. More broadly still, scholars of legal pluralism remind us that law is not solely produced by the state. From this perspective, law includes other forms of norms and dispute resolution. Non-state religious law, along with customary law and councils (like the *panchayat, mel,* or *salish*) reached into rural and non-elite communities that may never have seen the inside of a courtroom. Legal 'folkways' were not always documented in written form, making oral history again of special value—for periods and episodes that live on in the memory of people alive today. Scholars of the administrative state may make a valid criticism against case law specialists, and scholars of legal pluralism in turn may make a similar point in relation to legal historians who draw exclusively from state-produced legal sources. In other words, there is a larger world of state and non-state law in India that is easily sidelined by legal histories focused on written records emanating from appellate courts.

These criticisms reflect a fundamental tension at the heart of Indian legal history. There is a disjunction between elite legal institutions (particularly courts), on the one hand, and most of the population, on the other.[55] How do we square

---

[53] On obstacles to gaining entry to Indian state archives generally, see Balachandran, Pinto (n. 30), 76–80.

[54] See S. Dube, *Stitches in Time: Colonial Textures and Postcolonial Tangles* (2004); R. Pant, 'Revisiting family and inheritance: old age endowments among peasant households in early twentieth century Garhwal' (2013) 29 *Nehru Mem. Museum Lib. Occ. Papers Hist. Soc.*, new series, 1 ff.; and R. Pant, 'Matrimonial Strategies among Peasant Women in Early 20th Century Garhwal' (2014) 48 *Contrib. Ind. Soc.* 1 ff.

[55] Partha Chatterjee makes a similar argument about 'civil society' in India. See his 'On Civil and Political Society in Postcolonial Democracies' in Sudipta Kaviraj, Sunil Khilnani (eds.), *Civil Society: History and Possibilities* (2001) 165 ff.

the English-language, common law work of appellate courts with the everyday lived experience of millions in over a dozen vernacular languages and often rural settings who arguably had little contact with such state institutions? State courts for most of Indian history remained remote and disconnected from the lives of many. There were exceptions—like the working-class women who obtained divorces in Bombay's colonial courts and the slum-dwellers who made their case before the Supreme Court in the 1980s.[56] In general, though, an unavoidable question for legal historians of India has been: how much did the courts reach into the lives of non-elites? This issue is a version of the question for legal historians of the Anglo-American world: were courts really arenas of conflict *for everyone?*

Even for those who did make it to court, there was delay. Since the colonial period, delay has been a major problem for the courts in India.[57] Here, even people who did go to court felt the force and reach of state law blunted. It could be years, or even decades, before litigation was concluded. The delays that plagued the Indian courts enabled an alternative use of litigation—not to win one's case, but simply to tie up the other side and its property for years. 'Punitive litigating' meant that the process itself was the punishment.

Equally, there remains the age-old issue for legal historians: even for the small number of people who did go to court, how could the voice of litigants themselves be recovered given that so many spoke through carefully planned scripts on the advice of lawyers? The history of the legal profession is a vibrant and promising area of Indian legal history, particularly when focusing on Indian lawyers who acted as intellectual and cultural intermediaries between the legal system and Indian populations. But when it is the litigant who is of interest, the challenge is to filter out the scripted narratives produced by the 'hired gun' lawyer, where those statements may simply reflect arguments that were most likely to succeed in court. The issue plagues legal historians writing about courtroom trials in almost all times and places. In the context of India, this phenomenon adds yet another layer of padding between law and social life.

Together, these issues suggest that studying formal law, particularly through appellate court records, may give little insight into law as a social institution. One counter-argument is that even when interactions with state law—filtered through bureaucracy or police—were rare, they could be life-shaping nonetheless. And even in the absence of consistent enforcement, regulation could and often did loom large in people's lives. The threat of interaction with police or other organs of the state in the clearance of illegal slums or street hawkers, for instance, meant that law *was* felt by people, even if they interacted only rarely with the state and never entered

---

[56] See Sharafi (n. 24) 193–236; *Olga Tellis and others v. Bombay Municipal Corporation and others,* AIR 1986 SC 180; and Mendelsohn, 253–4.

[57] E.g., see Sharafi (n. 33), 269–70. The problem persists today: see Marc Galanter, 'Foreword: World of Our Cousins' (2009–2010) 2 *Drexel L.R.* 368.

a courtroom. Scholars of the future should further explore such arguments about law's reach.

Another approach to the legal pluralism part of this discussion—the question of state and non-state law—is the interactive view. Rather than state and non-state law blocking each other out, one could argue that the two interacted constantly and shaped each other. Non-elites did have contact with state law, the argument goes, even if they interacted solely with non-state law. In north India today, caste councils known as *khap panchayats* have come into conflict with state law for allegedly ordering rape as a punishment and condoning honour killings for exogamy. However, the longer history of *panchayats* reflects a much more symbiotic relationship with the state. For much of the nineteenth century, for instance, the state worked to strengthen and broaden *panchayat* authority. Many in the independence movement embraced the *panchayat* as an institution, and post-colonial governments again experimented with state-bolstered versions in the twentieth century.[58]

Many questions remain: has the nature of sources for legal history structured views of law in the field, generating an excessive focus on litigation and state law? Has the reach of state law been broad and deep in India? Collaboration between scholars of Indian legal history may offer the field new ways to tackle questions like these.

D. Collaboration

Most scholars have focused on one end or the other of the legal pluralist spectrum—whether re-discovering the archival records of India's highest courts, on the one hand, or illuminating non-state dispute resolution in *panchayats* and non-state religious courts, on the other. How can the field bridge the space between state and non-state dispute resolution? How might scholars find a way to take advantage both of the written archival sources and the oral history (or ethnographic) research? Outside of legal history, some individual scholars have married historical and anthropological, archival and ethnographic, methods.[59] For most scholars, however, it may be more practical to team up with each other. For reasons rooted in the mysterious ways disciplinary cultures develop, legal historians—like historians and academic lawyers—rarely collaborate.[60]

---

[58] See Jaffe (n. 20).

[59] See Laura Bear, *Lines of the Nation: Indian Railway Workers, Bureaucracy, and the Intimate Historical Self* (2007); and Anupama Rao, *The Caste Question: Dalits and the Politics of Modern India* (2009).

[60] For recent exceptions, see Lauren Benton, Lisa Ford, *Rage for Order: The British Empire and the Origins of International Law, 1800–1850* (2016); and Amanda Nettelbeck, Russell Smandych, Louis A. Knafla, Robert Foster, *Fragile Settlements: Aboriginal Peoples, Law, and Resistance in South-West Australia and Prairie Canada* (2016).

Through co-authorship, scholars could produce truly interdisciplinary work that would bridge state and non-state dispute resolution, spanning law, history, and anthropology, for instance. A historian could equally collaborate with a legal practitioner in India today—particularly to assess the colonial continuities debate on anti-sodomy or -terrorism laws, for instance.[61] They could also assess materials in multiple languages. This is particularly appropriate in multilingual India, with more than twenty official languages recognized at state level and with its many scripts and countless regional dialects. India's multilingualism makes gaining access to a full range of voices all the more challenging, such that collaboration makes special sense for the study of more than one linguistic community or region, whether geographically adjacent or from different parts of India. For example, a scholar working with Gujarati sources could team up with another using Marathi for a project on the legal history of Western India. Or a historian working with Tamil sources could collaborate with another working in Burmese for a comparative study of law at colonial port cities Madras and Rangoon along the Bay of Bengal. Scholars with expertise in different bodies of law could also produce impressive work together. A scholar of Hindu law and another of Islamic law, for instance, could do comparative work across fields of personal law with the ability to engage with religious texts in multiple languages and traditions.

Admittedly, institutional pressures in the scholarly life cycle often dis-incentivize collaboration. Co-authorship requires added coordination challenges and only yields half of the 'credit' of a solo-authored piece. These concerns may be especially acute for junior scholars operating within a USA-style tenure system or for any scholar in a UK-style Research Assessment Exercise system. For those in a tenure system, it may be that collaboration makes most sense for mid-level and senior scholars—and such scholars should lead in modelling this type of research. Regardless, the intellectual returns for scholars at any stage seem potentially enormous and refreshing.

III. CONCLUSIONS

In the late twentieth century, collaboration was the topic of a heated debate among scholars of colonial India. By Subaltern Studies accounts, the Cambridge School of Indian history attributed responsibility for colonial rule to Indian traders and

---

[61] For a similar collaboration between a historian and legal academic, see Durba Mitra, Mrinal Satish, 'Testing Chastity, Evidencing Rape: Impact of Medical Jurisprudence on Rape Adjudication', (11 October 2014) 99 *Econ. Pol. Weekly* 51 ff.

others who cooperated with the British. It may be, though, that collaboration in a different sense—co-authorship—will allow the field of Indian legal history to move beyond the colonial and to enrich our understanding of the historical reach of law in Indian society. In addition, digital legal history raises new analytical and preservationist possibilities and the promise of better access to precious and fragile primary sources. And oral history offers new ways into the lived experience of law that are often absent from the written archive.

There is one other thing scholars in Indian legal history should aspire to do. They should continue to turn outward, connecting with fields beyond our own. For instance, they can do a better job of making South Asian legal history truly South Asian, so that 'South Asia' is not just a euphemism for India. They should examine lines of influence and interaction in legal culture between India and Pakistan, Afghanistan, Bangladesh, Sri Lanka, Myanmar, Nepal, Tibet, the Maldives, and Bhutan. Comparative historical research across South Asia could also contribute to the 'colonial continuities' debate, exploring the ways that a shared colonial past continues to reveal itself (or not) across jurisdictions.[62]

Scholars should also continue to reach into the history of the larger Indian Ocean region and British Empire.[63] British Indian legal culture spread to East Africa and Southeast Asia, particularly through legislation and personnel. Equally, the growth of the Indian diaspora worldwide meant that non-state Indian 'law ways' radiated outward from India. Co-authorship between specialists of these different regions would help capture the richness of these legal zones.[64]

Finally, Indian legal history should also contribute to conversations about legal history in the broader Anglophone world. As almost a fifth of the world's population and a nation that presents itself as the world's largest democracy, India is English-speaking and common-law at its upper institutional levels. Yet it is typically absent from comparative Anglophone historical assessments. Of special interest here are India's constitutionally mandated 'affirmative action' system of quotas or 'reservations' for disadvantaged populations; constitutionalism; and law's treatment of indigenous peoples.[65]

---

[62] By Harshan Kumarasingham, see *A Political Legacy of the British Empire: Power and the Parliamentary System in Post-Colonial India and Sri Lanka* (2013); and 'Eastminster—Decolonisation and State Building in British Asia', in H. Kumarasingham (ed.), *Constitution-Making in Asia: Decolonisation and State-Building in the Aftermath of the British Empire* (2016) 1 ff.

[63] See, e.g., Fahad Ahmad Bishara, *A Sea of Debt: Law and Economic Life in the Western Indian Ocean, 1870–1950* (2017).

[64] For a contemporary model, see Benjamin Schonthal, Matthew J. Walton, 'The (New) Buddhist Nationalisms? Symmetries and Specificities in Sri Lanka and Myanmar' (2016) 17 *Contemp. Buddhism: Interdisc. J.* 85 ff.

[65] For work that connects the Indian context with indigeneity studies of other parts of the English-speaking world, see Pooja Parmar, *Indigeneity and Legal Pluralism in India: Claims, Histories, Meanings* (2015).

The future of Indian legal history looks bright, particularly if scholars are willing to experiment and re-tool. By working together, turning outwards, and acquiring the skills to engage with new media and techniques, scholars can continue to re-imagine and re-invigorate the field of Indian legal history.

BIBLIOGRAPHY

Ritu Birla, *Stages of Capital: Law, Culture and Market Governance in Late Colonial India* (Duke University Press, 2009)

Indrani Chatterjee, *Gender, Slavery and Law in Colonial India* (Oxford University Press, 1999)

Nandini Chatterjee, *The Making of Indian Secularism: Empire, Law and Christianity, 1830–1960* (Palgrave Macmillan, 2011)

Bernard S. Cohn, *The Bernard Cohn Omnibus* (Oxford University Press, 2004)

Rohit De, *A People's Constitution: The Everyday Life of Law in the Indian Republic* (Princeton University Press, 2019)

J. D. M. Derrett, *Religion, Law and the State in India* (Oxford University Press, 1999)

Nasser Hussain, *The Jurisprudence of Emergency: Colonialism and the Rule of Law* (University of Michigan Press, 2003)

James Jaffe, *The Ironies of Colonial Governance: Law, Custom, and Justice in Colonial India* (Cambridge University Press, 2015)

Elizabeth Kolsky, *Colonial Justice in British India: White Violence and the Rule of Law* (Cambridge University Press, 2010)

Gregory Kozlowski, *Muslim Endowments and Society in British India* (Cambridge University Press, 1985)

Chandra Mallampalli, *Race, Religion and Law in Colonial India: Trials of an Interracial Family* (Cambridge University Press, 2011)

Mithi Mukherjee, *India in the Shadows of Empire: A Legal and Political History 1774–1950* (Oxford University Press, 2010)

Eleanor Newbigin, *The Hindu Family and the Emergence of Modern India: Law, Citizenship and Community* (Cambridge University Press, 2013)

Mitra Sharafi, *Law and Identity in Colonial South Asia: Parsi Legal Culture, 1772–1947* (Cambridge University Press, 2014)

Radhika Singha, *A Despotism of Law: Crime and Justice in Early Colonial India* (Oxford University Press, 1998)

Amrita Shodhan, *A Question of Community: Religious Groups and Colonial Law* (Samya, 2001)

Rachel Sturman, *The Government of Social Life in Colonial India: Liberalism, Religious Law, and Women's Rights* (Cambridge University Press, 2012)

CHAPTER 45

....

GOVERNANCE HISTORIES OF INTERNATIONAL LAW

....

DOREEN LUSTIG

I. INTRODUCTION

....

CHAPTER X in H. L. A. Hart's *The Concept of Law* is notorious among international lawyers for its dismissive account of international law as a modern system of law. Since its publication in 1961, international lawyers have developed a clearer account of its rule of recognition and have established enforcement mechanisms that answer some of Hart's concerns over compliance. Over time, the sense of urgency over proving Hart wrong seemed to diminish. International lawyers grew more attentive to how international law matters beyond compliance and recognition, and less apologetic about their field.[1] The surge in international legal institutions and the proliferation of international legal ideas in the decade or so following the end of the Cold War pushed some in the field even further beyond the apologetic frontiers to the utopias of human rights and a new world order. After years of relative insecurity and institutional instability, so the popular narrative goes, international lawyers became quite comfortable reflecting on their past and engaging in an introspective

---

[1] Robert Howse, Ruti Teitel, 'Beyond Compliance: Rethinking Why International Law Really Matters' (2010) 1 *Global Policy* 127.

critique on what has now unquestionably become an established sphere of legal practice and research.[2]

Yet while the tide in international legal scholarship took a historical turn, scholars retained a degree of loyalty to Hart in their choice of historical lens. International legal history has hitherto been a history of the ideas and practices of legal officials. The identity of legal officials has been primarily that of 'the international lawyer.' As the following analysis suggests, scholars have offered different interpretations of the identity of the international lawyer. While the classical historical research began with a heroic history of the founding fathers—Hugo Grotius, Thomas Hobbes, Emer de Vattel, or a history of clearly-distinguished 'epochs'[3]—later, more critical, accounts problematized the progressive aspects in the work of 'the founding fathers' or 'great thinkers' identified with the discipline,[4] or defined the interlocutors of the field more narrowly to include the founders of the modern discipline of international law.[5] The methodological choice to frame the history of international law as an intellectual history of the profession offered a new *mode of critique* on international law as an exercise of power and a *jurisprudential perspective* on what international law is: what international lawyers recognize as law. It left those interested in studying the history of international law with a clear mission: to reconstruct the perspectives of international lawyers by studying their life's work, ideas, and contributions.

This critical and jurisprudential standpoint drew inspiration from the visionary aspects of the field while confronting its 'civilizing' shadowy sides. The international

---

[2] The publication of numerous symposia in the *European Journal of International Law*—Georges Scelle (vol. 1), Hersch Lauterpacht (vol. 8[2]), Hans Kelsen (vol. 9[2]), James Lorimer (vol. 27[2]), and many others dedicated to the history of international legal thought—the 1999 establishment of the *Journal of the History of International Law*; the publication of the *Oxford Handbook of the History of International Law* in 2012; and the studies written at the Max Planck Institute for European Legal History in Frankfurt—constitute but a few of the signs of the emerging field. Alexandra Kemmerer, 'Völkerrechtsgeschichten—Histories of International Law', *E.J.I.L. Talk!* (6 January 2015).

[3] See, e.g., earlier 'heroic' accounts of the law of nations in the late eighteenth and nineteenth centuries by G. F. von Martens, Henry Wheaton and others, and a history of 'epochs' by Wilhelm Grewe, *The Epochs of International Law* (2000) [1984], and Carl Schmitt, *The Nomos of the Earth in the International Law of the Jus Publicum Europaeum* (2006). For further discussion, see Martti Koskenniemi, 'A History of International Law Histories', in B. Fassbinder, A. Peters (eds.), *The Oxford Handbook of the History of International Law* (2012) 943–71.

[4] Uday Singh Mehta, *Liberalism and Empire: A Study in Nineteenth Century British Thought* (1999); Sankar Muthu, *Enlightenment Against Empire* (2003); Jennifer Pitts, *A Turn to Empire: The Rise of Imperial Liberalism in Britain and France* (2005); D. S. Bell, 'Empire and International Relations in Victorian Political Thought' (2006) 49 *The Historical Journal* 281 ff.; Ian Hunter, 'Vattel in Revolutionary America', in Lisa Ford, Tim Rowse (eds.), *Between Indigenous and Settler Governance* (2012) 12 ff.; Karuna Mantena, *Alibis of Empire: Henry Maine and the Ends of Liberal Imperialism* (2011); Benedict Kingsbury, Benjamin Straumann (eds.), *The Roman Foundations of the Law of Nations: Alberico Gentili and the Justice of Empire* (2010); Andrew Fitzmaurice, *Sovereignty, Property and Empire 1500–2000* (2014); Edward Keene, *Beyond the Anarchical Society: Grotius, Colonialism and Order in World Politics* (2002).

[5] These intellectual histories often offered foundational critique of international law and its relation to empire. Mehta (n. 4); Bell (n. 4); Pitts (n. 4); Hunter (n. 4).

lawyer was at once the dark and the white knight, or at least a white knight working for a dark prince. The exposition of this *critical* component—the role of international lawyers in the establishment of hegemonic rule, exploitation, and suffering—positioned them closer to the source of power. This position implicitly conveyed confidence in their influence on world affairs: what they wrote and said was studied because it *mattered*. 'European jurists', as noted by Lauren Benton, 'with an occasional cameo appearance by Americans and jurists from other regions, carry the story's plot and exhaust its twists and turnings'.[6] But the question of who the international lawyer *is*, what his position of power means to our broader concept of international law, and whether the history of ideas is the only approach relevant to the writing of international legal history has gained little scholarly attention thus far.

This chapter problematizes the Hartian perspective in international law's historiography and explores how it may compound a narrow understanding of international law that concentrates on states and their practices as the main actors of relevance to international law (hereinafter: the statist bias). The chapter explores the potential of alternative perspectives loosely termed 'governance' for questions of agency in the history of international law. Section II provides a brief sketch of the state of the field and its main historiographical debates. Section III revisits the statist bias and how this has been confronted through competing visions of the international lawyer and the institutional and social arenas in which he or she operates. Section IV endeavours to unravel how these novel conceptions of agency correspond with key theoretical developments of the post-Cold War era: transnational and global historical writing and international legal theories on global governance. Drawing on the literature from these wide-ranging perspectives, this section argues for a broader scope for international legal history.[7]

II. Towards Critical International Legal History

Critical international legal history was first conceived as such by Martti Koskenniemi in his 2001 book, *The Gentle Civilizer of Nations*.[8] His work explored

---

[6] Lauren Benton and Lisa Ford, *Rage for Order: The British Empire and the Origins of International Law 1800–1850* (2016) 21.

[7] On questions of scope in the writing of legal history, see Christopher Tomlins, 'After Critical Legal History: Scope, Scale, Structure' (2012) 8 *Annual Review of Law and Social Science* 31 ff.

[8] Martti Koskenniemi, *The Gentle Civilizer of Nations: The Rise and Fall of International Law 1870—1960* (2001). Histories of international law were written by non-international lawyers before

the history of international law through the eyes of international lawyers, exposing a rich terrain of thought that challenged contemporary understandings of various aspects of international law and offered a critique on the standard evolutionary and progressive narrative on the history of international law.[9] It framed the history of international law as the history of ideas developed and practised by international lawyers. In taking this approach, Koskenniemi defined international law as a professional discipline shaped by a group of experts who share a political project. The book distinguished between the different perspectives and visions for the international legal project in different European jurisdictions (most prominently German, French, and English) and concluded with a critical chapter on American international law. This structure conveyed the plurality of international legal histories while sustaining their affiliation with national legal traditions.

Beyond different national sensibilities, the book conceived international law as one unified discipline whose members shared a vision and political sensibilities. The first source of commonality was institutional. The Introduction and Chapter I set the stage for the *professionalization* argument, which casts the book as a sociological history of international law. The disciplinary and professionalization lens regards international law as a relatively *recent* political project, initiated by a particular elitist group of legal experts ('the men of 1873'). Second, international lawyers shared a civilizing vision and a Eurocentric outlook on the world outside Europe and the United States. The intellectual history of international law as 'a civilizing project' and thus part-and-parcel of the colonial enterprise soon gained scholarly momentum until some, including Koskenniemi himself, considered the historical turn to be primarily a postcolonial one.[10]

The flourishing field of international legal history that followed[11] soon gave rise to historiographical debates over method and the appropriate relationship between

2001. Diplomatic history is an example of a historical field that addressed the history and theory of international legal sources and institutions. Similarly, international relations scholars have often alluded to historical research in their writing (e.g., the English School), while the history of ideas of prominent thinkers who are often affiliated with international law has been the subject of continuous and rigorous research among political theorists and historians such as Richard Tuck, Istvan Hont, and Anabel Brett. However, a critical history that addresses the legal discipline of international law and attempts to frame the field of international law itself as a subject of critical historical inquiry remained entirely unexplored until the publication of Koskenniemi's ground-breaking work.

[9] Koskenniemi developed the historiographical contribution of the book and its critique on earlier histories of international law in later publications. See, e.g., M. Koskenniemi, 'Histories of International Law: Significance and Problems for a Critical View' (2013) 27 *Temple International and Comparative L.J.* 215.

[10] For further discussion, see Liliana Obregón, 'Martti Koskenniemi's Critique of Eurocentrism in International Law', in W. Werner, A. Galán, M. de Hoon (eds.), *The Law of International Lawyers: Reading Martti Koskenniemi* (2015) 360 ff.

[11] Koskenniemi (n. 8); Benedict Kingsbury, 'Legal Positivism as Normative Politics: International Society, Balance of Power and Lassa Oppenheim's Positive International Law' (2002) 13 *E.J.I.L* 401 ff.; David Armitage, *Foundations of Modern International Thought* (2013); Pitts (n. 4); Mónica García-Salmones Rovira, *The Project of Positivism in International Law* (2013). Special attention has been paid

history and law in international law.[12] One strand in the historiographical debate addressed the question of anachronism—how one should approach the history of ideas: through the vernacular of the past, the present, or both? This debate exposed a tension between contextualist historiography (defined primarily by the Cambridge School method for the history of ideas) and critical historiography in the writing of international law (hereinafter: contextualism v. critique, or not only the past).[13] Another line of historiographical contestation addressed the question of Eurocentrism and empire and developed alternative approaches to the writing of international legal history. It sought to challenge the Eurocentric epistemology in international law, to undermine the centrality of European actors as the ultimate founding fathers of the discipline, or to expose the role of European international law in colonial domination (hereinafter: the Third World Approaches to International Law—TWAIL—critique, or not only Europe). A related line of historiographical critique addressed the question of statism or the statist bias in the writing of international legal histories, and challenged the centrality of interstate relations or sovereignty as the focal point for the history of international law, arguing for a broader terrain of concepts (hereinafter: the statist-bias critique, or not only the state).[14] This third historiographical debate—the statist-bias critique, or not only

to histories of international law, natural law, and human rights. See, e.g., Annabel Brett, *Changes of the State: Nature and Limits of the City in Early Modern Natural Law* (2011); Samuel Moyn, *The Last Utopia* (2010); Martti Koskenniemi, 'Rights, History, Critique', in Adam Etinson (ed.), *Human Rights: Moral or Political?* (forthcoming, 2018).

[12] For the earlier batch of historiographical accounts, see, e.g., George Rodrigo Bandeira Galindo, 'Martti Koskenniemi and the Historiographical Turn in International Law' (2005) 16 *E.J.I.L.* 539; Matthew Craven, 'Introduction: International Law and its Histories', in Matthew Craven, Malgosia Fitzmaurice, Maria Vogiatzi (eds.), *Time, History and International Law* (2007) 1; R. C. H. Lesaffer, 'International Law and its History: The Story of an Unrequited Love', in Matthew Craven, Malgosia Fitzmaurice, Maria Vogiatzi (eds.), *Time, History and International Law* (2006) 27; A. Kemmerer, 'Turning Aside: On International Law and its History', in R. Miller, R. Bratspies (eds.), *Progress in International Law* (2008), 71; T. Skouteris 'Engaging History in International Law', in J. M. Beneyto, D. Kennedy (eds.), *New Approaches to International Law* (2012).

[13] In a series of articles, Anne Orford called on international lawyers to go against the grain of historical method and embrace their anachronism as a means to sustain their critical edge ('the turn to history as method began to have a conservative effect on international law scholarship'). Anne Orford, 'International Law and the Limits of History', in W. Werner, A. Galán, M. de Hoon (eds.), *The Law of International Lawyers: Reading Martti Koskenniemi* (2015). Orford dedicated a series of publications to the question of method in the writing of history in international law. See, e.g., Anne Orford, 'Scientific Reason and the Discipline of International Law' 25 *E.J.I.L* (2014); Anne Orford, 'On International Legal Method' 1 *London Review of International Law* (2013); Anne Orford, 'The Past as Law or History? The Relevance of Imperialism for Modern International Law', in M. Toufayan et al. (eds.), *International Law and New Approaches to the Third World: Between Repetition and Renewal* (2013). On the question of text and context in the history of international law, see also Martti Koskenniemi, 'Vitoria and Us: Thoughts on Critical Histories of International Law' (2014) 22 *Rechtsgeschichte* 152.

[14] Ignacio de la Rasilla del Moral addresses the second (Eurocentric) and third (statist) strands as the two dominant exclusionary biases in contemporary international law's historiography. Ignacio de la Rasilla del Moral, 'The Shifting Origins of International Law' (2015) 28 *Leiden Journal of International Law* 419; Kemmerer, Alexandra, 'Towards a Global History of International Law? A Review Symposium

the state—is probably the most puzzling of the three and is the least explored in the literature thus far. Unsurprisingly, then, it is the core concern to which this chapter is devoted.

During virtually the same period in which international lawyers began to critically explore the history of their discipline, historians turned to the forgotten pasts of international legal institutions such as the League of Nations, the United Nations, the international human rights system, and related systems of global governance as subjects of historical inquiry,[15] while engaging in a vibrant debate over the meaning of their historiographical shift.[16] Historians describe the turn to the international as a challenge to methodological nationalism.[17] At the same time, international lawyers' turn to history remains locked within statist constraints,[18] provoking repeated calls for a 'global history' of international law.[19]

In what follows, the chapter draws attention to a further bias in the history of international law—the centrality of the history of ideas[20]—and argues that studying the history of international law from a history of ideas perspective involves

on Bardo Faßbender', Anne Peters et al. (eds.), The Oxford Handbook of the History of International Law (2012), Editor's Note (15 January 2014) E.J.I.L. 2014 25 (1): 287–95: as noted by Koskenniemi: '... whether supporters or critics, international lawyers have broadly agreed that the history of our field is the history of statehood, situated in the realm of the "international", conceptualized as a terrain of war and peace, diplomatic conflict, and cooperation'. Martti Koskenniemi, 'Expanding Histories of International Law' (2016) 56 American Journal of Legal History 104, 107.

[15] For a (non-exhaustive) list of these sources, see Mark Mazower, No Enchanted Palace: The End of Empire and the Ideological Origins of the United Nations (2009); M. Mazower, Governing the World: The History of an Idea, 1815 to the Present (2012); Susan Pedersen, The Guardians (2015); Moyn (n. 11); Armitage (n. 11); Patricia Clavin, Securing the World Economy (2013); Brett (n. 11); Lauren Benton, A Search for Sovereignty: Law and Geography in European Empires, 1400–1900 (2010); Lauren Benton, Law and Colonial Cultures: Legal Regimes in World History, 1400–1900 (2001); Glenda Sluga, Patricia Clavin (eds.), Internationalisms: A Twentieth-Century History (2017); Thomas Hippler and Miloš Vec, Paradoxes of Peace in Nineteenth Century Europe (2015).

[16] Sebastian Conrad, What is Global History? (2016); Lynn Hunt, Writing History in the Global Era (2014); Samuel Moyn, Andrew Sartori (eds.), Global Intellectual History (2013); Armitage (n. 11).

[17] Lynn Hunt described how history grew as a discipline 'in a symbiotic relationship with nationalism in the nineteenth and twentieth centuries. History provided new countries with a heritage that had been previously suppressed or ignored, and it shored up identity even in the oldest nation-states, such as England and France.' Hunt (n. 16) at 3. See also de la Rasilla del Moral (n. 14).

[18] Methodological nationalism and the statist position are quite distinct concepts. The former is centred on national, cultural, and political boundaries of a particular state while the statist position refers to the view of the state as the main entity relevant for international legal thought. It is concerned with the focus on states as the only structure of authority relevant to international law and the recognized source for international law rather than a particular national, cultural, or political context.

[19] See, e.g., A. Kemmerer, 'Towards a Global History of International Law? Editor's Note' (2014) 25 E.J.I.L. 287; T. Duve, 'European Legal History—Global Perspectives' (2013) Working Paper for the Colloquium 'European Normativity—Global Historical Perspectives' (Max-Planck Institute, 2–4 September 2013) No. 2013–06 accessible (accessed 2 May 2015).

[20] Will Hanley addressed this bias: '... the history of international law is dominated by Europe, by states, and by ideas (especially the ideas of great men)'. Will Hanley, 'Statelessness: An Invisible Theme in the History of International Law' (2014) 25 E.J.I.L. 326.

decisions on questions of agency that draw from theoretical predispositions on what international law *is*. The three historiographical debates in contemporary international legal history widely share a vision of international legal history as a history of ideas and, in various ways, the history of ideas as they were advocated and developed by international lawyers. Analysing the history of international law through the study of the work and thought of prominent international lawyers is tuned to telling a history of law through their theoretical, cultural, and sociological perspectives. This approach therefore remains loyal to their understanding of what international law *is* and the set of ideas, practices, and institutions they deem relevant for its understanding. The questions they are interested in and the concepts they develop become the questions and concepts we are studying: primarily questions about sovereignty and the interstate public order.

This methodological perspective provides an intriguing critical window onto international lawyers' imagined legal world at a particular time and place. However, telling the history of international law through the eyes of those who recognize nothing but states as relevant to their oeuvre could easily conflate between the historical perspective and the jurisprudential assumptions underpinning the historical inquiry. In turn, this could lead to an account of the international legal order as irrelevant to the fate of non-state actors such as corporations, NGOs, minorities, or stateless persons or to 'non-statist' aspects of social life such as economic relations or the family. As noted by Will Hanley: 'Those who do not speak for states rarely meet the threshold of inclusion in conventional histories of international law, despite their evident participation in the world of international law.'[21] Furthermore, ideas about law may not be confined to such mandarin legality and appear 'in non-traditional sites and texts such as the public square, the coffeehouse, the theater or the cinema, and newspapers and magazines'. Embracing such perspectives about the law may move beyond the history of ideas and open up the historical inquiry of international law to social and cultural histories[22] and revisit processes of change and influence in international legal historiography (e.g., away from presumed top-down processes to trickle-up possibilities).[23]

This chapter highlights the relevance of two particular facets of the Hartian perspective in our understanding of the writings on the history of international law. The first relates to the *scholar's* underlying assumptions on the theory of the law, and the second is the theory of law of the agents whose work, ideas, and practices the scholar studies. Bearing in mind the relevance of these theoretical perspectives to our understanding of the history of international law, the chapter explores the link between, on the one hand, the agent we choose to study and her/his theory of the law and, on the other, our own. It further inquires into how studies that move beyond the dominant traditional imagery of the international lawyer as the pre-eminent

---

[21] Ibid.   [22] See ch. 9 in this volume.
[23] Robert Gordon, 'Critical Legal Histories' (1984) 36 *Stanford L.R.* 56.

agent in international legal historiography could change our understanding of international legal history and how might such a shift in understanding, in turn, inform our theoretical predispositions on international law. These are the overarching questions of this chapter.

The starting point for a discussion on agency in international legal historiography is TWAIL. This innovative body of research on the histories of international law from the Global South is posited as *the* alternative to more Eurocentric and traditional accounts of international legal history. Yet, as others have shown before, TWAIL scholarship is not necessarily committed to a jurisprudential departure from positivism and its ramifications for the study of international law.[24] Against the backdrop of the TWAIL perspective in international legal history, Section III explores a few alternatives that embody a broader understanding of international legal agency (Section IV) and, with it, address the promise and risks of a governance perspective for the history of international law (Section V).

III. The Mandarin Legality of Non-European Histories of International Law

In the historical study of international law in its non-European contexts[25] the work of Charles Henry Alexandrowicz (1902–1975) in the late 1960s is a prominent precursor. In the introduction to the edited volume of his writings, David Armitage and Jennifer Pitts describe how 'Alexandrowicz recognized international law's complicity with European imperial expansion and sought in history resources for a more egalitarian and less Eurocentric international order'. In the era of decolonization, he used history to unsettle the 'orthodox view' that 'New States are faced with the fait accompli of the existing international legal order and must accept its principles as they find them'.[26] Alexandrowicz's work was studied and published in the heyday of decolonization, amid the struggles of newly-established states

---

[24] See, e.g., Martti Koskenniemi, 'Expanding Histories of International Law' (2016) 56 *American Journal of Legal History* 104, 105–6; Alexandra Kemmerer, 'We Do Not Need to Always Look at Westphalia …: A Conversation with Martti Koskenniemi and Anne Orford' (2015) 17 *Journal of the History of International Law* 1–14.

[25] For more on the term 'mandarin legality', see Gordon (n. 23).

[26] C. H. Alexandrowicz, David Armitage, Jennifer Pitts (eds.), *The Law of Nations in Global History* (2017) 3.

to gain stature and international support. Scholars following in Alexandrowicz's footsteps chose historical research to assert the political and legal claims of post-colonial states.[27] These earlier historical accounts were not meant to repudiate international law but to produce a universal vision of international law.[28]

More recently, Antony Anghie's *Imperialism, Sovereignty and the Making of International Law* marked a turning point towards a foundational critique of the role of international law in facilitating and legitimizing the exploitation of the Global South through colonization.[29] In the wake of Anghie's work, TWAIL histories sought to remedy the narrative that focused almost exclusively on Western international lawyers by including non-Western jurists in the international legal cannon or alternative non-European traditions. Arnulf Becker Lorca's work in this genre explains how this historical outlook unfolds a competing argument on the history of international law: rather than a Eurocentric project that originated in Europe, was developed by Europeans, and was used to assert European values and rule outside Europe, it 'suggests that international law emerged out of the interaction between Western and non-Western sovereigns, as well as from the professional rapports and debates between Western and non-Western international lawyers'.[30]

Beyond the particular histories of individual protagonists from the Global South, regional-historical accounts, which do not necessarily recognize themselves as part of the TWAIL corpus, presented non-European traditions of international law: Chinese, Russian, or Latin American, to mention but a few.[31] Some of these histories did not focus on particular international lawyers from the South but sought to expose the hegemonic role of the international law of the Global North: how international legal doctrines, institutions, and techniques were used to assert colonial rule before and after decolonization.[32]

---

[27] See, e.g., R. P. Anand, *New States and International Law* (1972); T. O. Elias, *New Horizons in International Law* (1978); Nagendra Singh, *India and International Law: Ancient and Mediaeval* (1973); S. P. Sinha, *New Nations and the Law of Nations* (1967); J. J. G. Syatauw, *Some Newly Established Asian States and the Development of International Law* (1961). For an overview of first generation third world legal scholars, see Karin Mickelson, 'Rhetoric and Rage: Third World Voices in International Legal Discourse' (1997) 16 *Wisconsin International L.J.* 353.

[28] For an introspective historiographical account on TWAIL see B. S. Chimni, 'The Past, Present and Future of International Law: A Critical Third World Approach' (2007) 8 *Melbourne Journal of International Law* 27.

[29] Antony Anghie, *Imperialism, Sovereignty and the Making of International Law* (2004).

[30] Arnulf Becker Lorca, *Mestizo International Law: A Global Intellectual History 1842–1933* (2010) 10–11.

[31] See, e.g., Phil C. W. Chan, 'China's Approaches to International Law Since the Opium War' (2014) 27 *Leiden Journal of International Law* 859; Lauri Mälksoo, *Russian Approaches to International Law* (2015); Juan Pablo Scarfi, *The Hidden History of International Law in the Americas* (2017).

[32] Furan Kyaogly, *Legal Imperialism: Sovereignty and Extraterritoriality in Japan, the Ottoman Empire, and China* (2010); Sandhuya Pahuja, *Decolonizing International Law: Development, Economic Growth and the Politics of Universality* (2011); Kate Miles, *The Origins of International Investment Law: Empire, Environment and the Safeguarding of Capital* (2013); Mamadou Hebie, *Souveraineté territoriale par traité: une Étude des accords entre puissances coloniales et entités politiques locales* (2015).

A recurring criticism of TWAIL histories was that writing them from the South did not amount to writing them 'from below'.[33] As noted by Umut Özsu, '[m]en like Takahashi and Calvo were rarely "of the people". Trained for and employed by the powerful ruling elites, they articulated and fought for political and economic interests favoured by dominant forces within their states.'[34] Both Eurocentric and TWAIL accounts suffered from the 'elite manipulation' view, due to their focus on the actions and influence of legal and economic elites with vested ideological (and often exclusive) interests.[35] Furthermore, problematizing international law's imperial past (and present) through the lens of conceptual debates over the civilizing mission runs the risk of reinstating 'familiar and seductive narratives' that exaggerate the ability of European powers to master colonial space and fail to capture the porous and contested aspects of this history.[36]

These histories of international lawyers from the Global North and South were not merely studies of 'great' international lawyers but often represented the cadre of international lawyers as 'communities of knowledge'—ideas of groups of elite thinkers that constituted the international legal discipline.[37] Against the backdrop of these existing accounts of the role of the European and non-European international lawyers as individuals or participants in a community of knowledge, alternative ways of thinking about—imageries of—the international legal official have emerged. The following analysis cannot encompass in full these fresh perspectives on agency in international legal history, but it will highlight a few intriguing directions that could complicate our perceptions of the international legal official and point to alternative models. By reconstructing the contribution of these studies through their outlooks on agency, I wish to examine how our choice of the agents we focus on for our historical inquiry relates to our underlying theories of law and whether a change in the identity of the agent may challenge the statist bias in the history of international law. The aim of expanding the historiographical perspective in this way is to use the plurality of agency to demonstrate the contestation and plurality of viewpoints, practices, and institutions that formed and transformed the international legal sphere, and thus to provide alternative ways to decipher the relevance and influence of international legal ideas, practices, and institutions for the architecture of global politics.

[33] See, e.g., Rajagopal's pioneering call for writing histories of international law from below. Balakrishnan Rajagopal, *International Law from Below: Development, Social Movements and Third World Resistance* (2003).

[34] Umut Özsu, 'Agency, Universality and the Politics of International Legal History' (2010) 52 *Harvard International L.J.* 58, 70.

[35] Sluga and Clavin (n. 15) at 7–8.

[36] For this line of critique, see Benton, *A Search for Sovereignty* (n. 15) at xii.

[37] On *The Gentle Civilizer* as a nuanced approach to the history of the discipline, see Orford (n. 14). For the classic sources on the history of the discipline, see Thomas Kuhn, *The Structure of Scientific Revolutions* (1962); Michel Foucault, *Les mots et les choses: Une archéologie des sciences humaines* (1966). For further analysis, see ch. 9, s. 4.

IV. THE AGENT IN INTERNATIONAL LEGAL HISTORY AND THE MOVE BEYOND

A. Bureaucrats and Unofficial Men

The so-called 'new era of globalization' is characterized by the rise of international institutions such as the World Bank, the World Trade Organization (WTO), the Security Council, and less rigidly-formalized governance regimes including the G7 or the Basel Committee on Banking Supervision. These governance regimes often go hand-in-hand with certain ideological sensibilities on the operation of markets and a managerial ethos that draws inspiration from the technical expert or the CEO as models of leadership in the context of reform and policy innovation. As convincingly argued by Jo Guldi and David Armitage, these transitions to global institutions are products of history and should 'be understood as historical watersheds, and what they mean and whether they have worked is a matter for critical thinking about long-term change'.[38] And so they have been. Mark Mazower's *Governing the World* (2012), Susan Pedersen's *The Guardians* (2015), and Patricia Clavin's *Securing the World Economy* (2013) are leading examples of historians' attempts to think critically and historically on 'what they mean and whether they have worked'.

Similarly, 'the turn to institutions', pioneered by David Kennedy in an article of that name,[39] later translated to a few important strands of work in international legal history. International lawyers shared historians' revived interest in the League of Nations,[40] explored economic governance regimes, their histories, and their related history of ideas,[41] and sought to unravel the meaning of the international organization as a concept and an institution.[42] Some used institutional settings to delve into key areas of policy-making and revisited their imagined traditions,[43]

---

[38] Jo Guldi and David Armitage, *The History Manifesto* (2014) 74.

[39] David Kennedy, 'The Move to Institutions' (1987) 8 *Cardozo L.R.* 841.

[40] For an early influential work on the League of Nations, see Nathaniel Berman, *Passion and Ambivalence: Colonialism, Nationalism and International Law* (2012).

[41] See, e.g., Pahuja (n. 32); Anne Orford, 'Food Security, Free Trade, and the Battle for the State' (2015) 11 *Journal International Law & International Relations* 1.

[42] Jan Klabbers, 'The EJIL Foreword: The Transformation of International Organizations Law' (2015) 26 *E.J.I.L.* 9.

[43] Ralph Wilde, *International Territorial Administration: How Trusteeship and the Civilizing Mission Never Went Away* (2008); Anne Orford, *International Authority and the State Responsibility to Protect* (2011); Guy Fiti Sinclair, *To Reform the World: International Organizations and the Making of Modern States* (2017); Karen Knop, *Diversity and Self-Determination in International Law* (2002).

while others studied neglected—even purposefully forgotten—policies and their enduring legacies.[44]

Authors writing on global institutions present various models for the 'international legal official'. In her critical history of the idea of the Common Heritage of Mankind and the concept of the Global Commons, Surabhi Ranganathan juxtaposed the more classical agent for a history of ideas—biologist Garrett Hardin—with the concepts articulated by diplomat Arvid Pardo to demonstrate how they responded to some of the most pressing issues of their time: decolonization, developed/ developing state relations, and the pressures of population and resource security, leading to problematic results.[45] Drawing on three studies on the role and impact of Dag Hammarskjöld,[46] Guy Sinclair highlighted competing attempts to theorize the contribution of the international civil servant, whether as a political leader, an international legal expert, or an agent operating within the wider intellectual context of the larger corps of UN functionaries. Tracking the work of the most senior figures in the administration and also that of post-holders further down the hierarchy, Susan Pedersen described the importance of studying 'the quiet persistence of a much less flamboyant and largely forgotten group of men' to understand the League of Nations:

Bureaucrats are unglamorous historical actors. But to turn programmes into practices, especially when the visionaries have either left the stage or turned petulant, demands a particular sort of character and capacity.... They had the support of key (mostly British) statesmen as well, but they considered the work their job and brought to the task all those skills—networking, planning, report-writing, alliance-building, compromising—on which successful administration depends. Bureaucracy, more than idealism, tamed the demons of power.[47]

Megan Donaldson's inspiring account of the history of secrecy and publicity in the interwar period similarly draws on a breadth of sources 'from within the Secretariat', the League Council meetings, and the broader public discourse (using parliamentary debates, publications of international associations, and the press). But Donaldson's history of ideas also moves beyond these sources and uncovers secret channels and informal communications between activists and the Secretariat staff to excavate the ideas of secrecy and publicity as they were *experienced* and

---

[44] Umut Özsu, *Formalizing Displacement International Law and Population Transfers* (2014) [on minority exchange].

[45] Surabhi Ranganathan, 'Global Commons', (2016) 27 *European Journal of International Law* 693.

[46] Guy Fiti Sinclair, 'The International Civil Servant in Theory and Practice: Law, Morality, and Expertise', Review of Carsten Stahn and Henning Melber (eds.), 'Peace Diplomacy, Global Justice and International Agency: Rethinking Human Security and Ethics in the Spirit of Dag Hammarskjöld'; Roger Lipsey, 'Hammarskjöld: A Life'; Lise Namikas, 'Battleground Africa: Cold War in the Congo, 1960–1965'; Anne Orford, 'International Authority and the Responsibility to Protect' (2015) 26 *E.J.I.L.* 747–66.

[47] Pedersen (n. 15) at 45–6.

practised by contemporary actors in ways that verbal iterations ultimately fail to capture.[48] By wedding together a history of ideas with a history of practice, she unravels unconscious predispositions alongside clear statements of policy and ideas; she exposes how 'juridical categories and practices are pressed into service or held at bay and the way in which law interacts with diplomatic culture and lay understandings to produce and encode particular positions'.[49]

While some of these bureaucratic histories focus on particular figures,[50] others are more interested in exploring the institutional culture and shared conceptual and normative sensibilities of particular discourse communities within international institutions[51] or between those who use such institutions to promote their political endeavours.[52] These accounts differ from the history of great thinkers or even the more recent histories of prominent international lawyers by shifting their attention to lower echelons of power and attempting to grasp the institutional cultures or shared consciousness of broader, and more loosely defined, discourse communities. But the line between these different 'types' of histories—the history of individual prominent legal officials and that of their shared consciousness—is not always rigid. It can be blurred by weaving these different approaches into the writing of history, as Anne Orford's influential work on the history of State Responsibility to Protect (R2P) demonstrates. In this book, Orford intertwined the history of great thinkers on sovereignty, such as Thomas Hobbes and Carl Schmitt, with the later diverse practices of peacekeeping, led by contemporary international lawyer and leading figure—UN Secretary-General, Dag Hammarskjöld. Orford's account challenged the prevailing contention that R2P was a very recent conceptual innovation and redefined it as a theoretical account of a body of practices prevalent since decolonization, reminiscent of earlier attempts to balance between legitimate authority, executive action, and civilian protection.[53]

The mirror image of the prominent or mundane bureaucrat working at the League is the outsider to such bureaucracies who used his institutional settings to pursue his political projects. Mira Siegelberger defined the agency of such outsiders with the term 'unofficial men', but we could get carried away by their boldness and romanticize them as the fringe heroes of international law. The archetypal fringe figure for such histories is the Jewish–Polish jurist Raphael Lemkin.[54] Lemkin's story

---

[48]   Megan Donaldson, 'From Secret Diplomacy to Diplomatic Secrecy: Secrecy and Publicity in the International Legal Order 1919–1950' (JSD Dissertation, NYU Law School, 2016).

[49]   Ibid., at page 11.   [50]   Mazower, *No Enchanted Palace* (n. 15).

[51]   Donaldson, (n. 49); Clavin (n. 15).

[52]   See, e.g., Liat Kozma, *Global Women, Colonial Ports: Regulated Prostitution in the Interwar Middle East* (SUNY Press, 2017)

[53]   Anne Orford, *International Authority and the Responsibility to Protect* (2011).

[54]   For different perspectives on Lemkin's life and work see Mazower, *No Enchanted Palace* (n. 15) at 126–33; Philippe Sands, *East West Street: On the Origins of Genocide and Crimes Against Humanity* (2017) 141–90; James Loeffler, Becoming Cleopatra: the Forgotten Zionism of Raphael Lemkin (2017) 19 *Journal of Genocide Research* 340–60, 351.

and other histories of fringe figures and their disruption of institutional culture and procedures tell us something about the importance of personal charisma and character in history's unfolding as it does. The study of their ideas further holds the potential to provide a unique window onto elusive notions of shared consciousness and the broader political, economic, or cultural circumstances that made their challenging endeavours possible.

B. Networks and Transnational Actors

The methodological landscape of *the turn to institutions* draws on global governance insights and uses them as a new historical lens. In that vein, the interwar period has proven particularly intriguing for historiographical attempts to contemplate the past in contemporary theoretical terms. In a landmark article published by Pedersen in *The American Historical Review* in 2007, she conceived of the League of Nations as the harbinger of global governance. This, she argued, was not merely confined to the practices of bureaucrats, but included a myriad of agents for whom the League served as a fruitful platform for political and legal experimentation.[55]

The historiography of the interwar era has indeed given rise to insightful accounts that extend our understanding of how the cohort of international lawyers experimented with alternative conceptualizations to the state and developed innovative frameworks for political and legal entities.[56] Scholars have also examined how such non-statist political and legal visions were operationalized and performed. Daniel Gorman identified in the League era campaigns the 'antecedents of the modern phenomena of international NGOs and global governance' and described the interwar 'trans-Atlantic international peace work of private foundations', such as the Carnegie Endowment for International Peace, as precursors to the non-state actors of the late-twentieth-century global governance era.[57] Moria Paz's history of the Alliance network[58] and James Loeffler's work on the campaign of the American

---

[55] Susan Pedersen, 'Back to the League of Nations' (2007) 112 *The American Historical Review* (2007).

[56] See, e.g., Natasha Wheatley, 'Spectral Legal Personality in Interwar International Law: On New Ways of Not Being a State' (2017) 35 *Law and History Review* 753; N. Wheatley, 'New Subjects in International Law and Order', in Sluga and Clavin, (n. 15) at 265; Mira Siegelberg, *Statelessness: A Modern History* (forthcoming, 2018).

[57] Daniel Gorman, *The Emergence of International Society in the 1920s* (2012).

[58] Moria Paz, 'States and Networks in the Formation of International Law' (2011) 26 *American University International L.R.* 1241. On the concept of networks in global governance literature, see, e.g., Anne-Marie Slaughter, 'Governing the Global Economy Through Government Networks', in Michael Byers (ed.), *The Role of Law in International Politics: Essays in International Relations and International Law* (2000) 177, 177–8 (writing about 'the disaggregated State that comes in place of the mythical unitary State').

Jewish Committee for the 1944 Declaration on Human Rights[59] are both set in the context of the inter- and post-war eras alongside work dedicated to classic examples of political projects organized in transnational networks, such as feminism[60] and socialism.[61] In *Women, Feminisms and Twentieth-Century Internationalisms,* Glenda Sluga demonstrates how these histories 'lead us to the mid- as well as high-level intellectual history of feminism, to the ideologies of popular social movements as well as elites, and non-Europeans and colonials as well as to the 'West'.[62]

The network prism is not the only suitable framework to decipher the relevance of non-state actors' perspectives to the history of international law. Works on Jewish international lawyers, women, or South American alliances tell the history of how ideas and practices in international law were shaped by agents whose perspectives drew considerably from their respective group identities. This trend may not be new to legal historians but is less common in the history of international law, which tended to focus on *national* legal traditions of international law—such as German, French, or American international law—rather than seeking particular cultural and political features that bring individuals together in their international legal approach, irrespective of their national affiliations.

Another line of work that pushes the boundaries of comparative international law can be found in the regional or 'hemispheric' perspective of Juan Pablo Scarfi in *The Hidden History of International Law in the Americas: Empire and Legal Networks* (OUP, 2017). Scarfi's book provides an eye-opening transnational history of international law in the American hemisphere and explores the history of international law through the lens of particular US–Latin American power relations. Scarfi explores the history of key institutions such as the American Institute of International Law and the Pan-American Movement through the networks they

---

[59] James Loeffler, 'The Particularist Pursuit of American Universalism: The American Jewish Committee's 1944 "Declaration on Human Rights"' (2015) 50 *Journal of Contemporary History* 274. This work is related to Loeffler's broader interest and contribution to the study of Jewish tradition of international lawyers. See, his forthcoming book, James Loeffler, *Rooted Cosmopolitans: Jews and Human Rights in the Twentieth Century* (forthcoming, 2018). For additional works in this vein see Rotem Giladi and Shabtai Rosenne, 'The Transformation of Sefton Rowson', in James Loeffler, Moriah Paz (eds.), *Law of Strangers: Critical Perspectives on Jewish Lawyering and International Legal Thought* (forthcoming); Eliav Lieblich, 'Assimilation through Law: Hans Kelsen and the Jewish Experience', in James Loeffler, Moriah Paz (eds.), *Law of Strangers: Critical Perspectives on Jewish Lawyering and International Legal Thought* (forthcoming).

[60] Glenda Sluga, 'Women, Feminisms, and Twentieth-Century Internationalisms', in Sluga and Clavin, (n. 15) at 61.

[61] See, e.g., Patricia Dogliani, 'The Fate of Socialist Internationalism', in Sluga and Clavin (n. 15) at 38.

[62] Sluga (n. 61), at 82. Deborah Whitehall's work on Rosa Luxemburg and the history of self-determination is at the intersection of socialism and feminist perspectives on the history of international law. Whitehall unravels an earlier history of the concept outside and prior to its known affiliation with liberal approaches to international law as a subject of debate between opposing socialist factions and a personal attempt to gain recognition as a thinker and activist. Deborah Whitehall, 'A Rival History of Self Determination' (2016) 27 *E.J.I.L.* 719.

fostered, reconstructing a history of international legal ideas and practices that derives from the dialogue and interactions between prominent figures (such as Elihu Root, James Brown Scott, and Alejandro Álvarez) and relatively unknown figures in international law.

Scarfi's examination of the Pan-American network joins the work of Mark Mazower and others on the rise and fall of the New International Economic Order as well as related TWAIL accounts of legal projects emerging from decentralized groups,[63] such as Natasha Wheatley's analysis of innovative group claims at the League of Nations,[64] and Samuel Moyn's groundbreaking work on the history of human rights.[65] As noted by Moyn: 'The world of the 1970s in human rights history, by contrast, is a world of delocalized grassroot agents making claims.... Unlike the 1940s, there was no center to developments, and indeed the cacophony of voices at the closure of decolonization raises the question of whether noise or music resulted.'[66] These studies all shift the locus of analysis away from methodological statism. Such histories of ideas and practices of transnational non-governmental organizations, individual activists, and networks blur the lines between the history of ideas, institutions, culture, and praxis. As a result, they illuminate how the participation of non-state groups and individuals in international legal forums or their experimentation with different political organizations are closely related to the novel conceptualizations they offer to their own (and others') international capacity, thus provoking alternative visions of the international order itself.[67] Despite these important challenges to the statist position, it should be noted that the practice and organization of non-state actors does not necessarily undermine statist *positions* and could actually enhance their relevance.[68]

---

[63] Mazower, *Governing the World* (n. 15); Pahuja, (n. 42); series of articles published in vol. 6(1) of *Humanity* in 2015; Luis Eslava, Michael Fakhri, Vasuki Nesiah (eds.), *Bandung, Global History and International Law: Critical Pasts and Pending Futures* (2017) to mention but a few.

[64] Natasha Wheatley, 'Mandatory Interpretation: Legal Hermeneutics and the New International Order in Order in Arab and Jewish Petitions to the League of Nations' (2015) 227 *Past and Present* 205: 'Minorities, nationalities, mandate territories, individuals, international organizations, indigenous peoples, colonies, dominions, races and religions all emerged as candidates for international legal capacity, with the League as the most obvious testing ground for such claims.'

[65] Moyn (n. 11).

[66] Moyn, *The Return of the Prodigal: The 1970s as a Turning Point in Human Rights History*, in *Human Rights and the Uses of History* (2014) 6.

[67] Wheatley, 'New Subjects' (n. 56) at 269. See also ibid., at 286: 'Practical and procedural measures sometimes ran far ahead of the conceptual world, leaving scholars to "discover" the great theoretical innovations of the former only belatedly ...'; Moyn's concept of international human rights is embedded and closely related to the transnational non-governmental organizations such as Amnesty that operationalized the concept. Moyn (n. 11). On different internationalisms, see Glenda Sluga and Patricia Clavin, 'Rethinking the History of Internationalism', in Sluga and Clavin, (n. 15) at 3.

[68] Glenda Sluga made this point in her study of nationalism as an internationalist project. Glenda Sluga, *Internationalism in the Age of Nationalism* (2013). Similar insights arise in the context of historical studies on the NIEO and the centrality its interlocutors attributed to the concept of sovereignty.

c. Economic Ideas, Institutions, and Actors

As noted earlier, the statist bias of international law historiography does not simply manifest in a tendency to focus on inter-state relations or state actors, but involves the endorsement of the statist *jurisprudential* perspective on the study of international law. This problem seems particularly acute in the context of economic relations. A classic vantage point on the relationship between international law and the economy can be found in the history of political economic concepts such as free trade and their conjunction with ideas associated with the history of ideas in international law regarding states and political ordering.[69] But, as Anne Orford demonstrates, to break out of the statist paradigm in the telling of such histories requires a shift in the methodological gaze to a broader set of agents, such as British colonial administrators, and to conversations beyond international lawyers alone to include their exchange with political economists and free trade ideologues.[70]

The institutional parallels to political economic concepts such as free trade or the free market in international law are global economic entities such as the WTO or the World Bank. We often think of these institutions as new and even unconventional, but such establishments carry with them imagined traditions and conceptual legacies in the context of trade, investment, or monetary policy that call for historical scrutiny and critique. The work of Patricia Clavin on the history of the League's Economic and Financial Organisation (EFO), the world's first intergovernmental organization devoted to the promotion of economic and monetary co-operation.[71] Kate Miles on investment,[72] and Andrew Lang and Michael Fahkri on trade[73] represent but a few examples of such critical histories of international economic governance regimes.

Another layer of history of international law and the economy would move beyond the *direct and stated* engagement of international law and economic regulation, towards the interplay between private law institutions, practices, and concepts.[74] In a series of articles, Martti Koskenniemi highlighted the relevance of historical accounts of the interplay between sovereignty and property to the history of international law.[75] In an article titled *Expanding Legal Histories*, he

---

[69] See Istvan Hont, *Jealousy of Trade: International Competition and the Nation-State in Historical Perspective* (2005).

[70] Anne Orford, 'Food Security, Free Trade, and the Battle for the State' (2015) 11 *Journal of International Law and International Relations* 1.

[71] Patricia Clavin, *Securing the World Economy: The Reinvention of the League of Nations, 1920–1946* (2nd edn., 2015).

[72] Miles (n. 33).

[73] Andrew Lang, *World Trade Law after Neoliberalism* (2011); Michael Fakhri, *Sugar and the Making of International Trade Law* (2014).

[74] For the role of private international law in forming the character of sovereignty or informing questions of legitimacy in situations of political conflict, see Karen Knop, Ralf Michaels, and Annelise Riles, Foreword to 'Transdisciplinary Conflict of Laws' (2008) 71 *Law and Contemporary Problems* 16.

[75] Koskenniemi (n. 13); Koskenniemi, 'Sovereignty, Property and Empire: Early Modern English Contexts' (2017) 18 *Theoretical Inquiries in Law* 355.

summarized his methodological point as follows: 'while international legal histories have meticulously traced the legal trajectories of the foreign policies of states, they have paid much less attention—virtually no attention—to the private law relations that undergird and support state action and that become visible only once analysis penetrates beyond the official statements or formal acts of governments and diplomatic chancelleries'.[76] Matthew Craven reiterated a similar concern as he highlighted 'the task of understanding the (historic) conditions that delimit the parameters of what may or may not be rendered as the past of international law today'.[77]

One actor puzzlingly absent from the past of international law as we know it today is the private business corporation. Despite its success as the leading economic institution of the twentieth-century global economy, it is curiously absent from international legal books until at least the 1970s and, since then, has been considered a failing subject of international regulation. A possible alternative would be to think of exploring the facilitative role of international legal doctrines, ideas, and practices in constituting the transnational regulatory space in which private business corporations were able to operate (and continue to do so).[78] Methodologically, discerning these elements requires a juxtaposition between the official perspectives of international lawyers and a better grasp of 'international law in practice' through the ideas and practices of lower-ranking colonial officials, bureaucrats in international organizations, and legal officials affiliated with the company—that is, international law as it is experienced by company men.

D. Pluralist Visions and Layered Ordering: Empire and the Disaggregated State

To unravel the related histories of international law and global economic policies presupposes the coexistence of, and interaction between, different normative orders. Such a jurisprudential perspective lends itself to a pluralist historical lens and a layered understanding of international law. Pluralist accounts manifested themselves in two discrete areas of historical research: 'international law and empire' and studies that linked internal processes within states to the history of international law.

---

[76] Koskenniemi (n. 24) at 109. For a similar statement, see also Koskenniemi (n. 9) at 235.

[77] Matthew Craven, 'Theorising the Turn to History in International Law', in Anne Orford, Florian Hoffmann (eds.), *The Oxford Handbook of the Theory of International Law* (2016) 21.

[78] Doreen Lustig, *The Regulation of Private Business Corporations in International Law: A History of Failure?* (forthcoming, 2018).

1. *International Law and Empire*

A diverse set of studies loosely labelled 'international law and empire' present an alternative model to statist accounts.[79] Thomas Duve notes: '"Empire" has emerged as an important analytical framework for breaking up national historiographies and understanding the larger spaces of governance since the 1990s.... Studies generally highlight the centrality of law in the construction of empires as well as the significance of both formal and informal empires as spaces of communication, fundamental for the evolution of law.'[80] These studies often challenge the post-Westphalian *periodization* of international law histories and convey the relevance of earlier imperial ordering to the history of international law.[81]

Some of these studies follow a history of ideas perspective to revisit the relationship between liberalism and empire,[82] while others engage in competing approaches to agency. In *Rage for Order*, Lauren Benton and Lisa Ford draw attention to the *interior workings of empire* and redefine intellectual influences as much more diffuse, as they are 'distributed across the empire in the writings, utterances, and acts of myriad participants in legal conflicts, all of whom understood their contests to have wider implications'.[83] Philip Stern's analysis of the East India Company (EIC) as an imperial political institution problematizes our conventional understanding of corporations as merely economic entities and the supposedly hierarchical distinction between superior states and corporations.[84] These studies complicate the image of state law as uniform and emphasize 'the multilayered and multicentric law of empire-states ... exhibiting patterns of jurisdictional complexity that persist into the era of robust claims about state legal hegemony'.[85]

[79] Lauren Benton and Lisa Ford, *Rage for Order: the British Empire and the Origins of International Law* (2016); Benton, *A Search for Sovereignty* (n. 15); Benton, *Law and Colonial Cultures: Legal Regimes in World History, 1400–1900* (2001); Kingsbury and Straumann (n. 4); Martti Koskenniemi, Walter Rech, Manuel Jimenez Fonseca (eds.), *International Law and Empire* (2017); Liliana Obregón, 'Between Civilisation and Barbarism: Creole Interventions in International Law' (2006) 27 *Third World Quarterly* 815, 820–4; Özsu (n. 45).

[80] Thomas Duve, 'European Legal History: Concepts, Methods, Challenges', in Thomas Duve (ed.), *Entanglements in Legal History: Conceptual Approaches* (2014) 29.

[81] For a general critique on the periodization of international law as post-Westphalian, see de la Rasilla del Moral (n. 14); Kingsbury and Straumann (n. 4), which explores the significance and implications of the use made of Roman legal concepts and of Roman just war theory and imperial practice by early modern European writers for natural law and the law of nations.

[82] Mehta (n. 4); Muthu (n. 4); Pitts (n. 4); Bell (n. 4); Mantena (n. 4).

[83] Benton and Ford (n. 80) at 189.

[84] Philip J. Stern, *The Company-State, Corporate Sovereignty and the Early Modern Foundations of the British Empire in India* (2011). See also Stern, 'Bundles of Hyphens': Corporations as Legal Communities in the Early Modern British Empire', in *Legal Pluralism and Empires 1500–1800* (2013).

[85] Lauren Benton and Richard Ross, *Legal Pluralism and Empires 1500–1800* (2013) 8.

2. *Disaggregating the Statist Position*

Meanwhile, in an even less cohesive list of works, scholars attempted to move further beyond an inter-state or even inter-polity perspective and illuminate how internal social and political processes within states shaped international legal processes. John Fabian Witt's *Lincoln's Code* explained how the Lieber Code came out of the imperatives of the emancipation of slaves in the U.S. For Witt, the laws of armed conflict were being driven by the two grand questions of political economy and politics of the era: slavery and freedom for all in the U.S.[86] In *The Verdict of Battle*, James Whitman demonstrated how the decline of dynastic succession shaped the meaning of war and the law that governed it.[87] A related study on the history of international humanitarian law in the formative era of the late-nineteenth century pointed to the spread of socialism, nationalism, and democracy and their political ramifications within European states as catalysts for the international codification of the laws of war in Europe.[88] These accounts consider the relevance of internal political and social processes to international legal developments.

Important theoretical insights used in the study of global governance prove particularly valuable in such historical inquiries that engage with inner-state processes and regard them as relevant explanatory avenues for developments in international law. For example, the histories of administrative, constitutional, and international law together as interrelated fields[89] provide a fruitful lens with which to move beyond the restrictions of an account of the law as divorced from other public (national and international) legal orders.[90] These attempts to pierce the sovereign veil to internal power relations and their influence on shaping international law could be conceived, through international relations theoretical terms, as institutionalist perspectives on the history of international law. They join more classical realist accounts of international legal histories that emphasize the relevance of power dynamics between powerful and weaker states and draw particular attention to hegemonic and counter-hegemonic forces.[91]

---

[86] John Fabian Witt, *Lincoln's Code: The Laws of War in American History* (2012).

[87] James Q. Whitman, *The Verdict of Battle* (2012) 224.

[88] Eyal Benvenisti and Doreen Lustig, 'Taming Democracy: Codifying the Laws of War to Restore the European Order 1856–1874' (on file with author).

[89] See J. H. H. Weiler, The International Society for Public Law [Mission Statement] 12 I-Con (2014).

[90] As Megan Donaldson's 'double-facing constitution' in the history of the League successfully demonstrates. Donaldson (n. 49).

[91] For an influential criticism of international law as being designed to protect strong states over weaker parties, see Roger Normand and Chris A. F. Jochnick, 'The Legitimation of Violence: A Critical Analysis of the Gulf War' (1994) 35 *Harvard International L.J.* 387.

V. JURISPRUDENTIAL ANACHRONISM
AND METHODOLOGICAL INNOVATION

The broadening of the question of agency could easily be associated with the theoretical terms of contemporary scholarship often termed 'global governance'—the innovative set of frameworks developed to think about the activities of international organizations, networks, hybrid public/private actors, and private entities.[92] Such broadening of the historical playing field holds the potential to embed our international histories of ideas in social histories, institutional histories, and histories of practice, and to present new and intriguing answers to the question of how to write an adequately nuanced global history of international law. The interplay of what is recognized by lawyers as international law and the aspects of life they ignore or exclude as irrelevant to its scope (such as economy, family, or political and social life within a state) is pivotal to our understanding of the role and influence of international law throughout history. More radical points of view may add material to ideational accounts to help us understand the developments in international law; emphasize the role and influence of structures of authority and modes of governance; or engage with the histories of contestation in international law, the roads not taken, and the struggles between the hegemonic and the counter-hegemonic—to include voices outside the chorus of great thinkers, institutionalized professionals, and high-ranking officials.

Such histories divert considerably from the history of prominent figures of the field, and yet remain loyal to the *professional* outlook of the 'legal official.' A more radical departure from the legal official would be to write a history of the knowledge of international law as disseminated to lay persons, or even a history of legal consciousness.[93] Such perspectives would inquire: 'what did ordinary people know about international law in different places and times, as reflected in the changing attitudes to the Nuremberg trials of different communities, for instance?'[94] Were people hopeful about the League of Nations in its inception, and how did their views change over time? The trends discussed in the previous section—international law

---

[92] Benedict Kingsbury, Nico Krisch, and Richard B. Stewart, 'The Emergence of Global Administrative Law' (2005) 68 *Law and Contemporary Problems* 15; Armin von Bogdandy, et al. (eds.), *The Exercise of Public Authority by International Institutions: Advancing International Institutional Law*, (Springer Science & Business Media, Vol. 210, 2010); Benedict Kingsbury and Lorenzo Casini, 'Global Administrative Law Dimensions of International Organizations Law', (2009) 6 *International Organizations L.R.* 319; Eyal Benvenisti, *The Law of Global Governance* (2014); D. Avant, M. Finnemore, S. Sell (eds.), *Who Governs the Globe?* (2010).

[93] See ch. 9.

[94] See, e.g., Leora Bilsky's work on popular perceptions of political trials, see Leora Bilsky, 'Political Trials', in N. J. Smelser, P. Baltes (eds.), *International Encyclopedia of the Social and Behavioral Sciences*, (2001) 11712–17.

and empire and the analysis of political, social, and cultural processes not confined to the state—may be further developed by drawing attention to such non-professional contexts, where legal consciousness evolves and could be enhanced by comparative analysis of the perspectives of different communities alongside similar international legal concepts or institutions.

The statist position is extremely important in exposing both a set of sensibilities and also a shared consciousness among international lawyers (at least those we identify as the leading figures of the discipline). And yet, as prisoners of their own time and place, their conceptual outlook and theoretical toolkit constitute only one set of perspectives in a multifaceted legal process that they and their counterparts around the world experience.

Our own jurisprudential consciousness and sensibilities render our reading of the past better tuned to a multilayered understanding of international law—to multiple, often contested, structures of authority that defy formal categorization. In a book review on Daniel Gorman's book, Natasha Wheatley succinctly captured the risks inherent in addressing old terms through the lens of later theories: 'Let us by all means recast old terms to capture new historiographical concerns, but in doing so remain reflective about how notions of 'society' worked to disconnect or differentiate parts of the world as much as we now see it bringing them together.'[95]

In a similar vein, Samuel Moyn warned against *sentimental fictions* in the history of the interwar period, the result of projecting our own era's hopes for international law.[96] Another reflection of contemporary law on our historical analysis is the fragmentation of international legal histories that probably permeates the wide range of writing in specific fields of international law, such as human rights[97] or international criminal law.[98] These fragmented accounts echo our governance-era tendencies to conceive international law through discrete fields of expertise. While such histories deepen our understanding of these respective fields, they may also result in a compartmentalized view of international law and its histories and remain blind to broader power relations or ideological sensibilities that run across and between different sub-fields of the discipline.

Guldi and Armitage attribute the return of the *longue durée* to changing questions of scale, and conclude: '... the new historians of the long durée should be inspired to use history to criticize the institutions around us and to return history to its mission as a critical social science.'[99] A conceptualization of international law as governance, a

---

[95] Natasha Wheatley, Review of Daniel Gorman, '*The Emergence of International Society in the 1920s*', H-Diplo, H-Net Reviews (November, 2013), available at <http://www.h-net.org/reviews/showrev.php?id=37488>.

[96] Samuel Moyn, *Martti Koskenniemi and the Historiography of International Law in the Age of the War on Terror* (2017) 350.

[97] Moyn (n. 11).

[98] See, e.g., Ziv Bohrer, 'International Criminal Law's Millennium of Forgotten History' (2016) 34 *Law and History* Review 393. On the history of international commissions of inquiry and their embrace of international criminal law, see Jan Lemnitzer, 'International Commissions of Inquiry and the North Sea Incident: A Model for a MH17 Tribunal?' (2016) 27 *E.J.I.L.* 923.

[99] Guldi and Armitage (n. 39) at 85.

public order that is not confined to the scripts of its positive sources, enables an outlook on its past that draws inspiration from the present. The author believes theoretical predispositions related to governance theory inform the historiographical choices of sites and agents in the studies in his survey, as well as the questions they choose to investigate as a window onto a legal past. As Justin Desautels-Stein noted, '[a]s much as we have strained to listen, texts of the past never speak to us; we can only speak the texts, shaping them from our own particular positions, our own particular times, our own particular figurations and orientations.'[100] These differences, as Hayden White emphasized, have much to do with how our intellectual orientations already prefigure what it is we are disposed to see.[101] The present, in that respect, provides us with a methodological window we could not have opened until just about now.

VI. LEGAL THEORY AS NORMATIVE POLITICS

In an article dedicated to the normative theories underpinning Lassa Oppenheim's theory of legal positivism, Benedict Kingsbury explored how 'Oppenheim's commitment to a positivist approach to international law was not simply an assertion that a positivist concept of law was the only coherent one, but also embodied a normative or ethical view ...'[102] This chapter seeks to engage in a similar exercise and add history to the relationship between politics and our theory of the law. It shows how a Hartian approach to international legal history—the choice of a particular group of agents as the lens through which we analyse the history of international law (international lawyers of particular elites in Europe and in the Global South)—is directly linked to the statist bias in the history of international law. But, as Kingsbury demonstrates in his analysis of Oppenheim's oeuvre, legal theory is often chosen (either consciously or not) to advance moral and political values. This is true not only for the subjects of historical inquiry (deciphering their theory of law would expose their normative and political inclinations), but also for those of us who study such histories. In a particularly memorable passage, Hart warned against a world governed by legal officials:

In an extreme case ... only officials might accept and use the system's criteria of legal validity. The society in which this was so might be deplorably sheeplike; and the sheep might end in the slaughter-house.[103]

---

[100] Justin Desautels-Stein, 'The Context for Legal History, or This is not your Father's Contextualism' (2016) 56 *American Journal of Legal History*, 29.

[101] Hayden White, *Metahistory: The Historical Imagination in Nineteenth Century Europe* (2014).

[102] Benedict Kingsbury, 'Legal Positivism as Normative Politics: International Society, Balance of Power and Lassa Oppenheim's Positive International Law' (2002) 13 *E.J.I.L.* 401, 431. For another study on the political theory underpinning Oppenheim's positivism, see García-Salmones Rovira (n. 11).

[103] H. L. A. Hart, *The Concept of Law* (1961) 117.

A historical landscape laid open to differing voices and counter-hegemonic resistance, while complicating our understanding of our histories, may helpfully usher us away from idealist accounts of the past and take us beyond the realist contention of an ongoing game between the powerful.

BIBLIOGRAPHY

Antony Anghie, *Imperialism, Sovereignty and the Making of International Law* (Cambridge University Press, 2004)

David Armitage, *Foundations of Modern International Thought* (Cambridge University Press, 2013)

David Armitage, *The History Manifesto* (Cambridge University Press, 2014) [with Jo Guldi]

Arnulf Becker Lorca, *Mestizo International Law: A Global Intellectual History 1842–1933* (Cambridge University Press, 2010)

Lauren Benton, *A Search for Sovereignty: Law and Geography in European Empires, 1400–1900* (Cambridge University Press, 2010)

Annabel Brett, *Changes of the State: Nature and Limits of the City in Early Modern Natural Law* (Princeton University Press, 2011)

Patricia Clavin, *Securing the World Economy* (Oxford University Press, 2013)

Thomas Duve (ed.), *Entanglements in Legal History: Conceptual Approaches* (Max Plunck Institute for European Legal History, 2014)

Istvan Hont, *Jealousy of Trade: International Competition and the Nation-State in Historical Perspective* (Harvard University Press, 2005)

Benedict Kingsbury, Benjamin Straumann (eds.), *The Roman Foundations of the Law of Nations: Alberico Gentili and the Justice of Empire* (Oxford University Press, 2010)

Martti Koskenniemi, *The Gentle Civilizer of Nations: The Rise and Fall of International Law 1870–1960* (Cambridge University Press, 2001)

Mark Mazower, *No Enchanted Palace: The End of Empire and the Ideological Origins of the United Nations* (Penguin Books, 2009)

Mark Mazower, *Governing the World: the History of an Idea, 1815 to the Present* (Princeton University Press, 2012)

Samuel Moyn, *The Last Utopia* (Harvard University Press, 2010)

Anne Orford, *International Authority and the Responsibility to Protect* (Oxford University Press, 2011)

Sandhuya Pahuja, *Decolonizing International Law: Development, Economic Growth and the Politics of Universality* (Cambridge University Press, 2011)

Susan Pedersen, *The Guardians* (Oxford University Press, 2015)

Jennifer Pitts, *A Turn to Empire: The Rise of Imperial Liberalism in Britain and France* (Princeton University Press, 2005)

Richard Tuck, *The Rights of War and Peace Political Thought and the International Order from Grotius to Kant* (Oxford University Press, 2001)

CHAPTER 46

IMPERIAL LAW

THE LEGAL HISTORIAN AND THE TRIALS AND TRIBULATIONS OF AN IMPERIAL PAST

PAUL G. MCHUGH

IN ancient Rome the term *imperium* referred to the supreme power, held especially by consuls and emperors, to command and administer in military, judicial, and civil affairs. Then, as now, 'empire' described a relationship of power through which an expansionist polity asserted and exerted ascendance over a far-flung subject population by force and/or non-violent means. The imperial legal system constructed its *imperium* to describe the reach and character of its authority afar as pursued and enforced by its officials, legal functionaries, tribunes, and armies. Colonialism refers to the practice of founding settlements and is rooted in Rome's *colonia*, meaning a farm or settlement in foreign territory on the basis that Roman citizenship would be retained. Colonies have been such an adjunct of empire that frequently the two practices—of building an empire and establishing colonies—have become almost interchangeable, though strictly colonies are a sign of empire which can manifest itself in other ways. Although the subjugating of one polity by another is not unusual in human history, the European domination of the non-European world is the most recent. Its technologies, those of distance in particular, gave these empires extents previously inconceivable. Imperialism and colonialism have become nouns imbued with intentionality that suggests an ideology of European expansionism that has had continuance into the twenty-first century.

The term 'imperial law' does not hold any distinctive meaning but it supposes historical practices emanating from an imperialist polity that were systemic, juridical, and inscribing a relation of ascendance and subjugation. The term supposes an imperialist legal system against which is counterposed a 'unit' or object in subjection to it. Often this ascendance will be over a distinct community with an alternative system of authority in the subjection or suppression of which the imperial one asserts its own as overriding. This dynamic of dominance and subjugation of a foreign region (periphery) is the hallmark of an authority relationship that is 'imperial'. Imperial law is the imprimatur legalism emanating from the metropolitan authority by and through which it seeks and asserts its authority in peripheries afar.

Besides the legally trained, the educational background of those at the forefront of today's busy and active field of imperial legal studies includes history, anthropology, and English literature. With law, these are forms of disciplinary practice that professionalized in the universities at the end of the nineteenth century and that situated empire in terms of those practices. The frequent description nowadays of imperial legal studies as 'interdisciplinary' supposes the appearance of the disciplinary fields and method to which the prefix attaches. The appearance of the university and the professionalization of (legal) knowledge occurred when the imperialist practices and competition of European nation-state were at a peak. The educational, academic, and professional merchandizing of knowledge both absorbed and reflected the imperialist setting of late nineteenth-century Europe. The specialization, segmentation, and territorialism of the faculty format and the denominational politics of method inside emergent disciplinary fields produced distinctive ways of looking at empire with aspiration frequently cast in terms of the scientific and universalistic. The currency of academic knowledge about empire and about law (and thus about imperial law) reflected the university's political mission within the world and the disciplinary jockeying of its inner life. The ambition of the university formed an easy and unforced alliance with the reorganizing and professionalizing of legal services, as both forms expanded and rebranded during the late nineteenth century. The commodification of legal knowledge and practice opened a gap between law and history, which now professed ostensibly distinct forms of knowledge and method. Law turned Langdellian and history became Rankean. This bordering of method obscured the continuance of a very similar attitude towards the use of the past. For lawyer and historian the professionalization of method made their pasts more didactic, more the habitat of the practical man to read backwards 'in order to explain his present world, to justify it, or to make it a more habitable and a less mysterious place'.[1] If European expansionism has left its stamp on much of the globe, then the knowledge priesthoods of its universities and legal profession have matched its imperialist form in their disciplinary and professional practices.

---

[1] Michael Oakeshott, 'The Activity of Being an Historian' in *Rationalism in Politics and other Essays* (1962) 147.

To situate imperial law in terms of legal historical research today it is necessary, then, to have a sense of the nature and orientation of disciplinary enquiry into empire as it developed in the universities from the late nineteenth century through to the rise of imperial legal studies in the 1990s. *Démodé* since the Second World War, by the 1990s imperial studies had mushroomed, much of the momentum coming from critical scholars. In the decade before, critical method had been describing, often vehemently, the persistence of the imperial condition in spite of its ostensible disavowal after the Second World War in the international community's rhetoric and gesturing of decolonization and universal human rights. The university became implicated as the intellectualizing mouthpiece of this old-style western domination that had rebranded but never disappeared.

The rise of global markets and their circuits of production as well as the militarism of the post-Cold War era fuelled the *fin de siècle* return of interest in empire. This was accompanied by constant announcement and counter-announcement of the passing of nation-state sovereignty with its deliberative and representative institutions and the emergence of a new logic of rule. This new logic flashed and pulsated with the technologies of its instantaneity that made the global and the local virtually interchangeable. Hardt and Negri's *Empire* (2000) was timely as the talking piece of this intellectual turn to empire as much for its contribution to the currency within the intelligentsia of political philosophers like Carl Schmitt, Walter Benjamin, and Hannah Arendt. There appeared a more theoretical field that showed and explored Foucauldian sensitivity to the role of historical research, such as in Giorgio Agamben's 'state of exception' and Sebastian Conrad's 'transnational history'. Epic, bigger boned, and wider haunched histories of the *longue durée* and empire returned to university and popular culture.

In the last decade of the twentieth century there appeared a rich and increasingly active historical field of 'imperial legal studies'. This research activity continues to flourish. Its *habitués* have not collectively designated themselves as a distinct field, nor indeed have bothered to ponder this point. Nor have they collectively pinned the 'interdisciplinary' tag to the activity—this is the outcome rather than the entry-point to this scholarship. Much of it could also fall into fields such as legal pluralism, the history of political thought, post-colonial studies, but such slotting is largely irrelevant to such multifarious research. Nonetheless it can be said that current historical legal research into imperial law can be described generally in terms of the fixating it has largely left behind. Old-style imperial legal studies were largely steered by what might be termed the historiography of reception. This older approach had its origins in late nineteenth-century European imperial practice, legalism (method, profession, and education), and the mission statement of the university. The historiography of reception saw the legalism of empire—its institutions and its doctrine—as its chief ideological export and the liberal nation-state its spawn. Reception took a national turn to regenerate in the post-War rhetoric of decolonization, universal human rights, and national civil rights. This historiography rendered histories of imperial law that were inherently institutional and/or doctrinal, which though affected by the particularities of time, place, and culture rendered the past by reference to the constitutional arrangement and agenda of imperial possession turned liberal nation-state.

Empire thus segued into histories of the constitutional politics of the post-imperial nation and it was in this light that the impact of the imperial experience was written. As the strife-ridden democracies of the new international order—those of the new Commonwealth in particular—entered the final quarter of the century, it dawned that the colonial legacy had an afterlife that the nation-makers and their historians but a generation before had rather under-estimated. Seeing the benighted political condition of the national polity drew its historians towards greater sensitivity and anger about that past. Here was the imperial state in its true colour: authoritarian and paternalistic; the lazy preference for administrative convenience (as in the drawing of boundaries) over longstanding local particularity; the instrumental use of law and military to inscribe overriding and paramount authority; factionalizing and the privileging of particular sectors for leadership, policing, trading, and brokering; the inconsistent treatment of pre-existing communities and their ongoing, known sensitivities. The colonial legacy showed itself in various ways, most often for legal historical researchers in the constitutional politics that played turbulently in post-colonial nations. Features such as the collapsed democracies and the one-party politics that followed, the return of martial law (a phenomenon supposed to have disappeared), ethnic and religious sectarianism prone to outbreaks of violence, the social and economic deprivation, the degradation, poor health, and incarceration rates of landless indigenous peoples. Reception thus had a sequence of several forms: as celebration of empire, as promise of liberal and democratic nationhood committed to diversity and equality, then as polity afflicted by colonial legacy in the crippled institutions of government (Africa and Asia) or in the crippling legacy of their failure (race and indigenous peoples).

Social history had always barked at the feet of the more dominant form of imperial and national political history, and in the 1980s began to bite. This style of history was becoming more prominent as the failed and struggling new democracies across the world faltered and fell into dictatorship, as the older ones became sclerotic, as new elites mobilized and concentrated wealth, as liberal diversity was exposed as delivering less than its rhetoric promised so accentuating the discriminations it had set out to eliminate and as new ones appeared, as refugee crises became more usual. It became subaltern legal studies, the sociology of resistance to the imposition of imperial law and the persistence of its legacy in what came after. Imperial studies of the twenty-first century may well have appeared in some interdisciplinary form without the impetus from critical and subaltern scholars. It is interested, however, in the sociology of the imposition of legal authority afar and across seas rather than the sociology of local and particular resistance that give the subaltern its historical identity. For the legal historical researcher into imperial law, the power of the subaltern critique lies (at its least) in the liberating and widening of the legal vista and the depiction of law not as closed institutional practice but as a site of continual and usually irresolute contest and struggle.[2]

The new-style imperial legal studies shed the historiography of reception's fixation upon imperial law as inherently imperative without also discarding the interest in institutional culture and its generation of legal meaning. Today's historian of imperial law will encounter terms such as 'governmentality', 'police', 'subaltern', 'office', 'borderlands' (or 'middle ground'), and (multiple) 'legality'. They will be seeing law as process and imbricated with other socially constructed activity rather than as fixed and closed (surprisingly enough, a past where law is as contingent and negotiated as we experience it today). They will be finding a travelling *imperium*, an ocean-going legalism with nodes and networks rather than one set sedentarily inside a series of fragmenting (and then fragmented) and territorialized proto-national peripheries.

The British Empire always presented and prided itself as being an Empire of Law. Until the 1990s sea-change, the history of this Empire of Law was recounted largely through the historiography of reception. This divided itself into complementary streams—the institutional and the doctrinal—that largely reflected the division of knowledge in the universities of the late-nineteenth century. The constitutional aspects of this Empire were left to the imperial-whigs, providing structure for broader political histories. In this tradition of imperial history, the Whig tale of the British polity took ocean-going form as the transplantation abroad of the institutional loci of that history—a representative legislature supplying responsible Ministers to provide advice and courts applying the rule of (common) law, the secular trinity of the three branches. Meanwhile a small band of Anglo-American legal historians of the late nineteenth century burrowed into the technicalities of the transmission of doctrine. The specificity as well as doctrinal nature of this attention reflected its occasional day-tripping nature. Seeley, the father of imperial history, and Maitland, the father of English legal history, were colleagues at Cambridge University in the late nineteenth century when these two forms of history were putting down roots. Meanwhile in Oxford, Edward Burnett Tylor was a key figure in the world of anthropology. His depiction of societies as running through three stages of savagism to barbarism then civilization nourished longstanding Victorian views about the static and foredoomed character of customary legalism. In this way primitive societies lacked any historical agency, cleaving instinctively to the static customary law without the deliberative mechanisms of legal change and advancement. Anthropologists were in places where reception had not occurred or where the ground was being softened for it to happen (as with Macaulay's Indian Penal Code (1835)).

---

[2] For the interdisciplinary see Markus Dubber, 'Critical Analysis of Law: Interdisciplinarity, Contextuality, and the Future of Legal Studies', (2014) 1 *Critical Analysis of Law: An International & Interdisciplinary Law Review* 1. Available at SSRN: <https://ssrn.com/abstract=2385656 or http://dx.doi.org/10.2139/ssrn.2385656> (accessed 26 April 2017).

Reception replicated the division of intellectual province in the universities of the late nineteenth century. For history, law, and anthropology as emergent academic disciplines, the Empire provided the means by which the British could learn of the world so as to be able to instruct it. Reception provided the intellectual tiller for imperial history (governmental institutions), legal history (doctrine), and anthropology (primitive).

The imperial-whig tradition had the longevity of the Empire itself, as it told the tale of a Parliamentary people under the rule of law planting these institutions overseas: as long as the Empire lasted in an effectual global sense so also did the imperial-whig tradition supply it with self-legitimating histories. This tradition weakened mid-century as the Empire itself weakened, being as much undermined by its American ally as attacked by its continental foes. The imperial federation movement towards the close of the nineteenth century nourished the imaginary of Greater Britain, as the Colonial Conferences became the mutual congratulatory of the Imperial Conferences that began the twentieth. The backslapping of this club underlined its exclusivity. Political resistance in Britain to Ireland and India's inclusion in the club of the self-governing Dominions hardened the nationalisms being expressed. Justification for this exclusion strained the imperial-whig narrative increasingly as the twentieth century rolled on, not only from the nationalist historians but also within the ranks of its own, Arthur Berriedale Keith most notably. As Ghandi's influence rose, the Montagu-Chelmsford Report (1918) formed the basis of the Government of India Act 1919 which contemplated gradual transition to self-government. Through arms and despite close-run dissention, the Irish Free State (1921) joined the club of self-governing dominions in the Empire. These accommodations and the Statute of Westminster gave the tradition breathing space that carried it through to the Second World War. However, it was by then expiring as with the Empire it was validating.

Meanwhile, at the beginning of the twentieth century English legal history was still the pursuit of a small band of English and American scholars with a heavily doctrinal approach aiming to assist the sourcing of positive legal authority and practical skills of the lawyer.[3] Maitland was the guru of this group though always in a class of his own. In turning his attention fleetingly to imperial law in his Rede Lecture (1901) he raised what he saw as a different, more preoccupying and perplexing reception question—the failure of the civil law to root in English soil. His imperial examples were a handful of imperial feudatories (Virginia, Maryland, Rupert's Land, Bombay) and the Blackstone that James Kent and John Marshall had taken 'straight to the Pacific'.[4] Crown charter, with its invocation of the imperial

---

[3] Jonathan Rose, 'Studying the Past: the Nature and Development of Legal History as an Academic Discipline' (2010) 31 *Journal of Legal History* 2 101–28 ff.

[4] Angela Fernandez, Markus D. Dubber (eds.), *Law Books in Action: Essays on the Anglo-American Legal Treatise.*

space both governed and owned by the sovereign (the Norman Yoke, reviled by the Founding Fathers, that fused *imperium* and *dominium*)—and the legal treatise were Maitland's insignia of the unity of the common law. Seemingly he lauded the hundred legislatures that the Empire had produced, 'little more or less building on that foundation [of the common law]: on the rock that was not submerged'. Yet he spoke in rueful realization that these legislatures were also causing the permanent submergence of his much-loved imperial rock.[5] As typical of Maitland, the past held the seed of its future but it is never one to be presumed will be sown or germinate.

The three-volume *Select Essays on Anglo-American Legal History* (1907–1909) were an American initiative. Two and, to a lesser extent, another of those essays in this collection have since become classics in the history of imperial law, those by Paul Reinsch (1869–1923, legally educated but with a PhD under the supervision of Frederick Jackson Turner and later a professor of political science), St George Leakin Sioussat (1878–1960, then a young historian), and Charles McLean Andrews (1863–1943, historian). Generally, however, the compilation kept to the Anglo-provenance of private law topics like the law merchant, insurance, corporations, and negotiable instruments. Though the historiographical style may have been more sophisticated than has been acknowledged,[6] the interest in sources was essentially positivist. The collection reflected consensus on the nature of legal method and its abstraction and organization by category through which the common law expressed its logic of experience and the practical man. It also reflected the ambition of the legal historian in university, profession, polity, and politeness. One sees in the *Select Essays* the miniaturist (academic essay in legal periodical), the manly and practical ethos of legal historicism (commerce and the transactional world of economic liberty enabled by the pragmatic common law), and the conjunction of pedagogic mission (betterment of legal method) with an unthreatening fraternal comparativism. This was the intellectualism and historicism of the doctrinal commonalities that bound rather than the public law differences that had sundered. Public law was for the most part avoided. To concentrate upon doctrine was also to concentrate mostly on courts and a transacting world of men of affairs, oiled if not greased by the common law. In that sense, in the validation of the common law as a form of institutional practice that encompassed and traversed like jurisdictions, the doctrinal legal historian shored up the wider institutional project.

At the beginning of the twentieth century, public law was a field in respect of which the British and American national and legal historiographical traditions were very differently oriented and which the courtesies of the *Select Essays* compilation did not press. Quite expectedly, these historiographical traditions supported their own constitutional order much as the imperial one validated the imperial.

---

[5] Maitland, *English Law and the Renaissance* (1901) 31–2 ff.
[6] David Rabban, *Law's History: American Legal Thought and the Transatlantic Turn to History* (2013).

Britain's national constitution was then in the jockeying of Lords and Commons in its supreme Parliament, and the Labour party rising from the aftershock of the *Taff Vale* case (1901).[7] The Queen who had reigned for sixty years lasted a year into the new century. By then Fenians, socialists, and suffragettes were besieging this constitution. Though the paramount political authority of the people (as represented in the House of Commons) was sealed with the passage of the Parliament Act 1911, its identity remained fundamentally monarchist. The British constitution remained constituted through its Crown and on no stronger footing than what its prime commentator Albert Venn Dicey termed convention, in particular, the pervasive convention of 'advice'.

On the other hand, the American invocation of 'We the People' put demos at the centre of national historiography. Frederick Jackson Turner's (1893) famously set the frontier as the elemental driving force of American history. 'Behind institutions, behind constitutional forms and modifications, lie the vital forces that call these organs into life and shape them to meet changing conditions.' Turner's historical generative, the enterprise and activity of its people, meshed with the laissez-faire constitutionalism of the Supreme Court in the (much talked about) *Lochner* era (1905). This was the pre-Depression period during which the Supreme Court interpreted the Fourteenth Amendment substantive due process clause to strike down state legislation that it saw as redistributive and infringing economic liberty. Oliver Wendell Holmes' brief and famous dissents in *Lochner* and *Adkins* (1923) may be seen not as differing in principle so much as the degree to which the people had empowered judicial interpretation. The social approach towards writing history (that Turner has often been associated with) became manifesto in Franklin Jameson's *The American Revolution Considered as a Social Movement* (1925). For Jameson, the Revolution was a social phenomenon that was levelling in its nature and that reordered the status of peoples, the land, industry, and commerce (his four categories). The year before, McIlwain's Pulitzer Prize-winning *The American Revolution: A Constitutional Interpretation* (1924) had described the Revolution as a clash of constitutional ideas and stressed the ways in which the American colonists saw the British after 1763 as interfering with their constitutional rights as Englishmen. For Jameson and other historians this was too lofty and theoretical, as well as insufficiently nationalist a way to explain the cataclysmic character of the breach. This reaction was indicative of how American intellectual history of this time—the legal included—resonated with the pragmatics of its millions knitting the empirical into its knowledge. One might instance the 'mood' that was American legal realism, the sociological jurisprudence of Roscoe Pound in the early twentieth century and the philosophy of John Dewey. It is impossible here to capture the sophistication of these historiographical and

---

[7] *Taff Vale Railway Co. v. Amalgamated Society of Railway Servants* [1901] UKHL 1.

jurisprudential traditions.[8] The point is the rather simple folkish one that the Americans built numerous intellectual traditions as a generative emanation from its people whereby the empirical became the ideological. And so was built the paradox long noted: that the imperialist character of American expansionism was built upon an anti-imperialist stance.

In terms of institutional foci, the nationalist historiographies of the old Commonwealth were essentially concerned with the articulation of a national sovereignty as the loyalist continuation from the imperial. Alternatively but on essentially the same lines were the independent nations who had escaped the clutch of Empire (rebelliously—the United States and Ireland) or had not to now inhabit its ruins (the colonial legacy afflicting the new Commonwealth). In all these styles of history imperial law was the precursor of the liberal nation-state and its institutions, acting as the spectral foreshadow of this future yet to happen and in respect of which its legacy would be cherished or detested. *Imperium* took some historiographic role as foundation or foil. It was imbued with an inherent evanescence and transitional character that for better or worse, in sickness or in health, sired the historicity of the nation-state that came after. It is less a case of all roads leading to Rome than of all the roads leading from it, headed towards the nation-state. This state was national and territorially-defined, its constitution articulating the means by which its three branches together and institutionally expressed the paramountcy of their political authority and the rights of its citizenry.

In associating imperial law with institutional form and practice, the reception historiography replicated English law's dualist separation of international and munici-pal law. Volume 14 of Holdsworth's *History of the Laws of England* treated imperial law as a distinct area in which the legal consequence of international law was a matter of British election. This was tempered with a touch of common law doctrine moderating the imperial prerogative in British possessions, Lord Mansfield's judgment in *Campbell v. Hall* (1774)[9] the key (and almost solitary) example. Nonetheless the reception historiography anointed the late-nineteenth-century view of the imperial as custodian in the meanwhile of civilized nationhood about to come. The talk of impermanence that becomes a kind of drumbeat for imperialist officialdom and rhetoric from the middle of the nineteenth century echoed into the reception historiography of imperial law. It pulled historical attention eyes up towards destination rather than on the mucky and perplexing circumstances of the march itself.

Generally speaking, today's historians do not perpetuate their predecessors' propelling of imperial law into its glory- or hell-bound afterlife in the liberal

---

[8] On the American tradition, for instance, through to recent times, see G. Edward White, 'The Arrival of History in Constitutional Scholarship' (2002) 88 *Virginia L.R.* 3, 485–633 ff; and 'Reflections on the Republican Revival: Interdisciplinary Scholarship in the Legal Academy' (1994) 6 *Yale J.L. & Human.* 1 ff; and Christopher Tomlins, 'The Consumption of History in the Legal Academy: Science and Synthesis, Perils and Prospects, Review Essay' (2011) 61 *J. Legal Educ.* 139 ff.

[9] *Campbell v. Hall* (1774) 1 Cowp 204, 98 ER 1045 (KB).

nation-state. The historical compass of imperial legal studies is broad as well as long, aerial as well as micro. Reception has long faded as the predominant concern, though many of the insights its historians offered into administrative history and office remain. The interest is in the historical culture of legal authority (as opposed to a subaltern one of resistance) and the sociology of its pursuit of ascendance. This law is lived in its moment. It is not legalism conducting itself to the teleology of its own transcendence into some eventual nationhood. It is perceptual, mobile, uneven in its travels and adaptation, improvisational. Its journeying has something of the picaresque wherein the politeness of the imperial court turns into the messiness of maritime distance, the ennui of journeying, and the ongoing need to police Empire. The researcher thus will see an imperial legal culture that is as imaginative and performative as well as imperative, one that can be recaptured through the ordinary lives of its functionaries so much as the heroics of peak officials.

The term 'governmentality' has been used to describe the emergence of the idea during the eighteenth century of humans as forming a kind of natural collectivity of living beings, this population having its own characteristics unlike those shaping individual wills. These populations were to be understood by specific knowledges and governed through techniques attuned to their condition. Foucault devised the term governmentality to describe a mentality that had become the common ground of political thought and action from the eighteenth century. It was the art of government, he argued an 'ensemble formed by the institutions, procedures, analyses and reflections, the calculations and tactics, that allow the exercise of this very specific albeit complex form of power ...' Increasingly through the nineteenth century populations became a site of knowledge and field of rising and intensifying regulation.[10] Governmentality is concerned with more than law, which it sees as a key part of the suite of technologies and strategies by which rationalizations occurred, that is to say the replacement of traditions, values, and emotions as motivators for behaviour within a population with rational, calculated ones. Governmentality describes the constructing, contesting, and managing of juridical space(s) through networks, authorities, groups, individuals, and institutions thinking, talking, and acting in ways that construct, validate, and change that space. This is activity governmental in its reach (albeit not necessarily always legal in character) by which the subject is co-opted into an ever-configuring mesh of relations situating them by reference to the freedom given them.

This freedom is put in the long arch by Christopher Tomlins' important book *Freedom Bound: Law, Labor, and Civic Identity in Colonizing English America, 1580–1865* (2010). Across nearly three centuries of Empire and the early republic, Tomlins describes the legal regimes of labour as an early imperial

---

[10] Nikolas Rose, Pat O'Malley, Mariana Valverde, 'Governmentality', Sydney Law School Legal Studies Research Paper No. 09/94 at 6-7 ff. Online at <http://ssrn.com/abstract=1474131>.

governmentality that becomes a national one constituting civic identity in what became the United States. He argues (p.5) that 'law supplied the arguments that enabled the colonizers to justify—to themselves, to their rivals, to those they displaced—taking what they could keep, and keeping what they had taken.... Law was integral to the creation and implementation of governance.' This law (p.7) was 'not only protean but plural in the extreme', drawing on many sources (Roman law, natural law, common law), all of which were distinct but connected. The legal culture of labour was also localized and regionalized, reflecting the origins of immigrant communities and their political influence. Slavery had become distinguished from servitude by the early eighteenth century, and the distinction had hardened to become everywhere regulated and recognizable. Indentured white labour largely ended after the American Revolution, yet there remained restrictive working regulations for 'free labour' and the slave trade flourished. Anglo-American slave law began in the 1660s by fusing 'intellectual arguments and justifications from *ius natural* and *gentium* with the peculiarly protean transactional capacities and policing technologies of English statute and common law' (at p. 419). Together, Tomlins continues, these 'furnished resources of transplantation and management easily mobilized, as the occasion demanded, to legitimize English colonizers' transactions, insure their investments and otherwise define the relativities of unfreedom in their settlements to whatever extent they found desirable'. For Tomlins there is no such thing as imperial law so much as a de-centred and heterogeneous pool of legal sources that equipped Anglo-American expansionism and subjugation with a key technology, one that had functionality either side of the Revolution.

Other historians—Hulsebosch and Bilder, for instance—have put imperial law into a similar continuity with less de-centring (of what Tomlins calls the 'intrastructure') but as much if not more attention to the inwardness and constructed nature of political authority. In ways quite different but in a manner complementary to Tomlins, these historians have shown that for most of those involved in empire and nation (at least in the thinking part of it) these were not mutually exclusive conditions of governance. Empire also signified a form of progress. Hulsebosch reminds us, for instance, that Alexander Hamilton famously opened *The Federalist* by telling his readers that in their hands rested 'the fate of an empire, in many respects, the most interesting in the world', not least because the outcome would prove 'whether societies of men are really capable or not, of establishing good government from reflection and choice, or whether they are forever destined to depend, for their political constitutions, on accident and force'. Thus the 'first developing nation was also an empire: it conquered territory occupied by native populations; it innovated ways to control far-flung settlements by translating the metropole from an immobile capital into a portable idea of governance; it allowed commercial behavior to outrun political management as a paradoxical means of building state power; and it embraced the law of nations as the traditional tool of managing friction between empires'.[11] Tomlins, Hulsebosch, and Bilder vary in the breadth they give what here is called imperial law. All open with a transoceanic imperial law and give it longevity as such, but it has nonetheless put down roots in American soil and the governmentality that grows over the longer arch of time necessarily becomes geographically and jurisdictionally national.

This is an approach to imperial law that sees it in terms of state formation whilst shedding a twentieth-century fixation with mere state form. The attention to the inner life of imperial law has also retrieved the language of police, notably in Tomlins also in Dubber and Valverde. In Blackstone's classic statement, police is the maintenance of 'due regulation and domestic order' in the state, whereby 'the individuals of the state, like members of a well-governed family, are bound to conform their general behaviour to the rules of propriety, good neighbourhood, and good manners; and to be decent, industrious and inoffensive in their respective stations.' The relation of law and police is the fraught one between autonomy and heteronomy. The tension between police and law is complicated by the liberal inclination to see the former as the resort of the state benevolently to lift its citizenry, by the inherent elusiveness of police, and in an Anglophone tradition where (empirically as well as institutionally) police and law are far from distinct.[12] Recent attention to police in its imperial setting reflects current anxieties about the nature of emergency powers and legal techniques for the self-preservation of a polity in reference to its overseas interests.

Benton and Ford's recent book *Rage for Order* is the manual for imperial legal studies today. The authors frame British imperial legalism of the late eighteenth and early nineteenth centuries in terms of the 'pursuit of imperial order', a frame that implicitly reflects the miscibility of law and police within the primary material. Their approach does not preclude a more theoretical perspective but that is not the one they take. In that respect their concentration upon the socio-legal culture of imperial law and the relaying of authority across the vastness of empire can enrich the discussion of the theorists in showing the legal techniques of the time. Unlike Tomlins, and to give another important unmentioned historian, Martin Chanock, Benton and Ford are less interested in the sites of resistance, not least as this would pull their narrative towards territorial fixities and away from an ocean-going imperial setting. Benton and Ford stress the importance of middling levels and the quotidian inner life of an imperial sphere—its networks of corridors, enclaves, institutional reporting, commissions of inquiry—that is in a state of endless self-consciousness and inter-imperial machination the goal of which, like a cat chasing its own tail, is the pursuit of its own order.

Imperial law was the product of an imperial legal culture in which the relaying of knowledge and the technological logistics of its transmission as well as the

---

[11] Daniel Hulsebosch, 'Constitution-making in the Shadow of Empire' (2016) 56 *American Journal of Legal History* 84, 85–6 ff.

[12] Christopher Tomlins, 'To Improve the State and Condition of Man: The Power to Police and the History of American Governance' (2005) 53 *Buffalo L.R.* 1215 ff.

social practice of its officialdom were as important as the formal assertions of authority and skirmishes and flashpoints in the field. The cultural settings of the formation of legal knowledge within the empire are as important for setting the bounds of governmentality as the actual instantiation through command of court, governor, or colonial legislator: these laws have to be imagined before they can be announced. This can turn the historian's interest to the middling strata of authority such as the officials or judges circulating about Empire, its inquisitorial commissions, its jurisdictional perplexities (of prize, pirates, slaves), the materiality and mobility of law libraries and books, the administrative structuring of appeals to the imperial centre, the role and incorporation of legal advice into Whitehall and bureaucratic circles, or the subculture of the legal profession locally, regionally and in the nature of their fraternal activity.[13]

In different ways, but both as historical studies into imperial law, Tomlins and Benton and Ford show why reception historiography has lost currency. Reception searches for the positivist's institutionalized insignia (or promise) of law's presence. It does not address the historical questions current today that have arisen from the nature of our hindsight and in the modern world of globalization and inter-connectedness. There are questions about how that imperial law encountered other legal systems and the dynamics of an engagement destined to last much longer than the imperialist and colonialist authorities and their public had expected. How did the imperialist polity imagine its authority in sites and ways available to it other than through (though always along with) governmental institution, so that the forms of this legalism would retain hold long after the imperial relation had gone?

The historian of imperial law must also historicize the nature of law and legal method in the constituting of politics of time and place(s). Imperial law is part of a history through which the changing conception of the province of law affects political practice and vice versa. Per Martin Loughlin, we may understand law as a means of conducting politics, when law is understood to be grounded in custom; as the instrument of politics, when law is understood as commands issued by the state; or as restraining politics, when law is understood to have institutionalised fundamental 'right' principles of justice, with which norms must cohere to be lawful. These historical staging points were neither a necessary chronological, nor an inexorable, process of evolution from one to the next.[14] Thus, for example, has Benton challenged the depiction of abolition as the origins of post-War universalistic human rights. To understand how law is present in the imperial past it is necessary to be clear how law was constituting the politics of that imperial past and vice versa. The historian of imperial law must not merely describe what law was doing or what it enabled but how it was thinking.

---

[13] E.g., W. Wesley Pue, *Lawyers' Empire: Legal Professions and Cultural Authority, 1780–1950*.

[14] Loughlin's concern is for law of the public sphere and his interest is more theoretical than historical. See Michael Gordon, 'A Basis for Positivist and Political Public Law: Reconciling Loughlin's Public Law with (Normative) Legal Positivism' (2015) 1 *Jurisprudence* 29 ff.

The British Crown routinely issued charters and royal instruments to facilitate the governance of its subjects abroad, but this was never something the monarch and ministers felt obliged to do. Securing a charter was not simply a matter of asking but required protracted ingratiation and supplication—what today is called lobbying—that could take years or end fruitless. The terminology of these charters and the circumstances of their issue evoked a legal order—or series of orders—of which this chartering partook and ostensibly encompassed but the imaginary of which was to worlds and places far beyond the sceptred isle and its earth of majesty.

There is in this chartering and there continued through the eighteenth century a sense of constitutional 'politeness' at the metropolitan centre, the protocols by which the Crown permitted its subjects to venture abroad and comported itself in the manner becoming a Christian prince. Comportment was a matter of election, the monarch's displaying the *dignitas regalis* of supreme prerogative to its subjects and to other Christian princes. The civility of the polity became the language by which Burke, for example, counselled caution in the Imperial Parliament's legislating for the thirteen colonies and by which he condemned the East India Company's rule. The sovereign power was expected to comport its dignity as to show restraint, consistency, benevolence, facilitation of commerce, courtesy to other monarchs and their plenipotenaries, and maintain the protestant succession and patronage of the aristocracy. This sense of comportment ran from the discovery of the New World through to the early nineteenth century, disappearing during the second quarter of the nineteenth century when the nature of British imperialism lost what traces of courtliness had survived the Napoleonic Wars. Comportment entailed a conceptualizing of the exercise of supreme power that cannot be meshed with a dualist international/municipal dichotomizing. Much of the imperial law was exemplary rather than of the imperative.

The shifting edifice of imperial law was built from these charters. All government was exercised in the Crown's name and chartering in all its various forms (and so on down) was the central organizing feature of British imperial administration and the foundation for its enduring self-conception as an Empire of Law. Necessarily any history of imperial law will work through the smaller-form, encompassed, purpose-led authorizing of 'office' and its internal mechanisms of discipline and surveillance. Office must be historicized and contextualized not just as formal practice but also as demonstrative of a prevailing worldview as to the nature of authority. The actors in this past did not build the multiple pyramids of office because there was an external rule or requirement by which they did what otherwise they would not. Their deferential and hierarchical world did not have the public and private spheres of today with separation of the religious and secular.[15] Office was reflexive. It only

---

[15] Conal Condren, 'Public, Private and the Idea of the "Public Sphere" in Early–Modern England' (2009) 19 *Intellectual History Review* 1 ff.

dawned gradually that there were other ways by which they might imagine the nature of authority.

The legal historical researcher of the British Empire will identify the network of office, the stratification, communication (including control of the flow of information), and activity of this composite body. The legalism animating the network will give much attention to remit of office as well in the mediations and ruminating as actual exercises, disciplining and reporting of it. The ramifying of office through the increasing specificities of commission and instruction, superior to subordinate, transmitted, and dispersed that authority vertically and horizontally in multiple ways especially through practices of administration and communication that can be seen as networks. Just as there were formal channels that attended office—commission, instruction, reporting back—and the sanctions of reprimand, there were also less formal. Authority manifested itself in the everyday routine of those on deck where decks were scrubbed and rigging checked, the lapping and tiding of this through indifferent weather so much as exceptional circumstances of skirmish or storm. There was leakage and informality throughout this system but especially at the middle levels, crucial in terms of any siphoning, condoning, blocking, or transgressing of imperial authority and the nature of the information that circulated within the body imperial. In *Rage for Order*, Benton and Ford explain and illustrate the importance of the mediate levels of imperial authority in setting the jurisdictional, bureaucratic, and administrative channelling and organizing.

Benton and Ford use protection to show features of imperial law in the early nineteenth century. Protection-talk became a feature of British imperial practice of the post-1815 period in relation to slavery and indigenous peoples decades before it became the Protectorate form of the Scramble.[16] It did so in ways that emphasized the status of those protected as British subjects less as the appearance of a humanitarian inflected conception of rights than as the juridical foundation for British authority. Subjecthood, less prominent in the last quarter of the eighteenth century,[17] became a stronger starting and organizing principle of imperial law and policy in the second quarter of the nineteenth century. When the Victorians distinguished classes of people by law it was not to endow with rights so much as disability. Not infrequently the British contrasted the subjecthood their imperial law gave slaves and its tribal peoples with the denial of it by the American republic, this counterpointing occurring during the mid-century decades of Reform, Mutiny, the American Civil War, Morant Bay, and Canadian Confederation. Protection had its legal particularities in the West Indies and settlement colonies of Southern Africa and Australasia. It also had recurrence, transmissions, and constitutional

---

[16] Lauren Benton, Lisa Ford, *Rage for Order*, 88 ff.

[17] C. L. Brown, 'Empire without Slaves: British Concepts of Emancipation in the Age of the American Revolution' (1999) 56 *W&M. Qly.* 2, 273–306 ff.

overtones for governmentality of its imperial sort and as more than the sum of its particular parts. One recent approach has been to describe protection in terms of the circulation around the Empire of key mid-level officials as protectors, and whose mission restated and sometimes deflated from one location to another.[18] This account gives less attention to the deeper constitutional origin of protection (in kingship) and the actual deployments of legal authority by protectors than might more directed legal research, though it does emphasize the Victorian preference for rectitude over rights. The authors' linking of mid-nineteenth-century protection of subject tribal peoples with contemporary humanitarian rights-based discourse is suggestive but lacks (and tends against) Benton and Ford's historicizing of rights-talk.

Historians such as Tomlins (labour and civic identity) and Benton and Ford (pursuit of imperial order) have described an imperial legalism that was essentially iterative, improvisational, heterogeneous, mobile, hierarchical, and trans-hemispheric whilst capable of highly localized effects and particularities. The historiography of the American Revolution (Bernard Bailyn, Gordon Wood, John Phillip Reid, Jack Greene) has been influential in showing this vernacular and multiple imperial constitution. Yet though this 'vernacular imperial constitution' has institutional loci it may figure historically in ways not necessarily on the road to statehood. Imperial law might be a vast resource frantically on the treadmills of its own search for order (Benton and Ford); a way of drawing upon juridical forms of occupation to justify expansionism (Fitzmaurice); a resource deployed opportunistically rather than coherently against the land prerogative and discretion of office (Hickford); the means of indicting at home a murderous colonial Governor (Kostal); an enquiry into the nature of customary law to build knowledge for the pursuit of colonial governmentality (Mantena); or persistently present in less noticed pockets of what becomes national constitutional life (Hulsebosch, Bilder). Imperial law and its colonialist manifestations may represent a field of resistance or a site of juridical knowledge as well as imposition of authority.[19] Tomlins and Chanock, as well as Hickford in his study of the legal politics of native title in the mid-nineteenth century, show the complexities and multiple agencies involved as those subject to imperial legalism devise their own strategies of habitation. Richard White's influential *The Middle Ground* (1991) is both a place (the *pays d'en haut* of the Great Lakes region between 1650–1815) and a process of mutual accommodation between Algonquian-speaking Indians and French, British, and Americans. This middle ground arises because imperial authority cannot police it but neither can the indigenous. Just as governmentality intensified as the activity of the territorialized

---

[18] Alan Lester, Fae Dussart, *Colonization and the Origins of Humanitarian Governance: Protecting Aborigines across the Nineteenth-Century British Empire* (2014).

[19] E.g., see essays in Saliha Belmessous (ed.), *Native Claims: Indigenous Law against Empire, 1500–1920* (2011).

liberal national-state, so did borderlands turn into borders, particularly with regard to tribal nations—bordered into the legislative compound of allotment, individualization of title and enfranchisement, elective modes of governance, measurement, surveillance, and political marginalization.[20] As rose the governmentality of the colonial state so fragmented and shattered the indigenous, the vernacular imperial constitution less the site for this activity than a resource on which its agents drew to legitimate an ascendance.

Imperial law can be seen not as a thing or finished product, but as an activity. This allows the historian to look at the culture of imperial authority in sources like commissions of inquiry, the endless petitioning of colonial governors, communication across political communities, travelogues, denominational jostling, the organizing of the legal profession in particular places, treaty-making with indigenous peoples, and the legal situating of religious minority communities. This legal culture within empire, sedentary or sea-going, at centre or periphery, was in constant pursuit of order, its governmentality largely the many and varied forms of office with all the hierarchy and circuitry these required and the disputation they generated. Imperial law was activity so multiple as to be at once ramshackle and rampaging.[21]

BIBLIOGRAPHY

David Armitage, Jennifer Pitts, (eds.), *The Law of Nations in Global History* (Oxford University Press, 2017) (re-publication of essays of C. H. A. Alexandrowicz, classic work from post-war period with editorial essay)

Lauren Benton, Lisa Ford, *Rage for Order: The British Empire and the Origins of International Law, 1800–1850* (Harvard University Press, 2016)

Mary Sarah Bilder, *The Transatlantic Constitution: Colonial Legal Culture and the Empire* (Harvard University Press, 2004)

Martin Chanock, *Law, Custom, and Social Order: Colonial Experience in Malawi and Zambia* (Cambridge University Press, 1985)

Shaunnagh Dorsett, John McLaren (eds.), *Legal Histories of the British Empire: Laws, Engagements and Legacies* (Routledge, 2014)

Andrew Fitzmaurice, *Sovereignty, Property and Empire, 1500–2000* (Cambridge University Press, 2014)

Lisa Ford, *Settler Sovereignty: Jurisdiction and Indigenous People in America and Australia, 1788–1836* (Harvard University Press, 2010)

---

[20] E.g., Jeremy Adelman, Stephen Aron, 'From Borderlands to Borders: Empires, Nation-States, and the Peoples in between in North American History' (1999) 104 *American Historical Review* 814–41 ff.

[21] J. M. McKenzie, 'The British Empire: Ramshackle or Rampaging? A Historiographical Reflection' (2015) 43 *Journal of Imperial and Commonwealth History* 1.

Mark Hickford, *Lords of the Land: Indigenous Property Rights and the Jurisprudence of Empire* (Oxford University Press, 2011/2012)

D. Hulsebosch, *Constituting Empire: New York and the Transformation of Constitutionalism in the Atlantic World, 1664–1830* (The University of North Carolina Press, 2005)

Rande A. Kostal, *Jurisprudence of Power: Victorian Empire and the Rule of Law* (Oxford University Press, 2008)

Alan Lester, Fae Dussart, *Colonization and the Origins of Humanitarian Governance: Protecting Aborigines across the Nineteenth-Century British Empire* (Cambridge University Press, 2014)

Karuna Mantena, *Alibis of Empire: Henry Maine and the Ends of Liberal Imperialism* (Princeton University Press, 2010)

Christopher Tomlins, *Freedom Bound: Law, Labor, and Civic Identity in Colonizing English America, 1580–1865* (Cambridge University Press, 2010)

PART V

ILLUSTRATIONS: DOING THINGS WITH LEGAL HISTORY

CHAPTER 47

A HISTORY OF VIOLENCE

AMERICAN CONSTITUTIONAL HISTORY AND THE CRIMINAL SYSTEM

GERALD LEONARD[*]

I. LAW AND VIOLENCE

NOBODY is in favour of 'police violence', a phrase redolent of unconstitutional abuse of power. Police are supposed to be agents of the law, acting only as the law authorizes, never in the service of unregulated power. When *USA Today* headlines an opinion piece in this way, 'On Father's Day, remember dads suffering loss because of police violence',[1] the obvious premise—sustained by the body of the piece—is that 'police violence' is unjustified, a violation of the victim's rights, inconsistent with law. Similarly, when *The Atlantic* runs a piece titled 'We, Too, Are

* Professor of Law, Boston University School of Law. The author is very grateful to Pnina Lahav for her careful reading of a draft of this chapter.

[1] https://www.usatoday.com/story/opinion/policing/spotlight/2017/06/18/policing-the-usa-violence-force-brutality-fathers-day-police-dads/102990688/ (accessed 7 March 2018).

Targets of Police Violence', arguing that black women, just as much as black men, are disproportionately victimized by 'police violence', the premise is the same.[2] The police are supposed to be the agents of law, not violence.

On the other hand, the law itself depends on violence. Few doubt the utility of a police force empowered to arrest and incarcerate dangerous criminals—that is, to wield violence in the service of the law. At least where the police are in possession of strong evidence that a person has committed a serious crime and would remain a danger to the community if allowed to run free, few people would object to an arrest done professionally and within the law. And, once a conviction is had for a serious offence, substantial punishment, usually including incarceration, is widely accepted as an appropriate tool of the law. In this sense, we endorse police violence and judicially authorized violence as routine expressions of the law.[3] To subdue, arrest, and cage a criminal is not assault and kidnapping but a defence of the rule of law itself.

These observations suggest that defenders of the rule of law prefer to obscure its violent nature. They prefer to separate the law from the violence it authorizes; from the very violence that makes it law rather than moral philosophy and moral exhortation; and indeed from the violence which gives birth to law and legal orders in the first place. Law is fully entwined with the violence of the police and other coercive institutions, and yet we do not call the police 'violent' when they enforce the law. We use that term only when we condemn 'police violence' for being outside the law. In 'a government of laws and not of men',[4] the very purpose of law is to substitute peaceful, rational, and impartial rules of social living for the violent domination of some persons by others. But is that substitution a mirage? Is it historically true that law tends to free a society from violence and arbitrary domination? Or, alternatively, does history demonstrate that violence itself sustains law as an efficient form of domination?

This chapter is about the violence of constitutional law, as verified by American constitutional history.[5] It does not claim that the law is wholly a mirage, that it merely obscures and facilitates the violence it purports to supplant. But it suggests that that is a lot of what it does. The next section of this chapter seeks to illuminate the centrality of violence to the history of American constitutional law generally. Although nothing could be easier than to find epic examples of injustice in

[2] 'We, Too, Are Targets of Police Violence', <https://www.theatlantic.com/politics/archive/2017/06/we-too-are-targets-of-police-violence/528579/> (accessed 7 March 2018).

[3] Decades ago, Robert Cover explained the seemingly obvious point that law is fundamentally institutional rather than philosophical and, therefore, fundamentally in the service of violence. Robert M. Cover, 'Violence and the Word' 95 *Yale L.J.* 1601 (1986).

[4] Massachusetts Constitution, Part the First, Article XXX.

[5] Much of this chapter was inspired by Christopher Tomlins, *Freedom Bound: Law, Labor, and Civic Identity in Colonizing English America, 1580–1865* (2010), especially ch. 10. I want to acknowledge that some of my most important points are influenced by that work without pretending that Tomlins would necessarily endorse any particular claim in this piece.

American constitutional history, my object is not to call out injustice as such but to illustrate the violence—justified or not—at the root of and in the continuing history of American constitutional law.[6] The balance of the chapter then turns specifically to the history of some current controversies in the American constitutional law of crime. It tries to demonstrate that the historical violence of American constitutional law illuminates the shape and trajectory, the limits and possibilities, of American constitutional law in the present.

II. Constitutional History as a History of Violence

Criminal law is the most conspicuous form of domestic state violence, so the constitutional law that frames the American criminal system is a focus of this chapter. Even in civil disputes, though, rights of enormous value are at stake. When the law vindicates one interest at the expense of another in cases petty and grand, it silently (usually) threatens to forcibly impose its notions of freedom, equality, well-being, and justice. And it exploits the resources, labour, and humanity of one party for the benefit of another. Indeed, no law is impartial but merely provides, at its best, relatively peaceful and predictable ways of vindicating some interests at the expense of others, with the threat of violence hidden as deep in the background as the rhetoric of the law can manage. This point is not philosophical[7] but historical. So we begin at the beginning of American constitutional law.

Every American constitution of the late eighteenth century was imposed by the violence of propertied white men directed at the disfranchised majority of women, the enslaved, non-whites, the unpropertied, the dependent, and the young. Of course, there were procedures, orderly legislative actions, majority votes of electorates and legislative bodies, and constitutional conventions. But, notwithstanding some measure of variety in the states, it was broadly true in the 1770s and 1780s that American state governments were created and recreated without the direct participation of the vast majority of the population. The overwhelming majority

---

[6] In this respect, I doubt that the constitutional law of the United States is distinct from that of any country that claims to adhere to a set of constitutional principles and institutions. Indeed, I doubt that the basic claim here is special to constitutional law, as opposed to other branches of law.

[7] So I do not feel the need to contend with various theoretical definitions of law and philosophies of law. Nevertheless, for a recent philosophical argument that I find consistent with my formulations in the text, see Joseph D'Agostino, 'Law's Violence' 22 *Texas Review of Law and Politics* 121 (2017).

of women could not vote (there were probably some exceptions in some town elections and a narrow and temporary exception in New Jersey's state elections). The overwhelming majority of black Americans, most of them enslaved, could not vote. The overwhelming majority of indigenous peoples could not vote. Among white men, the franchise was held remarkably broadly in some states, but those without meaningful property were widely disfranchised. By around 1790, only about 60 to 70 per cent of adult white males could vote.[8]

To the enfranchised, these exclusions generally did not have the flavour of violence because they appeared rational, just, and wise in that time and place, just as the exclusion of children and aliens from the franchise seems obviously prudent to most today. Yet, regardless of justice or injustice, the violence of these exclusions is clear. Most conspicuously, the subjection of so many black Americans to slavery was an exercise in overt violence of the first order. White interactions with Indian nations and individuals were complex and varied, but violence played a major role in the white American subjection of the indigenous to the rule of American law. Often less obvious to men was the equivalent violence suffered by women in the name of the patriarchal rights of men. If women lacked the vote and other civic rights as well as the right, in most cases, to control their own financial well-being and the course of their lives, the fundamental constraint was the threat of violence. The government might not send in the army nor apply slave law to white women. But women's uncompensated and unlimited labour was as firmly expected as the labour of the enslaved. And the violence of domestic discipline at the hands of the male head of household or the poverty that widely awaited the unmarried woman was violence as real as that experienced by the explicitly enslaved and by Indians in the way of white settlement. Even less conspicuous was the violence experienced by the unpropertied, but even the white men among this group were subject to poverty and then to public discipline if they should rebel against the structures that kept them in that state.

The federal Constitution of 1787 perpetuated all these forms of violence while constructing the national legal order anew. Wilfully disregarding the legal constraints imposed by the Articles of Confederation—that is, the requirement of unanimity among the states for any amendment to the Articles—the Framers of 1787 and the ratifiers of 1787–1788 simply replaced that legal order with one more amenable to their interests (that is, to 'justice' as they saw it). Again, that is not to make a judgment about the justice of the new Constitution, which was only replacing a prior structure that had itself been imposed on the nation by a narrow segment of the population. It is only to emphasize again the intertwining of violence and law. A white, male, propertied minority of the nation simply imposed a new Constitution that frankly embraced the enslavement of millions of Americans in

---

[8] Alexander Keyssar, *The Right to Vote: The Contested History of Democracy in the United States* (2000) 24 ff.

the Fugitive Slave Clause. It tacitly accepted the exclusion of, the subordination of, and the violence directed at free blacks, indigenous peoples, and women. And it openly favoured the propertied over the unpropertied in its structural design and in its incorporation of the Contracts Clause, designed to prevent the states from offering types of economic policy and relief inconsistent with the economic views of the well-propertied Framers.[9]

The process of ratifying the Constitution made clear that the only law involved was made up by the Framers and then by the enfranchised minority in each state. The Framers simply declared that the Constitution would be ratified as soon as nine states, not all thirteen, approved it. Then, each state gradually ratified the new Constitution. Although at least a few states dropped property requirements for voting for convention delegates,[10] the ratification electorate remained quite restricted. And, since many states contained large, anti-ratification minorities in and out of their conventions, it is fair to say that the Constitution was imposed by somewhat more than half of the nation's propertied, white men on a much larger population of propertied and unpropertied women and men of all races.

Of course, it is easy to ignore the violence of the process, because the founding constitutions established familiar institutions of peace. The founding documents created courts and legislatures, marked by civilized, dignified rituals putatively dedicated to peace, justice, and even equality. The resort to overtly violent enforcement was rare enough to be elided because the subordinated only rarely resorted to a violent resistance that they knew to be futile. Those who felt their economic marginalization did rise on rare occasions in the early years when the wake of the Revolution could still be felt: the Massachusetts debtors' uprising of 1786 known as Shays's Rebellion, for example; and the anti-tax Whiskey Rebellion of the early 1790s, which was put down by a show of overwhelming federal force. Rebellions of the enslaved were also widely feared, although in fact they occurred very rarely, on a small scale, and were suppressed ruthlessly. Resistance to the subordination of women took the most subtle, domestic form of all, bursting into public space only with the publication of the occasional proto-feminist writings of England's Mary Wollstonecraft or the American Federalist Judith Sargent Murray. And peaceful resistance by the disfranchised was of little effect since, to adapt an old adage, the state had monopolized the use of peace, through the establishment of courts and legislatures. These institutions were specifically designed to substitute peace for violence by monopolizing public authority. They acted in the name of freedom, equality, impartiality, and the public good but on

[9] See, among many others, Michael J. Klarman, *The Framers' Coup: The Making of the United States' Constitution* (2016); Jennifer Nedelsky, *Private Property and the Limits of American Constitutionalism: The Madisonian Framework and Its Legacy* (1990); Rosemarie Zagarri, *Revolutionary Backlash: Women and Politics in the Early American Republic* (2007); Gregory Ablavsky, 'The Savage Constitution' (2014) 63 *Duke L.J.* 999 ff.

[10] Pauline Maier, *Ratification: The People Debate the Constitution, 1787–1788* (2010) 134, 140, 327 ff.

behalf of the propertied white males who manned them and who had founded the state in the first place.

Even the appellate courts never operated as heroic defenders of equal rights, champions of universal liberty and equality against the partial interests of propertied white men. The courts were, after all, constructed and manned by that very group. And these legal institutions par excellence depended always on the support of other key institutions which were controlled, by definition, by the politically powerful. The history of the first decades under the Constitution reveals that the Supreme Court in particular learned quickly that its power depended on the approval of others: the majority of the enfranchised, legislatures, executive agencies, and political parties at both state and federal levels. Courts wielded power, but only as long as they adequately integrated themselves into the political dynamics and trajectories of other important institutions.

Thus, *Marbury v. Madison* (1803)[11] famously demonstrated the Supreme Court's dependence on the political branches, as well as the Court's own recognition of that dependence.[12] In *Marbury* and again in *Fletcher v. Peck*,[13] decided in 1810, Chief Justice John Marshall and the Supreme Court claimed a role for the Court as supreme interpreter of the Constitution, yet yielded to the de facto control of the political branches. In the case of *Marbury*, the Court both struck down a federal statute for unconstitutionality—vindicating its claim to supremacy in constitutional interpretation—and lectured President Jefferson on his obligation to recognize Mr. Marbury's legal right to the office of Justice of the Peace in the District of Columbia. The President and Congress had no objection to Marshall's striking down the federal statute, so they let that ruling stand, vindicating the judicial power of constitutional review. But Jefferson objected strongly to Marbury's claim to a judicial appointment left incomplete by the prior President, so he ignored that part of the opinion with impunity. Thus, the *Marbury* case cemented the Court's public image as defender of the law, but also demonstrated that that legal authority would extend only as far as the electorate and its representatives would permit.

In the case of *Fletcher*, the Marshall Court insisted that the common law of contracts as understood by the Court must control the question of title to tens of millions of acres of Georgia's hinterland; neither the people of Georgia nor Congress could question that judicial understanding, according to the Court. In fact, however, Georgia insisted on its own power to determine rights to that land, and Congress ultimately produced a compromise settlement. Congress's disposition of the Georgia land claims never accepted the *Fletcher* claimants' title nor depended

---

[11]   *Marbury v. Madison* (1803) 5 U.S. 137.

[12]   A classic analysis of *Marbury* along these lines appears within a larger account of the Supreme Court's embeddedness in American social and political development in Robert G. McCloskey, *The American Supreme Court* (1960). (McCloskey's classic is now periodically updated by Sanford Levinson with attention to constitutional developments since McCloskey's premature death in 1969.)

[13]   *Fletcher v. Peck* (1810) 10 U.S. 87.

on the *Fletcher* decision in any way.[14] Congress had no need to openly flout the Court's specific holding in *Fletcher*, but it freely went about its business in silent disregard of Marshall's claims.

The enduring lesson, again, was that the Court could only exercise such authority as the electorate and other public institutions would allow it. In both cases, the President and Congress were able to marginalize the Court's authority, ceding to it the nominal authority to control legal questions under the Constitution but in fact denying it control over public policy. In short, all involved recognized that constitutional questions could not be reliably reduced to matters of impartial judicial logic but would be determined by the will of electoral majorities and well-placed custodians of institutions like the presidency and Congress, as well as state governments and emergent political parties—all of which were expressions of the propertied white males who made the Constitution in the first place.[15]

Marshall knew this well but also recognized the value in clothing as many issues as possible in legal garb to forestall a return to the violence of the Revolution and the smaller rebellions still in recent memory. The dominance of propertied white men would not be questioned, but it would be obscured and facilitated by its decoration in the language of the law. Marshall made the lesson explicit in the great Indian cases late in his time on the Court, beginning with *Johnson v. M'Intosh*[16] (1823) and extending through the *Cherokee Cases* of the early 1830s.[17] The context of those cases was a past and a future of violent conflict among the Indian nations, the national government, the state governments, and westward-moving white settlers. The Constitution and the Washington Administration had ostensibly looked to a future of Indian relations governed by law rather than violence. The Constitution gave the federal government exclusive authority over commerce with the Indians, and the Administration advertised its determination to deal with the Indians on the basis of fair dealing through negotiated treaties and land sales. But the steady migration of white settlers westward since the seventeenth century and continuing through the nineteenth had always been marked by violence as much as by law. And the state and federal governments themselves often threatened violence as they relentlessly pressed the Indian nations for cessions and concessions.

In *Johnson*, Marshall reluctantly legitimated all of this violence by an inherited 'right of discovery'. That doctrine of law, according to Marshall, had granted to the British discoverers of the eastern seaboard ultimate title over all the land to the

---

[14] See C. Peter Magrath, *Yazoo: Law and Politics in the New Republic: The Case of Fletcher v. Peck* (1967); Gerald Leonard, 'Fletcher v. Peck and Constitutional Development in the Early United States' (2014) 47 *U. C. Davis L.R.* 1843 ff.

[15] See Gerald Leonard and Saul Cornell, *The Partisan Republic: Democracy, Exclusion, and the Fall of the Founders' Constitution, 1780s–1830s* (forthcoming).

[16] *Johnson v. M'Intosh* (1823) 21 U.S. 543.

[17] *Cherokee Nation v. Georgia* (1831) 30 U.S. 1; *Worcester v. Georgia* (1832) 31 U.S. 515.

interior of that seacoast. At the same time, though, the doctrine had somehow left the Indians legally entitled to exclusive habitation of the land until such time as they chose to sell that right to the British (and then to the United States after the Revolution). This odd, pragmatic line between the discoverers' 'title' to the land and the inhabitants' continuing 'right' of habitation illustrated the utter arbitrariness of the doctrine. Still, Marshall seized on it as a way of preserving some legal rooting for the Indian nations' land claims.

Marshall fully recognized the absurdity of discovery as a doctrine of law, observing dryly that Britain's 'claim of all the lands to the Pacific Ocean because she had discovered the country washed by the Atlantic, might . . . be deemed extravagant'.[18] He nevertheless deemed it law and even went so far as to explain how such 'law' emerges from violence. He explained how the magic wand of 'discovery' had long since obscured and legalized the violence by which the settlers and the colonial governments had extracted the indigenous peoples' lands: 'However extravagant the pretension, . . . if the principle has been asserted in the first instance, and afterwards sustained; if a country has been acquired and held under it; if the property of the great mass of the community originates in it, it becomes the law of the land and cannot be questioned.'[19]

Marshall thus recognized that such bald assertions of law are the mechanism by which violent seizures of power and resources are converted into founding acts of a durable legal order. That new legal order then obviates, usually, the need for continuing, overt violence and eliminates legal actors' capacity to question the unbalanced doctrines at the root of the legal order. It makes clear to a judge in, say, 1823 that he may adjudicate which group of propertied white men—these speculators in Indian lands over here or those representatives of the federal government over there—can claim property rights in those lands. But that judge cannot go back to first principles and say that the violently subjugated Indians actually have the full legal title to this land by right of some peaceful and impartial principle of law, such as their prior and continuous possession.

Indeed, when Marshall and a majority of the Court attempted a modest vindication of Indian rights in the Cherokee cases, they were unceremoniously swept aside. In *Worcester v. Georgia* (1832),[20] Marshall reaffirmed that the doctrine of discovery had left the Indian nations with a firm right of habitation in their lands, protected by the law until they should freely choose to sell that right to the United States. But the Court's judgment clashed with dominant public opinion, the relevant state governments, the President, and Congress, who asserted not simply their raw power to move the Cherokees out of the way but an interpretation of the Constitution that purported to legitimate removal of the Indians. That interpretation of the Constitution—or, rather the political and military force that it legitimated—won

---

[18] 21 U.S. at 582.   [19] 21 U.S. at 591.   [20] 31 U.S. 515.

the day and gave us the Trail of Tears, the evocative and enduring label for the forced removal of Indians from their lands.[21]

A generation later, in 1857, the *Dred Scott*[22] case too demonstrated the violence of the law both in its founding and in its continuing legitimation of violence by propertied white men. *Scott* denied an enslaved petitioner's claim to freedom, despite his having resided for a time in a free, federal territory. The Court held both that a black person could not be a citizen of the United States and that Congress could not constitutionally prevent white Americans from holding black Americans as property in the western territories. For both these reasons, the Court insisted it had no jurisdiction to hear Scott's claim to freedom and left him to his fate.

Scott is reflexively condemned by modern, American lawyers—and rightly so, but often for the wrong reasons. The majority's opinion is often criticized for being political, going out of its way to protect slavery and resolve a great national controversy rather than just adjudicating a case. But, of course, historical research has demonstrated repeatedly the political ambitions and manoeuvering of the Supreme Court. If the *Scott* majority did something unusual, it was in badly misreading the political space available for its intervention on a question of unusually high stakes. The Court was not able to tip the scales in some decisive way but only intensified the battle between the racist North and the slaveholding South in their competition for control of the western territories. Moreover, historians have demonstrated that the majority opinion comported with the norms of legal craftsmanship as well as one normally expects of Supreme Court opinions. That is, its slavery-embracing racism simply reflected the slavery-embracing racism of the Constitution itself, which had frankly affirmed the rights of slaveholders to their property in black Americans and left to the states the power to regulate such rights. And that racist Constitution continued in 1857 to reflect the slavery-embracing racism of the society that had developed alongside that Constitution. Slavery was legal in virtually all American states at the Founding, remained so in half the states in 1857, and was legitimated by the Constitution itself until the Civil War. Even non-slave states widely consigned blacks to distinctly subordinate civic status, while their white citizens mostly waited until the eve of the Civil War before turning against Southern slavery as such. This racial caste system was sustained through systematic state and private violence. But that violence was wielded in the name of the law, as *Scott* demonstrated.[23]

---

[21] See Tim Alan Garrison, *The Legal Ideology of Removal: The Southern Judiciary and the Sovereignty of Native American Nations* (2002); Jill Norgren, *The Cherokee Cases: Two Landmark Federal Decisions in the Fight for Sovereignty* (2004 [1996]).

[22] *Scott v. Sandford* (1857) 60 U.S. 393.

[23] The classic account of the case is Don Fehrenbacher, *The Dred Scott Case: Its Significance in American Law and Politics* (1978). Modern, revisionist accounts include Mark A. Graber, *Dred Scott and the Problem of Constitutional Evil* (2006); and Gerald Leonard, 'Law and Politics Reconsidered: A New Constitutional History of *Dred Scott*' (2009) 34 *Law and Social Inquiry* 747 ff.

Law has in the American past often legitimated race-based violence in ways we now find hard to credit as genuinely legal. We condemn *Dred Scott* and the political defiance directed at the Marshall Court that ended in the Trail of Tears. Again, we are right to do so, but not because such racist violence is inconsistent with the idea of law. Those actions were legitimated in their times by highly plausible arguments as to the implications of a Constitution written by and for propertied white men, who had gained the right to write that Constitution and make it 'law' by conquering black Americans, Indian nations, and others, who would have written very different constitutions and laws. The Constitution thus was burdened from the start, sometimes in its letter, sometimes in its implications, with the task of sustaining the social distribution of power as it was and as it might gradually evolve.

Before going further, I want to acknowledge that the distribution of power in American society has, of course, evolved over time and that that evolution has been aided importantly at times by law. That is, the Constitution and other sources of law have not simply protected some static and reified class of the powerful, but have at times offered tools to the aggrieved by which gradual shifts of power have been facilitated. In the period I have just been discussing, the move to nearly 'universal' suffrage among white men was facilitated by the possibility of reading the Constitution as a more democratic document than its authors had meant it to be. Later periods would see well-known advances for women and black Americans, sometimes making use of preexisting law to upset established structures of power.

In all these cases, however, meaningful changes in structures of power proceeded initially and mostly from social change and political activism, including a willingness on the part of the aggrieved to physically confront and expose the violence of the state. Such political action has sometimes altered the law, prompting the courts to fall in line. Judicial action then has sometimes added crucial support and facilitation of the change, but mostly continued to reflect dominant structures of power, even as those structures decisively changed.[24] Below, I will discuss briefly an example of how the Civil Rights struggle of the 1960s found some notable victories in constitutional litigation but mostly after forcing change from the outside, changing the law gradually by overcoming overt violence done (often) in the name of the law. So, while I do not want to simply reduce law to the violence authorized by established structures of domination—and there is no shortage elsewhere of plausible, historical narratives of the heroic work of the courts[25]—I do want to insist

[24] A monumental investigation of the ways in which courts function mainly at the margins of important changes in the structures of power, as well as the legalized state violence that activists must overcome to achieve such changes, is Michael J. Klarman, *From Jim Crow to Civil Rights: The Supreme Court and the Struggle for Racial Equality* (2004).

[25] In contrast to his work cited in (n. 24), Klarman himself came to recognize an unusually important and leading role for courts in social change in his account of the politics and litigation of the movement for same-sex marriage. Michael J. Klarman, *From the Closet to the Altar: Courts, Backlash, and the Struggle for Same-Sex Marriage* (2013).

that this sort of conservative, judicial legitimation of violence in defence of the powerful is a major and indisputable function of law, for better and worse.

III. CONSTITUTIONAL RIGHTS AND THE VIOLENCE OF THE CRIMINAL SYSTEM

If American constitutional history suggests that law is always imbued with violence and pre-existing power relations, it may be unsurprising to learn that the law of crime, constitutional and otherwise, represents a durable example of law as violence. Consider the arrestee charged with a third instance of driving on a revoked licence who faces jail without a lawyer, a not uncommon scenario in the American system of prosecution. The threat of being forcibly confined in a cage is not a threat of violence, the system supposes, because the threat is legalized by the statute that authorizes the arrest and jail time, by the police officer who implements the statute, by the judge who ensures fair proceedings for the accused (who has legally waived her right to a lawyer), by the jailer whose unlimited control over the conditions of the arrestee's life is not really totalitarian because the jail is putatively an institution of law.

Of course, innumerable defendants in this position have little sense of law in operation but a distinct sense of the violence to which they are subjected. That sense may be a function of the general principle, memorably argued by Thomas Hobbes, that no one is ever obliged to accept her or his subjection to violence, no matter how legally proper that violence: '[N]o man can transfer or lay down his right to save himself from death, wounds, and imprisonment (the avoiding whereof is the only end of laying down any right) . . . And this is granted to be true by all men, in that they lead criminals to execution, and prison, with armed men, notwithstanding that such criminals have consented to the law, by which they are condemned.'[26] Or the defendant's sensation of violence may be a function of particular conditions that convince some, though not all, that they have been treated unfairly, not in accord with the law at all.

Perhaps, any society of any complexity cannot do without some version of this violence. Perhaps, this violence is rarer, milder, and a better protector of most members of society to the extent that it is carried out in the name and in the frame of law. Still, it remains violence, whether the violence of the law itself or the violence that demonstrates the absence of law.

[26] Thomas Hobbes, *Leviathan* (2009 [1651]) 395 ff. See Alice Ristroph, 'Sovereignty and Subversion' (2015) 101 *Virginia L.R.* 1029–53 ff.

If the infusion of law into such violence marks a civilized society,[27] one should never assume that the law has supplanted violence. History demonstrates the commonsensical point that violence is indispensable to the founding of a legal order and persists as fundamental to its maintenance. Indeed, violence tends to remain in the hands of those dominant groups who triumphed in the violent contest to enshrine a legal order in the first place. If the American Constitution represented, as it did, the triumph of propertied white men and the subjugation in varying ways of women, black Americans, indigenous peoples, and the unpropertied, then it should not be surprising that the 'impartial law' and the 'justice' that it generated has often felt more like violence to those who have been largely excluded from its making. That is not to say that the American system of constitutional law is not really law, nor that its legal character is mere charade; it is to say that the system, founded in violent subjugation, can never fully substitute impartial justice for violence and domination.

Today, the violence that runs through and around American law appears most conspicuously in the criminal system. The system purports to legitimate its practices by pointing to the right of every defendant to a lawyer, assuring the targets of that violence that they will be caged and disciplined only according to the impartial principles of the law. The American Constitution embraced a right to counsel in criminal cases from its (almost) earliest days. But 170 years passed before the Supreme Court of the United States held in *Gideon v. Wainwright* (1963)[28] that the state violence of the criminal law required a state-funded guarantee of defence counsel to legalize that violence. And it took that long because fully enfranchised Americans took that long to recognize the extra-legal violence that characterized important aspects of the criminal system.

The history of the constitutional right to counsel reaffirms the limits of impartial judicial principles in constitutional history more generally. It demonstrates again that the Supreme Court's understanding of the constitutional law that converts American state violence into marks of civilization depends substantially on the support of other courts and institutions (who will choose whether and how to implement the Court's pronouncements), as well as the will of the majority of the enfranchised. Since 1963, those running the criminal system have substantially undermined the promise of *Gideon*. History has thus demonstrated the ways in which the constitutional right to counsel promulgated by the courts has done less to control that violence than to obscure and legitimate it for the comfortable folks who are least vulnerable to it. Today, for better or worse, a large proportion of the criminally accused still faces the violence of the system without meaningful

---

[27] See Gerald Leonard, 'Civilizing Darwin: Holmes on Criminal Law', in Markus Dubber and Lindsay Farmer (eds.), *Modern Histories of Crime and Punishment* (2007).

[28] *Gideon v. Wainwright* (1963) 372 U.S. 335.

counsel, or with no counsel at all, a fact that has taken half a century to begin showing up in public consciousness.

It is unclear what the right to counsel looked like in practice for most of the nineteenth century, but it seems unlikely that the indigent accused had meaningful representation except in very serious cases.[29] A campaign to establish a state-funded infrastructure of public defence began only in the 1890s. About the same time, a few courts began to suggest that ineffective assistance of counsel might be grounds for revisiting a prisoner's conviction. Clara Foltz, a pioneering female lawyer whose arbitrary exclusion from prestigious law practice forced her to rely partly on low-level criminal cases for her living, launched the idea of publicly funded criminal defence in a speech at the Congress of Jurisprudence and Law Reform (at the Chicago World's Fair) in 1893. She had seen the worse than useless defence with which most criminal defendants were saddled. In her experience, 'meet "em" and plead "em" defenders' predominated (as they do in many places today), and no defender had to fear that the appellate courts would hold them to any standard of competence. So Foltz argued that the states had an obligation to pay for competent criminal defence for every accused on the same principle by which they were obligated to provide courthouses, judges, juries, and all of the paraphernalia of a criminal system. Gradually, her idea gained adherents, and state-funded public defence organizations were established in Los Angeles in 1913 and, with time, in numerous other cities and states.[30]

Along with the emergence of a handful of public defender offices came a handful of state cases that pioneered the idea that ineffective assistance of counsel could be grounds for reversal of a criminal conviction. But only starting in 1924 did the practice of reversing convictions for ineffective assistance gain some momentum, climaxing in the Supreme Court case of *Powell v. Alabama* in 1932.[31] That case bore headline-worthy marks of grotesque injustice and racism as nine young black men and boys were convicted capitally for rapes of two young white women that probably never happened. Evidently, it took that sort of extreme abuse of the state's monopoly on violence to induce the Court to announce the obvious: that no lay

---

[29] See, e.g., Allen Steinberg, *The Transformation of Criminal Justice: Philadelphia, 1800–1880* (1989). The supposition that defence counsel were rare and inadequate is noted and questioned by Mike McConville and Chester Mirsky, 'The Rise of Guilty Pleas: New York, 1800–1865' (1995) 22 *Journal of Law and Society* 443 ff. That article demonstrates that at least in the early part of the nineteenth century in indicted cases in New York, defendants were routinely represented by what appear to have been good quality lawyers, sometimes assigned by the court and working pro bono whenever necessary. But the article does not suggest that anything like that was true for less serious, non-indicted cases, nor that the practice survived the rapid rise in caseloads and guilty pleas unscathed, nor that any findings regarding New York City would be readily applicable anywhere else.

[30] Barbara Allen Babcock, 'Inventing the Public Defender' (2006) 43 *American Criminal Law Review* 1267 ff; Sara Mayeux, 'Ineffective Assistance of Counsel before *Powell v. Alabama*: Lessons from History for the Future of the Right to Counsel' (2014) 99 *Iowa L.R.* 2161 ff.

[31] *Powell v. Alabama* (1932) 287 U.S. 45. See ibid.

person could be expected to defend her- or himself against a criminal charge without a competent lawyer:

The right to be heard would be, in many cases, of little avail if it did not comprehend the right to be heard by counsel. Even the intelligent and educated layman has small and sometimes no skill in the science of law. If charged with crime, he is incapable, generally, of determining for himself whether the indictment is good or bad. He is unfamiliar with the rules of evidence. Left without the aid of counsel, he may be put on trial without a proper charge, and convicted upon incompetent evidence, or evidence irrelevant to the issue or otherwise inadmissible. He lacks both the skill and knowledge adequately to prepare his defense, even though he have a perfect one. He requires the guiding hand of counsel at every step in the proceedings against him. Without it, though he be not guilty, he faces the danger of conviction because he does not know how to establish his innocence. If that be true of men of intelligence, how much more true is it of the ignorant and illiterate, or those of feeble intellect.[32]

The Court's description of the plight of the lawyerless defendant was logically just as true during the first 140 years of the republic as it was in 1932 and just as applicable to most minor charges as to capital cases. For some reason, however, the Court was ready only in 1932 to acknowledge that truth and demand this basic constitutional guarantee of legality in the daily use of state violence.

Even in *Powell*, however, the Court did not clearly extend the right beyond capital cases, the most unambiguous cases of state violence. Its language finally embraced the idea that no lay person can be expected to navigate the system without competent representation, but it focused only on the extreme case of a capital conviction without counsel, which it declared the equivalent of 'judicial murder'. The facts of *Powell* laid bare the violence of the system as clearly as any case likely could—often a racist violence that reminded all that the law's impartiality primarily served the white, the male, and the resourced at the expense of most others—such that only the right to counsel could supply law to civilize that violence.

By the time of *Gideon v. Wainwright* in 1963, the great majority of states guaranteed counsel statutorily in serious felony cases while all states did so in capital cases. *Gideon* then held that all states must provide counsel to the indigent accused. But it is not clear how often the counsel being provided in these cases, before or after *Gideon*, was really better than no counsel at all. Nor did *Gideon* imply any particular standard for effective assistance or even explain exactly what sorts of cases it applied to (all felonies? misdemeanours, too?), though it was widely taken at least to compel the more reluctant states to pay for counsel in all cases of serious felonies.[33] And the *Argersinger* case of 1972[34] clarified that the *Gideon* right applied even to misdemeanours whenever the sentence included incarceration. Not until 1984, however, did the Court establish in *Strickland*

---

[32]   287 US at 68–9 ff.   [33]   Sara Mayeux, 'What *Gideon* Did' (2016) 116 *Columbia L.R.* 15 ff.
[34]   *Argersinger v. Hamlin* (1972) 407 U.S. 25.

v. Washington[35] a standard for ineffective assistance under the Sixth Amendment guarantee of a right to counsel, giving shape to the smattering of constitutional cases in lower courts that had tried to give life to *Powell, Gideon*, and *Argersinger*.

Still, to this day, claims of ineffective assistance overwhelmingly fail in court,[36] even though we know that the right to counsel remains an empty guarantee for large numbers of criminal defendants, maybe most. The reasons for the de facto denial of counsel are many: counsel may nominally be supplied by the state, but defenders often carry caseloads so unmanageable that the defender has neither the time nor the resources to investigate the facts, do meaningful legal research, or perform any service for the client beyond facilitating a quick guilty plea. A 2009 report of the National Association of Criminal Defense Lawyers assembled evidence of caseloads in a number of major American cities that limited defenders to no more than a couple hours' work on the average misdemeanour, sometimes an average of no more than a few minutes.[37] A careful study of misdemeanour processing in New York City concluded that daunting caseloads were part of the explanation for the emergence of a system of 'managerial justice', unconcerned with adjudicating guilt and innocence but only with processing defendants according to the number and types of 'marks' that any particular defendant had accumulated at the hands of the police.[38] Meanwhile, many jurisdictions provide public defence through contracts awarded sometimes to a single private attorney, who is paid a flat fee to handle all cases for a full year, thus creating strong incentives to maximize cost-saving rather than committed defence. Resource constraints have been sufficiently severe that the Chief Justice of the South Carolina Supreme Court openly flouted the United States Supreme Court's recent holding that the right to counsel applies even to suspended sentences (those involving no jail time unless the convicted person violates probation). Speaking to a state bar meeting, she announced openly that 'I have simply told my magistrates that we just don't have the resources' to 'adher[e] to *Alabama v. Shelton* in every situation.'[39] Courtroom observers have reported widespread, routine pressure by judges and prosecutors on defendants to waive representation in order to get charges disposed of quickly.[40] Such pressure is especially intense when the prosecutor has requested and the judge has imposed unaffordable bail, leaving the accused incarcerated indefinitely. The right to counsel is further undermined by policies of charging the indigent defendant an application fee to get a defender; by delaying the appointment of defence lawyers to incarcerated,

---

[35] *Strickland v. Washington* (1984) 466 U.S. 668.

[36] Joseph L. Hoffmann and Nancy J. King, 'Rethinking the Federal Role in State Criminal Justice' (2009) 84 *N.Y.U. L.R.* 791, 806–10 ff.

[37] Robert C. Boruchowitz, et al., *Minor Crimes, Massive Waste: The Terrible Toll of America's Broken Misdemeanor Courts* (2009) 21–2 ff.

[38] Issa Kohler-Hausmann, 'Managerial Justice and Mass Misdemeanors' (2014) 66 *Stanford L.R.* 611 ff.

[39] Quoted in Boruchowitz (n. 37) 15 ff.   [40] Boruchowitz (n. 37) 14–17 ff.

indigent defendants for weeks or months; by policies that nearly everywhere deny the indigent any right to choose their own lawyer; and by institutional realities that cause defenders often to be more loyal to the judges and prosecutors with whom they work every day than to clients who pass through for a few minutes.[41] All of these inadequacies of the right to counsel arguably render the criminal system not just violent but arbitrary in its violence.

But state violence happens even more overtly, of course, on the street, in the procedurally prior actions of the police. Thus, parallel to these developments in right to counsel—recognizing rights in court but failing to alter the realities of constitutional law in practice—the Supreme Court has nominally recognized, legalized, and disciplined the discretionary violence of the police on patrol. Yet, these cases, too, have used the Constitution more to legitimate police violence than to discipline it.

Risa Goluboff tells the story of the nominally successful campaign, climaxing in the 1960s and 1970s, to strike down widespread vagrancy statutes.[42] These state and local statutes gave the police authority to arrest and imprison anyone who could be portrayed as living on the margins of society. They were variously worded but tended to criminalize, in the words of the most famous of these statutes, the mere status of 'rogue', 'common drunkard', or 'habitual loafer', among many other options.[43] Incredibly, these statutes often did not require proof of any conduct whatsoever but only proof of one's status as a vagrant, a never well-defined condition that seemed to roll together judgments about one's capacity to support oneself, one's moral habits, and one's history of arrests (not even necessarily convictions). Once saddled with this status, the police might arrest you any time for any reason, and the courts might imprison you for days or even months at a time.

Only gradually did the Court come around to holding in the 1972 *Papachristou* decision[44] that such extraordinary discretion in the police use of violence was inconsistent with the Constitution. Indeed, the cases leading up to *Papachristou* mostly demonstrate not the Court's supreme control of the Constitution's meaning, but its timid acceptance of the established practices of other branches. Across the 1960s, one batch of civil rights protesters after another sought federal judicial relief from vagrancy prosecutions employed by Southern law enforcement to maintain local, racial discipline. The Supreme Court repeatedly found case-specific excuses for granting relief to the protesters while declining to address the constitutionality

---

[41] In addition to Boruchowitz (n. 37) and Kohler-Hausmann (n. 38), see Amy Bach, *Ordinary Injustice: How America Holds Court* (2009).

[42] Risa Goluboff, *Vagrant Nation: Police Power, Constitutional Change, and the Making of the 1960s* (2016).

[43] See the Jacksonville, Florida ordinance quoted in *Papachristou v. City of Jacksonville* (1972) 405 U.S. 156, 156.

[44] *Papachristou v. City of Jacksonville* (1972) 405 U.S. 156.

of the statutes themselves or their use generally against civil rights activists to defend racial segregation and subordination.

The Court only grew bold in confronting vagrancy statutes, and the police violence that they enabled after it had found a way to ratify similar police violence by other means. In *Terry v. Ohio* (1968),[45] the Court affirmed the authority of the police to detain anyone on the street and pat them down for weapons. *Terry* required of the police only that they be able to articulate some 'reasonable suspicion', after the fact, that criminality was afoot, a rule easily used to cover detentions driven by race, politics, or what have you.

Only after *Terry* had anchored discretionary police violence firmly in the Constitution did the Court decide the short sequence of cases that culminated in *Papachristou*. These cases purported to rein in the broad discretion of the police to restrain and confine people. The Court's own ad hoc civil rights rulings had revealed how readily such discretionary police violence could be abused, how easily it could be turned to the suppression of dissent and the imposition of arbitrary—often racist—lines of power and subordination. And so the Court ringingly rejected the vagrancy law for 'the unfettered discretion it places in the hands of the . . . police',[46] taking particular pains to indicate its concern that the police in that case had acted out of racist motives.

But the *Papachristou* Court never even mentioned *Terry*, even though that case was evidently a precondition for the Court's willingness to promulgate *Papachristou*. The result has been that stop-and-frisk policies have persisted to this day with recently well-documented evidence of arbitrariness and racism.[47] In fact, the police in New York City not only relied on *Terry* to authorize their large-scale program of discretionary street stops across the early 2000s (at least); their confidence in their authority to rule the streets also saw them freely deploying a municipal loitering law for decades after the courts had struck down that very law. They continued to justify thousands of arrests on the basis of that 'law' until finally confronting a successful federal lawsuit that concluded in 2012.[48] Today, thanks to a class action lawsuit and a settlement,[49] the New York City police stop and frisk far fewer New Yorkers than they did just a few years ago. However, all indications are that they still use this authorized violence disproportionately against black and Hispanic men,[50] despite the federal court's detailed findings of unjustified, race-based street stops.

[45] *Terry v. Ohio* (1968) 392 U.S. 1.

[46] *Papachristou v. City of Jacksonville* (1972) 405 U.S. 156, 168.

[47] See *Floyd v. City of New York* (2103) 959 F.Supp.2d 540 (S.D.N.Y.).

[48] William Glaberson, 'Long Fight Ends Over Arrests for Loitering' *New York Times*, 7 February 2012.

[49] *Floyd v. City of New York* (2103) 959 F.Supp.2d 540 (S.D.N.Y.).

[50] 'Street Stops by New York City Police Have Plummeted', <https://www.nytimes.com/2017/05/30/nyregion/nypd-stop-and-frisk.html> (accessed 7 March 2018).

IV. CONCLUSIONS

Law is partial, then, and it is violent. It represents such complete domination by certain interests and certain structures of power as to make its violence often unnecessary and indeed virtually invisible to those who generally benefit from its use against others. In the criminal context, then, one has to ask whether the Constitution has ensured the civilizing of the violent practice of criminal justice— or if, instead, the Constitution (and the law more generally) have functioned mainly to legitimate the use of discretionary violence against whoever the police and prosecutors deem 'criminals'.

Gideon and *Papachristou* are celebrated landmarks of the Constitution's guarantee that state power will be exercised rationally and impartially in one of the areas that it is exercised most violently. If those cases have failed to impart to state violence the reliable rationality and impartiality that ostensibly make it not violent at all, is that because the courts and the lawyers and the politicians just have not worked hard enough? Or does the history of the Constitution suggest that that failure is all but inherent in law? If law is founded in the violent vanquishing of one group by another, then perhaps law is nothing more than the conversion of the new ascendancy into one that can dominate without routine recourse to violence.[51] So Chief Justice Marshall himself seemed to argue in *Johnson v. M'Intosh*.

What is the future of the right to counsel, of police discretion on the streets, and of other features of the criminal system in which announced constitutional principles seem in deep tension with the routine practice of law's violence? (See, for another example, the common incarceration of poor persons solely because of their inability to make bail or pay costs of the system.) Will class action lawsuits on behalf of the incarcerated poor or refusals by public defenders to accept excessive caseloads find vindication in the Constitution? Or, as history suggests, will the Constitution take its meaning less from intermittently high-minded courts and more from the majority of the electorate (safely on the outside of the criminal system), from legislators seeking re-election, from criminal court judges seeking to dispose of their caseloads, from prosecutors seeking to maintain high conviction rates, from police officers trying to prevent crime, limit disorder, and meet job-performance targets—few of them seeing the violence in what the Constitution authorizes them to do?

The constitutional law of right to counsel is not mostly *Gideon*, *Strickland*, and the rest of the Court's Sixth Amendment cases, as those cases' effects are commonly imagined. Rather, the right to counsel amounts to its real implementation in the institutions of the criminal system, where the right is often openly evaded or honoured with lip service. Similarly, the constitutional law regarding vague criminal

---

[51] Again, for a much fuller discussion of these sorts of questions, see Tomlins (n. 5) *Freedom Bound*, as well as Cover (n. 3) 'Violence and the Word'.

statutes and the right to be free of unreasonable police searches and seizures is not the world of carefully disciplined police discretion. It is the real practice of often-arbitrary detention and arrest. And the constitutional law of equal protection is not the right to equal justice for rich and poor but the reality that the poor will be incarcerated both before and after trial at much higher rates than the resourced, although both have done (or not done!) the very same conduct.

What then is the future of constitutional law in these areas? Can constitutional law civilize the violence that the criminal law visits on the marginalized, the constitutional heirs of those vanquished by the Founding Fathers? Or is law only for those who wield the violence, occasionally providing tools by which a few of the victims exchange places with the victimizers, thus forestalling the next revolution? History does not offer much hope for an escape from violence, but it does offer an awareness of the violence of the law, for better and worse.

Bibliography

Robert M. Cover, 'Violence and the Word' (1986) 95 *Yale L.J.* 1601

Risa Goluboff, *Vagrant Nation: Police Power, Constitutional Change, and the Making of the 1960s* (Oxford University Press, 2016)

Robert W. Gordon, 'Critical Legal Histories' (1984) 36 *Stanford L.R.* 57

Mark A. Graber, *Dred Scott and the Problem of Constitutional Evil* (Cambridge University Press, 2006)

Jeremy K. Kessler, 'The Political Economy of "Constitutional Political Economy"' (2016) 94 *Texas L.R.* 1527

Michael J. Klarman, *From Jim Crow to Civil Rights: The Supreme Court and the Struggle for Racial Equality* (Oxford University Press, 2004)

Michael J. Klarman, *The Framers' Coup: The Making of the United States' Constitution* (Oxford University Press, 2016)

Issa Kohler-Hausmann, 'Managerial Justice and Mass Misdemeanors' (2014) 66 *Stanford L.R.* 611

Gerald Leonard, 'Party as a "Political Safeguard of Federalism": Martin Van Buren and the Constitutional Theory of Party Politics' 54 *Rutgers Law Review* 221 (2001)

Gerald Leonard, Saul Cornell, *The Partisan Republic: Democracy, Exclusion, and the Fall of the Founders' Constitution, 1780s–1830s* (forthcoming, Cambridge University Press).

Sara Mayeux, 'Ineffective Assistance of Counsel before *Powell v. Alabama*: Lessons from History for the Future of the Right to Counsel' (2014) 99 *Iowa L.R.* 2161

Robert G. McCloskey, *The American Supreme Court* (University of Chicago Press, 1960)

Jennifer Nedelsky, *Private Property and the Limits of American Constitutionalism: The Madisonian Framework and Its Legacy* (University of Chicago Press, 1990)

Christopher Tomlins, *Freedom Bound: Law, Labor, and Civic Identity in Colonizing English America, 1580–1865* (Cambridge University Press, 2010)

Keith E. Whittington, *Political Foundations of Judicial Supremacy: The Presidency, the Supreme Court, and Constitutional Leadership in U.S. History* (Princeton University Press, 2007)

CHAPTER 48

....

DOING THINGS WITH LEGAL HISTORY

HISTORICAL ANALYSIS IN PROPERTY LAW

....

ALFRED L. BROPHY*

I. INTRODUCTION

....

PROPERTY law is almost necessarily among the areas of law most concerned with history. For title to property turns on the history of who had title before the current claimants and on what the current claimants did to acquire title. But this is not just a question of individual owners' claims. The legal history of property also addresses larger questions, such as what a nation has done to achieve sovereignty over property. On those big picture questions of sovereignty, contemporary jurisprudence is mostly concerned with history as an explanation of why the law is the way it is. That is, history is a tool for understanding the evolution of law. However, throughout a lot of the United States' legal history, historical analysis also justified sovereignty over land and ownership of human beings, for judges and lawyers frequently turned to historical analysis to justify the property rights as they

* University of Alabama School of Law.

were. That is, while contemporary jurisprudence frequently uses history as a mode of critique, often history has been used to justify and support the distribution of property as it is.

This dual nature of the role of historical analysis in property law—as an explanation of how we get to where we are and as a justification for the (perhaps unjust) distribution of property—appears in two of Chief Justice John Marshall's property opinions. His 1823 opinion in *Johnson v. M'Intosh* involves Native American sovereignty, and his 1825 opinion in *The Antelope* involves the international slave trade. Both cases address big-picture questions of why a nation might be able to assert a claim to property (in one case over land taken from Natives and in another to human beings). Those opinions also address why a particular claimant has a right to property in a piece of land or a human. In both cases the answer turns on the Court's recitation of history over centuries: how nations have agreed to a particular property regime and how rights have grown up around those agreements. There is a sense borne of economics and of history that rules long followed must continue to be followed. Property's history tells us about who owns and controls land and humans. We can also turn to it to understand what has happened. Legal history, then, is both a tool and a guide. History provides arguments about what *should* be done and a way of understanding what *has* been done.

The reason that 'historical analysis in property' helps us 'do' things with legal history is because history is used, at various times in American legal history, to justify the way property is already distributed. At other times, history is used to undermine that distribution of wealth. For particularly from the early twentieth century onwards, the history of property rights has sometimes been used to show the inequality of the current distribution and to justify another distribution, or at least to suggest that a different distribution is desirable. Thus, history is a tool that yields different results depending on who is wielding it.

II. HISTORY'S USE IN JUSTIFYING PROPERTY RIGHTS: NATIVE AMERICANS AND SLAVERY

In the nineteenth century, as judges began writing expansive opinions that surveyed broadly the justifications of their outcomes, they frequently turned to history to elaborate a particular property rule: what does it tell us about sovereignty and about individuals' titles to land? Here, cases like *Johnson v. M'Intosh* and a handful of state cases related to it are useful in explaining how nineteenth-century Americans saw sovereignty over property.[1] The issue at the centre of *Johnson* was a dispute between two groups of claimants—both were groups of whites people. By the time this case reached the U.S. Supreme Court, there were no Native Americans involved, but the case dealt with whether a Native American tribe could convey title to land they inhabited—or whether their title had been extinguished by conquest. A Native American tribe had sold property in what is now Indiana to white settlers before the American Revolution. The successors to those purchasers claimed they had a superior title to those who claimed they had acquired title from a later grant by the United States government. Marshall, thus, had a dispute between those who supported the rights of Natives to control and sell their property and those who thought that the Natives had no such rights and that only the federal government had those rights.

Marshall framed the issue in *Johnson* as whether the Natives had sovereignty over the land. He looked to a lot of different factors to conclude that they did not. Marshall looked to history to help settle the question. He found that the settled usages of European nations for generations regarding sovereignty over land was that those nations that first 'discovered' the land had a right to perfect their rights to the property by either conquest of the natives or by purchasing from them. Thus, once conquered, the native tribes could not convey their land, and in this case those claiming from the pre-Revolutionary grant from the Natives had to lose. But Marshall also confirmed this result by looking at the Native Americans' agricultural practices. Where Europeans farmed, Natives made less productive use of the land—they were hunters, largely. Thus Marshall joined a history of property law with his understanding of Native Americans' use of the land to justify taking the land away from them. This is a form of what one might call 'applied legal history.' It was a historical argument grounded in a vision of white supremacy and power that justified taking away rights from natives to control their land.

Some state cases followed *Johnson v. M'Intosh* in dealing with questions of Native American sovereignty. Those cases did not always involve issues of property rights, but they involved at least issues of sovereignty over land.[2] Those cases reveal that sovereignty turned on long-term usage of land, on agricultural uses, and on expectations of the market. This is drawn from Blackstone's arguments about the claims of countries to land that they use.[3]

The ideas about the origins of property rights, their grounding in long-term practices, and their centrality to economic development appeared in cases involving

---

[1] *Johnson v. M'Intosh*, 21 U.S. (8 Wheat.) 543 (1823).

[2] *State v. Forman*, 16 Tenn. (8 Yearg.) 256 (1835); *Georgia v. Corn Tassels*, 1 Dud. 229 (Ga. 1830); *Caldwell v. Alabama* 2 Stew. & P. 327 (Ala. 1831).

[3] William Blackstone, *Commentaries on the Laws of England*, vol. 2 (1765) *6.

humans as well. Two years after *Johnson v. M'Intosh*, Marshall decided another case using similar reasoning. This time, in *The Antelope*, the case involved the international slave trade.[4] Though the United States had outlawed the importation of slaves, in this case Marshall was dealing with the rights of Spanish claimants to humans who had been taken off a Spanish ship by people variously described as pirates and privateers and then brought to the Florida coast, where *The Antelope* was preparing to land them and sell them. If the slaves had been owned by US citizens, they would have been freed because United States citizens were not permitted to engage in the international slave trade. But Spain had not yet outlawed the trade, so there was a question about the rights of Spanish citizens to slaves taken from their ships.

As with *Johnson*, Marshall looked to the history of the law of slavery to understand the rule to apply. As with *Johnson*, the common usages of European nations for generations were the basis for Marshall's decision. They had all agreed that nothing would be outlawed by international law until all nations agreed.[5] This playing to the lowest common denominator had been the practice of European nations for generations; again, history and long-established patterns of usage dictated the boundaries of property law. While he criticized slavery in the opinion and stated that it was inconsistent with the law of nature[6]—a proposition other southern jurists disputed in the coming decades—Marshall believed that property rights in humans had been established law and had been accepted for generations.[7] 'Slavery, then', he wrote, 'has its origin in force; but as the world has agreed that it is a legitimate result of force, the state of things which is thus produced by general consent cannot be pronounced unlawful.'[8] In the end, Marshall concluded that the slaves taken from Spanish ships had to be returned, though in a move that was perhaps subtly anti-slavery, Marshall demanded that the Spanish claimants be able to identify the people who were taken from their ships before they could claim them as slaves.[9]

The use of history to justify property rights in humans appeared frequently in pro-slavery arguments. In fact, some of the most comprehensive theorizing about the relationship between history, society, and property occurred in the context of debates over slavery. For this, let us turn first to the debates that took place in the wake of the Nat Turner rebellion of August 1831 in Southampton County, Virginia. In the spring of 1831 the Virginia legislature took up debate around a petition filed by Quakers in Virginia's Charles City County, where more than half of the population was enslaved, that asked the legislature to do something to end slavery in

---

[4] *The Antelope*, 23 U.S. (10 Wheat.) 66 (1825).   [5] Ibid., 122.   [6] Ibid., 120.

[7] Ibid., 115. (Slave trade had 'all the sanction which could be derived from long usage and general acquiescence').

[8] Ibid., 121. '[A] jurist must search for its legal solution in those principles of action which are sanctioned by the usages, the national acts, and the general assent of that portion of the world of which he considers himself as a part and to whose law the appeal is made.' Ibid.

[9] Ibid., 128–9.

the commonwealth.[10] What followed was a wide range of ideas about the utility of slavery and property in Virginia society.

Much of the anti-slavery arguments in the debates were about grand Enlightenment theories of universal freedom, as well as the dangers that enslaved people posed to white Virginians. The rebellion, after all, reminded everyone of the possibility of widespread violence. The pro-slavery side utilized a series of related arguments, including the economic necessity of slave labour, the difficulty of removing freed people from the state (there was no sense that the enslaved would be freed and allowed to remain in Virginia), and also what one member of the Virginia House of Delegates called 'sacred' rights of property.[11] As the delegates explained that latter point they articulated a detailed picture of how they saw property's role in history and its centrality to human society.

One of the most zealous defenders of property rights in the Virginia debates was James Gholson, who represented a county where sixty percent of the population was enslaved. He argued that if slavery were terminated 'the bands which bind society together would at once dissolve—the relations of husband and wife, parent and child, master and apprentice, and even our present deliberations would be "most strange and unnatural" '.[12] Gholson, property owners' rights were indispensable to the continuation of society. Gholson believed that property rights were a key foundation of society and that such rights were more fundamental even than the Constitution. 'This sacred principle of meum and tuem does not derive its sanctions from conventional charters—it has its foundations laid deep in principles of justice—it is the very ligament which binds society together . . . . Without this principle, there is no civilization—no government.'[13] The legislature threatened the sacred and long-standing rights of property on the basis of claims of necessity. Gholson found such justifications hollow:

Gentlemen, in the heat of their own intemperance, and by the aid of their own disturbed and distempered fancies, raise spirits and spectres at pleasure—gaze at them with horror, and then set about to show their skill in exorcism. These spirits and spectres they call 'necessity', 'self-preservation', 'public safety'. The exorcism is the simple process of taking eighty or one-hundred millions of private property for public use, without compensation.[14]

Another delegate who spoke about the importance of property rights was Thomas Marshall, the son of Chief Justice John Marshall, author of the *Johnson v. M'Intosh* and *Antelope* opinions discussed earlier in this chapter. Thomas Marshall thought that property in humans could not be taken away unless the owners were paid compensation. 'Whenever the tranquility and security of society shall imperiously

---

[10] See Eva Sheppard Wolf, *Race and Liberty in the New Nation: Emancipation in Virginia from Revolution to Nat Turner's Rebellion* (2006) 231–3.

[11] 'House of Delegates', *Richmond Enquirer* 24 January 1832 at 2.

[12] 'House of Delegates', *Richmond Enquirer* 21 January 1832 at 2.   [13] Ibid.

[14] 'House of Delegates', *Richmond Enquirer*, 24 January 1832 at 2.

demand this sacrifice, the rights of property must yield to the preservation of happiness and life; but still it is a sacrifice, and one for which compensation should be made', Marshall said.[15] The defence of property was placed, then, on its importance to American society and on Constitutional principles. All of this was based on the delegates' understanding of history.

A young history professor at the College of William and Mary, Thomas R. Dew, explored these ideas about property's importance in some depth after the legislative debate was over. He wrote a short treatise, *Review of the Debates in the Virginia Legislature*, which summarized and critiqued the debate. He focused on the role of property in civilizing human society. The anti-slavery legislators, Dew charged, were of a 'wild and intemperate nature'.[16] Their arguments were 'based on false principles . . . subversive of the rights of property and the order and tranquility of society, portending to the whole slave-holding community . . . inevitable and ruinous consequences'.[17] Dew turned to the 'most dangerous of all the wild doctrines advanced by abolitionists in the Virginia legislature': '*that property is the creature of civil society, and is subject to its action even to destruction*'.[18] By singling out the attack on property as the 'most dangerous' of the anti-slavery arguments, Dew connected property ownership to the pro-slavery argument.

Dew was responding to anti-slavery legislators who argued that slavery was not constitutionally protected private property, that the state could regulate or even abolish property rights in slaves. One delegate from western Virginia provided a forceful statement of the power of the state to abolish slavery without paying compensation, based on the harm that slave property caused:

when [property] loses its utility, when it no longer contributes to the personal benefits and wants of its holders in any equal degree with the expense or risk or the danger of keeping it, much more when it jeopardizes the security of the public;—when this is the case, then the original purpose for which it is authorized is lost, its character of property in the just and beneficial sense of it is gone, and it may be regulated without private injustice, in any manner which the general good of the community, by whose laws it was licensed, may require.[19]

That argument was a restatement of the common law doctrine that the state may regulate dangerous property.[20] Thus the debates aired arguments that supported broad protection for private property, as well as broad limitation of it. This reflects the dispute about the nature of the state's power to regulate property and the desirability of doing so.

---

[15] Ibid., 14 February 1832 at 4.

[16] Thomas Dew, *Review of the Debate in the Virginia Legislature of 1831 and 1832* (1832) 8.

[17] Ibid.   [18] Ibid., 64.

[19] Ibid., 65 (citing 'McDowell's Speech', *Richmond Whig*, 24 March 1832).

[20] See William Novak, *The People's Welfare: Law and Regulation in Nineteenth Century America* (1996).

Dew's vision of political theory did not treat property so lightly. Such anti-slavery doctrine, Dew thought, 'so far from being true in its application, is not true in theory'.[21] Like Representative Gholson, Dew thought property was the foundation of government and the object of government is the protection of property. '[F]rom the days of the patriarchs down to the present time', Dew wrote, 'the great desideratum has been to find out the most efficient mode of protecting property'.[22] Contemporary history supported Dew's argument, too. 'There is not a government at this moment in Christendom, whose peculiar practical character is not the result of the state of property'.[23] In Dew's view, it was property that preceded and created government, not the other way around.

Later in his career, Dew put together a series of lectures for his students, which were published posthumously in 1852 under the grand title, *A Digest of the Laws, Customs, Manners, and Institutions of the Ancient and Modern Nations*. That book was essentially a legal history of Western civilization. Dew assigned pride of place in the progress of civilization to the institution of property. Dew told a story of the growth of liberty from the feudal system. One leading cause in the changing conception of liberty was the centrality of property ownership to the feudal system. The feudal lord had the same 'sentiment of *personality*, of individual liberty, which the barbarian had in the forest'.[24] Moreover, as the 'chief of the family and master of those who surround him', he felt an 'immense superiority'.[25] The feudal lord had 'no equal around him, with no superior above him'. The Lord's 'will was law—he was restrained by no external power—he was the center and the soul of the baronial government—in fine, [the] feudal lord must have been the *proudest being on earth*'.[26] Dew reviewed his argument: 'all disputes turned on questions about landed property. The lord lived in his castle and defended his property till it seemed part of himself—it is this sacredness of property—this notion of *meum and tuum* caused by the feudal system, that lies at the bottom of those obstinate struggles made by the English barons against usurpation of kings'.[27] The feudal system gave a sacredness to property, as demonstrated by the feudal law books that marked out in precise detail 'the reciprocity of obligations between lord and vassal, . . . and the administration of justice by one's peers'.[28]

From the relation between lord and vassal came sentiments of loyalty, which were analogous to patriotism in modern republics—and, one suspects, to the harmonious sentiments that Dew believed existed on slave plantations. Dew's meta-history, taken from Englishman Henry Hallam's *History of the Middle Ages*, credits feudalism with the rise of liberty.

---

[21] Ibid., 66.   [22] Ibid.   [23] Ibid.
[24] Thomas R. Dew, *The Laws, Customs, Manners, and Institutions of the Ancient and Modern Nations* (1852) 331.
[25] Ibid.   [26] Ibid.   [27] Ibid.   [28] Ibid., 340.

In England freedom arose from the conjunction between the people and the feudal lords against the king, which led to the House of Commons.[29] Soon after 1066, the lords and king had been united against the natives—much as the whites in the South were united against the slaves—but as the fear of revolution subsided, divisions emerged between king and lords. Parliament was the result of the king's need for money. 'Some of the best laws of England, [even] *Magna Charta* itself . . . were *literally purchased with money.*'[30] Parliament's development showed the problem that perplexed Rome—how to balance patricians and plebeians, property, and numbers.[31] In one of his most eloquent paragraphs, Dew described the balance that property helped achieve in English freedom:

He who examines the British constitution will see a beautiful exemplification of the virtue of perseverance and the necessity of continued, unwearied vigilance in the defence of liberty—the struggle against the royal prerogative was like that of the waterman against a rapid stream—the slightest relaxation of exertion and the fruit of years of labor would be swept away—under weak princes the principal acquisitions were made—under the able ones liberty would be regulated and restrained.[32]

'From this beginning, so unpropitious to liberty, the fabric of English freedom rose, step by step, through toil and sacrifice, each generation adding something to the security of the work, until the whole fabric was completed.'[33] The story in Dew's mind and that of many other pre-Civil War thinkers was that property was central to civilization and that it was a key driver of further civilization and freedom.

Several decades after Dew's *Review of the Debates* appeared, a young lawyer in Georgia, Thomas R. R. Cobb, published *An Inquiry into the Law of Negro Slavery*, the most comprehensive pro-slavery legal treatise ever written. Like Dew, Cobb was deeply interested in history. Cobb drew on historical examples from ancient Egypt through the Revolution in Haiti and the emancipation in the West Indies—which had not even been completed when Dew was writing—to suggest that African slavery was consistent with natural law and that any attempts at emancipation would lead to disastrous economic and demographic results. That is, Cobb drew deeply upon historical examples to make the case for property rights in humans. For Cobb maintained that history, stretching back across thousands of years, demonstrated that Africans were enslaved, that slavery was their natural state, and that there could be no successful emancipation.[34]

As an adjunct of the pro-slavery thought based on history, pro-slavery writers also looked to other evidence—often pseudo-science but sometimes contemporary sociology and economics—to further support property in humans. Looked at in this light, the history of property in humans was one piece of the empirical evidence that supported continued slavery. History, economics, and contemporary

[29] Ibid., 465.   [30] Ibid., 485.   [31] Ibid., 484.   [32] Ibid., 485.   [33] Ibid., 485–6.
[34] Thomas R. R. Cobb, *An Inquiry into the Law of Negro Slavery* (1858).

sociology all were harnessed to make the argument in favour of slavery. History was part of the turn to empiricism that American law was making in the middle of the nineteenth century.

And yet, empirical evidence was also harnessed by slavery's opponents. Thus, while slavery's history over centuries was used as a justification of its appropriateness, anti-slavery writers pointed to the harshness of slavery, particularly of contemporary slavery, to undermine it. Frequently it was shown that owners of human property were allowed to do as they wished with their enslaved human property and, as a result of the state's hands-off policy, that owners tortured and brutalized their human property. Moreover, there was question about the morality of the common law and the right to own other people. In an address in 1851 in Concord, Massachusetts, Ralph Waldo Emerson turned to ancient authors in the common law tradition to suggest that the common law incorporated values of morality that limited the rights of property in humans.[35] The pro-slavery and anti-slavery forces conducted a robust debate about the extent of property rights and, in comparison, human rights. The debate was carried, for a while, by the pro-slavery side. Ultimately, the American Civil War changed the balance and the power of property rights diminished by the emancipation of four million humans.[36]

III. Property's History
in Fictional Literature

The fictional literature of the pre-American Civil War era often entered the debate over the extent of property ownership and the exclusion of non-owners from property. Probably the best known work along these lines was James Fenimore Cooper's 1823 novel, *The Pioneers*.[37] It revolved around a judge, Marmaduke Temple, who owned about 60,000 acres of land. A recently enacted law prohibited hunting of deer out of season. This was of particular problem to the hero of the story, Leather-stocking (also known as Natty Bumppo), a man who hunted only

---

[35] Ralph Waldo Emerson, 'The Fugitive Slave Law—Address at Concord', in *Ralph Waldo Emerson: The Complete Works: Miscellanies*, vol. 11 (1904) 179, 190.

[36] Even a century later, in debate over the Civil Rights Act of 1964, some Senators recognized and celebrated the effects of emancipation on property rights. 'Slaves were treated as items of private property, yet surely no man dedicated to the cause of individual freedom could contend that individual freedom and liberty suffered by emancipation of the slaves.' Civil Rights Act of 1964, Senate Rep. No. 88-872 (1964) 15.

[37] James Fenimore Cooper, *The Pioneers, Or the Sources of the Susquehanna* (1823).

when necessary, took no more from the land than he needed, and treated others with respect. Though Leather-Stocking had been hunting for decades without interference, he was confronted by the owner of the land where he hunted and even charged with hunting out of season.[38] *The Pioneers* reflects a conflict in American property law—some thought they should be able to use the property, as had been done for generations, presumably, to hunt at will; others were claiming ownership and thus putting a stop to such hunting (and trespassing). This represented a conflict between established rights of property and those who asserted customary rights and thought they should be able to roam and hunt as they pleased.

One of Judge Temple's supporters urged him to seek the prosecution of Leather-Stocking. He asked the judge rhetorically:

Do you not own the mountains as well as the valleys? are not the woods your own? what right has this chap, or the Leather-stocking, to shoot in your woods, without your permission? . . . Now, if a man has a right to do this on a farm of a hundred acres, what power must a landlord have who owns sixty thousand—aye, for the matter of that, including the late purchases, a hundred thousand?[39]

Leather-stocking was eventually convicted of hunting out of season and assaulting a magistrate who came to inspect his home for the carcass of a deer.

The Pioneers also sets up a conflict between property and justice, for Leather-Stocking rescues Judge Temple's daughter from a mountain lion.[40] The hero here, then, is a person motivated by sentiments of honour and right treatment of other Americans, while the judge and the magistrate who convict Leather-Stocking of hunting out of season represent the rights of property. This conflict of the individual seeking to roam and use property and the rights of established owners is also illustrated by Ralph Waldo Emerson's statement in his address 'The Conservative', that 'I find this vast network, which you call property, extended over the whole planet. I cannot occupy the bleakest crag of the White Hills or the Allegheny Range, but some man or corporation steps up to me to show me that it is his.'[41] Thus, while the fictional literature explored the nature of property rights—often historically—it also offered a critique of those values of exclusion.

Maybe the best-known example of the exploration of property's history and its critique comes in Nathaniel Hawthorne's *The House of Seven Gables*. The multi-generational saga was set in motion by a dispute over land in Salem, Massachusetts. A small but desirable plot of land was owned by Matthew Maule, the man who first settled it. The land was coveted by Colonel Pynchon, a wealthy and unscrupulous neighbour, who accused Maule of witchcraft during the Salem witch trials. Maule was sentenced to execution as a result, and Pynchon benefitted from the execution because he ended up with Maule's property. On that rather unjust foundation

---

[38] Ibid., ch. 27.   [39] Ibid., ch. 28.   [40] Ibid.
[41] Ralph Waldo Emerson, 'The Conservative', in *Nature, Addresses, and Lectures* (1883) 239, 249.

was laid the Pynchon's family's house and fortune into the nineteenth century. Hawthorne thus sets his book in motion by a story of property's unseemly and uncertain origins. Yet, after so many generations the ownership of that property could not be questioned.[42]

Hawthorne echoed the great treatise writer William Blackstone, who began the second volume of his *Commentaries on the Laws of England,* on property, by discussing the seeming reverence that many had for long-term customs in establishing property rights. Yet, even Blackstone was aware that we are often hesitant to look too closely at the origins of property. For Blackstone wrote that 'we seem afraid to look back to the means by which it was acquired', recognizing that title to property often rested on uncertain moral ground, if one looked closely enough. And in that regard Blackstone was joined by many in the United States who—while they generally worshipped property ownership—were sceptical of the power that property exercised as well. They were sceptical of the power that property's owners exercised over their neighbours. While many Americans revered property, many others feared it.

The landscape art of the pre-Civil War era, like the literature, likewise reflected the ambivalence of Americans towards robust protection of property rights in all cases. Often landscape art celebrated Americans' development of nature. Landscapes depicted the farms cleared from the forests, as well as the canals, railroads, and buildings that Americans built. One of the most famous of the pre-Civil War landscapes, Asher Durand's *Progress,* for instance, is filled with images of progress—including steamboats, railroads, canals, towns, even telegraph wires—along with a small group of Native Americans in the lower left corner, looking out from a patch of trees, in wonder and amazement at the civilization.[43] While *Progress* and other landscape art celebrated property's contribution to economic development, other landscapes reflected many Americans' ambivalence towards development of property. For instance, Thomas Cole's *Notch in the White Mountains* shows a horse and rider going through a field with a cut stump, towards a house. The recently cleared field does not have the beauty of many other parts of nature. *Notch* reflects, then, the sense that development had negative as well as positive aspects. Yet, the central tendency of Americans was acquisition of private property. Emerson caricatured this in his essay 'The Conservative': 'Yonder sun in heaven you would pluck down from shining on the universe, and make him a property and privacy, if you could; and the moon and the north star you would quickly have occasion for in your closet and bed-chamber.'[44]

---

[42] Nathaniel Hawthorne, *The House of Seven Gables* (1851).

[43] Alfred L. Brophy, 'Property and Progress: Antebellum Landscape Art and Property Law' *McGeorge L.R.* 40 (2009) 647–8.

[44] Emerson, 'The Conservative' 250.

IV. ALTERNATIVE VISIONS OF PROPERTY AND COMMUNITY RIGHTS

Much of how we think about property in American history, and especially in the nineteenth century, is a vision of rugged individualism, in which each owner is responsible for their own property; they can police their property as they like, and if there are losses, those losses are borne by the individual property owner. And there is a lot to this vision. However, there are also alternative traditions that have been drawn upon to suggest the government was more engaged in regulation—and sometimes support for those who lost.

Some of these alternative visions of property appeared in the debate over slavery, as well as in the fictional literature and the landscape art discussed above. They also appeared in what was known as the Anti-Rent Movement, which swept through the Hudson River Valley from the late 1830s to the 1850s. The movement centred around disputes between 'tenants' who owed annual payments or services to their 'landlords', the most prominent one of whom was the case of Stephen Van Rensselaer. In actuality, the 'tenants' were owners of their property, but the property was subject to covenants that required, variously, some obligations to their 'landlords'. The obligations had been put on the property when it was first sold back in the eighteenth century. Presumably the property was sold for less than it would have been without the obligations; that is, the obligations were a financing device. The obligations ranged from paying a portion of the sale price of their property to landlords, to annual payments, to a small numbers of days of labour each year. While many of these obligations were relatively minor, Van Rensselaer (a descendant of one of the original sellers of the property) had for many years allowed 'tenants' to skip their services. When he died in 1838, however, his heirs began to try to enforce the obligations and obtain the back 'rent'. This led to protests, increasing tensions, more law enforcement presence, and ultimately some violence, in which a few law enforcement officers were killed. The anti-renters argued that they should not have to pay feudal dues on their property; the landlords argued that the property obligations had to be respected.[45]

The anti-rent dispute took place in many places—from farms along the Hudson River Valley, where tenants disguised themselves as Native Americans and clashed with law enforcement officials, to the ballot box, where the anti-renters elected members of the New York Assembly and Senate, to the courthouses, where the anti-renters challenged the rights of landlords. The anti-renters met with some

---

[45] Charles McCurdy, *The Anti-Rent Era in New York Law and Politics, 1839–1865* (2001); Reeve Huston, *Land and Freedom: Rural Society, Popular Protest, and Party Politics in Antebellum New York* (2000).

success in each of those places. A lower court in New York, for instance, concluded that the rent obligations were feudal incidents that were inappropriate in the United States. Here the court drew a distinction between the English law of feudalism and American property law, which favoured free alienability of property. This was one place that property's history in the United States was turned against what was styled as the English law of feudalism.[46] That opinion was modified on appeal, but the appellate court reached the same ultimate conclusion: that some of the obligations should not be enforced against the 'tenants'.[47]

A robust literature grew up around the competing visions of property. Representatives of the landlords spoke forcefully about the obligations of property and the ways that property secured the nation from excesses of democracy.[48] The ultimate resolution was to allow many tenants to buy out their on-going obligations. In many ways this resolution was a defeat for the anti-rent ideology, because the anti-renters had initially wanted to have their obligations simply removed. However, in other ways this reflected the increasing power of the tenants to control property they occupied and owned.

One obscure, but in some ways illuminating, story emerges from the Nat Turner rebellion in 1831. A number of rebels—and suspected rebels—were killed during the rebellion. Their owners then petitioned the Virginia legislature to ask for compensation for the slaves. (Had the rebels survived and then been tried and executed, the state would have paid the owners compensation.) Several of the petitions base their request for relief on the idea that the Virginia legislature had for generations recognized the public good from killing runaway (or outlawed) slaves without a trial. The petitions point up an important conflict in property rights—should the state compensate individual owners who suffered loss that in some way 'benefitted' (or was perceived to benefit) the public, or should individual owners of property bear the loss themselves? The petitions—which were unsuccessful—reveal the conflict between individual property rights and collective liability.[49] Quite frequently, nineteenth-century property law is perceived as a regime that allows individual owners to profit from their ownership, with a minimum of government interference. But they are also seen bearing the risk of loss.

Some recent—and even not so recent—research challenges this picture and depicts both substantial regulation of property and also substantial government support for property rights and protection of property owners. In slavery, especially, the state took great interest in regulation of property—especially in requiring owners to treat enslaved humans as slaves. This appeared in two types of cases involving attempts at emancipation. First, in some cases owners of slaves left their

---

[46] *Overbaugh v. Patrie*, 8 Barb. 28 (N.Y. Sup. Ct. 1850).

[47] *De Peyster v. Michael*, 6 N.Y. 467 (1852).

[48] Daniel Barnard, 'The "Anti-Rent" Movement and Outbreak in New York' *Whig Review* 2 (1845) 577.

[49] Alfred L. Brophy, 'The Nat Turner Trials' *North Carolina L.R.* (2013) 1817, 1831–4.

property to friends (or members of a religious society) with the understanding that the new 'owners' of the slaves would allow the 'slaves' to work for their own account and to be, in essence, free. Those wills, which courts often referred to as cases of 'quasi-freedom' or 'quasi-slavery', were challenged by relatives of the testator who claimed that the slaves needed to be treated as slaves and that any time they were treated as quasi-free people the state should step in, invalidate the devise, and return the slaves to the testator's estate. When one lawyer argued—on behalf of the testator—that the new owners did not need to try to make a profit off of the slaves and that the slaves could be permitted to work on their own account, the North Carolina Supreme Court concluded that, in fact, the owners did need to treat the slaves as slaves. The Court invalidated the quasi-freedom arrangement because such treatment might lead other slaves to resent their servitude. In the end, it might even result in a rebellion. Such was the approach to the testator's property rights: the property had to be used in a way consistent with the state's need to protect slavery.[50] Once the quasi-slavery arrangement was defeated, they would be returned to the testator's estate and his relatives would return them to a state of full slavery.

A second set of cases involved outright attempts at emancipation, where owners (who were often also the fathers of the enslaved people they sought to set free) made an outright bequest of freedom. Over the course of the pre-Civil War period, southern courts also became substantially more sceptical of such attempts to free slaves via will. As with attempts at quasi-slavery, southern courts routinely and increasingly spoke of the need to protect slavery and thus restrict the emancipation of slaves via will. One Alabama jurist was explicit about the public's interest in the continuance of slavery. 'As a measure of expediency, the State owes it to its citizens at large, to protect their interest, by throwing suitable guards around the institution of slavery,' he wrote. The state's interest thus justified restrictions on emancipation. 'If emancipation were allowed, at the mere volition of the master, consequences, disastrous to the quiet of the country would likely result,—the public would be burthened with the charge of more paupers than it would be convenient to support, and slaves, themselves, would be turned loose upon society. . .'[51] Southern state regulation of slavery is consonant with William Novak's research that reveals a robust spirit of property regulation by the state.[52]

Given the centrality of the economy to the United States, no one should be surprised to learn that the state and federal governments had policies to promote the acquisition of land from Natives and other countries, and then encouraged its

---

[50] See *Trustees of Quaker Society of Contentnea v. Dickenson*, 12 N.C. (1 Dev.) 189, 192 (1827); see also *Sorrey v. Bright*, 21 N.C. 113, 115 (1835); Alfred L. Brophy, 'The Market, Utility, and Slavery in Southern Legal Thought,' in Sven Beckert and Seth Rockman, *Slavery's Capitalism: A New History of American Economic Development* (2016) 262, 268–9 (discussing southern courts' responses to quasi-slavery cases).

[51] *Trotter v. Blocker*, 6 Porter 269 (Ala. June term 1837).

[52] William Novak, *The People's Welfare: Law and Regulation in Nineteenth-Century America* (1996).

development. Nor should we be surprised to learn that the common law of property evolved to protect the interests of owners, such as allowing easy recording of title and mortgages and providing for efficient foreclosure of mortgages.[53] There was often conflict between competing users of property over who had the right to use it. This often emerged as a debate between longer-term users and more recent arrivals. For instance, one famous dispute that went to the United States Supreme Court was the 1836 case of *Charles River Bridge v. Warren Bridge*. In that case the Charles River Bridge Company, which had a state charter authorizing it to charge a fee to cross its bridge, claimed that the chartering of a nearby, competing bridge infringed the Charles River Bridge's contract rights. This set up a conflict between a prior user, the Charles River Bridge, and a new entrant into the market, the Warren Bridge. The Supreme Court construed the Charles River Bridge Company's contract rights narrowly. While the Supreme Court limited the rights of the earlier user, it protected the rights of the newer user.[54] Such conflicts between competing uses of property were, unsurprisingly, common.[55]

Thus, property was seen as a cornerstone of American, indeed human, society, and property rights were robustly protected. Property was seen this way, in part, because of its long history as a part of civilization; it was also seen as a way of justifying the current distribution of property. That use of history to justify the current distribution of property continued through the final three-quarters of the nineteenth century, when the use of history began to shift. By the twentieth century the history of property law was used in some ways to indict and limit the scope of property rather than to promote it. Therein lies a story about the shifting value of historical analysis in law—from the power it had to restrain change in the eighteenth and early nineteenth century—to its power to indict and discredit the majesty of the law from Oliver Wendell Holmes' era forward.

V. PROGRESSIVE ERA AND CIVIL RIGHTS ERA PROPERTY RIGHTS THOUGHT

Pre-Civil War lawyers celebrated property's role in the progress of civilization and used such imagery to oppose efforts at redistribution of property. This was part of

---

[53] See, e.g., Claire Priest, 'Creating an American Property Law: Alienability and Its Limits in American History' *Harv. L.R.* 120 (2008) 385.

[54] 36 U.S. 420 (1837).

[55] See, e.g., Morton J. Horwitz, *The Transformation of American Law, 1780–1860* (1977) 47–53 (discussing the Mill Acts, which adjusted rights between earlier and more recent users of water).

the historical jurisprudence school that turned to history for guidance of what the law was. By the late nineteenth century, the role that history served was changing. It was no longer the prop to the present system that it had been. It became a tool for critique, for history might do more than say that whatever was, was right. History might also show the long-term irrationality, maybe even unfairness, of what had evolved. It might show that the rationale for a rule had disappeared. History, as Oliver Wendell Holmes' *The Common Law* suggested, might be a tool of reformers, as well as those who justified the present.

The Progressive Era and then the Civil Rights Era turned to a new narrative about property's history, which emphasized the ways that property rights are constrained by the interests of the community. (There were certainly hints of this alternative use of history starting in the late nineteenth century, most notably Oliver Wendell Holmes' aphorism that the life of law had not been logic, it had been experience.[56] And then later, in 1921, his remark that 'a page of history is worth a volume of logic'.[57]) This strand of thinking and action then turned to history to destabilize property rights. For while many continued to speak of the importance of property rights, courts, legal realists, and individuals increasingly advanced a different vision of the relationship of human rights and property rights. The talk of human rights versus property rights was popularized by Theodore Roosevelt[58] and carried onward by Woodrow Wilson in the context of foreign relations.[59] In a series of decisions in the 1940s, the right of employers to exclude Union organizers and religious dissenters was limited. Moreover, in 1948 in *Shelley v. Kraemer*, the Supreme Court limited the property rights of neighbours to enforce a restrictive covenant to exclude African American homeowners.[60] The theme of human rights limiting the scope of property rights flowered during the Civil Rights Movement. James Reston of the *New York Times*, for instance, appealed to the idea that property should serve human rights in June 1963 as part of the debate over what became known as the Civil Rights Act of 1964, as the opponents of the bill argued that it interfered with the rights of property owners.[61]

Harper Lee's recently published novel *Go Set a Watchman* illustrates the challenge that the civil rights movement posed to established property rights. In that novel,

---

[56] Oliver Wendell Holmes, *The Common Law* (1881) 1.

[57] *New York Trust Co. v. Eisner*, 256 U.S. 345, 349 (1921).

[58] *See* Harold Howland, *Theodore Roosevelt and His Times* (1921) 114. ('Ordinarily, and in the great majority of cases, human rights and property rights are fundamentally and in the long run identical; but when it clearly appears that there is a real conflict between them, human rights must have the upper hand, for property belongs to man and not man to property.')

[59] James Peck, *Ideal Illusions: How the U.S. Government Co-Opted Human Rights* (2010) 60–1.

[60] *See Republic Aviation Corp. v. Labor Board*, 324 U.S. 793 (1945); *Marsh v. Alabama*, 326 U.S. 501 (1946); *Shelley v. Kraemer*, 334 US 1 (1948).

[61] James Reston, 'Property vs. Human Rights: The Big Issue' *New York Times*, 21 June 1963.

the central character, Jean Louise Finch, was told by her uncle that respect for property rights had declined:

The time-honored, common-law concept of property—a man's interest in and duties to that property—has become almost extinct. People's attitudes toward the duties of a government have changed. The have-nots have risen and have demanded and received their due—sometimes more than their due. The haves are restricted from getting more. You are protected from the winter winds of old age, not by yourself voluntarily, but by a government that says we do not trust you to provide for yourself, therefore we will make you save.[62]

What emerged from the Civil Rights Act of 1964 was a new understanding of the relationship of owners of property and the rights of non-owners. In the wake of the Civil Rights Movement, there have appeared in property jurisprudence some common law fragments that help to rebalance the right to regulate, to force the transfer of rights to neighbours, and even in some cases to require landowners to allow others onto their property.[63] The best-known example of the judicial recognition of the changing balance between property rights and human rights is a case from the New Jersey Supreme Court in 1971, *State v. Shack*, which allowed lawyers and physicians to visit migrant farm workers who were residing on a farm, even though the farm-owner told them that they could not visit the workers.[64]

VI. CONCLUSION

The two competing visions of the right to exclude and the community's rights in private property have been in existence since the colonial era, but the former has been largely dominant in each era. The central tendency of American property law has been towards respect, even reverence, for property owners.

The history of property has been used, quite effectively, to offer support for property rights. Their long history makes the distribution of property look normal, indeed, natural and something that cannot or should not be challenged. There have, however, been competing visions of property throughout the history of the United States. At certain times, and particularly in the period from the Progressive era onward, the history of property has been used to show the unequal distribution of property and to offer an alternative vision that expands the rights of non-owners

---

[62] Harper Lee, *Go Set a Watchman: A Novel* (2015) ch. 14.

[63] See, e.g., *United States v. Platt*, 730 F. Supp. 318 (D. Ariz. 1990) (permitting Zuni Tribe a prescriptive easement over property they have used for generations).

[64] *State v. Shack*, 277 A.2d 369 (N.J. 1971).

of property. The understanding that there has been a history of robust protection of property owners is often used to justify further protection of property rights. Conversely, and particularly in the late twentieth and early twenty-first century, the history of opposition to feudalism and protection of the rights of non-owners is sometimes used to protect the rights of non-owners. Thus, the history of property has been a tool of judges and legislators to support property rights and it has also been, less frequently, a tool of critique.

BIBLIOGRAPHY

Gregory Alexander, *Commodity & Propriety: Competing Visions of Property in American Legal Thought, 1776–1970* (University of Chicago Press, 1997)

James W. Ely, *The Guardian of Every Other Right: A Constitutional History of Property Rights* (Oxford University Press, 3rd edn. 2007)

Eric T. Freyfogle, *On Private Property: Finding Common Ground on the Ownership of Land* (Beacon Press, 2007)

Daniel W. Hamilton, *The Limits of Sovereignty: Property Confiscation in the Union and the Confederacy During the Civil War* (University of Chicago Press, 2007)

William J. Novak, *The People's Welfare: Law and Regulation in Nineteenth-Century America* (University of North Carolina Press, 1996)

Stephen Siegel, 'Understanding the Nineteenth Century Contract Clause: The Role of the Property-Privilege Distinction and "Takings" Clause Jurisprudence' *So. Cal. L.R.* 60 (1986) 1

G. Edward White, *Oliver Wendell Holmes Devise History of the Supreme Court of the United States: The Marshall Court and Cultural Change, 1815–1835* vols. 3–4 (Oxford University Press, 1988)

CHAPTER 49

WHAT DO CONTRACTS HISTORIES TELL US ABOUT CAPITALISM?

FROM ORIGINS AND DISTRIBUTION, TO THE BODY AND THE NATION

ANAT ROSENBERG*

I. CONTRACTS HISTORIES AS HISTORIES OF THE CAPITALIST ORDER

CONTRACTS histories are inextricable from the history of capitalism. Not only functionally is capitalist life dependent on contracts for labour, capital, and

* Radzyner Law School, The Interdisciplinary Center (IDC) Herzliya; For helpful comments the author is grateful to participants at the private law workshop of IDC, UPF, and MacGill, 2017, and at the Berg legal history workshop, TAU, 2017. The author thanks Ron Harris, Moran Ofir, and Ronit Levine-Schnur for thoughtful discussions about this chapter, and Noa Nitzan for excellent research assistance.

consumer goods and services, but conceptually, too. By the Age of Capital, as Eric Hobsbawn called the era of global advance of capitalism towards the mid-nineteenth century,[1] the cultural association of the concept of contract with ideas of markets and economic liberalism superseded an earlier dominance of contract as a principle of political sovereignty handed down by social contract philosophers, which itself overshadowed associations of contract with covenant theology and natural law jurisprudence.[2] These resonances of contract remain valid. One way of grasping the field of contracts histories and its deep significance, thus, is by reading it as a set of debates about historical capitalism, rather than reviewing histories either chronologically or methodologically.

This chapter reads contracts histories as discussions about capitalism. What do histories tell us about capitalism? What kind of concerns do they betray about it? The chapter's case study is Britain, the first capitalist nation, in the late eighteenth and nineteenth centuries; the era is known in contracts scholarship as the high point of the classical model of contract, which remains influential still.[3] Histories of contracts of this era, viewed as a whole, address capitalism within two established modes of political-economic debate, which consider the origins of capitalism and its distributive effects. The first part of the chapter describes these two dominating concerns, and the way in which existing contracts histories, coming from a variety of historical schools, have significantly coalesced around them. The second part of the chapter seeks to move beyond these concerns, and offers two other perspectives on contracts and capitalism: embodiment and nationalism.

II. Dominating Concerns

Two organizing questions have long informed histories of capitalism: *origins*— when capitalism emerged, a question intertwined with determining what elements were fundamental to it; and *distribution*—questions of economic, social, and cultural equality in capitalism. Contracts histories of Britain in the

---

[1] E. J. Hobsbawm, *The Age of Capital, 1848–1875* (2004).

[2] Victoria Ann Kahn, *Wayward Contracts: The Crisis of Political Obligation in England, 1640–1674* (2004).

[3] The term 'classical' might confuse given incongruent uses among historical schools, only some of which distinguish within the model between stages of development. It might also confuse given the lateness in history of the model, which is anachronistically termed 'classical'. The author uses it for convenience, given that in popular discussions of contracts it is familiar. The crucial dimensions are mentioned below.

late eighteenth and particularly nineteenth centuries have largely corresponded with these themes.

To examine the themes of origins and distribution in contracts histories, they are separated and simplified. The themes are not, of course, mutually exclusive, nor uncomplicated. From the perspective of contracts, the themes come loaded with law-related complications beyond those which typify histories of capitalism in general; among such complications are tensions between material and ideational effects of law, disagreements about the role of law in capitalism in relation to law's internal history, and mixed normative evaluations of legal developments. The discussion cannot do justice to all of these; it instead takes a broad view to highlight thick points of controversy and research. It points to the methodological and theoretical richness of existing work, and yet to the significant extent to which that richness is oriented towards the long-standing intellectual concerns with origins and distribution.

A. Origins

The origins debate addresses the *when* and *what* of capitalism (or, more often, specific phases, such as industrial and financial capitalism): when did it arise historically? What defines it—what are its terms of art and key conceptual, technological, institutional, and practical elements? From the perspective of contracts, two areas of research, which do not converse very often, have been dominant: legal histories of ideas and doctrines, and economic histories. Both examine questions which speak to the origins debate.

The debate about the classical model of contract among legal historians might be read as a specialized instance of the debate about the origins of capitalism. Admittedly, legal historians tend to resist swift moves between contract law and capitalism. Depending on the historical school, their resistance is rooted in theories of law's partial autonomy, claims of indeterminacy, or commitments to complexity, multiplicity, or resistance to hegemonic ideologies and powers. Despite such resistances, much in the history of the classical model contributes to the question of origins.

The classical model of contract, a generalized conceptual structure which superseded a once-dispersed understanding of common law forms, is often interpreted as an idealist capitalist scheme reaching its zenith in the nineteenth century. To recount the most familiar pillars,[4] the model offered a picture of the social order at the centre of which lies a sphere of free competitive economic

---

[4] For a detailed review see Anat Rosenberg, *Liberalizing Contracts: Nineteenth Century Promises Through Literature, Law and History* (2018) ch. 1 ff.

activity conducted by autonomous contracting individuals who are rational maximizers of economic interest. It was founded on clear divisions between public and private, both vertically, between the state and civil society, and horizontally, between economic and intimate relations within civil society. The role of politics was not necessarily a laissez-faire picture, but legitimate government activity was to encourage economic competition and individual self-reliance. The judiciary was viewed as a protector of rights, the goal being to ensure mutual respect of rights among individuals and, thus, adequate spaces for self-realization. Central to the model, on most accounts, was the will theory of contract, yet it is important to appreciate the difference between the abstraction of free will and the modelling of a capitalist market; in clashes between protecting subjective positions and a market vision, the classical model gave priority to the latter.

The formulation of the will theory came from Civilian jurisprudence, but the reasons for the receptivity to Civilian ideas are matters of disagreement. At stake here are two intertwined questions: periodization and causality. To put it simply, historians are split on whether the classical model was revolutionary or evolutionary, and their answers to that question are bound up with causal explanations about its crystallization in the nineteenth century. The debate thus echoes and indeed contributes to the origin of capitalism question.

One interpretive camp sees the late eighteenth century, and even more the nineteenth century, as revolutionary in contracts. Among dominant figures here are Patrick Atiyah and historians associated with Critical Legal Studies (CLS), such as Duncan Kennedy and Roberto Unger, who often work on the two sides of the Atlantic at least in terms of contract theory.[5] Internal disagreements notwithstanding, historians who tend to the revolutionary side see contract law as intertwined with the economic, cultural, or social conditions of capitalism in this era.

The other interpretive camp consists of a diverse group of historians, among them the late Brian Simpson, James Gordley, David Ibbetson, John Baker, Phillip Hamburger, Warren Swain, and earlier figures like Frederic Maitland and Francis Montague.[6] While divergent in many ways, historians in this group tend to find the consensual elements of the classical model in periods much earlier than the late eighteenth and the nineteenth centuries. They offer myriad explanations for the sense of newness in the nineteenth century, which share an internalist

---

[5] Patrick S. Atiyah, *The Rise and Fall of Freedom of Contract* (1979); Duncan Kennedy, *The Rise and Fall of Classical Legal Thought* (2006); Roberto Mangabeira Unger, *The Critical Legal Studies Movement: Another Time, A Greater Task* (1986).

[6] A representative text by each: A. W. B. Simpson, 'Innovation in Nineteenth-Century Contract Law' (1975) 91 *L.Q.R.* 247 ff; James Gordley, *The Philosophical Origins of Modern Contract Doctrine* (1991); David J. Ibbetson, *A Historical Introduction to the Law of Obligations* (1999); J. H. Baker, 'Book Review of *The Rise and Fall of Freedom of Contract* by P. S. Atiyah' (1980) 43 *Modern L.R.* 467–9 ff; Philip A. Hamburger, 'The Development of the Nineteenth-Century Consensus Theory of Contract' (1989) 7 *Law and History Review* 241–329 ff; Warren Swain, *The Law of Contract 1670–1870* (2015); Frederic W. Maitland, Francis C. Montague, *A Sketch of English Legal History* (ed. James F. Colby, 1915).

orientation (not exclusive, but dominant) focused on *legal* elements; for instance, a jurisprudential crisis, selective assimilation of Civilian influence by English jurists, the emergence of treatise literature which systematized doctrines and became the first common law theory of contract, or the decline of jury trial which pushed judges to articulate legal principles. These historians typically do not dispute, and sometimes confirm, capitalist echoes in the classical model; such echoes might speak to the earlier origins of capitalism; on some accounts they explain the classical model's salience (rather than newness) in the nineteenth century, when they resonated with the era's capitalist developments.[7]

Links with capitalism become more explicit, while less oriented towards conceptual and ideological shifts, in the realm of economic histories, the second dominant historical field dealing extensively with contracts and concerned with the origins of capitalism.

Economic historians seek to explain the emergent pattern of sustained growth in late modern Britain.[8] In doing so, they sometimes examine formal contract law and court proceedings in terms of the institutional infrastructure of economic development, asking, for instance, about the level of security (reduction of uncertainty), or regulation of transactions (e.g., oversight of contractual terms in areas such as labor or consumer services) provided by formal law. Contractual practice, including structures of contractual relations, has also been examined through the institutional framework. For instance, historical networks of credit, structures of subcontracting in manufacturing industries, culturally-based informal enforcement of contracts, or guild structures which contextualized and framed apprenticeship contracts, are examined for their role in encouraging trust, reducing risks, monitoring performance, and lowering costs of entry into a trade, or transaction costs.[9] The broad question in all of these cases is the extent of growth-inducing cooperative behavior undergirded by contractual or contract-related institutions.

Contractual practice has also been a test case for the existence of capitalist institutions, or for the dominance of specific capitalist rationalities. When those are found beyond the geographical or temporal boundaries of a specific capitalist phase, or are missing within them, the periodization or theoretical definition of capitalism come into question. For instance, historians find sophisticated practices of finance and trade which predated financial capitalism, or existed outside its Western

---

[7]   Some histories fall between the two directionalites, assessing the rise of the classical model as a process of intensification, e.g., James Oldham, *English Common Law in the Age of Mansfield* (2004); Allan E. Farnsworth, 'The Past of Promise: An Historical Introduction to Contract' (1969) 69 *Columbia L.R.* 576–607 ff; Roscoe Pound, 'The Role of the Will in Law' (1954) 68 *Harvard L.R.* 1–19 ff.

[8]   And related questions, among them the British lead among other Western economies and its consequent decline, and the divergence from the East.

[9]   E.g., Pat Hudson, 'Industrial Organisation and Structure', in Roderick Floud, Paul Johnson (eds.), *The Cambridge Economic History of Modern Britain* (2004) 28–55 ff; Joel Mokyr, Hans-Joachim Voth, 'Understanding Growth in Europe, 1700–1870: Theory and Evidence', in Stephen Broadberry, Kevin H. O'Rourke (eds.), *The Cambridge Economic History of Modern Europe*, Vol. 1 (2010) 7–42 ff. Further examples appear below.

core; date capitalism to early modernity based on the contractual organization of agriculture through land rental and wage labour; observe an absence of ideas like shareholders' primacy in the contractual organization of companies late into the nineteenth century; or note the ongoing role of familial and informal economic relations.[10] Such findings imply either a broader scope of capitalism in space and time, or a need to rethink the essential characteristics of particular capitalist phases.

Finally, contractual practice is also part of histories of trades, services, industries, and other contract-based economic activities, examined for their contribution to growth. Contracts are viewed here in functional terms, typically not as an independent theme but as elements of economic activity within a broader debate about the historical causes and turning points of capitalist development.

B. Distribution

Alongside debates about the origins of capitalism, its distributive effects have long preoccupied historians. The debate about distribution, as defined here, is not limited to economic capital; it includes cultural capital as well, and examines questions of social equality in gender as well as class terms, and sometimes in terms of other group dimensions, such as professions. In contracts histories, it unfolds through two more focused debates along the conceptual axis of late modern British history: *status-liberalism (the classical model of contract)-welfarism*. (Conceptual axis, not necessarily temporal; most historians are not committed to the axis as a matter of linear historical progression, but they do confirm the significance of its categories.)

One debate addresses the persistence of status hierarchies (status-liberalism), the other the socialization of contracts (liberalism-welfarism); both are essentially debates about the hegemony of the classical model as a distributive scheme. In distributive terms, the classical model may be read either as a promise of new equalities, premised on new freedoms for individuals, or as a creation of modern hierarchies; I discuss both options as I review the debates, drawing on a wide array of histories which include not only work centred on traditional legal texts, but also, when relevant, social and economic histories interested in contractual practice and mundane relations, cultural histories examining varied representations of contracts, and intellectual histories of political and economic thought.

---

[10] E.g., Morten Jerven, 'The Emergence of African Capitalism', in Larry Neal, Jeffrey G. Williamson (eds.), *The Cambridge History of Capitalism*, Vol. 1 (2014) 431–54 ff; C. Knoick Harley, 'British and European Industrialization', in Neal and Williamson, ibid., 491–532 ff; Timothy W. Guinnane et al., 'Contractual Freedom and Corporate Governance in Britain in the Late Nineteenth and Early Twentieth Centuries' (2017) 91 *Business History Review* 227–77; see discussion in text accompanying (nn. 18–21) ff.

1. *Status-Liberalism*

Conceptually, the classical model established a distinction between status and contract. Contract represented a set of freely chosen, self-imposed obligations of abstract (i.e., socially undefined—conceptually disembedded) individuals, unlike status which represented obligations imposed a priori, without an individual's consent, based on ascription: a preassigned social position based on ascribed characteristics.[11] Henry Maine's formulation of the difference as progress remains unsurpassed still: 'Not many of us are so unobservant as not to perceive that in innumerable cases where old law fixed a man's social position irreversibly at his birth, modern law allows him to create it for himself by convention.'[12] Set against this impression of history, historians ask, *had status really lost the day*?[13]

When viewed from the perspective of contract doctrine, the answer often implies 'yes.' Legal thinking shifted from associating contractual rules with sets of relationships (landlord and tenant, master and servant, etc.), to an abstraction focused on the general conditions under which individually-willed content would be enforceable. CLS work has been particularly effective in showing how statuses lost their operative power as sources for the generation of legal rules and interpretation. The point, however, is also confirmed in some social histories. Craig Muldrew's work on credit, for instance, depicts a break between two relatively distinct stages in conceptualizations of contract, of early and late modern capitalism. Early modernity was characterized by tangled interpersonal obligation, where distinctions between economically rational transactions and other social transactions such as courtship, sex, patronage, or parenthood made no sense. A language of duty and trust involving notions of household virtue dominated credit relations and served as justification for hierarchy. This system was replaced by a utilitarian ethos centred on the individual self only in late modernity, as capitalist economic systems grew more complex and the bureaucratic state began to emerge.[14]

There is sometimes a sense of lament over a lost world of communal solidarity in the move away from statuses, yet lament is a question of perspective. Consider for

[11] 'Status' is sometimes used to refer to state- as opposed to individually-determined content of relations, hence we often see a 'back to status' account of the history of contracts. However, ascription carries sociological and cultural implications, closer to questions of identity, that the simple fact of state regulation does not, in itself, carry. Modern regulation, moreover, is premised, at its best, on substantive equality, while ascription is tied with hierarchy, typically appearing as unequal legal capacities based on inherited positions. The question of state regulation is customarily viewed as part of the legal framework of late modern capitalism, and integral to contracts, unlike ascription. Therefore, despite obvious overlap, the two meanings are separated here.

[12] Henry Sumner Maine, *Ancient Law: Its Connection with the Early History of Society and Its Relation to Modern Ideas* (1906) 295 ff.

[13] While I focus on late modernity, the status/contract conceptual distinction is integral to analyses of capitalism generally: contractual institutions mark capitalist development.

[14] Craig Muldrew, *The Economy of Obligation: The Culture of Credit and Social Relations in Early Modern England* (1998). Also, Hudson (n. 9).

instance the exclusion of domestic relations from contract law under the classical model. From the perspective of doctrine, the exclusion radicalized contract as an arms-length market relation, which marginalizes communal and intimate ties; that is a hostile picture of contracts. However, the other side of status communities was hierarchy. Feminist histories thus often recount efforts to introduce the language of contract and arms-length equality into a patriarchal world; that is a hostile picture of statuses.[15] Be the normative evaluation what it may, these interpretations trace how statuses were excluded from contracts.

The other interpretive direction in histories concerned with the status-liberalism axis, reveals the limits of classical contract's victory. Such histories often focus on specific types of contracts central to the modern capitalist order, such as credit, employment, or marriage, and reveal the viability of status ascriptions in the era of liberal contracts. They show how contractual practice, interpretation, and doctrine sustained myriad inequalities; they trace how contract law, broadly understood, ensured that employees did not negotiate on a footing with employers; and that gender and class informed the treatment of credit contracts on all levels: legislation, judicial interpretation, enforcement, institutional structures, and practice. Historians have also recovered the conceptual foundations of these trends in the codependence of contract and hierarchy for both private and public ordering in key texts of political philosophy.[16]

As with conclusions about classical contract's victory, so with findings about statuses' persistence, an attendant debate involves normative tones. Historians who doubt contract's victory tend to emphasize hierarchy over solidarity and so see the persistence of statuses as problematic. Given that persistence is a source of concern, the question becomes, what does it tell us about capitalism? The viability of statuses is interpreted by liberally-leaning historians as a partial or sometimes complete failure of capitalism to deliver on its promises of equality. The radically-leaning, meanwhile, see here a confirmation of the real meaning of capitalism as a modern complex of hierarchies; from the latter perspective, no surprise attaches, for instance, to the state imposition of criminal sanctions on labourers' contractual breaches, or to the gendered doctrinal structures of the promise of marriage, for capitalism is built on such forms of exploitation and power.

2. Liberalism-Welfarism

'Socialization' implies the introduction of principles that acknowledge and correct power and information disparities and, more broadly, introduce fairness, solidarity,

---

[15] E.g. Staves argues that eighteenth-century courts withdrew the applicability of contractual ideology from domestic relations because of its subversive potential. Susan Staves, *Married Women's Separate Property in England, 1660–1833* (1990).

[16] Carole Pateman, *The Sexual Contract* (1988); Christopher Tomlins, *Freedom Bound: Law, Labor, and Civic Identity in Colonizing English America, 1580–1865* (2012) ch. 8 ff.

and known dependencies into contracts. For those who see the classical model of contract as a blindness to socio-economic disparities, the question is, *was classical contract socialized?* Here too we find 'yes' and 'no' camps. Yet, it bears clarifying that the debate can also be read through two different historical understandings of socialization that cut across these answers. I explain them first and then return to yes/no positions on the question of socialization.

In one group there are historians who treat socialization as a matter of linear timeline: first there was classical contract, then it was socialized. This is essentially a history of the rise of the welfare state and of welfarist understandings of contracts in the second half of the nineteenth century.

A different group of historians challenges the linearity of the narrative. One way to challenge linearity is to retrospectively read indeterminacy into law and recognize social elements within classical doctrine. This is a theoretical project known as the internal critique of contract, which carries historical implications.[17] Another challenge to linearity recovers social elements in contracts which coexisted with the classical model. For instance, cultural history recovers relational commitments in both practice, for example of personal credit contracts, and in dominant cultural representations of contracts.[18] Historians also observe the continuing role of equity which span ideas of fairness and dependence until the Judicature Acts of 1873–1875 (although originally status-inspired).[19] Many histories point to a gap between judicial practice and theory, the former never becoming atomistic as theory was, or to complexities within judicial practice which was never wholly transformed to radical individualism.[20] All of these speak to a level of socialization existing within contracts all along.

With these distinctions between linear and nonlinear historical assessments of socialization, I turn to the 'yes' and 'no' directionalities to the question of socialization: did socialization undermine the classical model?

The 'yes, socialized' camp can be read through two dominant insights. One has been in dialogue with the linear narrative, telling the story of the fall of classical contract. The story describes historical efforts, dating from mid-nineteenth century onward, to mitigate the unwanted effects of the unrestrained pursuit of self-interest,

---

[17] E.g., Duncan Kennedy, 'From the Will Theory to the Principle of Private Autonomy: Lon Fuller's "Consideration and Form"' (2000) 100 *Columbia L.R.* 94–175 ff; Alan Brudner, *The Unity of the Common Law* (2nd edn., 2013).

[18] E.g., Margot Finn, *The Character of Credit: Personal Debt in English Culture, 1740–1914* (2003); Rosenberg (n. 4) Part 1 ff.

[19] E.g., W. R. Cornish, G. Clark, *Law and Society in England 1750–1950* (1989).

[20] E.g., James Gordley, 'Contract, Property and the Will—The Civil Law and Common Law Tradition', in Harry N. Scheiber (ed.), *The State and Freedom of Contract* (1998) 66–88 ff; R. B. Ferguson, 'The Horwitz Thesis and Common Law Discourse in England' (1983) 3 *Oxford Journal of Legal Studies* 34–58 ff; Ron Harris, 'Government and the Economy, 1688–1850', in Floud and Johnson (n. 9), 204–37 ff. That case law was not consistently shaped by theory is generally acknowledged, Swain (n. 6) although the point in itself does not speak to a competing welfarist outlook.

mostly reliant on state regulation, whether as part of a radical or a liberal political program. No commentator since Albert Venn Dicey has argued for a laissez faire age, or for an absence of state before the welfarist era; rather, the story recovers a change in political sympathies and a growing state administration, which led to a socialization of contracts. Legislation began to apply special rules to types of ordinary contracts (labour, corporate, consumer, etc.). Alongside legislative growth, judges showed increasing willingness to counteract power disparities in contracts, and tort law expanded to compensate for reliance damages.

Another socialization route is nonlinear and emphasizes classical contract's failure to achieve hegemony in the first place, pointing to significant social approaches to contract, as explained above.

The 'not socialized' interpretive camp is implied in three dominant insights. The first one, in dialogue with the linear narrative, suggests that if welfarism is viewed as a specific historical stage beginning in the second half of the nineteenth century, the socialization of contracts, well into the twentieth century (when legal theory, at least, was pluralized), functioned as a palliative rather than alternative to the classical model; both the consensual idea and the conceptual separations between private and public were maintained as cornerstones. This point has been confirmed by virtually every historian who considered the question, but has not been consistently conceived as a failure of socialization. The reason is that socialization is theorized in functionalist terms which examine the overall effect of legal change; from this perspective, the question is how the legal regime functions in distributive terms to correct for unequal power, whether or not the effects are achieved through the category of contract alone. However, if the drama of the 'fall of contract' was not a dispute about the meaning of contract in its classical formulation, but rather only about contract's desirability or workability, the implication is that the category of contract itself remained little reformed by social law.

Second, and again in a linear vein, some historians suggest that socialization was marginal in its effects and indeed in its intentions, dominated well into the twentieth century by liberal rather than radical sentiments, and on some versions functioning as little more than market apologetics. The rise of internal critique, which found the social within classical contract, is itself best understood as a theory—rather than history—of contracts, which only began to be developed in the twentieth century with the rise of Legal Realism.[21]

---

[21] E.g., Ibbetson (n. 6) ch. 13 argues that real collectivism arrived only toward the end of the twentieth century, and only then an argument emerged that perhaps principles of substantive fairness underlay contractual liability; Harry N. Scheiber, 'Economic Liberty and the Modern State', in Scheiber (n. 20), 122–60, notes the involvement of English liberals in important 'interventionist' legislation ff; Richard A Epstein, 'Contracts Small and Contract Large: Contract Law Through the Lens of Laissez-Faire', in F. H. Buckley (ed.), *The Fall and Rise of Freedom of Contract* (1999) 25–61, argues that nineteenth-century collectivist changes were not inconsistent with laissez-faire ff; Eric A. Posner, 'The Decline of Formality in Contract Law', in Buckley, ibid., 61–78, supports Epstein's analysis ff.

Finally, some historians point out that social alternatives were strongly resisted or overshadowed. For instance, Cornish and Clark argue that Equity was not a real threat for most of the nineteenth century and that when it became one, at the same time that legislative activity intensified in welfarist directions, case law responded by consolidating its individualist ideology. Other accounts speak to mistrust of the state. For instance, Marc Steinberg shows working-class leaders' support of liberal models, having encountered state support of capitalist interests.[22] Other histories of socialized versions of contract are open to interpretation in terms of the historical dominance of the alternatives that they recover.

As a matter of emphasis, debates about socialization (liberalism-welfarism) are often narrower in scope than those dealing with statuses (status-liberalism), because their focus is mostly economic distribution, rather than the broader questions of identity and cultural struggle that typify histories concerned with status hierarchies. The distinctions, however, are tenuous. Viewed as a whole, histories debating the *status-liberalism-welfarism* axis have gone wide and deep in terms of sources, methodological approaches, types of contracts, identities of parties, contexts, and conceptual perspectives on the very scope of the field of contracts. Yet as discussions of capitalism they are largely interested in distributive justice.

As Ellen Meiksins Wood said about the history of capitalism, how we understand history 'has a great effect on how we understand the thing itself'.[23] The next section speculatively explores what contracts might tell us about capitalism, beyond the now well-developed issues of origins and distribution.

III. Contracts and Capitalism, Redirected

This section explores two possible routes: embodiment and nationalism. These foci are unexhausted by political-economic questions of origins and distribution. Embodiment calls attention to lived experience, to perspectives of persons which are not clarified by questions of socio-cultural and economic distribution, all the less by intellectual and economic developments. The national framework calls attention to a circumscribing background assumption of debates about distribution: they are largely limited to distributive trends within the state political unit. Questions of

---

[22] Marc W. Steinberg, *England's Great Transformation: Law, Labor, and the Industrial Revolution* (2016).

[23] Ellen Meiksins Wood, *The Origin of Capitalism: A Longer View* (1999) 34 ff.

origins, meanwhile, sometimes touch the history of the nation state, but do not make it their theoretical focus in relation to contracts. Both foci are revealing of historical capitalist structures and logic and ultimately tie together into the broader picture of the capitalist order. Both are already embedded to an extent in existing histories; they require fleshing out, reconceptualization, and more research, but seem viable.

A. Bodies

Body studies are a multi- and interdisciplinary endeavour pulling together a number of overlapping trajectories: the material body to be fed and maintained, associated with industrial capitalism and classical political economy's focus on production and reproduction; the social body to be perfected and displayed, associated with consumer capitalism; the cultural body constituted by historical social forces, a question for all kinds of identity studies; and finally, drawing on the previous ones, the body broken down to parts available for analysis, discipline, usage, alteration, and sale, a theme engaging questions of modern science, technology, disability studies, labour studies, feminism, political theory, commodification theory, theories of organizations and occupations (divisions of labour in tending to bodies; occupations involving bodily contact/analysis), and issues of risk, accident, and safety, among others. Embodiment[24] is a potentially limitless theoretical perspective in studies of humanity. Legal historical scholarship has been slower than normative and sociological legal scholarship in embracing embodiment as an analytical perspective. Contracts seem the least likely area, and foremost the classical model given the dominance of abstraction at its core, but precisely for this reason it is apt for exciting re-conceptualization.

Three trajectories of the body in relation to capitalism in the late eighteenth and nineteenth centuries, which implicate contracts, might be considered: the body as object of exchange, as means of exchange, and as driver of exchange. Two theoretical concerns cut across them. *First*, the body as a locus of disempowerment and, conversely, empowerment. As David Harvey observes, body politics become disempowering in the most common trajectories of body theory, namely, sexuality and labour.[25] And we should add race, perhaps the clearest case of disempowerment based on, or projected through, the body.[26] While those are important to contracts, if the body is not to be rediscovered in history only to be lost again, histories of empowered bodies should also come into

---

[24]   A term gesturing at the social construction involved in the experience and role of bodies.

[25]   David Harvey, 'The Body as an Accumulation Strategy' (1998) 16 *Environment and Planning D: Society and Space* 401–21, 414 ff.

[26]   Even if performativity is part of the picture.

view.[27] Second, and relatedly, the problem of Cartesian dualism. The conceptual separation of mind from body, and the identification of the mind as humans' true essence, has been challenged in body studies through the alternative of embodied individuals and embodied agency, where the body is not an object external to consciousness but rather its grounds (subject). The classical model of contract, centred on the will theory and operating through abstraction, is a paradigmatic example of privileging mind over body; recovering bodies in contracts history might enable significant additions and reappraisals. Together, these two questions invite an effort to *historicize* the conceptualization of the body as weakness—and its consequent disappearance, from contracts, and so rely on contracts to rethink embodiment in capitalism.

1. *The Body as Object of Exchange*

Body sale is a long-standing locus of debate about the implications of capitalist exchange: is alienation of bodies as saleable commodities a manifestation of structured subordination, or an instance of self-possession? The theme is embedded in histories of trade in body organs and in bodily capacities, yet historical perspectives framed through contracts have not been dominant in the debate.

Trade in bodies can range to include body fluids, organs, services like surrogacy or personal care, and much else. Two contractual contexts, however, have been identified as constitutive of capitalism: labour, drawing on employees' bodies (labour power), and marriage, drawing on women's sexuality. (In classical contract theory, only the promise of marriage was theorized as a contract, yet popular and political debates routinely assumed that marriage raised questions of contract.) Labour has been integral to both mainstream and radical political economy. Meanwhile, marriage, or more broadly the traffic in women, as Gayle Rubin put it,[28] was historically theorized as part of the capitalist economy by outsiders to economic theory,[29] and became a mainstay of feminist history.

Labour and marriage have respective boundary marks: the contractually-unenforceable relations of slavery and prostitution.[30] Work on these boundaries can historicize the role of the body as a negation of contract, and of contract as a negation of the body: the association of slaves and prostitutes with mere bodies[31] implied that contract began when something *more* than the body was involved. To take this one step further, work on the slippery boundaries of slavery and prostitution, and on the

---

[27]   Furthermore, while Harvey points to analytical mainstays (with Judith Butler and Michel Foucault chiefly in mind), sex and labour themselves are not uniform trajectories.

[28]   Gayle Rubin, 'The Traffic in Women: Notes on the "Political Economy" of Sex', in Rayna R. Reiter (ed.), *Toward an Anthropology of Women* (1975).

[29]   Noam Yuran, 'Finance and Prostitution: On the Libidinal Economy of Capitalism', (2017) 28 *Differences* 136–165.

[30]   Only formally, of course. These contracts have a social reality.

[31]   Tomlins (n. 16); Pateman (n. 16).

fear of slippage, can uncover historical efforts to locate contract in the mind, and challenge their coherence. For example, the stringent guarding of female sexuality in the nineteenth century can be read through the question of contract and its dissociation from embodiment: contracts to marry, which were premised on female sexual purity and could be negated if that condition was violated, might be interpreted as a historical effort to maintain a guarded distance from bodily drives through contract, as critical for women who were traditionally suspected of being unable to do so.

The history of contracts also speaks to the logic of capitalism, which demands at least the semblance of agency in the process of human commodification. The one thing that seems increasingly hard to do is to turn bodies into commodities without the embodied person's involvement as agent. To see this through a contractual lens we might consider, for instance, the emergent requirement of 'insurable interest' in life insurance; this requirement essentially forbade contracting on lives unrelated to the insured. While cast as a problem of speculation, we might read this history through the lens of commodification of bodies without the embodied person's agency. The point is perhaps more apparent in a different area, that of cargo insurance involving slaves and indentured laborers, where challenges of interpretation and enforcement of these contracts fed into abolition.[32] Whether the capitalist resistance to exchange in bodies without the agency of the embodied is humanitarian or monstrous given expanding markets for bodies is a question that can be addressed more fully with the aid of contracts histories addressing the boundary lines of exchange in bodies.

The body is typically identified as a locus of disempowerment, despite histories of embodied resistance and agency, and for good historical reasons. To recover empowerment and locate the body at the centre of contracts, attention to empowered bodies is in order. We might turn to the male body, and in paradigmatic contexts of business. Cultural representations of masculinity in business contracts raise questions that can be asked of more traditional legal sources: what kind of masculine imperatives were businessmen or capitalists operating under in negotiating, performing, and litigating contracts? How did these assumptions infiltrate doctrine and theory? The role of powerful bodies in contracts is yet to be examined.[33]

2. The Body as Means of Exchange

Putting your body on the line as implicit contractual guarantee was integral to the capitalist credit economy. Sean O'Connell, for instance, points to the body's role as one indicator of working-class debtors' creditworthiness.[34] Indeed, notions of able-bodiedness undergirded financial support more broadly. Friendly societies had over four million members, joining contractually, by 1850—about one half of

---

[32] See, e.g., the discussions in symposium issue 28 of the *Journal of Legal History*, on the Zong case.

[33] E.g., Rosenberg (n. 4) ch. 4 ff.

[34] Sean O'Connell, *Credit and Community: Working-Class Debt in the UK Since 1880* (2009).

the adult male population. Penelope Ismay's work on their history shows how able-bodiedness became a factor in the structures that protected members from life-cycle poverty. That logic later disappeared into ideas of industriousness, a process which speaks to a disappearance of the body as an openly acknowledged constitutive element in contracts.[35]

The role of the body as contractual guarantee becomes dramatic in the history of imprisonment for debt: that history reveals an economy in which credit was issued on the assumption that enforcement against the body guaranteed repayment. Debtors' prisons were gradually reformed from the late eighteenth century and through the nineteenth century, from asylums with porous boundaries, associated with upper no less than lower classes, to penal institutions aimed almost exclusively at the working classes.[36] The history of imprisonment for debt is typically viewed as a disciplining mechanism and a class story and therefore invokes the association of embodiment with disempowerment. However, this history seems more broadly related to shifting conceptualizations of the role of the body in contracts, and specifically to the body's gradual marginalization.

A number of legal reforms of the second half of the nineteenth century are worth considering together as a dramatic disruption of the association of contracts with bodies: general limited liability legislation, the expansion of bankruptcy to consumers (previously applicable only to traders), the abolition of imprisonment for large debts, married women's separate property against which creditors could increasingly proceed, and the repeal of imprisonment under master and servant laws, which served historically to enforce employment contracts. Read together, these reforms introduced mechanisms which limited contractual enforcement against bodies. Many of the reforms have been viewed as an Enlightenment trajectory, but they also speak to a particular contracts history which is yet to be told: Until late in the nineteenth century, the sense that the body was implicated in the very essence contract found popular, formal, and theoretical resonance;[37] disembodiment was a late arrival, which required extensive legal reforms. Viewed through embodiment, an anti-Cartesian history of contracts emerges.

3. The Body as Driver of Exchange

Need recalls the body. Hunger for food or sex; pain, sickness, impending death. Desires of other kinds, too, might involve the body as a locus of maintenance,

---

[35] Penelope Gwynn Ismay, 'Trust Among Strangers: Securing British Modernity "by way of friendly society" 1780s–1870s' (PhD dissertation, UC-Berkley, 2010).

[36] Finn (n. 18).

[37] E.g., Frederick Pollock, *Principles of Contract at Law and in Equity* (1876) 66 ff. ('Engagement' is different from a contract in as much as it gives rise to no personal remedy against a married woman but only against her separate property.)

cultivation, and adornment. Since these ideas resurrect the full array of options in capitalism, we might narrow them down by thinking through particular areas of contracts, where indications of disappearing corporeality abound.

Bodily drives emerge in history as signs of disorder and justifications for discipline and marginalization. In the context of credit contracts, for instance, the working classes were subjected to what Paul Johnson described as evolutionary metaphors centred on biological drives: animal appetites and savage needs unrestrained by reason were perceptions informing legal responses which prejudiced working classes' 'efforts at money management'.[38] The same is true of women's representations as unrestrained consumers, which justified disciplinary responses to their contracts.[39] In these cases, treatments of contracts reveal a sense of its incompatibility with embodied agency. Yet the body as driver of exchange exceeds these traditional topics.

Life insurance, historically rooted in maritime pursuits, involves fear, or at least consciousness, of death, a point that could guide insurance contracts' histories. At a less general level, consider two interesting and related trajectories. First, the late eighteenth and nineteenth centuries saw a process of rationalization typified by the rise of modern actuarial science as the informational basis of contracts. Dominant historical work on insurance reads these processes within the story of capitalism's culture of risk, most familiar in contracts as the 'contract vs. wager' dilemma. Yet, statistical knowledge replaced direct and non-professionalized observations of bodies which were relied on to determine health and life expectancy, a process that may be thought of as a case of the body's disappearance.[40] Second, as Timothy Alborn observes of the modernizing science of insurance, it was a locale in which conceptions of what is normal in bodies converged with what is normal in curves and prices, as insurers employed experts in medicine, probability theory, and economics to assess risks of mortality. And yet, Alborn also argues that insurance companies diverted experts to their own profit-oriented ends in deciding what was insurable and at what premium, turning themselves into the producers of normalcy, and with less tendency to pathologize and exclude than academic disciplines.[41] From the perspective of contracts, such research reveals how a contractual practice became a dominant generator of the experience of embodiment in market contexts, even as its procedures claimed to rely on expert mediation rather than lay perceptions of bodies.

---

[38]   Paul Johnson, 'Class Law in Victorian England' (1993) 141 *Past & Present* 147–69 ff.

[39]   E.g., Erika Rappaport, *Shopping for Pleasure: Women in the Making of London's West End* (2000); Anat Rosenberg, 'Rational Households: Consumption Between Love and Hate' *Georgetown Journal of Gender and the Law* (forthcoming 2018) ff.

[40]   Robin Pearson, 'Moral Hazard and the Assessment of Insurance Risk in Eighteenth- and Early-Nineteenth-Century Britain' (2002) 76 *The Business History Review* 1–35 ff. On the lateness of modern actuarial practices see Geoffrey Wilson Clark, *Betting on Lives: The Culture of Life Insurance in England, 1695–1775* (1999).

[41]   Timothy Alborn, 'Normal Bodies, Normal Prices: Interdisciplinarity in Victorian Life Insurance' (2008) 49 *Romanticism and Victorianism on the Net* ff.

For a final example in a different vein we might turn to advertising targeting the body, which expanded rapidly from the late eighteenth century onwards. Advertisements of quack medicine, which Thomas Richards described as a constitution of the human body as a commodity,[42] were a thriving industry by the late nineteenth century and attracted public attention and legislative activity. This area is most familiar in contracts history from the case of *Carlill v. Carbolic Smoke Ball Company*,[43] concerned with medicine advertised as preventing influenza. The case became a staple of contract doctrine (unilateral offer) and a comic relief, yet the corporeal element has largely disappeared[44] and remains to be conceptualized, as do other developments of late modern contract law implicating bodies.[45]

B. Nationalism

Like engagements with the body, hints of nationalism—taken as a dynamically constituted consciousness of collective identity on a principle of congruence with the state political unit—can be glimpsed from contracts histories, but nationalism, like embodiment, is not a consistent conceptual lens.[46]

The era of classical contract is intriguing as a specific historical stage of nation formation. To mention some milestones: on the outside, changes in imperial scope, the American independence, and the European outbreak of peace as Linda Colley called it,[47] which ended a warring religiosity, all put pressure on the meaning of national identity. On the inside, on many accounts England was an early instance of a relatively centralized state, with significant national consciousness and nationwide economic and political systems by the seventeenth century, and part of a United Kingdom from 1707. Yet, processes of harmonization of decentralized powers were drawn out, and provincial autonomy lingered. The bureaucratic state, increasingly involved in civic life, was a nineteenth century legacy, as were the coming of new transportation and communication modes, importantly the railway and telegraph, and new communication media, which undermined localism, and

[42] Thomas Richards, *The Commodity Culture of Victorian England: Advertising and Spectacle, 1851–1914* (1990) ch. 4 ff.

[43] *Carlill v. Carbolic Smoke Ball Co.* (1893) 1 QB 256.

[44] Simpson's history of the case highlighted issues of health and medical science, but it was not driven by a theoretical perspective on embodiment. A. W. B. Simpson, 'Quackery and Contract Law: The Case of the Carbolic Smoke Ball' (1985) 14 *The Journal of Legal Studies* 345–89 ff.

[45] For instance, work on promises of marriage, the doctrinal framework of which developed in this era, is abound with issues of embodiment: women's sexuality and men's good health.

[46] The discussion which follows takes nationalism to be a modern phenomenon, and emphasizes civic over ethnic dimensions, although ethnicity too had a role to play (for instance in the faultlines between Britain and England). While familiar assumptions, they are not uncontested. On competing paradigms see, e.g., Anthony D. Smith, *Nationalism and Modernism* (1998).

[47] Linda Colley, *Britons: Forging the Nation, 1707–1837* (2010) 321 ff.

the slow expansion of democracy which turned more people into citizens. The same era also saw a globalizing capitalism, free trade policies, and an expanding system of international trade, alongside movements for international legal harmonization.[48] Globalization processes, on some analyses, should have undermined the nation-state. That both continued to thrive requires explaining and has sparked a debate among historians. Contract law and practice, by virtue of their mundane relation to individual experience as well as the state legal infrastructure, might offer a rich angle on the extent to which nationalism and a globalizing capitalism were reconciled.

Contracts' role is particularly intriguing if it lent support to nation-building, because the abstract universalism of the classical model has not seemed to depend on specifically English or British attributes, as it has on specifically male and specifically middle class ones; indeed, as we have seen, it had civil law roots. Liberal universalism has been re-read for nationalist biases, but the realm of contracts remains at the margins of the discussion.[49] Moreover, the nationalist character of private law is usually associated with codification projects.[50] The common law does have its own claim to a deep-rooted national character,[51] yet contract law specifically has not been an object of examination.

To begin charting directions, I consider two perspectives on the relation of contracts to nationalism: from within, harmonization of local legal cultures, speaking to the formation of national consciousness and practice answering to capitalist tenets. From without, difference maintenance, that is, contracts' role in constituting national differences and making borders, real or imagined, matter in global capitalist trade. If future research ultimately finds them to be negligible or overshadowed rather than important, that too is important for the debate on capitalism and nationalism.

1. Inside Borders: National Harmonization

A number of strands in scholarship suggest at least mutual support between contracts and nationalism.

Theoretically, Benedict Anderson's classic theory of imagined communities is an apt starting point. It turned on a forged relation among strangers who learned

---

[48] Ron Harris, 'Spread of Legal Innovations Defining Private and Public Domains', in Neal and Williamson, Vol. 2 (n. 10) 127–68 ff.

[49] E.g., Uday Singh Mehta, *Liberalism and Empire: A Study in Nineteenth-Century British Liberal Thought* (2nd edn., 1999), argues for the national (or at least European) bias of self-proclaimed universalist liberal thought of major liberal theorists, Mehta also points to that bias in social contract philosophy. For arguments about nationalist biases in British free trade policy see, e.g., Hannes Lacher and Julian Germann, 'Before Hegemony: Britain, Free Trade, and Nineteenth-Century World Order Revisited' (2012) 14 *International Studies Review* 99–124 ff; Boyd Hilton, *The Age of Atonement* (1986).

[50] Guido Comparato, *Nationalism and Private Law in Europe* (2014).

[51] Peter Goodrich, 'Poor Illiterate Reason: History, Nationalism and Common Law' (1992) 1 *Social & Legal Studies* 7–28 ff.

to experience a community characterized by being horizontal, secular, within an empty homogenous time measured by calendar and clock. The classical model, which idealized contract as a tool of formal equality, was centred on immanent ties and was premised on linear modern temporality, is a perfect conceptual fit, hardly considered for its role in the links that Anderson charted between nationalism and capitalism.[52]

Not only conceptually, but in the content of theory and doctrine and in contracting practices, we might think of contract as an agent of harmonization. In theoretical content, the classical model was notable for its level of generalization. The era of abstract monistic theories of legal categories has been regarded as a paradigm of modern thought and criticized, as we have seen, for its universalist blindness to distributive injustice. Viewed from the perspective of historical localism, however, it can also be studied for its role in imposing a sense of likeness on immense difference. The private/public divide at the heart of the classical model was part of a theory of state; its role in turning contract law—the centre of the private—into a nation-building project might be historicized alongside debates about its capitalist tenets.

In doctrinal content, innovations which concretized expanding networks of trade and credit and shortened spatiotemporal distances were arguably important for a national consciousness. For instance, the postal rule (a contract is formed upon posting a letter of acceptance), often discussed as an exemplary instantiation of the idea of contract as bilateral exchange, and now an archaism, became significant in the era which opened the mail system to public use and created a fiction of instantaneous communication over geographical and temporal distance.[53]

Anonymity was one of the threatening implications of developments which brought strangers into economic contact. In contractual practice and doctrine we see efforts to rationalize assessments of credit-worthiness for anonymous transactions.[54] Rationalizations tended to rely on capitalist numerical assessment, yet might also be historicized as suppliers of links and common denominators which overcame distance and estrangement and forged a national imagined community.

A different practice of harmonization which overcame regional cultures was the imposition of a culture of work through contracts backed by a penal state regime.[55]

---

[52] Benedict Anderson, *Imagined Communities: Reflections on the Origin and Spread of Nationalism* (1983).

[53] Peter Goodrich, 'The Posthumous Life of the Postal Rule: Requiem and Revival of *Adams v. Lindsell*', in Linda Mulcahy, Sally Wheeler (eds.), *Feminist Perspectives on Contract Law* (2005) 75–90 ff. The *Carlill* decision, which found a contract upon performance unknown to the advertiser, can be read for the same effects of flattening the national space. For additional examples see Atiyah (n. 5) 460–61 (Atiyah reads them through the prism of reliance) ff.

[54] More broadly, in economic history, generalized contractual enforcement is often theorized as a historical substitute for familiarity.

[55] Tomlins (n. 16) ch. 6 ff.

The regime has been criticized from perspectives of distributive justice (i.e., class inequality); however, it also speaks to the role of contracts in overcoming local differences and forging the capitalist nation.

Two significant court reforms in the nineteenth century impacted contracts: the 1846 establishment of the County Courts, which superseded a network of local courts and communal justice, and largely dealt with contractual consumer debts, and the 1873–1875 Judicature Acts, which unified the common law courts with the courts of chancery and brought the common law's classical model to national dominance.[56] The model's hegemony is contested, as we have seen. Nonetheless, the question of how consistently contractual paradigms were interpreted and applied would not even arise without the move to a nation-wide unification. The debate about class law (i.e., distribution), in which the County Courts loomed large, was likewise a question asked against the background of the utilitarian effort to create a universal and rational legal administration on the national level. Institutional economists see in harmonization of contractual litigation a functional contribution to industrialism through the reduction of transaction costs.[57] It seems but a small step to consider the question in cultural terms of forging a sense of belonging to a capitalist nation—the national pride at being the 'workshop of the world', and a financial centre, which was stimulated by these reforms.

A different perspective on the relation of contracts and nationalism turns on the ideological view of contracts, foremost the labour contract, as the opposite of dependence, and the tie between dependence and the denial of citizenship. The Poor Law reform of 1834 famously sought to limit state relief to those unable to contract their labour even on the worst of terms and disenfranchised those who entered the system. The logic thus tied political participation with contract. The idea of contract, in other words, functioned to create the national community by means of inclusion and exclusion of men (specifically) as citizens. This point can be complicated by attention to the actual administration of the reform, which was more lenient than the conceptual structure suggests.

The relation of contract and citizenship can also be considered through work on consumption and (as) citizenship, which examines consumer practices as political speech and action, consumer culture as a post-class political configuration, and the rights and duties of citizens as actual and as metaphoric consumers. Within this context, the role of rural consumer contracts in processes of harmonization and nation-building are particularly revealing. Margot Finn's work on itinerant traders known as the Scotch Drapers shows their effects in pulling plebian households into the modern market economy and, at the same time, the national and ethnic

---

[56] E.g., Paul Johnson, *Making the Market: Victorian Origins of Corporate Capitalism* (2010) ch. 2 ff.

[57] Paul Johnson, 'Creditors, Debtors, and the Law in Victorian and Edwardian England', in Willibald Steinmetz (ed.), *Private Law and Social Inequality in the Industrial Age: Comparing Legal Cultures in Britain, France, Germany, and the United States* (2000) 485–504 ff.

lines which were iterated through popular and political debates about the trade's contractual practices.[58]

2. Outside Borders: Difference Maintenance

Did contracts have a role in constituting and maintaining national borders?

One entry point into the question is the prevalent distinction between contract and status. Karnua Mantena's work on Maine's influence on British imperial policy shows that the opposition between contract and status underlay an emergent view of foundational differences between peoples and transformed practices of imperial rule.[59] Mantena concentrates on Maine's account of status, that is, so-called traditional societies, which justified ideas of difference; the other side of the same coin, which awaits further development, is the implication of contract as a nationalist, or more loosely an exclusionary, nation-sensitive construct.[60] In similar vein, research on emancipation in British colonies shows that the move from slave to contractual labour was conditioned on a prior acculturation into the capitalist ethos; assumptions of difference, in other words, translated into policies which shaped and were shaped by the idealized contours of capitalist contracts and marked colonial labour relations as backwards.[61]

Research on risk assessment might also reveal the maintenance of national difference, because perceptions of risk are culturally-loaded. For instance, the category of 'moral hazard' and its assessment in insurance contracts practice, was bound with a sense of the local and the foreign, not least within Britain itself. Robin Pearson shows that English insurers had difficulty in assessing the riskiness of Irish drinking habits, particularly the cultural boundaries between convivial social tippling and alcoholism.[62]

The law of negotiable instruments is another area of boundary-making. Historians tend to describe a process in which the common law allowed the negotiability of debts and so eventually, if grudgingly, underwrote a credit-based expanding economy.[63] For economic historians, negotiable instruments were key in global financial capitalism, utilized to reduce the risks of international trade.[64] Yet, the argument in itself also bespeaks issues of trust, and it appears that cross-border negotiability remained more difficult than British transactions.[65] Conceptually no

---

[58] Margot C. Finn, 'Scotch Drapers and the Politics of Modernity: Gender, Class and National Identity in the Victorian Tally Trade', in Martin Daunton, Matthew Hilton (eds.), *The Politics of Consumption: Material Culture and Citizenship in Europe and America* (2001) 89–108 ff.

[59] Karuna Mantena, *Alibis of Empire: Henry Maine and the Ends of Liberal Imperialism* (2010). Mantena offers a corrective to claims that British imperialism was premised on universalist liberal assumptions.

[60] Realist literature certainly recognized this point. Rosenberg (n. 4) ch. 2 ff.

[61] Thomas C. Holt, *The Problem of Freedom: Race, Labor, and Politics in Jamaica and Britain, 1832–1938* (1992).

[62] Pearson (2002) 76 *The Business History Review* 25 ff.   [63] E.g., Atiyah (n. 5) 135–8 ff.

[64] Ronald Michie, 'Financial Capitalism', in Neal and Williamson, Vol. 2 (n. 10) ff.

[65] E.g., Swain (n. 6) 79 ff.

less than practically, so-called inland instruments were distinguished from foreign ones. While the typical account of such distinctions presents them as practical accommodations for other national legal systems, the question of (dis)trust in international contracts merits research. A somewhat similar point applies to the observation that negotiable instruments were experienced as remote and almost incomprehensible for most people.[66] Here, too, the typical account is functional and points to the small clustering of international financial activity in professional trade and banking centres. Yet, once again, the effect on national consciousness is worth contemplating.

The law of contract itself was not easily exported across borders even to British colonies. Here, too, historians point to practical difficulties such as differences in expertise, communications, and local legal cultures.[67] Yet in an era of trade globalization, the effect may be worth considering as a reinforcement of national boundaries.

Even under an interpretation of an ultimately global spread of law dominating the governance of international markets, a comparison to later periods should inform our understanding. Grégoire Mallard and Jérôme Sgard observe that only in the Interwar period did an international law of markets produced by transnational actors and institutions such as the International Chamber of Commerce (ICC) come to dominate international contracting. Until then, English law ruled trade. The rule of English law, interpreted by English courts, into the twentieth century, speaks to the history of nationalism no less than imperialism and might be explored in such terms.[68]

What if we read contracts history as a linguistic project with implications for national consciousness? A dual or triple link is required, between work on contracts and language, both theoretical and historical,[69] and work on language and nationalism. Anderson saw print languages, in their relation to industry, commerce, and bureaucracy, as the source of cohesion of late modern nations, with local languages increasingly shared by the state apparatus and the population. The question of contractual language, mediating between parties, and between formal legal institutions and the everyday of persons and organizations, seems likewise important. Conferring authority on individual utterances through contract operates at once in two directions, to forge a sense of belonging through the successful use of language and to legitimate national institutions by this operation. As the writ

---

[66]   Michie (n. 64).   [67]   Harris (n. 48).

[68]   Grégoire Mallard, Jérôme Sgard (eds.), *Contractual Knowledge: One Hundred Years of Legal Experimentation in Global Markets* (2016).

[69]   E.g., Marianne Constable, *Our Word is Our Bond: How Legal Speech Acts* (2014); Peter Goodrich, *Legal Discourse: Studies in Linguistics, Rhetoric and Legal Analysis* (1987). In the context of nineteenth century England, Randall Craig has worked on promises of marriage: Randal Craig, *Promising Language: Betrothal in Victorian Law and Fiction* (2000).

system was replaced with the modern category of contract, popular language became a determinant of legal implications, without the need to fit into state-prescribed forms. Such a perspective might also extend work on public finance as part of the history of nation-building: it can add to the picture private finance (credit being of the most prevalent forms of contract) and its changing practices.[70]

More concretely, objectivist interpretations of contractual language, for which the classical era is famed, might be examined for their effects in consolidating a vernacular variety inside borders and marking the conditions and limits of assimilation and communication across them. Indeed, considering contractual language in terms of nation-building might offer a different response to the historical puzzle of objectivism in a theory centred on individual intention. The puzzle has usually been resolved by historians by pointing to the market ideologies which undergirded objectivism.[71] There might be another explanation: both in and across borders, processes of objectivist interpretation carry on, as it were, the assembling, fixing, and differentiating functions of languages that Anderson described as the effects of print capitalism.[72]

CONCLUSION

The robust perspectives on the *when* and *what* of late modern capitalism as viewed through contracts, and on its distributive effects, are a consequence of decades of historical work. Yet origins and distribution are not the only concerns to be addressed. As contracts became the taken-for-granted infrastructure of capitalism, both functional and conceptual, they implicated additional levels of capitalist life, among them embodied experience and national consciousness, issues that historians of contracts engage only at the margins. This chapter pulled out some threads, to gesture at possibilities. In that sense, the future of contracts histories still lies ahead.

---

[70] Nineteenth-century commentators were not oblivious to the connection between credit contracts and national life. E.g., Select Committee on Debtors (Imprisonment), Report, HC 1909-239, at iv ff. See Mallard and Sgard (n. 70) for such an analysis applied to the twentieth century, including a discussion of standardization in contractual interpretation in the context of global trade.

[71] See also Tucker's work on Holmes' objectivist analysis of *Raffles v. Wichelhaus* (1864) EHC Exch. J19, which notes that normalizing expectations of a national language turned contract into an active tool which generates a cultural consensus delimiting possible behaviours. Irene Tucker, *A Probable State: The Novel, The Contract and the Jews* (1995).

[72] Anderson (n. 52).

Bibliography

Patrick S. Atiyah, *The Rise and Fall of Freedom of Contract* (Clarendon, 1979)

Margot Finn, *The Character of Credit: Personal Debt in English Culture, 1740–1914* (Cambridge University Press, 2003)

James Gordley, *The Philosophical Origins of Modern Contract Doctrine* (Clarendon, 1991)

David J. Ibbetson, *A Historical Introduction to the Law of Obligations* (Oxford University Press, 1999)

Duncan Kennedy, *The Rise and Fall of Classical Legal Thought* (Beard, 2006)

Saskia Lettmaier, *Broken Engagements: The Action for Breach of Promise of Marriage and the Feminine Ideal, 1800–1940* (Oxford University Press, 2010)

Larry Neal, Jeffrey G. Williamson, (eds.), *The Cambridge History of Capitalism*, Vols. 1 and 2 (Cambridge University Press, 2014)

Carole Pateman, *The Sexual Contract* (Stanford University Press, 1988)

Anat Rosenberg, *Liberalizing Contracts: Nineteenth Century Promises Through Literature, Law and History* (Routledge, 2018)

Harry N. Scheiber, (ed.), *The State and Freedom of Contract* (Stanford University Press, 1998)

Marc W. Steinberg, *England's Great Transformation: Law, Labor, and the Industrial Revolution* (University of Chicago Press, 2016)

Warren Swain, *The Law of Contract 1670–1870* (Cambridge University Press, 2015)

CHAPTER 50

HISTORICAL ANALYSIS IN CRIMINAL LAW

A COUNTER-HISTORY OF CRIMINAL TRIAL VERDICTS

ARLIE LOUGHNAN*

I. INTRODUCTION

HISTORICAL analysis in criminal law is experiencing a recent flowering. Such scholarly work takes seriously the temporal, institutional, and other conditions of possibility of the development of criminal law rules and practices. Criminal law scholars have adopted historical research methods (and allied methods such as socio-legal studies approaches) to develop fascinating and provocative accounts of issues in criminal law, including the key issues of criminal responsibility and criminalization. In this growing body of work, responsibility for crime and the criminalization of conduct are understood not as 'thin' or abstract products of certain rules or moral norms (as is the case in legal-philosophical analysis

* I would like to thank Mark Coen, Kevin Crosby, Markus Dubber, and Chloe Kennedy for comments on an earlier version of this chapter, and Alexandra Chappell, Natalie Czapski, and Louisa Vaupel for research assistance.

of criminal law, the type of scholarship inspired by normative philosophical thinking), but as complex sets of practices that take place in particular contexts and at particular moments in time.

Historical analysis in criminal law may be organized into several broad strands. The first strand comprises work that is in close dialogue with legal-philosophical analysis, and which exposes the limitations of, and contingencies in, that analysis. A pre-eminent example is Nicola Lacey's work on criminal responsibility. Lacey pushes scholars to move beyond the standard focus on what criminal responsibility 'is', and ask what it is 'for', a question that, for Lacey, exposes its centrality to criminal law as a system of regulation governing individual and group behaviour, and structuring the interaction of people and systems.[1] The second strand of historical analysis consists of works that offer alternative methods of analytical inquiry. Here, a prominent example is Lindsay Farmer's scholarship on criminalization. Farmer's inquiry is framed not by interest in which principles should guide the determination of the appropriate reach and limits of the criminal law, but by 'the prior question', 'how is it that the question of criminalization has come to be framed in these terms?'[2] A third strand of historical analysis seeks to contextualize major developments in criminal law and process, by presenting close and careful accounts of change over time. This strand of scholarly research, where historians are better represented than lawyers, boasts several significant works on diverse topics.[3] Across these three strands of scholarship, historical analysis in criminal law deploys diverse methodological approaches, including social history and legal biography, and draw on a wide range of primary sources, including literary sources, historical archives, and cultural materials.

A fourth strand of historical analysis in criminal law is what we can call counter-history. Here, counter-history is understood in a broad way, as the sort of scholarship that challenges dominant narratives about the historical development of the criminal law. Work within this strand of historical analysis focuses on paths not taken at significant junctures in the development of the criminal law, and offers alternative narratives of legal developments via a focus on otherwise occluded aspects of the development of the law over time. Like work falling within other strands of historical analysis in criminal law, counter-histories of criminal law may serve various aims—including developing alternative methods of analytical inquiry, and contextualizing developments in criminal law and process—but such work offers a novel and creative means by

---

[1] See, e.g., Nicola Lacey, *In Search of Criminal Responsibility: Ideas, Interests and Institutions* (2016) 178–9.

[2] Lindsay Farmer, *Making of the Modern Criminal Law: Civil Order and Criminalization* (2016) 1.

[3] For just two examples, see, e.g., Joel P. Eigen, *Mad-Doctors in the Dock: Defending the Diagnosis, 1760–1913* (2016); Martin Wiener, *Reconstructing the Criminal: Culture, Law, and Policy in England, 1830–1914* (1990).

which to advance the knowledge and understanding of criminal law principles and practices.

This chapter presents an analysis that falls into this fourth strand of historical analysis in criminal law. It offers a counter-history of criminal trial verdicts, restoring special verdicts—findings of fact, where the jury fails to conclude questions of law—to the story typically told about trial verdicts. According to this typical story, the dominance of the general verdict—'guilty' or 'not guilty', a determination of both the factual and legal issues at trial—is thought to be both inevitable and right. While special verdicts are now virtually unknown in English trial process, during the period of the development of the modern criminal trial they played a greater role in criminal process, functioning as a means by which the seismic changes associated with the appearance of the modern criminal trial were negotiated in the courtroom. Bringing to light the all-but-forgotten past of trial verdicts opens the way to think again about verdicts in the current era, considering the possibilities for the restoration of a meaningful role for special verdicts.

II. The Modern Criminal Trial and the General Verdict

The modern adversarial criminal trial developed over the 'long' eighteenth century—the period from the end of the 1600s up to the first decades of the 1800s.[4] This development entailed major changes in the relationships between actors in the criminal courtroom, significant development of legal principles, and radical changes to practices of evidence and proof. Many of the hallmarks of the adversarial trial appeared in the 1700s. These included the involvement of prosecution and defence counsel (although the latter had a limited role until the nineteenth century); a distinction between fact and law; and the rudiments of laws of evidence and procedure.[5] During the century, the increasing presence of prosecution and defence counsel gave 'more structure to criminal trials' which 'encouraged evidential objections and the recognition of burdens of proof'.[6] This development

---

[4] On the periodization of a 'long' eighteenth century, see Frank O'Gorman, *The Long Eighteenth Century: British Political and Social History 1688–1832* (1997).

[5] See David J. A. Cairns, *Advocacy and the Making of the Adversarial Criminal Trial 1800–1865* (1998) ch. 4; John Langbein, *The Origins of Adversary Criminal Trial* (2003) ch. 3; see also J. M. Beattie, *Crime and the Courts in England: 1660–1800* (1986).

[6] Cairns (n. 5) 30.

brought trained, legal counsel, rather than judges and defendants, to the foreground and paved the way for the modern 'mode' of trial, the adversary trial, in which the defence tests the prosecution case.[7]

The appearance of the modern criminal trial was a political development. The modern criminal trial took shape against the backdrop of late seventeenth-century constitutional struggles concerning religious and political freedoms. Criminal trials were at the forefront of these struggles because political opponents were dealt with via the criminal law, and because trial by jury was implicated in debates about constitutional freedoms. During these struggles, the process of trial by jury, and the balance of power between jury and judicial decision-making, took on political significance. In this context, some of the mechanisms by which criminal trial juries could be controlled came under criticism. Most prominently, following a series of high-profile criminal prosecutions of Quakers in the 1660s, where recalcitrant juries that refused to convict were fined,[8] *Bushell's Case* (1670) established the principle that jurors could not be threatened or punished for their verdicts.[9] This decision, which both reflected and advanced the wider politicization of criminal trial by jury, heralded a sustained period in which the relationship between criminal trial judges and juries was much debated and contested.

The trial verdict represented the fulcrum of the interaction between judges and juries, and the politicization of criminal trial by jury pushed trial verdicts to the forefront of wider debates about criminal justice. The development of the modern criminal trial brought with it the dominance of the general verdict— 'guilty' or 'not guilty'. The standard historical account of this period suggests that there was something inevitable and right about this development. According to this account, in this period, the general verdict came to be closely implicated in the right to trial by jury, which was regarded as a safeguard against government tyranny. As Thomas Green argues, in the 1700s, defending the practice of juries of tempering or moderating the criminal law, and mitigating punishment, came to entail defending the general verdict.[10] That is, arguments and agitation *against* government tyranny became arguments *for* the general verdict. The expansion of the jury's role over the period to the end of the 'long' eighteenth century—via the increase in the number of capital offences, and the advent of transportation as an alternative sentence to death—resulted in efforts to consolidate the administration of the criminal law, and bring jury practices under greater control.[11] These efforts

---

[7] Langbein (n. 5) 253.

[8] See Thomas Green, *Verdict According to Conscience: Perspectives on the English Criminal Trial Jury, 1200–1800* (1985) 209, and 208–21 more generally; see also E. M. Morgan, 'A Brief History of Special Verdicts and Special Interrogatories' (1923) 32(6) *Yale L.J.* 575.

[9] *Bushell's Case* (1671) 124 Eng. Rep. 1006. See Kevin Crosby, '*Bushell's Case* and the Juror's Soul' (2012) 33(3) *Journal of Legal History* 251.

[10] Green (n. 8) 347.   [11] Ibid., ch. 7.

formalized the jury's role in the criminal trial, and, because of the association of the general verdict and protection from tyranny, cemented the dominance of the general verdict.[12]

This account obscures the part played by special verdicts in this period, and risks reducing the significance of such verdicts to a circumscribed and short-lived story of curiosity value only. But special verdicts deserve more careful consideration. Special verdicts, which, as mentioned above, include statements of facts, and fail to conclude the questions of law, became a feature of criminal trial process in the medieval era, when, for instance, they presented a way of dealing with matters of justification and excuse in cases of homicide, which were all tried as murder.[13] Over time, special verdicts came to be used for a variety of purposes, as I discuss below. Writing in the seventeenth century, Lord Coke stated that jurors are best placed to advise the judge on the facts, and that the special verdict represented the ideal type of verdict for judge–jury relationships.[14] In the period under discussion in this chapter, Sir Matthew Hale referred to the value of special verdicts in trials for murder where the accused had killed in self-defence or as a result of an accident.[15] Special verdicts remained a familiar if relatively uncommon result of criminal trial process in the 'long' eighteenth century, with such verdicts returned in small but consistent numbers throughout this period.[16] This suggests that special verdicts were regarded as a legitimate option for the judge and jury, and as an appropriate outcome of criminal trial process.

A counter-history of trial verdicts restores the place of special verdicts in the story of trial process, and opens up consideration of their potential part in criminal process in the current era. In the current era, special verdicts have been returned in only a handful of trials in England and Wales over recent decades: it has been held that 'special verdicts ought to be found only in the most exceptional circumstances'.[17] Rather than a legitimate option for the judge and jury, and an appropriate conclusion to criminal process, in the current era, special verdicts now seem to have a whiff of the failure of criminal process, on the basis a trial *should* result in the standard general verdict. Given that the status of special verdicts has changed profoundly from the time of Coke and Hale, we can ask: under what conditions were special verdicts a useful outcome of criminal process? And is it possible to envisage a meaningful role for special verdicts once again?

---

[12] Ibid.   [13] See generally Green (n. 8) 53–9.

[14] See for discussion, Crosby (n. 9) 271 ff.

[15] Sir Matthew Hale, *The History of the Pleas of the Crown* (London, vol. 1, 1736), 471.

[16] According to the Old Bailey Proceedings (OBP) database (see n. 18), there were 113 special verdicts returned between 1674 and 1830. This is a small fraction of the total number of trial records in the database, although it represents an under-estimation of the numbers of special verdicts (in part because the OBP coding excludes verdicts of self-defence and accident, see (n. 18)).

[17] *R v. Bourne* (1952) 36 Cr App R 125, 127.

III. Reclaiming Special Verdicts

Special verdicts functioned as a means by which the seismic changes associated with the development of the modern criminal trial were negotiated in the courtroom. A study of the trial records contained in the *Old Bailey Proceedings* (OBPs)[18] shows that special verdicts were deployed by various actors, and for various purposes, in a way that indicates that the special verdict served diverse interests and functions. I assess the three main functions of special verdicts: accommodating the changing division of labour between actors in the criminal courtroom; negotiating the formalization of criminal legal principles; and facilitating the acceptance of modern practices of evidence and proof in the criminal trial.

A. Accommodating the Changing Division of Labour between Actors in the Criminal Courtroom

The development of the modern criminal trial entailed major changes in the division of labour between actors in the criminal courtroom. In this context, special verdicts were deployed by both judges *and* juries as a way of accruing *and* divesting power in the courtroom. This seemingly contradictory use of special verdicts reflected the fluidity in the roles of judges and juries in this period, and the adjustment required as lawyers entered the courtroom and an emergent appellate review process came to sit above adjudication at trial.

Even as their power diminished over the course of the 1700s, judges dominated criminal trials, and a judge could do a great deal to assist a prisoner if he so chose.[19] Alongside the more familiar 'narrow construction of the criminal law' as a form of mitigation,[20] directing the jury to return a special verdict enabled judges to take control of the trial outcome. A judicial direction to the jury 'to bring it in Special' occurred in two kinds of cases. The first kind of case concerned a point of law arising in the matter ('perverting justice': 'the Jury consider'd the Matter, and brought him in guilty of the Fact. But the Court being of opinion that some point of Law would arise, directed the Jury to find it Special, which they did'; forgery: 'a Point of Law arising, the Court directed the Jury to bring it in Special'; murder: 'Some Points of

---

[18] See *OBPs Online*, <http://www.oldbaileyonline.org/static/Proceedings.jsp> (accessed 16 July 2017). The OBPs are a digitized collection of trials that took place at the Old Bailey, London's main criminal court, between 1674 and 1913. The OBPs database contains almost 200,000 trial records. Like any sources, the OBPs must be read carefully: see further Arlie Loughnan, 'Reading the Old Bailey Proceedings' (2013) *Australia and New Zealand Law and History E-Journal* 1–14.

[19] Beattie (n. 5) 343, 346.   [20] Green (n. 8) 276.

Law arising from the Evidence, the Jury gave in a Special Verdict').[21] The second kind of case featured in judicial directions to the jury to return a special verdict concerned those cases in which a question arose as to whether all the requisite elements of the offence had been proved ('whether under all the circumstances of the case it amounts to murder or no [sic]'; whether there had been a taking and carrying away of property as required for the offence of larceny).[22]

Like judges, juries also utilized the special verdict as a means to accumulate power in the courtroom. Reflecting the already established tradition of 'merciful application of the law' by juries,[23] juries used the special verdict to temper the harshness of the criminal law: although a special verdict did not prevent a prisoner from being tried and convicted at a later time, there was a chance the prisoner would be reprieved. Although less well known than partial verdicts (convicting on a lesser charge), special verdicts seem to have been an important merciful tool for the jury. An illustration of this sort of use of the special verdict is provided by Mary Anson's trial, in 1769, for the manslaughter of her husband 'by biting his little finger'.[24] The OBP trial record includes a discussion of the cause of death (which followed amputation of the finger three months after the injury), and the medical witness is recorded as stating 'we have the greatest reason to suppose he [the victim] might have died by the scratch of a pin, as he was in so bad a habit of body'.[25] When combined with the possibility that the prisoner was responding to violence from her husband when 'the finger was bit', a jury attempt at leniency provides some explanation of the result—'Special'. There were several other special verdicts that represented jury efforts to temper the law.[26]

The division of labour between judges and juries was altered by the appearance of defence and prosecution counsel from the early decades of the 1700s.[27] At this time, the role of defence counsel was still emerging (they could not address the jury or offer a defence but they could cross-examine prosecution witnesses), and the government had only begun to pay prosecutors who secured convictions in ordinary felony trials and to engage lawyers to ensure certain serious cases were prosecuted effectively.[28] This was the context for those special verdicts that appear to have been initiated by counsel. Defence arguments leading to special verdicts

---

[21] See trial of John Wilder, 6 September 1710, t17100906-24; trial of John Seal, 12 October 1715, t17151012-16; trial of John Oneby, 2 March 1726, t17260302-36, respectively.

[22] See Trial of Mary Adey, 15 September 1779, t17790915-74, and Trial of James Lapier, 26 May 1784, t17840526-19, respectively.

[23] Green (n. 8) 200.   [24] Trial of Mary Anson, 6 September 1769, t17690906-102.

[25] Ibid.

[26] See e.g., trial of James Wolden, 9 April 1684, t16840409-1; trial of C-D, 6 April 1687, t16870406-38.

[27] See Peter King, *Crime, Justice and Discretion in England, 1740–1820* (2000) 227–8.

[28] See Clive Emsley, *Crime and Society in England 1750–1900* (Harlow, 3rd edn., 2005), 183; Peter King, 'Decision-Makers and Decision-Making in the English Criminal Law, 1750–1800' (1984) 27(1) *The Historical Journal* 25, 32–3, and J. M. Beattie, 'Scales of Justice: Defense Counsel and the English Criminal Trial in the Eighteenth and Nineteenth Centuries' (1991) 9(2) *Law and History Review* 221, 225.

varied, and included, for example, that a client did not fall within the scope of the relevant statute, or that the facts did not support a conviction.[29] A useful illustration of the role of counsel in prompting special verdicts is provided by the trial of John Bigg for forgery of a Bill of the Bank of England in 1715. The defence was summarized in the following way:

> The Prisoner did not deny the Fact; but being allow'd Council, they argu'd, that Mr. Odam [the victim] was not a Servant qualify'd to make out such Bills, unless authoriz'd by the Corporation-Seal; That writing with Red Ink on the Inside of the Bill, cannot be call'd an Indorsement; Nor, if that were an Indorsement, can be call'd raising or altering. . . . whereupon the Court were of Opinion, that Mr. Odam is a Servant qualify'd to make out such Bills for the Governor and Company of the Bank of England, but the other two Articles are referr'd to a special Verdict.[30]

The technical nature of forgery seems to have invited such close argument, and to have produced quite a few special verdicts. I discuss forgery below, in relation to the appearance of modern practices of evidence and proof.

At the same time as juries and judges were utilizing the special verdict as a means to accumulate power in the courtroom, it also appears that special verdicts were being deployed by juries and judges to divest themselves of decision-making responsibility. Juries deployed the special verdict in order to assign tasks to the judge. Examples of this divestment of power include assigning the task of determining whether something was a felony or a misdemeanour, which involved a determination of whether the accused would face capital punishment ('The Jury found him Guilty of the Fact upon the Evidence, which was very full, and that he was very Notorious in those vile Practices, and Married all his Wives with a Felonious Intent to Rob them of their Money and Goods, and as to the Indictment found a special Verdict whether the Fact was Felony or not.'[31]). Juries also used the special verdict to divest themselves of power where the facts were unclear ('whether the facts charged were within the statutes . . . they knew not, and therefore prayed the assistance of the court. So it was made Special').[32] Cases of unlawful killing—where the issue was whether the accused would be convicted of murder or manslaughter—featured in this use of the special verdict, as I discuss in the next section of this chapter.

Judges also used special verdicts to divest themselves of decision-making responsibility. Judges appear to have relied on special verdicts in order to send a matter for review, a then still emergent practice that was coming to sit above adjudication at trial. Originally reliant on the writ of *certiorari*, by the early eighteenth century, the judges of the King's Bench were reviewing judgments and orders made

---

[29] E.g., trial of Joseph Sloper, 9 January 1772, t17720109-60; trial of Robert Classon and Thomas Whittocks, 11 September 1799, t17990911-16, respectively.

[30] Trial of John Bigg, 2 June 1715, t17150602-10.

[31] Trial of Robert Booth, 25 May 1721, t17210525-55.

[32] E.g., Trial of Stephen M'Daniel, John Berry, James Egan, 1 March 1755, t17550301-1.

by any inferior jurisdiction (including justices of the peace).[33] Deployment of special verdicts fed into the development of a nascent practice of judicial review, and may have aided the doctrinal development of the common law by providing a space for judges to discuss the law.[34] The option of a special verdict meant that challenging questions of law could be left to a bench of twelve justices for consideration. Judges appear to have directed the jury to return a special verdict in a number of instances in which they sought 'the opinion of the twelve judges'.[35] Special verdicts acted as a means of bringing particular cases to the attention of the review body, and relieving the judge of responsibility for making difficult or controversial decisions.

B. Negotiating the Formalization of Legal Principles

The development of the modern criminal trial brought with it the formalization of criminal legal principles, according to which key legal principles, such as conduct and fault, were subject to conceptual elaboration.[36] In the 'long' eighteenth century, this process of formalization included the early development of two closely related dimensions of criminal fault: the 'factualization' of *mens rea* (explained below), and the elaboration of a subjective pattern of criminality, whereby the defendant's intent became 'the central question in assessing liability'.[37] Special verdicts played a role in the negotiation of these two changes in legal principles in the criminal courtroom.

At the beginning of the period of the 'long' eighteenth century, the notion of criminal fault was largely undeveloped, as fault was assumed and not subject to investigation at trial. As Farmer argues, fault was based on the wrongfulness of the act, and because 'legal guilt was equivalent to moral wrong', the degree of intention of the actor did not have to be explicitly proved as a condition of liability.[38] As statutory offences, some of which contained an express fault element, were introduced in increasing numbers over the 1700s, it became necessary to prove fault specifically. This development depended on the 'factualization' of *mens rea*—the process by which interior mental states came to be regarded as amenable to proof as a question

---

[33] See Norman Landau, *The Justices of the Peace, 1679–1760* (Berkeley, 1984) 345–8. The Court of Crown Cases Reserved, which became the Court of Criminal Appeal, was only established in 1848: see Philip Handler, 'The Court for Crown Cases Reserved, 1848–1908' (2011) 29(1) *Law and History Review* 259–88.

[34] James Q. Whitman, *The Origins of Reasonable Doubt: Theological Roots of the Criminal Trial* (Yale University Press, 2008) 258.

[35] See trial of William Wynn, 26 April 1786, t17860426-14; see also trial of Isaac Cockwaine, 10 December 1788, t17881210-91; *Rex v. Pedley* (1784) 168 ER 224.

[36] On formalization, see Arlie Loughnan, *Manifest Madness: Mental Incapacity in Criminal Law* (2012) ch. 2.

[37] George Fletcher, *Rethinking Criminal Law* (2000) 89.

[38] Lindsay Farmer, *Criminal Law, Tradition and Legal Order: Crime and the Genius of Scots Law 1747 to the Present* (1997) 132.

of fact.[39] The 'factualization' of *mens rea* was part of the broader development according to which fault came to be identified as an express dimension of criminal offences, and an essential aspect of the prosecution case. And, as Lacey argues, the 'factualization' of *mens rea* formed the basis for the subsequent development of a 'primarily capacity-based and heavily psychologized notion of mens rea' that marked 'the core of the late modern general part of the criminal law'.[40]

Special verdicts played a role in negotiating, or perhaps institutionalizing, the 'factualization' of *mens rea*. A number of OBP trials resulting in special verdicts focused on the prisoner's mental state, and the issue of whether it had been proved to the satisfaction of the court. For example, in Robert Munday's trial for the theft of 200lbs of lead in 1799, Munday was found guilty, but, in addition, the judge asked the jury to determine whether the prisoner entered into a contract for the lease of the house from which the theft was committed in order to get fraudulent possession of the house, a matter which had come up in the course of the trial.[41] The jury found that Munday did enter into the contract for a fraudulent purpose, and, perhaps because this finding of fact exposed the prisoner to an additional charge, the court reserved the case for 'the opinion of the Judges' (a reference to the emergent practice of review, referred to above). Another example is provided by the trial of Thomas Field for fraud in 1785. In Field's trial, the jury had to determine if Field 'unlawfully, fraudulently and feloniously' took the stamp off a writ to use again, with intent to defraud the King. The judge directed the jury that, if it found the accused guilty of taking the stamp off, and selling it, then it was to specifically state for what purpose the accused acted, 'besides finding the prisoner guilty'. The jury concluded that Field was guilty of 'taking a stamp from a certain instrument, and of affixing it to another, with an intent that it should be used by others'. [42] This verdict meant judgment in the case was 'arrested', preventing sentence being handed down, and sparing the prisoner from punishment (at least temporarily).

The other major change on the level of legal principle in the 'long' eighteenth century was the gradual and piecemeal elaboration of a subjective pattern of criminality, which depended on the 'factualization' of *mens rea*. A subjectivist conception of fault orients the legal evaluation of liability around what an individual knew, perceived, or intended at the time of the offence.[43] This type of criminal liability rose to the fore at the end of the eighteenth century and is emblematic of the late modern criminal law. As Lacey argues, prior to the eighteenth century, a defendant's capacities were 'merely components of [his or her] character which was the object

---

[39] Nicola Lacey, 'Responsibility and Modernity in Criminal Law' (2001) 9(3) *Journal of Political Philosophy* 249, 268.

[40] Ibid., 266.   [41] Trial of Robert Munday, 20 February 1799, t17990220-47.

[42] Trial of Thomas Field, 11 May 1785, t17850511-76.

[43] See Jeremy Horder, 'Criminal Law', in Peter Cane, Mark Tushnet (eds.), *Oxford Handbook of Legal Studies* (2003) 226–49.

of evaluation' during a trial.[44] Between the eighteenth and twentieth centuries, the English criminal process was marked by 'a broad movement from ideas of responsibility as founded in character to conceptions of responsibility as founded in capacity', where the concept of capacity-responsibility was a subjective one.[45] The development of subjective liability did not take place on an intellectual level only, but, as Farmer argues, was linked to changes in state and social organization (such as organized policing).[46]

The rise of subjectivism was reflected in, and in turn enhanced by, the more finely tuned grading of offences according to culpability, a process in which special verdicts were implicated. The OBPs records reveal the historical existence of two verdicts that are appropriately included among special verdicts, although they would later be subsumed into more formalized defence categories: the verdict that a killing had occurred *se defendendo* (in self-defence), or *per misfortunam* or *per infortuniam* (by accident). Lord Hale identified these verdicts as special verdicts, stipulating that the jury was required not just to state that the killing occurred in this manner, but to state how it was done.[47] The practice of distinguishing killings that occurred *se defendendo* or *per infortuniam* was premised on the status of all unlawful killings as prima facie murder. As the indictment was likely to allege murder, it was up to the prisoner to provide evidence that the death was not murder.[48] In the absence of a positive requirement of fault or a formalized law of self-defence, which would have meant that evidence of accident or self-defence would be a failure of the prosecution case, the finding that a prisoner charged with murder had killed by accident or in self-defence was a finding of fact for the jury. Such a finding was stipulated in the special verdict, remaining separate from any conclusion on questions of law.

A number of verdicts of *se defendendo* and *per infortuniam* are recorded in the OBPs database.[49] These special verdicts evidenced the growing appreciation of a subjective conceptualization of fault as they allowed certain types of killings to be distinguished from other killings. In relation to self-defence, some of the trial records provide little information ('The Jury considering the whole Matter, brought it in Se Defendendo.' 'Upon a full hearing of the Matter, the Jury acquitted him of all three Indictments, bringing in their Verdict, Se Defendendo.'[50]), but it seems clear that all the circumstances of the killing impacted on the trials in which the jury

---

[44]   Lacey (n. 39) 263; see also Lacey (n. 1).   [45]   Ibid., 250, 268.

[46]   See Farmer (n. 2) 77 ff.   [47]   Hale (n. 15) 471.

[48]   See *Rex v. Oneby* (1795) 2 Ld. Raym. 1485; see also Beattie (n. 5) 80.

[49]   The OBPs record thirty-one of these verdicts over 1674–1830. This is probably an underestimate of the number of trials for murder in which the jury found self-defence, as some of these may have been recorded as chance medley or manslaughter: see Bernard J. Brown, 'The Demise of Chance Medley and the Recognition of Provocation as a Defence to Murder in English Law' (1963) 7(4) *American Journal of Legal History* 310.

[50]   Trial of Isaac Causabon, 8 December 1708, t17081208-38; trial of Charles Harrison, 12 August 1724, t17208I2-50, respectively.

returned *se defendendo* verdicts ('Upon a full hearing, the Jury gave their Verdict that it was done in his own Defence.'[51]). In relation to killings that were determined to be accidental, special verdicts presented a way of explaining a decision not to convict ('The Witnesses swore, That the Prisoner and the deceased, were intimate Friends; and Ingle having a Pistol in her Hand, drew the Cock in Jest, and it went off and shot Townsend, but it was done unwillingly, and she did not know it was Charged; so the Verdict, was found Special.' 'The Evidence swore, That the Prisoner was driving along Bow-street in Bloomsbury, and the Child appeared to be in the way, and accidentally run over it . . . The Jury found the Matter Special.')[52] The findings of fact of self-defence or accident would later develop into stand-alone legal doctrines—self-defence as a defence to a criminal charge, and accident as the absence of *mens rea*—but, in advance of the development of these doctrines, special verdicts functioned to distinguish the reduced culpability of those accused of these types of killings.

c. Facilitating the Acceptance of Modern Practices of Evidence and Proof

The development of the modern criminal trial entailed a revolution in evidence and proof. Special verdicts facilitated this revolution, helping to smooth the way towards the high standard of proof that was coming to be required in criminal trials, and to demarcate the then still solidifying boundary between law and fact.

In relation to proof, the 'long' eighteenth century was marked by the transition from the 'altercation' trial of the early modern period—an adjudicative process that centred on the idea that the direct confrontation of the accused with his or her charge was the best means of discovering the truth of the allegation—to the adversarial trial familiar in the current era.[53] In the period from 1700, proof gradually became 'internal to the legal proceedings', subject to the arguments presented by each of the parties (and counsel) and the limitations on admissible evidence.[54] Changing evidentiary and procedural norms were associated with changes in scientific practices in the eighteenth century.[55] Over the 'long' eighteenth century, the criminal trial came to be oriented around an increasingly formalized and high standard of proof, and, before the end of the century, references to the 'beyond reasonable doubt' standard

---

[51] Trial of Patrick French, 10 September 1712, t17120910-28.

[52] E.g., trial of Mary Ingle, 22 April 1691, t16910422-17; trial of Thomas Banks, 9 September 1691, t16910909-21, respectively; see also trial of Ralph Kemp, 30 August 1694, t16940830-32.

[53] On the 'altercation' trial, see Anthony Duff, Lindsay Farmer, Sandra Marshall, Victor Tadros, *The Trial on Trial: Vol. 3: Towards a Normative Theory of the Criminal Trial* (2007) 31–2.

[54] Ibid., 44.

[55] See generally, Barbara Shapiro, *A Culture of Fact, England, 1550–1720* (2000).

had appeared.[56] This was a gradual and uneven development, led by the 'very high threshold of proof' required for conviction of capital offences.[57] The presumption of innocence crystallized by the end of the 1700s, but, before then, it was widely accepted that any doubts about the case should be resolved in the accused's favour.[58]

Special verdicts were issued in several trials in which the OBPs records reveal that the court held doubts about proof. An example is provided by William Bird's trial for the murder of Mary Maurice in 1742. The trial record indicates that the jury was tasked with determining whether the victim, who suffocated as a result of being detained in a 'Close-Room' of St Martin's Round-House called 'the Hole', died because she was forced to go into the room, or because, after she went in voluntarily, the prisoner did not respond to her cries to let her out. The jury 'found the Verdict Special' and the trial ends with a lengthy, narrative style verdict cataloguing those facts the jury had accepted (that the defendant was the keeper of the Round-House, that Mary Maurice was in the Hole for about two hours, and that she was held against her will, etc.). The jury found all 'Matters and Circumstances' necessary for 'bringing the point in Issue before the Court', but, as to whether William Bird was guilty of 'Felony and Murder in the said Indictment supposed', the jury concluded 'we know not'.[59] There were several other trial records resulting in special verdicts that suggest doubts about proof.[60]

Like attitudes to, and standards of, proof in criminal process, understanding of the relationship between law and fact changed significantly in the 'long' eighteenth century. The idea of a distinction between fact and law firmed over this period, developing along with the changing division of courtroom labour (canvassed above). But the distinction between law and fact remained highly charged throughout the century, something that may have contributed to the sustained use of the special verdict over the period. As Green argues, even as late as the eighteenth century, whether the jury 'found', as opposed to merely applied, the law in its decision-making, and the question of whether the law was such that every man could know it, continued to be live issues.[61] These issues lurked behind eighteenth century criminal justice: the established tradition that part of the jury's role was to be merciful generated anxiety and debate about whether exercising that role amounted to law-finding.[62]

---

[56] Thomas Green, 'A Retrospective on the Criminal Trial Jury', in J. S. Cockburn, Thomas Green (eds.), *Twelve Good Men and True: The Criminal Jury Trial in England, 1200–1800* (1988) 394–5.

[57] See King (n. 28) 233, and Green (n. 8) 280–1, 286, respectively.

[58] Beattie (n. 28) 248–9; see also Green (n. 8) 272–4.

[59] Trial of William Bird, 9 September 1742, t17420909-37; see also *Hazel's Case* (1785) 1 Leach CC 368; *Mackalley's Case* (1610) 9 Co. Rep. 61[b].

[60] See e.g., Trial of John Godson, 5 June 1690, t16900605-5; trial of George Duffus, 6 December 1721, t17211206-20; and trial of John Huggins, 21 May 1729, t17210521-49.

[61] Green (n. 8) 260–2; Green (n. 56) 398–9.

[62] Green (n. 9) 310, and, more generally, ch. 7.

These issues with the distinction between fact and law came to a head in the last decades of the eighteenth century, in relation to the common law offence of seditious libel, the intentional publication of material that 'scandalized' the government (that is, subverted its authority).[63] The political and religious conflicts that generated trials for seditious libel in this period meant that they were subject to high levels of interest. Juries were central to seditious libel trials: because the question of whether a publication was seditious was regarded as a matter of law, if a jury found as a matter of fact that the accused 'intentionally published the writing' and that 'the writing bore the meaning alleged by the prosecution' (known as innuendo), it had to convict (truth was not a defence to seditious libel). With a number of high-profile acquittals running against the letter of the law in the decades from the turn of the eighteenth century, seditious libel became a lightning rod for debates, taking place both within and beyond Parliament, about free speech and free press, the scope of the role of the jury, its autonomy, and its place in the English constitution.[64]

Special verdicts were at the heart of the controversy surrounding seditious libel—although their significance was obscured—and thus at the centre of the then still solidifying boundary between law and fact. The law of seditious libel was such that juries had to return a guilty verdict even if they thought that the publication was harmless, or that the accused did not have any seditious intent; alternatively, they were forced into nullifying the law by finding the defendant not guilty even in the face of proof of publication.[65] The effect of the law of seditious libel was that questions of fact were cast as questions of law, and general verdicts in effect masked particular findings of fact, with the jury asked to 'render what amounted to a special verdict in the form of a general verdict of "guilty"'.[66] Thus, in the OBPs, seditious libel trials generally resulted in general verdicts of 'guilty' or 'not guilty'.[67] As this suggests, in seditious libel trials, the role of the jury was tightly circumscribed, provoking consternation and placing additional pressure on trial verdicts.

The debates about seditious libel culminated in the passage of *Fox's Libel Act* in 1792, an Act which is associated with the widespread acceptance in England of the principle of freedom of political communication, said to mark the 'formal installation' of the idea that 'political expression should be relatively unhindered'.[68] This Act was presented as a declaration of the common law, rather than an attempt to change it, but it altered the relationship between fact and law in seditious libel. The Act provided that, in seditious libel cases, judges were to give directions to the jury 'in like manner as in other criminal cases': it did not specifically state that questions of intent or seditiousness were to be understood as questions of fact, but

---

[63]   Ibid., 319; see also James Oldham, *English Common Law in the Age of Mansfield* (2004) ch. 10.

[64]   See for discussion Green (n. 8) 320–31.   [65]   See Oldham (n. 63) 211.

[66]   See Green (n. 8) 319.

[67]   According to the OBP database, there were sixty-six trials for seditious libel held at the Old Bailey between 1674 and 1830.

[68]   Oldham (n. 63) 209.

affirmed the jury's right to return a general verdict.[69] This Act has been interpreted as an admission that 'discretionary lay fact-finding was central to the administration of justice', and a vindication of the historic role of the jury as a safeguard against tyranny by the executive.[70] According to Green, with the central place of the jury, and its role, reinforced, the distinction between fact and law hardened.[71] Thus, against a backdrop of the political use of trial verdicts in seditious libel, with questions of fact cast as questions of law, the 1792 Act's affirmation of the general verdict further raised its profile and status, at the expense of the special verdict.

IV. HISTORY AND COUNTER-HISTORY IN CRIMINAL LAW

This chapter presented a counter-history of trial verdicts, restoring the place of special verdicts in the historical story. While special verdicts are now virtually unknown, over the period of the development of the modern criminal trial, they played a greater role, operating as a means by which the seismic changes associated with the development of the modern criminal trial were negotiated in the courtroom. A study of the use of special verdicts in the *Old Bailey Proceedings* shows that they were deployed by various actors, and for various purposes, in a way that indicates that the special verdict served diverse interests and functions. This counter-history opens the way to think again about trial verdicts in the current era, considering the possibilities for the restoration of a meaningful role for special verdicts.

A counter-history of the general verdict casts a fresh, critical perspective on the present. First, in an era of ever-increasing complexity in criminal law, the special verdict might be thought to represent a welcome recalibration of the relationship between judge and jury, and conclusions of law and of fact, in favour of newly sharp and clear boundaries and demarcations. Second, while the formalized rules of evidence and proof that developed in the nineteenth century, and which now govern criminal process, are aimed at restricting 'the potential of the jury to err',[72] errors occur, and juror misconduct and miscarriages of justice draw popular and political condemnation and negatively affect the legitimacy of criminal trials. The focus on particular facts in issue that is entailed in special verdicts seems to present a valuable option for ensuring accuracy and fairness in trial process. Third, viewed in light of more and more elaborate laws on sentencing, and the recurring question

---

[69] Extracted in Green (n. 8) 330.   [70] Ibid., 353.   [71] Ibid., 355.
[72] See Langbein (n. 5) 330.

of lay involvement in deciding punishment,[73] special verdicts may be seen as a way of enhancing the communicative power of trial verdicts.

The story told in this chapter of the history of special verdicts shows their utility under the dynamic conditions associated with the development of the modern criminal trial. It has been suggested that the general verdict, 'the great procedural opiate', is valued for what it does—covering up errors—rather than for what it is.[74] The peculiarity of general verdicts has been said to be 'the merger into a single indivisible residuum of all matters, however numerous, whether of law or fact'.[75] The inarticulateness of the general verdict is infamous—and perhaps increasingly untenable. The contrast between special verdicts and general verdicts may be taken to indicate that it is actually the latter that are odd. Indeed, the story told here, of the utility of special verdicts at the time of the development of the modern criminal trial, suggests that such verdicts may come to be regarded as a useful option for reform of criminal process again at some point.

Historical analysis in criminal law represents a rich and expanding scholarly terrain. This chapter presented a strand of historical analysis in criminal law, counter-history, focusing on paths not taken at significant junctures in the development of the criminal law, and offering alternative narratives of legal developments via a focus on otherwise occluded aspects of legal history. Counter-history represents a distinctive and valuable addition to historical analysis. Such history encourages legal scholars to take seriously the cul-de-sacs as well as the apparently straight roads we find in the historical development of the criminal law. And, like the most innovative and sophisticated contributions that fall within the wider set of historical analysis in criminal law, counter-history invites us to think again about received historical wisdom, opens up possibilities for re-thinking the present, and perhaps goes some way towards encouraging us to imagine counter-futures.

Bibliography

Markus Dubber, Lindsay Farmer (eds.), *Modern Histories of Crime and Punishment* (Stanford University Press, 2007)

Markus Dubber (ed.), *Foundational Texts in Modern Criminal Law* (Oxford University Press, 2014)

Anthony Duff, Lindsay Farmer, Sandra Marshall, Victor Tadros, *The Trial on Trial: Vol. 3: Towards a Normative Theory of the Criminal Trial* (Oxford University Press, 2007)

---

[73] See, e.g., Chris Kemmitt, 'Function Over Form: Reviving the Criminal Jury's Historical Role as a Sentencing Body' (2006) 40 *University of Michigan Journal of Law Reform* 93.

[74] E. R. Sunderland, 'Verdicts, General and Special' (1920) 24(3) *Yale L.J.* 253, 258, 262.

[75] Ibid., 258; see also Larry Laudan, 'Need Verdicts Come in Pairs?' (2010) 14(1) *International Journal of Evidence & Proof.*

Lindsay Farmer, *Making of the Modern Criminal Law: Civil Order and Criminalization* (Oxford University Press, 2016)

George Fletcher, *Rethinking Criminal Law* (Oxford University Press, 2000)

Michel Foucault, *Discipline and Punish: The Birth of the Prison* (Pantheon Books, 1977)

Thomas Green, *Verdict According to Conscience: Perspectives on the English Criminal Trial Jury, 1200–1800* (University of Chicago Press, 1985)

Douglas Hay, Peter Linebaugh, John G. Rule, E. P. Thompson, Cal Winslow, *Albion's Fatal Tree: Crime and Society in Eighteenth Century England* (Allen Lane, 1975)

Nicola Lacey, *In Search of Criminal Responsibility: Ideas, Interests and Institutions* (Oxford University Press, 2016)

Barbara Shapiro, *A Culture of Fact, England, 1550–1720* (Cornell University Press, 2000)

James Q. Whitman, *The Origins of Reasonable Doubt: Theological Roots of the Criminal Trial* (Yale University Press, 2008)

CHAPTER 51

....

THE HISTORICAL METHOD IN PUBLIC LAW

....

MARTIN LOUGHLIN[*]

I. INTRODUCTION

....

IN his classic study on *The Elementary Forms of Religious Life* in 1912, Émile Durkheim demonstrated that the key to understanding contemporary religions is to trace them to their most primitive forms. Only by this genetic method of locating their originating causes can the constituent elements of any institution be exposed and only then might we appreciate how an institution comes to assume its present more complex form. Following Durkheim's injunction, the objective of this chapter is to highlight the importance of the historical method in public law by showing the way that public law was established as a distinct field of knowledge in European jurisprudence. Since developments in French legal thought in the sixteenth century provided the catalyst for generating this modern concept of public law, this is the focus of the chapter. This approach exposes the constituent elements of public law and shows how the historical method becomes a central element of the modern practice of public law.

Modern practice exhibits an ineradicable tension between the claims of reason and history. This tension is played out in many forms, including those between rationalism and empiricism, the universal and the particular, nomocratic and teleocratic ordering,

* London School of Economics & Political Science.

rights and utility, legitimacy and effectiveness, normativism and functionalism, and so on. The competing influences vary according to the circumstances of the time. Today, it would appear, the claims of reason are again in the ascendancy. This shapes our understanding of public law, which increasingly is being conceived as a universal set of principles of constitutional morality. But when we turn to origins, we see that public law was formed in opposition to this type of claim: its establishment came about through a shift in legal thinking from the transcendental to the institutional. The modern idea of public law was created as a local, contextual, source-based practice in opposition to the universal metaphysics of medieval scholasticism. It was established by setting in place a conception of law as a body of practical knowledge that is historical in orientation and geared to the concerns of civil government.

II. The Humanist Challenge to the Authority of Roman Law

The revival of Roman law in late eleventh-century western Europe ignited a new era of scientific jurisprudence. The great task became that of assimilating Justinian's Code, a challenge primarily taken up by a school of jurists known as the Glossators. Centred on Bologna, their methods were exegetical and anti-historical. Their objective was to make the *Corpus Juris Civilis* available as the authoritative common law (*ius commune*) of that sphere of Europe that had been incorporated into the Roman Empire. And throughout parts of Europe this met with some success, with Roman law being applied in court as a default rule whenever the law of the local jurisdiction was silent.

The Glossators treated the *Corpus Juris* as a comprehensive and binding code and they promoted a method of legal science based on close analysis of that authoritative text. This scholastic method quickly established itself as the predominant method of late-medieval jurists. Their method was dictated by the sheer scale of their adopted task, which was to convert the vast and sprawling materials of the *Corpus Juris* into a set of useable rules. Since they felt obliged to treat the *Corpus Juris* as a comprehensive and perfect code, its meaning could be derived only through a skilful exercise in logical analysis. Innovation henceforth could only be a product of textual interpretation.[1]

---

[1] See Donald Kelley, 'Civil Science in the Renaissance: The Problem of Interpretation' in Anthony Pagden (ed.), *The Languages of Political Theory in Early-Modern Europe* (1987) 57–78.

Roman law was concerned primarily with private law, but by borrowing from the work of canon lawyers on the authority structure of the medieval church, the scholastic jurists combined it with a hierocratic conception of secular governmental authority. The effect of this conjunction was to bolster the legal authority of the Holy Roman Empire. When during the fourteenth century certain conflicts arose as a result of a struggle by the cities of Lombardy and Tuscany against imperial claims, these conflicts were also fought out among the jurists. From these struggles emerged the great school of post-Glossators, led by Bartolus and his pupil, Baldus.

The main contribution of the post-Glossators was methodological. In Skinner's words, Bartolus 'abandoned the cardinal assumption of the Glossators to the effect that, when the law appears to be out of line with the legal facts, the facts must be adjusted to meet a literal interpretation of the law' and 'instead made it his basic precept that, when the law and the facts collide, it is the law which must be brought into conformity with the facts'.[2] Accepting that the Emperor is *dominus mundi* and wields the *merum imperium*, Bartolus nevertheless identified cities as an independent class of *civitates* and argued that the Emperor had no power of rule within the cities since he was master of the whole *qua* whole and not the ruler of each of its particular parts. Through this casuistic and dialectical procedure, the post-Glossators were able to challenge some of the literalism of Roman law scholarship and to open up the method of inquiry into the sources of governmental authority.

After technological developments in printing aided the diffusion of Renaissance values, the work of the post-Glossators was built upon, and by the beginning of the sixteenth century this led to the emergence a humanist culture across northern Europe. Returning to classical sources and seeking to restore classical ideals, the northern humanists applied techniques of philological and historical criticism to challenge the intellectual authority of the *Corpus Juris*. By demonstrating that the codification of Justinian was less than comprehensive, that it had been put together in a fragmentary way, and that the methods of interpretation used to reinforce its authority were highly dubious and often based on ignorance of the classical sources, they were able to mount a decisive attack on scholastic jurisprudence. The implications of this challenge to the authority of Roman law, a challenge which also extended to the more flexible methods of Bartolus and the post-Glossators, gradually permeated politico-legal thinking. But if the precepts of public law were no longer to be derived from an explication of Roman law principles, where were they to be found?

---

[2] Quentin Skinner, *The Foundations of Modern Political Thought* (1978) vol. I, 9.

III. The Work of the French Legists

The answer to that question was first provided by a prominent group of French jurists. By the sixteenth century, the law schools of Angers, Bourges, and Toulouse had grown into leading centres of European jurisprudence and the French legists in general 'constituted in themselves a great school of writers, the finest of their profession to be found in Europe during the century'.[3] These scholars addressed the question of the source of governmental authority during a critical period in which political ideas were losing their theological complexion, when the intellectual authority of Roman law was being undermined, and also when across Europe the nation-state was emerging as the primary territorial unit of allegiance.

By examining the pressing political issues of their day through the prism of law, these French scholars were obliged to develop new accounts of the framework of governmental ordering. This, in turn, called for new methods of legal analysis. Their investigations led to a break not only with Romanist conceptions of authority but also with the traditions of medieval constitutionalism. The methodological innovation they effected, which constituted a central element of what has been called 'juridical nationalism',[4] proved to be the decisive break that laid the ground for the emergence of the modern idea of public law.

The French legists argued that public law principles were to be found not within Justinian's Code but through historical investigation of the legal and political practices of European states. Such scientific laws as could be derived were therefore to be acquired from the application of a comparative method to these historical experiences of governmental ordering. This argument marked a decisive historical turn of inquiry, one that led to the *lex terrae* emerging alongside Roman law and canon law as an alternative source of juristic authority. The treatises of the French legists played a pivotal role in enabling law to be de-theologized. And by promoting this historical method, they were also able to undermine the authority of the medieval hierarchical and corporational scheme. From their perspective, the determinative public law relationship was one in which all subjects were brought into immediate subordination under the king.

The pioneering work of the French legists reached a critical stage during the first decade of the French wars of religion in the 1560s. Against the background of this crisis, one that threatened to weaken the French state, three scholars—François

---

[3] William Farr Church, *Constitutional Thought in Sixteenth-Century France: A Study in the Evolution of Ideas* (1941) 4.

[4] See Kelley (n. 1) 71.

Hotman, François Baudouin, and Jean Bodin—made particularly important methodological contributions to public law. Their work deserves further consideration.

The most militant anti-Romanism is to be found in Hotman's Calvinist writing. In *Anti-Tribonian* (1567), he argued that, being drawn up by Greeks and Byzantines in the fifth century, the *Corpus Juris* was written after the collapse of the Roman state and by writers 'who were estranged from the Roman spirit by nation, place, and time'.[5] The codifiers 'altered much and what they did not alter they scattered and rearranged' and 'what they did not retain they destroyed'.[6] In Pocock's summation of Hotman's arguments, the Codes and Digests 'are useless to the lawyer because they bear no relation to modern society' and 'they are useless to the historian because they are not the law that was practised at Rome at any time in its history'.[7] Echoing Bartolus, Hotman had opened *Anti-Tribonian* with the claim that: 'The learned men of every age have observed and voiced approval of the rule that the laws should be accommodated to the form and condition of the commonwealth, not the commonwealth to the laws.'[8] But Hotman drew a more radical message: different laws may be required for states that differ according to nature, history, culture, or contemporary circumstances. For Hotman, the study of the constitutional law required historical investigation into the distinctive practices of particular regimes.

Hotman had contended in particular that Roman law was irrelevant to the task of seeking to understand the constitution of the French state. Through historical investigation, he showed that the original *francsgaulois* had devised an ancient constitution that protected the people against tyranny and had preserved their liberties. These inquiries had an obvious contemporary purpose: the ancient constitution, he argued, had been able to reconcile authority and liberty by making French kings subject to the constraints of the law and by requiring them to respect the will of the people expressed through the Estates General.[9]

Hotman's historical investigations into customary law formed part of a general movement that sought to supplant the authority of Roman law with that of the *lex terrae*. This had specific implications for juristic method. While Roman law was fixed and written and had thus given rise to formal scholastic methods of interpretation, the folkways of customary law (*lex terrae*), being unwritten, were

---

[5] Julian H. Franklin, *Jean Bodin and the Sixteenth-Century Revolution in the Methodology of Law and History* (1963) 54 (paraphrasing Hotman's argument in *Anti-Tribonian*). Tribonian was the jurist who, at the command of Justinian, had supervised the production of the *Corpus Civilis*.

[6] J. G. A. Pocock, *The Ancient Constitution and the Feudal Law: A Study of English Historical Thought in the Seventeenth Century* (1987) 12; see also Skinner (n. 2) vol. II 270.

[7] Pocock (n. 6).   [8] Hotman, *Anti-Tribonian*; cited in Franklin (n. 5) 46.

[9] François Hotman, *Francogallia* [1573] Ralph E. Giesey, J. H. M. Salmon (eds.), (1972).

the subject of the more creative interpretative techniques of judges. Roman law was universal, fixed, and formal, whereas customary law was particular, fluid, and informal. In particular, being evolutionary in character, customary law was able to keep attuned to contemporary requirements. Customary law, in a trope that is resonant of the period, was held to be *tam antique et tam nova*, always immemorial and always up-to-date.

Hotman's work is an expression of a general reordering of the methods of political jurisprudence away from exegesis of a fixed authority and towards a more historically orientated and sociologically informed theory of law and legislation. The pedagogical aspects of this movement were most fully brought out by Baudouin in his work of 1561, *Prolegomenon on the Teaching of Universal History and its Conjunction with Jurisprudence*.

For our purposes, the most important message of Baudouin's work was his argument that the university law curriculum had become focused almost entirely on private law and this offered an altogether inadequate training for a jurisconsult. A jurisconsult called on to offer advice on affairs of state requires training in the arts of governing. If we are to train students in 'fostering the commonwealth and for the governance of empires', public not private law must be studied, and this means that 'history [should] be called on first of all'. Law is insufficient for training in statecraft: the study of history teaches how regimes are built and destroyed and only from these historical experiences can students acquire an education in the arts of prudence.

iv. The Birth of Modern Public Law

This line of legal scholarship culminates in work of Bodin who argued, contrary to the French legists of the early sixteenth century, that there is no irreconcilable conflict between the claim of absolute authority of the crown and the maintenance of traditional local liberties. Bodin maintained that those liberties were underpinned and guaranteed by the authority of the crown itself. This conception of the crown as both absolute by right but limited by practice could not easily be accounted for in a Roman public law based on the maxim *princeps legibus solutus est*. The line of argument that the French legists were striving to make led to the conclusion that the authority of the French monarch was based not on any enacted code but on historic practices of governing. By synthesizing this line of argument and radicalizing its implications, Bodin was able to establish the foundations of the modern idea of public law.

A. The *Methodus*

Bodin's method was first displayed in his *Methodus ad facilem historiarum cognitionem* (*Method for the Easy Comprehension of History*) of 1566.[10] Notwithstanding its title, Bodin was not interested in the study of history for its own sake. His objective was to promote historical inquiry for the purpose of revealing the main precepts of the art of governing. History provided the key to understanding public law. The nature of public law could be revealed only through a comparative and historical investigation into the laws, customs, and practices of particular governing regimes.

This juristic objective was evident in his introduction, which opened with a full-fronted attack on Roman law's claim to constitute the *ratio scripta* of universal law. Bodin argued that Justinian's Code was drafted during a period 'when all things suffered from the crudest barbarism' and by lawyers who 'so disturbed the sources of legislation that almost nothing pure is dragged forth from the filth and mud'. Its recent interpreters, Bodin continued, 'assume a false reputation of knowledge and none of equity' and they 'think that the state is served, judgments decided, and lawsuits settled by the quantities of syllables'. Those who 'ought gently to have cleaned the stains and spots from the old record, so that the ancient scene would be recognized, have with a steel pen so heavily glossed all books with worthless and, indeed, misleading notes that almost no image of antiquity remains'.[11] In place of jurisconsults, Bodin complained that the leading French jurists had become mere grammarians.

The message promoted by the *Methodus* is that the path of progress is to be discovered through the study of history; it is here that 'the best part of universal law lies hidden'.[12] Since history is for the most part concerned with politics, Bodin argued that the good historian must be familiar with the art of statecraft. This knowledge is most readily acquired from experience, from participation 'in public counsels, executive power, or legal decisions'. However, since 'without books we can hardly attain the very complex knowledge of governing the state', a man becomes even more skilled 'if he has added to this practice the profound study of letters and public law'.[13] The knowledge required for directing the state is derived from a comparative study of the laws and customs of peoples (*jus gentium*).

The *Methodus* is not so much a guide to the study of history as the prospectus for a new type of jurisprudence. Having rejected as absurd the attempt 'to establish principles of universal jurisprudence from the Roman decrees', Bodin advocated a comparative method in which 'wise men should bring together and compare the legal framework of all states . . . and from them compile the best kind'.[14] The study

---

[10] Jean Bodin, *Method for the Easy Comprehension of History*, trans. Beatrice Reynolds (1945) 43: 'The best writers are fully equipped . . . if only they could rid themselves of all emotion in writing history.'

[11] Ibid., 4.   [12] Ibid., 8.   [13] Ibid., 43.   [14] Ibid., 2.

of history thus had a specific purpose: his historical inquiry aims to show 'the way in which one should cull flowers from history to gather thereof the sweetest fruits'.[15] This new type of political jurisprudence required a new style of legal education. Rather than focusing on instruction in the finer points of court practice, a broader humanist curriculum aimed at educating jurisconsults skilled in the art of governing the state was needed.

The recurrent theme of the *Methodus* is that a state's destiny is determined by the character of its people. What therefore drives Bodin's comparative method is the search for those factors that shape the character of a people. The key factors he highlights are those of climate and geography. Notwithstanding some eccentricities, his achievement here was to have introduced a comparative method that, especially in the work of Montesquieu, was to flourish in the eighteenth century, and which provides the basis on which a sociological understanding of law was able to evolve.

The principal section of the *Methodus* examines the main forms of government and includes surveys of the constitutional history of the major states. In this section, we find the core of his research on comparative jurisprudence and an exposition of the *jus gentium*, the common law of nations. These central chapters provide a detailed first draft of the argument that Bodin in 1576 was to develop in his *Six Livres de la République*. But because the *République* is often credited with being the originating source of a modern conception of sovereignty, Bodin's later work has been fated to be interpreted mainly from the perspective of his successors. One consequence is that his writings often have not been analysed on their own terms, so that the lines of continuity with the French legists are underplayed and the organizing premises of the *République*, which were already outlined in the *Methodus* ten years earlier, have been overlooked. The achievement of the *République* can be appreciated only by examining the structure of the treatise as a whole.

B. *De la République*

Most commentators, for understandable reasons, have focused on the first of the six books of Bodin's *République*. Its opening words offer some sense of the scope of his inquiry: 'A commonwealth is a lawful government (*droit gouvernement*) of many families, and of that which unto them in common belongs, with a sovereign power.'[16] He then analyses each of these components, distinguishing in particular between rightful and disordered government and between public and private, defining sovereign power as the highest power of command, and emphasizing

---

[15] Ibid., 2, 1.
[16] Jean Bodin, *The Six Bookes of a Commonweale*, trans. Richard Knolles, ed. Kenneth Douglas McRae, (1962).

the common subjection of citizens to the sovereign. The aim in the first book is to outline the parameters of public law.

Notwithstanding the originality of Book I, the remaining five books cannot be overlooked without distorting Bodin's purpose. The main objectives of these books are to offer an analysis by way of comparisons drawn from history of the various forms of government and the jurisdiction of its officers (Books II and III), of the various factors that cause states to grow, flourish, and decline, and thence to derive prudential maxims that should enable governors to maintain their state (Books IV–VI). As a whole, the *République* provides a comprehensive and systematic account of the 'fundamental laws' at work in the public realm. By use of examples drawn from history, Bodin seeks to expose the sociological laws of governmental development and the ways in which they can be rightfully harnessed (the art of governing). Bodin's *République* gives us the first systematic account of modern public law.

Of particular significance for public law is the distinction drawn in Book II between sovereignty and government. There is a 'great difference between the state and the government of the state' and this, he claims, is 'a rule in policy (to my knowledge) not before touched on by any man'.[17] Thus, the commonwealth of ancient Rome was democratic in sovereignty, but aristocratic in its form of government. Similarly, the state may be a monarchy and yet the government popular, 'if the king do distribute all places of command, magistracy, offices and preferments indifferently unto all men, without regard of their nobility, wealth or virtue'.[18] This distinction provides the basis on which the claim to the autonomy of public law can be differentiated from its institutional formation.

In the later books Bodin proceeds, in orderly progression, to distil the precepts of the art of governing and, from the materials of universal history, to sketch the rudiments of a sociological theory of the development of public law. Bodin rehearses his theory of climate and of astrology and numbers. Interspersed amongst the various discussions on the art of governing are many maxims that have become powerful tropes of modern political thought. These include: power corrupts; on the necessity of ensuring a separation of the legislative and executive power; that relative equality in wealth distribution promotes the stability of the state; that wars sustain democracies; that most self-styled democracies are disguised aristocracies; and that 'the less the power of the sovereignty is (the true marks of majesty thereunto still reserved), the more it is assured'. The *République* concludes with Bodin's analysis of the three types of mathematical progression: arithmetic; geometric; and harmonic. Arithmetic progression, denoting equality and representing order, is consonant with the interests of democracies; geometric progression, representing justice, is expressive of aristocratic government; and the harmonic ratio, portraying the ruler–ruled relationship and representing peace, was attuned to monarchies.

---

[17] Ibid., 199.   [18] Ibid..

The *République*, 'arguably the most original and influential work of political philosophy to be written in the sixteenth century',[19] represents the highest achievement of the movement of French jurists in mid-century to displace the authority of Roman law and to establish a modern conception of public law founded on civil wisdom and derived from a comparative and historical inquiry into the governing practices of European states. Public law is conceived as a set of basic rules, principles, and practices that establish, sustain, and regulate the activity of governing the state.

V. THE METHOD OF MODERN PUBLIC LAW

Modern public law is established as a consequence of this basic shift in juristic method. The practices of public law are to be found in the *lex terrae*, a type of law that cannot be identified by the scholastic method of exegesis but only by historical investigation. This provides us with a concept of public law as a type of historico-political discourse. And the establishment of public law as historico-political discourse has important implications, of which three might be highlighted.

The first is that this discourse draws on a much broader range of sources of knowledge than Romanist techniques; it recognizes that in order to discern the meaning of public law it is necessary to extend beyond the forms of official legal texts and assess those innumerable informal understandings that condition the ways in which authority is understood to be properly exercised. Jurist-law must accommodate the ways of folk-law, and this makes the exercise of discerning meaning more flexible, and also more contestable.

Secondly, and related to this first point, the adoption of public law as a type of historico-political discourse inevitably leads to the past being treated in an ideological manner. This is unavoidable because history thereby becomes bound up with a discourse of power. We see, for example, that wrapped up in the anti-Romanist discourse of the French jurists is a strong strain of Protestant historiography that seeks to press its claims against royal (Catholic) absolutism. It might also be noted that, at the same time as French jurists were developing these arguments, lawyers in Britain were beginning to use similar modes of discourse in their own disputes over the power of the sovereign.[20] This historico-political discourse reached its zenith

---

[19] Skinner (n. 2) vol. I 208.

[20] See, e.g., Adam Blackwood, *Adversus Georgii Buchanani dialogum, de jure regni apud Scotus, pro regibus apologia, Pictavis, apud Pagaeum* (1581). Blackwood uses historical arguments to bolster the rights of the sovereign and to challenge the abstract arguments of Buchanan.

in England in the myth of the ancient constitution, the claim that there existed an original Anglo-Saxon constitution under which kings were elected to an office of limited authority, and which constitution operated to protect ancient liberties.[21] During the early seventeenth century, this doctrine of the ancient constitution was invoked by common lawyers, notably Sir Edward Coke, to complain about the erosion of English liberties by the exercise of the prerogative powers of Stuart kings.[22] The structure of this discourse—of Saxon right versus Norman statecraft—established a tension that turned into a regular refrain,[23] and later provides the master narrative of Whig constitutional history.[24]

The last implication to be highlighted is the most complex and perhaps also the most important. As is signalled by the fact that Bodin opens the *République* not with an account of the sovereign but with that of the commonwealth, this historico-political discourse shifts the focus of its inquiry. In Foucault's words, this discourse 'is no longer the State [sc. sovereign] talking about itself; it is something else talking about itself, and the something else that speaks in history and takes itself as the object of its own historical narrative is a sort of new entity known as the nation'.[25] Bodin's disquisition on the character of peoples, for example, illustrates his general argument that a good ruler must first understand the nature of the people. By opening up for consideration the relation between the people and their institutions of government, this historico-political discourse shifts the conception of power from that of the highest power of command (Bodin, Book I) to a relational notion

[21] See Pocock (n. 6); Corinne C. Weston, 'England: Ancient Constitution and Common Law' in J. H. Burns (ed.), *The Cambridge History of Political Thought, 1450–1700* (1991) 374–411. This was part of a more general move in European political thought of the period. It might therefore be noted that in *De antiquitate Reipublicae Batavicae* (1610), Grotius made a similar appeal to an ancient Batavian constitution to justify Dutch revolt against the Spanish: see Annabel S. Brett, 'The Development of the Idea of Citizen's Rights' in Quentin Skinner, Bo Stråth (eds.), *States and Citizens: History, Theory, Prospects* (2003) 97–112, 109. A related argument was pursued by Spener when in the early eighteenth century he sought to rid the study of German imperial public law of all foreign influences and attempted to restore an edifice of Germanic principles rooted in German legal history: Jacob Karl Spener, *Teutsches Ius Publicum, oder des Heilige Römisch-teutschen Reichs* (7 vols., 1723–1733).

[22] See, e.g., Pocock (n. 6) 32: 'In the first decade of the new century . . . English lawyers were prepared to define common law as custom and to defend custom against written law in language which recalls certain French ideas of an earlier generation.'

[23] See J. G. A. Pocock, 'Burke and the Ancient Constitution—A Problem in the History of Ideas' (1960) 3 *Historical Journal* 125–43; Christopher Hill, 'The Norman Yoke' in his *Puritanism and Revolution* (1958) 50–122.

[24] See J. W. Burrow, *A Liberal Descent: Victorian Historians and the English Past* (1981).

[25] Michel Foucault, *Society Must Be Defended: Lectures at the Collège de France, 1975–1976*, trans. David Macey (2003) 142. See further Francis D. Wormuth, *The Royal Prerogative, 1603–1649: A Study in English Political and Constitutional Ideas* (1939) 31: 'Every nation, by virtue of its individuality, had a peculiar history, a peculiar population, peculiar customs from which arose these fundamental laws. The fundamental laws were justified, not by their logicality and universality, but precisely by reason of their local character; they were justified because they came from a particular milieu and were adapted to it.'

in which power is understood to be generated in a field of forces (Bodin, Book VI, harmonic proportion).

The struggle that subsequently took place in the period between the sixteenth and eighteenth centuries is that between the rival claims of absolutism (the sovereign) and constitutionalism (the people). The struggle was vital primarily because of the growth in the extent and intensity of governing power. In this situation, the claim of absolutism presents itself not as a conservative argument of seeking to bolster the authority of ancient arrangements, but as a novel argument born of the necessity of maintaining order in a changing world. The absolute sovereign should not to be confused with the figure of the despot or tyrant, the ruler who wields an unrestrained power that can be exercised in an arbitrary manner. Absolutism was a rationalist argument tied to the emerging modern concept of sovereignty. Its contentious character is heightened by virtue of having to make the claim in a secularizing world, one in which the sovereign has ceased to embody the link between heaven and earth. Absolutism is the crucible in which the modern concept of sovereignty is forged. So even though this concept is eventually wrested from the figure of the sovereign and vested in 'the nation', the idea of the nation as the ultimate repository of sovereign authority continues to draw its power from the transcendental image of monarchy.

Bodin again provides guidance. For much of the sixteenth century, the French legists had been developing sophisticated constitutional theories and Bodin had adopted their constitutionalist method in the *Methodus*. But ten years later, he shifted his position and in the *République* produced a systematic account of sovereignty that laid the foundation for a theory of absolutism. He argues in the *République* that every viable state must possess a single, supreme centre of authority that contains all governmental powers, and this is 'the most necessary point for the understanding of the nature of a commonwealth'. The phenomenon to which he refers is defined as 'the most high, absolute, and perpetual power over the citizens and subjects in a commonwealth'. This is what he calls sovereignty, 'the greatest power of command', which is 'not limited either in power, charge, or time certain'.[26] This sovereign authority, which Bodin explicates by identifying the 'true marks of sovereignty',[27] is vested in the sovereign ruler.

Bodin's account thus signalled an abrupt break not only in the general movement in European public law thought but also with his earlier work. It can be explained ideologically as a response to the upheavals that threatened to undermine the French state and which were triggered by the St Bartholomew's Day Massacre of 1572 and the threat of religion-inspired civil war. After the massacre, the Huguenots proclaimed the king a tyrant, resorted to armed action, and their

---

[26] Bodin (n. 16) 84–5.   [27] Ibid., Bk. I, ch. 10.

supporters claimed the right of legitimate resistance to tyrannical authority. Hotman's treatise, *Francogallia*, drafted in the 1560s but published only in 1573, was a principal inspiration. In this work, Hotman unearthed the ancient French constitution, a framework of government in which kings had been elected, were law-bounded, and created by the ultimate authority of the people meeting in the public council of the realm. Hotman's contemporary message was clear.

Bodin's shift towards an absolutist conception of sovereignty can be attributed to his reaction to the Huguenot doctrines of legitimate resistance. This is seen most explicitly in his preface to the first edition of *République*, which begins by explaining how he has written this treatise on the commonwealth precisely because the 'ship of state, rocked by a violent tempest, is in imminent danger of foundering'. Bodin explained the need to place a study of the state at the heart of politics, precisely because certain writers display ignorance of 'laws and of public right' that establish and maintain the state. There are, in particular, two types of writers who 'have profaned the sacred mysteries of political philosophy'. First, the followers of Machiavelli, 'the most perfidious son of a priest that ever lived', who taught princes the 'rules of injustice in order through tyranny to consolidate their power'. This, Bodin argued, is a disastrous foundation and will lead to the ruin of princes and their state. Secondly, he argued against those who have taken the opposite view but are 'no less dangerous': those who 'under the pretext of exemption from duties . . . induce the subjects to rebel against their natural princes, opening the door to a licentious anarchy, which is worse than the harshest tyranny in the world'.[28] By negotiating his way between the threats of tyranny and anarchy, Bodin lays down the basis for a modern understanding of public law.

Sovereignty is necessarily absolute and indivisible but it is also apparently limited. These limitations, Bodin suggests, are of two main types: those that concern the 'fundamental laws' that establish and maintain the office of the sovereign, and those 'natural laws' that condition the sovereign's treatment of his subjects. This is puzzling. But when we examine these carefully we see that these fundamental rules are not to be conceived as imposing limitations on the sovereign: they are rules that define the nature of the office. The innovative first book of the *République* should thus be viewed as the earliest attempt to specify the constitutive rules for the establishment of a commonwealth or state. These rules establish the nature of the undertaking: that of governing the public realm by means of positive law, with such law-making power being vested in an absolute authority. This is a major achievement: it outlines for the first time the constitution of sovereignty.

---

[28] Ibid., A69–70.

But Bodin also recognized that these constitutive rules merely establish the basic institutional forms and that, for the regime to work, these constitutive rules need to be supplemented by a set of regulative rules, rules which seek to regulate actual political behaviour in the world. In the remaining five books of the *République*, as we have seen, Bodin elaborates these regulative rules of state-building practice. Thus, although sovereign authority formally vests in the crown, Bodin recognizes that parliaments and assemblies are essential aids: 'the just monarchy hath not any more assured foundation or stay, than the estates of the people, communities, corporations, and colleges'.[29] The importance of Bodin's concept of sovereignty thus lies not so much in Bodin's own expectations as to how government would actually operate, since his views on this matter are conventional. Rather, its significance is to be found in its treatment of the legal norm.

We can go one stage further and suggest that Bodin elaborates both the formal logic of sovereignty (the relation of legal norms) and conditions for the generation of power through that framework (the importance of various regulative rules and practices). Both are necessary elements of public law. Bodin was the first to grasp this and to try to integrate logic and practice—reason and history—into a system of universal jurisprudence that analyses both the formalities of state-building and the conditions for maintaining the state. That is, Bodin is concerned not only with establishing the formalities of the right to rule but also with elaborating the practices that can enhance the sovereign's capacity to rule.

This aspect of Bodin's work is well drawn out by Holmes, who argues that 'Bodin treats restrictions on power, unconventionally, as a set of authority-reinforcing, will-empowering, and possibility-expanding rules.' It is precisely because Bodin was interested in political practice as well as legal theory that he was able 'to redescribe traditional limits on royal power as conditions for the successful exercise of royal power' and explain how the ruler could be 'a sovereign in fact as well as in law'. Holmes notes especially that Bodin 'redefines natural law as a set of prudential maxims for avoiding revolution' and replaces crude Machiavellism with a strategy that recognizes that 'authority is strengthened when its jurisdiction is narrowed'.[30] In the context of the religious wars that ravaged France between 1562 and 1598, Bodin's teaching conveyed a precise if paradoxical message: in order to preserve absolute authority, the sovereign was obliged to differentiate between public and private—between matters of state and matters of religion—and actively to promote a policy of religious toleration. Through his precise definition of the supreme authority, his determination of its scope, and his analysis of the conditions for its exercise, Bodin was able to turn public law into a scientific discipline.

[29] Bodin (n. 16) 384.
[30] Stephen Holmes, 'The Constitution of Sovereignty in Jean Bodin' in his *Passions and Constraints: On the Theory of Liberal Democracy* (1995) 100–33, at 110–13.

vi. The Historical Method in Modern Practice

The main implications to be derived from examining this critical period of birth of the modern concept of public law can now be signalled.

First, a juristic revolution was initiated by the French legists who, challenging the hierocratic and imperial assumptions of Romanism, advanced the argument that constitutional law (*droit gouvernement*) should be understood as forming a set of rules, customs, and practices through which the several territorially based regimes of rule had been established and the governing framework has evolved. This led to the formation of a modern concept of public law and, on this modern understanding, its meaning can be grasped only by examining the historical experience of a people.

Secondly, the historical method of modern public law generates less dogmatic legal methodologies and this enables legal discourse more readily to serve contemporary needs. The historical method in public law invariably serves present purposes. We have seen, for example, that in the context of the French religious wars it was their respective judgments on the nature of these political controversies that caused Bodin and Hotman, equal pioneers of the methodological shift, to adopt opposing positions on the question of the authority of the sovereign. Politics is the place where law and history meet.

Thirdly, among the French legists, it was Bodin who most clearly spoke in a modern voice: only by arguing that the sovereign possessed an absolute power to make law and by claiming that its authority was permanent and indivisible could the principle of representation complete the work of transforming the hierarchical notions of medieval rulership into the immanent logic of the governing regime of the modern state. Destruction of the old regime could be achieved only by way of elevation. But the logic of modern sovereignty is very different from the medieval notion of rule. While medieval government was anchored by the principle of hierarchy, the modern concept of sovereignty is immanent in nature. The driving force of modern sovereignty is to be found in the immanent necessities that maintain the existence of the political entity of the state. The modern concept expresses an egalitarian and democratic ethos and this type of framework is no longer intrinsically organized in a hierarchical fashion. Transcendence is opposed by immanence; divine right is supplanted by the general will.

Fourthly, this shift has a specific juristic consequence: although the transition to a modern concept of sovereignty was set in train by historically orientated jurists who sought to anchor constitutional ordering in the 'fundamental laws' of the ancient constitution, in a strict sense the immanent logic of modern sovereignty can have no place for fundamental law. The idea of fundamental law makes sense only when the regime is externally determined by a higher authority; only in this manner are we able to appeal to an authoritative past. But when the regime is no longer externally authorized, we are required to turn to the future as the source of legitimacy. In this unsettling situation, modern regimes of sovereign states are obliged to borrow the old forms of religiosity in the guise of a 'civil religion'. Modern public law operates in an age of ideology, in which the quest for future salvation offers a justification for present sacrifices.

Fifthly, although the problem of dealing with this tension between law and history—of distilling the *jus gentium* from comparative historical investigation—has already been touched on, the general tension between the universal and the particular is symptomatic of a larger and more general issue that has come to bedevil modern public law. This is sometimes expressed as the tension between reason and history or, specifically, the quest to integrate conceptually the rational and the empirical, the normative and the factual. But one message from this study of origins is that public law emerged only by acknowledging the distinction between natural law and positive law. And once the essential unity of the two is broken, and the explanatory power of natural law is restricted: law and ethics are distinct disciplines.

Sixthly, with this rupture, there is a temptation to confine the remit of legal study to the structure of positive law. But if public law is to retain its explanatory power, this offers no solution. The entire structure of Bodin's *République* demonstrates that *droit public* rests not only on the commands of the sovereign but on the conditions through which the sovereign is able to maintain authority. Transposing this insight into modern terminology, it might be said that public law acquires its identity not from the figure of the sovereign but from the modern concept of sovereignty, not from the formal law-giver but from the immanent logic that binds together the political entity of the state.

Seventhly, this, ultimately, is the significance of the methodological turn in the late sixteenth century. Expressing scepticism over the applicability of universal principles of morality to governmental issues, the anti-scholastic scholars sought lessons in history. Only from such historical study, which today must be extended to include empirical or sociological investigation, can the 'real' interests of states be discerned. This line of analysis, which stretches from Machiavelli and through the work of Bodin and Pufendorf, culminates in the doctrine of *raison d'état*. It is in this transformation of natural jurisprudence, effected during the seventeenth century, that we locate the emergence of public law as an autonomous field, that is, as the arrangements that sustain the modern immanent concept of sovereignty.[31]

Eighthly, once this system of territorially based sovereign states that replaced the Romanist theological-political construct of the empire and the papacy had been set in place, the modern framework of international relations and international law was able to emerge. The *jus publicum europaeum* of the modern era was built on

---

[31] See Martin Loughlin, 'Reason of State/State of Reason' in Loughlin, *Political Jurisprudence* (2017) ch. 8.

the foundation of mutual respect of the inviolable domestic authority of sovereign states and mutual recognition of autonomous states in the international arena. Not being subject to any common higher authority and possessing the right to make war (*jus ad bellum*), the nature of the inter-state law that evolved implied the subordination of morality to politics. Public international law emerges as a form of political jurisprudence operating to govern inter-state relations.

Ninthly, the claim that reason of state supplies the underlying logic of modern public law stands directly opposed to Kantian-inspired philosophies that deploy rationalist political metaphysics to derive a formal transcendental law from the precepts of critical reason. And it is these Kantian-inspired philosophies that have fuelled the present movement of treating law as the elaboration of reason. The historical method, it is argued, enables us to situate matters of public law in an appropriate intellectual framework. Public law must bring the rational into an appropriate alignment with empirical claims. This makes the subject both ambiguous and complex: since the tensions are intrinsic and irresolvable, public law remains an ambiguous and impermanent discourse.

BIBLIOGRAPHY

Jean Bodin, *Method for the Easy Comprehension of History* [1566] trans. Beatrice Reynolds (Columbia University Press, 1945)

Jean Bodin, *The Six Bookes of a Commonweale*, trans. Richard Knolles ed. Kenneth Douglas McRae (Harvard University Press, 1962)

William Farr Church, *Constitutional Thought in Sixteenth-Century France: A Study in the Evolution of Ideas* (Harvard University Press, 1941)

Julian H. Franklin, *Jean Bodin and the Sixteenth-Century Revolution in the Methodology of Law and History* (Columbia University Press, 1963)

Stephen Holmes, 'The Constitution of Sovereignty in Jean Bodin' in his *Passions and Constraints: On the Theory of Liberal Democracy* (University of Chicago Press,1995)

Donald R. Kelley, *Foundations of Modern Historical Scholarship: Language, Law, and History in the French Renaissance* (Columbia University Press, 1970)

Martin Loughlin, *Foundations of Public Law* (Oxford University Press, 2010)

Martin Loughlin, 'Reason of State/State of Reason' in *Political Jurisprudence* (Oxford University Press, 2017) ch. 8

Quentin Skinner, *The Foundations of Modern Political Thought* (Cambridge University Press, 1978) 2 vols

CHAPTER 52

HISTORICAL ANALYSIS IN ENVIRONMENTAL LAW

DAVID B. SCHORR*

ENVIRONMENTAL law has no history: this is not to say environmental law has no past; indeed, scholars are beginning to uncover its historical roots. Having no history means, first, that there is a general feeling, common to legal historians and environmental lawyers (particularly in the United States), that environmental law is something new under the sun, having emerged in the 1970s from the environmental crises of the preceding decade (such as the Cuyahoga River catching fire) and a contemporaneous sharpening of ecological consciousness (spurred, most prominently, by Rachel Carson's *Silent Spring*). Modern environmental law lacks connection both to earlier periods and to the great themes and trends of legal history.

The general view of environmental law's history is that before circa 1970 environmental regulation as we think of it today—a branch of public law in which the regulator sets standards for activities with environmental impacts—was insignificant. Rather, it is taught, the environment was regulated through nuisance law—a system relying on private parties, or sometimes the government, bringing a lawsuit to enjoin environmentally harmful activities or obtain damages

* Thanks to Rona Wollack for research assistance, and to Lorenzo Gagliardi, Joshua Getzler, Ron Harris, Noga Morag-Levine, Silvia Schiavo, Lehua Yim, and participants in a workshop at TAU Law on chapters in this volume for their helpful comments. Funding was provided by the Israel Science Foundation (grant no. 1822/16) and U.S. National Endowment for the Humanities.

for environmental harm: 'Prior to the explosion of environmental legislation in the 1970s, the common law was the legal system's primary vehicle for responding to environmental problems . . . The common law relied largely on nuisance law doctrines to resolve environmental controversies . . .'[1] Some look to this period as a lost golden age; others see it as having been a workable system for its time; while yet others condemn it as a failure.[2]

This view of modern environmental law being created *ex nihilo* in a moment of crisis is, first and foremost, inherently implausible. One need only peruse the hundreds of pages of the 1970s-era *United States Statutes at Large* dedicated to environmental legislation to intuit that the legislators and draftsmen who created the laws, talented as they may have been, did not pull these legal regimes out of thin air. Some of the legal forms, classifications, and terms may have been new, but most were not. (One might also point out that some obvious continuities with earlier law are evident on the face of much of the legislation: the Clean Air Act and Clean Water Act—the centrepieces of the supposedly new American environmental law— were actually officially named the 'Clean Air Amendments of 1970' and the 'Federal Water Pollution Control Act Amendments of 1972', thus signalling their continuity with earlier pollution control law.)[3]

Though a recent wave of research (some of it surveyed below) has made progress in exposing some earlier statutory regulation of industrial pollution, this valuable work has yet to make a serious impression on environmental lawyers or legal historians. Moreover, other historical sources of modern environmental law have been almost entirely neglected, certainly by legal historians.

This lack of a felt historical anchor, of a back story, is of course unfortunate for the historical ignorance it perpetuates, though this is perhaps a matter that primarily concerns academics and antiquarians. What should concern broader circles, it will be argued in this chapter, is that the lack of a historical sensibility with regard to the field severely impedes understanding of environmental law's form and substance, at the same time leaving a yawning gap in legal histories precisely where one would hope to find engagement with the legal-environmental roots of present challenges.

Environmental law has no history in a second, sense, too; it lacks history as a mode of argument or analysis. Beyond a sea of baroque doctrinal and literature

---

[1] Robert V. Percival, Christopher H. Schroeder, Alan S. Miller, James P. Leape, *Environmental Regulation: Law, Science, and Policy* (6th edn. 2009) 63.

[2] See, e.g., Richard A. Epstein, 'From Common Law to Environmental Protection: How the Modern Environmental Movement Has Lost Its Way' (2015) 23 *Supreme Court Economic Review* 141 ff (golden age); Ben Pontin, 'Nuisance Law and the Industrial Revolution: A Reinterpretation of Doctrine and Institutional Competence' (2012) 75 *Modern L.R.* 1010 ff (workable system); John P. S. McLaren, 'Nuisance Law and the Industrial Revolution—Some Lessons from Social History' (1983) 3 *O.J.L.S.* 155 ff (failure).

[3] Pub. L. No. 91-604, 84 Stat.1676 ff; Pub L. No. 92-500, 86 Stat. 816 ff.

that typifies a field dominated by complex legislation, the primary critical modes of contemporary analysis of environmental law are those of neoclassical economics and two branches of environmental ethics—'environmental justice' and eco-centrism. In legal cultures in which precedent and history are often what make a winning argument, the unavailability of historical analysis as a mode of legal discourse—as it is, for instance, in constitutional and property law (two fields in which environmental legal disputes are often entangled)—means that environmental values are often forced to retreat in the face of others.

For these reasons, environmental law needs both heightened historical analysis and a sense of its own historical roots. This chapter aims to sketch current, possible, and desirable directions for future research into the history of environmental law. Before doing so, it notes a current scholarly pathology.

I. 'THE ONE CAME NOT NEAR THE OTHER ALL THE NIGHT'

In May 2010 *Environmental History*, the leading journal in its field, published an article by Aaron Sachs on antebellum environmental thought as expressed in contemporary American cemeteries.[4] A few months later legal historian Alfred Brophy published a blog post on American antebellum constitutionalism as expressed in speeches made in cemeteries.[5] Though both pieces focused on the same cemeteries, with rich discussions of the political, social, and cultural contexts in which they operated, neither work made any reference to the other, nor, indeed, to the literature or historical sub-discipline in which the other was located. Three years later, both pieces were released in expanded form, again with no interaction between them or their scholarly worlds.[6]

This was not an isolated (non-)incident. Though the fields of environmental history and legal history seemingly share a wealth of common interests—the histories of capitalism, slavery, and the administrative state are a few of the topics

---

[4] Aaron Sachs, 'American Arcadia: Mount Auburn Cemetery and the Nineteenth-Century Landscape Tradition' (2010) 15 *Environmental History* 206 ff.

[5] Alfred Brophy, 'Constitutionalism and the Antebellum Cemetery', The Faculty Lounge, 20 December 2010 <http://www.thefacultylounge.org/2010/12/constitutionalism-and-the-antebellum-cemetery.html>.

[6] Alfred L. Brophy, '"These Great and Beautiful Republics of the Dead": Public Constitutionalism and the Antebellum Cemetery' SSRN, 12 August 2013 <https://ssrn.com/abstract=2304305>; Aaron Sachs, *Arcadian America: The Death and Life of an Environmental Tradition* (2013).

receiving intense attention in both fields in recent years—the two fields move through parallel intellectual universes with nary a glance at one another.

If there is a certain symmetry in the blissful ignorance in which each field operates with regard to the scholarship of its sister field, the same cannot be said of the relative interest each takes in the subject matter of the other. In the last decade (2007–2016) *Law and History Review,* the leading English-language legal history journal, published only three articles that might be described as engaging with environmental issues; and only one of these—its author an environmental historian, not a legal one—was directly on an environmental topic.[7] Meanwhile the situation in *Environmental History,* the leading journal in its field, in the same period was radically different; counting conservatively, over twenty-five articles in this journal engaged significantly with legal issues, on a wide variety of topics, including a collection of essays dedicated to a single environmental statute.[8] A similar picture emerges from an examination of leading European journals in the two fields: on the one hand, *Journal of Legal History* with two articles dealing with issues of public property that might be tagged as environmental and *Rechtsgechichte* with three on environmental topics;[9] on the other, *Environment and History* with close to thirty articles with significant treatment of legal issues.

The situation with regard to monographs is harder to measure, but with them, too, the impression is that few legal historians have incorporated environmental law into their work, while the recent work of many environmental historians has been foregrounding legal issues such as property regimes in natural resources, regulation of pollution, and racial discrimination.[10] For instance, environmental historians have identified the American New Deal as a key moment in environmental history, a leading historian characterizing the period as 'the decade of incipient U.S. hegemony in the domains later grouped under environmental policy'.[11] Yet while American legal historians display an ongoing and intense interest in the

---

[7]   Paul Sabin, 'Environmental Law and the End of the New Deal Order' (2015) 33 *Law and History Review* 965 ff. The other two articles were Harry N. Scheiber, 'Taking Legal Realism Offshore: The Contributions of Joseph Walter Bingham to American Jurisprudence and to the Reform of Modern Ocean Law' (2008) 26 *Law and History Review* 649 ff; Brian Sawers, 'Property Law as Labor Control in the Postbellum South' (2015) 33 *Law and History Review* 351 ff.

[8]   'Reflections on the Wilderness Act at Fifty' (2014) 19 *Environmental History* 714 ff.

[9]   See Andrea Loux Jarman, 'Customary Rights in Scots Law: Test Cases on Access to Land in the Nineteenth Century' (2007) 28 *Journal of Legal History* 207 ff; Huw Pryce, Gwilym Owen, 'Medieval Welsh Law and the Mid-Victorian Foreshore' (2014) 35 *Journal of Legal History* 172 ff; Henning Schmidgen, '*Die Gletscher haben keine Zei*' (2007) 10 *Rechtsgeschichte* 74 ff; Osvaldo Cavallar, 'The Wheels of Watermills and the Wheel of Fortune: A *consilium* of Donatus Ricchi de Aldighieris' (2008) 13 *Rechtsgeschichte* 80 ff.; Daniel Damler, '*Das Meer im Recht*' (2010) 16 *Rechtsgeschichte* 258 ff.

[10]   See, e.g., Stefania Barca, *Enclosing Water: Nature and Political Economy in a Mediterranean Valley, 1796–1916* (2010); William M. Cavert, *The Smoke of London: Energy and Environment in the Early Modern City* (2016); William E. O'Brien, *State Parks and Jim Crow in the American South: The Untold Story of Segregation in State Parks* (2015).

[11]   Joachim Radkau, *The Age of Ecology: A Global History,* trans. Patrick Camiller (2014) 52–3.

New Deal, the environmental aspects of the legal history of this period have been notably absent from their work.

The reasons for this asymmetry are unclear, and yet more puzzling if we take into account that the American field of legal history traces its origins to James Willard Hurst, whose work was firmly planted in an environmental context.[12] Perhaps law is simply so pervasive that other sub-fields of history have no choice but to actively engage legal issues; yet one might be forgiven for thinking that the environment, too, is always physically present and needing to be accounted for. Alternatively, perhaps the imbalance reflects the salience of law in modern environmentalism bleeding over into the related historical discipline. Whatever the reason, the fact remains that while environmental historians as a group take a keen interest in legal issues, legal historians seem to be almost wilfully ignorant of environmental issues and the way the environment might enrich their scholarship.

II. Winds of Change

Nonetheless, recent years have seen deepening interest in the history of environmental law, with a few scholars highlighting the connections between the supposedly foundational environmental legislation of the 1970s and earlier law. One prominent work in this genre of pushing back environmental law's start date is Karl Boyd Brooks's *Before Earth Day*.[13] Brooks's book is notable not only for identifying the statutory precursors of modern environmental regulation, but for its attempt to trace the manifold legal, personal, and institutional connections between legislation and litigation, and between pollution control law and the law of nature protection, two areas of modern environmental law that might be assumed to have distinct, even antagonistic, origins.

Another front opened recently regards the relationship between modern environmental law as it coalesced in the 1970s and the New Deal administrative state. On the one hand, Arthur McEvoy has argued that environmental law was a project of the New Deal regime, and that after the early 1970s it declined

---

[12] See James Willard Hurst, *Law and Economic Growth: The Legal History of the Lumber Industry in Wisconsin, 1836–1915* (1964). For Hurst as the founding father of the discipline in the US, see Kunal M. Parker, 'Writing Legal History Then and Now: A Brief Reflection' (2016) 56 *American Journal of Legal History* 168 ff.

[13] Karl Boyd Brooks, *Before Earth Day: The Origins of American Environmental Law, 1945–1970* (2012).

along with the wider regime.[14] On the other, two recent articles have argued that the environmental law of the 1970s marked a break with New Deal liberalism. Paul Sabin explains the era's public interest law organizations as growing out of environmentalists' increasing disillusionment with the state as an engine of public-minded environmental protection, spurring a turn to an oppositional and litigious stance.[15] Jedediah Purdy, meanwhile, sees the salient federal legislation of the 1970s and the organizations that grew up around it as departing from an earlier tradition that viewed environmental issues in a wider context of social and economic justice. Mainstream environmental lawyers, he argues, were lulled by the shrinking economic inequality of the postwar period into focusing on elite and professional advocacy and environmental issues narrowly defined, forsaking issues, such as the disproportionate impacts of environmental harms (and environmental regulation) on minorities and workers, that would later come to be labelled 'environmental justice'.[16]

Yet while these works do the valuable service of suggesting connections to wider themes of legal history such as the rise of—and reaction to—the administrative state, they push back the start of environmental law by only a few decades. They also make no connections to environmental regulation before the twentieth century, outside the US, or indeed outside the arena of federal regulation.

It bears noting that the relative dearth of historical work on environmental law, as well as the relatively narrow jurisdictional and chronological frames of what work there is, are far more marked in the American context than in the European. For instance, scholars have produced a significant body of work on French regulation of early industrial pollution,[17] and quite a few British legal historians have given significant attention to environmental issues.[18] Noga Morag-Levine's work has bridged some of these bodies of scholarship, compellingly arguing that English and Continental approaches to pollution control in the nineteenth century continue to inform current American debates over issues such as the appropriateness of the

---

[14]   Arthur F. McEvoy, 'Environmental Law and the Collapse of New Deal Constitutionalism' (2013) 46 *Akron L.R.* 881 ff.

[15]   Sabin (2015) 33 *Law and History Review* 965 ff.

[16]   Jedediah Purdy, 'The Long Environmental Justice Movement', (2018) 44 *Ecology Law Quarterly* 809 ff.

[17]   See, e.g., Geneviève Massard-Guilbaud, 'La régulation des nuisances industrielles urbaines (1800–1940)' (1999) 64 *Vingtième Siècle* 53 ff; Pierre Claude Reynard, 'Public Order and Privilege: Eighteenth-Century French Roots of Environmental Regulation' (2002) 43 *Technology and Culture* 1 ff.

[18]   See, e.g., Pontin (2012) 75 *Modern L.R.* 1010 ff; Ben Pontin, 'Integrated Pollution Control in Victorian Britain: Rethinking Progress Within the History of Environmental Law' (2007) 19 *Journal of Environmental Law* 173 ff; Michael Lobban, 'Nuisance', in *The Oxford History of the Laws of England: Volume XII: 1820–1914 Private Law* (2010) 1068 ff; Raymond Cocks, 'Health for the Public', in *The Oxford History of the Laws of England: Volume XIII: 1820–1914 Fields of Development* (2010) 535 ff; Leona J. Skelton, *Tyne After Tyne: An Environmental History of a River's Battle for Protection, 1529–2015* (2017).

precautionary principle or feasibility standards.[19] The blindness as to the history of environmental law may be a particularly American disease. (To the extent it is, this exceptionalism is itself a topic worthy of research.)

The work that perhaps treats American environmental law in the most comprehensive manner is Betsy Mendelsohn's chapter on law and the environment in *The Cambridge History of Law in America*,[20] which notes in its opening section:

Environmental law cannot be understood apart from the long-established debates and tensions that define the traditions of American law as a whole: individual rights and the extent of state power, the authority of law and its means of implementation. Long before the midtwentieth century, American law was fully engaged with such matters as, for example, the private use of common resources, such as wildlife and rivers; private activity that injured public health and welfare, such as the emission of industrial wastes; and the municipal assumption of administrative power to build networked sanitary infrastructure. Courts had accepted science-based rationales to authorize law that limited private rights. Governments had engaged in interstate responses to environmental problems that crossed jurisdictional boundaries.

Two essential categories of environmental law and litigation, nuisance and natural resources, are ancient and capacious: they have occupied courts, legislatures, and other governmental authority for centuries.[21]

Mendelsohn then goes on to trace environmental regulation—including legal regimes designed to encourage exploitation of the environment—from colonial times, through the growth of the administrative state in the nineteenth and twentieth centuries, to the environmental law of the postwar period.

Yet Mendelsohn's article stands alone. Few legal historians have followed her example, whether in uncovering the legal roots of contemporary environmental law or in making the lateral connections between historical environmental law and other historical topics. The field remains in need of extensive work in both of these directions.

III. WHAT IS TO BE DONE?

I would like to suggest that of these two dimensions—we might think of them as longitudinal and lateral—the first order of business should be longitudinal, deepening the temporal dimension of environmental law. We will be hard

[19] Noga Morag-Levine, *Chasing the Wind: Regulating Air Pollution in the Common Law State* (2003); Noga Morag-Levine, 'Is Precautionary Regulation a Civil Law Instrument? Lessons from the History of the Alkali Act' (2011) 23 *Journal of Environmental Law* 1 ff.

[20] Betsy Mendelshon, 'Law and the Environment', in Michael Grossberg, Christopher Tomlins (eds.), *Cambridge History of Law in America* vol. 3 (2008) 472 ff.

[21] Ibid. 472.

pressed to assess the significance of historical environmental law or its interactions with other areas of law and life without knowing what it was or what people thought about it. However, given that 'environmental law' is a recently coined term, where are we to look for historical environmental law? This chapter offers several directions of inquiry, some of them already explored by environmental and other historians, though often without the sensitivity to legal dimensions that might be expected were more legal historians to take up the task.[22] (Not all work on historic environmental regulation is necessarily relevant to understanding the sources of current environmental law. For instance, scholars have investigated environmental regulation in Roman law and Jewish law, but it would be difficult to claim that these ancient legal systems were the source of modern environmental law.[23])

One obvious place to look is to the history of that most well-worn of metaphors for environmental problems—*the commons*. As is well known by now, the actual medieval and early modern European commons caricatured in Garrett Hardin's parable of the tragedy of the commons were not the rule-free disaster zones he depicted,[24] but rather highly regulated sites of interaction between humans and nature. Environmental historians have studied the laws governing the woodland and pasture commons, though not necessarily in the framework of 'environmental law' or with an eye to the type of questions a lawyer might ask of the sources.[25] In particular, historians of environmental law might want to investigate broad issues such as the conceptions of law, justice, right, and property reflected in the commons regulations, as well as narrower ones such as the types of rules, standards, adjudicatory procedures, and remedies applied to various forms of environmental conflicts and their possible influence on later legal rules.

For instance, the principle of 'necessary use'—'that the actions of others should not deprive one of the basic materials needed to sustain one's enterprise'—was apparently ubiquitous in early modern German commons by-laws, as it was in the rules governing water allocation in the nineteenth century western United States.[26] It is also arguably the motivating principle behind the feasibility standard

---

[22] For a list of the sources of modern environmentalism similar to the below list of possible sources of environmental law, see Radkau (n. 11) 11 ff and 118 ff.

[23] See Rena van den Bergh, 'Roman Origins of Environmental Law' (1999) *Journal of South African Law* 495 ff; Ora R. Sheinson, 'Lessons from the Jewish Law of Property Rights for the Modern American Takings Debate' (2001) 26 *Columbia Journal of Environmental Law* 483 ff.

[24] Garrett Hardin, 'The Tragedy of the Commons' (1968) 162 *Science* 1243 ff.

[25] See, e.g., Paul Warde, 'Imposition, Emulation and Adaptation: Regulatory Regimes in the Commons of Early Modern Germany' (2013) 19 *Environment and History* 313 ff. For an overview of the commons in recent historical writing, see Giacomo Bonan, 'Confronting Hardin: Trends and Approaches to the Commons in Historiography' (2018) 19 *Theoretical Inquiries in Law* (forthcoming, 2018).

[26] For commons, see Warde (2013) 19 *Environment and History* 333. For water, see David Schorr, *The Colorado Doctrine: Water Rights, Corporations, and Distributive Justice on the American Frontier* (2012).

so pervasive in modern environmental regulation, which requires a polluter to use the best available technology only to the extent it is economically feasible.[27] While a theorist might use this commonality to support a normative or positive argument about property in natural resources or pollution regulation, a historian might profitably search for the common roots of these norms or the paths through which they travelled in time and space, and the ways people justified or criticized them over time.

Moreover, legal fights against enclosure of the commons were clearly a precursor of more recent legal protections for open spaces, an alternative source to the commonly accepted stories about the Romantic and preservationist roots of this area of law, and one with a more socially oriented tint.[28] Investigation of the commons preservation movement and anti-enclosure movements in general are likely to yield insights into the political valence of some of the historical building blocks of environmental preservation law.

A related field demanding study is *forest law*. It is practically a commonplace among environmental historians that the concept of sustainability, so central to contemporary environmental law, originated in early modern forest management, and historians have shown that intensive forest regulation in Europe goes back to the medieval period.[29] Environmental historian Richard Grove has made the connection between colonial forest management and concerns over climate change, and my own work has connected this concern to colonial forest regulation.[30] E. P. Thompson's *Whigs and Hunters* highlighted the way early modern English forest law was both a tool of enclosure on behalf of landed elites and a site of resistance for commoners, and similar points have been made about English law in the medieval period.[31] Other works have examined the historic interplay of private, common,

---

[27] See David M. Driesen, 'Distributing the Costs of Environmental, Health, and Safety Protection: The Feasibility Principle, Cost-Benefit Analysis, and Regulatory Reform' (2005) 32 *Boston College Environmental Affairs L.R.* 1 ff.

[28] See Antony Taylor, '"Commons-Stealers", "Land-Grabbers" and "Jerry-Builders": Space, Popular Radicalism and the Politics of Public Access in London, 1848–1880' (1995) 40 *International Review of Social History* 383 ff; G. Shaw Lefevre, *English Commons and Forests: The Story of the Battle During the Last Thirty Years for Public Rights over the Commons and Forests of England and Wales* (1894); Gregory S. Alexander, 'The Sporting Life: Democratic Culture and the Historical Origins of the Scottish Right to Roam' (2016) *University of Illinois L.R.* 321 ff.

[29] See Klaus Bosselmann, *The Principle of Sustainability: Transforming Law and Governance* (2nd edn., 2017) 12–13; Peter Sand, 'Sustainability: Of Forests, Ships, and Law' (2007) 37 *Environmental Policy and Law* 202 ff; Richard Keyser, 'The Transformation of Traditional Woodland Management: Commercial Sylviculture in Medieval Champagne' 32 (2009) *French Historical Studies* 353 ff.

[30] Richard H. Grove, *Green Imperialism: Colonial Expansion, Tropical Island Edens and the Origins of Environmentalism, 1600–1860* (1996); David B. Schorr, 'Forest Law in the Palestine Mandate: Colonial Conservation in a Unique Context', in Uwe Luebken, Frank Uekötter (eds.), *Managing the Unknown: Essays on Environmental Ignorance* (2014) 71 ff.

[31] E. P. Thompson, *Whigs and Hunters: The Origins of the Black Act* (1975); Nicholas A. Robinson, 'The Charter of the Forest: Evolving Human Rights in Nature', in Daniel Barstow Magraw, Andrea Martinez, Roy E. Brownell II (eds.), *Magna Carta and the Rule of Law* (2015).

and state property in forests and varying conceptions of conservation that were expressed in their regulation.[32] These are all themes that continue to resonate in modern environmental debates. Further research might shed light on how forest law variously worked to preserve forests or facilitate their destruction, as well as on how this regulatory field influenced other areas of environmental law, including modern debates over the commons and enclosure.

Both these bodies of law are connected to a third, broad one (though some would deny it the distinction of being considered 'law'): so-called *'police' regulation*. This flexible and capacious form of regulation, justified in terms of its promotion of good government and the common welfare, has had many points of contact with environmental issues since early modern times, through its protections for public health and safety and rules for management of natural resources.[33]

While critics (most recently Markus Dubber) have impugned police for its broad discretion and patriarchal foundations,[34] these very elements were powerful enablers of environmental regulation in the public interest. Moreover, the opposing tradition that Dubber identifies—the Enlightenment ideal of the 'rule of law'—has often used the liberal ideal of private property to frustrate public-minded environmental regulation. In any case, police regulations, with their wide remit and geographic dispersion,[35] are natural places to look for sources of modern environmental law. Noga Morag-Levine has indeed made the connection between early modern 'science of police' and later regulation of air pollution,[36] but it is likely that 'police' was—for better or worse—a fertile source of much more of environmental regulation than we yet realize.

An important sub-set of police regulation was the *public health law* that grew up in the Victorian age as a response to the urbanization and industrialization of the period, giving expression to the sanitary movement's concern with the effects of environmental degradation on human health and welfare, particularly of the working classes. Public health statutes, bylaws, regulations, and licences regulated issues such as smoke pollution, industrial odours, and sewage disposal.[37] This highly developed area of law could be investigated for its influences on later environmental law, including its emphasis on technical solutions to pollution problems and the

---

[32] See, e.g., Kieko Matteson, *Forests in Revolutionary France: Conservation, Community, and Conflict, 1669–1848* (2015).

[33] See Marc Raeff, *The Well-Ordered Police State: Social and Institutional Change through Law in the Germanies and Russia, 1600–1800* (1983) 92 ff.

[34] See, e.g., Markus D. Dubber, 'New Historical Jurisprudence: Legal History as Critical Analysis of Law' (2015) 2 *Critical Analysis of Law* 1 ff.

[35] See Heikki Pihlajamäki, 'The Westernization of Police Regulation: Spanish and British Colonial Laws Compared', in Thomas Duve, Heikki Pihlajamäki (eds.), *New Horizons in Spanish Colonial Law: Contributions to Transnational Early Modern Legal History* (2015) 97 ff.

[36] Morag-Levine (n. 19).

[37] See Cocks (n. 18).

division of labour between central and local regulation that continue to characterize the field. Public health law is also likely responsible for the creation of a bureaucracy of professionals with expertise in the health and engineering aspects of pollution that would form the core professional staff of modern environmental regulators.

Associated with public health law in the Anglo-American world was the law of *statutory nuisances*.[38] Statutory nuisances allowed for private and public administrative and criminal enforcement of prohibitions on various forms of pollution and encroachment on the public domain, and thus are a likely source of much modern environmental law. Moreover, this area of law may be a source of the prevalent confusion over the role of nuisance law in the pre-1970 area. It may be true that 'nuisance law' was the dominant vehicle for environmental regulation in this period; yet the category of 'nuisance' included not only a common law variant (private and public, the latter of which could be criminally prosecuted), but also statutory nuisance, with its explicit prohibitions on specific types of environmental harms and risks, such as discharges of pollution into water sources and emissions of 'noxious vapours'. If the law of nuisance one imagines is the private, common law of nuisance usually thought of, modern environmental legislation might indeed seem to represent a major revolution. If, on the other hand, statutory nuisance is given its due, the environmental legislation of the 1970s may look more like an elaboration of existing law.

The issue of incompatible land uses also spurred development of the modern law of *planning and zoning*. Beyond the obvious environmental ramifications (both positive and negative) of this area of law, it likely influenced modern environmental regulation in several ways. Not only has it served as an important tool for protection of open space and nature, but it may also have been a complementary source of regulation of classic environmental issues such as water and air pollution. For not only did zoning law mandate separation of uses (a principle much denounced by contemporary critics), it also created a process by which the environmentally harmful land uses could be enjoined at the land-use permitting stage, or else conditioned on meeting environmental requirements.[39]

Note that most of the above areas of proto-environmental law were centred on local rather than central governments. Even environmental regulation more recognizable as modern, such as permitting systems, often developed at the local level before the national one.[40] The 1970 start date for even modern environmental

---

[38] See Rosalind Malcolm and John Pointing, 'Statutory Nuisance: The Sanitary Paradigm and Judicial Conservatism' (2006) 18 *Journal of Environmental Law* 37 ff.

[39] See, e.g., David Schorr, 'A Prolonged Recessional: The Continuing Influence of British Rule on Israeli Environmental Law', in Dan Orenstein, Char Miller, Alon Tal (eds.), *Between Ruin and Restoration: Chapters in Israel's Environmental History* (2013) 218 ff.

[40] See, e.g., N. William Hines, 'Nor Any Drop to Drink: Public Regulation of Water Quality Part I: State Pollution Control Programs' (1966) 52 *Iowa L.R.* 186 ff; Frank Uekoetter, *The Age of Smoke: Environmental Policy in Germany and the United States, 1880–1970* (2009).

regulation would thus look even more tenuous were we to widen the scope of research to include local governments; many key provisions are likely to be revealed as not much more than the adoption of local legal norms and their application across a jurisdiction with a wider geographical scope. On the other hand, the shortcomings and failures of local government and local solutions might be investigated as motivating factors behind the development of modern, nationally based systems of environmental regulations.

Another apparent historical font of environmental law is *labour law*, particularly the legal protections for the health of workers.[41] The place of workers in nature conservation law is a related theme that would benefit from further research.[42] Like several of the sources of environmental law surveyed above, this one, too, might provide valuable insight into the class politics of the field, helping to revise a prevalent view that associates environmental law with elite interests and values.

Finally, in keeping with Assaf Likhovski's chapter in this volume, a promising avenue of research lies not in the search for environmental law's sources in positive law, but in historical, legal, and environmental *literature*. Treatises on water law, forest law, and other environmental-legal topics go back several hundred years; on pollution law at least to the nineteenth century. Relatedly, this author has elsewhere suggested that the history of environmental law might be studied through visual art and literature.[43] Studies of past scholarly and artistic works, including the arguments about law and regulation in environmental writings, can help not only to put historical environmental law in context, but also to reveal some of the intellectual and cultural roots of developments in the law over time.

The above desiderata call for a clarification: this chapter does not mean to suggest that in this search for origins of environmental law we should wish or expect to find unbroken continuity between environmental-legal regimes or the environmental attitudes that motivated them; nor can we assume that the meaning of terms such as 'environment' or 'conservation' in the past denoted the same things they do today. Ideas and concerns about the natural environment obviously changed from place to place and from time to time, and it would be foolish to think that the cultural meanings of smoke emissions or the commons in the Victorian era (to give but two examples) were the same as today. Nor can we assume

[41] See, e.g., Christopher C. Sellers, *Hazards of the Job: From Industrial Disease to Environmental Health Science* (1999); Katrin MacPhee, 'Canadian Working-Class Environmentalism, 1965–1985' (2014) 74 *Labour/Le Travail* 123 ff; Josiah Rector, 'Environmental Justice at Work: The UAW, the War on Cancer, and the Right to Equal Protection from Toxic Hazards in Postwar America' (2014) 101 *Journal of American History* 480 ff.

[42] See, e.g., Erik Loomis, 'When Loggers Were Green: Lumber, Labor, and Conservation, 1937–1948' (2015) 46 *Western Historical Quarterly* 1937–1948 421 ff.

[43] David B. Schorr, 'Art and the History of Environmental Law' (2015) 2 *Critical Analysis of Law* 322 ff.

that the law regulated these issues in different eras for identical reasons or in identical ways.

Yet this chapter does mean to suggest that the past may not be as foreign a country as we sometimes think. Some of the basic motivations behind modern environmental law—public health and safety, conservation of resources to allow future use, aesthetics, and so on—are evident in much historical law, even as their meanings and particular expressions change over time. Moreover, even when societal attitudes and motivations have changed, available legal technologies—permitting processes based on best available techniques, requirements for studies of environmental impacts, demands for sustainability—may have survived and been applied to purposes both old and new. Without denying that environmental law may have seen a major change around 1970 (and at other historical inflection points yet to be identified), it was just that—a change—not the birth of a field of law out of thin air.

So much for the longitudinal axis; on the lateral axis, a brief comment only. Once the various areas of environmental law *avant la lettre* have been fleshed out, they need to be contextualized. Who pushed for these legal regimes and who opposed them? What material and economic interests were at stake? Which conceptions of justice, political ideologies, and environmental attitudes were reflected in the law, and which rejected? What were the effects of the law, not only on 'the environment' but also on society, economy, and culture? What changes occurred in the field, and why? These questions will be kept in mind in the next and final section of this chapter.

iv. What Is at Stake

This final section tentatively offers some thoughts on why the historical exploration of environmental law matters.

First of all, history can help us better understand current environmental law. For instance, David Driesen has recently advanced a positive theory of environmental law, attempting to explain its salient features, such as reliance on certain types of standards.[44] Notably missing from his account are historical explanations for these aspects of environmental law, explanations which might be provided by works such as those of Morag-Levine.[45] Or take the argument of 'free market environmentalists'

---

[44] See, e.g., David M. Driesen, 'The Ends and Means of Pollution Control: Toward a Positive Theory of Environmental Law' (2017) *Utah L.R.* 57 ff.

[45] Morag-Levine (n. 19).

that private law would do a better job of protecting the environment than modern regulation;[46] this type of argument could be checked against the historical experience of legal systems that have relied on private law for this purpose.

Second, the history of environmental law is a topic that offers an opportunity to bridge the material and the abstract, or to take up environmental historian Linda Nash's challenge 'to show how what is presumed to be social or cultural is thoroughly intertwined with the natural'.[47] Such an endeavour would be beneficial to both environmental history and legal history, as legal doctrines, institutions, and ideologies—social and cultural artefacts—developed with regard to the natural, may circulate beyond the narrow confines of environmental law to other legal contexts. One thinks, for instance, of Pigouvian taxes, cost-benefit analyses, and feasibility standards, all developed 'intertwined with the natural' but spreading their branches far afield.

Environmentalists often portray themselves as acting in the name of an apolitical public interest. Nevertheless, environmentalism and environmentalists are often seen as highly political; accused on the one hand of advocating an anti-capitalist, anti-market, state-interventionist agenda, while at the same time accused by others of elitism, putting the aesthetic and recreational values of the (white) upper classes ahead of the basic economic interests or needs of the working classes, indigenous peoples, and racial minorities. The history of environmental law provides an interesting arena for the study of class and race politics and environmentalism on the one hand, and law on the other.

Historical analysis of environmental law is likely to show that there is some truth to the elitist charge, as in recent work by Ben Pontin identifying a strain of 'old Tory', aristocratic environmentalism in nineteenth-century Britain, or in the work of Mario Prost and Yoriko Otomo showing the imperialist and racist sources of international wildlife protection law.[48] Yet in other contexts environmental law may be shown to have lined up with the working classes and minorities, whether in the commons preservation movement that fought for access by the British working classes to environmental amenities, the alliances with occupational health regulation and trade unions, or in the proto-environmental justice aspects of the American wilderness movement recently explored by Jed Purdy.[49] Further research will no doubt reveal more complex, even ambiguous political colouring of environmental law, thus deepening analysis of the political and distributional aspects of both the environment and the law.

---

[46] See Terry L. Anderson, Donald R. Leal, *Free Market Environmentalism* (1991).

[47] Linda Nash, 'Furthering the Environmental Turn' (2013) 100 *Journal of American History* 131, 134.

[48] Ben Pontin, 'Environmental Law-Making Public Opinion in Victorian Britain: The Cross-Currents of Bentham's and Coleridge's Ideas' (2014) 34 *O.J.L.S.* 1 ff; Mario Prost, Yoriko Otomo, 'British Influences on International Environmental Law: The Case of Wildlife Conservation', in Robert McCorquodale, Jean-Pierre Gauci (eds.), *British Influences on International Law, 1915–2015* (2016) 192 ff.

[49] Purdy (n. 16).

Finally, politics and distributional issues bring us to the potential of the history of environmental law to enrich our understanding of two of the most important historical issues of our time: empire and capitalism. Empire and colonialism have become central to our understanding of environmental history, from Alfred Crosby's *Columbian Exchange* to Richard Grove's *Green Imperialism.*[50] Recent years have also seen a surge of interest in the legal histories of empires (though rarely with any attention to the environmental aspects of those histories).[51] We need to ask what the role of law was in the environmental transformations wrought by empire, and what the effect the varied environments of empire had on the development of law. These questions need to be asked not only with regard to imperial peripheries, but also for imperial centres, as well as for the jurisdictions that were not formally part of empires but were nonetheless caught up in their economic, cultural, and ecological webs.

As for capitalism, it is impossible to imagine it without the material capital originating in the environment, and without law to facilitate the exploitation of the environment. Environmental historian Steven Stoll has written, 'Documenting the effects of capital without confronting its architecture and foundation seems like an ineffective scholarly project.'[52] Environmental law is an important part of this architecture and foundation; it must have enabled exploitation of the environment and possibly legitimated it, but at other times regulated and even stymied it. How, where, when, and why these various scenarios played out, who benefited and who lost, and under what conditions the worst excesses of capitalism were curbed, are questions whose answers might not only enrich our historical understanding, but our current environmental law and politics as well.

BIBLIOGRAPHY

Karl Boyd Brooks, *Before Earth Day: The Origins of American Environmental Law, 1945–1970* (University Press of Kansas, 2012)

[50] Alfred W. Crosby, Jr., *The Columbian Exchange: Biological and Cultural Consequences of 1492* (1972); Grove (n. 30).

[51] For examples of histories of environmental law in imperial contexts see, e.g., Prost and Otomo (n. 48); Vinita Damodaran, 'Indigenous Agency: Customary Rights and Tribal Protection in Eastern India, 1830–1930' (2013) 76 *History Workshop Journal* 85 ff; and Schorr (n. 30); Schorr (n. 39); David Schorr, 'Riparian Rights in Lower Canada and Canada East: Inter-imperial Legal Influences', in Roland Cvetkovski, Volker Barth (eds.), *Imperial Co-operation and Transfer, 1870–1930: Empires and Encounters* (2015) 107 ff.

[52] Steven Stoll, 'A Metabolism of Society: Capitalism for Environmental Historians', in Andrew C. Isenberg (ed.), *Oxford Handbook of Environmental History* (2014) 369.

Betsy Mendelsohn, 'Law and the Environment', in Michael Grossberg, Christopher Tomlins (eds.), *Cambridge History of Law in America*, vol. 3 (Cambridge University Press, 2008) 472 ff

Noga Morag-Levine, *Chasing the Wind: Regulating Air Pollution in the Common Law State* (Princeton University Press, 2003)

Ben Pontin, 'Integrated Pollution Control in Victorian Britain: Rethinking Progress Within the History of Environmental Law' (2007) 19 *Journal of Environmental Law* 173 ff

Jedediah Purdy, 'The Long Environmental Justice Movement', (2018) 44 *Ecology Law Quarterly* 809 ff

Pierre Claude Reynard, 'Public Order and Privilege: Eighteenth-Century French Roots of Environmental Regulation' (2002) 43 *Technology and Culture* 1 ff

Peter Sand (ed.), *The History and Origin of International Environmental Law* (Edward Elgar Publishing, 2015)

E. P. Thompson, *Whigs and Hunters: The Origins of the Black Act* (Pantheon Books, 1975)

CHAPTER 53

....

REDEEMING THE AMERICAN FOUNDING?

....

NORMAN W. SPAULDING[*]

This Fourth of July is yours, not mine.[1]
—Frederick Douglass, 4 July 1852

The end to be attained justifies the means, we are willing to believe;
but the sight of these pictures is a commentary on civilization
such as a savage might well triumph to show its missionaries.
Yet through such martyrdom must come our redemption. War
is the surgery of crime. Bad as it is in itself, it always implies
that something worse has gone before. Where is the American,
worthy of his privileges, who does not now recognize the fact, if
never until now, that the disease of our nation was organic, not
functional, calling for the knife, and not for washes and anodyne?[2]

Oliver Wendell Homes, Sr., July 1863

---

[*] Thoughtful alternative accounts of redemption in American legal thought can be found in Amy Kapczynski's 'Historicism, Progress, and the Redemptive Constitution' (2005) 26 *Cardozo L.R.* 1041 ff (drawing on Walter Benjamin's concept of redemption), and J. M. Balkin, *Constitutional Redemption: Political Faith in an Unjust World* (2011). This chapter develops a more sceptical claim about redemptivism.

[1] Frederick Douglass, 'The Meaning of the Fourth of July', Speech at Rochester, New York, 4 July 1852, reprinted in, Philip S. Foner, Yuval Taylor (eds.), *Frederick Douglass: Selected Speeches and Writings* (1999) 188 ff.

[2] Oliver Wendell Holmes, Sr., 'Doings of the Sunbeam' (1863) 12 *The Atlantic Monthly* 1, 12 ff.

I.

ALTHOUGH separated by more than a decade, the remarks of Holmes and Douglass address the same subject: the American founding. Douglass indicts. Holmes convicts.

Douglass' use of the second person plural pronoun throughout the first part of his speech 'What to the Slave is the Fourth of July?' merges all the traditional elements of an indictment—caption, commencement, statement, and conclusion—into a single word. *Yours.* 'Fellow citizens, pardon me, allow me to ask', the speech begins, 'What have I, or those I represent, to do with *your* national independence?'[3] Running back to the founding itself, indeed to the antecedents of the Revolution in colonial opposition to Crown policies, African Americans had levelled the same indictment in the same grammar. Weeks before the first continental congress would convene in 1774 in opposition to the 'Intolerable Acts' passed by the British Parliament as punishment for the Boston Tea Party, the *Essex Journal and Merrimack Packet* published an 'Essay on Slavery'.[4] Its author, Caesar Sarter, a freedman with 'no less than eleven relatives suffering in bondage' insisted that African Americans be emancipated '[a]s the first step' in the burgeoning independence movement.[5] '[T]hen and not till then', he insisted, 'may *you* with confidence and consistency of conduct, look to Heaven for a blessing on your endeavors to knock the shackles with which your task masters are hampering you, from your own feet.'[6] For Sarter, protesting so-called political slavery was an 'absurdity . . . while you have slaves in your homes.'[7]

The metaphor of political slavery was not Sarter's. It belonged most prominently to Locke, who in his *Second Treatise on Government* sought to justify resistance and revolution against tyranny by characterizing legislation contrary to the natural rights of the people as enslavement:

It can never be supposed to be the will of the people of the society that the legislature should have a power to destroy what everyone aimed to keep safe by entering into society and submitting themselves to legislators of their own making. So when the legislators try to take away and destroy the property of the people or to reduce them to slavery, they put themselves into a state of war with the people, who are thereby absolved from any further obedience and are left to the common escape that God has provided for all men against force and violence.[8]

From Locke and other opposition Whigs the metaphor of political slavery entered into American revolutionary discourse leading up to the war as a justification for rebellion and it remained salient through the debates on ratification of the Constitution more

---

[3] Douglass (n. 1) 188 ff.

[4] Caesar Sarter, 'Essay on Slavery', *The Essex Journal and Merrymack Packet*, 17 August 1774, reprinted in Gary B. Nash, *Race and Revolution* (1990) 167 ff.

[5] Ibid., 170 ff.   [6] Ibid. (emphasis added).   [7] Ibid.

[8] John Locke, *Second Treatise of Government* (1980) § 222, 111 ff. See also Preface and §§ 17, 135, 210 ff.

than a decade later.[9] Americans were thus acutely aware of the basic contradiction named by Douglass in the disjunctive grammar of his Independence Day oration not only before the founding of the republic, but in and through it.[10]

Holmes' statement on the American Civil War and the crime of slavery is drawn from an essay on the new science of photography. In it he describes a series of pictures taken by Alexander Gardner of fallen soldiers strewn about the battlefield at Antietam in September 1863—see Figure 53.1.

Figure 53.1 [image: Library of Congress; Photographer Alexander Garner; Antietam: "Dead Soldiers in Ditch on the Right Wing Where Kimball's Brigade Fought so Desperately." September 1862.]

[9] See David Waldstreicher, *Slavery's Constitution: From Revolution to Ratification* (2009) 31, 131, 142, 146 ff; Eric Slauter, *The State as a Work of Art: The Cultural Origins of the Constitution* (2009) 176–80, 184 ff.

[10] On contemporaneous attempts to reason away the contradiction by turning to theories of white supremacy, see ibid., 177 ff.

Antietam was the single 'costliest day of combat in American history, leaving twenty-five thousand Americans dead or wounded'.[11] The battle was significant, not so much for its immediate tactical outcome as for the massive bloodshed ('more than twice as many Americans were killed in a single day than in every other nineteenth century American war' combined[12]) and the 'revolutionary' transformation in the terms of the war that ensued.[13] As Richard Slotkin has observed, '[b]efore Antietam it was still possible for Americans to imagine a compromise settlement of sectional differences' and Lincoln welcomed such a settlement to preserve the Union even if it meant preserving slavery.[14] 'After Antietam', and Lincoln's pivotal decision to use the victory to announce the Emancipation Proclamation, 'the only way the war could end was by the outright victory of one side over the other'.[15] For the North, the effort to end secession and restore the Union 'as it was' became instead 'a war of *subjugation*, aimed at destroying the South's ability to resist and uprooting its fundamental institution'.[16] The South, now facing a genuine mortal threat to its very 'social fabric' would brook no compromise. As a consequence, and as the bloodshed at Antietam itself suggested, 'the conflict would become something like "total war"'.[17] 'Events would pressure both Lincoln and Davis to stretch their constitutional authority to or beyond the breaking point, to intensify the scope of combat operations beyond all precedent, and to inflict loss and suffering on civilian populations as an instrument of policy'.[18]

We know the outcome of these revolutionary convulsions, but during the autumn and early winter of 1862, the North remained demoralized. Antietam was in Maryland after all—Union territory. Pushing Lee back across the Potomac was a modest and scarcely reassuring accomplishment following the string of embarrassing Union defeats that brought Lee into the North and so close to Washington, D.C., in the first place. And with such high casualties, '[t]he struggle began to seem to many Northerners a suicide mission. Mixed with this was the suspicion that Northern lives were being wasted because of mismanagement and political meddling'.[19] Nor was there great enthusiasm for the Emancipation Proclamation in mainstream Republican circles; northern Democratic opposition was in fact galvanized by the announcement and the Republican party suffered stinging defeats in the mid-term elections.[20]

---

[11] Richard Slotkin, *The Long Road to Antietam: How the Civil War Became a Revolution* (2012) 357 ff.

[12] Louis Menand, *The Metaphysical Club: A Story of Ideas in America* (2001) 42 ff.

[13] Slotkin (n. 11) xv–xvi ff.

[14] Ibid., xiv ff. On Lincoln's support in 1861 of an amendment to permanently insulate slavery from federal interference, see Daniel W. Crofts, *Lincoln and the Politics of Slavery* (2016), and Norman W. Spaulding, 'Paradoxes of Constitutional Faith: Federalism, Emancipation, and the Original Thirteenth Amendment' (2016) 3 *Critical Analysis of Law* 306 ff.

[15] Slotkin (n. 11) xiv ff.   [16] Ibid., 88, 395 ff.   [17] Ibid., 395 ff.   [18] Ibid., xv ff.

[19] Menand (n. 12) 42 ff.   [20] Spaulding (n. 14).

It is against this backdrop that Gardner's morbid photographs reached the public. He arrived at Antietam two days after the battle ended when bodies were still strewn about. His exhibit in October of 1962, *The Dead of Antietam*, sponsored by fellow Civil War photographer Mathew Brady in his New York studio, 'was the first time in history that the general public was able to see the true carnage of war',[21] because it was the 'first time an American battlefield had ever been photographed before the dead had been buried'.[22] Audiences were 'both horrified and fascinated'.[23] Holmes Sr. not only saw the photographs, he had travelled to Antietam himself just a few days after the battle to search for his son (and future Supreme Court Justice), a captain of the Twentieth Massachusetts Regiment who had been shot through the neck and 'left for dead' behind enemy lines for part of the battle.[24] The 'martyrdom' requisite to any potential 'redemption' for the nation's crimes was thus no abstraction for Holmes Sr. Certainly the desire to both convict the nation for its crimes and to identify redemptive meaning in such a scene of death would have been palpable for him.

In his essay, Holmes Sr. is at pains to establish the verisimilitude of the photographs, and not merely the respects in which they 'bear witness to the accuracy of' his own published account of the scene as he searched for his son.[25] He insisted that the new medium of photography exposed as 'fanciful' the grand battle scenes painted by the prominent nineteenth-century French rivals Baron Gros and Horace Vernet.[26] Gros was celebrated for his heroic depictions of Napoleon at war and Vernet was recognized for depicting French military gallantry in the Bourbon Restoration, the colonization of Algeria, and the Second Empire under Napoleon III.[27] The work of Gros and Vernet, Holmes Sr. charged, was produced 'to please an imperial master'.[28] Rather than romanticize military conflict, images of 'war and battles should have truth for their delineator'.[29] We should have 'some conception of what a repulsive, brutal, sickening, hideous thing it is, this dashing together of two frantic mobs to which we give the name of armies'.[30]

---

[21] Terry L. Jones, 'The Dead of Antietam', *New York Times*, 24 September 2012; Arthur Schlesinger Jr., 'Mathew B. Brady, Photographer', *New York Times*, 10 February 1946 at 114, 125 ff; see generally Anthony W. Lee, Elizabeth Young, *On Alexander Gardner's Photographic Sketch Book of the Civil War* (2007).

[22] <www.nps.gov/anti/learn/photosmultimedia/gardnerphotos.htm> (accessed 1 August, 2017).

[23] Jones (n. 21).

[24] James McPherson, *Battle Cry of Freedom: The Civil War Era* (1988) 541 ff. See also Menand (n. 12) 3 ff. Holmes Sr. published an account of his journey in, 'My Hunt After the Captain' (1862) 10 *The Atlantic Monthly* 738 ff.

[25] Holmes Sr., ibid., 11 ff.   [26] Ibid., 12 ff.

[27] On the development of history paintings as propaganda, see David O'Brien, *After the Revolution: Antoine-Jean Gros: Painting and Propaganda Under Napoleon* (2006); see also Daniel Harkett, Katie Hornstein (eds.), *Horace Vernet and the Thresholds of Nineteenth-Century Visual Culture* (2017).

[28] Holmes Sr. (n. 24), 12 ff.   [29] Ibid.

[30] Ibid. But see O'Brien (n. 27) 155 ff.

The Antietam battlefield was equal to this demand. Front line units found themselves in what Slotkin describes as a 'meat grinder'—as soon as either side seized the advantage and moved forward it came within range of the deadly defensive artillery of the enemy.[31] In just the morning phase of the battle west of Antietam Creek and north of Lee's headquarters in the town of Sharpsburg a 'dreadful slaughter raged' leaving '[t]welve thousand men . . . dead and wounded'.[32] In one of the most striking passages in James McPherson's *Battle Cry Freedom*, he quotes the vivid recollections of 'a norther soldier' regarding the stark terror and 'fighting madness' he and others experienced at Antietam:

'The truth is, when bullets are whacking against tree-trunks and solid shot are cracking skulls like egg-shells, the consuming passion in the breast of the average man is to get out of the way. Between the physical fear of going forward and the moral fear of turning back, there is a predicament of exceptional awkwardness.' But when the order came to go forward, his regiment did not falter. 'In a second the air was full of the hiss of bullets and the hurdle of grape-shot. The mental strain was so great that I saw . . . the whole landscape for an instant turned slightly red.' This psychological state produced a sort of fighting madness in many men, a superadrenalized fury that turned them into mindless killing machines heedless of the normal instinct of self-preservation. This frenzy seems to have prevailed at Antietam on a greater scale than in any previous Civil War battle. 'The men are loading and firing with demoniacal fury and shouting and laughing hysterically', wrote a Union officer in the present tense a quarter-century later as if that moment of red-sky madness lived in him yet.[33]

Of course, Gardner's photographs are of the aftermath, not the battle itself, and the composition of prints such as 'Federal Buried, Confederate Unburied, Where They Fell', belies any claim that what the viewer sees is unmediated—see Figure 53.2. It is a *scene* of death in the theatre of war, framed in every meaningful sense by Gardner's lens. The juxtaposition of the two bodies and the eerie presence of a northerner likely charged with burial duties prompts questions about what, if anything, the unburied Confederate soldier is owed, whether he will be laid to rest, and the consequences of failing to do so.[34]

But even if war and battles cannot have 'truth for their delineator' via photography or any other medium, Holmes Sr. is right to identify the strange reluctance of a supposedly civilized society to look plainly upon the uncivilized realities of a fratricidal war and the temptation, all the more strong after having seen Gardner's series of seventy prints 'and dreamed of its horrors . . . to lock it up in some secret drawer'.[35]

---

[31] Slotkin (n. 11) 266 ff; see also McPherson (n. 24) 540 ff (noting that 'fighting at Antietam was among the hardest of the war').

[32] McPherson (n. 24) 541 ff.

[33] Ibid., 540 ff (quoting Rufus R. Dawes of the 6th Wisconsin regiment, which 'lost 40 men killed and 112 wounded out of about 300 engaged at Antietam').

[34] On the relationship between the 'partiality', 'belatedness', and 'eerie suggestions of loss[,] mourning and melancholy' in Garner's photographs, on the one hand, and the technical capacities of mid-nineteenth-century cameras, on the other, see Lee and Young (n. 21) 29–32 ff.

[35] Holmes Sr. (n. 25) 12 ff.

Figure 53.2 Federal Buried, Confederate Unburied, Where They Fell

Demoniacal fury, hysteria, and red-sky madness may be recognizable psychological conditions, even recognizable social and political conditions of transformative or revolutionary states—the very stuff of which foundings are made. But we do tend to lock them up, to insist that the awkward predicaments, convulsive violence, madness, uncertainty, and contradictions these uncivilized states invite remain transitory even as their outcomes are celebrated and valour is retroactively assigned to the confused and terrified protagonists. Holmes Sr.'s drawer is decidedly allegorical—crime, conviction, a sentence of blood sacrifice, and national redemption (made all the more personally gratifying no doubt by the fact of his son's survival). Holmes Jr., Menand suggests, fashioned a rather different drawer altogether. From his physical wounds he recovered, but '[t]he effects of the mental ordeal were permanent. He had gone off to fight because of his moral beliefs, which he held with singular fervor. The war did more than make him lose those beliefs. It made him lose his belief in beliefs. It impressed on his mind, in the most graphic and indelible way, a certain idea about the limits of ideas.'[36]

---

[36] Menand (n. 12) 4 ff.

II.

Every revolutionary liberal democratic founding has its secret drawers where one can find the illiberal ideas and mnemonic traces of illiberal acts in and through which the state came into being and sustains itself. This chapter began with the disjunctive African-American grammar on the hollowness of liberty and the carnage of Antietam, distant as they are in time from the American founding, because they disrupt conventional legal and historiographic approaches towards 1776 and 1789. Conventional approaches to the American founding either ignore the American Civil War altogether, or attempt to render it continuous with the constitution of 1789 by arguing that, apart from the abolition of slavery, the Union survived the war intact. As the author has argued elsewhere, although many contemporaries (including Lincoln) clung desperately to the idea that the Union 'as it was' had been saved, and although this is true in a strictly geographic sense, as a constitutional matter it is a position that demands indifference bordering on outright denial regarding the paradoxical terms on which emancipation, abolition, the suppression of northern dissent, and the ratification of the Reconstruction Amendments occurred.[37]

Even revisionist scholars who see the American Civil War and Reconstruction Amendments as a kind of re-founding seek to align the trajectory of the period's convulsions with the natural rights identified in the Declaration of Independence. That requires accounting for the return to 'home rule' after the contested presidential election of 1876, and the long, long wait through Jim Crow segregation for partial vindication of those natural rights in the lives of African Americans nearly a century later. It is a difficult task.[38] As unchristian as the thought may be, redemption delayed at some point is redemption denied. But for most Americans (particularly white Americans) this thought is unbearable. Indeed, it is unthinkable. Hence the continuing allure of the conventional account. Better, all things considered, to keep the drawer closed.

This section seeks not only to hold the drawer open, but to inquire whether it is possible to develop an account of the founding in which the drawer is left open. Although the focus is on the American founding, it is worth noting that similar interpretive challenges attend the English and French revolutions. Steve Pincus contends that although England's Glorious Revolution 'marked a fundamental break in the history of the British state', was widely understood at the time as 'inaugurating a new age of liberty', 'a new order of things', and was, 'like all other

---

[37] Spaulding (n. 14) 306 ff.
[38] See Mark E. Brandon, *Free in the World: American Slavery and Constitutional Failure* (1998) 201–2, 213–15, 219–20 ff.

revolutions, violent, popular, and divisive', over time its place in English history was systematically transformed by both Whigs and Tories.[39] In the 'hegemonic "neoconservative interpretation"', an interpretation that now dominates both popular imagination and professional historical treatments, 'James had been the innovator; the revolutionaries were conservative and virtuous defenders of the ancient constitution.'[40] Whigs such as Edmond Burke insisted that unlike the French and other European revolutions, in the Glorious Revolution 'there had been no innovation, no revolution, but merely a sensible and backward-looking restoration of the old order', and that it should accordingly be 'celebrated less as a turning point in British history than as an event that distinguished Britain from the Continent and the rest of the world.'[41] By the mid-nineteenth century, with the upheavals of 1848 in full view, Thomas Babington Macaulay would charge that it was 'almost an abuse of terms to call a proceeding, conducted with so much deliberation, with so much sobriety, and with such minute attention to prescriptive etiquette, by the terrible name of revolution.'[42] And by the twentieth century, this mere '"proceeding"' would be characterized as '"a victory of moderation"', a 'non-event', notable precisely because it 'prevented a real revolution from happening in Britain.'[43] Having locked the drawer, the key was thrown away.

In France, by contrast, the Terror has always posed a barrier to revisionism of this kind. To begin with, there is, at least in conventional accounts of the French Revolution, no denying a radical break with the past. As François Furet describes, '1789 became the birth date, the year zero of a new world founded on equality.'[44] But precisely because of the conjunction of the 'birth of equality' with the Terror—a superadrenalized, lethal fury—the historian of the French Revolution is always obliged to 'show his colors'.[45] And once shown, he is promptly 'labelled a royalist, a liberal, or a Jacobin. . . . There is no such thing as "innocent" historical interpretation, and written history is itself located in history . . . [as] the product of an inherently unstable relationship between the present and the past.'[46] At the same time, these competing histories, 'which have bitterly fought each other for the last two hundred years in the name of the origins of their opposition, in fact share a common ground: they are all histories in quest of identity'.[47] There is not only powerful personal and ideological identification on the part of historians with their revolutionary subjects (their 'heroes') but an effort to manifest France's national identity in their struggles.[48] Each narrative seeks to establish the '"true" origin for the nation' and each, in its own way, plays upon the 'infinite capacity for commemoration' the period offers to the nation.[49]

[39] Steve Pincus, *1688: The First Modern Revolution* (2009) 8, 13 ff.   [40] Ibid., 14, 17 ff.
[41] Ibid., 23–4 ff.   [42] Ibid., 25 ff.   [43] Ibid., 14, 25 ff.
[44] Francois Furet, *Interpreting the French Revolution* (1981) 2 ff.   [45] Ibid., 1 ff.
[46] Ibid.   [47] Ibid., 10 ff.   [48] Ibid.   [49] Ibid., 3, 9 ff.

'No Frenchman living in the second half of the twentieth century can perceive the French Revolution *from the outside*.'[50] A dresser full of drawers, in tricolor, and no locks.

Like the French Revolution, the American Revolution is conventionally interpreted and celebrated as a transformative liberal democratic break with the past—a year zero. Happily, though, Americans are supposed to have avoided the spasms of violence and red-sky madness associated with the Terror. In the canonical treatments by Bernard Bailyn and Gordon Wood, the American Revolution was a revolution of *ideas*, led by visionary philosopher statesmen. Even if economic interests and other parochial concerns were present, nothing like the stark material deprivation that motivated lower class participation in the more convulsive European revolutions existed in the colonies. There may have been hints of 'paranoia',[51] but the overall impression is of a deliberative, legalistic process—in particular, a steady collective escalation of resistance to objectionable Crown policies more or less precisely calibrated to the nature of the perceived infringements on the natural rights and 'rights of Englishmen' the colonists believed they held.[52] Revolution arrived only when those more modest efforts to seek redress of grievances failed.

Finally, the innovation of a written constitution establishing a republican form of government served as ' "ideological fulfillment of the American Revolution" ', proving that it was 'reasonable, its violence defensible, its limits necessary', much as Burke and Macaulay would later characterize the Glorious Revolution.[53] The morally vexed 'limits' (regarding the protections given to chattel slavery) were, on this view, 'at most a side issue' deftly handled by 'creative statecraft' leading to a series of constitutional compromises that left its future status ambiguous and therefore open to revision.[54] And these compromises were real achievements, we are told, given the fact of white racism, the depth of southern attachment to the peculiar institution, and the supposed absence of a meaningful anti-slavery movement in the 1780s.[55] A more seductive tableau, in the style of Gros or Vernet, could scarcely be imagined.

---

[50] Ibid., 10 ff.

[51] Gordon Wood, *The Creation of the American Republic: 1776–1787* (1969) 16–17 ff.

[52] See Pauline Maier, *From Resistance to Revolution: Colonial Radicals and the Development of American Opposition to Britain, 1756–1776* (1991). Here historians have adopted the self-serving statements of the protagonists. See Robert G. Parkinson, *The Common Cause: Creating Race and Nation in the American Revolution* (2016) 8 ff (noting the influence of John Adams claim that the war 'was no part of the Revolution . . . The Revolution was in the Minds of the People, and this was effected, from 1760 to 1775').

[53] Waldstreicher (n. 9) 11 ff (referencing the famous Bernard Bailyn essay of the same title).

[54] Ibid., 10–11 ff.   [55] Ibid., 12–13 ff.

III.

Over the last few decades, revisionist histories have drawn nearly every aspect of the conventional portrait into doubt. First, against the assumption of an epochal break leading to unprecedented constitutional innovation, revisionist scholars have detailed extensive evidence of continuity with British common law and the constitutional thought, rhetoric, and practice of the British Empire.[56] They also have shown the extent to which American constitutional law supported an imperial project not unlike Britain's,[57] the absence of contemporaneous consensus regarding the meaning of the constitution as ratified,[58] and the extent to which American constitutional law is, in fact, unwritten.[59]

Second, against the assumption of restraint and contained violence, Holger Hoock's *Scars of Independence: America's Violent Birth* shows that when the independence movement 'escalated':

Patriots targeted both their outspoken opponents and the as-yet-uncommitted—and they did so with threats and physical violence. There was no guillotine in Boston, New York, or Charleston, as there would be in Paris two decades later. Yet forging the new American nation entailed the forced exclusion not only of black slaves and Native Americans but also of white[s] . . . who did not subscribe to the Revolutionary project. The Revolution's noble ideas aside, violent incidents were not the unfortunate exceptions to an orderly, restrained revolution. Rather, and especially where Loyalists were concerned, they were the norm.[60]

Moreover, '[n]arratives of violence, as much as ideology, helped shape allegiances and mobilize support . . . Stories of persecution, suffering, and sacrifice empowered American Patriots and Loyalists—and also Britons—to make sense of the Revolution.'[61]

---

[56] See Daniel J. Hulsebosch, *Constituting Empire: New York and the Transformation of Constitutionalism in the Atlantic World: 1664–1830* (2005) 304–5 ff; Mary Sarah Bilder, *The Transatlantic Constitution: Colonial Legal Culture and the Empire* (2004) 186 ff.

[57] See Aziz Rana, *The Two Faces of American Freedom* (2010); Hulsebosch (n. 56).

[58] See Saul Cornell, 'Meaning and Understanding in the History of Constitutional Ideas: The Intellectual History Alternative to Originalism', (2013) 82 *Fordham L.R.* 721, 724 ff ('Early American history was not characterized by broad agreement on constitutional matters, but rather was deeply divided on a variety of fundamental issues . . .'); Slauter (n. 9) 18–26 ff.

[59] See Sanford Levinson (ed.), *Responding to Imperfection: The Theory and Practice of Constitutional Amendment* (1995); Thomas C. Grey, 'Origins of the Unwritten Constitution: Fundamental Law in American Revolutionary Thought' (1978) 30 *Stanford L.R.* 843 ff.

[60] Hoock, *Scars of Independence* (2017) 18 ff. See also ibid., 74 ff (describing British allegations that American tactics and conduct 'violated the codes of civilized warfare'); ibid., 288–9 ff (discussing violence against Native Americans on the western front of the war); Thomas B. Allen, *Tories: Fighting for the King in America's First Civil War* (2010).

[61] Hoock, 18–19 ff.

Third, and relatedly, against the assumption that lofty civic republican ideas motivated the American Revolution, scholars such as Robert G. Parkinson have shown the extent to which American elites manipulated public opinion by demonizing the opposition and racializing patriotism.[62] This included not only the occasional use of ' "black propaganda" (hoaxes intentionally meant to deceive and agitate)' but much more pervasively the construction and dissemination of tendentious newsprint stories about slave rebellions ' "instegat[ed]" ' by the British, 'Indian "massacres" ' supported by the British on the western front, and 'Hessian "atrocities" ' to 'shore up an unstable political union'.[63] 'These stories were based, at some level, on real events but heightened for effect precisely because the patriots' political and military situation was tenuous at the start and grew more desperate as the conflict deepened.'[64] In order to convince enough people that the revolution was a worthy 'common cause', that their status as British subjects was a 'foreign' shell to be cast off, and that their Loyalist neighbours and the British were '[s]uspicious foreigners', ideas about civic republican decay and corruption in England helped. But when the conflict came to bullets and bayonets, Parkinson contends, their very '[s]urvival depended on convincing enough people they were right'.[65]

That meant severing bonds of emotional attachment and forging new identities, not merely offering universal principles to justify violent revolution in the abstract language of natural rights. 'To accomplish this vital, difficult task, they embraced the most powerful weapons in the colonial cultural arsenal: stereotypes, prejudices, expectations, and fears about violent Indians and Africans . . . A true patriot was not just anti-British, but anti-slave, anti-savage, and anti-mercenary, as well.'[66] These hyperbolized narratives not only helped to constitute the necessary 'common cause' during the war, they forged the identity of the nation in difference, 'supplying patriotic ammunition for attacking Indians and expanding west' long after the war ended, and providing 'rhetorical cover for those who sought to deepen and extend the slave system . . . and counter abolitionist claims'.[67] In this way, hyperbolized stories in the revolutionary newsprint public relations campaign became 'founding stories', deeply 'bound up with theories of self-government and the ongoing construction of a republican regime'.[68]

Finally, as David Waldstreicher and others have shown, slavery and the contradiction inherent in waging a revolution against political slavery while protecting chattel slavery, were not mere 'side issues' in the drafting and ratification

---

[62] Parkinson (n. 52); see also Carrol Smith-Rosenberg, *This Violent Empire: The Birth of an American Empire* (2010).

[63] Parkinson (n. 52) 20–1 ff.   [64] Ibid., 21 ff.   [65] Ibid.   [66] Ibid., 21–2 ff.

[67] Ibid., 23 ff. On the influence of concerns about slave revolts in the drafting and ratification of the constitution, see Waldstreicher (n. 9) 38, 44, 47, 56, 94, 99, 113, 120, 127–33, 144 ff.

[68] Parkinson (n. 52) 23 ff.

of the constitution.[69] During the revolution it was primarily the British who emancipated slaves—'liberty', for most African Americans, was thus a right to be claimed by escaping behind *British* lines.[70] In the constitution, six clauses are 'directly concerned with slaves and their owners. Five others had implications for slavery that were considered and debated by the delegates to the 1787 Constitutional Convention and the citizens of the states during ratification . . . All but one of these clauses protects slavery; only one points to a possible future power by which the institution might be ended.'[71] As importantly, resolution of two of the most significant obstacles at the Convention—how to count the population and thus structure representation in the national government and how to structure taxation and other national powers over the economy—was profoundly influenced by debates over slavery. 'Every time a major decision was made about the nature of representation, which the delegates rightly assumed would critically shape taxation, the slavery question came to the fore again, shifting votes and muddying the waters.'[72] In this way, Waldstreicher argues, slavery was central to the most significant design elements and innovations of the new republican form of government.

It is no accident then that, during ratification, anti-slavery advocates saw the extent of the constitution's protection of slavery (even going so far as to require states that had abolished slavery to aid in putting down slave insurrections in other states) as a flat betrayal of the revolution.[73] And they were quick to take up the metaphor of political slavery. '[O]ld patriots' such as Benjamin Gale of Connecticut argued that '"[t]here would be no need to extend the slave trade for twenty-one years or half that time"' given the powers conferred on the national government by the constitution:

sooner than that, '3/4 of us will be slaves to all intents and purposes whatsoever without any trouble or expense of sending to Africa for slaves, for it is as perfect a system of slavery as I ever saw planned out by any nation, kingdom or state whatever. For what have we been contending and shedding our blood and wasting our substance, but to support the natural rights of men.'[74]

Quaker minister John Neal protested at the Massachusetts convention that '"Americans deserved to be enslaved if they agreed to a compact that legalized the slave trade."'[75]

---

[69] See Waldstreicher (n. 9) 11 ff; Nash (n. 4) 7–8, 25 ff. For a survey of revisionist scholarship on slavery and the founding, see ibid., 161–8 ff.

[70] See Manisha Sinha, *The Slave's Cause: A History of Abolition* (2016) 41, 48–50, 67–8 ff; Cassandra Pybus, *Epic Journeys of Freedom: Runaway Slaves of the American Revolution and Their Global Quest for Freedom* (2006) 29–30 ff; Sylvia R. Frey, *Water From the Rock: Black Resistance in a Revolutionary Age* (1991); Edmund S. Morgan, 'Slavery and Freedom: The American Paradox' (1972) 59 J. American History 5 ff.

[71] Waldstreicher (n. 9) 3 ff. On the failure of northern opponents of slavery to press their case at the convention, see ibid., 70–1, 103–4 ff; and Nash (n. 4) 26, 30 ff.

[72] Ibid., 77 ff.   [73] Ibid., 118, 126–8, 146 ff.   [74] Ibid., 122 ff.

[75] Ibid., 122–3, 131, 142 ff. Northern proponents of ratification, for their part, resorted to alternative pleading stressing the virtues of compromise, 'admit[ing] the presence of necessary evils . . . project[ing]

IV.

With but a few notable exceptions, these powerful revisionist critiques have failed to penetrate into popular consciousness or judicial interpretation of the founding. Twenty-first-century Americans may be prepared to do some kinds of memory work—to remove from public spaces certain Confederate monuments,[76] to accept evidence of moral failure on the part of individual founders, and to strip the names of slaveholders from certain university buildings.[77] However this kind of memory work generally travels under the banner of vindicating the ideals of the Declaration of Independence—rearranging the structure and nomenclature of public space precisely in order to bend reality towards the trajectory of the nation's revolutionary ideals. In this way, the dissociation of slavery from the founding is paradoxically recapitulated in the very revisionist memory work supposedly addressed to the perverse relationship between the two. There is finally a Museum of African American History on the Mall, but no one contemplates enshrining Sarter's *Essay* or Douglass's speech next to the Declaration of Independence at the National Archives.[78]

Part of the failure of revisionist critiques of the founding to penetrate popular consciousness and judicial interpretation is historiographic. Collective memory and history interact in complex ways which historians have just begun rigorously to probe.[79] This is nowhere more evident than in the decidedly mixed record of attempts by professional historians to shape collective memory by participating in the design and messaging of 'lieux de memoire' such as famous battlefields and national monuments managed by the National Park Service.[80] The tendency is ever to replace one set of heroes with another, one triumphalist narrative with another.

blame onto the Deep South', . . . and capitalizing on the document's silences to 'exaggerate the Constitution's antislavery implications.' Ibid., 108.

[76] Jelani Cobb, 'The Battle over Confederate Monuments in New Orleans', *The New Yorker*, 12 May 2017; Ned Oliver, 'Mayor Stoney: Richmond's Confederate Monuments Can Stay, But 'Whole Story' Must Be Told', *Richmond Times-Dispatch*, 22 June 2017.

[77] See 'Report of The Working Group on Slavery, Memory, and Reconciliation to the President of Georgetown University', Washington, D.C., Summer 2016.

[78] On the Supreme Court's resistance to the implications of the American Civil War for traditional federalism doctrine, see Spaulding (n. 14) 306; Norman W. Spaulding, 'Constitution as Counter-Monument: Federalism, Reconstruction, and the Problem of Collective Memory' (2003) 103 *Colum. L. R.* 1292 ff.

[79] The seminal text on which modern studies are grounded is Maurice Halbwach, *On Collective Memory*, Lewis A. Coser (ed.) (1992). On law and collective memory, see Joachim J. Savelsberg, Ryan D. King, 'Law and Collective Memory' (2007) 3 *Annual Review of Law and Social Science* 189 ff; Norman W. Spaulding, 'Resistance, Counter-Memory Justice' (2014) 41 *Critical Inquiry* 132 ff.

[80] See Norman W. Spaulding, 'Remembering Our Second Revolution: Sesquicentennial Reflections on Civil War Historiography', in Neil H. Cogan (ed.), *Union & States' Rights: A History and Interpretation of Interposition, Nullification, and Secession 150 Years After Fort Sumter* (2014) 260 ff.

As importantly, over the last few decades the discipline of history has moved gradually but decisively away from the study of political history and towards broader analysis of social life.[81] Insofar as political history had dominated the field, this shift is not only long overdue but quite salutary, particularly as social historians have elevated the voices and experiences of people excluded from political office and elite political debate. They have also produced remarkable work informing and complicating our understanding of the founding, most prominently by revealing the ways in which social, economic, and cultural practices, along with the elements of material culture, reflect, subvert, and ramify in the formal settings of law and politics.[82]

On the other hand, this important methodological turn has been accompanied by increasingly narrow specialization and occasional neglect of or indifference towards politics.[83] And these developments in the field of history have coincided with a sharp turn towards empirical studies in political science departments (foxes have been replaced by abacus-wielding hedgehogs) as well as a retreat from grand synthetic analysis on the part of prominent constitutional law scholars.[84] So the academic audience with the expertise to take up, reconcile, translate, and amplify the implications of revisionist critiques for public consumption appears to have diminished even as the field of *legal* history blossoms and ordinary briefing before the Supreme Court is increasingly and enthusiastically supplemented with historians' briefs attempting to correct (or play into) the Court's originalist impulses.[85] Moreover, there has always been an anti-establishment tradition in American public life, a tradition defined by scepticism of professional expertise and authority. The tradition is often associated with populism,[86] but its political and epistemological roots are revolutionary—in the idea that 'the people' know best.[87]

[81] On the 'demise of political history', see Mark E. Neely Jr., *The Boundaries of American Political Culture in the Civil War Era* (2005) vii–viii ff.

[82] See Annette Gordon Reed, *The Hemingses of Monticello* (2008); T. H. Breen, *The Marketplace of Revolution: How Consumer Politics Shaped American Independence* (2004); Slauter (n. 9).

[83] See Neely (n. 81) 3–5 ff.

[84] See Isaiah Berlin, *The Hedgehog and the Fox: An Essay on Tolstoy's View of History* (2014). On the rise of empiricism, see Robert Adcock, Mark Bevir, Shannon C. Stimson, 'A History of Political Science: How? What? Why?', in Adcock, Bevir, Stimson (eds.), *Modern Political Science: Anglo-American Exchanges Since 1880* (2007) 9 ff. On the retreat to 'minimalist' theories of the constitution, see Cass R. Sunstein, 'Problems with Minimalism', (2010) 58 *Stanford L.R.* 1899 ff; Lawrence H. Tribe, 'An Open Letter to Interested Readers of *American Constitutional Law*' 29 April 2005, reprinted in (2005) 8 *Green Bag* 291, 293–5 ff ('no treatise, in my sense of that term, can be true to this moment in our constitutional history—to its conflicts, innovations, and complexities').

[85] See Joshua Stein, 'Historians Before the Bench: Friends of the Court, Foes of Originalism' (2013) 25 *Yale J. Law and Humanities* 359 ff. On originalism as a theory of constitutional interpretation, see Cornell (n. 58); Lawrence B. Solum, Robert W. Bennett, *Constitutional Originalism: A Debate* (2011).

[86] See Lawrence Friedman, *A History of American Law* (2010), 304 ff ('with the rise of Jeffersonian and Jacksonian democracy, the leading political party opposed the idea of government by experts').

[87] Ibid. On eighteenth-century views about public opinion, see Mark G. Schmeller, *Invisible Sovereign: Imagining Public Opinion from the Revolution to Reconstruction* (2016).

In any event, the twenty-first-century strain is particularly robust. At the same time, conservative legal scholars, judges, and public figures have drawn upon and supplemented the conventional account of the founding in an effort to shape public opinion and to characterize revisionism as both irresponsible and unpatriotic.[88] All in all, one suspects that even if foxes were not an endangered species in the academy, their influence would be limited.

A perhaps more fundamental issue is that relatively widespread popular and judicial consensus about the genius and restraint of the revolution, if not the integrity of each and every founder, seems to provide a kind of scaffolding for pitched modern debates about the meaning of the constitution and methods of constitutional interpretation. It would be an exaggeration to say that Americans can debate and litigate their constitution so vigorously because they so enthusiastically celebrate their revolutionary heritage. But the longstanding practice of omitting inconvenient facts about the revolutionary experience from modern interpretive debates about the constitution is conspicuous. Resistance to revisionism may indeed be a mainstay of American constitutional faith.

This is precisely what makes Frederick Douglass' Independence Day oration such a jarring and compelling indictment. On the one hand, it appears to reverse the ordinary terms of debate by levelling a direct challenge to the nation's revolutionary ideals. And yet, as the second half of his speech ultimately makes clear, the question of who is free to celebrate Independence Day is posed in the service of a redemptive dialectic whose movement is defined in terms of those very ideals. Having abandoned disunionism by 1852, and with it the Garrisonian reading of the constitution as a pro-slavery instrument, Douglass 'draw[s] encouragement from the Declaration of Independence, the great principles it contains, and the genius of American institutions' in concluding that certain 'forces in operation . . . must inevitably work the downfall of slavery'.[89] Diametrically opposed as their positions on the constitution had become, one can read even William Lloyd Garrison's disunionism, embodied most radically in his burning of a copy of the constitution in 1854 (along with a copy of the Fugitive Slave Act and a judicial opinion enforcing it), as engaging the same redemptive dialectic.[90] His antinomian pyrotechnic display was staged, after all, at an anti-slavery rally on Independence Day. Even if it was aimed at promoting

[88] On efforts to influence public opinion, see Nicole Hemmer, *Messengers of the Right: Conservative Media and the Transformation of American Politics* (2016); Kim Phillips-Fein, *Invisible Hands: The Making of the Conservative Movement From the New Deal to Reagan* (2009). For an example of resistance to 'revisionism' and the attempt to characterize *both* liberal and conservative alternatives to originalism as revisionist, see Robert Bork, *The Tempting of America: The Political Seduction of the Law* (1990) 187, 223 ff.

[89] Douglass (n. 1) 204–5 ff.

[90] Garrison offers an account of his actions in *The Liberator*, Vol. 27 7 July 1854 at 106 ff.

disunion *in fact*, if it cannot be interpreted as a species of high political theatre designed to heighten commitment to the abolition of slavery *among unionists*, utopian separatism can trace its lineage not just to the revolutionary ideals of the 1770s, but to Plymouth Rock.[91]

To charge Garrison with disloyalty, as he was at the time, this lineage either has to be denied, distinguished, or deemed to have terminated in the revolution itself. And of course one must blink at Garrison's 1844 prediction that an anti-slavery interpretation of the constitution 'never can be carried into effect without dissolving the Union by provoking a civil war'.[92] Notice the paradox. Garrison, the incendiary radical, admonished his fellow abolitionists that the more politically and legally engaged the abolition movement became, the more it insisted that the constitution supported resistance to slavery, the more likely it would be to provoke violent conflict with the South. One need not subscribe to the 'irrepressible conflict' thesis to appreciate that, if he was correct, the raw materials for the superadrenalized fury that fed the 'meat grinder' at Antietam fell into place well before the election of Lincoln and the firing on Fort Sumter.[93]

Remarkably, once the war broke out, and 'even after it became clear how deadly it was going to be', Garrisonian abolitionists who 'had been pacifists', and therefore *opposed* forcing the South to remain in the Union, 'reconciled themselves to the war'.[94] George M. Frederickson sees complex motivations for this shift in attitudes towards the use of force by abolitionists formerly committed to non-violence and moral persuasion. He emphasizes abolitionists' underlying ' "martyr complex"', the respects in which death was viewed in religious terms as a 'revelation of perfection', and their keen interest in the war as a means of bringing about emancipation.[95] He points to anti-slavery activist Gail Hamilton's essay in the *Atlantic Monthly*, published a few months before Holmes Sr.'s on the Garner photographs of Antietam, admonishing women of the North to:

[c]onsecrate to a holy cause not only the incidentals of life, but life itself. Father, husband, child,—I do not say give them up to toil, exposure, suffering, death, without a murmur—that implies reluctance. I rather say, Urge them to the offering; fill them with sacred fury. . . . Be large and lofty. Count it all joy that you are reckoned worthy to suffer in a grand and glorious cause.[96]

---

[91] See David D. Hall, *The Antinomian Controversy, 1636–1638: A Documentary History* (1990).

[92] W. L. Garrison, 'Editorial Reply to a Subscriber's Letter', Vol. 14, *The Liberator* 28 June 1844 103 ff. On whether the lineage of separatism reached its terminus in the Civil War, see Sanford Levinson (ed.), *Nullification and Secession in Modern Constitutional Thought* (2016).

[93] William H. Seward, 'On the Irrepressible Conflict', Speech at Rochester, N.Y., 25 October 1858.

[94] George M. Fredrickson, *The Inner Civil War: Northern Intellectuals and the Crisis of the Union* (1993) 81 ff. On Garrison's support for the war, see ibid., 61 ff.

[95] Ibid., 82–3 ff; see also 57, 63 ff.   [96] Ibid., 83–4 ff.

At the very same time, death on a mass scale taught many 'to act and think like a machine', to value 'impersonal efficiency' over the humanitarian emotions that had animated the abolition movement before the war.[97] And 'since there were clear limitations to what could actually be accomplished for the relief of the wounded and the dying, a stoical and fatalistic sense of the inevitability of large-scale suffering was also being inculcated'.[98]

Garner's photographs notwithstanding, the scale of violence produced by the admixture of secessionism, Southern pride, 'sacred fury', mechanistic efficiency, and fatalism remains, to this day, difficult to fathom. The vastness of this scene of death and the horrors of slavery account in no small measure for modern resistance to revisionist theories of the founding. It is difficult, to say the least, to conclude that what the founders bequeathed to the nation was a set of contradictions that made suffering and death on such a scale possible, difficult to conclude that the constitution was, in fact, 'a covenant with death'.[99] Instead, from the start of the war there was talk, as Henry David Thoreau put it to a friend, ' "of the moral regeneration of the nation" '.[100] Others would insist that the desire to preserve the Union affirmed 'the people's "conservative love of order, government, and law" ', and that the military conflict would diminish fanaticism and revive self-restraint on both sides of the Mason-Dixon line.[101] Even as the casualties mounted, Holmes Sr.'s reaction was more common than Holmes Jr.'s loss of 'belief in belief'. And as the war and Reconstruction passed from active memory into professional history, a striking historiographic consensus emerged blaming the scale of death and the conflicts over Reconstruction on the failures of statesmanship of the Civil War generation, *not* the founders. Even modern revisionists, acutely aware of what followed the retreat from Reconstruction and keen on rehabilitating the image of abolitionists and Radical Republicans, resist the thought that the contradictions of the founding cannot be solved, that time and perseverance may not yet make the Union more perfect. Redemptive dialectics *feed* upon this resistance.

We are now in a position to appreciate the singular elasticity and resilience of the ideals of the American revolution, their capacity to support divergent starting points for redemptive projects, and, we could add with Furet, the seemingly 'infinite capacity for commemoration' of the revolution. So much the better, one might reasonably conclude, as long as the bloodshed on battlefields like Antietam is not forgotten—as long, that is, as the elasticity of our revolutionary ideals and the divergent trajectories of redemption supported by them are channelled into the ordinary forms of constitutional debate.

---

[97] Ibid., 90 ff.   [98] Ibid.

[99] The phrase is Garrison's; see Phillip S. Paludan, *Covenant with Death: The Constitution, Law, and Equality in the Civil War Era* (1975).

[100] Fredrickson (n. 94) 73 ff.   [101] Ibid., 55, 69 ff.

V.

Still, anyone sensitive to the pathologies of repetition compulsion must wonder if there is not something missing in this approach to the founding, if there is not a toll associated with failing to escape what Furet called 'the tyranny of the historical actors' own conception of their experience and the myth of origins'.[102] To explain this 'tyranny' in the French context, Furet contrasts the famous history of the French Revolution written by Jules Michelet with Alexis de Tocqueville's less celebrated critique. Notwithstanding the deeply held egalitarian *ambitions* of the revolutionaries, Tocqueville had argued that the most significant practical effect of their *actions* was to complete the centralization of state power begun by the monarchy during the ancien regime. Focusing on the writings of the revolutionaries in the manner of Michelet, seeking to reveal and validate their aspirations through the primary source material, and attempting thereby to canonize one or another triumphalist national narrative, obscures the extent to which the supposed ruptures and innovations of the revolution merely 'accelerat[ed] a prior political and social trend' initiated by Richelieu and Louis XIV.[103] Furet continues:

It seems to me that historians of the Revolution have, and always will have, to make a choice between Michelet and Tocqueville. By that I do not mean the choice between a republican and a conservative interpretation of the French Revolution, for those two kinds of history would still be linked together in a common definition of the problem, which is precisely what Tocqueville rejected. What separates Michelet and Tocqueville is something else: it is that Michelet brings the Revolution back to life from the inside, that he communes and commemorates, while Tocqueville constantly examines the discrepancy he discerns between the intentions of the actors and the historical role they played. Michelet installed himself in the visible or transparent Revolution; he celebrated the memorable coincidence between values, the people and men's actions. Tocqueville not only questioned that transparency or coincidence, [he thought that it actually masked a fundamental disconnect between human action and its real meaning (sens réel), a disconnect that arises precisely from, and is indeed, characteristic of, the role played by democratic ideology in a period of revolutionary upheaval.] For Tocqueville, there was a gulf between the Revolution's true outcome and the revolutionaries' intentions.[104]

Furet insists that Tocqueville's methodological turn is the 'most important' in the 'entire historiography of the French Revolution', and, tellingly, the very reason why his book has been ignored—treated 'for more than a century [as] the stepchild of that historiography, more often cited than read, and more read than understood' .[105] There

---

[102] Furet (n. 44) 16 ff. See also Parkinson (n. 52) 24 ff. [103] Ibid., 15 ff.

[104] Ibid., 16 ff. The bracketed text is translated directly from François Furet, *Penser la Révolution Francaise* (1978) 35 ff ('Il pense qu'elles masquent une opacité maximale entre l'action humaine et son sens réel, opacité caractéristique de la Révolution comme période historique, de par le role qu'y joue l'idéologie démocratique.').

[105] Ibid., 16 ff.

is apparently little appetite in France for lingering on the respects in which the French Revolution betrayed its own ideals and consummated longstanding monarchic aspirations to centralize administrative control of the levers of state power.

The point is not just that Tocqueville looked for continuities where most historians of the French Revolution have taken for granted a radical break with the ançien regime. Nor is it just that shockingly inegalitarian consequences resulted from radical egalitarian aspirations, or that concentrating on an archive filled with the ideas and arguments of revolutionary protagonists will, in both obvious and quite subtle ways, draw the historian (whether conventional or revisionist, left or right leaning) into the struggle of those protagonists.[106] Beyond these important points, Furet suggests that liberal democratic revolutions become legible as historical phenomena through, *not in spite of,* their contradictions. As long as these contradictions remain obscure or are swept up into redemptive dialectics, the nation's founding will be misunderstood. The historian remains caught in a 'game of mirrors . . . bound to execrate or to celebrate, *both of which are ways of commemorating*'.[107] And in the process, the Revolution itself is transformed into history's chief 'protagonist, the absolutely trustworthy Antigone of the new era'.[108]

In the American context, described above, revisionists have made the methodological turn to expose continuities as well as the failure of egalitarian aspirations. But the habit of approaching the founding through the 'protagonists' archive' has proved harder to break. Seminal texts produced by those who led the revolution and most enthusiastically supported ratification of the constitution (Madison's notes on the debates at the constitutional convention, and the *Federalist Papers*) continue to exert gravitational pull even when counterbalanced by the writings of opponents and lesser known source material that draws the views of non-elites into relief and reveals the extent to which the constitution is polysemic.[109] The assignment of moral authority and agency is different for revisionists, but they share with conventional accounts the same 'definition of the problem', the same logic of 'commemoration'. Finally, although discrete inconsistencies and contradictions are more commonly raised, they are almost invariably swept up into redemptive dialectics.

Consider the contradiction between chattel slavery and the Declaration of Independence. Rather than interrogating liberty and slavery as mutually interdependent categories—rather than examining the ways in which servitude operates as a condition of certain exercises of liberty, the ways in which ordered liberty itself entails (inescapably?) violent bondage—chattel slavery is consistently figured as the normatively and diachronically transitory and subordinate half of a hierarchically arranged pair. A temporally limited practice, not an unavoidable or enduring complement to liberty, and certainly not a principle equal in significance

---

[106]   Ibid.   [107]   Ibid., 17 ff (emphasis added).   [108]   Ibid.
[109]   Parkinson (n. 52) 24 ff; Cornell (n. 58) 724, 736–7 ff.

to the principle of liberty. Whatever else modern Americans understand about their founding and the Civil War, they are certain that they live *after* slavery, not with it.

As importantly, chattel slavery is often figured as a singular injustice, radically different not only from other forms of bondage or servitude, but also from the very social, political, legal, and economic consequences of slavery that outlasted abolition and Reconstruction.[110] In this way, the protean metaphor of political slavery, so significant to American revolutionaries and opponents of the constitution ratified in 1789, is rendered anachronistic. Moreover, by reading chattel slavery through the interpretive framework of redemptive dialectics, the ideals of the revolutionary period are paradoxically acquitted in the same revisionist accounts that charge the founders with moral and political failure. One consequence of this is that, notwithstanding the deep political salience of redemptive dialectics in American culture, they tend to obscure the problem of irredeemably unjust acts, injustices so grave as to draw these ideals into doubt. Indeed, by promising movement beyond these injustices—movement that, by definition, cannot be completed—redemptive dialectics may actually exacerbate the problem.

Or consider the difficulties associated with explaining the relationship between the illiberal excesses of revolutionary violence, on the one hand, and the role of popular sovereignty in liberal democratic government, on the other. In the conventional account, as we have seen, the violence of the revolution is not only said to be justified by the lofty ideals for which the war was fought, it is characterized as valiant, clever (given the might of the British Imperial forces) and restrained; excesses are either ignored altogether or explained away as unfortunate but necessary responses to exigent circumstances. The constitution 'fulfils' the revolution by transforming its ideals and the underlying principle of popular sovereignty into a durable framework of governance. The representative branches of government channel the voice of the people, and the judicial branch resolves both public and private 'cases and controversies'. The sovereign status of 'the people' may be implicated in voting and in the occasional ratification of amendments, but the genius of the constitutional design lies precisely in the disaggregation of sovereignty from governance. Following ratification 'the people' can get on with their private affairs. While there may have been lingering debts, property disputes, and treaty obligations to adjudicate from the revolutionary period, ratification of the constitution also formally separated the sovereign acts associated with establishing a system of governance from the antecedent violence of the revolution.

In the revisionist account offered by proponents of popular constitutionalism, 'the people' never completely ceded interpretive authority regarding either ordinary or fundamental law to the courts and they remained active in the machinery of governance through service in legal entities such as the jury (in which nullification

---

[110] Cf. Douglas A. Blackmon, *Slavery by Another Name: The Re-Enslavement of Black Americans From the Civil War to World War II* (2012).

was recognized), the grand jury (in which a prosecutor's request for an unlawful or otherwise unfair indictment might be refused), the posse comitatus (including, critically, refusal to serve), the militia, and alternatively, as a 'last resort . . . crowd action'.[111] In this way, controversial state action could be inhibited or stopped in its tracks by popular will. The reference to crowd action is particularly important as it underscores the connection all too often suppressed in conventional accounts between the ordinary operation of law and the tradition of revolutionary resistance. On the other hand, as in conventional accounts, extra-judicial interpretation of law by 'the people' is still framed in terms of a rationally calibrated hierarchy of techniques of resistance; violent excesses may be acknowledged, but they are typically framed as discrete, unfortunate, and transitory exceptions that draw 'the people's' sobriety and commitment to restraint into even sharper relief.

The difficulty is that duelling, courthouse burnings, rioting, lynching, slave revolts, wildcat strikes, and other forms of popular violence described elsewhere by this author as 'impersonation of justice' are generally excluded from consideration.[112] These forms of social action do not fit comfortably within a rationally calculated hierarchy of techniques of resistance to law (though they cannot be described as completely antinomian either), they were not necessarily viewed as means of last resort by participants, and they raise exceedingly complex and interesting questions about the relationship between restraint and excess, the limitations and failures of formal adjudication in court, who possesses the social and reputational capital to impersonate justice, and who has the authority to determine whether or not an official act is lawful. Precisely because these forms of impersonation raise the question of who has authority to determine the legality of an official act, they must also be read in light of the widespread public hostility towards lawyers, judges, and the legal system at the founding,[113] as well as the surprisingly active role that members of the legal profession sometimes played in violent, extra-judicial impersonation of justice.[114]

Missing even from the revisionist accounts, then, is not just a fully articulated theory of the respects in which law is constituted in and through popular resistance, but also an understanding of how excess, violent excess, and above all the *terror* of violent excess, influences both the ordinary operation of law and the state's legal and political responses to exigent circumstances. Charles Tilly has written

[111] Larry Kramer, *The People Themselves: Popular Constitutionalism and Judicial Review* (2004) 27 ff. 'Whether enforcing morality or law, eighteenth-century Whig mobs were generally conservative: organized to uphold community values against indifferent or ineffective public officials and illegal or unconstitutional government action. . . . These mobs demonstrated a "remarkable single-mindedness and discriminating purposefulness" in selecting their targets and in taking care not to inflict collateral damage.' Ibid.

[112] Norman W. Spaulding, 'The Impersonation of Justice: Lynching, Dueling, and Wildcat Strikes in Nineteenth Century America', in Nan Goodman, Simon Stern (eds.), *The Routledge Research Companion to Law and Humanities in Nineteenth Century America* (2017) 163 ff.

[113] See Friedman (n. 86) 303–4 ff.   [114] Spaulding (n. 112).

that 'revolutionary situations consist in the convergence of variable political conditions . . . that appear widely outside of revolutions'.[115] The same can be said of revolutionary resistance.[116] We simply cannot understand the American revolution or the legal order established by the American constitution (of either 1789 *or 1865*) as long as revolutionary resistance and its various legacies, remainders, and analogues are treated as aberrant, antinomian exceptions.

VI.

> I confess that there are several parts of this constitution which I do not at present approve, but I am not sure I shall never approve them: For having lived long, I have experienced many instances of being obliged by better information on fuller consideration, to change opinions even on important subjects, which I once thought right, but found to be otherwise. . . . Most men indeed as well as most sects in Religion, think themselves in possession of all truth, and that wherever others differ from them it is so far error. Steele, a Protestant in a Dedication tells the Pope, that the only difference between our Churches in their opinions of the certainty of their doctrines is, the Church of Rome is infallible and the Church of England is never wrong.[117]

These words are taken from a speech by Benjamin Franklin read on the last day of the constitutional convention seventy-five years, to the day, before the battle of Antietam. Historians and other commentators have focused more on an offhand remark by Franklin at the close of the convention comparing 'the result of that summer's deliberations to a half-eclipsed sun painted on George Washington's chair'.[118] Franklin mused that at different points in the deliberations of the convention during the summer he had looked at the emblem with trepidation, '"[b]ut now at length I have the happiness to know that it is a rising and not a setting sun."'[119] The speech, however, is about fallibility, not redemption. It is about not knowing, or rather knowing that one is prone to error and that one must act in the face of that debilitating knowledge. Franklin sounds considerably more like Holmes Jr. than Holmes Sr.

It is also a deeply political speech. Franklin was the head of the Pennsylvania Abolition Society in 1787 and had long promised to '"act in concert" with anti-slavery activists'.[120] In that capacity he had agreed to present a petition opposing the

---

[115] Charles Tilly, *European Revolutions, 1492–1992* (1993) 11 ff.   [116] Ibid., 39 ff.

[117] Max Farrand (ed.), *The Records of the Federal Convention of 1787* (1911) vol. 2, 642 ff.

[118] Slauter (n. 9) 1 ff.   [119] Ibid.   [120] Waldstreicher (n. 9) 70 ff.

slave trade at the constitutional convention, a pledge he failed to keep.[121] This was not a change of opinion over time and after deep reflection, but the subordination of one firmly held (or at least professed) conviction to another. He also believed that ratification of the constitution, such as it was, would be aided if, on the last day of the convention, all of its drafters signed the instrument. So his speech was crafted to convince delegates whose doubts about the enterprise ran even deeper than his may have been. Hence the emphasis on fallibility:

I cannot help expressing a wish that every member of the Convention who may still have objections to it, would with me, on this occasion doubt a little of his own infallibility—and to make manifest our unanimity, put his name to this instrument.[122]

As Eric Slauter has observed, Franklin's ensuing motion was carefully formulated to indicate that signing represented a mere witnessing of the fact that the instrument had been drafted by representatives of the states 'present' (not *all* the states, because Rhode Island had appointed no delegation, and not all delegates since, 'for one reason or another, almost a quarter of the members had left the Convention, and only four states still possessed their full delegations').[123] More than a few of those who remained were opposed, for various reasons, to the constitution. It was therefore critical to avoid the implication that signing represented endorsement, and yet equally critical to project to the public an appearance of 'unanimous consent' in a group that had strayed radically from its limited mandate to consider mere revisions to the Articles of Confederation.[124]

Franklin's motion passed and all but three delegates affixed their signatures.[125] Yet it is readily apparent from the notes of the debate that the delegates remained in profound disagreement about what signing either did or did not signify. Some proponents of the constitution announced that their signatures were not just endorsements of the constitution but a solemn 'pledge' to *support* ratification; others, while supporting the motion, emphasized that refusal to sign would be read publicly as *opposition* to the instrument.[126] Slauter is right to observe how easy it is 'for modern readers to forget the lack of unanimity during the 'founding period', to ignore strategies of compromise that framers like Franklin employed to produce a veneer of consensus, or to overlook the lengths to which historians . . . have sometimes gone to cover over dissent'.[127] An 'unsettled ambiguity' rests in the very signatures of the framers to the instrument of their making.[128]

---

[121] Ibid., 103–4 ff.   [122] Farrand (n. 117) 643 ff.   [123] Slauter (n. 9) 5 ff.
[124] Farrand (n. 117) 643 ff.   [125] Slauter (n. 9) 6 ff.   [126] Ibid., 645–7 ff.
[127] Ibid., 6–7 ff.

[128] Ibid. And of course even cursory study of the positions taken by the framers *over time* reveals not just ambiguity, but, as with Frederick Douglass, shifts, internal discord, and contradiction. For a noble effort to reconcile James Madison's shifts, see 'How to Maintain a Constitution: The Virginia and Kentucky Resolutions and James Madison's Struggle with the Problem of Constitutional Maintenance', in Levinson (n. 92) 53 ff.

Franklin's invocation of fallibilism may have been strategic, and less hard won than Holmes Jr.'s. Given his decision to pocket the anti-slavery petition he was charged with presenting, it can hardly be seen as heroic. But for just that reason—because of the disjunction between its purpose, its language, and the contemporaneous actions and omissions of its author—it warrants closer analysis in histories of the founding. It is indeed emblematic of the founding. The charge of the historian, and perhaps too the constitutional lawyer, is not to redeem the founding, nor is it merely to reveal 'unsettled ambiguities'. The charge is to see ambiguity, contradiction, and error as constitutive, to constantly test the paradox of unanimity made manifest in doubt. That entails reading the constitution, the written text itself, as an expression of fallibilism, not the canonization of one set of beliefs or another (what Holmes Jr. famously called 'fighting faiths'[129]), and certainly not as the 'ideological fulfilment' or flat betrayal of revolutionary ideals. A history that meets this charge is no mere supplement to the text and structure of the constitution, it is their measure, a condition of their legibility.

BIBLIOGRAPHY

Max Farrand (ed.), *The Records of the Federal Convention of 1787* (1911)

Francois Furet, *Interpreting the French Revolution* (1981)

Thomas C. Grey, 'Origins of the Unwritten Constitution: Fundamental Law in American Revolutionary Thought' (1978) 30 *Stanford L. R.* 843

Sanford Levinson (ed.), *Responding to Imperfection: The Theory and Practice of Constitutional Amendment* (1995)

Garry B. Nash, *Race and Revolution* (1990)

Robert G. Parkinson, *The Common Cause: Creating Race and Nation in the American Revolution* (2016)

Steve Pincus, *1688: The First Modern Revolution* (2009)

Eric Slauter, *The State as a Work of Art: The Cultural Origins of the Constitution* (2009)

Richard Slotkin, *The Long Road to Antietam: How the Civil War Became a Revolution* (2012)

Norman W. Spaulding, 'Paradoxes of Constitutional Faith: Federalism, Emancipation, and the Original Thirteenth Amendment' (2016) 3 *Critical Analysis of Law* 306

David Waldstreicher, *Slavery's Constitution: From Revolution to Ratification* (2009)

Gordon Wood, *The Creation of the American Republic: 1776–1787* (1969)

[129] Menand (n. 12) 430 ff.

CHAPTER 54

....

FOUNDINGS

EUROPEAN INTEGRATION

....

PETER LINDSETH

I.

....

THE catastrophe of 1933–1945—indeed of 1914–1945—is rightly seen as a central impetus behind the founding of European integration in the 1950s. A crucial dimension of that founding, however, also relates to the advent of the modern administrative state in twentieth-century Europe—what we may call the 'postwar constitutional settlement of administrative governance' after 1945.[1]

Beyond the functional demands of postwar reconstruction,[2] along with the desire to transcend the excesses of nationalism,[3] the postwar period was also the moment in Western European history when the constitutional foundations of modern administrative governance were also secured. In the decades following the end of the Second World War, the major Western European countries had arguably found the formula for the 'new form of governance' designed to meet a 'larger pattern

[1] See Peter L. Lindseth, *Power and Legitimacy: Reconciling Europe and the Nation-State* (2010) ch. 2 ff; see also Peter L. Lindseth, 'The Paradox of Parliamentary Supremacy: Delegation, Democracy, and Dictatorship in Germany and France, 1920s–1950s' (2004) 113 *Yale L.J.* 1341 ff.

[2] See, e.g., Alan S. Milward, *The Reconstruction of Western Europe, 1945–1951* (1984).

[3] See, e.g., Walter Lipgens, *Documents on the History of European Integration: Continental Plans for European Union 1939–1945* (1985).

of obligations' in the emergent welfare state, something they had actively been seeking since the end of the First World War.[4] This 'new form of governance' built on a transformed understanding of the legitimacy of regulatory power delegated to the executive and administrative spheres, combined with checks exercised by parliaments and judicial institutions—in effect, a reconciliation of democracy and bureaucracy.[5] It was no coincidence—given the fundamentally executive and technocratic character of European integration—that several of the prime movers in the process of European integration in the 1950s (e.g., Jean Monnet, Robert Schuman, Konrad Adenauer) had also been major players in the construction of their respective national postwar administrative states as well.

After the disaster of two world wars, all the major countries in Western Europe sought to reconcile the increased functional demand for delegated regulatory power with their historical experiences and constitutional traditions. Although the legal and institutional approaches to the problem would differ in particulars, each country's solution followed the same basic pattern: the vast majority of rules of general application would no longer be in the form of traditional legislation passed by parliament but would now take the form of regulations or other subordinate legislation produced within the executive and administrative spheres, adopted pursuant to 'enabling legislation' or 'framework laws'. The democratic legitimation of these rules would no longer be directly through a vote of individual legislators as such but rather through their initial vote on the enabling legislation combined with subsequent hierarchical oversight of the administrative sphere by government ministers (who were in turn responsible before parliament). Supplementing these forms of oversight were legal controls enforced by courts or other court-like administrative tribunals, which served as 'commitment mechanisms'—to use the language of principal-agent theory— to ensure that administrative governance remained within the confines of both statutory and constitutional bounds.

At almost the same historical moment that these *national* forms of administrative governance were consolidated in Western Europe, however, administrative governance also began to take on an additional *supranational* dimension. This new dimension involved the shift of regulatory power, both in terms of rulemaking and enforcement/adjudication, to institutions operating *outside* the confines of the nation-state. Beginning with the establishment of the European Coal and Steel Community (ECSC) in 1951, and continuing with the founding of the European Economic Community (EEC) and the European Atomic Energy Community (Euratom) in 1957, European integration built directly on several key elements of administrative governance as it was emerging on the national and supranational levels in the aftermath of the Second World War.

[4] Alan S. Milward, *The European Rescue of the Nation-State* (2000) 4.
[5] Lindseth, 'The Paradox of Parliamentary Supremacy' (n. 1).

As a political matter, integration built most importantly on the constitutional predominance of the national executive, not merely as a 'legislator' in its own right, but also as the first line of democratic legitimation over policy-making in the administrative sphere, whether national or supranational. Integration further depended on the political and institutional ascendance within the administrative sphere of the technocrat, whose primary bases for legitimacy were a combination of seemingly 'depoliticized' expertise, ministerial oversight, as well as a (judicially enforced) respect for the tenets of administrative legality. Additionally, European integration built on enabling legislation in a new guise—the various Community treaties and related agreements—which, like enabling legislation and framework laws on the national level, did not specify most regulatory norms directly but rather delegated this normative power to executive and technocratic institutions, albeit ones which now extended beyond the strict confines of the nation-state. Finally, the process of European integration entailed an important judicial 'commitment mechanism'—the European Court of Justice (ECJ)—not merely to review the legality of Community norms but also, somewhat more unexpectedly, to scrutinize the conformity of Member State laws with the goals of market integration as set forth in the treaties.

In seeking to understand the founding of integration, it is equally crucial, however, to remember that the new supranational apparatus not only *depended upon*, but also *disrupted*, the forms of administrative governance that were emerging on the national level in the postwar decades. The dependence could be seen primarily in the crucial role played by national executives in providing shared control and oversight of supranational technocrats. At the inception of European integration in the early 1950s, what distinguished supranational administrative governance from its national counterparts was the ambiguous legal role of national executives in the legitimation of technocratic norms produced at the Community level. Although committed European federalists like Jean Monnet saw the essence of supranationalism as technocratic autonomy from even national executive control, much of the institutional politics of European integration in its first three decades would centre around the largely *successful* effort by national executives to assert their hierarchical legal authority (either severally and collectively) over Community rule-making.[6] The legitimacy of regulatory norm-production at the Community level was primarily mediated through cabinet ministers, and especially through the plebiscitary leadership of chief executives, just as in the administrative state.

By contrast, nationally mediated legitimacy was much more difficult to maintain in the supranational judicial context, which in turn gave rise to a significant *disruption* of the postwar constitutional settlement in the process of European integration. On the national level, courts and court-like *juridictions administratives* (for example,

---

[6] See Peter L. Lindseth, 'Transatlantic Functionalism: New Deal Models and European Integration' (2015) 2 *Critical Analysis of Law* 83 ff.

the French Conseil d'État) saw one of their main functions to be constraining the normative autonomy of the administrative sphere in certain key areas. These constraints took the form of principles of natural justice designed to protect individual rights, or, more importantly, the application of constitutional limits on delegation designed to protect certain core democratic functions of the national legislature. The very purpose of courts and court-like *juridictions administratives* in the postwar constitutional settlement was thus to serve as an independent check on the exercise of executive and administrative power in the interest of legislatively and constitutionally defined policy goals.

When this independent check was transferred to the supranational level, however, certain contradictions arose. On the one hand, consistent with the postwar constitutional settlement, the ECJ sought to advance the rule of law on the supranational level through the enforcement of procedural protections on behalf of private parties in the face of Community action. (Although, it should be noted, the Court would prove to be parsimonious in granting broad standing to private parties against certain kinds of regulatory conduct at the Community level.)[7] On the other hand, in a break with the postwar constitutional settlement, the Court consistently geared its case law towards *promoting* the normative autonomy of Community institutions—including, most importantly, the Court's own autonomy—from any kind of specifically national control that might impair the achievement of the 'Community interest' as the Court defined it.

Thus, while national executives were working hard after the 1950s to reinforce Member State control over regulatory decision-making in the Community—in a manner consistent, arguably, with the executive element of the postwar constitutional settlement—the ECJ was laying the groundwork for a very different understanding of the nature of European integration. Implicit in the Court's jurisprudence in the early decades of integration was a conception of the Community as an autonomous level of governance in a federal-type system, with a 'constitutional' legitimacy of its own independent of the Member States (rather than merely a mediated 'administrative' legitimacy as the Member States' regulatory agent). The ECJ became the driving force behind the effort to transform the Community, conceptually, from a legal arrangement among individual sovereign states governed by international law into a vertically integrated 'new legal order'—a kind of autonomously constitutional order—as the Court so boldly announced in 1963 in its celebrated judgment in *Van Gend & Loos*.[8]

This 'constitutional' approach has no doubt deeply influenced how lawyers and legal scholars have come to understand the process of European integration over the last half-century. Nonetheless, the flaw in the Court's approach has

---

[7] See Case 25/62, *Plaumann & Co. v. Commission*, 1963 E.C.R. 95.

[8] Case 26/62, *Van Gend & Loos v. Nederlands Administratie der Belastingen*, 1963 E.C.R. 1. For further discussion, see below nn. 49–51 and accompanying text.

always been that it assumes what is fundamentally in historical doubt—i.e., that the supranational apparatus has in fact attained its own democratic and constitutional legitimacy. To be sure, European integration possesses various other kinds of legitimacy (legal, technocratic, and functional) and these have been crucial to supporting the now-vast regulatory power of the European Union (EU). Nonetheless, EU governance today still depends on the Member States to supply the most robust forms of democratic and constitutional legitimacy, precisely as one would expect of a system in which the 'principals'—in an ultimate legitimacy sense—remain national, while the regulatory 'agents' are increasingly supranational. This disconnect between the extent of the EU's regulatory *power* and its sources for robust democratic and constitutional *legitimacy* on the national level (lacking such legitimacy in its own right) has deeply shaped the evolution of European public law since its inception.

II.

For Western European elites faced with the daunting task of reconstruction in the aftermath of Second World War, the New Deal in the United States seemed to offer a successful model of institutional and regulatory innovation in the face of devastating crisis. '[T]he situation at the end of this war will resemble that in America in 1933, though on a wider and deeper scale,' wrote David Mitrany, a Romanian-born, naturalized-British scholar of international relations, in 1943. 'And for the same reasons the path pursued by Mr. Roosevelt in 1933 offers the best, perhaps the only chance for getting a new international life going.'[9] Mitrany's wartime pamphlet, *A Working Peace System*, was appropriately subtitled *An Argument for the Functional Development of International Organization*. This alluded to the developing ideal that all public institutions should evolve as a 'function' of the problems they were established to solve, rather than being governed by traditional normative or constitutional commitments (e.g., on the national level, 'separation of powers' or, on the international level, 'national sovereignty'). The emergence of 'specific administrative agencies' of the New Deal-type, Mitrany argued, was 'the peculiar trait and indeed the foundation of modern government', whose purpose and power was being 'determined less by constitutional norms than by practical requirements'.[10] Mitrany hoped to harness this functionalist dynamic in service of

[9] David Mitrany, *A Working Peace System: An Argument for the Functional Development of International Organization* (4th edn., 1946) 30 (1st edn., 1943) ff.
[10] Ibid., 28 ff.

peaceful change *among states*, allowing New Deal-type administrative governance to 'do internationally what it does nationally'.[11] The key would be the creation of 'a detached international civil service', with 'a new conscience' of independence and practical problem-solving on a transnational scale.[12]

The same mindset guided the leading advocates of European integration in the 1950s. The most important those, of course, was Jean Monnet, who on behalf of the French government led the drafting of integration's founding document: the Schuman Declaration of May 1950.[13] The only institution actually mentioned in the Schuman Declaration was an independent technocratic body, the so-called High Authority, a name intentionally evocative of administrative agencies on the New Deal model (like the Tennessee Valley Authority). Paul Reuter, a law professor who was a member of Monnet's drafting team, later acknowledged that the proposal for a High Authority stood 'in a disquieting solitude'.[14] According to Reuter, the High Authority's independence 'was in some sense a desperate solution', because there was 'neither a European parliament, nor government, nor people'[15] on which to build an integrated polity or market. Reuter argued that the only way 'to build Europe without Europeans' was 'to address ourselves to independent personalities',[16] whose decisions would then be binding on national governments. Reuter would later recall that he 'knew a bit of the American system', the principal virtue of which in his view was how it conferred power on 'independent men' to exercise a variety of functions, 'be they "quasi-judicial", administrative, even economic . . . When I proposed [this formula] to Monnet, using the American term "Authority", he accepted it immediately'.[17]

Thus, in the original French proposal the High Authority was to serve, in effect, as a kind of autonomous regulatory agency of an extraordinarily novel type, one that possessed normative power delegated from national parliaments but would otherwise be freed from having its decisions legitimized by subsequent national oversight (notably via the national executive). This formula, however, proved unachievable, at least in a political sense. Over the course of the negotiations of the Treaty of Paris of 1951 establishing the ECSC, other countries pressed for the establishment of a Council of Ministers drawn from national executives to oversee the High Authority's activities politically, a new Court of Justice to oversee its activities legally, as well as a Common Assembly—the future 'European Parliament'—whose members would be drawn from national parliamentarians

---

[11] Ibid., 34 ff.   [12] Ibid., 48 ff.

[13] The Schuman Declaration—9 May 1950, <https://europa.eu/european-union/about-eu/symbols/europe-day/schuman-declaration_en>, accessed 23 April 2018.

[14] Paul Reuter, *La Communauté européenne du charbon et de l'acier* (1953) 51 ff.

[15] Ibid., 51–2 ff.   [16] Ibid., 51 ff.

[17] Paul Reuter, 'Aux Origines du Plan Schuman' in Pierre-Henri Teitgen (ed.), *Mélanges Fernand Dehousse*, vol. 2 (1979) 67 ff.

in order to provide some modicum of parliamentary representation at the supranational level.[18]

What the ECSC negotiations suggested was the fundamental impossibility of separating the purportedly 'technical' from the 'political'—a central distinction of the functionalist framework for supranationalism. The weakness of functionalism was perhaps one reason why it was eventually displaced by so-called neo-functionalist theory, a newer framework that had the virtue of recognizing that the initial decision to delegate to supranational bodies was the by-product of a highly political rather than merely functional/technical process. But like the functionalists before them, the neo-functionalists of the 1950s (most importantly Ernst Haas)[19] still foresaw that the driving force behind any *subsequent* expansion of the supranational regulatory competences would be the neutral imperatives of functional problem-solving (the infamous 'spill-over' effect). This spill-over would be driven, it was theorized, by lower level technocrats, operating in relative autonomy from political control by national executives, and in alliance with sub-national economic interests committed to expanding integration. Walter Hallstein, a German negotiator in the integration process in the 1950s and later the President of the European Commission in the 1960s, grounded his faith in Europe's federal destiny in its purportedly ever-expanding *Sachlogik*, or substantive logic, entailing precisely this neofunctionalist 'spill over' of integration from one interdependent domain to the next.[20]

And yet, even with neo-functionalism's refinement to account for the role of politics (at least initially), the theory still did not prove to be a robust explanation of the integration phenomenon, as the subsequent workings of the ECSC demonstrated. The basic premise of the establishment of a Council of Ministers was that technical decision-making at the Community level would inevitably impinge on political questions of values or the allocation of scarce resources, for which more legitimate political oversight would be necessary.[21] Thus, in the negotiations of the Treaty of Paris, organizational questions were intimately bound up with the intergovernmental effort 'to determine as far as possible the extent and direction of national gain and loss before the High Authority began to function.'[22] Given the legal framework within which the High Authority was supposed to operate, it is hardly surprising that this supranational technocracy did not subsequently act 'as

---

[18] See generally Anne Boerger-De Smedt, 'Negotiating the Foundations of European Law, 1950–57: The Legal History of the Treaties of Paris and Rome' (2012) 21 *Contemporary European History* 339 ff.

[19] Ernst B. Haas, *The Uniting of Europe: Political, Social, and Economic Forces, 1950–1957* (1958).

[20] Walter Hallstein, *Europe in the Making* (1972); Robert Marjolin, *Architect of European Unity: Memoirs 1911–1986* (1989) 256–66 ff; Matthias Schönwald, 'Walter Hallstein and the "Empty Chair" Crisis 1965/66', in Wilfried Loth (ed.), *Crises and Compromises: The European Project 1963–1969* (2001) 164 ff.

[21] Dirk Spierenburg and Raymond Poidevin, *Histoire de la Haute Autorité de la Communauté européenne du charbon et de l'acier: Une Expérience supranationale* (1993) 20 ff.

[22] Milward (n. 2) 498 ff.

a neutral functional regulator as [the neo-functionalists] claimed'.[23] The organs of the ECSC arguably came into existence in the legal form they did—including, most importantly, with a key role played by the Council of Ministers drawing from national executives—'precisely because the issues involved could not be reduced to the merely functional level'.[24]

Although the functionalist and neofunctionalist advocates of integration no doubt underestimated the genuinely political character of the ECSC's regulatory activities, their emphasis on the technical character of the Community corresponded to reality in at least one important sense: precisely because the coal and steel sector was broadly *perceived* to involve regulatory issues of a largely technical or functional nature, supranational delegation was less *politically* problematic, requiring little or no parliamentary involvement, whether nationally or supranationally.[25] The same sort of stratagem was unavailable, of course, once the process of European integration shifted to national defence and control of the armed forces. The French proposal in the fall of 1950 for a European Defence Community (EDC), culminating in the signing of the proposed EDC Treaty in May 1952, quickly revealed the limits of political support for supranational delegation. Ironically, it would be the French National Assembly that would ultimately kill the EDC in 1954, but the concerns over unbridled supranational power that the EDC raised would shadow integration for the remainder of the decade. The Treaties of Rome of 1957, most importantly that establishing the European Economic Community (EEC), would retain the quadripartite organizational *form* of the ECSC (a national-executive Council of Ministers, a supranational technocratic body now called the 'European Commission', a parliamentary 'Assembly', and a Court of Justice). But there would be one major *substantive* difference between the institutional structures of the new EEC and the old ECSC: the legal balance of power under the EEC would shift formally and decisively towards the Council of Ministers, which gained the final say in most aspects of legislative norm-production at the Community level.

---

[23] Milward (n. 4) 15 ff; Karen J. Alter, David Steinberg, 'The Theory and Reality of the European Coal and Steel Community', in Sophie Meunier, Kathleen R. McNamara (eds.), *Making History: European Integration and Institutional Change at Fifty—State of the European Union* (2007) 89 ff.

[24] Milward (n. 4) 15 ff.

[25] In the debate over the Treaty of Paris in the French National Assembly, for example, a Gaullist deputy complained that French sovereignty was being 'abandon[ed] . . . to a stateless and uncontrolled technocracy'. Jacques Soustelle, Journal officiel, Débats parlementaires, Assemblée nationale 8881 (6 December 1951). However, a centre-right supporter of the ECSC could offer the more comforting argument that the High Authority was 'merely the organ for the administration of common rules', with delegated normative powers subject to the detailed and precise terms of the treaty. Alfred Coste-Floret, ibid., at 8854. Outside of those strictly delimited and largely technical realms, Coste-Floret implied, national governments and parliaments retained the full prerogatives of sovereignty. For a discussion of the parliamentary debates, see Henry L. Mason, *The European Coal and Steel Community: Experiment in Supranationalism* (1955) 22–3 ff.

This did not mean, however, that the effort to define the treaty balance between the Council and the other institutions would be easy. The task was given over to a group of nationally designated legal experts—the *groupe juridique*—which was responsible for drafting the institutional and legal provisions in the Treaties of Rome.[26] Given the ultimate decisional power in the Council, the *groupe juridique* inserted a provision designed to protect, at least, the Commission's unfettered discretion in making legislative proposals (the cornerstone of the so-called 'Community method').[27] Although largely ignored at the time, these decisions would eventually prove controversial, particularly in France after de Gaulle's return to power in 1958. The same would also be true of the planned shift to qualified-majority voting in the Council over the course of the 'transition period', which was to last twelve years from the entry into force of the treaty, divided equally into three parts. As De Gaulle would later assert, to accept majority voting after 'we had decided to take destiny into our own hands' at home would leave France 'exposed to the possibility of being overruled in any economic matter whatsoever, and therefore in social and sometimes political matters' as well.[28]

De Gaulle, however, held off his battle over qualified-majority voting until the final year of the second stage, in 1965, by which time he had secured his principal policy goal from integration: generous, Community-based support for French agriculture under the terms of the common agricultural policy (CAP). De Gaulle had long recognized, however, that the move to qualified-majority voting in the third stage would greatly strengthen the position of the Commission—'this embryonic technocracy, for the most part foreign'[29]—which would no longer need to satisfy each and every Member State in order to see its legislative proposals adopted in the Council. The episode that followed—the so-called 'empty chair' crisis of 1965 culminating in the 'Luxembourg Compromise' of January 1966—was often construed in subsequent decades as introducing a right of national veto into the Community's early legislative procedure, in which any Member State could

---

[26] The major questions of policy were the responsibility of the other two main negotiating groups, for the common market and atomic affairs respectively. The legal group was assembled originally as a drafting group (*groupe de rédaction*) responsible for putting into legal forms the agreements over political and economic substance made by the other groups. It took on, however, a key role in the actual negotiation of the institutional provisions. See generally Pierre Pescatore, 'Les travaux du "groupe juridique" dans les négociations des Traités de Rome' (1981) 34 *Studia Diplomatica* 159 ff. See also Boerger-De Smedt (n. 18).

[27] Article 149 thus provided that, as long as the Council had not acted, the Commission remained free to alter its proposal at any time. By contrast, for the Council to amend a proposal of the Commission, Article 149 required unanimity of the Member State representatives. In this respect, the legal group borrowed from the model established by the ECSC Treaty, in which a Council unanimity requirement was actually often used to augment the normative autonomy of the Commission (although the Council still retained the ultimate power of decision in most cases, in striking contrast to the Treaty of Paris).

[28] Press Conference, 9 September 1965 (quoted in Anthony L. Teasdale, 'The Life and Death of the Luxembourg Compromise' (1993) 31 *Journal of Common Market Studies* 567, 568 ff).

[29] Ibid.

demand a Council decision by unanimity when it believed that 'a very important national interest' was at stake.[30] This understanding, however, is something of a historical misconception. The Luxembourg Compromise arguably only codified the traditional practice of consensus politics in the Council,[31] thus marking the *reassertion* of an older set of ground rules for European integration: Community norm-production needed to be mediated in some way through national executives, just as in the administrative state.

The culmination of this institutional reinforcement of national-executive oversight at the supranational level would occur just under ten years later, in 1974, in a development with significant long-term effects for the political life of European integration. At the initiative of French President Valéry Giscard d'Estaing and German Chancellor Helmut Schmidt, the heads of state and government of the Member States formed themselves into the 'European Council'—a body initially outside the confines of treaty law[32]—to serve as a forum for the chief executives of the Member States to decide on the future direction of integration policy. Assembling in (then) semi-annual summit meetings, the purpose of the European Council was to provide political guidance to Europe's supranational regulatory process.

In its seemingly blatant inter-governmentalism, the European Council appeared to federalists and other pro-Europeans as a fundamental reversal of the progress towards integration. This view assumed, however, that the most important measure of such progress was the degree of supranational normative autonomy in Community decision-making. The more persuasive historical interpretation is that, 'rather than reversing the process of European integration', the establishment of the Council 'actually signifie[d] a wish to extend Community decision-making to new areas in response to changes in national policy objectives arising from the fundamental change in economic circumstances of the western European countries after 1974'.[33] The establishment of the European Council suggested that, for the process of European integration to have any hope of continued development with the end of the three decades of steady postwar expansion (the 'trentes glorieuses'), clear *political* backing by the national chief executives would be needed. Technocratic policy development in the Commission (the 'Community model'), even under ministerial supervision in the Council of Ministers, would not be enough; some form of leadership by heads of state or government was required.

---

[30] See Bulletin of the European Communities 8–10 (March 1966).

[31] See generally Jean-Marie Palayret, Helen Wallace, Pascaline Winand (eds.), *Visions, Votes, and Vetoes: The Empty Chair Crisis and the Luxembourg Compromise Forty Years On* (2006).

[32] The European Council would not be formally established until the Single European Act of 1986.

[33] Alan S. Milward and Vibeke Sørensen, 'Interdependence or Integration? A National Choice' in Alan S. Milward et al. (eds.), *The Frontier of National Sovereignty: History and Theory, 1945–1992* (1993) 24–5 ff.

III.

While this reinforcement of national-executive oversight undoubtedly made it difficult for the Commission to play the role that the neo-functionalists envisioned for it—a kind of supranational vanguard of the integration process—there was another supranational institution that enjoyed considerably more freedom to pursue the same goal: the ECJ. In what Joseph Weiler famously termed the 'dual character of supranationalism' over the course of the 1960s and 1970s,[34] integration came to be characterized by 'the apparently paradoxical emergence of two conflicting trends'—an expansive 'normative' (judicial) supranationalism, on the one hand, and much more constrained, if not outright diminishing, 'decisional' (political) supranationalism, on the other.[35]

Lawyers and judges clearly played a major role in the development of the 'normative' side of European supranationalism in the founding period. Perhaps one of the most important dimensions of the historiography of European integration over the last two decades has been the emergence of work that deepens our understanding of the intellectual mind-set and social practices of the European legal elite in the early years of integration. The supranational legal professionals in and around the ECJ viewed themselves, as one historical sociologist has put it, as 'the institutionalised carriers of the European idea' in the face of political resistance or reluctance.[36] Further historical research has since uncovered the extent to which jurists pursued a conscious political strategy to advance the integration process through judicial means.[37] By establishing itself as a defender of a new patrimony of rights (generally market-based) against national encroachments, the Court was able to draw on the perception that it was 'simply a continuation of the traditional role of European courts and, indeed, liberal courts everywhere: the protection of individual rights against the state'.[38] The Court's efforts laid the foundation for a dynamic of integration that corresponded remarkably well to the particulars

[34] J. H. H. Weiler, 'The Community System: The Dual Character of Supranationalism' (1982) 1 *Yearbook of European Law* 267 ff.

[35] Ibid., 273 ff.

[36] Antoine Vauchez, '"Integration-through-Law": Contribution to a Socio-History of EU Political Commonsense' (*Robert Schuman Centre for Advanced Studies, EUI Working Papers, RSCAS 2008/10*, 2008) <http://cadmus.iue.it/dspace/handle/1814/8307> 16, citing the statement of Judge Donner (as quoted in Werner Feld, *The Court of the European Communities: New Dimensions in International Adjudication* (1964) 116; see also (Judge) Robert Lecourt, 'L'unification du droit européen est aussi un moyen de construire l'Europe', *France-Forum* (1963) 27–31, 31 ff.

[37] See, e.g., Morten Rasmussen, 'Establishing a Constitutional Practice of European Law: The History of the Legal Service of the European Executive, 1952–65' (2012) 21 *Contemporary European History* 375 ff.

[38] Anne-Marie Burley, Walter Mattli, 'Europe Before the Court: A Political-Theory of Legal Integration' (1993) 47 *International Organization* 41, 64 ff.

of the neo-functionalist theory, with two major differences. First, it was the law that 'function[ed] as a mask for politics, precisely the role neofunctionalists originally forecast for economics'.[39] Second, it was the Court of Justice that took the lead in forging an effective supranational alliance with national interest groups (private litigants, their lawyers, and lower national courts) to push the boundaries of integration—the role the neo-functionalists originally envisioned for the Commission.[40]

The foundations for this 'legal neo-functionalist' dynamic, if you will, were in fact laid during the negotiation of the Treaty of Rome, again through the efforts of the *groupe juridique* mentioned above.[41] Especially helpful to our understanding here are the published recollections of Pierre Pescatore, a Luxembourg jurist who served on the *groupe* and would later become a judge on the ECJ in the 1960s.[42] As Pescatore explained it, despite a mandate limited to dealing with 'general', 'nontechnical', and therefore presumably 'nonpolitical' aspects of the treaty, the *groupe juridique* in fact operated with great autonomy and considerable (if not well-recognized) influence over the institutional design of supranational bodies, most importantly the ECJ. According to Pescatore, the effectiveness of the *groupe juridique* depended, in important part, on a shared sense of legal culture of its members: '[G]iven the essentially legal character of our discussions, conflicts of interest hardly arose between us.'[43] Rather, '[w]e were all jurists and, in spite of our national origins, we therefore participated in a world of common values'.[44] The group's juristic 'common values' manifested themselves in several of the 'general' and 'nontechnical' provisions which would figure directly in the Court's subsequent jurisprudence seeking to 'constitutionalise' the Community legal order. These included, most notably, 'the preamble and the preliminary articles which defined the mission of the Community'[45] (which would also have a strong influence on the Court's subsequent interpretation of the treaty), as well as Article 5, which defined the Member State's duty of loyalty and cooperation to the Community (and which would form the basis for the Court's doctrine of the primacy of Community law in the coming years).[46]

Pescatore's recollections further suggest that, during the negotiation of the Treaty of Rome, the *groupe juridique* exploited the same political-cultural environment that the ECJ would come to enjoy in the coming decades, making possible the 'legal neo-functionalism' noted above.[47] It was an environment of deference to the law and legal expertise that permitted the transformation of essentially political questions into legal ones, which could then be resolved in relative autonomy by legal professionals—lawyers and judges—according to their own professional 'language and logic'.[48] Indeed, the most important of all the provisions inserted

---

[39] Ibid., 44 ff.   [40] For an overview, see Lindseth, *Power and Legitimacy* (n. 1) 137–52 ff.
[41] See above nn. 25–6 and accompanying text.   [42] Pescatore (n. 26).   [43] Ibid., 166 ff.
[44] Ibid., 165 ff.   [45] Ibid., 173–4 ff.   [46] Ibid., 174 ff.
[47] See above nn. 37–9 and accompanying text.   [48] Burley, Mattli (n. 38) 44 ff.

by the *groupe juridique* into the Treaty of Rome was the preliminary reference mechanism of Article 177—the option (and, in some cases, the duty) of national courts to refer questions on 'the interpretation of this Treaty' to the Community's own supranational adjudicative body, the Court of Justice. Article 177 would eventually provide the procedural basis for the Court's claimed power to review the conformity of Member State law with Community law in actions brought by private parties.

The cornerstone of this jurisprudence was a method of treaty interpretation— the so-called 'teleological method'—that viewed the commitment set out in the preamble to the Treaty of Rome to 'an ever closer union among the peoples of Europe' as the very purpose—the *telos*—of European integration. The Court used the teleological approach, as well as the related doctrine of *effet utile* (a functionalist notion to be sure), to overcome textual obstacles, ambiguities, or silences in the treaties to achieve the aims of integration as the judges understood them, looking to what they regarded as the 'spirit' and 'general scheme', and not just the 'wording' of the treaty.[49] From this perspective, as a member of the Court would later put it, the drafters of the treaties purportedly built a 'preference for Europe' into 'the genetic code transmitted to the Court'.[50]

No judgment of the ECJ from the founding period better demonstrates this approach than what may be fairly regarded as the *Marbury v. Madison* of EU law: the *Van Gend & Loos* judgment of 1963. In that case the Court recognized de facto private-party standing to bring claims of Member State nonconformity with supranational law by way of a preliminary reference from a national court under Article 177. In this way, the Court avoided the seeming restrictions that the Member States had placed on the infringement procedure under Articles 169 and 170, which limited standing to the Commission or another Member State. As the Court held: 'The vigilance of individuals concerned to protect their rights amounts to an

---

[49] *Van Gend & Loos*, 1963 E.C.R. 1, at 12. The teleological method and *effet utile* are now so closely identified with the ECJ that observers often overlook their essentially functionalist character, born of the same jurisprudential mindset that rationalized the restructuring of the administrative state (and unprecedented intervention into society) from the 1920s to the 1950s. In interwar Britain, for example, Harold Laski called for a similar method of statutory interpretation 'less analytical and more functional in character', which 'should seek to discover the effect of the legislative precept in action'. Committee on Ministers' Powers, 'Report' (Stationery Office Cmd 4060 1932), Annex V, 137. Robert Lecourt, who is reputed to have written the judgment in *Van Gend & Loos*, wrote a 1931 doctoral dissertation reflected the functionalist spirit of the interwar period. See Robert Lecourt, 'Nature juridique de l'action en réintégrande: Etude de la jurisprudence française' (Université de Caen, 1931) 282–3 (describing the action to re-establish possession of property after violent dispossession as 'a remarkable example of a purely judicial construction necessitated by equity and practical circumstances'). He would later argue that instrumental-functional concerns should guide all legal interpretation, because law was inherently 'in the service of an objective' and '[t]he goal is the engine of the law.' Robert Lecourt, *L'Europe des juges* (1976) 305 ff.

[50] G. Federico Mancini, David T. Keeling, 'Democracy and the European Court of Justice' (1994) 57 *Modern Law Review* 175, 186 ff.

effective supervision in addition to the supervision entrusted by [the infringement procedure] to the diligence of the Commission and of the Member States.' The decision further stated: 'A restriction of the guarantees against infringement . . . by Member States to the procedures under Article 169 and 170 would remove all direct protection of the individual rights of their nationals.' More importantly, Article 169 and 170 would be 'ineffective' if recourse to them was made 'after the implementation of a national decision taken contrary to the provisions of the Treaty'.[51]

From the perspective of the *Van Gend & Loos* court, in other words, the Treaty of Rome did not provide the right tools for the Court to pursue the purported 'preference for Europe'. The Court's broad interpretation of standing under the preliminary reference procedure —and hence its own jurisdiction—would provide the framework within which the Court could articulate the major substantive 'constitutional' doctrines of EU law: direct effect and supremacy. As for Article 177 itself, Pescatore would later claim that the *groupe juridique* inserted this provision into the Treaty without any awareness 'of the importance of th[e] innovation'.[52] Subsequent archival research, however, has suggested a slightly more considered effort at 'constitutionalising' the ECJ, at least in part.[53] The apparent model was an analogous preliminary reference mechanism to the Italian constitutional court (although a similar mechanism existed in Germany). Thus, drawing on these post-war constitutional examples, this small group of elite lawyers and legal scholars helped to expand the scope of the Community system of judicial remedies and in so doing laid the foundation for the subsequent transformation of the public law of European integration. Originally modelled on the greatest of all *juridictions administratives*—the French *Conseil d'État*—the ECJ now possessed the procedural tool to become, in effect, a 'constitutional court' vis-à-vis the member states, a kind of supranational *Bundesverfassungsgericht*.

IV.

As one historian of integration has aptly put it, *Van Gend & Loos* was 'a revolution in the case law of the ECJ and a final endorsement of the constitutional approach to European law'.[54] This conventional understanding, which from the perspective of judges, lawyers, and law professors was something to be celebrated, has increasingly

---

[51] 1963 E.C.R. at 13 ff.   [52] Pescatore (n. 26) 173 ff.   [53] Boerger-De Smedt (n. 18) ff.
[54] Morten Rasmussen, 'Revolutionizing European Law: A History of the *Van Gend en Loos* Judgment' (2014) 12 *International Journal of Constitutional Law* 136, 156 ff.

become the object of historical analysis and legal critique in recent decades. On the occasion of the fiftieth anniversary of *Van Gend & Loos*, the EU found itself mired in the Eurozone crisis. And in this context, perhaps the EU's leading legal commentator of the prior three decades, Joseph Weiler, provocatively claimed that the *Van Gend & Loos* case was in many respects the 'fountainhead' of the legitimacy problems that had long plagued European integration.[55] Although initially seen as 'a response to non-functioning dimensions of the [supranational] political process', the case presupposed that supranational politics would eventually gain a robust democratic legitimacy of its own.[56] This has not happened. Even the eventual expansion of the legislative role of an elected European Parliament (making it an effective co-legislator with the Council, which since the 1980s operated largely through qualified majority voting), has not helped. As Weiler concluded, the 'manifestations of the so-called democracy deficit are persistent, and no endless repetition of the powers of the European Parliament will remove them'.[57]

The problem, however, has not simply been one of misdirected institutional engineering, which has somehow failed to translate, 'at the Union level, even the imperfect habits of governmental control, parliamentary accountability, and administrative responsibility that are practiced with different modalities in the various member states'.[58] Rather, the problem goes deeper, to the socio-historical level, to the absence of an as-yet coherent European 'demos' upon which to construct genuinely 'constitutional' bodies on the EU level. The emergence of a demos depends on an intertwined democratic and constitutional self-consciousness,[59] on a sense of mutual entitlement and solidarity that makes representative government possible. Ignoring this socio-historical dimension, the ECJ approached questions of supranational authority—again, most importantly its own—primarily as a matter of legal logic, guided by the functional demands of uniformity and autonomy of the integration process. The problem with this approach—converting functional demand into constitutional principle—is that it has proceeded 'as if' the EU possesses this robust form of legitimacy in its own right, in defiance of the EU's actual socio-historical character.[60]

---

[55] J. H. H. Weiler, '*Van Gend en Loos*: The Individual as Subject and Object and the Dilemma of European Legitimacy' (2014) 12 *International Journal of Constitutional Law* 94, 99 ff. On the ongoing legitimacy challenges, see, e.g., Claudia Sternberg, *The Struggle for EU Legitimacy: Public Contestation, 1950–2005* (2013).

[56] Weiler (n. 55) 99 ff.   [57] Ibid., 100 ff.

[58] Ibid., citing Neil Walker, 'Postnational Constitutionalism and the Problem of Translation' in J. H. H. Weiler, Marlene Wind (eds.), *European Constitutionalism Beyond the State* (2003).

[59] Cf. Jed Rubenfeld, *Freedom and Time: A Theory of Constitutional Self-Government* (2001); Bruce A. Ackerman, *We the People: Foundations* (1991).

[60] Peter L. Lindseth, 'The Perils of "As If" European Constitutionalism' (2016) 22 *European Law Journal* 696 ff.

What the chronic legitimacy crisis of the EU of the last several decades demonstrates, however, is that, *despite* what EU judges, lawyers, and law professors have maintained since the founding of integration, there have proven to be numerous features of EU public law that are not merely in tension with, but also that directly contradict, the dominant constitutionalist discourse. First and foremost, the EU remains almost entirely dependent on the Member States for the *sine qua non* of genuine constitutional power: the legitimate, compulsory capacity to extract and redirect—i.e., 'mobilize'—either fiscal resources (taxing and spending) or human resources (policing and defence) for the benefit of the polity as a whole.[61] Secondly, even with regard to regulatory power that falls short of compulsory resource mobilization—particularly rule-making and adjudicative power—the EU remains dependent on mechanisms of national oversight and intermediation that channel the more robust democratic and constitutional legitimacy of national institutions to the EU level. These mechanisms of 'mediated legitimacy'—drawing importantly on models developed in the postwar administrative state—have been central features of the institutional development of EU governance since its inception.[62]

These shortfalls in the EU's legitimacy, which we can fairly trace to the founding period of integration in the 1950s and 1960s, have proven to have particular significance in the period of crisis since 2010, whether as to the Eurozone, the influx of refugees, or the increased terrorist threat. All these crises point to an essential truth articulated by the Italian political theorist Stefano Bartolini in 2005: 'the risk of miscalculating the extent to which true legitimacy surrounds the European institutions and their decisions . . . may lead to the overestimating of the capacity of the EU to overcome major economic and security crises.'[63] In responding to its various challenges of the last decade, the EU has been forced to rely on a strategy whereby all essential costs—political and economic—have been borne internally, by the individual states, because that is where legitimate compulsory mobilization powers still reside. This is not to deny that transnational coordination has been necessary, but that coordination has been primarily national and intergovernmental rather than supranational (that is, most definitely not via the Commission and Court but rather via the European Council or the Eurogroup finance ministers). The primary exception has, of course, been the European Central Bank (ECB), but its sometimes 'heroic' role has been driven by the incapacity of the EU and Member States to mobilize fiscal resources

[61] Peter L. Lindseth, 'Between the "Real" and the "Right": Explorations Along the Institutional-Constitutional Frontier' in Maurice Adams, Ernst Hirsch Ballin, Anne Meuwese (eds.), *Constitutionalism and the Rule of Law: Bridging Idealism and Realism* (2017).

[62] Lindseth *Power and Legitimacy* (n. 1).

[63] Stefano Bartolini, *Restructuring Europe: Centre Formation, System Building, and Political Structuring between the Nation State and the European Union* (2005) 175 ff.

on a coordinated, supranational scale commensurate with the demands of the Eurozone crisis.[64]

In short, the continued locus of true democratic and constitutional legitimacy at the national level has had a direct bearing on the scope of power that could be successfully transferred to the EU institutions, a fact true of integration since its inception. We can call this the *power-legitimacy nexus* in European public law. Understanding how this power-legitimacy nexus affects what the EU can realistically achieve, as well as how its law should be interpreted, is not just a legal-theoretical exercise. Rather, it is crucial to the sustainability and success of European integration over the long term, something that European elites—particularly EU judges, lawyers, and legal scholars—ignore at their peril.

BIBLIOGRAPHY

In addition to the sources cited in the notes above, the reader may also find the following useful:

A. Cohen, 'Constitutionalism Without Constitution: Transnational Elites Between Political Mobilization and Legal Expertise in the Making of a Constitution for Europe (1940s–1960s)' (2007) 32 *Law & Social Inquiry* 109

A. Cohen, M. R. Madsen, 'Cold War Law: Legal Entrepreneurs and the Emergence of a European Legal Field (1945–1965)' in Volkmar Gessner, David Nelken (eds.), *European Ways of Law: Toward a European Sociology of Law* (Hart, 2007)

B. Davies, *Resisting the European Court of Justice: West Germany's Confrontation with European Law, 1949–1979* (Cambridge University Press, 2012)

B. Davies, M. Rasmussen, 'Towards a New History of European Law' (2012) 21 *Contemporary European History* 305

A. Deighton (ed.), *Building Postwar Europe: National Decision-Makers and European Institutions 1948–1963* (St Martin's Press, 1995)

W. Kaiser, B. Leucht, M. Rasmussen (eds.), *The History of the European Union: Origins of a Trans- and Supranational Polity 1950–1972* (Routledge, 2008)

W. Loth, *Building Europe: A History of European Unification* (Walter de Gruyter GmbH & Co KG, 2015)

N. P. Ludlow, *The European Community and the Crises of the 1960s: Negotiating the Gaullist Challenge* (Routledge, 2006)

M. R. Madsen, A. Vauchez 'European Constitutionalism at the Cradle: Law and Lawyers in the Construction of European Political Orders (1920–1960),' in Alex Jettinghoff, Harm

---

[64] See generally Peter L. Lindseth, 'Power and Legitimacy in the Eurozone: Can Integration and Democracy Be Reconciled?' in Maurice Adams, Federico Fabbrini, Pierre Larouche (eds.), *The Constitutionalization of European Budgetary Constraints* (2014).

Schepel, *Lawyers' Circles: Lawyers and European Legal Integration* (Special Issue of *Recht der Werkelikheid*, 2005)

A. Moravcsik, *The Choice for Europe: Social Purpose and State Power from Messina to Maastricht* (Cornell University Press, 1998)

C. Parsons, *A Certain Idea of Europe* (Cornell University Press, 2003)

H. Schepel, R. Wesseling, 'The Legal Community: Judges, Lawyers, Officials and Clerks in the Writing of Europe' (1997) 3 *European Law Journal* 165

K. Schwabe (ed.), *Die Anfänge des Schuman-Plans, 1950/51: Beiträge des Kolloquiums in Aachen, 28.-30. Mai 1986*, vol 1. Aufl. (1988)

E. Serra (ed.), *Il Rilancio dell'Europa e i Trattati di Roma: La relance européenne et les Traités de Rome: Actes du Colloque de Rome 25–28 Mars 1987* (1989)

A. Vauchez, *Brokering Europe* (Cambridge University Press, 2015)

CHAPTER 55

ADJUDICATION OF INDIGENOUS-SETTLER RELATIONS

RICHARD P. BOAST

I. SETTLER SOCIETIES

THIS chapter is concerned with the connections between the field of legal history and various ways in which claims against states by indigenous groups in the present day are adjudicated and resolved. The focus of the chapter is on 'indigenous' and 'settler' relationships and, thus, on legal processes in 'settler' societies. But the latter term has its uncertainties. What are 'settler' societies? Most commentators using this term would have in mind those parts of the world settled by European immigrants in the nineteenth century, notably the United States, Canada, Australia, and New Zealand. These four countries seem to have certain features in common. The importance of nineteenth-century rural settlement by English-speaking migrants in all four is undeniable. No less striking is an *ideology* of settlement, not only historically, but also in the present day. In the art, historiography, and literature of all four countries, the image of the white settler frontier in the national psyche has loomed large historically and continues to do so.[1]

---

[1] There are numerous comparative studies of Canada, Australia, New Zealand, and the United States, some of which consider legal institutions to varying extents: see, e.g., Peter Karsten, *Between*

Nonetheless there are some difficulties in confining 'settler' societies to these four countries. There were many other frontiers of European settlement. It is not obvious why South Africa should be excluded from the group, for example: although its first European colonists were from the Netherlands, it, too, was part of an expanding British colonial world in the nineteenth century, and it has developed some important methods of adjudication of indigenous-settler relations today using special tribunals which have many affinities with the Native Title Tribunal in Australia or New Zealand's Waitangi Tribunal. The only real difference between South Africa and (say) Australia is that in the former, the settler community never became the majority population, not necessarily a criterion of difference that makes any logical sense. Other standard examples of 'settler' societies are Argentina and Uruguay, also countries where the agrarian frontier looms large in historical and economic importance and in national self-definition. To see Argentina as a 'settler' society and Colombia or Mexico as not implies a distinctiveness about Argentina within the overall framework of Latin American history. Although Argentina was a long established colony and Buenos Aires became the capital of a viceroyalty in 1776, nevertheless Argentina, along with Uruguay, is usually perceived as an essentially nineteenth-century construction compared to older colonial societies such as Peru and Mexico. Argentina and Uruguay took national shape in the nineteenth century with large-scale immigration from Europe, resulting in the mushrooming growth of Buenos Aires and Montevideo, both cities which can plausibly be said to have many affinities with other settler capitals such as Toronto, Johannesburg, or Melbourne, rather than with older Spanish American cities like Quito or Bogota. Significantly, Mario Rappoport and María Seoane date the origins of modern Buenos Aires from 1880–1914.[2] (Nonetheless large-scale European migration to Spanish America in the nineteenth century was not *confined* to the River Plate region—many went to other countries as diverse as Costa Rica and Chile.) The distinctiveness of Uruguay and Argentina is a matter of scale, however, of self-definition and also of national historiographies. There is a well-developed tradition in economic history of analysing the contrasting performance of Australia and New Zealand on the one hand and Argentina and Uruguay on the other, based on the plausible view that this group of countries have a number of similarities: rapid economic growth in the nineteenth century, high standards of living as at circa 1900, the importance of British investment, economies based on the export of

---

Law and Custom: "High and "Low" Legal Cultures in the Lands of the British Diaspora—the United States, Canada, Australia, and New Zealand (2002); John C. Weaver, *The Great Land Rush and the Making of the Modern World* (2003); Paul G. McHugh, *Aboriginal Societies and the Common Law* (2004); James Belich, *Replenishing the Earth: The Settler Revolution and the Rise of the Angloworld* (2011). For a more theoretical perspective see Lorenzo, Veracini, *Settler Colonialism: A Theoretical Overview* (2010).

[2] Mario Rapoport, María Seoane, *Buenos Aires: Historia de una ciudad*, vol. 1 (2007) 51–260.

primary products to Europe, a frontier of settlement—and displacement of the former indigenous occupiers.[3]

But other countries could qualify as well. What of Brazil? While Brazil has a long colonial history, like the Rio de la Plata countries it too received a massive influx of immigrants from southern Europe in the nineteenth century. São Paulo, while also possessing a long colonial history, is another nineteenth-century boom city, a South American equivalent of Melbourne or San Francisco. There was certainly a Brazilian frontier, and indigenous peoples were—and continue to be—displaced.[4] There has been no shortage of 'adjudication' in contemporary Brazil. There is thus no justifiable case for excluding Brazil from the class of 'settler societies'. There are other possibilities. Siberia could qualify as a 'settler' country, and so can Taiwan, undoubtedly settled by Han Chinese people and where adjudication of 'settler-indigenous relations' is happening today. The reality is that the field covered by this chapter is of uncertain scope. The main focus will in fact be on Australia and New Zealand, but this should not be seen as endorsing any kind of narrow approach to the subject. I suggest that what is normally meant by 'settler societies' are societies outside of Europe which today are largely products of nineteenth-century migration from Europe—whether from southern Europe (Argentina, Uruguay), northern Europe (Canada, Australia, New Zealand, South Africa), or both (the United States).

II. Modes of Adjudication

In many countries indigenous groups have made, or are still in the process of making, claims for redress against the states in which they live, seeking outcomes of various kinds for historic injustices. Typically these claims relate to land, but there are some which do not—as in the case of the 'stolen generations' controversy in Australia or tribunal-based claims relating to the Maori language and legal rights with respect to flora and fauna in New Zealand.

As this chapter is focused on adjudication, the focus will be on court or tribunal-related processes of resolution of indigenous claims. It is certainly the case,

---

[3] Jorge Álvarez, Luis Bértola, Gabriel Porcile, *Primos Ricos y Empobrecidos: Crecimiento, distribución del Ingreso e instituciones en Australia-Nueva Zelanda vs Argentina-Uruguay* (2007). There is a substantial literature on the agrarian history of Argentina: for an overview see Eric Van Young, 'Rural History' in Jose C. Moya (ed.), *The Oxford Handbook of Latin American History* (2011) 309–41. On indigenous peoples in southern South America in the nineteenth century see Carmen Bernand, *Les Indiens face à la construction de l'État-nation: Mexique-Argentine 1810–1917* (2013).

[4] See John Hemming, *Die if you Must: Brazilian Indians in the Twentieth Century* (2003).

however, that non-court systems of negotiation and settlement of historic claims can require comprehensive historical research, as is the position in New Zealand (the complexities of the New Zealand institutional arrangements are discussed fully below). A further complexity lies within the field of judicial adjudication itself. Broadly, the primary distinction is between adjudication in the ordinary courts of a country using the ordinary processes and legal discourses of private and public law—of which Canada is a principal example—or the utilization of special-purpose tribunals set up by particular statutes to adjudicate on historical or contemporary claims, examples including South Africa, Australia, and New Zealand. A quite different adjudicatory framework occurs when indigenous groups bring claims against their own governments before international courts or arbitral bodies rather than via domestic courts or tribunals. Typically, indigenous groups resort to international courts when their own countries fail to establish trustworthy mechanisms of domestic grievance resolution, although not necessarily: some Maori groups in New Zealand, for example, have brought claims to the International Convention on the Elimination of All Forms of Racial Discrimination Committee in Geneva notwithstanding the existence of the Waitangi Tribunal in that country and the willingness of its national courts to recognize and give effect to Maori legal claims. This chapter will not be considering legal-historical research before international courts or committees, but it is nevertheless important to recognize that cases brought to such bodies will often require comprehensive input from specialists in legal history.

Canada, the United States, Australia, and New Zealand are all countries which have a long history of cases being brought by indigenous plaintiffs in the ordinary courts. The principal problem with the ordinary courts as a forum, however, is that cases can become almost impossibly complex and expensive, largely because of the technical rules relating to the hearing of evidence in such courts and the elaborate cross-examination of witnesses. A number of countries have experimented with special-purpose tribunals set up by statutes such as the Native Title Act 1993 (Australia) or the Treaty of Waitangi Act 1975 (NZ). Both statutes set up special tribunals with jurisdiction to deal with indigenous claims (the Native Tribunal and the Waitangi Tribunal). In neither case was the establishment of these bodies primarily driven by the need to hear claims more cheaply and more expeditiously than the ordinary courts, although that was probably seen as desirable. However, the Waitangi Tribunal process is a comparatively cheap process for claimants compared with the ordinary courts in New Zealand, partly because it is relatively easy to obtain legal aid as compared to the ordinary courts, which also impose substantial hearing fees on litigants (the Waitangi Tribunal does not). Nevertheless, in both countries such special purpose tribunals do not exclude cases relating to indigenous-settler relations being heard by the ordinary courts in these countries, and in both New Zealand and Australia the ordinary courts have continued to play a pivotal role.

The limitations of the Courts as a means of redress are not only practical, but also legal and constitutional. Courts in Australia, Canada, and New Zealand apply the Common Law of their respective countries, built on the foundations of English law but in each case modified by statutes, constitutional documents, and judicial decisions in their respective countries, the latter sometimes deviating from established English precedent. Alternatively the Courts of the former settler colonies have to develop solutions of their own to legal issues peculiar to their respective countries, of which the status of indigenous peoples is the most obvious example. Canadian and English Common Law are not the same. Nonetheless the bedrock of the Common Law, its techniques and ways of thinking, remain. As will be seen, the High Court of Australia's *Mabo* decision did not disrupt Australian common law, but rather reintegrated Australia into a common law framework, drawing on authorities from other parts of the common law world, New Zealand included. But this continual refashioning of the common law has its limits. Australian Courts have been able to say that the doctrine of Native Title fits within the fundamental framework of Australian law. The New Zealand Courts, on the other hand, have not been able to say that the Treaty of Waitangi of 1840 is generally enforceable of itself in the New Zealand Courts, although they have sometimes come close to this. In New Zealand the issue has been readily circumvented by the simple expedient of setting up a special purpose tribunal and directing that body to apply the principles of the Treaty of Waitangi to cases that come before it.

The special tribunals set up in Australia and New Zealand were not the products of any constitutional or political transition and have no kind of embedded constitutional status (indeed New Zealand, in contrast to Australia, does not have a written constitution at all). They are simply tribunals, not different in kind from specialist tribunals dealing with, for instance, environmental permits or mining and prospecting licences. They can be contrasted with their South African equivalents set up under the Restitution of Land Rights Act 1994, enacted in compliance with the 1993 Interim Constitution of South Africa.[5] Although the Waitangi Tribunal and the Native Title Tribunal have some affinities to transitional justice institutions, such a comparison is of limited value given that neither Australia nor New Zealand was in any noticeable state of transition when their respective bodies were established. It makes more sense to see the two tribunals as arising from a particular conjuncture of historical and legal circumstances in each country, unique in each case—and indeed the two antipodean special-purpose bodies are quite different. In New Zealand, the Waitangi Tribunal can be seen as a response to an upsurge in Maori political activism in the 1970s; the Native Title Tribunal, on the other hand, was much more of a response to a particular judicial decision that caused a political and constitutional crisis in Australia. That two somewhat similar societies, settled

---

[5] See generally Liesle Theron, 'Healing the Past: A Comparative Analysis of the Waitangi Tribunal and the South African Land Claims System' (1998) 28 *Victoria University of Wellington L.R.* 311.

at roughly the same time, can produce radically different legal solutions proves the inherent variety of 'indigenous-settler relations' in various countries and the ways in which redress can be provided. What Australia and New Zealand have in common, however, is a sense that redress *should* be provided, and sufficient political will for redress-oriented institutions to be established. This does not, on the other hand, guarantee that such institutions will work well or that they will be immune from criticism, either from those who believe that such redress was unnecessary in the first place or from indigenous scholars who believe that the institutions that have been established are inadequate or problematic. Bringing cases within a particular legal framework implies a submission to that very framework and operating within such room for manoeuvre as it might have. As J. G. A. Pocock puts it, '[t]here is a good case for the view that common law has always been an instrument of the individualization of tenure, leading towards the commodification of the *whenua* [Maori for 'land', but carrying a charge of its own]; some substance, therefore, in the radical and post-Marxist charge that, in appealing to the courts, we are placing ourselves in the power of a sovereign legislature which cannot reverse its course towards the commodification of rights.'[6]

III. Particular Jurisdictions

A. The *Mabo* Decision and the Native Title Tribunal in Australia

In Australia the emergence of a special tribunal is closely linked to a decision of the ordinary Courts, the High Court of Australia decision in *Mabo v. Queensland* (1992).[7] This case was an application of the English common law rules relating to aboriginal title, previously thought not to apply in Australia on the basis that it was a colony of settlement.[8] In *Mabo* the High Court of Australia, following the decision of the Supreme Court of Canada in *Calder v. A-G (British Columbia)*,[9] decided that

---

[6] J. G. A. Pocock, 'Tangata Whenua and Enlightenment Anthropology' (1992) 26 *New Zealand Journal of History* 28, 50. As can be seen, Pocock notes that there is only 'some substance' in this claim. The tenor of his article is that matters are much more complex.

[7] *Mabo v. Queensland (No. 2)* 175 CLR 1.

[8] On the common law of aboriginal native title see Kent McNeil, *Common Law Aboriginal Title* (1989). The principal pre-*Mabo* case on native title in Australia is *Milirrpum v. Nabalco Pty Ltd* (1971) 17 FLR 141 (SC(NT)).

[9] (1973) 34 DLR (3d) 145 (SC(Can)).

the doctrine of aboriginal or native title was part of the common law of Australia, meaning that such a title could be recognized and enforced in the Australian courts provided that the title had not been validly extinguished. No formal recognition of Native Title by the state was required as it was an integral aspect of the framework of Australian common law. The High Court did not 'abolish' the settled colony rule or the doctrine of *terra nullius*: rather, it concluded that in a settled colony such as Australia the common law doctrine of aboriginal title applied with the acquisition of British sovereignty and in this way brought Australia into line with the law as it was understood in Canada and New Zealand.[10] It so happened that the plaintiff was not an Australian Aboriginal but a Torres Strait Islander, belonging to an indigenous culture that had a very different political economy from the Aboriginal peoples of the mainland. The High Court of Australia could have decided the case by distinguishing the Torres Strait islanders from Australian Aborigines, but instead took advantage of the opportunity provided by the case to restate Australian common law as a whole. The High Court saw aboriginal title as a 'burden' on the Crown's radical title, or to put it another way, recognition of native title is not incompatible with the sovereignty of the Crown.

The lead judgment was given by Brennan J, who saw native title as deriving from the continued maintenance of aboriginal customary law. In a much-quoted passage, Brennan J observed:[11]

Native title has its origin and is given its content by the traditional laws acknowledged by the traditional customs observed by the Indigenous inhabitants of a territory. The nature and incidents of native title must be ascertained as a matter of reference to those laws and customs.

Brennan J stated that when 'a clan or group' had continued 'to acknowledge the laws and ... to observe the customs' of the group 'whereby their traditional connexion with the land has been substantially maintained', then the title remains in existence:

However, when the tide of history has washed away any real acknowledgment of traditional law and any real acknowledgment of traditional customs, the foundation of native title has disappeared. A native title which has ceased with the abandoning of laws and customs based on tradition cannot be revived for contemporary recognition.

The *Mabo* decision was a revolutionary event in the legal history of Australia, as until 1992 native or aboriginal title had in practice not been recognized by either the Federal or state governments, although some states had set aside substantial areas as Aboriginal reserves. Complex issues arose as to whether state legislation was incompatible with the law as stated in *Mabo*. The government of the day, confronted with the risk of a proliferation of cases against the Crown in the ordinary courts chose to establish a specialist tribunal, given the name of the Native Title Tribunal,

---

[10] See Richard Bartlett, *Native Title in Australia* (2000) 24.   [11] *Mabo (No. 2)* at 57.

set up by the Native Title Act 1993 (Cth), enacted eighteen months after the release of the *Mabo* judgment. The new tribunal was set up to give effect to native title rights. Such rights were defined in s. 223 of the Act, a key provision which has been the subject of repeated scrutiny of the Australian Courts. Section 223 essentially translated into statutory form the principal components of Native Title as defined in the Australian Courts. The tribunal has gone on to make many determinations of native title to particular areas. Cases relating to Aboriginal rights have, however, continued to feature in the Australian courts, typically relating to the extent of the Native Title Tribunal's jurisdiction over problematic categories of land, for example pastoral leases[12] or the territorial sea.[13] A vast structure of precedent and academic commentary has been built up since *Mabo*.

B. The Waitangi Tribunal in the Context of the New Zealand Legal System

Of all the 'settler' societies, it is in New Zealand that relationships between the government and an indigenous people have been most central to law-making and to national politics. The country's history takes its starting point from the Treaty of Waitangi (1840), a treaty negotiated between representatives of the British government and the Maori people. The document is written in both the Maori and English languages, and the two texts have some significant differences in meaning. In the nineteenth century the Maori *iwi* (tribes) were formidable opponents of the colonial regime, albeit that the Maori world was divided in its allegiances with some of the tribes supporting the colonial government.[14] Today the Maori people form about 14% of the national population, and many Maori people are active in politics, the professions, the media, the arts, and in academia. An indigenous Maori monarchical movement, the *Kingitanga* (the King movement), continues to thrive, although not all sections of the Maori world regard themselves as owing allegiance to the Maori king. In addition, New Zealand has long had a special court of record dealing with Maori land matters, the Maori Land Court, originally established in 1865, and there also exists a separate system of Maori land tenure governed by a

---

[12] *Wik Peoples v. State of Queensland* (1996) 187 CLR 1.

[13] *Commonwealth v. Yarmirr* (2001) 208 CLR 1; (2001) 184 ALR 113. This case was concerned with waters and land in the territorial sea on the seaward side of low water mark. In the Federal Court of Australia, Olney J, exercising the Federal Court's powers under the Native Title Act, determined that while the applicants did have native title within the claimed area, the nature of these rights were very limited in nature and did not confer exclusive possession. Olney J's decision was upheld by the High Court of Australia (Kirby J dissenting), which held that exclusive native title rights to the area in issue were incompatible with other public rights and the right of innocent passage.

[14] Ron Crosby, *Kūpapa: The Bitter Legacy of Māori Alliances with the Crown* (2015).

special statutory regime, which applies to about 14% of the North Island.[15] The records of the Native/Maori Land Court, in continuous operation since 1865, are a key source for ethnohistorical research in New Zealand and are often utilized by historians carrying out research for Maori groups to support their claims against the government. The Maori people were, and still are, divided into numerous tribes (the Maori term is *iwi,* which also means 'bones'), themselves divided into smaller social units in ways which are much too complex to explain here. Some *iwi* are very large: over 100,000 people affiliate to the Ngapuhi *iwi* of the Northland region, for example.

The Waitangi Tribunal is another unique component of the New Zealand legal and constitutional structure.[16] The Waitangi Tribunal was established in 1975, but it did not begin to become significant until 1983, when it released its first major report dealing with an area in North Taranaki. At first, the tribunal's jurisdiction was confined to government actions arising after 1975, but in 1985 its jurisdiction was substantially enlarged to all acts or omissions of the Crown since 1840. The tribunal's principal function is to issue non-binding recommendations to the state as to whether any act or omission of the Crown since 1840 is contrary to the principles of the Treaty of Waitangi.[17] Legally, it is a permanent, or standing, commission of inquiry. Most of the judges of the Maori Land Court, a number of whom are Maori themselves, are members of the Waitangi Tribunal; being legally qualified it is they who usually preside over the tribunal's inquiries. But the tribunal is also comprised of many members who while not legally qualified may be experts or specialists in other disciplines such as anthropology, history, Maori studies, and linguistics. It is a bicultural body: many of its members are Maori *kaumatua* (elders, experts in custom and Maori language and oratory). There are some tribunal members who have the status of both Māori *kaumatua* and academic specialists, an example being the late Hirini Moko Mead, a *kaumatua* of the Ngati Awa people of the Bay of Plenty who was an academic specialist in Maori art and Polynesian archaeology. The tribunal's functions derive entirely from statute, and the Treaty of Waitangi Act 1975 is just an ordinary act of parliament, which can be amended by parliament at any time; it has been amended and modified by parliament on many occasions. In effect claims in the tribunal are essentially civil actions by Maori claimants against the state ('the Crown') which participates in the process basically as a defendant. The 'law', however, by which the state is held accountable, is not ordinary public or private law, but rather that of the 'principles of the Treaty of Waitangi'. The Treaty

---

[15] On the origins of the Native Land Court and for a selection of its early case law see R. P. Boast, *The Native Land Court 1862–1887: A Historical Study, Cases and Commentary* (2013). On the Maori land law system, which in New Zealand is based on statute, see Richard Boast, Andrew Erueti, Doug McPhail, Norman Smith, *Maori Land Law*, 2nd edn., (2004).

[16] For a general guide see Janine Hayward, Nicola Wheen (eds.), *The Waitangi Tribunal: Te Roopu Whakamana i te Tiriti o Waitangi*, (2004).

[17] Treaty of Waitangi Act 1975, s. 6.

of Waitangi Act does not attempt to define the 'principles of the Treaty of Waitangi', and merely requires the Tribunal to 'have regard' to the Maori and English texts of the Treaty (both reproduced in a Schedule to the Act.) There is no developed body of material on what these principles are, apart from some very basic concepts developed by the ordinary courts in the 1980s,[18] and so the Waitangi Tribunal, as well as conducting its very elaborate inquiries, has also itself had to create the meta-law by which the state is to be held accountable. It is thus something of an enclosed process, built not on the existing public law legal norms (natural justice, for instance), still less on the norms of international law (these the Tribunal only discusses in passing) but on norms it has created itself and which apply only to its own adjudicative system.

The tribunal has been procedurally innovative. (The following description is based largely on my own observations, having appeared as counsel or as an expert witness before the tribunal on numerous occasions.) Claimant hearings are usually heard on the claimant group's own *marae*. A *marae* is a Maori ceremonial centre, and there are hundreds of these all over the country which are in constant use for meetings (*hui*), funerals (*tangi*), and other events. *Marae* are linked conceptually to particular descent groups, and the meeting house and dining room will be given the names of particular ancestors connected with that group. Spatially and architecturally, a *marae* is a complex of buildings enclosed within a perimeter fence and includes always a meeting house (*wharenui* or *whare whakairo*), a dining room, and kitchen, and sometimes a Maori-language kindergarten (*kohanga reo*: 'language nest') and a church. Many of the meeting-houses are beautifully carved and painted and are famous works of architecture. Some *marae* are in urban areas, others are in remote rural localities; some are very substantial and impressive in every way, others are relatively humble, but all are very important to their home communities. Each tribunal hearing lasts for about a week, the day beginning and ending with prayers and Maori ceremonial, and all participants have meals together in the *marae* dining room. The hearings are open to the public. Usually the tribunal will sit in the meeting house, with tables set aside for Crown and claimant counsel. Evidence can be given in the Maori language and often is, but in practice most testimony, questioning, and cross-examination is conducted in English. Cross-examination is routine, especially of commissioned historians. Crown counsel do not aggressively cross-examine Maori witnesses drawn from the claimant group speaking on traditional history or on the personal impacts of Crown policy, but often cross-examine at some length expert witnesses giving historical evidence on behalf of claimant groups. In many respects Waitangi Tribunal procedure is more or less the same as that which operates in the ordinary courts or other special purpose tribunals, such as the Environment Court. Nevertheless, the Tribunal's practice of hearing claims on *marae*, the fact that Tribunal panels usually have two

---

[18] *New Zealand Maori Council v. Attorney-General* [1987] 1 NZLR 641.

or three Maori members out of five, and the use of Maori ceremonial to open and close each day and week of the hearing all combine to give a special flavour to the hearings and are an important component of the Waitangi Tribunal's success. Some hearings have been very tense and confrontational, but most are not. The tribunal commands widespread legitimacy and respect and is now a routine, rather than controversial, component of the New Zealand legal system. Most of the time the New Zealand media pays little attention to it. This is understandable. Much of the evidence given to the tribunal is technical in nature and relates to surveys, Native Land Court cases, the details of government land purchasing, and so forth, and can be somewhat boring. Waitangi Tribunal hearings are heard all over the country, but its home base is in Wellington, where its registry staff, research teams, and library facilities can be found.

Hearings before the Waitangi Tribunal are typically multi-party. The tribunal does not hear historical claims one by one, but instead groups claims into large regional clusters, and then inquires into all the claims in a region (for example the northern South Island, the central North Island, the Whanganui region) over a lengthy investigative process that can last from five to six years. At the end of an inquiry the tribunal prepares its report, which is recommendatory only, which can itself take some years to write. The tribunal can also deal with one-off urgency claims using a more abbreviated process. Claims are based on written statements of claim analogous to those used in civil proceedings. There can be several dozen claimants or claimant groups in one regional historical inquiry, who may all have their own counsel, although it is more usual for claimant counsel to act for a number of groups. There tend, therefore, to be a large number of lawyers present—in fact many of the lawyers are Maori themselves. There will also always be a team of senior lawyers from the Crown Law Office to represent the government, and the government will typically commission historical evidence prepared by professional historians to counterbalance that commissioned by the claimants. This multi-party dimension of the process can cause procedural problems when it comes to the management of cross-examination and open and closing submissions: claimant counsel, who mostly know one another well, manage these matters themselves on a co-operative basis. There can however sometimes be real tensions amongst claimants, and many claimant groups will be divided politically inter se, with different factions or groupings bringing separate claims. Inter-Maori politics remain intense in New Zealand, and neighbouring groups can have very different interpretations of the relevant history. The tribunal is by now accustomed to the complexities of Maori society. The tribunal process is very thorough and meticulous, but it is also time-consuming and elaborate. With the Waitangi Tribunal, New Zealand has chosen an adjudicative path which is based on solid research, lengthy hearings, and comprehensive but not binding reports, and which has become dominated by lawyers and expert witnesses at an extent not foreseen when the tribunal's empowering legislation was enacted in 1975. Some claimant groups do not mind that tribunal inquiries take a lot of time and value the opportunity to have long-standing grievances patiently considered by a specialist tribunal; others find it too slow and seek to either by-pass it altogether or at least circumvent aspects of it and proceed directly to negotiations with the state.

The New Zealand government in the present day is also engaged in a very active programme of negotiating and settling Maori historic claims. There is a special agency with the responsibility of implementing the process known as the Office of Treaty Settlements (OTS),[19] a section of the Justice Department in Wellington, and also a Minister of the Crown in charge of the process generally. The historic settlements, although they cannot amount to full *restitutio in integrum*—this could bankrupt the state—can still be very substantial. The largest settlements are in the range of $NZ170 million; others range from $NZ20–$NZ100 million. This programme of large-scale settlements has been going on since the late 1990s. Settlements are with *iwi* (tribes), or at least with substantial sections of tribes ('large natural groupings'). The settlements are meant to provide redress for historic breaches of the treaty by 'the Crown' with respect to that group. The settlements are partly in cash, partly in land and other kinds of landed assets, and partly take the form of 'cultural redress': the latter can include particular rights of consultation with respect to areas of land and water in public ownership. The process has become a very elaborate one and is one of the largest-scale processes of settlement of historic grievances with indigenous people going on the world at the present time. It will cost several $NZ billion by the time it is complete, a sum which the New Zealand government can, however, well afford. The settlements are given effect by deed (written contract), which are very lengthy—hundreds of pages—and then implemented by an Act of Parliament, which gives the agreement unchallengeable legal effect. The first such settlement acts were enacted in the 1990s (Waikato Raupatu Claims Settlement Act 1995, Ngai Tahu Claims Settlement Act 1998); there are now a large number of them. The legislation will deem the relevant Waitangi Tribunal claims to be fully and finally settled, and they can no longer be raised again with the Waitangi Tribunal subsequently.[20] In New Zealand, resolution of historic grievances is not merely a component of the government's Maori policy; it is in fact *central* to it. Whether this has been a wise move remains to be seen. The New Zealand state invests significantly in Maori health and education, but it is legitimate to ask whether the additional resources that have been devoted to the resolution of historic claims might have been better spent on additional funding in these other sectors. In the case of some settlements there has been little discernible benefit to ordinary Maori people affiliating to the claimant body. In some respects the 'settlement' is a type of seed capital made available to the collective group, the

---

[19] The Office of Treaty Settlements was first established in 1995.

[20] The formal mechanism by which this is achieved is that each settlement act results in an amendment to s. 6 of the Treaty of Waitangi Act 1975.

precise amount reflecting the size of the group and the significance of its historical grievances. All that can be said at this stage is that the state's willingness to negotiate and settle historic claims, which is undoubted, has not been matched into any real inquiry as to the practical results of the process.

The Waitangi Tribunal operates within a complex legal structure in New Zealand. It is not the sole means by which Maori groups can seek to obtain redress. The tribunal has not replaced the ordinary courts. The doctrine of Native Title exists in New Zealand as in Australia, and the courts have played an important role in some recent controversies. There have been important cases in recent decades which have considered the status and meaning of the Treaty of Waitangi, aspects of the government's negotiation and settlement system, ownership of rivers, and the extent to which the state is required to act as a fiduciary in the course of managing certain classes of Maori lands. Probably the most important recent controversy was concerned with the foreshore and seabed, the subject of a decision of the New Zealand Court of Appeal in 2003.[21] The Court of Appeal found that the Maori Land Court had jurisdiction to investigate Maori land claims relating to land in the intertidal zone and the bed of the territorial sea, which could have led to the award of Maori land titles to this area. The decision caused a great deal of controversy, and the government of the day responded with a statute extinguishing Maori claims to the foreshore and seabed at common law and under the Maori land legislation, replacing the former legal options with new processes for recognizing Maori claims to what was now referred to as the Marine and Coastal area. The outcome was thus somewhat similar to what happened in Australia after the *Mabo* decision in that various legal rights and options recognized by the ordinary courts were recast into a statutory framework. The government's statutory vehicle, the Foreshore and Seabed Act 2004 was widely criticized and was replaced by new legislation in 2011.[22] It is still unclear whether the 2011 Act provides a workable or effective solution.

IV. THE ROLE OF HISTORIANS

A. Historical Research and Evidence

The extent to which specialists in legal history play a role in adjudication of settler-indigenous relations turns on the nature of the adjudicatory mechanisms

---

[21] *Ngati Apa v. Attorney-General* [2003] 3 NZLR 643.
[22] Foreshore and Seabed Act 2004; Marine and Coastal Area (Takutai Moana) Act 2011. See generally R. P. Boast, *Foreshore and Seabed* (2004).

established in various countries and the legal parameters within which such bodies operate. In this respect, Australia's Native Title Tribunal and New Zealand's Waitangi Tribunal are quite different. In Australia, indigenous groups need to show the maintenance of customary practices down to the present day. This has meant that the role of historians as expert witnesses in Australia is comparatively limited; the expertise that is required, rather, is provided by ethnographers and anthropologists, many of whom work as consultants who have built up high levels of practical experience in giving evidence before the Native Title Tribunal.[23] In New Zealand, by contrast, the legal tests relate to breaches of the principles of the Treaty of Waitangi after 1840. Such breaches are a matter of historical evidence and interpretation, and as a result specialist historians have played a dominant role as expert witnesses in the Waitangi Tribunal. The amount of historical research that has been commissioned and presented in New Zealand is extraordinary in terms of its scale and range, and practically every aspect of Maori interaction with settlers and the colonial state has now been explored comprehensively, but arguably somewhat narrowly.

In New Zealand, research has been funded generously: claimants in the Waitangi Tribunal are not required to pay for it themselves. There are now hundreds of elaborate research reports on such subjects as government land purchasing, confiscation of land by the Crown in some parts of the country during and after the New Zealand wars era (1860–1872), the Native Land Court (established in 1865), state management of waterways and forests, management of reserves, and various socio-economic trends. Many of these research reports have been authored by academic specialists drawn from the country's history departments and law schools. Much of the research has focused on legal developments in the nineteenth century, including the statutes relating to land confiscation and the functioning of the Native Land Court. The tribunal's hearings have also led to the emergence, for the first time, of a number of practising public historians in New Zealand, who make a living working on research contracts. All this work has also led to an upsurge in published historical works on indigenous-settler relationships in the country, especially in the nineteenth century, as historians contracted to prepare research reports for the Waitangi Tribunal go on to turn their research into works of history written for the general public.[24] New Zealand historiography is in a flourishing state at the present time, and this is partly a result of the upsurge in primary research generated by the

---

[23] For an anthropological analysis of the Native Title process see Peter Sutton, *Native Title in Australia: An Ethnographic Perspective* (2003).

[24] One example is Judith Binney, *Encircled Lands: Te Urewera, 1820–1920* (2009). This book, a comprehensive study of the Tuhoe people, was derived from comprehensive evidence prepared by Professor Binney for the Tuhoe claimants in the Waitangi Tribunal's Te Urewera inquiry. Another is Vincent O'Malley, *The Great War for New Zealand: Waikato 1800–2000* (2015), deriving to some degree from O'Malley's research prepared for the Waitangi Tribunal's Rohe Potae (King Country) regional inquiry.

Waitangi Tribunal process. Here, another contrast with Australia can be noted. In Australia, the historiography of the colonial encounter is a battleground and has become highly politicized; in New Zealand, it is not.

Historians are commissioned to prepare specialist reports on particular issues or questions arising out of pending Waitangi Tribunal inquiries. Examples might be the effects of confiscation in Taranaki or the Bay of Plenty, pre-emptive Crown purchasing in Hawke's Bay or the northern South Island, or the Native Land Court in the Hauraki region, Northland, or in the Central North Island. The reports can be very substantial documents, much larger sometimes than the average PhD, and very thoroughly referenced to primary materials. The contracting historians will typically prepare 'document banks' which are filed at the same time as their reports: the document banks, which tend to be even more bulky than the commissioned research reports, are collections of photocopied primary sources. Historians can be commissioned by claimants, by the Crown, and sometimes by the Waitangi Tribunal itself. The reports are distributed in advance to the claimant and Crown counsel. The historians are also required to give evidence before the tribunal, and for this purpose will produce written briefs of evidence summarizing their research and findings. At tribunal hearings the historians will read out or speak to their briefs of evidence and will then be cross-examined, sometimes at considerable length, by claimant or Crown counsel, and will typically be questioned in addition by the Waitangi Tribunal panel as well. Thus the extent of material placed for the tribunal in any one regional inquiry is very substantial, far beyond the capacity of any individual member of the tribunal panel to read and absorb. This material is supplemented by memoranda filed by claimant and Crown counsel during the hearings, written tribunal directions on points of evidence and procedure, and a substantial transcript of the oral evidence and cross-examination. Proceedings on this scale, as indicated earlier, would be impossibly expensive in the ordinary courts, but the burdens are still daunting even for a special purpose body such as the Waitangi Tribunal. As a result of the scale of the evidence and the wide range of issues that need to be reported on, tribunal reports on regional historical inquiries will themselves be very bulky texts that can take years to prepare. Any jurisdiction that experiments with the New Zealand Tribunal-based model will quickly find that judicial or semi-judicial inquiries into indigenous historical grievances create significant problems with the management of documentary evidence and testimony.

B. 'Retrospective Utopias': Claims-Related Research and the Writing of History

As bodies such as the Native Title Tribunal or the Waitangi Tribunal have become established features of the legal and constitutional order in their respective countries, there has been a growing debate about the historical assumptions that underpin their reports and decisions. A number of writers have suggested that the Waitangi Tribunal's approach to history is 'presentist' or teleological, or that it applies inappropriate and over-rigorous canons of behaviour to government actions in the past. According to W. H. Oliver, one of New Zealand's leading academic historians, the Waitangi Tribunal has constructed a 'retrospective Utopia' by applying the idealistic standards of the present day to the actions of colonial regimes in the nineteenth century.[25] The argument is that the standard of the 'principles of the Treaty of Waitangi' is a contemporary construction, one that it is essentially meaningless to apply to the actions of governments and officials in the past.

Another critic is Giselle Byrnes, author of a monograph on Waitangi Tribunal historiography published in 2004.[26] In this book Byrnes argues that the Waitangi Tribunal, an institution which constructs reports that are essentially lengthy historical analyses, is caught in a contradiction by which it seeks to demonstrate that Maori were autonomous actors in nineteenth century New Zealand (that is, they were not merely passive victims of government policies) but on the other hand were fated to be overwhelmed by those same policies. Maori could protest, and struggle for autonomy, but were always destined to defeat. Moreover, the tribunal, Byrnes claims, tends to avoid discussing inter-tribal conflict, of which there was a great deal, and presents a 'one-dimensional' picture of Europeans, making little effort to understand competing attitudes amongst the Pakeha (non-Maori New Zealanders) or the varying policies of particular governments. Moreover '[a]ccording to the Tribunal, European perceptions were, on the whole, monocultural and narrow-minded.' The tribunal presents history which is essentially crude and lacking in historical sensitivity:[27]

The representation of Maori and non-Maori world views as being fundamental opposites, and the positing of these two intellectual traditions and habits of thought as separate but unequal, ultimately leads to the creation of good and bad stereotypes, and the passing of moral judgments. This kind of interpretation has serious problems. First, colonial encounters are reduced to a series of binary opposites. Second, this approach does justice to neither party: it allows Maori and non-Maori to be typecast, and does not permit change over time.

Not all academic historians in New Zealand accept this analysis, pointing out that many of the policies the tribunal criticizes, such as confiscation of land as a punishment for 'rebellion', were denounced in their day by opposition politicians, missionaries, or pressure groups such as the Aborigines Protection Society in

---

[25] W. H. Oliver 'The Future Behind Us: The Waitangi Tribunal's Retrospective Utopia' in Andrew Sharp, Paul McHugh (eds.), *Histories Power and Loss: Uses of the Past—A New Zealand Commentary* (2001) 9–29.

[26] Giselle Byrnes, *The Waitangi Tribunal and New Zealand History* (2004).

[27] Ibid., 127–8.

Britain.[28] Moreover, the Waitangi Tribunal is not a free agent, nor is it conducting research seminars: it is directed by its own empowering statute to report on acts or omissions of the Crown that were in breach of the principles of the Treaty of Waitangi. In many respects, moreover, the debates over Waitangi Tribunal historiography in New Zealand simply reflect interpretive debates within the historiography of Western-indigenous encounters generally, and are therefore unsurprising. The debate over 'tribunal' history in New Zealand echoes the debates over so-called 'fatal impact' historiography in the field of Pacific history, or that over native agency in the United States and Latin America. Moreover, the Waitangi Tribunal does not have a monopoly over the production of history in New Zealand, which has long had, and still has, a lively historiography examining the country's race relations history from many diverse perspectives. Some works seek to contextualize New Zealand's constitutional and legal history, including the history of the Treaty of Waitangi, within contemporary discourses of political thought and constitutionalism in the nineteenth century.[29] It probably is the case that the reports of judicial bodies such as the Waitangi Tribunal, here resembling the productions of transitional justice institutions, cannot escape their essentially legal nature, which explains their tendency to evaluate the behaviours of governments by reference to legal standards such as fairness, standards of consultation, or the principles of international law, or—in the New Zealand case—a treaty text which is generally interpreted to exemplify universal standards in any event.

Left out of account in such historico-legal narratives are wider social, environmental, and economic changes which cannot easily be attributed to particular governments or individuals, as they may well be global in nature and to some extent beyond the control of particular states. In the Waitangi Tribunal, for example, it is common for historians to be commissioned to prepare reports dealing with the 'social impacts' of government policies. Evidence of this kind is usually supplementary to the main research focusing on legislative, legal, and policy developments. It may seem obvious that massive land loss by indigenous peoples will generate poverty, but this can be harder to demonstrate in a judicial forum than it might seem: in fact, in the New Zealand case at least, the reverse situation applies, in that Maori were poor and marginalized to begin with and sold their land as a result.[30] It is clear that the social and economic plight of Maori people in the later nineteenth century was dire,

---

[28] Jim McAloon, 'By Which Standards? History and the Waitangi Tribunal' (2006) 40 New Zealand Journal of History 194; Byrnes, 'By Which Standards? History and the Waitangi Tribunal: A Reply' (2006) 40 New Zealand Journal of History 214.

[29] See Mark Hickford, Lords of the Land: Indigenous Property Rights and the Jurisprudence of Empire (2011).

[30] I argue this in Buying the Land, Selling the Land (2015). The Native Lands Acts created saleable individual interests in Maori land blocks. Given the economic plight of many Maori people in the nineteenth century, their willingness to trade individual shares for cash, often to government land purchase officers, is readily understandable.

but linking the clear evidence of widespread immiseration to particular government actions and policies, some of which were aimed at ameliorating Maori poverty and distress, has proved difficult in practice. This is partly because wider, indeed global, transformations set in play by colonialism and the spread of international capitalism, played an important role in transforming the lives and economies of indigenous peoples around the world, not excluding Maori people in New Zealand. However, global transformations are not easily translated into the legal discourses that operate either in Courts or in special purpose tribunals, which are focused on apportioning blame at the state level. Thus the need for historiographies of international change, such as those provided by Fernand Braudel or Immanuel Wallerstein, can never be diminished by single-jurisdiction tribunals. It is historiographies of the latter kind which may at the end of the day have far greater explanatory power. National tribunals are ill-placed to consider international trends. For example New Zealand's Native Lands Acts of 1862–1866, which individualized Maori customary lands, derive from the same ideological underpinnings as do the *Reforma* laws in Mexico, General Allotment in the United States, and the abolition of customary tenures in Ireland. A particularly close parallel with New Zealand is Hawai'i, where a number of enactments of the Hawaiian monarchy—in particular the *Kuleana* Act of 6 August 1850—have many similarities to the Native Lands Acts of 1862 and 1865 in New Zealand.[31] Confiscation of the land of Maori in 'a state of rebellion' against the Crown in the 1860s has its parallels with Crown policies in Ireland in the seventeenth century.[32] National adjudicative tribunals cannot and do not inquire into parallels of this kind. More than the risk of presentism, which can be exaggerated, the historiography generated by special purpose national tribunals will always be only partial given that the supranational and the global will always be outside its gaze. The real risk of a historiography arising from adjudicative mechanisms is not so much presentism as it is insularity.

V. CONCLUSIONS

This brief survey has considered the problem of what is meant by 'settler' societies and has focused on redress mechanisms in two countries, Australia and

---

[31] On the Hawaiian legislation see Melody Kapilialoha MacKenzie, 'Historical Background', in Melody Kapilialoha MacKenzie, Susan K. Serrano, D. Kapua'ala Sproat, *Native Hawaiian Law: A Treatise* (2015) 5–74.

[32] On confiscation in New Zealand see Richard P. Boast, Richard Hill (eds.), *Raupatu: The Confiscation of Maori Land* (2009); O'Malley, *Great War for New Zealand* (n. 24) 407–511. There is a large literature on the Irish confiscations. See, e.g., Nicholas Canny, *Making Ireland British 1580–1650* (2001).

New Zealand. In both cases the establishment of such mechanisms arose out of political and legal conjunctures within each country and owed little to developments in international law. The Waitangi Tribunal in New Zealand and the Native Title Tribunal in Australia have very different functions, utilize different kinds of expert evidence, and operate in very different political and constitutional settings. While both bodies require expert evidence typically provided by non-indigenous specialist researchers, the required expertise in each case is different: anthropology in the Australian case, and history in the case of New Zealand. In Australia, the Aboriginal people have long been marginalized and comprise only a small percentage of the national population. In New Zealand, by contrast, a significant percentage of the population is Maori, and relations between Maori and the state have always been central to national politics. In both countries, on the other hand, although specialist tribunals have been established to adjudicate on government-indigenous relations, in neither case do these bodies monopolize legal adjudication in this field, and in both the ordinary courts they have continued to play an important role. As a general conclusion, redress mechanisms such as the Native Title Tribunal and the Waitangi Tribunal cannot be properly understood in the absence of a full consideration of the historical, political, and legal contexts that operate in their respective countries.

Bibliography

Jorge Álvarez, Luis Bértola, Gabriel Porcile, *Primos Ricos y Empobrecidos: Crecimiento, distribución del Ingreso e instituciones en Australia-Nueva Zealanda vs Argentina-Uruguay* (Fin de siglo, 2007)

Richard H. Bartlett, *Native Title in Australia* (Butterworths, 2000)

James Belich, *Replenishing the Earth: The Settler Revolution and the Rise of the Angloworld* (Oxford University Press, 2011)

Carmen Bernand, *Les Indiens face à la construction de l'État-nation: Mexique-Argentine 1810–1917* (Éditions Atlande, 2013)

Judith Binney, *Encircled Lands: Te Urewera, 1820–1921* (Bridget Williams Books, 2009)

Richard Boast, *Foreshore and Seabed* (LexisNexis, 2004)

Richard Boast, *Buying the Land, Selling the Land: Governments and Maori Land in the North Island 1865–1921* (Victoria University Press, 2008)

Richard Boast, *The Native Land Court 1862–1887: A Historical Study, Cases and Commentary* (Thomson Reuters, 2013)

Richard Boast, Andrew Erueti, Doug McPhail, Norman F. Smith, *Maori Land Law* (LexisNexis, 2004)

Richard Boast, Richard Hill, *Raupatu: The Confiscation of Maori Land* (Victoria University Press, 2009)

Giselle Byrnes, *The Waitangi Tribunal and New Zealand History* (Oxford University Press, 2004)

Giselle Byrnes, 'By Which Standards? History and the Waitangi Tribunal: A Reply' (2006) 40 *New Zealand Journal of History* 214

Nicholas Canny, *Making Ireland British 1580–1650* (Oxford University Press, 2001)

Ron Crosby, *Kūpapa: The Bitter Legacy of Māori Alliances with the Crown* (Penguin Books, 2015)

Janine Hayward, Nicola Wheen (eds.), *The Waitangi Tribunal: Te Roopu Whakamana i te Tiriti o Waitangi* (Bridget Williams Books, 2004)

John Hemming, *Die if you Must: Brazilian Indians in the Twentieth Century* (Pan Macmillan, 2003)

Hickford, Mark, *Lords of the Land: Indigenous Property Rights and the Jurisprudence of Empire* Oxford University Press, 2011)

Peter Karsten, *Between Law and Custom* (Cambridge University Press, 2003)

Jim McAloon, 'By Which Standards? History and the Waitangi Tribunal' (2006) 40 *New Zealand Journal of History* 194

Paul McHugh, *Aboriginal Societies and the Common Law* (Oxford University Press, 2004)

Melody Kapilialoha MacKenzie, 'Historical Background', in Melody Kapilialoha MacKenzie; Susan K. Serrano, Sproat D. Kapuaʻala, (ed.), *Native Hawaiian Law: A Treatise* (Kamehameha Publishing, 2015) 5–74

W. H. Oliver, 'The Future Behind Us: The Waitangi Tribunal's Retrospective Utopia' in Andrew Sharp, Paul McHugh (eds.), *Histories Power and Loss: Uses of the Past—A New Zealand Commentary* (Bridget Williams Books, 2001) 9–29

Vincent O'Malley, *The Great War for New Zealand: Waikato 1800–2000* (Bridget Williams Books, 2015)

J. G. A. Pocock, 'Tangata Whenua and Enlightenment Anthropology' (1992) 26 New Zealand Journal of History 28

Mario Rapoport, María Seoane, *Buenos Aires: Historia de una ciudad*, vol. 1 (Editorial Planeta, 2007)

Peter Sutton, *Native Title in Australia: An Ethnographic Perspective* (Cambridge University Press, 2003)

Eric Van Young, 'Rural History', in José C. Moya (ed.), *The Oxford Handbook of Latin American History* (2011) 309–41

Lorenzo Veracino, *Settler Colonialism: A Theoretical Overview* (Palgrave Macmillan, 2010)

John C. Weaver, *The Great Land Rush and the Making of the Modern World* (McGill-Queen's University Press, 2003)

Simon Young, *The Trouble with Tradition: Native Title and Cultural Change* (Federation Press, 2008)

CHAPTER 56

CULTURAL GENOCIDE

BETWEEN LAW AND HISTORY*

LEORA BILSKY AND RACHEL KLAGSBRUN

TODAY, when one thinks about the term 'cultural genocide', the immediate thought is of indigenous peoples, whose culture has been erased over decades and centuries by white colonial settlers. Immediate suspects are Canada, Australia, and South America. This particular wrong adds to other wrongs wrought by the West/North on the East and South and is part of the continuous discourse, ever since decolonization started, about the history of colonization. Specifically, this wrong is claimed by the survivors of colonization practices who term the disappearance of their cultures and languages 'cultural genocide'. Yet, as a legal claim, this is still a contentious one. The discussion that ensued during the debates around the drafting of the *United Nations Declaration on the Rights of Indigenous Peoples* (2007) is a case in point. A draft article that included the thorny words was eventually amended to exclude them. The arguments were legal in nature, mainly claiming that such term was not defined in international law.

This chapter sets out to depict in broad brushstrokes the development of the term 'cultural genocide', its connection to the term 'genocide', and what this can teach us about the relationship between law and history. The puzzle that the crime of genocide

* This essay grew out of a research project on the history of cultural genocide. For a comprehensive and extended elaboration of our findings see, L. Bilsky, R. Klagsbrun, 'The Return of Cultural Genocide?' (forthcoming *European Journal of International Law*, 2018).

posits, in a nutshell, is this: how is it that a crime that was originally designed to deal with a new historical occurrence—a systemic attempt to completely erase a cultural group—turned from an encompassing concept of genocide to one limited to its physical and biological aspects? How was the cultural essence of genocide reduced to attack on 'cultural heritage' and then detached from the international crime of genocide and relegated to human rights and minority law under the control of nation states?

In order to answer this puzzle, this chapter lets go of a binary approach positing law and history opposite each other. First, it adopts an approach that sees the plurality in law: litigation, legislation, international conventions, both international and national. This pluralistic view allows us to deviate from the conventional understanding that sees history as a complex and flexible discipline—one that can study long-term processes, take account of myriad of motives, and go beyond legal definitions of protected groups to account for hybrid groups—as opposed to law, which is regarded as rigid, doctrinal, and procedural. For these reasons, law restricts the crime of genocide to the most serious acts and by that, limits genocide to the physical and biological aspects, requiring a special intent or a plan directed at the destruction of a group as such and affording protection to only limited classes of groups. Instead, the authors examine the dialectics between law and history to show the occasions when law becomes the main tool to address a new historical phenomenon, and those times in which law's categories and doctrines obscure the novelty in history and force new practices into familiar boxes. The chapter adopts a critical approach to law—one that brings the political dimensions to the centre of the discourse and claims that we cannot understand the tension between law and history as one detached from politics. Conversely, it claims that politics alone—without understanding precedents and legal doctrines or historical traditions and methodologies—cannot explain the transformations in the meaning of genocide.

Prior to the involvement of states and their political considerations, it was mostly the endeavour of one man, Raphael Lemkin, that gave rise to the idea of genocide in the first place. What influenced Lemkin in devising his theory of genocide is the subject of many historical-legal researches. Among other influences writers have identified the Armenian genocide; the South American *conquistadors*; the Zionist movement; the trial of Sholem Shvartsbard; his academic work as a comparative criminal lawyer; and his own personal experiences during the Second World War— as leading factors.[1] For the authors, what is missing in this debate about the origins

---

[1] See, inter alia, Elisa Novic, *The Concept of Cultural Genocide: An International Law Perspective* (2016) 20–1 ff; Alexa Stiller, 'Semantics of Extermination: The Use of the New Term of Genocide in the Nuremberg Trials and the Genesis of A Master Narrative', in K. C. Priemel, Alexa Stiller (eds.), *Reassessing The Nuremberg Military Tribunals* (2012) 104, 106 ff; Ana Filipa Vrdoljak, *International Law, Museums and the Return of Cultural Objects* (2006) 168 ff; Ana Vrdoljak, 'Human Rights and Genocide: The Work of Lauterpacht and Lemkin in Modern International Law' (2009) 20(4) *European Journal of International Law* 1163 ff; James Loeffler, 'Becoming Cleopatra: The Forgotten Zionism of Raphael Lemkin' (2017) *Journal of Genocide Research* 340; A. Dirk Moses, 'Lemkin, Culture, and the Concept of Genocide', in

of Lemkin's concept of genocide, is a discussion of the method he employed in identifying and mapping the new historical phenomenon. This refers to Lemkin's rigorous collection of legislation—orders, decrees, and laws—enacted by the Nazis in every country they have occupied—which later became the basis to his book *Axis Rule in Occupied Europe* (1944). This method—that we term 'legal philology'— allowed Lemkin to expose the grand plan of the Nazis: not just physical annihilation of individuals—and long before such was executed—but a systemic and holistic dispossession of entire groups, through legislation that applies to every aspect of life: from the right to freely use trams or parks to the right to possess real estate and other property; from the right to employ Arian help to the right to freely marry or to have intimate relations; from the obligation to wear a yellow star, to the obligation to add the name Sarah to one's identity card. By collecting and amassing these decrees one by one, Lemkin came to realize the depth of the Nazi plan and how it had targeted groups. He understood that people were not persecuted because any individual trait they might have—other than their belonging to a certain group that was a target of persecution. The ingenuity of this approach, explains Philippe Sands, lies in its piecemeal method: 'Individually, each decree looked innocuous, but when they were taken together and examined across borders, a broader purpose emerged.'[2]

For Lemkin, what was most disturbing was the way the Nazis sought to destroy these groups' cultures: by enforcing German as the formal language of daily life and as a teaching language; by enforcing Nazi curriculum to the exclusion of local or liberal ones; and by destroying synagogues and confiscating libraries. Culture, the glue that keeps a group together, was being destroyed, and this led to the destruction of the group. This need not necessarily be accompanied with physical destruction—although in the case of the Holocaust it was. But as opposed to current understanding of the terms physical genocide and cultural genocide—as different 'types' of genocide—Lemkin saw all the varied ways in which the Nazis employed their plan as 'techniques' of genocide. In his book he enumerated eight of these techniques—political, social, cultural, economic, biological, physical, religious, and moral.[3] These are not 'degrees' of genocide: for Lemkin the cultural technique was as bad as any of the others. It was an aim in itself and not a by-product of another technique. Another important aspect of this proposition is that these techniques are what differentiates between genocide and mass murder: following Lemkin, one can say that if the phenomenon could be reduced to mass murder, a new crime would not have to be defined, as such a crime is already prohibited by national and international legislation and the only problem it presents is jurisdictional, owing to

---

Donald Bloxham, A. Dirk Moses (eds.), *The Oxford Handbook of Genocide Studies* (2010) 19 ff; Philippe Sands, *East West Street: On the Origins of Genocide and Crimes Against Humanity* (2016).

[2] Sands (n. 1) 168–9 ff.

[3] For an elaboration of each of these techniques see Raphael Lemkin, *Axis Rule in Occupied Europe: Laws of Occupation, Analysis of Government, Proposals for Redress* (1944) 82–90 ff.

state immunity. This problem can be solved by creating an international or universal jurisdiction to adjudicate such a crime and does not necessitate the definition of a new crime. But if one understands the crime as targeting a group as such then the protected value is different and a different solution is called for.

Another important aspect that Lemkin learned from his meticulous work was that genocide has two stages: a 'negative' one, which is the destruction and annihilation of a national group inhabiting a conquered land; and a 'positive' one, which is the imposition of the national pattern of the oppressor on the oppressed— the people (if they are worthy of it) or their land. This analysis led him to see the insufficiency of law as it stood at the time—and to a large extent as it stands today. This is the first moment in our account where we meet law as a limiting, obscuring force, that lacks the adequate tools to catch new historical phenomena because of its rigid distinctions. International law is very much a statist project: states are immune from intervening in their internal affairs, and international humanitarian law was manifestly lacking in its treatment, as the Hague Regulations only protect individuals and not groups and do so only during wartime; civilians attacked by their own states are left unprotected. Moreover, the war crimes approach favours a discrete approach that prohibits certain crimes without presenting the link between them. What Lemkin saw as the essence of the crime was left untreated by current legal protection.

We see that in the 'discovery' of genocide, law played a dual role, both as an aiding tool in revealing the crime (legal philology) and as a limiting and obscuring factor (i.e.—statist bias of international law). As to the former, what is interesting for us in terms of understanding the link between law and history is the fact that Lemkin developed his sophisticated understanding of genocide by mostly studying legal documents, without having access to minutes of secret meetings or the subjective state of mind of the leaders. The law itself reveals the system, because the system *needs* the law in order to operate: since the target is a group and since every aspect of group life is affected, a coordination must be achieved between all arms of government and private sectors to create a total exclusion, disintegration and eventually—annihilation of a group.

How did genocide and cultural genocide fair in the courtroom? The next significant stop in our journey is the International Military Tribunal (IMT) at Nuremberg. Although Lemkin (as well as Jewish organizations) tried to influence the design of the indictment (and even suggested a separate trial be dedicated to the Jewish Holocaust), eventually the aggressive war paradigm persisted in a way that prevented a significant change in the capacity of law to cope with the new type of criminality that unfolded. Significant for cultural genocide was the fact that the required link to aggressive war (through art. 6(c) of the London Charter) meant that most of the acts considered by Lemkin to be techniques of genocide were left outside the temporal scope of the indictment (1939–1945). And so we are left with a legacy of international criminal law that cannot release itself from legalistic constraints of precedents and the criminal law rule of *nullum crimen sine lege*. Yet law alone cannot explain the difficulty of addressing the new historical phenomenon of genocide because one can find behind the legalistic considerations a deeper, political concern about creating a precedent that will undermine state sovereignty. Such was Robert Jackson's concern regarding interference in a state's internal affairs (the U.S. treatment of its black population, for instance).[4]

Another factor raised by legal historians to account for the blindness of the trial in relation to genocide is the absence of victims' testimonies from the Nuremberg proceedings, a fact that some scholars have connected with the perceived marginality of genocide in Nuremberg. New historical research reveals the many attempts of Jewish organizations to join the process, not only as witnesses but also as prosecutors, *amici curiae*, and as the ones that suggested to designate a special crime 'against the Jewish people' or even dedicating a separate trial to the Holocaust.[5] The underlying assumption of such revisionist history is that had the victims participated in the trials in a meaningful way, genocide would have taken a more central place. Yet recent historical research reveals a process by which law has gradually grasped the centrality of genocide, as the trial progressed and new evidence was revealed—despite the relative lack of survivor witnesses.

Such research reveals that the Holocaust was not entirely absent from the proceedings. To give a few examples: Kim Priemel shows that it was very much present in the deliberations as they are reflected in the trial sessions' transcripts and that it had influenced sentencing. Lawrence Douglas shows that in the subsequent trials by the Nuremberg Military Tribunal (NMT), crimes against humanity was the prevalent category: as the facts of the magnitude of Nazi criminality unfolded, law was being adapted; Control Council Law No. 10 severed the link to aggressive war and provided a more comprehensive definition of crimes against humanity than the London Charter. Regarding cultural genocide in Nuremberg, Alexa Stiller studied the NMT trials and, specifically, the Race and Settlement Main Office of the SS (*Rasse- und Siedlungshauptamt der SS*, RuSHA) trial. She shows that the prosecution was well aware of Lemkin's theory, quoted from his book, and specifically dedicated the trial to the 'positive' aspect of genocide—positing it as a complementary to the IMT, which dealt with the 'negative' aspect. Yet these efforts did not bear the hoped fruit: the judges were not persuaded that the crime of genocide was indeed part of international law and hence did not use it as a legal category. Instead, they particularized the Germanization plan into discrete war crimes. Likewise, the mass murder of the Jews underwent de-contextualization—from a broad Nazi policy

---

[4] Lawrence Douglas, *The Memory of Judgment: Making Law and History in the Trials of the Holocaust* (2001) 50 ff.

[5] This demand for a 'Holocaust trial' stood in opposition to the functional/structural approach of the prosecution in the NMT (devoting different trials to the involvement of various sectors.) Mark Lewis devotes a chapter in his book to the World Jewish Congress' (WJC) efforts to instigate a 'new justice' paradigm; Mark Lewis, *The Birth of the New Justice* (2014) 150–80 ff.

executed in stages and by various techniques to a narrow perception of murder only, perpetrated by SS men. Again, the available legal tools and legal imagination were inadequate to capture the realities of the atrocities that pervaded Europe only a few years earlier.[6]

Was the fact that almost no Jewish survivors have testified at the IMT a decisive factor in the tribunal's comprehension of the essence of genocide as mass murder? Historians believe that the tribunal was not disposed to hearing testimonies about the cultural destruction that befell European Jewry.[7] This is especially evident in the testimony of one of the only Jewish survivors, who was summoned by the Russian prosecution to give testimony. Abraham Sutzkever, the famous Jewish-Lithuanian Yiddish poet who lost most of his family, also had a central role in the efforts to rescue Jewish cultural property in Vilna during and immediately after the war. Despite this unique role in relation to the Jewish cultural genocide, Sutzkever's testimony focused on the collective murder, and he was not asked about the cultural destruction nor his efforts in cultural rescue.[8] One remote echo for the cultural side of the genocide appeared in Sutzkever's request to testify in Yiddish—the language of most of the murdered Jewish victims—a request that was denied as Yiddish was not one of the four official languages of the trial, and hence no translator from this language was available.[9]

The IMT and NMT were not the only trials that dealt with the Nazi atrocities. Soon after the war, Poland had established a tribunal to judge major Nazi criminals active in Poland during the occupation, in accordance with international and Polish criminal law. Being a national tribunal of the persecuted group, it was much more sensitive to the cultural destruction and Germanization that set upon Poland and the Polish population. This was manifested in the trial of Gauleiter Artur Greiser, where the tribunal found that the German occupation in Poland was manifested, among other things, in religious and cultural repression—both termed 'genocidal' and both found to be part of the Germanization of Poland. Moreover, both negative

---

[6] Lawrence Douglas, 'Crimes of Atrocity, the Problem of Punishment and the Situ of Law', in Predrag Dojčinović (ed.), *Propaganda, War Crimes Trials and International Law* (2012) 269, 271, 272 ff; Kim Priemel, 'Beyond the Saturation Point of Horror: The Holocaust at Nuremberg Revisited', in Daniel Hedinger, Daniel Siemens (eds.), *The Trials of Nuremberg and Tokyo revisited* (2016) 522 ff; Alexa Stiller, 'Semantics of Extermination: The Use of the New Term of Genocide in the Nuremberg Trials and the Genesis of A Master Narrative', in K. C. Priemel, A. Stiller (eds.), *Reassessing The Nuremberg Military Tribunals* (2012) 104 ff.

[7] Donald Bloxham, *Genocide on Trial: War Crimes Trials and the Formation of Holocaust History and Memory* (2001).

[8] *Nuremberg Trial Proceedings* Vol. 8, 27 February 1946, 301–7 ff. Despite the focal point of the testimony being the physical destruction, Sutzkever did not fail to mention by name a few figures of Jewish cultural life—a scientist, the president of the Jewish Society of Vilna, a historian, and a writer— that were murdered by the Nazis in Vilna, so as to hint at the grave cultural destruction obscured by the sheer number of murdered victims (Ibid., 303, 305).

[9] Laura Jockusch, 'Justice at Nuremberg? Jewish Responses to Nazi War-Crime Trials in Allied-Occupied Germany' (2012) 19(1) *Jewish Social Studies* 107, 108 ff.

and positive aspects of Nazi persecution were considered by the tribunal, following Lemkin's structural analysis of the crime. We see then that in this case, cultural genocide came to the fore, inter alia, due to the willingness of the court to hear survivor witnesses, to introduce historians as expert-witnesses (expanding the narrow understanding of eyewitness), and adopting Lemkin's theory of genocide, notwithstanding the official mandate to investigate 'war crimes.' Again, it was not only law or history that played a role in revealing cultural genocide, but to no small account, also the political will of the Polish authorities.

Can we assume then that national courts of the victims' group are more favourable towards the prosecution of cultural genocide? Not necessarily so.

Another famous national trial was that of Adolf Eichmann in 1961, in Israel. Although here, too, the trial was conducted by the victim group, and the testimonies of survivors were given centre stage, the narrative that came out of this trial was very different. To understand that, we need to listen to the voices that were not heard and to the voices that were heard but were dismissed and forgotten. The poet Abraham Sutzkever—whom we met as a witness at Nuremberg—was not called to the stand in the Eichmann trial (although by that time he had already moved to Israel). The historian Salo Baron of Columbia University testified at length as expert historian, but his testimony, which was rather long, is not etched into the collective memory of the trial. Rachel Auerbach, a prominent figure among survivors, testified to the cultural destruction and cultural and spiritual resistance at the Warsaw ghetto, but her testimony, too, did not resonate in the judgment or collective memory of the trial. What is common to these three individuals that can explain such forgetfulness? We claim that their prominence in the domain of cultural salvage and rejuvenation made them less attractive in the eyes of the Israeli prosecution. The latter had a very clear view of the trajectory of the story which can be summarized in the motto 'from Holocaust to Revival' (*Mi'Shoa le'Tkuma.*) The narrative centred on the importance of the establishment of the state of Israel, and the trial emphasized the physical aspect of both parts: physical genocide and military resistance.

Apart from his cultural salvage efforts during and after the war, in Israel, Sutzkever was a leading Yiddish poet and publicist. To him, the fact that Yiddish was absent from the trial—the proceedings were not simultaneously translated into the language that many survivors and families of victims spoke—was a lamentable fact, as he saw the Yiddish itself as another victim of the Nazis. This—as well as the marginal place of cultural genocide in the trial—was criticized by other survivors as well.[10]

Professor Baron, who testified at length to the destruction of Jewry in Europe, tried also to convey the enormous cultural destruction: libraries and collections that were compiled throughout many generations erased with one throwing of

---

[10] Gali Drucker Bar-Am, 'The Holy Tongue and the Tongue of the Martyrs: The Eichmann Trial as Reflected in Letste Nayes' (2014) 28(1) *Dapim: Studies on the Holocaust* 17 ff.

a torch. To him, the genocide was not less cultural than it was physical, and the revival, too, needs to be achieved on both planes. In his testimony, Baron tried again and again to bring up cultural genocide and referred to the organized Jewish campaign for cultural restitution and reconstruction. By doing so he produced a subversive narrative of the Jewish genocide, in competition with that promoted by the prosecution, as for him revival could also be achieved outside Israel. Significantly, one of the only times he mentions the term genocide is in reference to the plunder of Jewish libraries for the purpose of 'scientifically' proving their inferiority.[11]

Another fascinating testimony was that given by Rachel Auerbach, who was also a prominent figure among the survivors and who has dedicated her life to the recording of testimonies from the Holocaust. In fact, she had already begun this enterprise during the war, in the Warsaw ghetto, and continued it after the war in the Central Jewish Historical Commission in Poland[12] and later in Israel, in Yad VaShem (the central Holocaust memorial institute in Israel). Auerbach, who was a journalist, was a careful observant of Jewish life in Warsaw from the 1920s until after the war. This span allowed her to witness first the vibrant and rich Jewish life that existed in Warsaw prior to the war and then the Nazi attempts to obliterate it. Her testimony offers a shrewd understanding of the goal the Nazis had tried to achieve by issuing edicts prohibiting religious, educational, and cultural activities: 'Coinciding with the administrative and economic restrictions designed to cut us off from all sources of livelihood, *they wanted to break us from the spiritual point of view.*' This understanding shares with Lemkin's holistic notion of genocide: '*this was also a prelude to physical destruction, to humiliate us and to convince their own people and the world at large that this was a nation of parasites who were not fit to live in the world,* that they were a kind of gypsies'. Auerbach also testified at length to the creative activities that were happening in the ghetto (in which she played an active role), despite the prohibitions—and probably with an urgency owing to them.[13] During her testimony, the prosecution did relate to these activities as 'keep[ing] together body and soul of the Jews' but in the judgment the emphasis is on the 'inconceivable feats of heroism performed by ghetto-fighters, by those who mutinied in the camps, and by Jewish partisans'. One wonders whether this extends also to the activities of spiritual resistance of the kind Auerbach

---

[11] Testimony of Salo Baron, Session no. 13 (24 April 1961) 158 ff (English translation available from <http://www.nizkor.org/hweb/people/e/eichmann-adolf/transcripts/Sessions/Session-013-01.html>, accessed 2 February 2017).

[12] Laura Jockusch, 'Historiography in Transit: Survivor Historians and the Writing of History in the Late 1940s', *Leo Baeck Institute Year Book* vol. 58, (2013) 75–94 ff. [Immediately after the war Jews in fourteen countries established historical commissions for the purpose of researching the recent annihilation of European Jews. The Jewish historical commission in Poland was headed by historian Philip Friedman, and Rachel Auerbach joined it.]

[13] Testimony of Rachel Auerbach, Session no. 26 (3 May 1961) 361 ff (English translation available from <http://www.nizkor.org/hweb/people/e/eichmann-adolf/transcripts/Sessions/Session-026-01.html>, accessed 10 July 2017).

described, which she viewed as equal to military resistance and an important counter-measure to cultural genocide.

Thus we see that although the occasion for highlighting cultural genocide was present in the Eichmann trial, it was nevertheless marginalized, mainly because it did not fit the hegemonic-ideological perception advanced by the trial.

Perhaps the fact that the *crime against the Jewish people* which Eichmann was indicted of was based on the model of the *Convention on the Prevention and Punishment of the Crime of Genocide* was a factor in the prosecution's ignorance of cultural genocide, although it is important to mention that the Israeli law was broader than the Convention in respect to cultural genocide and included subsections: (5) forcibly transferring Jewish children to another national or religious group; and (6) destroying or desecrating Jewish religious or cultural assets or values.[14] Yet, Eichmann was not charged with any of these.

The Genocide Convention in its final form presents only an echo of the attempt to include cultural genocide, i.e. the prohibition of 'Forcibly transferring children of the group to another group' (Art. II, para. e). Yet cultural genocide was the subject of several debates during the drafting of the Convention. This is no surprise, as Lemkin was appointed as one of the three legal experts to help design the Convention. Not only because what was for him a disappointing outcome of the IMT, Lemkin had always believed that a concerted international effort was needed in order to prevent the destruction of groups.[15] Loyal to his view, he, of course, endorsed the inclusion of cultural genocide as one technique of destroying a group among others. But his position was opposed to from the beginning, first by the other two experts. They opined what later became a recurrent theme in the objection to the inclusion of cultural genocide in a treaty to prevent genocide: cultural genocide is an undue extension of 'pure' genocide and is just an attempt to revive the (failed) pre-war minorities protection regime. Cultural genocide nevertheless entered the draft they had proposed, together with the other seven techniques enumerated by Lemkin, grouped under three categories—physical (causing death), biological (preventing births), and cultural (destroying a group's specific characteristics).[16]

---

[14] The Nazis and Nazi Collaborators (Punishment) Law 5710-1950 [Nazis Punishment Law]. The preparation work of the Nazis Punishment Law shows that the drafters were aware that the cultural element was absent from the Convention and wanted to rectify such omission by adding sub-para. 6. See Orna Ben-Naftali and Yogev Tuval, 'Punishing International Crimes Committed by the Persecuted' (2006) 4 *Journal of International Criminal Justice* 128, 133 ff.

[15] This is present in his 1933 attempt to advocate for the international prohibition on the crimes of 'vandalism' (attacks on culture and heritage) and 'barbarity' (the destruction of groups) and the application of universal jurisdiction on them. Raphael Lemkin, 'Acts Constituting a General (Transnational) Danger Considered as Offences Against the Law of Nations', *Additional Explications to the Special Report Presented to the 5th Conference for the Unification of Penal Law in Madrid (14–20 October 1933)* available at <http://www.preventgenocide.org/lemkin/madrid1933-english.htm> (accessed 29 January 2017).

[16] UN Doc. E/447 26 June 1947 Draft Convention on the Crime of Genocide, Art. I, para. II, sub-ss. 1, 2, and 3. Cultural genocide was explained in the draft as consisting 'not in the destruction of

A later draft devoted a separate article to cultural genocide, and this draft was debated and voted on by the Sixth Committee of the UNGA. These debates show a clear chasm between the supporters of the inclusion and the objectors to it. And although the claims were cloaked with legalist arguments, the fault line between the two groups lies very much in the path of the historical experience of the countries these delegates represented. In the supporters group, we can thus find, for example, the delegates of Czechoslovakia and Pakistan, whose arguments were that a group can be destroyed by destroying its cultural foundations; or even that not only were physical and cultural genocide intrinsically linked, cultural genocide was the aim, whereas physical genocide was the means. The arguments of the objecting delegates reveal their fear that actions that their states routinely do and see as perfectly benign and required—such as assimilation practices—even forced ones—of minorities or indigenous groups living within their territory, or efforts made overseas, in the colonies—be captured by the Convention and be regarded as criminal.[17]

Eventually the article fell, with the formal reasoning that the Genocide Convention was not the adequate instrument. Rather, an instrument dedicated to the protection of human rights (such as the protection of language, religion, and culture under the Universal Declaration of Human Rights) or the respective national constitutional and criminal legislation protecting national minorities are more suitable. This, in fact, brought an end to the effort to establish an international criminal prohibition on cultural genocide. For us, what is fascinating about this endeavour is the way this exclusion shapes our understanding of genocide as we know it today: genocide is a plan of a rogue, authoritarian regime to exterminate a group within its control. Actions taken by a democratic state within its borders, or in its colonies, which do not amount to systemic killing but that nevertheless destroy whole groups, do not amount to genocide, and the legal treatment—if any—is left to other instruments.

Where in law today can we nevertheless find treatment of cultural destruction? Today, cultural destruction can be prosecuted as a war crime in and of itself (as was recently done in the ICC's *Al-Mahdi* case), and it can serve as an evidentiary tool to prove the special intent needed to commit genocide in international criminal law trials.[18] Current international criminal law also allows for compensation, through the system of the ICC: art. 75 of the Rome Statute envisions compensation to victims, and art. 79 established the Trust Fund for Victims (TFV) whose mandate is inter alia to implement Court-Ordered reparations. Yet the

members of a group nor in restrictions on birth, but in the destruction by brutal means of the specific characteristics of a group'. Ibid., 26 ff.

[17] UN Doc. A/C.6/SR Third Session of the General Assembly, Sixth Committee, Eighty-Third Session 25 October 1948 193–207.

[18] See Schabas' review of this point in William Schabas, *Genocide in International Law: The Crime of Crimes* (2009) 2nd edn., 216–19 ff.

earlier exclusion of cultural genocide means that compensation—if given—will be limited to physical genocide.[19]

CONCLUSION

This chapter explored the relations between law and history by following the transformations in the concept of cultural genocide in the period of its inception during the 1940s. While many claim that the difficulty to understand the varied histories of genocide comes from a 'definitionalist' approach that tries to fit the historical case to a strict legal definition, it points to the creative potential of the law and how it was initially used to understand the novelty of genocide as a crime targeting a group. The chapter showed that both at Nuremberg and during the Convention deliberations, the struggle was simultaneously an attempt to recognize a new crime and also to keep it in strict boundaries so that it will not be used to review the discriminatory policies of democratic states against domestic minorities and indigenous peoples. Since the concept of cultural genocide undermined the clear distinction between authoritarian states and democratic states, it is no wonder that the opposition to its inclusion both in the Nuremberg trial and in the Convention was very strong. However, when the victim group managed to conduct criminal domestic trials, there was more room for cultural genocide.

In conclusion, mention must be made of a recent case argued before the ICC that demonstrates law's continuous struggle to recognize cultural genocide. In September 2016, the ICC rendered its first verdict that deals entirely with cultural destruction, *Prosecutor v. Al Mahdi*.[20] The decision was lauded for its recognition of the link between an attack on a group's culture and its destruction and for the precedential value of such recognition in international criminal law. As one commentator noticed: 'The courts have been slow to recognize this, but there is a clear link between crimes committed against people and attacks on their cultural heritage.'[21] However, in so doing, the court did not invoke the crime of genocide that

---

[19] This, without relating to the 'reparations gap' identified by scholars, by which reparations are not 'a natural dimension of criminal law' and that it is almost impossible for victims of convicted perpetrators to receive compensation in civil courts. Novic (n. 1) 203–4 ff.

[20] *The Prosecutor v. Ahmad Al Faqi Al Mahdi*, ICC-01/12-01/15-171, Judgment and Sentence (27 September 2016).

[21] Marlise Simons, *Extremist Pleads Guilty in Hague Court to Destroying Cultural Sites in Timbuktu*, New York Times, 23 August 2016, at A8, citing Andras Riedlmayer, a scholar of Islamic art and architecture at Harvard. This article is also available online at <http://www.nytimes.com/2016/08/23/world/europe/ahmed-al-mahdi-hague-trial.html?_r=0> (accessed 6 May 2018).

deals with the destruction of groups and indicted the accused for the more limited war crime of destruction of cultural property.[22] We thus find that despite the growing public recognition in the importance of the prohibition of cultural genocide—for instance, in relation to the wars in Iraq and Syria, as in the struggles of indigenous peoples to recognize their cultural genocide—the law is still struggling to adjust itself to deal with the historic phenomenon of cultural genocide.

Moreover, lately the process for compensation in the Al-Mahdi case has started: 135 applications for reparations were submitted, and two documents of observations have been filed: one by *Fédération internationale des ligues des droits de l'Homme* and *Association malienne des droits de l'Homme*, the other by the defence. The former points to a vast array of victims, starting from the mausoleums' guardian families and extending to the people of Mali, and discusses material as well as mental harm, referring to the point made by the Chamber regarding the bond between the people of Timbuktu and its mausoleums. The defence's document lays down the principles for reparations, pointing to the fact that 'the attacked mausoleums neither had their own legal personality, nor were they the property of determined natural persons', and that 'Mr Al Mahdi's liability and capacity cannot be measured against those of a State', eventually asking that collective reparations shall be set. We see in these both an attempt to view cultural property as intrinsic to the group's self perception and central to its identity (in the first document), as well as a recent demonstration of the 'reparations gap' in ICL (in the second document). The fact that the buildings that were ruined are also valuable to the common heritage of mankind is evident in the restoration work performed through UNESCO.[23] In August 2017, the ICC has rendered its Reparations Order in this case.[24] It appears to be an understanding by the Court that protection of culture is intrinsically linked to the protection of groups, as the Court favours collectivist compensation over individual one. Two main factors hinder the Court's action, though: the first is that the indictment was for War Crimes (and not genocide), and the second is that the Rome Statute's framework is an individualistic one—and moreover, criminal and not civil. Therefore, the Court devised a dual model, by which direct victims who suffered exclusive harm (such as those whose livelihood exclusively depended on the buildings, or those whose ancestors were buried in the destroyed graves) are

---

[22] Al Mahdi was convicted of a war crime under the Rome Statute of the International Criminal Court, 17 July 1998, 2187 U.N.T.S. 38544, Art. 8(2)(e)(iv). Art. 8(2)(e) refers to war crimes committed in the context of a non-international armed conflict. Para. (iv) criminalizes acts: 'Intentionally directing attacks against buildings dedicated to religion, education, art, science or charitable purposes, historic monuments, hospitals and places where the sick and wounded are collected, provided they are not military objectives.'

[23] 'Reconstruction of Timbuktu mausoleums nears completion' 30 June 2015 <http://whc.unesco.org/en/news/1307/> (accessed 29 June 2017).

[24] *The Prosecutor v. Ahmad Al Faqi Al Mahdi*, ICC-01/12-01/15-236, Reparations Order (17 August 2017).

entitled to individual compensation. As to other victims—whose claims the Court has accepted as belonging to the wider circles of harm—the Court ordered they should be collectively compensated. Thus, in this recent case, it is revealed how almost seventy years after the adoption of the Genocide Convention, international law is still struggling with the concept of cultural genocide, trying to fit it to the available rubrics of state, individual, and humanity. Lost is the earlier understanding of the need to recognize the cultural group or the heritage community by allowing for a more participatory model of engaging the persecuted group in the struggle to bridge the gap between law and history.

Bibliography

Donald Bloxham, A. Dirk Moses (eds.), *The Oxford Handbook of Genocide Studies* (Oxford University Press, 2010)

Raphael Lemkin, *Axis Rule in Occupied Europe: Laws of Occupation, Analysis of Government, Proposals for Redress* (Carnegie Endowment for International Peace, Division of International Law, 1944)

Mark Levene, *Genocide in the Age of the Nation-State*, vols. I and II (Tauris, 2005)

Mark Lewis, *The Birth of the New Justice* (Oxford University Press, 2014)

Elisa Novic, *The Concept of Cultural Genocide: An International Law Perspective* (Oxford University Press, 2016)

K. C. Priemel, A. Stiller (eds.), *Reassessing The Nuremberg Military Tribunals* (Berghahn Books, 2012)

William Schabas, *Genocide in International Law: The Crime of Crimes* 2nd edn. (Cambridge University Press, 2009)

Ana Filipa Vrdoljak, *International Law, Museums and the Return of Cultural Objects* (Cambridge University Press, 2006)

Hannah Yablonka, *The State of Israel Vs. Adolf Eichmann* (Schocken Books, 2004)

CHAPTER 57

HISTORIANS' AMICUS BRIEFS

PRACTICE AND PROSPECT

SAM ERMAN AND
NATHAN PERL-ROSENTHAL

I. INTRODUCTION

THE authors began their collaboration as friends of the court. In 2014, they organized colleagues to address the federal court contemplating whether natives of American Samoa who are born owing full allegiance to the United States are ipso facto U.S. citizens. Their historical brief in support of the Samoan plaintiffs argued that the United States in the nineteenth century had a strong presumption in favour of *jus soli* citizenship, rooted in the English precedent of *Calvin's Case* (1608): a U.S. citizen was any person who was born on lands over which national sovereignty extended and who owed allegiance to the nation. The only means the U.S. Supreme Court found to limit this rule, they argued, was by recourse to explicitly racist arguments. That was the Court's approach in the notorious *Dred Scott* decision (1857) and the *Insular Cases* (1901–1925). It is an approach that is no longer acceptable to today's jurists.

The experience of writing the brief was simultaneously thrilling and unsettling. The authors found themselves engaged in a kind of work quite different from their usual fare. Accustomed to writing for fellow scholars and with no ulterior agenda, as authors of an amicus brief, they found themselves trying to make an argument that could have immediate consequences for the citizenship status of thousands of Americans. Their readership of judges was tiny, known in advance, and focused on a very specific set of questions. The authors worked hard to translate their scholarship into language that they thought would be appreciated by this very specialized audience. The historian's tendency to work alone gave way, in this project, to a cross-disciplinary collaboration that included working lawyers.

As the authors talked to colleagues about the process of amicus briefing, they started to see that they shared both excitement and ambivalence about the project. Again and again, colleagues would express their enthusiasm for the work being undertaken, then immediately add, 'I didn't think we historians did that sort of thing.' The authors found themselves in conversations about the ethics and strategy of the project, how legal and historical institutions interacted (and did not), and what distinguished the ways that jurists and historians conceived of the past and used it.

This chapter seeks to use the historians' toolkit to understand why historians often find amicus brief writing so vexed and how historians have navigated the challenges that it poses. It begins with a conceptual analysis of the historians' amicus brief, in two parts, focused on the problem of expertise. Courts permit historians to participate as friends of the court because they believe that scholars' knowledge of the past and its relationship to the present are valuable to their juridical work. Yet there are two troublesome questions about expertise that threaten this cross-disciplinary collaboration. One is the nature of historians' expertise: about which things, exactly, are historians 'experts?' The second is that the courts' work and expertise also concern relating the past to the present, especially where precedent is concerned. So where does the expertise of historians end and that of courts begin?

The chapter then turns to a history of high-profile amicus briefs by historians in the post-Second World War period. Although *Brown v. Board of Education* (1954) was an early and influential instance of historians' participation in Supreme Court deliberations, the modern debate over the historian's amicus brief dates to the late 1980s. The pace of such brief writing only really accelerated in the twenty-first century. During those three decades, brief writers became more adept at choosing disputes and framing arguments that provide courts with historical narratives that are both relevant to them and conform to the norms of historical scholarship.

In conclusion, the chapter briefly considers what these analyses can tell us about the prospects for future amicus briefs. Because historians' amicus briefs are encounters between the judiciary and academic history, the trajectory, ethics, and practices of each discipline shape the interaction. Lawyers and historians have distinct codes of scholarly ethics, and the historian friend of the court must grapple with both. And since both legal and historical scholarship are dynamic, the interface is a moving target. The authors nonetheless identify a few concrete strategies that have been consistently useful for friends of the court as they aim to bring historical scholarship into the juridical process.

To keep the topic manageable, several limitations are required. Though the chapter is concerned here with the place of history in jurisprudence, this is not about originalism. Historians and originalists both engage the past, but they do so in different ways that have been exhaustively catalogued elsewhere. Here, it is enough to say that originalist work rarely counts as good academic history, and vice-versa. This chapter is also not about historians' expert testimony. Such testimony is subject to cross-examination and other forms of testing at trial, which alleviates some concerns about amicus briefs and raises other concerns all its own. Finally, the focus in this chapter is on amicus briefs filed with the Supreme Court. These have been the most influential among both lawyers and judges, so they offer a useful point of entry into the subject.

II. The Historian Amicus: A Brief Conceptual Analysis

The institution of the *amicus curiae*, or friend-of-the-court brief, is at once an admission of humility by the court and a gauntlet thrown down by it. It is a statement of humility because it represents judges' acknowledgment that their knowledge of a case—whether of the relevant doctrines or of the factual context—may be imperfect. By accepting the contributions of amici, they declare themselves willing to accept the help of outsiders in order to find the right answer to a legal problem. But it is also a gauntlet that they throw down: the amici are challenged to prove to the court that they have knowledge or authority that the court ought to respect. What distinguishes the scholarly *amicus curiae* from a mere citizen petitioning the court is the claim (often made explicit) that the amicus possesses some expert knowledge not otherwise available to the court.[1]

---

[1] For discussions, see Linda Sandstrom Simard, 'An Empirical Study of Amici Curiae in Federal Court: A Fine Balance of Access, Efficiency and Adversarialism' (2008) 27 *Review of Litigation* 669, 675 ff; Samuel Krislov, 'The Amicus Brief: From Friendship to Advocacy' (1963) 72 *Yale L.J.* 694 ff; Paul M. Collins, Jr., 'Friends of the Court: Examining the Influence of Amicus Curiae Participation

The juxtaposition of these two faces of the *amicus curiae* is what makes *amicus curiae* briefs in general, and the historians' amicus brief in particular, difficult to carry off. Amici must thread fine conceptual and psychological needles in order to participate successfully in a court's proceedings. They have to be authoritative and provide expertise that the court recognizes in order to vault over the barrier that divides the ordinary non-party from the *amicus curiae*. Yet they must do so without overstepping the sphere in which the court welcomes their input and without offending the court's sense of its own authority.

The problem of competition with the jurists' expertise is hardly unique to historians or other humanist amici. Amici in every field, no matter what kind of expertise they claim to supply, face the same problem. One might imagine that humanists, whose knowledge is less obviously technical than that which is supplied by social or natural scientists, would have a harder time presenting themselves as additive to the courts' own expertise. Yet the courts over time acquire technical expertise in any area in which they are frequently called to practice, forcing experts in even the most technical fields to take care not to overplay their authority.

It is true, nevertheless, that history as a discipline faces some special hurdles in establishing its authority over an intellectual domain distinct from that of courts. The exact nature of historical methodology is fluid—one might even say unclear—even to many practising historians.[2] The kinds of expertise that we are able to offer the court can thus be difficult to pinpoint with precision. The paucity of quantitative methods in today's historical scholarship, moreover, puts historians at something of a disadvantage. Our culture's 'trust in numbers' confers value on arguments framed in terms of quantitative evidence.[3] And because interpreting the past is a central role of the common law judge, especially when he or she analyses precedent, judges may be particularly resistant to the historian amicus who claims to be able to present a (or *the*) authoritative narrative of the law's history.

---

in U.S. Supreme Court Litigation' (2004) 38 *Law and Society Review* 804, 810–11, 825–6 ff. The double character of the amicus is well reflected in the court rules governing them. Rule of the Supreme Court of the United States 37(1), for instance, instructs prospective friends that the line between the contribution of 'considerable help' and that which 'burdens' the Court is whether the brief provides new, relevant information.

[2] Classic discussions of historical methodology have described history as a 'craft' or an 'art' and emphasize its subjective elements and the flexibility of the tools that historians employ. See, e.g., E. H. Carr, *What Is History?* (1961); Marc Bloch, *The Historians' Craft* (1953).

[3] See Daniel Klerman, 'Quantitative Legal History', in Markus D. Dubber, Christopher Tomlins, (eds.), *The Oxford Handbook of Legal History* (2018); Theodore M. Porter, *Trust in Numbers: The Pursuit of Objectivity in Science and Public Life* (1996).

III. THE BRIEF OF BRIEFERS, OR WHAT DO HISTORIANS KNOW, ANYWAY?

What expertise can historians offer to the courts? There are at least three analytically distinct problems lurking within this question. The first is how historians demonstrate to the courts that they have expertise—that is, that they have a legitimate role as amici. A second question that arises is about which specific kinds of expertise historians can supply to the courts. What, in other words, is the nature of the historians' expertise as it is relevant to the law? Third, what are the limits of the expertise that historians can offer to the courts? In other terms: which elements or aspects of the expertise that we offer will the courts regard as adding to their knowledge rather than overlapping with their own rightful sphere of knowledge?

On the face of it, it would seem that historians have not had much difficulty gaining access to the courts as amici; their status as experts seems to be a matter of mutual agreement. Yet historians and the courts mean different things when they talk about expertise. When an historian talks about his or her 'expertise', it is usually in reference to a well-delimited area of geographic and temporal specialization. The level of a scholar's 'expertise' within this field depends on the quality of the scholarship, linguistic and archival accomplishments, and the scholar's influence in setting the agenda for her field. Courts are far less attuned to these measures of expertise. Judges have limited capacity either to examine the prior scholarship of amicus briefers to assess whether their work is good or to test the expertise evident in the amicus briefs themselves by checking footnotes or evaluating arguments. Judges rely on the disciplines themselves to do the vetting. If a field has shown itself to be an authorized area of expertise, its certified practitioners (in this case, usually holders of a PhD in history) tend to be considered by the courts to be experts.

These different understandings of expertise are consequential. They can set up broader misunderstandings between the courts and the amicus briefers about who has what expertise and in which domains it might be relevant. For the courts, it is an academic discipline's general prestige and social-intellectual role that confers expert authority on its practitioners. Credentialled historians thus have a clear path into court as experts. But the road is deceptively smooth. Precisely because they have no trouble gaining admittance in this fashion, historians have neither the need—nor, really, the opportunity—to explain to the courts the precise nature of the expertise they bring. This can lead to a situation in which the courts' understanding of what historians have to offer and historians' own notion of their potential contribution are at odds.

What is the nature of historians' expertise, as it is understood by the courts and by scholars themselves? Many jurists seem to regard knowledge of facts about the past as a primary component of historians' expertise. In this regard, judges share a view of historians and their work that is widespread among the non-academic public. Naturally, courts have access to facts immediately pertinent to the case before them. What they sometimes lack is a broader factual context, either temporal or geographic, and knowledge of more obscure but pertinent past events. As a rule, courts are ready and willing to seek the expertise of historians to fill in such gaps: to be provided, that is, with a set of facts about the past curated by experts.[4] They are ready to accord historians entry to the courtroom in order to benefit from this knowledge.

Historians have not hesitated to seize on the proffered role as experts in the facts of the past. Many historians' briefs, including the one that we spearheaded in 2014 in *Tuaua*, see communicating wider historical contexts to the court as a useful part of the exercise. Our brief, for instance, supplemented the factual record of the case by laying out the deeper history of citizenship law in the United States.[5] The historian amici in *Dollar General Corp. v. Mississippi Band of Choctaw Indians* (2015), similarly, informed the Court about the long and relatively little-known history of tribal courts with the right to 'exercise some forms of civil jurisdiction over non-Indians'.[6]

Professional historians, however, see themselves not primarily as repositories of historical facts, but as interpreters of historical events. It is the interpretation of the past, most scholars would argue, that constitutes the real expertise of the historian. Such a self-identification implies that historians possess additional types of expertise that they might wish to share with the courts as amici. One is the use of specialized tools or hermeneutic practices for studying past events. This includes archival methods as well as ways of reading documents in context and evaluating their meaning and significance. A second area of expertise is in historical narration. Historians' training centres on how to assemble plausible narratives, a process that involves knowing how to evaluate the relative importance of various causal factors as well as skill applying the discipline's notions about the relationship between

---

[4] This role has come under some degree of pressure, especially in constitutional law cases, from the publication and digitization of relevant sources. Scholarly editions of primary sources from the founding era have made available to jurists the papers of many political leaders as well as more obscure items, from the records of ratifying conventions to tracts by Anti-Federalists. The digitization of many other primary sources during the past decade, from newspapers to pamphlet literature, has made them far less difficult to use. As jurists have an easier time using and citing these sources, they may be less willing to cede to historians a role as guardians or curators of knowledge about them.

[5] Brief of Amici Curiae Scholars of Constitutional Law and Legal History in Support of Neither Party, No. 13-5272, *Tuana v. United States*, 788 F.3d 300 (D.C. 12 May 2014).

[6] Brief for Amici Curiae Historians and Legal Scholars in Support of Respondents, No. 13-1496, *Dollar General Corp. v. Mississippi Band of Choctaw Indians*, 579 U.S. ___ (22 October 2015). In *Brown v. Board of Education*, historians acted as curators for the NAACP Legal Defense Fund rather than the Court. According to Jonathan D. Martin, 'Historians at the Gate: Accommodating Expert Historical Testimony in Federal Courts' (2003) 78 *New York University L.J.* 1518, 'the historians incorporated the encouraging facts they could find respecting the Amendment's intent into a story the NAACP could take to the Supreme Court' ff.

causes and effects.[7] It is to these two domains of the historian's expertise, and their role before the courts, that this chapter now turns.

Some historian amici have tried to share expertise in historical methods with the courts. As with factual information, historians have a relatively clear route to persuading the courts to accept their authority as experts in historical methods. Courts are accustomed to drawing on technical experts and to receiving expert opinions. Insofar as historians present themselves as the experts in the use of a set of specific methodological tools that can illuminate the past, they are likely to receive a favourable hearing from the court. The historian friend of the court benefits here from playing a familiar role, similar to that of a special master in a complex and obscure area of law.

Expertise in historical methods has been a main form of assistance proffered in amicus briefs regarding Native American history. A recent law review article noted that a large number of the Indian law cases reaching the U.S. Supreme Court drew amicus briefs.[8] The vast majority of these briefs offered additional support for merits claims already made by the parties (most favoured the Native side of the litigation), frequently in the form of additional details and interpretation of historical evidence. Canadian courts have been particularly willing to draw on historians' expert testimony and amicus briefs in order to adjudicate cases involving Native land claims. An important recent case, *Tsilhqot'in Nation v. British Columbia*, ultimately decided on appeal by the Supreme Court of Canada in 2014, offers an illustration. A crucial part of the trial record was expert testimony by historians concerning the size, depth, and character of the plaintiffs' historical claim to land in British Columbia. Much of this testimony rested on the expertise of historians able to make sense of technically difficult sources such as oral testimony and treaties.[9]

Yet historian amici may find that claiming methodological expertise provides only a rather narrow doorway to influence over the courts. As *Tsilhqot'in Nation* suggests, much of the potential need for expert historical methodology to elucidate the facts of the case may already have been met in the form of expert testimony submitted by the parties themselves. Insofar as the case record already reflects this expertise, it is not clear what historian amici are able to add. If such material has not yet been introduced, the judge or the parties may object to attempts to smuggle in what should have been trial evidence via appellate briefs instead. The parties will lose their usual rights to test such evidence. The court will lose the benefit of such

---

[7] These two forms of expertise correspond very roughly to the schema of historical explanation outlined in David H. Fischer, *Historians' Fallacies: Toward a Logic of Historical Thought* (1970).

[8] Matthew L. M. Fletcher, 'The Utility of Amicus Briefs in the Supreme Court's Indian Cases' (2013) 2 *American Indian L.J.* 38 ff.

[9] See *Tsilhqot'in Nation v. British Columbia*, 2014 SCC 44; *Xeni Gwet'in First Nations v. British Columbia*, 2007 BCSC 1700. For a note on different ways of discussing amicus curiae in Canada and in the United States, see Helen A. Anderson, 'Frenemies of the Court: The Many Faces of Amicus Curiae' (2015) 49 *University of Richmond L.J.* 361, n. 7 ff.

adversarial inquiry. Thus, the late-arriving amici's right to involvement may rest on a weak foundation.

There are two other roadblocks, one internal to the discipline and one external to it, that can limit the success of historian amici in wielding their methodological expertise to influence the courts. One problem is that changes in how history is done over the past forty years have raised new doubts about the usefulness of historical research to the courts. The linguistic and cultural turns of the 1980s, by calling into question whether historians can claim to be describing past 'realities' in any simple sense, can be seen as undermining the claim of historical research to be part of the courts' reasoning.[10] In a broader sense, scholarship influenced by the new cultural history rests in part on a willingness to use evidence that is more anecdotal, exceptional, or incomplete than might once have been deemed acceptable. This has allowed scholars to open up new doors and to see many more actors than earlier scholarship did. Yet it comes at a cost: for non-specialists, the truth status of claims based on this sort of evidence may seem far less secure than that which was based on more 'traditional' historical evidence.[11]

A second kind of trouble can arise when historians claim that their specialized methods enable them to arrive at the most accurate account of a past *legal* question. The amicus brief submitted by a group of historians in *Patterson v. McLean Credit Union* (SCOTUS, 1989) illustrates the problem. The historian amici in that case claimed that a review of new scholarship showed that the 1866 statute at the heart of the case, the Civil Rights Act of 1866, reached private discrimination.[12] Yet historians' efforts to make claims about the past status of legal questions, as they did in *Patterson*, can quickly run up against the courts' well-developed sense of their own expertise and authority concerning the interpretation of law in the past. Common law courts, which derive their authority and the law they apply from the past, understand the elucidation of precedent to be part of *their* expertise. When historian amici try to elucidate past law for them, they may be asking the court to humble itself just a bit too much for comfort.

Another kind of know-how that historians may offer courts is expertise in historical narration: ways of describing historical causation and reconstructing how past events unfolded. In many cases, the fundamental premise of the historian's narrative art is the notion that there is a significant disjuncture between past and present, and that the historian's task is to explain how change occurs. The chain of historical causation that explains change over time, as historians understand it, is invariably multiple in nature. Understanding it thus involves detecting and

---

[10] See e.g., the influential Joan W. Scott, 'Gender: A Useful Category of Historical Analysis' (1986).

[11] For discussions of these issues, see Joyce Appleby et al., *Telling the Truth About History* (1995). To be clear, we do not endorse these non-specialists' doubts about the truth status of cultural or social histories.

[12] Brief Amicus Curiae of Eric Foner, John H. Franklin, Louis R. Harlan, Stanley N. Katz, Leon F. Litwack, C. Vann Woodward, and Mary Frances Berry, No. 87-107, *Patterson*, 491 U.S. 164 (22 June 1988).

integrating multiple causes into a plausible account of how past events occurred. Doing this requires both observing and noting the 'complexity' of the past and determining which causes were major and which ones were minor in a particular historical moment.

Historical narratives can provide back stories for legal rules and categories or examine how such legal items have themselves changed across time. An example of the first approach is the historians' amicus brief in the *District of Columbia v. Heller* (2008), a dispute over the meaning of the Second Amendment right to bear arms. The brief presented a causally attuned narrative history of that guarantee and its antecedents. During the colonial, revolutionary, and Founding eras, the concerns animating each such provision were not an individual right to self-defence, but rather the ability of one governmental institution to use control of an armed militia as a check against aggrandizement by a competing governmental institution. Hence, the historians concluded, 'the authors of the Second Amendment would be flabbergasted to learn' that their work was also 'precluding restrictions on such potentially dangerous property as firearms'. Historian amici took the second approach in *Obergefell v. Hodges* (2015), which involved a potential constitutional right to same-sex marriage. Describing instances of the historical changeability of marriage, they declared that 'recognizing the right of individuals of the same sex to marry' was consistent with 'this historical trend'.[13]

Though such displays of expertise in historical narration comport well with the historian's sense of the work they do, they face a triple challenge in being accepted by the courts. For one, historians may find themselves asked to justify the status of this form of expertise *as* expertise, because it is not generally regarded by laypeople as typical of historians' knowledge. Historians themselves must bear some of the responsibility for this confusion. The profession's commitment to speaking to general audiences has often led historians to bury or conceal methodological discussions that other disciplines (especially in the social sciences) are at pains to make explicit. While every historian weighs causes and considers how to narrate, the norm in large swathes of the discipline has been to do this silently rather than overtly, even in scholarly monographs.[14]

A second and more serious challenge for historians-as-narrators arises when the subject of their narration skirts close to legal interpretation. When it comes to the meaning of past legal pronouncements, judges jealously guard their own, competing methods of historical narration. Common law courts are essentially historical institutions: the law that they interpret, and indeed their authority as an institution,

---

[13] Brief for Jack N. Rakove, Saul Cornell, David T. Konig, William J. Novak, Lois G. Schwoerer et al. in Support of Petitioner, No. 07-290, *Heller*, 554 U.S. 570 (11 January 2008), 36 and throughout; Brief of Historians of Marriage and the American Historical Association as *Amici Curiae* in Support of Petitioners, No. 14-556, *Obergefell*, 576 U.S. ___ (6 March 2015) 23–4 and throughout.

[14] There are exceptions; see, e.g., Robert Darnton, *The Great Cat Massacre and Other Episodes in French Cultural History* (1984); Natalie Davis, *The Return of Martin Guerre* (1983).

are both rooted in continuity with the past. As a result, jurists have resisted notions of a radical disjuncture between past and present, which would cut the common law courts off from their own source of legitimacy. They have instead offered their own narration of the law's history, built on an assumption of broad-gauge continuity. This has not prevented courts from imagining change over time. But it does mean that historical narratives that can be integrated into judges' interpretations of the past may face less resistance than those that mount a frontal assault.

The recent rise of originalism in American law presents a third and related challenge. Like amicus briefs by historians, originalism has a political history. At the risk of oversimplification, it has proceeded through three postwar incarnations: the proto-originalism of Justice Hugo Black's textualism and the rebriefing in *Brown v. Board of Education* (1954), the original intent jurisprudence (originalism 1.0) that attacked the Warren Court's decisions, and the original public meaning jurisprudence (originalism 2.0) that is a focus of current efforts to deconstruct the New Deal state.[15] In spite of the significant differences among them, originalists of all stripes are committed to the notion that law has a fixed 'meaning' that 'should remain the same', invariant through time. To the extent that courts take up such interpretive approaches, the space for historical narratives of the changing meaning of legal dictates will shrink to the vanishing point.[16]

IV. HISTORIANS' AMICUS BRIEFS, C. 1950S TO 2015

A survey of key Supreme Court cases involving historians' amicus briefs over the past century reveals the crucial role that ideas about the relative expertise of jurists and their historians friends have had on scholars' success (or not) in speaking to the courts. The institution of the amicus brief is a relatively late-blooming phenomenon in American law. During the nineteenth century and the first decades of the twentieth century, amicus briefs were rare. In the years after the Second World War,

---

[15] The authors are grateful to Saul Cornell for suggesting this formulation.

[16] Randy Barnett, 'The Gravitational Force of Originalism' (2013) 82 *Fordham L.J.* 412 ff. For a helpful overview of the lines of differentiation between several historians (see, especially, Jonathan Gienapp's criticisms of 'Originalism 2.0') and their originalist interlocutors, see Randy Barnett, 'Originalism's Teachable Moment' (2017) *Washington Post*, <https://www.washingtonpost.com/news/volokh-conspiracy/wp/2017/04/05/originalism-teachable-moment-update/?utm_term=.6dd2cd1f63ff> (accessed 7 May 2018). See also Jonathan Gienapp, 'Historicism and Holism: Failures of Originalist Translation' (2015) 84 *Fordham L.J.* 935 ff.

the number of amicus briefs filed in federal courts grew larger, and the numbers have expanded substantially over the seventy years since.[17] Yet even as the amicus brief became more common, historians were laggards: recent counts suggest that as late as the 1990s, fewer than one historian amicus brief was filed per year before the Supreme Court. Historians' amicus briefs have proliferated in the decade and a half since 2001: between 2006 and 2012, historians presented over thirty to the Supreme Court alone.[18]

One of the earliest uses of historians' expertise in Supreme Court briefs came in *Brown v. Board of Education* (1954). Though there was no brief by independent historians, the NAACP drew on a group of historians in order to write the historical portions of their argument on plaintiffs' behalf in opposition to segregation. Spurred by the Court's questions about the relationship of the Reconstruction amendments to segregation, they went to historians in the hopes of finding evidence that the two had been at odds. Unable to cite strong evidence that the framers of the Reconstruction Amendments had in fact intended to bar racial segregation, the historians instead offered studied ambiguity. Their argument came down, in essence, to a claim that the history of Reconstruction was complex enough that the Court could not reasonably draw firm conclusions from it either way.[19]

In spite of the historians' best efforts, however, it might not be unfair to characterize their intervention in *Brown* as a failure. Perhaps influenced by the historians' agnosticism about the lessons of the past, the Court turned to social science (psychology), not history, to resolve the case. As a result, the historians who participated in the case did not exert a strong influence on its outcome, at least in a positive sense. The failure of historians in this case had effects that went well beyond missing an opportunity for influence. The social-scientific basis on which the Court ultimately decided *Brown* has long been a source of concern to some, who have insisted that constitutional principles should rest on more enduring and abstract grounds. A decision based on the historical record—for instance, one that unmasked the intentions of Jim Crow's framers to re-establish racial caste throughout the former Confederacy—might have set the whole edifice of racial justice on a firmer footing in the later twentieth century.

The experience of *Brown* suggests some of the lasting difficulties that arose as historians have intervened as amici. One was historians' relative lack of prestige, especially by comparison to social scientists. This can be linked, of course, to the relative prestige attached to their methods, especially at the height of the post-war

---

[17] For discussion, see Joseph D. Kearney, Thomas W. Merrill, 'The Influence of Amicus Curiae Briefs on the Supreme Court' (2000) 148 *University of Pennsylvania L.J.* 752 ff; Michael E. Solimine, 'Retooling the Amicus Machine' (2016) 102 *Virginia L.J. Online* 151 ff.

[18] See Joshua Stein, 'Historians Before the Bench: Friends of the Court, Foes of Originalism' (2013) 25 *Yale Journal of Law & the Humanities* 359, for discussion of historian participation in amicus briefs ff.

[19] Jonathan Martin, 'Historians at the Gate' (2003) 78 *New York University L.J.* 1518 ff.

science boom. The psychological research on which the *Brown* Court drew in deciding the case presented itself as not only expert, but *decisive* as well. As became clearer in the years after *Brown*, historians were not always comfortable becoming advocates. A number of the historians involved in *Brown*, both at the time and later on, expressed concern that performing advocacy had caused them to distort their historical work. They worried that, spurred on by their desire to reach a particular outcome, they had drawn conclusions that were not warranted by strict historical methods. In effect, the historians came to doubt their ability to maintain their expertise in the context of the courtroom. This form of methodological self-doubt would be a persistent issue among historians writing amicus briefs and may have played a role in undermining the breadth, scope, and success of their arguments over time.

Historians again saw an opportunity to intervene productively in the Supreme Court's work in two high-profile cases in the late 1980s, in *Webster v. Reproductive Health Services* (1989) and *Patterson v. McLean Credit Union* (1989). The historian amici in each of these cases sought to make an argument about how doctrines that drew legitimacy from history ought to be interpreted. The timing of the high-profile briefs reflected broader trends in the academy and at the Court. The 1980s had seen originalism explode onto the scene as a method of constitutional interpretation. As courts seemed increasingly open to historically grounded argumentations, some historians had grown accustomed to addressing the relationship between history and law. Relatedly, legal history was emerging as a major subfield distinct from originalism and often housed in law schools.[20]

Webster addressed state rules restricting the use of state funds for abortion-related activities. The Supreme Court had previously rooted such fundamental rights and their limits in the history and traditions of the United States.[21] More than 200 historians now co-signed an amicus brief, presenting the Court with a family of historical narratives intended to favour abortion rights. Some supported a tradition of permitting abortion; others undermined arguments that there was any tradition to the contrary, as the government argued. The amici here deployed a range of forms of historical expertise. Justices learned novel historical facts and context, including religious authorities' prior reluctance to campaign against abortion. The brief walked them through historical methods of analysis such as the conclusion that unenforced anti-abortion laws revealed widespread lack of moral concern with the issue. It also rebutted opponents' claim of a longstanding U.S. concern with fetal life by presenting a historical narrative in which factors such as sexism, racism, and

---

[20] Michael Grossberg, 'Friends of the Court: A New Role for Historians' (2010) 40 *Perspectives on History* 27 ff.

[21] The classic formulation comes from *Snyder v. Commonwealth* (1934), which forbade any state's act that 'offends some principle of justice so rooted in the traditions and conscience of our people as to be ranked as fundamental'.

professional chauvinism had driven much more of the ebb and flow of restrictions on abortion.[22]

The briefers in *Webster* self-consciously understood themselves as engaging in advocacy as well as history. Yet some participants still came to worry that the brief had been better lawyering than historical scholarship. Several participants, writing later in *The Public Historian*, attempted to redefine their claim to expertise by arguing that their role as amici was to be expert advocates: that is, they aimed to make only true, historically defensible claims, but they focused attention selectively with the goal of influencing the outcome. According to a central participant in the brief, the historian James C. Mohr, that Janus-faced role did not need to be expressly mentioned in the brief because that was what it was to be an amicus. As a legal argument, the brief succeeded: *Webster* did not overturn *Roe v. Wade*. The brief was also well-received by the media throughout the pendency of the case. But the participants' doubts about the status of their expertise when they were acting as advocates spread, too. As Jane E. Larson and Clyde Spillenger recalled of their experiences as attorneys on the brief, some signatories worried that the 'unqualified nature of some of the briefs arguments and assertions' jeopardized their claim to historical expertise. Just as serious, as George Will argued, to the extent that policy preferences drove the historian's conclusion, the historian could be seen as intruding on the judge's domain.[23]

The experience of the amici in *Patterson* reveals more vividly still the tenuous position of historians' expertise when it comes under suspicion of being shaped by advocacy. The case asked whether a protection against race discrimination in the Enforcement Act of 1866 (as amended) covered discrimination by private individuals, or only discrimination attributable to a public official. The Court had previously signalled that the meaning of the act at the moment of its passage would determine its meaning today. As the author of the definitive monograph on Reconstruction, Eric Foner filed an amicus brief with several other historians. It observed that the sharp line the Court had come to draw between private and public acts was of relatively recent vintage. The framers of the Enforcement Act did not think in those terms. With that proviso made, the brief advanced 'one inescapable conclusion: the framers of the Act intended . . . to prohibit certain forms of private activity'. Though framed in absolute language, it was a modest claim. At a time when lawmakers did not sharply divide public and private in today's terms, they passed a law that covered at least some material in both domains.[24]

---

[22] Clyde Spillenger et al., 'Brief of 281 American Historians as Amici Curiae Supporting Appellees' (1990) 12 *The Public Historian* 57 ff.

[23] Jane E. Larson, Clyde Spillenger, '"That's Not History": The Boundaries of Advocacy and Scholarship' (1990) 12 *The Public Historian* 40 ff; the rest of (1990) 12 *The Public Historian*; George F. Will, 'Abortion is a State Question' (1989) *Washington Post*.

[24] Brief Amicus Curiae of Eric Foner et al., *Patterson*, 24 and throughout; Pamela Brandwein, *Rethinking the Judicial Settlement of Reconstruction* (2011).

The seeming modesty of the *Patterson* amici's argument, however, could not protect it from suspicion that the authors had crafted an historical narrative to support their preferred disposition of the case. More than one observer noticed that the brief was selective in its narration of the Civil Rights Bill of 1866. Foner himself, in *Reconstruction: America's Unfinished Revolution*, had argued that the Bill 'was primarily directed against public, not private, acts of injustice'.[25] Even before the Court issued its opinion, Harvard Law Professor Randall Kennedy had noted the 'sharp contrast' between the 'ambivalent, nuanced, and tentative treatment of the issue' in his book and the 'unambiguous assertions' of the brief.[26] It later became known that Justice Anthony Kennedy had told his colleagues that he found the gap between Foner's treatment of the issue in his monograph and the brief to be 'highly misleading'.[27]

Together, the *Patterson* and *Webster* amicus briefs became a cautionary tale about the perils for historians of seeking to divide labour with judges. To leave all judgment to the judges would be to author a brief that helped no one. The authors of the *Webster* brief forthrightly acknowledged as much. But if one let one's policy preferences guide one's scholarly work, as some suspected the amici had done in these cases, then their claim to expertise became shakier, and the line between their expertise and that of the judges less sharp, to their detriment. Conversely, as *Patterson* suggests, to intrude too deeply into the realm of judgment is to invite judicial backlash. At some undefined point in the process, historical expertise must give way to judicial expertise. In *Patterson*, Justice Kennedy reacted to what he understood to be Foner's attempt to shade the history to his preferred policy outcome. What was less clear from these cases, however, was how historians could find a way to achieve respectful relevance within the bounds of what they understood to be their expertise.

Historians seemed to find firmer footing when they submitted briefs in early-twenty-first-century cases involving same-sex relationships. The historian Nancy Cott was at the centre of the effort, which spanned more than a decade. The success of the amicus briefers in those cases can be attributed to several factors. They began to lay the groundwork for their briefs very early. They identified and leveraged the authority of areas of historical consensus. Individuals who spanned the legal-historical divide joined the effort. Their briefs aimed to facilitate rather than oppose the doctrinal changes that the Court seemed inclined to make. And, perhaps most fortuitously, their opponents' arguments rested on highly dubious historical foundations.

The path to the marriage equality amicus briefs was unusually long. In 2000, Cott published her groundbreaking history of American marriage, *Public Vows*.

---

[25] Eric Foner, *Reconstruction: America's Unfinished Revolution, 1863–1877* (2002 [1988]) 245.

[26] Randall Kennedy, 'Reconstruction and the Politics of Scholarship' (1989) 98 *Yale L.J.* 538 n. 70.

[27] James F. Simon, *The Center Holds: The Power Struggle Inside the Rehnquist Court* (1995) 55.

As its title suggested, it argued that marriage was first and foremost a public institution—not, as people often conceive it, natural, private, and eternal. Cott also reminded her readers of marriage's long history as an instrument of coercion and oppression. Two years later, Cott joined an amicus brief in *Lawrence v. Texas* (2003), authored by a handful of historians whose work focused on sexual orientation. The issue in the case was whether to overturn the holding in *Bowers v. Hardwick* (1986) that the Constitution permitted states to criminalize same-sex sodomy. The *Bowers* decision had rested on the assertion that such bans had 'ancient roots', an implicit acknowledgement of the difficulty identifying secular justifications for a practice that legal thinkers had long treated as a victimless crime.[28] The *Lawrence* brief contested that claim, arguing that singling out same-sex sexual conduct for particular opprobrium was a twentieth-century innovation that had begun to decline even before the century had ended. In overturning *Bowers*, the *Lawrence* Court cribbed repeatedly from the historians' brief.[29]

A dozen years later, Cott co-authored an amicus brief in *Obergefell v. Hodges* (2015). The signatories—a select group of historians of marriage, family, and law—included scholars who were expert in the languages of both historians and judges. The case presented the question whether the Constitution included a right to same-sex marriage. Unable to muster social-science evidence that associated same-sex marriage with measurable harms, opponents sought refuge in history. They argued that marriage was an unchanging institution eternally focused on promoting procreation. The historians' brief answered by discussing the many public purposes marriage has served and the many public forms it has taken. The Court's opinion declaring the right to same-sex marriage cited *Public Vows* repeatedly.[30]

Cott's two interventions were undoubted successes, perhaps among the most successful interventions by historian amici in the Supreme Court's jurisprudence. Yet it may prove difficult for other scholars to repeat the success of those briefs; Cott may have ridden the unicorn. Rare indeed are the cases where opponents can identify no convincing secular reason in favour of their argument. Few are the scholars who will write a book that so clearly foreshadows a major constitutional litigation campaign. Yet there are some elements of those briefs that are replicable: the ability to identify and convey historical consensuses, to find scholars who can speak history to courts, and to write with an ear to what the Court is prepared to hear.

Kristin Collins replicated elements of the above strategy during the second decade of the twenty-first century in cases concerning sex discrimination and

---

[28] *The Wolfenden Report: Report of the Committee on Homosexual Offenses and Prostitution* (1958 [1957]) 115 ff; American Law Institute, *Model Penal Code Tentative Draft No. 4* (1955) 276 ff.

[29] Brief of Professors of History George Chauncey, Nancy F. Cott, John D'Emilio, Estelle B. Freedman, Thomas C. Holt, John Howard, Lynn Hunt, Mark D. Jordan, Elizabeth Lapovsky Kennedy, and Linda P. Kerber as Amici Curiae in Support of Petitioners, No. 02-102, *Lawrence*, 539 U.S. 558 (16 January 2003); *Lawrence*, 539 U.S., 567–8, 571.

[30] Brief of Historians of Marriage, *Obergefell*; *Obergefell*, 576 U.S. ___, slip op. 6, 7, 16.

intergenerational transmission of citizenship. *Flores-Villar v. United States* (2011) featured a challenge to a federal statute making it easier for unmarried U.S.-citizen women to transmit citizenship to children whose other parent was an alien than for unmarried U.S.-citizen men to do the same. Collins spearheaded a brief presenting the substantial historical scholarship on the role of gender stereotypes in sex-differentiated citizenship laws. After Justice Elena Kagan's recusal caused the Court to divide evenly in 2011, the issue returned to the Court in *Sessions v. Morales-Santana* (2017). In the interim, Collins returned to the archive, then published an influential legal-historical article in the *Yale Law Journal* that became the basis for the revised brief she and colleagues offered the Court in *Morales-Santana*. The article revealed that the facial sex discrimination of citizenship laws often served racist nativist policy aims. It also demonstrated that racial chauvinism and gender stereotypes were animating concerns for the framers of the specific laws at issue before the justices. When the Court struck down such laws in *Morales-Santana*, Collins's analysis was central to its reasoning.[31]

A very different but no less successful model of historians' intervention in the Court's jurisprudence arose, in the period between *Lawrence* and *Obergefell*, with the litigation of detainees at Guantánamo Bay. Despite the myriad doctrinal tangles that those cases raised, they all unfolded against the same basic backdrop, the doctrine of the separation of powers. Specifically, the cases raised the question of aggrandizement. Was the executive claiming unprecedented powers? Were the political branches seeking to subjugate the judiciary? Or was the judiciary on the brink of transforming itself into a political actor?

In amicus briefs filed in a series of the detention cases historians argued that legitimate questions of executive overreach were at issue and sought to reassure the Court that the steps it was being asked to take were not unprecedented. One brief authored by scholars of *Ex parte Quirin* (1942), a Supreme Court case that granted the executive broad discretion over prisoners during wartime, argued that *Quirin* had been riddled by 'bias, conflicts of interest, undue executive influence, judicial haste, and lack of authority'. To rest upon it again would be to legitimize the executive's prior power grab and the Court's prior abdication of authority. Another brief contended that though the Early Republic faced undeclared wars, difficulties of identification, and irregular conflict, it had adhered to normal law. The implication was that the executive was now seeking powers that his predecessors in similar circumstances had done without. Other historian amici reassured the justices that

---

[31] Brief Amici Curiae of Professors of History, Political Science, and Law in Support of Petitioner, No. 09-5801, *Flores-Villar*, 564 U.S. 210 (25 June 2010); Kristin A. Collins, 'Illegitimate Borders: Jus Sanguinis Citizenship and the Legal Construction of Family, Race, and Nation' (2014) 123 *Yale L.J.* 2134 ff; Brief Amici Curiae of Professors of History, Political Science, and Law in Support of Respondent, No. 15-1191, *Morales-Santana*, 582 U.S. ___ (4 October 2016); *Morales-Santana*, 582 U.S. ___, slip op. 10, 12, 20–1. Not coincidentally, Cott was a signatory to both briefs. One author of this essay, Sam Erman, participated in Collins's second brief.

judges had long been called upon to review detentions in similar circumstances. There was nothing unusual about taking on such a role in the instant cases.[32]

The Court was broadly receptive to the arguments of the amici: it rejected the military tribunals that the executive unilaterally sought to establish and it affirmed its ability to review the constitutionality of the prisoners' detentions. What did these scholars do right? One part of the answer is surely that the historian amici in these cases offered up one of the more modest forms of expertise they had to provide— the small gift of historical context. In these cases, they could be effective simply by offering the Court an account of its own jurisprudence and the executive branch's actions over the previous two hundred plus years. That was sufficient to give the justices the confidence that their intervention would be more preservative than disruptive of the separation-of-powers status quo. In this sense, the historian amici were lucky, too: the nature of the case meant that they could influence the outcome without needing (like the amici in *Patterson*) to claim that they could elucidate the past state of a legal principle.[33] As with the briefs in *Obergefell* and *Lawrence*, moreover, the amici in the detainee cases were at pains to enlist select groups of specialists, including historians situated at law schools. This strategy enabled them to maximize their chances of speaking with an authoritative historical voice that would still be comprehensible to the justices.

v. Whither the Historians' Amicus Brief?

Though the primary goal of this chapter has been to reflect on the practice of amicus briefing by historians, the authors' analysis suggests a few ways in which historians can best make use of their expertise before the courts. These thoughts are offered by way of conclusion, in the full knowledge that they are necessarily preliminary in nature.

---

[32] Brief of Legal Scholars and Historians as Amici Curiae in Support of Petitioner, No. 05-184, *Hamdan v. Rumsfeld*, 548 U.S. 557 (6 January 2006) 2 and throughout; Brief of Lawrence M. Friedman, Jonathan Lurie, and Alfred P. Rubin as Amici Curiae in Support of Petitioner, *Hamdan* (6 January 2006); Brief Amici Curiae of Legal Historians Listed Herein in Support of the Petitioners, No. 03-334, *Rasul v. Bush*, 542 U.S. 466 (14 January 2004).

[33] The Court responded with scepticism to the claim in another historical amicus brief that de facto control rather than de jure sovereignty set the borders of habeas corpus review under Founding-Era common law. See Brief of Legal Historians as Amici Curiae in Support of Petitioners, No. 06-1195, *Boumediene v. Bush*, 553 U.S. 723 (24 August 2007); *Boumediene*, 553 U.S. 746 (2008).

The historian who acts as the friend of the court aims to influence the law's development by participating in a judicial institution as an outside expert. Such a stance carries ethical obligations. The court permits the historian's participation in cases on the presumption that the historian has expertise that the court values, and that the historian aims to assist the court in doing its duty. Fulfilling this role will often require historians to speak in a language legible to courts on matters of concern to them, while respecting the court's distinct areas of authority. Threading these various needles, as our analytic and historical overviews of historians' briefs suggests, is not easy.

One set of strategies that historians would do well to adopt in writing amicus briefs is to focus on respecting the disciplinary divide between historians and judges. Historians will do well to stop short of purporting to decide legal questions. Judges often understand their role to include (at a minimum) the final disposition of the case. That makes sense, for if an historical account wholly decides a dispute, then the division of labour between judge and historian has ceased to be any such thing. Seeking to find a line between what history can say and the ultimate issue in the case can also be an effective way to discipline scholars' tendency to let policy preferences cloud our better judgment and impair our claims to expertise.

Respecting the disciplinary divide is not only a matter of content; it is also a matter of personnel. Limiting participation in amicus briefs to experts on the specific topic at issue has proven to be beneficial in gaining the attention of judges. Busy judges, besieged by filings, may view a brief with hundreds of signatories more as citizen lobbying than as an expert submission. Curating participation is also a way to increase the likelihood that participants critically read and fully stand behind the submission to the court.

Another set of strategies, conversely, calls for attempts to *bridge* that disciplinary divide. Here, intermediaries are often key. Lawyers familiar with history, historians of both law and history, legal historians who understand law well, or historians willing to learn about law all contribute to briefs that judges may understand and use. A historian can also increase the likelihood that a judge will find her brief helpful by providing the judge with multiple points of entry into the argument. Some of the successful briefs we have discussed above argue both that history runs contrary to the claim some other party or amicus is making *and* that there are good reasons to think that history supports the result for which the amicus advocates. Another approach is to try and identify what types of historical narratives a judge may be tempted to use and then to provide her analyses of the relative historical validity of one or another such approach.

By the same token, historian amici should do more in their briefs to set out explicitly for the courts the methodological assumptions underlying their arguments. An historian amicus might work out in detail for the court why he or she believes a particular event occurred, or why a text was intended in a particular way. By making their methods explicit, they can work to re-valorize them as expertise. That is doubly important when one considers that courts frequently muster historical narratives as support for their legal reasoning. Courts are expert in understanding what sorts of historical narratives potentially have this legitimizing function. But they are less expert in understanding which of those narratives will withstand historians' scrutiny. Historians can thus provide courts information on the historical credibility of various potentially attractive historical narratives.[34]

Finally, it is worth bearing in mind that amicus briefing is not just a one-way street in which historians aim to serve the court and get nothing in return. Participating in judicial proceedings as a friend of the court can also lead to new research questions and to sharper formulations of old ones. Like Collins's contribution to the *Yale Law Journal*—just one example of many—the concerns that drive historians to write amicus briefs are continuous with the ones that lead to innovative historical research. The discipline that the legal process imposes may even serve to stimulate new thinking.[35] The authors' own experience attests to the potential scholarly benefits to be reaped from participating in the judicial process. Their brief in *Tuaua*, though it did not succeed in persuading the court, did get them wondering about the surprising fact that there seemed to be a uniform (though racially discriminatory) *jus soli* citizenship rule for the first century of the Republic. The authors have since embarked on what promises to be a long-term research project on the history of the *jus soli* concept, focused on how it came into being in the nineteenth century and the legal conflicts and complexities that it sought to obscure. The authors hope, then, for themselves and for others as well, becoming friends of the court can lead beyond the win-lose proposition of a case's disposition and into the richer realms of new scholarly sleuthing.

Bibliography

Brief of Historians of Marriage and the American Historical Association as *Amici Curiae* in Support of Petitioners, No. 14-556, *Obergefell v. Hodges*, 576 U.S. ___ (6 March 2015)

Brief of Legal Historians as Amici Curiae in Support of Petitioners, No. 06-1195, *Boumediene v. Bush*, 553 U.S. 723 (24 August 2007)

Brief of Professors of History George Chauncey, Nancy F. Cott, John D'Emilio, Estelle B. Freedman, Thomas C. Holt, John Howard, Lynn Hunt, Mark D. Jordan, Elizabeth Lapovsky Kennedy, and Linda P. Kerber as Amici Curiae in Support of Petitioners, No. 02-102, *Lawrence v. Texas*, 539 U.S. 558 (16 January 2003)

Kristin A. Collins, 'Illegitimate Borders: Jus Sanguinis Citizenship and the Legal Construction of Family, Race, and Nation' (2014) 123 *Yale L.J.* 2134

---

[34] E.g., historian amici provided such evaluations of the plausibility of various possible historical narratives in *District of Columbia v. Heller* (2008). See Brief for Jack N. Rakove et al., *Heller*.

[35] Paul D. Halliday, *Habeas Corpus: From England to Empire* (2010); Cott, *Public Vows* (2000).

Paul M. Collins Jr., 'Friends of the Court: Examining the Influence of Amicus Curiae Participation in U.S. Supreme Court Litigation' (2004) 38 *Law and Society Review* 804

Nancy F. Cott, *Public Vows: A History of Marriage and the Nation* (Harvard University Press, 2000)

Matthew L. M. Fletcher, 'The Utility of Amicus Briefs in the Supreme Court's Indian Cases' (2013) 2 *American Indian L.J.* 38

Otis L. Graham (ed.), Roundtable, 'Historians and the *Webster* Case' (1990) 12 *The Public Historian* 9

Michael Grossberg, 'Friends of the Court: A New Role for Historians' (2010) 48 *Perspectives on History* 27

Paul D. Halliday, *Habeas Corpus: From England to Empire* (Harvard University Press, 2010)

Randall Kennedy, 'Reconstruction and the Politics of Scholarship' (1989) 98 *Yale L.R.* 521

Joshua Stein, 'Historians Before the Bench: Friends of the Court, Foes of Originalism' (2013) 25 *Yale Journal of Law & the Humanities* 359

INDEX

A

Printed and bound by CPI Group (UK) Ltd, Croydon, CR0 4YY